DogFriendly.com's

# United States and Canada Dog Travel Guide
# 5th Edition

by
Len Kain
DogFriendly.com, Inc.

DogFriendly.com's United States and Canada Dog Travel Guide
by Len Kain

DogFriendly.com, Inc.
PO Box 1017 Anchor Point AK 99556
1-877-475-2275
email: email@dogfriendly.com
http://www.dogfriendly.com

## PLEASE NOTE
Although the author and publisher have tried to make the information as accurate as possible,  they do not assume, and hereby disclaim, any liability for any loss or damage caused by errors, omissions, misleading information or potential travel problems caused by this book, even if such errors or omissions result from negligence, accident or any other cause.

## CHECK AHEAD
We remind you, as always, to call ahead and confirm that the applicable establishment is still "dog-friendly" and that it will accommodate your pet.

## DOGS OF ALL SIZES
If your dog is over 75-80 pounds, then please call the individual establishment to make sure that they allow your dog. Please be aware that establishments and local governments may also not allow particular breeds.

## OTHER PARTIES DESCRIPTIONS
This book is a work for hire. Some of the descriptions have been provided  to us by our web site advertisers, paid researchers or other parties. Part of the introductions and descriptions were contributed to by former DogFriendly.com president Tara Kain.

ISBN 13 - 9780979555169

Printed in the United States of America


Cover Photographs (top to bottom, left to right):
Lafayette Park, Washington D.C.
Garden of the Gods, Colorado Springs, CO

Back Cover Photographs (top to bottom):
Bar Harbor, ME
Dallas, TX

# TABLE OF CONTENTS

*Beaches that allow dogs, most require leashes, some are off-leash, some have restricted hours or seasons.*

*Policies for subways, buses, local air service, ferries and other transportation for you and your dog.*

*What to see with your dogs and dog policies at the National Parks.*

*Tourist sites, museums, boat tours, city tours, historical sites, amusement parks, cross-country skiing, shopping centers, wineries and other places that allow your dog.*

*Restaurants and coffee shops with outdoor patios or tables that allow your dog to accompany you. In some establishments you pick up your own food and in others they serve you outdoors.*

*Areas in parks that are authorized for off-leash playtime for your dog. Some are fenced, some are not fenced. Some may have restricted hours or other restrictions.*

*Where to find emergency and off-hours pet medical care while traveling.*

## Introduction

DogFriendly.com's guides have helped millions of dog lovers plan vacations and trips with their dogs. The ultimate in Dog Travel Guides, our United States and Canada Dog Travel Guide includes dog-friendly lodging and attractions such as tours, historical places and more. Also included are restaurants with outdoor patio dining where your dog is welcome, national parks, information about the airlines, subways, buses and other transportation systems that permit dogs and emergency veterinarians just in case. The guide gives detailed pet policies for most places, including how many dogs may be allowed per room, weight limits, fees and other useful information. In many cases, toll-free numbers and websites are given. Also very importantly, our lodging guide focuses on those places that allow dogs of all sizes and do not restrict dogs to smoking rooms only. Not included in this guide are places that allow, for example, only dogs up to ten pounds or require that your dog be carried or in a carrier while on the premises. Also, we do not think that places that require dog owners to stay in smoking rooms are dog-friendly and we do not include them. Accommodations in this book have been called by DogFriendly.com to verify pet policies although these policies do change often. Thank you for selecting our pet travel guide and we hope you spend less time researching and more time actually going places with your dog. Enjoy your dog-friendly travels!

## About Author Len Kain

Len Kain began traveling with his dog when he was young. His family traveled with a camping trailer and brought along their standard poodle, Ricky. On trips, he found places and attractions that welcomed his best friend. When Len grew up and got his own dog, he continued the tradition of bringing his dog on trips with him. Len and his family have traveled over 200,000 miles across the country on road trips. Today he continues to travel and find fun and exciting dog-friendly places.

Currently, Len serves as DogFriendly.com's President. Len has been quoted numerous times in print, on radio and television about issues relating to traveling with dogs. Prior to joining DogFriendly.com Len served in various executive and management positions in several Silicon Valley and Internet Companies. Len holds a Bachelor of Engineering degree from Stevens Tech in New Jersey, a Master of Science degree from Stanford University and an MBA from the University of Phoenix. Len resides in Anchor Point, Alaska.

## Your Comments and Feedback

We value and appreciate your feedback and comments. If you want to recommend a dog-friendly place or establishment, let us know. If you find a place that is no longer dog-friendly, allows small dogs only or allows dogs in smoking rooms only, please let us know. You can contact us using the following information.

Mailing Address and Contact Information:
DogFriendly.com, Inc.
PO Box 1017 Anchor Point, AK 99556 USA
Toll free phone: 1-877-475-2275
email: email@ dogfriendly.com
http://www.dogfriendly.com

**How To Use This Guide**

*General Guidelines*

1. Please only travel with a well-behaved dog that is comfortable around other people and especially children. Dogs should also be potty trained and not bark excessively.

2. Always keep your dog leashed unless management specifically tells you otherwise.

3. Establishments listed in this book should allow well-behaved dogs of ALL sizes (at least up to 75 pounds) and in non-smoking rooms. If your dog is over 75-80 pounds, then please call the individual establishment to make sure they will allow your dog. We have listed some establishments which only allow dogs up to 50 pounds, but we try our best to make a note in the comments about the restrictions. All restaurants and attractions we list should allow dogs of all sizes.

4. Accommodations listed do not allow dogs to be left alone in the room unless specified by hotel management. If the establishment does not allow pets to be left alone, try hiring a local pet sitter to watch your dog in the room.

5. All restaurants listed as dog-friendly refer to outdoor seating only. While dogs are not permitted to sit in a chair at a restaurant's outdoor dining table, they should be allowed to sit or lay next to your table. We do not list outdoor restaurants that require your dog to be tied outside of a fenced area (with you at the dining table on one side and your dog on the other side of the fence). In our opinion, those are not truly dog-friendly restaurants. Restaurants listed may have seasonal outdoor seating.

6. Pet policies and management change often, especially within the lodging and restaurant industries. Please always call ahead to make sure an establishment still exists and is still dog-friendly.

**Preparation for a Road Trip**

*A Month Before*

If you don't already have one, get a pet identification tag for your dog. It should have your dog's name, your name and phone number. Consider using a cell phone number, a home number and, if possible, the number of where you will be staying.

Get a first aid kit for your dog. It comes in very handy if you need to remove any ticks. The kits are usually available at a pet store, a veterinary office or on the Internet.

If you do not already have a dog harness for riding the car, consider purchasing one for your dog's and your own safety. A loose dog in the car can fly into the windshield, out of the car, or into you and injure you or cause you to lose control of the car. Dog harnesses are usually sold at pet stores or on the Internet.

Make a trip to the vet if necessary for the following:

- A current rabies tag for your dog's collar. Also get paperwork with proof of the rabies vaccine.
- Dogs can possibly get heartworm from mosquitoes in the mountains, rural areas or on hikes. Research or talk to your vet and ask him or her if the area you are traveling to has a high risk of heartworm disease. The vet may suggest placing your dog on a monthly heartworm preventative medicine.
- Consider using some type of flea preventative for your dog, preferably a natural remedy. This is out of courtesy for the dog-friendly hotels plus for the comfort of your pooch.
- Make sure your dog is in good health.

*Several Days Before*

Make sure you have enough dog food for the duration of the trip.

If your dog is on any medication, remember to bring it along.

Some dog owners will also purchase bottled water for the trip, because some dogs can get sick from drinking water they are not used to. Talk to your vet for more information.

*The Day Before*

Do not forget to review DogFriendly.com's Etiquette for the Traveling Dog!

*Road Trip Day*

Remember to pack all of your dog's necessities: food, water, dog dishes, leash, snacks and goodies, several favorite toys, brush, towels for dirty paws, plastic bags for cleaning up after your dog, doggie first aid kit, possibly dog booties if you are venturing to an especially cold or hot region, and bring any medicine your dog might be taking.

Before you head out, put on that doggie seat belt harness.

*On The Road*

Keep it cool and well ventilated in the car for your dog.

Stop at least every 2-3 hours so your dog can relieve him or herself. Also offer him or her water during the stops.

Never leave your pet alone in a parked car - even in the shade with the window cracked open. According to the Los Angeles SPCA, on a hot day, a car can heat up to 160 degrees in minutes, potentially causing your pet (or child) heat stroke, brain damage, and even death.

If your dog needs medical attention during your trip, check the yellow pages phone book in the area and look under Veterinarians. If you do not see an emergency vet listed, call any local vet even   during the evening hours and they can usually inform you of the closest emergency vet.

## Etiquette for the Traveling Dog

So you have found the perfect getaway spot that allows dogs, but maybe you have never traveled with your dog. Or maybe you are a seasoned dog traveler. But do you know all of your doggie etiquette? Basic courtesy rules, like your dog should be leashed unless a place specifically allows your dog to be leash-free. And do you ask for a paper bowl or cup for your thirsty pooch at an outdoor restaurant instead of letting him or her drink from your water glass?

There are many do's and don'ts when traveling with your best friend. We encourage all dog owners to follow a basic code of doggie etiquette, so places will continue to allow and welcome our best friends. Unfortunately all it takes is one bad experience for an establishment to stop allowing dogs. Let's all try to be on our best behavior to keep and, heck, even encourage new places to allow our pooches.

*Everywhere...*

- Well-Behaved Dogs. Only travel or go around town with a well-behaved dog that is friendly to people and especially children. If your dog is not comfortable around other people, you might consider taking your dog to obedience classes or hiring a professional trainer. Your well-behaved dog should also be potty trained and not bark excessively in a hotel or other lodging room. We believe that dogs should be kept on leash. If a dog is on leash, he or she is easier to bring under control. Also, many establishments require that dogs be on leash and many people around you will feel more comfortable as well. And last, please never leave your dog alone in a hotel or other lodging room unless you have the approval from the establishment's management.

- Leashed Dogs. Please always keep your dog leashed, unless management specifically states otherwise. Most establishments (including lodging, outdoor restaurants, attractions, parks, beaches, stores and festivals) require that your dog be on leash. Plus most cities and counties have an official leash law that requires pets to be leashed at all times when not on your property. Keeping your dog on leash will also prevent any unwanted contact with other people that are afraid of dogs, people that do not appreciate strange dogs coming up to them, and even other dog owners who have a leashed dog. Even when on leash, do not let your pooch visit with other people or dogs unless welcomed. Keeping dogs on leash will also protect  them from running into traffic, running away, or getting injured by wildlife or other dogs. Even the most well-behaved and trained dogs can be startled by something, especially in a new environment.

- Be Considerate. Always clean up after your dog. Pet stores sell pooper scooper bags. You can also buy sandwich bags from your local grocery store. They work quite well and are cheap!

*At Hotels or Other Types of Lodging...*

- Unless it is obvious, ask the hotel clerk if dogs are allowed in the hotel lobby. Also, because of health codes, dogs are usually not allowed into a lobby area while it is being used for serving food like continental breakfast. Dogs may be allowed into the area once there is no food being served, but check with management first.

- Never leave your dog alone in the hotel room without the permission of management. The number one reason hotel management does not allow dogs is because some people leave them in the room alone. Some dogs, no matter how well-trained, can cause damage, bark continuously or scare the housekeepers. Unless the hotel management allows it, please make sure your dog is never left alone in the room. If you need to leave your dog in the room, consider hiring a local pet sitter.

- While you are in the room with your dog, place the Do Not Disturb sign on the door or keep the deadbolt locked. Many housekeepers have been surprised or scared by dogs when entering a room.

- In general, do not let your pet on the bed or chairs, especially if your dog sheds easily and might leave pet hair on the furniture. Some very pet-friendly accommodations will actually give you a sheet to lay over the bed so your pet can join you. If your pet cannot resist coming hopping onto the furniture with you, bring your own sheet.

- When your dog needs to go to the bathroom, take him or her away from the hotel rooms and the bushes located right next to the rooms. Try to find some dirt or bushes near the parking lot. Some hotels have a designated pet walk area.

*At Outdoor Restaurants...*

- Tie your dog to your chair, not the table (unless the table is secured to the ground). If your dog decides to get up and move away from the table, he or she will not take the entire table.

- If you want to give your dog some water, please ask the waiter/waitress to bring a paper cup or bowl of water for your dog. Do not use your own water glass. Many restaurants and even other guests frown upon this.

- Your pooch should lay or sit next to your table. At restaurants, dogs are not allowed to sit on the chairs or tables, or eat off the tables. This type of activity could make a restaurant owner or manager ban dogs. And do not let your pooch beg from other customers. Unfortunately, not everyone loves dogs!

- About Restaurant Laws regarding dogs at restaurants
State health codes in the United States prohibit all animals except for service animals inside indoor sections  of restaurants. In recent years some health departments have begun banning dogs from some outdoor restaurant areas. It is complicated to determine where dogs are and are not allowed outdoors because most State laws are vague. They state something such as "Animals are not allowed on the premises of a food establishment". These laws also define animals to include "birds, vermin and insects" which are always present at outdoor restaurants. Various health departments have various interpretations of where the premises start and stop. Some allow dogs at outdoor areas where food is served, some allow dogs at outdoor areas only where you bring your own food to the table. Some will allow special pet-friendly areas or will allow dogs on the outside of the outer most tables. Any city or county can issue a variance to State law if it wants to allow dogs into outdoor (or indoor) restaurants. This can be done in two ways, directly by the local health department or through a vote of the local government. If a restaurant that you are visiting with your dog cites some  curious requirement it is probably due to the health code. Please also understand that in all places the owner of a restaurant has the choice to not allow dogs with the exception of service dogs. Nationally, Austin, Dallas, Orlando, Chicago, Denver and Alexandria forced law changes to allow dogs at outdoor restaurants when their health departments went too far in banning dogs from outdoor seats. Dogs are now allowed in outdoor areas in these cities through variances (or in Orlando's case) changing Florida state law. For up to date information please see http://www.dogfriendly.com/dining . The laws are in a state of flux at the moment so please understand that they may change.

*At Retail Stores...*

- Keep a close eye on your dog and make sure he or she does not go to the bathroom in the store. Store owners that allow dogs inside assume that responsible dog owners will be entering their store. Before entering a dog-friendly store, visit your local pet store first. They are by far the most forgiving. If your dog does not go to the bathroom there, then you are off to a great start! If your dog does make a mistake in any store, clean it up. Ask the store clerk for paper towels or something similar so you can clean up any mess.

- In most states dogs are allowed in stores, shops and other private buildings with the exception of grocery stores and restaurants. The decision to allow dogs is the business owner's and you can always ask if you may bring your dog inside. Also in most states packaged foods (bottled sodas, waters, bags of cookies or boxes of snacks) does not cause a store to be classified as a grocery. Even pet stores do sell these items . In many states, drinks such as coffee, tea and water are also allowed. You can order food from a restaurant to a pet-friendly establishment (so long as the establishment is not also the restaurant with the kitchen) in most areas.

*At Festivals and Outdoor Events...*

Make sure your dog has relieved himself or herself before entering a festival or event area. The number one reason that most festival coordinators do not allow dogs is because some dogs go to the bathroom on a vendor's booth or in areas where people might sit.

## Breed Specific Laws and the Effect of These Laws on Travel With Dogs

There has been a trend in cities, counties, states and provinces towards what is known as Breed-Specific Laws (BSL) in which a municipality bans or restricts the freedoms of dog owners with specific breeds of dogs. These laws vary from place to place and are effecting a greater number of dog owners every year. Most people may think that these laws effect only the "Pit Bull" but this is not always the case. Although the majority of dogs effected are pit-bulls other breeds of dogs as well as mixed breeds that include targeted breeds are also  named in the various laws in North America. These laws range from registration requirements and leash or muzzle requirements to extreme laws in which the breed is banned from the municipality outright. Some places may even be permitted to confiscate a visitor's dog who unknowingly enters the region with a banned breed.

As of August 29, 2005 the province of Ontario, Canada (including Toronto, Niagara Falls, and Ottawa) passed a very broad breed-specific law banning Pit Bulls and "similar" dogs from the province. The law allows for confiscation of visiting dogs as well as dogs living in Ontario. It is extremely important that people visiting Ontario make sure that they are able to prove that their dog is not a Pit Bull with other documentation. Various cities throughout the U.S. and Canada have muzzle requirements for Pit Bulls and other restrictions on targeted breeds as well. Breed-specific laws do get repealed as well. In October, 2005 the city of Vancouver, BC removed its requirement that Pit Bulls be muzzled in public and now only requires dogs with a known history of aggressiveness to be muzzled.

The breed specific laws usually effect pit bull type dogs but are often vaguely written and may also effect mixed breed dogs that resemble the targeted breeds. These laws are always changing and can be passed by cities, counties and even states and provinces. We recommend that travelers with dogs check into whether they are effected by such laws. You may check www.DogFriendly.com/bsl for links to further information on BSL.

DogFriendly.com does not support breed-specific laws. Most people who take their dogs out in public are responsible and those that choose to train a dog to be viscous will simply choose another breed, causing other breeds to be banned or regulated in the future.

## Customs Information for Traveling Between the United States and Canada

If you will be traveling between the United States and Canada, identification for Customs and Immigration is required. U.S. and Canadian citizens traveling across the border need the following:

*People*

- A passport or passport card is now required to move between the U.S. and Canada. Children also need a passport of their own now.

*Dogs*

- Dogs must be free of evidence of diseases communicable to humans when possibly examined at the port of entry.

- Valid rabies vaccination certificate (including an expiration date usually up to 3 years from the actual vaccine date and a veterinarian's signature). If no expiration date is specified on the certificate, then the certificate is acceptable if the date of the vaccination is not more than 12 months before the date of arrival. The certificate must show that the dog had the rabies vaccine at least 30 days prior to entry.

- Young puppies must be confined at a place of the owner's choosing until they are three months old, then they must be vaccinated. They must remain in confinement for 30 days after the vaccination.

## Chain Hotel Websites

| | | |
|---|---|---|
| Best Western: bestwestern.com | Candlewood Suites: ichotelsgroup.com | Clarion: choicehotels.com |
| Comfort Inn: choicehotels.com | Days Inn: daysinn.com | Drury Inn: druryhotels.com |
| Extended Stay: extendedstayhotels.com | Hilton: hilton.com | Holiday Inn: ichotelsgroup.com |
| Howard Johnson: hojo.com | Kimpton Group: kimptonhotels.com | La Quinta: lq.com |
| Loews Hotels: loewshotels.com | Marriott: marriott.com | Motel 6: motel6.com |
| Quality Inn: www.choicehotels.com | Red Roof Inn: redroof.com | Residence Inn: residenceinn.com |
| Sheraton: starwoodhotels.com | Sleep Inn: choicehotels.com | Staybridge Suites: ichotelsgroup.com |
| Super 8: super8.com | Townplace Suites: towneplaceSuites.com | Westin: starwoodhotels.com |

## Traveling with a Dog By Air

Many commercial airlines allow dogs to be transported with the traveling public. Small dogs, usually no more than 15 to 20 pounds and with shorter legs, may travel in a carrier in the cabin with you. They must usually be kept under the seat. Any larger dogs must travel in a kennel in the cargo hold. It can be difficult for dogs to travel in the cargo hold of airplanes. Most airlines restrict cargo hold pet transportation during very hot and cold periods. Most require that you notify them when making reservations about the pet as they limit the number of pets allowed on each plane and the size of the carriers may vary depending on what type of plane is being used. There are no commercial airlines that we are aware of today that will allow dogs larger than those that fit in a carrier under a seat to fly in the cabin. Service animals are allowed in the cabin and are harnessed during takeoff and landing. The FAA is now tracking pet injury and death information from airline cargo section pet travel. Their monthly reports are at the website airconsumer.ost.dot.gov/reports. In the past we have been more concerned with larger dogs in the cargo hold of airplanes. However, with the newer jets, it is becoming safer and more common, although incidents can happen.

*Charters and Shared Charters:*

A charter airline flight is a flight reserved by an individual, a company or a small party or club to transport in smaller jets or other small aircraft their group on a schedule and route selected by them. This option is always available to people traveling with dogs but is very expensive. A charter is a flight reserved by you. A shared charter is when you "hitch" a ride on a charter set up by another party. This is still quite expensive, but less so than a solo charter. Many charter aircraft will allow your dog of all sizes on board.

*Commercial Airlines:*

| Airline | Cabin – Small Dogs Allowed | Cargo – Dogs Allowed | Phone | Fees (US) (each way) | General Information (For more updated information see: dogfriendly.com/airlines) |
|---|---|---|---|---|---|
| Air Canada | Yes | Yes | 888-247-2262 (US) | $50 to $60 each way (cabin) - $105 to $120 each way (cargo) - North America more elsewhere | Pets are allowed on domestic Canadian/North American flights; Health Cert rqd plus some shots |
| Alaska Air | Yes | Yes | 800-252-7522 | $100 each way (cabin), $100 each way (cargo) | Pets not allowed as Chked Bags during winter months; Health Cert within 30 days; |
| American | Yes | Yes | 800-433-7300 | $125 each way (cabin), $200 each way (cargo) | Dogs, including the kennel, can weigh no more than 100 pounds for the cargo area. Dogs are not allowed in the cabin for International flights. |
| Delta | Yes | Yes | 800-221-1212 | $125 each way (cabin), $200 each way domestic $ more each way Int'l (cargo) | Only a limited # of pets allowed per flight, so check ahead. There is no cert required for domestic flights. |
| Frontier | Yes | No | 800-432-1359 | $75 each way small/ medium kennels, | Dogs may not be transported in cargo. |
| Jet Blue | Yes | No | 800-538-2583 | $100 each way (cabin only) | 4 pets allowed per flight; 20 lbs or less (with kennel) in cabin |
| Southwest | Yes | No | 800-IFLY-SWA | $95 each way (cabin only) | Dogs in cabin must fit in a carrier under the seat. Reservations with pets must be made by phone. |
| United | Yes | Yes | 800-241-6522 | $125 each way (cabin), $169 to $210 each way (cargo) | 800-825-3788 to ship unaccompanied pets; Pets must be booked within 7 days of flight; 30 day health certificate; Short nosed dogs not allowed in summer |
| Virgin America | Yes | No | 877-359-8474 | $100 each way | Pets can only be booked in the Main Cabin (Coach) and can not weigh over 20 pounds. |

## Traveling with a Pet On Amtrak

Dogs and cats up to 20 pounds are now allowed to travel with you on certain United States Amtrak routes. There are certain restrictions, however. Only certain train routes allow pets. Pet travel is restricted to routes under 7 hours long. There is a maximum of five pets per train and it is first come first serve with regard to buying pet tickets. So you should make your reservation as soon as possible. A passenger may only take one pet. There is a $25 pet fee for each travel segment. In the event of a service disruption, Amtrak will try to make accommodations at a pet-friendly hotel but will not guarantee that they can. The dog must remain in a pet carrier at all times on the train. The pet carrier counts as one of your pieces of baggage allowed.

At check-in at the station you must arrive 30 minutes before departure to allow the staff to verify eligibility of your pet. They will verify the size and weight, see that the pet is not distruptive such as non-stop barking or growling and have you sign a pet document. The pet must be at least 8 weeks old. You will need to certify that your pet is up to date on vaccinations.

Pets may not be shipped on Amtrak or checked as baggage. They must travel with a person.

Here are the routes that pets are allowed on at this time. You should check at www.amtrak.com/pets for updates as your trip approaches.

Northeast Routes:
Acela Express (Weekends and Holidays Only), Adirondack (excluding Canada), Downeaster, Empire Service, Ethan Allen Express, Maple Leaf (excluding Canada), Northeast Regional, Vermonter

Eastern Routes:
Capitol Limited, Carolinian, Cardinal, Crescent, Lake Shore Limited, Piedmont, Palmetto, Silver Star, Silver Meteor

Midwest Routes:
California Zephyr, Capitol Limited, Cardinal, City of New Orleans, Empire Builder, Heartland Flyer, Hiawatha, Hossier State, Carl Sandburg, Illinois Zephyr, Illini, Saluki, Pere Marquette, Wolverine, Blue Water, Lake Shore Limited, Missouri River Runner, Southwest Chief, Texas Eagle

Western Routes:
Amrtak Cascades (excluding Canada), California Zephyr, Coast Starlight, Southwest Chief, Sunset Limited, Texas Eagle

To make reservations call 1-800-USA-RAIL or visit a staffed station. At this time, you cannot make your pet reservations online. Service animals are allowed on all trains and routes for no fee.


VIA Rail in Canada

In Canada, dogs of all sizes are allowed to be taken as baggage on the VIA trains that serve the entire country. They are not allowed in passenger cars regardless of their size. So the train must offer baggage service for you to take your dog. Since the baggage cars are not air-conditioned pets are not allowed between June 1 and September 22. The fee for taking a dog in a carrier is between $30 and $50.

You are allowed to take your pet on longer train routes in Canada – including cross country. It will be your responsibility to take your pet out at station stops for a quick bathroom break and to feed and give water to your pet. You can access the pet at the stations and many of the stops are 5 – 15 minutes long allowing you time for this. It appears that you should have no more than about 5 hours between stops on normal schedules.

For reservations and to check if a route allows pets call VIA Rail at 888-842-7245. For more online information see www.viarail.ca/en/travel-info/baggage/travelling-with-pets


Intercity Buses

Unfortunately, Greyhound and all intercity bus routes and lines in the United States do not allow any pets of any size. Only service dogs are allowed. This policy has been in place for years.

Chapter 1

# Dog-Friendly Lodging

# Alabama Listings

Candlewood Suites Alabaster
1004 Balmoral Drive
Alabaster, AL
205-620-0188

Quality Inn Alexander City
2945 Highway 280
Alexander City, AL
256-234-5900

Sleep Inn Athens
1115 Audubon Lane
Athens, AL
256-232-4700

Super 8 - Athens
1325 Us Highway 72 East
Athens, AL

256-233-1446

Holiday Inn Express Atmore
111 Lakeview Circle
Atmore, AL
251-368-1585

Days Inn - Attalla
801 Cleveland Avenue
Attalla, AL
256-538-7861

Homelodge - Attalla
901 Cleveland Avenue
Attalla, AL

256-538-4003

Relax Inn
915 East 5th Avenue
Attalla, AL

256-570-0117

Econo Lodge Auburn
2145 South College St.
Auburn, AL
334-826-8900

Microtel Inn & Suites By Wyndham
Auburn
2174 South College Street
Auburn, AL

334-826-1444

Best Western Plus Bessemer Hotel &
Suites
5041 Academy Lane
Bessemer, AL
205-481-1950

Best Western Plus Carlton Suites
140 State Farm Parkway
Birmingham, AL
205-940-9990

Candlewood Suites Birmingham
600 Corporate Ridge
Birmingham, AL

205-991-0272

Days Inn Birmingham
905, 11th Court West
Birmingham, AL

205-324-4510

Days Inn Birmingham, Al
1485 Montgomery Highway
Birmingham, AL

205-823-4300

Days Inn Galleria-Birmingham
1800 Riverchase Drive  ;
Birmingham, AL

205-985-7500

Drury Inn & Suites Birmingham
Southeast
3510 Grandview Parkway
Birmingham, AL

205-967-2450

Drury Inn & Suites Birmingham
Southwest
160 State Farm Parkway
Birmingham, AL

205-940-9500

Embassy Suites Hotel Birmingham
2300 Woodcrest Place
Birmingham, AL

205-879-7400

Extended Stay America -
Birmingham - Perimeter Park South
12 Perimeter Park South
Birmingham, AL

205-967-3800

Homewood Suites By HiltonÂ®
Birmingham-South/Inverness, Al
215 Inverness Center Drive
Birmingham, AL

205-995-9823

Red Roof Inn Birmingham South
1466 Montgomery Highway
Birmingham, AL

205-822-2224

Residence Inn Birmingham
Downtown Uab
821 20th Street South
Birmingham, AL

205-731-9595

Residence Inn By Marriott
Birmingham Homewood

50 State Farm Parkway
Birmingham, AL

205-943-0044

Residence Inn By Marriott
Birmingham Inverness
3 Greenhill Parkway, At Us Highway
280
Birmingham, AL

205-991-8686

Sheraton Birmingham
2101 Richard Arrington Junior
Boulevard North
Birmingham, AL

205-324-5000

Towneplace Suites By Marriott
Birmingham Homewood
500 Wildwood Circle
Birmingham, AL

205-943-0114

Westin Birmingham
2221 Richard Arrington Jr. Boulevard
North
Birmingham, AL

205-307-3600

Quality Inn Calera
357 Highway 304
Calera, AL
205-668-3641

Days Inn Of Centre
1585 West Main Street
Centre, AL
256-927-1090

Days Inn - Childersburg
33669 Us Highway 280
Childersburg, AL
256-378-6007

Days Inn Clanton Al
2000 Big M Blvd
Clanton, AL
205-755-2420

Americas Best Value Inn
6349 AL Highway 157
Cullman, AL
256-734-8854

Econo Lodge Cullman
1655 County Road 437
Cullman, AL

256-734-2691

Econo Lodge Inn & Suites Fort
Rucker
444 N Daleville Ave
Daleville, AL
334-598-6304

Best Western River City Hotel
1305 Front Avenue Southwest
Decatur, AL
256-301-1388

Microtel Inn & Suites By Wyndham
Decatur
2226 Beltline Road Southwest
Decatur, AL

256-301-9995

Super 8 - Decatur-Priceville
70 Marco Drive
Decatur, AL

256-355-2525

Best Western Plus Two Rivers Hotel
& Suites
662 Highway 80 West
Demopolis, AL
334-289-2611

Days Inn Demopolis
1005 Us Hwy 80 East
Demopolis, AL

334-289-2500

Comfort Suites Dothan
1650 Westgate Parkway
Dothan, AL
334-792-9000

Days Inn Dothan
3071 Ross Clark Circle
Dothan, AL

334-671-3700

Econo Lodge Dothan
2910 Ross Clark Circle
Dothan, AL

334-673-8000

Residence Inn Dothan
186 Hospitality Lane
Dothan, AL

334-793-1030

Candlewood Suites Enterprise
203 Brabham Drive
Enterprise, AL
334-308-1102

Holiday Inn Express Hotel & Suites
Enterprise
9 North Pointe Boulevard
Enterprise, AL

334-347-2211

Rodeway Inn & Suites Enterprise
615 Boll Weevil Circle
Enterprise, AL

334-393-2304

Comfort Suites Eufaula

12 Paul Lee Pkwy
Eufaula, AL
334-616-0114

Days Inn Eufaula
1521 S Eufaula Avenue
Eufaula, AL

334-687-1000

Econo Lodge Eufaula
1243 ;North Eufaula Avenue
Eufaula, AL

334-687-0166

Quality Inn & Suites Eufaula
631 East Barbour Street
Eufaula, AL

334-687-4414

Econo Lodge Inn & Suites
Evergreen
215 Highway 83
Evergreen, AL
251-578-2100

Quality Inn Evergreen
1571 Ted Bates Road
Evergreen, AL

251-578-4701

Holiday Inn Express Fairhope - Point
Clear
19751 Greeno Road
Fairhope, AL
251-928-9191

Oak Haven Cottages
355 S Mobile Street
Fairhope, AL

251-928-5431

Knights Inn Florence
1915 Florence Blvd
Florence, AL
256-766-2620

Marriott Shoals Hotel And Spa
800 Cox Creek Parkway South
Florence, AL

256-246-3600

Residence Inn By Marriott Florence
1000 Sweetwater Avenue
Florence, AL

256-764-9966

Super 8 Motel - Florence
101 Florence Blvd.
Florence, AL

256-757-2167

Adam's Outdoors Cherokee Camp
6110 Cherokee County Road #103
Fort Payne, AL

256-845-2988

Days Inn Fultondale
616 Decatur Highway
Fultondale, AL
205-849-0111

Comfort Suites Gadsden
96 Walker Street
Gadsden, AL
256-538-5770

Rodeway Inn Gadsden
3909 West Meighan Blvd
Gadsden, AL

256-543-0323

Best Western Inn
56 Cahaba Road
Greenville, AL
334-382-9200

Days Inn - Greenville
946 Fort Dale
Greenville, AL

334-382-3118

Magnuson Inn And Suites Gulf
Shores
3049 W 1st Street
Gulf Shores, AL
251-968-8604

Staybridge Suites Gulf Shores
3947 State Highway 59
Gulf Shores, AL

251-975-1030

Lake Guntersville State Park
Cottages and Chalets
7966 H 227
Guntersville, AL
256-571-5440

Wyndham Garden Lake Guntersville
2140 Gunter Avenue
Guntersville, AL

256-582-2220

Days Inn Hamilton
1849 Military Street
Hamilton, AL
205-921-1790

Econo Lodge Inn & Suites Hamilton
2031 Military Street South
Hamilton, AL

205-921-7831

Quality Inn Homewood
155 Vulcan Road
Homewood, AL
205-945-9600

Super 8 Homewood Birmingham
Area

Dog-Friendly Lodging - Please always call ahead to make sure an establishment is still dog-friendly.

140 Vulcan Road
Homewood, AL

205-945-9888

Homewood Suites By Hilton
Birmingham Sw/Riverchase Galleria
121 Riverchase Parkway East
Hoover, AL
205-637-2900

Residence Inn Marriott Hoover
2725 John Hawkins Pkwy
Hoover, AL

205-733-1655

Candlewood Suites Huntsville
201 Exchange Place
Huntsville, AL
256-830-8222

Extended Stay America -Huntsville -
U.S. Space And Rocket Center
4751 Govenors House Dr.
Huntsville, AL

256-830-9110

Microtel Inn & Suites By Wyndham
Huntsville
1820 Chase Creek Row
Huntsville, AL

256-859-6655

Residence Inn By Marriott Huntsville
6305 Residence Inn Road
Huntsville, AL

256-895-0444

Towneplace Suites By Marriott
Huntsville
1125 Mcmurtrie Drive
Huntsville, AL

256-971-5277

Knights Inn Lanett
2314 South Broad Avenue
Lanett, AL
334-644-2181

Leeds-Days Inn
1838 Asheville Road
Leeds, AL
205-699-9833

Adam's Outdoors;""; Cherokee Camp
and Yellow River Cottage
6110 H 103
Mentone, AL
256-845-2988

Candlewood Suites Mobile
121 North Royal Street
Mobile, AL
251-690-7818

Drury Inn Mobile

824 West I-65 Service Road South
Mobile, AL

251-344-7700

Extended Stay America - Mobile -
Spring Hill
508 Spring Hill Plaza Ct.
Mobile, AL

251-344-2514

Holiday Inn Mobile West - I-10
5465 Hwy 90 W Government Blvd
Mobile, AL

251-666-5600

Quality Inn & Suites Mobile
150 West I-65 Service Road
Mobile, AL

251-343-4949

Residence Inn By Marriott Mobile
950 S Beltline Highway
Mobile, AL

251-304-0570

THE BATTLE HOUSE
RENAISSANCE MOBILE HOTEL &
SPA, A Marriott Luxury & Lifestyle
Hotel
26 North Royal Street
Mobile, AL

251-338-2000

Towneplace Suites By Marriott
Mobile
1075 Montlimar Drive
Mobile, AL

251-345-9588

Best Western Inn
4419 South Alabama Avenue
Monroeville, AL
251-575-9999

Mockingbird Inn & Suites
4389 South Alabama Avenue
Monroeville, AL

251-743-3297

Baymont Inn & Suites Montgomery
5837 Monticello Drive
Montgomery, AL
334-277-4442

Baymont Inn & Suites Montgomery
South
4273 Troy Highway
Montgomery, AL

334-288-8844

Candlewood Suites Montgomery-
North
9151 Boyd Cooper Parkway

Montgomery, AL

334-277-0677

Doubletree By Hilton Montgomery
Downtown
120 Madison Avenue
Montgomery, AL

334-264-2231

Drury Inn & Suites Montgomery
1124 Eastern Boulevard
Montgomery, AL

334-273-1101

Embassy Suites Hotel Montgomery-
Conference Center
300 Tallapoosa Street
Montgomery, AL

334-269-5055

Extended Stay America -
Montgomery - Eastern Blvd.
2491 Eastern Boulevard
Montgomery, AL

334-279-1204

Home-Towne Suites Montgomery
5047 Towneplace Drive
Montgomery, AL

334-396-5505

Homewood Suites By HiltonÂ®
Montgomery
1800 Interstate Park Drive
Montgomery, AL

334-272-3010

Knights Inn Montgomery East
1185 Eastern Boulevard
Montgomery, AL

334-356-3335

Red Roof Inn Montgomery - Midtown
2625 Zelda Road
Montgomery, AL

334-269-9611

Residence Inn Montgomery
1200 Hilmar Court
Montgomery, AL

334-270-3300

Staybridge Suites Montgomery-
Eastchase
7800 Eastchase Parkway
Montgomery, AL

334-277-9383

Super 8 Moody
2451 Moody Parkway
Moody, AL
205-640-7091

Dog-Friendly Lodging - Please always call ahead to make sure an establishment is still dog-friendly.

Days Inn Opelika
1014 Anand Avenue
Opelika, AL
334-749-5080

Magnuson Hotel Opelika
1002 Columbus Parkway
Opelika, AL
334-749-1461

Americas Best Value Inn Oxford
Anniston
3 Recreation Drive
Oxford, AL
256-835-0300

Hampton Inn & Suites Oxford-
Anniston, Al
210 Colonial Drive
Oxford, AL
256-831-8958

Holiday Inn Express Hotel & Suites
Anniston/Oxford
160 Colonial Drive
Oxford, AL
256-835-8768

Red Roof Inn & Suites Oxford
138 Elm Street
Oxford, AL
256-831-0860

Super 8 Oxford
1600 Alabama Highway 21 South
Oxford, AL
265-835-1492

Quality Inn & Suites
858 Us Hwy. 231 South
Ozark, AL
334-774-7300

Quality Inn Prattville
797 Business Park Drive
Prattville, AL
334-365-6003

Days Inn - Priceville
63 Marco Drive
Priceville, AL
256-355-3297

Joe Wheeler State Park
201 McLean Drive
Rogersville, AL
256-685-2656

Microtel Inn & Suites By Wyndham
Saraland/North Mobile
1124 Shelton Beach Road
Saraland, AL
251-675-5045

Econo Lodge Scottsboro

23945 John T Reid Parkway
Scottsboro, AL
256-574-1212

Selma Hotel
1710 West Highland Avenue
Selma, AL

Days Inn Shorter
450 Main Street
Shorter, AL
334-727-6034

Red Roof Inn Sylacauga
40770 Highway 280
Sylacauga, AL
256-249-4321

Super 8 - Talladega
220 Haynes Street
Talladega, AL
256-315-9511

Days Inn Troy
1260 Hwy 231 South
Troy, AL
334-566-1630

Econo Lodge Troy
811 Us 231 Bypass
Troy, AL
334-566-7799

Candlewood Suites Tuscaloosa
651 Skyland Boulevard East
Tuscaloosa, AL
205-722-0999

Centerstone Inn Tuscaloosa
4700 Doris Pate Drive
Tuscaloosa, AL
205-556-3232

Jameson Inn
5021 Oscar Baxter Drive
Tuscaloosa, AL
205-345-5024

Wingate By Wyndham Tuscaloosa
4918 Skyland Blvd. E.
Tuscaloosa, AL
205-553-5400

Americas Best Inn & Suites York
17700 Highway 17 North
York, AL
205-392-9675

# Alaska Listings

America's Best Suites
4110 Spenard Road
Anchorage, AK
907-243-3433

Comfort Inn Downtown - Ship Creek
111 West Ship Creek Avenue
Anchorage, AK
907-277-6887

Guesthouse Inn & Suites Anchorage
321 East 5th Avenue
Anchorage, AK
907-276-7226

Hilton Anchorage
500 West Third Avenue
Anchorage, AK
907-272-7411

Long House Alaskan Hotel
4335 Wisconsin Street
Anchorage, AK
907-243-2133

Merrill Field Inn
420 Sitka Street
Anchorage, AK
907-276-4547

Microtel Inn & Suites By Wyndham
Anchorage Airport
5205 Northwood Drive
Anchorage, AK
907-245-5002

Parkwood Inn Extended Stay
4455 Juneau Street
Anchorage, AK
907-563-3590

Puffin Inn Anchorage
4400 Spenard Road
Anchorage, AK
907-243-4044

Residence Inn By Marriott Anchorage
Midtown
1025 35th Avenue
Anchorage, AK
907-563-9844

Sheraton Anchorage Hotel and Spa
401 East Sixth Avenue
Anchorage, AK
907-276-8700

Sourdough Lodge
801 Erickson Street
Anchorage, AK
907-279-4148

Super 8 Anchorage
3501 Minnesota Drive
Anchorage, AK
907-276-8884

Dog-Friendly Lodging - Please always call ahead to make sure an establishment is still dog-friendly.

The Lakefront Anchorage - A
Millennium Hotel
4800 Spenard Road
Anchorage, AK
907-243-2300

Long House Bethel Hotel
751 3rd Avenue
Bethel, AK
907-486-4300

Border City Motel & RV Park
Mile 1225 Alaska Hwy
Border City, AK
907-774-2205

Backwoods Lodge
At George Parks Hwy, Milepost 210
Cantwell, AK
907-768-2232

Chena Hot Springs
56.5 Chena Hot Springs Road
Chena Hot Springs, AK
907-451-8104

Alaska 7 Motel
Mile 270 Richardson Hwy
Delta Junction, AK
907-895-4848

Alaskan Steak House & Motel
265 Richardson Hwy
Delta Junction, AK

907-895-5175

Clearwater Lodge
7028 Remington Rd
Delta Junction, AK

907-895-5152

McKinley Chalet Resort
Milepost 238 George Parks H
Denali, AK
907-267-7234

McKinley Village Lodge
Mile 231 Alaska H3
Denali, AK

907-683-8900

Microtel Inn & Suites By Wyndham
Eagle River/Anchorage Area
13049 Old Glenn Highway
Eagle River, AK
907-622-6000

Golden North Motel
4888 Old Airport Way
Fairbanks, AK
907-479-6201

Pike's Waterfront Lodge
1850 Hoselton Rd
Fairbanks, AK

907-456-4500

The New Caribou Hotel
Box 329
Glennallen, AK
907-822-3302

Glacier Bay Lodge and Tours
179 Bartlett Cove
Gustavus, AK
888-BAY-TOUR

Captain's Choice
108 2nd Avenue North
Haines, AK
907-766-3111

Eagle's Nest Motel
1069 Haines Hwy
Haines, AK

907-766-2891

Fort Seward Lodge
39 Mud Bay Rd
Haines, AK

907-766-2009

Hotel Halsingland
13 Fort Seward Dr
Haines, AK

907-766-2000

Thunderbird Motel
216 Dalton Street
Haines, AK

907-766-2131

Denail Park Hotel
Otto Lake Road and Parks Highway
Healy, AK
907-683-1800

Best Western Bidarka Inn
575 Sterling Highway
Homer, AK
907-235-8148

Driftwood Inn
135 W Bunnell Avenue
Homer, AK

907-235-8019

Good Karma Inn
57480 Taku Avenue
Homer, AK

907-235-4728

Heritage Hotel
147 E Pioneer Avenue
Homer, AK

907-235-7787

Homer Seaside Cottages
58901 East End Road

Homer, AK

907-235-2716

Jenny Lane Cottage
353 D Jenny Lane
Homer, AK

907-235-5434

Lakewood Inn Bed and Breakfast
984 Ocean Dr #1
Homer, AK

907-235-6144

Otter Cove Resort
PO Box 2543
Homer, AK

907-235-7770

Extended Stay America - Juneau -
Shell Simmons Drive
1800 Shell Simmons Drive
Juneau, AK
907-790-6435

Juneau Hotel
1250 W 9th Street
Juneau, AK

907-586-5666

Prospector Hotel Juneau
375 Whittier Street
Juneau, AK

907-586-3737

Super 8 Motel - Juneau
2295 Trout Street
Juneau, AK

907-789-4858

The Driftwood Hotel
435 Willoughby Avenue
Juneau, AK

907-586-2280

Best Western Plus Landing
3434 Tongass Avenue
Ketchikan, AK
907-225-5166

Ketchikan`s Black Bear Inn - Bed And
Breakfast
5528 North Tongass Highway
Ketchikan, AK

907-225-4343

Super 8 Ketchikan
2151 Sea Level Drive
Ketchikan, AK

907-225-9088

The Narrows Inn, Restaurant and
Marina

4871 N Tongass H/H 7
Ketchikan, AK

907-247-2600

King Salmon Inn
MP 13, Alaska Peninsula H
King Salmon, AK
907-246-3444

Shelikof Lodge
211 Thorsheim Street
Kodiak, AK
907-486-4141

A Cottage on the Bay
13710 Beach Drive
Lowell Point, AK
907-224-8237

Gold Miners Hotel
918 South Colony Way
Palmer, AK
907-745-6160

Paxson Inn and Lodge
Mile 185 Richardson H
Paxson, AK
907-822-3330

Scandia House
110 N Nordic Drive
Petersburg, AK
907-772-4281

Marina Motel
Mile 1 Seward H
Seward, AK
907-224-5518

New Seward Hotel
217 5th Avenue
Seward, AK

907-224-8001

Seward Cabins
31730 Bronze Avenue
Seward, AK

907-224-4891

Super 8 Sitka
404 Sawmill Creek Road
Sitka, AK
907-747-8804

Sgt Preston's Lodge
370 6th Ave
Skagway, AK
907-983-2521

Westmark Inn Skagway
Third and Spring Streets
Skagway, AK

907-983-6000

Talkeetna Inn
25 Coffee Lane
Talkeetna, AK

907-733-7530

Burnt Paw Cabins
Box 7
Tok, AK
907-883-4121

Cleft on the Rock Bed and Breakfast
Mile 0.5 Sundog Trail
Tok, AK

907-883-4219

Showshoe Motel
Mile 1314 Alaska Hwy
Tok, AK

907-883-4511

Westmark Tok Hotel
Alaska Hwy & Glenn Hwy
Tok, AK

907-883-5174

Young's Motel
Box 482
Tok, AK

907-883-4411

The Grand Aleutian
498 Salmon Way
Unalaska, AK
907-581-3844

Totem Hotel & Suites
144 East Egan Drive
Valdez, AK
907-835-4443

Best Western Lake Lucille Inn
1300 West Lake Lucille Drive
Wasilla, AK
907-373-1776

# Arizona Listings

Motel 6 Apache Junction
251 East 29th Avenue
Apache Junction, AZ
480-288-8888

Best Western Quail Hollow Inn
699 North Ocotillo Road
Benson, AZ
520-586-3646

Super 8 Benson
855 North Ocotillo Rd
Benson, AZ

520-586-1530

The Gardens at Mile High Ranch
901 Tombstone Canyon Road
Bisbee, AZ
520-432-3866

The Sleepy Dog Guest House
212A Opera Drive
Bisbee, AZ

520-432-3057

Days Inn Buckeye
25205 W Yuma Rd
Buckeye, AZ
623-386-5400

Days Inn Bullhead City
1126 Highway 95
Bullhead City, AZ
928-754-3000

El Rio Waterfront Resort & RV Park
1641 H 95
Bullhead City, AZ
928-763-4385

Comfort Inn Camp Verde
340 North Goswick Way
Camp Verde, AZ
928-567-9000

Days Inn Camp Verde, Arizona
1640 West Highway 260
Camp Verde, AZ
928-567-3700

The Boulders Resort & Spa, Curio
Collection By Hilton
34631 N. Tom Darlington Drive
Carefree, AZ
480-488-9009

Super 8 Motel - Casa Grande
2066 East Florence Boulevard
Casa Grande, AZ
520-836-8800

Comfort Inn Chandler
255 N. Kyrene Road
Chandler, AZ
480-705-8882

Comfort Inn Chandler
7400 West Boston Street
Chandler, AZ

480-857-4969

Crowne Plaza Phoenix - Chandler
Golf Resort
One San Marcos Place
Chandler, AZ

480-812-0900

Hilton Phoenix - Chandler
2929 Frye Road
Chandler, AZ

480-899-7400

Homewood Suites By Hilton Phoenix
Chandler Fashion Center
1221 S. Spectrum Blvd.

Chandler, AZ

480-963-5700

Homewood Suites By Hilton
Phoenix/Chandler
7373 West Detroit Street
Chandler, AZ

480-753-6200

Hyatt Place Phoenix/Chandler
Fashion-Center
3535 West Chandler Boulevard
Chandler, AZ

480-812-9600

Quality Inn Chandler
255 North Kyrene Road
Chandler, AZ

480-705-8882

Residence Inn Phoenix Chandler
200 North Federal Street
Chandler, AZ

480-782-1551

Sheraton Grand at Wild Horse Pass
5594 W Wild Horse Pass Blvd
Chandler, AZ

602-225-0100

Super 8 Chandler
7171 West Chandler Boulevard
Chandler, AZ

480-961-3888

Best Western Desert Oasis
I-10 Exit 1 South Frontage Road
Cibola, AZ
928-923-9711

Days Inn Casa Grande
5300 South Sunland Gin Road
Eloy, AZ
520-426-9240

Quality Inn Eloy
7190 S Sunland Gin Road
Eloy, AZ

520-836-5000

Super 8 Eloy
4015 West Outer Drive
Eloy, AZ

520-466-2522

Best Western Pony Soldier Inn And
Suites
3030 East Route 66
Flagstaff, AZ
928-526-2388

Comfort Inn I-17 & I-40
2355 South Beulah Boulevard

Flagstaff, AZ

928-774-2225

Days Hotel Flagstaff
2200 East Butler Avenue
Flagstaff, AZ

Days Inn And Suites
3601 East Lockett Road
Flagstaff, AZ

928-527-1477

Days Inn Flagstaff - West Route 66
1000 West Hwy 66/I-40
Flagstaff, AZ

928-774-5221

Drury Inn & Suites Flagstaff
300 S Milton Rd
Flagstaff, AZ

928-773-4900

Econo Lodge University
914 South Milton Road
Flagstaff, AZ

928-774-7326

Howard Johnson Inn - Flagstaff
3300 East Route 66
Flagstaff, AZ

928-526-1826

Knights Inn Flagstaff
224 S. Mikes Pike
Flagstaff, AZ

928-774-8888

Quality Inn Flagstaff
2500 East Lucky Lane
Flagstaff, AZ

928-226-7111

Quality Inn I-40 & I-17
2000 South Milton Road
Flagstaff, AZ

928-774-8771

Ramada Flagstaff East
2350 East Lucky Lane
Flagstaff, AZ

928-779-3614

Springhill Suites By Marriott
Flagstaff
2455 South Beulah Boulevard
Flagstaff, AZ

928-774-8042

Super 8 Flagstaff I-40 Ex 198 Lucky
Lane
2540 East Lucky Lane
Flagstaff, AZ

928-773-4888

Super 8 I-40 Flagstaff Mall
3725 Kasper Avenue
Flagstaff, AZ

928-526-0818

Travelodge Flagstaff
1560 East Route 66
Flagstaff, AZ

928-774-7186

Best Western Space Age Lodge
401 East Pima
Gila Bend, AZ
928-683-2273

Knights Inn Gila Bend
1046 East Pima Street
Gila Bend, AZ

928-683-6303

Comfort Suites Univ. Of Phoenix
Stadium Area
9824 West Camelback Road
Glendale, AZ
623-271-9005

Residence Inn By Marriott Phoenix
Glendale Sport & Entertainment
7350 N. Zanjero Boulevard
Glendale, AZ

623-772-8900

Staybridge Suites Phoenix-Glendale
9340 West Cabela Drive
Glendale, AZ

623-842-0000

Best Western Plus Phoenix
Goodyear Inn
55 North Litchfield Road
Goodyear, AZ
623-932-3210

Comfort Suites Goodyear
15575 West Roosevelt Street
Goodyear, AZ

623-266-2884

Hampton Inn & Suites Goodyear
2000 North Litchfield Road
Goodyear, AZ

623-536-1313

Holiday Inn Express Goodyear
1313 North Litchfield Road
Goodyear, AZ

623-535-1313

Holiday Inn Hotel & Suites Goodyear
- West Phoenix Area
1188 North Dysart Road

Goodyear, AZ
623-547-1313

Residence Inn By Marriott Phoenix
Goodyear
2020 North Litchfield Road
Goodyear, AZ
623-866-1313

Towneplace Suites By Marriott
Phoenix Goodyear
13971 West Fillmore Street
Goodyear, AZ
623-535-5009

Red Feather Lodge
Highway 64
Grand Canyon, AZ
800-538-2345

Best Western Green Valley Inn
111 South la Canada Drive
Green Valley, AZ
520-625-2250

Comfort Inn Green Valley
90 West Esperanza
Green Valley, AZ
520-399-3736

Big Ten Resort Cabins
45 Main Street
Greer, AZ
928-735-7578

Best Western Arizonian Inn
2508 Navajo Boulevard
Holbrook, AZ
928-524-2611

Howard Johnson Holbrook
2608 E. Navajo Blvd
Holbrook, AZ
928-524-2566

Quality Inn Holbrook
2602 East Navajo Boulevard
Holbrook, AZ
928-524-6131

Ghost City Inn
541 Main Street
Jerome, AZ
928-634-4678

Best Western Plus King's Inn And
Suites
2930 East Andy Devine Avenue
Kingman, AZ
928-753-6101

Comfort Inn Kingman
3129 E Andy Devine
Kingman, AZ
928-718-1717

Days Inn Kingman East
3381 East Andy Devine
Kingman, AZ
928-757-7337

Days Inn Kingman West
3023 East Andy Devine
Kingman, AZ
928-753-7500

Econo Lodge Kingman
3421 East Andy Devine Avenue
Kingman, AZ
928-757-7878

Holiday Inn Express Hotel & Suites
Kingman, Az
3031 E. Andy Devine Ave.
Kingman, AZ
928-718-4343

Kingman I-40 Travelodge
3275 East Andy Devine
Kingman, AZ
928-757-1188

Quality Inn Kingman
1400 E Andy Devine Avenue
Kingman, AZ
928-753-4747

Rodeway Inn Kingman
3016 East Andy Devine Avenue
Kingman, AZ
928-753-9555

Springhill Suites By Marriott
Kingman Route 66
3101 E. Andy Devine Ave.
Kingman, AZ
928-753-8766

Super 8 Kingman
3401 East Andy Devine Avenue
Kingman, AZ
928-757-4808

Hampton Inn Lake Havasu City
245 London Bridge Road
Lake Havasu City, AZ
928-855-4071

Island Inn Hotel
1300 W McCulloch Blvd
Lake Havasu City, AZ
928-680-0606

Lake Havasu Travelodge
480 London Bridge Road
Lake Havasu City, AZ
928-680-9202

Quality Inn & Suites Lake Havasu
City
271 Lake Havasu Avenue South
Lake Havasu City, AZ
928-855-1111

Super 8 Lake Havasu City
305 London Bridge Road
Lake Havasu City, AZ
928-855-8844

Arizona Golf Resort, Spa &
Conference Center - Phoenix, Mesa
425 South Power Road
Mesa, AZ
480-832-3202

Best Western Superstition Springs
Inn
1342 S Power Road
Mesa, AZ
480-641-1164

Days Inn Mesa
333 West Juanita Avenue
Mesa, AZ
480-844-8900

Extended Stay America - Phoenix -
Mesa
455 W. Baseline Rd.
Mesa, AZ
480-632-0201

Extended Stay America - Phoenix -
Mesa - West
1920 W. Isabella
Mesa, AZ
480-752-2266

Hilton Phoenix/Mesa
1011 West Holmes Avenue
Mesa, AZ
480-833-5555

Mesa Travelodge Suites
4244 East Main Street
Mesa, AZ
480-832-5961

Quality Inn & Suites
1410 South Country Club Drive
Mesa, AZ
480-964-2897

Residence Inn Phoenix-Mesa
941 West Grove Avenue
Mesa, AZ
480-610-0100

Sleep Inn Mesa Superstition Springs

6347 East Southern Avenue
Mesa, AZ

480-807-7760

Super 8 Motel - Phoenix/Mesa/Gilbert Road
1550 South Gilbert Road
Mesa, AZ

480-545-0888

Super 8 Motel - Phoenix/Mesa/Power & Main
6733 E. Main Street
Mesa, AZ

480-981-6181

Candlewood Suites Nogales
875 North Frank Reed Road
Nogales, AZ
520-281-1111

Days Inn And Suites Page/Lake Powell
961 North Highway 89
Page, AZ
928-645-2800

Quality Inn At Lake Powell
287 North Lake Powell Boulevard
Page, AZ

928-645-8851

Super 8 Page
649 South Lake Powell Boulevard
Page, AZ

928-645-5858

Travelodge Page
207 North Lake Powell Boulevard
Page, AZ

928-645-2451

Wahweap Lodge and Marina
100 Lakeshore Drive
Page, AZ

928-645-2433

The Hermosa Inn
5532 North Palo Cristi Road
Paradise Valley, AZ
602-955-8614

Best Western Parker Inn
1012 Geronimo Avenue
Parker, AZ
928-669-6060

Quality Inn Payson
801 North Beeline Highway
Payson, AZ
928-474-3241

Comfort Suites Peoria Sports Complex
8473 West Paradise Lane

Peoria, AZ
623-334-3993

Days Hotel Peoria Glendale Area
8955 W Grand Avenue
Peoria, AZ

623-979-7200

Extended Stay America - Phoenix - Peoria
7345 W. Bell Rd.
Peoria, AZ

623-487-0020

Residence Inn By Marriott Phoenix Glendale Peoria
8435 West Paradise Lane
Peoria, AZ

623-979-2074

Arizona Biltmore, A Waldorf Astoria Hotel
2400 East Missouri Avenue
Phoenix, AZ
602-955-6600

Best Western Innsuites Phoenix Hotel & Suites
1615 East Northern Avenue
Phoenix, AZ

602-997-6285

Best Western Phoenix I-17 Metrocenter
8101 North Black Canyon Highway
Phoenix, AZ

602-864-6233

Candlewood Suites Phoenix
11411 North Black Canyon Highway
Phoenix, AZ

602-861-4900

Comfort Inn North Phoenix
2641 West Union Hills Drive
Phoenix, AZ

602-978-2222

Comfort Suites At Metro Center Phoenix
10210 North 26th Drive
Phoenix, AZ

602-861-3900

Crossland Economy Studios - Phoenix - Metro - Dunlap Ave.
2102 West Dunlap Ave
Phoenix, AZ

602-944-7828

Crosslands Phoenix - Metro - Black Canyon Highway
11211 N. Black Canyon Hwy

Phoenix, AZ

602-870-2999

Crowne Plaza Phoenix - Phx Airport
4300 East Washington Street
Phoenix, AZ

602-273-7778

Drury Inn & Suites Phoenix Happy Valley
2335 West Pinnacle Peak Road
Phoenix, AZ

623-879-8800

Embassy Suites Hotel Phoenix - Airport At 24th Street
2333 East Thomas Road
Phoenix, AZ

602-957-1910

Embassy Suites Hotel Phoenix-Biltmore
2630 East Camelback
Phoenix, AZ

602-955-3992

Embassy Suites Hotel Phoenix-North
2577 West Greenway Road
Phoenix, AZ

602-375-1777

Extended Stay America - Phoenix - Airport
3421 E. Elwood St.
Phoenix, AZ

602-438-2900

Extended Stay America - Phoenix - Airport - E. Oak St.
4357 East Oak St
Phoenix, AZ

602-225-2998

Extended Stay America - Phoenix - Chandler
14245 S. 50th St.
Phoenix, AZ

480-785-0464

Extended Stay America - Phoenix - Chandler - E. Chandler Blvd.
5035 E. Chandler Blvd
Phoenix, AZ

480-753-6700

Extended Stay America - Phoenix - Deer Valley
20827 N. 27th Ave
Phoenix, AZ

623-879-6609

Four Points by Sheraton Phoenix

North
2532 West Peoria Avenue
Phoenix, AZ

602-943-2341

Four Points by Sheraton Phoenix
North
2532 West Peoria Avenue
Phoenix, AZ

602-943-2341

Hilton Suites Phoenix
10 East Thomas Road
Phoenix, AZ

602-222-1111

Holiday Inn North Phoenix
12027 North 28th Drive
Phoenix, AZ

602-548-6000

Homewood Suites By Hilton Phoenix
North-Happy Valley
2470 West Charlotte Drive
Phoenix, AZ

623-580-1800

Homewood Suites By HiltonÂ®
Phoenix-Biltmore
2001 East Highland Avenue
Phoenix, AZ

602-508-0937

Homewood Suites Phoenix-Metro
Center
2536 West Beryl Avenue
Phoenix, AZ

602-674-8900

Hotel 502
502 West Camelback Road
Phoenix, AZ

602-264-9290

Howard Johnson Airport Downtown
4120 East Van Buren
Phoenix, AZ

602-275-5746

Kimpton Palomar Hotel
2 East Jefferson Street
Phoenix, AZ

602-253-6633

Knights Inn Fairground-Phoenix
1624 N. Black Canyon Highway
Phoenix, AZ

602-269-6281

Pointe Hilton Squaw Peak Resort
7677 North 16th Street
Phoenix, AZ

602-997-2626

Pointe Hilton Tapatio Cliffs Resort
11111 North 7th Street
Phoenix, AZ

602-866-7500

Pointe Hilton Tapatio Cliffs Resort
11111 North 7th Street
Phoenix, AZ

602-866-7500

Quality Hotel Phoenix - Chandler
5121 East la Puente Avenue
Phoenix, AZ

480-893-3900

Red Roof Inn - Phoenix West
5215 West Willetta Street
Phoenix, AZ

602-233-8004

Red Roof Inn Phoenix North - Bell
Road
17222 North Black Canyon Highway
Phoenix, AZ

602-866-1049

Residence Inn By Marriott Phoenix
8242 North Black Canyon Freeway
Phoenix, AZ

602-864-1900

Residence Inn Phoenix Airport
801 North 44th Street
Phoenix, AZ

602-273-9220

Residence Inn Phoenix Desert View
At Mayo Clinic
5665 E. Mayo Boulevard
Phoenix, AZ

480-563-1500

Residence Inn Phoenix North/Happy
Valley
2035 West Whispering Wind Drive
Phoenix, AZ

623-580-8833

Sheraton Crescent Hotel
2620 West Dunlap Avenue
Phoenix, AZ

602-943-8200

Sheraton Grand Phoenix
340 North 3rd Street
Phoenix, AZ

602-262-2500

Sleep Inn Phoenix Airport

2621 South 47th Place
Phoenix, AZ

480-967-7100

Towneplace Suites By Marriott
Phoenix
9425 N. Black Canyon Highway
Phoenix, AZ

602-943-9510

Vacation Inn Phoenix
2420 West Thomas Road
Phoenix, AZ

602-257-0801

Best Western Inn Of Pinetop
404 East White Mountain Blvd.
Pinetop, AZ
928-367-6667

Buck Springs Resort
6126 Buck Springs Road
Pinetop, AZ

928-369-3554

Best Western Prescottonian
1317 East Gurley Street
Prescott, AZ
928-445-3096

Comfort Inn At Ponderosa Pines
1290 White Spar Road
Prescott, AZ

928-778-5770

Forest Villas Hotel
3645 Lee Circle
Prescott, AZ

928-717-1200

Prescott Cabin Rentals
SR69 and Onyx Rd
Prescott, AZ

928-778-9573

Residence Inn Prescott
3599 Lee Circle
Prescott, AZ

928-775-2232

Springhill Suites By Marriott Prescott
200 East Sheldon Street
Prescott, AZ

928-776-0998

Arizona Inn
7875 East Highway 69
Prescott Valley, AZ
928-772-8600

Comfort Suites Prescott Valley
2601 North Crownpointe Drive
Prescott Valley, AZ

928-771-2100

Super 8 Quartzsite
2050 Dome Rock Road
Quartzsite, AZ
928-927-8080

Best Western Desert Inn
1391 W Thatcher Boulevard
Safford, AZ
928-428-0521

Days Inn Safford
520 East Highway 70
Safford, AZ

928-428-5000

Quality Inn And Suites
420 E. Hwy 70
Safford, AZ

928-428-3200

Best Western Plus Sundial
7320 E Camelback Road
Scottsdale, AZ
480-994-4170

Comfort Suites Old Town
3275 North Drinkwater Boulevard
Scottsdale, AZ

480-946-1111

Days Inn And Suites Scottsdale North
7330 North Pima Road
Scottsdale, AZ

480-948-3800

Doubletree Paradise Valley
Resort/Scottsdale
5401 North Scottsdale Road
Scottsdale, AZ

480-947-5400

Extended Stay America - Phoenix -
Scottsdale - North
15501 N. Scottsdale Rd.
Scottsdale, AZ

480-607-3767

Extended Stay America - Phoenix -
Scottsdale - Old Town
3560 North Marshall Way
Scottsdale, AZ

480-994-0297

Fairmont Scottsdale Princess
7575 East Princess Drive
Scottsdale, AZ

480-585-4848

Hampton Inn Phoenix/Scottsdale At
Shea Blvd.
10101 North Scottsdale Road

Scottsdale, AZ
480-443-3233

Hilton Scottsdale Resort And Villas
6333 North Scottsdale Road
Scottsdale, AZ

480-948-7750

Homewood Suites By HiltonÂ®
Phoenix/Scottsdale
9880 N Scottsdale Rd
Scottsdale, AZ

480-368-1200

Hyatt Regency Scottsdale Resort &
Spa
7500 East Doubletree Ranch Road
Scottsdale, AZ

480-444-1234

Kimpton Firesky Resort & Spa
4925 North Scottsdale Road
Scottsdale, AZ

480-945-7666

Marriott Scottsdale Mcdowell
Mountain
16770 North Perimeter Drive
Scottsdale, AZ

480-502-3836

Residence Inn By Marriott
Scottsdale North
17011 N. Scottsdale Road
Scottsdale, AZ

480-563-4120

Residence Inn Scottsdale Paradise
Valley
6040 North Scottsdale Road
Scottsdale, AZ

480-948-8666

Springhill Suites By Marriott
Scottsdale North
17020 North Scottsdale Road
Scottsdale, AZ

480-922-8700

The Phoenician A Luxury Collection
Resort Scottsdale
6000 East Camelback Road
Scottsdale, AZ

480-941-8200

Towneplace Suites By Marriott
Scottsdale
10740 North 90th Street
Scottsdale, AZ

480-551-1100

W Scottsdale

7277 East Camelback Road
Scottsdale, AZ

480-970-2100

Amara Resort & Spa A Kimpton Hotel
100 Amara Lane
Sedona, AZ
928-282-4828

Best Western Plus Inn Of Sedona
1200 West Highway 89a
Sedona, AZ

928-282-3072

Kings Ransom Sedona
771 Hwy 179 P.o. Box 180
Sedona, AZ

928-282-7151

Matterhorn Motor Lodge
230 Apple Ave
Sedona, AZ

928-282-7176

Oak Creek Terrace Resort
4548 N. Hwy. 89A
Sedona, AZ

928-282-3562

Red Agave Resort
120 Canyon Circle Drive
Sedona, AZ

928-284-9327

Sedona Real Inn & Suites
95 Arroyo Pinon
Sedona, AZ

928-282-1414

Sky Ranch Lodge
1105 Airport Road
Sedona, AZ

928-282-6400

Super 8 Sedona
2545 West Highway 89a
Sedona, AZ

928-282-1533

Best Western Paint Pony Lodge
581 W Deuce Of Clubs
Show Low, AZ
928-537-5773

Days Inn Show Low
480 West Deuce Of Clubs
Show Low, AZ

928-537-4356

Super 8 Show Low
1751 West Deuce Of Clubs
Show Low, AZ

928-532-7323

Candlewood Suites Sierra Vista
1904 South Highway 92
Sierra Vista, AZ
520-439-8200

Holiday Inn Express Sierra Vista
1902 S. Hwy 92
Sierra Vista, AZ
520-439-8800

Quality Inn Sierra Vista
1631 South Highway 92
Sierra Vista, AZ

520-458-7900

Towneplace Suites By Marriott Sierra
Vista
3399 Rodeo Drive
Sierra Vista, AZ

520-515-9900

Travelodge Inn And Suites Sierra
Vista
201 West Fry Boulevard
Sierra Vista, AZ

520-458-6711

Americas Best Value Inn Snowflake
2055 South Main Street
Snowflake, AZ
928-536-3888

Days Inn St. Johns
125 E Commercial St.
St Johns, AZ
928-337-4422

Days Inn & Suites Surprise
12477 West Bell Road
Surprise, AZ
623-933-4000

Hampton Inn & Suites Phoenix-
Surprise, Az
14783 West Grand Avenue
Surprise, AZ

623-537-9122

Quality Inn And Suites
16741 N Greasewood St
Surprise, AZ

623-583-3500

Residence Inn Phoenix Nw/Surprise
16418 North Bullard Avenue
Surprise, AZ

623-249-6333

Aloft Tempe
951 East Playa Del Norte Drive
Tempe, AZ
480-621-3300

Best Western Inn Of Tempe
670 North Scottsdale Road
Tempe, AZ

480 784-2233

Best Western Plus Tempe By The
Mall
5300 South Priest Drive
Tempe, AZ

480-820-7500

Candlewood Suites Tempe
1335 West Baseline Road
Tempe, AZ

480-777-0440

Days Inn & Suites Tempe
1660 West Elliot Road
Tempe, AZ

480-345-8585

Extended Stay America - Phoenix -
Airport - Tempe
2165 West 15th
Tempe, AZ

480-557-8880

Quality Inn Airport
1550 S. 52nd St.
Tempe, AZ

480-967-3000

Quality Suites Near Old Town
Scottsdale
1635 North Scottsdale Road
Tempe, AZ

480-947-3711

Red Lion Inn & Suites
Phoenix/Tempe - Asu
1429 North Scottsdale Road
Tempe, AZ

480-675-9799

Red Roof Inn Tempe - Phoenix
Airport
2135 West 15th Street
Tempe, AZ

480-449-3205

Residence Inn Tempe
5075 South Priest Drive
Tempe, AZ

480-756-2122

Super 8 Tempe/Asu/Airport
1020 E. Apache Boulevard
Tempe, AZ

480-967-8891

Towneplace Suites By Marriott

Tempe
5223 South Priest Drive
Tempe, AZ

480-345-7889

Trail Rider's Inn Motel
13 North 7th Street
Tombstone, AZ
520-457-3573

Quality Inn Tuba City
10 North Main Street (Main St And
Moanave Rd)
Tuba City, AZ
928-283-4545

Aloft Tucson University
1900 East Speedway Boulevard
Tucson, AZ
520-908-6800

Best Western Innsuites Tucson
Foothills Hotel & Suites
6201 N. Oracle Rd.
Tucson, AZ

520-297-8111

Best Western Royal Sun Inn & Suites
1015 N. Stone Ave.
Tucson, AZ

520-622-8871

Clarion Hotel
4550 S Palo Verde Road
Tucson, AZ

520-746-1161

Comfort Suites At Sabino Canyon
7007 East Tanque Verde Road
Tucson, AZ

520-298-2300

Comfort Suites At Tucson Mall
515 West Automall Drive
Tucson, AZ

520-888-6676

Doubletree Hotel Tucson-Reid Park
445 South Alvernon Way
Tucson, AZ

520-881-4200

Econo Lodge Tucson
3020 South 6th Avenue
Tucson, AZ

520-623-5881

Econo Lodge University
1136 North Stone Avenue
Tucson, AZ

520-622-6714

Extended Stay America - Tucson -

Dog-Friendly Lodging - Please always call ahead to make sure an establishment is still dog-friendly.

Grant Road
5050 E. Grant Rd.
Tucson, AZ

520-795-9510

Hampton Inn Tucson-North
1375 West Grant Road
Tucson, AZ

520-206-0602

Hilton Tucson El Conquistador Golf
And Tennis Resort
10000 North Oracle Road
Tucson, AZ

520-544-5000

Holiday Inn Express Tucson-Airport
2548 East Medina Road
Tucson, AZ

520-889-6600

Loews Ventana Canyon Resort
7000 North Resort Drive
Tucson, AZ

520-299-2020

Motel 6 Tucson Airport
1025 East Benson Highway
Tucson, AZ

520-623-7792

Quality Inn Airport
2803 East Valencia Road
Tucson, AZ

520-294-2500

Quality Inn Flamingo Tucson
1300 North Stone Avenue
Tucson, AZ

520-770-1910

Red Lion Inn And Suites Tucson
North Foothills
7411 North Oracle Road
Tucson, AZ

520-575-9255

Red Roof Inn Tucson North - Marana
4940 West Ina Road
Tucson, AZ

520-744-8199

Red Roof Inn Tucson South
3704 East Irvington Road
Tucson, AZ

520-571-1400

Residence Inn Tucson Airport
2660 East Medina Road
Tucson, AZ

520-294-5522

Residence Inn Tucson Williams
Centre
5400 East Williams Circle
Tucson, AZ

520-790-6100

Sheraton Tucson Hotel And Suites
5151 East Grant Road
Tucson, AZ

520-323-6262

Sonesta Es Suites Tucson
6477 East Speedway Boulevard
Tucson, AZ

520-721-0991

Staybridge Suites Tucson Airport
2705 Executive Drive
Tucson, AZ

520-807-1004

The Hotel Congress
311 E Congress Street
Tucson, AZ

520-622-8848

Towneplace Suites By Marriott
Tucson Airport
6595 South Bay Colony Drive
Tucson, AZ

520-294-6677

Towneplace Suites Tucson
405 West Rudasill Road
Tucson, AZ

520-292-9617

Westward Look Resort
245 East Ina Road
Tucson, AZ

520-297-1151

Windmill All Suites In Surprise
12545 West Bell Road
Tucson, AZ

623-583-0133

Microtel Inn & Suites by Wyndham
Wellton
28784 Commerce Way
Wellton, AZ
928-785-3777

Best Western Rancho Grande
293 E. Wickenburg Way
Wickenburg, AZ
928-684-5445

Super 8 Wickenburg Az
1021 North Tegner
Wickenburg, AZ

928-684-0808

Days Inn Willcox
724 North Bisbee Ave
Willcox, AZ
520-384-4222

Holiday Inn Express Hotel & Suites
Willcox
1251 North Virginia Avenue
Willcox, AZ

520-384-3333

Super 8 Willcox
1500 West Fort Grant Road
Willcox, AZ

520-384-0888

Best Western Plus Inn Of Williams
2600 West Route 66
Williams, AZ
928-635-4400

Days Inn Williams
2488 West Route 66,I-40 &; Route 66
Exit 161
Williams, AZ

928-635-4051

Mountain Ranch Resort At Beacon
Hill
6701 East Mountain Ranch Road
Williams, AZ

928-635-2693

Ramada Williams/Grand Canyon
Area
950 North Grand Canyon Boulevard
Williams, AZ

928-635-4114

Williams Grand Canyon Travelodge
430 E Bill Williams Ave
Williams, AZ

928-635-2651

Quality Inn Navajo Nation Capital
48 West Highway 264
Window Rock, AZ
928-871-4108

La Posada
303 E 2nd Street
Winslow, AZ
928-289-4366

Oak Tree Inn Winslow
1706 North Park Drive
Winslow, AZ

928-289-4687

Quality Inn Winslow
1701 North Park Drive
Winslow, AZ

928-289-4638

Rodeway Inn Winslow
1916 W. 3rd Street
Winslow, AZ

928-289-4606

Best Western Inn & Suites Of Sun
City
11201 Grand Avenue
Youngtown, AZ
623-933-8211

Americas Best Value Inn - Yuma
300 East 32nd Street
Yuma, AZ
928-344-1050

Best Western Innsuites Yuma Mall
Hotel & Suites
1450 S Castle Dome Ave
Yuma, AZ

928-783-8341

Candlewood Suites Yuma
2036 South Avenue 3e
Yuma, AZ

928-726-2800

Coronado Motor Hotel
233 South 4th Avenue
Yuma, AZ

928-783-4453

Homewood Suites Yuma
1955 East 16th Street
Yuma, AZ

928-782-4100

Howard Johnson Inn Yuma
3181 South 4th Avenue
Yuma, AZ

928-344-1420

Microtel Inn & Suites By Wyndham
Yuma
11274 South Fortuna Road
Yuma, AZ

928-345-1777

Quality Inn & Suites Yuma
1691 South Riley Avenue
Yuma, AZ

928-782-1200

Shilo Inn Yuma
1550 South Castle Dome Road
Yuma, AZ

928-782-9511

Super 8 Yuma
1688 South Riley Avenue

Yuma, AZ
928-782-2000

TownePlace Suites Yuma
1726 South Sunridge Drive
Yuma, AZ

928-783-6900

Yuma Airport Inn
711 East 32nd Street
Yuma, AZ

# Arkansas Listings

Days Inn Alma
250 North Us Hwy 71
Alma, AR
479-632-4595

Quality Inn & Suites Alma
439 Highway 71 North
Alma, AR

479-632-4141

Comfort Inn Arkadelphia
100 Crystal Palace
Arkadelphia, AR
870-246-3800

Days Inn Arkadelphia
137 Valley Drive
Arkadelphia, AR

870-246-3031

Super 8 Arkadelphia Caddo Valley
Area
118 Valley Street
Arkadelphia, AR

870-246-8585

Ramada Batesville Arkansas
1325 North Saint Louis Street
Batesville, AR
870-698-1800

Super 8 Batesville
1287 North Saint Louis
Batesville, AR

870-793-5888

Days Inn Beebe
100 Tammy Lane
Beebe, AR
501-882-2008

Best Western Benton Inn
17036 Interstate 30
Benton, AR
501-778-9695

Days Inn Benton
17701 I-30

Benton, AR

501-776-3200

Econo Lodge Benton
16732 Interstate 30
Benton, AR

501-776-1900

Comfort Suites Bentonville
2011 Se Walton Blvd
Bentonville, AR
479-254-9099

Towneplace Suites By Marriott
Bentonville
3100 Southeast 14th Street
Bentonville, AR

479-621-0202

Wingate By Wyndham Bentonville Ar
7400 Sw Old Farm Boulevard
Bentonville, AR

479-418-5400

Comfort Inn & Suites Blytheville
1510 East Main Street
Blytheville, AR
870-763-0900

Days Inn Blytheville
102 South Porter Drive
Blytheville, AR

870-763-1241

Quality Inn Blytheville
1520 E. Main St.
Blytheville, AR

870-763-7081

Days Inn And Suites Brinkley
1815 North Main Street
Brinkley, AR
870-734-4300

Econo Lodge & Suites Brinkley
2203 N. Main Street
Brinkley, AR

870-734-1052

Super 8 Bryant Little Rock Area
201 Dell Dr
Bryant, AR
501-847-7888

Days Inn & Suites Cabot
1302 West Locust Street
Cabot, AR
501-605-1810

Super 8 Cabot
15 Ryeland Drive
Cabot, AR

501-941-3748

Dog-Friendly Lodging - Please always call ahead to make sure an establishment is still dog-friendly.

Holiday Inn Express And Suites
Arkadelphia Caddo Valley
7 Frost Road
Caddo Valley, AR
870-403-0880

Americas Best Value Inn
942 Adams Avenue South
Camden, AR
870-836-2535

Sunset Inn Clarksville
2600 West Main Street
Clarksville, AR
479-754-8555

Super 8 Clarksville
1238 South Rogers Avenue
Clarksville, AR

479-754-8800

Best Western Hillside Inn
1025 Highway 65 B
Clinton, AR
501-745-4700

Candlewood Suites Conway
2360 Sanders Street
Conway, AR
501-329-8551

Days Inn Conway
1002 East Oak Street
Conway, AR

501-450-7575

Quality Inn Conway
150 Skyline Drive
Conway, AR

501-329-0300

Econo Lodge Conference Center
1920 Junction City Rd.
El Dorado, AR
870-862-5191

Super 8 El Dorado
1925 Junction City Road
El Dorado, AR

870-862-1000

1886 Crescent Hotel & Spa
75 Prospect Avenue
Eureka Springs, AR
479-253-9766

5 Ojo Inn
5 Ojo Street
Eureka Springs, AR

479-253-6734

Best Western Inn Of The Ozarks
207 W Van Buren
Eureka Springs, AR

479-253-9768

GuestHouse Inn Swiss Holiday
Resort
2015 East Van Buren
Eureka Springs, AR

479-253-9501

Lazee Daze
5432 H 23 S
Eureka Springs, AR

479-253-7026

Roadrunner Inn
3034 Mundell Road
Eureka Springs, AR

479-253-8166

Best Western Windsor Suites
1122 South Futrall Drive
Fayetteville, AR
479-301-2882

Candlewood Suites Fayetteville
2270 West Martin Luther King Junior
Boulevard
Fayetteville, AR

479-856-6262

Econo Lodge Fayetteville
1000 South Futrall Drive
Fayetteville, AR

479-442-3041

Sleep Inn Fayetteville
728 Millsap Road
Fayetteville, AR

479-587-8700

Staybridge Suites Fayetteville
1577 West 15th Street
Fayetteville, AR

479-695-2400

Baymont Inn & Suites Fort Smith
2123 Burnham Road
Fort Smith, AR
479-484-5770

Candlewood Suites Fort Smith
7501 Madison Street
Fort Smith, AR

479-424-3800

Courtyard By Marriott Downtown Ft.
Smith
900 Rogers Avenue
Fort Smith, AR

479-783-2100

Holiday Inn Express Fort Smith
6813 Phoenix Avenue
Fort Smith, AR

479-452-7500

Quality Inn Fort Smith
2120 Burnham Road
Fort Smith, AR

479-484-0227

Residence Inn By Marriott Fort Smith
3005 South 74th Street
Fort Smith, AR

479-478-8300

Riverfront Inn
1021 Garrison Avenue
Fort Smith, AR

479-783-0548

The Executive Hotel At City Center
700 Rogers Ave
Fort Smith, AR

479-783-1000

Blue Lady Resort and Winery
149 Country Road 820
Gamaliel, AR
870-421-2076

Days Inn Harrison
1425 Hwy 62-65 North
Harrison, AR
870-391-3297

Quality Inn Harrison
1210 Us 62/65 N
Harrison, AR

870-741-7676

Super 8 Hazen
4167 Highway 63 North
Hazen, AR
870-255-2888

Lake and River Inn
2322 H 25 B
Heber Springs, AR
501-362-3161

Best Western Of Hope
1800 Holiday Drive
Hope, AR
870-777-9222

Holiday Inn Express Hope
2600 North Hervey
Hope, AR

870-722-6262

Super 8 Hope
I-30 Exit 30 At Hwy 4
Hope, AR

870-777-8601

Arlington Resort Hotel and Spa
101 Park Avenue/H 7

Hot Springs, AR
501-623-5511

Candlewood Suites Hot Springs
3404 Central Avenue
Hot Springs, AR

501-624-4000

Embassy Suites Hotel Hot Springs,
Ar
400 Convention Blvd
Hot Springs, AR

501-624-9200

Lake Hamilton Resort
2803 Albert Pike Road/H 270
Hot Springs, AR

501-767-8606

Park Hotel Hot Springs
211 Fountain Street
Hot Springs, AR

501-624-5323

Staybridge Suites Hot Springs
103 Lookout Circle
Hot Springs, AR

501-525-6500

Velda Rose Resort Hotel and Spa
218 Park Avenue/H 7
Hot Springs, AR

501-623-3311

Days Inn Jacksonville
1414 John Harden Drive
Jacksonville, AR
501-982-1543

Candlewood Suites Jonesboro
2906 Kazi Street
Jonesboro, AR
870-336-6500

Econo Lodge Jonesboro
2406 Phillips Drive
Jonesboro, AR

870-932-9339

Fairbridge Inn & Suites Jonesboro
3006 South Caraway Road
Jonesboro, AR

870-935-2030

Super 8 Jonesboro
2500 South Caraway Road
Jonesboro, AR

870-972-0849

Gaston's White River Resort
1777 River Rd
Lakeview, AR
870-431-5202

Candlewood Suites West Little Rock
10520 West Markham
Little Rock, AR
501-975-3800

Clarion Hotel Medical Center
925 South University Avenue
Little Rock, AR
501-664-5020

Comfort Inn & Suites Little Rock
Airport
4301 East Roosevelt
Little Rock, AR

501-376-2466

Days Inn And Suites Little Rock
3200 Bankhead Drive
Little Rock, AR

501-490-2010

Embassy Suites Hotel Little Rock
11301 Financial Centre Parkway
Little Rock, AR

501-312-9000

Extended Stay America - Little Rock
- Financial Centre Parkway
600 Hardin Rd
Little Rock, AR

501-954-9199

Four Points by Sheraton Little Rock
Midtown
925 South University Avenue
Little Rock, AR

501-664-5020

Holiday Inn Express Little Rock-
Airport
3121 Bankhead Dr
Little Rock, AR

501-490-4000

Holiday Inn Little Rock-Arpt-Conf Ctr
3201 Bankhead Drive
Little Rock, AR

501-490-1000

Little Rock Airport Travelodge
7615 Fluid Drive
Little Rock, AR

501-490-2200

Quality Inn And Suites Little Rock
6100 Mitchell Drive
Little Rock, AR

501-562-6667

Residence Inn By Marriott Little
Rock

1401 South Shackleford Road
Little Rock, AR

501-312-0200

Rodeway Inn & Suites Little Rock
2401 West 65th Street
Little Rock, AR

501-801-0188

Towneplace Suites By Marriott Little
Rock West
12 Crossings Court
Little Rock, AR

501-225-6700

Best Western Plus Lonoke Hotel
102 Dee Dee Lane
Lonoke, AR
501-676-8880

Days Inn Lonoke
105 Dee Dee Lnterstate 40 Highway
31
Lonoke, AR

501-676-5138

Super 8 Malvern
3445 Oliver Lancaster Blvd.
Malvern, AR
501-332-5755

Days Inn Forrest City
200 Holiday Drive
Maumelle, AR
501-851-4422

Best Western Mcgehee
1202 Highway 65 North
Mc Gehee, AR
870-222-3564

Super 8 Monticello, Ar
306 Highway 425 North
Monticello, AR
870-367-6271

Comfort Inn Mountain Home
1031 Highland Circle
Mountain Home, AR
870-424-9000

Days Inn Mountain Home
1746 Hwy 62 East B
Mountain Home, AR

870-425-1010

Holiday Inn Express Hotel & Suites
Mountain Home
1005 Coley Drive
Mountain Home, AR

870-425-6200

Ramada Mountain Home
1127 North East Highway 62
Mountain Home, AR

870-425-9191

Teal Point Resort
715 Teal Point Rd
Mountain Home, AR
870-492-5145

Days Inn Mountain View
703 East Main Street
Mountain View, AR
870-269-3287

Red Roof Inn Little Rock JFK
120 W. Pershing Blvd.
North Little Rock, AR
501-758-1851

Red Roof Inn North Little Rock
5711 Pritchard Drive
North Little Rock, AR

501-945-0080

Residence Inn Little Rock North
4110 Health Care Drive
North Little Rock, AR

501-945-7777

Super 8 Motel - Little
Rock/North/Airport
1 Gray Rd
North Little Rock, AR

501-945-0141

Black Oak Resort
8543 Oakland Road
Oakland, AR
870-431-8363

Americas Best Value Inn Ozark
105 Airport Road
Ozark, AR
479-667-2530

Ozark Mountain Meadows
2669 Country Road 4021
Ozark, AR

479-497-2127

Econo Lodge Inn & Suites Paragould
2310 West Kingshighway
Paragould, AR
870-239-2121

Quality Inn & Suites Pine Bluff
2809 Pines Mall Dr.
Pine Bluff, AR
870-535-5300

Days Inn & Suites Pocahontas
2805 Hwy 67 South
Pocahontas, AR
870-892-9500

Candlewood Suites Rogers
4601 West Rozell Street

Rogers, AR
479-636-2783

Embassy Suites Hotel Northwest
Arkansas
3303 Pinnacle Hills Parkway
Rogers, AR

479-254-8400

Homewood Suites By Hilton
Bentonville-Rogers, Ar
4302 West Walnut Street
Rogers, AR

479-636-5656

Residence Inn By Marriott Rogers
4611 West Locust Street
Rogers, AR

479-636-5900

Staybridge Suites Bentonville -
Rogers
1801 South 52nd Street
Rogers, AR

479-845-5701

Quality Inn Russellville
3019 East Parkway Drive
Russellville, AR
479-967-7500

Super 8 Motel - Russellville
2404 N. Arkansas Avenue
Russellville, AR

479-968-8898

Extended Stay America -
Fayetteville - Springdale
5000 Luvene Ave
Springdale, AR
479-872-1490

Hampton Inn And Suites Springdale
1700 South 48th Street
Springdale, AR

479-756-3500

Residence Inn By Marriott
Springdale
1740 South 48th Street
Springdale, AR

479-872-9100

Towneplace Suites By Marriott
Fayetteville North/Springdale
5437 S 48th Street
Springdale, AR

479-966-4400

Days Inn and Suites Stuttgart
708 West Michigan Street
Stuttgart, AR
870-673-3616

Super 8 Stuttgart
701 West Michigan Street
Stuttgart, AR

870-673-2611

Luxury Inn and Suites
5210 N. Stateline Ave.
Texarkana, AR
870-772-0070

Days Inn Trumann Ar
400 Commerce Drive
Trumann, AR
870-483-8383

Best Western Van Buren Inn
1903 North 6th Street
Van Buren, AR
479-474-8100

Holiday Inn Express And Suites Van
Buren-Ft Smith Area
1637 N. 12th Court
Van Buren, AR

479-471-7300

Super 8 Van Buren
106 North Plaza Court
Van Buren, AR

479-471-8888

Red Roof Inn West Memphis
1401 North Ingram Boulevard
West Memphis, AR
870-735-7100

Super 8 West Memphis
901 Martin Luther King Jr Dr
West Memphis, AR

870-735-8818

# California Listings

California Inn Hotel and Suites
11628 Bartlett Avenue
Adelanto, CA
760-246-8777

Extended Stay America - Oakland -
Alameda
1350 Marina Village Pkwy
Alameda, CA
510-864-1333

Timber Cove Inn
21780 North Coast Highway 1
Albion, CA
707-937-9200

Best Western Trailside Inn
343 N. Main St.
Alturas, CA
530-233-4111

Super 8 Alturas

511 N Main Street
Alturas, CA

530-233-3545

Holiday Inn Express And Suites Napa
Valley-American Canyon
5001 Main Street
American Canyon, CA
+17-075-5281

Clarion Hotel Anaheim Resort
616 Convention Way
Anaheim, CA
714-750-3131

Extended Stay America - Orange
County - Anaheim Convention Cente
1742 S. Clementine St
Anaheim, CA

714-502-9988

Extended Stay America - Orange
County - Anaheim Hills
1031 N. Pacificenter Drive
Anaheim, CA

714-630-4006

Hotel Indigo Anaheim Maingate
435 West Katella
Anaheim, CA

714-772-7755

Hotel Menage
1221 South Harbor Blvd
Anaheim, CA

714-758-0900

Residence Inn Anaheim Maingate
1700 South Clementine Street
Anaheim, CA

714-533-3555

Staybridge Suites Anaheim Resort
Area
1855 South Manchester Avenue
Anaheim, CA
714-748-7700

Residence Inn By Marriott Anaheim
Hills Yorba Linda
125 South Festival Drive
Anaheim Hills, CA
714-974-8880

Baymont Inn & Suites Anderson
2040 Factory Outlets Drive
Anderson, CA
530-365-6100

Best Western Anderson Inn
2688 Gateway Drive
Anderson, CA

530-365-2753

Ramada Inn Antioch
2436 Mahogany Way
Antioch, CA
925-754-6600

Apple Lane Inn B&B
6265 Soquel Drive
Aptos, CA
831-475-6868

Extended Stay America - Los
Angeles - Arcadia
401 E Santa Clara St
Arcadia, CA
626-446-6422

Residence Inn Arcadia
321 East Hungtington Drive
Arcadia, CA

626-446-6500

Best Western Arcata Inn
4827 Valley West Blvd.
Arcata, CA
707-826-0313

Days Inn And Suites Arcata Ca
4701 Valley West Boulevard
Arcata, CA

707-826-2827

Quality Inn Arcata
3535 Janes Road
Arcata, CA

707-822-0409

Red Roof Inn Arcata
4975 Valley West Boulevard
Arcata, CA

707-822-4861

Super 8 Arcata
4887 Valley West Boulevard
Arcata, CA

707-822-8888

Ebbetts Pass Lodge
1173 Highway 4, Box 2591
Arnold, CA
209-795-1563

Best Western Casa Grande Inn
850 Oak Park Boulevard
Arroyo Grande, CA
805-481-7398

Best Western Golden Key
13450 Lincoln Way
Auburn, CA
530-885-8611

Foothills Motel
13431 Bowman Road
Auburn, CA

530-885-8444

Super 8 Auburn
140 East Hillcrest Drive
Auburn, CA

530-888-8808

Best Economy Inn & Suites
5200 Olive Tree Court
Bakersfield, CA

Best Western Heritage Inn
253 Trask Street
Bakersfield, CA

661-764-6268

Best Western Plus Hill House
700 Truxtun Avenue
Bakersfield, CA

661-327-4064

Historic Downtowner Inn
1301 Chester Avenue
Bakersfield, CA

661-327-7122

Hotel Rosedale
2400 Camino Del Rio Court
Bakersfield, CA

661-327-0681

Howard Johnson Express Inn -
Bakersfield
2700 White Lane
Bakersfield, CA

661-396-1425

Ramada Limited Bakersfield Central
830 Wible Road
Bakersfield, CA

661-831-1922

Residence Inn Bakersfield
4241 Chester Lane
Bakersfield, CA

661-321-9800

Sleep Inn And Suites
6257 Knudsen Drive
Bakersfield, CA

661-399-2100

Super 8 Bakersfield/Central
901 Real Road
Bakersfield, CA

661-322-1012

Travelodge Motel Bakersfield
1011 Oak St
Bakersfield, CA

661-325-0772

Days Inn Banning

Dog-Friendly Lodging - Please always call ahead to make sure an establishment is still dog-friendly.

2320 W. Ramsey St.
Banning, CA
951-849-0092

Quality Inn Banning I-10
1690 West Ramsey Rd
Banning, CA

951-849-8888

Travelodge Banning
1700 West Ramsey Street
Banning, CA

951-849-1000

Best Western Desert Villa Inn
1984 East Main Street
Barstow, CA
760-256-1781

Days Inn South Lenwood
2551 Commerce Parkway
Barstow, CA

760-253-2121

Econo Lodge On Historic Route 66
1230 E Main St
Barstow, CA

760-256-2133

Hampton Inn & Suites Barstow
2710 Lenwood Road
Barstow, CA

760-253-2600

Holiday Inn Express Hotel & Suites
Barstow
2700 Lenwood Road
Barstow, CA

760-253-9200

Ramada Inn Barstow
1511 East Main Street
Barstow, CA

760-256-5673

Sleep Inn On Historic Route 66
1861 W. Main St.
Barstow, CA

760-256-1300

Super 8 Barstow
170 Coolwater Lane
Barstow, CA

760-256-8443

Travelodge Barstow
1630 E Main St
Barstow, CA

760-256-8931

The Pines Resort
54432 Road 432

Bass Lake, CA
559-642-3121

Rodeway Inn Beaumont
1265 E. 6th Street
Beaumont, CA
951-845-1436

Extended Stay America - San
Francisco - Belmont
120 Sem Lane
Belmont, CA
650-654-0344

Best Western Plus Heritage Inn
1955 East Second Street
Benicia, CA
707-746-0401

Americas Best Value Inn
1620 San Pablo Ave
Berkeley, CA
510-525-6770

Blue Sky Hotel
2520 Durant Avenue
Berkeley, CA

510-540-7688

Doubletree By Hilton Berkeley
Marina
200 Marina Boulevard
Berkeley, CA

510-548-7920

Lake Oroville Bed and Breakfast
240 Sunday Drive
Berry Creek, CA
530-589-0700

Best Western Big Bear Chateau
42200 Moonridge Road
Big Bear Lake, CA
909-866-6666

Eagle's Nest Lodge
41675 Big Bear Blvd.
Big Bear Lake, CA

909-866-6465

Golden Bear Cottages
39367 Big Bear Blvd/H 18
Big Bear Lake, CA

805-226-0102

Majestic Moose Lodge
39328 Big Bear Blvd/H 18
Big Bear Lake, CA

909-866-9586

Shore Acres Lodge
40090 Lakeview Drive
Big Bear Lake, CA

909-866-8200

Timber Haven Lodge
877 Tulip Lane
Big Bear Lake, CA

909-866-7207

Timberline Lodge
39921 Big Bear Blvd.
Big Bear Lake, CA

909-866-4141

Big Pine Motel
370 S Main St
Big Pine, CA
760-938-2282

Bristlecone Motel
101 North Main Street
Big Pine, CA

760-938-2067

Big Sur Vacation Retreat
off Highway One
Big Sur, CA
831-624-5339 Ext 13

Best Western Bishop Lodge
1025 North Main Street
Bishop, CA
760-873-3543

Bishop Village Motel
286 W Elm Street
Bishop, CA

888-668-5546

Comfort Inn Bishop
805 N. Main St.
Bishop, CA

760-873-4284

Days Inn Bishop
724 West Line Street
Bishop, CA

760-872-1095

Econo Lodge Bishop
150 East Elm Street
Bishop, CA

760-873-3564

Holiday Inn Express Hotel And Suites
Bishop
636 North Main Street
Bishop, CA

760-872-2423

Super 8 Bishop
535 South Main Street
Bishop, CA

760-872-1386

Travelodge Bishop
155 East Elm Street

Bishop, CA
760-872-1771

Vagabond Inn Bishop
1030 North Main Street
Bishop, CA
760-873-6351

Knights Inn Blythe
1127 East Hobsonway
Blythe, CA
760-922-4126

M-Star Inn And Suites Blythe
9232 E Hobsonway
Blythe, CA
760-922-3334

Super 8 Blythe
550 West Donlon Street
Blythe, CA
760-922-8881

Bodega Bay and Beyond
575 Coastal H One
Bodega Bay, CA
707-875-3942

Redwood Croft B&B
275 Northwest Drive
Bonny Doon, CA
831-458-1939

Pleasure Cove Marina, a Forever
Resort
6100 Highway 128
Boonville, CA
707-895-2210

Chase Suites Hotel Brea
3100 East Imperial Hwy
Brea, CA
714-579-3200

Extended Stay America - Orange
County - Brea
3050 E. Imperial Highway
Brea, CA
714-528-2500

Walker River Lodge
100 Main Street
Bridgeport, CA
760-932-7021

Quality Inn Santa Ynez Valley
630 Avenue Of The Flags
Buellton, CA
805-688-0022

Santa Ynez Valley Marriott
555 Mcmurray Road
Buellton, CA
805-688-1000

Colony Inn
7800 Crescent Avenue
Buena Park, CA
714-527-2201

Extended Stay America - Los
Angeles - Burbank Airport
2200 Empire Ave
Burbank, CA
818-567-0952

Residence Inn Los Angeles
Burbank/Downtown
321 S. First Street
Burbank, CA
818-260-8787

Safari Inn, a Coast Hotel
1911 West Olive Avenue
Burbank, CA
818-845-8586

Crowne Plaza San Francisco Airport
1177 Airport Boulevard
Burlingame, CA
650-342-9200

Doubletree Hotel San Francisco
Airport
835 Airport Boulevard
Burlingame, CA
650-344-5500

Embassy Suites San Francisco
Airport Burlingame Hotel
150 Anza Boulevard
Burlingame, CA
650-342-4600

Red Roof Inn San Francisco Airport
777 Airport Boulevard
Burlingame, CA
650-342-7772

San Francisco Airport Marriott
Waterfront
1800 Old Bayshore Hwy
Burlingame, CA
650-692-9100

Vagabond Inn Executive San
Francisco Airport
1640 Bayshore Hwy.
Burlingame, CA
650-692-4040

Econo Lodge Inn & Suites I-5 At
Route 58
20688 Tracy Avenue
Buttonwillow, CA
661-764-5207

Motel 6 Buttonwillow Central
20645 Tracy Avenue
Buttonwillow, CA

661-764-5121

Super 8 Buttonwillow
20681 Tracy Avenue
Buttonwillow, CA
661-764-5117

Motel 6 San Bernardino South
111 West Redlands Boulevard
CA, CA

Calistoga Ranch
580 Lommel Road
Calistoga, CA
707-254-2800

Meadowlark Inn
601 Petrified Forest Road
Calistoga, CA
707-942-5651

The Pink Mansion - Bed And
Breakfast - Adult Only
1415 Foothill Boulevard
Calistoga, CA
707-942-0558

Best Western Camarillo Inn
295 E Daily Dr
Camarillo, CA
805-987-4991

Residence Inn Camarillo
2912 Petit Street
Camarillo, CA
805-388-7997

Cambria Pines Lodge
2905 Burton Drive
Cambria, CA
805-927-4200

Cambria Shores Inn
6276 Moonstone Beach Drive
Cambria, CA
805-927-8644

Coastal Escapes Inc.
778 Main Street
Cambria, CA
805-927-3182

Fog Catcher Inn
6400 Moonstone Beach Drive
Cambria, CA
805-927-1400

The Big Red House
370- B Chelsea Lane
Cambria, CA
805-927-1390

Quality Inn & Suites Cameron Park

Dog-Friendly Lodging - Please always call ahead to make sure an establishment is still dog-friendly.

3361 Coach Lane
Cameron Park, CA
530-677-2203

Residence Inn San Jose Campbell
2761 South Bascom Avenue
Campbell, CA
408-559-1551

Towneplace Suites By Marriott San
Jose Campbell
700 East Campbell Avenue
Campbell, CA
408-370-4510

Holiday Inn Express Encinitas-Cardiff
Beach Area
1661 Villa Cardiff Drive
Cardiff By The Sea, CA
760-944-0427

Extended Stay America - San Diego -
Carlsbad Village By The Sea
1050 Grand Avenue
Carlsbad, CA
760-729-9380

Homewood Suites By Hilton
Carlsbad-North San Diego County
2223 Palomar Airport Road
Carlsbad, CA
760-431-2266

Ramada Carlsbad
751 Macadamia Drive
Carlsbad, CA
760-438-2285

Residence Inn By Marriott Carlsbad
2000 Faraday Avenue
Carlsbad, CA
760-431-9999

Sheraton Carlsbad Resort & Spa
5480 Grand Pacific Drive
Carlsbad, CA
760-827-2400

West Inn And Suites
4970 Avenida Encinas
Carlsbad, CA
760-208-4929

West Inn And Suites
4970 Avenida Encinas
Carlsbad, CA
760-448-4500

West Inn And Suites
4970 Avenida Encinas
Carlsbad, CA
760-448-4500

Briarwood Inn Bed and Breakfast

San Carlos Street between 4th and
5th Streets
Carmel, CA
831-626-9056

Carmel Country Inn
Dolores Street & Third Avenue
Carmel, CA
831-625-3263

Carmel Mission Inn
3665 Rio Rd.
Carmel, CA
831-624-1841

Carmel Valley Ranch
One Old Ranch Road
Carmel, CA
831-625-9500

Coachman's Inn
San Carlos St. & 7th
Carmel, CA
831-624-6421

Cypress Inn
7th Avenue &; Lincoln Street
Carmel, CA
831-624-3871

Happy Landing Inn
Monte Verde at 6th
Carmel, CA
831-624-7917

Hofsas House Hotel
3rd &; 4th Street At San Carlos
Carmel, CA
831-624-2745

Hofsas House Hotel
3rd &; 4th Street At San Carlos
Carmel, CA
831-624-4862

Lamp Lighter Inn
Camino Real and Ocean Ave
Carmel, CA
831-624-4884

Monte Verde Inn
Monte Verde Street at Ocean
Avenue
Carmel, CA
831-624-2429

Vagabond's House Inn B&B
PO Box 2747
Carmel, CA
831-624-7738

Carmel Valley Lodge

8 Ford Road
Carmel Valley, CA
831-659-2261

Los Laureles Lodge
313 W Carmel Valley Road
Carmel Valley, CA
831-659-2233

Carmel Green Lantern Inn
Casanova & 7th Avenue
Carmel by The Sea, CA
831-624-4392

Forest Lodge Cottages
Corner of Ocean and Torres
Carmel by the Sea, CA
831-624-7023

Tradewinds Carmel
Mission Street at 3rd Avenue
Carmel-by-the-Sea, CA
831-624-2776

Holiday Inn Express Hotel & Suites
Carpinteria
5606 Carpinteria Avenue
Carpinteria, CA
805-566-9499

Extended Stay America - Los
Angeles - Carson
401 E. Albertoni St.
Carson, CA
310-323-2080

Desert Princess Palm Springs Golf
Resort
67967 Vista Chino
Cathedral City, CA
760-322-7000

Red Lion Inn & Suites - Cathedral
City - Palm Springs
69151 East Palm Canyon Drive
Cathedral City, CA
760-324-5939

Cayucos Beach Inn
333 South Ocean Avenue
Cayucos, CA
805-995-2828

Cypress Tree Motel
125 S. Ocean Avenue
Cayucos, CA
805-995-3917

Shoreline Inn...on the beach
1 North Ocean Avenue
Cayucos, CA
805-995-3681

The Dolphin Inn
399 South Ocean Avenue
Cayucos, CA

805-995-3810

Sunrise Motel & RV Park
54889 Highway 200 West
Cedarville, CA
530-279-2161

Sheraton Cerritos
12725 Center Court Drive
Cerritos, CA
562-809-1500

Ramada Inn Chatsworth
21340 Devonshire Street
Chatsworth, CA
818-998-5289

Staybridge Suites Chatsworth
21902 Lassen St
Chatsworth, CA

818-773-0707

Music Express Inn Bed and Breakfast
1091 El Monte Avenue
Chico, CA
530-891-9833

Oxford Suites Chico
2035 Business Lane
Chico, CA

530-899-9090

Ramada Plaza Chico
685 Manzanita Ct
Chico, CA

530-345-2491

Residence Inn By Marriott Chico
2485 Carmichael Drive
Chico, CA

530-894-5500

Super 8 Motel - Chico
655 Manzanita Ct.
Chico, CA

530-345-2533

Extended Stay America - Los
Angeles - Chino Valley
4325 Corporate Center Ave
Chino, CA
909-597-8675

Days Inn Chowchilla Gateway To
Yosemite
220 East Robertson Blvd
Chowchilla, CA
559-665-4821

Pacific Palms Conference Resort
One Industry Hills Parkway
City of Industry, CA
626-810-4455

Clear Lake Cottages & Marina

13885 Lakeshore Drive
Clearlake, CA
707-995-5253

Homewood Suites Clovis
835 Gettysburg Ave
Clovis, CA
559-292-4004

Best Western Big Country Inn
25020 West Dorris Avenue
Coalinga, CA
559-935-0866

Coalinga Travelodge
25278 West Dorris Avenue
Coalinga, CA

559-935-2063

Becker's Bounty Lodge and Cottage
HCR #2 Box 4659
Coffee Creek, CA
530-266-3277

Andruss Motel
106964 Us Highway 395
Coleville, CA
530-495-2216

Golden Lotus Bed and Breakfast Inn
1006 Lotus Road
Coloma, CA
530-621-4562

Columbia Gem Motel
22131 Parrotts Ferry Rd
Columbia, CA
209-532-4508

Hilton Concord
1970 Diamond Boulevard
Concord, CA
925-827-2000

Best Western Plus Corning Inn
910 Highway 99 W
Corning, CA
530-824-5200

Econo Lodge Inn & Suites Corning
3475 South Highway 99 West
Corning, CA

530-824-2000

Holiday Inn Express Corning
3350 Sunrise Way
Corning, CA

530-824-6400

Best Western Corona
1084 Pomona Road
Corona, CA
951-734-4241

Residence Inn By Marriott Corona
Riverside
1015 Montecito Drive

Corona, CA
951-371-0107

Crown City Inn Coronado
520 Orange Avenue
Coronado, CA
619-435-3116

Avenue of the Arts Costa Mesa a
Tribute Portfolio Hotel
3350 Avenue Of The Arts
Costa Mesa, CA
714-751-5100

Residence Inn Costa Mesa
881 West Baker Street
Costa Mesa, CA

714-241-8800

Vagabond Inn Costa Mesa
3205 Harbor Blvd
Costa Mesa, CA

714-557-8360

Yosemite Gold Country Lodge
10407 Highway 49 North
Coulterville, CA
209-878-3400

Quality Inn & Suites Redwood Coast
100 Walton Street
Crescent City, CA
707-464-3885

Town House Motel
444 US H 101S
Crescent City, CA

707-464-4176

The Four Points By Sheraton Culver
City
5990 Green Valley Circle
Culver City, CA
310-641-7740

Extended Stay America - Orange
County - Cypress
5990 Corporate Avenue
Cypress, CA
714-761-2766

Woodfin Suite Hotel
5905 Corporate Ave
Cypress, CA

714-828-4000

Best Western Plus Marina Shores
Hotel
34280 Pacific Coast Highway
Dana Point, CA
949-248-1000

Doubletree Suites By Hilton Doheny
Beach - Dana Point
34402 Pacific Coast Highway
Dana Point, CA

949-661-1100

Best Western Danville Sycamore Inn
803 Camino Ramon
Danville, CA
925-855-8888

Econo Lodge Davis
221 D Street
Davis, CA
530-756-1040

University Inn Bed and Breakfast
340 A Street
Davis, CA

530-756-8648

University Park Inn & Suites
1111 Richards Boulevard
Davis, CA

530-756-0910

Stovepipe Wells Village Motel
H 190
Death Valley, CA
760-786-2387

Hilton San Diego/Del Mar
15575 Jimmy Durante Boulevard
Del Mar, CA
858-792-5200

Les Artistes Inn
944 Camino Del Mar
Del Mar, CA

858-755-4646

Americas Best Value Inn Delano
2231 Girard Street
Delano, CA
661-725-7551

Best Western Liberty Inn
14394 County Line Road
Delano, CA

661-725-0976

Rodeway Inn Delano
2211 Girard Street
Delano, CA

661-725-1022

Holiday Inn Express Hotel & Suites
Dinuba West
375 S. Alta Ave.
Dinuba, CA
559-595-1500

Best Western Plus Inn Dixon
1345 Commercial Way
Dixon, CA
707-678-1400

Embassy Suites Los Angeles
Downey Hotel

8425 Firestone Blvd
Downey, CA
562-861-1900

Downieville Loft
208 Main Street
Downieville, CA
510-501-2516

Old Well Motel
15947 State Highway 49
Drytown, CA
209-245-6467

Extended Stay America - Dublin -
Hacienda Dr.
4500 Dublin Blvd
Dublin, CA
925-875-9556

Holiday Inn Dublin
6680 Regional Street
Dublin, CA

925-828-7750

Dunsmuir Lodge
6604 Dunsmuir Avenue
Dunsmuir, CA
530-235-2884

Railroad Park Resort
100 Railroad Park Road
Dunsmuir, CA

530-235-4440

Best Western Courtesy Inn
1355 East Main Street
El Cajon, CA
619-440-7378

Relax Inn And Suites
1220 West Main Street
El Cajon, CA
619-442-2576

Travelodge El Cajon
425 West Main Street
El Cajon, CA
619-441-8250

Towneplace Suites By Marriott El
Centro
3003 South Dogwood Avenue
El Centro, CA
760-370-3800

Value Inn & Suites
2030 Cottonwood Circle
El Centro, CA
760-353-7750

The Monarch
5059 Highway 140
El Portal, CA
209-379-2681

Extended Stay America Los Angeles
- LAX Airport - El Segundo
1910 E Mariposa Ave
El Segundo, CA
310-607-4000

Residence Inn By Marriott El
Segundo
2135 East El Segundo Blvd
El Segundo, CA

310-333-0888

Elk Cove Inn & Spa
6300 California 1
Elk, CA
707-877-3321

The Greenwood Pier Inn
5928 S H 1
Elk, CA

707-877-9997

The Griffin House Inn
5910 S H 1
Elk, CA

707-877-1820

Extended Stay America - Sacramento
- Elk Grove
2201 Long Port Court
Elk Grove, CA
916-683-3753

Fairfield Inn & Suites By Marriott
Sacramento Elk Grove
8058 Orchard Loop Lane
Elk Grove, CA

916-681-5400

Holiday Inn Express & Suites Elk
Grove - Sacramento
2460 Maritime Drive
Elk Grove, CA

916-478-4000

Holiday Inn Express Hotel & Suites
Elk Grove
9175 W. Stockton Blvd.
Elk Grove, CA

916-478-9000

Best Western Encinitas Inn & Suites
At Moonlight Beach
85 Encinitas Blvd
Encinitas, CA
760-942-7455

Casa Leucadia
Call to Arrange
Encinitas, CA

760-633-4497

Quality Inn Encinitas Near Legoland
607 Leucadia Boulevard
Encinitas, CA

760-944-3800

Palm Tree Lodge Motel
425 W Mission Avenue
Escondido, CA
760-745-7613

Rodeway Inn Escondido
250 West El Norte Parkway
Escondido, CA

760-746-0441

Tuscany Hills Retreat
29850 Circle R Way
Escondido, CA

760-751-8800

Carter House Inns
301 L Street
Eureka, CA
707-444-8062

Discovery Inn - Eureka
2832 Broadway Street
Eureka, CA

707-441-8442

Quality Inn Eureka
1209 Fourth Street
Eureka, CA

707-443-1601

Extended Stay America - Fairfield -
Napa Valley
1019 Oliver Rd
Fairfield, CA
707-438-0932

Homewood Suites By Hilton Fairfield
4755 Business Center Drive
Fairfield, CA

707-863-0300

Pala Mesa Golf Resort
2001 Old Highway 395
Fallbrook, CA
760-728-5881

Quail Cove
39117 Northshore Drive
Fawnskin, CA
800-595-2683

Best Western La Posada Motel
827 W Ventura Street
Fillmore, CA
805-524-0440

Narrow Gauge Inn
48571 Highway 41
Fish Camp, CA
559-683-7720

Lake Natoma Inn
702 Gold Lake Drive

Folsom, CA
916-351-1500

Residence Inn By Marriott
Sacramento Folsom
2555 Iron Point Road
Folsom, CA

916-983-7289

Beachcomber Motel
1111 North Main Street
Fort Bragg, CA
707-964-2402

Cleone Gardens Inn
24600 N. Hwy 1
Fort Bragg, CA

707-964-2788

Harbor View Seasonal Rental
Call to arrange.
Fort Bragg, CA

760-438-2563

Holiday Inn Express Ft Bragg
250 West Highway 20
Fort Bragg, CA

707-964-1100

Motel 6 Fort Bragg
400 South Main Street
Fort Bragg, CA

707-964-4761

Pine Beach Inn
16801 N H 1
Fort Bragg, CA

888-987-8388

Super 8 Fort Bragg
888 South Main Street
Fort Bragg, CA

707-964-4003

The Rendezvous Inn and
Restaurant
647 North Main Street
Fort Bragg, CA

707-964-8142

Best Western Country Inn Fortuna
2025 Riverwalk Drive
Fortuna, CA
707-725-6822

The Redwood Fortuna Riverwalk
Hotel
1859 Alamar Way
Fortuna, CA

707-725-5500

Residence Inn Huntington Beach
Fountain Valley

9930 Slater Ave
Fountain Valley, CA
714-965-8000

Best Western Plus Garden Court Inn
5400 Mowry Avenue
Fremont, CA
510-792-4300

Extended Stay America - Fremont -
Warm Springs
46312 Mission Blvd
Fremont, CA

510-979-1222

Extended Stay America Fremont -
Fremont Blvd. South
46080 Fremont Blvd
Fremont, CA

510-353-1664

Residence Inn Fremont Silicon Valley
5400 Farwell Place
Fremont, CA

510-794-5900

Ashlan Inn
4278 West Ashlan Avenue
Fresno, CA
559-275-2727

Best Western Village Inn
3110 North Blackstone Avenue
Fresno, CA

559-226-2110

Days Inn Fresno South
2640 South 2nd Street
Fresno, CA

559-237-6644

Econo Lodge Fresno
445 North Parkway Drive
Fresno, CA

559-485-5019

Extended Stay America - Fresno -
North
7135 North Fresno Street
Fresno, CA

559-438-7105

Fresno-Days Inn
1101 N Parkway Drive
Fresno, CA

559-268-6211

Parkway Inn
959 North Parkway Drive
Fresno, CA

559-445-0322

Ramada Fresno Northwest

5046 North Barcus Avenue
Fresno, CA

559-277-5700

Residence Inn Fresno
5322 N Diana Ave
Fresno, CA

559-222-8900

Super 8 Fresno Convention Center
2127 Inyo Street
Fresno, CA

559-268-0621

Towneplace Suites By Marriott
Fresno
7127 Fresno Street
Fresno, CA

559-435-4600

University Inn Fresno
2655 East Shaw Avenue
Fresno, CA

559-294-0224

Fullerton Marriott At California State
University
2701 East Nutwood Avenue
Fullerton, CA
714-738-7800

Best Western Plus Humboldt House
Inn
701 Redwood Dr.
Garberville, CA
707-923-2771

Anaheim Marriott Suites
12015 Harbor Boulevard
Garden Grove, CA
714-750-1000

Candlewood Suites Anaheim South
12901 Garden Grove Blvd
Garden Grove, CA

714-539-4200

Residence Inn Garden Grove
11931 Harbor Boulevard
Garden Grove, CA

714-591-4000

Sheraton Garden Grove-Anaheim
South
12221 Harbor Boulevard
Garden Grove, CA

714-703-8400

Extended Stay America - Los
Angeles - South
18602 South Vermont Avenue
Gardena, CA
310-515-5139

American River Bed and Breakfast
Inn
Main and Orleans Streets
Georgetown, CA
530-333-4499

Best Western Plus Forest Park Inn
375 Leavesley Road
Gilroy, CA
408-848-5144

Quality Inn & Suites
8430 Murray Ave
Gilroy, CA

408-847-5500

Extended Stay America - Los
Angeles - Glendale
1377 W Glenoaks Blvd
Glendale, CA
818-956-6665

Hilton Los Angeles North/Glendale
And Executive Meeting Ctr
100 West Glenoaks Blvd
Glendale, CA

818-956-5466

Vagabond Inn Glendale
120 W. Colorado Street
Glendale, CA

818-240-1700

Kimpton Goodland
5650 Calle Real
Goleta, CA
805-964-6241

Econo Lodge Gorman
49713 Gorman Post Road
Gorman, CA
661-248-6411

Gray Eagle Lodge
5000 Gold Lake Rd.
Graeagle, CA
800-635-8778

Best Western Gold Country Inn
972 Sutton Way
Grass Valley, CA
530-273-1393

Grass Valley Courtyard Suites
210 North Auburn Street
Grass Valley, CA

530-272-7696

Holiday Inn Express Hotel & Suites
Gold Miners Inn-Grass Valley
121 Bank Street
Grass Valley, CA

530-477-1700

Swan Levine House Bed and
Breakfast

328 South Church Street
Grass Valley, CA

916-272-1873

Hotel Charlotte
18736 Main Street
Groveland, CA
209-962-6455

Hotel Charlotte
18736 Main Street
Groveland, CA

209-962-6455

Sunset Inn
33569 Hardin Flat Rd.
Groveland, CA

209-962-4360

The Groveland Hotel
18767 Main Street
Groveland, CA

209-962-4000

Yosemite Pines RV Resort & Family
Lodging
20450 Old Highway 120
Groveland, CA

209-962-7690

Mar Vista Cottages
35101 S H 1
Gualala, CA
707-884-3522

Ocean View Properties
P.O. Box 1285
Gualala, CA

707-884-3538

Sea Ranch Vacation Homes
P.O. Box 246
Gualala, CA

707-884-4235

Serenisea Vacation Homes
36100 Highway 1 S.
Gualala, CA

707-884-3836

Surf Inn
39170 South Highway 1
Gualala, CA

707-884-3571

Cottages On River Road
14880 River Road
Guerneville, CA
888-342-2624

Creekside Inn & Resort
16180 Neeley Rd
Guerneville, CA

707-869-3623

Ferngrove Cottages
16650 H 116
Guerneville, CA

707-869-8105

Super 8 Hanford
918 E Lacey Blvd
Hanford, CA
559-582-1736

Towneplace Suites By Marriott LAX
Manhattan Beach
14400 Aviation Blvd
Hawthorne, CA
310-725-9696

Best Western Dry Creek Inn
198 Dry Creek Road
Healdsburg, CA
707-433-0300

Duchamp Hotel
421 Foss Street
Healdsburg, CA

707-431-1300

Russian River Adventures Canoe
Rentals
20 Healdsburg Ave
Healdsburg, CA

707-433-5599

Best Western Plus Diamond Valley
Inn
3510 West Florida Avenue
Hemet, CA
951-658-2281

Americas Best Value Inn - Hesperia
12033 Oakwood Avenue
Hesperia, CA
760-949-3231

Days Suites
14865 Bear Valley Rd
Hesperia, CA

760-948-0600

Chateau Marmont
8221 Sunset Boulevard
Hollywood, CA
323-656-1010

Sorensen's Resort
14255 Highway 88
Hope Valley, CA
530-694-2203

Extended Stay America - Orange
County - Huntington Beach
5050 Skylab West Circle
Huntington Beach, CA
714-799-4887

Kimpton Shorebreak Hotel
500 Pacific Coast Highway
Huntington Beach, CA

714-861-4470

The Waterfront Beach Resort, a
Hilton Hotel
21100 Pacific Coast Highway
Huntington Beach, CA

714-845-8000

Tahquitz Inn
25840 Highway 243
Idyllwild, CA
909-659-4554

The Fireside Inn
54540 N Circle Drive
Idyllwild, CA

877-797-FIRE (3473)

Independence Courthouse Motel
157 N Edwards Street
Independence, CA
760-878-2732

Best Western Date Tree Hotel
81909 Indio Boulevard
Indio, CA
760-347-3421

Palm Shadow Inn
80-761 Highway 111
Indio, CA

760-347-3476

Royal Plaza Inn
82347 Highway 111
Indio, CA

760-347-0911

Super 8 Indio
81-753 Highway 111
Indio, CA

760-342-0264

Rosemary Cottage
75 Balboa Ave
Inverness, CA
415-663-9338

Candlewood Suites Spectrum
16150 Sand Canyon Ave
Irvine, CA
949-788-0500

Extended Stay America - Orange
County - Irvine Spectrum
30 Technology Dr
Irvine, CA

949-727-4228

Hilton Irvine/Orange County Airport
18800 Macarthur Blvd
Irvine, CA

949-833-9999

Hilton Irvine/Orange County Airport
18800 Macarthur Blvd
Irvine, CA

949-833-9999

Residence Inn Irvine John Wayne
Airport
2855 Main Street
Irvine, CA

949-261-2020

Residence Inn Irvine Spectrum
10 Morgan Street
Irvine, CA

949-380-3000

Amador Motel
12408 Kennedy Flat Rd
Jackson, CA
209-223-0970

Dog & Pony Ranch
East Clinton Rd.
Jackson, CA

408-471-8757

The Jackson Lodge
850 North State Highway 49
Jackson, CA

209-223-0486

Historic National Hotel & Restaurant
18183 Main Street
Jamestown, CA
209-984-3446

Historic National Hotel & Restaurant
18183 Main Street
Jamestown, CA

209-984-3446

Jenner Inn
10400 H 1
Jenner, CA
707-865-2377

Joshua Tree
6426 Valley View Street
Joshua Tree, CA
760-366-2212

Apple Tree Inn
4360 Highway 78
Julian, CA
800-410-8683

Big Rock Resort
Big Rock Road at Boulder Drive
June Lake, CA
760-648-7717

Double Eagle Resort and Spa

Dog-Friendly Lodging - Please always call ahead to make sure an establishment is still dog-friendly.

5587 Highway 158
June Lake, CA

760-648-7004

June Lake Villager Inn
Boulder Dr & Knoll Ave
June Lake, CA

760-648-7712

Edgewater Resort and RV Park
6420 Soda Bay Road
Kelseyville, CA
707-279-0208

Casa Bella Inn
8790 Highway 12
Kenwood, CA
707-833-6996

River View Lodge
2 Sirreta Street
Kernville, CA
760-376-6019

Motel 6 Kingsburg
401 Sierra Street
Kingsburg, CA
559-897-1022

Motel Trees
15495 Highway 101 South
Klamath, CA
707-482-3152

Sierra Inn
13666 Highway Us 50
Kyburz, CA
530-293-3382

Hotel La Jolla, A Kimpton Hotel
7955 la Jolla Shores Drive
La Jolla, CA
858-551-3600

La Jolla Village Lodge
1141 Silverado Street
La Jolla, CA

858-551-2001

La Valencia Hotel
1132 Prospect Street
La Jolla, CA

858-454-0771

Residence Inn La Jolla
8901 Gilman Drive
La Jolla, CA

858-587-1770

San Diego Marriott La Jolla
4240 la Jolla Village Drive
La Jolla, CA

858-587-1414

Sheraton La Jolla

3299 Holiday Court
La Jolla, CA

858-453-5550

Extended Stay America - Los
Angeles - La Mirada
14775 Firestone Blvd
La Mirada, CA
714-670-8579

Residence Inn By Marriott La
Mirada-Buena Park
14419 Firestone Blvd
La Mirada, CA

714-523-2800

La Porte Cabin Rentals
Main Street and Pike Road/P. O.
Box 225
La Porte, CA
530-675-0850

La Quinta Resort & Club, A Waldorf
Astoria Resort
49-499 Eisenhower Drive
La Quinta, CA
760-564-4111

Arrowhead Saddleback Inn
PO Box 1890
Lake Arrowhead, CA
800-858-3334

Prophet's Paradise B&B
26845 Modoc Lane
Lake Arrowhead, CA

909-336-1969

Candlewood Suites Irvine East
3 South Pointe Drive
Lake Forest, CA
949-598-9105

Extended Stay America - Orange
County - Lake Forest
20251 Lake Forest Dr
Lake Forest, CA

949-598-1898

Quality Inn & Suites Irvine Spectrum
23702 Rockfield Boulevard
Lake Forest, CA

949-458-1900

Staybridge Suites Irvine East/Lake
Forest
2 Orchard
Lake Forest, CA

949-462-9500

Lakehouse Hotel And Resort
1025 la Bonita Drive
Lake San Marcos, CA
760-744-0120

The Beach Retreat & Lodge at Tahoe
3411 Lake Tahoe Boulevard
Lake Tahoe, CA
530-541-6722

Sugarloaf Cottages Resort
19667 Lakeshore Drive
Lakehead, CA
800-953-4432

Tsasdi Resort Cabins
19990 Lakeshore Dr.
Lakehead, CA

530-238-2575

Homewood Suites Lancaster
2320 Double Play Way
Lancaster, CA
661-723-8040

Days Inn Lathrop
14750 S. Harlan Road
Lathrop, CA
209-982-1959

Holiday Inn Express Lathrop - South
Stockton
15688 South Harlan Road
Lathrop, CA

209-373-2700

Holiday Inn Express Hotel Frazier
Park
612 Wainwright Court
Lebec, CA
661-248-1600

Ramada Limited Lebec
9000 Countryside Ct
Lebec, CA

661-248-1530

Murphey's Hotel
51493 Hwy 395
Lee Vining, CA
760-647-6316

Travelodge Lemoore
877 East D Street
Lemoore, CA
559-924-1261

Lewiston Valley RV Park
4789 Trinity Dam Blvd.
Lewiston, CA
530-778-3942

S. S. Seafoam Lodge
6751 N H 1
Littleriver, CA
707-937-1827

Extended Stay America - Livermore -
Airway Blvd.
2380 Nissen Dr
Livermore, CA
925-373-1700

Microtel Inn & Suites By Wyndham
Lodi/North Stockton
6428 West Banner Street
Lodi, CA
209-367-9700

Inn Of Lompoc
1122 North H Street
Lompoc, CA
805-735-7744

Travelodge Lompoc California
1415 E Ocean Avenue
Lompoc, CA

805-736-6514

Best Western Plus Frontier Motel
1008 South Main Street
Lone Pine, CA
760-876-5571

Comfort Inn Lone Pine
1920 South Main Street
Lone Pine, CA

760-876-8700

Extended Stay America - Los
Angeles - Long Beach Airport
4105 E. Willow St.
Long Beach, CA
562-989-4601

Hilton Long Beach & Executive
Meeting Center Hotel
701 West Ocean Boulevard
Long Beach, CA

562-983-3400

Hotel Current
5325 E Pacific Coast Highway
Long Beach, CA

562-597-1341

Residence Inn By Marriott Long
Beach
4111 East Willow Street
Long Beach, CA

562-595-0909

Residence Inn Long Beach
Downtown
600 Queensway Drive
Long Beach, CA

562-495-0700

Residence Inn Cypress Los Alamitos
4931 Katella Avenue
Los Alamitos, CA
714-484-5700

Residence Inn By Marriott Palo Alto
4460 El Camino Real
Los Altos, CA
650-559-7890

Best Western Plus Dragon Gate Inn
818 N. Hill St.
Los Angeles, CA
213-617-3077

Best Western Plus Hollywood Hills
Hotel
6141 Franklin Avenue
Los Angeles, CA

323-464-5181

Beverly Laurel Motor Hotel
8018 Beverly Boulevard
Los Angeles, CA

323-651-2441

Extended Stay America - Los
Angeles - LAX Airport
6531 S Sepulveda Blvd
Los Angeles, CA

310-568-9337

Hilton Checkers Los Angeles
535 South Grand Avenue
Los Angeles, CA

213-624-0000

Kimpton Everly Hotel
1800 Argyle Avenue
Los Angeles, CA

213-279-3532

Kimpton Hotel Palomar Los Angeles
Beverly Hills
10740 Wilshire Boulevard
Los Angeles, CA

310-475-8711

Kimpton Hotel Wilshire
6317 Wilshire Boulevard
Los Angeles, CA

323-852-6000

Residence Inn Beverly Hills
1177 South Beverly Drive
Los Angeles, CA

310-228-4100

Sheraton Grand Los Angeles
711 South Hope Street
Los Angeles, CA

213-488-3500

Sofitel Los Angeles At Beverly Hills
8555 Beverly Boulevard
Los Angeles, CA

310-278-5444

Super 8 Motel - Los
Angeles/Alhambra
5350 S. Huntington Dr.

Los Angeles, CA

323-225-2310

Travelodge Hotel At LAX Airport
5547 W. Century Blvd
Los Angeles, CA

310-649-4000

Best Western Executive Inn
301 W. Pacheco Boulevard
Los Banos, CA
209-827-0954

Maple Inn and Suites Los Banos
1621 East Pacheco Boulevard
Los Banos, CA

209-827-4600

Red Roof Inn Los Banos
2169 East Pacheco Boulevard
Los Banos, CA

209-826-9690

Sun Star Inn
839 West Pacheco Boulevard
Los Banos, CA

209-826-3805

Days Inn Lost Hills
14684 Aloma Street
Lost Hills, CA
661-797-2371

Gateway Inn
2095 West Kennedy Street
Madera, CA
559-674-8817

Super 8 Madera
1855 West Cleveland Avenue
Madera, CA

559-661-1131

Convict Lake Resort
2000 Convict Lake Road
Mammoth Lakes, CA
760-934-3800

Crystal Crag Lodge
P.O. Box 88
Mammoth Lakes, CA

760-934-2436

Edelweiss Lodge
1872 Old Mammoth Road
Mammoth Lakes, CA

760-934-2445

Rodeway Inn Wildwood Inn
3626 Main Street
Mammoth Lakes, CA

760-934-6855

Dog-Friendly Lodging - Please always call ahead to make sure an establishment is still dog-friendly.

Shilo Inn Mammoth Lakes
2963 Main Street
Mammoth Lakes, CA

760-934-4500

Sierra Lodge
3540 Main Street
Mammoth Lakes, CA

760-934-8881

Swiss Chalet
3776 Viewpoint Road
Mammoth Lakes, CA

760-934-2403

Tamarack Lodge
P.O. Box 69/Lake Mary Road
Mammoth Lakes, CA

760-934-2442

The Mammoth Creek Inn
663 Old Mammoth Road
Mammoth Lakes, CA

760-934-6162

The Westin Monache Resort
Mammoth
50 Hillside Drive
Mammoth Lakes, CA

760-934-0400

Travelodge Mammoth Lakes
54 Sierra Blvd
Mammoth Lakes, CA

760-934-8892

Manhattan Beach Marriott
1400 Parkview Avenue
Manhattan Beach, CA
810-546-7511

Residence Inn Los Angeles
LAX/Manhattan Beach
1700 North Sepulveda Boulevard
Manhattan Beach, CA

310-421-3100

Best Western Plus Executive Inn And
Suites
1415 East Yosemite Avenue
Manteca, CA
209-825-1415

Hotel Mdr Marina Del Rey- A
Doubletree By Hilton
13480 Maxella Avenue
Marina Del Rey, CA

Hotel Mdr Marina Del Rey- A
Doubletree By Hilton
13480 Maxella Avenue
Marina Del Rey, CA

Americas Best Value Inn Mariposa

Lodge
5052 Highway 140
Mariposa, CA
209-966-3607

Yosemite's SierraScape Vacation
Rentals
Please call to reserve
Mariposa, CA

209-966-4945

Best Western Plus John Muir Inn
445 Muir Station Road
Martinez, CA
925-229-1010

Comfort Suites Beale Air Force
Base Area
1034 North Beale Road
Marysville, CA
530-742-9200

Century House Inn
433 Lawndale Court
McCloud, CA
530-964-2206

Stoney Brook Inn
309 W Colombero Road
McCloud, CA

800-369-6118

Sunset Ranch Oasis
69-520 South Lincoln
Mecca, CA
626-705-3273

Coastal Getaways
10501 Ford Street POB1355
Mendocino, CA
707-937-9200

Cottages at Little River Cove
7533 N. Highway 1
Mendocino, CA

707-937-5339

Inn at Schoolhouse Creek
7051 N. Highway 1
Mendocino, CA

707-937-5525

Mendocino Seaside Cottages
10940 Lansing St
Mendocino, CA

707-485-0239

Stanford Inn by the Sea and Spa
44850 Comptche Ukiah Rd and
Highway One
Mendocino, CA

707-937-5615

Sweetwater Inn and Spa
44840 Main Street

Mendocino, CA

707-937-4076

The Blair House Inn
45110 Little Lake Street
Mendocino, CA

707-937-1800

Best Western Apricot Inn
46290 West Panoche Road
Mendota, CA
559-659-1444

Americas Best Value Inn
1213 V Street
Merced, CA
209-723-3711

Best Western Plus Inn
1033 Motel Drive
Merced, CA

209-723-2163

Merced Inn & Suites
2010 E Childs Ave
Merced, CA

209-723-3121

Motel 6 Merced
1983 East Childs Avenue
Merced, CA

209-384-1303

Travelodge Merced Yosemite
1260 Yosemite Parkway
Merced, CA

209-722-6224

Child's Meadow Resort
41500 Highway 36E
Mill Creek, CA
530-595-3383

Aloft San Francisco Airport
401 East Millbrae Avenue
Millbrae, CA
650-692-6363

Westin San Francisco Airport
One Bayshore Highway
Millbrae, CA

650-692-3500

Best Western Plus Brookside Inn
400 Valley Way
Milpitas, CA
408-263-5566

Crowne Plaza Hotel San Jose-Silicon
Valley
777 Bellew Drive
Milpitas, CA

408-321-9500

Extended Stay America - San Jose - Milpitas
1000 Hillview Court
Milpitas, CA

408-941-9977

Extended Stay America San Jose - Milpitas - Mccarthy Ranch
330 Cypress Drive
Milpitas, CA

408-433-9700

Residence Inn Milpitas Silicon Valley
1501 California Circle
Milpitas, CA

408-941-9222

Sheraton San Jose Hotel
1801 Barber Lane
Milpitas, CA

408-943-0600

Staybridge Suites Silicon Valley-Milpitas
321 Cypress Drive
Milpitas, CA

408-383-9500

Towneplace Suites By Marriott Milpitas
1428 Falcon Drive
Milpitas, CA

408-719-1959

Miranda Gardens Resort
6766 Avenue of the Giants
Miranda, CA
707-943-3011

Baymont Inn & Suites Modesto Salida
4100 Salida Blvd
Modesto, CA
209-543-9000

Days Inn Modesto
1312 Mchenry Avenue
Modesto, CA

209-527-1010

Quality Inn Modesto
500 Kansas Avenue
Modesto, CA

209-578-5400

Microtel Inn & Suites By Wyndham Modesto Ceres
1760 Herndon Road
Modesto Ceres, CA
209-538-6466

Motel 6 Mojave - Airport
16100 Sierra Highway
Mojave, CA
661-824-2421

Extended Stay America - Los Angeles-Monrovia
930 S Fifth Ave
Monrovia, CA
626-256-6999

Grandma's House Bed and Breakfast
20280 River Blvd
Monte Rio, CA
707-865-1865

San Ysidro Ranch
900 San Ysidro Lane
Montecito, CA
805-969-5046

Bay Park Hotel
1425 Munras Avenue
Monterey, CA
831-649-1020

Best Western Plus Victorian Inn
487 Foam Street
Monterey, CA

831-373-8000

Inn By the Bay Monterey
936 Munras Avenue
Monterey, CA

831-372-5409

Monterey Bay Lodge
55 Camino Aquaiito/H 1
Monterey, CA

831-372-8057

Monterey Bay Travelodge
2030 North Fremont Street
Monterey, CA

Monterey Fireside Lodge
1131 Tenth Street
Monterey, CA

831-373-4172

Monterey Tides
2600 Sand Dunes Dr.
Monterey, CA

831-394-3321

Floral Inn
1560 Monterey Pass Road
Monterey Park, CA
323-263-9888

Comfort Inn Moreno Valley
23330 Sunnymead Blvd.
Moreno Valley, CA
951-242-0699

Extended Stay America - San Jose - Morgan Hill
605 Jarvis Drive
Morgan Hill, CA

408-779-9660

Residence Inn San Jose South Morgan Hill
18620 Madrone Parkway
Morgan Hill, CA

408-782-8311

Bayfront Inn
1150 Embarcadero
Morro Bay, CA
805-772-5607

Days Inn Morro Bay
1095 Main Street
Morro Bay, CA

805-772-2711

La Serena Inn
990 Morro Ave
Morro Bay, CA

805-772-5665

Morro Bay Sandpiper Inn
540 Main Street
Morro Bay, CA

805-772-7503

Pleasant Inn
235 Harbor Street
Morro Bay, CA

805-772-8521

Dream Inn Bed and Breakfast
326 Chestnut Street
Mount Shasta, CA
530-926-1536

Mount Shasta Ranch Bed and Breakfast
1008 W. A. Barr Rd.
Mount Shasta, CA

530-926-3870

Swiss Holiday Lodge
2400 S. Mt. Shasta Blvd.
Mount Shasta, CA

530-926-3446

The Woodsman Lodge
1121 S Mount Shasta Boulevard
Mount Shasta, CA

530-926-3411

Extended Stay America San Jose-Mountain View
190 East El Camino Real
Mountain View, CA
650-962-1500

Residence Inn Palo Alto Mountain View
1854 El Camino Real West
Mountain View, CA

650-940-1300

Tropicana Lodge
1720 El Camino Real
Mountain View, CA

650-961-0220

Chablis Inn Napa Valley
3360 Solano Ave
Napa, CA
707-257-1944

Embassy Suites Hotel Napa Valley
1075 California Boulevard
Napa, CA

707-253-9540

Napa River Inn
500 Main Street
Napa, CA

707-251-8500

The Inn On First
1938 First Street
Napa, CA

707-253-1331

The Napa Inn Bed and Breakfast
1137 Warren Street
Napa, CA

707-257-1444

The Westin Verasa Napa
1314 Mckinstry Street
Napa, CA

707-257-1800

Best Western Plus Marina Gateway
800 Bay Marina Drive
National City, CA
619-259-2800

Best Western Colorado River Inn
2371 West Broadway
Needles, CA
760-326-4552

Rodeway Inn Needles
1195 3rd Street
Needles, CA

760-326-4900

The Outside Inn
575 E. Broad Street
Nevada City, CA
530-265-2233

Doubletree By Hilton Newark -
Fremont
39900 Balentine Drive
Newark, CA
510-490-8390

Homewood Suites By HiltonÂ®

Newark/Fremont, Ca
39270 Cedar Blvd
Newark, CA

510-791-7700

Residence Inn By Marriott Newark
Silicon Valley
35466 Dumbarton Court
Newark, CA

510-739-6000

Woodfin Suite Hotel
39150 Cedar Blvd.
Newark, CA

510-795-1200

Extended Stay America Orange
County - John Wayne Airport
4881 Birch St.
Newport Beach, CA
949-851-2711

Dog Friendly Tahoe Rentals
Call to Arrange
North Lake Tahoe, CA
530-546-4256

Enchanted Vacation Properties
Call to Arrange
North Lake Tahoe, CA
530-546-2066

Extended Stay America - Los
Angeles - Northridge
19325 Londelius St.
Northridge, CA
818-734-1787

Inn Marin
250 Entrada Drive
Novato, CA
415-883-5952

San Francisco-Days Inn Novato
8141 Redwood Boulevard
Novato, CA

415-897-7111

Oakridge Inn
780 North Ventura Avenue
Oak View, CA
805-649-4018

Best Western Plus Yosemite
Gateway Inn
40530 Highway 41
Oakhurst, CA
559-683-2378

Comfort Inn Yosemite Area
40489 Highway 41
Oakhurst, CA

559-683-8282

High Sierra RV & Mobile Park

40389 H 41
Oakhurst, CA

559-683-7662

Pine Rose Inn Bed and Breakfast
41703 Road 222
Oakhurst, CA

559-642-2800

Extended Stay America - Oakland -
Emeryville
3650 Mandela Pkwy
Oakland, CA
510-923-1481

Hilton Oakland Airport
1 Hegenberger Road
Oakland, CA

510-635-5000

Homewood Suites By HiltonÂ®
Oakland-Waterfront
1103 Embarcadero
Oakland, CA

510-663-2700

Best Western Plus Delta Hotel
5549 Bridgehead Road
Oakley, CA
925-755-1222

Inn At Occidental Of Sonoma Wine
Country - Bed And Breakfast
3657 Church Street
Occidental, CA
707-874-1047

Occidental Hotel
3610 Bohemian Highway
Occidental, CA

707-874-3623

Beachfront Only Vacation Rentals
1821 S Coast Hwy
Oceanside, CA
858-759-0381

Extended Stay America - San Diego -
Oceanside
3190 Vista Way
Oceanside, CA

760-439-1499

Ramada Oceanside
1440 Mission Avenue
Oceanside, CA

760-967-4100

Residence Inn By Marriott San Diego
Oceanside
3603 Ocean Ranch Blvd.
Oceanside, CA

760-722-9600

Lavender Inn
210 E Matilija Street
Ojai, CA
805-646-6635

Ojai Valley Inn and Spa
905 Country Club Road
Ojai, CA

805-646-2420

Ranch Motel
2051 S Highway 395
Olancha, CA
760-764-2387

Olema Inn
10,000 Sir Francis Drake Blvd
Olema, CA
415-663-9559

Best Western Plus Innsuites Ontario
Airport E Hotel & Suites
3400 Shelby Street
Ontario, CA
909-466-9600

Doubletree Hotel Ontario Airport
222 North Vineyard
Ontario, CA

909-937-0900

Econo Lodge Ontario
1655 East 4th Street
Ontario, CA

909-986-7000

Extended Stay America - Los
Angeles - Ontario Airport
3990 East Inland Empire Blvd.
Ontario, CA

909-944-8900

Knights Inn Ontario
1120 East Holt Blvd
Ontario, CA

909-984-9655

Ontario Airport Hotel
700 North Haven Avenue
Ontario, CA

909-980-0400

Red Roof Inn Ontario Airport
1818 East Holt Blvd
Ontario, CA

909-988-8466

Residence Inn Ontario
2025 Convention Center Way
Ontario, CA

909-937-6788

Doubletree Hotel Anaheim/Orange
County

100 The City Drive
Orange, CA
714-634-4500

Extended Stay America Orange
County - Katella Ave.
1635 West Katella Avenue
Orange, CA

714-639-8608

Redwood Parks Lodge Company
7 Valley Green Camp Road
Orick, CA
866-733-9637

Days Inn Oroville
1745 Feather River Boulevard
Oroville, CA
530-533-3297

Super 8 Oroville
1470 Feather River Boulevard
Oroville, CA

530-533-9673

Best Western Oxnard Inn
1156 South Oxnard Blvd.
Oxnard, CA
805-483-9581

Residence Inn By Marriott Oxnard
River Ridge
2101 W Vineyard Ave
Oxnard, CA

805-278-2200

Vagabond Inn Oxnard
1245 North Oxnard Boulevard
Oxnard, CA

805-983-0251

Andril Fireplace Cottages
569 Asilomar Blvd
Pacific Grove, CA
831-375-0994

Lighthouse Lodge And Cottages
1150 &; 1249 Lighthouse Avenue
Pacific Grove, CA

831-655-2111

Best Western Plus Palm Desert
Resort
74695 Highway 111
Palm Desert, CA
760-340-4441

Holiday Inn Express Palm Desert
74675 Highway 111
Palm Desert, CA

760-340-4303

Residence Inn By Marriott Palm
Desert
38-305 Cook Street

Palm Desert, CA

760-776-0050

The Inn At Deep Canyon
74-470 Abronia Trail
Palm Desert, CA

760-346-8061

Ace Hotel And Swim Club
701 East Palm Canyon Drive
Palm Springs, CA
760-325-9900

Best Western Inn At Palm Springs
1633 S. Palm Canyon Drive
Palm Springs, CA

760-325-9177

Casa Cody
175 South Cahuilla Rd
Palm Springs, CA

760-320-9346

Extended Stay America - Palm
Springs - Airport
1400 E. Tahquitz Canyon Way
Palm Springs, CA

760-416-0084

Hilton Palm Springs Resort
400 East Tahquitz Canyon Way
Palm Springs, CA

760-320-6868

Musicland Hotel
1342 South Palm Canyon Drive
Palm Springs, CA

760-325-1326

Orchid Tree Inn
261 South Belardo Road
Palm Springs, CA

760-325-2791

Palm Springs Hotels Caliente Tropics
Resort
411 E. Palm Canyon Drive
Palm Springs, CA

800-658-5975

Parker Palm Springs
4200 East Palm Canyon Drive
Palm Springs, CA

760-770-5000

Quality Inn Palm Springs
1269 E Palm Canyon Dr
Palm Springs, CA

760-323-2775

RENAISSANCE PALM SPRINGS
HOTEL, A Marriott Luxury & Lifestyle

Hotel
888 Tahquitz Canyon Way
Palm Springs, CA

760-322-6000

The Riviera Palm Springs a Tribute
Portfolio Resort
1600 North Indian Canyon Drive
Palm Springs, CA

760-327-8311

Vacation Palm Springs
1401 N Palm Canyon Drive, Suite
201
Palm Springs, CA

760-778-7832

Red Roof Inn Palmdale - Lancaster
200 West Palmdale Boulevard
Palmdale, CA
661-273-8000

Residence Inn Palmdale
514 West Rancho Vista Boulevard
(Avenue P)
Palmdale, CA

661-947-4204

Comfort Inn Palo Alto
3945 El Camino Real
Palo Alto, CA
650-493-3141

Crowne Plaza Cabana Palo Alto
4290 El Camino Real
Palo Alto, CA

650-857-0787

The Nest Hotel
3901 El Camino Real
Palo Alto, CA

650-493-2760

Panamint Springs Resort
Highway 190
Panamint Springs, CA
775-482-7680

Comfort Inn Central Paradise
5475 Clark Road
Paradise, CA
530-876-0191

Ponderosa Gardens Motel
7010 The Skyway
Paradise, CA

530-872-9094

Hotel Le Reve Pasadena
3321 East Colorado Boulevard
Pasadena, CA
626-796-9291

Bestway Inn
2701 Spring Street

Paso Robles, CA

Holiday Inn Express Hotel & Suites -
Paso Robles
2455 Riverside Avenue
Paso Robles, CA

805-238-6500

The Lodge At Pebble Beach
1700 Seventeen Mile Drive
Pebble Beach, CA
831-624-3811

Red Lion Inn & Suites Perris
480 South Redlands Avenue
Perris, CA
951-943-5577

Best Western Petaluma Inn
200 S. Mcdowell Blvd
Petaluma, CA
707-763-0994

Quality Inn Petaluma
5100 Montero Way
Petaluma, CA

707-664-1155

Sheraton Sonoma County Petaluma
745 Baywood Drive
Petaluma, CA

707-283-2888

Anderson Valley Inn
8480 H 128
Philo, CA
707-895-3325

Highland Ranch
18941 Philo Greenwood Rd.
Philo, CA

707-895-3600

Pioneer Town Motel
5040 Curtis Road
Pioneertown, CA
760-365-4879

Cottage Inn By The Sea
2351 Price St.
Pismo Beach, CA
805-773-4617

Oxford Suites Pismo Beach
651 Five Cities Drive
Pismo Beach, CA

805-773-3773

Sea Gypsy Motel
1020 Cypress Street
Pismo Beach, CA

805-773-1801

Spyglass Inn
2703 Spyglass Drive

Pismo Beach, CA

805-773-4855

Residence Inn Placentia Fullerton
700 West Kimberly Avenue
Placentia, CA
714-996-0555

Best Western Plus Placerville Inn
6850 Greenleaf Drive
Placerville, CA
530-622-9100

Fleming Jones Homestead B&B
3170 Newtown Road
Placerville, CA

530-344-0943

The Seasons B&B
2934 Bedford Avenue
Placerville, CA

530-626-4420

Extended Stay America - Pleasant
Hill - Buskirk Ave.
3220 Buskirk Ave
Pleasant Hill, CA
925-945-6788

Residence Inn By Marriott Pleasant
Hill Concord
700 Ellinwood Way
Pleasant Hill, CA

925-689-1010

Best Western Plus Pleasanton Inn
5375 Owens Court
Pleasanton, CA
925-463-1300

Residence Inn By Marriott Pleasanton
11920 Dublin Canyon Road
Pleasanton, CA

925-227-0500

Sheraton Pleasanton
5990 Stoneridge Mall Road
Pleasanton, CA

925-463-3330

Point Reyes Station Inn Bed and
Breakfast
11591 Highway One, Box 824
Point Reyes Station, CA
415-663-9372

Tree House Bed and Breakfast Inn
73 Drake Summit, P.O. Box 1075
Point Reyes Station, CA

415-663-8720

La Quinta Inn & Suites Pomona - Cal
Poly
3200 W Temple Ave
Pomona, CA

909-598-0073

Sheraton Fairplex Hotel &
Conference Center
601 W Mckinley Avenue
Pomona, CA

909-622-2220

Best Western Porterville Inn
350 West Montgomery Avenue
Porterville, CA
559-781-7411

Best Western Poway/San Diego
Hotel
13845 Poway Road
Poway, CA
858-748-6320

Ramada Poway
12448 Poway Road
Poway, CA

858-748-7311

Bucks Lake Lodge
23685 Bucks Lake
Quincy, CA
530-283-2262

Comfort Inn & Suites Near Folsom
Lake Rancho Cordova
12249 Folsom Boulevard
Rancho Cordova, CA
916-351-1213

Comfort Inn & Suites Near Folsom
Lake Rancho Cordova
12249 Folsom Boulevard
Rancho Cordova, CA

916-351-1213

Extended Stay America - Sacramento
- White Rock Rd.
10721 White Rock Rd
Rancho Cordova, CA

916-635-2363

Fairfield Inn And Suites By Marriott
Sacramento Rancho Cordova
10745 Gold Center Drive
Rancho Cordova, CA

916-858-8680

Red Roof Inn Rancho Cordova
10800 Olson Drive
Rancho Cordova, CA

916-638-2500

Residence Inn Sacramento Rancho
Cordova
2779 Prospect Park Drive
Rancho Cordova, CA

916-851-1550

Four Points By Sheraton Ontario-

Rancho Cucamonga
11960 Foothill Boulevard
Rancho Cucamonga, CA
909-204-6100

Homewood Suites By HiltonÂ®
Ontario-Rancho Cucamonga, Ca
11433 Mission Vista Drive
Rancho Cucamonga, CA

909-481-6480

Towneplace Suites By Marriott
Ontario Airport
9625 Milliken Avenue
Rancho Cucamonga, CA

909-466-2200

Agua Caliente Casino Resort Spa
32-250 Bob Hope Drive
Rancho Mirage, CA
888-999-1995

The Inn At Rancho Santa Fe
5951 Linea Del Cielo
Rancho Santa Fe, CA
858-756-1131

Best Western Antelope Inn
203 Antelope Boulevard
Red Bluff, CA
530-527-8882

Comfort Inn Red Bluff
90 Sale Lane
Red Bluff, CA

530-529-7060

Days Inn Red Bluff
5 Sutter Street
Red Bluff, CA

530-527-6130

Riverbank Inn Red Bluff / South Of
Redding
38 Antelope Boulevard
Red Bluff, CA

530-527-6020

Sportsman Lodge Red Bluff
768 Antelope Boulevard
Red Bluff, CA

530-527-2888

Super 8 Red Bluff
30 Gilmore Road
Red Bluff, CA

530-529-2028

Best Western Plus Twin View Inn &
Suites
1080 Twin View Boulevard
Redding, CA
530-241-5500

Bridge Bay Resort

10300 Bridge Bay Road
Redding, CA

530-275-3021

Fawndale Lodge and RV Resort
15215 Fawndale Road
Redding, CA

800-338-0941

Holiday Inn Redding
1900 Hilltop Drive
Redding, CA

530-221-7500

Ramada Limited Redding
1286 Twin View Boulevard
Redding, CA

530-246-2222

Red Lion Hotel Redding
1830 Hilltop Drive
Redding, CA

530-221-8700

River Inn
1835 Park Marina Drive
Redding, CA

530-241-9500

Shasta Lodge
1245 Pine Street
Redding, CA

530-243-6133

Dean Creek Resort
4112 Redwood Drive
Redway, CA
707-923-2555

Towneplace Suites By Marriott
Redwood City
1000 Twin Dolphin Drive
Redwood City, CA
650-593-4100

Extended Stay America - Richmond -
Hilltop Mall
3170 Garrity Way
Richmond, CA
510-222-7383

Marina Bay Inn & Suites
915 West Cutting Boulevard
Richmond, CA

510-237-3000

Best Western China Lake Inn
400 S China Lake Blvd
Ridgecrest, CA
760-371-2300

Econo Lodge Inn & Suites Ridgecrest
201 West Inyokern Road
Ridgecrest, CA

760-446-2551

Travel Inn Ridgecrest
131 West Upjohn Avenue
Ridgecrest, CA

760-384-3575

Riverside Inn & Suites
10705 Magnolia
Riverside, CA
951-351-2424

Rodeway Inn Riverside
10518 Magnolia Avenue
Riverside, CA

951-359-0770

Staybridge Suites Rocklin
6664 Lonetree Blvd
Rocklin, CA
916-781-7500

Best Western Inn Rohnert Park
6500 Redwood Drive
Rohnert Park, CA
707-584-7435

Doubletree Hotel Sonoma Wine
Country
One Doubletree Drive
Rohnert Park, CA

707-584-5466

Best Western Roseville Inn
220 Harding Boulevard
Roseville, CA
916-782-4434

Extended Stay America - Sacramento
- Roseville
1000 Lead Hill Blvd
Roseville, CA

916-781-9001

Residence Inn Roseville
1930 Taylor Road
Roseville, CA

916-772-5500

Towneplace Suites Sacramento
Roseville
10569 Fairway Drive
Roseville, CA

916-782-2232

Best Western Sandman Motel
236 Jibboom Street
Sacramento, CA
916-443-6515

Canterbury Inn Hotel
1900 Canterbury Rd
Sacramento, CA

916-927-0927

Days Inn Sacramento Downtown
228 Jibboom Street
Sacramento, CA

916-443-4811

Doubletree By Hilton Sacramento
2001 Point West Way
Sacramento, CA

916-929-8855

Econo Lodge Sacramento
711 16th Street
Sacramento, CA

916-443-6631

Extended Stay America -
Sacramento - Arden Way
2100 Harvard Street
Sacramento, CA

916-921-9942

Extended Stay America -
Sacramento - South Natomas
2810 Gateway Oaks Drive
Sacramento, CA

916-564-7500

Residence Inn By Marriott
Sacramento Downtown At Capitol
Park
1121 15th Street
Sacramento, CA

916-443-0500

Residence Inn Sacramento Airport
Natomas
2410 West El Camino Avenue
Sacramento, CA

916-649-1300

Residence Inn Sacramento Airport
Natomas
2410 West El Camino Avenue
Sacramento, CA

916-649-1300

Residence Inn Sacramento Cal
Expo
1530 Howe Ave
Sacramento, CA

916-920-9111

Sacramento Inn And Suites
1401 Arden Way, Suite 1
Sacramento, CA

916-922-8041

Sheraton Grand Sacramento Hotel
1230 J Street
Sacramento, CA

916-447-1700

Staybridge Suites Sacramento Airport
Natomas
140 Promenade Circle
Sacramento, CA

916-575-7907

Towneplace Suites By Marriott
Sacramento Cal Expo
1784 Tribute Road
Sacramento, CA

916-920-5400

Residence Inn By Marriott Salinas
Monterey
17215 El Rancho Way
Salinas, CA
831-775-0410

Best Western Hospitality Lane
294 East Hospitality Lane
San Bernardino, CA
909-381-1681

DoubleTree by Hilton San Bernardino
285 East Hospitality Lane
San Bernardino, CA

909-889-0133

HILLS GARDEN HOTEL
2000 Ostrems Way
San Bernardino, CA

909-880-8425

Quality Inn San Bernardino
1750 South Waterman Avenue
San Bernardino, CA

909-888-4827

Residence Inn San Bernardino
1040 East Harriman Place
San Bernardino, CA

909-382-4564

Super 8 San Bernadino-E. Hospitality
225 East Hospitality Lane
San Bernardino, CA

909-888-6777

Extended Stay America San
Francisco - San Carlos
3 Circle Star Way
San Carlos, CA
650-368-2600

Best Western Plus Casablanca Inn
1601 North El Camino Real
San Clemente, CA
949-361-1644

Holiday Inn San Clemente
111 South Avenue de la Estrella
San Clemente, CA

949-361-3000

Best Western Lamplighter Inn &
Suites At Sdsu
6474 El Cajon Boulevard
San Diego, CA
619-582-3088

Best Western Plus Hacienda Suites-
Old Town
4041 Harney Street
San Diego, CA

619-298-4707

Crowne Plaza Hotel San Diego -
Mission Valley
2270 Hotel Circle North
San Diego, CA

619-297-1101

Doubletree Hotel San Diego/Del Mar
11915 El Camino Real
San Diego, CA

858-481-5900

Extended Stay America - San Diego -
Fashion Valley
7444 Mission Valley Road
San Diego, CA

619-299-2292

Extended Stay America - San Diego -
Hotel Circle
2087 Hotel Circle South
San Diego, CA

619-296-5570

Extended Stay America - San Diego -
Mission Valley - Stadium
3860 Murphy Canyon Road
San Diego, CA

858-292-8927

Extended Stay America - San Diego -
Sorrento Mesa
9880 Pacific Heights Blvd
San Diego, CA

858-623-0100

Hampton Inn San Diego Del Mar
11920 Camino Real
San Diego, CA

858-792-5557

Harborview Inn And Suites
550 West Grape Street
San Diego, CA

619-233-7799

Heritage Inn San Diego - Sea World
3333 Channel Way
San Diego, CA

619-223-9500

Hilton San Diego Airport/Harbor
Island
1960 Harbor Island Drive
San Diego, CA

619-291-6700

Hilton San Diego Bayfront
1 Park Boulevard
San Diego, CA

619-564-3333

Hilton San Diego Gaslamp Quarter
401 K Street
San Diego, CA

619-231-4040

Hilton San Diego Mission Valley
901 Camino Del Rio South
San Diego, CA

619-543-9000

Hilton San Diego Resort
1775 East Mission Bay Drive
San Diego, CA

619-276-4010

Hotel Indigo San Diego Gaslamp
Quarter
509 9th Avenue
San Diego, CA

619-727-4000

Ocean Villa Inn
5142 West Point Loma Blvd
San Diego, CA

619-224-3481

Old Town Inn
4444 Pacific Highway
San Diego, CA

619-260-8024

Pacific Inn and Suites-Convention
Center-Gaslamp-Seaworld
1655 Pacific Highway
San Diego, CA

619-232-6391

Palomar San Diego, A Kimpton
Hotel
1047 5th Avenue
San Diego, CA

619-515-3000

Quality Inn San Diego Miramar
9350 Kearny Mesa Road
San Diego, CA

858-578-4350

Renaissance San Diego Hotel A
Marriott Luxury & Lifestyle Hotel

421 West B Street
San Diego, CA

619-398-3100

Residence Inn By Marriott Rancho
Bernardo / Scripps Poway
12011 Scripps Highland Drive
San Diego, CA

858-635-5724

Residence Inn By Marriott San Diego
Downtown
1747 Pacific Highway
San Diego, CA

619-338-8200

Residence Inn By Marriott San Diego
Downtown/Gaslamp Quarter
356 6th Avenue
San Diego, CA

619-487-1200

Residence Inn Rancho Bernardo
Carmel Mountain
11002 Rancho Carmel Drive
San Diego, CA

858-673-1900

Residence Inn San Diego Mission
Valley
1865 Hotel Circle South
San Diego, CA

619-881-3600

Residence Inn San Diego Sorrento
Mesa/Sorrento Valley
5995 Pacific Mesa Court
San Diego, CA

858-552-9100

San Diego Marriott Del Mar
11966 El Camino Real
San Diego, CA

858-523-1700

Solamar, A Kimpton Hotel
435 6th Avenue
San Diego, CA

619-531-8740

Staybridge Suites Carmel Mountain
11855 Avenue Of Industry
San Diego, CA

858-487-0900

Staybridge Suites Sorrento Mesa
6639 Mira Mesa Blvd
San Diego, CA

858-453-5343

The Us Grant, A Luxury Collection
Hotel, San Diego

326 Broadway
San Diego, CA

619-232-3121

The Westin San Diego Gaslamp
Quarter
910 Broadway Circle
San Diego, CA

619-937-8461

The Wine Pub
2907 Shelter Island Dr. #108
San Diego, CA

619-758-9325

Town and Country San Diego
500 Hotel Circle North
San Diego, CA

619-291-7131

Vagabond Inn San Diego
Airport/Marina
1325 Scott Street
San Diego, CA

619-224-3371

Wyndham San Diego Bayside
1355 North Harbor Drive
San Diego, CA

619-232-3861

Extended Stay America - Los
Angeles - San Dimas
601 W. Bonita Ave
San Dimas, CA
909-394-1022

Red Roof Inn San Dimas
204 North Village Court
San Dimas, CA

909-599-2362

Argonaut Hotel
495 Jefferson Street
San Francisco, CA
415-563-0800

Beresford Arms
701 Post Street
San Francisco, CA

415-673-2600

Best Western Plus Americania
121 Seventh Street
San Francisco, CA

415-626-0200

Best Western Plus The Tuscan
425 North Point Street
San Francisco, CA

415-561-1100

Best Western Plus The Tuscan
425 North Point Street
San Francisco, CA

415-561-1100

Fairmont Heritage Place, Ghirardelli
Square
900 N Point, Suite D100
San Francisco, CA

415-268-5706

Harbor Court Hotel
165 Steuart St
San Francisco, CA

415-882-1300

Hilton San Francisco
333 Ofarrell Street
San Francisco, CA

415-771-1400

Hilton San Francisco Financial
District
750 Kearny Street
San Francisco, CA

415-433-6600

Hotel Triton
342 Grant Ave
San Francisco, CA

415-394-0500

Hotel Vitale-embarcadero
Eight Mission Street
San Francisco, CA

415-278-3700

Hotel Zelos
12 Fourth Street, San Francisco, CA
San Francisco, CA

415-348-1111

Hotel Zeppelin San Francisco
545 Post Street
San Francisco, CA

415-563-0303

Intercontinental San Francisco
888 Howard Street
San Francisco, CA

415-616-6500

Kimpton Buchanan Hotel
1800 Sutter Street
San Francisco, CA

415-921-4000

Laurel Inn, a Joie de Vivre Hotel
444 Presidio Ave
San Francisco, CA

415-567-8467

Le Meridien San Francisco
333 Battery Street
San Francisco, CA

415-296-2900

Loews Regency San Francisco Hotel
222 Sansome Street
San Francisco, CA

415-276-9888

San Francisco Lofts
1501 Mariposa, Suite 328
San Francisco, CA

415-355-1018

San Francisco Marriott Fisherman's
Wharf
1250 Columbus Avenue
San Francisco, CA

415-775-7555

Serrano Hotel
405 Taylor Street
San Francisco, CA

415-885-2500

Sir Francis Drake, A Kimpton Hotel
450 Powell Street
San Francisco, CA

415-392-7755

Taj Campton Place
340 Stockton Street
San Francisco, CA

415-781-5555

The Inn San Francisco
943 S Van Ness Avenue
San Francisco, CA

415-641-0188

The Marker San Francisco
501 Geary Street
San Francisco, CA

415-292-0100

Hilton Los Angeles - San Gabriel
225 West Valley Boulevard
San Gabriel, CA
626-270-2700

The-Eco-NEST
Sir Francis Drake
San Geronimo, CA
415-323-3601

Doubletree By Hilton San Jose
2050 Gateway Place
San Jose, CA
408-453-4000

Extended Stay America - San Jose -

Edenvale - North
6199 San Ignacio Avenue
San Jose, CA

408-226-4499

Extended Stay America - San Jose -
Santa Clara
2131 Gold Street
San Jose, CA

408-262-0401

Extended Stay America San Jose-
Downtown
1560 North First Street
San Jose, CA

408-573-0648

Hilton San Jose
300 Almaden Boulevard
San Jose, CA

408-287-2100

Homewood Suites by Hilton San Jose
Airport-Silicon Valley
10 West Trimble Road
San Jose, CA

408-428-9900

Residence Inn San Jose South
6111 San Ignacio Avenue
San Jose, CA

408-226-7676

San Jose Marriott
301 South Market Street
San Jose, CA

408-280-1300

The Fairmont San Jose
170 South Market Street
San Jose, CA

408-998-1900

San Juan Inn
410 The Alameda #156
San Juan Bautista, CA
831-623-4380

Best Western Plus Royal Oak Hotel
214 Madonna Road
San Luis Obispo, CA
805-544-4410

Sands Inn & Suites
1930 Monterey Street
San Luis Obispo, CA

805-544-0500

Super 8 Motel - San Luis Obispo
1951 Monterey Street
San Luis Obispo, CA

805-544-6888

Vagabond Inn San Luis Obispo
210 Madonna Road
San Luis Obispo, CA

805-544-4710

Residence Inn By Marriott San
Diego North/San Marcos
1245 Los Vallecitos Boulevard
San Marcos, CA
760-591-9828

Extended Stay America San
Francisco - San Mateo - Sfo
1830 Gateway Drive
San Mateo, CA
650-574-1744

Residence Inn San Mateo
2000 Winward Way
San Mateo, CA

650-574-4700

The Lemon Tree Hotel
1600 East Lincoln Avenue
San Rafael, CA
415-456-4975

Extended Stay America - San
Ramon - Bishop Ranch - East
2100 Camino Ramon
San Ramon, CA
925-242-0991

Extended Stay America San Ramon
- Bishop Ranch - West
18000 San Ramon Valley Blvd
San Ramon, CA

925-277-0833

Marriott San Ramon
2600 Bishop Drive
San Ramon, CA

925-867-9200

Best Western Plus Cavalier
Oceanfront Resort
9415 Hearst Drive
San Simeon, CA
805-927-4688

Silver Surf Motel
9390 Castillo Drive
San Simeon, CA

805-927-4661

Candlewood Suites Orange County
2600 South Red Hill Avenue
Santa Ana, CA
949-250-0404

Red Roof Inn - Santa Ana
2600 North Main Street
Santa Ana, CA

714-542-0311

Best Western Beachside Inn
336 West Cabrillo Boulevard
Santa Barbara, CA
805 965-6556

Casa Del Mar Inn - Bed And
Breakfast
18 Bath Street
Santa Barbara, CA

805-963-4418

Extended Stay America - Santa
Barbara - Calle Real
4870 Calle Real
Santa Barbara, CA

805-692-1882

Kimpton Canary Hotel
31 West Carrillo Street
Santa Barbara, CA

805-884-0300

San Ysidro Ranch
900 San Ysidro Lane
Santa Barbara, CA

805-969-5046

Candlewood Suites Silicon Valley
San Jose
481 El Camino Real
Santa Clara, CA
408-241-9305

Vagabond Inn Santa Clara
3580 El Camino Real
Santa Clara, CA

408-241-0771

Fairfield Inn By Marriott Santa Clarita
Valencia
25340 The Old Road
Santa Clarita, CA
661-290-2828

Residence Inn By Marriott Santa
Clarita Valencia
25320 The Old Road
Santa Clarita, CA

661-290-2800

Bucks Beach Bungalow
341 35th Avenue
Santa Cruz, CA
831-476-0170

Edgewater Beach Motel
525 Second Street
Santa Cruz, CA

831-423-0440

Hilton Santa Cruz / Scotts Valley
6001 la Madrona Dr.
Santa Cruz, CA

831-440-1000

Pacific Inn Santa Cruz
330 Ocean Street
Santa Cruz, CA

831-425-3722

Redtail Ranch by the Sea
Call to Arrange.
Santa Cruz, CA

831-429-1322

Best Western Plus Big America
1725 North Broadway
Santa Maria, CA
805-922-5200

Candlewood Suites Santa Maria
2079 N. Roemer Court
Santa Maria, CA

805-928-4155

Holiday Inn Hotel & Suites Santa
Maria
2100 North Broadway
Santa Maria, CA

805-928-6000

Fairmont Miramar Hotel & Bungalows
101 Wilshire Boulevard
Santa Monica, CA
310-576-7777

Le Meridien Delfina Santa Monica
530 Pico Boulevard
Santa Monica, CA

310-399-9344

Loews Santa Monica Beach Hotel
1700 Ocean Avenue
Santa Monica, CA

310-458-6700

Viceroy Santa Monica
1819 Ocean Avenue
Santa Monica, CA

310-260-7500

Quality Inn Santa Nella
28976 West Plaza Drive
Santa Nella, CA
209-826-8282

Americas Best Value Inn - Santa
Rosa
1800 Santa Rosa Avenue
Santa Rosa, CA
707-523-3480

Best Western Garden Inn
1500 Santa Rosa Avenue
Santa Rosa, CA

707-546-4031

Best Western Plus Wine Country
Inn & Suites
870 Hopper Avenue
Santa Rosa, CA

707-545-9000

Extended Stay America - Santa
Rosa - North
100 Fountain Grove Pkwy
Santa Rosa, CA

707-541-0959

Extended Stay America - Santa
Rosa - South
2600 Corby Ave
Santa Rosa, CA

707-546-4808

Hilton Sonoma Wine Country
3555 Round Barn Boulevard
Santa Rosa, CA

707-523-7555

Quality Inn & Suites Santa Rosa
3000 Santa Rosa Avenue
Santa Rosa, CA

707-521-2100

Rodeway Inn Santa Rosa
2632 Cleveland Avenue
Santa Rosa, CA

707-542-5544

Travelodge Santa Rosa
1815 Santa Rosa Avenue
Santa Rosa, CA

707-542-3472

Best Western Santee Lodge
10726 Woodside Avenue
Santee, CA
619-449-2626

Best Western Plus Inn Scotts Valley
6020 Scotts Valley Drive
Scotts Valley, CA
831-438-6666

Sea Ranch Lodge
60 Sea Walk Drive
Sea Ranch, CA
707-785-2371

Super 8 Selma/Fresno Area
3142 S Highland Ave
Selma, CA
559-896-2800

Mill Creek Eco Resort
7185 Mill Creek Road
Shingletown, CA
530-474-4415

Herrington's Sierra Pines Resort
104 Main Street/H 49
Sierra City, CA
530-862-1151

Extended Stay America - Los
Angeles - Simi Valley
2498 Stearns St.
Simi Valley, CA
805-584-8880

Royal Copenhagen Inn
1579 Mission Drive
Solvang, CA
800-624-6604

The Meadowlark Inn
2644 Mission Drive/H 246
Solvang, CA

805-688-4631

Wine Valley Inn
1564 Copenhagen Drive
Solvang, CA

805-688-2111

THE LODGE AT SONOMA
RENAISSANCE RESORT & SPA, A
Marriott Luxury & Lifestyle Hotel
1325 Broadway
Sonoma, CA
707-935-6600

Best Western Plus Sonora Oaks
Hotel & Conference Center
19551 Hess Avenue
Sonora, CA
209-533-4400

Sonora Aladdin Motor Inn
14260 Mono Way (Hwy 108)
Sonora, CA

209-533-4971

Alder Inn
1072 Ski Run Blvd
South Lake Tahoe, CA
530-544-4485

Colony Inn at South Lake Tahoe
3794 Montreal Road
South Lake Tahoe, CA

530-544-6481

Heavenly Valley Lodge Bed &
Breakfast
1261 Ski Run Boulevard
South Lake Tahoe, CA

530-544-4244

Knights Inn South Lake Tahoe
3600 Lake Tahoe Boulevard
South Lake Tahoe, CA

530-544-3476

Rodeway Inn Casino Center
4127 Pine Boulevard
South Lake Tahoe, CA

530-541-7150

Sunray Tahoe
2659 Lake Tahoe Boulevard
South Lake Tahoe, CA

530-544-3959

The Nash Cabin
3595 Betty Ray
South Lake Tahoe, CA

415-759-6583

Residence Inn San Francisco Airport
Oyster Point Waterfront
1350 Veterns Boulevard
South San Francisco, CA
650-837-9000

Harvest Inn by Charlie Palmer
One Main Street
St Helena, CA
707-963-9463

Route 66 Motel
195 West Main Street
St Helena, CA

707-963-3216

Extended Stay America - Los
Angeles - Valencia
24940 W. Pico Canyon Rd
Stevenson Ranch, CA
661-255-1044

Beach Front Retreat
90 Calle Del Ribera
Stinson Beach, CA
415-383-7870

Redwoods Haus Beach
1 Belvedere
Stinson Beach, CA

415-868-9828

Days Inn Stockton
550 West Charter Way
Stockton, CA
209-948-0321

Econo Lodge Stockton
2654 West March Lane
Stockton, CA

209-478-4300

Extended Stay America - Stockton -
March Lane
2844 W. March Lane
Stockton, CA

209-472-7588

Red Roof Inn Stockton
1707 West Freemont St

Stockton, CA

209-466-7777

Residence Inn By Marriott Stockton
3240 March Lane
Stockton, CA

209-472-9800

Extended Stay America San Jose-
Sunnyvale
1255 Orleans Drive
Sunnyvale, CA
408-734-3431

Quality Inn Santa Clara Convention
Center
1280 Persian Drive
Sunnyvale, CA

408-744-1100

Residence Inn Silicon Valley I
750 Lakeway Drive
Sunnyvale, CA

408-720-1000

Residence Inn Silicon Valley Ii
1080 Stewart Drive
Sunnyvale, CA

408-720-8893

Staybridge Suites Sunnyvale
900 Hamlin Court
Sunnyvale, CA

408-745-1515

Towneplace Suites By Marriott
Sunnyvale Mountain View
606 South Bernardo Avenue
Sunnyvale, CA

408-733-4200

Woodfin Suite Hotel
635 E. El Camino Real
Sunnyvale, CA

408-738-1700

Budget Host Frontier Inn
2685 Main Street
Susanville, CA
530-257-4141

River Inn
1710 Main Street
Susanville, CA

530-257-6051

Super 8 Motel - Susanville
2975 Johnstonville Rd.
Susanville, CA

530-257-2782

Days Inn Sutter Creek

271 Hanford Street
Sutter Creek, CA
209-267-9177

Tahoe Moon Properties
P.O. Box 7521
Tahoe City, CA
530-581-2771

Holiday House
7276 North Lake Blvd
Tahoe Vista, CA
530-546-2369

Rustic Cottages
7449 N Lake Blvd
Tahoe Vista, CA

530-546-3523

Waters of Tahoe Vacation Properties
PO Box 312
Tahoe Vista, CA

530-546-8904

Norfolk Woods Inn
6941 West Lake Blvd.
Tahoma, CA
530-525-5000

Tahoma Lodge
7018 West Lake Blvd
Tahoma, CA

530-525-7721

Tahoma Meadows Bed and Breakfast
6821 W. Lake Blvd.
Tahoma, CA

530-525-1553

La Quinta Inn Tehachapi
500 East Steuber Road
Tehachapi, CA

Extended Stay America - Temecula -
Wine Country
27622 Jefferson Avenue
Temecula, CA
951-587-8881

TownePlace Suites Thousand Oaks
Ventura County
1712 Newbury Road
Thousand Oaks, CA
805-499-3111

Red Roof Inn Palm Springs -
Thousand Palms
72215 Varner Rd
Thousand Palms, CA
760-343-1381

Buckeye Tree Lodge
46,000 Sierra Drive/H 198
Three Rivers, CA
559-561-5900

Sequoia Village Inn

45971 Sierra Drive/H 198
Three Rivers, CA

559-561-3652

Days Inn Torrance Redondo Beach
4111 Pacific Coast Highway
Torrance, CA
310-378-8511

Extended Stay America - Los
Angeles - Torrance - Del Amo Circle
3995 Carson St
Torrance, CA

310-543-0048

Extended Stay America - Los
Angeles - Torrance Blvd.
3525 Torrance Blvd
Torrance, CA

310-540-5442

Extended Stay America - Los
Angeles - Torrance Harbor Gateway
19200 Harbor Gtwy
Torrance, CA

310-328-6000

Holiday Inn Torrance
19800 S Vermont
Torrance, CA

310-781-9100

Residence Inn By Marriott Torrance
Redondo Beach
3701 Torrance Blvd
Torrance, CA

310-543-4566

Staybridge Suites Torrance
19901 Prairie Ave
Torrance, CA

310-371-8525

Econo Lodge Tracy
3511 North Tracy Boulevard
Tracy, CA
209-835-1335

Extended Stay America - Stockton -
Tracy
2526 Pavilion Pwky
Tracy, CA

209-832-4700

Microtel Inn & Suites By Wyndham
Tracy
861 W Clover Road
Tracy, CA

209-229-1201

Best Western Town & Country Lodge
1051 North Blackstone
Tulare, CA

559-688-7537

Quality Inn Tulare
1010 East Prosperity Avenue
Tulare, CA

559-686-3432

Red Roof Inn Tulare
1183 North Blackstone
Tulare, CA

559-686-0985

Candlewood Suites Turlock
1000 Powers Court
Turlock, CA
209-250-1501

Comfort Suites Turlock
191 North Tully Road
Turlock, CA

209-667-7777

Travelodge Turlock Ca
201 West Glenwood Avenue
Turlock, CA

209-668-3400

29 Palms Inn
73950 Inn Avenue
Twentynine Palms, CA
760-367-3505

Harmony Hotel
71161 29 Palms H/H 62
Twentynine Palms, CA

760-367-3351

Four Seasons Chalet #1373

UNKNOWN, CA

Best Western Orchard Inn
555 South Orchard Avenue
Ukiah, CA
707-462-1514

Days Inn Ukiah/Gateway To
Redwoods Wine Country
950 North State Street
Ukiah, CA

707-462-7584

Quality Inn Ukiah
1050 South State St
Ukiah, CA

707-462-2906

Super 8 Ukiah
693 South Orchard Avenue
Ukiah, CA

707-468-8181

Extended Stay America - Union City
- Dyer St.

31950 Dyer St
Union City, CA
510-441-9616

Hilton Los Angeles/Universal City
555 Universal Terrace Parkway
Universal City, CA
818-506-2500

Super 8 Upper Lake
450 East Highway 20
Upper Lake, CA
707-275-0888

Best Western Heritage Inn
1420 E Monte Vista Ave
Vacaville, CA
707-448-8453

Extended Stay America - Sacramento
- Vacaville
799 Orange Drive
Vacaville, CA

707-469-1371

Hampton Inn & Suites Vacaville, Ca
800 Mason Street
Vacaville, CA

707-469-6200

Quality Inn & Suites Vacaville
1050 Orange Drive
Vacaville, CA

707-446-8888

Residence Inn By Marriott Vacaville
360 Orange Drive
Vacaville, CA

707-469-0300

Super 8 Vacaville
101 Allison Court
Vacaville, CA

707-449-8884

Best Western Valencia Inn
27413 Wayne Mills Place
Valencia, CA
661-255-0555

Best Western Inn And Suites At
Discovery Kingdom
1596 Fairgrounds Drive
Vallejo, CA
707-554-9655

Courtyard By Marriott Vallejo Napa
Valley
1000 Fairgrounds Drive
Vallejo, CA

707-644-1200

Ramada Inn Vallejo / Napa Valley
Area
1000 Admiral Callaghan Lane

Vallejo, CA
707-643-2700

Best Western Plus Carriage Inn
5525 Sepulveda Boulevard
Van Nuys, CA
818-787-2300

Crowne Plaza Ventura
450 East Harbor Boulevard
Ventura, CA
805-648-2100

Four Points By Sheraton Ventura
Harbor Resort
1050 Schooner Drive
Ventura, CA

805-658-1212

Holiday Inn Express Hotel & Suites
Ventura Harbor
1080 Navigator Drive
Ventura, CA

805-856-9533

Vagabond Inn Ventura
756 East Thompson Boulevard
Ventura, CA

805-648-5371

Days Inn Victorville
15401 Park Avenue East
Victorville, CA
760-241-7516

Red Roof Inn Victorville
13409 Mariposa Road
Victorville, CA

760-241-1577

Travelodge Victorville
12175 Mariposa Road
Victorville, CA

760-241-7200

Super 8 Visalia
4801 West Noble Avenue
Visalia, CA
559-627-2885

Visalia Marriott At The Convention
Center
300 South Court Street
Visalia, CA

559-636-1111

Wyndham Visalia
9000 West Airport Drive
Visalia, CA

559-651-5000

Towneplace Suites By Marriott San
Diego Carlsbad-Vista
2201 South Melrose Drive

Vista, CA
760-216-6010

The St. George Hotel
16104 Main Street
Volcano, CA
209-296-4458

Quality Inn & Suites Walnut
1170 Fairway Drive
Walnut, CA

Best Western Rose Garden Inn
740 Freedom Boulevard
Watsonville, CA
831-724-3367

Comfort Inn Watsonville
112 Airport Boulevard
Watsonville, CA

831-728-2300

RODEWAY INN WATSONVILLE
1620 W. Beach Street
Watsonville, CA

831-740-4520

Comfort Inn Mount Shasta Area
1844 Shastina Dr
Weed, CA
530-938-1982

Lake Shastina Golf Resort
5925 Country Club Drive
Weed, CA

530-938-3201

Quality Inn & Suites Weed
1830 Black Butte Drive
Weed, CA

530-938-1308

Le Montrose Suite Hotel
900 Hammond Street
West Hollywood, CA
310-855-1115

Extended Stay America -
Sacramento - West Sacramento
795 Stillwater Rd
West Sacramento, CA
916-371-1270

Residence Inn Los Angeles
Westlake Village
30950 Russell Ranch Road
Westlake Village, CA
818-707-4411

Holiday Inn Express Westley
4525 Howard Road
Westley, CA
209-894-8940

Howard Creek Ranch Inn B&B
40501 N. Highway 1
Westport, CA

707-964-6725

Econo Lodge Williams
400 C Street
Williams, CA
530-473-2381

Best Western Willows Inn
475 North Humboldt Avenue
Willows, CA
530-934-4444

Holiday Inn Express Hotel & Suites
Willows
545 Humboldt Avenue
Willows, CA

530-934-8900

Wickyup Bed and Breakfast Cottage
22702 Avenue 344
Woodlake, CA
559-564-8898

Holiday Inn Express Sacramento
Airport Woodland
2070 Freeway Drive
Woodland, CA
530-662-7750

Extended Stay America - Los
Angeles - Woodland Hills
20205 Ventura Blvd.
Woodland Hills, CA
818-710-1170

Hilton Woodland Hills
6360 Canoga Ave
Woodland Hills, CA

818-595-1000

Best Western Cajon Pass
8317 Us Highway 138
Wrightwood, CA
760-249-6777

Extended Stay America - Orange
County - Yorba Linda
22711 Oakcrest Circle
Yorba Linda, CA
714-998-9060

The Other Place and the Long Valley
Ranch
P.O. Box 49
Yorkville, CA
707-894-5322

The Redwoods In Yosemite
PO Box 2085; Wawona Station
Yosemite National Park, CA
209-375-6666

The Vintage Inn
6541 Washington Street
Yountville, CA
707-944-1112

Best Western Miners Inn

122 East Miner Street
Yreka, CA
530-842-4355

Comfort Inn Yreka
1804 B Fort Jones Rd
Yreka, CA

530-842-1612

Econo Lodge Yreka
526 South Main Street
Yreka, CA

530-842-4404

Relax Inn Yreka
1210 South Main Street
Yreka, CA

530-842-2791

Rodeway Inn Yreka
1235 South Main Street
Yreka, CA

530-842-4412

Days Inn - Yuba City
700 North Palora Ave
Yuba City, CA
530-674-1711

Econo Lodge Inn & Suites
730 Palora Ave.
Yuba City, CA

530-674-1592

# Colorado Listings

Best Western Alamosa Inn
2005 Main Street
Alamosa, CO
719-589-2567

Comfort Inn & Suites Alamosa
6301 Us Highway 160
Alamosa, CO

719-587-9000

Days Inn Alamosa
223 Santa Fe Avenue
Alamosa, CO

719-589-9037

Super 8 Alamosa
2505 West Main Street
Alamosa, CO

719-589-6447

Harmel's Ranch Resort
P.O. Box 399
Almont, CO
970-641-1740

Hotel Aspen

110 West Main Street
Aspen, CO
970-925-3441

Hotel Jerome An Auberge Resort
330 East Main Street
Aspen, CO

970-920-1000

Limelight Hotel
355 South Monarch Street
Aspen, CO

970-928-3025

Little Nell
675 E Durant Street
Aspen, CO

970-920-4600

Sky Hotel, A Kimpton Hotel
709 East Durant Avenue
Aspen, CO

970-925-6760

St. Regis Resort Aspen
315 East Dean Street
Aspen, CO

970-920-3300

St. Regis Resort Aspen
315 East Dean Street
Aspen, CO

970-920-3300

Best Western Plus Gateway Inn &
Suites
800 South Abilene Street
Aurora, CO
720-748-4800

Econo Lodge Denver International
Airport
15900 East 40th Avenue
Aurora, CO

303-373-1616

Extended Stay America - Denver -
Aurora South
13941 East Harvard Ave
Aurora, CO

303-750-9116

Residence Inn By Marriott Denver
Airport
16490 East 40th Circle
Aurora, CO

303-459-8000

Comfort Inn Near Vail Beaver Creek
0161 West Beaver Creek Boulevard
Avon, CO
970-949-5511

The Westin Riverfront Resort & Spa
at Beaver Creek Mountain
126 Riverfront Lane
Avon, CO

970-790-6000

Glen Isle Resort
Highway 285 (near milepost marker
221)
Bailey, CO
303-838-5461

Best Western Plus Boulder Inn
770 28th Street
Boulder, CO
303-449-3800

Boulder Outlook Hotel And Suites
800 28th Street
Boulder, CO

303-443-3322

Foot of the Mountain Motel
200 Arapahoe Ave.
Boulder, CO

303-442-5688

Holiday Inn Express Boulder
4777 North Broadway
Boulder, CO

303-442-6600

Homewood Suites By Hilton®
Boulder
4950 Baseline Road
Boulder, CO

303-499-9922

Homewood Suites By Hilton®
Boulder
4950 Baseline Road
Boulder, CO

303-499-9922

Quality Inn & Suites Boulder Creek
2020 Arapahoe Avenue
Boulder, CO

303-449-7550

Residence Inn By Marriott Boulder
3030 Center Green Drive
Boulder, CO

303-449-5545

Doubletree By Hilton Breckenridge
550 Village Road
Breckenridge, CO
970-547-5550

Super 8 Motel - Brighton
15040 Brighton Road
Brighton, CO
303-659-6063

Dog-Friendly Lodging - Please always call ahead to make sure an establishment is still dog-friendly.

Towneplace Suites By Marriott
Boulder Broomfield
480 Flatiron Boulevard
Broomfield, CO
303-466-2200

Econo Lodge Brush
1208 N. Colorado Ave.
Brush, CO
970-842-5146

Comfort Inn Burlington
282 S. Lincoln
Burlington, CO
719-346-7676

Econo Lodge Calhan
15 5th Street
Calhan, CO
719-347-9589

Quality Inn & Suites
3075 E. Us 50
Canon City, CO
719-275-8676

Comfort Inn & Suites Carbondale
920 Cowen Drive
Carbondale, CO
970-963-8880

Days Inn Carbondale
950 Cowen Drive
Carbondale, CO

970-963-9111

Best Western Plus Castle Rock
595 Genoa Way
Castle Rock, CO
303-814-8800

Comfort Suites Castle Rock
4755 Castleton Way
Castle Rock, CO

303-814-9999

Days Inn & Suites Castle Rock
4691 Castleton Way
Castle Rock, CO

303-814-5825

Super 8 Castle Rock Colorado
1020 Park Street
Castle Rock, CO

303-688-0880

Hawthorn Suites by Wyndham
Denver Tech Center
6780 South Galena Street
Centennial, CO
303-792-5393

Staybridge Suites Denver Tech
Center
7150 South Clinton Street
Centennial, CO

303-858-9990

Steamboat Lake Marina Camper
Cabins
P. O. Box 867/H 62
Clark, CO
970-879-7019

Days Inn Colorado
6670 West Highway 165
Colorado City, CO
719-676-2340

Comfort Inn North - Air Force
Academy Area
6450 Corporate Drive
Colorado Springs, CO
719-262-9000

Days Inn Colorado Springs
2409 East Pikes Peak Avenue
Colorado Springs, CO

719-471-0990

Days Inn Colorado Springs
2409 East Pikes Peak Avenue
Colorado Springs, CO

719-471-0990

Doubletree By Hilton Colorado
Springs
1775 East Cheyenne Mountain
Boulevard
Colorado Springs, CO

719-576-8900

Econo Lodge Inn and Suites World
Arena
1623 South Nevada
Colorado Springs, CO

719-632-6651

Extended Stay America - Colorado
Springs - West
5855 Corporate Dr
Colorado Springs, CO

719-266-4206

Fairfield Inn & Suites By Marriott
Colorado Springs South
2725 Geyser Drive
Colorado Springs, CO

719-576-1717

Hampton Inn & Suites Colorado
Springs Air Force Academy/I-25 N
1307 Republic Drive
Colorado Springs, CO

719-598-6911

Holiday Inn Express Hotel & Suites
Colorado Springs-Air Force
7110 Commerce Center Drive
Colorado Springs, CO

719-592-9800

Homewood Suites By Hilton®
Colorado Springs Airport
2875 Zeppelin Road
Colorado Springs, CO

719-574-2701

Homewood Suites By Hilton®
Colorado Springs-North
9130 Explorer Drive
Colorado Springs, CO

719-265-6600

Hotel Elegante Conference and Event
Center
2886 South Circle Drive
Colorado Springs, CO

719-576-5900

Howard Johnson Colorado Springs
8280 Highway 83, Academy
Boulevard North
Colorado Springs, CO

Knights Inn Colorado Springs
2850 S Circle Dr
Colorado Springs, CO

719-527-0800

Pine Tree Hotel
520 North Murray Boulevard
Colorado Springs, CO

719-596-7660

Plaza Inn Colorado Springs
8155 North Academy Boulevard
Colorado Springs, CO

719-598-2500

Quality Inn South
1410 Harrison Road
Colorado Springs, CO

719-579-6900

Radisson Hotel Colorado Springs
Airport
1645 North Newport Road
Colorado Springs, CO

719-597-7000

Residence Inn By Marriott Colorado
Springs North
9805 Federal Drive
Colorado Springs, CO

719-388-9300

Residence Inn By Marriott Colorado
Springs South
2765 Geyser Drive
Colorado Springs, CO

719-576-0101

Rodeway Inn & Suites Colorado Springs
1623 South Nevada Avenue
Colorado Springs, CO

719-623-2300

Sonesta Es Suites Colorado Springs
3880 North Academy Boulevard
Colorado Springs, CO

719-574-0370

Staybridge Suites Colorado Springs-Air Force Academy
7130 Commerce Center Drive
Colorado Springs, CO

719-590-7829

Super 8 Colorado Springs Airport
1790 Aeroplaza Drive
Colorado Springs, CO

719-570-0505

Super 8 Colorado Springs/Afa Area
8135 N Academy Blvd (5)
Colorado Springs, CO

719-528-7100

Super 8 Cos/Hwy. 24 E/Pafb Area
605 Peterson Rd
Colorado Springs, CO

719-597-4100

The Academy Hotel Colorado Springs
8110 North Academy Boulevard
Colorado Springs, CO

719-598-5770

The Antlers Hotel
4 South Cascade Avenue
Colorado Springs, CO

719-955-5600

The Cheyenne Canon Inn
2030 W Cheyenne Blvd
Colorado Springs, CO

800-633-0625

Towneplace Suites By Marriott Colorado Springs
4760 Centennial Boulevard
Colorado Springs, CO

719-594-4447

Towneplace Suites By Marriott Colorado Springs South
1530 North Newport Road
Colorado Springs, CO

719-638-0800

Baymont Inn & Suites Cortez
2279 Hawkins Street

Cortez, CO
970-565-3400

Best Western Turquoise Inn And Suites
535 East Main Street
Cortez, CO

970-565-3778

Cortez Mesa Verde Inn
640 South Broadway
Cortez, CO

970-565-3773

Days Inn Cortez
430 N State Hwy 145
Cortez, CO

970-565-8577

Econo Lodge Cortez
2020 East Main Street
Cortez, CO

970-565-3474

Super 8 Cortez/Mesa Verde Area
505 E Main St
Cortez, CO

970-565-8888

Best Western Plus Deer Park Inn & Suites
262 Commerce Street (Hwy 13)
Craig, CO
970-824-9282

Candlewood Suites Craig-Northwest
92 Commerce Street
Craig, CO

970-824-8400

Clarion Inn & Suites Craig
300 South Colorado Highway 13
Craig, CO

970-824-4000

The Ruby of Crested Butte
624 Gothic Avenue
Crested Butte, CO
970-349-1338

Quality Inn Delta
180 Gunnison River Drive
Delta, CO
970-874-1000

Best Western Denver Southwest
3440 South Vance Street
Denver, CO
303-989-5500

Cameron Motel
4500 E Evans
Denver, CO

303-757-2100

Comfort Inn Central
401 East 58th Avenue
Denver, CO

303-297-1717

Comfort Inn Denver
4380 Peoria Street
Denver, CO

303-373-1983

Courtyard By Marriott Denver Stapleton
7415 East 41st Avenue
Denver, CO

303-333-3303

Crowne Plaza Denver Airport Convention Ctr
15500 East 40th Avenue
Denver, CO

303-371-9494

Extended Stay America - Denver - Tech Center - North
4885 South Quebec St
Denver, CO

303-689-9443

Hampton Inn And Suites Denver Tech Center
5001 S. Ulster Street
Denver, CO

303-804-9900

Holiday Inn Denver East - Stapleton
3333 Quebec Street
Denver, CO

303-321-3500

Holiday Inn Express Denver Downtown
401 17th Street
Denver, CO

303-296-0400

Hotel Teatro
1100 Fourteenth Street
Denver, CO

303-228-1100

Hyatt Place Denver Cherry Creek
4150 East Mississippi Avenue
Denver, CO

303-782-9300

Inn at Cherry Creek
233 Clayton Street
Denver, CO

303-377-8577

JW Marriott Denver Cherry Creek

150 Clayton Lane
Denver, CO

303-316-2700

Kimpton Hotel Born
1600 Wewatta Street
Denver, CO

303-323-0024

Kimpton Hotel Monaco Denver
1717 Champa Street At 17th Street
Denver, CO

303-296-1717

Marriott TownePlace Suites -
Downtown
685 Speer Blvd
Denver, CO

303-722-2322

Microtel Inn By Wyndham Denver
18600 East 63rd Avenue
Denver, CO

303-371-8300

Oxford Hotel
1600 17th St
Denver, CO

303-628-5400

Quality Inn & Suites Denver
3737 Quebec Street
Denver, CO

303-388-6161

Quality Inn & Suites Denver
3737 Quebec Street
Denver, CO

303-388-6161

Quality Inn & Suites Denver
International Airport
6890 Tower Road
Denver, CO

303-371-5300

Quality Inn Denver Central
200 West 48th Avenue
Denver, CO

303-296-4000

RENAISSANCE DENVER
STAPLETON HOTEL, A Marriott
Luxury & Lifestyle Hotel
3801 Quebec Street
Denver, CO

303-399-7500

Ramada Inn Denver Downtown
1150 East Colfax Avenue
Denver, CO

303-831-7700

Ramada Plaza & Convention Center
Denver North
10 East 120th Avenue
Denver, CO

303-452-4100

Residence Inn By Marriott Denver
City Center
1725 Champa Street
Denver, CO

303-296-3444

Residence Inn Denver Downtown
2777 Zuni Street
Denver, CO

303-458-5318

Rodeway Inn Denver
3975 Peoria Way
Denver, CO

303-371-5640

Staybridge Suites Denver
International Airport
6951 Tower Road
Denver, CO

303-574-0888

Super 8 Denver
5888 North Broadway
Denver, CO

303-296-3100

Super 8 Denver Midtown
2601 Zuni B Street
Denver, CO

303-433-8586

Super 8 Denver Midtown
2601 Zuni B Street
Denver, CO

303-433-6677

Super 8 Denver Stapleton
7201 East 36th Avenue
Denver, CO

303-393-7666

The Curtis A Doubletree Hotel
1405 Curtis Street
Denver, CO

800-525-6651

The Magnolia Hotel Denver
818 17th Street
Denver, CO

303-607-9000

The Timbers Hotel

4411 Peoria Street
Denver, CO

303-373-1444

Towneplace Suites By Marriott
Denver Southeast
3699 South Monaco Parkway
Denver, CO

303-759-9393

Towneplace Suites By Marriott
Downtown Denver
685 Speer Boulevard
Denver, CO

303-722-2322

Best Western Ptarmigan Lodge
652 Lake Dillon Drive
Dillon, CO
970-468-2341

Doubletree Hotel Durango
501 Camino Del Rio
Durango, CO
970-259-6580

Quality Inn Durango
2930 Main Ave.
Durango, CO

970-259-5373

Residence Inn By Marriott Durango
21691 Us Hwy 160 West
Durango, CO

970-259-6200

Rochester Hotel
726 E. Second Ave.
Durango, CO

970-385-1920

Super 8 Durango
20 Stewart Drive
Durango, CO

970-259-0590

Travelodge Of Durango
2970 Main Avenue
Durango, CO

970-247-1741

Holiday Inn Express Eagle
0075 Pond Road
Eagle, CO
970-328-8088

Candlewood Suites Meridian
Business Park
10535 El Diente Ct
Englewood, CO
303-858-9900

Days Inn Englewood Denver Tech
Center

9719 East Geddes Avenue
Englewood, CO

303-768-9400

Drury Inn & Suites Denver Tech
Center
9445 East Dry Creek Road
Englewood, CO

303-694-3400

Extended Stay America - Denver -
Tech Center South - Inverness
9650 East Geddes Ave
Englewood, CO

303-708-8888

Ramada Hotel and Suites
Englewood/Denver South
7770 South Peoria Street
Englewood, CO

303-790-7770

Residence Inn By Marriott Denver
South/Park Meadows Mall
8322 South Valley Highway
Englewood, CO

720-895-0200

Residence Inn Denver Tech Center
6565 S Yosemite St.
Englewood, CO

303-740-7177

Towneplace Suites By Marriott
Denver Tech Center
7877 South Chester Street
Englewood, CO

720-875-1113

Cliffside Cottages
2445 H 66
Estes Park, CO
970-586-4839

Rodeway Inn Estes Park
1701 North Lake Avenue
Estes Park, CO

970-586-5363

YMCA of the Rockies
2515 Tunnel Road/H 66
Estes Park, CO

800-777-9622

Comfort Suites Golden West On
Evergreen Parkway
29300 Us Highway 40
Evergreen, CO
303-526-2000

Comfort Suites Longmont Firestone
11292 Business Park Circle
Firestone, CO

720-864-2970

Super 8 Florence Canon City A
4540 State Hwy 67
Florence, CO
719-784-4800

Best Western Kiva Inn
1638 East Mulberry Street
Fort Collins, CO
970 484-2444

Best Western University Inn
914 South College Avenue
Fort Collins, CO

970-484-1984

Comfort Suites Fort Collins
1415 Oakridge Drive
Fort Collins, CO

970-206-4597

Courtyard Fort Collins
1200 Oakridge Drive
Fort Collins, CO

970-282-1700

Days Inn Fort Collins
3625 East Mulberry/I-25
Fort Collins, CO

970-221-5490

Fort Collins Marriott
350 East Horsetooth Rd
Fort Collins, CO

970-226-5200

Hampton Inn Ft. Collins
1620 Oakridge Drive
Fort Collins, CO

970-229-5927

Hilton Fort Collins
425 West Prospect Road
Fort Collins, CO

970-482-2626

Holiday Inn Express Hotel & Suites
Fort Collins
1426 Oakridge Drive
Fort Collins, CO

970-225-2200

Homewood Suites By Hilton Fort
Collins
1521 Oakridge Drive
Fort Collins, CO

970-225-2400

Residence Inn By Marriott Fort
Collins
1127 Oakridge Drive
Fort Collins, CO

970-223-5700

Super 8 Fort Collins
409 Centro Way
Fort Collins, CO

970-493-7701

Rodeway Inn Ft. Morgan
1409 Barlow Road
Fort Morgan, CO
970-867-9481

Super 8 Fountain
6120 East Champlin Drive
Fountain, CO
719-382-4610

Best Western Alpenglo Lodge
78665 Us Highway 40
Fraser, CO
970-726-8088

Baymont Inn & Suites Frisco Lake
Dillon
1202 Summit Boulevard
Frisco, CO
970-668-5094

Hotel Frisco
308 Main Street
Frisco, CO

970-668-5009

Ramada Limited Frisco
990 Lakepoint Drive
Frisco, CO

970-668-8783

Comfort Inn Fruita
400 Jurassic Ave
Fruita, CO
970-858-1333

Super 8 Fruita
399 Jurassic Ave
Fruita, CO

970-858-0808

Super 8 Georgetown
1600 Argentine St
Georgetown, CO
303-569-3211

Extended Stay America - Denver -
Cherry Creek
4444 Leetsdale Dr
Glendale, CO
303-388-3880

Hotel Colorado
526 Pine Street
Glenwood Springs, CO
970-945-6511

Quality Inn & Suites On The River
2650 Gilstrap Court

Glenwood Springs, CO
970-945-5995

Ramada Inn & Suites Glenwood
Springs
124 West 6th Street
Glenwood Springs, CO
970-945-2500

Red Mountain Inn
51637 H 6/24
Glenwood Springs, CO
970-945-6353

Residence Inn Glenwood Springs
125 Wulfsohn Road
Glenwood Springs, CO
970-928-0900

Candlewood Suites Denver
Lakewood
895 Tabor Street
Golden, CO
303-232-7171

Residence Inn Denver West Golden
14600 W. 6th Ave Frontage Road
Golden, CO
303-271-0909

The Golden Hotel Near Coors, An
Ascend Hotel Collection Member
800 11th Street
Golden, CO
303-279-0100

Towneplace Suites By Marriott
Denver West /Federal Center
800 Tabor Street
Golden, CO
303-232-7790

Snow Mountain Ranch
1101 County Road 53
Granby, CO
800-777-9622

Snow Mountain Ranch
1101 H 53
Granby, CO
970-887-2152

Best Western Grande River Inn &
Suites
3228 I-70 Business Loop
Grand Junction, CO
970-434-3400

Candlewood Suites Grand Junction
654 Market Street
Grand Junction, CO
970-255-8093

Clarion Inn Grand Junction
755 Horizon Drive
Grand Junction, CO
970-243-6790

Days Inn Grand Junction
708 Horizon Drive
Grand Junction, CO
970-243-4150

Knights Inn Grand Junction
141 N 1st St
Grand Junction, CO
970-245-8585

Ramada Inn Grand Junction
752 Horizon Drive
Grand Junction, CO
970-243-5150

Residence Inn By Marriott Grand
Junction
767 Horizon Drive
Grand Junction, CO
970-263-4004

Super 8 Grand Junction Colorado
728 Horizon Drive
Grand Junction, CO
970-248-8080

Mountain Lakes Lodge
10480 H 34
Grand Lake, CO
970-627-8448

Clarion Hotel And Conference
Center Greeley
701 8th Street
Greeley, CO
970-353-8444

Comfort Inn Greeley
2467 West 29th Street
Greeley, CO
970-330-6380

Days Inn Greeley
5630 West 10th Street
Greeley, CO
970-392-1530

Super 8 Motel - Greeley
2423 West 29th Street
Greeley, CO
970-330-8880

Best Western Plus Denver Tech
Center Hotel
9231 East Arapahoe Road
Greenwood Village, CO
303-792-9999

Extended Stay America - Denver -
Tech Center - Central
5200 S. Quebec St
Greenwood Village, CO
303-220-8448

Sheraton Hotel Denver Tech Center
7007 South Clinton Street
Greenwood Village, CO
303-799-6200

Extended Stay America-Denver-Tech
Center South-Greenwood Village
9253 E. Costilla Ave
Greenwood Villiage, CO
303-858-1669

Days Inn Gunnison
701 West Highway 50
Gunnison, CO
970-641-0608

Econo Lodge Gunnison
411 East Tomichi Avenue
Gunnison, CO
970-641-3068

Quality Inn Gunnison
400 East Tomichi Avenue
Gunnison, CO
970-641-1237

Comfort Suites Highlands Ranch
Denver Tech Center Area
7060 East County Line Road
Highlands Ranch, CO
303-770-5400

Residence Inn Highlands Ranch
93 West Centennial Boulevard
Highlands Ranch, CO
303-683-5500

Comfort Suites Southwest Lakewood
7260 West Jefferson
Lakewood, CO
303-988-8600

Crossland Economy Studios - Denver
- Lakewood West
715 Kipling St
Lakewood, CO
303-275-0840

Extended Stay America - Denver -
Lakewood South
7393 W Jefferson Ave
Lakewood, CO
303-986-8300

Quality Inn Lakewood
7240 W. Jefferson Avenue
Lakewood, CO
303-989-4600

Residence Inn By Marriott Denver
Southwest/Lakewood
7050 West Hampden Avenue
Lakewood, CO

303-985-7676

Sheraton Denver West Hotel
360 Union Boulevard
Lakewood, CO

303-987-2000

Holiday Inn Express Hotel & Suites
Lamar
1304 N. Main Street
Lamar, CO
719-931-4010

Super 8 Lamar
1202 North Main Street
Lamar, CO

719-336-3427

Holiday Inn Express Littleton
12683 West Indore Place
Littleton, CO
720-981-1000

Homewood Suites By Hilton Denver -
Littleton
7630 Shaffer Parkway
Littleton, CO

720-981-4763

Towneplace Suites By Marriott
Denver Southwest
10902 West Toller Drive
Littleton, CO

303-972-0555

Element Denver Park Meadows
9985 Park Meadows Drive
Lone Tree, CO
303-790-2100

Extended Stay America - Denver -
Park Meadows
8752 S Yosemite St
Lone Tree, CO

303-662-1511

Staybridge Suites Denver South-Park
Meadows
7820 Park Meadows Dr.
Lone Tree, CO

303-649-1010

Holiday Inn Express Hotel & Suites
Longmont
1355 Dry Creek Drive
Longmont, CO
303-684-0404

Residence Inn By Marriott Boulder
Longmont

1450 Dry Creek Drive
Longmont, CO

303-702-9933

Super 8 Longmont/Del Camino
10805 Turner Blvd
Longmont, CO

303-772-0888

Super 8 Longmont/Twin Peaks
2446 North Main Street
Longmont, CO

303-772-8106

Travelodge Longmont
3820 Highway 119
Longmont, CO

303-651-6999

Best Western Plus Louisville Inn
And Suites
960 West Dillon Road
Louisville, CO
303-327-1215

Best Western Plus Louisville Inn
And Suites
960 West Dillon Road
Louisville, CO

303-327-1215

Quality Inn Denver-Boulder Turnpike
1196 Dillon Road
Louisville, CO

303-604-0181

Residence Inn By Marriott Boulder
Louisville
845 Coal Creek Circle
Louisville, CO

303-665-2661

Best Western Plus Crossroads Inn
& Conference Center
5542 E Us Highway 34
Loveland, CO
970-667-7810

Candlewood Suites Loveland
6046 East Crossroads Blvd
Loveland, CO

970-667-5444

Embassy Suites Loveland Hotel,
Spa & Conference Center
4705 Clydesdale Parkway
Loveland, CO

970-593-6200

Residence Inn By Marriott Loveland
Fort Collins
5450 Mcwhinney Boulevard
Loveland, CO

970-622-7000

Travelodge Loveland/Fort Collins
Area
1655 E Eisenhower Blvd
Loveland, CO

970-663-7000

Far View Lodge
Mesa Verde National Park
Mancos, CO
970-529-4421

Morefield Lodge and Campground
34879 H 160
Mancos, CO

800-449-2288

Best Western Movie Manor
2830 Us Highway 160 West
Monte Vista, CO
719-852-5921

Black Canyon Motel
1605 East Main Street
Montrose, CO
970-249-3495

Days Inn Montrose
1417 East Main Street
Montrose, CO

970-249-4507

Hampton Inn Montrose, Co
1980 North Townsend Avenue
Montrose, CO

970-252-3300

Quality Inn & Suites Montrose
2751 Commercial Way
Montrose, CO

970-249-1011

Super 8 Montrose Co
1705 East Main Street
Montrose, CO

970-249-9294

The Grand Lodge Crested Butte
Hotel
600 Gothic Road/Gunnison National
Forest/H
Mount Crested Butte, CO
800-810-7669

Econo Lodge Inn & Suites New
Castle
781 Burning Mountain Avenue
New Castle, CO
970-984-2363

Comfort Inn Ouray
191 5th Ave
Ouray, CO
970-325-7203

Rivers Edge Motel Lodge & Resort
110 7th Avenue
Ouray, CO

970-325-4621

Econo Lodge Pagosa Springs
315 Navajo Trail Drive
Pagosa Springs, CO
970-731-2701

Fireside Inn
1600 E Hwy 160
Pagosa Springs, CO

970-264-9204

High Country Lodge
3821 East Hwy 160
Pagosa Springs, CO

970-264-4181

Quality Inn Pagosa Springs
158 Hot Springs Boulevard
Pagosa Springs, CO

866-472-4672

Candlewood Suites Parachute
233 Grand Valley Way
Parachute, CO
970-285-9880

Holiday Inn Denver-Parker-
E470/Parker Rd
19308 Cottonwood Drive
Parker, CO
303-248-2147

Super 8 Parker
6230 East Pine Lane
Parker, CO

720-851-2644

Baymont Inn & Suites Pueblo
3626 N Freeway Rd
Pueblo, CO
719-583-4000

Best Western Plus Eagleridge Inn &
Suites
4727 N. Elizabeth St.
Pueblo, CO

719-543-4644

Holiday Inn Express Hotel & Suites
Pueblo North
4530 Dillon Drive
Pueblo, CO

719-542-8888

Microtel Inn & Suites By Wyndham
Pueblo
3343 Gateway Drive
Pueblo, CO

719-242-2020

Ramada Inn Pueblo
4703 North Freeway
Pueblo, CO

719-544-4700

Rodeway Inn Pueblo
960 West Us Highway 50
Pueblo, CO

719-583-0333

Super 8 Pueblo
1100 Hwy 50 W
Pueblo, CO

719-545-4104

Sundance Trail Guest Ranch
17931 Red Feather Lakes Road/H
74E
Red Feather, CO
970-224-1222

Sundance Trail Guest Ranch
17931 Red Feather Lakes Road
Red Feather Lakes, CO
970-224-1222

Buckskin Inn
101 Ray Avenue
Rifle, CO
970-625-1741

Comfort Inn And Suites Rifle
301 South 7th Street
Rifle, CO

970-625-9912

Great Western Colorado Lodge
352 W Rainbow Blvd/H 50
Salida, CO
719-539-2514

San Isabel Bed & Breakfast
15914 H 260
Salida, CO

719-539-5432

Super 8 Salida
525 West Rainbow Road
Salida, CO

719-539-6689

Tudor Rose Chalets
6720 County Road 104
Salida, CO

719-539-2002

Woodland Motel
903 W 1st Street
Salida, CO

719-539-4980

Quality Inn & Suites Summit County
530 Silverthorne Lane

Silverthorne, CO
970-513-1222

Silverthorne Days Inn
580 Silverthorne Lane
Silverthorne, CO

970-468-8661

Canyon View Motel
661 Greene Street
Silverton, CO
970-387-5400

The Wyman Hotel & Inn
1371 Greene Street
Silverton, CO

970-387-5372

Alpiner Lodge
424 Lincoln Ave
Steamboat Springs, CO
970-879-1430

Fairfield Inn & Suites Steamboat
Springs
3200 South Lincoln Avenue
Steamboat Springs, CO

970-870-9000

Holiday Inn Steamboat Springs
3190 South Lincoln Avenue
Steamboat Springs, CO

970-879-2250

Quality Inn & Suites Steamboat
Springs
1055 Walton Creek Road
Steamboat Springs, CO

970-879-6669

Rabbit Ears Motel
201 Lincoln Avenue
Steamboat Springs, CO

970-879-1150

Best Western Sundowner Motel
125 Overland Trail
Sterling, CO
970-522-6265

Ramada Inn
22246 East Hwy 6
Sterling, CO

970-522-2625

Super 8 Sterling Co
12883 Highway 61
Sterling, CO

970-522-0300

Hotel Columbia by Telluride Alpine
Lodging
301 West San Juan Avenue
Telluride, CO

970-728-0660

Mountain Lodge Telluride
457 Mountain Village Blvd.
Telluride, CO

866-368-6867

The Peaks Resort and Spa
136 Country Club Drive
Telluride, CO

970-728-6800

Econo Lodge Thornton - Denver
North
12101 Grant Street
Thornton, CO
303-280-9818

Days Inn And Suites Trinidad
900 West Adams Street
Trinidad, CO
719-846-2215

Holiday Inn Hotel & Suites Trinidad
3130 Santa Fe Trail Drive
Trinidad, CO

719-845-8400

Super 8 Trinidad
1924 Freedom Road
Trinidad, CO

719-846-8280

Antlers at Vail
680 W. Lionshead Place
Vail, CO
970-476-2471

Holiday Inn Vail
2211 North Frontage Road
Vail, CO

970-476-2739

Hotel Talisa Vail
1300 Westhaven Drive
Vail, CO

800-420-2424

Sonnenalp
20 Vail Road
Vail, CO

970-479-5441

The Lift House Lodge
555 East Lionshead Circle
Vail, CO

970-476-2340

The Sebastian - Vail
16 Vail Road
Vail, CO

970-477-8000

Days Inn Wellington
7860 6th Street
Wellington, CO
970-568-0444

Jack's Cabin
30 County Road 388
Wentmore, CO
719-784-3160

Doubletree By Hilton Hotel Denver
North
8773 Yates Drive
Westminster, CO
303-427-4000

Extended Stay America - Denver -
Westminster
1291 W. 120th Ave
Westminster, CO

303-280-0111

Residence Inn By Marriott Denver
North/Westminster
5010 West 88th Place
Westminster, CO

303-427-9500

Super 8 Westminister Denver North
12055 Melody Drive
Westminster, CO

303-451-7200

The Westin Westminster
10600 Westminster Boulevard
Westminster, CO

303-410-5000

Super 8 Denver West
4700 Kipling Street
Wheat Ridge, CO
303-423-4000

Howard Johnson Denver West
12100 W 44th Ave
Wheatridge, CO
303-467-2400

Super 8 Windsor
1265 Main Street
Windsor, CO
970-686-5996

Beaver Village Lodge
79303 Us Highway 40
Winter Park, CO
970-726-5741

Winter Park Resort
85 Parsenn Road
Winter Park, CO

970-726-5514

# Connecticut

# Listings

Residence Inn By Marriott Hartford
Avon
55 Simsbury Road
Avon, CT
860-678-1666

Days Inn Berlin Ct
2387 Berlin Turnpike
Berlin, CT
860-828-4181

Days Inn Bethel - Danbury
18 Stony Hill Road
Bethel, CT
203-743-5990

Microtel Inn & Suites By Wyndham
Bethel/Danbury
80 Benedict Road
Bethel, CT

203-748-8318

Baymont Inn And Suites Branford
3 Business Park Drive
Branford, CT
203-488-4991

Newbury Inn
1030 Federal Road
Brookfield, CT
203-775-0220

Radisson Hotel Cromwell
100 Berlin Road
Cromwell, CT
860-635-2000

Residence Inn Danbury
22 Segar Street
Danbury, CT
203-797-1256

Comfort Inn & Suites Dayville
16 Tracy Road
Dayville, CT
860-779-3200

Econo Lodge East Hartford
490 Main Street
East Hartford, CT
860-569-1100

Quality Inn East Haven - New Haven
30 Frontage Road
East Haven, CT
203-469-5321

Baymont Inn & Suites East Windsor
CT
260 Main Street
East Windsor, CT
860-627-6585

Rodeway Inn & Suites East Windsor
161 Bridge Street
East Windsor, CT

Dog-Friendly Lodging - Please always call ahead to make sure an establishment is still dog-friendly.

860-623-9411

Red Roof Inn Enfield
5 Hazard Avenue
Enfield, CT
860-741-2571

Best Western Plus Black Rock Inn
100 Kings Highway Cutoff
Fairfield, CT
203-659-2200

Homewood Suites By Hilton®
Hartford-Farmington
2 Farm Glen Boulevard
Farmington, CT
860-321-0000

Homewood Suites Hartford South
Glastonbury
65 Glastonbury Boulevard
Glastonbury, CT
860-652-8111

Homespun Farm Bed and Breakfast
306 Preston Road/H 164
Griswold, CT
860-376-5178

Ramada Groton
156 Kings Highway
Groton, CT
860-446-0660

Hilton Hartford
315 Trumbull Street
Hartford, CT
860-728-5151

Homewood Suites Hartford
338 Asylum Street
Hartford, CT

860-524-0223

Red Roof Plus+ Hartford Downtown
440 Asylum Street
Hartford, CT

860-246-9900

Residence Inn Hartford Downtown
942 Main Street
Hartford, CT

860-524-5550

The Copper Beech Inn
46 Main Street
Ivoryton, CT
860-767-0330

Best Western Plus New England Inn
& Suites
2253 Berlin Turnpike
Kensington, CT
860-828-3000

Abbey's Lantern Hill Inn
780 Lantern Hill Road

Ledyard, CT
860-572-0483

Extended Stay America - Hartford -
Manchester
340 Tolland Tpke.
Manchester, CT
860-643-5140

Residence Inn Manchester
201 Hale Road
Manchester, CT

860-432-4242

Extended Stay America - Hartford -
Meriden
366 Bee St.
Meriden, CT
203-630-1927

Four Points By Sheraton Meriden
275 Research Pkwy.
Meriden, CT

203-238-2380

Hawthorn Suites By Wyndham
Hartford Meriden
1151 East Main Street
Meriden, CT

203-379-5048

Red Roof Inn Milford
10 Rowe Avenue
Milford, CT
203-877-6060

Residence Inn Milford
62 Rowe Avenue
Milford, CT

203-283-2100

Econo Lodge Mystic
251 Greenmanville Avenue
Mystic, CT
860-536-9666

Hampton Inn & Suites Mystic
6 Hendel Drive
Mystic, CT

860-536-2536

Harbour Inne & Cottage
15 Edgemont Street
Mystic, CT

860-572-9253

Quality Inn Mystic
48 Whitehall Avenue
Mystic, CT

860-572-8531

Residence Inn By Marriott Mystic
Groton
40 Whitehall Avenue
Mystic, CT

860-536-5150

New Haven Inn
100 Pond Lily Ave.
New Haven, CT
203-387-6651

New Haven Premiere Hotel And
Suites
3 Long Wharf Drive
New Haven, CT

203-777-5337

Red Roof Inn Mystic - New London
707 Coleman Street
New London, CT
860-444-0001

High Acres
222 NW Corner Road
North Stonington, CT
860-887-4355

Extended Stay America - Norwalk -
Stamford
400 Main Ave
Norwalk, CT
203-847-6888

Liberty Inn Old Saybrook
55 Springbrook Road
Old Saybrook, CT
860-388-1777

Quality Inn Plainfield
55 Lathrop Road
Plainfield, CT
860-564-4021

Kings Inn Putnam
5 Heritage Road
Putnam, CT
860-928-7961

Days Inn Ridgefield
296 Ethan Allen Highway (Rt 7)
Ridgefield, CT
203-438-3781

Residence Inn Hartford Rocky Hill
680 Cromwell Avenue
Rocky Hill, CT
860-257-7500

Sheraton Hartford South
100 Capital Boulevard
Rocky Hill, CT

860-257-6000

Super 8 Hartford South - Rocky Hill
1499 Silas Deane Highway
Rocky Hill, CT

860-372-4636

Extended Stay America - Shelton -
Fairfield County
945 Bridgeport Ave

Shelton, CT
203-926-6868

Residence Inn Fairfield
County/Shelton
1001 Bridgeport Avenue
Shelton, CT

203-926-9000

Iron Horse Inn
969 Hopmeadow Street
Simsbury, CT
860-658-2216

Crowne Plaza Hotel Southbury
1284 Strongtown Road
Southbury, CT
203-598-7600

Residence Inn By Marriott
Southington
778 West St.
Southington, CT
860-621-4440

Hilton Stamford Hotel And Executive
Meeting Center
One First Stamford Place
Stamford, CT
203-967-2222

Sheraton Stamford Hotel
700 East Main Street
Stamford, CT

203-358-8400

Stamford Marriott Hotel And Spa
243 Tresser Blvd
Stamford, CT

203-357-9555

Super 8 Stamford
32 Grenhart Road
Stamford, CT

203-324-8887

Homewood Suites By Hilton®
Stratford, Ct
6905 Main Street
Stratford, CT
203-377-3322

Days Inn Vernon
451 Hartford Turnpike
Vernon, CT
860-875-0781

Homewood Suites Wallingford-
Meriden
90 Miles Drive
Wallingford, CT
203-284-2600

Rodeway Inn Waterford
211 Parkway North
Waterford, CT
860-442-7227

Residence Inn Hartford
100 Dunfey Lane
Windsor, CT
860-688-7474

Candlewood Suites Windsor Locks,
Ct
149 Ella Grasso Turnpike
Windsor Locks, CT
860-623-2000

Econo Lodge Inn & Suites
34 Old County Road
Windsor Locks, CT

860-623-2533

Sheraton Hartford Hotel At Bradley
Airport
1 Bradley International Airport
Windsor Locks, CT

860-627-5311

Elias Child House
50 Perrin Road
Woodstock, CT
860-974-9836

# D.C. Listings

Crowne Plaza Hamilton
1001 14th Street Nw And K St
Washington, DC
202-682-0111

Fairmont Washington DC
Georgetown
2401 M Street Northwest
Washington, DC

202-429-2400

Harrington Hotel
11th And E Streets Nw
Washington, DC

202-628-8140

Hotel Madera
1310 New Hampshire Avenue
Northwest
Washington, DC

202-296-7600

Howard Johnson Inn Washington
DC
600 New York Avenue North East
Washington, DC

202-546-9200

Kimpton Donovan Hotel
1155 14th Street Northwest
Washington, DC

202-737-1200

Kimpton Donovan Hotel
1155 14th Street Northwest
Washington, DC

202-737-1200

Kimpton Glover Park Hotel
2505 Wisconsin Avenue Nw
Washington, DC

202-337-9700

Kimpton Hotel Monaco Washington
DC
700 F Street Northwest
Washington, DC

202-628-7177

Kimpton Hotel Palomar Washington,
DC
2121 P Street Northwest
Washington, DC

202-448-1800

Kimpton Mason & Rook Hotel
1430 Rhode Island Avenue North
West
Washington, DC

202-462-9001

Loews Madison Hotel
1177 15th Street Nw
Washington, DC

202-862-1600

Residence Inn By Marriott
Washington, DC Downtown
1199 Vermont Avenue Nw
Washington, DC

202-898-1100

Residence Inn By Marriott
Washington, DC/Capitol
333 E Street Sw
Washington, DC

202-484-8280

Residence Inn By Marriott
Washington, DC/Dupont Circle
2120 P Street Northwest
Washington, DC

202-466-6800

Rouge, A Kimpton Hotel
1315 Sixteenth Street Northwest
Washington, DC

202-232-8000

Sofitel Washington DC Lafayette
Square Hotel
806 15Th Street
Washington, DC

202-730-8441

THE MAYFLOWER HOTEL,
AUTOGRAPH COLLECTION, A
Marriott Luxury & Lifestyle Hotel
1127 Connecticut Avenue Northwest
Washington, DC

202-347-3000

The Embassy Row Hotel
2015 Massachusetts Avenue
Northwest
Washington, DC

202-265-1600

The George, A Kimpton Hotel
15 E Street Nw
Washington, DC

202-347-4200

Topaz, A Kimpton Hotel
1733 N Street Northwest
Washington, DC

202-393-3000

Washington Hilton
1919 Connecticut Ave Northwest
Washington, DC

202-483-3000

Willard Intercontinental
1401 Pennsylvania Avenue Nw
Washington, DC

202-628-9100

# Delaware Listings

Bethany Beach House
Off Central Avenue
Bethany Beach, DE
443-621-6649

Lagoon Front/#125307
217 Belle Road
Bethany Beach, DE

954-782-8277

Atlantic Oceanside Hotel
1700 Coastal H
Dewey Beach, DE
302-227-8811

Ocean Block #47227
given at time of reservations
Dewey Beach, DE

302-542-3570

Sea-Esta Motel I
2306 Hwy 1
Dewey Beach, DE

302-227-7666

Days Inn Dover
272 North Dupont Highway

Dover, DE
302-674-8002

Hampton Inn Dover
1568 North Dupont Highway
Dover, DE

302-736-3500

Home2 Suites By Hilton Dover
222 South Dupont Highway
Dover, DE

302-674-3300

Red Roof Inn Dover
652 North Dupont Highway
Dover, DE

302-730-8009

Residence Inn By Marriott Dover
600 Jefferic Blvd
Dover, DE

302-677-0777

Sleep Inn & Suites Dover
1784 N. Dupont Hwy
Dover, DE

302-735-7770

Rodeway Inn
111 S Dupont Hwy
Dutch Inn, DE
302-328-6246

Comfort Inn & Suites Georgetown
20530 Dupont Blvd
Georgetown, DE
302-854-9400

Clarion Hotel The Belle
1612 North Dupont Highway
New Castle, DE
302-428-1000

Quality Inn And Suites Skyways
147 North Dupont Highway
New Castle, DE

302-328-6666

Courtyard By Marriott Newark-
University Of Delaware
400 David Hollowell Drive
Newark, DE
302-737-0900

Days Inn Newark Delaware
900 Churchmans Road
Newark, DE

302-368-2400

Extended Stay America Newark -
Christiana - Wilmington
333 Continental Drive
Newark, DE

302-283-0800

Four Points By Sheraton Newark
56 S. Old Baltimore Pike
Newark, DE

302-266-6600

Hilton Wilmington/Christiana
100 Continental Drive
Newark, DE

302-454-1500

Homewood Suites By Hilton®
Newark/Wilmington South
640 South College Avenue
Newark, DE

302-453-9700

Red Roof Inn And Suites Newark -
University
1119 South College Avenue
Newark, DE

302-368-8521

Red Roof Plus Wilmington De
415 Stanton Christiana Road
Newark, DE

302-292-2870

Residence Inn By Marriott Wilmington
Newark/Christiana
240 Chapman Road
Newark, DE

302-453-9200

Rodeway Inn University
1120 South College Avenue
Newark, DE

302-731-3131

Towneplace Suites By Marriott
Wilmington Newark/Christiana
410 Eagle Run Road
Newark, DE

302-369-6212

Americinn Rehoboth Beach
36012 Airport Road
Rehoboth, DE
302-226-0700

Bewitched & BEDazzled B&B
67 Lake Ave
Rehoboth Beach, DE
302-226-3900

Sea Esta Motel III
1409 DE 1
Rehoboth Beach, DE

302-227-4343

The Homestead at Rehoboth
35060 Warrington Road
Rehoboth Beach, DE

302-226-7625

Quality Inn
225 N. Dual Hwy
Seaford, DE
302-629-8385

Sheraton Suites Wilmington
Downtown
422 Delaware Avenue
Wilmington, DE
302-654-8300

# Florida Listings

Econo Lodge Alachua
15920 Northwest Us Highway 441
Alachua, FL
386-462-2414

Quality Inn I-75 At Exit 399
15960 Northwest Us Highway 441
Alachua, FL

386-462-2244

Days Inn And Suites Altamonte
Springs
150 South Westmonte Drive
Altamonte Springs, FL
407-788-1411

Embassy Suites Hotel Orlando-North
225 Shorecrest Drive
Altamonte Springs, FL

407-834-2400

Extended Stay America - Orlando -
Altamonte Springs
302 Northlake Blvd.
Altamonte Springs, FL

407-332-9300

Ramada Altamonte Springs
150 Douglas Avenue
Altamonte Springs, FL

407-862-8200

Residence Inn Orlando Altamonte
Springs
270 Douglas Ave
Altamonte Springs, FL

407-788-7991

Days Inn And Suites Amelia Island
2707 Sadler Road
Amelia Island, FL
904-277-2300

Rancho Inn
240 Hwy 98
Apalachicola, FL
850-653-9435

The Gibson Inn

Market St and Avenue C
Apalachicola, FL

850-653-2191

Knights Inn Arcadia
504 S Brevard Ave
Arcadia, FL
863-494-4884

Residence Inn By Marriott Miami
Aventura Mall
19900 West Country Club
Aventura, FL
786-528-1001

Econo Lodge Sebring
2511 Us 27 South
Avon Park, FL
863-453-2000

Extended Stay America Boca Raton
- Commerce
501 Northwest 77th Street
Boca Raton, FL
561-994-2599

Fairfield Inn & Suites By Marriott
Boca Raton
3400 Airport Road
Boca Raton, FL

561-417-8585

Holiday Inn Express Boca Raton
West
8144 Glades Road
Boca Raton, FL

561-482-7070

Residence Inn Boca Raton
525 Northwest 77th Street
Boca Raton, FL

561-994-3222

Towneplace Suites Boca Raton
5110 Northwest 8th Avenue
Boca Raton, FL

561-994-7232

Holiday Inn Express Bonita Springs
27891 Crown Lake Boulevard
Bonita Springs, FL
239-948-0699

Courtyard Bradenton
Sarasota/Riverfront
100 Riverfront Dr. West
Bradenton, FL

Days Inn Bradenton Near The Gulf
3506 1st Street West
Bradenton, FL

941-746-1141

Extended Stay America - Tampa -
Brandon

330 Grand Regency Blvd.
Brandon, FL
813-643-5900

Days Inn Brooksville
6320 Windmere Road
Brooksville, FL
352-796-9486

Holiday Inn Express Hotel & Suites
Brooksville
30455 Cortez Boulevard
Brooksville, FL

352-796-0455

Microtel Inn & Suites By Wyndham
Brooksville
6298 Nature Coast Blvd
Brooksville, FL

352-796-9025

Quality Inn Weeki Wachee
9373 Cortez Boulevard
Brooksville, FL

352-596-9000

Residence Inn Cape Canaveral
Cocoa Beach
8959 Astronaut Boulevard
Cape Canaveral, FL
321-323-1100

Cape Escape Vacation Rentals - Pet
Friendly Beach & Rentals
Barrier Dunes: Gulf Front, Gated
Neighborhood.
Cape San Blas, FL
678-523-1161

Pristine Properties Pet Friendly
Vacation Rentals on Cape San Blas
Call to Arrange
Cape San Blas, FL

877-378-1273

Sunset Reflections Vacation Rentals
Call to Arrange
Cape San Blas, FL

850-227-5432

Quality Inn Chiefland
1125 North Young Boulevard
Chiefland, FL
352-493-0663

Super 8 Chipley
1150 Motel Drive
Chipley, FL
850-638-8530

Candlewood Suites Clearwater - St.
Petersburg
13231 49th Street North
Clearwater, FL
727-573-3344

Express Inn & Suites Clearwater
11333 Us Highway 19
Clearwater, FL

727-572-4929

Extended Stay America - Clearwater -
Carillon Park
2311 Ulmerton Rd.
Clearwater, FL

727-572-4800

Extended Stay America - St.
Petersburg - Clearwater - Executive
Dr.
3089 Executive Drive
Clearwater, FL

727-561-9032

Holiday Inn St Petersburg N -
Clearwater
3535 Ulmerton Road
Clearwater, FL

727-577-9100

Homewood Suites By HiltonÂ®
Clearwater
2233 Ulmerton Road
Clearwater, FL

727-573-1500

Residence Inn By Marriott Clearwater
Downtown
940 Court Street
Clearwater, FL

727-562-5400

Residence Inn St Petersburg
Clearwater
5050 Ulmerton Road
Clearwater, FL

727-573-4444

Rodeway Inn Clearwater
16405 Us Highway 19 North
Clearwater, FL

727-535-0505

Super 8 Clearwater/U.S. Hwy 19 N
22950 Us Hwy 19 North
Clearwater, FL

727-799-2678

Sea Spray Inn
331 Coronado Drive
Clearwater Beach, FL
727-442-0432

Fairfield Inn & Suites Clermont
1750 Hunt Trace
Clermont, FL
352-394-6585

Secluded Sunsets

10616 South Phillips Road
Clermont, FL

352-429-0512

The Ever After Estate
9512 Oak Island
Clermont, FL

800-792-0447

Best Western Ocean Beach Hotel &
Suites
5600 North Alantic Avenue
Cocoa Beach, FL
321-783-7621

Surf Studio Beach Resort
1801 South Atlantic Avenue
Cocoa Beach, FL

321-783-7100

Residence Inn Miami Coconut
Grove
2835 Tigertail Avenue
Coconut Grove, FL
305-285-9303

Hotel Colonnade Coral Gables a
Tribute Portfolio Hotel
180 Aragon Avenue
Coral Gables, FL
305-441-2600

Americas Best Value Inn
4255 South Ferdon Boulevard
Crestview, FL
850-682-8842

Super 8 Crestview
3925 South Ferdon Boulevard
Crestview, FL

850-682-9649

Best Western Crystal River Resort
614 Northwest Us Highway 19
Crystal River, FL
352-795-3171

Days Inn Crystal River
2380 Northwest Highway 19
Crystal River, FL

352-795-2111

Le Meridien Fort Lauderdale Airport
and Cruise Port Hotel
1825 Griffin Road
Dania, FL
954-920-3500

Extended Stay America - Fort
Lauderdale - Davie
7550 State Road 84
Davie, FL
954-476-1211

Hilton Daytona Beach/Ocean Walk
Village

100 North Atlantic Avenue
Daytona Beach, FL
386-254-8200

Homewood Suites By Hilton Daytona
Beach Speedway-Airport
165 Bill France Boulevard
Daytona Beach, FL

386-258-2828

Residence Inn Daytona Beach
Speedway/Airport
1725 Richard Petty Boulevard
Daytona Beach, FL

386-252-3949

The Shores Resort And Spa
2637 South Atlantic Avenue
Daytona Beach Shores, FL
386-760-3651

Doubletree Deerfield Beach-Boca
Raton
100 Fairway Drive
Deerfield Beach, FL
954-427-7700

Extended Stay America - Fort
Lauderdale - Deerfield Beach
1200 Fau Research Park Blvd
Deerfield Beach, FL

954-428-5997

Regency Inn and Suites
472 Hugh Adams Road
Defuniak Springs, FL
850-892-6115

Delray Breakers on the Ocean
1875 S. Ocean Blvd
Delray Beach, FL
561-278-4501

Residence Inn Delray Beach
1111 East Atlantic Avenue
Delray Beach, FL

561-276-7441

Candlewood Suites Destin-Sandestin
Area
11396 Us 98 West
Destin, FL
850-337-3770

Days Inn Destin
1029 Highway 98 East
Destin, FL

850-837-2599

DestinFLRentals.com
Call to Arrange
Destin, FL

850-650-5524

Extended Stay America Destin - Us

98 - Emerald Coast Pkwy.
4615 Opa Locka Lane
Destin, FL

850-837-9830

Newman-Dailey Resort Properties
12815 Highway 98 W Suite 100
Destin, FL

800-225-7652

Ocean Reef Resorts
10221 Emerald Coast Parkway
Destin, FL

800-782-8736

Residence Inn by Marriott Sandestin
at Grand Boulevard
300 Grand Boulevard
Destin, FL

850-650-7811

Best Western Plus Yacht Harbor Inn
150 Marina Plaza
Dunedin, FL
727-733-4121

Quality Inn Elkton -St. Augustine
South
2625 Sr 207
Elkton, FL
904-829-3435

Red Roof Inn Ellenton
4915 17th Street East
Ellenton, FL
941-729-0600

Sleep Inn & Suites Riverfront
5605 18th Street East
Ellenton, FL

941-721-4933

Hampton Inn Amelia Island
2549 Sadler Road
Fernandina Beach, FL
904-321-1111

Residence Inn Amelia Island
2301 Sadler Road
Fernandina Beach, FL

904-277-2440

Topaz Motel - Flagler Beach
1224 South Oceanshore Boulevard
Flagler Beach, FL
386-439-3301

Whale Watch Motel
2448 S Oceanshore Blvd
Flagler Beach, FL

386-439-2545

Ramada Florida City
124 East Palm Drive
Florida City, FL

305-247-8833

Best Western Ft. Lauderdale I-95
Inn
4800 Powerline Road
Fort Lauderdale, FL
954-776-6333

Candlewood Suites Ft. Lauderdale
Air/ Seaport
1120 West State Road 84
Fort Lauderdale, FL
954-522-8822

Embassy Suites Hotel Ft.
Lauderdale-17th Street
1100 Se 17th Street
Fort Lauderdale, FL
954-527-2700

Extended Stay America - Fort
Lauderdale - Plantation
7755 Sw 6th Street
Fort Lauderdale, FL
954-382-8888

Extended Stay America Fort
Lauderdale-Cypress Creek-Andrews
Ave.
5851 N. Andrews Ave Ext.
Fort Lauderdale, FL

954-776-9447

Extended Stay America-Fort
Lauderdale-Convention Ctr-Cruise
Port
1450 Southeast 17th Street
Causeway
Fort Lauderdale, FL

954-761-9055

Rodeway Inn & Suites Airport/Cruise
Port
2440 West State Road 84
Fort Lauderdale, FL

954-792-8181

Towneplace Suites Fort Lauderdale
West
3100 West Prospect Rd
Fort Lauderdale, FL

954-484-2214

Allure Suites Of Fort Myers
9200 College Pkwy
Fort Myers, FL
239-454-6363

Best Western Fort Myers Waterfront
13021 North Cleveland Avenue
Fort Myers, FL

239-997-5511

Candlewood Suites Ft. Myers North

I-75
3626 Colonial Court
Fort Myers, FL

239-344-4400

Residence Inn By Marriott Fort Myers
2960 Colonial Blvd
Fort Myers, FL

239-936-0110

Residence Inn By Marriott Fort Myers
Sanibel
20371 Summerlin Road
Fort Myers, FL

239-415-4150

Travelodge Fort Myers Airport
13661 Indian Paint Lane
Fort Myers, FL

Americas Best Value Inn
6651 Darter Ct
Fort Pierce, FL
772-466-4066

Royal Inn Beach Hotel Hutchinson
Island
222 Hernando Street
Fort Pierce, FL

772-672-8888

Days Inn - Fort Walton Beach
135 Miracle Strip Pkwy Sw
Fort Walton Beach, FL
850-244-6184

Baymont Inn & Suites Gainesville
6901 Northwest 4th Boulevard
Gainesville, FL
352-332-8292

Best Western Gateway Grand
4200 Nw 97th Boulevard
Gainesville, FL

352-331-3336

Comfort Inn University Gainesville
3440 Southwest 40th Boulevard
Gainesville, FL

352-264-1771

Days Inn Gainesville University
1901 Southwest 13th Street
Gainesville, FL

352-376-2222

Extended Stay America - Gainesville
- I-75
3600 Sw 42nd St
Gainesville, FL

352-375-0073

Hilton University Of Florida
Conference Center Gainesville

Dog-Friendly Lodging - Please always call ahead to make sure an establishment is still dog-friendly.

1714 Sw 34th St.
Gainesville, FL

352-371-3600

Homewood Suites Gainesville
3333 Sw 42nd Street
Gainesville, FL

352-335-3133

Magnolia Plantation Bed and
Breakfast
305 SE 7th Street
Gainesville, FL

352-375-6653

Red Roof Plus+ Gainesville
3500 Southwest 42nd Street
Gainesville, FL

352-336-3311

Residence Inn Gainesville I-75
3275 Sw 40th Boulevard
Gainesville, FL

352-264-0000

Super 8 Gainesville
4202 Sw 40th Blvd
Gainesville, FL

352-378-3888

Sun Cruz Inn
340 Desoto St.
Hollywood, FL
954-925-7272

Sun Cruz Inn
340 Desoto St.
Hollywood, FL

954-925-7272

Swan/Mermaid Motel
319 Pierce Street (office)
Hollywood Beach, FL
954-921-4097

Barrett Beach Bungalows
19646 Gulf Blvd
Indian Shores, FL
727-455-2832

La Siesta Resort & Marina
80241 Overseas Highway, Mile
Marker 80.5
Islamorada, FL
877-926-6329

Postcard Inn Beach Resort & Marina
at Holiday Isle
84001 Overseas Highway
Islamorada, FL

305-664-2321

Candlewood Suites Jacksonville
Southpoint

4990 Belfort Road
Jacksonville, FL
904-296-7785

Days Inn Jacksonville Bay Meadows
8255 Dix Ellis Trail
Jacksonville, FL

Extended Stay America -
Jacksonville - Baymeadows
8300 Western Way
Jacksonville, FL

904-739-1881

Extended Stay America -
Jacksonville - Lenoir Avenue East
6961 Lenoir Ave
Jacksonville, FL

904-296-0181

Extended Stay America -
Jacksonville - Salisbury Rd -
Southpoint
4693 Salisbury Road
Jacksonville, FL

904-296-0661

Extended Stay America-
Jacksonville-Riverwalk -Convention
Center
1413 Prudential Drive
Jacksonville, FL

904-396-1777

Extended Stay America-
Jacksonville-Southside-St. Johns
Towne Ctr
10020 Skinner Lake Drive
Jacksonville, FL

904-642-9911

Hampton Inn & Suites Jacksonville-
Deerwood Park, Fl
4415 Southside Blvd
Jacksonville, FL

904-997-9100

Holiday Inn Express Hotel & Suites
Chaffee-Jacksonville West
537 Chaffee Point Boulevard
Jacksonville, FL

904-652-2782

Holiday Inn Express Jacksonville
Mayport/Beach
2040 Mayport Road
Jacksonville, FL

904-435-0700

Hometown Inn & Suites Jacksonville
Butler Blvd./Southpoint
4940 Mustang Road
Jacksonville, FL

904-281-2244

Homewood Suites by Hilton
Jacksonville Southside Deerwood
Park
8511 Touchton Road
Jacksonville, FL

904-253-7120

Hotel Indigo Jacksonville-Deerwood
Park
9840 Tapestry Park Circle
Jacksonville, FL

904-996-7199

Ramada Conference Center
Mandarin
3130 Hartley Road
Jacksonville, FL

904-268-8080

Red Roof Inn - Jacksonville - Orange
Park
6099 Youngerman Circle
Jacksonville, FL

904-777-1000

Red Roof Inn Jacksonville Airport
1063 Airport Road
Jacksonville, FL

904-741-4488

Red Roof Inn Jacksonville Southpoint
6969 Lenoir Avenue East
Jacksonville, FL

904-296-1006

Residence Inn By Marriott
Jacksonville Airport
1310 Airport Road
Jacksonville, FL

904-741-6550

Residence Inn By Marriott
Jacksonville Butler Boulevard
10551 Deerwood Park Blvd
Jacksonville, FL

904-996-8900

Residence Inn Jacksonville
Baymeadows
8365 Dix Ellis Trail
Jacksonville, FL

904-733-8088

Sheraton Jacksonville Hotel
10605 Deerwood Park Boulevard
Jacksonville, FL

904-564-4772

Towneplace Suites By Marriott
Jacksonville Butler Boulevard

4801 Lenoir Ave
Jacksonville, FL

904-296-1661

Holiday Inn Express North Palm
Beach-Oceanview
13950 U.S. Hwy 1
Juno Beach, FL
561-622-4366

Dream Bay Resort
4 Woodward Way
Key Largo, FL
305-393-0634

Marina del Mar Resort & Marina
527 Caribbean Drive
Key Largo, FL

305-451-4107

Ambrosia House Tropical Lodging
622 Fleming Street
Key West, FL
305-296-9838

Banana Bay Resort and Marina
2319 N. Roosevelt Blvd/H 1
Key West, FL

305-296-6925

Best Western Key Ambassador
Resort Inn
3755 S. Roosevelt Blvd.
Key West, FL

305-296-3500

Casa 325 Guesthouse
325 Duval Street
Key West, FL

305-292-0011

Courtney's Place Historic Cottages &
Inns
720 Whitmarsh Lane
Key West, FL

305-294-3480

Francis Street Bottle Inn
535 Francis Street
Key West, FL

305-294-8530

Key West's Travelers Palm - Inn and
Cottages
915 Center Street
Key West, FL

800-294-9560

Old Town Manor
511 Eaton Street
Key West, FL

305-292-2170

Pelican Landing Resort and Marina
915 Eisenhower Drive
Key West, FL

305-296-9976

Blue Inn Lake Buena Vista South
4970 Kyngs Heath Road
Kissimmee, FL
407-396-0065

Ramada Hotel Gateway
7470 W Irlo Bronson
Kissimmee, FL

407-396-4400

The Palms Hotel and Villas
3100 Parkway Blvd
Kissimmee, FL

407-396-2229

Oaks 'N Pines RV/Campground
3864 N H 441
Lake City, FL
386-752-0830

Ramada Limited
3340 W. Us Hwy 90
Lake City, FL

386-752-6262

Rodeway Inn Lake City
205 Sw Commerce Dr.
Lake City, FL

386-755-5203

Candlewood Suites Lake Mary
1130 Greenwood Boulevard
Lake Mary, FL
407-585-3000

Extended Stay America - Orlando -
Lake Mary -1036 Greenwood Blvd
1036 Greenwood Blvd.
Lake Mary, FL

407-833-0011

Extended Stay America - Orlando -
Lake Mary -1040 Greenwood Blvd
1040 Greenwood Blvd
Lake Mary, FL

407-829-2332

Homewood Suites By Hilton® Lake
Mary
755 Currency Circle
Lake Mary, FL

407-805-9111

Residence Inn Orlando Lake Mary
825 Heathrow Park Lane
Lake Mary, FL

407-995-3400

Residence Inn Lakeland
3701 Harden Boulevard
Lakeland, FL
863-680-2323

Holiday Inn Express Hotel & Suites
Inverness
903 E Gulf To Lake Highway
Lecanto, FL
352-341-3515

Best Western Plus Chain Of Lakes
Inn & Suites
1321 North 14th Street
Leesburg, FL
352-460-0118

Residence Inn Marriott Tampa
Suncoast Pkwy Northpointe Village
2101 Northpointe Parkway
Lutz, FL
813-792-8400

Wingate By Wyndham Panama City
Area Lynn Haven
2610 Lynn Haven Parkway
Lynn Haven, FL
850-248-8080

Travelodge Suites Macclenny
1651 S 6th Street
MacClenny, FL
904-259-6408

Changing Tides Cottages
225 Boca Ciega Dr
Madeira Beach, FL
727-397-7706

Island Paradise Cottages of Madeira
Beach
13215 2nd Street East
Madeira Beach, FL

727-395-9751

Super 8 Madison
6246 State Rd. 53 South
Madison, FL
850-973-6267

Homewood Suites By Hilton®
Orlando-Maitland
290 Southhall Lane
Maitland, FL
407-875-8777

Quality Inn Marianna
2175 Hwy 71 South
Marianna, FL
850-526-5600

Candlewood Suites Melbourne-Viera
2930 Pineda Causeway
Melbourne, FL
321-821-9009

Days Inn Melbourne
4500 West New Haven Avenue
Melbourne, FL

321-724-2051

Residence Inn By Marriott Melbourne
1430 South Babcock Street
Melbourne, FL

321-723-5740

Candlewood Suites Miami Airport
West
8855 Nw 27th Street
Miami, FL
305-591-9099

Element Miami International Airport
3525 Northwest 25th Street
Miami, FL

305-636-1600

Epic Miami, A Kimpton Hotel
270 Biscayne Boulevard Way
Miami, FL

305-424-5226

Extended Stay America - Miami -
Airport - Blue Lagoon
6605 Northwest 7th Street
Miami, FL

305-260-0085

Extended Stay America - Miami -
Airport - Doral
8720 Nw 33rd Street
Miami, FL

305-436-1811

Extended Stay America - Miami -
Airport - Doral
8720 Nw 33rd Street
Miami, FL

305-436-1811

Extended Stay America - Miami -
Airport - Miami Springs
101 Fairway Drive
Miami, FL

305-870-0448

Extended Stay America - Miami -
Airport-Doral 87th Avenue South
8655 Northwest 21st Terrace
Miami, FL

786-331-7717

Extended Stay America - Miami -
Downtown Brickell - Cruise Port
298 Sw 15th Road
Miami, FL

305-856-3700

Extended Stay America Miami - Coral
Gables
3640 Sw 22nd Street
Miami, FL

305-443-7444

Hilton Miami Downtown
1601 Biscayne Boulevard
Miami, FL

305-374-0000

Red Roof Plus Miami Airport
3401 Nw Lejeune Road
Miami, FL

305-871-4221

Residence Inn Miami Airport
1201 Nw 42nd Avenue
Miami, FL

305-642-8570

Staybridge Suites Miami Doral Area
3265 Nw 87th Avenue
Miami, FL

305-500-9100

Towneplace Suites By Marriott
Miami Airport West
10505 Nw 36th Street
Miami, FL

305-718-4144

Brigham Gardens Guesthouse
1411 Collins Avenue
Miami Beach, FL
305-531-1331

Brigham Gardens Guesthouse
1411 Collins Avenue
Miami Beach, FL

305-531-1331

Hotel Leon
841 Collins Avenue
Miami Beach, FL

305-673-3767

Hotel Ocean
1230 Ocean Drive
Miami Beach, FL

800-783-1725

Surfcomber Hotel, A Kimpton Hotel
1717 Collins Ave
Miami Beach, FL

305-532-7715

Milton Inn and Suites
8936 Highway 87 South
Milton, FL
850-623-1511

Red Roof Inn Pensacola East -
Milton
2672 Avalon Boulevard
Milton, FL

850-995-6100

Residence Inn By Marriott Fort
Lauderdale Sw/Miramar
14700 Hotel Road
Miramar, FL
954-450-2717

Beach Condos in Destin
2606 Scenic Gulf Drive
Miramar Beach, FL
850-269-3342

Super 8 Monticello
140 Pafford Rd
Monticello, FL
850-997-8888

Red Roof Plus+ & Suites Naples
1925 Davis Boulevard
Naples, FL
239-774-3117

Residence Inn Naples
4075 Tamiami Trail North
Naples, FL

239-659-1300

Staybridge Suites Naples-Gulf Coast
4805 Tamiami Trail North
Naples, FL

239-643-8002

Days Inn Ocala
3811 Nw Blitchton Rd
Ocala, FL
352-629-7041

Hilton Ocala
3600 Southwest 36th Avenue
Ocala, FL

352-854-1400

Microtel Inn & Suites By Wyndham
Ocala
1770 Southwest 134th Street
Ocala, FL

352-307-1166

Red Roof Inn and Suites Ocala
120 Northwest 40th Avenue
Ocala, FL

352-732-4590

Residence Inn By Marriott Ocala
3610 South West 38th Avenue
Ocala, FL

352-547-1600

Super 8 Ocala
3924 W Silver Spring Blvd
Ocala, FL

352-629-8794

Dog-Friendly Lodging - Please always call ahead to make sure an establishment is still dog-friendly.

Residence Inn By Marriott Tampa Oldsmar
4012 Tampa Road
Oldsmar, FL
813-818-9400

Quality Inn Orange City
445 South Volusia Avenue
Orange City, FL
386-775-7444

Best Western Orlando East Inn & Suites
8750 East Colonial Drive
Orlando, FL
407-282-3900

Days Inn And Suites Orlando/Ucf Research Park
11639 East Colonial Drive
Orlando, FL
407-282-2777

Days Inn Orlando Universal North
2500 W 33rd St
Orlando, FL
407-841-3731

Extended Stay America - Orlando - Convention Ctr - 6451 Westwood
6451 Westwood Boulevard
Orlando, FL
407-352-3454

Extended Stay America - Orlando - Maitland - 1760 Pembrook Dr.
1760 Pembrook Drive
Orlando, FL
407-667-0474

Extended Stay America - Orlando - Southpark - Equity Row
4101 Equity Row
Orlando, FL
407-352-5577

Extended Stay America - Orlando Theme Parks - Major Blvd.
5620 Major Boulevard
Orlando, FL
407-351-1788

Hyatt Regency Grand Cypress
One Grand Cypress Blvd
Orlando, FL
407-239-1234

Red Roof Inn Orlando South Florida Mall
8296 South Orange Blossom Trail
Orlando, FL
407-240-0570

Red Roof Inn Orlando-International

Dr/Convention
9922 Hawaiian Court
Orlando, FL
407-352-1507

Residence Inn By Marriott Orlando At Seaworld
11000 Westwood Boulevard
Orlando, FL
407-313-3600

Residence Inn By Marriott Orlando Convention Center
8800 Universal Boulevard
Orlando, FL
407-226-0288

Residence Inn By Marriott Orlando Convention Center
8800 Universal Boulevard
Orlando, FL
407-226-0288

Residence Inn By Marriott Orlando East/Ucf
11651 University Boulevard
Orlando, FL
407-513-9000

Residence Inn By Marriott Orlando Lake Buena Vista
11450 Marbella Palms Court
Orlando, FL
407-465-0075

Residence Inn Orlando Airport
7024 Augusta National Drive
Orlando, FL
407-856-2444

Residence Inn SeaWorld
11000 Westwood Blvd.
Orlando, FL
407-313-3600

Residence Inn SeaWorld
11000 Westwood Blvd.
Orlando, FL
407-313-3600

Rosen Inn At Pointe Orlando
9000 International Drive
Orlando, FL
407-996-8585

Rosen Inn Closest To Universal
6327 International Drive
Orlando, FL
407-996-4444

Rosen Inn International
7600 International Drive

Orlando, FL
407-996-1600

Sheraton Lake Buena Vista Resort
12205 S Apopka Vineland Rd.
Orlando, FL
407-239-0444

Sheraton Lake Buena Vista Resort
12205 S. Apopka Vineland Road
Orlando, FL
407-239-0444

Sheraton Suites Orlando Airport
7550 Augusta National Drive
Orlando, FL
407-240-5555

Staybridge Suites Orlando Airport South
7450 Augusta National Drive
Orlando, FL
407-438-2121

Universal's Hard Rock Hotel
5800 Universal Boulevard
Orlando, FL
407-503-7625

Universal's Loews Portofino Bay Hotel
5601 Universal Boulevard
Orlando, FL
407-503-1000

Universal's Loews Royal Pacific Resort
6300 Hollywood Way
Orlando, FL
407-503-3000

Chesterfield Hotel
363 Cocoanut Row
Palm Beach, FL
561-659-5800

Quality Inn & Conference Center
1013 East 23rd Street
Panama City, FL
850-769-6969

Red Roof Inn Panama City
217 North Us Hwy 231
Panama City, FL
850-215-2727

Towneplace Suites By Marriott Panama City
903 East 23rd Place
Panama City, FL
850-747-0609

Extended Stay America Pensacola -
University Mall
809 Bloodworth Lane
Pensacola, FL
850-473-9323

Red Roof Inn Pensacola West Florida
Hospital
7340 Plantation Road
Pensacola, FL

850-476-7960

Residence Inn By Marriott Pensacola
Downtown
601 East Chase Street
Pensacola, FL

850-432-0202

Towneplace Suites By Marriott
Pensacola
481 Creighton Road
Pensacola, FL

850-484-7022

Days Inn Perry
2277 South Byron Butler Pkwy
Perry, FL
850-584-5311

Knights Inn Plant City
301 South Frontage Rd
Plant City, FL
813-752-0570

Residence Inn By Marriott Fort
Lauderdale Plantation
130 North University Drive
Plantation, FL
954-723-0300

Staybridge Suites Ft. Lauderdale-
Plantation
410 North Pine Island Road
Plantation, FL

954-577-9696

Residence Inn Fort Lauderdale
Pompano Beach/Oceanfront
1350 N Ocean Blvd
Pompano Beach, FL
954-590-1000

Sawgrass Marriott Golf Resort & Spa
1000 Pga Tour Boulevard
Ponte Vedra Beach, FL

Knights Inn Port Charlotte
4100 Tamiami Trail
Port Charlotte, FL
941-743-2442

Sleep Inn & Suites Port Charlotte
806 Kings Highway
Port Charlotte, FL

941-613-6300

Homewood Suites By Hilton Tampa-
Port Richey
11115 Us Highway 19 North
Port Richey, FL
727-819-1000

Homewood Suites Port St Lucie
10301 Sw Innovation Way
Port St Lucie, FL
772-345-5300

Residence Inn Port St. Lucie
1920 Sw Fountainview Blvd
Port St Lucie, FL

772-344-7814

Best Western Plus Sanford
Airport/Lake Mary Hotel
3401 S. Orlando Drive
Sanford, FL
407-320-0845

Signal Inn
1811 Olde Middle Gulf Drive
Sanibel, FL
800-992-4690

Tropical Winds Beachfront Motel
and Cottages
4819 Tradewinds Drive
Sanibel Island, FL
239-472-1765

Coquina On the Beach Resort
1008 Ben Franklin Drive
Sarasota, FL
941-388-2141

Holiday Inn Lido Beach
233 Ben Franklin Drive
Sarasota, FL

941-388-5555

Residence Inn By Marriott Sarasota
Bradenton
1040 University Pkwy
Sarasota, FL

941-358-1468

Americas Best Value Inn
180 Highway A1a
Satellite Beach, FL
321-777-3552

Residence Inn Sebring
3221 Tubbs Road
Sebring, FL
863-314-9100

Flip Flop Cottages - Siesta Key
8254 Midnight Pass Road
Siesta Key, FL
941-346-0113

Microtel Inn & Suites By Wyndham
Spring Hill/Weeki Wachee
4881 Commericial Way
Spring Hill, FL

352-596-3444

Bayfront Marin House
142 Avenida Menendez
St Augustine, FL
904-824-4301

Inn at Camachee Harbor
201 Yacht Club Dr.
St Augustine, FL

904-825-0003

Our Beach Lodgings of St. Augustine
Florida
279 Saint George Street (Check-In
Location Only)
St Augustine, FL

904-824-6068

Saint Augustine Beach House
10 Vilano Road
St Augustine, FL

904-829-5939

Quality Inn & Suites Saint Augustine
901 A1a Beach Boulevard
St Augustine Beach, FL
904-471-1474

Loews Don Cesar Hotel
3400 Gulf Boulevard
St Pete Beach, FL
727-360-1881

Postcard Inn on the Beach
6300 Gulf Boulevard
St Pete Beach, FL

727-367-2711

TradeWinds Island Resorts
5500 Gulf Blvd
St Pete Beach, FL

888-794-0070

Days Inn St. Petersburg North
5005 34th Street North
St Petersburg, FL

Valley Forge Motel
6825 Central Avenue
St Petersburg, FL

727-345-0135

Americas Best Value Inn Starke
880 North Temple Avenue
Starke, FL
904-964-7357

Best Western Starke
1290 N. Temple Ave.
Starke, FL

904-964-6744

Legacy Inn -Starke

1101 North Temple Avenue
Starke, FL

904-964-7600

Best Western Downtown Stuart
1209 S Federal Highway
Stuart, FL
772-287-6200

Courtyard By Marriott Stuart
7615 Sw Lost River Road
Stuart, FL

772-781-3344

Pirate's Cove Resort and Marina -
Stuart
4307 Southeast Bayview Street
Stuart, FL

772-287-2500

Aloft Tallahasee Downtown
200 North Monroe Street
Tallahassee, FL
850-513-0313

Best Western Pride Inn And Suites
2016 Apalachee Parkway
Tallahassee, FL

850-656-6312

Days Inn University Center-
Tallahassee
1350 West Tennessee Street
Tallahassee, FL

850-222-3219

Homewood Suites By HiltonÂ®
Tallahassee
2987 Apalachee Parkway
Tallahassee, FL

850-402-9400

Red Roof Inn Tallahassee
2930 Hospitality Street
Tallahassee, FL

850-385-7884

Residence Inn By Marriott
Tallahassee North Capital Circle
1880 Raymond Diehl Road
Tallahassee, FL

850-422-0093

Residence Inn Tallahassee
Universities At The Capitol
600 West Gaines Street
Tallahassee, FL

850-329-9080

Staybridge Suites Tallahassee I-10
East
1600 Summit Lake Drive
Tallahassee, FL

850-219-7000

Suburban Extended Stay
Tallahassee
522 Silver Slipper Lane
Tallahassee, FL

850-386-2121

Travelodge Inn & Suites
Tallahassee North
2801 North Monroe Street
Tallahassee, FL

850-386-8286

Extended Stay America - Fort
Lauderdale - Tamarac
3873 West Commercial Blvd
Tamarac, FL
954-733-6644

Econo Lodge Airport At RJ Stadium
4732 North Dale Mabry
Tampa, FL
813-874-6700

Extended Stay America - Tampa -
Airport - Spruce Street
4312 W. Spruce Street
Tampa, FL

813-873-2850

Extended Stay America - Tampa -
North Airport
5401 Beaumont Ctr. Blvd. East
Tampa, FL

813-243-1913

Holiday Inn Express Hotel & Suites
Tampa-Fairgrounds-Casino
8610 Elm Fair Boulevard
Tampa, FL

813-490-1000

Homewood Suites Tampa Brandon
10240 Palm River Road
Tampa, FL

813-685-7099

Homewood Suites by Hilton Tampa
Airport-Westshore
5325 Avion Park Drive
Tampa, FL

813-282-1950

Howard Johnson Hotel - Tampa
Near Airport Stadium
2055 North Dale Mabry Highway
Tampa, FL

813-875-8818

Red Roof Inn Tampa Brandon
10121 Horace Avenue
Tampa, FL

813-681-8484

Red Roof Inn Tampa Fairgrounds
5001 North Us 301
Tampa, FL

813-623-5245

Residence Inn By Marriott Tampa
Downtown
101 East Tyler Street
Tampa, FL

813-221-4224

Residence Inn By Marriott Tampa
Sabal Park/Brandon
9719 Princess Palm Way
Tampa, FL

813-627-8855

Residence Inn By Marriott Tampa
Westshore/Airport
4312 W. Boy Scout Boulevard
Tampa, FL

813-877-7988

Residence Inn Tampa North/I-75
Fletcher
13420 North Telecom Parkway
Tampa, FL

813-972-4400

Sheraton Suites Tampa Airport
Westshore
4400 West Cypress Street
Tampa, FL

813-873-8675

Sheraton Tampa Riverwalk Hotel
200 N. Ashley Drive
Tampa, FL

813-223-2222

Staybridge Suites Tampa East-
Brandon
3624 North Falkenburg Road
Tampa, FL

813-227-4000

Super 8 Tampa U.S.F. Near Busch
Gardens Downtown
321 E Fletcher Ave
Tampa, FL

813-933-4545

Towneplace Suites By Marriott
Tampa North/I-75 Fletcher
6800 Woodstork Road
Tampa, FL

813-975-9777

Towneplace Suites By Marriott
Tampa Westshore/Airport

5302 Avion Park Drive
Tampa, FL
813-282-1081

Travelodge Near Busch Gardens - Tampa
2901 East Busch Boulevard
Tampa, FL
813-933-6471

Best Western Plus Lake County Inn & Suites
1380 E Burleigh Boulevard
Tavares, FL
352-253-2378

Extended Stay America - Tampa - North - USF - Attractions
12242 Morris Bridge Rd.
Temple Terrace, FL
813-989-2264

Comfort Suites The Villages
1202 Avenida Central
The Villages, FL
352-259-6578

Towneplace Suites By Marriott The Villages
1141 Alonzo Avenue
The Villages, FL
352-753-8686

Best Western Space Shuttle Inn
3455 Cheney Highway
Titusville, FL
321-269-9100

Days Inn Kennedy Space Center
3755 Cheney Highway
Titusville, FL
321-269-4480

Executive Garden Titusville Hotel
3480 Garden Street
Titusville, FL
321-269-9310

Holiday Inn Titusville - Kennedy Space Ctr
4715 Helen Hauser Blvd.
Titusville, FL
321-383-0200

Quality Inn Kennedy Space Center
3655 Cheney Highway
Titusville, FL
321-269-7110

Ramada Inn Kennedy Space Center
3500 Cheney Highway
Titusville, FL
321-269-5510

Lorelei Resort Motel
10273 Gulf Blvd
Treasure Island, FL
727-360-4351

South Beach Motel & Resort
1705 South Ocean Drive
Vero Beach, FL
772-231-5366

Vero Beach Hotel & Spa, A Kimpton Hotel
3500 Ocean Drive
Vero Beach, FL
772-231-5666

Best Western Palm Beach Lakes Inn
1800 Palm Beach Lakes Boulevard
West Palm Beach, FL
561-683-8810

Homewood Suites By Hilton West Palm Beach
2455 Metrocentre Boulevard
West Palm Beach, FL
561-682-9188

Red Roof PLUS+ West Palm Beach
2421 Metrocentre Blvd East
West Palm Beach, FL
561-697-7710

Residence Inn By Marriott West Palm Beach
2461 Metrocentre Blvd East
West Palm Beach, FL
561-687-4747

West Palm Beach - Days Inn Airport North
2300 W 45th St
West Palm Beach, FL
561-689-0450

Residence Inn by Marriott Fort Lauderdale Weston
2605 Weston Road
Weston, FL
954-659-8585

Towneplace Suites By Marriott Fort Lauderdale Weston
1545 Three Village Road
Weston, FL
954-659-2234

Howard Johnson Inn - Winter Haven
1300 3rd Street Sw
Winter Haven, FL
863-294-7321

Microtel Inn & Suites By Wyndham Zephyrhills
7839 Gall Boulevard

Zephyrhills, FL
813-783-2211

Ramada Zephyrhills
6815 Gall Blvd.
Zephyrhills, FL
813-762-2000

# Georgia Listings

Best Western Acworth Inn
5155 Cowan Road
Acworth, GA
770-974-0116

Econo Lodge Acworth
4980 Cowan Road
Acworth, GA
770-974-1922

Super 8 Acworth
4970 Cowan Road
Acworth, GA
770-966-9700

Ramada Limited - Adairsville
500 Georgia North Circle
Adairsville, GA
770-769-9726

Days Inn-Adel-South Georgia-Motorsports Park
1204 West 4th Street
Adel, GA
229-896-4574

Hampton Inn Adel
1500 West 4th Street
Adel, GA
229-896-3099

Days Inn Albany
422 W. Oglethorpe Blvd.
Albany, GA
229-888-2632

Kings Inn - Albany
1201 Schley Avenue
Albany, GA
229-888-9600

Super 8 Albany
2444 North Slappy Boulevard
Albany, GA
229-888-8388

Days Inn Alma
930 South Pierce Street Highway 1 And 23 South
Alma, GA
912-632-7000

Extended Stay America - Atlanta - Alpharetta - Rock Mill Rd.

Dog-Friendly Lodging - Please always call ahead to make sure an establishment is still dog-friendly.

1950 Rock Mill Road
Alpharetta, GA
770-475-2676

Residence Inn By Marriott Atlanta
Alpharetta/North Point Mall
1325 Northpoint Drive
Alpharetta, GA

770-587-1151

Residence Inn By Marriott Atlanta
Alpharetta/Windward
5465 Windward Pkwy
Alpharetta, GA

770-664-0664

Staybridge Suites Alpharetta North
Point
3980 North Point Park
Alpharetta, GA

770-569-7200

Wingate By Wyndham - Alpharetta
1005 Kingswood Place
Alpharetta, GA

770-649-0955

Wingate By Wyndham - Alpharetta
1005 Kingswood Place
Alpharetta, GA

770-649-0955

Knights Inn Americus
1007 Martin Luther King Boulevard
Americus, GA
229-924-3613

Super 8 Motel Ashburn
749 East Washington Avenue
Ashburn, GA
229-567-4688

Best Western Athens
170 North Milledge Avenue
Athens, GA
706-546-7311

Hotel Indigo Athens - University Area
500 College Avenue
Athens, GA

706-546-0430

Hotel Indigo Athens - University Area
500 College Avenue
Athens, GA

706-546-0430

Sleep Inn &""; Suites

Athens, GA

706-850-1261

Aloft Atlanta Downtown
300 Spring Street Nw

Atlanta, GA

Americas Best Value Inn Downtown
Midtown
1641 Peachtree Street Northeast
Atlanta, GA

404-873-5731

Crowne Plaza Atlanta Airport
1325 Virginia Ave
Atlanta, GA

404-768-6660

Extended Stay America - Atlanta -
Clairmont
3115 Clairmont Rd.
Atlanta, GA

404-679-4333

Extended Stay America - Atlanta -
Perimeter - Crestline
905 Crestline Pkwy
Atlanta, GA

770-396-5600

Extended Stay America - Atlanta -
Perimeter - Hammond Drive
1050 Hammond Drive
Atlanta, GA

770-522-0025

Hawthorn Suites By Wyndham
Atlanta Perimeter Center
6096 Barfield Road Ne
Atlanta, GA

404-252-5066

Hilton Atlanta
255 Courtland Street Ne
Atlanta, GA

404-659-2000

Hilton Atlanta Airport
1031 Virginia Avenue
Atlanta, GA

404-767-9000

Holiday Inn Atlanta-
Perimeter/Dunwoody
4386 Chamblee Dunwoody Road
Atlanta, GA

770-457-6363

Homewood Suites By HiltonÂ®
Atlanta-Galleria/Cumberland
3200 Cobb Parkway S W
Atlanta, GA

770-988-9449

Homewood Suites By HiltonÂ®
Atlanta/Buckhead
3566 Piedmont Rd
Atlanta, GA

404-365-0001

Hotel Indigo - Atlanta Midtown
683 Peachtree Street Ne
Atlanta, GA

404-874-9200

Inn at the Peachtrees
330 W Peachtree St Nw
Atlanta, GA

404-577-6970

La Quinta Inn & Suites Atlanta Airport
North
1200 Virginia Ave
Atlanta, GA

404-209-1800

Le Meridien Atlanta Perimeter
111 Perimeter Center West
Atlanta, GA

770-396-6800

Loews Atlanta Hotel
1065 Peachtree Street
Atlanta, GA

404-745-5000

Motel 6 Atlanta Downtown
311 Courtland Street Northeast
Atlanta, GA

404-659-4545

Red Roof PLUS Atlanta - Buckhead
1960 North Druid Hills Road
Atlanta, GA

404-321-1653

Residence Inn Atlanta Buckhead
2960 Piedmont Rd Northeast
Atlanta, GA

404-239-0677

Residence Inn Atlanta Downtown
134 Peachtree Street Nw
Atlanta, GA

404-522-0950

Residence Inn Atlanta
Midtown/Georgia Tech
1041 West Peachtree Street
Atlanta, GA

404-872-8885

Residence Inn By Marriott Atlanta
Buckhead/Lenox Park
2220 Lake Blvd
Atlanta, GA

404-467-1660

Residence Inn By Marriott Atlanta

Midtown/Peachtree At 17th
1365 Peachtree St
Atlanta, GA

404-745-1000

Sheraton Atlanta Airport Hotel
1900 Sullivan Road
Atlanta, GA

770-997-1100

Sheraton Atlanta Perimeter North
800 Hammond Drive Northeast
Atlanta, GA

404-564-3000

Sonesta Es Suites Atlanta Perimeter
Center
760 Mount Vernon Highway
Northeast
Atlanta, GA

404-250-0110

Staybridge Suites Atlanta Perimeter
4601 Ridgeview Road
Atlanta, GA

678-320-0111

Staybridge Suites Buckhead
540 Pharr
Atlanta, GA

404-842-0800

Super 8 Atlanta
3701 Jonesboro Road
Atlanta, GA

404-361-1111

Towneplace Suites By Marriott
Atlanta Northlake
3300 Northlake Parkway
Atlanta, GA

770-938-0408

W Hotel Atlanta Midtown
188 14th St N.E.
Atlanta, GA

404-892-6000

Augusta Marriott at the Convention
Center
Two Tenth Street
Augusta, GA
706-722-8900

Augusta Travelodge
3039 Washington Rd
Augusta, GA

706-868-6930

Candlewood Suites Augusta
1080 Claussen Road
Augusta, GA

706-733-3300

Econo Lodge Fort Gordon
2051 Gordon Highway
Augusta, GA

706-738-6565

Econo Lodge Martinez
4090 Belair Rd
Augusta, GA

706-863-0777

Quality Inn At Fort Gordon
4073 Jimmie Dyess Parkway
Augusta, GA

706-855-2088

Sheraton Augusta Hotel
1069 Stevens Creek Road
Augusta, GA

706-396-1000

Super 8 Augusta
456 Parkwest Drive
Augusta, GA

706-396-1600

Guest Inn
95 South Service Road
Austell, GA

Misty Mountain Inn & Cottages - Bed
And Breakfast
55 Misty Mountain Lane
Blairsville, GA
706-745-4786

1 My Mountain Cabin Rentals
P.O. Box 388
Blue Ridge, GA
800-844-4939

Avenair Mtn Cabin Rentals North
Georgia
1862 Old Highway 76
Blue Ridge, GA

706-632-0318

Black Bear Cabin Rentals
21 High Park Drive Ste 7
Blue Ridge, GA

888-902-2246

Comfort Inn & Suites Blue Ridge
83 Blue Ride Overlook
Blue Ridge, GA

706-946-3333

Douglas Inn & Suites, Blue Ridge,
GA
1192 Windy Ridge Road
Blue Ridge, GA

706-258-3600

Tica Cabin Rentals Inc.
699 East Main Street
Blue Ridge, GA

706-632-4448

Candlewood Suites Athens
156 Classic Road
Bogart, GA
706-548-9663

Econo Lodge Brunswick
2300 Perry Lane Rd
Brunswick, GA
912-264-8666

M Star Brunswick
450 Warren Mason Boulevard
Brunswick, GA

912-267-6500

Red Roof Inn And Suites Brunswick I-
95
25 Tourist Drive
Brunswick, GA

912-264-4720

Super 8 Brunswick/St Simons Island
Area
5280 New Jesup Highway
Brunswick, GA

912-264-8800

America's Comfort Lodge
12009 Watson Boulevard
Byron, GA
478-956-5300

Quality Inn Byron
115 Chapman Rd.
Byron, GA

478-956-1600

Best Western Executive Inn
2800 Us Highway 84 E
Cairo, GA
229-377-8000

Econo Lodge Calhoun
915 Hwy 53 East Se
Calhoun, GA
706-629-9501

Econo Lodge Inn & Suites Canton
138 Keith Drive
Canton, GA
770-345-1994

Country Hearth Inns And Suites
Cartersville
25 Carson Loop Northwest
Cartersville, GA
770-386-0700

Days Inn Cartersville
5618 Highway 20 Southeast
Cartersville, GA

770-382-1824

Econo Lodge Cartersville
41 State Route 20 Spur Southeast
Cartersville, GA

770-382-8881

Quality Inn & Suites
2385 Aubrey Lake Rd
Cartersville, GA

770-382-7011

Super 8 Cartersville
45 Highway 20 Spur Se
Cartersville, GA

770-382-1515

Residence Inn By Marriott Atlanta
Perimeter Center
1901 Savoy Drive
Chamblee, GA
770-455-4446

Days Inn Airport Best Road
4505 Best Road
College Park, GA
404-767-1224

Microtel Inn By Wyndham Atlanta
Airport
4839 Massachusetts Boulevard
College Park, GA

770-994-3003

Super 8 College Park/Atlanta Airport
2010 Sullivan Road
College Park, GA

770-991-8985

Extended Stay America - Columbus -
Airport
5020 Armour Road
Columbus, GA
706-653-0131

Extended Stay America - Columbus -
Bradley Park
1721 Rollins Way
Columbus, GA

706-653-9938

Hawthorn Suites by Wyndham
Columbus Fort Benning
3662 Victory Drive
Columbus, GA

706-687-7515

Holiday Inn Columbus
2800 Manchester Expressway
Columbus, GA

706-324-0231

Residence Inn Columbus
2670 Adams Farm Drive
Columbus, GA

706-494-0050

Staybridge Suites Columbus - Fort
Benning
1678 Whittlesey Road
Columbus, GA

706-507-7700

Super 8 Columbus Airport
2935 Warm Springs Road
Columbus, GA

706-322-6580

Best Western Commerce Inn
157 Eisenhower Drive
Commerce, GA
706-335-3640

Howard Johnson Inn Commerce Ga
148 Eisenhower Drive
Commerce, GA

706-335-5581

Red Roof Inn And Suites Commerce
30747 Highway 441 South
Commerce, GA

706-335-5183

Super 8 Commerce, Ga
152 Eisenhower Drive
Commerce, GA

706-336-8008

Hampton Inn Conyers
1340 Dogwood Drive Se
Conyers, GA
770-483-8838

Jameson Inn Conyers
1070 Dogwood Drive
Conyers, GA

770-760-0777

Best Western Colonial Inn
1706 East 16th Avenue
Cordele, GA
229-273-5420

Lake Blackshear Resort and Golf
Club
2459-H US Highway 280 West
Cordele, GA

229-276-1004

Quality Inn Cordele
1601 East 16th Avenue
Cordele, GA

229-273-2371

Ramada Cordele
2016 16th Avenue East
Cordele, GA

229-273-5000

Travelodge Cordele
1618 East 16th Avenue
Cordele, GA

Hampton Inn Covington
14460 Paras Drive Ne
Covington, GA
678-212-2500

Super 8 Covington
10130 Alcovy Road
Covington, GA

770-786-5800

Bend of the River Cabins and Chalets
319 Horseshoe Lane
Dahlonega, GA
706-219-2040

Hidden River Cabin
1104 Horseshoe Bend Rd.
Dahlonega, GA

770-518-9942

Days Inn Dalton
1518 West Walnut Avenue
Dalton, GA
706-278-0850

Quality Inn Dalton
875 College Drive
Dalton, GA

706-278-0500

Comfort Inn Darien
12924 GA Hwy 251 I-95 Exit 49
Darien, GA
912-437-4200

Comfort Inn Darien
12924 GA Hwy 251 I-95 Exit 49
Darien, GA

912-437-6660

Country Hearth Inns And Suites
Dawson
938 Forrester Drive South East
Dawson, GA
229-995-5725

Dawson Village Inn
76 North Georgia Avenue
Dawsonville, GA
706-216-4410

Quality Inn & Suites Dawsonville
127 Beartooth Parkway
Dawsonville, GA

Dog-Friendly Lodging - Please always call ahead to make sure an establishment is still dog-friendly.

706-216-1900

Knights Inn Dillard
3 Best Inn Way
Dillard, GA
706-746-5321

Econo Lodge Donalsonville
208 West 3rd Street
Donalsonville, GA
229-524-2185

Executive Inn
415 W 3rd Street
Donalsonville, GA

229-524-8695

Econo Lodge Douglas
1750 South Peterson Avenue
Douglas, GA
912-383-0433

Days Inn Douglasville-Atlanta-Fairburn Road
5489 Westmoreland Plaza
Douglasville, GA
770-949-1499

Candlewood Suites Atlanta Gwinnett Place
3665 Shackleford Road
Duluth, GA
678-380-0414

Holiday Inn Gwinnett Center
6310 Sugarloaf Parkway
Duluth, GA

770-476-2022

Quality Inn Duluth
3500 Venture Parkway
Duluth, GA

770-623-9300

Residence Inn Atlanta Gwinnett Place
1760 Pineland Road
Duluth, GA

770-921-2202

Wyndham Garden Duluth
1948 Day Drive
Duluth, GA

770-814-2800

Living on Mountain Tyme
Call to Arrange
Ellijay, GA
855-636-2226

Econo Lodge Forest Park
5060 Frontage Rd.
Forest Park, GA
404-363-6429

Super 8 Forest Park

410 Old Dixie Way I-75 South Exit 235
Forest Park, GA

404-363-8811

Travelodge Forest Park Atlanta South
6025 Old Dixie Road
Forest Park, GA

404-361-3600

Comfort Inn Forsyth
333 Harold G. Clark Pkwy
Forsyth, GA
478-994-3400

Days Inn Forsyth
343 North Lee Street
Forsyth, GA

478-994-2900

Econo Lodge Forsyth
320 Cabiness Road
Forsyth, GA

Motel 6 Forsyth
480 Holiday Circle
Forsyth, GA

478-994-5691

The Guest Lodge Gainesville
520 Queen City Pkwy Sw
Gainesville, GA
770-535-8100

Express Inn & Suites - Griffin
1690 North Expressway
Griffin, GA
770-227-1516

Residence Inn By Marriott Atlanta Airport North/Virginia
3401 International Blvd
Hapeville, GA
404-761-0511

Best Western Lake Hartwell Inn And Suites
1357 E Franklin St
Hartwell, GA
706-376-4700

Travelodge Hinesville
738 East Oglethorpe Highway
Hinesville, GA
912-368-4146

The Blue Goose
128 E. Main Street
Irwinton, GA
478-946-1501

Seventy-Four Ranch - Bed And Breakfast
9205 Highway 53 West
Jasper, GA
706-692-0123

Oceanside Inn And Suites
711 North Beachview Drive
Jekyll Island, GA
912-635-2211

Quality Inn & Suites Jekyll Island
700 North Beachview Drive
Jekyll Island, GA

912-635-2202

Villas by the Sea
1175 N Beachview Drive
Jekyll Island, GA

800-841-6262

Best Western Kennesaw Inn
3375 Busbee Drive Nw
Kennesaw, GA
770-424-7666

Days Inn Kennesaw/Atlanta
760 Cobb Place Boulevard
Kennesaw, GA

770-419-1576

Extended Stay America - Atlanta - Kennesaw Town Center
3000 Busbee Pkwy
Kennesaw, GA

770-422-1403

Quality Inn Kennesaw
750 Cobb Place
Kennesaw, GA

770-419-1530

Red Roof Inn - Kennesaw
520 Roberts Court Northwest
Kennesaw, GA

770-429-0323

Towneplace Suites By Marriott Kennesaw
1074 Cobb Place Blvd., Nw
Kennesaw, GA

770-794-8282

Econo Lodge Cumberland
1135 East King Avenue
Kingsland, GA
912-673-7336

Microtel Inn & Suites By Wyndham Kingsland
1325 East King Avenue
Kingsland, GA

912-729-1555

Motel 6 - Kingsland/Kings Bay Naval Base Area
120 Robert L. Edenfield Drive
Kingsland, GA

912-729-6888

Quality Inn Kingsland
111 Robert L. Edenfield Dr.
Kingsland, GA
912-729-6979

Red Roof Inn Kingsland
1363 Highway 40 East
Kingsland, GA
912-729-1130

Rodeway Inn Kingsland
1311 E. King Ave
Kingsland, GA
912-729-5454

Days Inn La Grange
2606 Whitesville Road
La Grange, GA
706-882-8881

Americas Best Value Inn & Suites
2209 North Main Street
LaFayette, GA
706-639-9362

Baymont Inn & Suites Lagrange
107 Hoffman Drive
Lagrange, GA
706-885-9002

Americas Best Value Inn -
Valdosta/Lake Park
4907 Timber Drive
Lake Park, GA
229-559-8111

Days Inn Lake Park/Valdosta
4913 Timber Drive
Lake Park, GA

229-559-0229

Quality Inn Lake Park
1198 Lakes Boulevard
Lake Park, GA

229-559-5181

Travelodge Lake Park/ Valdosta Area
4912 Timber Drive
Lake Park, GA

Super 8 Lavonia
14227 Jones Street
Lavonia, GA
706-356-8848

Crossland Economy Studios - Atlanta
- Lawrenceville
474 W. Pike St.
Lawrenceville, GA
770-962-5660

Days Inn Lawrenceville
731 Duluth Hwy. Sr / I-85 &; GA 316

Lawrenceville, GA
770-995-7782

Red Roof Inn Lithonia
5400 Fairington Road
Lithonia, GA
770-322-1400

Red Roof Inn Locust Grove
4840 Bill Gardner Parkway
Locust Grove, GA
678-583-0004

Super 8 Locust Grove
4605 Bill Gardners Parkway I-75
East
Locust Grove, GA

770-957-2936

Americas Best Value Inn And Suites
Macon
4951 Romeiser Drive
Macon, GA
478-474-1661

Baymont Inn & Suites Macon
150 Plantation Inn Drive
Macon, GA

478-474-8004

Best Western Inn And Suites Of
Macon
4681 Chambers Road
Macon, GA

478 781-5300

Best Western Riverside Inn
2400 Riverside Dr.
Macon, GA

478-743-6311

Candlewood Suites Macon
3957 Riverplace Dr
Macon, GA

478-254-3530

Days Inn Macon I-475
4999 Eisenhower Pkwy
Macon, GA

478-781-4343

Econo Lodge Macon
1990 Riverside Drive
Macon, GA

478-746-6221

Quality Inn Macon
4630 Chambers Rd.
Macon, GA

478-781-7000

Ramada Macon
4755 Chambers Road

Macon, GA
478-788--0120

Red Roof Inn - Macon Ga
3950 River Place Drive
Macon, GA

478-477-7477

Residence Inn By Marriott Macon
3900 Sheraton Drive
Macon, GA

478-475-4280

Deerfield Inn & Suites
2080 Eatonton Road
Madison, GA
706-342-3433

Days Inn Marietta-Whitewater
753 N. Marietta Parkway
Marietta, GA
678-797-0233

Drury Inn & Suites Atlanta Marietta
1170 Powers Ferry Place
Marietta, GA

770-612-0900

Extended Stay America - Atlanta -
Marietta - Powers Ferry Rd.
2239 Powers Ferry Road
Marietta, GA

770-303-0043

Extended Stay America - Atlanta -
Marietta - Windy Hill
1967 Leland Dr.
Marietta, GA

770-690-9477

Hilton Atlanta/Marietta Conference
Center
500 Powder Springs Street
Marietta, GA

770-427-2500

Ramada Limited Marietta Suites
630 Franklin Road
Marietta, GA

770-919-7878

Rodeway Inn & Suites Marietta
2375 Delk Road Southeast
Marietta, GA

770-951-1144

Super 8 Marietta/West/Atl Area
610 Franklin Rd
Marietta, GA

770-919-2340

Days Inn Mcdonough

744 Hwy 155 S
McDonough, GA
770-957-5261

Quality Inn & Suites Conference
Center Mcdonough
930 Highway 155 South
McDonough, GA

770-957-5291

Days Inn Milledgeville
2551 North Columbia Street
Milledgeville, GA
478-453-8471

Traveler's Rest - Bed And Breakfast
318 North Dooly Street
Montezuma, GA
478-472-0085

Americas Best Value Inn & Suites
Atlanta South
2185 Mount Zion Parkway
Morrow, GA
770-472-9800

Best Western Southlake Inn
6437 Jonesboro Road
Morrow, GA

770-961-6300

Drury Inn & Suites Atlanta Morrow
6520 South Lee Street
Morrow, GA

770-960-0500

Extended Stay America - Atlanta -
Morrow
2265 Mt. Zion Pkwy
Morrow, GA

770-472-0727

Red Roof Inn Atlanta South - Morrow
1348 Southlake Plaza Drive
Morrow, GA

770-968-1483

Americas Best Value Inn Newnan
1344 Highway 29 South
Newnan, GA
770-253-8550

Economy Inn Newnan
1310 Highway 29 South
Newnan, GA

770-683-1499

Homelodge Newnan
1344 South Highway 29 Suite B
Newnan, GA

678-854-0501

Crossland Economy Studios - Atlanta
- Jimmy Carter Blvd.
6295 Jimmy Carter Boulevard

Norcross, GA
770-446-9245

Crossland Economy Studios -
Atlanta - Norcross
200 Lawrenceville St.
Norcross, GA

770-729-8100

Crossland Economy Studios -
Atlanta - Peachtree Corners
7049 Jimmy Carter Blvd.
Norcross, GA

770-449-9966

Hampton Inn Norcross
5655 Jimmy Carter Blvd.
Norcross, GA

770-729-0060

Homewood Suites by Hilton Atlanta
Peachtree Corners
450 Technology Parkway
Norcross, GA

770-448-4663

Knights Inn Norcross
5122 Brook Hollow Parkway
Norcross, GA

770-446-5490

Red Roof Inn Norcross
5171 Brook Hollow Parkway
Norcross, GA

770-448-8944

Residence Inn Atlanta
Norcross/Peachtree Corners
5500 Triangle Drive
Norcross, GA

770-447-1714

Towneplace Suites Atlanta
Norcross/Peachtree Corners
6640 Bay Circle
Norcross, GA

770-447-8446

Best Western Plus Lake Lanier
Gainesville Hotel & Suites
4535 Oakwood Road
Oakwood, GA
770-535-8080

Days Inn And Suites Peachtree City
976 Crosstown Road
Peachtree City, GA
770-632-9700

Holiday Inn Hotel And Suites
Peachtree City
203 Newgate Road
Peachtree City, GA

770-487-4646

Knights Inn Perry
704 Mason Terrance
Perry, GA
478-987-1515

New Perry Hotel & Motel
800 Main Street
Perry, GA

478-987-1000

Rodeway Inn
110 Perimeter Road
Perry, GA

478-987-4454

Super 8 Perry Ga
102 Plaza Drive
Perry, GA

478-987-0999

Econo Lodge
500 E. US 80
Pooler, GA
912-748-4124

Econo Lodge Pooler
500 E. Us 80
Pooler, GA

912-748-4124

Red Roof Inn And Suites Savannah
Airport - Pooler
20 Mill Creek Circle
Pooler, GA

912-748-4050

Travelodge Suites Savannah Pooler
130 Continental Boulevard
Pooler, GA

912-748-6363

Super 8 Port Wentworth/Savannah
Area
7200 Highway 21 North
Port Wentworth, GA
912-965-9393

Travelodge Port Wentworth
Savannah Area
110 Travelers Way
Port Wentworth, GA

912-964-6060

Best Western Plus Richmond Hill Inn
4564 Us Highway 17
Richmond Hill, GA
912-756-7070

Days Inn Richmond Hill/Savannah
3926 Highway 17
Richmond Hill, GA

912-756-3371

Quality Inn Richmond Hill
4300 Us Highway 17 South
Richmond Hill, GA
912-756-3351

Travelodge Savannah
Area/Richmond Hill
4120 Highway 17
Richmond Hill, GA
912-756-3325

Sunrise Inn Rome
1610 Martha Berry Boulevard
Rome, GA
706-291-1994

Doubletree Hotel Atlanta Roswell
1075 Holcomb Bridge Road
Roswell, GA
770-992-9600

Best Western Plus Savannah Historic
District
412 West Bay Street
Savannah, GA
912-233-1011

Best Western Savannah Gateway
1 Gateway Boulevard East
Savannah, GA
912-925-2420

Candlewood Suites Savannah Airport
50 Stephen S Green Dr.
Savannah, GA
912-966-9644

Comfort Suites Historic District
Savannah
630 West Bay Street
Savannah, GA
912-629-2001

Days Inn Airport Savannah
2500 Dean Forest Road
Savannah, GA
912-966-5000

Days Inn And Suites Savannah
6 Gateway Boulevard East
Savannah, GA
912-925-6666

Days Inn Southside
11750 Abercorn Street
Savannah, GA
912-927-7720

East Bay Inn
225 E Bay Street/H 25
Savannah, GA

912-0238-1225

Econo Lodge Savannah South
3 Gateway Blvd South
Savannah, GA
912-925-2770

Extended Stay America - Savannah
- Midtown
5511 Abercorn St
Savannah, GA
912-692-0076

Foley House Inn
14 West Hull Street
Savannah, GA
912-232-6622

Joan's on Joan
17 W Jones Street
Savannah, GA
912-234-3863

Kimpton Brice Hotel
601 East Bay Street
Savannah, GA
912-238-1200

Motel 6 - Savannah Midtown
201 Stephenson Avenue
Savannah, GA
912-355-4100

Olde Harbour Inn
508 East Factors Walk
Savannah, GA
912-234-4100

Quality Inn Gateway
17007 Abercorn Street
Savannah, GA

Quality Inn Heart Of Savannah
300 W Bay St
Savannah, GA
912-236-6321

Quality Inn Midtown Savannah
7100 Abercorn Street
Savannah, GA
912-352-7100

Red Roof Inn And Suites Savannah
Gateway
405 Al Henderson Boulevard
Savannah, GA
912-920-3535

Residence Inn By Marriott Savannah
Downtown Historic District
500 West Charlton Street
Savannah, GA

912-233-9996

Residence Inn By Marriott Savannah
Midtown
5710 White Bluff Road
Savannah, GA
912-356-3266

Rodeway Inn

Savannah, GA
912-356-1234

Staybridge Suites Savannah Historic
District
301 East Bay Street
Savannah, GA
912-721-9000

Super 8 Savannah
387 Canebrake Rd
Savannah, GA
912-925-6996

THE BOHEMIAN HOTEL
SAVANNAH RIVERFRONT,
AUTOGRAPH COLLECTION, A
Marriott Luxury & Lifestyle Hotel
102 West Bay Street
Savannah, GA
912-721-3800

The Brice, A Kimpton Hotel
601 East Bay Street
Savannah, GA
912-238-1200

The Thunderbird Inn
611 West Oglethorpe Avenue
Savannah, GA
912-232-2661

Towneplace Suites By Marriott
Savannah Airport
4 Jay R Turner Drive
Savannah, GA
912-629-7775

Towneplace Suites By Marriott
Savannah Midtown
11309 Abercorn Street
Savannah, GA
912-920-9080

Wingate By Wyndham Savannah
Airport
50 Sylvester C Formey Drive
Savannah, GA
912-544-1180

Wingate By Wyndham Savannah
Airport

50 Sylvester C Formey Drive
Savannah, GA

912-544-1180

Extended Stay America - Atlanta -
Cumberland Mall
3103 Sports Ave.
Smyrna, GA
770-432-4000

Red Roof Inn Atlanta Smyrna
2200 Corporate Plaza
Smyrna, GA

770-952-6966

Residence Inn by Marriott Atlanta
Cumberland/Galleria
2771 Cumberland Boulevard
Smyrna, GA

770-433-8877

Howard Johnson Inn - Statesboro Ga
316 South Main Street
Statesboro, GA
912-489-2626

Knights Inn Statesboro
461 South Main Street
Statesboro, GA

912-764-5666

Super 8 Statesboro
1 Jameson Avenue
Statesboro, GA

912-681-7900

FairBridge Inn Express at Eagles
Landing
100 North Park Court
Stockbridge, GA
770-507-6500

Red Roof Inn Atlanta Southeast
637 State Route 138 West
Stockbridge, GA

678-782-4100

Quality Inn Suwanee
2945 Lawrenceville Suwanee
Suwanee, GA
770-945-1608

Best Western Bradford Inn
688 South Main Street
Swainsboro, GA
478-237-2400

Days Inn Thomaston
1211 Highway 19 North
Thomaston, GA
706-648-9260

Econo Lodge Thomaston
1207 Highway 19 North
Thomaston, GA

706-648-2900

Days Inn Thomasville
15375 Us 19 South
Thomasville, GA
229-226-6025

Rodeway Inn Thomasville
14866 Us Highway 19 South
Thomasville, GA

229-228-5555

Days Inn Tifton
1199 Highway 82 West
Tifton, GA
229-382-8505

Econo Lodge Tifton
1025 West 2nd Street
Tifton, GA

229-382-0280

Hampton Inn And Suites Tifton
720 U.S. Hwy 319 South
Tifton, GA

229-382-8800

Motel 6 Tifton
1103 King Road
Tifton, GA

229-382-0395

Super 8 Tifton
1022 W. 2nd Street
Tifton, GA

229-382-9500

Econo Lodge Union City
7410 Oakley Road
Union City, GA
770-964-9999

Microtel Inn & Suites By Wyndham
Union City/Atlanta Airport
6690 Shannon Parkway
Union City, GA

770-306-3800

Best Western Plus Valdosta Hotel &
Suites
4025 Northlake Drive
Valdosta, GA
229-241-9221

Courtyard By Marriott Valdosta
1564 Baytree Road
Valdosta, GA

Howard Johnson Valdosta North
4598 North Valdosta Road
Valdosta, GA

229-244-4460

Kinderlou Inn

2101 Us Hwy 84
Valdosta, GA

229-242-1212

Quality Inn South
1902 W Hill Ave
Valdosta, GA

229-244-4520

Super 8 Valdosta/Conf Center Area
1825 West Hill Avenue
Valdosta, GA

229-249-8000

Valdosta Days Inn Conference Center
1827 West Hill Avenue
Valdosta, GA

229-249-8800

Days Inn Villa Rica
195 Highway 61 Connector
Villa Rica, GA
770-459-8888

Fairbridge Inn Express Villa Rica
128 Highway 61 Connector
Villa Rica, GA

770-459-8000

Candlewood Suites Warner
Robins/Robins Afb
110 Willie Lee Parkway
Warner Robins, GA
478-333-6850

Days Inn & Suites Warner Robins
Near Robins AFB
2739 Watson Boulevard
Warner Robins, GA

478 953-3800

Ramada Warner Robins
2024 Watson Blvd
Warner Robins, GA

478-923-8871

Suburban Extended Stay Warner
Robins
2727 Watson Blvd
Warner Robins, GA

478-953-5100

Super 8 Warner Robins
105 Woodcrest Blvd
Warner Robins, GA

478-923-8600

Holiday Inn Express Hotel & Suites
Waycross
1761 Memorial Drive
Waycross, GA
912-548-0720

Quality Inn & Suites Waycross
1725 Memorial Drive
Waycross, GA

912-283-4490

QUALITY INN WINDER
177 W Athens St
Winder, GA
770-868-5303

# Hawaii Listings

Mahina Kai Ocean Villa
4933 Aliomanu Road
Anahola, HI
808-822-9451

Haiku Private Home Rental
Call to Arrange.
Haiku, HI
808-575-9610

North Shore Vacation Rental
Call to Arrange.
Haiku, HI

307-733-3903

Bjornen's Mac Nut Farm and
Vacation Rental
805 Kauhi Ula Road
Hilo, HI
808-969-7753

Hilo Seaside Retreat Rentals
Call to Arrange.
Hilo, HI

808-961-6178

Hilo Vacation Rental
Call to Arrange.
Hilo, HI

707-865-1200

The Inn at Kulaniapia Falls
100 Kulaniapia Drive
Hilo, HI

808-935-6789

Dragonfly Ranch
PO Box 675
Honaunau, HI
808-328-2159

Airport Honolulu Hotel
3401 North Nimitz Highway
Honolulu, HI
808-836-0661

Best Western The Plaza Hotel
3253 North Nimitz Highway
Honolulu, HI

808-836-3636

White Sands Hotel Honolulu

431 Nohonani Street
Honolulu, HI

808-924-7263

Paradise Cottage Vacation Rental
Call to Arrange.
Kaihua, HI
808-254-3332

Kailua Beach Vacation Home
Call to Arrange.
Kailua, HI
808-230-2176

Garden Island Inn
3445 Wilcox Road
Kalapaki Beach - Lihue, HI
808-245-7227

Paradise Bay Resort
47-039 Lihikai Drive
Kaneohe, HI
808-239-5711

Makaleha Mountain Retreat
Call to Arrange.
Kapaa, HI
808-822-5131

Ohia Kai Cottage
4566 Ohia Street
Kapaa, HI

808-822-5955

Sheraton Kauai Resort
2440 Hoonani Road Poipu Beach
Koloa, HI
808-742-1661

Tiki Moon Villas
55-367 Kamehameha H/H 83
Laie, HI
808-371-4507

Garden Island Inn
3445 Wilcox Road
Lihue, HI
808-245-7227

Coco's Kauai B&B Rental
Call to Arrange.
Makaweli, HI
808-338-0722

LavaBeds Hawaii Bed and Breakfast
P.O. Box 1120
Pahoa, HI
808-315-2256

Aloha Junction Bed & Breakfast
19-4037 Olapalapa Road
Volcano, HI
808-967-7289

# Idaho Listings

High Country Inn

4232 Old Ahsahka Grade
Ahsahka, ID
208-476-7570

Cedar Mountain Farm B&B
25249 N. Hatch Road
Athol, ID
208-683-0752

Best Western Blackfoot Inn
750 Jensen Grove Drive
Blackfoot, ID
208-785-4144

Super 8 Blackfoot
1279 Parkway Drive
Blackfoot, ID

208-785-9333

Best Western Airport Inn
2660 Airport Way
Boise, ID
208-384-5000

Best Western Northwest Lodge
6989 South Federal Way
Boise, ID

208-287-2300

Best Western Vista Inn At The Airport
2645 Airport Way
Boise, ID

208-336-8100

Candlewood Suites Boise - Towne
Square
700 North Cole Road
Boise, ID

208-322-4300

Extended Stay America - Boise -
Airport
2500 S Vista Ave.
Boise, ID

208-363-9040

Holiday Inn Express University Area
475 West Parkcenter Boulevard
Boise, ID

208-345-2002

La Quinta Inn & Suites Boise Airport
2613 South Vista Avenue
Boise, ID

208-388-0800

Red Lion Hotel Boise Downtown
1800 Fairview Avenue
Boise, ID

208-344-7691

Residence Inn By Marriott Boise
Downtown
1401 Lusk Avenue

Boise, ID
208-344-1200

Residence Inn By Marriott Boise West
7303 West Denton Street
Boise, ID
208-385-9000

Springhill Suites By Marriott Boise Parkcenter
424 East Parkcenter Blvd
Boise, ID
208-342-1044

Super 8 Boise
2773 Elder Street
Boise, ID
208-344-8871

The Riverside Hotel
2900 West Chinden Boulevard
Boise, ID
208-343-1871

Towneplace Suites By Marriott Boise
1455 S. Capitol Blvd.
Boise, ID
208-429-8881

Best Western Plus Burley Inn & Convention Center
800 N Overland Avenue
Burley, ID
208-678-3501

Super 8 Heyburn Burley Area
336 South 600 West
Burley, ID
208-678-7000

Best Western Plus Caldwell Inn & Suites
908 Specht Avenue
Caldwell, ID
208 454-7225

Best Western Plus Coeur D'Alene Inn
506 West Appleway Avenue
Coeur D Alene, ID
208-765-3200

Days Inn Coeur d'Alene
2200 Northwest Blvd
Coeur D'Alene, ID
208-667-8668

Holiday Inn Express Hotel & Suites Coeur Dalene
2300 West Seltice Way
Coeur D'Alene, ID
208-667-3100

Shilo Inn Suites Hotel - Coeur

D'Alene
702 West Appleway
Coeur D'Alene, ID
208-664-2300

Super 8 Coeur D'Alene
505 West Appleway
Coeur D'Alene, ID
208-765-8880

Coeur d'Alene Resort
115 S 2nd Street
Coeur d'Alene, ID
208-765-4000

Ramada Coeur D'Alene
2303 North 4th Street
Coeur d'Alene, ID
208-664-1649

Dog Bark Park Inn
2421 H 95
Cottonwood, ID
208-962-3647

Dover Bay Resort Sandpoint
659 Lakeshore Avenue
Dover, ID
208-263-5493

Pine Motel Guest House
105 S MainH33
Driggs, ID
208-354-2774

Woods River Inn
601 Main Street/H 75
Hailey, ID
208-578-0600

Triple Play Resort Hotel & Suites
151 West Orchard Street
Hayden, ID
208-772-7900

Best Western Driftwood Inn
575 River Parkway
Idaho Falls, ID
208-523-2242

Best Western Plus Cottontree Inn
900 Lindsay Boulevard
Idaho Falls, ID
208-523-6000

Candlewood Suites Idaho Falls
665 Pancheri Drive
Idaho Falls, ID
208-525-9800

Comfort Inn Idaho Falls
195 S Colorado Ave
Idaho Falls, ID
208-528-2804

Rodeway Inn Idaho Falls
525 River Parkway
Idaho Falls, ID
208-523-8000

Shilo Inn Suites - Idaho Falls
780 Lindsay Boulevard
Idaho Falls, ID
208-523-0088

Super 8 Idaho Falls
705 Lindsay Boulevard
Idaho Falls, ID
208-522-8880

Best Western Sawtooth Inn And Suites
2653 South Lincoln Avenue
Jerome, ID
208-324-9200

Morning Star Lodge
602 Bunker Avenue
Kellogg, ID
208-783-1111

Silverhorn Motor Lodge
699 W Cameron Avenue
Kellogg, ID
208-783-1151

Comfort Inn Lewiston
2128 8th Avenue
Lewiston, ID
208-798-8090

Days Inn - Lewiston
3120 North South Highway
Lewiston, ID
208-743-8808

GuestHouse Inn & Suites Lewiston
1325 Main Street
Lewiston, ID
208-746-1393

Holiday Inn Express Lewiston
2425 Nez Perce Drive
Lewiston, ID
208-750-1600

Red Lion Hotel Lewiston
621 21st Street
Lewiston, ID
208-799-1000

Best Western Plus Mccall Lodge And Suites
211 South 3rd Street
Mc Call, ID
208-634-2230

Brundage Inn
1005 W Lake Street/H 55

Dog-Friendly Lodging - Please always call ahead to make sure an establishment is still dog-friendly.

McCall, ID
208-634-2344

Super 8 McCall
303 South 3rd St
McCall, ID
208-634-4637

Candlewood Suites Meridian
1855 S. Silverstone Way
Meridian, ID
208-888-5121

Best Western Plus University Inn
1516 Pullman Road
Moscow, ID
208-882-0550

Hillcrest Motel
706 North Main Street
Moscow, ID

208-882-7579

Motel 6 Moscow
101 Baker Street
Moscow, ID

208-882-5511

Super 8 Motel - Moscow
175 Peterson Drive
Moscow, ID

208-883-1503

Rodeway Inn & Suites Nampa
130 Shannon Drive
Nampa, ID
208-442-0800

Super 8 Nampa Idaho
624 Northside Boulevard
Nampa, ID

208-467-2888

Elkin's Resort on Priest Lake
404 Elkins Road
Nordman, ID
208-443-2432

Helgeson Place Hotel Suites
125 Johnson Avenue
Orofino, ID
208-476-5729

Best Western Pocatello Inn
1415 Bench Rd.
Pocatello, ID
208-237-7650

Comfort Inn Pocatello
1333 Bench Road
Pocatello, ID

208-237-8155

Red Lion Hotel Pocatello
1555 Pocatello Creek Road

Pocatello, ID

208-233-2200

Rodeway Inn University Pocatello
835 South 5th Avenue
Pocatello, ID

208-233-0451

Super 8 Pocatello
1330 Bench Road
Pocatello, ID

208-234-0888

Towneplace Suites By Marriott
Pocatello
2376 Via Caporatti Drive
Pocatello, ID

208-478-7000

Days Inn Sandpoint
363 Bonner Mall Way
Ponderay, ID
208-263-1222

Holiday Inn Express Hotel & Suites
Sandpoint North
477326 Highway 95 North
Ponderay, ID

208-255-4500

Hotel Ruby Ponderay
477255 Highway 95 North
Ponderay, ID

208-263-5383

Quality Inn Post Falls
3175 East Seltice Way
Post Falls, ID
208-773-8900

Red Lion Templin's Hotel On The River
414 East First Avenue
Post Falls, ID

208-773-1611

Sleep Inn Post Falls
157 S. Pleasant View Road
Post Falls, ID

208-777-9394

Hill's Resort
4777 W. Lakeshore Rd.
Priest Lake, ID
208-443-2551

Hill's Resort
4777 W Lakeshore Road
Priest Lake, ID

208-443-2551

Quality Inn Rexburg
885 W. Main St.

Rexburg, ID
208-359-1311

Salmon River Motel
1203 S H 95
Riggins, ID
208-628-3231

Bottle Bay Resort Marina
115 Resort Road
Sagle, ID
208-263-5916

Best Western Edgewater Resort
56 Bridge Street
Sandpoint, ID
208-263-3194

Guesthouse Lodge Sandpoint
476841 Highway 95 North
Sandpoint, ID

208-263-2210

Quality Inn Sandpoint
807 North 5th Avenue
Sandpoint, ID

208-263-2111

Schweitzer Mountain Resort
10,000 Schweitzer Mountain Drive
Sandpoint, ID

208-255-3081

Mountain Village Resort
P. O. Box 150/ @ H 75/21
Stanley, ID
208-774-3661

Best Western Plus Twin Falls Hotel
1377 Blue Lakes Boulevard N
Twin Falls, ID
208-736-8000

Quality Inn & Suites Twin Falls
1910 Fillmore Street North
Twin Falls, ID

208-734-7494

Red Lion Hotel Canyon Springs/Twin Falls
1357 Blue Lakes Blvd., North
Twin Falls, ID

208-734-5000

Super 8 Twin Falls
1260 Blue Lakes Blvd. N
Twin Falls, ID

208-734-5801

Hells Canyon Jet Boat Trips and Lodging
1 mile S of White Bird on Old H 95
White Bird, ID
800-469-8757

Coeur d' Alene Casino Resort Hotel
27068 S H 95
Worley, ID
800-523-2464

# Illinois Listings

Baymont Inn & Suites Chicago/Alsip
12801 South Cicero
Alsip, IL
708-597-3900

Days Inn Alsip
5150 West 127th Street
Alsip, IL

708-371-5600

Super 8 Altamont
3091 E. Mill Rd.
Altamont, IL
618-483-6300

Atrium Hotel And Conference Center
3800 Homer Adams Parkway
Alton, IL
618-462-1220

Best Western Plus Parkway Hotel
1900 Homer Adams Parkway
Alton, IL

618-433-9900

Comfort Inn Alton
11 Crossroads Ct.
Alton, IL

618-465-9999

Super 8 Motel Alton
1800 Homer Adams Parkway
Alton, IL

618-465-8885

Comfort Inn Arcola
610 East Springfield
Arcola, IL
217-268-4000

Doubletree Hotel Chicago Arlington
Heights
75 West Algonquin Road
Arlington Heights, IL
847-364-7600

Red Roof Inn Chicago O'Hare Airport
22 West Algonquin Road
Arlington Heights, IL

847-228-6650

Candlewood Suites Chicago/Aurora
2625 West Sullivan Rd
Aurora, IL
630-907-9977

Staybridge Suites Naperville
4320 Meridian Parkway

Aurora, IL

630-978-2222

Americas Best Value Inn
Barrington/Chicago West
405 W Northwest Hwy
Barrington, IL
847-381-2640

Americas Best Value Inn
Beardstown
9918 Grand Avenue
Beardstown, IL
217-323-5858

Extended Stay America - Chicago -
Midway
7524 State Road
Bedford Park, IL
708-496-8211

Residence Inn By Marriott Chicago
Midway Airport
6638 South Cicero Avenue
Bedford Park, IL

708-458-7790

Super 8 Belleville
600 East Main Street
Belleville, IL
618-234-9670

Magnuson Hotel Benton
711 West Main Street
Benton, IL
618-439-3183

Magnuson Hotel Benton
711 West Main Street
Benton, IL

618-438-8205

Hilton Chicago Indian Lakes Resort
250 West Schick Road
Bloomingdale, IL
630-529-0200

Residence Inn By Marriott Chicago
Bloomingdale
295 Knollwood Drive
Bloomingdale, IL

630-893-9200

Doubletree Hotel Bloomington
10 Brickyard Drive
Bloomington, IL
309-664-6446

Extended Stay America -
Bloomington
1805 South Veterans Parkway
Bloomington, IL

309-662-8533

Holiday Inn Hotel & Suites
Bloomington-Airport

3202 East Empire Street
Bloomington, IL

309-662-4700

Quality Inn & Suites Bloomington
1803 East Empire Street
Bloomington, IL

309-662-7100

Quality Inn & Suites Bloomington
1707 West Market Street
Bloomington, IL

309-829-6292

Ramada Limited And Suites
Bloomington
919 Maple Hill Road
Bloomington, IL

309-828-0900

Super 8 Bloomington
818 Iaa Drive
Bloomington, IL

309-663-2388

Holiday Inn Express Hotel & Suites
Bourbonnais (Kankakee/Bradley
62 Ken Hayes Drive
Bourbonnais, IL
815-932-4411

Motel 6 Bridgeview
9625 South 76th Avenue
Bridgeview, IL
708-430-1818

Extended Stay America Chicago -
Buffalo Grove - Deerfield
1525 Busch Parkway
Buffalo Grove, IL
847-215-0641

Extended Stay America - Chicago -
Burr Ridge
15 West 122nd South Frontage Road
Burr Ridge, IL
630-323-6630

Quality Inn Cairo
13201 Kessler Road Route 3 And I-
57
Cairo, IL
618-734-0215

Super 8 Canton II
2110 Main Street
Canton, IL
309-647-1888

Days Inn & Suites Carbondale
2400 Reed Station Parkway
Carbondale, IL
618-529-2720

Super 8 Carbondale
1180 East Main

Carbondale, IL
618-457-8822

Centerstone Inn & Suites
1371 Williams Road
Carlyle, IL
618-594-8888

Hampton Inn Chicago-Carol Stream
Hotel
205 West North Avenue
Carol Stream, IL
630-681-9200

Days Inn And Suites Casey
933 North Route 49
Casey, IL
217-932-2212

Baymont Inn & Suites Champaign-
Urbana
302 West Anthony Drive
Champaign, IL
217-356-8900

Candlewood Suites Champaign-
Urbana Univ Area
1917 Moreland Boulevard
Champaign, IL
217-398-1000

Days Inn Champaign / Urbana
914 W. Bloomington Road
Champaign, IL
217-356-6000

Drury Inn & Suites Champaign
905 West Anthony Drive
Champaign, IL
217-398-0030

Extended Stay America - Champaign
- Urbana
610 West Marketview Drive
Champaign, IL
217-351-8899

Homewood Suites By Hilton
Champaign-Urbana
1417 South Neil Street
Champaign, IL
217-352-9960

Red Roof Inn - Champaign II
212 West Anthony Drive
Champaign, IL
217-352-0101

Super 8 Champaign
202 Marketview Drive
Champaign, IL
217-359-2388

Americas Best Value Inn Chenoa

505 Hoselton Drive
Chenoa, IL
815-945-5900

Allegro Chicago, A Kimpton Hotel
171 West Randolph Street
Chicago, IL
312-236-0123

Chicago Joe's
2256 West Irving Park Road
Chicago, IL

773-478-7000

Hilton Chicago
720 South Michigan Avenue
Chicago, IL

312-922-4400

Hilton Chicago O' Hare Airport
O Hare International Airport
Chicago, IL

773-686-8000

Hilton Suites Chicago/Magnificent
Mile
198 E. Delaware Place
Chicago, IL

312-664-1100

Holiday Inn Chicago O'Hare Area
5615 North Cumberland Avenue
Chicago, IL

773-693-5800

Homewood Suites By Hilton
Chicago Downtown
40 East Grand Street
Chicago, IL

312-644-2222

Intercontinental Chicago
505 North Michigan Avenue
Chicago, IL

312-944-4100

Loews Chicago Hotel
455 North Park Drive
Chicago, IL

312-840-6600

Monaco Chicago, A Kimpton Hotel
225 N Wabash Ave At Wacker
Chicago, IL

312-960-8500

Palomar Chicago, A Kimpton Hotel
505 North State Street
Chicago, IL

312-755-9703

RENAISSANCE BLACKSTONE

CHICAGO HOTEL, A Marriott Luxury
& Lifestyle Hotel
636 South Michigan Avenue
Chicago, IL

312-447-0955

Red Roof Inn Chicago Downtown
162 East Ontario Street
Chicago, IL

312-787-3580

Residence Inn By Marriott Chicago
Downtown/Magnificent Mile
201 East Walton Place
Chicago, IL

312-943-9800

Residence Inn By Marriott Chicago
Downtown/River North
410 North Dearborn Street
Chicago, IL

312-494-9301

Sheraton Grand Chicago
301 East North Water Street
Chicago, IL

312-464-1000

The Drake Hotel
140 East Walton Place
Chicago, IL

312-787-2200

The Gwen, a Luxury Collection Hotel,
Chicago
521 North Rush Street
Chicago, IL

312-327-0664

The James Chicago
55 East Ontario
Chicago, IL

877-526-3755

The Palmer House Hilton
17 East Monroe Street
Chicago, IL

312-726-7500

The Robey
2018 W North Avenue
Chicago, IL

872-315-3050

The Westin Michigan Avenue
Chicago
909 North Michigan Avenue
Chicago, IL

312-943-7200

Super 8 - Chillicothe
615 South 4th Street

Chillicothe, IL
309-274-2568

Drury Inn St. Louis Collinsville
602 North Bluff Road
Collinsville, IL
618-345-7700

Super 8 Motel - Collinsville/Il St Louis
Mo Area
2 Gateway Drive
Collinsville, IL

618-345-8008

Hampton Inn St. Louis-Columbia,Il
165 Admiral Trost Drive
Columbia, IL
618-281-9000

Super 8 Crystal Lake
577 Crystal Point Drive
Crystal Lake, IL
815-788-8888

Best Western Regency Inn
360 Eastgate Drive
Danville, IL
217-446-2111

Quality Inn Danville
383 Lynch Drive
Danville, IL

217-443-8004

Super 8 Danville
377 Lynch Drive
Danville, IL

217-443-4499

Extended Stay America Chicago -
Darien
2345 Sokol Court
Darien, IL
630-985-4708

Super 8 DeKalb IL
800 W. Fairview Dr
DeKalb, IL
815-748-4688

Americas Best Value Inn
333 North Wyckles Road
Decatur, IL
217-422-5900

Ramada Limited Decatur
355 E Hickory Point Rd.
Decatur, IL

217-876-8011

Sleep Inn Decatur
3920 E Hospitality Lane
Decatur, IL

217-872-7700

Red Roof Inn Chicago -

Northbrook/Deerfield
340 South Waukegan Road
Deerfield, IL
847-205-1755

Residence Inn Deerfield/Chicago
530 Lake Cook Rd
Deerfield, IL

847-940-4644

Comfort Inn Ohare
2175 East Touhy Avenue
Des Plaines, IL
847-635-1300

Extended Stay America - Chicago -
O'Hare
1201 East Touhy Avenue
Des Plaines, IL

847-294-9693

Comfort Inn Dixon
136 Plaza Drive
Dixon, IL
815-284-0500

Extended Stay America - Downers
Grove
3150 Finley Road
Downers Grove, IL
630-810-4124

Holiday Inn Express Downers Grove
3031 Finley Rd
Downers Grove, IL

630-810-9500

Red Roof Inn Chicago - Downers
Grove
1113 Butterfield Road
Downers Grove, IL

630-963-4205

Super 8 Duquoin
1010 S. Jefferson
Du Quoin, IL
618-542-4335

Super 8 Dwight
14 East Northbrook Drive
Dwight, IL
815-584-1888

Super 8 East Moline
2201 John Deere Road
East Moline, IL
309-796-1999

Embassy Peoria East Peoria
100 Conference Center Drive
East Peoria, IL
309-694-0200

Super 8 Peoria East
725 Taylor Street
East Peoria, IL

309-698-8889

Comfort Suites Effingham
1310 West Fayette Road
Effingham, IL
217-342-3151

Econo Lodge Effingham
1412 W. Fayette Ave.
Effingham, IL

217-342-9271

Quality Inn Effingham
1304 West Evergreen Drive
Effingham, IL

217-347-5050

Rodeway Inn Effingham
1205 North Keller Drive
Effingham, IL

217-347-7515

Rodeway Inn Effingham
1205 North Keller Drive
Effingham, IL

217-347-7131

Super 8 Motel - Effingham
1400 Thelma Keller Avenue
Effingham, IL

217-342-6888

Days Inn El Paso
630 West Main St
El Paso, IL
309-527-7070

Candlewood Suites Elgin Nw -
Chicago
1780 Capital Street
Elgin, IL
847-888-0600

Quality Inn Elgin
500 Tollgate Road
Elgin, IL

847-608-7300

Rim Rock's Dogwood Cabins
Karbers Ridge/Pounds Hollow
blacktop
Elizabethtown, IL
618-264-6036

Days Inn Elk Grove
Village/Chicago/Ohare Airport West
1920 East Higgins Road
Elk Grove Village, IL
847-437-1650

Motel 6 Elk Grove Village
1000 West Devon Avenue
Elk Grove Village, IL

847-895-2085

Dog-Friendly Lodging - Please always call ahead to make sure an establishment is still dog-friendly.

Sheraton Suites Chicago Elk Grove
121 Northwest Point Boulevard
Elk Grove Village, IL

847-290-1600

Super 8 Chicago Ohare Airport
2951 Touhy Ave.
Elk Grove Village, IL

847-827-3133

Extended Stay America - Chicago -
Elmhurst - O'Hare
550 West Grand Avenue
Elmhurst, IL
630-530-4353

Comfort Suites Fairview Heights
137 Ludwig Drive
Fairview Heights, IL
618-394-0202

Drury Inn & Suites St. Louis Fairview
Heights
12 Ludwig Drive
Fairview Heights, IL

618-398-8530

Four Points By Sheraton St Louis -
Fairview Heights
319 Fountains Parkway
Fairview Heights, IL

Super 8 Motel Fairview Heights
45 Ludwig Drive
Fairview Heights, IL

618-398-8338

Days Inn Farmer City
975 East Clinton Avenue
Farmer City, IL
309-928-9434

Hampton Inn Decatur/Forsyth
1429 Hickory Point Drive
Forsyth, IL
217-877-5577

Rodeway Inn & Suites O'Hare South
3001 N. Mannheim Road
Franklin Park, IL
847-233-9292

Baymont Inn And Suites Freeport
1060 Riverside Drive
Freeport, IL
815-599-8510

Cloran Mansion
1237 Franklin Street
Galena, IL
815-777-0583

Eagle Ridge Resort and Spa
444 Eagle Ridge Drive
Galena, IL

815-777-2444

Galena Rentals
95 Heatherdowns Lane
Galena, IL

773-631-5253

Grant Hills Motel
9372 W H 20
Galena, IL

877-421-0924

Best Western Prairie Inn &
Conference Center
300 South Soangetaha Road
Galesburg, IL
309-343-7151

Econo Lodge Galesburg
907 W. Carl Sandburg Dr.
Galesburg, IL

309-344-5445

Super 8 Galesburg II
737 Knox Hwy 10
Galesburg, IL

309-289-2100

Americas Best Value Inn Geneseo
765 West Main Street
Geneseo, IL
309-945-1898

Super 8 Gilman
1301 S. Crescent St.
Gilman, IL
815-265-7000

Crowne Plaza Glen Ellyn Lombard
1250 Roosevelt Road
Glen Ellyn, IL
630-629-6000

Staybridge Suites Glenview
2600 Lehigh Avenue
Glenview, IL
847-657-0002

Comfort Suites Grayslake
1775 East Belvidere Road
Grayslake, IL
847-223-5050

Super 8 Grayville
2060 County Road 2450 North
Grayville, IL
618-375-7288

Comfort Inn Gurnee
6080 Gurnee Mills Circle E.
Gurnee, IL
847-855-8866

Extended Stay America Chicago -
Gurnee
5724 Northridge Drive

Gurnee, IL

847-662-3060

Super 8 Hampshire II
115 Arrowhead Drive
Hampshire, IL
847-683-0888

Extended Stay America - Chicago -
Hanover Park
1075 Lake Street
Hanover Park, IL
630-893-4823

Best Western Plus Chicago Hillside
4400 Frontage Road
Hillside, IL
708-544-9300

Extended Stay America - Chicago -
Hillside
4575 Frontage Road
Hillside, IL

708-544-4409

Hawthorn Suites By Wyndham
Chicago Hoffman Estates
2875 Greenspoint Parkway
Hoffman Estates, IL
847-490-1686

Red Roof Inn Chicago South
Barrington
2500 Hassell Road
Hoffman Estates, IL

847-885-7877

Extended Stay America Chicago -
Itasca
1181 Rohlwing Road
Itasca, IL
630-250-1111

Westin Chicago Northwest
400 Park Boulevard
Itasca, IL

630-773-4000

Holiday Inn Express & Suites
Jacksonville
2501 Holliday Lane
Jacksonville, IL
217-245-6500

Super 8 - Jacksonville
1003 West Morton Road
Jacksonville, IL

217-479-0303

Super 8 Jerseyville
1303 State Highway 109
Jerseyville, IL
618-498-7888

Red Roof Inn Joliet
1750 Mcdonough Street

Dog-Friendly Lodging - Please always call ahead to make sure an establishment is still dog-friendly.

Joliet, IL
815-741-2304

Towneplace Suites By Marriott Joliet
South
1515 Riverboat Center Drive
Joliet, IL

815-741-2400

FairBridge Inn Express Kewanee
901 South Tenney Street
Kewanee, IL
309-853-8800

Holiday Inn Express Hotel And Suites
Lake Zurich Barrington
197 South Rand Road
Lake Zurich, IL
847-726-7500

Extended Stay America - Chicago -
Lansing
2520 173rd Street
Lansing, IL
708-895-6402

Red Roof Inn Lansing
2450 East 173rd Street
Lansing, IL

708-895-9570

Days Inn Le Roy/Bloomington
Southeast
1 Demma Dr
Le Roy, IL
309-962-4700

Holiday Inn Express Le Roy
705 South Persimmons Court
Le Roy, IL

309-962-4439

Candlewood Suites Libertyville
1100 North Us Route 45
Libertyville, IL
847-247-9900

Days Inn Libertyville
1809 North Milwaukee Avenue
Libertyville, IL

847-816-8006

Best Western Plus Lincoln Inn
1750 5th Street
Lincoln, IL
217-732-9641

Hampton Inn Lincoln
1019 North Heitmann Drive
Lincoln, IL

217-732-6729

Staybridge Suites Lincolnshire
100 Barclay Blvd
Lincolnshire, IL
847-821-0002

Extended Stay America - Chicago -
Lisle
445 Warrenville Road
Lisle, IL
630-434-7710

Baymont Inn & Suites Litchfield
1405 West Hudson Drive
Litchfield, IL
217-324-4556

Hampton Inn Litchfield
11 Thunderbird Circle
Litchfield, IL

217-324-4441

Super 8 Litchfield
211 Ohren Lane
Litchfield, IL

217-324-7788

Embassy Suites Hotel Chicago-
Lombard/Oak Brook
707 E Butterfield Road
Lombard, IL
630-969-7500

Extended Stay America - Chicago -
Lombard - Oakbrook
2701 Technology Drive
Lombard, IL

630-928-0202

Residence Inn Lombard
2001 South ;Highland Ave
Lombard, IL

630-629-7800

The Westin Lombard Yorktown
Center
70 Yorktown Center
Lombard, IL

630-719-8000

Towneplace Suites By Marriott
Lombard
455 East 22nd Street
Lombard, IL

630-932-4400

Quality Inn Macomb
1646 N Lafayette St
Macomb, IL
309-837-2220

Americas Best Value Inn Marion
1802 Bittle Place
Marion, IL
618-997-1351

Drury Inn Marion
2706 West Deyoung Street
Marion, IL

618 997-9600

Econo Lodge Marion
1806 Bittle Place
Marion, IL

618-993-1644

OldSquat Inn
14160 Liberty School Road
Marion, IL

618-982-2916

Super 8 Marion
2601 Vernell Road
Marion, IL

618-993-5577

Rodeway Inn Maryville Illinois
2701 Maryville Road
Maryville, IL
618-345-5720

Holiday Inn Express Hotel & Suites
Mattoon
121 Swords Drive
Mattoon, IL
217-235-2060

Super 8 - Mclean/Bloomington
Southwest
503 E South Street
McLean, IL
309-874-2366

Comfort Inn Mendota Illinois
1307 Kailash Drive
Mendota, IL
815-538-3355

Super 8 Motel Mendota
2601 East 12th Street
Mendota, IL

815-539-7429

Americas Best Value Inn Metropolis
1415 East 5th Street
Metropolis, IL
618-524-9341

Baymont Inn And Suites Metropolis
203 East Front Street
Metropolis, IL

618-524-5678

Residence Inn By Marriott Chicago
Lake Forest/Mettawa
26325 N Riverwoods Boulevard
Mettawa, IL
847-615-2701

Super 8 Mokena
9485 West 191st Street
Mokena, IL
708-479-7808

Motel 6 Moline
2501 52nd Avenue

Moline, IL
309-797-5580

Quality Inn & Suites Moline
6910 27th Street
Moline, IL

309-762-8300

Residence Inn By Marriott Moline
Quad Cities
4600 53rd Street
Moline, IL

309-796-4244

Best Western Monticello Gateway Inn
805 Iron Horse Place
Monticello, IL
217 762-9436

Comfort Inn Morris
70 Gore Road West
Morris, IL
815-942-1433

Days Inn And Suites Of Morris
80 Hampton Road
Morris, IL

815-942-9000

Quality Inn Morris
200 Gore Road
Morris, IL

815-942-6600

Super 8 Morris
70 Green Acres Drive
Morris, IL

815-942-3200

Americas Best Value Inn Morton
Peoria
150 West Ashland Street
Morton, IL
309-266-9933

Baymont Inn And Suites Morton
210 East Ashland Street
Morton, IL

309-266-8888

Holiday Inn Express Hotel & Suites
Morton Peoria Area
140 Ashland Street
Morton, IL

309-263-4400

Quality Inn Morton
115 East Ashland
Morton, IL

309-266-8310

Comfort Suites Mount Vernon
404 South 44th Street
Mount Vernon, IL

618-244-2700

Drury Inn & Suites Mt. Vernon
145 North 44th Street
Mount Vernon, IL

618-244-4550

Holiday Inn Mount Vernon
222 Potomac Boulevard
Mount Vernon, IL

618-244-7100

Motel 6 Mount Vernon
220 South 44th Street
Mount Vernon, IL

618-242-1200

Super 8 Motel - Mt. Vernon
401 S. 44th St.
Mount Vernon, IL

618-242-8800

Super 8 Mundelein Libertyville Area
1950 S. Lake Street
Mundelein, IL
847-949-8842

Best Western Naperville Inn
1617 N Naperville Rd
Naperville, IL
630-505-0200

Extended Stay America - Chicago -
Naperville - East
1827 Centre Point Circle
Naperville, IL

630-577-0200

Extended Stay America - Chicago -
Naperville - West
1575 Bond Street
Naperville, IL

630-983-0000

Red Roof Plus Chicago Naperville
1698 West Diehl Road
Naperville, IL

630-369-2500

Sleep Inn Naperville
1831 West Diehl Road
Naperville, IL

630-778-5900

Towneplace Suites By Marriott
Chicago Naperville
1843 West Diehl Road
Naperville, IL

630-548-0881

Candlewood Suites Bloomington-
Normal
203 Susan Drive

Normal, IL
309-862-4100

Motel 6 Normal
202 Landmark Drive
Normal, IL

309-454-6600

Super 8 Normal/Bloomington Area
2 Traders Circle
Normal, IL

309-454-5858

Baymont Inn & Suites - North Aurora
308 South Lincolnway Street
North Aurora, IL
630-897-7695

Hilton Northbrook
2855 N Milwaukee Avenue
Northbrook, IL
847-480-7500

RENAISSANCE CHICAGO NORTH
SHORE HOTEL, A Marriott Luxury &
Lifestyle Hotel
933 Skokie Boulevard
Northbrook, IL

847-498-6500

Sheraton Chicago Northbrook Hotel
1110 Willow Road
Northbrook, IL

847-480-1900

Extended Stay America - St. Louis -
O' Fallon, Il
154 Regency Park
O'Fallon, IL
618-624-1757

Quality Inn O'Fallon
1409 West Us Highway 50
O'Fallon, IL

618-628-8895

Days Inn O'Fallon
1320 Park Plaza Drive
OFallon, IL
618-628-9700

Residence Inn By Marriott Chicago
Oak Brook
790 Jorie Boulevard
Oak Brook, IL
630-571-1200

Holiday Inn Oak Brook
17 West 350 22nd Street
Oakbrook Terrace, IL
630-833-3600

Staybridge Suites Oakbrook Terrace
200 Royce Blvd
Oakbrook Terrace, IL

630-953-9393

Candlewood Suites Ofallon, Il - St.
Louis Area
1332 Park Plaza Drive
Ofallon, IL
618-622-9555

Best Western Oglesby Inn
900 Holiday Street
Oglesby, IL
815-883-3535

Days Inn Oglesby/Starved Rock
120 North Lewis Avenue
Oglesby, IL

815-883-9600

Homewood Suites By Hilton Orland
Park
16245 S la Grange Road
Orland Park, IL
708-364-9411

Holiday Inn Express Chicago-
Palatine/North Arlington Heights
1550 East Dundee Road
Palatine, IL
847-934-4900

Super 8 Paris II
11642 IL Highway 1
Paris, IL
217-463-8888

Econo Lodge & Suites Pekin
3240 North Vandever Avenue
Pekin, IL
309-353-4047

Candlewood Suites Peoria At Grand
Prairie
5300 W. Landens Way
Peoria, IL
309-691-1690

Comfort Suites Peoria
1812 West War Memorial Drive
Peoria, IL

309-688-3800

Extended Stay America - Peoria -
North
4306 North Brandywine Drive
Peoria, IL

309-688-3110

Hampton Inn And Suites Peoria-West
7806 N. Route 91
Peoria, IL

309-589-0001

Mark Twain Hotel
225 Northeast Adams Street
Peoria, IL

309-676-3600

Quality Inn & Suites Peoria
4112 North Brandywine Drive
Peoria, IL

309-685-2556

Red Roof Inn Peoria
1822 West War Memorial Drive
Peoria, IL

309-685-3911

Residence Inn Peoria
2000 West War Memorial Drive
Peoria, IL

309-681-9000

Staybridge Suites Peoria Downtown
300 West Romeo B Garrett Avenue
Peoria, IL

309-673-7829

Super 8 Peoria
1816 West War Memorial Drive
Peoria, IL

309-688-8074

Holiday Inn Express Hotel & Suites
Peru - Lasalle Area
5253 Trompeter Rd
Peru, IL
815-224-2500

Super 8 Peru Starved Rock State
Park
1851 May Rd.
Peru, IL

815-223-1848

Americas Best Value Inn & Suites
Pickneyville
5700 State Route 154
Pinckneyville, IL
618-357-5600

Best Western Pontiac Inn
1821 W Reynolds St
Pontiac, IL
815-842-2777

Three Roses Bed and Breakfast
209 E. Howard Street/H 116
Pontiac, IL

815-844-3404

Super 8 Motel - Pontoon Beach,
Il/St. Louis, Mo Area
4141 Timberlake Drive
Pontoon Beach, IL
618-931-8808

Days Inn Princeton
2238 North Main Street
Princeton, IL

815-875-3371

Econo Lodge Princeton
2200 North Main Street
Princeton, IL

815-872-3300

Motel 6 Prospect Heights
540 North Milwaukee Avenue
Prospect Heights, IL
847-459-0545

Budget Host Inn
200 Maine Street
Quincy, IL
217-223-6610

Comfort Inn Quincy
4122 Broadway Street
Quincy, IL

217-228-2700

Microtel Inn & Suites By Wyndham
Quincy
200 South 3rd Street
Quincy, IL

217-222-5620

Quincy Inn & Suites
224 North 36th Street
Quincy, IL

217-228-8808

Days Inn Rantoul
801 W Champaign Ave
Rantoul, IL
217-893-0700

Super 8 Rantoul
207 South Murray Road
Rantoul, IL

217-893-8888

Best Western Robinson Inn
1500 W. Main Street
Robinson, IL
618-544-8448

Comfort Inn & Suites Rochelle
1133 North 7th Street
Rochelle, IL
815-562-5551

Baymont Inn & Suites Rockford
662 N. Lyford Road
Rockford, IL
815-229-8200

Candlewood Suites Rockford
7555 Walton Street
Rockford, IL

815-229-9300

Comfort Inn Rockford
7392 Argus Drive

Rockford, IL
815-398-7061

Days Inn Rockford
220 South Lyford Road
Rockford, IL

815-332-4915

Extended Stay America - Rockford -
I-90
653 Clark Drive
Rockford, IL

815-226-8969

Red Roof Inn Rockford
7434 East State Street
Rockford, IL

815-398-9750

Rockford Residence Inn By Marriott
7542 Colosseum Dr
Rockford, IL

815-227-0013

Sleep Inn Rockford
725 Clark Drive
Rockford, IL

815-398-8900

Staybridge Suites Rockford
633 North Bell School Road
Rockford, IL

815-397-0200

Super 8 Rockford
7646 Colosseum Drive
Rockford, IL

815-229-5522

Extended Stay America - Chicago -
Rolling Meadows
2400 Golf Road
Rolling Meadows, IL
847-357-1000

Holiday Inn Express Rolling Meadows
3477 Algonquin Road
Rolling Meadows, IL

847-259-6600

Extended Stay America - Chicago -
Romeoville -Bollingbrook
1225 Lakeview Drive
Romeoville, IL
630-226-8966

Super 8 Romeoville/Bolingbrook
1301 Marquette Drive
Romeoville, IL

630-759-8880

Crowne Plaza Chicago O Hare Hotel

And Conference Center
5440 North River Road
Rosemont, IL
847-671-6350

Doubletree Hotel Chicago O Hare
Airport Rosemont
5460 North River Road
Rosemont, IL

847-292-9100

Embassy Suites Hotel Chicago-O'
Hare Rosemont
5500 North River Road
Rosemont, IL

847-678-4000

Hilton Rosemont/Chicago O Hare
5550 North River Road
Rosemont, IL

847-678-4488

Loews Chicago O'Hare Hotel
5300 North River Road
Rosemont, IL

847-544-5300

Residence Inn O' Hare Rosemont
7101 Chestnut Street
Rosemont, IL

847-375-9000

The Westin O' Hare
6100 North River Road
Rosemont, IL

847-698-6000

Super 8 Motel - Salem
118 Woods Lane
Salem, IL
618-548-5882

L & M Motel
2000 N Oakton Road
Savanna, IL
815-273-7728

Savanna Inn & Suites
101 Valley View Drive
Savanna, IL

815-273-2288

The Oscar Swan Country Inn
3315 Elizabeth-Scales Road
Scales Mound, IL
815-541-0653

Extended Stay America - Chicago -
Schaumburg - Convention Center
51 East State Parkway
Schaumburg, IL
847-882-6900

Extended Stay America - Chicago -
Schaumburg - I-90

2000 North Roselle Road
Schaumburg, IL

847-882-7011

Extended Stay America - Chicago -
Woodfield Mall
1200 American Lane
Schaumburg, IL

847-517-7255

Hawthorn Suites By Wyndham
Chicago Schaumburg
1200 East Bank Drive
Schaumburg, IL

847-517-7644

Hawthorn Suites Schaumburg
1251 E. American Lane
Schaumburg, IL

847-706-9007

Homewood Suites By Hilton®
Chicago/Schaumburg
815 East American Lane
Schaumburg, IL

847-605-0400

Residence Inn By Marriott Chicago
Schaumburg
1610 Mcconnor Parkway
Schaumburg, IL

847-517-9200

Sonesta Es Suites Chicago
Schaumburg
901 East Woodfield Office Court
Schaumburg, IL

847-619-6677

Candlewood Suites Chicago - O'Hare
4021 North Mannheim Road
Schiller Park, IL
847-671-4663

Comfort Suites O' Hare Airport
4200 N. River Road
Schiller Park, IL

847-233-9000

Four Points By Sheraton Chicago
O'Hare Airport
10249 West Irving Park Road
Schiller Park, IL

847-671-6000

Extended Stay America - Chicago -
Skokie
5211 Old Orchard Road
Skokie, IL
847-663-9031

Holiday Inn Chicago North Shore
Skokie

5300 West Touhy Avenue
Skokie, IL
847-679-8900

Rodeway Inn
9333 Skokie Boulevard
Skokie, IL
847-679-4200

Comfort Inn South Jacksonville
200 Comfort Drive
South Jacksonville, IL
217-245-8372

Baymont Inn & Suites Springfield
5871 South 6th St. Frontage Rd
Springfield, IL
217-529-6655

Best Western Clearlake Plaza
3440 East Clear Lake Avenue
Springfield, IL
217-525-7420

Candlewood Suites Springfield
2501 Sunrise Drive
Springfield, IL
217-522-5100

Holiday Inn Express And Suites Hotel
Springfield
3050 South Dirksen Parkway
Springfield, IL
217-529-7771

Howard Johnson Inn And Suites
Springfield
1701 J. David Jones Parkway
Springfield, IL
217-541-8762

Mansion View Inn and Suites
529 S 4th Street
Springfield, IL
800-252-1083

Quality Inn & Suites Springfield
3442 Freedom Drive
Springfield, IL
217-787-2250

Red Roof Inn Springfield
3200 Singer Avenue
Springfield, IL
217-753-4302

Signature Inn Springfield
3090 Stevenson Drive
Springfield, IL
217-529-6611

Sleep Inn Springfield

3470 Freedom Dr
Springfield, IL
217-787-6200

Staybridge Suites Hotel Springfield
South
4231 Schooner Drive
Springfield, IL
217-793-6700

Wyndham Springfield City Centre
700 East Adams Street
Springfield, IL
217-789-1530

Courtyard By Marriott St. Charles
700 Courtyard Dr
St Charles, IL
630-377-6370

Geneva Motel Inn
100 South Tyler Road
St Charles, IL
630-513-6500

Quality Inn & Suites Saint Charles
1600 East Main Street
St Charles, IL
630-584-5300

Super 8 St. Charles
1520 E Main St
St Charles, IL
630-377-8388

Super 8 Staunton
1527 Herman Road
Staunton, IL
618-635-5353

Red Roof Inn St Louis - Troy
2030 Formosa Road
Troy, IL
618-667-2222

Super 8 Troy
910 Edwardsville Road
Troy, IL
618-667-8888

Holiday Inn Express Tuscola, Illinois
1201 Tuscola Blvd
Tuscola, IL
217-253-6363

Super 8 Tuscola
1007 E. Southline Drive
Tuscola, IL
217-253-5488

Ramada Urbana/Champaign
902 West Killarney Street
Urbana, IL
217-328-4400

Sleep Inn Urbana
1908 N. Lincoln Ave.
Urbana, IL
217-367-6000

Americas Best Value Inn Vandalia
1920 North Kennedy Boulevard
Vandalia, IL
618-283-4400

Economy Inn - Vandalia
1500 North 6th Street
Vandalia, IL
618-283-2363

Holiday Inn Express Hotel & Suites
Vandalia
21 Mattes Avenue
Vandalia, IL
618-283-0010

Extended Stay America - Chicago -
Vernon Hills - Lake Forest
215 N Milwaukee Ave
Vernon Hills, IL
847-821-7101

Extended Stay America - Chicago -
Vernon Hills - Lincolnshire
675 Woodlands Pkwy
Vernon Hills, IL
847-955-1111

Holiday Inn Express Chicago Nw-
Vernon Hills
975 North Lakeview Parkway
Vernon Hills, IL
847-367-8031

Hotel Indigo Chicago - Vernon Hills
450 North Milwaukee Avenue
Vernon Hills, IL
847-918-1400

Candlewood Suites Warrenville
27 West 300 Warrenville Road
Warrenville, IL
630-836-1650

Residence Inn By Marriott Chicago
Naperville/Warrenville
28500 Bella Vista Parkway
Warrenville, IL
630-393-3444

Super 8 Motel - Washington/Peoria
Area
1884 Washington Road
Washington, IL
309-444-8881

Super 8 Watseka
710 West Walnut St
Watseka, IL

815-432-6000

Candlewood Suites Chicago
Waukegan
1151 S Waukegan Road
Waukegan, IL
847-578-5250

Econo Lodge Waukegan
630 N Green Bay Rd
Waukegan, IL
847-249-2388

Residence Inn Chicago
Waukegan/Gurnee
1440 South White Oak Drive
Waukegan, IL

847-689-9240

Travelodge Waukegan Gurnee
3633 North Lewis Avenue
Waukegan, IL

847-249-7778

Americas Best Value Inn Wenona
5 Cavalry Drive
Wenona, IL
815-853-4371

Extended Stay America - Chicago -
Westmont - Oak Brook
855 Pasquinelli Drive
Westmont, IL
630-323-9292

Hawthorn Suites By Wyndham
Northbrook Wheeling
8000 Capitol Drive
Wheeling, IL
847-520-1684

Econo Lodge Willowbrook
820 West 79th Street
Willowbrook, IL
630-789-6300

Red Roof Plus+ Chicago -
Willowbrook
7535 Kingery Hwy State Rte 83
Willowbrook, IL

630-323-8811

Super 8 Woodstock
1220 Davis Rd
Woodstock, IL
815-337-8808

# Indiana Listings

Best Western Plus Anderson
2114 E 59th Street
Anderson, IN
765-649-2500

Super 8 Anderson

2215 East 59th Street
Anderson, IN

765-642-2222

Ramada Inn Angola
3855 North State Road 127
Angola, IN
260-665-9471

Days Inn Auburn
1115  ;W 7th St
Auburn, IN
260-925-1316

Holiday Inn Express Auburn
404 Touring Drive
Auburn, IN

260-925-1900

Super 8 Motel - Auburn
503 Ley Drive
Auburn, IN

260-927-8800

Hampton Inn Batesville
1030 State Road 229 N.
Batesville, IN
812-934-6262

Holiday Inn Express Hotel And
Suites Bedford
2800 Express Lane
Bedford, IN
812-279-1206

Super 8 Bedford
501 Bell Back Road
Bedford, IN

812-275-8881

A Summerhouse Inn
4501 East Third Street
Bloomington, IN
812-332-2141

Americas Best Value Inn
Bloomington
1722 North Walnut Street
Bloomington, IN

812-339-1919

Hampton Inn Bloomington
2100 N Walnut Street
Bloomington, IN

812-334-2100

Towneplace Suites By Marriott
Bloomington West
105 South Franklin Road
Bloomington, IN

812-334-1234

Quality Inn & Suites Brownsburg
31 Maplehurst Drive
Brownsburg, IN

317-852-5353

Super 8 Brownsburg/Indianapolis
Area
1100 North Green Street, I-74 Exit 66
Brownsburg, IN

317-852-5211

Residence Inn Indianapolis Carmel
11895 North Meridian Street
Carmel, IN
317-846-2000

Super 8 Centerville-Richmond
2407 N. Centerville Rd
Centerville, IN
765-855-5461

Econo Lodge Chesterton
713 Plaza Drive
Chesterton, IN
219-929-4416

Best Western Green Tree Inn
1425 Broadway Street
Clarksville, IN
812-288-9281

Candlewood Suites Louisville-North
1419 Bales Lane
Clarksville, IN

812-284-6113

Clarion Hotel Conference Center
Louisville North
505 Marriott Drive
Clarksville, IN

us8-122-8344

Days Inn Cloverdale
1031 North Main Street
Cloverdale, IN
765-795-6400

Super 8 Cloverdale
1020 North Main Street
Cloverdale, IN

765-795-7373

Days Inn Columbus Indiana
3445 Jonathan Moore Pike
Columbus, IN
812-376-9951

Hotel Indigo Columbus Architectural
Center
400 Brown Street
Columbus, IN

812-375-9100

Residence Inn Columbus
4525 West State Road 46
Columbus, IN

812-342-2400

Baymont Inn And Suites Corydon
2495 Landmark Avenue North East
Corydon, IN
812-738-1500

Super 8 Corydon In
168 Pacer Drive
Corydon, IN

812-738-8887

Comfort Inn Crawfordsville
2991 North Gandhi Street
Crawfordsville, IN
765-361-0665

Hampton Inn & Suites Crawfordsville
2895 Gandhi Drive
Crawfordsville, IN

765-362-8884

Baymont Inn & Suites Decatur
1201 South 13th Street
Decatur, IN
260-728-4600

Ohio River Cabins
13445 N H 66
Derby, IN
812-836-2289

Candlewood Suites Elkhart
300 North Pointe Blvd.
Elkhart, IN
574-262-8600

Econo Lodge Elkhart
3440 Cassopolis Street
Elkhart, IN

574-262-0540

Red Roof Inn Elkhart
2902 Cassopolis Street
Elkhart, IN

574-262-3691

Staybridge Suites Elkhart North
3252 Cassopolis Street
Elkhart, IN

574-970-8488

Super 8 Elkhart
345 Windsor Avenue
Elkhart, IN

574-262-0000

Drury Inn & Suites Evansville East
100 Cross Pointe Boulevard
Evansville, IN
812-471-3400

Econo Lodge Evansville
2508 Highway 41 North
Evansville, IN

812-425-1092

Econo Lodge Inn & Suites
Evansville
1930 Cross Pointe Boulevard
Evansville, IN

812-471-9340

Holiday Inn Express Evansville -
West
5737 Pearl Drive
Evansville, IN

812-421-9773

Quality Inn East Evansville
5006 East Morgan Avenue
Evansville, IN

812-477-2211

Red Roof Inn Evansville
19600 Elpers Road
Evansville, IN

812-867-1100

Residence Inn By Marriott Evansville
East
8283 East Walnut
Evansville, IN

812-471-7191

Super 8 Evansville East
4600 East Morgan Avenue
Evansville, IN

812-476-4008

Super 8 Motel - Evansville North
19601 Elpers Rd
Evansville, IN

812-867-8500

Red Roof Inn & Suites Ferdinand
440 South Main Street
Ferdinand, IN
812-367-1122

Baymont Inn & Suites Fishers /
Indianapolis Area
9790 North By Northeast Boulevard
Fishers, IN
317-578-2000

Best Western Luxbury Inn-Fort
Wayne
5501 Coventry Lane
Fort Wayne, IN
260-436-0242

Candlewood Suites Fort Wayne -
Nw
5251 Distribution Drive
Fort Wayne, IN

260-484-1400

Comfort Inn Fort Wayne
1005 West Washington Center

Road
Fort Wayne, IN

260-489-2220

Extended Stay America - Fort Wayne
- South
8309 W. Jefferson Blvd
Fort Wayne, IN

260-432-1916

Hawthorn Suites By Wyndham Fort
Wayne
4919 Lima Road
Fort Wayne, IN

260-484-4700

Hilton Fort Wayne At The Grand
Wayne Center
1020 South Calhoun Street
Fort Wayne, IN

260-420-1100

Holiday Inn Fort Wayne - Ipfw &
Coliseum
4111 Paul Shaffer Drive
Fort Wayne, IN

260-482-3800

Knights Inn Ft. Wayne
2901 Goshen Rd
Fort Wayne, IN

260-484-2669

Residence Inn By Marriott Fort
Wayne
7811 West Jefferson Boulevard
Fort Wayne, IN

260-432-8000

Rodeway Inn Fort Wayne
2920 Goshen Road
Fort Wayne, IN

260-484-8641

Staybridge Suites Fort Wayne
5925 Ellison Road
Fort Wayne, IN

260-432-2427

Super 8 Fort Wayne
5710 Challenger Parkway
Fort Wayne, IN

260-489-0050

Towneplace Suites Fort Wayne North
3949 Ice Way Drive
Fort Wayne, IN

260-483-1160

Holiday Inn Express Fremont (Angola
Area)
6245 North Old 27 Suite 400

Fremont, IN
260-833-6464

Comfort Suites French Lick
9530 West State Road 56
French Lick, IN
812-936-5300

Super 8 Gas City/Marion Area
5172 Kaybee Drive
Gas City, IN
765-998-6800

Best Western Inn
900 Lincolnway E
Goshen, IN
574-533-0408

Red Roof Inn Mishawaka - Notre
Dame
1325 E University Dr Ct
Granger, IN
574-271-4800

Quality Inn And Suites Greenfield
Hotel
2270 North State Street
Greenfield, IN
317-462-7112

Holiday Inn Express Greensburg
915 Ann Boulevard
Greensburg, IN
812-663-5500

Candlewood Suites Indianapolis
South
1190 N Graham Road
Greenwood, IN
317-882-4300

La Quinta Inn & Suites Greenwood
1281 South Park Drive
Greenwood, IN

317-865-0100

Red Roof Greenwood, In
110 Sheek Road
Greenwood, IN

317-887-1515

Residence Inn Chicago
Southeast/Hammond, In
7740 Corinne Drive
Hammond, IN
219-844-8440

Baymont Inn & Suites Evansville
North
12798 Access 1250 South
Haubstadt, IN
812-768-5878

Holiday Inn Express Howe/Sturgis
45 W. 750 N.
Howe, IN
260-562-3660

Super 8 Motel - Huntington
2801 Guilford Street
Huntington, IN
260-358-8888

Baymont Inn & Suites Indianapolis
Northeast
5755 N. German Church Rd.
Indianapolis, IN
317-823-7700

Baymont Inn And Suites
Indianapolis
1540 Brookville Crossing Way
Indianapolis, IN
317-322-2000

Best Western Airport Suites
55 South Highschool Road
Indianapolis, IN
317-246-1505

Best Western Country Suites
3871 West 92nd Street
Indianapolis, IN
317-879-1700

Candlewood Suites Indianapolis
8111 Bash Street
Indianapolis, IN
317-595-9292

Candlewood Suites Indianapolis
Airport
5250 West Bradbury Street
Indianapolis, IN
317-241-9595

Candlewood Suites Indianapolis City
Centre
1152 N White River Pkwy, West
Drive
Indianapolis, IN
317-536-7700

Candlewood Suites Indianapolis
East
7040 East 21st Street
Indianapolis, IN
317-495-6600

Candlewood Suites Indianapolis
Northwest
7455 Woodland Drive
Indianapolis, IN
317-298-8000

Clarion Hotel Indianapolis
6990 East 21st Street
Indianapolis, IN
317-359-5341

Comfort Inn Indianapolis East

2295 North Shadeland Avenue
Indianapolis, IN

317-359-9999

Comfort Stay Inn
7610 Old Trails Road
Indianapolis, IN

317-353-6966

Comfort Suites Ne Indianapolis
Fishers
9760 Crosspoint Blvd.
Indianapolis, IN

317-578-1200

Days Inn- Indianapolis
2150 North Post Road
Indianapolis, IN

317-899-2100

Drury Inn & Suites Indianapolis
Northeast
8180 North Shadeland Avenue
Indianapolis, IN

317-849-8900

Drury Inn Indianapolis Northwest
9320 North Michigan Road
Indianapolis, IN

317-876-9777

Extended Stay America - Indianapolis
- Airport
2730 Fortune Circle W.
Indianapolis, IN

317-248-0465

Extended Stay America - Indianapolis
- North - Carmel
9750 Lake Shore Drive
Indianapolis, IN

317-843-1181

Extended Stay America - Indianapolis
- Northwest - College Park
9030 Wesleyan Road
Indianapolis, IN

317-872-3090

Extended Stay America - Indianapolis
- West 86th St.
8520 Northwest Blvd
Indianapolis, IN

317-334-7829

Extended Stay America - Indianapolis
Â¿ Castleton
7940 North Shadeland Ave
Indianapolis, IN

317-596-1288

Hilton Indianapolis Hotel & Suites

Dog-Friendly Lodging - Please always call ahead to make sure an establishment is still dog-friendly.

120 West Market Street
Indianapolis, IN

317-972-0600

Holiday Inn Express Indianapolis
South
5151 South East Street
Indianapolis, IN

317-783-5151

Homewood Suites By Hilton®
Indianapolis-At The Crossing
2501 East 86th Street
Indianapolis, IN

317-253-1919

Knights Inn Indianapolis South
4909 Knights Way
Indianapolis, IN

317-788-0125

Quality Inn & Suites Airport
2631 South Lynhurst Drive
Indianapolis, IN

317-381-1000

Quality Inn & Suites Indianapolis
4345 Southport Crossing Way
Indianapolis, IN

317-859-8888

Quality Inn- Indianapolis North
9251 Wesleyan Road
Indianapolis, IN

317-879-9100

Ramada Airport Indianapolis
5601 Fortune Circle West
Indianapolis, IN

317-244-1221

Ramada Limited Indianapolis West
3851 Shore Drive
Indianapolis, IN

317-297-1848

Red Roof Inn Indianapolis North -
College Park
9520 Valparaiso Court
Indianapolis, IN

317-872-3030

Red Roof Inn Indianapolis South
5221 Victory Drive
Indianapolis, IN

317-788-9551

Residence Inn Indianapolis Airport
5224 West Southern Avenue
Indianapolis, IN

317-244-1500

Residence Inn Indianapolis
Downtown On The Canal
350 West New York Street
Indianapolis, IN

317-822-0840

Residence Inn Indianapolis
Northwest
6220 Digital Way
Indianapolis, IN

317-275-6000

Residence Inn Indianapolis/ Fishers
9765 Crosspoint Boulevard
Indianapolis, IN

317-842-1111

Sheraton Indianapolis Hotel At
Keystone Crossing
8787 Keystone Crossing
Indianapolis, IN

317-846-2700

Staybridge Suites Indianapolis City
Centre
535 S. West Street
Indianapolis, IN

317-536-7500

Staybridge Suites Indianapolis-
Carmel
10675 N. Pennsylvania Street
Indianapolis, IN

317-582-1500

Staybridge Suites Indianapolis-
Fishers
9780 Crosspoint Boulevard
Indianapolis, IN

317-577-9500

Suburban Extended Stay Northeast
8055 Bash Street
Indianapolis, IN

317-598-1914

Super 8 Indianapolis South
450 Bixler Road
Indianapolis, IN

317-788-0811

Super 8
Indianapolis/Northeast/Castleton
7202 East 82nd Street
Indianapolis, IN

317-841-8585

Super 8 Motel -
Indianapolis/Emerson Ave.
4530 S. Emerson Ave.
Indianapolis, IN

317-788-0955

The Westin Indianapolis
50 South Capitol Avenue
Indianapolis, IN

317-262-8100

Towneplace Suites By Marriott
Indianapolis Keystone
8468 Union Chapel Road
Indianapolis, IN

317-255-3700

Towneplace Suites By Marriott
Indianapolis Park 100
5802 West 71st Street
Indianapolis, IN

317-290-8900

Travelodge Indianapolis Castleton
8275 Craig Street
Indianapolis, IN

317-841-9700

Wingate By Wyndham - Indianapolis
Airport
5797 Rockville Road
Indianapolis, IN

317-243-8310

Wingate By Wyndham - Indianapolis
Airport
5797 Rockville Road
Indianapolis, IN

317-243-8310

Days Inn And Suites Jeffersonville In
354 Eastern Boulevard
Jeffersonville, IN
812-288-7100

Hawthorn Suites by Wyndham
Louisville North
703 N Shore Drive
Jeffersonville, IN
812-280-8200

Sheraton Louisville Riverside Hotel
700 West Riverside Drive
Jeffersonville, IN
812-284-6711

Comfort Inn Kokomo
522 Essex Drive
Kokomo, IN
765-452-5050

Days Inn Kokomo
3980 South Reed Road
Kokomo, IN

765-453-7100

Hampton Inn And Suites Kokomo
2920 S Reed Rd
Kokomo, IN

765-455-2900

Super 8 Kokomo
5110 Clinton Drive
Kokomo, IN

765-455-3288

Baymont Inn And Suites Lafayette
201 Frontage Road
Lafayette, IN

Best Western Lafayette Executive
Plaza & Conference Center
4343 South Street
Lafayette, IN

765-447-0575

Candlewood Suites Lafayette
240 Meijer Drive
Lafayette, IN

765-807-5735

Comfort Suites Lafayette
31 Frontage Rd
Lafayette, IN

765-447-0016

Days Inn & Suites Lafayette IN
151 Frontage Road
Lafayette, IN

765-446-8558

Homewood Suites By Hilton®
Lafayette
3939 State Road 26 East
Lafayette, IN

765-448-9700

Knights Inn Lafayette Midwest
4110 State Road 26 East
Lafayette, IN

765-447-5611

Red Roof Inn Lafayette
4201 State Route 26 East
Lafayette, IN

765-448-4671

Super 8 Lafayette
4301 State Road 26
Lafayette, IN

765-447-5551

Towneplace Suites By Marriott
Lafayette
163 Frontage Road
Lafayette, IN

765-446-8668

Holiday Inn Express La Porte
100 East Shore Court
Laporte, IN
219-326-7900

Baymont Inn & Suites Lawrenceburg
1000 East Eads Parkway
Lawrenceburg, IN
812-539-4770

Comfort Inn Lebanon
210 Sam Ralston Road
Lebanon, IN
765-482-4800

Econo Lodge Lebanon
1245 West State Road 32
Lebanon, IN

765-482-9611

Holiday Inn Express Lebanon
335 North Mt. Zion Road
Lebanon, IN

765-483-4100

Quality Inn Conference Center
3550 E. Market St.
Logansport, IN
574-753-6351

Super 8 Logansport
3801 East Market Street
Logansport, IN

574-722-1273

Comfort Suites Marion
1345 North Baldwin Avenue
Marion, IN
765-651-1006

Econo Lodge Marion
1615 North Baldwin Ave
Marion, IN

765-664-9100

Econo Lodge Markle
610 Annette Drive
Markle, IN
260-758-8888

Holiday Inn Express Bloomington
North-Martinsville
2233 Burton Lane
Martinsville, IN
765-813-3999

Super 8 Martinsville
55 Bills Boulevard
Martinsville, IN

765-349-2222

Candlewood Suites Merrillville
8339 Ohio Street
Merrillville, IN
219-791-9100

Extended Stay America - Merrillville -
Us Rte. 30
1355 East 83rd Avenue
Merrillville, IN

219-769-4740

Red Roof Inn Merrillville
8290 Georgia Street
Merrillville, IN

219-738-2430

Residence Inn Merrillville
8018 Delaware Place
Merrillville, IN

219-791-9000

Super 8 Motel - Merrillville/Gary Area
8300 Louisiana Street
Merrillville, IN

219-736-8383

Duneland Beach Inn
3311 Pottawattamie Trail
Michigan City, IN
219-874-7729

Knights Inn Michigan City
201 W. Kieffer Rd.
Michigan City, IN

219-878-8100

Red Roof Inn Michigan City
110 West Kieffer Road
Michigan City, IN

219-874-5251

Tryon Farm Guest House - Bed And
Breakfast
1400 Tryon Road
Michigan City, IN

219-879-3618

Extended Stay America - South Bend
- Mishawaka - North
5305 North Main
Mishawaka, IN
574-277-9912

Holiday Inn Express Mishawaka
(South Bend Area)
420 West University Drive
Mishawaka, IN

574-277-2520

Residence Inn By Marriott South
Bend Mishawaka
231 Park Place
Mishawaka, IN

574-271-9283

Super 8 Mishawaka/South Bend Area
535 West University Drive
Mishawaka, IN

574-247-0888

Days Inn Muncie
3509 North Everbrook Lane
Muncie, IN
765-288-2311

Super 8 Muncie
3601 West Foxridge Lane
Muncie, IN

765-286-4333

Baymont Inn & Suites Noblesville
16025 Prosperity Drive
Noblesville, IN
317-770-6772

Super 8 Motel - Noblesville
17070 Dragonfly Lane
Noblesville, IN

317-776-7088

Best Western Circus City Inn
2642 S Business 31
Peru, IN
765 473-8800

Knights Inn Peru
2661 South Business 31
Peru, IN

765-472-3971

Baymont Plainfield
6010 Gateway Drive
Plainfield, IN
317-837-9000

Days Inn Plainfield
2245 East Perry Road
Plainfield, IN

317-839-5000

Staybridge Suites Indianapolis-Airport
6295 Cambridge Way
Plainfield, IN

317-839-2700

Days Inn Plymouth
2229 North Michigan Street
Plymouth, IN
574-935-4276

Comfort Inn Portage
2300 Willowcreek Road
Portage, IN
219-763-7177

Holiday Inn Express Portage
2323 Willowcreek
Portage, IN

219-762-7777

Super 8 Portage
6118 Melton Rd

Portage, IN
219-762-8857

Best Western Classic Inn
533 West Eaton Pike
Richmond, IN
765-939-9500

Days Inn - Richmond
5775 National Road East
Richmond, IN

765-966-4900

Motel 6 Richmond
6030 National Road East
Richmond, IN

765-966-6559

Richmond Inn and Suites
3020 East Main Street
Richmond, IN

765-966-1505

Quality Inn Rochester
289 Mcdonald Dr
Rochester, IN
574-223-7300

Econo Lodge Rockville
1659 East Us Highway 36
Rockville, IN
765-569-3430

Comfort Inn Rushville
320 Conrad Harcourt Way
Rushville, IN
765-932-2999

Travelodge Sellersburg
7618 Old State Road 60
Sellersburg, IN
812-246-4451

Econo Lodge Seymour
220 Commerce Drive
Seymour, IN
812-522-8000

Seymour Days Inn
302 South Commerce Drive
Seymour, IN

812-522-3678

Travelodge Seymour
306 S Commerce Dr
Seymour, IN

812-519-2578

Comfort Inn Shelbyville
36 West Rampart
Shelbyville, IN
317-398-8044

Super 8 Shipshewana
740 South Vanburen Street

Shipshewana, IN
260-768-4004

Candlewood Suites South Bend
Airport
3916 Lincolnway West
South Bend, IN
574-968-1072

Comfort Suites University Area
52939 U.S. 933 North
South Bend, IN

574-272-1500

Cushing Manor Inn
508 West Washington
South Bend, IN

574-288-1990

Econo Lodge
515 North Dixie Highway
South Bend, IN

574-272-6600

Economy Inn Airport South Bend
3233 Lincoln Way West
South Bend, IN

574-232-9019

Oliver Inn
630 W Washington Street
South Bend, IN

574-232-4545

Residence Inn By Marriott South
Bend
716 N Niles Ave
South Bend, IN

574-289-5555

Sleep Inn South Bend
4134 Lincolnway West
South Bend, IN

574-232-3200

Staybridge Suites South Bend-
University Area
52860 S.R. 933
South Bend, IN

574-968-7440

Suburban Extended Stay Hotel South
Bend
52825 Indiana Route 933 North
South Bend, IN

574-968-4737

Days Inn Sullivan
907 W State Road 154
Sullivan, IN
812-268-6391

Red Roof Inn Columbus - Taylorsville

10330 N Us Hwy 31
Taylorsville, IN
812-526-9747

Candlewood Suites Terre Haute
721 Wabash Avenue
Terre Haute, IN
812-234-3400

Days Inn & Suites Terre Haute
101 East Margaret Ave
Terre Haute, IN

812-232-8006

Drury Inn Terre Haute
3040 South Us Highway 41
Terre Haute, IN

812-238-1206

Econo Lodge Terre Haute
401 East Margaret Avenue
Terre Haute, IN

812-234-9931

Holiday Inn Express Hotel & Suites
Terre Haute
2645 South Joe Fox Street
Terre Haute, IN

812-234-3200

Motel 6 Terre Haute
1 W Honey Creek Drive
Terre Haute, IN

812-238-1586

Super 8 Terre Haute
3089 South First Street
Terre Haute, IN

812-232-4890

Terre Haute Travelodge
530 South 3rd Street
Terre Haute, IN

812-232-7075

Rosemont Inn
806 W Market Street
Vevay, IN
812-427-3050

Econo Lodge Vincennes
600 Old Wheatland Rd, Bldg. A
Vincennes, IN
812-882-1479

Four Points By Sheraton West
Lafayette
1600 Cumberland Avenue
W Lafayette, IN
765-463-5511

Comfort Inn & Suites Warsaw
3328 East Center Street
Warsaw, IN
574-269-6655

Holiday Inn Express Hotel & Suites
Warsaw
3825 Lake City Highway
Warsaw, IN

574-268-1600

Wyndham Garden Warsaw
2519 E Center Street
Warsaw, IN

574-269-2323

Holiday Inn Express Washington
1808 East National Highway
Washington, IN
812-254-6666

Econo Lodge West Lafayette
2030 Northgate Drive
West Lafayette, IN
765-567-7100

# Iowa Listings

Super 8 Adair IA
111 S 5th Street
Adair, IA
641-742-5251

Super 8 Algona
210 E Norwood Dr
Algona, IA
515-295-7225

Microtel Inn & Suites By Wyndham
Ames
2216 South East 16th Street
Ames, IA
515-233-4444

Quality Inn & Suites Starlite Village
Conference Center
2601 East 13th Street
Ames, IA

515-232-9260

Super 8 Ames
1418 S Dayton Place
Ames, IA

515-232-6510

Super 8 Anamosa
100 Grant Wood Drive
Anamosa, IA
319-462-3888

Days Inn Ankeny
103 Ne Delaware Ave
Ankeny, IA
515-965-1995

Super 8 Atlantic
1902 East 7th Street
Atlantic, IA
712-243-4723

Econo Lodge Inn & Suites Bettendorf
815 Golden Valley Drive
Bettendorf, IA
563-355-6336

Ramada Bettendorf
3020 Utica Ridge Road
Bettendorf, IA

563-355-7575

Super 8 Bettendorf
890 Golden Valley Drive
Bettendorf, IA

563-355-7341

Super 8 Boone
1715 South Story Street
Boone, IA
515-432-8890

Comfort Suites Burlington
1780 Stonegate Center Drive
Burlington, IA
319-753-1300

Quality Inn Burlington
3051 Kirkwood
Burlington, IA

319-753-0000

Super 8 Burlington
3001 Kirkwood Street
Burlington, IA

319-752-9806

Super 8 Carroll North
1757 Highway 71 North
Carroll, IA
712-792-4753

Super 8 Omaha Eppley Airport/Carter
Lake
3000 Airport Drive
Carter Lake, IA
712-347-5588

Comfort Suites Cedar Falls
7402 Nordic Drive
Cedar Falls, IA
319-273-9999

Baymont Inn & Suites Cedar Rapids
1220 Park Place
Cedar Rapids, IA
319-378-8000

Best Western Coopers Mill Hotel
100 F Avenue Northwest
Cedar Rapids, IA

319-366-5323

Best Western Plus Longbranch Hotel
& Convention Center
90 Twixt Town Road North East
Cedar Rapids, IA

319-377-6386

Clarion Hotel & Convention Center
Near Hawkeye Downs
525 33rd Avenue, Southwest
Cedar Rapids, IA

319-366-8671

Econo Lodge Cedar Rapids
622 33rd Avenue Southwest
Cedar Rapids, IA

319-363-8888

Mainstay Suites Cedar Rapids
5145 Rockwell Drive Northeast
Cedar Rapids, IA

319-363-7829

Motel 6 Cedar Rapids Airport
616 33rd Avenue Southwest
Cedar Rapids, IA

319-366-2475

Quality Inn At Collins Road
5055 Rockwell Drive
Cedar Rapids, IA

319-393-8247

Quality Inn North Cedar Rapids
4747 1st Avenue Southeast
Cedar Rapids, IA

319-393-8800

Quality Inn South Cedar Rapids
390 33rd Avenue Southwest
Cedar Rapids, IA

319-363-7934

Red Roof Cedar Rapids
3243 Southridge Dr Sw
Cedar Rapids, IA

319-364-2000

Residence Inn Cedar Rapids
1900 Dodge Road Ne
Cedar Rapids, IA

319-395-0111

Super 8 Cedar Rapids East
400 33rd Avenue South West
Cedar Rapids, IA

319-363-1755

Super 8 Cedar Rapids West
720 33rd Avenue South West
Cedar Rapids, IA

319-362-6002

Super 8 Clarinda
1203 South 12th Street
Clarinda, IA

712-542-6333

Microtel Inn & Suites By Wyndham
Clear Lake
1305 North 25th Street
Clear Lake, IA
641-357-0966

Super 8 Clear Lake
2809 4th Ave. South
Clear Lake, IA

641-357-7521

Country Inn And Suites By Carlson
Clinton
2224 Lincoln Way
Clinton, IA
563-244-9922

Super 8 Motel - Clinton
1711 Lincoln Way
Clinton, IA

563-242-8870

Best Western Plus Des Moines
West Inn And Suites
1450 Northwest 118th Street
Clive, IA
515-221-2345

Chase Suite Hotel by Woodfin
11 428 Forest Ave.
Clive, IA

515-223-7700

Colfax Inn
1402 North Walnut Street
Colfax, IA
515-674-4455

Microtel Inn & Suites By Wyndham
Colfax
11000 Federal Avenue
Colfax, IA

515-674-0600

Baymont Inn & Suites Coralville
200 6th Street
Coralville, IA
319-337-9797

Super 8 Motel - Iowa City Coralville
611 1st ;Avenue
Coralville, IA

319-337-8388

Best Western Crossroads Of The
Bluffs
2216 27th Avenue
Council Bluffs, IA
712-322-3150

Days Inn Council Bluffs
3619 9th Avenue
Council Bluffs, IA

712-323-2200

Days Inn Council Bluffs-Lake
Manawa
3208 South 7th Street
Council Bluffs, IA

712-366-9699

Microtel Inn & Suites By Wyndham
Council Bluffs
2141 South 35th Street
Council Bluffs, IA

712-256-2900

Quality Inn & Suites
3537 West Broadway
Council Bluffs, IA

712-328-3171

Cresco Motel
620 2nd Avenue SE/H 9E
Cresco, IA
563-547-2240

Super 8 Cresco Ia
511 Second Ave Se
Cresco, IA

563-547-9988

Baymont Inn And Suites Davenport
400 Jason Way Court
Davenport, IA
563-386-1600

Country Inn & Suites By Carlson,
Davenport, Ia
140 East 55th Street
Davenport, IA

563-388-6444

Days Inn And Suites Davenport East
3202 East Kimberly Road
Davenport, IA

563-359-7165

Hotel Davenport And Conference
Center
5202 Brady Street
Davenport, IA

563-391-1230

Quality Inn & Suites Davenport
6605 North Brady Street
Davenport, IA

563-386-8336

Residence Inn Davenport
120 E 55th St
Davenport, IA

563-391-8877

Staybridge Suites Davenport

Dog-Friendly Lodging - Please always call ahead to make sure an establishment is still dog-friendly.

4729 Progress Drive
Davenport, IA

563-359-7829

Travelodge Denison
502 Boyer Valley Road
Denison, IA
712-263-5081

Econo Lodge Inn & Suites Des
Moines
4755 Merle Hay Road
Des Moines, IA
515-278-8858

Quality Inn & Suites Des Moines
Airport
5231 Fleur Drive
Des Moines, IA

515-287-3434

Quality Inn & Suites Event Center
Des Moines
929 3rd Street
Des Moines, IA

515-282-5251

Rodeway Inn Des Moines
5020 Ne 14th Street
Des Moines, IA

515-265-7511

Days Inn Dubuque
1111 Dodge Street
Dubuque, IA
563-583-3297

Holiday Inn Dubuque Galena
450 Main Street
Dubuque, IA

563-556-2000

Holiday Inn Express Hotel & Suites -
Dubuque West
2080 Holiday Drive
Dubuque, IA

563-556-4600

Quality Inn Dubuque
4055 Mcdonald Drive
Dubuque, IA

563-556-3006

Super 8 Dubuque
2730 Dodge Street
Dubuque, IA

563-582-8898

Super 8 Dyersville
925 15th Avenue Se
Dyersville, IA
563-875-8885

Quality Inn & Suites Eldridge

1000 East Iowa Street
Eldridge, IA
563-285-4600

Super 8 Emmetsburg
3501 Main Street
Emmetsburg, IA
712-852-2667

Estherville Hotel & Suites
2008 Central Avenue
Estherville, IA
712-362-5522

Super 8 Estherville
1919 Central Avenue
Estherville, IA

712-362-2400

Days Inn Evansdale Waterloo
450 Evansdale Drive
Evansdale, IA
319-235-1111

Best Western Fairfield Inn
2200 W Burlington Avenue
Fairfield, IA
641-472-2200

Super 8 Fairfield
3001 W Burlington Ave
Fairfield, IA

641-469-2000

Comfort Inn Fort Dodge
2938 5th Ave. S.
Fort Dodge, IA
515-573-5000

Comfort Inn & Suites
6169 Reve Court
Fort Madison, IA
319-372-6800

Super 8 Fort Madison
5107 Avenue ";o";
Fort Madison, IA

319-372-8500

Comfort Inn & Suites Grinnell
1630 West Street South
Grinnell, IA
641-236-5236

Super 8 Motel - Grinnell
2111 West Street South
Grinnell, IA

641-236-7888

Super 8 Ida Grove
90 East Highway 175
Ida Grove, IA
712-364-3988

Super 8 Independence
2000 1st Street West
Independence, IA

319-334-7041

Quality Inn Indianola
1701 North Jefferson Way
Indianola, IA
515-961-0058

Alexis Park Inn And Suites
1165 South Riverside Drive
Iowa City, IA
319 337-8665

Sheraton Iowa City
210 S Dubuque St
Iowa City, IA

319-337-4058

Travelodge Iowa City
2216 North Dodge St
Iowa City, IA

319-351-1010

Super 8 Iowa Falls
839 S Oak Hwy 65 S
Iowa Falls, IA
641-648-4618

Americinn Johnston
5050 Merle Hay Road
Johnston, IA
515-270-1111

Towneplace Suites By Marriott Des
Moines Urbandale
8800 Northpark Drive
Johnston, IA

515-727-4066

Super 8 Motel - Keokuk
3511 Main Street
Keokuk, IA
319-524-3888

Comfort Inn & Suites Riverview
902 Mississippi View Court
Le Claire, IA
563-289-4747

Holiday Inn Express Le Claire
Riverfront-Davenport
1201 Canal Shore Drive
Le Claire, IA

563-289-9978

Super 8 Le Claire/Quad Cities
1552 Welcome Center Drive
Le Claire, IA

563-289-5888

Baymont Inn Le Mars
1314 12th Street Southwest
Le Mars, IA
712-548-4910

Econo Lodge Le Mars
1201 Hawkeye Ave Sw

94

Le Mars, IA
712-546-8800

Comfort Inn Marshalltown
2613 South Center Street
Marshalltown, IA
641-752-6000

Clarion Inn
2101 4th Street Sw
Mason City, IA
641-423-1640

Super 8 Mason City
3010 4th Street Southwest
Mason City, IA
641-423-8855

Desoto Inn & Suites
1967 Highway 30
Missouri Valley, IA
712-642-4003

Super 8 Missouri Valley
3167 Joliet Avenue
Missouri Valley, IA
712-642-4788

Ramada Limited
1200 East Baker St.
Mount Pleasant, IA
319-385-0571

Super 8 Mt. Pleasant
1000 North Grand Avenue
Mount Pleasant, IA
319-385-8888

Sleep Inn & Suites Mount Vernon
310 Virgil Avenue
Mount Vernon, IA
319-895-0055

Super 8 Muscatine
2900 North Highway 61
Muscatine, IA
563-263-9100

Travelodge Inn & Suites - Muscatine
2402 Park Avenue
Muscatine, IA
563-264-3337

Super 8 New Hampton
825 S Linn St
New Hampton, IA
641-394-3838

Best Western Holiday Manor
208 West 4th Street North
Newton, IA
641-792-3333

Days Inn Newton
1605 West 19th Street South
Newton, IA

641-792-2330

Econo Lodge Inn & Suites Newton
1405 West 19th Street South
Newton, IA

641-792-8100

Holiday Inn Express And Suites
Northwood
4712 Wheelerwood Road
Northwood, IA
641-323-7500

Super 8 Oelwein
210 10th Street Southeast
Oelwein, IA
319-283-2888

Super 8 Osage
1530 E Main Street
Osage, IA
641-732-1800

Lakeside Hotel Casino
777 Casino Drive
Osceola, IA
641-342-9511

Quality Inn Osceola
710 Warren Avenue
Osceola, IA

641-342-6666

Super 8 Osceola
720 Warren Avenue
Osceola, IA

641-342-6594

Comfort Inn Oskaloosa
2401 A Avenue West
Oskaloosa, IA
641-676-6000

Super 8 Oskaloosa
306 South 17th Street
Oskaloosa, IA

641-673-8481

Super 8 - Pella
105 East Oskaloosa Street
Pella, IA
641-628-8181

Super 8 Nebraska City
2103 249th Street
Percival, IA
712-382-2828

Sleep Inn & Suites Pleasant Hill
5850 Morning Star Court
Pleasant Hill, IA
515-299-9922

Econo Lodge Sergeant Bluff
103 Sergeant Square
Sergeant Bluff, IA

712-943-5079

Holiday Inn Express Hotel & Suites
Sheldon
201 34th Avenue
Sheldon, IA
712-324-3000

Super 8 Motel - Sheldon
210 N. 2nd Avenue
Sheldon, IA

712-324-8400

Sibley Inn
1108 2nd Avenue
Sibley, IA
712-754-3603

Holiday Inn Express Hotel & Suites
Sioux Center
100 Saint Andrews Way
Sioux Center, IA
712-722-3500

Comfort Inn Sioux City
4202 South Lakeport Street
Sioux City, IA
712-274-1300

Days Inn Sioux City Ia
3000 Singing Hills Boulevard
Sioux City, IA

712-258-8000

Quality Inn & Suites Sioux City
4230 South Lakeport Street
Sioux City, IA

712-274-1400

Super 8 Spirit Lake/Okoboji
2203 Circle Drive West
Spirit Lake, IA
712-336-4901

Comfort Inn Story City
425 Timberland Drive
Story City, IA
515-733-6363

Super 8 Story City
515 Factory Outlet Drive
Story City, IA

515-733-5281

Americas Best Value Inn And Suites
Stuart
203 Se 7th Street
Stuart, IA
515-523-2888

Super 8 Toledo
207 Hwy 30 W
Toledo, IA
641-484-5888

Extended Stay America - Des Moines
- Urbandale

3940 114th Street
Urbandale, IA
515-276-1929

Sleep Inn Urbandale
11211 Hickman Road
Urbandale, IA

515-270-2424

Super 8 Urbandale/Des Moines Area
5900 Sutton Drive
Urbandale, IA

515-270-1037

Sheraton West Des Moines Hotel
1800 50th Street
W Des Moines, IA
515-223-1800

Americas Best Value Inn Walcott
Davenport
241 Interstate Street
Walcott, IA
563-284-5083

Comfort Inn Walcott
501 Walker Street
Walcott, IA

563-284-9000

Days Inn Walcott Davenport
2889 North Plainview Road
Walcott, IA

563-284-6600

Econo Lodge Inn & Suites Walnut
1614 Antique City Drive
Walnut, IA
712-784-2233

Super 8 Walnut
2109 Antique City Drive
Walnut, IA

712-784-2221

Baymont Inn & Suites - Waterloo
1945 la Porte Road
Waterloo, IA
319-234-7411

Howard Johnson Waterloo
3052 Marnie Avenue
Waterloo, IA

319-232-7467

Motel 6 Crossroads Mall-Waterloo-
Cedar Falls
2141 Laporte Road
Waterloo, IA

319-233-9191

Quality Inn & Suites Waterloo
226 West 5th Street
Waterloo, IA

319-235-0301

Ramada Waterloo Hotel And
Convention Center
205 West 4th Street
Waterloo, IA

319-233-7560

Super 8 Waterloo
1825 la Porte Road
Waterloo, IA

319-233-1800

Comfort Inn Waverly
404 29th Avenue Southwest
Waverly, IA
319-352-0399

Super 8 Webster City
305 Closz Drive
Webster City, IA
515-832-2000

Candlewood Suites West Des
Moines
7625 Office Plaza Drive North
West Des Moines, IA
515-221-0001

Drury Inn & Suites West Des Moines
5505 Mills Civic Parkway
West Des Moines, IA

515-457-9500

Residence Inn By Marriott Des
Moines West
160 South Jordan Creek Parkway
West Des Moines, IA

515-267-0338

Staybridge Suites West Des Moines
6905 Lake Drive
West Des Moines, IA

515-223-0000

West Des Moines Marriott
1250 Jordan Creek Parkway
West Des Moines, IA

515-267-1500

Econo Lodge West Liberty
1943 Garfield Avenue
West Liberty, IA
319-627-2171

Super 8 Winterset
1312 Cedar Bridge Road
Winterset, IA
515-462-4888

# Kansas Listings

Holiday Inn Express Hotel & Suites

Abilene
110 East Lafayette Ave.
Abilene, KS
785-263-4049

Super 8 Abilene Ks
2207 N. Buckeye Ave
Abilene, KS

785-263-4545

Super 8 Arkansas City
3228 North Summit Street
Arkansas City, KS
620-442-8880

The Inn on Oak Street
1003 L Street
Atchison, KS
913-367-1515

Americas Best Value Inn Belleville
1616 Us Highway 36
Belleville, KS
785-527-2112

Super 8 Bonner Springs
13041 Ridge Avenue
Bonner Springs, KS
913-721-3877

Best Western Bricktown Lodge
605 Northeast Street
Caney, KS
620-251-3700

Comfort Inn Colby
2225 S Range
Colby, KS
785-462-3833

Days Inn Colby
1925 South Range
Colby, KS

785-462-8691

Holiday Inn Express Hotel & Suites
Colby
645 West Willow Road
Colby, KS

785-462-8787

Quality Inn Colby
1950 South Range Avenue
Colby, KS

785-462-3933

Sleep Inn & Suites Colby
2075 Sewell Avenue
Colby, KS

785-460-0310

Rodeway Inn Concordia
89 Lincoln Street
Concordia, KS
785-243-4545

Dog-Friendly Lodging - Please always call ahead to make sure an establishment is still dog-friendly.

Super 8 Concordia
1320 Lincoln Highway
Concordia, KS

785-243-4200

The Cottage House Hotel
25 North Neosho
Council Grove, KS
620-767-6828

Super 8 Motel - De Soto
34085 Commerce Drive
De Soto, KS
913-583-3880

Hampton Inn Derby
1701 Cambridge Street
Derby, KS
316-425-7900

Boot Hill Bed and Breakfast
603 W Spruce
Dodge City, KS
620-225-0111

Quality Inn Dodge City
2000 West Wyatt Earp Boulevard
Dodge City, KS

620-338-8700

Stay Suites of America - Dodge City
2320 West Wyatt Earp
Dodge City, KS

620-227-5000

Super 8 Dodge City
1708 W Wyatt Earp Blvd
Dodge City, KS

620-225-3924

Kuhrt Prairie Castle Guest House and
Lodge
2735 Road 75
Edson, KS
785-899-5306

Super 8 El Dorado
2530 W Central
El Dorado, KS
316-321-4888

America's Best Inn and Suites
Emporia
3181 West Highway 50
Emporia, KS
620-342-7820

Best Western Hospitality House
3021 West Highway 50
Emporia, KS

620-342-7587

Candlewood Suites Emporia
2602 Candlewood Drive
Emporia, KS

620-343-7756

Comfort Inn Emporia
2836 W. 18th Ave.
Emporia, KS

620-342-9700

Days Inn Emporia
3032 West Highway 50
Emporia, KS

620-342-1787

Econo Lodge Emporia
2511 West 18th Avenue
Emporia, KS

620-343-7750

Clarion Inn Garden City
1911 East Kansas Avenue
Garden City, KS
620-275-7471

Comfort Inn Garden City
2608 East Kansas Avenue
Garden City, KS

620-275-5800

Super 8 Gardner
2001 East Santa Fe
Gardner, KS
913-856-8887

Comfort Inn Goodland
2519 Enterprise Rd
Goodland, KS
785-899-7181

Super 8 Goodland
2520 Commerce Road
Goodland, KS

785-890-7566

Best Western Angus Inn
2920 10th Street
Great Bend, KS
620-792-3541

Days Inn Great Bend
4701 10th Street
Great Bend, KS

620-792-8235

Great Bend Travelodge
3200 10th Street ; ; ; ; ; ; ;
Great Bend, KS

620-792-7219

Best Western Plus Night Watchman
Inn & Suites
515 W. Kansas Ave.
Greensburg, KS
620-723-2244

Days Inn Hays

3205 Vine/I-70
Hays, KS
785-628-8261

Quality Inn Hays
2810 Vine Street
Hays, KS

785-628-8008

Red Roof Inn Holton
115 Us Highway 75
Holton, KS
785-364-3172

Atrium Hotel And Conference Center
1400 North Lorraine
Hutchinson, KS
620-669-9311

Days Inn Hutchinson
1420 North Lorraine Street
Hutchinson, KS

620-665-3700

Knights Inn Independence
3222 West Main Street
Independence, KS
620-331-7300

Microtel Inn & Suites By Wyndham
Independence
2917 West Main Street
Independence, KS

620-331-0088

Americas Best Value Inn Iola
1315 North State Street
Iola, KS
620-365-5161

Log Cabin Retreat
250 Xavier Road
Jamestown, KS
620-241-2981

Best Western J. C. Inn
604 East Chestnut Street
Junction City, KS
785-210-1212

Candlewood Suites Junction City - Ft.
Riley
100 South Hammons Drive
Junction City, KS

785-238-1454

Holiday Inn Express Junction City
120 East Street
Junction City, KS

785-762-4200

Super 8 Junction City
1133 South Washington Street
Junction City, KS

785-238-1141

Dog-Friendly Lodging - Please always call ahead to make sure an establishment is still dog-friendly.

Candlewood Suites Kansas City
10920 Parallel Parkway
Kansas City, KS
913-788-9929

Days Inn - Kansas Speedway
7721 Elizabeth Avenue
Kansas City, KS

913-334-3028

Oak Tree Inn Kansas City
501 Southwest Boulevard
Kansas City, KS

913-677-3060

Windy Heights Inn
607 Country Heights Road
Lakin, KS
620-355-7699

Econo Lodge Lansing - Leavenworth
504 North Main Street
Lansing, KS
913-727-2777

Best Western Lawrence
2309 Iowa Street
Lawrence, KS
785-843-9100

Days Inn Ku Lawrence
730 South Iowa Street
Lawrence, KS

785-841-6500

Quality Inn Lawrence
801 Iowa Street
Lawrence, KS

785-842-5100

Rodeway Inn Lawrence
2222 West Sixth Street
Lawrence, KS

785-842-7030

The Lawrence Hotel and Convention
Center
200 Mcdonald Drive
Lawrence, KS

785-841-7077

Americas Best Value Inn
303 Montana Court
Leavenworth, KS
913-682-0744

Days Inn Leavenworth
3211 South 4th Street
Leavenworth, KS

913-651-6000

Extended Stay America - Kansas City
- Lenexa - 87th St.

8015 Lenexa Drive
Lenexa, KS
913-894-5550

Kansas City - Lenexa - 95th St
9775 Lenexa Drive
Lenexa, KS

913-541-4000

Super 8 Lenexa Overland Park Area
9601 Westgate
Lenexa, KS

913-888-8899

Days Inn Liberal Ks
405 E Pancake
Liberal, KS
620-626-7377

Quality Inn Liberal
720 East Pancake Boulevard
Liberal, KS

620-624-0242

Super 8 Liberal Ks
747 E Pancake Blvd
Liberal, KS

620-624-8880

Best Western Manhattan Inn
601 East Poyntz Avenue
Manhattan, KS
785-537-8300

Four Points By Sheraton Manhattan
530 Richards Drive
Manhattan, KS

785-539-5311

Holiday Inn MANHATTAN AT THE
CAMPUS
1641 Anderson Avenue
Manhattan, KS

785-539-7531

Quality Inn & Suites Manhattan
150 East Poyntz Avenue
Manhattan, KS

785-770-8000

Econo Lodge Mcpherson
2111 East Kansas Avenue
McPherson, KS
620-241-6960

Extended Stay America - Kansas
City - Shawnee Mission
6451 East Frontage Road
Merriam, KS
913-236-6006

Knights Inn Oakley
3506 Us Highway 40
Oakley, KS
785-672-3254

Sleep Inn & Suites Oakley
3596 East Highway 40
Oakley, KS

785-671-1111

Best Western Plus Olathe Hotel &
Suites
1580 South Hamilton Circle
Olathe, KS
913-440-9762

Candlewood Suites Olathe
15490 South Rogers Road
Olathe, KS

913-768-8888

Days Inn Olathe Medical Center
20662 West 151st Street
Olathe, KS

913-390-9500

Econo Lodge South Olathe
209 East Flaming Road
Olathe, KS

913-829-1312

Quality Inn & Suites Olathe
15475 S. Rogers Rd
Olathe, KS

913-948-9000

Residence Inn By Marriott Kansas
City Olathe
12215 S Strang Line Rd
Olathe, KS

913-829-6700

Rodeway Inn & Suites Olathe
211 North Rawhide Drive
Olathe, KS

913-782-4343

Best Western Ottawa Inn
212 East 23rd Street
Ottawa, KS
785-242-2224

Econo Lodge Ottawa
2331 South Cedar
Ottawa, KS

785-242-3400

Knights Inn Ottawa
1641 South Main Street
Ottawa, KS

785-242-4842

Candlewood Suites Kansas
City/Overland Park
11001 Oakmont
Overland Park, KS
913-469-5557

Chase Suite Hotel
6300 W 110th Street
Overland Park, KS

913-491-3333

Days Inn Overland Park
6800 West 108th Street
Overland Park, KS

913-341-0100

Drury Inn & Suites Overland Park
10963 Metcalf Avenue
Overland Park, KS

913-345-1500

Extended Stay America - Kansas City
- Overland Park - Nall Ave.
5401 West 110th Street
Overland Park, KS

913-661-7111

Extended Stay America - Kansas City
- Overland Park - Quivira Rd
10750 Quivira Road
Overland Park, KS

913-661-9299

Knights Inn Overland Park
7240 B Shawnee Mission Parkway
Overland Park, KS

913-262-9100

Residence Inn Kansas City Overland
Park
12010 Blue Valley Parkway
Overland Park, KS

913-491-4444

Super 8 Motel - Overland Park/S
Kansas City Area
10750 Barkley Street
Overland Park, KS

913-341-4440

Super 8 Park City/North Wichita Area
6075 Air Cap Drive
Park City, KS
316-744-2071

Best Western Parsons Inn
101 Main Street
Parsons, KS
620-423-0303

Rodeway Inn & Suites Parsons
1807 Harding Drive
Parsons, KS

620-421-6126

Super 8 Parsons
229 East Main St.
Parsons, KS

620-421-8000

Super 8 Motel - Pittsburg
3108 North Broadway
Pittsburg, KS
620-232-1881

Comfort Suites Pratt
704 Allison
Pratt, KS
620-672-9999

Days Inn Pratt
1901 E First Street
Pratt, KS

620-672-9465

Holiday Inn Express Hotel & Suites
Pratt
1903 Paulene Place
Pratt, KS

620-508-6350

Super 8 Pratt
1906 East 1st Street
Pratt, KS

620-672-5945

Days Inn - Russell
1225 South Fossil Street
Russell, KS
785-483-6660

Candlewood Suites Salina
2650 Planet Avenue
Salina, KS
785-823-6939

Hunters Leigh
4109 E North Street
Salina, KS

785-823-6750

Quality Inn & Suites Salina
2110 West Crawford Street
Salina, KS

785-825-2111

Salina Ambassador Hotel &
Conference Center
1616 West Crawford Street
Salina, KS

785-823-1739

Sleep Inn & Suites
3932 South 9th Street
Salina, KS

785-404-6777

Super 8 Motel - Salina/I-70 And 9th
Street
120 East Diamond Drive
Salina, KS

785-823-8808

Value Inn & Suites Salina
1640 West Crawford Street
Salina, KS

785-823-9215

Best Western Topeka Inn & Suites
700 Southwest Fairlawn Road
Topeka, KS
785-228-2223

Econo Lodge Topeka
2950 Southwest Topeka Boulevard
Topeka, KS

785-267-1681

Econo Lodge Topeka
1518 Southwest Wanamaker Road
Topeka, KS

Quality Inn Topeka
1240 S W Wanamaker Rd
Topeka, KS

785-273-6969

Ramada Convention Center,
Downtown Topeka
420 Southeast 6th Ave.
Topeka, KS

785-234-5400

Residence Inn By Marriott Topeka
1620 Sw Westport Drive
Topeka, KS

785-271-8903

Sleep Inn And Suites Topeka
1024 Sw Wanamaker Rd
Topeka, KS

785-228-2500

Studio 6 Topeka
914 Sw Henderson Road
Topeka, KS

785-271-7822

Super 8 Motel Topeka At Forbes
Landing
5922 Southwest Topeka Blvd
Topeka, KS

785-862-2222

Super 8 Topeka/Wanamaker Rd/I-70
5968 S.W. 10th Ave.
Topeka, KS

785-273-5100

Topeka Days Inn
1510 Southwest Wanamaker Road
Topeka, KS

785-272-8538

Dog-Friendly Lodging - Please always call ahead to make sure an establishment is still dog-friendly.

Best Western Plus Wakeeney Inn &
Suites
525 S 1st Street
Wa Keeney, KS
785-743-2700

Butterfield Trail Bunkhouse
RR 2 Box 86, 23033 T Road
WaKeeney, KS
785-743-2322

Super 8 Wakeeney
709 S 13th Street
Wakeeney, KS
785-743-6442

Simmer Motel
1215 West Us Highway 24
Wamego, KS
785-456-2304

Best Western Wichita North Hotel &
Suites
915 E 53rd Street N
Wichita, KS
316-832-9387

Candlewood Suites Wichita - Airport
570 S Julia
Wichita, KS

316-942-0400

Candlewood Suites Wichita
Northeast
3141 North Webb Road
Wichita, KS

316-634-6070

Clarion Inn & Suites Airport Wichita
5805 West Kellogg
Wichita, KS

316-942-7911

Comfort Inn East
9525 East Corporate Hills
Wichita, KS

316-686-2844

Doubletree By Hilton Wichita Airport
2098 Airport Road
Wichita, KS

316-945-5272

Homewood Suites By Hilton® At
The Waterfront
1550 North Waterfront Parkway
Wichita, KS

316-260-8844

Quality Inn South
4849 South Laura
Wichita, KS

316-522-1800

Residence Inn Wichita East At
Plazzio
1212 N. Greenwich
Wichita, KS

316-682-7300

Staybridge Suites Wichita
2250 North Greenwich Road
Wichita, KS

316-927-3888

Towneplace Suites By Marriott
Wichita East
9444 East 29th Street North
Wichita, KS

316-631-3773

Wyndham Garden Wichita
Downtown
221 East Kellogg Street
Wichita, KS

316-269-2090

Econo Lodge Winfield
1710 Main Street
Winfield, KS
620-221-9050

# Kentucky Listings

Knights Inn Ashland
7216 State Route 60
Ashland, KY
606-928-9501

General Nelson Inn
411 West Stephen Foster Avenue
Bardstown, KY
502-348-3977

Hampton Inn Bardstown
985 Chambers Blvd
Bardstown, KY

502-349-0100

Super Inn Downtown
523 N 3rd Street
Bardstown, KY

502-349-0363

Quality Inn & Suites Benton -
Draffenville
173 Carroll Road
Benton, KY
270-527-5300

Americas Best Value Inn Berea
196 Prince Royal Drive
Berea, KY
859-986-8426

Econo Lodge Berea
254 Paint Lick Road

Berea, KY
859-986-9324

Historic Boone Tavern
100 Main Street North
Berea, KY

606-986-9358

Holiday Inn Express Berea
219 Paint Lick Road
Berea, KY

859-985-5500

Motel 6 Berea
1029 Cooper Drive
Berea, KY

859-986-7373

Baymont Inn & Suites Bowling Green
1919 Mel Browning Street
Bowling Green, KY
270-846-4588

Candlewood Suites Bowling Green
540 Wall Street
Bowling Green, KY

270-843-5505

Drury Inn Bowling Green
3250 Scottsville Road
Bowling Green, KY

270-842-7100

Holiday Inn University Plaza-Bowling
Green
1021 Wilkinson Trace
Bowling Green, KY

270-745-0088

Red Roof Inn Bowling Green
3140 Scottsville Road
Bowling Green, KY

270-781-6550

Baymont Inn And Suites Brooks
149 Willabrook Drive
Brooks, KY
502-957-6900

Super 8 Cadiz
154 Hospitality Lane
Cadiz, KY
270-522-7007

Days Inn Calvert City
75 Campbell Drive
Calvert City, KY
270-395-7162

Super 8 Campbellsville Ky
100 Albion Way
Campbellsville, KY
270-789-0808

100

Red Roof Inn Carrollton
10 Slumber Lane
Carrollton, KY
502-732-8444

Super 8 Carrollton
130 Slumber Lane
Carrollton, KY

502-732-0252

Baymont Inn & Suites Cave City
799 Mammoth Cave Street
Cave City, KY
270-773-2500

Best Western Columbia Inn
710 Bomar Heights
Columbia, KY
270-384-9744

Best Western Corbin Inn
2630 Cumberland Falls Hwy
Corbin, KY
606-528-2100

Knights Inn Corbin
37 Highway 770
Corbin, KY

606-523-1500

Super 8 Motel - Corbin/London
171 W. Cumberland Gap Parkway
Corbin, KY

606-528-8888

Extended Stay America - Cincinnati -
Covington
650 West 3rd Street
Covington, KY
859-581-3000

Comfort Suites Danville
864 Ben-Ali Drive
Danville, KY
859-936-9300

Super 8 Danville
3663 Hwy 150/127 Bypass
Danville, KY

859-236-8881

Comfort Inn Dry Ridge
1050 Fashion Ridge Road
Dry Ridge, KY
859-824-7121

Microtel Inn By Wyndham Dry Ridge
79 Blackburn Lane
Dry Ridge, KY

859-824-2000

Value Stay Dry Ridge
88 Blackburn Lane
Dry Ridge, KY

859-824-3700

Eddy Creek Marina Resort
7612 H 93S
Eddyville, KY
270-388-2271

Baymont Inn & Suites Elizabethtown
209 Commerce Drive
Elizabethtown, KY
270-769-9616

Days Inn Elizabethtown
2010 North Mulberry Street
Elizabethtown, KY

270-769-5522

Quality Inn & Suites Elizabethtown
2009 N. Mulberry St.
Elizabethtown, KY

270-765-4166

Super 8 Elizabethtown
2028 North Mulberry Street
Elizabethtown, KY

270-737-1088

Econo Lodge Erlanger
633 Donaldson Rd
Erlanger, KY
859-342-5500

Red Roof Inn Cincinnati Airport
Erlanger Ky
630 Donaldson Road
Erlanger, KY

859-727-3400

Residence Inn By Marriott Cincinnati
Airport
2811 Circleport Dr
Erlanger, KY

859-282-7400

Best Western Inn Florence
7821 Commerce Drive
Florence, KY
859-525-0090

Comfort Inn Airport Turfway Road
7454 Turfway Road
Florence, KY

859-647-2700

Extended Stay America - Cincinnati
- Florence - Turfway Rd.
7350 Turfway Road
Florence, KY

859-282-7829

Florence Inn (Formerly Knights Inn)
8049 Dream Street
Florence, KY

859-371-9711

Hilton Cincinnati Airport
7373 Turfway Road
Florence, KY

859-371-4400

Microtel Inn & Suites By Wyndham
Florence/Cincinnati Airport
7490 Woodspoint Drive
Florence, KY

Quality Inn & Suites
7915 Us Highway 42
Florence, KY

859-371-4700

Super 8 Florence
7928 Dream Street
Florence, KY

859-283-1221

Super 8 Fort Mitchell
2350 Royal Drive
Fort Mitchell, KY
859-341-2090

Days Inn Frankfort
1051 Us 127 South
Frankfort, KY
502-875-2200

Days Inn Franklin
103 Trotter Lane
Franklin, KY
270-598-0163

Quality Inn Franklin
3794 Nashville Road
Franklin, KY

270-586-6100

Super 8 Franklin Hwy 31
3811 Nashville Road
Franklin, KY

270-586-5090

Baymont Inn & Suites Georgetown
250 Outlet Center Drive
Georgetown, KY
502-867-1648

Best Western Plus Georgetown
Corporate Center Hotel
132 Darby Drive
Georgetown, KY

502-868-0055

Georgetown Days Inn North Of
Lexington
385 Cherry Blossom Way
Georgetown, KY

502-863-5000

Holiday Inn Express Lexington North-
Georgetown
140 Osborne Way

Dog-Friendly Lodging - Please always call ahead to make sure an establishment is still dog-friendly.

Georgetown, KY

502-570-0220

Comfort Inn Glasgow
210 Cavalry Dr.
Glasgow, KY
270-651-9099

Days Inn - Grayson
650 Cw Stevens Boulevard
Grayson, KY
606-475-3224

Quality Inn Grayson
205 State Hwy 1947
Grayson, KY

606-474-7854

Super 8 Grayson
125 Super Eight Lane
Grayson, KY

606-474-8811

Days Inn Harrodsburg
1680 Danville Road
Harrodsburg, KY
859-734-9431

Super 8 Hazard Ky
125 Village Lane
Hazard, KY
606-436-8888

Economy Inn & Suites
2030 Us Highway 41 North
Henderson, KY
270-827-5611

Holiday Inn Hopkinsville
2910 Fort Campbell Boulevard
Hopkinsville, KY
270-886-4413

First Farm Inn
2510 Stevens Road
Idlewild, KY
859-586-0199

Days Inn Kuttawa
139 Days Inn Drive
Kuttawa, KY
270-388-4060

Comfort Inn & Suites La Grange
1001 Paige Place
La Grange, KY
502-222-5678

Quality Suites La Grange
1500 Crystal Drive East
La Grange, KY

502-225-4125

Hampton Inn Lebanon, Ky
1125 Loretto Road
Lebanon, KY
270-699-4000

Candlewood Suites Lexington
603 Ad Color Drive
Lexington, KY
859-967-1940

Clarion Hotel Conference Center -
South
5532 Athens Boonesboro Rd
Lexington, KY

859-263-5241

Comfort Suites Lexington
3060 Fieldstone Way
Lexington, KY

859-296-4446

Crossland Economy Studios -
Lexington - Patchen Village
2750 Gribbin Drive
Lexington, KY
859-266-4800

Days Inn & Suites Lexington
1987 N. Broadway
Lexington, KY

859-299-1202

Econo Lodge Lexington
5527 Athens-Boonesboro Rd.
Lexington, KY

859-263-5101

Extended Stay America - Lexington -
Tates Creek
3575 Tates Creek Road
Lexington, KY

859-271-6160

Extended Stay America Lexington -
Nicholasville Road
2650 Wilhite Drive
Lexington, KY

859-278-9600

Four Points Sheraton Lexington
1938 Stanton Way
Lexington, KY

859-259-1311

Griffin Gate Marriott Resort & Spa
1800 Newtown Pike
Lexington, KY

859-231-5100

Hampton Inn Lexington - I-75
2251 Elkhorn Road
Lexington, KY

859-299-2613

Hilton Lexington Suites
245 Lexington Green Circle

Lexington, KY

859-271-4000

La Quinta Inn And Suites Lexington
South / Hamburg
100 Canebrake Drive
Lexington, KY

859-543-1877

Lexington-Days Inn South
5575 Athens Boonesboro Road
Lexington, KY

859-263-3100

Microtel Inn By Wyndham Lexington
2240 Buena Vista
Lexington, KY

859-299-9600

Ramada Inn And Conference Center-
Lexington
2143 North Broadway
Lexington, KY

859-299-1261

Red Roof Inn - Lexington South
2651 Wilhite Drive
Lexington, KY

606-277-9400

Red Roof Inn Lexington
1980 Haggard Court
Lexington, KY

859-293-2626

Residence Inn Lexington
1080 Newtown Pike
Lexington, KY

859-231-6191

Residence Inn Lexington
Keeneland/Airport
3110 Wall Street
Lexington, KY

859-296-0460

Residence Inn Lexington South
Hamburg Place
2688 Pink Pigeon Parkway
Lexington, KY

859-263-9979

Sleep Inn Lexington
1920 Plaudit Pl.
Lexington, KY

859-543-8400

Super 8 Lexington Winchester Rd
2351 Buena Vista Road
Lexington, KY

859-299-6241

Days Inn - London
207 Highway 80 West
London, KY
606-864-2222

Econo Lodge London
105 Melcon Lane
London, KY
606-877-9700

Red Roof Inn London I-75
110 Melcon Lane
London, KY
606-862-8844

Super 8 Louisa
191 Falls Creek Drive
Louisa, KY
606-638-7888

Aloft Louisville Downtown
102 West Main Street
Louisville, KY
502-583-1888

Baymont Inn Louisville East
9400 Blairwood Road
Louisville, KY
502-339-1900

Breckinridge Inn
2800 Breckenridge Lane
Louisville, KY
502-456-5050

Candlewood Suites-Louisville Airport
1367 Gardiner Lane
Louisville, KY
502-357-.357

Cottonwood Suites Louisville Fair &
Expo Center
4110 Dixie Highway
Louisville, KY
502-448-2020

Crossland Economy Studios -
Louisville - St. Matthews
1401 Browns Lane
Louisville, KY
502-897-2559

Crowne Plaza Louisville-Arpt Ky Expo
Ctr
830 Phillips Lane
Louisville, KY
502-367-2251

Days Inn - Hurstbourne
9340 Blairwood Road
Louisville, KY
502-425-8010

Days Inn Airport/Fair & Expo Center
- Louisville
2905 Fern Valley Road
Louisville, KY
502-968-8124

Days Inn Louisville Central
University & Expo Center
1620 Arthur Street
Louisville, KY
502-636-3781

Drury Inn & Suites Louisville East
9501 Blairwood Road
Louisville, KY
502-326-4170

Extended Stay America - Louisville -
Alliant Avenue
1650 Alliant Avenue
Louisville, KY
502-267-4454

Extended Stay America - Louisville -
Dutchman
6101 Dutchmans Lane
Louisville, KY
502-895-7707

Extended Stay America - Louisville -
Hurstbourne
9801 Bunsen Parkway
Louisville, KY
502-499-6215

Hawthorn Suites By Wyndham
Louisville
11762 Commonwealth Drive
Louisville, KY
502-261-0085

La Quinta Inn & Suites Louisville
East
1501 Alliant Avenue
Louisville, KY
502-267-8889

Microtel Inn By Wyndham Louisville
East
1221 Kentucky Mills Lane
Louisville, KY
502-266-6590

Ramada Limited & Suites
Airport/Fair/Expo Center
2912 Crittenden Drive
Louisville, KY
502-637-6336

Red Roof Inn Louisville East
Hurstbourne
9330 Blairwood Rd

Louisville, KY
502-426-7621

Red Roof Inn Louisville Expo Airport
4704 Preston Highway
Louisville, KY
502-968-0151

Red Roof Inn Louisville Fair And
Expo
3322 Red Roof Inn Place
Louisville, KY
502-456-2993

Residence Inn By Marriott Louisville
Airport
700 Phillips Lane
Louisville, KY
502-363-8800

Residence Inn By Marriott Louisville
Downtown
333 East Market Street
Louisville, KY
502-589-8998

Residence Inn By Marriott Louisville
East
120 North Hurstbourne Parkway
Louisville, KY
502-425-1821

Residence Inn By Marriott Louisville
Northeast
3500 Sprimghurst Commons Drive
Louisville, KY
502-412-1311

Sleep Inn Louisville East
1850 Priority Way
Louisville, KY
502-266-6776

Staybridge Suites Louisville-East
11711 Gateworth Way
Louisville, KY
502-244-9511

Super 8 Louisville Airport
4800 Preston Highway
Louisville, KY
502-968-0088

The Seelbach Hilton Louisville
500 Fourth Street
Louisville, KY
502-585-3200

Days Inn Madisonville
1900 Lantaff Boulevard
Madisonville, KY
270-821-8620

Dog-Friendly Lodging - Please always call ahead to make sure an establishment is still dog-friendly.

Days Inn Maysville
84 Moody Drive
Maysville, KY
606-564-6793

Super 8 Maysville Ky
550 Tucker Drive
Maysville, KY
606-759-8888

Comfort Inn & Suites Morehead
2650 KY 801 North
Morehead, KY
606-780-7378

Red Roof Inn Morehead
175 Toms Drive
Morehead, KY
606-784-2220

Ramada Limited/Conference Center-
Mt. Sterling
115 Stone Trace Drive
Mount Sterling, KY
859-497-9400

Days Inn Mt. Vernon Renfro Valley
1630 Richmond Street
Mount Vernon, KY
606-256-3300

Best Western University Inn
1503 North 12th Street
Murray, KY
270-753-5353

Days Inn Owensboro
3720 New Hartford Road
Owensboro, KY
270-684-9621

Candlewood Suites Paducah
3940 Coleman Crossing Circle
Paducah, KY
270-442-3969

Days Inn Paducah
3901 Hinkleville Road
Paducah, KY
270-442-7500

Drury Inn Paducah
3975 Hinkleville Road
Paducah, KY
270-443-3313

Drury Suites Paducah
2930 James Sanders Boulevard
Paducah, KY
270-441-0024

Residence Inn Paducah
3900 Coleman Crossing Circle
Paducah, KY

270-444-3966

Thrifty Inn Paducah
5002 Hinkleville Road
Paducah, KY

270-444-0157

Super 8 Prestonsburg
550 Us 23 South
Prestonsburg, KY
606-886-3355

Candlewood Suites Radcliff-Fort
Knox
100 Endeavour Way
Radcliff, KY
270-351-3333

Comfort Suites Richmond
2007 Colby Taylor Dr.
Richmond, KY
859-624-0770

Days Inn Richmond
2109 Belmont Drive
Richmond, KY

859-624-5769

Red Roof Inn Lexington - Richmond
111 Bahama Court
Richmond, KY

859-625-0084

Super 8 Richmond
107 North Keeneland Drive
Richmond, KY

859-624-1550

Best Western River Cities
31 Russell Plaza Drive
Russell, KY
606-326-0357

Best Western Shelbyville Lodge
115 Isaac Shelby Drive
Shelbyville, KY
502-633-4400

Red Roof Inn Shelbyville
101 Howard Drive
Shelbyville, KY

502-633-4005

Sleep Inn & Suites Shepherdsville
130 Spring Pointe Drive
Shepherdsville, KY
502-921-1001

Red Roof Inn Somerset
1201 South Hwy 27
Somerset, KY
606-678-8115

Ramada Sparta Ky
525 Dale Drive

Sparta, KY
859-567-7223

Barthell Coal Mining Camp Lodging
552 Barthell Road
Sterns, KY
606-376-8749

Rose Hill Inn
233 Rose Hill Avenue
Versailles, KY
859-873-5957

Days Inn West Liberty
1613 West Main
West Liberty, KY
606-743-4206

Super 8 Motel - Whitesburg
377a Hazard Road And Route 15
Whitesburg, KY
606-633-8888

Super 8 Williamsburg
30 West Highway 92
Williamsburg, KY
606-549-3450

Sunrise Inn Williamstown
211 KY Hwy 36 West
Williamstown, KY
859-824-5025

Best Western Winchester Hotel
1307 West Lexington Avenue
Winchester, KY
859-744-7210

Quality Inn & Suites Winchester
960 Interstate Drive
Winchester, KY
859-737-3990

# Louisiana Listings

Best Western Of Alexandria Inn &
Suites & Conference Center
2720 North Macarthur Drive
Alexandria, LA
318-445-5530

Ramada Inn Alexandria
742 Macarthur Drive
Alexandria, LA
318-448-1611

Super 8 Alexandria
700 Macarthur Drive
Alexandria, LA
318-445-6541

Candlewood Suites Avondale-New
Orleans
3079 Highway 90
Avondale, LA
504-875-3500

Best Western Plus Richmond Inn & Suites-Baton Rouge
2683 Energy Drive
Baton Rouge, LA
225-924-6500

Chase Suites By Woodfin
5522 Corporate Blvd
Baton Rouge, LA

225-927-5630

Crossland Economy Studios - Baton Rouge - Sherwood Forest
11140 Boardwalk Dr.
Baton Rouge, LA

225-274-8997

Drury Inn & Suites Baton Rouge
7939 Essen Park Avenue
Baton Rouge, LA

225-766-2022

Extended Stay America - Baton Rouge - Citiplace
6250 Corporate Blvd.
Baton Rouge, LA

225-201-0330

Hilton Baton Rouge Capitol Center
201 Lafayette Street
Baton Rouge, LA

225-344-5866

Holiday Inn Baton Rouge College Drive I-10
4848 Constitution Avenue
Baton Rouge, LA

225-448-2030

Hotel Indigo Baton Rouge Downtown
200 Convention Street
Baton Rouge, LA

225-343-1515

Knights Inn Baton Rouge
9919 Gwenadele Ave
Baton Rouge, LA

225-364-3520

Magnuson Hotel Baton Rouge
9999 Gwenadelle Drive
Baton Rouge, LA

225-925-8399

Radisson Hotel Baton Rouge
2445 South Acadian Thruway
Baton Rouge, LA

225-236-4000

Red Roof Inn Baton Rouge
11314 Boardwalk Drive

Baton Rouge, LA

225-275-6600

Residence Inn By Marriott Baton Rouge Siegen Lane
10333 North Mall Drive
Baton Rouge, LA

225-293-8700

Residence Inn By Marriott Baton Rouge Towne Ctr At Cedar Lodge
7061 Commerce Circle
Baton Rouge, LA

225-925-9100

Staybridge Suites Baton Rouge-University At Southgate
4001 Nicholson Drive
Baton Rouge, LA

225-456-5430

Towneplace Suites Baton Rouge South
8735 Summa Avenue
Baton Rouge, LA

225-819-2112

Days Inn Bossier City
200 John Wesley Blvd
Bossier City, LA
318-742-9200

Microtel Inn & Suites By Wyndham Bossier City
2713 Village Lane
Bossier City, LA

318-742-7882

The Shreveport Country Inn
1984 Airline Drive
Bossier City, LA

Towneplace Suites By Marriott Shreveport-Bossier City
1009 Gould Drive
Bossier City, LA

318-741-9090

Holiday Inn Express Breaux Bridge
2942 H. Grand Point Highway
Breaux Bridge, LA
337-667-8913

Best Western Northpark Inn
625 North Highway 190
Covington, LA
985-892-2681

Residence Inn New Orleans Covington/North Shore
101 Park Place Blvd
Covington, LA

985-246-7222

Staybridge Suites Covington
140 Holiday Blvd
Covington, LA

985-892-0003

Days Inn Crowley
9571 Egan Highway
Crowley, LA
337-783-2378

Candlewood Suites Denham Springs
246 Rushing Road
Denham Springs, LA
225-271-0300

Best Western Hammond Inn & Suites
107 Duo Drive
Hammond, LA
985-419-2001

Magnuson Grand Hotel And Conference Center Hammond
2000 South Morrison Boulevard
Hammond, LA

985-345-0556

Towneplace Suites By Marriott New Orleans Metairie
5424 Citrus Blvd
Harahan, LA
504-818-2400

Crochet House
301 Midland Drive
Houma, LA
985-879-3033

Extended Stay America - New Orleans - Airport
2300 Veterans Blvd
Kenner, LA
504-465-8300

Best Western Inn At Coushatta
12102 Us Highway 165
Kinder, LA
337-738-4800

Econo Lodge Kinder
13894 Highway 165
Kinder, LA

337-738-3240

Best Western La Place Inn
4289 Main Street
La Place, LA
985-651-4000

Best Western Lafayette Inn
2207 Nw Evangeline Thruway
Lafayette, LA
337-769-2900

Candlewood Suites Lafayette
2105 Kaliste Saloom Road
Lafayette, LA

337-984-6900

Dog-Friendly Lodging - Please always call ahead to make sure an establishment is still dog-friendly.

Days Inn Lafayette/Airport
2501 Se Evangeline Thruway
Lafayette, LA

337-769-8000

Days Inn Lafayette/University
1620 North University Ave
Lafayette, LA

337-237-8880

Drury Inn & Suites Lafayette
120 Alcide Dominique Drive
Lafayette, LA

337-262-0202

Extended Stay America - Lafayette -
Airport
807 S. Hugh Wallis Rd
Lafayette, LA

337-232-8313

Pear Tree Inn Lafayette
126 Alcide Dominique Drive
Lafayette, LA

337-289-9907

Ramada Lafayette Conference
Center
2032 Ne Evangeline Trwy
Lafayette, LA

337-233-6815

Red Roof Inn Lafayette
1718 North University Avenue
Lafayette, LA

337-233-3339

Residence Inn Lafayette Airport
128 James Comeaux Road
Lafayette, LA

337-232-3341

Staybridge Suites Lafayette-Airport
129 E Kaliste Saloom Road
Lafayette, LA

337-267-4666

C.A.'s House
624 Ford Street
Lake Charles, LA
337-439-6672

Red Roof Inn Lake Charles
269 Highway 397
Lake Charles, LA

337-990-0165

Extended Stay America New Orleans
- Metairie
3300 Interstate 10 Service Road
West

Metairie, LA
504-837-5599

Residence Inn Metairie/New Orleans
3 Galleria Blvd
Metairie, LA

504-832-0888

Sheraton Hotel Metairie New
Orleans
4 Galleria Boulevard
Metairie, LA

504-837-6707

Best Western Minden Inn
1411 Sibley Road
Minden, LA
318-377-1001

Residence Inn Monroe
4960 Millhaven Rd
Monroe, LA
318-387-0210

Holiday Inn Morgan City
520 Roderick St
Morgan City, LA
985-385-2200

Americas Best Value Inn
Natchitoches
7624 Highway 1 Bypass
Natchitoches, LA

Best Western Natchitoches Inn
5131 University Pkwy
Natchitoches, LA

318-352-6655

Super 8 Natchitoches
5821 Highway 1 Bypass
Natchitoches, LA

318-352-1700

Madewood Plantation
4250 H 308
Nepolianville, LA
985-369-7151

Candlewood Suites New Iberia
2600 Hwy 14
New Iberia, LA
337-256-8113

Ramada Conference Center New
Iberia
2915 Highway 14
New Iberia, LA

337-367-1201

Best Western Patio Downtown Motel
2820 Tulane Avenue
New Orleans, LA
504-822-0200

Best Western Plus St. Charles Inn

3636 Saint Charles Avenue
New Orleans, LA

504-899-8888

Best Western Plus St. Christopher
Hotel
114 Magazine Street
New Orleans, LA

504-648-0444

Chimes Bed and Breakfast
Constantinople St & Coliseum St
New Orleans, LA

504-899-2621

Creole Gardens Guesthouse and Inn
1415 Prytania Street
New Orleans, LA

504-569-8700

Creole Gardens Guesthouse and Inn
1415 Prytania Street
New Orleans, LA

504-569-8700

Drury Inn & Suites New Orleans
820 Poydras Street
New Orleans, LA

504-529-7800

Elysian Fields Inn
930 Elysian Fields
New Orleans, LA

504-948-9420

Hilton New Orleans/St. Charles Ave.
French Quarter Area
333 St. Charles Avenue
New Orleans, LA

504-524-8890

Hotel Monteleone
214 Royal Street
New Orleans, LA

504-523-3341

Lions Inn
2517 Chartres Street
New Orleans, LA

504-945-2339

Loews New Orleans Hotel
300 Poydras Street
New Orleans, LA

504-595-3300

New Orleans Courtyard Hotel
1101 North Rampart Street
New Orleans, LA

504-522-7333

Pontchartrain Hotel
2031 St. Charles Avenue
New Orleans, LA

504-524-0581

Rathbone Mansion
1244 Esplanade Avenue
New Orleans, LA

504-309-4479

Residence Inn New Orleans
Downtown
345 St. Joseph
New Orleans, LA

504-522-1300

Sheraton New Orleans Hotel
500 Canal Street
New Orleans, LA

504-525-2500

Windsor Court Hotel
300 Gravier Street
New Orleans, LA

504-523-6000

Super 8 Opelousas
5791 I-49 S Service Road
Opelousas, LA
337-942-6250

Microtel Inn & Suites By Wyndham
Pearl River/Slidell
63537 Highway 1090
Pearl River, LA
877-827-8441

Microtel Inn & Suites By Wyndham
Ponchatoula/Hammond
727 West Pine Street
Ponchatoula, LA

Days Inn Rayne
1125 Church Point Hwy
Rayne, LA
337-334-0000

Days Inn Shreveport Airport
4935 West Monkhouse Drive
Shreveport, LA
318-636-0080

Fairfield Place Inn
2221 Fairfield Avenue
Shreveport, LA

866-432-2632

Homewood Suites By Hilton
Shreveport
5485 Financial Plaza
Shreveport, LA

318-549-2000

Howard Johnson Shreveport
6715 Rasberry Lane

Shreveport, LA

318-671-0731

Residence Inn By Marriott
Shreveport Airport
4910 West Monkhouse Drive
Shreveport, LA

318-635-8000

Rodeway Inn & Suites Shreveport
5101 Westwood Park Drive
Shreveport, LA

318-631-2000

Studio 6 Shreveport
5020 Hollywood Avenue
Shreveport, LA

318-635-8062

Super 8 Shreveport
4911 Monkhouse Drive
Shreveport, LA

318-636-0771

Candlewood Suites Slidell
Northshore
100 Holiday Boulevard
Slidell, LA
985-326-0120

Holiday Inn Hotel & Suites Slidell
372 Voters Road
Slidell, LA

985-639-0890

Butler Greenwood Plantation
8345 H 61
St Francisville, LA
225-635-6312

Lake Rosemound Inn
10473 Lindsey Lane
St Francisville, LA

504-899-0701

Candlewood Suites Lake Charles-
Sulphur
320 Arena Road
Sulphur, LA
337-528-5777

Red Roof Inn - West Monroe
102 Constitution Drive
West Monroe, LA
318-388-2420

Best Western Zachary Inn
4030 Highway 19
Zachary, LA
225-658-2550

# Maine Listings

Oceanside Meadows Inn
Prospect Harbor Road
Acadia Schoodic, ME
207-963-5557

Arundel Meadows Inn
1024 Portland Road
Arundel, ME
207-985-3770

Best Western Plus Augusta Civic
Center Inn
110 Community Drive
Augusta, ME
207-622-4751

Comfort Inn Civic Center
281 Civic Center Drive
Augusta, ME

207-623-1000

Best Western White House Inn
Bangor
155 Littlefield Avenue
Bangor, ME
207-862-3737

Days Inn Bangor
250 Odlin Road
Bangor, ME

207-942-8272

Four Points By Sheraton Bangor
Airport
308 Godfrey Boulevard
Bangor, ME

207-947-6721

Holiday Inn Bangor Odlin Road
404 Odlin Rd &; 395 At Hermon
Bangor, ME

207-947-0101

Howard Johnson Inn Bangor
336 Odlin Road I-95
Bangor, ME

207-942-5251

Quality Inn Bangor
750 Hogan Rd.
Bangor, ME

207-942-7899

Rodeway Inn Bangor
327 Odlin Rd
Bangor, ME

207-945-0111

Travelodge Bangor
482 Odlin Road
Bangor, ME

207-942-6301

Travelodge Bangor

482 Odlin Road
Bangor, ME

Acadia Acres
205 Knox Road
Bar Harbor, ME
207-288-5055

Balance Rock Inn
21 Albert Meadow
Bar Harbor, ME

207-288-2610

Bar Harbor Acadia Cottage Rentals
P.O. Box 265
Bar Harbor, ME

207-288-0307

Days Inn Bar Harbor
120 Eden Street
Bar Harbor, ME

207-288-3321

Gale's Gardens Guesthouses
Daylily Lane
Bar Harbor, ME

207-733-8811

Hanscom's Motel and Cottages
273 H 3
Bar Harbor, ME

207-288-3744

Hutchins Mountain View Cottages
286 H 3
Bar Harbor, ME

207-288-4833

Rose Eden Cottages
864 State Highway 3
Bar Harbor, ME

207-288-3038

Ryan Estate Rentals
700 Eagle Lake Road
Bar Harbor, ME

207-288-5154

Summertime Cottages
1 Bloomfield Road
Bar Harbor, ME

207-288-2893

The Ledgelawn Inn
66 Mount Desert Street
Bar Harbor, ME

207-288-4596

Town and Country Cottage
230 H 3
Bar Harbor, ME

207-288-3439

The Inn at Bath
969 Washington Street
Bath, ME
207-443-4294

Day Lily Cottage
Call to Arrange
Belfast, ME
207-342-5444

Fireside Inn & Suites Belfast
159 Searsport Avenue
Belfast, ME

207-338-2090

Bethel Inn and Country Club
7 Broad Street
Bethel, ME
207-824-2175

Sudbury Inn
151 Main Street
Bethel, ME

207-824-2174

The Inn at the Rostay
186 Mayville Road
Bethel, ME

888-754-0072

Rodeway Inn & Suites Brunswick
287 Bath Road
Brunswick, ME
207-729-6661

Calais Motor Inn
293 Main Street
Calais, ME
207-454-7111

International Motel
276 Main Street
Calais, ME

207-454-7515

Blue Harbor House
67 Elm Street
Camden, ME
207-236-3196

Fisherman's Cottage
113 Bayview Street
Camden, ME

207-342-5444

Grand Harbor Inn
14 Bay View Landing
Camden, ME

207-230-7177

Lord Camden Inn
24 Main Street
Camden, ME

207-236-4325

Inn By the Sea
40 Bowery Beach Road
Cape Elizabeth, ME
207-799-3134

Inn by the Sea
40 Bowery Beach Road/H 77
Cape Elizabeth, ME

207-799-3134

Castine Harbor Lodge
147 Perkins Street
Castine, ME
207-326-4335

The Pilgrim's Inn
20 Main Street
Deer Isle, ME
207-348-6615

Milliken House
29 Washington Street
Eastport, ME
207-853-2955

Sheepscot Harbour Village & Resort
306 Eddy Road
Edgecomb, ME
207-882-6343

Ramada Ellsworth
215 High Street
Ellsworth, ME
207-667-9341

Best Western Freeport Inn
31 U.S. Route 1
Freeport, ME
207-865-3106

Harraseeket Inn
162 Main Street Cumberland
Freeport, ME

207-865-9377

The Main Idyll Motor Court
1411 H 1
Freeport, ME

207-865-4201

Sagadahoc Bay Campground
9 Molly Point Lane
Georgetown Island, ME
207-371-2014

The Crocker House
967 Point Road
Hancock, ME
207-422-6808

The Hounds Tooth Inn
82 Summer Street
Kennebunk, ME
207-985-0117

Lodge At Turbat's Creek
Turbats Creek Rd at Ocean Avenue
Kennebunkport, ME
207-967-8700

The Colony Hotel
140 Ocean Avenue
Kennebunkport, ME

207-967-3331

The Yachtsman Lodge And Marina
57 Ocean Avenue
Kennebunkport, ME

207-967-2511

Enchanted Nights B&B
29 Wentworth Street
Kittery, ME
207-439-1489

Enchanted Nights B&B
29 Wentworth Street
Kittery, ME

207-439-1489

Pine Grove Cottages
2076 Atlantic H
Lincolnville, ME
207-236-2929

Gateway Inn
Route 157
Medway, ME
207-746-3193

Wolf Cove Inn
5 Jordan Shore Drive
Poland, ME
207-998-4976

Clarion Hotel Airport Portland
1230 Congress Street
Portland, ME
207-774-5611

Embassy Suites Hotel Portland
1050 Westbrook St
Portland, ME

207-775-2200

Hilton Garden Inn Portland Downtown
Waterfront
65 Commerical Street
Portland, ME

207-780-0780

Inn at St John
939 Congress Street
Portland, ME

207-773-6481

Ramada Plaza Portland
155 Riverside Street
Portland, ME

207-774-5861

Westin Portland Harborview
157 High Street
Portland, ME

207-775-2872

Old Granite Inn
546 Main Street
Rockland, ME
207-594-9036

Country Inn at Camden/Rockport
8 Country Inn Way
Rockport, ME
207-236-2725

The Birches Resort
281 Birches Road
Rockwood, ME
http://www.birches.com

Linnel Motel
986 Prospect Avenue
Rumford, ME
207-364-4511

The Perennial Inn
141 Jed Martin Road
Rumford Point, ME
207-369-0309

Hampton Inn Saco/Biddeford
48 Industrial Park Road
Saco, ME
207-282-7222

Ramada Saco
352 North Street
Saco, ME

207-286-9600

Extended Stay America - Portland -
Scarborough
2 Ashley Dr.
Scarborough, ME
207-883-0554

Homewood Suites By Hilton
Portland
200 Southborough Drive
Scarborough, ME

207-775-2700

Best Western Merry Manor Inn
700 Main Street
South Portland, ME
207-774-6151

Days Inn South Portland
461 Maine Mall Road I-95 Exit
South Portland, ME

207-772-3450

Hampton Inn Portland-Airport
171 Philbrook Ave
South Portland, ME

207-773-4400

Holiday Inn Express Hotel & Suites
South Portland
303 Sable Oaks Drive
South Portland, ME

207-775-3900

Howard Johnson Hotel Portland
South
675 Main Street
South Portland, ME

207-775-5343

Portland Marriott At Sable Oaks
200 Sable Oaks Drive
South Portland, ME

207-871-8000

The Willard Beach House
14 Myrtle Avenue
South Portland, ME

207-799-9824

Flander's Bay Cabins
22 Harbor View Drive
Sullivan, ME
207-422-6408

Harbor Watch Motel

Swans Island, ME
207-526-4563

The East Wind Inn
21 Mechanic Street
Tenants Harbor, ME
207-372-6366

Best Western Plus Waterville Grand
Hotel
375 Main Street
Waterville, ME
207-873-0111

Comfort Inn And Suites
332 Main Street
Waterville, ME

207-873-2777

Comfort Inn & Suites
1026 Us Route 2 East
Wilton, ME
207-645-5155

York Harbor Inn
480 York St.
York Harbor, ME
207-363-5119

# Maryland Listings

Merit Hotel And Suites
980 Hospitality Way

Dog-Friendly Lodging - Please always call ahead to make sure an establishment is still dog-friendly.

Aberdeen, MD
410-273-6300

Red Roof Inn Aberdeen
988 Hospitality Way
Aberdeen, MD

410-273-7800

Super 8 Motel - Aberdeen
1008 Beards Hill Road
Aberdeen, MD

410-272-5420

Travelodge Hotel Aberdeen
820 West Bel Air Avenue
Aberdeen, MD

410-272-5500

Extended Stay America - Annapolis -
Admiral Cochrane Drive
120 Admiral Cochrane Drive
Annapolis, MD
410-571-6600

Extended Stay America - Annapolis -
Womack Drive
1 Womack Drive
Annapolis, MD

410-571-9988

Loews Annapolis Hotel
126 West Street
Annapolis, MD

410-263-7777

Towneplace Suites By Marriott
Baltimore/ Fort Meade
120 National Business Parkway
Annapolis Junction, MD
301-498-7477

Admiral Fell Inn, An Ascend Hotel
Collection Member
888 South Broadway
Baltimore, MD
410-522-7377

Best Western Plus Bwi Airport North
Inn & Suites
6055 Belle Grove Road
Baltimore, MD

410-789-7223

Brookshire Suites
120 East Lombard Street
Baltimore, MD

410-625-1300

Hilton Baltimore Convention Center
401 West Pratt Street
Baltimore, MD

443-573-8700

Holiday Inn Express Baltimore

Downtown
221 North Gay Street
Baltimore, MD

410-400-8045

Homewood Suites By Hilton
Baltimore
625-A South President Street
Baltimore, MD

410-234-0999

Monaco Baltimore, A Kimpton Hotel
2 North Charles Street
Baltimore, MD

443-692-6170

Pier 5, An Ascend Hotel Collection
Member
711 Eastern Avenue
Baltimore, MD

410-539-2000

Radisson Hotel Baltimore
Downtown-Inner Harbor
101 West Fayette Street
Baltimore, MD

410-752-1100

Sheraton Baltimore North Hotel
903 Dulaney Valley Road
Baltimore, MD

410-321-7400

Sleep Inn & Suites Downtown Inner
Harbor
301 Fallsway
Baltimore, MD

410-779-6166

Tremont Park Hotel
8 East Pleasant Street
Baltimore, MD

410-576-1200

Candlewood Suites Bel Air
4216 Philadelphia Road
Bel Air, MD
410-914-3060

Extended Stay America Baltimore -
Bel Air - Aberdeen
1361 James Way
Bel Air, MD

410-273-0194

Homewood Bel Air
4170 Philadelphia Road
Bel Air, MD

410-297-8585

Comfort Inn Capital Beltway/I-95
North
4050 Powder Mill Road

Beltsville, MD
301-572-7100

Towneplace Suites By Marriott Bowie
Town Center
3700 Town Center Boulevard
Bowie, MD
301-262-8045

Super 8 Lexington Park/California
Area
22801 Three Notch Road
California, MD
301-862-9822

Comfort Inn & Suites Cambridge
2936 Ocean Gateway
Cambridge, MD
410-901-0926

Super 8 Camp Springs/Andrews Afb
DC Area
5151b Allentown Road
Camp Spring, MD
301-702-0099

Quality Inn Camp Springs
4783 Allentown Road
Camp Springs, MD
301-420-2800

Brampton Bed And Breakfast Inn
25227 Chestertown Road
Chestertown, MD
410-778-1860

Holiday Inn Express Hotel & Suites
Chestertown
150 Scheeler Road
Chestertown, MD

410-778-0778

Howard Johnson Washington DC
North / Bw Parkway
5811 Annapolis Road
Cheverly, MD
301-779-7700

Comfort Inn At Joint Base Andrews
7979 Malcolm Rd.
Clinton, MD
301-856-5200

Chase Suite Hotel by Woodfin
10710 Beaver Dam Road
Cockeysville, MD
410-584-7370

Extended Stay America Columbia -
Columbia Parkway
8870 Columbia 100 Parkway
Columbia, MD
410-772-8800

Homewood Suites By Hilton®
Columbia
8320 Benson Drive
Columbia, MD

410-872-9200

Sheraton Columbia Town Center
10207 Wincopin Circle
Columbia, MD
410-730-3900

Sonesta Es Suites Baltimore
Columbia
8844 Columbia 100 Parkway
Columbia, MD
410-964-9494

Best Western Braddock Motor Inn
1268 National Hwy.
Cumberland, MD
301-729-3300

Ramada Cumberland Downtown
100 South George Street
Cumberland, MD
301-724-8800

Railey Mountain Lake Vacations
5 Vacation Way
Deep Creek Lake, MD
301-387-2124

Days Inn Easton
7018 Ocean Gateway
Easton, MD
410-822-4600

The Tidewater Inn
101 East Dover Street
Easton, MD
410-822-1300

Days Inn Elkton
311 Belle Hill Road
Elkton, MD
410-392-5010

Comfort Inn Frederick
7300 Executive Way
Frederick, MD
301-668-7272

Country Inn & Suites By Carlson,
Frederick, Md
5579 Spectrum Drive
Frederick, MD
301-695-2881

Econo Lodge Frederick
6021 Francis Scott Key Drive
Frederick, MD
301-698-0555

Extended Stay America Frederick -
Westview Dr.
5240 Westview Drive
Frederick, MD
301-668-0808

Holiday Inn Frederick-Conf Ctr At
Francis Scott Key Mall
5400 Holiday Drive * I-270 &; Route
85
Frederick, MD
301-694-7500

Mainstay Suites Frederick
7310 Executive Way
Frederick, MD
301-668-4600

Super 8 Frederick
20 Monocacy Road
Frederick, MD
301-663-0500

Yough Valley Motel
138 Walnut Street
Friendsville, MD
301-746-5700

Days Inn And Suites Frostburg
11100 New George Creek Road
Frostburg, MD
301-689-2050

The Savage River Lodge
1600 Mount Aetna Rd
Frostburg, MD
301-689-3200

Comfort Inn At Shady Grove
16216 Frederick Rd
Gaithersburg, MD
301-330-0023

Extended Stay America
Washington, D.C. - Gaithersburg
205 Professional Drive
Gaithersburg, MD
301-869-9814

Hilton Washington DC
North/Gaithersburg
620 Perry Parkway
Gaithersburg, MD
301-977-8900

Towneplace Suites By Marriott
Gaithersburg
212 Perry Parkway
Gaithersburg, MD
301-590-2300

Extended Stay America -
Washington, D.C. - Germantown -
Mileston
12450 Milestone Center Drive
Germantown, MD
301-540-9369

Extended Stay America
-Washington, D.C.-Germantown-

Town Center
20141 Century Boulevard
Germantown, MD
301-515-4500

Days Inn Glen Burnie
6600 Ritchie Hwy
Glen Burnie, MD
410-761-8300

Extended Stay America Baltimore -
Glen Burnie
104 Chesapeake Centre Court
Glen Burnie, MD
410-761-2708

Holiday Inn Express Hotel & Suites
Hagerstown
241 Railway Lane
Hagerstown, MD
301-745-5644

Homewood Suites By Hilton
Hagerstown
1650 Pullman Lane
Hagerstown, MD
301-665-3816

Sleep Inn And Suites Hagerstown
18216 Colonel H K Douglas Dr
Hagerstown, MD
301-766-9449

Super 8 Hagerstown/Halfway
16805 Blake Road
Hagerstown, MD
301-582-1992

Super 8 Motel Hancock Md
118 Limestone Road
Hancock, MD
301-678-6101

Aloft Arundel Mills
7520 Teague Road
Hanover, MD
443-577-0077

Element Arundel Mills
7522 Teague Rd
Hanover, MD
443-577-0050

Homewood Baltimore Arundel Mills
7491-B New Ridge Road
Hanover, MD
410-878-7201

Red Roof PLUS BW Parkway
7306 Parkway Drive South
Hanover, MD
410-712-4070

Super 8 Motel - Havre De Grace

929 Pulaski Highway
Havre De Grace, MD
410-939-1880

Super 8 Indian Head
4694 Indian Head Highway
Indian Head, MD
301-753-8100

Extended Stay America Columbia -
Laurel - Ft. Meade
8550 Washington Boulevard
Jessup, MD
301-725-3877

Quality Inn Near Ft. Meade
8828 Washington Boulevard Rt. 1
Jessup, MD

410-880-3133

Red Roof Inn Washington DC
(Columbia-Jessup)
8000 Washington Boulevard
Jessup, MD

410-796-0380

Super 8 La Vale/Cumberland
1301 National Highway
La Vale, MD
301-729-6265

Econo Lodge Lavale
12310 Winchester Road, Sw
LaVale, MD
301-729-6700

Extended Stay America Washington,
D.C. - Landover
9401 Largo Drive West
Landover, MD
301-333-9139

Red Roof Inn Washington DC
Lanham Md
9050 Lanham Severn Road
Lanham, MD
301-731-8830

DoubleTree by Hilton Laurel
15101 Sweitzer Lane
Laurel, MD
301-776-5300

Red Roof Inn Washington DC -
Laurel
12525 Laurel Bowie Road
Laurel, MD

301-498-8811

Americas Best Value Inn and Suites
Lexington Park
21847 Three Notch Road
Lexington Park, MD
301-863-6666

Extended Stay America Lexington
Park - Pax River
46565 Expedition Park Drive

Lexington Park, MD

240-725-0100

Towneplace Suites Lexington Park
Patuxent River Naval Air Statio
22520 Three Notch Road
Lexington Park, MD

301-863-1111

Aloft Bwi Baltimore Washington
International Airport
1741 West Nursery Road
Linthicum, MD
410-691-6969

Candlewood Suites Baltimore -
Linthicum
1247 Winterson Road
Linthicum, MD

410-850-9214

Extended Stay America - Baltimore -
Bwi Airport - Aero Dr.
1500 Aero Drive
Linthicum, MD

410-850-0400

Hampton Inn Baltimore-Washington
International Airport
829 Elkridge Landing Rd
Linthicum, MD

410-850-0600

Staybridge Suites Baltimore Bwi
Airport
1301 Winterson Road
Linthicum, MD

410-850-5666

Towneplace Suites By Marriott
Baltimore Bwi Airport
1171 Winterson Road
Linthicum, MD

410-694-0060

Extended Stay America - Baltimore -
Bwi Airport - International
939 International Drive
Linthicum Heights, MD
410-691-2500

Holiday Inn Baltimore Bwi Airport
Area
815 Elkridge Landing Road
Linthicum Heights, MD

410-691-1000

Red Roof PLUS Baltimore
Washington DC-BWI Airport
827 Elkridge Landing Road
Linthicum Heights, MD

410-850-7600

Deep Creek Lake Resort Vacation
Rentals
23789 Garrett Highway, Suite 3
McHenry, MD
301-387-5832

WISP Resort & Conference Center
296 Marsh Hill Road
McHenry, MD

301-387-4911

The Westin National Harbor
171 Waterfront Street
National Harbor, MD
301-567-3999

Best Western North East Inn
39 Elwoods Road
North East, MD
410-287-5450

Swallow Falls Inn
1691 Swallow Falls Rd
Oakland, MD
301-387-9348

Barefoot Mailman
16 35th Street
Ocean City, MD
410-289-5343

Beach Getaways Management
4th, 5th and 8th Street Call to
Arrange
Ocean City, MD

410-289-8531

Comfort Suites Ocean City
12718 Ocean Gateway
Ocean City, MD

410-213-7171

Parrot Bay Condos
405 N Philadelphia Ave
Ocean City, MD

410-289-8531

Serene Hotel and Suites
12004 Coastal H
Ocean City, MD

410-250-4000

Combsberry - Bed And Breakfast
4837 Evergreen Rd
Oxford, MD
410-226-5353

Days Inn Perryville
61 Heather Lane
Perryville, MD
410-642-2866

Americas Best Value Inn Pocomoke
City
1540 Ocean Highway
Pocomoke, MD

410-957-3000

Econo Lodge Pocomoke City
825 Ocean Hwy.
Pocomoke City, MD
410-957-1300

Econo Lodge Princess Anne
10936 Market Lane
Princess Anne, MD
410-651-9400

Huntingfield Manor Bed & Breakfast
4928 Eastern Neck Rd
Rock Hall, MD
410-639-7779

Mariners Motel
5681 Hawthorne Avenue
Rock Hall, MD

410-639-2291

Extended Stay America - Washington
D.C. - Rockville
2621 Research Blvd
Rockville, MD
301-987-9100

Hilton Washington DC Rockville
Executive Meeting Center
1750 Rockville Pike
Rockville, MD

301-468-1100

Red Roof Plus Washington DC -
Rockville
16001 Shady Grove Road
Rockville, MD

301-987-0965

Sheraton Rockville Hotel
920 King Farm Boulevard
Rockville, MD

240-912-8200

Woodfin Suite Hotel
1380 Piccard Drive
Rockville, MD

301-590-9880

Best Western Salisbury Plaza
1735 N Salisbury Boulevard
Salisbury, MD
410-546-1300

Days Inn Salisbury
2525 N Salisbury Boulevard
Salisbury, MD

410-749-6200

La Quinta Inn & Suites Salisbury
300 South Salisbury Boulevard
Salisbury, MD

410-546-4400

Quality Inn Salisbury
2701 N. Salisbury Blvd.
Salisbury, MD

410-543-4666

Sheraton Silver Spring Hotel
8777 Georgia Avenue
Silver Spring, MD
301-589-0800

River House Inn Bed and Breakfast
201 E Market St
Snow Hill, MD
410-632-2722

Five Gables Inn and Spa
209 North Talbot Street
St Michaels, MD
410-745-0100

Inn at Perry Cabin by Belmond
308 Watkins Lane
St Michaels, MD

410-745-2200

Super 8 Thurmont
300 Tippin Drive
Thurmont, MD
301-271-7888

The Tilghman Island Inn
21384 Coopertown Road
Tilghman Island, MD
401-886-2141

Extended Stay America Baltimore -
Timonium
9704 Beaver Dam Road
Timonium, MD
410-628-1088

Red Roof PLUS Baltimore -
Timonium Fairgrounds
111 W Timonium Road
Timonium, MD

410-666-0380

Holiday Inn Express Waldorf
11370 Days Court
Waldorf, MD
301-932-9200

Best Western Westminster Catering
& Conference Center
451 Wmc Dr
Westminster, MD
410-857-1900

# Massachusetts Listings

Homewood Suites By Hilton Boston
Andover Hotel
4 Riverside Drive

Andover, MA
978-475-6000

Residence Inn By Marriott Boston
Andover
500 Minuteman Road
Andover, MA

978-683-0382

Sonesta Es Suites Boston Andover
4 Tech Drive
Andover, MA

978-686-2000

Homewood Suites By Hilton®
Boston-Billerica/Bedford
35 Middlesex Turnpike
Billerica, MA
978-670-7111

Aloft Boston Seaport
401-403 D Street
Boston, MA
617-530-1600

Best Western Plus Roundhouse
Suites
891 Massachusetts Avenue
Boston, MA

617-989-1000

Boston Harbor Hotel
70 Rowes Wharf On Atlantic Ave
Boston, MA

617-439-7000

Boston Park Plaza Hotel

Boston, MA

617-426-2000

Element Boston Seaport
391-395 D Street
Boston, MA

617-530-1700

Fairmont Copley Plaza
138 Saint James Avenue
Boston, MA

617-267-5300

Hilton Boston Downtown/Faneuil Hall
89 Broad Street
Boston, MA

617-556-0006

Hilton Boston Logan Airport
One Hotel Drive
Boston, MA

617-568-6700

Hyatt Regency Boston
One Avenue de Lafayette

Boston, MA

617-912-1234

Loews Boston Hotel
154 Berkeley Street
Boston, MA

617-266-7200

Nine Zero, A Kimpton Hotel
90 Tremont Street
Boston, MA

617-772-5800

Onyx, A Kimpton Hotel
155 Portland Street
Boston, MA

617-557-9955

Residence Inn By Marriott Boston
Harbor On Tudor Wharf
34-44 Charles River Avenue
Boston, MA

617-242-9000

Sheraton Boston Hotel
39 Dalton Street
Boston, MA

617-236-2000

Taj Boston
15 Arlington Street
Boston, MA

617-536-5700

The Eliot Hotel
370 Commonwealth Avenue
Boston, MA

617-267-1607

The Liberty A Starwood Luxury
Collection Hotel
215 Charles Street
Boston, MA

617-224-4000

The Ritz-Carlton Boston Common
10 Avery Street
Boston, MA

617-574-7100

The Westin Boston Waterfront
425 Summer Street
Boston, MA

617-532-4600

Holiday Inn Boxborough (I-495 Exit
28)
242 Adams Place
Boxborough, MA
978-263-8701

Candlewood Suites Boston-Braintree

235 Wood Rd
Braintree, MA
781-849-7450

Extended Stay America - Boston -
Braintree
20 Rockdale St.
Braintree, MA

781-356-8333

Hampton Inn Boston/Braintree
215 Wood Road
Braintree, MA

781-380-3300

Residence Inn By Marriott Brockton
124 Liberty Street
Brockton, MA
508-583-3600

Rodeway Inn Brockton
1005 Belmont Street
Brockton, MA

508-588-3333

Holiday Inn Boston-Brookline
1200 Beacon Street
Brookline, MA
617-277-1200

Candlewood Suites Burlington
Boston
130 Middlesex Turnpike
Burlington, MA
781-229-4300

Extended Stay America - Boston -
Burlington
40 South Ave.
Burlington, MA

781-359-9099

Sonesta Es Suites Boston
Burlington
11 Old Concord Road
Burlington, MA

781-221-2233

Bay Motor Inn
223 Main St
Buzzards Bay, MA
508-759-3989

Best Western Plus Hotel Tria
220 Alewife Brook Parkway
Cambridge, MA
617-491-8000

Le Meridien Cambridge-M.I.T.
20 Sidney Street
Cambridge, MA

617-577-0200

Marlowe, A Kimpton Hotel
25 Edwin H Land Boulevard

Cambridge, MA

617-868-8000

Sheraton Commander Hotel
16 Garden Street
Cambridge, MA

617-547-4800

The Charles Hotel
One Bennett Street
Cambridge, MA

617-864-1200

Brentwood Motor Inn
961 H 28
Cape Cod, MA
800-328-8812

Days Inn Springfield/Chicopee, Ma
450 Memorial Drive
Chicopee, MA
413-739-7311

Econo Lodge Chicopee
357 Burnett Rd.
Chicopee, MA

413-592-9101

Best Western At Historic Concord
740 Elm Street
Concord, MA
978-369-6100

Residence Inn By Marriott Boston
North Shore/Danvers
51 Newbury Street Route 1
Danvers, MA
978-777-7171

Towneplace Suites By Marriott
Boston North Shore/Danvers
238 Andover Street
Danvers, MA

978-777-6222

Green Harbor Cape Cod Lodging
134 Acapesket Road
East Falmouth, MA
508-548-4747

Anchorage on the Cove
450 State Hwy.
Eastham, MA
508-255-1442

Four Points By Sheraton Eastham
Cape Cod
3800 State Highway
Eastham, MA

508-255-5000

Ocean Park Inn
3900 State Highway
Eastham, MA

508-255-1132

Colonial Inn
38 North Water Street
Edgartown, MA
508-627-4711

Martha's Vineyard Vacation Homes
Call to Arrange.
Edgartown, MA

800-544-2044

Shiverick Inn
5 Pease Point Way
Edgartown, MA

508-627-3797

Comfort Inn & Suites Fall River
360 Airport Road
Fall River, MA
508-672-0011

Foley Real Estate
703 Main Street/H28
Falmouth, MA
508-548-3415

Residence Inn Foxborough
250 Foxborough Boulevard
Foxborough, MA
508-698-2800

Red Roof Inn Boston Framingham
650 Cochituate Road
Framingham, MA
508-872-4499

Sheraton Framingham Hotel
1657 Worcester Road
Framingham, MA

508-879-7200

Residence Inn By Marriott Boston
Franklin
4 Forge Parkway
Franklin, MA
508-541-8188

Super 8 Gardner
22 North Pearson Boulevard
Gardner, MA
978-630-2888

Cape Ann Motor Inn
33 Rockport Road
Gloucester, MA
978-281-2900

Quality Inn Greenfield
125 Mohawk Trail
Greenfield, MA
413-774-2211

Comfort Inn Hadley
237 Russell St.
Hadley, MA
413-584-9816

Knights Inn Hadley
208 Russell Street
Hadley, MA

413-585-1552

Best Western Merrimack Valley
401 Lowell Avenue
Haverhill, MA
978-373-1511

Hampton Inn Haverhill
106 Bank Road
Haverhill, MA

978-374-7755

Homewood Suites Holyoke-
Springfield
375 Whitney Avenue
Holyoke, MA
413-532-3100

Comfort Inn Cape Cod
1470 Iyannough Rd
Hyannis, MA
508-771-4804

Simmons Homestead Inn
288 Scudder Ave.
Hyannis Port, MA
800-637-1649

Holiday Inn Express Lawrence-
Andover
224 Winthrop Avenue
Lawrence, MA
978-975-4050

Sally's Place
160 Orchard Street
Lee, MA
413-243-1982

Seven Hills Inn
40 Plunkett Street
Lenox, MA
413-637-0060

Walker House
64 Walker Street
Lenox, MA

413-637-1271

Aloft Lexington
727 Marrett Road - A
Lexington, MA
781-761-1700

Element Lexington
727 Marret Road - B
Lexington, MA

781-761-1750

Quality Inn And Suites Lexington
440 Bedford Street
Lexington, MA

781-861-0850

Red Roof Inn - Mansfield/Foxboro
60 Forbes Boulevard
Mansfield, MA
508-339-2323

Best Western Royal Plaza Hotel And
Trade Center
181 Boston Post Road West
Marlborough, MA
508-460-0700

Courtyard By Marriott Boston
Marlborough
75 Felton Street
Marlborough, MA

508-480-0015

Embassy Suites Hotel
Boston/Marlborough
123 Boston Post Road West
Marlborough, MA

508-485-5900

Extended Stay America - Boston -
Marlborough
19 Northboro Rd East
Marlborough, MA

508-490-9911

Residence Inn By Marriott Boston
Marlborough
112 Donald Lynch Boulevard
Marlborough, MA

508-481-1500

Days Hotel And Conference Center
159 Pelham Street
Methuen, MA
978-686-2971

Days Inn Middleboro
30 East Clark Street
Middleboro, MA
508-946-4400

Holiday Inn Express Milford
50 Fortune Boulevard
Milford, MA
508-634-1054

Brass Lantern Inn
11 North Water Street
Nantucket, MA
508-228-4064

Quidnuck Vacation Rental
Call to Arrange.
Nantucket, MA

202-663-8439

Safe Harbor Guest House
2 Harbor View Way
Nantucket, MA

508-228-3222

Dog-Friendly Lodging - Please always call ahead to make sure an establishment is still dog-friendly.

The Cottages and Lofts at the Boat Basin
24 Old South Wharf
Nantucket, MA

508-325-1499

The Cottages at Nantucket Boat Basin
24 Old South Wharf
Nantucket, MA

508-325-1499

Crowne Plaza Boston - Natick
1360 Worcester Street
Natick, MA
508-653-8800

Sheraton Needham Hotel
100 Cabot Street
Needham, MA
781-444-1110

Captain Haskell's Octagon House
347 Union Street
New Bedford, MA
508-999-3933

New Bedford Inn and Suites
500 Hathaway Road
New Bedford, MA

508-997-1231

Hotel Indigo Boston - Newton Riverside
399 Grove Street
Newton, MA
617-969-5300

The Porches Inn at Mass MoCA
231 River Street.
North Adams, MA
413-664-0400

Residence Inn By Marriott New Bedford Dartmouth
181 Faunce Corner Road
North Dartmouth, MA
508-984-5858

The Provincetown Inn
1 Commercial Street
North Truro, MA
508-487-9500

Econo Lodge Inn & Suites Northborough
380 Southwest Cutoff
Northborough, MA
508-842-8941

Extended Stay America - Foxboro - Norton
280 S. Washington Street
Norton, MA
508-285-7800

Residence Inn Boston Norwood
275 Norwood Park South
Norwood, MA
781-278-9595

Martha's Vineyard Surfside Hotel
7 Oak Bluffs Avenue
Oak Bluffs, MA
508-693-2500

Extended Stay America - Boston - Peabody
200 Jubilee Dr
Peabody, MA
978-531-6632

Homewood Suites By Hilton®
Boston-Peabody
57 Newbury Street
Peabody, MA

978-536-5050

Hampton Inn & Suites Plymouth
10 Plaza Way
Plymouth, MA
508-747-5000

BayShore on the Water
493 Commercial Street
Provincetown, MA
508-487-9133

Cape Inn Resort
698-716 Commercial Street
Provincetown, MA

508-487-1711

Crowne Pointe Historic Inn & Spa
82 Bradford Street
Provincetown, MA

508-487-6767

Surfside Hotel and Suites
543 Commercial Street
Provincetown, MA

508-487-1726

The Provincetown Hotel at Gabriel's
102 Bradford Street
Provincetown, MA

508-487-3232

The Sandpiper Beach House
165 Commercial Street
Provincetown, MA

508-487-1928

White Wind Inn
174 Commercial St
Provincetown, MA

508-487-1526

Quality Inn Raynham
164 New State Hwy Rt 44 1 Mi
Raynham, MA

508-824-8647

Comfort Inn & Suites Logan International Airport
85 American Legion Highway
Revere, MA
781-485-3600

Hawthorne Hotel
18 Washington Square West
Salem, MA
978-744-4080

Stephen Daniels House
1 Daniels Street
Salem, MA

978-744-5709

Sandwich Lodge
54 Route 6a
Sandwich, MA
508-888-2275

The Earl of Sandwich Motor Manor
378 Rt 6A
Sandwich, MA

508-888-1415

Red Roof Plus Boston - Logan
920 Broadway
Saugus, MA
781-941-1400

Comfort Inn Seekonk
341 Highland Avenue
Seekonk, MA
508-336-7900

Birch Hill Bed and Breakfast
254 S Undermountain Road/H 41
Sheffield, MA
413-229-2143

Econo Lodge Hyannis
59 East Main St
Sheffield, MA

413-229-2129

Riverview Inn & Suites
1878 Wilbur Ave
Somerset, MA
508-678-4545

Red Roof PLUS+ South Deerfield
9 Greenfield Road
South Deerfield, MA
413-665-7161

Red Roof Inn Boston - Southborough/Worcester
367 Turnpike Road
Southborough, MA
508-481-3904

Vienna Historic Inn
14 South Street
Southbridge, MA

508-764-0700

Sheraton Springfield Monarch Place
Hotel
1 Monarch Place
Springfield, MA
413-781-1010

The Red Lion Inn
30 Main Street
Stockbridge, MA
413-298-5545

Days Inn Sturbridge
400 Route 15
Sturbridge, MA
508-347-1978

Super 8 Sturbridge
358 Main Street
Sturbridge, MA

508-347-9000

Extended Stay America - Boston -
Tewksbury
1910 Andover St.
Tewksbury, MA
978-863-9888

Towneplace Suites By Marriott
Boston Tewksbury/Andover
20 International Place
Tewksbury, MA

978-863-9800

Mansion House
9 Main Street
Vineyard Haven, MA
508-693-2200

Martha's Vineyard Rental Houses
Call to Arrange.
Vineyard Haven, MA

508-693-6222

Four Points By Sheraton Wakefield
Boston Hotel & Conference Ctr
One Audubon Road
Wakefield, MA
781-245-9300

Courtyard By Marriott Boston
Waltham
387 Winter Street
Waltham, MA
781-419-0900

Extended Stay America - Boston -
Waltham - 52 4th Ave
52 Fourth Ave.
Waltham, MA

781-890-1333

Holiday Inn Express Waltham
385 Winter Street
Waltham, MA

781-890-2800

The Westin Waltham Boston
70 Third Avenue
Waltham, MA

781-290-5600

Candlewood Suites-West Springfield
572 Riverdale Street
West Springfield, MA
413-739-1122

Hampton Inn West Springfield
1011 Riverdale Street
West Springfield, MA

413-732-1300

Quality Inn West Springfield
1150 Riverdale Street
West Springfield, MA

413-739-7261

Red Roof Plus+ West Springfield
1254 Riverdale Street
West Springfield, MA

413-731-1010

Econo Lodge Hyannis
59 East Main St
West Yarmouth, MA
508-771-0699

Extended Stay America - Boston -
Westborough - Connector Road
19 Connector Rd.
Westborough, MA
508-616-0155

Quality Inn Westfield
2 Southampton Road
Westfield, MA
413-568-2821

Rodeway Inn Westminster
183 Main Street
Westminster, MA
978-874-5951

Clover Hill Farm
249 Adams Rd
Williamstown, MA
413-458-3376

Cozy Corner Motel
284 Sand Spring Road
Williamstown, MA

413-458-8006

Best Western Plus New Englander
1 Rainin Road
Woburn, MA
781-935-8160

Hilton Boston Woburn
2 Forbes Road

Woburn, MA

781-932-0999

Red Roof Plus Boston - Woburn
19 Commerce Way
Woburn, MA

781-935-7110

Quality Inn & Suites Worcester
50 Oriol Drive
Worcester, MA
508-852-2800

Colonial House Inn and Restaurant
277 Main Street Route 6a
Yarmouth, MA
508-347-3313

Colonial House
Old Kings Hwy
Yarmouth Port, MA
508-362-4348

# Michigan Listings

Linda's Lighthouse Inn
5965 Pointe Tremble Road/H 29
Algonac, MI
810-794-2992

Castle in the Country
340 H 40S
Allegan, MI
269-673-8054

Best Western Greenfield Inn
3000 Enterprise Drive
Allen Park, MI
313-271-1600

Petticoat Inn
2454 W Monroe Road/H 46
Alma, MI
989-681-5728

Days Inn Alpena
1496 M-32 West
Alpena, MI
989-356-6118

Sanctuary Inn And Conference
Center
1000 Us 23 North
Alpena, MI

989-356-2151

Candlewood Suites-Detroit Ann Arbor
701 Waymarket Way
Ann Arbor, MI
734-663-2818

Comfort Inn & Suites Ann Arbor
2376 Carpenter Road
Ann Arbor, MI

734-477-9977

Dog-Friendly Lodging - Please always call ahead to make sure an establishment is still dog-friendly.

Days Inn Ann Arbor
2380 Carpenter Road
Ann Arbor, MI

734-971-0700

Extended Stay America - Detroit -
Ann Arbor - Briarwood Mall
1501 Briarwood Circle Drive
Ann Arbor, MI

734-332-1980

Holiday Inn Ann Arbor-Near The
Univ. Of Mi
3600 Plymouth Road
Ann Arbor, MI

734-769-9800

Red Roof Inn Ann Arbor University
South
3505 S. State Street
Ann Arbor, MI

734-665-3500

Red Roof Inn Plus Ann Arbor Univ Of
Michigan North
3621 Plymouth Road
Ann Arbor, MI

734-996-5800

Residence Inn Ann Arbor
800 Victors Way
Ann Arbor, MI

734-996-5666

Crystal Inn Hotel - Suites
4955 South Garfield Road
Auburn, MI
989-662-7888

Extended Stay America - Detroit -
Auburn Hills - I -75
1180 Doris Road
Auburn Hills, MI
248-373-1355

Extended Stay America - Detroit -
Auburn Hills - University Dr
3315 University Drive
Auburn Hills, MI

248-340-8888

Hilton Suites Auburn Hills
2300 Featherstone Road
Auburn Hills, MI

248-334-2222

Sonesta Es Suites Detroit Auburn
Hills
2050 Featherstone Road
Auburn Hills, MI

248-322-4600

Baymont Inn & Suites Battle Creek
4725 Beckley Road
Battle Creek, MI
269-979-5400

Econo Lodge Battle Creek
165 Capital Ave S W
Battle Creek, MI

269-965-3976

Knights Inn Battle Creek Mi
2595 Capital Avenue Southwest
Battle Creek, MI

269-964-2600

Red Roof Inn & Suites Battle Creek
5050 Beckley Road
Battle Creek, MI

269-979-1100

Travelodge Of Battle Creek
5395 Beckley Road
Battle Creek, MI

269-979-1828

Travelodge Of Battle Creek
5395 Beckley Road
Battle Creek, MI

269-979-1828

Americinn Bay City
3915 3 Mile Road
Bay City, MI
989-671-0071

Holiday Inn Express Hotel & Suites
Bay City
3959 Traxler Court
Bay City, MI

989-667-3800

Comfort Inn Belleville
45945 South I-94 Service Drive
Belleville, MI
734-697-8556

Holiday Inn Express Hotel & Suites
Belleville (Airport Area)
46194 North I-94 Service Drive
Belleville, MI

734-857-6200

Red Roof Inn Detroit Metro Airport
West
45501 North I-94 Service Dr
Belleville, MI

734-697-2244

Red Roof Inn Benton Harbor - St.
Joseph
1630 Mall Drive
Benton Harbor, MI
269-927-2484

Bluffs Inn - Ironwood
707 West Us Hwy 2
Bessemer, MI
906-667-0311

Best Western Scenic Hill Resort
1400 Us Highway 31
Beulah, MI
231-882-7754

Quality Inn & Suites Big Rapids
1705 South State Street
Big Rapids, MI
231-592-5150

Americas Best Value Inn
9235 East Birch Run Road
Birch Run, MI
989-624-4440

Best Western Of Birch
Run/Frankenmuth
9087 E Birch Run Road
Birch Run, MI

989-624-9395

Holiday Inn Express Birch Run
12150 Dixie Highway
Birch Run, MI

989-624-9300

Insel Haus
HCR 1, Box 157
Bois Blanc Island, MI
231-634-7393

Baymont Inn & Suites
Bridgeport/Frankenmuth
6460 Dixie Hwy
Bridgeport, MI
989-777-3000

Courtyard By Marriott Detroit Brighton
7799 Conference Center Drive
Brighton, MI
810-225-9200

Dewey Lake Manor
11811 Laird Road
Brooklyn, MI
517-467-7122

Evergreen Resort
7880 Mackinaw Trail
Cadillac, MI
231-775-9947

Days Inn Canton
40500 Michigan Avenue
Canton, MI
734-721-5200

Extended Stay America - Detroit -
Canton
2000 Haggerty Road
Canton, MI

734-844-6725

Super 8 Canton/Livonia Area
3933 Lotz Road
Canton, MI

734-722-8880

Charlevoix Inn & Suites
800 Petoskey Ave.
Charlevoix, MI
231-547-0300

Lodge
120 Michigan Avenue
Charlevoix, MI

231-547-6565

Pointes North Inn By Resort Bookings
101 Michigan Avenue
Charlevoix, MI

231-547-0055

Best Western River Terrace
847 South Main Street
Cheboygan, MI
231-627-5688

Comfort Inn Chelsea
1645 Commerce Park Drive
Chelsea, MI
734-433-8000

Waterloo Gardens
7600 Werkener Road
Chelsea, MI

734-433-1612

Best Western Plus Coldwater Hotel
630 East Chicago Street
Coldwater, MI
517-279-0900

Comfort Inn & Suites Coldwater
1000 Orleans Boulevard
Coldwater, MI

517-278-2017

Red Roof Inn Coldwater
348 S Willowbrook Rd
Coldwater, MI

517-279-1199

Super 8 Coldwater
600 Orleans Boulevard
Coldwater, MI

517-278-8833

Extended Stay America - Detroit -
Dearborn
260 Town Center Drive
Dearborn, MI
313-336-0021

Red Roof Inn Dearborn
24130 Michigan Avenue

Dearborn, MI

313-278-9732

THE HENRY, AUTOGRAPH
COLLECTION, A Marriott Luxury &
Lifestyle Hotel
300 Town Center Drive
Dearborn, MI

313-441-2000

THE HENRY, AUTOGRAPH
COLLECTION, A Marriott Luxury &
Lifestyle Hotel
300 Town Center Drive
Dearborn, MI

313-441-2000

Towneplace Suites By Marriott
Dearborn
6141 Mercury Drive
Dearborn, MI

313-271-0200

Holiday Inn Express Downtown
Detroit
1020 Washington Boulevard
Detroit, MI
313-887-7000

Drummond Island Resort &
Conference Center
33494 S Maxton Road
Drummond Island, MI
906-493-1000

H & H Resort
33185 S Water Street
Drummond Island, MI

800-543-4743

Days Inn & Suites Dundee
130 Outer Dr Us 23 &; M-50
Dundee, MI
734-529-5505

Quality Inn Dundee
111 Waterstradt Commerce Drive
Dundee, MI

734-529-5240

Hampton Inn East Lansing
2500 Coolidge Road
East Lansing, MI
517-324-2072

Towneplace Suites East Lansing
2855 Hannah Boulevard
East Lansing, MI

517-203-1000

Extended Stay America - Detroit -
Farmington Hills
27775 Stansbury Boulevard
Farmington Hills, MI
248-473-4000

Hawthorn Suites By Wyndham Detroit
Farmington Hills
37555 Hills Tech Drive
Farmington Hills, MI

248-324-0540

Red Roof Inn Detroit - Farmington
Hills
24300 Sinacola Court Ne
Farmington Hills, MI

248-478-8640

Glenn Country Inn
1286 64th Street
Fennville, MI
888-237-3009

Sleep Inn Flat Rock
29101 Commerce Drive
Flat Rock, MI
734-782-9898

Baymont Inn & Suites Flint
4160 Pier North Boulevard
Flint, MI
810-732-2300

Holiday Inn Express Flint-Campus
Area
1150 Robert T. Longway Boulevard
Flint, MI

810-238-7744

Red Roof Inn Flint - Bishop Airport
G - 3219 Miller Road
Flint, MI

810-733-1660

Residence Inn Flint
2202 West Hill Road
Flint, MI

810-424-7000

Super 8 Burton/Flint
1343 South Center Road
Flint, MI

810-743-8850

Drury Inn & Suites Frankenmuth
260 South Main Street
Frankenmuth, MI
989-652-2800

Valentine's Bay Lodge
8191 H 183
Garden, MI
906-644-5012

Baymont Inn & Suites Gaylord
510 South Wisconsin Avenue
Gaylord, MI
989-731-6331

Quality Inn Gaylord

137 West St.
Gaylord, MI

989-732-7541

Norway Pines Motel
7111 US 2, 41 and M-35
Gladstone, MI
906-786-5119

131 Hotel-Plaza
255 28th Street Sw
Grand Rapids, MI
616-241-6444

Best Western Hospitality Hotel &
Suites
5500 28th Street Se
Grand Rapids, MI

616-949-8400

Clarion Inn And Suites Grand Rapids
4981 28th Street Southeast
Grand Rapids, MI

616-956-9304

Comfort Inn Airport Grand Rapids
4155 28th Street Southeast
Grand Rapids, MI

616-957-2080

Econo Lodge & Suites
2985 Kraft Avenue Southeast
Grand Rapids, MI

616-940-1777

Holiday Inn Express Hotel & Suites
Grand Rapids Airport
5401 28th Street Court Se
Grand Rapids, MI

616-940-8100

Holiday Inn Grand Rapids Downtown
310 Pearl Street Nw
Grand Rapids, MI

616-235-7611

Holiday Inn Grand Rapids Downtown
310 Pearl Street Nw
Grand Rapids, MI

616-235-7611

Homewood Suites By Hilton Grand
Rapids
3920 Stahl Drive Se
Grand Rapids, MI

616-285-7100

Homewood Suites By Hilton Grand
Rapids
3920 Stahl Drive Se
Grand Rapids, MI

616-285-7100

Motel 6 Grand Rapids Airport
4855 28th Street Southeast
Grand Rapids, MI

616-957-3000

Red Roof Inn Grand Rapids
5131 28th Street South East
Grand Rapids, MI

616-942-0800

Riverfront Hotel-Grand Rapids
270 Ann Street Northwest
Grand Rapids, MI

616-363-9001

Sleep Inn And Suites Grand Rapids
4284 29th Street Southeast
Grand Rapids, MI

616-975-9000

Staybridge Suites Grand Rapids
3000 Lake Eastbrook Boulevard
Southeast
Grand Rapids, MI

616-464-3200

Residence Inn Grand Rapids West
3451 Rivertown Point Court Sw
Grandville, MI
616-538-1100

Days Inn Grayling
2556 Business Loop South
Grayling, MI
989-344-0204

Ramada Grayling Conference
Center
2650 I-75 Business Loop
Grayling, MI

989-348-7611

Super 8 Grayling
5828 Nelson A. Miles Parkway
Grayling, MI

989-348-8888

Birchwood Inn
7077 S. Lake Shore Dr.
Harbor Springs, MI
231-526-2151

Comfort Inn Hart
2248 North Comfort Drive
Hart, MI
231-873-3456

Best Western Of Hartland
10087 M-59
Hartland, MI
810-632-7177

Days Inn Holland

717 Hastings Avenue
Holland, MI
616-392-7001

Microtel Inn & Suites By Wyndham
Holland
643 Hastings Avenue
Holland, MI

616-392-3235

Residence Inn By Marriott Holland
631 Southpointe Ridge Road
Holland, MI

616-393-6900

Holiday Inn Express Houghton-
Keweenaw
1110 Century Way
Houghton, MI
906-482-1066

Travelodge Houghton
215 Shelden Avenue
Houghton, MI

906-482-1400

Baymont Inn & Suites
Howell/Brighton
4120 Lambert Drive
Howell, MI
517-546-0712

Magnuson Hotel Howell
1500 Pinckney Rd.
Howell, MI

517-548-2900

Quality Inn Hudsonville
3301 Highland Drive
Hudsonville, MI
616-662-4000

Travelodge Hudsonville
3005 Corporate Grove Drive
Hudsonville, MI

616-896-6710

Days Inn Imlay City
6692 Newark Road
Imlay City, MI
810-724-8005

Super 8 Imlay City
6951 Newark Road
Imlay City, MI

810-724-8700

Super 8 Ionia Mi
7245 South State Road
Ionia, MI
616-527-2828

Comfort Inn Iron Mountain
1565 North Stephenson Avenue
Iron Mountain, MI

Dog-Friendly Lodging - Please always call ahead to make sure an establishment is still dog-friendly.

906-774-5505

Days Inn Iron Mountain
2001 South Stephenson Avenue
Iron Mountain, MI

906-774-2181

Super 8 Iron Mountain
2702 North Stephenson Avenue
Iron Mountain, MI

906-774-3400

Magnuson Country Inn Ishpeming
850 Us Highway 41 West
Ishpeming, MI
906-485-6345

Baymont Inn & Suites Jackson
2035 Bondsteel Drive
Jackson, MI
517-789-6000

Hampton Inn Jackson
2225 Shirley Drive
Jackson, MI

517-789-5151

Baymont Inn And Suites Kalamazoo
2203 South 11th Street
Kalamazoo, MI
269-372-7999

Candlewood Suites Kalamazoo
3443 Retail Place Drive
Kalamazoo, MI

269-270-3203

Econo Lodge Kalamazoo
3750 Easy Street
Kalamazoo, MI

269-388-3551

Four Points By Sheraton Kalamazoo
3600 East Cork Street Court
Kalamazoo, MI

269-385-3922

Holiday Inn Kalamazoo West
2747 South 11th Street
Kalamazoo, MI

269-375-6000

Quality Inn Kalamazoo
3820 Sprinkle Road
Kalamazoo, MI

269-381-7000

Red Roof Inn Kalamazoo East
3701 East Cork Street
Kalamazoo, MI

3826350

Red Roof Inn Kalamazoo West -

Western Michigan U
5425 West Michigan Avenue
Kalamazoo, MI

269-375-7400

Residence Inn By Marriott
Kalamazoo East
1500 East Kilgore Road
Kalamazoo, MI

269-349-0855

Staybridge Suites Kalamazoo
2001 Seneca Lane
Kalamazoo, MI

269-372-8000

Super 8 Kalamazoo
618 Maple Hill Drive
Kalamazoo, MI

269-345-0146

Towneplace Suites By Marriott
Kalamazoo
5683 South 9th Street
Kalamazoo, MI

269-353-1500

Extended Stay America - Grand
Rapids - Kentwood
3747 29th Street Southeast
Kentwood, MI
616-977-6750

Crooked Lake Resort and Bait Shop
8071 Mystic Lake Drive
Lake, MI
989-544-2383

The White Rabbit Inn
14634 Red Arrow H
Lakeside, MI
269-469-4620

Comfort Inn Lansing
525 North Canal Road
Lansing, MI
517-627-8381

Courtyard By Marriott Lansing
2710 Lake Lansing Road
Lansing, MI

517-482-0500

Quality Suites Lansing
901 Delta Commerce Drive
Lansing, MI

517-886-0600

Ramada Lansing Hotel And
Conference Center
7501 West Saginaw Highway
Lansing, MI

517-627-3211

Red Roof Inn Lansing East -
Michigan State University
3615 Dunckel Road
Lansing, MI

517-332-2575

Red Roof Inn Lansing West
7412 West Saginaw Highway
Lansing, MI

517-321-7246

Residence Inn West Lansing
922 Delta Commerce Drive
Lansing, MI

517-886-5030

Super 8 Lansing
910 American Road
Lansing, MI

517-393-8008

Residence Inn Livonia
17250 Fox Drive
Livonia, MI
734-462-4201

Towneplace Suites By Marriott
Livonia
17450 Fox Drive
Livonia, MI

734-542-7400

Americas Best Value Inn - Ludington
5095 West Us 10
Ludington, MI
231-843-2233

Candlelight Inn
709 E Ludington Avenue/H 10
Ludington, MI

231-845-8074

Holiday Inn Express Ludington
5323 W. Us 10
Ludington, MI

231-845-7004

Nader's Lake Shore Motor Lodge
612 N Lakeshore Dr
Ludington, MI

231-843-8757

Super 8 Luna Pier/Monroe/Toledo
Area
4163 Super 8 Drive
Luna Pier, MI
734-848-8880

Comfort Inn & Suites and Conference
Center
2424 South Mission Street
Mackinac Island, MI
231-881-3343

Harbor Place Studio Suites
7439 Main Street
Mackinac Island, MI

800-626-6304

Mission Point Resort
One Lakeshore Drive
Mackinac Island, MI

906-847-3312

Baymont Inn And Suites Mackinaw City
109 South Nicolet Street
Mackinaw City, MI
231-436-7737

Econo Lodge Mackinaw City
712 S. Huron
Mackinaw City, MI

231-436-5777

Knights Inn Mackinaw City
412 North Nicolet Street
Mackinaw City, MI

231-436-5026

Super 8 Mackinaw City/Beachfront Area
519 South Huro
Mackinaw City, MI

231-436-7111

Extended Stay America - Detroit - Madison Heights
32690 Stephenson Highway
Madison Heights, MI
248-583-5522

Red Roof Inn Detroit Royal Oak
Madison Heights
32511 Concord Dr
Madison Heights, MI

248-583-4700

Residence Inn Troy Southeast
32650 Stephenson Hwy
Madison Heights, MI

248-583-4322

Econo Lodge Lakeside
2050 South Us 41
Marquette, MI
906-225-1305

Ramada Inn Marquette
412 West Washington Street
Marquette, MI

906-228-6000

Arbor Inn
15435 W Michigan Avenue
Marshall, MI
269-781-7772

Comfort Inn Marshall
204 Winston Drive
Marshall, MI

269-789-7890

Holiday Inn Express Marshall
329 Sam Hill Drive
Marshall, MI

269-789-9301

Mendon Country Inn
440 E Main Street/H 60
Mendon, MI
269-496-8132

Econo Lodge On The Bay
2516 10th Street
Menominee, MI
906-863-4431

Baymont Inn & Suites Midland
2200 West Wackerly Street
Midland, MI
517-631-0070

Best Western Valley Plaza Inn
5221 Bay City Road
Midland, MI

989-496-2700

Sleep Inn Midland
2100 West Wackerly Street
Midland, MI

989-837-1010

Sleep Inn & Suites Milan
1230 Dexter St
Milan, MI
734-439-1400

Baymont Inn Monroe
14774 la Plaisance Road
Monroe, MI
734-384-1600

Knights Inn - Monroe
1250 North Dixie Highway
Monroe, MI

734-243-0597

Comfort Inn & Suites and Conference Center
2424 South Mission Street
Mount Pleasant, MI
989-772-4000

Super 8 Mt. Pleasant
2323 S Mission St
Mount Pleasant, MI

989-773-8888

Americas Best Value Inn - Marquette
1010 State Highway M-28 East
Munising, MI

906-387-2493

Holiday Inn Express Munising-Lakeview
E8990 M-28
Munising, MI

906-387-4800

AmericInn Charlevoix
11800 US 31 North
N Charlevoix, MI
231-237-0988

New Buffalo Inn and Spa
231 E Buffalo Street/H 12
New Buffalo, MI
269-469-1000

The Rainbow Lodge
9706 County Road 423
Newberry, MI
906-658-3357

Extended Stay America - Detroit - Novi - Haggerty Road
21555 Haggerty Road
Novi, MI
248-305-9955

Residence Inn By Marriott Detroit Novi
27477 Cabaret Drive
Novi, MI

248-735-7400

Sheraton Detroit Novi
21111 Haggerty Road
Novi, MI

248-349-4000

Towneplace Suites Detroit Novi
42600 Eleven Mile Rd
Novi, MI

248-305-5533

Comfort Inn Okemos
2187 University Park Drive
Okemos, MI
517-347-6690

Holiday Inn Express & Suites Lansing-Okemos (Msu Area)
2209 University Park Drive
Okemos, MI

517-349-8700

Staybridge Suites Lansing-Okemos
3553 Meridian Crossing
Okemos, MI

517-347-3044

Comfort Inn & Suites Paw Paw
153 Ampey Road
Paw Paw, MI
269-655-0303

Econo Lodge Paw Paw
139 Ampey Road
Paw Paw, MI

269-657-2578

Comfort Inn Petoskey
1314 Us 31 North
Petoskey, MI
231-347-3220

Grace Grange Lodge and Stable
8000 Newson Road
Petoskey, MI

231-347-5869

Red Roof Inn Plymouth
39700 Ann Arbor Road
Plymouth, MI
734-459-3300

Baymont Inn & Suites Port Huron
1611 Range Road
Port Huron, MI
810-364-8000

Comfort Inn Port Huron
1700 Yeager Street
Port Huron, MI

810-982-5500

Days Inn Port Huron
2908 Pine Grove Avenue
Port Huron, MI

810-984-1522

East Bay Lakefront Lodge
125 Twelfth Street P.o. Box 914
Prudenville, MI
989-366-5910

Red Roof Inn Detroit Auburn Hills
Rochester Hills
2580 Crooks Road
Rochester Hills, MI
248-853-6400

Baymont Inn & Suites Detroit Airport
Romulus
9000 Wickham Road
Romulus, MI
734-722-6000

Extended Stay America - Detroit -
Metropolitan Airport
30325 Flynn Drive
Romulus, MI

734-722-7780

Rodeway Inn Metro Airport
8500 Wickham Rd.
Romulus, MI

734-595-1990

Days Inn And Suites Roseville

31327 Gratiot Avenue
Roseville, MI
586-294-0400

Extended Stay America Detroit -
Roseville
20200 Thirteen Mile Road
Roseville, MI

586-294-0141

Holiday Inn Express Hotel & Suites
Roseville
31900 Little Mack Avenue
Roseville, MI

586-285-5800

Microtel Inn & Suites By Wyndham
Roseville/Detroit Area
20313 13 Mile Road
Roseville, MI

586-415-1000

Red Roof Inn Detroit St. Clair
Shores
31800 Little Mack Road
Roseville, MI

586-296-0310

Comfort Suites Saginaw
5180 Fashion Square Boulevard
Saginaw, MI
989-797-8000

Knights Inn Saginaw
2225 Tittabawassee Road
Saginaw, MI

989-791-1411

Quality Inn Saint Ignace
561 Boulevard Drive
Saint Ignace, MI
906-643-9700

Comfort Inn Sault Sainte Marie
4404 I-75 Business Spur
Sault Sainte Marie, MI
906-635-1118

Best Value Inn
3411 I-75 Business Spur
Sault Ste Marie, MI
906-635-9190

Days Inn Sault Ste Marie
3651 I-75 Business Spur
Sault Ste Marie, MI

906-635-5200

Ramada Plaza Hotel Ojibway
240 West Portage
Sault Ste Marie, MI

906-632-4100

Americas Best Value Inn
3826 I-75 Business Spur

Sault Ste. Marie, MI
906-632-8882

Comfort Suites South Haven
1755 Phoenix Street
South Haven, MI
269-639-2014

Candlewood Suites Detroit Southfield
1 Corporate Drive
Southfield, MI
248-945-0010

Extended Stay America - Detroit -
Southfield - I-696
26250 American Drive
Southfield, MI

248-355-2115

Extended Stay America - Detroit -
Southfield - Northwestern High
28500 Northwestern Highway
Southfield, MI

248-213-4500

Red Roof Inn Detroit - Southfield
27660 Northwestern Highway
Southfield, MI

248-353-7200

Holiday Inn Grand Haven-Spring
Lake
940 West Savidge Street
Spring Lake, MI
616-846-1000

Quality Inn Saint Ignace
561 Boulevard Drive
St Ignace, MI
906-643-9700

Americas Best Value Inn & Suites
Benton Harbor
798 Ferguson Drive
St Joseph, MI
269-927-1172

Extended Stay America - Detroit -
Sterling Heights
33400 Van Dyke Road
Sterling Heights, MI
586-983-3773

Towneplace Suites By Marriott
Sterling Heights
14800 Lakeside Circle
Sterling Heights, MI

586-566-0900

Baymont Inn & Suites St. Joseph -
Stevensville
2601 West Marquette Woods Road
Stevensville, MI
269-428-9111

Tawas Motel
1124 W. Lake St.

Dog-Friendly Lodging - Please always call ahead to make sure an establishment is still dog-friendly.

Tawas City, MI
989-362-3822

Red Roof Inn Detroit Southwest
Taylor
21230 Eureka Road
Taylor, MI
734-374-1150

Super 8 Taylor Detroit Area
15101 Huron St.
Taylor, MI
734-283-8830

Crystal Mountain
12500 Crystal Mountain Drive
Thompsonville, MI
800-968-7686

Best Western Four Seasons
305 Munson Avenue
Traverse City, MI
231-946-8424

Blue Lakes Vacation Rentals
3704 Avery Trail
Traverse City, MI
231-632-0833

Boarders Inn Traverse City
1870 Us 31 North
Traverse City, MI
231-938-1887

Country Inn & Suites Of Traverse City
420 Munson Avenue
Traverse City, MI
231-941-0208

Econo Lodge Traverse City
1065 M-37 South
Traverse City, MI
231-943-3040

Quality Inn By The Bay
1492 Us 31 North
Traverse City, MI
231-929-4423

Traverse City Travelodge
704 Munson Avenue
Traverse City, MI
231-922-9111

Best Western Woodhaven Inn
21700 West Road
Trenton, MI
734-676-8000

Candlewood Suites Detroit-Troy
2550 Troy Center Dr
Troy, MI
248-269-6600

Drury Inn & Suites Troy
575 W Big Beaver Road
Troy, MI
248-528-3330

Red Roof Inn Detroit Troy
2350 Rochester Court
Troy, MI
248-689-4391

Staybridge Suites Detroit-Utica
46155 Utica Park Blvd.
Utica, MI
586-323-0101

Quality Inn Walker Grand Rapids North
2171 Holton Court
Walker, MI
616-791-8500

Candlewood Suites Detroit Warren
7010 Convention Boulevard
Warren, MI
586-978-1261

Red Roof Inn Detroit - Warren
26300 Dequindre Road
Warren, MI
586-573-4300

Residence Inn Detroit Warren
30120 Civic Center Blvd
Warren, MI
586-558-8050

Quality Inn & Suites Waterford
7076 Highland Road
Waterford, MI
248-666-8555

The Wren's Nest
7405 W Maple Street
West Bloomfield, MI
248-624-6874

Best Western Of Whitmore Lake
9897 Main Street
Whitmore Lake, MI
734-449-2058

The Knollwood Motel
5777 H 31N
Williamsburg, MI
231-938-2040

Super 8 Motel - Wyoming/Grand Rapids Area
727 44th St Sw
Wyoming, MI
616-530-8588

# Minnesota Listings

Best Western Plus Albert Lea I-90/I-

35 Hotel
821 E Plaza Street
Albert Lea, MN
507-373-4000

Best Western Alexandria Inn
508 Twin Boulevard
Alexandria, MN
320-762-5161

Holiday Inn Alexandria
5637 Highway 29 South
Alexandria, MN
320-763-6577

Super 8 Alexandria MN
4620 Hwy 29 S
Alexandria, MN
320-763-6552

Holiday Inn Austin
1701 4th Street Northwest
Austin, MN
507-433-1000

Rodeway Inn & Suites Austin
805 21st Street Northeast
Austin, MN
507-433-9254

Super 8 Austin
1401 14th Street Northwest
Austin, MN
507-433-1801

The Westin Minneapolis

Babbitt, MN
218-827-3682

Country Inn And Suites Baxter
15058 Dellwood Drive
Baxter, MN
218-828-2161

Rodeway Inn Baxter
7836 Fairview Road
Baxter, MN
218-829-0391

Super 8 Baxter/Brainerd Area
14341 Edgewood Drive
Baxter, MN
218-828-4288

Super 8 Becker
13804 First Street
Becker, MN
763-262-8880

Best Western Bemidji Inn
2420 Paul Bunyan Drive Northwest
Bemidji, MN
218-751-0390

124

Holiday Inn Express Bemidji
2422 Ridgeway Avenue, Northwest
Bemidji, MN

218-751-2487

Quality Inn Bemidji
3500 Moberg Dr. Nw
Bemidji, MN

218-444-7700

Days Inn Bloomington
7851 Normandale Boulevard
Bloomington, MN
952-835-7400

Extended Stay America - Minneapolis
- Bloomington
7956 Lyndale Ave. S
Bloomington, MN

952-884-1400

Hilton Minneapolis Bloomington
3900 American Boulevard West
Bloomington, MN

952-893-9500

Hilton Minneapolis St. Paul Airport
Mall Of America
3800 American Boulevard East
Bloomington, MN

952-854-2100

Homewood Suites By HiltonÂ®
Minneapolis-Mall Of America
2261 Killebrew Drive
Bloomington, MN

952-854-0900

Residence Inn by Marriott
Bloomington by Mall of America
7850 Bloomington Ave South
Bloomington, MN

952-876-0900

Staybridge Suites Minneapolis-
Bloomington
5150 American Blvd West
Bloomington, MN

952-831-7900

Super 8 Bloomington/Airport
7800 2nd Avenue South
Bloomington, MN

952-888-8800

Americas Best Value Inn Brainerd
11617 Andrew Street
Brainerd, MN
218-828-0027

Days Inn Brooklyn Center
6415 James Circle North
Brooklyn Center, MN

763-561-8400

Extended Stay America -
Minneapolis - Brooklyn Center
2701 Freeway Boulevard
Brooklyn Center, MN

763-549-5571

Quality Inn Brooklyn Center
1600 James Circle North
Brooklyn Center, MN

763-560-7464

Super 8 Brooklyn Center/Mpls
6445 James Circle
Brooklyn Center, MN

763-566-9810

Super 8 Buffalo
303 10th Ave S
Buffalo, MN
763-682-5930

Americinn & Suites Burnsville
14331 Nicollet Court
Burnsville, MN
952-892-1900

Norwood Inn & Suites
12920 Aldrich Avenue South
Burnsville, MN

952-890-7431

Pehrson Lodge
2746 Vermilion Drive/H 24
Cook, MN
218-666-5478

Voyagaire Lodge and Houseboats
7576 Gold Coast Road
Crane Lake, MN
218-993-2266

Best Western Plus Holland House
615 Highway 10 E
Detroit Lakes, MN
218-847-4483

Holiday Inn Detroit Lakes
1155 Highway 10 East
Detroit Lakes, MN

218-847-2121

Days Inn Duluth/By Miller Hill Mall
909 Cottonwood Avenue
Duluth, MN
218-727-3110

Residence Inn Duluth
517 West Central Entrance
Duluth, MN

218-279-2885

Sheraton Duluth Hotel
301 East Superior Street

Duluth, MN

218-733-5660

Willard Munger Inn
7408 Grand Avenue
Duluth, MN

218-624-4814

Days Inn Eagan Minneapolis Near
Mall Of America
4510 Erin Drive
Eagan, MN
651-681-1770

Extended Stay America - Minneapolis
- Airport - Eagan - North
3015 Denmark Avenue
Eagan, MN

651-905-1778

Extended Stay America - Minneapolis
Airport - Eagan
3384 Norwest Court
Eagan, MN

651-681-9991

Sonesta Es Suites Minneapolis - St.
Paul Airport
3040 Eagandale Place
Eagan, MN

651-688-0363

Staybridge Suites Eagan-Mall Of
America
4675 Rahncliff Road
Eagan, MN

651-994-7810

TownePlace Suites Minneapolis-St.
Paul Airport/Eagan
3615 Crestridge Drive
Eagan, MN

651-994-4600

Best Western Eden Prairie Inn
11500 West 78th Street
Eden Prairie, MN
952-829-0888

Extended Stay America -
Minneapolis-Eden Prairie-Technology
Dr
11905 Technology Drive
Eden Prairie, MN

952-942-6818

Extended Stay America -
Minneapolis-Eden Prairie-Valley View
Rd
7550 Office Ridge Circle
Eden Prairie, MN

952-941-1113

Residence Inn Eden Prairie
7780 Flying Cloud Drive
Eden Prairie, MN

952-829-0033

Towneplace Suites By Marriott
Minneapolis Eden Prairie
11588 Leona Road
Eden Prairie, MN

952-942-6001

Residence Inn Minneapolis Edina
3400 Edinborough Way
Edina, MN
952-893-9300

Paddle Inn
1314 E Sheridan Street
Ely, MN
218-365-6036

Super 8 Eveleth
1080 Industrial Park Drive, Hwy 53
Eveleth, MN
218-744-1661

Holiday Inn Fairmont
1201 Torgerson Drive
Fairmont, MN
507-238-4771

Quality Inn Fairmont
2225 N. State St.
Fairmont, MN

507-238-5444

Quality Inn Fairmont
2225 N. State St.
Fairmont, MN

507-235-2626

Super 8 Fairmont
1200 Torgerson Drive
Fairmont, MN

507-238-9444

Days Inn Faribault
1920 Cardinal Lane
Faribault, MN
507-334-6835

Comfort Inn Fergus Falls
425 Western Avenue
Fergus Falls, MN
218-736-5787

Super 8 Fergus Falls
2454 College Way
Fergus Falls, MN

218-739-3261

Aspen Lodge
310 East U.S. Hwy. 61
Grand Marais, MN
218-387-2500

Best Western Plus Superior Inn &
Suites
104 1st Avenue E Us Highway 61 E
Grand Marais, MN

218-387-2240

Clearwater Lodge
774 Clearwater Rd
Grand Marais, MN

218-388-2254

East Bay Suites
21 Wisconsin Street/H 61
Grand Marais, MN

218-387-2800

Gunflint Lodge
143 South Gunflint Lake
Grand Marais, MN

800-328-3325

Gunflint Lodge
143 South Gunflint Lake
Grand Marais, MN

218-388-2294

The Outpost Motel
2935 E H 61
Grand Marais, MN

218-387-1833

Country Inn By Carlson Grand
Rapids
2601 S Highway 169
Grand Rapids, MN
218-327-4960

Super 8 Grand Rapids
1702 S Pokegama Ave
Grand Rapids, MN

218-327-1108

Dakota Lodge
40497 H 48
Hinckley, MN
320-384-6052

Days Inn Hinckley
104 Grindstone Court
Hinckley, MN

320-384-7751

Americas Best Value Inn & Suites
International Falls
2326 Highway 53
International Falls, MN
218-283-8811

Days Inn International Falls
2331 U.S. Hwy 53 South
International Falls, MN

218-283-9441

Microtel Inn & Suites By Wyndham
Inver Grove Heights/Minneapolis
5681 Bishop Avenue
Inver Grove Heights, MN
651-552-0555

Econo Lodge Jackson
2007 Highway 71 North
Jackson, MN
507-847-3110

Super 8 Jackson Mn
2025 Highway 71 North
Jackson, MN

507-847-3498

Kahneetah Cottages
4210 W H 61
Lutsen, MN
218-387-2585

Solbakken Resort
4874 W H 61
Lutsen, MN

218-663-7566

Super 8 Luverne
1202 South Kniss Avenue
Luverne, MN
507-283-9541

Baymont Inn & Suites Mankato
131 Apache Place
Mankato, MN
507-388-5107

Best Western Hotel & Restaurant
1111 Range Street
Mankato, MN

507-625-9333

Holiday Inn Express Hotel & Suites
Mankato East
2051 Adams Street
Mankato, MN

507-388-1880

Mankato-Days Inn
1285 Range Street
Mankato, MN

507-387-3332

Microtel Inn & Suites By Wyndham
Mankato
200 St Andrews Dr
Mankato, MN

507-388-2818

Extended Stay America - Minneapolis
- Maple Grove
12970 63rd Avenue North
Maple Grove, MN
763-694-9747

Staybridge Suites Minneapolis Maple Grove
7821 Elm Creek Blvd
Maple Grove, MN

763-494-8856

Comfort Inn Marshall
1511 E College Dr
Marshall, MN
507-532-3070

Ramada Marshall
1500 East College Drive
Marshall, MN

507-532-3221

Super 8 Marshall Mn
1106 E Main St
Marshall, MN

507-537-1461

Super 8 Melrose
231 E County Road 173
Melrose, MN
320-256-4261

Best Western Plus The Normandy Inn & Suites
405 South 8th Street
Minneapolis, MN
612-370-1400

Days Hotel Minneapolis - University Of Minnesota
2407 University Ave Se
Minneapolis, MN

612-623-3999

Le Meridien Chambers Minneapolis
901 Hennepin Avenue
Minneapolis, MN

612-767-6900

Loews Minneapolis Hotel
601 First Avenue North
Minneapolis, MN

612-677-1100

Millennium Hotel Minneapolis
1313 Nicollett Mall
Minneapolis, MN

612-332-6000

Minneapolis Marriott City Center
30 South 7th Street
Minneapolis, MN

612-349-4000

RENAISSANCE THE DEPOT MINNEAPOLIS HOTEL, A Marriott Luxury & Lifestyle Hotel
225 South 3rd Avenue
Minneapolis, MN

Ramada Plymouth Hotel and Conference Center
2705 North Annapolis Lane
Minneapolis, MN

763-553-1600

Residence Inn By Marriott Minneapolis Downtown/City Center
45 S Eight Street
Minneapolis, MN

612-677-1000

Residence Inn Minneapolis At The Depot
425 South 2nd St
Minneapolis, MN

612-340-1300

Sheraton Bloomington Hotel
5601 West 78th Street
Minneapolis, MN

952-835-1900

Sheraton Hotel Minneapolis Midtown
2901 Chicago Avenue South
Minneapolis, MN

612-821-7600

THE HOTEL MINNEAPOLIS, AUTOGRAPH COLLECTION, A Marriott Luxury & Lifestyle Hotel
215 4th Street South
Minneapolis, MN

612-340-2000

The Grand Hotel Minneapolis, A Kimpton Hotel
615 2nd Avenue South
Minneapolis, MN

612-339-3655

The Marquette By Hilton
710 Marquette Avenue
Minneapolis, MN

612-333-4545

The Westin Minneapolis
88 South 6th Street
Minneapolis, MN

612-333-4006

TownePlace Suites by Marriott Minneapolis Downtown/North Loop
525 2nd Street North
Minneapolis, MN

612-340-1000

W Hotel Minneapolis The Foshay
821 Marquette Avenue
Minneapolis, MN

612-215-3700

La Quinta Inn & Suites Minneapolis-Minnetonka
10420 Wayzata Boulevard
Minnetonka, MN
952-541-1094

Sheraton Minneapolis West
12201 Ridgedale Dr
Minnetonka, MN

952-593-0000

Best Western Chelsea Inn & Suites
89 Chelsea Road
Monticello, MN
763-271-8880

Super 8 Moorhead
3621 South 8th Street
Moorhead, MN
218-233-8880

Days Inn Mounds View Twin Cities North
2149 Program Avenue
Mounds View, MN
763-786-9151

Holiday Inn Express Mountain Iron-Virginia
8570 Rock Ridge Drive
Mountain Iron, MN
218-741-7411

Microtel Inn & Suites By Wyndham New Ulm
424 20th South Street
New Ulm, MN
507-354-9800

Americas Best Value Inn
1420 Riverview Drive
Northfield, MN
507-663-0371

Econo Lodge Ortonville
650 Us Hwy. 75
Ortonville, MN
320-839-2414

Comfort Inn Owatonna
2345 43rd Street Northwest
Owatonna, MN
507-444-0818

Microtel Inn & Suites By Wyndham Owatonna
150 Saint John Drive
Owatonna, MN

507-446-0228

Super 8 Owatonna
1150 West Frontage Road
Owatonna, MN

507-451-0380

Rodeway Inn Pine River
2684 State Hwy 371 Sw
Pine River, MN

218-587-4499

Dancing Bear Resort
17025 Sitka Drive NW
Pinewood, MN
218-243-2700

Crowne Plaza Minneapolis West
3131 Campus Drive
Plymouth, MN
763-559-6600

Days Inn Minneapolis West Plymouth
2955 Empire Lane
Plymouth, MN

763-559-2400

Red Roof Inn Minneapolis Plymouth
2600 Annapolis Lane North
Plymouth, MN

763-553-1751

Residence Inn By Marriott
Minneapolis Plymouth
2750 Annapolis Circle
Plymouth, MN

763-577-1600

Star Lake Forest Rentals
14450 Bowers Drive
Ramsey, MN
866-888-8265

Rainy Lake Inn and Suites at Tara's
Wharf
2065 Spruce Street Landing
Ranier, MN
218-286-5699

Days Inn Red Wing
955 East 7th Street
Red Wing, MN
651-388-3568

Super 8 Red Wing
232 Withers Harbor Drive
Red Wing, MN

651-388-0491

Candlewood Suites Minneapolis
Airport
351 W 77th Street
Richfield, MN
612-869-7704

Four Points by Sheraton Mall of
America Minneapolis Airport
7745 Lyndale Avenue South
Richfield, MN

612-861-1000

Centerstone Plaza Hotel
401 6th Street Sw
Rochester, MN
507-288-2677

Clarion Inn Rochester
1630 South Broadway
Rochester, MN

507-288-1844

Comfort Inn Rochester
5708 Bandel Road Northwest
Rochester, MN

507-289-3344

Days Inn Rochester Downtown
1st Ave Nw
Rochester, MN

507-282-3801

Extended Stay America - Rochester
- North
2814 43rd St. Nw
Rochester, MN

507-289-7444

Extended Stay America - Rochester
- South
55 Wood Lake Drive S.E.
Rochester, MN

507-536-7444

Residence Inn By Marriott Rochester
Mayo Clinic Area
441 West Center Street
Rochester, MN

507-292-1400

Rochester Marriott Mayo Clinic Area
101 First Ave Sw
Rochester, MN

507-280-6000

Super 8 Rochester/Fairgrounds
Area
1230 South Broadway
Rochester, MN

507-288-8288

Towneplace Suites By Marriott
Rochester
2829 43rd Street Nw
Rochester, MN

507-281-1200

Key Inn
2550 Cleveland Ave North
Roseville, MN
651-636-6730

Red Roof Inn Minneapolis-Roseville
2401 Prior Avenue North
Roseville, MN

651-636-8888

Residence Inn By Marriott
Minneapolis St. Paul/Roseville
2985 Centre Pointe Drive

Roseville, MN
651-636-0680

Best Western Plus Kelly Inn
100 4th Avenue South
Saint Cloud, MN
320-253-0606

Homewood Minneapolis St Louis
Park
5305 Wayzata Boulevard
Saint Louis Park, MN
952-544-0495

Best Western Plus Bandana Square
1010 Bandana Boulevard W
Saint Paul, MN
651-647-1637

Best Western Plus Capitol Ridge
161 Saint Anthony Avenue
Saint Paul, MN

651-227-8711

Best Western Plus Dakota Ridge
3450 Washington Drive
Saint Paul, MN

651-452-0100

Best Western Plus White Bear
Country Inn
4940 Highway 61 North
Saint Paul, MN

651-429-5393

Homewood Minneapolis New
Brighton
1815 Old Highway 8 Nw
Saint Paul, MN

651-631-8002

Quality Inn Savage
4601 West Hwy 13
Savage, MN
952-894-6124

Best Western Shakopee Inn
511 Marschall Rd
Shakopee, MN
952-445-9779

Americinn Of Silver Bay, Mn
150 Mensing Drive
Silver Bay, MN
218-226-4300

Days Inn St Cloud
70 South 37th Avenue
St Cloud, MN
320-253-4444

Holiday Inn Express St. Cloud
4322 Clearwater Road
St Cloud, MN

320-240-8000

Super 8 St. Cloud
50 Park Avenue South
St Cloud, MN

320-253-5530

Super 8 St. James
1210 Heckman Court
St James, MN
507-375-4708

Towneplace Suites By Marriott
Minneapolis West/St. Louis Park
1400 Zarthan Avenue South
St Louis Park, MN
952-847-6900

Days Inn St. Paul-Minneapolis-
Midway
1964 University Ave W
St Paul, MN
651-645-8681

Super 8 Stillwater/St Paul
2190 W Frontage Rd.
Stillwater, MN
651-430-3990

The Springs Country Inn
361 Government St
Taylors Falls, MN
651-465-6565

Bluefin Bay Resort
7192 H 61W
Tofte, MN
1-800-BLUEFIN (258-3346)

Loghouse and Homestead
44854 Fred Holm Road
Vergas, MN
218-342-2318

Best Western Plus Willmar
2100 Highway 12 East
Willmar, MN
320-235-6060

Super 8 Willmar
2655 S 1st Street
Willmar, MN

320-235-4444

Red Carpet Inn - Windom
222 3rd Avenue South
Windom, MN
507-831-1120

Holiday Inn Express Hotel & Suites
Winona
1128 Homer Road
Winona, MN
507-474-1700

Quality Inn Winona
956 Mankato Ave
Winona, MN

507-454-4390

Extended Stay America -
Minneapolis - Woodbury
10020 Hudson Road
Woodbury, MN
651-501-1085

Red Roof Inn - St Paul Woodbury
1806 Wooddale Drive
Woodbury, MN
651-738-7160

Sheraton Hotel St. Paul Woodbury
676 Bielenberg Drive
Woodbury, MN
651-209-3280

Days Inn Worthington
207 Oxford Street
Worthington, MN
507-376-6155

Super 8 Worthington
850 Lucy Drive
Worthington, MN
507-372-7755

Travelodge Worthington
2015 North Humiston Avenue
Worthington, MN
507-372-2991

Americas Best Value Inn Zumbrota
1435 Northstar Drive
Zumbrota, MN
507-732-7852

# Mississippi Listings

Days Inn Batesville
280 Power Drive
Batesville, MS
662-563-4999

Quality Inn Batesville
290 Power Drive
Batesville, MS
662-563-1188

Edgewater Inn - Biloxi
1936 Beach Boulevard
Biloxi, MS
228-388-1100

Ramada Limited Ocean Springs
8011 Tucker Road
Biloxi/Ocean Springs, MS
228-872-2323

Drury Inn & Suites Jackson -
Ridgeland

610 East County Line Road
Brandon, MS
601-956-6100

Red Roof Inn And Suites Jackson -
Brandon
280 Old Highway 80
Brandon, MS

601-824-3839

Super 8 - Brookhaven
344 Dunn Ratcliff Road Northwest
Brookhaven, MS
601-833-8580

Best Western Canton Inn
137 Soldier Colony Road
Canton, MS
601-859-8600

Super 8 Canton
145 Soldier Colony Road
Canton, MS

601-859-7575

Drury Inn & Suites Jackson -
Ridgeland
610 East County Line Road
Clinton, MS
601-956-6100

Quality Inn Corinth
2101 Highway 72 West
Corinth, MS
662-287-4421

Econo Lodge Inn & Suites
441 Yacht Club Drive
Diamondhead, MS
228-586-0210

Candlewood Suites Flowood, Ms
3810 Flowood Drive
Flowood, MS
601-326-3600

Drury Inn & Suites Jackson -
Ridgeland
610 East County Line Road
Flowood, MS

601-956-6100

Americas Best Value Inn Forest
1846 Highway 35 South
Forest, MS
601-469-2640

Relax Inn Grenada
1632 Sunset Drive
Grenada, MS
662-226-8888

Best Western Plus Seaway Inn
9475 Highway 49
Gulfport, MS
228-864-0050

Quality Inn Gulfport
9435 Highway 49
Gulfport, MS

228-864-7222

Residence Inn By Marriott Gulfport-
Biloxi Airport
14100 Airport Road
Gulfport, MS

228-867-1722

Candlewood Suites Hattiesburg
9 Gateway Drive
Hattiesburg, MS
601-264-9666

Clarion Inn University Hattiesburg
6541 Highway 49
Hattiesburg, MS

601-264-1881

Residence Inn Hattiesburg
116 Grand Drive
Hattiesburg, MS

601-264-9202

Days Inn Hernando
943 East Commerce Street
Hernando, MS
662-429-0000

Super 8 Hernando
2425 Sloans Way
Hernando, MS

662-429-5334

Days Inn - Holly Springs
120 Heritage Drive
Holly Springs, MS
662-252-1120

Drury Inn & Suites Memphis
Southaven
735 Goodman Road West
Horn Lake, MS
662-349-6622

Sleep Inn Horn Lake
708 Desoto Cove
Horn Lake, MS

662-349-2773

Drury Inn & Suites Jackson -
Ridgeland
610 East County Line Road
Jackson, MS
601-956-6100

Extended Stay America - Jackson -
North
5354 I-55n
Jackson, MS

601-956-4312

Hilton Jackson

1001 East County Line Road
Jackson, MS

601-957-2800

Red Roof Inn Jackson Downtown
Fairgrounds
700 Larson Street
Jackson, MS

601-969-5006

Drury Inn & Suites Jackson -
Ridgeland
610 East County Line Road
Madison, MS
601-956-6100

Days Inn McComb MS
2298 Delaware Avenue
McComb, MS
601-684-5566

Drury Inn & Suites Meridian
112 Highway 11 And 80
Meridian, MS
601-483-5570

Days Inn Natchez
109 Highway 61 South
Natchez, MS
601-445-8291

Glenfield Plantation Bed and
Breakfast
6 Providence Road
Natchez, MS

601-442-1002

Holiday Inn Express Hotel & Suites
New Albany
300 Highway 30 West
New Albany, MS
662-534-8870

Days Inn Ocean Springs
7305 Washington Avenue
Ocean Spring, MS
228-872-8255

Magnuson Hotel Ocean Springs
7304 Washington Avenue
Ocean Springs, MS
228-875-7555

Candlewood Suites Olive Branch
7448 Craft Goodman Road
Olive Branch, MS
662-890-7491

Super 8 Oxford
2201 Jackson Avenue West
Oxford, MS
662-234-7013

Candlewood Suites Pearl
632 Pearson Road
Pearl, MS
601-936-3442

Drury Inn & Suites Jackson -
Ridgeland
610 East County Line Road
Pearl, MS

601-956-6100

Americas Best Value Inn Pontotoc
217 Highway 15 North
Pontotoc, MS
662-489-5200

Drury Inn & Suites Jackson -
Ridgeland
610 East County Line Road
Richland, MS
601-956-6100

Drury Inn & Suites Jackson -
Ridgeland
610 East County Line Road
Ridgeland, MS
601-956-6100

Red Roof Inn Ridgeland
810 Adcock Street
Ridgeland, MS

601-956-7707

Residence Inn Jackson Ridgeland
855 Centre St
Ridgeland, MS

601-206-7755

Staybridge Suites Jackson
801 Ridgewood Road
Ridgeland, MS

601-206-9190

Best Western Ripley
922 City Avenue South
Ripley, MS
662-837-0002

Microtel Inn & Suites By Wyndham
Tunica Resorts
2131 Casino Strip Blvd
Robinsonville, MS

Residence Inn By Marriott Memphis
Southaven
7165 Sleepy Hollow Drive
Southaven, MS
662-996-1500

Comfort Suites Starkville
801 Russell Street
Starkville, MS
662-324-9595

Days Inn And Suites Starkville
119 Hwy 12 W &; 25 N
Starkville, MS

662-324-5555

Hampton Inn Starkville

700 Highway 12
Starkville, MS

662-324-1333

Super 8 Tupelo Airport
3898 Mccullough Boulevard
Tupelo, MS
662-842-0448

Anchuca Mansion
1010 First East Street
Vicksburg, MS
601-661-0111

Battlefield Inn A Vista Collection Hotel
4137 I-20 North Frontage Road
Vicksburg, MS

601-638-5811

Best Western Vicksburg
2445 North Frontage Road
Vicksburg, MS

601-636-5800

Cedar Grove Inn
2200 Oak Street
Vicksburg, MS

601-636-1000

Duff Green Mansion
1114 First east street
Vicksburg, MS

601-638-6662

Econo Lodge Vicksburg
3959 East Clay Street
Vicksburg, MS

601-634-8438

Quality Inn & Suites Vicksburg
3332 Clay Street
Vicksburg, MS

601-636-0804

Rodeway Inn Vicksburg
2 Pemberton Place
Vicksburg, MS

601-634-1622

The Corners Bed and Breakfast Inn
601 Klien St
Vicksburg, MS

601-636-7421

Holiday Inn Express Hotel & Suites
Winona North
413 Se Frontage Road
Winona, MS
662-283-9992

# Missouri Listings

Econo Lodge Anderson
491 E Highway 76
Anderson, MO
417-845-4888

Cottages on Stouts Creek
H 72
Arcadia, MO
573-546-4036

Drury Inn & Suites St. Louis
Southwest
5 Lambert Drury Place
Arnold, MO
636-861-8300

Pear Tree Inn St. Louis - Arnold
1201 Drury Lane
Arnold, MO

636-296-9600

Super 8 Ava
1711 South Jefferson Street
Ava, MO
417-683-1343

Comfort Inn Bethany
496 South 39th Street
Bethany, MO
660-425-8006

Super 8 Bethany Mo
811 South 38th Street
Bethany, MO

660-425-8881

Pine Ridge Log Cabins
5704 MO-86
Blue Eye, MO
417-331-1556

Days Inn Blue Springs
451 Nw Jefferson Street
Blue Springs, MO
816-224-1199

Hampton Inn Kansas City/Blue
Springs
900 Nw South Outer Road
Blue Springs, MO

816-220-3844

Super 8 Bonne Terre
8 Northwood Drive
Bonne Terre, MO
573-358-5888

Days Inn Boonville
2401 Pioneer
Boonville, MO
660-882-8624

Super 8 Bowling Green
1216 East Champ Clark Drive
Bowling Green, MO
573-324-6000

Branson Inn
448 MO 248
Branson, MO
417-334-5121

Emory Creek Victorian Bed &
Breakfast and Gift shop
143 Arizona Drive
Branson, MO

417-334-3805

Hampton Inn Branson - Branson Hills
200 South Payne Stewart Drive
Branson, MO

417-243-7800

Hilton Branson Convention Center
200 East Main Street
Branson, MO

417-336-5400

Hilton Promenade At Branson
Landing
3 Branson Landing
Branson, MO

417-336-5500

Hotel Grand Victorian
2325 West Highway 76
Branson, MO

417-336-2935

Quality Inn On The Strip
2834 West Sr 76
Branson, MO

417-334-1194

Ramada Branson Hotel And Resort
1700 West Highway 76
Branson, MO

Residence Inn By Marriott Branson
280 Wildwood Drive South
Branson, MO

417-336-4077

Stone Castle Hotel
3050 Green Mt Dr
Branson, MO

417-335-4700

Extended Stay America - St. Louis
Airport - Central
11252 Lone Eagle Drive
Bridgeton, MO
314-739-0600

Days Inn Butler
100 South Fran Avenue
Butler, MO
660-679-4544

Super 8 Butler
1114 West Fort Scott Street

Butler, MO

660-679-6183

Econo Lodge Cameron
220 East Grand
Cameron, MO
816-632-6571

Super 8 Cameron
1710 N Walnut Street
Cameron, MO

816-632-8888

Centerstone Inn Canton
1701 Oak Street
Canton, MO
573-288-8800

Candlewood Suites Cape Girardeau
485 South Mount Auburn Road
Cape Girardeau, MO
573-334-6868

Drury Lodge Cape Girardeau
104 South Vantage Drive
Cape Girardeau, MO

573-334-7151

Econo Lodge Carthage
1441 West Central
Carthage, MO
417-358-3900

Precious Moments Hotel
2701 Hazel Street
Carthage, MO

417-359-5900

Super 8 Motel - Carthage
416 West Fir Road
Carthage, MO

417-359-9000

Quality Inn Charleston
102 Drake Street
Charleston, MO
573-683-4200

Drury Inn & Suites St. Louis
Southwest
5 Lambert Drury Place
Chesterfield, MO
636-861-8300

Drury Plaza Hotel St. Louis
Chesterfield
355 Chesterfield Center East
Chesterfield, MO

636-532-3300

Hampton Inn St. Louis/Chesterfield
16201 Swingley Ridge Rd
Chesterfield, MO

636-537-2500

Homewood Suites Chesterfield
840 North Chesterfield Pkwy West
Chesterfield, MO

636-530-0305

Residence Inn By Marriott St. Louis
Chesterfield
15431 Conway Road
Chesterfield, MO

636-537-1444

Econo Lodge Inn & Suites
Chillicothe
1020 South Washington
Chillicothe, MO
660-646-0572

Super 8 Motel - Chillicothe
500 Business Hwy 36 East
Chillicothe, MO

660-646-7888

Clayton Plaza Hotel
7750 Carondelet Avenue
Clayton, MO
314-726-5400

Americas Best Value Inn Columbia
Mall
1900 I-70 Drive Southwest
Columbia, MO
573-445-8511

Budget Host Columbia
900 Vandiver Drive
Columbia, MO

573-449-1065

Days Inn Columbia I-70
900 I-70 Drive Sw
Columbia, MO

573-442-1191

Drury Inn Columbia
1000 Knipp Street
Columbia, MO

573-445-1800

Extended Stay America - Columbia -
Stadium Boulevard
2000 West Business Loop 70
Columbia, MO

573-445-6800

Howard Johnson Inn Columbia
3100 I-70 Dr Se
Columbia, MO

573-474-6161

Quality Inn Columbia
1612 North Providence Road
Columbia, MO

573-449-2491

Ramada Columbia Mo
901 Conley Road
Columbia, MO

573-443-4141

Red Roof Inn Columbia
201 East Texas Avenue
Columbia, MO

573-442-0145

Residence Inn By Marriott Columbia
1100 Woodland Springs Court
Columbia, MO

573-442-5601

Staybridge Suites Columbia-Highway
63 & I-70
805 Keene Street
Columbia, MO

573-442-8600

Suburban Extended Stay Hotel
Columbia - Hwy 63 & I-70
3100 Wingate Court
Columbia, MO

573-817-0525

Super 8 Columbia Clark Lane
3216 Clark Lane
Columbia, MO

573-474-8488

Super 8 Columbia East
5700 Freedom Drive
Columbia, MO

573-474-8307

Days Inn Concordia
301 Nw 3rd Street
Concordia, MO
660-463-7987

Travelodge Concordia
406 Nw 2nd Street
Concordia, MO

660-463-2114

Econo Lodge - Cuba
246 Highway P
Cuba, MO
573-885-7707

Super 8 Cuba
28 Hwy P
Cuba, MO

573-885-2087

Best Western Montis Inn
14086 Highway Z
Dixon, MO

573-336-4299

Rock Eddy Bluff Farm
10245 Maries Road 511
Dixon, MO

573-759-6081

Candlewood Suites St Louis
3250 Rider Trail South
Earth City, MO
314-770-2744

Residence Inn St Louis Airport
3290 Rider Trail South
Earth City, MO

314-209-0995

Lake Ozark Vacation Rentals
35 Kristy Road
Eldon, MO
573-365-1600

Drury Inn & Suites St. Louis
Southwest
5 Lambert Drury Place
Eureka, MO
636-861-8300

Holiday Inn Saint Louis West Six
Flags
4901 Six Flags Road
Eureka, MO

636-938-6661

Quality Inn Farmington
1400 W Liberty Street
Farmington, MO
573-756-8951

Drury Inn & Suites St. Louis
Southwest
5 Lambert Drury Place
Fenton, MO
636-861-8300

Pear Tree Inn St. Louis Fenton
1100 South Highway Drive
Fenton, MO

636-343-8820

Towneplace Suites By Marriott St.
Louis Fenton
1662 Fenton Business Park Ct
Fenton, MO

636-305-7000

Motel 6 Florissant Missouri
307 Dunn Road
Florissant, MO
314-831-7900

Baymont Inn & Suites Fulton
2205 Cardinal Drive
Fulton, MO
573-642-2600

Travelodge Six Flags - Gray Summit
2875 Highway 100
Gray Summit, MO
800-782-8487

Super 8 Hannibal
120 Huckleberry Heights Drive
Hannibal, MO
573-221-5863

Comfort Inn Hayti
1500 Highway 84
Hayti, MO
573-359-2200

Crosslands St. Louis - Airport - N.
Lindbergh Blvd.
6065 North Lindbergh Boulevard
Hazelwood, MO
314-731-2991

Super 8 Higginsville
I-70 And Hwy 13
Higginsville, MO
660-584-7781

Best Western Truman Inn
4048 S Lynn Court
Independence, MO
816-254-0100

Comfort Suites Independence -
Kansas City
19751 East Valley View Parkway
Independence, MO

816-373-9880

Holiday Inn Express Suites
Independence
19901 East Valley View Parkway
Independence, MO

816-795-8889

Quality Inn & Suites East
4200 South Noland Road
Independence, MO

816-373-8856

Residence Inn Independence
3700 South Arrowhead Avenue
Independence, MO

816-795-6466

Staybridge Suites Kansas City-
Independence
19400 E. 39th Place South
Independence, MO

816-994-2700

Super 8 Motel -
Independence/Kansas City Area
4032 South Lynn Court Drive
Independence, MO

816-833-1888

Candlewood Suites Jefferson City
3514 Amazonas Drive
Jefferson City, MO
573-634-8822

Oak Tree Inn
1710 Jefferson Street
Jefferson City, MO

573-636-5456

Best Western Oasis Inn And Suites
3508 South Rangeline Road
Joplin, MO
417-781-6776

Candlewood Suites Joplin
3512 South Rangeline
Joplin, MO

417-623-9595

Days Inn Joplin
3500 Rangeline Road
Joplin, MO

417-623-0100

Drury Inn & Suites Joplin
3601 Rangeline Road
Joplin, MO

417-781-8000

Residence Inn Joplin
3128 East Hammons Boulevard
Joplin, MO

417-782-0908

Sleep Inn Joplin
I 44 And Sr 43 S
Joplin, MO

417-782-1212

Super 8 Joplin
2830 East 36th Street
Joplin, MO

417-782-8765

Towneplace Suites By Marriott Joplin
4026 South Arizona Avenue
Joplin, MO

417-659-8111

816 Hotel
801 Westport Road
Kansas City, MO
816-931-1000

Adams Mark Hotel And Conference
Center
9103 East 39th Street
Kansas City, MO

816-737-0200

Best Western Country Inn-North
2633 Ne 43rd Street

Kansas City, MO
816-459-7222

Best Western Plus Seville Plaza Hotel
4309 Main Street
Kansas City, MO
816-561-9600

Candlewood Suites Kansas City Airport
11110 Nw Ambassador
Kansas City, MO
816-886-9700

Candlewood Suites Kansas City Northeast
4450 Randolph Rd
Kansas City, MO
816-886-9311

Chase Suite Hotel
9900 NW Prairie View Road
Kansas City, MO
816-891-9009

Days Inn & Suites Kansas City South
8601 Hillcrest Road
Kansas City, MO
816-822-7000

Days Inn Kansas City
7100 N.E. Parvin Road
Kansas City, MO
816-453-3355

Days Inn Kansas City Intl Airport
11120 Nw Ambassador Dr
Kansas City, MO
816-746-1666

Drury Inn & Suites Kansas City Airport
7900 Northwest Tiffany Springs Parkway
Kansas City, MO
816-880-9700

Drury Inn & Suites Kansas City Stadium
3830 Blue Ridge Cutoff
Kansas City, MO
816-923-3000

Extended Stay America - Kansas City - Airport - Plaza Circle
11712 N.W. Plaza Circle
Kansas City, MO
816-270-7829

Extended Stay America - Kansas City - Airport - Tiffany Springs

9701 N. Shannon Ave
Kansas City, MO
816-891-8500

Extended Stay America - Kansas City - Country Club Plaza
4535 Main St
Kansas City, MO
816-531-2212

Extended Stay America - Kansas City - South
550 East 105th St
Kansas City, MO
816-943-1315

Four Points By Sheraton Kansas City - Sports Complex
4011 Blue Ridge Cut-Off
Kansas City, MO
816-353-5300

Hilton Kansas City Airport
8801 Northwest 112th Street
Kansas City, MO
816-891-8900

Holiday Inn At The Plaza
One East 45th Street
Kansas City, MO
816-753-7400

Holiday Inn Kansas City Airport
11728 Nw Ambassador Drive
Kansas City, MO
816-801-8400

Holiday Inn Kansas City Northeast I-435 North
7333 Parvin Rd
Kansas City, MO
816-455-1060

Homewood Suites By Hilton®
Kansas City-Airport
7312 Nw Polo Drive
Kansas City, MO
816-880-9880

Howard Johnson Plaza Kansas City Hotel And Conference Center
1601 North Universal Avenue
Kansas City, MO
816-245-5500

Microtel Inn & Suites By Wyndham Kansas City Airport
11831 Northwest Plaza Circle
Kansas City, MO
816-270-1200

Residence Inn By Marriott Kansas

City Downtown/Union Hill
2975 Main Street
Kansas City, MO
816-561-3000

Residence Inn Kansas City Airport
10300 North Ambassador Drive
Kansas City, MO
816-741-2300

Residence Inn Kansas City Country Club Plaza
4601 Broadway
Kansas City, MO
816-753-0033

Sheraton Suites Country Club Plaza
770 West 47th Street
Kansas City, MO
816-931-4400

Sleep Inn Kansas City Airport
7611 Nw 97th Terrace
Kansas City, MO
816-891-0111

Su Casa B&B
9004 E. 92nd Street
Kansas City, MO
816-916-3444

Comfort Inn Kearney
400 South Platte Clay Way
Kearney, MO
816-628-2288

Econo Lodge Kearney
505 Shanks Avenue
Kearney, MO
816-628-5111

Super 8 Kearney/Kc Area
210 Platte Clay Way
Kearney, MO
816-628-6800

Days Inn Kennett
110 Independence Avenue
Kennett, MO
573-888-9860

Super 8 Kennett
1808 First Street, Highway 412 &; 25
Kennett, MO
573-888-8800

Days Inn Kingdom City
3391 County Road 211
Kingdom City, MO
573-642-0050

Super 8 Kingdom City
3370 Gold Avenue

Kingdom City, MO
573-642-2888

Budget Host Village Inn
1304 South Baltimore Street
Kirksville, MO
660-665-3722

Super 8 Kirksville
1101 Country Club Drive
Kirksville, MO

660-665-8826

Americas Best Value Inn
10600 Veterans Memorial Parkway
Lake St Louis, MO
636-625-1711

Days Inn Lebanon
2071 West Elm Street
Lebanon, MO
417-532-7111

Super 8 Liberty/Ne Kansas City Area
115 North Stewart Road
Liberty, MO
816-781-9400

Americas Best Value Inn And Suites
28933 Sunset Drive
Macon, MO
660-385-2125

Super 8 Macon
203 East Briggs Road
Macon, MO

660-385-5788

Super 8 Marshall
1355 W College Street
Marshall, MO
660-886-3359

Holiday Inn Express Marshfield -
Springfield Area
1301 Banning Street
Marshfield, MO
417-859-6000

Hunter Lodge
501 Southeast Outer Road
Marston, MO
573-643-9888

Drury Inn & Suites Westport
12220 Dorsett Road
Maryland Heights, MO
314-576-9966

Extended Stay America - St. Louis -
Westport - East Lackland Rd.
11827 Lackland Rd
Maryland Heights, MO

314-993-6868

Americas Best Value Inn Maryville
222 East Summit Street

Maryville, MO
660-582-8088

Super 8 Moberly
300 Hwy 24 East
Moberly, MO
660-263-8862

Royal Inn & Suites
111 East 17th Street
Mountain Grove, MO
417-926-3152

Best Western Big Spring Lodge
1810 Southern View Drive
Neosho, MO
417-455-2300

Super 8 Neosho
3085 Gardner Edgewood Drive
Neosho, MO

417-455-1888

Super 8 Nevada
2301 E Austin Blvd
Nevada, MO
417-667-8888

Super 8 Nixa/Springfield Area
418 North Massey Boulevard
Nixa, MO
417-725-0880

Comfort Inn & Suites
100 Comfort Inn Court
O'Fallon, MO
636-696-8000

Residence Inn By Marriott St Louis
O Fallon
101 Progress Point Ct
OFallon, MO
636-300-3535

Econo Lodge Oak Grove
410 Southeast 1st Street
Oak Grove, MO
816-690-3681

Oak Grove Inn
101 North Locust Street
Oak Grove, MO

816-690-8700

Holiday Inn Express Hotel & Suites
St. Louis West-O'Fallon
1175 Technology Drive
Ofallon, MO
636-300-4844

Staybridge Suites Ofallon
Chesterfield
1155 Technology Drive
Ofallon, MO

636-300-0999

Country Hearth Inn Osage Beach

Hotel
3518 H 54S
Osage Beach, MO

Econo Lodge Inn & Suites Lake Of
The Ozarks
5760 Highway 54
Osage Beach, MO

573-348-1781

Comfort Inn Ozark
1900 West Evangel Street
Ozark, MO
417-485-6688

Comfort Inn Near Six Flags St. Louis
1320 Thornton Street
Pacific, MO
636-257-4600

Super 8 Motel - Platte City/Kci Airport
2500 Northwest Prairie View Road
Platte City, MO
816-858-2888

Travelodge Airport Platte City
504 Prairie View Road
Platte City, MO

816-858-4588

Comfort Inn Poplar Bluff
2582 North Westwood Boulevard
Poplar Bluff, MO
573-686-5200

Super 8 Poplar Bluff
Highway 67 North
Poplar Bluff, MO

573-785-0176

Super 8 - Potosi
820 East High Street
Potosi, MO
573-438-8888

Super 8 Riverside/Kansas City
800 NW Argosy Parkway
Riverside, MO
816-505-2888

Days Inn Rolla
1207 Kingshighway Street
Rolla, MO
573-341-3700

Econo Lodge Rolla
1417 Martin Spring Drive
Rolla, MO

573-341-3130

Pear Tree Inn Rolla
2006 North Bishop Avenue
Rolla, MO

573-364-4000

Pear Tree Inn St. Louis Airport

10810 Pear Tree Lane
Saint Ann, MO
314-427-3400

Comfort Suites Saint Charles
1400 South Fifth Street
Saint Charles, MO
636-949-0694

Drury Inn & Suites St Joseph
4213 Frederick Boulevard
Saint Joseph, MO
816-364-4700

Best Western Kirkwood Inn
1200 South Kirkwood Road
Saint Louis, MO
314-821-3950

Best Western St. Louis Inn
6224 Heimos Industrial Park Drive
Saint Louis, MO

314-416-7639

Drury Inn & Suites St. Louis
Convention Center
711 North Broadway
Saint Louis, MO

314-231-8100

Drury Inn & Suites St. Louis Creve
Coeur
11980 Olive Boulevard
Saint Louis, MO

314-989-1100

Drury Inn & Suites St. Louis Forest
Park
2111 Sulphur Avenue
Saint Louis, MO

314-646-0770

Drury Inn & Suites St. Louis
Southwest
5 Lambert Drury Place
Saint Louis, MO

636-861-8300

Drury Inn St. Louis Airport
10490 Natural Bridge Road
Saint Louis, MO

314-423-7700

Drury Inn St. Louis at Union Station
201 South 20th Street
Saint Louis, MO

314-231-3900

Drury Plaza St. Louis At The Arch
2 South 4th Street
Saint Louis, MO

314-231-3003

Hampton Inn St. Louis Southwest, Mo

9 Lambert Drury Place
Saint Louis, MO

636-529-9020

Pear Tree Inn St. Louis Near Union
Station
2211 Market Street
Saint Louis, MO

314-241-3200

Drury Inn St. Louis St. Peters
170 Mid Rivers Mall Circle
Saint Peters, MO
636-397-9700

Mainstay Suites St. Robert - Fort
Leonard Wood
227 St. Robert Boulevard
Saint Robert, MO
573-451-2700

Best Western State Fair Inn
3120 S Limit
Sedalia, MO
660-826-6100

Hotel Bothwell, An Ascend Hotel
Collection Member
103 East 4th Street
Sedalia, MO

660-826-5588

Motel 6 Hotel State Fair
3402 West Broadway Boulevard
Sedalia, MO

660-827-5890

Green Cocoon
On Farm Road 2212
Shell Knob, MO
417-858-8800

Days Inn Sikeston
1330 South Main Street
Sikeston, MO
573-471-3930

Drury Inn & Suites Sikeston
2608 East Malone Avenue
Sikeston, MO

573-472-2299

Pear Tree Inn Sikeston
2602 East Malone Avenue
Sikeston, MO

573-471-4100

Super 8 - Sikeston
2609 East Malone Avenue
Sikeston, MO

573-471-7944

Super 8 Smithville Lake
112 Cuttings Drive
Smithville, MO

816-532-3088

Baymont Inn & Suites Springfield
South Highway 65
3343 E Battlefield St
Springfield, MO
417-887-2323

Best Western Plus Coach House
2535 N. Glenstone Avenue
Springfield, MO

417-862-0701

Best Western Route 66 Rail Haven
203 South Glenstone Avenue
Springfield, MO

417-866-1963

Candlewood Suites Springfield
1920 East Kerr Street
Springfield, MO

417-866-4242

Candlewood Suites Springfield South
1035 East Republic Road
Springfield, MO

417-881-8500

Courtyard By Marriott Springfield
Airport
3527 West Kearney
Springfield, MO

417-869-6700

Days Inn South Springfield Missouri
621 W Sunshine
Springfield, MO

417-862-0153

Days Inn Springfield East
3260 East Montclair Street
Springfield, MO

417-882-9484

Drury Inn & Suites Springfield Mo
2715 North Glenstone Avenue
Springfield, MO

417-863-8400

Extended Stay America - Springfield -
South
1333 East Kingsley Street
Springfield, MO

417-823-9100

La Quinta Inn And Suites Springfield
Airport Plaza
2445 North Airport Plaza Avenue
Springfield, MO

417-447 4466

Quality Inn & Suites North Springfield

2745 North Glenstone Ave
Springfield, MO

417-869-0001

Quality Inn South
3330 E. Battlefield Rd.
Springfield, MO

417-889-6300

Residence Inn Springfield
1303 East Kingsley Street
Springfield, MO

417-890-0020

Sleep Inn Medical District
233 El Camino Alto Center
Springfield, MO

417-886-2464

Boone's Lick Trail Inn
1000 S Main Street
St Charles, MO
636-947-7000

Red Roof Inn St Louis/St Charles
2010 Zumbehl Road
St Charles, MO

636-947-7770

Towneplace Suites By Marriott St.
Louis - St. Charles
1800 Zumbehl Road
St Charles, MO

636-949-6800

Super 8 Saint Clair
1010 South Outer Road
St Clair, MO
636-629-8080

Americas Best Value Inn St. Joseph
4024 Frederick Avenue
St Joseph, MO
816-364-3031

Radisson Hotel St. Joseph
102 South Third Street
St Joseph, MO

816-279-8000

Radisson Hotel St. Joseph
102 South Third Street
St Joseph, MO

816-279-8000

Ramada St. Joseph
4016 Fredrick Blvd
St Joseph, MO

816-233-6192

Clayton on the Park
8025 Bonhomme Avenue
St Louis, MO

314-290-1500

Econo Lodge Southwest
3730 South Lindbergh Boulevard
St Louis, MO

314-842-1200

Extended Stay America - St. Louis -
Westport - Central
12161 Lackland Rd
St Louis, MO

314-878-8777

Hawthorn Suites By Wyndham St.
Louis Westport Plaza
1881 Craigshire Road
St Louis, MO

314-469-0060

Hilton St. Louis Airport
10330 Natural Bridge Road
St Louis, MO

314-426-5500

Hilton St. Louis At The Ballpark
One South Broadway
St Louis, MO

314-421-1776

Hilton St. Louis Downtown At The
Arch
400 Olive Street
St Louis, MO

314-436-0002

Holiday Inn Saint Louis Forest Park
5915 Wilson Avenue
St Louis, MO

314-645-0700

Magnolia Hotel St. Louis a Tribute
Portfolio Hotel
421 North 8th Street
St Louis, MO

314-436-9000

Marriott St. Louis Airport
10700 Pear Tree Lane
St Louis, MO

314-423-9700

Quality Inn Airport
10232 Natural Bridge Road
St Louis, MO

314-427-5955

Red Roof Inn - St Louis Westport
11837 Lackland Road
St Louis, MO

314-991-4900

Red Roof Plus+ St Louis - Forest

Park/Hampton Ave
5823 Wilson Avenue
St Louis, MO

314-645-0101

Residence Inn By Marriott St. Louis
Galleria
8011 Galleria Parkway
St Louis, MO

314-862-1900

Residence Inn Saint Louis Downtown
525 South Jefferson Avenue
St Louis, MO

314-289-7500

Sheraton Clayton Plaza Hotel
7730 Bonhomme Avenue
St Louis, MO

314-863-0400

Sheraton Westport Chalet Hotel St.
Louis
191 West Port Plaza
St Louis, MO

314-878-1500

Sheraton Westport Plaza
900 West Port Plaza
St Louis, MO

314-878-1500

Sonesta Es Suites St. Louis Westport
1855 Craigshire Rd
St Louis, MO

314-878-1555

The Westin Saint Louis
811 Spruce Street
St Louis, MO

314-621-2000

Extended Stay America - Saint Louis
- Saint Peters
5555 Veterans Memorial Parkway
St Peters, MO
636-926-2800

Candlewood Suites St. Robert
140 Carmel Valley Way
St Robert, MO
573-451-2500

Days Inn St. Robert
14125 Highway Z
St Robert, MO

573-336-5556

Red Roof Inn St. Robert - Ft. Leonard
Wood
129 Saint Robert Boulevard
St Robert, MO

583-336-2510

Super 8 St. Robert/Fort Leonard Wood Area
107 Mckinnon Street
St Robert, MO

573-451-2888

Microtel Inn & Suites By Wyndham, Ste. Genevieve
21958 Highway 32
Ste Genevieve, MO
573-883-8884

Hyatt Regency St. Louis At The Arch
315 Chestnut Street
Strafford, MO
417-736-3883

Baymont Inn & Suites - Sullivan
275 North Service Road
Sullivan, MO
573-860-3333

Super 8 Sullivan
601 North Service Road
Sullivan, MO

573-468-8076

Dogwood Acres Resort
14 Lamp Post Ct
Sunrise Beach, MO
573-374-5956

Rodeway Inn Sweet Springs
208 West Highway 40
Sweet Springs, MO
660-335-4888

Drury Inn & Suites St. Louis Southwest
5 Lambert Drury Place
Valley Park, MO
636-861-8300

Days Inn Warrensburg
204 East Cleveland Street
Warrensburg, MO
660-429-2400

Americas Best Value Inn Warrenton
220 Arlington Way
Warrenton, MO
636-456-4301

Quality Inn West Plains
220 Jan Howard Expressway
West Plains, MO
417-257-2711

Super 8 - West Plains
1210 Porter Wagoner Boulevard
West Plains, MO

417-256-8088

# Montana Listings

River's Edge Resort
22 S Frontage Road
Alberton, MT
406-722-3375

Super 8 Belgrade/ Bozeman Airport
6450 Jackrabbit Lane
Belgrade, MT
406-388-1493

Super 8 Big Timber
20a Big Timber Loop
Big Timber, MT
406-932-8888

Timbers Motel - Big Fork
8540 Hwy 35 South
Bigfork, MT
406-837-6200

The Islander Inn
14729 Shore Acres Drive
Bighorn, MT
406-837-5472

Best Western Plus Clocktower Inn
2511 First Ave., North
Billings, MT
406-259-5511

Best Western Plus Kelly Inn & Suites
4915 Southgate Drive
Billings, MT

406-256-9400

Days Inn Billings
843 Parkway Lane
Billings, MT

406-252-4007

Dude Rancher Lodge
415 North 29th Street
Billings, MT

406-259-5561

Econo Lodge Billings
5425 Midland Road
Billings, MT

406-252-2700

Extended Stay America - Billings - West End
4950 Southgate Drive
Billings, MT

406-245-3980

Hilltop Inn by Riversage
1116 North Broadway
Billings, MT

406-245-5000

Howard Johnson Billings
1345 Mullowney Lane
Billings, MT

406-252-2584

Kelly Inn Billings
5610 South Frontage Road
Billings, MT

406-248-9800

Motel 6 Billings - North
5353 Midland Road
Billings, MT

406-248-7551

Quality Inn Homestead Park Billings
2036 Overland Avenue
Billings, MT

406-652-1320

Residence Inn Billings
956 South 25th Street West
Billings, MT

406-656-3900

Riversage Billings Inn
880 North 29th Street
Billings, MT

406-252-6800

Sleep Inn Billings
4904 Southgate Drive
Billings, MT

406-254-0013

The Vegas Hotel
2612 Belknap Avenue
Billings, MT

406-248-7761

Best Western Plus Gran Tree Inn
1325 North Seventh Avenue
Bozeman, MT
406-587-5261

Days Inn And Suites Bozeman
1321 North 7th Avenue
Bozeman, MT

406-587-5251

Holiday Inn Bozeman
5 East Baxter Lane
Bozeman, MT

406-587-4561

Motel 6 of Bozeman
817 Wheat Drive
Bozeman, MT

406-585-7888

Ramada Bozeman
2020 Wheat Drive
Bozeman, MT

406-585-2626

Residence Inn By Marriott Bozeman
6195 East Valley Center Road
Bozeman, MT

406-522-1535

Super 8 Bozeman
800 Wheat Drive
Bozeman, MT

406-586-1521

Western Heritage Inn
1200 East Main Street
Bozeman, MT

406-586-8534

Best Western Plus Butte Plaza Inn
2900 Harrison Avenue
Butte, MT
406-494-3500

Comfort Inn Butte
2777 Harrison Avenue
Butte, MT

406-494-8850

Super 8 Butte
2929 Harrison Avenue
Butte, MT

406-494-6000

Super 8 Columbus
602 8th Avenue North
Columbus, MT
406-322-4101

Super 8 Conrad
215 North Main Street
Conrad, MT
406-278-7676

Travelodge Deer Lodge Montana
1150 N Main St
Deer Lodge, MT
406-846-2370

Americas Best Value Inn
550 North Montana Street
Dillon, MT
406-683-4288

Best Western Paradise Inn
650 North Montana Street
Dillon, MT

406-683-4214

Comfort Inn Dillon
450 North Interchange
Dillon, MT

406-683-6831

Dancing Bears Inn
40 Montana Avenue
East Glacier Park, MT

406-226-4402

Covered Wagon Ranch
34035 Gallatin Road/Highway191
Gallatin Gateway, MT
406-995-4237

Super 8 Gardiner/Yellowstone Park
Area
702 Scott St. West
Gardiner, MT
406-848-7401

Cottonwood Inn
45 1st Avenue NE
Glasgow, MT
800-321-8213

Days Inn Glendive
2000 N. Merrill Ave/I-94
Glendive, MT
406-365-6011

Super 8 Glendive
1904 N Merrill Ave
Glendive, MT

406-365-5671

Best Western Plus Heritage Inn
1700 Fox Farm Road
Great Falls, MT
406-761-1900

Comfort Inn Great Falls
1120 9th Street South
Great Falls, MT

406-454-2727

Days Inn Great Falls
101 14th Avenue Northwest
Great Falls, MT

406-727-6565

Extended Stay America - Great Falls
- Missouri River
800 River Drive South
Great Falls, MT

406-761-7524

Hampton Inn Great Falls, Mt
2301 14th Street Sw
Great Falls, MT

406-453-2675

Holiday Inn Great Falls
400 10th Ave. South
Great Falls, MT

406-727-7200

Staybridge Suites Great Falls
201 3rd Street Northwest
Great Falls, MT

406-761-4903

Super 8 Great Falls Mt
1214 13th Street South
Great Falls, MT

406-727-7600

Townhouse Inn Great Falls
1411 10th Avenue South
Great Falls, MT

406-761-4600

Paws Up Resort
40060 Paws Up Road
Greenough, MT
406-244-5200

Motel 6 Hamilton
409 South First Street
Hamilton, MT
406-363-2142

Western Motel Hardin
830 West 3rd Street
Hardin, MT
406-665-2296

Super 8 Havre
1901 Highway 2 West
Havre, MT
406-265-1411

Townhouse Inn Of Havre
601 West First Street
Havre, MT

406-265-6711

Barrister Bed and Breakfast
416 North Ewing
Helena, MT
406-443-7330

Baymont Inn & Suites Helena
750 Fee Street
Helena, MT

406-443-1000

Holiday Inn Helena
22 North Last Chance Gulch
Helena, MT

406-443-2200

Howard Johnson Helena
2101 East 11th Avenue
Helena, MT

406-443-2300

Lamplighter Motel
1006 Madison Avenue
Helena, MT

406-442-9200

Quality Inn Helena
2300 North Oaks
Helena, MT

406-442-3064

Dog-Friendly Lodging - Please always call ahead to make sure an establishment is still dog-friendly.

Radisson Colonial Hotel Helena
2301 Colonial Drive
Helena, MT

406-443-2100


Residence Inn By Marriott Helena
2500 East Custer Avenue
Helena, MT

406-443-8010


Shilo Inn Suites Hotel - Helena
2020 Prospect Avenue
Helena, MT

406-442-0320


Super 8 Helena
2200 11th Avenue
Helena, MT

406-443-2450


Wingate By Wyndham - Helena
2007 North Oakes
Helena, MT

406-449-3000


Wingate By Wyndham - Helena
2007 North Oakes
Helena, MT

406-449-3000


Comfort Inn Big Sky
1330 Us Highway 2 West
Kalispell, MT
406-755-6700


Econo Lodge Inn & Suites Kalispell
1680 Highway 93 South
Kalispell, MT

406-752-3467


Holiday Inn Express Hotel & Suites
Kalispell
275 Treeline Road
Kalispell, MT

406-755-7405


Kalispell Grand Hotel
100 Main Street
Kalispell, MT

406-755-8100


Red Lion Hotel Kalispell
20 North Main Street
Kalispell, MT

406-752-6660


Red Lion Hotel Kalispell
20 North Main Street
Kalispell, MT

406-751-5050


Super 8 Kalispell
1341 1st Avenue East
Kalispell, MT

406-755-1888


Travelodge Kalispell
350 North Main Street
Kalispell, MT

406-755-6123


Best Western Yellowstone Crossing
205 Se 4th Street
Laurel, MT
406-628-6888


Pelican Motel & RV Park
11360 S Frontage
Laurel, MT

406-628-4324


Caboose Motel
Us Hwy 2 West 714 W. 9th Street
Libby, MT
406-293-6201


Quality Inn Livingston
111 Rogers Lane
Livingston, MT
406-222-0555


Rodeway Inn Livingston
102 Rogers Lane
Livingston, MT

406-222-6320


Super 8 Livingston
105 Centennial Drive
Livingston, MT

406-222-7711


Yellowstone Pioneer Lodge
1515 West Park Street
Livingston, MT

406-222-6110


Days Inn & Suites Lolo
11225 Highway 93 South
Lolo, MT
406-273-2121


Best Western War Bonnet Inn
1015 South Haynes Avenue
Miles City, MT
406-234-4560


Econo Lodge Miles City
1209 South Haynes Avenue
Miles City, MT

406-232-8880


Best Western Plus Grant Creek Inn
5280 Grant Creek Road
Missoula, MT
406-543-0700


Days Inn Missoula Airport
8600 Truck Stop Road
Missoula, MT

406-721-9776


Doubletree By Hilton Missoula
Edgewater
100 Madison
Missoula, MT

406-728-3100


Econo Lodge Missoula
4953 North Reserve Street
Missoula, MT

406-542-7550


GuestHouse Inn & Conference
Center Missoula
3803 Brooks Street
Missoula, MT

406-251-2665


Hampton Inn Missoula
4805 N Reserve St
Missoula, MT

406-549-1800


Holiday Inn Downtown At The Park
200 South Pattee Street
Missoula, MT

406-721-8550


Howard Johnson Missoula
3530 Brooks Street
Missoula, MT

406-252-2250


Quality Inn & Suites Missoula
4545 North Reserve Street
Missoula, MT

406-542-0888


Red Lion Inn Missoula
700 West Broadway
Missoula, MT

406-728-3300


Staybridge Suites Missoula
120 Expressway
Missoula, MT

406-830-3900


Wingate By Wyndham - Missoula Mt
5252 Airway Boulevard
Missoula, MT

406-541-8000


Wingate By Wyndham - Missoula Mt
5252 Airway Boulevard
Missoula, MT

406-541-8000

Nevada City Hotel and Cabins
H 287
Nevada City, MT
406-843-5377

Chico Hot Springs Resort
#1 Chico Road
Pray, MT
406-333-4933

Comfort Inn Red Lodge
612 North Broadway
Red Lodge, MT
406-446-4469

Comfort Inn Shelby
455 Mckinley
Shelby, MT
406-434-2212

Clubhouse Inn
105 South Electric Street
West Yellowstone, MT
406-646-4892

Crosswinds Inn
201 Firehole Avenue
West Yellowstone, MT

406-646-9557

Hibernation Station
212 Grey Wolf Avenue
West Yellowstone, MT

406-646-4200

Holiday Inn West Yellowstone
315 Yellowstone Avenue
West Yellowstone, MT

406-646-7365

Kelly Inn West Yellowstone
104 South Canyon Street
West Yellowstone, MT

406-646-4544

Pioneer Motel
515 Madison Avenue
West Yellowstone, MT

406-646-9705

Whispering Pines Motel
321 Canyon Street
West Yellowstone, MT

406-646-1172

Best Western Rocky Mountain Lodge
6510 Highway 93 South
Whitefish, MT
406-862-2569

Gaynors River Bend Ranch Resort
1992 K M Ranch Road

Whitefish, MT
406-862-3802

Grouse Mountain Lodge
2 Fairway Drive
Whitefish, MT

406-862-3000

Stillwater Mountain Lodge
750 Beaver Lake Road
Whitefish, MT

406-862-7004

Rodeway Inn Whitehall
515 N. Whitehall St. Box 1003
Whitehall, MT
406-287-5588

# Nebraska Listings

Alliance Hotel And Suites
117 Cody Avenue
Alliance, NE
308-762-8000

Econo Lodge Beatrice
3210 North 6th Street
Beatrice, NE
402-223-3536

Holiday Inn Express Hotel And
Suites Beatrice
4005 North Sixth Street
Beatrice, NE

402-228-7000

Best Western White House Inn
305 North Fort Crook Road
Bellevue, NE
402-293-1600

Candlewood Suites Bellevue
10902 South 15th Street
Bellevue, NE

402-932-8144

Microtel Inn & Suites By Wyndham
Bellevue
3008 Samson Way
Bellevue, NE

402-292-0191

Best Western West Hills Inn
1100 West 10th Street
Chadron, NE
308-432-3305

Super 8 Chadron Ne
840 W. Hwy 20
Chadron, NE

308-432-4471

Americas Best Value Inn Columbus
3803 23rd Street
Columbus, NE
402-564-9955

Sleep Inn & Suites Columbus
303 23rd St
Columbus, NE

402-562-5200

Super 8 Columbus
3324 20th Street
Columbus, NE

402-563-3456

Rodeway Inn Cozad
809 South Meridian
Cozad, NE
308-784-4900

Super 8 Crete
1880 West 12th Street
Crete, NE
402-826-3600

Howard Johnson Gothenburg
401 Platte River Drive
Gothenburg, NE
308-537-2684

Days Inn Grand Island West
2620 North Diers Avenue
Grand Island, NE
308-384-8624

Quality Inn And Conference Center
Grand Island
7838 South Highway 281
Grand Island, NE

308-384-7770

Rodeway Inn
3205 S. Locust St.
Grand Island, NE

308-384-1333

Super 8 Grand Island
2603 South Locust St
Grand Island, NE

Dog-Friendly Lodging - Please always call ahead to make sure an establishment is still dog-friendly.

308-384-4380

Rodeway Inn Hastings
2424 Osborne Drive East
Hastings, NE
402-463-1422

Super 8 Motel - Hastings
2200 North Kansas Avenue
Hastings, NE

402-463-8888

Econo Lodge Kearney
709 East 2nd Avenue
Kearney, NE
308-237-2671

Howard Johnson Kearney
619 2nd Avenue East
Kearney, NE

308-234-5699

Microtel Inn & Suites - Kearney
104 Talmadge
Kearney, NE

308-698-3003

Quality Inn Kearney
121 3rd Avenue
Kearney, NE

308-237-0838

Rodeway Inn & Suites Kearney
411 2nd Avenue
Kearney, NE

308-698-2810

Super 8 Kearney
15 W 8th Street
Kearney, NE

308-234-5513

Days Inn Kimball
611 East Third Street
Kimball, NE
308-235-4671

Holiday Inn Express Hotel & Suites
Lexington
2605 Plum Creek Parkway
Lexington, NE
308-324-9900

Baymont Inn & Suites Lincoln
1133 Belmont Avenue
Lincoln, NE
402-435-0200

Candlewood Suites Lincoln
4100 Pioneer Woods Drive
Lincoln, NE

402-420-0330

Comfort Suites Lincoln

4231 Industrial Avenue
Lincoln, NE

402-476-8080

Country Inn & Suites By Carlson
Lincoln North
5353 North 27th Street
Lincoln, NE

402-476-5353

Days Inn And Suites Lincoln Ne
2001 West O Street
Lincoln, NE

402-477-4488

Holiday Inn Express Hotel & Suites
Lincoln Airport
1101 West Commerce Way
Lincoln, NE

402-464-0588

Holiday Inn Express Hotel & Suites
Lincoln South
8801 Amber Hill Court
Lincoln, NE

402-423-1176

Knights Inn Lincoln Airport
2920 Nw 12th Street
Lincoln, NE

402-475-3616

Microtel Inn & Suites By Wyndham
Lincoln
2505 Fairfield Street
Lincoln, NE

402-476-2591

Motel 6 Lincoln
6501 North 28th Street
Lincoln, NE

402-438-4700

Quality Inn & Suites Lincoln
1511 Center Park Road South
Lincoln, NE

402-423-3131

Residence Inn Lincoln South
5865 Boboli Lane
Lincoln, NE

402-423-1555

Staybridge Suites Lincoln
2701 Fletcher Avenue
Lincoln, NE

402-438-7829

Super 8 Lincoln - West
2635 West O Street
Lincoln, NE

402-476-8887

Super 8 Lincoln Cornhusker Highway
2545 Cornhusker Highway
Lincoln, NE

402-467-4488

TownHouse Extended Stay Hotel
Downtown
1744 M Street
Lincoln, NE

402-475-3000

Travelodge Lincoln
1101 West Bond Street
Lincoln, NE

Days Inn Mccook
901 North Highway 83
McCook, NE
308-345-7115

Pioneer Village Motel
224 E H 6
Minden, NE
800-445-4447

Super 8 Norfolk
1223 Omaha Avenue
Norfolk, NE
402-379-2220

Best Western Plus North Platte Inn &
Suites
3201 S Jeffers Street
North Platte, NE
308-534-3120

Howard Johnson Inn North Platte
1209 South Dewey Street
North Platte, NE

308-532-0130

Quality Inn And Suites North Platte
2102 South Jeffers
North Platte, NE

308-532-9090

Rodeway Inn North Platte
920 North Jeffers
North Platte, NE

308-532-2313

Super 8 North Platte
220 Eugene Avenue
North Platte, NE

308-532-4224

Days Inn Ogallala
601 Stage Coach Trail
Ogallala, NE
308-284-6365

Super 8 Ogallala

500 East A Street South
Ogallala, NE

308-284-2076

Americas Best Value Inn - Omaha
7101 Grover Street
Omaha, NE
402-391-5757

Baymont Inn & Suites Omaha Ne
3301 South 72nd Street
Omaha, NE

402-391-8129

Best Western Plus Kelly Inn
4706 South 108th Street
Omaha, NE

402-339-7400

Candlewood Suites Omaha Airport
2601 Abbott Plaza
Omaha, NE

402-342-2500

Econo Lodge Inn & Suites West
9595 S 145th St
Omaha, NE

402-896-6300

Econo Lodge West Dodge Omaha
7833 West Dodge Road
Omaha, NE

402-391-7100

Hawthorn Suites By Wyndham
Omaha / Old Mill
360 South 108th Avenue
Omaha, NE

402-758-2848

Hilton Omaha
1001 Cass
Omaha, NE

402-998-3400

Hilton Omaha
1001 Cass
Omaha, NE

402-998-3400

Holiday Inn Express & Suites Omaha
West
17677 Wright Street
Omaha, NE

402-333-5566

Holiday Inn Express Omaha West -
90th Street
8736 West Dodge Road
Omaha, NE

402-343-1000

New Victorian Inn & Suites
10728 L Street
Omaha, NE

402-593-2380

Sleep Inn & Suites Airport
2525 Abbott Dr
Omaha, NE

402-342-2525

Sonesta Es Suites Omaha
6990 Dodge Street
Omaha, NE

402-553-8898

Staybridge Suites Omaha 80th And
Dodge
7825 Davenport Street
Omaha, NE

402-933-8901

Towneplace Suites Omaha West
10865 West Dodge Road
Omaha, NE

402-590-2800

Days Inn Paxton
851 Paxton Elise Road
Paxton, NE
308-239-4510

Comfort Inn Scottsbluff
1902 21st Ave.
Scottsbluff, NE
308-632-7510

Days Inn Scottsbluff
1901 21st Avenue
Scottsbluff, NE

308-635-3111

Lamplighter American Inn
606 E 27th St
Scottsbluff, NE

308-632-7108

Super 8 Scottsbluff
2202 Delta Drive
Scottsbluff, NE

308-635-1600

Sunset Inn And Suites
3629 Progressive Road
Seward, NE
402-643-3388

Country Inn & Suites By Carlson,
Sidney, Ne
664 Chase Boulevard
Sidney, NE
308-254-2000

Super 8 Valentine
223 East Highway 20

Valentine, NE
402-376-1250

Super 8-West Point
1211 North Lincoln Street
West Point, NE
402-372-3998

Wood River Motel
11774 S H 11
Wood River, NE
308-583-2256

Best Western Plus York Hotel And
Conference Center
4619 South Lincoln Avenue
York, NE
402-362-6661

Super 8 York NE
4112 South Lincoln Avenue
York, NE

402-362-3388

# Nevada Listings

Super 8 Battle Mountain
825 Super 8 Dr.
Battle Mountain, NV
775-635-8808

Americas Best Value Inn/Carson City
2731 S. Carson St.
Carson City, NV
775-882-2007

Days Inn Carson City
3103 North Carson Street
Carson City, NV

775-883-3343

Holiday Inn Express Hotel & Suites
Carson City
4055 North Carson Street
Carson City, NV

775-283-4055

Rodeway Inn At Nevada State Capitol
1300 North Carson Street
Carson City, NV

775-883-7300

Super 8 Carson City
2829 South Carson Street
Carson City, NV

775-883-7800

Best Western Elko Inn
1930 Idaho Street
Elko, NV
775-738-8787

High Desert Inn
3015 Idaho Street
Elko, NV

775-738-8425

Quality Inn & Suites Elko
3320 East Idaho Street
Elko, NV
775-777-8000

Red Lion Hotel And Casino Elko
2065 Idaho Street
Elko, NV
775-738-2111

Rodeway Inn Elko
736 Idaho Street
Elko, NV
775-738-7152

Shilo Inn Elko
2401 Mountain City Highway
Elko, NV
775-738-5522

Super 8 Elko
1755 Idaho Street
Elko, NV
775-738-8488

Travelodge Elko
1785 Idaho Street
Elko, NV
775-753-7747

Jailhouse Motel and Casino
211 5th Street
Ely, NV
775-289-3033

Magnuson Hotel Park Vue
930 W. Aultman Street
Ely, NV
775-289-4497

Ramada Ely
805 Great Basin Boulevard
Ely, NV
775-289-4884

Best Western Fallon Inn & Suites
1035 West Williams Avenue
Fallon, NV
775-423-6005

Comfort Inn Near Fallon Naval Air
Station
1830 West Williams Avenue
Fallon, NV
775-423-5554

Holiday Inn Express Fallon
55 Commercial Way
Fallon, NV
775-428-2588

Best Western Fernley Inn
1405 Newlands Drive E
Fernley, NV
775-575-6776

Best Western Topaz Lake Inn
3410 Sandy Bowers Avenue
Gardnerville, NV
7752664661

Super 8 Gardnerville/Minden
1979 Highway 395 South
Gardnerville, NV
775-266-3338

Soldier Meadows Guest Ranch and
Lodge
Soldier Meadows Rd
Gerlach, NV
775-849-1666

Best Western Plus Henderson Hotel
1553 North Boulder Highway
Henderson, NV
702-564-9200

Hampton Inn And Suites Las Vegas
- Henderson
421 Astaire Drive
Henderson, NV
702-992-9292

Holiday Inn Express Hotel & Suites
Henderson
441 Astaire Drive
Henderson, NV
702-990-2323

Railroad Pass Hotel & Casino
2800 S Boulder H/H 528
Henderson, NV
702-294-5000

Residence Inn By Marriott Las
Vegas Henderson/Green Valley
2190 Olympic Avenue
Henderson, NV
702-434-2700

Towneplace Suites By Marriott Las
Vegas Henderson
1471 Paseo Verde Parkway
Henderson, NV
702-896-2900

Westin Lake Las Vegas Resort &
Spa
101 Montelago Boulevard
Henderson, NV
702-567-6000

Americas Best Value Inn
167 East Tropicana Avenue
Las Vegas, NV

702-795-3311

Americas Best Value Inn Downtown
Las Vegas
1000 N. Main Street
Las Vegas, NV
702-382-3455

Bally's Las Vegas
3645 Las Vegas Blvd S
Las Vegas, NV
877-603-4390

Baymont Inn And Suites Airport
South Las Vegas
55 East Robindale Road
Las Vegas, NV
702-273-2500

Best Western Plus Las Vegas West
8669 West Sahara Avenue
Las Vegas, NV
702-256-3766

Caesars Palace Las Vegas
3570 Las Vegas Boulevard
Las Vegas, NV
800-HARRAHS

Candlewood Suites Las Vegas
4034 South Paradise Road
Las Vegas, NV
702-836-3660

Crossland Economy Studios - Las
Vegas - Boulder Highway
4240 Boulder Highway
Las Vegas, NV
702-433-1788

Delano Las Vegas At Mandalay Bay
3940 Las Vegas Blvd South
Las Vegas, NV
702-632-7777

Element Las Vegas Summerlin
10555 Discovery Drive
Las Vegas, NV
702-589-2000

Extended Stay America - Las Vegas -
Midtown
3045 South Maryland Parkway
Las Vegas, NV
702-369-1414

Extended Stay America Las Vegas -
Valley View
4270 South Valley View Boulevard
Las Vegas, NV
702-221-7600

Flamingo Las Vegas
3555 Las Vegas Blvd S
Las Vegas, NV

888-902-9929

Fortune Hotel & Suites
325 East Flamingo Road
Las Vegas, NV

702-732-9100

Four Seasons Hotel Las Vegas
3960 Las Vegas Boulevard South
Las Vegas, NV

702-632-5000

Harrah's Las Vegas
3475 Las Vegas Blvd S
Las Vegas, NV

800-214-9110

Holiday Inn Express Las Vegas-Nellis
4035 North Nellis Boulevard
Las Vegas, NV

702-644-5700

Mount Charleston Lodge
1200 Old Park Road
Las Vegas, NV

702-872-5408

Paris Las Vegas
3655 Las Vegas Blvd S
Las Vegas, NV

702-946-7000

Planet Hollywood Resort And Casino
3667 Las Vegas Boulevard South
Las Vegas, NV

702-785-5555

Plaza Hotel Las Vegas
230 Plaza St
Las Vegas, NV

505-425-3591

Residence Inn By Marriott Las Vegas
Convention Center
3225 Paradise Road
Las Vegas, NV

702-796-9300

Residence Inn By Marriott Las Vegas
Hughes Center
370 Hughes Center Drive
Las Vegas, NV

702-650-0040

Residence Inn Las Vegas South
5875 Dean Martin Drive
Las Vegas, NV

702-795-7378

Rio All Suite Hotel and Casino
3700 W Flamingo Road/H 592
Las Vegas, NV

3700 W Flamingo Road

Siegel Suites Select Convention
Center
220 Convention Center Drive
Las Vegas, NV

702-735-4151

Staybridge Suites Las Vegas
5735 Dean Martin Drive
Las Vegas, NV

702-259-2663

The Cosmopolitan Of Las Vegas,
Autograph Collection
3708 South Las Vegas Boulevard
Las Vegas, NV

702-698-7000

The Platinum Hotel
211 East Flamingo Road
Las Vegas, NV

702-365-5000

The Quad Resort And Casino
Located Next To Flamingo
3535 LAS Vegas Boulevard South
Las Vegas, NV

702-731-3311

Travelodge Las Vegas
2830 Las Vegas Boulevard South
Las Vegas, NV

702-735-4222

Vdara Hotel & Spa At Aria Las
Vegas
2600 W Harmon Ave
Las Vegas, NV

702-590-2111

Harrahs Laughlin
2900 S Casino Drive
Laughlin, NV
702-298-4600

Pioneer Hotel And Gambling Hall
2200 South Casino Drive
Laughlin, NV

702-298-2442

Best Western Mesquite Inn
390 N Sandhill Boulevard
Mesquite, NV
702-346-7444

Virgin River Hotel and Casino
100 Pionner Blvd
Mesquite, NV

800-346-7721

Holiday Inn Express Hotel & Suites
Minden
1659 Hwy 88
Minden, NV
775-782-7500

Mount Charleston Lodge and Cabins
HCR 38 Box 325
Mount Charleston, NV
800-955-1314

Best Western Plus North Las Vegas
Inn & Suites
4540 Donovan Way
North Las Vegas, NV
702-649-3000

Lucky Club Casino And Hotel
3227 Civic Center Drive
North Las Vegas, NV

702-399-3297

Best Western Pahrump Oasis
1101 South Highway 160
Pahrump, NV
775-727-5100

Overland Hotel
85 Main Street
Pioche, NV
775-962-5895

Baymont Inn and Suites Reno
2050 B Market Street
Reno, NV
775-786-2506

Best Western Airport Plaza Hotel
1981 Terminal Way
Reno, NV

775-348-6370

Days Inn Reno
701 East 7th St.
Reno, NV

775-786-4070

Extended Stay America - Reno -
South Meadows
9795 Gateway Drive
Reno, NV

775-852-5611

Holiday Inn Express Hotel & Suites
Reno
2375 Market Street
Reno, NV

775-229-7070

Homewood Suites By Hilton Reno
5450 Kietzke Lane
Reno, NV

775-853-7100

Ramada Reno Hotel & Casino
1000 East Sixth Street
Reno, NV

775-786-5151

Residence Inn Reno
9845 Gateway Drive
Reno, NV

775-853-8800

Sands Regency Hotel And Casino
345 North Arlington Ave
Reno, NV

775-348-2200

University Inn
1651 North Virginia Street
Reno, NV

775-329-3464

Vagabond Inn Executive Reno
3131 S. Virginia St.
Reno, NV

775-825-7134

Holiday Inn Reno-Sparks
55 East Nugget Avenue
Sparks, NV
775-358-6900

Super 8 Sparks
1900 East Greg Street
Sparks, NV

775-358-8884

Western Village Inn And Casino
815 Nichols Boulevard
Sparks, NV

800-648-1170

Tonopah Station Hotel and Casino
1137 South Main Street
Tonopah, NV
775-482-9777

Silver Queen Hotel
28 North C Street/H 341
Virginia City, NV
775-847-0440

Silverland Inn and Suites
100 N E Street
Virginia City, NV

775-847-4484

Super 8 Wells
Box 302, I-80 Exit 352
Wells, NV
775-752-3384

Best Western Plus Gold Country Inn
921 West Winnemucca Boulevard
Winnemucca, NV

775-623-6999

Days Inn Winnemucca
511 W. Winnemucca Blvd
Winnemucca, NV

775-623-3661

Santa Fe Inn Winnemucca
1620 West Winnemucca Blvd
Winnemucca, NV

775-623-1119

Super 8 Winnemucca
1157 West Winnemucca Boulevard
Winnemucca, NV

775-625-1818

Winnemucca Inn
741 West Winnemucca Boulevard
Winnemucca, NV

775-623-2565

# New Hampshire Listings

Comfort Inn Ashland
53 West St.
Ashland, NH
603-968-7668

The Glynn House Inn
59 Highland Street
Ashland, NH

603-968-3775

Villager Motel
I 93N at H 3
Bartlett, NH
603-374-2742

Mountain Lake Inn
2871 Route 114
Bradford, NH
603-938-2136

Bretton Arms Country Inn
Route 302
Bretton Woods, NH
603-278-3000

Days Inn Campton
1513 Daniel Webster Hwy
Campton, NH
603-536-3520

Lazy Dog Inn
201 White Mountain H/H 16
Chocorua Village, NH
603-323-8350

Claremont Motor Lodge
Beauregard St, near SR 103
Claremont, NH
603-542-2540

Rodeway Inn Claremont
24 Sullivan Street
Claremont, NH

603-542-9567

Northern Comfort Motel
RR 1, Box 520
Colebrook, NH
603-237-4440

Best Western Concord Inn & Suites
97 Hall Street
Concord, NH
603-228-4300

Comfort Inn Concord
71 Hall Street
Concord, NH
603-226-4100

Residence Inn Concord
91 Hall Street
Concord, NH

603-226-0012

Foothills Farm
P. O. Box 1368
Conway, NH
207-935-3799

Tanglewood Motel and Cottages
1681 H 16
Conway, NH

603-447-5932

Comfort Inn & Suites
10 Hotel Dr.
Dover, NH
603-750-7507

Days Inn Dover Durham Downtown
481 Central Avenue
Dover, NH

603-742-0400

Homewood Suites By Hilton Dover
21 Members Way
Dover, NH

603-516-0929

Hickory Pond Inn & Golf Course
1 Stagecoach Rd
Durham, NH
603-659-2227

Holiday Inn Express Durham - Unh
2 Main Street
Durham, NH

603-868-1234

Paradise Point Cottages
Paradise Point Road
Errol, NH

603-482-3834

Hampton Inn And Suites Exeter
59 Portsmouth Avenue
Exeter, NH
603-658-5555

The Inn at Crotched Mountain
534 Mountain Road
Francestown, NH
603-588-6840

Best Western White Mountain Inn
87 Wallace Hill Road
Franconia, NH
603-823-7422

Franconia Notch Vacations
Call or email to Arrange.
Franconia, NH

800-247-5536

Horse & Hound
205 Wells Rd
Franconia, NH

603-823-5501

Lovetts Inn by Lafayette Brook
SR 18
Franconia, NH

603-823-7761

Westwind Vacation Cottages
1614 Profile Road
Franconia, NH

603-823-5532

Towneplace Suites By Marriott Gilford
14 Sawmill Road
Gilford, NH
603-524-5533

Top Notch Inn
265 Main Street
Gorham, NH
603-466-5496

Town And Country Motor Inn
20 State Route 2
Gorham, NH

603-466-3315

Chieftain Motor Inn
84 Lyme Road
Hanover, NH
603-643-2550

Franconia Notch Motel
572 Us Route 3
Holderness, NH
603-968-3535

Swiss Chalets Village Inn
Old Route 16A
Intervale, NH
603-356-2232

Dana Place Inn
SR 16
Jackson, NH
603-383-6822

The Village House
PO Box 359 Rt 16A
Jackson, NH

603-383-6666

Kearsarge Inn - Bed And Breakfast
42 Seavey Street
Jackson Village, NH
603-356-8700

Applebrook
110 Meadows Road/H 115A
Jefferson, NH
603-586-7713

Best Western Plus Sovereign Hotel
401 Winchester Street
Keene, NH
603-357-3038

Courtyard By Marriott Keene
Downtown
75 Railroad Square
Keene, NH

603-354-7900

Days Inn Keene
3 Ashbrook Road
Keene, NH

603-352-9780

Holiday Inn Express Keene
175 Key Road
Keene, NH

603-352-7616

The Lake Opechee Inn and Spa
62 Doris Ray Court
Laconia, NH
603-524-0111

Element Hanover - Lebanon
25 Foothill Street
Lebanon, NH
603-448-5000

Residence Inn By Marriott Hanover
Lebanon
32 Centerra Parkway
Lebanon, NH

603-643-4511

Econo Lodge Inn & Suites Lincoln
381 U.S. Route 3
Lincoln, NH
603-745-3661

Express Inn & Suites Lincoln
21 Railroad Street
Lincoln, NH

603-745-6700

Pemi Cabins
460 H 3
Lincoln, NH

800-865-8323

The Beal House Inn
2 W Main Street
Littleton, NH
603-444-2661

Loudon Inn
2 Staniels Rd
Loudon, NH
603-225-8399

Dowds County Inn
On the Common, Box 58
Lyme, NH
603-795-4712

Loch Lyme Lodge
70 Orford Road
Lyme, NH

603-795-2141

Best Western Plus Executive Court
Inn & Conference Center
13500 South Willow Street
Manchester, NH
603-627-2525

Econo Lodge Manchester
75 West Hancock Street
Manchester, NH

603-624-0111

Holiday Inn Express Hotel & Suites
Manchester-Airport
1298 South Porter Street
Manchester, NH

603-669-6800

Homewood Suites By Hilton®
Manchester/Airport, Nh
1000 N. Perimeter Road
Manchester, NH

603-668-2200

La Quinta Inn & Suites Manchester
21 Front Street
Manchester, NH

603-669-2660

Towneplace Suites By Marriott
Manchester-Boston Regional Airport
686 Huse Road
Manchester, NH
603-641-2288

Hawthorn Suites By Wyndham
Merrimack/Nashua Area
246 Daniel Webster Highway

Merrimack, NH
603-424-8100

Extended Stay America - Nashua - Manchester
2000 Southwood Dr.
Nashua, NH
603-577-9900

Hampton Inn Nashua
407 Amherst Street
Nashua, NH

603-883-5333

Sunapee Harbor Cottages (Lake Station Realty
1066 H 103
Newbury, NH
603-763-3033

Adventure Suites
3440 White Mountain Highway
North Conway, NH
603-356-9744

Hampton Inn & Suites North Conway
1788 White Mountain Highway
North Conway, NH

603-356-7736

Residence Inn North Conway
1801 White Mountain Highway
North Conway, NH

603-356-3024

Spruce Moose Lodge and Cottages
207 Seavey Street
North Conway, NH

603-356-6239

The Glen
77 The Glen Rd
Pittsburg, NH
603-538-6500

Econo Lodge Near Plymouth State University
304 Main Street
Plymouth, NH
603-536-2330

The Common Man Inn & Spa
231 Main Street
Plymouth, NH

603-536-2200

Hampton Inn Portsmouth Central
99 Durgin Lane
Portsmouth, NH
603-431-6111

Homewood Suites By Hilton Portsmouth
100 Portsmouth Boulevard
Portsmouth, NH

603-427-5400

Meadowbrook Inn
Portsmouth Traffic Circle
Portsmouth, NH

603-436-2700

Residence Inn By Marriott Portsmouth
1 International Drive
Portsmouth, NH

603-436-8880

Residence Inn Portsmouth Downtown/Waterfront
100 Deer Street
Portsmouth, NH

603-422-9200

Sheraton Portsmouth Harborside Hotel
250 Market Street
Portsmouth, NH

603-431-2300

Anchorage Inn Rochester
13 Wadleigh Road
Rochester, NH
603-332-3350

Holiday Inn Express Hotel & Suites Rochester
77 Farmington Road
Rochester, NH

603-994-1175

Red Roof Inn Salem
15 Red Roof Lane
Salem, NH
603-898-6422

The Hilltop Inn
9 Norton Lane
Sugar Hill, NH
603-823-5695

Tamworth Inn
Tamworth Village
Tamworth, NH
603-323-7721

The Inn at East Hill Farm
460 Monadnock Street
Troy, NH
603-588-6495

Johnson Motel and Cottages
364 H 3
Twin Mountain, NH
888-244-5561

Victorian Cottage
#30 Veterans Ave
Weirs Beach, NH
603-279-4583

Baymont Inn West Lebanon
45 Airport Road
West Lebanon, NH
603-298-8888

Fireside Inn & Suites West Lebanon
25 Airport Road
West Lebanon, NH

877-258-5900

All Seasons Motel
36 Smith St
Woodsville, NH
603-747-2157

# New Jersey Listings

Quality Inn & Suites Atlantic City Marina District
328 East White Horse Pike
Absecon, NJ
609-652-3300

Sheraton Atlantic City Convention Center Hotel
Two Convention Boulevard
Atlantic City, NJ
609-344-3535

Showboat Atlantic City
801 Boardwalk
Atlantic City, NJ

609-343-4000

Ramada Limited Atlantic City West
8037 Black Horse Pike
Atlantic City West, NJ
609-646-5220

Avon Manor Cottages
322 Sylvania Ave
Avon-by-the-Sea, NJ
732-776-7770

Hotel Indigo Basking Ridge
80 Allen Road
Basking Ridge, NJ
908-580-1300

Hotel Indigo Basking Ridge
80 Allen Road
Basking Ridge, NJ

908-580-1300

Engleside Inn
30 Engleside Avenue
Beach Haven, NJ
609-492-1251

The Sea Shell Motel, Restaurant & Beach Club
10 S. Atlantic Ave.
Beach Haven, NJ

609-492-4611

Howard Johnson Express Inn -
Blackwood
832 N Black Horse Pike
Blackwood, NJ
856-228-4040

Best Western Bordentown Inn
1068 Route 206
Bordentown, NJ
609-298-8000

Candlewood Suites Bordentown-
Trenton
200 Rising Sun Road
Bordentown, NJ

609-291-1010

Residence Inn By Marriott
Bridgewater Branchburg
3241 Route 22 East
Branchburg, NJ
908 725 9812

Somerset Hills Hotel
200 Liberty Corners Road
Bridgewater, NJ
908-647-6700

Motel 6 Brooklawn
801 Route 130 South
Brooklawn, NJ
856-456-6688

Extended Stay America - Mt. Olive -
Budd Lake
71 International Dr. South
Budd Lake, NJ
973-347-5522

Beach Shack
205 Beach Avenue
Cape May, NJ
877-742-2507

Marquis De Lafayette Hotel
501 Beach Avenue
Cape May, NJ

609-884-3500

Comfort Inn & Suites Carneys Point
634 Soders Road
Carneys Point, NJ
856-299-8282

Holiday Inn Express Hotel & Suites
Carneys Point Nj Trnpk Exit 1
506 Pennsville Auburn Road
Carneys Point, NJ

856-351-9222

Extended Stay America - Philadelphia
- Cherry Hill
1653 East State Highway No. 70
Cherry Hill, NJ
856-616-1200

Holiday Inn Cherry Hill
2175 West Marlton Pike
Cherry Hill, NJ

856-663-5300

Residence Inn Cherry Hill
Philadelphia
1821 Old Cuthbert Road
Cherry Hill, NJ

856-429-6111

Hampton Inn Clinton
16 Frontage Drive
Clinton, NJ
908-713-4800

Holiday Inn Clinton
111 West Main Street
Clinton, NJ

908-735-5111

Courtyard By Marriott Cranbury
South Brunswick
420 Forsgate Drive
Cranbury, NJ
609-655-9950

Residence Inn Cranbury South
Brunswick
2662 Route 130
Cranbury, NJ

609-395-9447

Staybridge Suites Cranbury
1272 South River Road
Cranbury, NJ

609-409-7181

Homewood Suites By HiltonÂ®
Newark-Cranford
2 Jackson Drive
Cranford, NJ
908-709-1980

Residence Inn Deptford
1154 Hurffville
Deptford, NJ
856-686-9188

Homewood Suites By Hilton Dover
Rockaway
2 Commerce Center Drive
Dover, NJ
973-989-8899

Best Western East Brunswick Inn
764 Route 18
East Brunswick, NJ
732-238-4900

Extended Stay America -
Meadowlands - East Rutherford
300 State Highway, Route 3 East
East Rutherford, NJ
201-939-8866

Residence Inn By Marriott East
Rutherford Meadowlands
10 Murray Hill Parkway
East Rutherford, NJ

201-939-0020

Quality Inn East Windsor
351 Franklin Street
East Windsor, NJ
609-448-7399

Homewood Suites by Hilton
Eatontown
4 Industrial Way East
Eatontown, NJ
732-380-9300

Extended Stay America - Edison -
Raritan Center
1 Fieldcrest Ave.
Edison, NJ
732-346-9366

Red Roof Inn Edison
860 New Durham Road.
Edison, NJ

732-248-9300

Sheraton Edison Hotel Raritan Center
125 Raritan Center Parkway
Edison, NJ

732-225-8300

Residence Inn Marriott Atlantic City
Airport Egg Harbor Township
3022 Fire Road
Egg Harbor Township, NJ
609-813-2344

Extended Stay America Elizabeth -
Newark Airport
45 International Boulevard
Elizabeth, NJ
908-355-4300

Residence Inn Newark Elizabeth
Liberty Intl Airport
83 Glimcher Realty Way
Elizabeth, NJ

908-352-4300

Element By Westin Ewing Princeton
1000 Sam Weinroth Road East
Ewing, NJ
609-671-0050

Ramada Flemington
250 Highway 202
Flemington, NJ
908-782-7472

Extended Stay America - Somerset -
Franklin
30 Worlds Fair Drive
Franklin, NJ
732-469-8080

The Widow McCrea House
53 Kingwood Avenue
Frenchtown, NJ
908-996-4999

Element By Westin Harrison-Newark
399 Somerset Street
Harrison, NJ
973-484-1500

Days Inn Hillsboro
118 Route 206 South
Hillsborough, NJ
908-685-9000

The Inn at Millrace Pond
313 Johnsonburg Road/H 519N
Hope, NJ
908-459-4884

APA Hotel Woodbridge
120 Wood Avenue South
Iselin, NJ
732-494-6200

Candlewood Suites Jersey City
Exchange Place
21 Second Street
Jersey City, NJ
201-659-2500

Howard Johnson -
Princeton/Lawrenceville
2995 Brunswick Pike
Lawrenceville, NJ
609-896-1100

Red Roof Inn Princeton - Ewing
3203 Brunswick Pike
Lawrenceville, NJ

609-896-3388

Quality Inn Ledgewood
1691 Route 46 East
Ledgewood, NJ
973-347-5100

Ocean Place Resort
1 Ocean Blvd
Long Branch, NJ
732-571-4000

Homewood Suites By HiltonÂ®
Mahwah, Nj
375 Corporate Drive
Mahwah, NJ·
201-760-9994

Sheraton Mahwah
1 International Boulevard
Mahwah, NJ

201-529-1660

Super 8 Mahwah
160 State Route 17 South
Mahwah, NJ

201-512-0800

Days Inn Monmouth Junction
Princeton
208 New Road
Monmouth Junction, NJ
732-821-8800

Candlewood Suites Parsippany-
Morris Plains
100 Candlewood Drive
Morris Plains, NJ
973-984-9960

Candlewood Suites Philadelphia Mt.
Laurel
4000 Crawford Place
Mount Laurel, NJ
856-642-7567

Extended Stay America
-Philadelphia - Mt. Laurel -Crawford
Place
101 Diemer Drive
Mount Laurel, NJ

856-778-4100

Red Roof Inn Mt Laurel
603 Fellowship Rd
Mount Laurel, NJ

856-234-5589

Residence Inn By Marriott Mt. Laurel
At Bishop's Gate
1000 Bishops Gate Boulevard
Mount Laurel, NJ

856-234-1025

Staybridge Suites-
Philadelphia/Mount Laurel
4115 Church Road
Mount Laurel, NJ

856-722-1900

Towneplace Suites By Marriott Mt
Laurel
450 Century Parkway
Mount Laurel, NJ

856-778-8221

Residence Inn Mount Olive At The
International Trade Center
271 Continental Drive
Mount Olive, NJ
973-691-1720

Red Roof Inn Neptune
3310 Highway 33
Neptune, NJ
732-643-8888

Residence Inn By Marriott Neptune
At Gateway Centre
230 Jumping Brook Road
Neptune, NJ

732-643-9350

Econo Lodge Newton
448 Route 206 South
Newton, NJ
973-383-3922

Meadowland View Hotel
2750 Tonnelle Avenue
North Bergen, NJ
201-348-3600

Surf 16 Motel
1600 Surf Avenue
North Wildwood, NJ
609-522-1010

Red Roof Inn Parsippany
855 Us 46
Parsippany, NJ
973-334-3737

Residence Inn Parsippany
3 Gatehall Drive
Parsippany, NJ

973-984-3313

Sonesta Es Suites Parsippany
61 Interpace Parkway
Parsippany, NJ

973-334-2907

Embassy Suites Hotel Piscataway-
Somerset
121 Centennial Avenue
Piscataway, NJ
732-980-0500

The Pillars of Plainfield
922 Central Avenue
Plainfield, NJ
908-753-0922

Extended Stay America - Princeton -
West Windsor
3450 Brunswick Pike
Princeton, NJ
609-919-9000

Hampton Inn Princeton, Nj
4385 Us 1 South
Princeton, NJ

609-951-0066

Holiday Inn Princeton
100 Independence Way
Princeton, NJ

609-520-1200

Residence Inn Princeton At Carnegie
Center
3563 Us Route 1
Princeton, NJ

609-799-0550

Residence Inn Princeton At Carnegie
Center

3563 Us Route 1
Princeton, NJ
609-799-0550

Sonesta ES Suites South Brunswick -
Princeton
4225 Us Highway 1
Princeton, NJ
732-329-9600

Sonesta Es Suites Princeton
4375 Us Route 1 South
Princeton, NJ
609-951-0009

Best Western Inn At Ramsey
1315 Route 17 South
Ramsey, NJ
201-327-6700

Extended Stay America Ramsey -
Upper Saddle River
112 State Highway 17
Ramsey, NJ
201-236-9996

Extended Stay America - Red Bank -
Middletown
329 Newman Springs Road
Red Bank, NJ
732-450-8688

Extended Stay America -
Meadowlands - Rutherford
750 Edwin L. Ward Hwy
Rutherford, NJ
201-635-0266

Residence Inn Saddle River
7 Boroline Road
Saddle River, NJ
201-934-4144

Candlewood Suites Secaucus
279 Secaucus Road
Secaucus, NJ
201-865-3900

Extended Stay America - Secaucus -
Meadowlands
1 Meadowlands Pkwy
Secaucus, NJ
201-617-1711

Extended Stay America - Secaucus -
New York City Area
One Plaza Drive
Secaucus, NJ
201-553-9700

Red Roof PLUS Secaucus -
Meadowlands - NYC
15 Meadowlands Parkway
Secaucus, NJ
201-319-1000

Sonesta Es Suites Somers Point
900 Mays Landing Road
Somers Point, NJ
609-927-6400

Candlewood Suites Somerset
41 Worlds Fair Drive
Somerset, NJ
732-748-1400

Holiday Inn Somerset
195 Davidson Avenue
Somerset, NJ
732-356-1700

Homewood Suites By HiltonÂ®
Somerset Nj
101 Pierce Street
Somerset, NJ
732-868-9155

Residence Inn Somerset
37 Worlds Fair Drive
Somerset, NJ
732-627-0881

Sonesta Es Suites Somerset
260 Davidson Avenue
Somerset, NJ
732-356-8000

Extended Stay America Princeton -
South Brunswick
4230 Us Route 1
South Brunswick, NJ
732-438-5010

Woolverton Inn
6 Woolverton Rd
Stockton, NJ
877-411-3436

Hampton Inn
Philadelphia/Bridgeport
2 Pureland Drive
Swedesboro, NJ
856-467-6200

Holiday Inn Philadelphia South -
Swedesboro
1 Pureland Drive
Swedesboro, NJ
856-467-3322

Residence Inn Tinton Falls
90 Park Road
Tinton Falls, NJ
732-389-8100

TP Hotel
2 West Water Street
Toms River, NJ
732-341-6700

TP Hotel

2 West Water Street
Toms River, NJ
732-341-6700

Rodeway Inn Vineland
998 West Landis Ave
Vineland, NJ
856-696-3030

Residence Inn Wayne
30 Nevins Road
Wayne, NJ
973-872-7100

Sheraton Lincoln Harbor Hotel
500 Harbour Boulevard
Weehawken, NJ
201-617-5600

The Highland House
131 N Broadway
West Cape May, NJ
609-898-1198

Residence Inn By Marriott West
Orange
107 Prospect Avenue
West Orange, NJ
973-669-4700

Extended Stay America - Hanover -
Parsippany
125 Rt 10 East
Whippany, NJ
973-463-1999

Tide Winds Motel
231 East Davis Avenue
Wildwood, NJ
690-522-0901 - off season 609-522-
4740

Extended Stay America - Newark -
Woodbridge
1 Hoover Way
Woodbridge, NJ
732-442-8333

# New Mexico Listings

Albuquerque Inn & Suites
1635 Candelaria Boulevard Northeast
Albuquerque, NM
505-344-5311

Amberly Courtyard Inn and Suites
25 1/2 Hotel Circle Northeast
Albuquerque, NM
505-314-2525

Amberly Courtyard Inn and Suites
25 1/2 Hotel Circle Northeast
Albuquerque, NM
505-271-1000

Americas Best Value Inn Midtown
Albuquerque
2108 Menaul Boulevard Ne
Albuquerque, NM

505-884-2480

Baymont Inn And Suites Albuquerque
Downtown
411 Mcknight Avenue Northwest
Albuquerque, NM

505-242-5228

Best Western Airport Albuquerque
Innsuites Hotel & Suites
2400 Yale Boulevard Se
Albuquerque, NM

505-242-7022

Best Western Plus Rio Grande Inn
1015 Rio Grande Boulevard Nw
Albuquerque, NM

505-843-9500

Brittania & W.E. Mauger Estate B&B
701 Roma Avenue Northwest
Albuquerque, NM

505-242-8755

Candlewood Suites Albuquerque
3025 Menaul Blvd Ne
Albuquerque, NM

505-888-3424

Casita Chamisa Bed & Breakfast
850 Chamisal Road Nw
Albuquerque, NM

505-897-4644

Comfort Inn And Suites North
5811 Signal Avenue Northeast
Albuquerque, NM

505-822-1090

Comfort Suites Albuquerque
5251 San Antonio Blvd
Albuquerque, NM

505-797-0850

Days Inn & Suites Albuquerque North
5101 Ellison Northeast
Albuquerque, NM

505-344-1555

Days Inn Midtown Abq
2120 Menaul Ne
Albuquerque, NM

505-884-0250

Days Inn West Albuquerque
6031 Iliff Road Northwest
Albuquerque, NM

505-836-3297

Drury Inn & Suites Albuquerque
North
4310 The 25 Way Northeast
Albuquerque, NM

505-341-3600

Econo Lodge Downtown
817 Central Ave. N.E.
Albuquerque, NM

505-243-1321

Econo Lodge East
13211 Central Ave N E
Albuquerque, NM

505-292-7600

Econo Lodge Midtown
2412 Carlisle Blvd N E
Albuquerque, NM

505-880-0080

Econo Lodge Old Town
Albuquerque
2321 Central Avenue Northwest
Albuquerque, NM

505-243-8475

Econo Lodge West - Coors Blvd
5712 Iliff Rd Nw
Albuquerque, NM

505-836-0011

Extended Stay America -
Albuquerque - Airport
2321 International Ave. Se
Albuquerque, NM

505-244-0414

Holiday Inn Express Albuquerque (I-
40 Eubank)
10330 Hotel Ave Northeast
Albuquerque, NM

505-275-8900

Homewood Suites By Hilton
Albuquerque Uptown
7101 Arvada Ave Ne
Albuquerque, NM

505-881-7300

Howard Johnson Albuquerque
Midtown
900 Medical Arts Avenue Ne
Albuquerque, NM

505-243-5693

Howard Johnson Express
Albuquerque
7630 Pan American North East
Albuquerque, NM

505-828-1600

Microtel Inn & Suites By Wyndham
Albuquerque West
9910 Avalon Road Northwest
Albuquerque, NM

505-836-1686

Quality Inn & Suites Albuquerque
West
6100 West Iliff Road
Albuquerque, NM

505-836-8600

Quality Inn University
2015 Menaul Boulevard Northeast
Albuquerque, NM

Residence Inn Albuquerque
3300 Prospect Ave Northeast
Albuquerque, NM

505-881-2661

Residence Inn Albuquerque Airport
2301 International Ave Se
Albuquerque, NM

505-242-2844

Residence Inn Albuquerque North
4331 The Lane At 25 Northeast
Albuquerque, NM

505-761-0200

Sheraton Uptown Albuquerque Hotel
2600 Louisiana Blvd Northeast
Albuquerque, NM

505-881-0000

Sleep Inn Airport Albuquerque
2300 International Avenue Southeast
Albuquerque, NM

505-244-3325

Staybridge Suites Albuquerque -
Airport
1350 Sunport Place Se
Albuquerque, NM

505-338-3900

Staybridge Suites Albuquerque North
5817 Signal Avenue Ne &; Alameda
Albuquerque, NM

505-266-7829

Suburban Extended Stay
Albuquerque
2401 Wellesley Drive Ne
Albuquerque, NM

505-883-8888

Super 8 Motel - Albuquerque East
450 Paisano St Ne

Albuquerque, NM
505-271-4807

Super 8 Motel - Albuquerque/West
6030 Iliff Nw
Albuquerque, NM
505-836-5560

Super 8 Motel Albuquerque/Midtown
2500 University Boulevard Ne
Albuquerque, NM
505-888-4884

Super 8 Motel Albuquerque/Midtown
2500 University Boulevard Ne
Albuquerque, NM
505-314-7148

The Hotel Cascada
2500 Carlisle Boulevard Northeast
Albuquerque, NM
505-888-3311

Towneplace Suites By Marriott
Albuquerque Airport
2400 Centre Avenue Southeast
Albuquerque, NM
505-232-5800

Angel Fire Resort
10 Miller Lane
Angel Fire, NM
575-377-6401

Best Western Pecos Inn
2209 W. Main St.
Artesia, NM
575-748-3324

Super 8 Belen
428 South Main Street
Belen, NM
505-864-8188

Days Inn Bernalillo / Albuquerque
North
107 North Camino Del Pueblo Drive
Bernalillo, NM
505-771-7000

Super 8 Motel - Bernalillo
265 East Hwy 550
Bernalillo, NM

505-771-4700

Super 8 Bloomfield
525 West Broadway
Bloomfield, NM
505-632-8886

Days Inn Carlsbad
3910 National Park Hwy
Carlsbad, NM
575-887-7800

High Feather Ranch
29 High Feather Ranch Road
Cerrillos, NM
505-424-1333

Best Western Kokopelli Lodge
702 South First St.
Clayton, NM
575-374-2589

Days Inn & Suites Of Clayton
1120 South 1st Street
Clayton, NM

575-374-0133

Super 8 Clayton
S Hwy 87
Clayton, NM

575-374-8127

The Lodge Resort
#1 Corona Place
Cloudcroft, NM
575-682-2566

Econo Lodge Clovis
1400 E. Mabry Drive
Clovis, NM
575-763-3439

Quality Inn Clovis
2920 Mabry Drive
Clovis, NM

Best Western Deming Southwest
Inn
1500 West Pine Street
Deming, NM
575-546-4544

Comfort Inn & Suites Deming
1010 West Pine Street
Deming, NM

575-544-3600

Deming - Days Inn
1601 E. Pine Street
Deming, NM

575-546-8813

Hampton Inn Deming
3751 E Cedar Street
Deming, NM

575-546-2022

Quality Inn Deming
4600 East Pine Street
Deming, NM

575-546-2661

Econo Lodge Eagle Nest
715 Highway 64 East
Eagle Nest, NM
575-377-6813

Hotel Luna Mystica
25 ABC Mesa Rd
El Prado, NM
575-613-1411

Rodeway Inn Espanola
604-B South Riverside Drive
Espanola, NM
505-753-2419

Comfort Inn Farmington
555 Scott Avenue
Farmington, NM
505-325-2626

Rodeway Inn Farmington
1601 East Broadway
Farmington, NM

505-325-1813

Towneplace Suites By Marriott
Farmington
4200 Sierra Vista Drive
Farmington, NM

505-327-2442

Days Inn Gallup East
1603 W. Highway 66
Gallup, NM
505-863-3891

Econo Lodge Gallup
3101 W Us 66
Gallup, NM

505-722-3800

Knights Inn & Suites Gallup
3208 West Highway 66
Gallup, NM

505-722-0982

Quality Inn & Suites Gallup
1500 West Maloney
Gallup, NM

505-726-1000

Red Roof Inn Gallup
3304 West Highway 66
Gallup, NM

505-722-7765

Rodeway Inn Gallup
1709 West Highway 66
Gallup, NM

505-863-9301

Sleep Inn Gallup
3820 E Highway 66
Gallup, NM

505-863-3535

Days Inn Grants
1504 East Santa Fe Avenue

Grants, NM
505-287-8883

Best Western Executive Inn
309 North Marland Boulevard
Hobbs, NM
575-397-7171

Days Inn Hobbs
211 North Marland Boulevard
Hobbs, NM

575-397-6541

Econo Lodge Hobbs
619 North Marland Boulevard
Hobbs, NM

575-397-3591

Sleep Inn And Suites Hobbs
4630 North Lovington Highway
Hobbs, NM

575-393-3355

Laughing Lizard Inn and Cafe
17526 H 4
Jemez Springs, NM
575-829-3108

Americas Best Value Inn And Suites
Las Cruces
901 Avenida de Mesilla
Las Cruces, NM
575-524-8603

Best Western Mission Inn
1765 South Main Street
Las Cruces, NM

575-524-8591

Comfort Suites University Las Cruces
2101 South Triviz
Las Cruces, NM

575-522-1300

Days Inn Las Cruces
755 Avenida de Mesilla
Las Cruces, NM

575-526-8311

Drury Inn & Suites Las Cruces
1631 Hickory Loop
Las Cruces, NM

575-523-4100

Hotel Encanto de Las Cruces
705 South Telshor Blvd.
Las Cruces, NM

575-522-4300

Lundeen Inn of the Arts
618 South Alameda
Las Cruces, NM

575-526-3326

Quality Inn & Suites Las Cruces
2200 South Valley Drive
Las Cruces, NM

575-524-4663

Ramada Palms De Las Cruces
201 East University Avenue
Las Cruces, NM

575-526-4411

Sleep Inn University
2121 South Triviz
Las Cruces, NM

575-522-1700

Staybridge Suites Las Cruces
2651 Northrise Drive
Las Cruces, NM

575-521-7999

Super 8 Las Cruces / La Posada
Lane
245 la Posada Lane
Las Cruces, NM

575-523-8695

Super 8 Las Cruces/White Sands
Area
3405 Bataan Memorial West
Las Cruces, NM

575-382-1490

Teakwood Inn and Suites
2600 S Valley Drive
Las Cruces, NM

575-526-4441

The Coachlight Inn and RV Park
301 S Motel Blvd
Las Cruces, NM

575-526-3301

Towneplace Suites By Marriott Las
Cruces
2143 Telshor Court
Las Cruces, NM

575-532-6500

Comfort Inn Las Vegas
2500 North Grand Avenue
Las Vegas, NM
505-425-1100

Holiday Inn Express Hotel & Suites
Las Vegas
816 South Grand Avenue
Las Vegas, NM

505-426-8182

Plaza Hotel Las Vegas
230 Plaza St

Las Vegas, NM

505-425-3591

Super 8 Las Vegas
2029 N Grand Ave
Las Vegas, NM

505-425-5288

Econo Lodge Lordsburg
1408 South Main Street
Lordsburg, NM
575-542-3666

Hampton Inn Lordsburg Nm
412 Wabash
Lordsburg, NM

575-542-8900

Holiday Inn Express Hotel & Suites
Los Alamos Entrada Park
60 Entrada Drive
Los Alamos, NM
505-661-2646

Days Inn Los Lunas
1919 Main St
Los Lunas, NM
505-865-5995

Best Western Moriarty Heritage Inn
111 Anaya Boulevard 87035
Moriarty, NM
505-832-5000

Comfort Inn Moriarty
119 Route 66 East
Moriarty, NM

505-832-6666

Super 8 Moriarty
1611 Old Route 66
Moriarty, NM

505-832-6730

Bear Creek Cabins
88 Main Street/H 15
Pinos Altos, NM
575-388-4501

Best Western Rivers Edge
301 W. River Street
Questa, NM
575-754-1766

Best Western Plus Raton Hotel
473 Clayton Road
Raton, NM
575-445-8501

Holiday Inn Express Hotel & Suites
Raton
101 Card Avenue
Raton, NM

575-445-1500

Microtel Inn & Suites by Wyndham Raton
1640 Cedar Street
Raton, NM

575-445-9100

Golden Eagle Lodge Red River
1100 East Main Street
Red River, NM
575-754-2227

Terrace Towers Lodge
712 West Main Street
Red River, NM

800-695-6343

Days Inn Rio Rancho
4200 Crestview Dr
Rio Rancho, NM
505-892-8800

Extended Stay America -
Albuquerque - Rio Rancho
2608 The American Rd. Nw
Rio Rancho, NM

505-792-1338

Best Western El Rancho Palacio
2205 N Main St
Roswell, NM
575-622-2721

Candlewood Suites Roswell New Mexico
4 Military Heights Drive
Roswell, NM

575-623-4300

Cozy Cowboy Cottage Rentals
804 W 4th Street
Roswell, NM

575-624-3258

Days Inn - Roswell
1310 North Main Street
Roswell, NM

575-623-4021

Frontier Motel
3010 N Main St
Roswell, NM

575-622-1400

Holiday Inn Express Roswell
2300 N Main Street
Roswell, NM

575-627-9900

Rodeway Inn Roswell
2803 West 2nd Street
Roswell, NM

575-623-9440

Alto Hombre Gordito Hideout
H 37 @ MM 3 N
Ruidoso, NM
575-336-7877

Apache Village Cabins
311 Mechem Drive
Ruidoso, NM

575-257-2435

Best Western Pine Springs Inn
111 Pine Springs Drive
Ruidoso, NM

575-378-8100

Casey's Cabins
2640 Suddereth
Ruidoso, NM

575-257-6355

Sierra Blanca Cabins
215 Country Club Drive
Ruidoso, NM

575-257-2103

The Lodge at Sierra Blanca
1451 Meecham Drive
Ruidoso, NM

575-258-3333

Whispering Pines Cabins
422 Main Road
Ruidoso, NM

575-257-4311

10,000 Waves Japanese Spa and Resort
3451 Hyde Park Road
Santa Fe, NM
505-992-5003

Alexander's Inn Vacation Rentals
106 East Faithway Street
Santa Fe, NM

505-986-1431

Best Western Plus Inn Of Santa Fe
3650 Cerrillos Road
Santa Fe, NM

505 438-3822

Comfort Inn Santa Fe
4312 Cerrillos Road
Santa Fe, NM

505-474-7330

Eldorado Hotel & Spa
309 W San Francisco Street
Santa Fe, NM

505-988-4455

Hacienda Nicholas

320 Marcy C
Santa Fe, NM

505-992-8385

Hampton Inn Santa Fe
3625 Cerrillos Road
Santa Fe, NM

505-474-3900

Hilton Santa Fe Historic Plaza
100 Sandoval Street
Santa Fe, NM

505-988-2811

Hilton Santa Fe Resort & Spa At Buffalo Thunder
20 Buffalo Thunder Trail
Santa Fe, NM

505-455-5555

Hotel Chimayo de Santa Fe
125 Washington Avenue
Santa Fe, NM

505-988-4900

Hotel Santa Fe & Spa
1501 Paseo de Peralta
Santa Fe, NM

505-982-1200

Hotel St. Francis
210 Don Gaspar Avenue
Santa Fe, NM

505-983-5700

Inn of the Turquoise Bear
342 E Buena Vista St.
Santa Fe, NM

505-983-0798

La Posada de Santa Fe A Tribute Portfolio Resort & Spa
330 East Palace Avenue
Santa Fe, NM

505-986-0000

Motel 6 Santa Fe Central
3470 Cerrillos Road
Santa Fe, NM

505-471-4000

Pecos Trail Inn
2239 Old Pecos Trail
Santa Fe, NM

505-982-1943

Residence Inn Santa Fe
1698 Galisteo Street
Santa Fe, NM

505-988-7300

Santa Fe Sage Inn
725 Cerrillos Road
Santa Fe, NM

505-982-5952

The Inn and Spa at Loretto
11 Old Santa Fe Trail
Santa Fe, NM

800-727-5531

The Inn of Five Graces
150 East Devargas Street
Santa Fe, NM

505-992-0957

The Lodge at Santa Fe
750 North St. Francis Drive
Santa Fe, NM

505-992-5800

Two Casitas, Vacation Rentals Pet
Friendly
30 homes. Walk to the Plaza &
Canyon Rd
Santa Fe, NM

505-984-2270

Comfort Inn Santa Rosa
2524 East Historic Route 66
Santa Rosa, NM
575-472-2663

Quality Inn Santa Rosa
2533 Historic Route 66
Santa Rosa, NM

575-472-5570

Comfort Inn Silver City
1060 E Us Hwy 180
Silver City, NM
575-534-1883

Econo Lodge Silver City
1120 Highway 180 East
Silver City, NM

575-534-1111

Holiday Inn Express Silver City
1103 Superior Street
Silver City, NM

575-538-2525

Motel 6 Silver City
1040 East Highway 180
Silver City, NM

575-388-1983

Rodeway Inn Silver City
3420 Highway 180 East
Silver City, NM

575-538-3711

Americas Best Value Inn
1009 North California Street
Socorro, NM
575-835-0276

Best Western Socorro Hotel &
Suites
1100 North California Street
Socorro, NM

575-838-0556

Comfort Inn & Suites Socorro
1259 Frontage Road Northwest
Socorro, NM

575-838-4400

Days Inn Socorro
507 North California Ave
Socorro, NM

575-835-0230

Super 8 Socorro
1121 Frontage Rd Nw
Socorro, NM

575-835-4626

Adobe and Pines Inn
4107 H 68
Taos, NM
575-751-0947

Alpine Village Suites
PO Box 917
Taos, NM

505-776-8540

American Artist Gallery House
132 Frontier Lane
Taos, NM

505-758-4446

Casa Europa
840 Upper Ranchitos Road (HC68,
Box 3F)
Taos, NM

575-758-9798

La Dona Luz Inn
206 Des Georges Lane
Taos, NM

575-758-9000

Palacio de Marquesa
405 Cordoba Road
Taos, NM

575-758-4777

Quality Inn Taos
1043 Paseo Del Pueblo Sur
Taos, NM

575-758-2200

San Geronimo Lodge
1101 Witt Road
Taos, NM

575-751-3776

Comfort Inn & Suites Truth Or
Consequences
2205 North Date Street
Truth Or Consequences, NM
575-894-1660

Best Western Discovery Inn
200 East Estrella Avenue
Tucumcari, NM
575-461-4884

Econo Lodge Tucumcari
3400 E. Tucumcari Boulevard
Tucumcari, NM

575-461-4194

Super 8 Tucumcari
4001 East Tucumcari Boulevard
Tucumcari, NM

575-461-4444

Rodeway Inn Whites City
6 Carlsbad Cavern Highway
Whites City, NM
575-785-2296

# New York Listings

Luxury Furnished Apartments In
Columbus Ave New York
808 Columbus Avenue
Acra, NY
888-K9-CLUBG (592-5824)

Best Western Albany Airport Inn
200 Wolf Road
Albany, NY
518-458-1000

Best Western Sovereign Hotel Albany
1228 Western Avenue
Albany, NY

518 489 2981

Cresthill Suites Hotel - Albany
1415 Washington Avenue
Albany, NY

518-454-0007

Days Inn Albany Guilderland
1230 Western Avenue
Albany, NY

518-489-4423

Days Inn And Suites Albany
1606 Central Ave
Albany, NY

518-869-5327

Dog-Friendly Lodging - Please always call ahead to make sure an establishment is still dog-friendly.

Econo Lodge Colonie Center Mall
1630 Central Avenue
Albany, NY

518-456-0222

Extended Stay America - Albany -
Suny
1395 Washington Ave.
Albany, NY

518-446-0680

Hampton Inn & Suites Albany-
Downtown, NY
25 Chapel Street
Albany, NY

518-432-7000

Radisson Hotel Albany
205 Wolf Road
Albany, NY

518-458-7250

Red Roof Inn Albany
188 Wolf Road
Albany, NY

518-459-1971

Towneplace Suites By Marriott
Albany University Area
1379 Washington Avenue
Albany, NY

518-435-1900

Gansett Green Manor
273 Main Street
Amagansett, NY
631-267-3133

Candlewood Suites Buffalo Amherst
20 Flint Road
Amherst, NY
716-688-2100

Comfort Inn University
1 Flint Road
Amherst, NY

716-688-0811

Extended Stay America - Buffalo -
Amherst
125 Inn Keepers Lane
Amherst, NY

716-564-0620

Lord Amherst Hotel
5000 Main Street
Amherst, NY

716-839-2200

Red Roof Plus University At Buffalo
Amherst
42 Flint Road

Amherst, NY

716-689-7474

Quality Inn Binghamton West
7666 Route 434
Apalachin, NY
607-625-4441

Days Inn Auburn/Finger Lakes
Region
37 William St.
Auburn, NY
315-252-7567

Super 8 Auburn
19 Mcmaster Street
Auburn, NY

315-253-8886

Caboose Motel
8620 State Route 415
Avoca, NY
607-566-2216

Microtel Inn & Suites By Wyndham
Baldwinsville/Syracuse
131 Downer Street
Baldwinsville, NY
315-635-9556

Batavia-Days Inn
200 Oak Street
Batavia, NY
585-343-6000

La Quinta Inn & Suites Batavia
8200 Park Road
Batavia, NY

585-344-7000

Red Roof Inn Batavia
8204 Park Road
Batavia, NY

585-343-1000

Days Inn Bath
330 West Morris Street
Bath, NY
607-776-7644

Microtel Inn & Suites By Wyndham
Bath
370 West Morris St.
Bath, NY

607-776-5333

Extended Stay America - Long
Island - Bethpage
905 South Oyster Bay Road
Bethpage, NY
516-349-8759

Comfort Inn Binghamton
1000 Upper Front Street
Binghamton, NY
607-724-3297

Econo Lodge Inn & Suites
Binghamton
690 Old Front Street
Binghamton, NY

607-724-1341

Holiday Inn Binghamton-Downtown
Hawley Street
2-8 Hawley Street
Binghamton, NY

607-722-1212

Red Roof Inn Binghamton North
650 Old Front Street
Binghamton, NY

607-773-8111

Red Roof Inn Buffalo Niagara Airport
146 Maple Drive
Bowmansville, NY
716-633-1100

Econo Lodge Brockport
6575 4th Section Road
Brockport, NY
585-637-3157

Holiday Inn Express Brooklyn
625 Union Street
Brooklyn, NY
718-797-1133

Econo Lodge South Buffalo
4344 Milestrip Rd.
Buffalo, NY
716-825-7530

Homewood Suites By Hilton®
Buffalo-Amherst, NY
1138 Millersport Highway
Buffalo, NY

716-833-2277

Residence Inn By Marriott Buffalo
Amherst
100 Maple Road
Buffalo, NY

716-632-6622

Residence Inn By Marriott Buffalo
Galleria Mall
107 Anderson Road
Buffalo, NY

716-892-5410

Cedar Terrace Resort
665 Main Street
Cairo, NY
518-622-9313

Microtel Inn By Wyndham Calcium
8000 Virginia Smith Drive
Calcium, NY
315-629-5000

Dog-Friendly Lodging - Please always call ahead to make sure an establishment is still dog-friendly.

Blue Harbor House
67 Elm Street
Camden, NY
207-236-3196

The Inn at The Shaker Mill Farm
40 Cherry Lane
Canaan, NY
518-794-9345

Days Inn Canastota/Syracuse
377 North Peterboro Street
Canastota, NY
315-697-3309

Mountain View Log Home
Hunter Mountain
Catskills, NY
212-381-2375

Lincklaen House
79 Albany St
Cazenovia, NY
315-655-3461

Crabtree`s Kittle House Restaurant &
Inn - Bed And Breakfast
11 Kittle Road
Chappaqua, NY
914-666-8044

Comfort Inn Near Walden Galleria
Mall
475 Dingens St
Cheektowaga, NY
716-896-2800

Holiday Inn Buffalo International
Airport
4600 Genesee Street
Cheektowaga, NY
716-634-6969

Homewood Suites By HiltonÂ®
Buffalo-Airport
760 Dick Road
Cheektowaga, NY
716-685-0700

Asa Ransom House - Bed And
Breakfast
10529 Main Street-Route 5
Clarence, NY
716-759-2315

Staybridge Suites Buffalo Airport
8005 Sheridan Drive
Clarence, NY
716-810-7829

Best Western Inn Of Cobleskill
121 Burgin Drive
Cobleskill, NY
518-234-4321

Super 8 Cobleskill

955 East Main Street
Cobleskill, NY
518-234-4888

Econo Lodge Darien Lakes
8493 Alleghany Road
Corfu, NY
585-599-4681

Staybridge Suites Corning
201 Townley Avenue
Corning, NY
607-936-7800

Stiles Motel
9239 Victory Highway
Corning, NY
607-962-5221

Comfort Inn Cortland
2 1/2 Locust Ave.
Cortland, NY
607-753-7721

Quality Inn Cortland
188 Clinton Ave.
Cortland, NY
607-756-5622

Ramada Cortland
2 River Street
Cortland, NY
607-756-4431

Days Inn Cortland/Mcgraw
3775 Us Rt 11
Cortland / Mc Graw, NY
607-753-7594

Econo Lodge Cuba
1 North Branch Road
Cuba, NY
585-968-1992

Econo Lodge Dewitt
3400 Erie Boulevard East
DeWitt, NY
315-446-3300

Best Western Plus Dunkirk &
Fredonia Inn
3912 Vineyard Drive
Dunkirk, NY
716-366-7100

Comfort Inn Dunkirk
3925 Vineyard Dr
Dunkirk, NY
716-672-4450

Residence Inn by Marriott Albany
East Greenbush/Tech Valley
3 Tech Valley Drive
East Greenbush, NY
518-720-3600

Bend In the Road Guest House
58 Spring Close H
East Hampton, NY
631-324-4592

Mill House Inn
31 N Main Street
East Hampton, NY
631-324-9766

The Bassett House Inn
128 Montauk H
East Hampton, NY
631-324-6127

The Maidstone
207 Main Street/H 27
East Hampton, NY
631-324-5006

The Mill House Inn
31 North Main Street
East Hampton, NY
631-324-9766

Americas Best Value Inn - East
Syracuse
6608 Old Collamer Road
East Syracuse, NY
315-437-3500

Candlewood Suites East Syracuse
6550 Baptist Way
East Syracuse, NY
315-432-1684

Extended Stay America - Syracuse -
Dewitt
6630 Old Collamer Rd
East Syracuse, NY
315-463-1958

Quality Inn East Syracuse
6611 Old Collamer Rd South
East Syracuse, NY
315-432-9333

Ramada East Syracuse Carrier Circle
6555 Old Collamer Road South
East Syracuse, NY
315-437-2761

Residence Inn By Marriott Syracuse
Carrier Circle
6420 Yorktown Circle
East Syracuse, NY
315-432-4488

The Jefferson Inn
3 Jefferson Street
Ellicottville, NY
716-699-5869

Extended Stay America - White
Plains - Elmsford
118 West Main Street
Elmsford, NY
914-347-8073

Red Carpet Inn Endicott
749 West Main Street
Endicott, NY

Knights Inn Endwell/Binghamton
2603 East Main Street
Endwell, NY
607-754-8020

Candlewood Suites Watertown-Fort
Drum
26513 Herrick Drive
Evans Mills, NY
315-629-6990

Towneplace Suites Republic Airport
Long Island/Farmingdale
1 Marriott Plaza
Farmingdale, NY
631-454-0080

Extended Stay America - Fishkill -
Route 9
25 Merritt Blvd
Fishkill, NY
845-897-2800

Extended Stay America - Fishkill -
Westage Center
55 W. Merritt Blvd
Fishkill, NY

845-896-0592

Hawthorn Suites By Wyndham
Fishkill/Poughkeepsie Area
14 Schuyler Boulevard
Fishkill, NY

845-896-5210

The River Run
882 Main Street
Fleischmanns, NY
845-254-4884

Sheraton Laguardia East Hotel
135 20 39th Avenue
Flushing, NY
718-460-6666

Inn at Lake Joseph
162 Saint Josephs Road
Forestburgh, NY
845-791-9506

Brookside Manor
3728 Route 83
Fredonia, NY
716-672-7721

Days Inn Fredonia/Dunkirk
10455 Bennett Road Rt 60
Fredonia, NY

716-673-1351

Quality Inn Geneseo
4242 Lakeville Road
Geneseo, NY
585-243-0500

Cobtree Vacation Rental Homes
440-450 Armstrong Road
Geneva, NY
315-789-1144

Microtel Inn And Suites By
Wyndham - Geneva
550 Hamilton Street
Geneva, NY

315-789-7890

Ramada Geneva Lakefront
41 Lakefront Drive
Geneva, NY

Days Inn And Suites
Glenmont/Albany
15 Frontage Road
Glenmont, NY
518-449-5181

Quality Inn Queensbury
547 Aviation Road
Glens Falls, NY
518-793-3800

Super 8 Queensbury, Glens Falls
191 Corinth Road
Glens Falls, NY

518-761-9780

Chateau Motor Lodge
1810 Grand Island Boulevard
Grand Island, NY
716-773-2868

The Trout House Village Resort
9117 Lakeshore Drive
Hague, NY
518-543-6088

Comfort Inn & Suites Hamburg
3615 Commerce Place
Hamburg, NY
716-648-2922

Red Roof Inn Buffalo - Hamburg
5370 Camp Road
Hamburg, NY

716-648-7222

Bowen's by the Bays
177 West Montauk Highway
Hampton Bays, NY
631-728-1158

Residence Inn Hauppauge
850 Veterans Memorial Highway
Hauppauge, NY
631-724-4188

Red Roof Inn Rochester - Henrietta
4820 West Henrietta Road
Henrietta, NY
585-359-1100

Super 8 Motel - Henrietta/Rochester
Area
1000 Lehigh Station Road
Henrietta, NY

585-359-1630

Red Roof Inn & Suites Herkimer
100 Marginal Road,
Herkimer, NY
315-866-0490

Super 8 Highland NY
3423 Route 9 West
Highland, NY
845-691-6888

Fairbridge Inn & Suites Highland Falls
17 Main Street
Highland Falls, NY
845-446-9400

Comfort Inn & Suites Adj To
Akwesasne Mohawk Casino
865 State Route 37
Hogansburg, NY
518-358-1000

Residence Inn By Marriott Long
Island Holtsville
25 Middle Avenue
Holtsville, NY
631-475-9500

Days Inn Hornell NY
Route 36 &; Webb Crossing
Hornell, NY
607-324-6222

Econo Lodge Hornell
7462 Seneca Rd N
Hornell, NY

607-324-0800

Hunter Inn
7344 Main Street
Hunter, NY
518-263-3777

Finger Lakes Home
7750 County Road 153
Interlaken, NY
607-532-4770

Best Western University Inn
1020 Ellis Hollow Road
Ithaca, NY
607-272-6100

Courtyard Ithaca Airport/University
29 Thornwood Drive
Ithaca, NY

607-330-1000

Econo Lodge Ithaca
2303 N. Triphammer Rd.
Ithaca, NY

607-257-1400

Homewood Suites Ithaca
36 Cinema Drive
Ithaca, NY

607-266-0000

Log Country Inn
South Danby and La Rue Roads
Ithaca, NY

607-589-4771

Quality Inn Ithaca
356 Elmira Road
Ithaca, NY

607-272-0100

The William Henry Miller Inn
303 N Aurora Street
Ithaca, NY

607-256-4553

Trip Hotel Ithaca
One Sheraton Drive
Ithaca, NY

607-257-2000

Comfort Inn Jamestown
2800 North Main Street Extension
Jamestown, NY
716-664-5920

Fourpeaks
Stonehouse Road
Jay, NY
518-524-6726

Best Western Plus Of Johnson City
569 Harry L Drive
Johnson City, NY
607-729-9194

Red Roof Inn Binghamton - Johnson
City
590 Fairview Street
Johnson City, NY

607-729-8940

Holiday Inn Johnstown-Gloversville
308 North Comrie Ave
Johnstown, NY
518-762-4686

Trails End Inn
62 Trails End Way
Keene Valley, NY
518-576-9860

Villa Rosa B&B Inn

121 Highland Street
Kings Park, NY
631-724-4872

Best Western Plus Kingston Hotel
And Conference Center
503 Washington Avenue
Kingston, NY
845-338-0400

Rodeway Inn Skytop
239 Forest Hill Drive
Kingston, NY

845-331-2900

Lake George Gardens Motel
2107 H 9N
Lake George, NY
518-668-2232

Super 8 Lake George/Warrensburg
Area
3619 State Route 9
Lake George, NY

518-623-2811

Luzerne Court
508 Lake Ave
Lake Luzerne, NY
518-696-2734

Art Devline's Olympic
350 Main St
Lake Placid, NY
518-523-3700

Crowne Plaza Lake Placid
101 Olympic Drive
Lake Placid, NY

518-523-2556

Lake Placid Lodge
Whiteface Inn Road
Lake Placid, NY

518-523-2700

Quality Inn Lake Placid
2125 Saranac Ave.
Lake Placid, NY

518-523-9555

Rodeway Inn Lakeville
6001 Big Tree Road
Lakeville, NY
585-346-2330

Days Inn & Suites Latham/Troy
954 New Loudon Road
Latham, NY
518-783-6162

Microtel Inn By Wyndham Albany
Airport
7 Rensselaer Avenue
Latham, NY

518-782-9161

Quality Inn & Suites Albany Airport
611 Troy-Schenectady Rd
Latham, NY

518-785-5891

Residence Inn By Marriott Albany
Airport
1 Residence Inn Drive
Latham, NY

518-783-0600

The Century House, An Ascend Hotel
Collection Member
997 New Loudon Rd.
Latham, NY

518-785-0931

The Century House, An Ascend Hotel
Collection Member
997 New Loudon Rd.
Latham, NY

518-785-0931

The Century House, An Ascend Hotel
Collection Member
997 New Loudon Rd.
Latham, NY

518-785-0931

Howard Johnson Inn Liberty
2067 Route 52 East
Liberty, NY
845-292-7171

Travelodge Little Falls
20 Albany Street
Little Falls, NY
315-823-4954

Best Western Plus Liverpool Grace
Inn & Suites
136 Transistor Parkway
Liverpool, NY
315-701-4400

Homewood Suites By Hilton®
Syracuse/Liverpool
275 Elwood Davis Road
Liverpool, NY

315-451-3800

Knights Inn Syracuse/Liverpool
430 Electronics Parkway
Liverpool, NY

315-453-6330

Staybridge Suites Syracuse/Liverpool
439 Electronics Parkway
Liverpool, NY

315-457-1900

Super 8 Liverpool/Clay/Syracuse
Area
7360 Oswego Rd Off Ex 38
Liverpool, NY

315-451-8550

The Guest House
408 Debruce Road
Livingston Manor, NY
845-439-4000

Quality Inn Lockport
551 South Transit Street
Lockport, NY
716-434-4411

Aloft Long Island City-Manhattan
View
27-45 Jackson Avenue
Long Island City, NY
718-433-9305

Econo Lodge Malone
227 W. Main St.
Malone, NY
518-483-0500

Econo Lodge Massena
15054 State Highway 37
Massena, NY
315-764-0246

Extended Stay America Long Island -
Melville
100 Spagnoli Road
Melville, NY
631-777-3999

Hampton Inn Middletown
20 Crystal Run Crossing
Middletown, NY
845-344-3400

Howard Johnson Middletown
551 Rte 211 East I 84 Route 17
Middletown, NY

845-342-5822

Super 8 Motel - Middletown
563 Route 211 East
Middletown, NY

845-692-5828

Buttermilk Inn and Spa
220 North Road
Milton, NY
845-795-1310

Hither House Cottages
10 Lincoln Road
Montauk, NY
631-668-2714

Super 8 Montgomery
207 Montgomery Road
Montgomery, NY
845-457-3143

Super 8 Monticello NY
290 East Broadway
Monticello, NY
845-791-1690

Glen Highland Farm
217 Pegg Road
Morris, NY
607-263-5415

Emerson Resort and Spa
5340 H 28
Mount Tremper, NY
845-688-2828

Candlewood Suites Nanuet
20 Overlook Boulevard
Nanuet, NY
845-371-4445

Days Inn Nanuet Spring Valley
367 West Route 59
Nanuet, NY

845-623-4567

DoubleTree by Hilton Hotel Nanuet
425 E. Route 59
Nanuet, NY

845-623-6000

The Vagabond Inn
3300 Sliter Road
Naples, NY
585-554-6271

Ramada New Hartford
141 New Hartford Street
New Hartford, NY

LeFevre House
14 Southside Avenue
New Paltz, NY
845-255-4747

Residence Inn New Rochelle
35 le Count Place
New Rochelle, NY
914-636-7888

Residence Inn New Rochelle
35 le Count Place
New Rochelle, NY

914-636-7888

Residence Inn New Rochelle
35 le Count Place
New Rochelle, NY

914-636-7888

Econo Lodge Near Stewart
International Airport
310 Windsor Hwy Sr 32
New Windsor, NY
845-561-6620

Homewood Suites By Hilton

Newburgh-Stewart Airport
180 Breunig Road
New Windsor, NY

845-567-2700

Bentley Hotel
500 East 62nd Street
New York, NY
212-644-6000

Conrad New York
102 North End Avenue
New York, NY

212-945-0100

Courtyard By Marriott New York
Manhattan/Times Square
114 West 40th Street
New York, NY

212-391-0088

Element New York Times Square
West
311 West 39th Street
New York, NY

212-643-0770

Eventi, A Kimpton Hotel
851 Avenue Of The Americas
New York, NY

212-564-4567

Flatiron Hotel
9 West 26th Street 1141 Broadway
Ave
New York, NY

212-839-8000

Hilton Times Square
234 West 42nd Street
New York, NY

212-840-8222

Hotel 48LEX New York
517 Lexington Avenue
New York, NY

212-888-3500

Hotel Americano
518 West 27th Street
New York, NY

212-216-0000

Ink48, A Kimpton Hotel
653 11th Avenue
New York, NY

212-757-0088

Le Parker Meridien New York
119 West 56th Street
New York, NY

212-245-5000

Loews Regency New York Hotel
540 Park Avenue At 61st Street
New York, NY

212-759-4100

New York Hilton Midtown
1335 Avenue Of Americas
New York, NY

212-586-7000

RENAISSANCE NEW YORK HOTEL
57, A Marriott Luxury & Lifestyle Hotel
130 East 57th Street
New York, NY

212-753-8841

RENAISSANCE NEW YORK TIMES
SQUARE HOTEL, A Marriott Luxury
& Lifestyle Hotel
714 7th Avenue
New York, NY

212-765-7676

Residence Inn By Marriott New York
Manhattan/Times Square
1033 Avenue Of The Americas
New York, NY

212-768-0007

Sheraton Tribeca New York Hotel
370 Canal Street
New York, NY

212-966-3400

Sofitel New York
45 West 44th Street
New York, NY

212-354-8844

Soho Grand Hotel
310 West Broadway
New York, NY

212-965-3000

THE ALGONQUIN HOTEL TIMES
SQUARE, AUTOGRAPH
COLLECTION, A Marriott Luxury &
Lifestyle Hotel
59 West 44th Street
New York, NY

212-840-6800

The Chatwal A Luxury Collection
Hotel
130 West 44th Street
New York, NY

212-764-6200

The James New York
27 Grand Street
New York, NY

212-465-2000

The Marmara Manhattan
301 East 94th Street
New York, NY

212-427-3100

The Muse New York, A Kimpton
Hotel
130 West 46th Street
New York, NY

212-485-2400

The Ritz-Carlton New York Central
Park
50 Central Park South
New York, NY

212-308-9100

Tribeca Grand Hotel
Two Avenue Of The Americas
New York, NY

212-519-6600

Best Western Plus Seaport Inn
Downtown
33 Peck Slip
New York City, NY
212-766-6600

Candlewood Suites New York City-
Times Square
339 W. 39th Street
New York City, NY

212-967-2254

Holiday Inn Express NYC Madison
Square Garden
232 West 29th Street
New York City, NY

212-695-7200

Holiday Inn Express New York City
Fifth Avenue
15 West 45th Street
New York City, NY

212-302-9088

Holiday Inn NYC Wall Street
51 Nassau Street
New York City, NY

212-227-3007

Hotel Indigo Chelsea New York
127 West 28th Street
New York City, NY

212-973-9000

InterContinental NEW YORK
BARCLAY - Newly Renovated
111 East 48th Street
New York City, NY

212-755-5900

InterContinental NEW YORK
BARCLAY - Newly Renovated
111 East 48th Street
New York City, NY

212-755-5900

Intercontinental New York Times
Square
300 West 44th Street
New York City, NY

212-803-4500

Staybridge Suites Times Square -
New York City
340 West 40th Street
New York City, NY

212-757-9000

Newark Garden Hotel
125 N Main St
Newark, NY
315-331-9500

Super 8 Motel - Newburgh
1287 Route 300
Newburgh, NY
845-564-5700

Holiday Inn Express Hotel & Suites
Niagara Falls
10111 Niagara Falls Boulevard
Niagara Falls, NY
716-298-4500

Howard Johnson Closest To The
Falls And Casino
454 Main Street
Niagara Falls, NY

716-285-5261

Quality Hotel & Suites At The Falls
240 First Street
Niagara Falls, NY

716-282-1212

Howard Johnson Hotel - Norwich
75 North Broad Street
Norwich, NY
607-334-2200

Super 8 Norwich
6067 State Highway 12
Norwich, NY

607-336-8880

Quality Inn Gran-View
6765 State Hwy. 37
Ogdensburg, NY
315-393-4550

Microtel Inn & Suites By Wyndham
Olean
3234 Nys Route 417

Olean, NY
716-373-5333

Holiday Inn Oneonta
5206 State Highway 23
Oneonta, NY
607-433-2250

Super 8 Oneonta/Cooperstown
4973 St Hwy 23
Oneonta, NY

607-432-9505

Hotel Oriskany
5920 Airport Road
Oriskany, NY

Knights Inn Oswego East
101 State Route 104
Oswego, NY
315-343-3136

Tillinghast Manor
7246 S Main Street
Ovid, NY
716-869-3584

Econo Lodge Painted Post
200 Robert Dann Drive
Painted Post, NY
607-962-4444

Ramada Painted Post
304 South Hamilton Street
Painted Post, NY

607-962-5021

Best Western Plus Vineyard Inn &
Suites
142 Lake Street
Penn Yan, NY
315-536-8473

Rufus Tanner House
60 Sagetown Road
Pine City, NY
607-732-0213

Homewood Suites By Hilton Melville,
NY
1585 Round Swamp Road
Plainview, NY
516-293-4663

Residence Inn Plainview Long Island
9 Gerhard Road
Plainview, NY

516-433-6200

Residence Inn Plainview Long Island
9 Gerhard Road
Plainview, NY

516-433-6200

Best Western Plus The Inn At
Smithfield
446 Route 3

Plattsburgh, NY
5185617750

Best Western Plus The Inn & Suites
At The Falls
50 Red Oaks Mill Road
Poughkeepsie, NY
845-462-5770

Days Inn Poughkeepsie
536 Haight Avenue
Poughkeepsie, NY

845-454-1010

Mercury Grand Hotel
2170 South Road Rt 9
Poughkeepsie, NY

845-462-4600

Red Roof Inn Poughkeepsie
2349 South Road
Poughkeepsie, NY

845-462-7800

Residence Inn By Marriott
Poughkeepsie
2525 South Road
Poughkeepsie, NY

845-463-4343

Holiday Inn Express East End
1707 Old Country Road, Route 58
Riverhead, NY
631-548-1000

Comfort Inn West Rochester
1501 West Ridge Road
Rochester, NY
585-621-5700

Days Inn Rochester Thruway /
Henrietta
4853 West Henrietta Road
Rochester, NY

585-334-9300

Extended Stay America - Rochester
- Greece
600 Center Place Drive
Rochester, NY

585-663-5558

Extended Stay America - Rochester
- Henrietta
700 Commons Way
Rochester, NY

585-427-7580

Hampton Inn Rochester-North
500 Center Place Drive
Rochester, NY

585-663-6070

Holiday Inn Express Irondequoit

2200 Goodman St ;North
Rochester, NY

585-342-0430

Homewood Suites By Hilton
Rochester/Henrietta
2095 Hylan Drive
Rochester, NY

585-334-9150

Quality Inn Rochester Airport
1273 Chili Avenue
Rochester, NY

585-464-8800

Residence Inn Rochester Henrietta
1300 Jefferson Road
Rochester, NY

585-272-8850

Residence Inn Rochester West
500 Paddy Creek Circle
Rochester, NY

585-865-2090

Staybridge Suites Rochester
University
1000 Genesee Street
Rochester, NY

585-527-9110

Hilton Westchester
699 Westchester Avenue
Rye Brook, NY
914-939-6300

Best Western Mountain Lake Inn
487 Lake Flower Avenue
Saranac Lake, NY
518-891-1970

Lake Flower Inn
15 Lake Flower Ave
Saranac Lake, NY

518-891-2310

Lake Side
27 Lake Flower Ave
Saranac Lake, NY

518-891-4333

Comfort Inn & Suites Saratoga
Springs
17 Old Gick Road
Saratoga Springs, NY
518-587-6244

Holiday Inn Saratoga Springs
232 Broadway
Saratoga Springs, NY

518-584-4550

Residence Inn Saratoga Springs

295 Excelsior Avenue
Saratoga Springs, NY

518-584-9600

Fire Island Real Estate Fire Island
Pines
P. O. Box 219
Sayville, NY
631-597-7575

Albany - Days Inn Schenectady
167 Nott Terrace
Schenectady, NY
518-370-3297

Super 8 - Schenectady
3083 Carman Road
Schenectady, NY

518-355-2190

Ramada Fishkill
542 Route 9
Schroon Lake, NY
518-532-7521

Starry Night Cabins
37 Fowler Avenue
Schroon Lake, NY

518-532-7907

Microtel Inn & Suites By Wyndham
Seneca Falls
1966 Route 5 And 20
Seneca Falls, NY
315-539-8438

Shelter Island House
11 Stearns Point Road
Shelter Island Heights, NY
631-749-1633

Bird's Nest
1601 E Genesee St
Skaneateles, NY
315-685-5641

Skaneateles Suites
4114 West Genesee Street Road
Skaneateles, NY

315-685-7568

Southampton Inn
91 Hill Street
Southampton, NY
631-283-6500

Microtel Inn & Suites By Wyndham
Springville
270 Cascade Drive
Springville, NY
716-592-3141

Hilton Garden Inn New York/Staten
Island
1100 South Avenue
Staten Island, NY
718-477-2400

Mountain House
150 Berkshire Way
Stephentown, NY
800-497-0176

Inn at Stone Ridge
Route 209
Stone Ridge, NY
845-687-0736

Crowne Plaza Hotel Suffern
3 Executive Boulevard
Suffern, NY
845-357-4800

Best Western Syracuse Airport Inn
900 Colonel Eileen Collins Blvd
Syracuse, NY
315-455-7362

Candlewood Suites Syracuse-
Airport
5414 South Bay Road
Syracuse, NY

315-454-8999

Comfort Inn & Suites Airport
Syracuse
6701 Buckley Road
Syracuse, NY

315-457-4000

Comfort Inn Carrier Circle
6491 Thompson Rd.
Syracuse, NY

315-437-0222

Comfort Inn Fairgrounds
7010 Interstate Island Road
Syracuse, NY

315-453-0045

Days Inn Syracuse University
6609 Thompson Road
Syracuse, NY

315-437-5998

Red Roof Inn Syracuse
6614 N. Thompson Road
Syracuse, NY

315-437-3309

Sheraton Syracuse University Hotel
And Conference Center
801 University Ave
Syracuse, NY

315-475-3000

Super 8 East Syracuse
6620 Old Collamer Road
Syracuse East, NY
315-432-5612

Circle Court
440 Montcalm St
Ticonderoga, NY
518-585-7660

Econo Lodge Tonawanda
2000 Niagara Falls Boulevard
Tonawanda, NY
716-694-6696

Best Western Plus Franklin Square
Inn Troy/Albany
1 4th Street
Troy, NY
518-274-8800

Best Western Tully Inn
5779 State Route 80
Tully, NY
315-696-6061

Luxury Furnished Apartments In
Columbus Ave New York
808 Columbus Avenue
UNKNOWN, NY

Knights Inn Utica
309 North Genesee Street
Utica, NY
315-797-0964

Red Roof Inn Utica
20 Weaver Street
Utica, NY

315-724-7128

Microtel Inn & Suites By Wyndham
Verona
5118 NY State Route 365
Verona, NY
315-363-1850

Residence Inn Binghamton
4610 Vestal Parkway East
Vestal, NY
607-770-8500

Hampton Inn & Suites
Rochester/Victor
7637 Newyork State Route 96
Victor, NY
585-924-4400

Homewood Suites By Hilton
Rochester - Victor
575 Fisher Station Drive
Victor, NY

585-869-7500

Microtel Inn By Wyndham
Victor/Rochester
7498 Main Street Fishers
Victor, NY

585-924-9240

The Cozy Cottages
395 Montauk Highway
Wainscott, NY

631-537-1160

Audrey's Farmhouse
2188 Brunswyck Road
Wallkill, NY
845-895-3440

Daggett Lake Campsites & Cabins
660 Glen Athol Rd
Warrensburg, NY
518-623-2198

MeadowLark Farm
180 Union Corners Road
Warwick, NY
845-651-4286

Best Western Watertown/Fort Drum
300 Washington Street
Watertown, NY
315-782-8000

Comfort Inn & Suites Watertown -
1000 Islands
110 Commerce Park Drive
Watertown, NY

315-782-2700

Rodeway Inn Watertown
652 Arsenal Street
Watertown, NY

Algonquin Motel
Box 528 H 30
Wells, NY
518-924-2751

Microtel Inn & Suites By Wyndham
Wellsville
30 West Dyke Street
Wellsville, NY
585-593-3449

Best Western New Baltimore Inn
12600 State Route 9w
West Coxsackie, NY
518-731-8100

Staybridge Suites Buffalo
164 Slade Avenue
West Seneca, NY
716-939-3100

Red Roof Inn Long Island
699 Dibblee Drive
Westbury, NY
516-794-2555

Hyatt House White Plains
101 Corporate Park Drive
White Plains, NY
914-251-9700

Residence Inn White Plains
5 Barker Avenue
White Plains, NY

914-761-7700

Willkommen Hof
5367 H 86
Whiteface, NY
518-946-SNOW (7669)

Extended Stay America - New York
City - Laguardia Airport
18-30 Whitestone Expressway
Whitestone, NY
718-357-3661

Knights Inn Williamsville Buffalo
Airport
50 Freeman Road
Williamsville, NY
716-633-6200

Hungry Trout Resort
(on Route 86)
Wilmington, NY
518-946-2217

Best Western Woodbury Inn
7940 Jericho Turnpike
Woodbury, NY
516-921-6900

Hampton Inn & Suites Yonkers
160 Corporate Blvd.
Yonkers, NY
914-377-1144

Residence Inn By Marriott, Yonkers
7 Executive Boulevard
Yonkers, NY

914-476-4600

# North Carolina Listings

Hampton Inn And Suites Southern
Pines/Pinehurst
200 Columbus Drive
Aberdeen, NC
910-693-4330

Quality Inn Albemarle
735 NC 24 27 Bypass East
Albemarle, NC
704-983-6990

Candlewood Suites Apex Raleigh
Area
1005 Marco Drive
Apex, NC
919-387-8595

Holiday Inn Express Hotel & Suites
High Point South
10050 North Main Street
Archdale, NC
336-861-3310

Holiday Inn Express Hotel And
Suites Asheboro
1113 E. Dixie Drive
Asheboro, NC

336-636-5222

Asheville Outlets
800 Brevard Rd.
Asheville, NC
828-667-2308

Best Western Of Asheville Biltmore
East
501 Tunnel Road
Asheville, NC

828-298-5562

Crowne Plaza Resort Asheville
1 Resort Drive
Asheville, NC

828-254-3211

Days Inn Asheville/Mall
201 Tunnel Road
Asheville, NC

828-252-4000

Days Inn Biltmore East
1435 Tunnel Road
Asheville, NC

828-298-4000

Engadine Cabins
2630 Smoky Park Highway
Asheville, NC

828-665-8325

Extended Stay America - Asheville -
Tunnel Rd.
6 Kenilworth Knoll
Asheville, NC

828-253-3483

Four Points By Sheraton Asheville
Downtown
22 Woodfin Street
Asheville, NC

828-253-1851

GRAND BOHEMIAN HOTEL
ASHEVILLE, AUTOGRAPH
COLLECTION, A Marriott Luxury &
Lifestyle Hotel
11 Boston Way
Asheville, NC

828-505-2949

Hilton Asheville Biltmore Park
43 Town Square Blvd
Asheville, NC

828-209-2700

Holiday Inn Biltmore East
1450 Tunnel Road
Asheville, NC

828-298-5611

Dog-Friendly Lodging - Please always call ahead to make sure an establishment is still dog-friendly.

Hotel Indigo Asheville Downtown
151 Haywood Street
Asheville, NC

828-239-0239

Quality Inn & Suites Biltmore East
1430 Tunnel Road
Asheville, NC

828-298-5519

RENAISSANCE ASHEVILLE
HOTEL, A Marriott Luxury & Lifestyle
Hotel
31 Woodfin Street
Asheville, NC

828-252-8211

Ramada Asheville / Biltmore West
275 Smokey Park Hwy
Asheville, NC

828-667-4501

Ramada Asheville Southeast
148 River Ford Parkway
Asheville, NC

Red Roof Inn Asheville West
16 Crowell Road
Asheville, NC

828-667-9803

Residence Inn By Marriott Asheville
Biltmore
701 Biltmore Ave
Asheville, NC

828-281-3361

Rodeway Inn
8 Crowell Road
Asheville, NC

828-667-8706

Rodeway Inn & Suites
9 Wedgefield Drive
Asheville, NC

828-670-8800

Super 8 Asheville
180 Tunnel Road
Asheville, NC

828-505-4648

The Cottage Asheville
Walking Distance to Downtown
Asheville
Asheville, NC

828-242-2454

Atlantis Lodge
123 Salter Path Road
Atlantic Beach, NC

252-726-5168

Outer Beaches Realty
Visit Website or Call to Arrange
Avon, NC
866-962-0409

Best Western Mountain Lodge At
Banner Elk
1615 Tynecastle Highway
Banner Elk, NC
828-898-4571

Econo Lodge North Battleboro
I-95 Exit 145
Battleboro, NC
252-972-9426

Quality Inn North Battleboro
7797 North Carolina Highway 48
Battleboro, NC

252-442-5111

Travelers Inn & Suites - I-95 exit 145
7568 NC Highway 48
Battleboro, NC

Country Home B&B
299 H 101
Beaufort, NC
252-728-4611

Days Inn Benson
202 N Honeycutt Street
Benson, NC
919-894-2031

Days Inn Biscoe
531 East Main Street
Biscoe, NC
910-428-2525

Quality Inn Black Mountain
585 Hwy 9
Black Mountain, NC
828-669-9950

Super 8 Black Mountain
101 Flat Creek Road
Black Mountain, NC

828-669-8076

DogWoods Retreat
164 Breckenridge Trail
Brevard, NC
828-507-3020

Holiday Inn Express Hotel And
Suites Brevard
2228 Asheville Hwy.
Brevard, NC

828-862-8900

Mountain Vista Log Cabins
300 Fernwood Drive
Bryson City, NC
828-508-4391

Econo Lodge Burlington
2133 West Hanford Road
Burlington, NC
336-227-1270

Red Roof Inn Burlington
2444 Maple Ave
Burlington, NC

336-229-5203

Blue Ridge Motel
204 West Blvd
Burnsville, NC
828-682-9100

Outer Banks Motel
2nd Motel on left on H 12
Buxton, NC
252-995-5601

Apple Blossom Cottage
46 Drawspring Road
Candler, NC
828-255-0704

Americas Best Value Inn Canton
1963 Champion Drive
Canton, NC
828-648-0300

Parkerton Inn
1184 Hwy 58
Cape Carteret, NC
252-393-9000

Best Western Plus Cary - Nc State
1722 Walnut St
Cary, NC
919-481-1200

Extended Stay America - Raleigh -
Cary - Regency Parkway North
1500 Regency Parkway
Cary, NC

919-468-5828

Red Roof Inn Raleigh Southwest -
Cary
1800 Walnut Street
Cary, NC

919-469-3400

Residence Inn By Marriott Raleigh
Cary
2900 Regency Parkway
Cary, NC

919-467-4080

Towneplace Suites By Marriott
Raleigh Cary/Weston Parkway
120 Sage Commons Way
Cary, NC

919-678-0005

Residence Inn Chapel Hill

Dog-Friendly Lodging - Please always call ahead to make sure an establishment is still dog-friendly.

101 Erwin Road
Chapel Hill, NC
919-933-4848

Sheraton Chapel Hill Hotel
1 Europa Drive
Chapel Hill, NC

919-968-4900

Candlewood Suites Charlotte -
University
8812 University East Drive
Charlotte, NC
704-598-9863

Charlotte Plaza Inn
3300 Queen City Drive
Charlotte, NC

704-392-2316

Comfort Inn Executive Park
5822 Westpark Drive
Charlotte, NC

704-525-2626

Comfort Suites Airport
3425 Mulberry Church Road
Charlotte, NC

704-971-4400

Days Inn Charlotte North-Speedway-
UNCC-Research Park
1408 West Sugar Creek Road
Charlotte, NC

704-597-8110

Doubletree Guest Suites Charlotte /
Southpark
6300 Morrison Boulevard
Charlotte, NC

704-364-2400

Drury Inn & Suites Charlotte
Northlake
6920 Northlake Mall Drive
Charlotte, NC

704-599-8882

Econo Lodge Inn & Suites Charlotte
3000 East Independence Bouleva
Charlotte, NC

704-377-1501

Extended Stay America - Charlotte -
Airport
710 Yorkmont Road
Charlotte, NC

704-676-0083

Extended Stay America - Charlotte -
Pineville - Park Rd.
10930 Park Road
Charlotte, NC

704-341-0929

Extended Stay America - Charlotte -
Tyvola Rd.
6035 Nations Ford Road
Charlotte, NC

704-676-0569

Extended Stay America - Charlotte -
University Place
8211 University Executive Park
Drive
Charlotte, NC

704-510-1636

Hawthorn Suites By Wyndham
Charlotte - Executive Center
5840 West Park Drive
Charlotte, NC

704-529-7500

Homewood Suites By Hilton
Charlotte-North/Univ Research Park
8340 N. Tryon St.
Charlotte, NC

704-549-8800

Homewood Suites By Hilton®
Charlotte Airport
2770 Yorkmont Road
Charlotte, NC

704-357-0500

Hyatt House Charlotte Airport
4920 South Tryon Street
Charlotte, NC

704-525-2600

Knights Inn Charlotte South
7901 Nations Ford Road
Charlotte, NC

704-522-0364

Mainstay Suites Charlotte
7926 Forest Pine Drive
Charlotte, NC

704-521-3232

Quality Inn & Suites Charlotte
Airport
3100 Queen City Drive
Charlotte, NC

704-393-5306

Residence Inn By Marriott Charlotte
Southpark
6030 Piedmont Row Drive South
Charlotte, NC

704-554-7001

Residence Inn Charlotte Piper Glen
5115 Piper Station Drive

Charlotte, NC

704-319-3900

Residence Inn Charlotte South
5816 Westpark Drive
Charlotte, NC

704-527-8110

Residence Inn Charlotte University
Research Park
8503 North Tryon Street
Charlotte, NC

704-547-1122

Residence Inn Uptown Charlotte
404 S. Mint Street
Charlotte, NC

704-340-4000

Sheraton Charlotte Airport Hotel
3315 Scott Futrell Drive
Charlotte, NC

704-392-1200

Sleep Inn Northlake
6300 Banner Elk Drive
Charlotte, NC

704-399-7778

Sleep Inn University Place Charlotte
8525 North Tryon Street
Charlotte, NC

704-549-4544

Sonesta Es Suites Charlotte
Arrowwood
7925 Forest Pine Drive
Charlotte, NC

704-527-6767

Staybridge Suites Ballantyne
15735 John J Delaney Drive
Charlotte, NC

704-248-5000

The Westin Charlotte
601 South College Street
Charlotte, NC

704-375-2600

Towneplace Suites By Marriott
Charlotte Arrowood
7805 Forest Point Blvd
Charlotte, NC

704-227-2000

Towneplace Suites By Marriott
Charlotte University Research Park
8710 Research Drive
Charlotte, NC

704-548-0388

Dog-Friendly Lodging - Please always call ahead to make sure an establishment is still dog-friendly.

Microtel Inn & Suites By Wyndham Cherokee
674 Casino Trail
Cherokee, NC

Baymont Inn & Suites Chocowinity/Washington
3635 Highway 17 South
Chocowinity, NC
252-946-8001

Days Inn Columbus/Tryon
626 West Mills Street
Columbus, NC
828-894-3303

Embassy Suites Hotel Concord, Nc
5400 John Q. Hammons Drive Nw
Concord, NC
704-455-8200

Howard Johnson Inn Concord
1601 Concord Pkwy N
Concord, NC

704-786-5181

Residence Inn Charlotte Concord
7601 Scott Padgett Pkwy
Concord, NC

704-454-7862

Sleep Inn Concord
1120 Copperfield Blvd
Concord, NC

704-788-2150

Suburban Extended Stay Concord
7725 Sossaman Lane
Concord, NC

704-979-5555

Clarion Inn Cornelius
19608 Liverpool Parkway
Cornelius, NC
704-896-0660

Comfort Inn & Suites Cornelius
19521 Liverpool Parkway
Cornelius, NC

704-896-7622

Days Inn Cornelius Lake Norman
19901 Holiday Lane
Cornelius, NC

704-892-9120

Econo Lodge & Suites Lake Norman
20740 Torrence Chapel Road
Cornelius, NC

704-892-3500

Microtel Inn By Wyndham
Cornelius/Lake Norman

20820 Torrence Chapel Rd
Cornelius, NC

704-895-1828

Brindley Beach Vacations and Sales
1023 Ocean Trail
Corolla, NC
877-642-3224

Carolina Designs Realty
Call to Arrange
Duck, NC
800-368-3825

Quality Inn Dunn
1011 East Cumberland Street
Dunn, NC
910-892-8101

Super 8 Dunn
1125 East Broad Sreet
Dunn, NC

910-892-1293

Candlewood Suites Durham
1818 East N C Highway 54
Durham, NC
919-484-9922

Comfort Inn Medical Park
1816 Hillandale Road
Durham, NC

919-471-6100

Comfort Inn Research Triangle Park
4507 NC 55/Apex Hwy
Durham, NC

919-361-2656

Extended Stay America - Durham - Research Triangle Park - Hwy 55
4515 NC Hwy 55
Durham, NC

919-544-9991

Extended Stay America - Durham - University
3105 Tower Blvd.
Durham, NC

919-489-8444

Extended Stay America - Durham - University - Ivy Creek Blvd.
1920 Ivy Creek Boulevard
Durham, NC

919-402-1700

Hilton Durham Near Duke University
3800 Hillsborough Road
Durham, NC

919-383-8033

Holiday Inn Express Durham
2516 Guess Road

Durham, NC

919-313-3244

Holiday Inn Express Hotel & Suites Research Triangle Park
4912 South Miami Boulevard
Durham, NC

919-474-9800

Homewood Suites Durham-Chapel Hill I-40
3600 Mount Moriah Road
Durham, NC

919-401-0610

Quality Inn & Suites Medical Park
3710 Hillsborough Road
Durham, NC

919-382-3388

Red Roof Inn Chapel Hill
5623 Durham-Chapel Hill Boulevard
Durham, NC

919-489-9421

Red Roof Inn Durham - Duke Univ.
Medical Center
1915 North Pointe Drive
Durham, NC

919-471-9882

Red Roof Inn Research Triangle Park
4405 Highway 55 East
Durham, NC

919-361-1950

Residence Inn Durham
201 Residence Inn Boulevard
Durham, NC

919-361-1266

Staybridge Suites Durham-Chapel Hill-Rtp
3704 Mt. Moriah Road
Durham, NC

919-401-9800

Super 8 Durham
2337 Guess Road
Durham, NC

919-286-7746

Econo Lodge Eden
110 East Arbor Lane
Eden, NC
336-627-5131

Econo Lodge Elizabeth City
522 South Hughes Boulevard B
Elizabeth City, NC
252-338-4124

Quality Inn Elizabeth
522 South Hughes Blvd
Elizabeth City, NC

252-338-3951

Candlewood Suites Fayetteville Fort Bragg
4108 Legend Avenue
Fayetteville, NC
910-868-0873

Comfort Inn Near Fort Bragg
1922 Skibo Road
Fayetteville, NC

910-867-1777

Econo Lodge Fayetteville
1952 Cedar Creek Road
Fayetteville, NC

910-433-2100

Extended Stay America - Fayetteville - Owen Dr.
408 Owen Dr.
Fayetteville, NC

910-485-2747

Holiday Inn Fayetteville I 95
1944 Cedar Creek Road
Fayetteville, NC

910-323-1600

Knights Inn Fayetteville/Fort Bragg
2848 Bragg Boulevard
Fayetteville, NC

910-485-4163

Residence Inn Fayetteville Cross Creek
1468 Skibo Road
Fayetteville, NC

910-868-9005

Rodeway Inn Fayetteville
1957 Cedar Creek Road
Fayetteville, NC

910-323-8333

Super 8 Fayetteville
1875 Cedar Creek Rd
Fayetteville, NC

910-323-3826

Towneplace Suites By Marriott Fayetteville Cross Creek
1464 Skibo Road
Fayetteville, NC

910-764-1100

Comfort Inn Asheville Airport
15 Rockwood Road
Fletcher, NC
828-687-9199

Days Inn Gastonia - West Of Charlotte Kings Mountain
1700 North Chester Street
Gastonia, NC
704-864-9981

Best Western Plus Goldsboro
909 North Spence Avenue
Goldsboro, NC
919-751-1999

Goldsboro Suites
2613 North Park Drive
Goldsboro, NC

919-759-0098

Baymont Inn & Suites Greensboro/Coliseum
2001 Veasley Street
Greensboro, NC
336-294-6220

Best Western Plus Greensboro Airport
7800 National Service Road
Greensboro, NC

336-454-0333

Best Western Plus Windsor Suites
2006 Veasley Street
Greensboro, NC

336-294-9100

Clarion Hotel Airport Greensboro
415 Swing Road
Greensboro, NC

336-299-7650

Days Inn Greensboro Airport
501 South Regional Road
Greensboro, NC

336-668-0476

Drury Inn & Suites Greensboro
3220 Gate City Blvd
Greensboro, NC

336-856-9696

Extended Stay America - Greensboro - Wendover Ave - Big Tree Way
4317 Big Tree Way
Greensboro, NC

336-299-0200

Hawthorn Suites By Wyndham Greensboro
7623 Thorndike Road
Greensboro, NC

336-454-0078

Quality Inn & Suites Airpark East
7067 Albert Pick Road

Greensboro, NC

336-668-3638

Red Roof Inn Greensboro Airport
615 Regional Road South
Greensboro, NC

336-271-2636

Red Roof Inn Greensboro Coliseum
2101 West Meadowview Road
Greensboro, NC

336-852-6560

Residence Inn Greensboro Airport
7616 Thorndike Road
Greensboro, NC

336-632-4666

Candlewood Suites Greenville West
1055 Waterford Commons Drive
Greenville, NC
252-317-3000

Hilton Greenville
207 Sw Greenville Blvd
Greenville, NC

252-355-5000

Holiday Inn Express Havelock Nw - New Bern
103 Branchside Drive
Havelock, NC
252-447-9000

Quality Inn Havelock
400 Us Hwy 70 West
Havelock, NC

252-444-1111

Econo Lodge Henderson
112 Parham Rd.
Henderson, NC
252-438-8511

Knights Inn Henderson
1052 Ruin Creek Rd
Henderson, NC

252-492-4041

Sleep Inn Henderson
18 Market Street
Henderson, NC

252-433-9449

Days Inn Hendersonville
102 Mitchell Drive
Hendersonville, NC
828-697-5899

Econo Lodge Hendersonville
206 Mitchelle Drive
Hendersonville, NC

828-693-8800

Ramada Hendersonville
150 Sugarloaf Rd
Hendersonville, NC
828-697-0006

Red Roof Inn Hendersonville
240 Mitchelle Drive
Hendersonville, NC
828-697-1223

Crowne Plaza Hotel Hickory
1385 Lenoir Rhyne Blvd Se
Hickory, NC
828-323-1000

Days Inn & Suites - Hickory
1725 13th Avenue Drive Northwest
Hickory, NC
828-431-2100

Red Roof Inn Hickory
1184 Lenior Rhyne Boulevard
Hickory, NC
828-323-1500

Best Western Plus Huntersville Inn &
Suites Near Lake Norman
13830 Statesville Road
Huntersville, NC
704-875-7880

Best Western Plus Huntersville Inn &
Suites Near Lake Norman
13830 Statesville Road
Huntersville, NC

704-875-7880

Candlewood Suites Huntersville
16530 Northcross Drive
Huntersville, NC

704-895-3434

Quality Inn Huntersville
16825 Caldwell Creek Drive
Huntersville, NC

704-892-6597

Residence Inn Lake Norman
16830 Kenton Dr
Huntersville, NC

704-584-0000

Candlewood Suites Jacksonville
119 Penny Lane
Jacksonville, NC
910-333-0494

Extended Stay America - Jacksonville
- Camp Lejeune
20 Mcdaniel Drive
Jacksonville, NC

910-347-7684

Towneplace Suites By Marriott
Jacksonville
400 Northwest Drive
Jacksonville, NC
910-478-9795

Comfort Inn Jonesville
1633 Winston Road
Jonesville, NC
336-835-9400

Days Inn Jonesville
1540 North Carolina 67 Highway
Jonesville, NC

336-526-6777

Super 8 Motel - Jonesville/Elkin
Area
5601 Us Highway 21
Jonesville, NC

336-835-1461

Days Inn Kenly
1139 Johnston Parkway
Kenly, NC
919-284-3400

Motel 6 Kenly
843 Johnston Parkway
Kenly, NC

919-284-3800

Quality Inn Kenly
405 S. Church Street
Kenly, NC

919-284-1000

Cavilier Motel
601 S Viriginia Dare Trail
Kill Devil Hills, NC
252-441-5585

Comfort Inn On The Ocean
1601 South Virginia Dare Trail
Kill Devil Hills, NC

252-441-6333

Comfort Inn On The Ocean
1601 South Virginia Dare Trail
Kill Devil Hills, NC

252-441-6333

Travelodge Nags Head Beach Hotel
804 North Virginia Dare Trail
Kill Devil Hills, NC

252-441-0411

Quality Inn - Kings Mountain
722 York Road
Kings Mountain, NC
704-739-7070

Atlantic Realty of the Outer Banks

Call to Arrange
Kitty Hawk, NC
855-766-2471

Beach Realty/Kitty Hawk Rentals
4820 N Croatan Hwy
Kitty Hawk, NC

252-441-7166

Carolina Shores Vacation Rentals
3600 N Croatan Hwy
Kitty Hawk, NC

866-418-5263

Outer Banks Blue
3732 North Croatan Highway
Kitty Hawk, NC

855-783-0925

The 1927 Lake Lure Inn and Spa
2771 Memorial H/H 9/64/74
Lake Lure, NC
828-625-2525

Best Western Plus Westgate Inn &
Suites
1120 Towne Lake Drive
Leland, NC
910-371-2858

Holiday Inn Express Leland -
Wilmington Area
1020 Grandiflora Drive
Leland, NC

910-383-3300

Days Inn & Suites - Lexington
1620 Cotton Grove Road
Lexington, NC
336-357-2333

Quality Inn Lexington
101 Plaza Parkway
Lexington, NC

336-243-2929

Comfort Inn Lincolnton
1550 East Main Street
Lincolnton, NC
704-732-0011

Days Inn Lincolnton
614 Clark Drive
Lincolnton, NC

704-735-8271

Best Western Lumberton
201 Jackson Court
Lumberton, NC
910-618-9799

Days Inn Lumberton-Outlet Mall
3030 North Roberts Avenue
Lumberton, NC

910-738-6401

Maggie Mountain
60 Twin Hickory
Maggie Valley, NC
828-926-4258

Americas Best Value Inn Marion
4248 Highway 221 South
Marion, NC
828-659-2567

Comfort Inn Marion
178 Us 70 West
Marion, NC
828-652-4888

Comfort Inn Mars Hill
167 J.F. Robinson Lane
Mars Hill, NC
828-689-9000

Country Inn & Suites Charlotte I-485
2001 Mount Harmony Church Road
Matthews, NC
704-846-8000

Econo Lodge Inn & Suites East
1938 Moore Road
Matthews, NC

704-847-5252

Quality Inn Mocksville
1500 Yadkinville Rd
Mocksville, NC
336-751-7310

Jameson Inn Monroe
608-E West Roosevelt Boulevard
Monroe, NC
704-289-1555

Holiday Inn Express Hotel & Suites
Mooresville-Lake Norman, Nc
130 Norman Station Boulevard
Mooresville, NC
704-662-6900

Sleep Inn Morganton
2400a South Sterling Street
Morganton, NC
828-433-9000

Extended Stay America - Raleigh -
Rdu Airport
2700 Slater Rd
Morrisville, NC
919-380-1499

Holiday Inn Express Raleigh-Durham
Airport
1014 Airport Boulevard
Morrisville, NC

919-653-2260

Holiday Inn Raleigh-Durham Airport
930 Airport Boulevard
Morrisville, NC

919-465-1910

Residence Inn by Marriott Raleigh-
Durham Airport/Morrisville
2020 Hospitality Ct
Morrisville, NC

919-467-8689

Staybridge Suites Raleigh-Durham
Airport
1012 Airport Boulevard
Morrisville, NC

919-468-0180

Holiday Inn Express Hotel & Suites
Mount Airy
1320 Ems Drive
Mount Airy, NC
336-719-1731

Quality Inn Mount Airy
2136 Rockford Street
Mount Airy, NC

336-789-2000

Best Western Of Murphy
1522 Andrews Road
Murphy, NC
828-837-3060

Days Inn Murphy
754 Us Highway 64 West
Murphy, NC

828-837-8030

Smoky Mountain Hideaway
Mary King Mountain
Murphy, NC

727-864-0526

Comfort Inn South Oceanfront
8031 Old Oregon Inlet Rd
Nags Head, NC
252-441-6315

Rodeway Inn & Suites Nags Head
7218 S Virginia Dare Trail
Nags Head, NC

252-441-5242

Sandbar Bed and Breakfast
Milepost 10.5
Nags Head, NC

252-489-1868

Stan White Realty
Call To Arrange
Nags Head, NC

800-338-3233

Village Realty OBX
5301 South Croatan Hwy
Nags Head, NC

252-480-2224

Candlewood Suites New Bern
3465 Dr Martin Luther King Jr. Blvd
New Bern, NC
252-638-8166

Doubletree By Hilton New Bern, Nc
100 Middle Street
New Bern, NC

252-638 3585

Oak Island Accommodations, Inc
8901 East Oak Island Drive
Oak Island, NC
910-278-6011

Oak Island Accommodations, Inc
8901 E Oak Island Drive
Oak Island, NC

910-278-6011

Blackbeard's Lodge
111 Back Road
Ocracoke Village, NC
252-928-2503

The Anchorage Inn
205 Irvin Garrish H/H 12
Ocracoke Village, NC

252-928-1101

The Island Inn
25 Lighthouse Road
Ocracoke Village, NC

252-928-4351

Comfort Inn & Suites
Oxford/Henderson
1000 Linden Avenue
Oxford, NC
919-692-1000

Holiday Inn Express Pembroke
605 Redmond Rd
Pembroke, NC
910-521-1311

Econo Lodge Inn & Suites Pilot
Mountain
711 S. Key Street
Pilot Mountain, NC
336-368-2237

Homewood Suites By Hilton®
Olmsted Village (Near Pinehurst)
250 Central Park Avenue
Pinehurst, NC
910-255-0300

Weddens Way, Too
231 Legra Rd
Piney Creek, NC
336-372-2985

Candlewood Suites Raleigh Crabtree

4433 Lead Mine Road
Raleigh, NC
919-789-4840

Days Inn Raleigh
3201 Wake Forest Road
Raleigh, NC

919-878-9310

Days Inn Raleigh, Glenwood-
Crabtree
6619 Glenwood Avenue
Raleigh, NC

919-782-8650

Extended Stay America - Raleigh -
Crabtree Valley
4810 Bluestone Drive
Raleigh, NC

919-510-8551

Extended Stay America - Raleigh -
North - Wake Forest Road
3531 Wake Forest Rd
Raleigh, NC

919-981-7353

Extended Stay America - Raleigh -
North Raleigh
911 Wake Towne Drive
Raleigh, NC

919-829-7271

Extended Stay America - Raleigh -
Northeast
2601 Appliance Court
Raleigh, NC

919-807-9970

Hampton Inn And Suites
Raleigh/Cary I-40 (Rbc Center)
111 Hampton Woods Lane
Raleigh, NC

919-233-1798

Hawthorn Suites By Wyndham-
Raleigh
1020 Buck Jones Road
Raleigh, NC

919-468-4222

Hilton North Raleigh-Midtown
3415 Wake Forest Road
Raleigh, NC

919-872-2323

Holiday Inn Express Hotel And Suites
Raleigh North - Wake Forest
11400 Common Oaks Drive
Raleigh, NC

919-570-5550

Knights Inn Raleigh Downtown East

3804 New Bern Avenue
Raleigh, NC

919-231-8818

Red Roof Inn Plus Raleigh Ncsu-
Convention Center
1813 South Saunders Street
Raleigh, NC

919-833-6005

Regency Suites North Raleigh
4400 Capital Boulevard
Raleigh, NC

919-876-2211

Residence Inn Raleigh Midtown
1000 Navaho Drive
Raleigh, NC

919-878-6100

Quality Inn Roanoke Rapids
1914 Julian R Allsbrook Highway
Roanoke Rapids, NC
252-537-9927

Sleep Inn Roanoke Rapids
101 Hampton Boulevard
Roanoke Rapids, NC

252-537-3141

Candlewood Suites Rocky Mount
688 English Road
Rocky Mount, NC
252-467-2550

Comfort Inn Rocky Mount
200 Gateway Boulevard
Rocky Mount, NC

252-937-7765

Days Inn Golden East
1340 N Wesleyan Blvd
Rocky Mount, NC

252-977-7766

Residence Inn Rocky Mount
230 Gateway Boulevard
Rocky Mount, NC

252-451-5600

Days Inn Salisbury
321 Bendix Drive
Salisbury, NC
704-633-5961

Econo Lodge Salisbury
1328 Jake Alexander Boulevard
South
Salisbury, NC

Hampton Inn Salisbury
1001 Klumac Road
Salisbury, NC

704-637-8000

Holiday Inn Express Hotel & Suites
Sanford
2110 Dalrymple Street
Sanford, NC
919-776-6600

Hummingbird Realty, Ltd.,
425 H 64W
Sapphire, NC
828-966-4737

Woodlands Inn of Sapphire
19259 Rosman H/64W
Sapphire, NC

828-966-4709

Fire Mountain Inn
On H 106
Scaley Mountain, NC
828-526-4446

Quality Inn Selma
1705 Industrial Park Drive
Selma, NC
919-965-5200

Days Inn Shelby
1431 West Dixon Boulevard
Shelby, NC
704-482-1800

Super 8 - Shelby
1716 East Dixon Blvd
Shelby, NC

704-484-2101

Super 8 Smithfield
735 Outlet Center Drive
Smithfield, NC
919-989-8988

Best Western Pinehurst Inn
1675 Us Highway 1 S
Southern Pines, NC
910-692-0640

Days Inn Conference Center
Southern Pines Pinehurst
805 South West Service Rd
Southern Pines, NC

910-692-8585

Econo Lodge & Suites Southern
Pines
408 W. Morganton Road
Southern Pines, NC

910-692-2063

Residence Inn By Marriott Southern
Pines
105 Brucewood Road
Southern Pines, NC

910-693-3400

Southern Shores Realty
Call to Arrange
Southern Shores, NC
252-261-2000

Comfort Suites Southport
4963 Southport Supply Road
Southport, NC
910-454-7444

Town and Country Inn Suites
Spindale
166 Reservation Drive
Spindale, NC
828-286-3681

Americas Best Value Inn
1125 Greenland Drive
Statesville, NC
704-878-9888

Best Western Statesville Inn
1121 Morland Drive
Statesville, NC
704-881-0111

Comfort Inn & Suites Statesville
1214 Greenland Drive
Statesville, NC

Courtyard Statesville
Mooresville/Lake Norman
1530 Cinema Drive
Statesville, NC
704-768-2400

Quality Inn Statesville
715 Sullivan Road
Statesville, NC
704-878-2721

Red Roof Plus+ Statesville
1508 East Broad Street
Statesville, NC
704-878-2051

Carawan's Motel
510 H 94/45
Swan Quarter, NC
252-926-5861

Comfort Inn Thomasville
895 Lake Road
Thomasville, NC
336-472-6600

Microtel Inn By Wyndham
Thomasville/High Point/Lexington
959 Lake Road
Thomasville, NC
336-474-4515

Valle Crucis Log Cabin Rentals
P.O. Box 554
Valle Crucis, NC

828-963-7774

Econo Lodge - Fayetteville North
3945 Goldsboro Road
Wade, NC
910-323-1255

Candlewood Suites Wake Forest-
Raleigh Area
12050 Retail Drive
Wake Forest, NC
919-554-6901

Days Inn Washington
916 Carolina Avenue
Washington, NC
252-946-6141

Econo Lodge North Washington
1220 W. 15th St.
Washington, NC

252-946-7781

Super 8 Motel Waynesville
79 Liner Cove Road
Waynesville, NC
828-454-9667

Days Inn Weldon Roanoke Rapids
1611 Julian R. Allsbrook Hwy
Weldon, NC
252-536-4867

Carolina Mountain Resort
8 N Jefferson Avenue
West Jefferson, NC
336-246-3010

Holiday Inn Express Williamston
1071 Cantle Court
Williamston, NC
252-799-0100

Baymont Inn & Suites Wilmington
306 South College Road
Wilmington, NC
910-392-6767

Best Western Plus Coastline Inn
503 Nutt Street
Wilmington, NC

910-763-2800

Camellia Cottage Bed and Breakfast
118 S. 4th Street
Wilmington, NC

910-763-9171

Days Inn Wilmington - Market Street
5040 Market Street
Wilmington, NC

910-799-6300

Extended Stay America -
Wilmington - New Centre Drive
4929 New Centre Dr.
Wilmington, NC

910-793-4508

Residence Inn Landfall
1200 Culbreth Dr
Wilmington, NC

910-256-0098

Staybridge Suites Wilmington East
5010 New Centre Drive
Wilmington, NC

910-202-8500

The Wilmingtonian
101 S 2nd St
Wilmington, NC

910-343-1800

Towneplace Suites By Marriott
Wilmington/Wrightsville Beach
305 Eastwood Road
Wilmington, NC

910-332-3326

Travelodge - Wilmington
4118 Market Street
Wilmington, NC

910-762-4426

Waterway Lodge
7246 Wrightsville Avenue
Wilmington, NC

910-256-3771

Candlewood Suites Wilson
2915 Independence Dr West
Wilson, NC
252-291-9494

Days Inn Wilson
1801 South Tarboro Street
Wilson, NC

252-291-2323

Microtel Inn By Wyndham Wilson
5013 Hayes Place
Wilson, NC

252-234-0444

Quality Inn University
5719 University Parkway
Winston Salem, NC
336-767-9009

Embassy Suites Hotel Winston-
Salem, Nc
460 North Cherry Street
Winston-Salem, NC
336-724-2300

Extended Stay America - Winston-
Salem - Hanes Mall Blvd.
1995 Hampton Inn Ct.
Winston-Salem, NC

336-768-0075

Quality Inn Coliseum
531 Akron Drive
Winston-Salem, NC

336-767-8240

Residence Inn Winston-Salem
University Area
7835 North Point Boulevard
Winston-Salem, NC

336-759-0777

Sleep Inn Hanes Mall
1985 Hampton Inn Court
Winston-Salem, NC

336-774-8020

WINSTON-SALEM HOTEL AND
SPA
3050 University Parkway
Winston-Salem, NC

336-723-2911

Days Inn Yanceyville
1858 NC Hwy 86 North
Yanceyville, NC
336-694-9494

# North Dakota
# Listings

Old School
400 Vine Street
Arnegard, ND
701-586-3595

Americas Best Value Inn And Suites
Bismarck
1505 Interchange Avenue
Bismarck, ND
701-223-8060

Best Western Plus Ramkota Hotel
800 South 3rd Street
Bismarck, ND

701-258-7700

Candlewood Suites Bismarck
4400 Skyline Crossings
Bismarck, ND

701-751-8900

Comfort Inn Bismarck
1030 E. Interstate Ave.
Bismarck, ND

701-223-1911

Days Inn Bismarck
1300 East Capitol Avenue
Bismarck, ND

701-223-9151

Kelly Inn Bismarck
1800 North 12th Street
Bismarck, ND

701-223-8001

Radisson Hotel Bismarck
605 East Broadway Avenue
Bismarck, ND

701-255-6000

Ramada Bismarck Hotel
1400 East Interchange Avenue
Bismarck, ND

701-258-7000

Ramada Limited Bismarck
3808 East Divide Avenue
Bismarck, ND

701-221-3030

Super 8 Bismarck
1124 East Capitol Ave
Bismarck, ND

701-255-1314

Super 8 Bowman
408 3rd Ave Sw
Bowman, ND
701-523-5613

Days Inn Fargo/Casselton
2050 Governors Drive
Casselton, ND
701-347-4524

Americas Best Value Inn Devils
Lake
1109 South Highway 20
Devils Lake, ND
701-662-5381

Holiday Inn Express Devils Lake
875 Hwy 2 East
Devils Lake, ND

701-665-3200

Woodland Resort
1012 Woodland Drive
Devils Lake, ND

701-662-5996

Comfort Inn Dickinson
493 Elk Drive
Dickinson, ND
701-264-7300

Motel 6 Dickinson
71 West Museum Drive
Dickinson, ND

701-225-9510

Americinn Lodge & Suites Of Fargo
1423 35th Street Sw
Fargo, ND
701-234-9946

Candlewood Suites Fargo-North
Dakota State University
1831 Ndsu Research Park Drive
Fargo, ND

701-235-8200

Days Inn Airport Dome Suites
1507 19th Ave N
Fargo, ND

701-232-0000

Econo Lodge East
1401 35th Street South
Fargo, ND

701-232-3412

Howard Johnson Inn Fargo
Downtown
301 3rd Avenue North
Fargo, ND

701-232-8850

Kelly Inn 13th Avenue Fargo
4207 13th Avenue Sw
Fargo, ND

701-277-8821

Mainstay Suites Fargo
1901 44th Street Southwest
Fargo, ND

701-277-4627

Quality Inn West Acres
1407 35th Street South
Fargo, ND

701-280-9666

Red Roof Inn Fargo
1921 44th Street Southwest
Fargo, ND

701-281-8240

Rodeway Inn Fargo
2202 South University Drive
Fargo, ND

701-239-8022

Staybridge Suites Fargo
4300 20th Avenue South
Fargo, ND

701-281-4900

Super 8 Fargo Airport
1101 38th St Nw
Fargo, ND

701-281-2109

Super 8 Fargo/I-29/West Acres Mall
3518 Interstate Blvd
Fargo, ND

701-232-9202

Econo Lodge Grand Forks
900 North 43rd Street
Grand Forks, ND
701-746-6666

Super 8 Grand Forks
1122 North 43rd Street
Grand Forks, ND

701-775-8138

Comfort Inn Jamestown
811 20th Street Southwest
Jamestown, ND
701-252-7125

Days Inn Jamestown
824 20th Street Southwest
Jamestown, ND

701-251-9085

Super 8 Jamestown
2623 Highway 281 South
Jamestown, ND

701-252-4715

Baymont Inn & Suites Mandan
Bismarck Area
2611 Old Red Trail
Mandan, ND
701-663-7401

Buffalo Gap Guest Ranch
2 1/2 miles south of Medora on gravel
road
Medora, ND
701-623-4200

Best Western Kelly Inn Minot
1510 26th Avenue Southwest
Minot, ND
701-852-4300

Candlewood Suites Minot
900 37th Ave Sw
Minot, ND

701-858-7700

Days Inn Minot
2100 4th St Sw
Minot, ND

701-852-3646

Grand Hotel
1505 North Broadway
Minot, ND

701-852-3161

Select Inn Minot
225 22nd Avenue Northwest
Minot, ND

701-852-3411

Sleep Inn & Suites
2400 10th Street Sw
Minot, ND

701-837-3100

Super 8 Minot
Hwy 83 N
Minot, ND

701-852-1817

Four Bears Lodge
SR 23W
New Town, ND
701-627-4018

Spirit Lake Casino and Resort
7889 H 57
St Michael, ND
701-766-4747

Americinn of Valley City
280 Wintershow Road Southeast
Valley City, ND
701-845-5551

Knights Inn Wahpeton
995 21st Ave North
Wahpeton, ND
701-642-8731

Rodeway Inn Wahpeton
209 13th Street South
Wahpeton, ND

701-642-1115

Howard Johnson West Fargo
525 Main Avenue East
West Fargo, ND
701-281-0000

Candlewood Suites Williston North
3716 6th Avenue West
Williston, ND
701-572-3716

Missouri Flats Inn
213 35th Street West
Williston, ND

701-572-4242

# Ohio Listings

Econo Lodge Akron
79 Rothrock Road
Akron, OH
330-666-8887

Hilton Akron/Fairlawn
3180 West Market Street
Akron, OH

330-867-5000

Red Roof Inn Akron South
2939 South Arlington Road
Akron, OH

330-644-7748

Americas Best Value Inn Alliance
2330 West State Street
Alliance, OH
330-821-5688

Comfort Inn Alliance
2500 W. State St.
Alliance, OH

330-821-5555

Days Inn Amherst Oh
934 N. Leavitt Rd
Amherst, OH
440-985-1428

Rodeway Inn Ashland
1423 County Road 1575
Ashland, OH
419-289-0101

Super 8 Ashland
736 Us Hwy 250 East
Ashland, OH

419-281-0567

Super 8 Athens
2091 East State Street
Athens, OH
740-594-4900

Comfort Inn Austintown
5425 Clarkins Drive
Austintown, OH
330-792-9740

Sleep Inn Austintown
5555 Interstate Blvd.
Austintown, OH

330-544-5555

Doubletree By Hilton Cleveland East
3663 Park East Drive
Beachwood, OH
216-464-5950

Extended Stay America - Cleveland -
Beachwood
3820 Orange Pl.
Beachwood, OH

216-595-9551

Extended Stay America-Cleveland-
Beachwood-Orange Place-North
3625 Orange Place
Beachwood, OH

216-896-5555

Residence Inn Cleveland Beachwood
3628 Park East Drive
Beachwood, OH

216-831-3030

Econo Lodge Beavercreek
2220 Heller Drive
Beavercreek, OH
937-426-5822

Residence Inn By Marriott
Beavercreek
2779 Fairfield Commons Blvd.
Beavercreek, OH

937-427-3914

Suburban Extended Stay Dayton-Wp
Afb
3845 Germany Lane
Beavercreek, OH

937-426-2608

Comfort Inn Bellefontaine
260 Northview
Bellefontaine, OH
937-599-5555

Mid Ohio Inn
880 State Route 97 West
Bellville, OH
419-886-3800

Extended Stay America - Cincinnati -
Blue Ash - Kenwood Road
11145 Kenwood Road
Blue Ash, OH
513-469-8900

Extended Stay America - Cincinnati -
Blue Ash - Reagan Hwy.
4260 Hunt Road
Blue Ash, OH

513-793-6750

Extended Stay America - Cincinnati -
Blue Ash - Reed Hartman
4630 Creek Road
Blue Ash, OH

513-985-9992

Hawthorn Suites By Wyndham
Cincinnati Blue Ash
10665 Techwoods Circle
Blue Ash, OH

513-733-0100

Residence Inn Cincinnati Blue Ash
11401 Reed Hartman Hwy
Blue Ash, OH

513-530-5060

Towneplace Suites By Marriott
Cincinnati Blue Ash
4650 Cornell Rd
Blue Ash, OH

513-469-8222

Comfort Inn Bluffton
117 Commerce Lane
Bluffton, OH
419-358-6000

Red Roof Inn Boardman
1051 Tiffany South
Boardman, OH
330-758-1999

Days Inn Bowling Green
1740 East Wooster Street
Bowling Green, OH
419-352-1520

Holiday Inn Express Hotel & Suites
Bowling Green
2150 Wooster Street
Bowling Green, OH

419-353-5500

Extended Stay America - Cleveland
- Brooklyn
10300 Cascade Crossing
Brooklyn, OH
216-267-7799

Best Western Airport Inn & Suites
Cleveland
16501 Snow Road
Brookpark, OH
216 267-9364

Howard Johnson Inn Cleveland
Airport
16644 Snow Road
Brookpark, OH

216-676-5200

Econo Lodge Buckeye Lake
10800 Hebron Rd
Buckeye Lake, OH
740-929-1015

Holiday Inn Express Hotel & Suites
Bucyrus
1575 North Sandusky Avenue
Bucyrus, OH
419-562-5664

Knights Inn Bucyrus
1515 North Sandusky Avenue
Bucyrus, OH

419-562-3737

Comfort Inn Cambridge
2327 Southgate Parkway
Cambridge, OH
740-435-3200

Days Inn Cambridge
2328 Southgate Parkway I-70
Cambridge, OH

740-432-5691

Residence Inn Canton
5280 Broadmoor Circle Nw

Canton, OH
330-493-0004

Days Inn Carrollton
1111 Canton Road
Carrollton, OH
330-627-9314

Staybridge Suites Cincinnati
North/West Chester
8955 Lakota Drive West
Chester, OH
513-874-1900

Quality Inn Chillicothe
20 N. Plaza Blvd.
Chillicothe, OH
740-775-3500

Best Western Clermont
4004 Williams Drive
Cincinnati, OH
513-528-7702

Clarion Hotel Cincinnati
3855 Hauck Road
Cincinnati, OH

513-563-8330

Days Inn Cincinnati East
4056 Mt Carmel Tobasco Road
Cincinnati, OH

513-528-3800

Drury Inn & Suites Cincinnati
Sharonville
2265 E Sharon Road
Cincinnati, OH

513-771-5601

Hampton Inn Cincinnati-Eastgate
858 Eastgate North Drive
Cincinnati, OH

513-752-8584

Holiday Inn Hotel & Suites Cincinnati-
Eastgate
4501 Eastgate Boulevard
Cincinnati, OH

513-752-4400

Red Roof Inn & Suites Cincinnati
North-Mason
8870 Governors Hill Drive
Cincinnati, OH

513-683-3086

Red Roof Inn - Cincinnati Blue Ash
5900 Pfeiffer Road
Cincinnati, OH

513-793-8811

Red Roof Inn Cincinnati East -
Beechmont
4035 Mount Carmel - Tobasco Road

176

Cincinnati, OH

513-528-2741

Residence Inn Cincinnati Downtown
506 East 4th Street
Cincinnati, OH

513-651-1234

Residence Inn Cincinnati
North/Sharonville
11689 Chester Rd
Cincinnati, OH

513-771-2525

Springdale Inn & Suites
400 Glensprings Drive
Cincinnati, OH

513-825-3129

Super 8 Cincinnati
330 Glensprings Drive
Cincinnati, OH

513-671-0556

TownePlace Suites by Marriott
Cincinnati Northeast/Mason
9369 Waterstone Boulevard
Cincinnati, OH

513-774-0610

Budget Host Inn Circleville
23897 Us Route 23 South
Circleville, OH
740-474-6006

Days Inn Of Lakewood
12019 Lake Avenue
Cleveland, OH
216-226-4800

Four Points by Sheraton Cleveland
Airport
4181 West 150th Street
Cleveland, OH

216-252-7700

Kimpton Schofield Hotel
2000 East Ninth Street
Cleveland, OH

216-357-3250

Residence Inn Cleveland Downtown
527 Prospect Avenue East
Cleveland, OH

216-443-9043

The Ritz-Carlton Cleveland
1515 West Third Street
Cleveland, OH

216-902-5223

Red Roof Inn Clyde

1363 West Mcpherson Highway
Clyde, OH
419-547-6660

Best Western Plus Columbus North
888 East Dublin-Granville Rd.
Columbus, OH
614-888-8230

Candlewood Suites Polaris
8515 Lyra Drive
Columbus, OH

614-436-6600

Comfort Inn & Suites Downtown
650 South High Street
Columbus, OH

614-228-6511

Comfort Suites Columbus
1690 Clara St
Columbus, OH

614-586-1001

Days Inn Columbus Fairgrounds
1700 Clara Street
Columbus, OH

614-299-4300

Drury Inn & Suites Columbus
Convention Center
88 East Nationwide Boulevard
Columbus, OH

614-221-7008

Embassy Suites Columbus Airport
2886 Airport Drive
Columbus, OH

614-536-0500

Extended Stay America - Columbus
- East
2200 Lake Club Drive
Columbus, OH

614-759-1451

Extended Stay America - Columbus
- Easton
4200 Stelzer Road
Columbus, OH

614-428-6022

Extended Stay America - Columbus
- North
6255 Zumstein Drive
Columbus, OH

614-431-0033

Extended Stay America - Columbus
- Worthington
7465 High Cross Boulevard
Columbus, OH

614-785-1006

Hilton Columbus
3900 Chagrin Drive
Columbus, OH

614-414-5000

Holiday Inn Columbus Downtown -
Capitol Square
175 East Town Street
Columbus, OH

614-221-3281

Knights Inn Downtown Columbus
1559 West Broad Street
Columbus, OH

614-275-0388

Quality Inn & Suites
4850 Frusta Drive
Columbus, OH

614-497-9600

Quality Inn And Suites North/Polaris
7500 Vantage Drive
Columbus, OH

614-436-0556

Ramada Columbus North
6767 Schrock Hill Ct.
Columbus, OH

614-890-8111

Red Roof Inn Columbus West
5001 Renner Road
Columbus, OH

614-878-9245

Red Roof Plus Columbus Downtown
111 East Nationwide Boulevard
Columbus, OH

614-224-6539

Red Roof Plus+ Columbus The Ohio
State University
441 Ackerman Road
Columbus, OH

614-267-9941

Residence Inn By Marriott Columbus
Downtown
36 E Gay Street
Columbus, OH

614-222-2610

Residence Inn Columbus Easton
3999 Easton Loop West
Columbus, OH

614-414-1000

Residence Inn Columbus
Worthington
7300 Huntington Park Drive

Columbus, OH
614-885-0799

Sheraton Suites Columbus
201 Hutchinson Avenue
Columbus, OH
614-436-0004

Super 8 Columbus North
1078 E. Dublin Granville Road
Columbus, OH
614-885-1601

Towneplace Suites By Marriott
Columbus-Gahanna
695 Taylor Road
Columbus, OH
614-861-1400

Towneplace Suites Columbus
Worthington
7272 Huntington Park Drive
Columbus, OH
614-885-1557

Towneplace Suites Columbus
Worthington
7272 Huntington Park Drive
Columbus, OH

Travelodge - Columbus
1551 West Broad Street
Columbus, OH
614-586-1750

University Plaza Hotel
3110 Olentangy River Road
Columbus, OH
614-267-7461

Days Inn Conneaut
600 Days Boulevard
Conneaut, OH
440-593-6000

Extended Stay America - Akron -
Copley - East
185 Montrose W. Ave.
Copley, OH
330-668-9818

Sheraton Suites Akron Cuyahoga
Falls
1989 Front Street
Cuyahoga Falls, OH
330-929-3000

Days Inn Hotel Huber Heights
7761 Old Country Court
Dayton, OH
937-233-1836

Drury Inn & Suites Dayton North
6616 Miller Lane
Dayton, OH

937-454-5200

Extended Stay America - Dayton -
North
6688 Miller Lane
Dayton, OH
937-898-9221

Extended Stay America - Dayton -
South
7851 Lois Circle
Dayton, OH
937-439-2022

Marriott at the University of Dayton
1414 South Patterson Boulevard
Dayton, OH
937-223-1000

Red Roof Inn Dayton North Airport
7370 Miller Lane
Dayton, OH
937-898-1054

Residence Inn Dayton North
7227 York Center Drive
Dayton, OH
937-890-2244

Towneplace Suites By Marriott
Dayton North
3642 Maxton Road
Dayton, OH
937-898-5700

Best Western Plus Delaware Inn
1720 Columbus Pike
Delaware, OH
740-363-3510

Quality Inn & Suites Delaware
1251 Columbus Pike
Delaware, OH
740-363-8869

Drury Inn & Suites Columbus Dublin
6170 Parkcenter Circle
Dublin, OH
614-798-8802

Extended Stay America - Columbus
- Dublin
450 Metro Place North
Dublin, OH
614-760-0053

Extended Stay America - Columbus
- Sawmill Rd.
6601 Reflections Drive
Dublin, OH
614-764-0159

Holiday Inn Express Columbus -
Dublin
5500 Tuttle Crossing Blvd.
Dublin, OH
614-793-5500

Homewood Suites By Hilton
Columbus-Dublin, Oh
5300 Park Center Avenue
Dublin, OH
614-791-8675

Quality Inn And Suites Dublin
3950 Tuller Road
Dublin, OH
614-764-0770

Red Roof PLUS Columbus - Dublin
5125 Post Road
Dublin, OH
614-764-3993

Sonesta Es Suites Columbus Dublin
435 Metro Place South
Dublin, OH
614-791-0403

Staybridge Suites Columbus-Dublin
6095 Emerald Parkway
Dublin, OH
614-734-9882

Woodfin Suite Hotel
4130 Tuller Road
Dublin, OH
614-766-7762

Quality Inn Elyria
739 Leona St.
Elyria, OH
440-324-7676

Red Roof Inn and Suites Cleveland
Elyria
621 Midway Boulevard
Elyria, OH
440-324-4444

Clarion Inn Dayton Airport Englewood
10 Rockridge Road
Englewood, OH
937-832-1234

Baymont Inn & Suites - Wright
Patterson Air Force Base
730 East Xenia Drive
Fairborn, OH
937-754-9109

Homewood Suites By Hilton Dayton-
Fairborn (Wright Patterson)
2750 Presidential Dr
Fairborn, OH

937-429-0600

Homewood Suites By Hilton Dayton-Fairborn (Wright Patterson)
2750 Presidential Dr
Fairborn, OH

937-429-0600

La Quinta Inn & Suites Fairborn
2540 University Blvd
Fairborn, OH

937-490-2000

Red Roof Inn Dayton Fairborn Nutter Center
2580 Colonel Glenn Highway
Fairborn, OH

937-426-6116

Extended Stay America - Cincinnati - Fairfield
9651 Seward Road
Fairfield, OH
513-860-5733

Drury Inn & Suites Findlay
820 Trenton Avenue
Findlay, OH
419-422-9700

Econo Lodge Findlay
316 Emma Street
Findlay, OH

419-422-0154

Holiday Inn Express Hotel & Suites Findlay
941 Interstate Drive
Findlay, OH

419-420-1776

Quality Inn Findlay
1020 Interstate Court
Findlay, QH

419-423-4303

Red Roof Inn Findlay
1951 Broad Avenue
Findlay, OH

419-424-0466

Towneplace Suites By Marriott Findlay
2501 Tiffin Avenue
Findlay, OH

419-425-9545

Best Western Fostoria Inn & Suites
1690 N Countyline Street
Fostoria, OH
419-436-3600

Drury Inn & Suites Middletown

3320 Village Drive
Franklin, OH
513-425-6650

Knights Inn Franklin/Middletown
8500 Claude-Thomas Rd.
Franklin, OH

937-746-2841

Comfort Inn & Suites Fremont
840 Sean Dr.
Fremont, OH
419-355-9300

Days Inn Fremont
3701 North State Route 53
Fremont, OH
419-334-9551

Travelodge Fremont
1750 Cedar Street
Fremont, OH

419-334-9517

Candlewood Suites Columbus - Gahanna
590 Taylor Road
Gahanna, OH
614-863-4033

Drury Inn & Suites Columbus Grove City
4109 Parkway Centre Drive
Grove City, OH
614-875-7000

Red Roof Inn Columbus - Grove City
4055 Jackpot Road
Grove City, OH

614-871-9617

Super 8 - Heath
1177 South Hebron Road
Heath, OH
740-788-9144

Red Roof Inn Columbus - Hebron
10668 Lancaster Road Southwest
Hebron, OH
740-467-7663

Hilliard Suites
3831 Park Mill Run Drive
Hilliard, OH
614-529-8118

Homewood Suites By Hilton® Columbus/Hilliard
3841 Park Mill Run Drive
Hilliard, OH

614-529-4100

Econo Lodge Holland
1201 East Mall Drive
Holland, OH
419-866-6565

Extended Stay America - Toledo - Holland
6155 West Trust Drive
Holland, OH

419-861-1133

Quality Inn Holland
1401 East Mall Dr.
Holland, OH

419-867-1144

Red Roof Inn Toledo/Holland
1214 Corporate Drive
Holland, OH

419-866-5512

Clarion Inn And Conference Center
6625 Dean Memorial Parkway
Hudson, OH
330-653-9191

Red Roof Inn Cleveland Independence
6020 Quarry Lane
Independence, OH
216-447-0030

Residence Inn Cleveland Independence
5101 West Creek Road
Independence, OH

216-520-1450

Quality Inn Jackson
605 E Main St
Jackson, OH
740-286-7581

Red Roof Inn Jackson
1000 Acy Ave
Jackson, OH

740-288-1200

Baymont Inn & Suites Washington Court House
11431 Allen Road N.W.
Jeffersonville, OH
740-948-2104

Econo Lodge Jeffersonville
9060 West Lancaster Road
Jeffersonville, OH

740-948-2332

Days Inn Kent - Akron
4422 Edson Road
Kent, OH
330-677-9400

Super 8 - Kent
4380 Edson Road
Kent, OH

330-678-8817

Knights Inn Lebanon
725 E. Main Street
Lebanon, OH
513-932-3034

Econo Lodge Lima
1250 Neubrecht Road
Lima, OH
419-227-6515

Howard Johnson Lima Oh
1920 Roschman Avenue
Lima, OH

419-222-0004

Days Inn Lisbon
40952 State Route 154
Lisbon, OH
330-420-0111

Old Man's Cave Chalets
18905 H 664S
Logan, OH
740-385-6517

Best Western Richland Inn-Mansfield
180 East Hanley Road
Mansfield, OH
419-756-6670

Heritage Inn Mansfield
1017 Koogle Rd
Mansfield, OH

419-589-3333

Quality Inn & Suites Mansfield
500 N. Trimble Rd.
Mansfield, OH

419-529-1000

Super 8 Mansfield
2425 Interstate Circle
Mansfield, OH

419-756-8875

Travelodge Mansfield
90 West Hanley Road
Mansfield, OH

419-756-7600

Majestic Motel
8629 Northshore Blvd
Marblehead, OH
419-798-4921

Quality Inn Marietta
700 Pike Street
Marietta, OH
740-374-8190

Comfort Inn Marysville
16420 Allenby Drive
Marysville, OH
937-644-0400

Super 8 Marysville
16510 Square Drive
Marysville, OH

937-644-8821

Super 8 Mason
5589 Kings Mills Road
Mason, OH
513-398-8075

Days Inn Maumee
1704 Tollgate Drive
Maumee, OH
419-897-6900

Homewood Suites By Hilton®
Toledo/Maumee
1410 Arrowhead Road
Maumee, OH

419-897-0980

Red Roof Inn Toledo Maumee
1570 South Reynolds Road
Maumee, OH

419-893-0292

Residence Inn By Marriott Toledo
Maumee
1370 Arrowhead Drive
Maumee, OH

419-891-2233

Staybridge Suites Toledo- Maumee
2300 Village Dr. Bldg. 1800
Maumee, OH

419-878-8999

Comfort Inn Mayfield Heights
Cleveland East
1421 Golden Gate Blvd
Mayfield Heights, OH

Comfort Inn Mayfield Heights
Cleveland East
1421 Golden Gate Blvd
Mayfield Heights, OH

440-442-8400

Staybridge Suites Cleveland
Mayfield Heights Beachwood
6103 Landerhaven Drive
Mayfield Heights, OH

440-442-9200

Red Roof Inn Medina, Oh
5021 Eastpointe Drive
Medina, OH
330-725-1395

Super 8 Medina
5161 Montville Drive.
Medina, OH

330-723-8118

Best Western Plus Lawnfield Inn And
Suites
8434 Mentor Avenue
Mentor, OH
440-205-7378

Residence Inn Mentor
5660 Emerald Ct
Mentor, OH

440-392-0800

Dayton South Knights Inn
185 Beyer Rd.
Miamisburg, OH
937-859-8797

Homewood Suites By Hilton®
Dayton-South
3100 Contemporary Lane
Miamisburg, OH

937-432-0000

Quality Inn & Suites Miamisburg
250 Byers Road
Miamisburg, OH

937-865-0077

Red Roof Inn Dayton South- I-75
Miamisburg
222 Byers Road
Miamisburg, OH

937-866-0705

Super 8 Miamisburg
155 Monarch Lane
Miamisburg, OH

937-866-5500

Comfort Inn Cleveland Airport
17550 Rosbough Drive
Middleburg Heights, OH
440-234-3131

Days Inn Cleveland Airport South
7233 Engle Road
Middleburg Heights, OH

440-243-2277

Red Roof Inn Cleveland Middleburg
Heights
17555 Bagley Road
Middleburg Heights, OH

440-243-2441

Sonesta ES Suites Cleveland Airport
17525 Rosbough Boulevard
Middleburg Heights, OH

440-234-6688

Towneplace Suites By Marriott
Cleveland Airport
7325 Engle Road
Middleburg Heights, OH

Dog-Friendly Lodging - Please always call ahead to make sure an establishment is still dog-friendly.

440-816-9300

Manchester Inn And Conference Center
1027 Manchester Avenue
Middletown, OH
513-422-5481

Super 8 Franklin/Middletown Area
3553 Commerce Drive
Middletown/Franklin, OH
513-422-4888

Red Roof Inn Sandusky - Milan
11303 Milan Road
Milan, OH
419-499-4347

Super 8 Motel -Milan/ Sandusky Area/South
11313 Milan Road
Milan, OH

419-499-4671

Homewood Suites By Hilton®
Cincinnati-Milford, Oh
600 Chamber Drive
Milford, OH
513-248-4663

Super 8 Millbury/Toledo
3491 Latcha Road
Millbury, OH
419-837-6409

Comfort Inn Millersburg
1102 Glen Drive
Millersburg, OH
330-674-7400

Quality Inn Bryan/Montpelier
13508 State Route 15
Montpelier, OH
419-485-5555

Knights Inn Dayton
2450 Dryden Road
Moraine, OH
937-298-0380

Knights Inn Mt. Gilead
5898 Route 95
Mount Gilead, OH
419-768-4217

Countryside Inn and Suites
100 Leininger Street
Mount Orab, OH
937-444-6666

Comfort Inn Mount Vernon
150 Howard Street
Mount Vernon, OH
740-392-6886

Super 8 Mt. Vernon
1000 Coshocton Ave.
Mount Vernon, OH

740-397-8885

Best Western Napoleon Inn & Suites
1290 Independence Drive
Napoleon, OH
419-599-0850

Econo Lodge Newton Falls
4248 Sr 5
Newton Falls, OH
330-872-0988

Red Roof Inn Canton
5353 Inn Circle Court Northwest
North Canton, OH
330-499-1970

Super 8 - North Lima
10076 Market Street
North Lima, OH
330-549-9190

Candlewood Suites Cleveland - N. Olmsted
24741 Country Club Blvd
North Olmsted, OH
440-716-0584

Extended Stay America - Cleveland - Airport - North Olmsted
24851 Country Club Blvd.
North Olmsted, OH

440-777-8585

Econo Lodge Norwalk
342 Milan Ave.
Norwalk, OH
419-668-5656

Oberlin Inn Ohio
7 North Main Street
Oberlin, OH
440-775-1111

Radisson Hotel Cleveland Airport
25070 Country Club Blvd
Olmsted, OH
440-734-5060

Sleep Inn & Suites Oregon
1761 Meijer Circle
Oregon, OH
419-697-7800

Baymont Inn & Suites Perrysburg
27441 Helen Drive
Perrysburg, OH
419-874-9181

Candlewood Suites Perrysburg
27350 Lake Vue Drive
Perrysburg, OH

419-872-6161

Econo Lodge Perrysburg
10667 Fremont Pike
Perrysburg, OH

419-874-8771

Budgetel Inn & Suites
902 Scott Drive
Piqua, OH
937-773-2314

Comfort Inn Miami Valley Centre Mall
987 E. Ash St.
Piqua, OH

937-778-8100

Residence Inn Youngstown Boardman/Poland
7396 Tiffany South
Poland, OH
330-726-1747

Best Western Port Clinton
1734 East Perry Street
Port Clinton, OH
419-734-2274

Holiday Village Resort
3247 N.E. Catawba Road
Port Clinton, OH

419-797-4732

Super 8 Motel Port Clinton
1704 Perry Street
Port Clinton, OH

419-734-4446

Holiday Inn Portsmouth Downtown
711 Second Street
Portsmouth, OH
740-354-7711

Super 8 Portsmouth
4266 Us Route 23 N
Portsmouth, OH

740-353-8880

Days Inn & Suites Columbus East Airport
2100 Brice Road
Reynoldsburg, OH
614-864-1280

Red Roof Inn Columbus East
Reynoldsburg
2449 Brice Road
Reynoldsburg, OH

614-864-3683

Super 8 Columbus
2055 Brice Road
Reynoldsburg, OH

614-864-3880

Super 8 Motel - Richfield Area
4845 Brecksville Road
Richfield, OH
330-659-6888

Dog-Friendly Lodging - Please always call ahead to make sure an establishment is still dog-friendly.

Knights Inn Sandusky
2405 Cleveland Road
Sandusky, OH
419-621-9000

Super 8 Sandusky North
5410 Milan Road
Sandusky, OH

419-625-7070

Comfort Inn Seaman
55 Stern Dr.
Seaman, OH
937-386-2511

Super 8 Seville
6116 Speedway Drive
Seville, OH
330-769-8880

Crosslands Cincinnati - Sharonville
11457 Chester Road
Sharonville, OH
513-771-7829

Red Roof Inn - Cincinnati Sharonville
2301 Sharon Road
Sharonville, OH

513-771-5552

Sonesta Es Suites Cincinnati
2670 East Kemper Road
Sharonville, OH

513-772-8888

Top O' The Caves Cabin Rentals
26780 Chapel Ridge Road
South Bloomingville, OH
800-967-2434

Crosland Economy Studios -
Cincinnati - Springdale - Tri-County
11645 Chesterdale Road
Springdale, OH
513-771-2457

Extended Stay America - Cincinnati -
Springdale - I-275
320 Glensprings Drive
Springdale, OH

513-671-4900

Baymont Inn & Suites Springfield
319 E Leffel Lane
Springfield, OH
937-328-0123

Courtyard By Marriott Springfield
Downtown
100 South Fountain Avenue
Springfield, OH

937-322-3600

Motel 6 Springfield
11 West Leffel Lane

Springfield, OH

937-322-4942

Red Roof Inn Springfield
155 West Leffel Lane
Springfield, OH

937-325-5356

Econo Lodge And Suites
51659 National Road
St Clairsville, OH
740-526-0128

Red Roof Inn St Clairsville -
Wheeling West
68301 Red Roof Lane
St Clairsville, OH

740-695-4057

Staybridge Suites Akron - Stow -
Cuyahoga Falls
4351 Steels Pointe Drive
Stow, OH
330-945-4180

Towneplace Suites By Marriott
Cleveland Streetsboro
795 Mondial Parkway
Streetsboro, OH
330-422-1855

Super 8 Strongsville
15385 Royalton Road
Strongsville, OH
440-238-0170

Americas Best Value Inn & Suites
Sunbury
7323 State Route 37 East
Sunbury, OH
740-362-6159

Holiday Inn Express Hotel & Suites
Sunbury-Columbus Area
7301 State Route 37
Sunbury, OH

740-362-3036

Days Inn Toledo Airport
10753 Airport Highway
Swanton, OH
419-865-2002

Days Inn Tiffin
1927 South State Route 53
Tiffin, OH
419-447-6313

Holiday Inn Express Tiffin
78 Shaffer Park Drive
Tiffin, OH

419-443-5100

Ramada Toledo Conference Center
3536 Secor Rd
Toledo, OH

419-535-7070

Red Roof Inn Toledo University
3530 Executive Parkway
Toledo, OH

419-536-0118

Rodeway Inn Toledo
445 E. Alexis Rd.
Toledo, OH

419-476-0170

Holiday Inn Express & Suites Troy
60 Troy Town Drive
Troy, OH
937-332-1700

Residence Inn By Marriott Dayton
Troy
87 Troy Town Drive
Troy, OH

937-440-9303

Comfort Suites Twinsburg
2716 Creekside Drive
Twinsburg, OH
330-963-5909

Super 8 Twinsburg/Cleveland Area
8848 Twin Hills Pkwy
Twinsburg, OH

330-425-2889

Red Roof Inn Uhrichsville
111 W Mccauley Dr I-77 At Us-250,
Exit #81
Uhrichsville, OH
740-922-0774

Super 8 Motel - Akron/Green/Canton
Area
1605 Corporate Woods Parkway
Uniontown, OH
330-899-9888

Comfort Inn Van Wert
840 North Washington Street
Van Wert, OH
419-232-6040

Super 8 Vandalia/Dayton
International Airport
550 East National Road
Vandalia, OH
937-898-7636

Holiday Inn Express Cleveland-
Vermilion
2417 State Route 60
Vermilion, OH
440-967-8770

Knights Inn Wapakoneta
1659 Bellefontaine Street
Wapakoneta, OH
419-738-2184

Best Western Del Mar
8319 State Highway 108
Wauseon, OH
419-335-1565

Residence Inn Cincinnati North/West
Chester
6240 Muhlhauser Road
West Chester, OH
513-341-4040

Staybridge Suites Cincinnati
North/West Chester
8955 Lakota Drive West
West Chester, OH

513-874-1900

Red Roof Inn Columbus Northeast
Westerville
909 South State Street
Westerville, OH
614-890-1244

Doubletree By Hilton Hotel Cleveland
- Westlake
1100 Crocker Road
Westlake, OH
440-871-6000

Red Roof Inn Westlake
29595 Clemens Road
Westlake, OH

440-892-7920

Sonesta ES Suites Cleveland
Westlake
30100 Clemens Road
Westlake, OH

440-892-2254

Super 8 Westlake/Cleveland
25200 Sperry Drive
Westlake, OH

440-871-3993

Towneplace Suites By Marriott
Cleveland Westlake
25052 Sperry Drive
Westlake, OH

440-892-4275

Quality Inn Wickliffe - Cleveland East
28611 Euclid Ave.
Wickliffe, OH
440-944-4030

Red Roof Inn Cleveland East -
Willoughby
4166 State Route 306
Willoughby, OH
440-946-9872

Travelodge Cleveland/Willoughby
34600 Maple Grove Road
Willoughby, OH

Hampton Inn & Suites Wilmington
201 Holiday Drive
Wilmington, OH
937-382-4400

Holiday Inn Wilmington
123 Gano Road
Wilmington, OH

937-283-3200

Super 8 Motel - Wooster
969 Timken Rd.
Wooster, OH
330-264-6211

Best Western Meander Inn
870 N Canfield Niles Rd
Youngstown, OH
330-544-2378

Econolodge Youngstown
5431 1/2 Seventy Six Drive
Youngstown, OH

330-270-2865

Rodeway Inn Youngstown
4250 Belmont Avenue
Youngstown, OH

330-759-0040

Super 8 Youngstown
5280 76 Drive
Youngstown, OH

330-793-7788

Baymont Inn And Suites Zanesville
230 Scenic Crest Drive
Zanesville, OH
740-454-9332

Best Western B. R. Guest
4929 East Pike
Zanesville, OH

740-453-6300

Comfort Inn Zanesville
500 Monroe St.
Zanesville, OH

740-454-4144

Motel 6 Zanesville
4645 East Pike
Zanesville, OH

Super 8 Zanesville
2440 National Road
Zanesville, OH

740-455-3124

Travel Inn Zanesville
58 North 6th Street
Zanesville, OH

# Oklahoma Listings

Days Inn Altus
2804 North Main Street
Altus, OK
580-482-9300

Hampton Inn & Suites Altus
3601 North Main Street
Altus, OK

580-482-1273

Americas Best Value Inn Ardmore
2519 Veterans Blvd.
Ardmore, OK
580-223-1234

Candlewood Suites Ardmore
2602 Rina Park Road
Ardmore, OK

580-226-0100

Comfort Inn & Suites
1502 South Mississippi Avenue
Atoka, OK
580-889-8999

Hiway Inn Express of Atoka
1101 South Mississippi Avenue
Atoka, OK

580-889-7300

Super 8 Atoka
2101 South Mississippi Avenue
Atoka, OK

580-889-7381

Candlewood Suites Bartlesville East
3812 Se Washington Place
Bartlesville, OK
918-766-0044

Holiday Inn Express Hotel & Suites
Oklahoma City - Bethany
7840 Nw 39 Expressway
Bethany, OK
405-787-6262

Econo Lodge Blackwell
1201 N. 44th St.
Blackwell, OK
580-363-7000

Super 8 Blackwell
1014 West Doolin Avenue
Blackwell, OK

580-363-5945

Towneplace Suites By Marriott Tulsa
Broken Arrow
2251 North Stone Wood Circle
Broken Arrow, OK
918-355-9600

Dog-Friendly Lodging - Please always call ahead to make sure an establishment is still dog-friendly.

Hampton Inn And Suites
Tulsa/Catoosa
100 Mcnabb Field Road
Catoosa, OK
918-739-3939

Lake Eufaula Inn
HC60 Box 1835
Checotah, OK
918-473-2376

Holiday Inn Express Hotel & Suites
Chickasha
2610 South 4th Street
Chickasha, OK
405-224-8883

Microtel Inn & Suites By Wyndham
Claremore
10600 East Mallard Lake Road
Claremore, OK
918-343-2868

Days Inn Clinton
1200 South 10th Street
Clinton, OK
580-323-5550

Holiday Inn Express And Suites
Clinton
2000 Boulevard Of Champions
Clinton, OK

580-323-1950

Ramada - Clinton
2140 West Gary Boulevard
Clinton, OK

580-323-2010

Magnolia Inn Durant
2121 West Main Street
Durant, OK
580-924-5432

Baymont Inn And Suites El Reno
1707 Southwest 27th Street
El Reno, OK
405-262-3050

Days Inn El Reno
2700 S Country Club
El Reno, OK

405-262-8720

Ramada Inn Elk City
102 Bj Hughes Access Road
Elk City, OK
580-225-8140

Baymont Inn & Suites Enid
3614 W Owen K. Garriott Road
Enid, OK
580-234-6800

Days Inn Enid
2818 S Van Buren St

Enid, OK
580 242-7110

Knights Inn Enid
2901 South Van Buren
Enid, OK
580-237-6000

Ramada Enid
3005 W Owen K Garriott Road
Enid, OK

580-234-0440

Days Inn Erick
1014 North Sheb Wooley Ave
Erick, OK
580-526-3315

Loyal Inn
300 Birkes Road
Eufaula, OK
918-689-9109

Best Western Glenpool/Tulsa
14831 S. Casper St.
Glenpool, OK
918-322-5201

Best Western Timberridge Inn
120 W 18th Street
Grove, OK
918 786-6900

Ambassador Inn
1909 North Hwy 64
Guymon, OK
580-338-5555

Gateway Inn
Hwy 75 and Trudgeon St
Henryetta, OK
918-652-4448

Comfort Suites Idabel
400 Se Lincoln Blvd.
Idabel, OK
580-286-9393

Baymont Inn & Suites Lawton
1203 Nw 40th Street
Lawton, OK
580-353-5581

Best Western Plus Lawton Hotel &
Convention Center
1125 East Gore Boulevard
Lawton, OK

580-353-0200

Knights Inn Lawton
2202 Nw Highway 277
Lawton, OK

580-353-0310

Quality Inn Lawton
3110 Cache Road

Lawton, OK
580-353-3104

Best Western Locust Grove Inn And
Suites
106 Holiday Lane
Locust Grove, OK
918-479-8082

Comfort Suites Mcalester
650 S. George Nigh Expy
McAlester, OK
918-302-0001

Econo Lodge Mcalester
731 S. George Nigh Expwy
McAlester, OK

918-426-4420

Best Western Inn Of Mcalester
1215 S George Nigh Expressway
Mcalester, OK
918-426-0115

Candlewood Suites Mcalester
425 S. George Nigh Expressway
Mcalester, OK

918-426-4171

Microtel Inn & Suites By Wyndham
Miami
2015 East Steve Owens Blvd
Miami, OK
918-540-3333

Travelers Inn Midwest City
6821 South East 29th Street
Midwest City, OK
405-737-8880

Candlewood Suites Oklahoma City-
Moore
1701 North Moore Avenue
Moore, OK
405-735-5151

Embassy Suites Norman - Hotel And
Conference Center
2501 Conference Drive
Norman, OK
405-364-8040

Super 8 Norman
2600 West Main Street
Norman, OK

405-329-1624

Travelodge Norman
225 North Interstate Drive
Norman, OK

405-329-7194

Days Inn Okemah
605 South Woody Guthrie Street
Okemah, OK
918-623-2200

Americas Best Value Inn Oklahoma City
12001 N. I-35 Service Road
Oklahoma City, OK
405-478-0400

Americas Best Value Inn-Oklahoma City I-35
3030 South Prospect Ave
Oklahoma City, OK
405-677-1000

Best Western Plus Broadway Inn And Suites
6101 N Santa Fe Avenue
Oklahoma City, OK
405-848-1919

Best Western Plus Greentree Inn & Suites
1811 North Moore Avenue
Oklahoma City, OK
405-912-8882

Best Western Plus Saddleback Inn And Conference Center
4300 South West Third Street
Oklahoma City, OK
405-947-7000

BudgetLodge Oklahoma City
11900 North I-35 Service Road
Oklahoma City, OK
405-478-2888

Candlewood Suites- Oklahoma City
4400 River Park Drive
Oklahoma City, OK
405-680-8770

Courtyard By Marriott Okalahoma City Downtown
2 West Reno Avenue
Oklahoma City, OK
405-232-2290

Days Inn Oklahoma City
12013 North Interstate 35 Service Road
Oklahoma City, OK
405-478-2554

Days Inn Oklahoma City Northwest
2801 Northwest 39th
Oklahoma City, OK
405-946-0741

Days Inn Oklahoma City South
2616 South Interstate 35 Service Road
Oklahoma City, OK
405-677-0521

Embassy Suites Hotel Oklahoma City-Will Rogers Airport
1815 South Meridian
Oklahoma City, OK
405-682-6000

Extended Stay America - Oklahoma City - Airport
4820 West Reno Ave.
Oklahoma City, OK
405-948-4443

Extended Stay America - Oklahoma City - Nw Expressway
2720 Northwest Expressway
Oklahoma City, OK
405-942-7441

Holiday Inn Express Hotel & Suites Oklahoma City Northwest
3520 Nw 135th St
Oklahoma City, OK
405-751-8900

Homewood Suites By Hilton Oklahoma City-West
6920 West Reno Avenue
Oklahoma City, OK
405-789-3600

Howard Johnson Oklahoma City Airport
400 S Meridian Ave
Oklahoma City, OK
405-943-9841

Microtel Inn & Suites By Wyndham Oklahoma City Airport
624 South Macarthur Blvd.
Oklahoma City, OK
405-942-0011

Motel 6 Oklahoma City
2727 West I-44 Service Road
Oklahoma City, OK
405-948-8000

Park Hill Inn and Suites
1400 North East 63rd Street
Oklahoma City, OK
405-478-5221

Ramada Oklahoma City Airport North
2200 S Meridian
Oklahoma City, OK
405-681-9000

Residence Inn Oklahoma City Downtown/Bricktown
400 East Reno Avenue
Oklahoma City, OK

405-601-1700

Residence Inn Oklahoma City South
1111 East I240 Service Road
Oklahoma City, OK
405-634-9696

Rodeway Inn Oklahoma City
8315 South I-35 Service Road
Oklahoma City, OK
405-631-8661

Sonesta Es Suites Oklahoma City
4361 West Reno Avenue
Oklahoma City, OK
405-942-4500

Staybridge Suites Oklahoma City
4411 Sw 15th
Oklahoma City, OK
405-429-4400

Staybridge Suites Oklahoma City-Quail Springs
2740 Nw 138th Street
Oklahoma City, OK
405-286-3800

The Skirvin Hilton Oklahoma City
One Park Avenue
Oklahoma City, OK
405-2723040

Best Western Okmulgee
3499 North Wood Drive
Okmulgee, OK
918-756-9200

Days Inn Okmulgee
1221 S Wood Drive
Okmulgee, OK
918-758-0660

Best Western Owasso Inn & Suites
7653 North Owasso Expressway
Owasso, OK
918-272-2000

Candlewood Suites Owasso
11699 E. 96th Street North
Owasso, OK
918-272-4334

Towneplace Suites By Marriott Tulsa North/Owasso
9355 North Owasso Expressway
Owasso, OK
918-376-4400

Comfort Inn & Suites Perry
3112 W. Fir Street
Perry, OK

Dog-Friendly Lodging - Please always call ahead to make sure an establishment is still dog-friendly.

580-336-3800

Comfort Inn & Suites Ponca City
3101 N. 14th Street
Ponca City, OK
580-765-2322

Holiday Inn Express Hotel & Suites
Poteau
201 Hillview Parkway
Poteau, OK
918-649-0123

Americas Best Value Inn Roland
824 South Paw Paw Road
Roland, OK
918-427-6600

Days Inn Sallisaw
710 South Kerr Boulevard
Sallisaw, OK
918-774-0400

Super 8 Sapulpa Tulsa Area
1505 New Sapulpa Road
Sapulpa, OK
918-227-3300

Super 8 Shawnee
4900 N Harrison St
Shawnee, OK
405-275-0089

Best Western Plus Cimarron Hotel &
Suites
315 North Husband Street
Stillwater, OK
405-372-2878

Days Inn Stillwater
5010 West 6th Street
Stillwater, OK

405-743-2570

Quality Inn Stillwater
2515 West 6th Avenue
Stillwater, OK

405-372-0800

Residence Inn Stillwater
800 South Murphy Street
Stillwater, OK

405-707-0588

Aloft Tulsa
6716 South 104th East Avenue
Tulsa, OK
918-949-9000

Americas Best Value Inn Tulsa West
5525 West Skelly Drive
Tulsa, OK

918-446-1561

Best Western Airport
222 N Garnett Rd
Tulsa, OK

918-438-0780

Candlewood Suites Tulsa
10008 East 73rd Street South
Tulsa, OK

918-294-9000

Comfort Inn Tulsa
4530 E. Skelly Drive
Tulsa, OK
918-488-8777

Country Inn & Suites By Carlson,
Tulsa Central, Ok
3209 South 79th East Avenue
Tulsa, OK

918-663-1000

Crowne Plaza Tulsa - Southern Hills
7902 South Lewis Avenue
Tulsa, OK
918-492-5000

Doubletree Hotel Tulsa At Warren
Place
6110 South Yale Avenue
Tulsa, OK
918-495-1000

Doubletree Hotel Tulsa-Downtown
616 West 7th Street
Tulsa, OK
918-587-8000

Extended Stay America - Tulsa -
Central
3414 South 79th East Ave.
Tulsa, OK
918-664-9494

Holiday Inn Hotel & Suites Tulsa
South
10020 East 81st Street
Tulsa, OK
918-994-5000

RENAISSANCE TULSA HOTEL &
CONVENTION CENTER, A Marriott
Luxury & Lifestyle Hotel
6808 South 107th East Avenue
Tulsa, OK
918-307-2600

Red Roof Inn Tulsa
4717 South Yale Avenue
Tulsa, OK
918-622-6776

Residence Inn Tulsa South
11025 East 73rd Street South
Tulsa, OK

918-250-4850

Rodeway Inn & Suites East / I-44
1737 S. 101st East Ave.
Tulsa, OK
918-628-0900

Staybridge Suites Tulsa-Woodland
Hills
11111 East 73rd Street South
Tulsa, OK
918-461-2100

Studio 6 Tulsa
8181 E 41st Street
Tulsa, OK
918-664-7241

Super 8 Motel - Tulsa/Arpt/St
Fairgrounds
6616 East Archer Street
Tulsa, OK
918-836-1981

Days Inn Woodward Ok
1212 North West Hwy 270
Woodward, OK
580-256-1546

Northwest Inn
3202 1st St
Woodward, OK
580-256-7600

Super 8 Woodward
4120 Williams Ave
Woodward, OK
580-254-2964

Wayfarer Inn
2901 Williams Avenue
Woodward, OK
580-256-5553

Best Western Plus Yukon
11440 West I-40 Service Road
Yukon, OK
405-265-2995

# Oregon Listings

Best Western Plus Prairie Inn
1100 Price Road South East
Albany, OR
541-928-5050

Comfort Suites Linn County
Fairground And Expo
100 Opal Court Northeast
Albany, OR
541-928-2053

Holiday Inn Express Hotel And Suites
Albany
105 Opal Court Ne
Albany, OR

541-928-8820

Rodeway Inn Albany
1212 Se Price Road
Albany, OR

541-926-0170

Super 8 Albany
315 Airport Road Se
Albany, OR

541-928-6322

The Inn at Arch Cape
79340 Highway 101 South
Arch Cape, OR
503-738-7373

Ashland Hills Hotel
2525 Ashland Street
Ashland, OR
541-482-8310

Best Western Bards Inn
132 North Main Street
Ashland, OR

541-482-0049

Best Western Windsor Inn
2520 Ashland Street
Ashland, OR

541-488-2330

Econo Lodge Ashland
50 Lowe Road
Ashland, OR

541-482-4700

Holiday Inn Express Hotel & Suites
Ashland
565 Clover Lane
Ashland, OR

541-201-0202

Best Western Lincoln Inn
555 Hamburg Avenue
Astoria, OR
503-325-2205

Crest Motel
5366 Leif Erikson Drive
Astoria, OR

503-325-3141

Holiday Inn Express Hotel & Suites
Astoria
204 West Marine Drive
Astoria, OR

503-325-6222

Hotel Elliott
357 12th Street
Astoria, OR

503-325-2222

Best Western Sunridge Inn
1 Sunridge Lane
Baker City, OR
541-523-6444

Rodeway Inn Baker City
810 Campbell Street
Baker City, OR

541-523-2242

Super 8 Baker City
250 Campbell Street
Baker City, OR

541-523-8282

Sunset Motel
1755 Beach Loop Rd
Bandon, OR
541-347-2453

Table Rock Motel
840 Beach Loop Road
Bandon, OR

541-347-2700

Extended Stay America - Portland -
Beaverton
875 Sw 158th Ave
Beaverton, OR
503-690-3600

Extended Stay America - Portland -
Beaverton - Eider Court
18665 Nw Eider Ct
Beaverton, OR

503-439-1515

HOMEWOOD SUITES
PORTLAND/BEAVERTON
15525 Northwest Gateway Court
Beaverton, OR

503-614-0900

Days Inn Bend Or
849 Northeast Third Street
Bend, OR
541-383-3776

Entrada Lodge
19221 Southwest Century Drive
Bend, OR

541-382-4080

Hillside Inn B&"";B
1744 Northwest 12th Street
Bend, OR

541-389-9660

Holiday Inn Express Bend

20615 Grandview Drive
Bend, OR

541-317-8500

McMenamins Old St. Francis School
700 NW Bond Street
Bend, OR

541-382-5174

Quality Inn Bend
20600 Grandview Drive
Bend, OR

541-318-0848

Red Lion Hotel Bend
1415 Ne Third Street
Bend, OR

541-382-7011

Rodeway Inn & Suites Bend
904 Southeast 3rd Street
Bend, OR

541-382-2111

Sleep Inn Bend
600 Northeast Bellevue Drive
Bend, OR

541-330-0050

Super 8 Bend
1275 Se 3rd St. OR Business 97
Bend, OR

541-388-6888

The Riverhouse Resort
3075 N Hwy 97
Bend, OR

541-389-3111

Towneplace Suites Bend Near Mt.
Bachelor
755 Southwest 13th Place
Bend, OR

541-382-5006

Whaleshead Beach Resort
19921 Whaleshead Road
Brookings, OR
541-469-7446

Silver Spur Motel
789 N Broadway Avenue
Burns, OR
541-573-2077

Hallmark Resort
1400 S Hemlock Street
Cannon Beach, OR
503-436-1566

Inn at Cannon Beach
3215 South Hemlock Street
Cannon Beach, OR

503-436-9085

Surfsand Resort
148 West Gower
Cannon Beach, OR

503-436-2274

The Ocean Lodge
2864 South Pacific Street
Cannon Beach, OR

503-436-2241

The Wayside Inn
3339 S. Hemlock Street
Cannon Beach, OR

503-436-1577

Tolovana Inn
3400 S Hemlock - Tolovana Park
Cannon Park, OR
800-333-8890

Holiday Inn Express Hotel & Suites
Canyonville
200 Creekside Drive
Canyonville, OR
541-839-4200

Best Western Plus Columbia River
Inn
735 Wanapa Street
Cascade Locks, OR
541-374-8777

Junction Inn
406 Redwood Hwy
Cave Junction, OR
541-592-3106

Holiday Inn Express Hotel & Suites
Medford-Central Point
285 Penninger Street
Central Point, OR
541-423-1010

Comfort Suites Clackamas
15929 Se Mckinley Ave
Clackamas, OR
503-723-3450

Motel 6 Clackamas
12855 South East 97th Avenue
Clackamas, OR

503-496-1000

Best Western Plus Holiday Hotel
411 North Bayshore Drive
Coos Bay, OR
541-269-5111

Red Lion Hotel Coos Bay
1313 North Bayshore Drive
Coos Bay, OR

541-267-4141

Super 8 Coos Bay/North Bend
1001 North Bayshore Drive
Coos Bay, OR

541-808-0704

Best Western Grand Manor Inn &
Suites
925 Northwest Garfield Ave.
Corvallis, OR
541-758-8571

Days Inn Corvallis
1113 Northwest 9th Street
Corvallis, OR

541-754-7474

Holiday Inn Express Corvallis-On
The River
781 Nw 2nd Street
Corvallis, OR

541-752-0800

Rodeway Inn Willamette River
345 N.W. 2nd St.
Corvallis, OR

541-752-9601

Quality Inn Cottage Grove
845 Gateway Boulevard
Cottage Grove, OR
541-942-9747

Super 8 Creswell
345 East Oregon Avenue
Creswell, OR
541-895-3341

Best Western Dallas Inn And Suites
250 Orchard Drive
Dallas, OR
503-623-6000

Trollers Lodge
355 SW H 101
Depoe Bay, OR
541-765-2287

Diamond Lake Resort
350 Resort Drive
Diamond Lake, OR
541-793-3333

Barking Mad Farm Bed and
Breakfast
65156 Powers Road, Enterprise,
Oregon 97828
Enterprise, OR
541-426-0360

Ponderosa Motel
102 E Greenwood
Enterprise, OR

541-426-3186

Days Inn Eugene
Downtown/University

1859 Franklin Boulevard
Eugene, OR
541-342-6383

Hilton Eugene
66 East Sixth Avenue
Eugene, OR

541-342-2000

Residence Inn Eugene
25 Club Road
Eugene, OR

541-342-7171

Valley River Inn
1000 Valley River Way
Eugene, OR

541-687-0123

Best Western Pier Point Inn
85625 Highway 101
Florence, OR
541-997-7191

Ocean Breeze Motel
85165 H 101S
Florence, OR

541-997-2642

Best Western University Inn & Suites
3933 Pacific Avenue
Forest Grove, OR
503-992-8888

Jo's Motel and Campground
52851 H 62
Fort Klamath, OR
541-381-2234

Econo Lodge Garibaldi
227 Garibaldi Avenue
Garibaldi, OR
503-322-2552

Gearhart Ocean Inn
67 North Cottage Avenue
Gearhart, OR
503-738-7373

Jot's Resort
94360 Wedderburn Loop
Gold Beach, OR
541-247-6676

Best Western Mt. Hood Inn
87450 East Government Camp Loop
Government Camp, OR
503-272-3205

Best Western Grants Pass Inn
111 N.E. Agness Ave.
Grants Pass, OR
541-476-1117

Holiday Inn Express Grants Pass
105 North East Agness Avenue
Grants Pass, OR

541-471-6144

Quality Inn Grants Pass
1889 Ne 6th St.
Grants Pass, OR

541-479-8301

Redwood Motel
815 NE 6th Street
Grants Pass, OR

541-476-0878

Super 8 Grants Pass
1949 North East 7th Street
Grants Pass, OR

541-474-0888

Days Inn & Suites Gresham
24124 Se Stark Street
Gresham, OR
503-465-1515

Super 8 Gresham/Portland Area Or
121 Ne 181st Ave
Gresham, OR

503-661-5100

Travelodge Pioneer Villa
33180 Highway 228
Halsey, OR

Comfort Inn Conference Center
Hillsboro
3500 Northeast Cornell Road
Hillsboro, OR
503-648-3500

Residence Inn By Marriott Portland
West/Hillsboro
18855 Nw Tanasbourne Dr.
Hillsboro, OR

503-531-3200

Towneplace Suites By Marriott
Portland Hillsboro
6550 Northeast Brighton Street
Hillsboro, OR

503-268-6000

Best Western Plus Hood River Inn
1108 East Marina Way
Hood River, OR
541-386-2200

Columbia Gorge Hotel
4000 Westcliff Drive
Hood River, OR

541-386-5566

Best Western John Day Inn
315 West Main Street
John Day, OR
541-575-1700

Mountain View Motel and RV Park
83450 Joseph H
Joseph, OR
541-432-2982

America's Best Inn and Suites
Klamath Falls
75 Main Street
Klamath Falls, OR
541-884-7735

Cimarron Motor Inn
3060 S Sixth St
Klamath Falls, OR

541-882-4601

CrystalWood Lodge
38625 Westside Road
Klamath Falls, OR

541-381-2322

Days Inn Klamath Falls
3612 South 6th Street
Klamath Falls, OR

541-882-8864

Quality Inn Klamath Falls
100 Main St
Klamath Falls, OR

541-882-4666

Shilo Suites Hotel Klamath Falls
2500 Almond Street
Klamath Falls, OR

541-885-7980

Super 8 Klamath Falls
3805 Hwy 97 N
Klamath Falls, OR

541-884-8880

Rodeway Inn La Grande
402 Adams Avenue
La Grande, OR
541-962-7143

Best Western Newberry Station
16515 Reed Road &; Highway 97
La Pine, OR
541-536-5130

Crowne Plaza Portland Lake
Oswego
14811 Kruse Oaks Drive
Lake Oswego, OR
503-624-8400

Residence Inn Portland South -
Lake Oswego
15200 Sw Bangy Road
Lake Oswego, OR

503-684-2603

Chinook Winds Casino Resort Hotel
1501 NW 40th Place

Lincoln City, OR
541-996-5825

Ester Lee Motel
3803 SW H 101
Lincoln City, OR

541-996-3606

Quality Inn Madras
12 Sw 4th St.
Madras, OR
541-475-6141

Comfort Inn Mcminnville
2520 Se Stratus Avenue
McMinnville, OR
503-472-1700

Red Lion Inn & Suites Mcminnville
2535 Ne Cumulus Avenue
McMinnville, OR

503-472-1500

GuestHouse Vineyard Inn Mc.
McMinnville
2035 South Highway 99 West
Mcminnville, OR
503-472-4900

Best Western Horizon Inn
1154 E Barnett Road
Medford, OR
541-779-5085

Candlewood Suites Medford
3548 Heathrow Way
Medford, OR

541-772-2800

Inn at the Commons
200 North Riverside
Medford, OR

541-779-5811

Medford Travelodge
954 Alba Drive
Medford, OR

Quality Inn & Suites Medford Airport
1950 Biddle Road
Medford, OR

541-779-0050

Ramada Medford & Convention
Center
2250 Biddle Road
Medford, OR

541-779-3141

Ramada Medford & Convention
Center
2250 Biddle Road
Medford, OR

541-779-3141

Towneplace Suites By Marriott Medford
1395 Center Drive
Medford, OR

541-842-5757

Sweet Virginia's Bed and Breakfast
407 6th Street
Metolius, OR
541-546-3031

Cooper Spur Mountain Resort
10755 Cooper Spur Road
Mount Hood, OR
541-352-6692

Terimore Lodging by the Sea
5105 Crab Avenue
Netarts Bay, OR
503-842-4623

Best Western Newberg Inn
2211 Portland Road
Newberg, OR
503 537-3000

Econo Lodge Newport
606 Sw Coast Hwy 101
Newport, OR
541-265-7723

Hallmark Resort - Newport
744 South West Elizabeth Street
Newport, OR

541-265-2600

Hallmark Resort - Newport
744 South West Elizabeth Street
Newport, OR

541-265-2600

Rogue Ales' House of Rogue
748 SW Bay Blvd
Newport, OR

541-265-3188

Shilo Inn Suites Newport
536 Southwest Elizabeth
Newport, OR

541-265-7701

Best Western Oakridge Inn
47433 Highway 58
Oakridge, OR
541-782-2212

Ontario Inn
1144 SW 4th Ave
Ontario, OR
541-823-2556

Super 8 Ontario
615 East Idaho Avenue
Ontario, OR

541-889-9188

Best Western Plus Rivershore Hotel
1900 Clackamette Drive
Oregon City, OR
503-655-7141

Inn at Cape Kiwanda
33105 Cape Kiwanda Drive
Pacific City, OR
503-965-7001

Howard Johnson Pendleton
105 Southeast Court Avenue
Pendleton, OR
541-276-3231

Knights Inn Pendleton
310 Se Dorion Ave
Pendleton, OR

541-276-6231

Pendleton Travelodge
411 Southwest Dorion Avenue
Pendleton, OR

541-276-7531

Red Lion Hotel Pendleton
304 Se Nye Avenue
Pendleton, OR

541-276-6111

Super 8 Pendleton
601 Southeast Nye Avenue
Pendleton, OR

541-276-8881

Best Western Inn At The Meadows
1215 North Hayden Meadows Drive
Portland, OR
503-286-9600

Best Western Pony Soldier Inn-Airport
9901 Ne Sandy Blvd
Portland, OR

503-256-1504

Candlewood Suites Portland-Airport
11250 N.E. Holman
Portland, OR

503-255-4003

Courtyard By Marriott Portland City Center
550 Sw Oak Street
Portland, OR

503-505-5000

Econo Lodge At Port Of Portland
9520 N E Sandy Blvd
Portland, OR

503-252-6666

Extended Stay America - Portland - Gresham
17777 Ne Sacramento St
Portland, OR

503-661-0226

Hilton Portland And Executive Tower
921 Sw Sixth Avenue
Portland, OR

503-226-1611

Holiday Inn Portland Airport
8439 Northeast Columbia Boulevard
Portland, OR

503-256-5000

Hotel Deluxe
729 Sw 15th Avenue
Portland, OR

503-223-6311

Hotel Lucia
400 Sw Broadway
Portland, OR

503-228-7221

Hotel Vintage Portland, A Kimpton Hotel
422 Southwest Broadway
Portland, OR

503-228-1212

Howard Johnson Portland Airport
8247 Ne Sandy Blvd
Portland, OR

503-256-4111

McMenamins Kennedy School
5736 Ne 33rd Ave
Portland, OR

503-249-3983

Monaco Portland, A Kimpton Hotel
506 Southwest Washington Street
Portland, OR

503-222-0001

Ramada Portland South I-205
9707 Southeast Stark
Portland, OR

503-252-7400

Red Roof Inn Portland
3828 Northeast 82nd Avenue
Portland, OR

503-256-2550

Residence Inn By Marriott Portland Airport At Cascade Station
9301 Ne Cascades Parkway
Portland, OR

503-284-1800

Residence Inn By Marriott Portland
Downtown/Lloyd Center
1710 Northeast Multnomah Street
Portland, OR

503-288-1400

Residence Inn By Marriott Portland
Downtown/Riverplace
2115 Sw River Parkway
Portland, OR

503-552-9500

Residence Inn By Marriott Portland
North Harbour
1250 North Anchor Way
Portland, OR

503-285-9888

Riverplace Hotel, A Kimpton Hotel
1510 Southwest Harbor Way
Portland, OR

503-288-3233

Staybridge Suites Portland-Airport
11936 Ne Glenn Widing Drive
Portland, OR

503-262-8888

Super 8 Portland Airport
11011 Ne Holman Lane
Portland, OR

503-257-8988

The Benson, a Coast Hotel
309 Southwest Broadway
Portland, OR

503-228-2000

The Heathman Hotel
1001 Southwest Broadway Ave
Portland, OR

503-241-4100

The Heathman Hotel
1001 Southwest Broadway Ave
Portland, OR

503-241-4100

The Mark Spencer Hotel
409 Southwest Eleventh Avenue
Portland, OR

503-224-3293

The Nines A Luxury Collection Hotel
Portland
525 Southwest Morrison
Portland, OR

877-229-9995

The Westin Portland
750 Sw Alder Street
Portland, OR

503-294-9000

Malheur Field Station
34848 Sodhouse Lane
Princeton, OR
541-493-2629

Comfort Suites Redmond Airport
2243 Southwest Yew Avenue
Redmond, OR
541-504-8900

Sleep Inn & Suites Redmond
1847 North Highway 97
Redmond, OR

541-504-1500

Sugarloaf Mountain Motel
62980 North Highway 97
Redmond, OR

541-548-8881

Economy Inn
1593 Highway 101
Reedsport, OR
541-271-3671

Loon Lake Lodge and RV Resort
9011 Loon Lake Rd
Reedsport, OR

541-599-2244

Ocean Locomotion
19130 Alder
Rockaway, OR
503-355-2093

Best Western Garden Villa Inn
760 Northwest Garden Valley
Boulevard
Roseburg, OR
541-672-1601

Holiday Inn Express Roseburg
375 West Harvard Boulevard
Roseburg, OR

541-673-7517

Quality Inn Central Roseburg
427 Northwest Garden Valley
Boulevard
Roseburg, OR

541-673-5561

Sleep Inn & Suites Roseburg
2855 Northwest Edenbower
Boulevard
Roseburg, OR

541-464-8338

Super 8 Roseburg
3200 North West Aviation Drive

Roseburg, OR

541-672-8880

Travelodge Roseburg
315 West Harvard Avenue
Roseburg, OR

541-672-4836

Windmill Inn Roseburg
1450 Nw Mulholland Dr.
Roseburg, OR

541-673-0901

Best Western Oak Meadows Inn
585 South Columbia River Highway
Saint Helens, OR
503-397-3000

Best Western Pacific Highway Inn
4646 Portland Road Northeast
Salem, OR
503-390-3200

Best Western Plus Mill Creek Inn
3125 Ryan Drive Southeast
Salem, OR

503-585-3332

Comfort Suites Airport Salem
630 Hawthorne Southeast
Salem, OR

503-585-9705

Howard Johnson Inn Salem
2250 Mission St. Se
Salem, OR

503-375-7710

Red Lion Hotel Salem
3301 Market Street Ne
Salem, OR

503-370-7888

Residence Inn By Marriott Salem
640 Hawthorne Avenue Southeast
Salem, OR

503-585-6500

Super 8 Salem
1288 Hawthorne Ne
Salem, OR

503-370-8888

Best Western Sandy Inn
37465 Highway 26
Sandy, OR
503-668-7100

Best Western Ocean View Resort
414 North Prom
Seaside, OR
503-738-3334

Comfort Inn & Suites By Seaside
Convention Center/Boardwalk
545 Broadway Avenue
Seaside, OR

503-738-3011

Holiday Inn Express Seaside-
Convention Center
34 North Holladay Drive
Seaside, OR

503-717-8000

Inn At Seaside
441 Second Avenue
Seaside, OR

503-738-9581

Sandy Cove Inn
241 Avenue U
Seaside, OR

503-738-7473

Best Western Grand Manor Inn
971 Kruse Way
Springfield, OR
541-726-4769

Comfort Suites Springfield
969 Kruse Way
Springfield, OR

541-746-5359

Holiday Inn Eugene North-Springfield
919 Kruse Way
Springfield, OR

541-284-0707

Holiday Inn Express
Eugene/Springfield-East (I-5)
3480 Hutton Street
Springfield, OR

541-746-8471

Quality Inn & Suites Springfield
3550 Gateway Street
Springfield, OR

541-726-9266

Sunset Realty
56805 Ventura Lane
Sunriver, OR
541-593-5018

Best Western Plus Hartford Lodge
150 Myrtle Street
Sutherlin, OR
541-459-1424

GuestHouse Inn & Suites Sutherlin
1400 Hospitality Way
Sutherlin, OR

800-467-6763

Comfort Inn Columbia Gorge
351 Lone Pine Drive
The Dalles, OR
541-298-2800

Super 8 The Dalles
609 Cherry Heights Road
The Dalles, OR

541-296-6888

Extended Stay America - Portland -
Tigard
13009 Sw 68th Parkway
Tigard, OR
503-670-0555

Comfort Inn Columbia Gorge
Gateway
1000 Northwest Graham Road
Troutdale, OR
503-492-2900

Holiday Inn Express Portland East -
Troutdale
477 Northwest Phoenix Drive
Troutdale, OR

503-669-6500

Comfort Inn & Suites Tualatin -
Portland South
7640 Sw Warm Springs Street
Tualatin, OR
503-612-9952

Shilo Inn Suites Warrenton
1609 East Harbor Drive
Warrenton, OR
503-861-2181

Guesthouse Inn & Suites Wilsonville
8855 Sw Citizens Dr.
Wilsonville, OR
503-682-9000

Motel 6 Portland - Wilsonville
25438 Sw Parkway Avenue
Wilsonville, OR

503-682-2088

Best Western Woodburn
2887 Newberg Highway
Woodburn, OR
503-982-6515

Super 8 Woodburn
821 Evergreen Rd.
Woodburn, OR

503-981-8881

Adobe Resort
1555 US 101
Yachats, OR
541-547-3141

Fireside Motel
1881 Hwy 101 North
Yachats, OR

541-547-3636

See Vue Hotel
95590 H 101
Yachats, OR

541-547-3227

# Puerto Rico Listings

Hotel La Cima & Suites Aguadil
Carretera 110 Kilometro 9.2
Aguadilla, PR
787-890-2016

Villa Montaña Beach Resort
Road 4466 Km 1.9 Interior Barrio
Bajuras
Isabela, PR
888-780-9195

Hotel Melia Ponce
Cristina Street #75
Ponce, PR
787-842-0260

St. Regis Bahia Beach Resort
State Road 187 Kilometer 4.2
Rio Grande, PR
787-809-8000

Sheraton Old San Juan Hotel
100 Brumbaugh Street
San Juan, PR
787-721-5100

W Retreat & Spa - Vieques Island
State Road 200
Vieques Island, PR
787-741-4100

Coqui Inn-formerly Green Isle Inn &
Casa Mathieson
36 Calle Uno Villamar
Villamar - Isla Verde, PR
787-726-4330

# Pennsylvania Listings

Adamstown Vacation Home
62 West Main Street
Adamstown, PA
717-484-0800

Black Forest Inn
500 Lancaster Ave
Adamstown, PA

717-484-4801

The Barnyard Inn
2145 Old Lancaster Pike
Adamstown, PA

717-484-1111

Boxwood Inn Bed & Breakfast
1320 Diamond St
Akron, PA
717-859-3466

Red Rose Inn
243 Meckesville Road
Albrightsville, PA
570-722-3526

Allenwood Motel
1058 Hausman Road
Allentown, PA
610-395-3707

Comfort Inn Lehigh Valley West
7625 Imperial Way
Allentown, PA
610-391-0344

Econo Lodge Conference Center
1151 Bulldog Drive
Allentown, PA
610-395-3731

Homewood Suites By Hilton
Allentown-West/Fogelsville
7686 Industrial Boulevard/Route 100
Allentown, PA
610-336-4860

Howard Johnson Inn And Suites -
Allentown
3220 Hamilton Blvd
Allentown, PA
610-439-4000

Knights Inn And Suites Allentown
1880 Steelstone Road
Allentown, PA
610-266-9070

Quality Inn Allentown
1715 Plaza Lane
Allentown, PA
610-435-7880

Red Roof Inn Allentown Airport
1846 Catasauqua Road
Allentown, PA
610-264-5404

Sleep Inn Allentown
327 Star Road
Allentown, PA
610-841-5100

Staybridge Suites Allentown Airprt
Lehigh Valley
1787a Airport Road
Allentown, PA

610-443-5000

Econo Lodge Altoona
2906 Pleasant Valley Blvd.
Altoona, PA
814-944-3555

Ramada Conference Center Altoona
Pa
1 Sheraton Drive
Altoona, PA

814-946-1631

Super 8 Motel - Altoona
3535 Fairway Drive
Altoona, PA

814-942-5350

Homewood Suites Valley Forge
681 Shannondell Boulevard
Audubon, PA
610-539-7300

Quality Inn Barkeyville
137 Gibb Road
Barkeyville, PA
814-786-7901

Baymont Inn & Suites Bartonsville
Poconos
116 Turtle Walk Lane
Bartonsville, PA
570-476-1500

Rimrock Country Cottages
Rimrock Drive
Bartonsville, PA

570-629-2360

Park Inn By Radisson Beaver Falls,
Pa
7195 Eastwood Road
Beaver Falls, PA
724-846-3700

Quality Inn Bedford
4407 Business Route 220
Bedford, PA
814-623-5188

Extended Stay America -
Philadelphia - Bensalem
3216 Tillman Drive
Bensalem, PA
215-633-6900

Best Western Garden Inn
101 Gosai Drive
Bentleyville, PA
724-239-4321

Residence Inn By Marriott Valley
Forge
600 West Swedesford Road
Berwyn, PA
610-640-9494

Comfort Inn Midway
41 Diner Road
Bethel, PA
717-933-8888

Best Western Lehigh Valley Hotel &
Conference Center
300 Gateway Drive
Bethlehem, PA
610-866-5800

Comfort Suites University Bethlehem
120 W. Third St.
Bethlehem, PA

610-882-9700

Extended Stay America - Allentown -
Bethlehem
3050 Schoenersville Rd
Bethlehem, PA

610-866-8480

Residence Inn Allentown
Bethlehem/Lehigh Valley Airport
2180 Motel Drive
Bethlehem, PA

610-317-2662

The View Inn & Suites Bethlehem /
Allentown / Lehigh Airport
3191 Highfield Drive
Bethlehem, PA

610-865-6300

Econo Lodge Bloomsburg
189 Columbia Mall Dr
Bloomsburg, PA
570-387-0490

Comfort Inn Bradford
76 Elm Street
Bradford, PA
814-368-6772

Econo Lodge Breezewood
16560 Lincoln Highway
Breezewood, PA
814-735-2200

Holiday Inn Allentown I-78 (Lehigh
Valley)
7736 Adrienne Drive
Breinigsville, PA
610-391-1000

Quality Inn Brookville
235 Allegheny Blvd.
Brookville, PA
814-849-8381

Super 8 Brookville
251 Allegheny Blvd.
Brookville, PA

814-849-8840

Days Inn Butler Conference Center

139 Pittsburgh Rd
Butler, PA
724-287-6761

Martinville Streamside Cottages
Box 323, H 390 N
Canadensis, PA
570-595-2489

The Merry Inn
H 390
Canadensis, PA

570-595-2011

Comfort Suites Downtown Carlisle
10 S. Hanover Street
Carlisle, PA
717-960-1000

Days Inn Carlisle
101 Alexander Spring Road
Carlisle, PA

717-258-4147

Hampton Inn Carlisle
1165 Harrisburg Pike
Carlisle, PA

717-240-0200

Knights Inn Carlisle
1245 Harrisburg Pike
Carlisle, PA

717-243-5411

Pheasant Field
150 Hickorytown Road
Carlisle, PA

717-258-0717

Residence Inn By Marriott Harrisburg
Carlisle
1 Hampton Court
Carlisle, PA

717-610-9050

Rodeway Inn Carlisle
1239 Harrisburg Pike
Carlisle, PA

717-249-2800

Sleep Inn Carlisle
5 East Garland Drive
Carlisle, PA

717-249-8863

Super 8 Carlisle North
1800 Harrisburg Pike
Carlisle, PA

717-249-7000

Super 8 Motel - Carlisle-South
100 Alexander Spring Road
Carlisle, PA

717-245-9898

Extended Stay America - Pittsburgh
- Carnegie
520 North Bell Avenue
Carnegie, PA
412-278-4001

The Pennsbury Inn
883 Baltimore Pike/H1
Chadds Ford, PA
610-388-1435

Best Western Chambersburg
211 Walker Road
Chambersburg, PA
717-262-4994

Candlewood Suites Chambersburg
231 Walker Road
Chambersburg, PA

717-263-2800

Chambersburg Travelodge
565 Lincoln Way East
Chambersburg, PA

717-264-4187

Comfort Inn Chambersburg
3301 Black Gap Road
Chambersburg, PA

717-263-6655

Days Inn Chambersburg
30 Falling Spring Road
Chambersburg, PA

717-263-1288

Sleep Inn & Suites Chambersburg
1435 Doron Drive
Chambersburg, PA

717-263-0596

Best Western Plus Philadelphia
Airport South At Widener Univ
1450 Providence Avenue
Chester, PA
610-872-8100

Hamanassett B&B and Carriage
House
Indian Springs Drive
Chester Heights, PA
610-459-3000

Comfort Inn Clarion
129 Dolby St.
Clarion, PA
814-226-5230

Mayfield Inn Clarion
135 Hotel Drive
Clarion, PA

814-226-4550

Monroe Heights Clarion
151 Hotel Drive
Clarion, PA

814-227-2700

Park Inn By Radisson Clarion, Pa
45 Holiday Inn Road
Clarion, PA

814-226-8850

Quality Inn & Suites
Route 68 And Interstate 80
Clarion, PA

814-226-8682

Econo Lodge Clarks Summit
649 Northern Blvd
Clarks Summit, PA
570-586-1211

Ramada - Clarks Summit
820 Northern Boulevard
Clarks Summit, PA

570-586-2730

Super 8 Clearfield
14597 Clearfield Shawville Hwy
Clearfield, PA
814-768-7580

Victorian Loft Bed and Breakfast
216 South Front Street
Clearfield, PA

814-765-4805

Residence Inn Conshohocken
191 Washington Street
Conshohocken, PA
610-828-8800

Embassy Suites Hotel Pittsburgh-
International Airport
550 Cherrington Parkway
Coraopolis, PA
412-269-9070

Pittsburgh Airport Marriott
777 Aten Road
Coraopolis, PA

412-788-8800

Sheraton Pittsburgh Airport Hotel
1160 Thorn Run Road
Coraopolis, PA

412-262-2400

Candlewood Suites Pittsburgh-
Cranberry
20036 Route 19 Oak Tree Place
Cranberry Township, PA
724-591-8666

Marriott Pittsburgh North

100 Cranberry Woods Drive
Cranberry Township, PA

Residence Inn By Marriott Cranberry
1308 Freedom Road
Cranberry Township, PA
724-779-1000

Red Roof Inn Pittsburgh North -
Cranberry Township
20009 Us Route 19 &; Marguerite
Road
Cranberry Twp., PA
724-776-5670

Quality Inn & Suites
15 Valley W. Road
Danville, PA
570-275-5100

Red Roof Inn Danville
300 Red Roof Road
Danville, PA

570-275-7600

Super 8 Danville
35 Sheraton Road
Danville, PA

570-275-4640

Super 8 Delmont
180 Sheffield Dr.
Delmont, PA
724-468-4888

Econo Lodge Inn & Suites
2031 N. Reading Rd.
Denver, PA
717-336-7000

Red Roof Inn Denver
2017 N. Reading Rd.
Denver, PA

717-336-4649

Residence Inn Scranton
947 Viewmont Drive
Dickson City, PA
570-343-5121

Econo Lodge Douglassville
387 Ben Franklin Hwy.
Douglassville, PA
610-385-3016

Best Western Plus Inn & Conference
Center
82 N. Park Place
Du Bois, PA
814-371-6200

Quality Inn Dunmore
1226 Oneill Highway
Dunmore, PA
570-348-6101

Sleep Inn & Suites Dunmore

102 Monahan Avenue
Dunmore, PA

570-961-1116

Echo Valley Cottages
1 Lower Lakeview Drive
E Stroudsburg, PA
570-223-0662

Budget Inn & Suites
320 Greentree Drive
East Stroudsburg, PA
570-424-5451

Super 8 Stroudsburg
I-80 Exit 308
East Stroudsburg, PA

570-424-7411

The Lafayette Inn
525 W. Monroe St.
Easton, PA
610-253-4500

Towneplace Suites By Marriott
Bethlehem Easton
3800 Easton/Nazareth Highway
Easton, PA

610-829-2000

Quality Inn Ebensburg
111 Cook Rd. Rt 22 And 219
Ebensburg, PA
814-472-6100

Holiday Inn Express Elizabethtown
147 Merts Drive
Elizabethtown, PA
717-367-4000

Comfort Inn & Suites Erie
8051 Peach St.
Erie, PA
814-866-6666

Days Inn Erie
7415 Schultz Road
Erie, PA

814-868-8521

Homewood Suites By HiltonÂ® Erie
2084 Interchange Road
Erie, PA

814-866-8292

Red Roof Inn Erie
7865 Perry Highway
Erie, PA

814-868-5246

Residence Inn by Marriott Erie
8061 Peach Street
Erie, PA

814-864-2500

Riviera Motel
3107 W Lake Road
Erie, PA

814-838-1997

Sheraton Erie Bayfront Hotel
55 West Bay Drive
Erie, PA

814-454-2005

Towneplace Suites By Marriott Erie
2090 Interchange Road
Erie, PA

814-866-7100

Wingate By Wyndham Erie
8060 Old Oliver Road
Erie, PA

814-860-3050

Wingate By Wyndham Erie
8060 Old Oliver Road
Erie, PA

814-860-3050

Golden Pheasant Inn
763 River Road/H 32S
Erwinna, PA
610-294-9595

Red Roof Plus Philadelphia Airport
49 Industrial Highway
Essington, PA
610-521-5090

Extended Stay America - Philadelphia
- Exton
877 N. Pottstown Pike (Rt 100)
Exton, PA
610-524-7185

Hampton Inn Downington/Exton
4 North Pottstown Pike
Exton, PA

610-363-5555

Residence Inn Philadelphia Great
Valley Exton
10 N Pottston Pike
Exton, PA

610-594-9705

Vacation Rental by Owner
5888 Path Valley Road
Fort Loudon, PA
717-369-3235

Best Western Fort Washington Inn
285 Commerce Drive
Fort Washington, PA
215 542-7930

Econo Lodge Frackville

501 S. Middle St.
Frackville, PA
570-874-3838

Super 8 Franklin
847 Allegheny Blvd
Franklin, PA
814-432-2101

Sheraton Great Valley Hotel
707 East Lancaster Avenue
Frazer, PA
610-524-5500

Americas Best Value Inn
301 Steinwehr Avenue
Gettysburg, PA
717-334-1188

Battlefield Bed & Breakfast
2264 Emmitsburg Road
Gettysburg, PA

717-334-8804

Comfort Inn Gettysburg
871 York Rd.
Gettysburg, PA

717-337-2400

Quality Inn & Suites North Gibsonia
5137 William Flynn Highway
Gibsonia, PA
724-444-8700

Staybridge Suites Wilmington -
Brandywine Valley
400 Evergreen Drive
Glen Mills, PA
610-358-2560

Sweetwater Inn
50 Sweetwater Road
Glen Mills, PA

610-459-4711

Days Inn Grantville
252 Bow Creek Road
Grantville, PA
717-469-0631

Holiday Inn Harrisburg Hershey Area
604 Station Road
Grantville, PA

717-469-0661

The Historic Greeley Inn
218 H 590
Greeley, PA
570-685-9997

Comfort Inn Greencastle
50 Pine Dr.
Greencastle, PA
717-597-8164

Knights Inn Greenburg
1215 S. Main Street

Greensburg, PA
724-836-7100

Old Arbor Rose
114 W Main Street
Grove City, PA
724-458-6425

Microtel Inn & Suites By Wyndham
Hamburg
50 Industrial Drive
Hamburg, PA
610-562-4234

Americas Best Value Inn
4125 North Front Street
Harrisburg, PA
717-233-5891

Candlewood Suites Harrisburg
504 North Mountain Road
Harrisburg, PA

717-652-7800

Hilton Harrisburg And Towers
1 North 2nd Street
Harrisburg, PA

717-233-6000

Holiday Inn Express Harrisburg East
4021 Union Deposit Road
Harrisburg, PA

717-561-8100

Red Lion Hotel Harrisburg Hershey
4751 Lindle Road
Harrisburg, PA

717-939-7841

Red Roof Harrisburg Hershey
950 Eisenhower Boulevard
Harrisburg, PA

717-939-1331

Red Roof Inn Harrisburg North
400 Corporate Circle
Harrisburg, PA

717-657-1445

Staybridge Suites Harrisburg
920 Wildwood Park Drive
Harrisburg, PA

717-233-3304

Falls Port Inn
330 Main Ave
Hawley, PA
570-226-2600

Best Western Hazleton Inn & Suites
1341 N Church Street
Hazleton, PA
570-454-2494

Candlewood Suites Hazleton
9 Bowmans Mill Road
Hazleton, PA

570-459-1600

Hazleton Motor Inn
615 East Broad St.
Hazleton, PA

570-459-1451

Ramada Hazleton
1221 North Church Street
Hazleton, PA

570-455-2061

Residence Inn Hazleton
1 Station Circle
Hazleton, PA

570-455-9555

Days Inn-Hershey
350 West Chocolate Ave Rt422
Hershey, PA
717-534-2162

Econo Lodge Hershey
115 Lucy Ave
Hershey, PA
717-533-2515

The Inn at Barley Sheaf Farm
5281 York Road/H 202/263
Holicong, PA
215-794-5104

Candlewood Suites Willow Grove
250 Business Center Drive
Horsham, PA
215-328-9119

Days Inn Horsham Philadelphia
245 Easton Road
Horsham, PA

215-674-2500

Extended Stay America - Philadelphia
- Horsham - Dresher Rd.
537 Dresher Road
Horsham, PA

215-956-9966

Extended Stay America - Philadelphia
- Horsham - Welsh Rd.
114 Welsh Road
Horsham, PA

215-784-9045

Residence Inn By Marriott Willow
Grove
3 Walnut Grove Drive
Horsham, PA

215-443-7330

Towneplace Suites By Marriott
Philadelphia Horsham
198 Precision Drive
Horsham, PA

215-323-9900

The Mill Stone Manor
11979 William Penn Highway
Huntingdon, PA
814-643-0108

Park Inn By Radisson Indiana, Pa
1395 Wayne Avenue
Indiana, PA
724-463-3561

Econo Lodge Johnstown
430 Napoleon Place
Johnstown, PA
814-536-1114

Holiday Inn Johnstown-Downtown
250 Market Street
Johnstown, PA

814-535-7777

Quality Inn & Suites Johnstown
455 Theatre Dr.
Johnstown, PA

814-266-3678

Sleep Inn Johnstown
453 Theatre Dr.
Johnstown, PA

814-262-9292

Comfort Inn Lebanon Valley-Ft.
Indiantown Gap
16 Marsanna Lane
Jonestown (Lebanon), PA
717-865-6600

Extended Stay America - Philadelphia
- King Of Prussia
400 American Avenue
King of Prussia, PA
610-962-9000

Quality Inn Royle
405 Butler Rd.
Kittanning, PA
724-543-1159

Holiday Inn Lansdale
1750 Sumneytown Pike
Kulpsville, PA
215-368-3800

Best Western PREMIER Eden Resort
& Suites
222 Eden Road
Lancaster, PA
717-569-6444

Days Inn And Suites Conference
Center
1492 Lititz Pike

Lancaster, PA

717-293-8400

Knights Inn Lancaster Pa
2151 Lincoln Highway East
Lancaster, PA

717-299-8971

Lancaster Amish Country
Travelodge
2101 Columbia Avenue
Lancaster, PA

717-397-4201

Lancaster Amish Country
Travelodge
2101 Columbia Avenue
Lancaster, PA

717-397-4201

Red Roof Inn Lancaster
2307 Lincoln Highway East
Lancaster, PA

717-299-9700

Super 8 Lancaster
2129 Lincoln Highway East
Lancaster, PA

717-393-8888

Red Roof Inn Philadelphia - Oxford
Valley
3100 Cabot Boulevard West
Langhorne, PA
215-750-6200

Residence Inn By Marriott
Philadelphia Langhorne
15 Cabot Blvd East
Langhorne, PA

215-946-6500

Sheraton Bucks County Hotel
400 Oxford Valley Road
Langhorne, PA

215-547-4100

Days Inn Lebanon Valley
625 Quentin Road
Lebanon, PA
717-273-6771

Holiday Inn Express Hotel & Suites
Lebanon
2205 East Cumberland Street
Lebanon, PA

717-273-9800

The Berry Patch
115 Moore Road
Lebanon, PA

717-865-7219

Days Inn Lebanon/Lickdale
3 Everest Lane
Lebanon/Jonestown, PA
717-865-4064

Mahoning Inn
71 Blakeslee Blvd/H 443
Lehighton, PA
610-377-1600

General Sutter Inn
14 E Main St
Lititz, PA
717-626-2115

Best Western Lock Haven
101 East Walnut Street
Lock Haven, PA
570-748-3297

Extended Stay America - Philadelphia
- Malvern - Great Valley
300 Moorehall Rd, Rt 29
Malvern, PA
610-240-0455

Extended Stay America - Philadelphia
- Malvern - Swedesford Rd.
8 E. Swedesford Road
Malvern, PA

610-695-9200

Homewood Suites By Hilton®
Philadelphia/Great Valley
12 East Swedesford Road
Malvern, PA

610-296-3500

Homewood Suites By Hilton®
Philadelphia/Great Valley
12 East Swedesford Road
Malvern, PA

610-296-3500

Sonesta Es Suites Valley Forge
Malvern
20 Morehall Road
Malvern, PA

610-296-4343

Best Western Lehigh Valley Hotel &
Conference Center
300 Gateway Drive
Mansfield, PA
570-662-3000

B. F. Hiestand House
722 E Market Street
Marietta, PA
717-426-8415

Comfort Inn Cranberry Twp.
924 Sheraton Drive
Mars, PA
724-772-2700

Super 8 Mars/Cranberry/Pittsburgh Area
929 Sheraton Drive
Mars, PA

724-776-9700

Best Western Inn At Hunts Landing
120 Routes 6 And 209
Matamoras, PA
570-491-2400

Days Inn Meadville Conference Center
18360 Conneaut Lake Road
Meadville, PA
814-337-4264

Quality Inn Meadville
17259 Conneaut Lake Road
Meadville, PA

814-333-8883

Comfort Inn Mechanicsburg - Harrisburg South
1012 Wesley Drive
Mechanicsburg, PA
717-766-3700

Hampton Inn Harrisburg-West
4950 Ritter Rd
Mechanicsburg, PA

717-691-1300

Holiday Inn Express Harrisburg Sw - Mechanicsburg
6325 Carlisle Pike
Mechanicsburg, PA

717-790-0924

Homewood Suites By Hilton®
Harrisburg West
5001 Ritter Road
Mechanicsburg, PA

717-697-4900

Super 8 Mifflinville
450 West 3rd Street I-80 Exit-242
Mifflinville, PA
570-759-6778

Black Walnut B&B Country Inn
179 Fire Tower Road
Milford, PA
570-296-6322

Hotel Fauchere
401 Broad Street
Milford, PA

570-409-1212

The New Muir House
102 H 2001
Milford, PA

570-722-3526

Quality Inn Mill Hall
31 Hospitality Lane
Mill Hall, PA
570-726-4901

Days Inn Monroeville Pittsburgh
2727 Mosside Boulevard
Monroeville, PA
412-856-1610

Extended Stay America - Pittsburgh - Monroeville
3851 Northern Pike
Monroeville, PA

412-856-8400

Hampton Inn Pittsburgh/Monroeville
3000 Mosside Blvd
Monroeville, PA

412-380-4000

Red Roof Plus Pittsburgh East - Monroeville
2729 Mosside Boulevard
Monroeville, PA

412-856-4738

QUALITY INN MONTGOMERYVILLE
678 Bethlehem Pike
Montgomeryville, PA
215-361-3600

Rodeway Inn Conference Center
969 Bethlehem Pike
Montgomeryville, PA

215-699-8800

Rodeway Inn Moosic
4130 Birney Ave.
Moosic, PA
570-457-6713

Towneplace Suites By Marriott Scranton Wilkes-Barre
26 Radcliffe Drive
Moosic, PA

570-207-8500

Holiday Inn Morgantown
6170 Morgantown Road
Morgantown, PA
610-286-3000

The Olde Square Inn
127 E Main Street
Mount Joy, PA
717-653-4525

Mainstay Suites Of Lancaster County
314 Primrose Lane
Mountville, PA
717-285-2500

Comfort Inn New Castle

1740 New Butler Rd.
New Castle, PA
724-658-7700

Quality Inn New Columbia
330 Commerce Park
New Columbia, PA
570-568-8000

The Hollander Motel
320 East Main Street
New Holland, PA
717-354-4377

1833 Umpleby House
111 W Bridge Street
New Hope, PA
215-862-3936

Wedgwood Inn
111 W Bridge Street
New Hope, PA

215-862-2570

Quality Inn New Kensington
300 Tarentum Bridge Road
New Kensington, PA
724-335-9171

Days Inn New Stanton
127 West Byers Avenue
New Stanton, PA
724-925-3591

Econo Lodge New Stanton
110 North Main Street And Byers Avenue
New Stanton, PA

724-925-6755

New Stanton Garden Inn
112 West Byers Avenue
New Stanton, PA

724-925-3511

Residence Inn By Marriott Philadelphia Montgomeryville
1110 Bethlehem Pike
North Wales, PA
267-468-0111

Quality Inn Pittsburgh Airport
7011 Old Steubenville Pike
Oakdale, PA
412-787-2600

Days Inn Oil City
1 Seneca Street
Oil City, PA
814-677-1221

Our Farm Under the Mimosa Tree
1487 Blue School Road
Perkasie, PA
215-249-9420

Aloft Philadelphia Airport

4301 Island Avenue
Philadelphia, PA
267-398-1700

Extended Stay America - Philadelphia - Airport - Tinicum Blvd.
9000 Tinicum Blvd
Philadelphia, PA

215-492-6766

Four Points By Sheraton Philadelphia Airport
4101a Island Avenue
Philadelphia, PA

215-492-0400

Kimpton Hotel Monaco Philadelphia
433 Chestnut Street
Philadelphia, PA

215-925-2111

Loews Philadelphia Hotel
1200 Market Street
Philadelphia, PA

215-627-1200

Palomar Philadelphia, A Kimpton Hotel
117 S. 17th Street
Philadelphia, PA

215-563-5006

Palomar Philadelphia, A Kimpton Hotel
117 S. 17th Street
Philadelphia, PA

215-563-5006

Residence Inn By Marriott Philadelphia Center City
One East Penn Square
Philadelphia, PA

215-557-0005

Sheraton Philadelphia Downtown Hotel
201 North 17th Street
Philadelphia, PA

215-448-2000

Sheraton Philadelphia Society Hill
One Dock Street 2nd And Walnut
Philadelphia, PA

215-238-6000

Sheraton Philadelphia University City Hotel
3549 Chestnut Street
Philadelphia, PA

215-387-8000

Sheraton Suites Philadelphia Airport
4101 B Island Avenue

Philadelphia, PA

215-365-6600

The Conwell Inn
1331 West Berks Street
Philadelphia, PA

215-235-6200

The Rittenhouse Hotel
210 West Rittenhouse Square
Philadelphia, PA

215-546-9000

Comfort Inn Pine Grove
433 Suedberg Road
Pine Grove, PA
570-345-8031

Econo Lodge Pine Grove
419 Suedberg Road
Pine Grove, PA

570-345-4099

Hampton Inn Pine Grove
481 Suedberg Road
Pine Grove, PA

570-345-4505

Candlewood Suites Pittsburgh Airport
100 Chauvet Dr
Pittsburgh, PA
412-787-7770

Comfort Inn Conference Center
699 Rodi Road
Pittsburgh, PA

412-244-1600

Crowne Plaza Hotel Pittsburgh South
164 Fort Couch Road
Pittsburgh, PA

412-833-5300

Hampton Inn Pittsburgh-University Center
3315 Hamlet Street
Pittsburgh, PA

412-681-1000

Kimpton Hotel Monaco Pittsburgh
620 William Penn Place
Pittsburgh, PA

412-471-1170

Morning Glory Inn
2119 Sarah Street
Pittsburgh, PA

412-431-1707

Quality Suites Pittsburgh

700 Mansfield Avenue
Pittsburgh, PA

412-279-6300

Red Roof Plus Pittsburgh South Airport
6404 Steubenville Pike
Pittsburgh, PA

412-787-7870

Residence Inn By Marriott Pittsburgh North Shore
574 West General Robinson Street
Pittsburgh, PA

412-321-2099

Residence Inn By Marriott Pittsburgh University/Medical Center
3896 Bigelow Boulevard
Pittsburgh, PA

412-621-2200

Residence Inn Pittsburgh Airport
1500 Park Lane Drive
Pittsburgh, PA

412-787-3300

Sheraton Pittsburgh Hotel At Station Square
300 West Station Square Drive
Pittsburgh, PA

412-261-2000

Super 8 Pittsburgh/Monroeville
1807 Route 286
Pittsburgh, PA

724-733-8008

Wyndham Garden Inn Pittsburgh Airport
1 Industry Lane
Pittsburgh, PA

724-695-0002

Wyndham Grand Pittsburgh Downtown
600 Commonwealth Place
Pittsburgh, PA

412-391-4600

Extended Stay America - Philadelphia - Plymouth Meeting
437 Irwins Lane
Plymouth Meeting, PA
610-260-0488

The Inn at Pocono Manor
H 314
Pocono Manor, PA
570-839-7111

Americas Best Value Inn Pottstown
29 East High Street

Pottstown, PA
610-970-1101

Comfort Inn & Suites Pottstown - Limerick
99 Robinson Street
Pottstown, PA
610-326-5000

Ramada Pottsville
101 South Progress Ave
Pottsville, PA
570-622-4600

Hampton Inn Quakertown
1915 John Fries Highway
Quakertown, PA
215-536-7779

Quality Inn & Suites
1905 John Fries Highway
Quakertown, PA
215-538-3000

Quality Inn & Suites Quakertown
1905 John Fries Highway
Quakertown, PA
215-538-3000

Quality Inn & Suites
1905 John Fries Highway
Quakertown - Phily Area, PA
215-538-3000

Jackson House Bed and Breakfast
6 East Main Street
Railroad, PA
717-227-2022

Best Western Plus Reading Inn & Suites
2299 Lancaster Pike
Reading, PA
610-777-7888

Candlewood Suites Reading
55 South 3rd Avenue
Reading, PA
610-898-1911

Homewood Suites By HiltonÂ®
Reading
2801 Papermill Road
Reading, PA
610-736-3100

Staybridge Suites Philadelphia Valley Forge 422
88 Anchor Parkway
Royersford, PA
610-792-9300

Best Western Grand Victorian Inn
255 Spring Street
Sayre, PA
570-888-7711

Days Inn Scranton Pa
1946 Scranton-Carbondale Hwy
Scranton, PA
570-383-9979

Econo Lodge Scranton
1175 Kane Street
Scranton, PA
570-348-1000

Hilton Scranton Hotel And Conference Center
100 Adams Avenue
Scranton, PA
570-343-3000

Econo Lodge Inn & Suites Shamokin Dam
3249 North Susquehanna Trail
Shamokin Dam, PA
570-743-1111

Whispering Winds Campground
277 Tollgate Road
Sheffield, PA
814-968-4377

Best Western Shippensburg Hotel
125 Walnut Bottom Road
Shippensburg, PA
717-532-5200

Rodeway Inn Shippensburg
10 Hershey Road
Shippensburg, PA
717-530-1234

Days Inn Somerset
220 Water Works Road
Somerset, PA
814-445-9200

Econo Lodge Somerset
125 Lewis Drive
Somerset, PA
814-445-8788

Quality Inn And Conference Center
215 Ramada Road
Somerset, PA
814-443-4646

Inn at Starlight Lake
289 Starlight Lake Road/H 4033
Starlight, PA
570-798-2519

The Inn at Starlight Lake
2890 Starlight Lake Road
Starlight, PA
570-798-2519

Days Inn State College
240 South Pugh Street

State College, PA
814-238-8454

Quality Inn State College
1274 N. Atherton Street
State College, PA
814-234-1600

Residence Inn By Marriott State College
1555 University Drive
State College, PA
814-235-6960

Super 8 Motel - State College
1663 South Atherton Street
State College, PA
814-237-8005

Clarion Inn Strasburg - Lancaster
1400 Historic Drive
Strasburg, PA
717-687-7691

Countryside Cottages
RR 11 Box 3002
Stroudsburg, PA
570-629-2131

River View Inn
103 Chestnut Street
Sunbury, PA
570-286-4800

Chateau Resort At Camelback
300 Camelback Road
Tannersville, PA
570-629-5900

Radisson Hotel Philadelphia NE
2400 Old Lincoln Highway
Trevose, PA
215-638-8300

Red Roof Inn - Philadelphia Trevose
3100 Lincoln Highway
Trevose, PA
215-244-9422

Park Inn By Radisson Uniontown, Pa
700 West Main Street
Uniontown, PA
724-437-2816

Holiday Inn Warren Kinzua Dam - Allegheny
210 Ludlow Street
Warren, PA
814-726-3000

Ramada Washington
1170 W Chestnut St
Washington, PA
724-225-9750

Red Roof Inn Washington
1399 W Chestnut St

Washington, PA
724-228-5750

Happy Acres Resort Cabins and
Campground
3332 Little Pine Creek Road
Waterville, PA
570-753-8000

Indian Rock Inn
155 Keen Lake
Waymart, PA
610-982-9600

Keen Lake Camping and Cottage
Resort
155 Keen Lake
Waymart, PA
570-488-5522

Days Inn Waynesboro
239 W Main St
Waynesboro, PA
717-762-9113

Kaltenbachs Inn
743 Stoney Fork Road
Wellsboro, PA
570-724-4954

Comfort Inn West Hazleton
58 State Route 93
West Hazleton, PA
570-455-9300

Extended Stay America - Pittsburgh -
West Mifflin
1303 Lebanon Church Road
West Mifflin, PA
412-650-9096

Best Western Genetti Hotel And
Convention Center
77 East Market Street
Wilkes Barre, PA
570-823-6152

Days Inn Wilkes-Barre
760 Kidder Street
Wilkes Barre, PA
570-826-0111

Econo Lodge Arena
1075 Wilkes-Barre Township Blvd Sr
309
Wilkes Barre, PA
570-823-0600

Quality Inn & Suites Conference
Center
880 Kidder Street
Wilkes Barre, PA
570-824-8901

The Woodlands Inn, An Ascend
Collection Hotel

1073 Highway 315
Wilkes Barre, PA
570-824-9831

Red Roof Inn Wilkes Barre Arena
1035 Highway 315
Wilkes-Barre, PA
570-829-6422

Best Western Williamsport Inn
1840 East 3rd Street
Williamsport, PA
570-326-1981

Candlewood Suites Williamsport
1836 East Third Street
Williamsport, PA
570-601-9100

Econo Lodge Williamsport
2019 E. Third St.
Williamsport, PA
570-326-1501

Econo Lodge Wormleysburg -
Harrisburg
860 N. Front St.
Wormleysburg, PA
717-763-7086

Comfort Inn & Suites York
2250 N. George St.
York, PA
717-699-1919

Holiday Inn Express York
140 Leader Heights Road
York, PA
717-741-1000

Quality Inn And Suites York
2600 East Market Street
York, PA
717-755-1966

Wyndham Garden York
2000 Loucks Road
York, PA
717-846-9500

# Rhode Island Listings

The Blue Dory Inn
Dodge Street
Block Island, RI
401-466-2254

The Island Home Inn
585 Beach Avenue
Block Island, RI
401-466-5944

Vacation Rentals by Owner
Calico Hill
Block Island, RI
401-497-0631

Econo Lodge Cranston
101 New London Ave
Cranston, RI
401-942-4200

Extended Stay America - Providence
- East Providence
1000 Warren Ave
East Providence, RI
401-272-1661

The Edith Pearl
250 W Main Road/H 77
Little Compton, RI
401-592-0053

Bartram's
94 Kane Avenue
Middletown, RI
401-846-2259

Howard Johnson Inn - Newport
Area/Middletown
351 West Main Road
Middletown, RI
401-849-2000

Quality Inn & Suites Middletown -
Newport
936 W. Main Road
Middletown, RI
401-846-7600

Residence Inn Newport Middletown
325 West Main Road
Middletown, RI
401-845-2005

Rodeway Inn Middletown
31 West Main Road
Middletown, RI
401-847-2735

Seaview Inn
240 Aquidneck Avenue/H 138A
Middletown, RI
888-534-9698

The Bay Willows Inn
1225 Aquidneck Avenue
Middletown, RI
401-847-8400

Admiral Sims' White House
73 Catherine Street
Newport, RI
401-841-0009

Dog-Friendly Lodging - Please always call ahead to make sure an establishment is still dog-friendly.

Almy Cottage
141 Coggeshall Ave
Newport, RI

401-864-0686

Banister Mansion
Pelham at Spring Street
Newport, RI

401-846-0059

Bannister's Wharf Guest Rooms
1 Bannister's Wharf
Newport, RI

401-846-4500

Beech Tree Inn And Cottage
34 Rhode Island Avenue
Newport, RI

401-847-9794

Chestnut Inn
99 3rd Street
Newport, RI

401-847-6949

Cooney Cottage
87 Memorial Blvd
Newport, RI

401-849-9114

Dun Rovin
7 Florence Ave.
Newport, RI

401-846-2294

Hawthorne House
71 Ruggles Avenue
Newport, RI

401-847-6340

Hotel Viking
One Bellevue Avenue
Newport, RI

401-847-3300

Hyatt Regency Newport
1 Goat Island
Newport, RI

401-851-1234

Sanford-Covell Villa Marina
72 Washington Street
Newport, RI

401-847-0206

Summer Cottage Guest House
21 Catherine Street
Newport, RI

401-842-7671

The Inn at Washington Square

39 Touro Street
Newport, RI

401-847-7319

The Poplar House
19 Poplar Avenue
Newport, RI

401-846-0976

Victorian Ladies Inn
63 Memorial Boulevard
Newport, RI

401-849-9960

Quality Inn Pawtucket
2 George Street
Pawtucket, RI
401-723-6700

Providence Marriott Downtown
1 Orms St
Providence, RI
401-272-2400

The Cady House
127 Power Street
Providence, RI

401-273-5398

Hampton Inn And Suites Smithfield
945 Douglas Pike Rd
Smithfield, RI
401-232-9200

The Kings' Rose
1747 Mooresfield Road
South Kingston, RI
401-783-5222

Best Western Airport Inn
2138 Post Road
Warwick, RI
401-737-7400

Comfort Inn Airport Warwick
1940 Post Rd
Warwick, RI

401-732-0470

Crowne Plaza Warwick
801 Greenwich Avenue
Warwick, RI

401-732-6000

Extended Stay America -
Providence - Airport
268 Metro Center Blvd
Warwick, RI

401-732-6667

Extended Stay America -
Providence - Warwick
245 W. Natick Rd
Warwick, RI

401-732-2547

Hampton Inn And Suites
Providence/Warwick-Airport
2100 Post Road
Warwick, RI

401-739-8888

Holiday Inn Express & Suites
Warwick
901 Jefferson Boulevard
Warwick, RI

401-736-5000

Homewood Suites By HiltonÂ®
Warwick, Ri
33 International Way
Warwick, RI

401-738-0008

Residence Inn Providence Warwick
500 Kilvert Street
Warwick, RI

401-737-7100

Sheraton Providence Airport Hotel
1850 Post Road
Warwick, RI

401-738-4000

Residence Inn Providence Coventry
725 Centre Of New England
Boulevard
West Greenwich, RI
401-828-1170

Extended Stay America - Providence
- West Warwick
1235 Division Road
West Warwick, RI
401-885-3161

# South Carolina Listings

Days Inn Aiken - Interstate Hwy 20
2654 Columbia Hwy North
Aiken, SC
803-642-5692

Days Inn Downtown Aiken
1204 Richland Ave West
Aiken, SC

803-649-5524

Howard Johnson Express Inn Aiken
1936 Wiskey Road South
Aiken, SC

803-649-5000

Quality Inn & Suites Aiken
3608 Richland Avenue West

Aiken, SC
803-641-1100

Days Inn Anderson
1007 Smith Mill Road
Anderson, SC
864-375-0375

Days Inn Barnwell
10747 Dunbarton Boulevard
Barnwell, SC
803-541-5000

Days Inn Port Royal
1660 Ribaut Road
Beaufort, SC
843-524-1551

Quality Inn At Town Center
2001 Boundary Street
Beaufort, SC

843-524-2144

Quality Inn Bennettsville
213 15-401 Bypass East
Bennettsville, SC
843-479-1700

Candlewood Suites Bluffton-Hilton
Head
5 Young Clyde Court
Bluffton, SC
843-705-9600

Holiday Inn Express Bluffton
35 Bluffton Road
Bluffton, SC

843-757-2002

Comfort Inn Blythewood
436 Mcnulty Street
Blythewood, SC
803-754-1441

Best Western Sweetgrass Inn
1540 Savannah Hwy.
Charleston, SC
843-571-6100

Charleston Cottage
Call to Arrange
Charleston, SC

207-342-5444

Indigo Inn
1 Maiden Lane
Charleston, SC

843-577-5900

Residence Inn By Marriott Charleston
Downtown/Riverview
90 Ripley Point Drive
Charleston, SC

843-571-7979

Days Inn Cheraw
820 Market Street
Cheraw, SC
843-537-5554

Days Inn Clinton-Presbyterian
College
I-26 And Highway 56
Clinton, SC
864-833-6600

Quality Inn Clinton
105 Trade Street
Clinton, SC

864-833-5558

Candlewood Suites Columbia-Ft.
Jackson
921 Atlas Road
Columbia, SC
803-727-1299

Days Inn Columbia
1144 Bush River Road
Columbia, SC

803-750-7550

Extended Stay America - Columbia -
Ft. Jackson
5430 Forest Dr.
Columbia, SC

803-782-2025

Extended Stay America - Columbia -
West - Interstate 126
450 Gracern Rd.
Columbia, SC

803-251-7878

Home-Towne Suites Columbia
350 Columbiana Drive
Columbia, SC

803-781-9391

Red Roof Inn Columbia East - Fort
Jackson
7580 Two Notch Road
Columbia, SC

803-736-0850

Red Roof Inn Columbia West
10 Berryhill Road
Columbia, SC

803-798-9220

Residence Inn By Marriott Columbia
Northeast
2320 Legrand Road
Columbia, SC

803-788-8850

Sheraton Columbia Downtown Hotel
1400 Main Street
Columbia, SC

803-988-1400

Staybridge Suites Columbia
1913 Huger St
Columbia, SC

803-451-5900

Super 8 Columbia
5719 Fairfield Road
Columbia, SC

803-735-0008

Towneplace Suites By Marriott
Columbia Southeast/Fort Jackson
250 East Exchange Boulevard
Columbia, SC

803-695-0062

Economy Inn Dillon
1223 Radford Boulevard, Interstate
95 , Exit 193
Dillon, SC
843-774-4181

Red Roof Inn - Dillon
810 Radford Boulevard
Dillon, SC

843-774-4137

South of the Border Motor Inn
H 301/501
Dillon, SC

843-774-2411

Holiday Inn Express & Suites
Greenville-Spartanburg (Duncan)
275 Frontage Road
Duncan, SC
864-486-9191

Quality Inn Duncan Spartanburg
West
1391 East Main Street
Duncan, SC

864-433-1333

Baymont Inn & Suites - Dunn
901 Jackson Road
Dunn, SC
910-891-5758

Days Inn Easley West Of
Greenville/Clemson Area
121 Days Inn Drive
Easley, SC
864-859-9902

Best Western Inn
1808 W Lucas Street
Florence, SC
843-678-9292

Days Inn Florence
2111 West Lucas Street
Florence, SC

843-665-4444

Econo Lodge Florence
1920 West Lucas Street
Florence, SC

843-665-4558

Florence Inn and Suites
3821 Bancroft Road
Florence, SC

877-665-9494

Quality Inn & Suites Civic Center
150 Dunbarton Drive
Florence, SC

843-664-2400

Ramada Florence Center
1819 West Lucas Street
Florence, SC

843-665-4555

Ramada Inn Florence Sc
3311 Meadors Road I-95 & Us 76 Exit
#157
Florence, SC

843-669-4171

Red Roof Inn Florence Civic Center
2690 David Mcleod Boulevard
Florence, SC

843-678-9000

Residence Inn Florence
2660 Hospitality Blvd.
Florence, SC

843-468-2800

Super 8 Florence
1832 1/2 Lucas Street
Florence, SC

843-661-7267

Thunderbird Inn Florence
2004 West Lucas Street
Florence, SC

843-669-1611

Travelodge Florence
3783a W. Palmetto St.
Florence, SC

843-673-0070

Comfort Inn Carowinds
3725 Avenue Of The Carolinas
Fort Mill, SC
803-548-5200

Days Inn Turbeville
7835 Myrtle Beach Highway
Gable, SC
843-659-8060

Quality Inn Gaffney
143 Corona Drive
Gaffney, SC
864-487-4200

Sleep Inn Gaffney
834 Windslow Avenue
Gaffney, SC

864-487-5337

Super 8 Gaffney
100 Ellis Ferry Avenue
Gaffney, SC

864-489-1699

Quality Inn Goose Creek
103 Red Bank Road
Goose Creek, SC
843-572-9500

Best Western Greenville Airport Inn
5009 Pelham Road
Greenville, SC
864-297-5353

Best Western Greenville Airport Inn
5009 Pelham Road
Greenville, SC

864-297-5353

Comfort Inn & Suites
831 Congaree Road
Greenville, SC

864-288-6221

Drury Inn & Suites Greenville
10 Carolina Point Parkway
Greenville, SC

864-288-4401

Extended Stay America - Greenville
- Airport
3715 Pelham Rd.
Greenville, SC

864-213-9698

Quality Inn & Suites Greenville
1314 South Pleasantburg Drive
Greenville, SC

864-770-3737

Quality Inn Executive Center
540 North Pleasantburg Drive
Greenville, SC

864-271-0060

Quality Inn Simpsonville
3755 Grandview Drive
Greenville, SC

864-963-2777

Red Roof Inn Greenville

91 Vision Court
Greenville, SC

864-297-4458

Residence Inn By Marriott Greenville-
Spartanburg Airport
120 Milestone Way
Greenville, SC

864-627-0001

Staybridge Suites
Greenville/Spartanburg
31 Market Point Drive
Greenville, SC

864-288-4448

Towneplace Suites By Marriott
Greenville Haywood Mall
75 Mall Connector Road
Greenville, SC

864-675-1670

Holiday Inn Express Hotel & Suites
Greenville Airport
2681 Dry Pocket Road
Greer, SC
864-213-9331

Mainstay Suites Greenville Airport
2671 Dry Pocket Road
Greer, SC

864-987-5566

Days Inn Hardeeville Interstate
Highway 95 State Line
16633 Whyte Hardee Boulevard
Hardeeville, SC
843-784-2281

Hardeeville Red Roof Inn
1122 Hummingbird Lane
Hardeeville, SC

843-784-2188

Quality Inn & Suites Hardeeville
19000 Whyte Hardee Boulevard
Hardeeville, SC

843-784-7060

Super 8 Hardeeville Sc
19289 Whyte Hardee Blvd
Hardeeville, SC

843-784-2151

Beachwalk Hotel & Condominiums
40 Waterside Drive
Hilton Head Island, SC
843-842-8888

Quality Inn South Forest Beach
2 Tanglewood Drive
Hilton Head Island, SC

843-842-6662

Ramada Hilton Head
200 Museum Street
Hilton Head Island, SC

843-681-3655

Red Roof Inn Hilton Head Island
5 Regency Parkway
Hilton Head Island, SC

843-686-6808

Kiawah Island Golf Resort
One Sanctuary Beach Drive
Kiawah Island, SC
843-768-2121

Best Western Magnolia Inn And
Suites
747 Treeland Drive
Ladson, SC
843-553-8888

Days Inn - Lake City
170 South Ron Mcnair Boulevard
Lake City, SC
843-394-3269

The Red Horse Inn
45 Winstons Chase Court
Landrum, SC
864-895-4968

Quality Inn & Suites Lexington
328 West Main Street
Lexington, SC
803-359-3099

Holiday Inn Express Hotel & Suites N.
Myrtle Beach-Little River
722 Highway 17
Little River, SC
843-281-9400

Camden West Inn
850 Us Highway 1 South
Lugoff, SC
803-438-9441

Days Inn Lugoff
542 Highway 601 South
Lugoff, SC

803-438-1807

Baymont Inn And Suites Manning
2284 Raccoon Rd.
Manning, SC
803-473-5334

Howard Johnson Manning
2816 Paxville Hwy
Manning, SC

803-473-5135

Quality Inn Manning
3031 Paxville Highway
Manning, SC

803-473-7550

Super 8 Manning
1062 Cross Road
Manning, SC

803-473-4646

Days Inn Mount Pleasant-
Charleston-Patriots Point
261 Johnnie Dodds Blvd
Mount Pleasant, SC
843-881-1800

Extended Stay America - Charleston
- Mt. Pleasant
304 Wingo Way
Mount Pleasant, SC

843-884-4453

Homewood Suites By Hilton®
Charleston - Mt. Pleasant
1998 Riviera Drive
Mount Pleasant, SC

843-881-6950

Masters Inn Charleston-mt. Pleasant
300 Wingo Way
Mount Pleasant, SC

843-884-2814

Red Roof Inn Mount Pleasant
301 Johnnie Dodds Boulevard
Mount Pleasant, SC

843-884-1411

Residence Inn Charleston Mount
Pleasant
1116 Isle Of Palms Connector
Mount Pleasant, SC

843-881-1599

Sleep Inn Mount Pleasant
299 Wingo Way
Mount Pleasant, SC

843-856-5000

Quality Inn Mullins
2693 E Hwy 76
Mullins, SC
843-423-0516

Holiday Inn Express Murrells Inlet
1303 A Tadlock Drive
Murrells Inlet, SC
843-357-0100

Best Western Plus Myrtle Beach
Hotel
9551 N Kings Highway
Myrtle Beach, SC
843-213-1440

Booe Realty
7728 N. Kings Hwy

Myrtle Beach, SC

800-845-0647

Comfort Suites Myrtle Beach
710 Frontage Rd. East
Myrtle Beach, SC

843-448-4884

Days Inn Myrtle Beach
3650 Waccamaw Boulevard
Myrtle Beach, SC

843-236-9888

Mariner Motel
7003 N Ocean Blvd
Myrtle Beach, SC

843-449-5281

Red Roof Inn Myrtle Beach Hotel -
Market Commons
2801 South Kings Highway
Myrtle Beach, SC

843-626-4444

Staybridge Suites Myrtle Beach -
West
303 Fantasy Harbour Blvd.
Myrtle Beach, SC

843-903-4000

The Sea Mist Resort
1200 S Ocean Blvd
Myrtle Beach, SC

843-448-1551

Vancouver Motel
2601 S Ocean Beach Blvd
Myrtle Beach, SC

843-448-4331

Days Inn Newberry
50 Thomas Griffin Road
Newberry, SC
803-276-2294

Econo Lodge Inn & Suites Newberry
1147 Wilson Road
Newberry, SC

803-276-1600

Candlewood Suites Charleston-
Ashley Phosphate
2177 Northwoods Boulevard
North Charleston, SC
843-797-3535

Days Inn Charleston - Airport
Coliseum
2998 West Montague Avenue
North Charleston, SC

843-747-4101

Extended Stay America - Charleston - Airport
5045 N. Arco Lane
North Charleston, SC

843-740-3440

Extended Stay America - Charleston - North Charleston
5059 N. Arco Lane
North Charleston, SC

843-747-3787

Hawthorn Suites by Wyndham North Charleston SC
7645 Northwoods Boulevard
North Charleston, SC

843-572-5757

Quality Inn North Charleston
7415 Northside Drive
North Charleston, SC

843-572-6677

Red Roof Inn North Charleston Coliseum
7480 Northwoods Blvd
North Charleston, SC

843-572-9100

Residence Inn By Marriott Charleston Airport
5035 International Boulevard
North Charleston, SC

843-266-3434

Sleep Inn Airport
7435 Northside Drive
North Charleston, SC

843-572-8400

Staybridge Suites North Charleston
7329 Mazyck Road
North Charleston, SC

843-377-4600

Retreat Myrtle Beach
Call to Arrange
North Myrtle Beach, SC
843-280-3015

Thomas Beach Vacations
Call to Arrange
North Myrtle Beach, SC

843-249-2100

Days Inn Orangeburg South
3402 Five Chop Road
Orangeburg, SC
803-534-0500

Quality Inn & Suites Orangeburg
3671 Saint Matthews Road
Orangeburg, SC

803-531-9200

Dieter Co. Vacation Rentals
13253 Ocean Hwy
Pawleys Island, SC
843-237-2813

Super 8 Motel - Greenville/Piedmont/Anderson
3104 Earl East Morris Hwy. 153
Piedmont, SC
864-220-1836

Econo Lodge Richburg
3190 Lancaster Highway
Richburg, SC
803-789-3000

Super 8 Motel Richburg/Chester
3085 Lancaster Highway
Richburg, SC

803-789-7888

Econo Lodge Ridgeland
511 James F Taylor Drive
Ridgeland, SC
843-726-6213

Quality Inn & Suites Ridgeland
221 James Taylor Road
Ridgeland, SC

843-726-2121

Howard Johnson Inn Rock Hill
911 Riverview Road
Rock Hill, SC
803-329-7900

Motel 6 Rock Hill
962 Riverview Road
Rock Hill, SC

803-329-3232

Super 8 Rock Hill
888 Riverview Road
Rock Hill, SC

803-980-0400

Towneplace Suites By Marriott Rock Hill
2135 Tabor Drive
Rock Hill, SC

803-327-0700

Comfort Inn Saint George
139 Motel Drive
Saint George, SC
843-563-4180

Quality Inn Saint George
6014 W Jim Bilton Blvd.
Saint George, SC

843-563-4581

Econo Lodge Santee
9112 Old Number 6 Highway
Santee, SC
803-854-3870

Quality Inn & Suites Santee
8929 Old Number Six Highway
Santee, SC

803-854-2121

Red Roof Inn Santee
9091 Old Highway 6
Santee, SC

803-854-3122

Super 8 Santee
9125 Old Hwy 6
Santee, SC

803-854-3456

Seabrook Exclusives
Call to Arrange
Seabrook Island, SC
843-768-0808

Days Inn Simpsonville
45 Ray East Talley Court
Simpsonville, SC
864-963-7701

Quality Inn Simpsonville
3755 Grandview Drive
Simpsonville, SC

864-963-2777

Comfort Inn And Suites
154 Candlenut Lane
Spartanburg, SC
864-814-2001

Crossland Economy Studios - Spartanburg - Asheville Hwy.
130 Mobile Drive
Spartanburg, SC

864-573-5949

Days Inn Spartanburg
115 Rogers Commerce Boulevard
Spartanburg, SC

864-814-0560

Red Roof Inn Spartanburg
6765 Pottery Road
Spartanburg, SC

864-587-0129

Residence Inn By Marriott Spartanburg
9011 Fairforest Road
Spartanburg, SC

864-576-3333

Super 8 Spartanburg
488 South Blackstock Road

Spartanburg, SC
864-576-2488

Knights Inn St George
114 Winningham Road
St George, SC
843-563-5551

Days Inn Summerton
400 Buff Blvd.
Summerton, SC
803-485-2865

Econo Lodge Summerville
110 Holiday Road
Summerville, SC
843-875-3022

Holiday Inn Exp Summerville
120 Holiday Inn Drive
Summerville, SC
843-875-3300

Quality Inn Summerville
1005 Jockey Court
Summerville, SC
843-851-2333

Sleep Inn Summerville
115 Holiday Drive
Summerville, SC
843-851-9595

Candlewood Suites Sumter
2541 Broad Street
Sumter, SC
803-469-4000

Econo Lodge Sumter
226 North Washington Street
Sumter, SC

Quality Inn Sumter
2390 Broad Street
Sumter, SC
803-469-9001

Travelers Rest Inn
110 Hawkins Road
Travelers Rest, SC
864-834-7040

Microtel Inn & Suites
130 Cane Branch Road
Walterboro, SC
843-539-5656

Microtel Inn & Suites By Wyndham
Walterboro
130 Cane Branch Road
Walterboro, SC
843-539-5656

Quality Inn & Suites Walterboro
1286 Sniders Highway

Walterboro, SC
843-538-5473

Ramada Inn - Walterboro
1245 Sniders Highway
Walterboro, SC
843-538-5403

Rice Planters Inn
I-95 and SR 63
Walterboro, SC
843-538-8964

Sleep Inn Walterboro
3043 Hiers Corner Road
Walterboro, SC
843-539-1199

Super 8 Walterboro
1972 Bells Highway 64
Walterboro, SC
843-538-5383

Clarion Inn Airport
500 Chris Drive
West Columbia, SC
803-794-9440

Quality Inn West Columbia
2516 Augusta Road
West Columbia, SC
803-791-5160

Americas Best Value Inn Winnsboro
1894 Us Hwy 321 Bypass
Winnsboro, SC
803-635-1447

Knights Inn Point South Yemassee
420 Campground Road
Yemassee, SC
843-726-8488

Super 8 Yemassee
409 Yemassee Highway
Yemassee, SC
843-589-2177

# South Dakota Listings

Best Western Ramkota Hotel
1400 8th Ave. N.W.
Aberdeen, SD
605-229-4040

Holiday Inn Express Hotel And
Suites Aberdeen
3310 7th Avenue Southeast
Aberdeen, SD
605-725-4000

Quality Inn Aberdeen
2923 6th Avenue South East
Aberdeen, SD
605-226-0097

Super 8 East Aberdeen
2405 Southeast 6th Avenue
Aberdeen, SD
605-229-5005

Super 8 North Aberdeen
1023 8th Avenue Northwest
Aberdeen, SD
605-226-2288

Super 8 West Aberdeen
714 South Highway 281
Aberdeen, SD
605-225-1711

The White House Inn
500 6th Avenue SW/H 12
Aberdeen, SD
605-225-5000

Super 8 Belle Fourche
501 National Street
Belle Fourche, SD
605-892-3361

Holiday Inn Express Hotel & Suites
Sioux Falls-Brandon
1103 N Splitrock Blvd
Brandon, SD
605-582-2901

Quality Inn Brandon
1105 North Splitrock Boulevard
Brandon, SD
605-582-5777

Days Inn Brookings
2500 E. 6th. St.
Brookings, SD
605-692-9471

Super 8 - Brookings
3034 Lefevre Drive
Brookings, SD
605-692-6920

Super 8 Chamberlain Sd
Box 36 Lakeview Heights
Chamberlain, SD
605-734-6548

Days Inn Oacoma
400 East Highway 16
Chamberlain/Oacoma, SD
605-734-4100

Best Western Buffalo Ridge Inn
310 W Mount Rushmore Road
Custer, SD
605-673-2275

Dog-Friendly Lodging - Please always call ahead to make sure an establishment is still dog-friendly.

Legion Lake Lodge
12967 Us Highway 16a
Custer, SD

605-255-4521

Quality Inn Oacoma
100 Highway 16
Custer, SD

605-255-4541

Black Hill Inn and Suites
206 Mt. Shadow Lane
Deadwood, SD
605-578-7791

Super 8 Hill City/Mt Rushmore/ Area
109 Main Street,
Hill City, SD
605-574-4141

Baymont Inn & Suites Hot Springs
737 South 6th Street
Hot Springs, SD
605-745-7378

Flatlron Coffee Bar, Grill and Guest
Suites
745 N River Street/H 385
Hot Springs, SD

605-745-5301

Super 8 Hot Springs
800 Mammoth Street
Hot Springs, SD

605-745-3888

Dakota Plains Inn
Highway 14E
Huron, SD
605-352-1400

Quality Inn Huron
100 21st Street Sw
Huron, SD

605-352-6655

Super 8 Huron
2189 Dakota Avenue South
Huron, SD

605-352-0740

Powder House Lodge
24125 H 16A
Keystone, SD
605-666-4646

Super 8 Madison
219 N Highland
Madison, SD
605-256-6931

Super 8 Miller
Hwy 14w And Hwy 45n
Miller, SD

605-853-2721

Americas Best Value Inn Mitchell
1001 South Burr Street
Mitchell, SD
605-996-5536

Days Inn Mitchell Sd
1506 South Burr
Mitchell, SD

605-996-6208

Econo Lodge Mitchell
1313 South Ohlman
Mitchell, SD

605-996-6647

Kelly Inn and Suites Mitchell
1010 Cabela Drive
Mitchell, SD

605-995-0500

Ramada Mitchell Hotel and
Conference Center
1525 West Havens Ave
Mitchell, SD

605-996-6501

Siesta Motel
1210 West Havens
Mitchell, SD

605-996-5544

Best Western Graham's
301 W. 5th St.
Murdo, SD
605-669-2441

Hampton Inn North Sioux City
101 S. Sodrac Drive
North Sioux City, SD
605-232-9739

Super 8 North Sioux City
108 Sodrac Drive
North Sioux City, SD

605-232-4716

Howard Johnson Inn & Suites
Oacoma
203 East Highway 16
Oacoma, SD
605-234-4222

Oasis Inn
1100 East Highway 16
Oacoma, SD

605-734-6061

Quality Inn Oacoma
100 Highway 16
Oacoma, SD

605-734-5593

Capitol Inn and Suites Pierre
815 East Wells Avenue
Pierre, SD
605-224-6387

Quality Inn Pierre
410 W. Sioux Ave.
Pierre, SD

605-224-0377

River Lodge
713 West Sioux Avenue
Pierre, SD

605-224-4140

Super 8 Pierre Sd
320 West Sioux Avenue
Pierre, SD

605-224-1617

Best Western Ramkota Hotel
2111 North Lacrosse Street
Rapid City, SD
605-343-8550

Econo Lodge Rapid City
625 E. Disk Dr.
Rapid City, SD

605-342-6400

Hillside Country Cottages
13315 S H 16
Rapid City, SD

605-342-4121

Holiday Inn Rushmore Plaza
505 North Fifth Street
Rapid City, SD

605-348-4000

Microtel Inn & Suites By Wyndham
Rapid City
1740 Rapp Street
Rapid City, SD

605-348-2523

Ramada Rapid City
1902 North la Crosse Street
Rapid City, SD

605-342-3322

Super 8 Rapid City
2124 Lacrosse Street
Rapid City, SD

605-348-8070

Super 8 Rapid City Rushmore Rd
2520 Tower Rd.
Rapid City, SD

605-342-4911

Travelodge Rapid City

2505 Mount Rushmore Road
Rapid City, SD

605-343-5383

Best Western Empire Towers
4100 West Shirley Place
Sioux Falls, SD
605-361-3118

Best Western Plus Ramkota Hotel
3200 West Maple Street
Sioux Falls, SD

605-336-0650

Comfort Suites Sioux Falls
3208 South Carolyn Ave.
Sioux Falls, SD

605-362-9711

Days Inn Sioux Falls
3401 Gateway Boulevard
Sioux Falls, SD

605-361-9240

Days Inn Sioux Falls
5001 North Cliff Avenue
Sioux Falls, SD

605-331-5959

Econo Lodge North Souix Falls
5100 North Cliff Avenue
Sioux Falls, SD

605-331-4490

GuestHouse Inn & Suites Sioux Falls
3101 West Russell Street
Sioux Falls, SD

605-338-6242

Holiday Inn City Center
100 W 8th St
Sioux Falls, SD

605-339-2000

Homewood Suites By Hilton® Sioux
Falls
3620 West Avera Drive
Sioux Falls, SD

605-338-8585

Quality Inn & Suites South
3216 S. Carolyn Ave.
Sioux Falls, SD

605-361-2822

Quality Inn And Suites Sioux Falls
5410 N. Granite Lane
Sioux Falls, SD

605-336-1900

Ramada Sioux Falls
407 Lyons Avenue

Sioux Falls, SD

605-330-0000

Red Roof Inn Sioux Falls
3500 Gateway Boulevard
Sioux Falls, SD

605-361-1864

Residence Inn Sioux Falls
4509 W Empire Place
Sioux Falls, SD

605-361-2202

Staybridge Suites Sioux Falls
2505 South Carolyn Avenue
Sioux Falls, SD

605-361-2298

Super 8 Airport
4808 North Cliff Avenue
Sioux Falls, SD

605-339-9212

Super 8 Sioux Falls
2616 East 10th Street
Sioux Falls, SD

605-338-8881

Super 8 Sioux Falls Near
Convention Center
1508 West Russell Street
Sioux Falls, SD

605-339-9330

Super 8 Sisseton
2104 SD Highway 10
Sisseton, SD
605-742-0808

Best Western Black Hills Lodge
540 East Jackson Boulevard
Spearfish, SD
605-642-7795

Days Inn Spearfish
240 Ryan Road
Spearfish, SD

605-642-7101

Holiday Inn Spearfish-Convention
Center
305 North 27th Street
Spearfish, SD

605-642-4683

Howard Johnson Inn-Spearfish
323 South 27th Street
Spearfish, SD

605-642-8105

Super 8 Spearfish
440 Heritage Drive

Spearfish, SD

605-642-4721

Prairie Sky Guest Ranch
44370 109th Street
Veblen, SD
605-738-2411

Best Western Vermillion Inn
701 West Cherry Street
Vermillion, SD
605-624-8333

The V
1208 East Cherry Street
Vermillion, SD

605-624-8005

Econo Lodge Wall
804 Glenn Street
Wall, SD
605-279-2121

Days Inn Watertown
2900 9th Ave Se
Watertown, SD
605-886-3500

Holiday Inn Express Hotel & Suites
Watertown
3901 9th Ave. S.E.
Watertown, SD

605-882-3636

Quality Inn & Suites Watertown
800 35th Street Circle
Watertown, SD

605-886-3010

Iron Horse Inn
600 Whitewood Service Road
Whitewood, SD
605-722-7574

Holiday Inn Express Hotel And Suites
Winner
1360 East Highway 44
Winner, SD
605-842-2255

Days Inn Yankton Sd
2410 Broadway
Yankton, SD
605-665-8717

Travelodge Yankton
1603 East Highway 50
Yankton, SD

605-665-6510

# Tennessee Listings

Candlewood Suites Knoxville Airport-
Alcoa
176 Cusick Road

Alcoa, TN
865-233-4411

Mainstay Suites Alcoa
361 Fountain View Circle
Alcoa, TN

865-379-7799

Motel 6 Alcoa
2962 Alcoa Hwy
Alcoa, TN

865-970-3060

Rodeway Inn & Suites Antioch
13010 Old Hickory Blvd
Antioch, TN
615-641-7721

Super 8 Antioch
1121 Bell Road
Antioch, TN

615-731-8440

Super 8 Athens
2541 Decatur Pike
Athens, TN
423-745-4500

Suburban Extended Stay Bartlett -
Memphis
7380 Stage Road Highway 64
Bartlett, TN
901-388-6000

Candlewood Suites Nashville -
Brentwood
5129 Virginia Way
Brentwood, TN
615-309-0600

Extended Stay America - Nashville -
Brentwood - South
9020 Church Street East
Brentwood, TN

615-377-7847

Mainstay Suites Brentwood
107 Brentwood Boulevard
Brentwood, TN

615-371-8477

Residence Inn Nashville-Brentwood
206 Ward Circle
Brentwood, TN

615-371-0100

Sleep Inn Brentwood - Nashville -
Cool Springs
1611 Galleria Blvd
Brentwood, TN

615-376-2122

Days Inn Bristol Parkway
536 Volunteer Pkwy
Bristol, TN

423-968-2171

Days Inn Brownsville
2530 Anderson Avenue
Brownsville, TN
731-772-3297

Paris Landing Inn
16055 H 79N
Buchanan, TN
731-642-4311

Super 8 - Bulls Gap
90 Speedway Lane
Bulls Gap, TN
423-235-4112

Montgomery Bell Resort and
Conference Center
1020 Jackson Hill Road
Burns, TN
615-797-3101

Iron Mountain Inn B & B And
Cottages
138 Moreland Drive
Butler, TN
423-768-2446

Iron Mountain Inn B & B And
Cottages
138 Moreland Drive
Butler, TN

423-768-2446

Super 8 Caryville
200 John Mcghee Blvd.
Caryville, TN
423-562-8476

Cedar Hill Resort
2371 Cedar Hill Road
Celina, TN
931-243-3201

Baymont Inn and Suites
Chattanooga
3540 Cummings Highway
Chattanooga, TN
423-821-1090

Best Western Royal Inn
3644 Cummings Highway
Chattanooga, TN

423-821-6840

Chattanooga Choo Choo
1400 Market Street/H 8
Chattanooga, TN

800-TRACK-29 (872-2529)

Extended Stay America -
Chattanooga - Airport
6240 Airpark Dr.
Chattanooga, TN

423-892-1315

La Quinta Inn & Suites Chattanooga -
East Ridge
6650 Ringgold Rd.
Chattanooga, TN

423-894-1860

Quality Inn Lookout Mountain
3109 Parker Lane
Chattanooga, TN

423-821-1499

Red Roof Inn Chattanooga - Lookout
Mountain
30 Birmingham Highway
Chattanooga, TN

423-821-7162

Red Roof Inn Chattanooga Airport
7014 Shallowford Road
Chattanooga, TN

423-899-0143

Residence Inn By Marriott
Chattanooga Downtown
215 Chestnut Street
Chattanooga, TN

423-266-0600

Residence Inn Chattanooga Near
Hamilton Place
2340 Center Street
Chattanooga, TN

423-468-7700

Rodeway Inn Chattanooga
7620 Hamilton Park Drive
Chattanooga, TN

423-499-1993

Staybridge Suites Chattanooga
Downtown - Convention Center
1300 Carter Street
Chattanooga, TN

423-267-0900

Super 8 Chattanooga
7024 Mccutcheon Road
Chattanooga, TN

423-490-8560

The Read House Historic Inn And
Suites
827 Broad St. Chattanooga TN 37402
Chattanooga, TN

423-266-4121

Baymont Inn & Suites Clarksville
1112 Highway 76
Clarksville, TN
931-358-2020

Candlewood Suites Clarksville
3050 Clay Lewis Road

Clarksville, TN
931-906-0900

Days Inn Clarksville North
130 Westfield Court
Clarksville, TN
931-552-1155

Days Inn Clarksville Tn
1100 Hwy 76/I-24
Clarksville, TN
931-358-3194

Econo Lodge Inn & Suite Clarksville
3065 Wilma Rudolph Blvd
Clarksville, TN
931-647-2002

Mainstay Suites Fort Campbell
115 Fairbrook Place
Clarksville, TN
931-648-3400

Quality Inn Exit 4
3095 Wilma Rudolph Blvd
Clarksville, TN
931-648-4848

Red Roof Inn Clarksville
197 Holiday Drive
Clarksville, TN
931-905-1555

Days Inn Cleveland
2550 Georgetown Road
Cleveland, TN
423-476-2112

Howard Johnson Cleveland Tn
2595 Georgetown Road
Cleveland, TN
423-476-8511

Super 8 Cleveland
163 Bernham Drive
Cleveland, TN
423-476-5555

Travelodge Cleveland
156 James Asbury Drive
Cleveland, TN
423-472-5566

Americas Best Value Inn Nashville
Hermitage

Clinton, TN

Super 8 Clinton
720 Park Place
Clinton, TN
865-457-2311

Days Inn Collierville Tn
1230 W. Poplar Avenue
Collierville, TN
901-853-1235

Hampton Inn Memphis/Collierville
1280 W Poplar Ave
Collierville, TN
901-854-9400

Days Inn Columbia
1504 Nashville Highway
Columbia, TN
931-381-3297

Alpine Lodge & Suites
2021 East Spring Street
Cookeville, TN
931-526-3333

Best Western Thunderbird Motel
900 South Jefferson Avenue
Cookeville, TN
931-526-7115

Country Inn & Suites By Carlson,
Cookeville, Tn
1151 South Jefferson Avenue
Cookeville, TN
931-525-6668

Quality Suites Cordova
8166 Varnavas Dr.
Cordova, TN
901-386-4600

Econo Lodge Cornersville
3731 Pulaski Hwy.
Cornersville, TN
931-293-2111

Quality Inn Crossville
4035 Highway 127 North
Crossville, TN
931-484-1551

Red Roof Inn Crossville
105 Executive Drive
Crossville, TN
931-484-9691

Holiday Inn Express Dandridge
119 Sharon Drive
Dandridge, TN
865-397-1910

Mountain Harbor Inn
1199 H 139
Dandridge, TN
865-397-1313

Super 8 - Dandridge
125 Sharon Drive
Dandridge, TN

865-397-1200

Best Western Executive Inn Dickson
2338 Highway 46 South
Dickson, TN
615-446-0541

Days Inn Dickson
2415 Highway 46 South
Dickson, TN
615-740-7475

Econo Lodge Inn And Suites
1025 East Christi Drive
Dickson, TN
615-441-5252

Holiday Inn Express Hotel & Suites
Dickson
100 Barzani Boulevard
Dickson, TN
615-446-2781

Rodeway Inn & Suites Dickson
1055 E. Christi Drive
Dickson, TN
615-740-0074

Super 8 Dickson
150 Suzanne Drive
Dickson, TN
615-446-1923

Americas Best Value Inn Fayetteville
1653 Huntsville Highway
Fayetteville, TN
931-433-6121

Best Western Franklin Inn
1308 Murfreesboro Road
Franklin, TN
615-790-0570

Comfort Inn Franklin
4202 Franklin Commons Court
Franklin, TN
615-591-6660

Days Inn Franklin
3915 Carothers Parkway
Franklin, TN
615-790-1140

Extended Stay America - Nashville -
Franklin - Cool Springs
680 Bakers Bridge Ave.
Franklin, TN
615-771-7600

Quality Inn & Suites
1307 Murfreesboro Road
Franklin, TN

615-794-7591

Residence Inn By Marriott Franklin
Cool Springs
2009 Meridian Blvd.
Franklin, TN

615-778-0002

Garden Plaza Hotel
520 Historic Nature Trail
Gatlinburg, TN
865-436-9201

Greenbrier Valley Resorts
Greenbrier Valley Resorts
Gatlinburg, TN

865-436-2015

Mountain Shadows Resort
1625 Hidden Hills Road
Gatlinburg, TN

865-430-9201

Homewood Suites By Hilton®
Memphis-Germantown
7855 Wolf River Parkway
Germantown, TN
901-751-2500

Quality Inn & Suites Germantown
7787 Wolf River Blvd.
Germantown, TN

901-757-7800

Residence Inn Memphis-Germantown
9314 Poplar Pike
Germantown, TN

901-752-0900

Days Inn Goodlettsville
909 Conference Drive
Goodlettsville, TN
615-851-6600

Fairwinds Inn
100 Northcreek Boulevard
Goodlettsville, TN

615-851-1067

Quality Inn Goodlettsville
925 Conference Drive
Goodlettsville, TN

615-859-5400

Red Roof Inn Nashville North -
Goodlettsville
110 Northgate Drive
Goodlettsville, TN

615-859-2537

Econo Lodge Greeneville
1790 East Andrew Johnson Hwy
Greeneville, TN

423-639-4185

Super 8 Motel - Hermitage Nashville
Area Tn
1414 Princeton Place
Hermitage, TN
615-871-4545

Days Inn Holladay
13845 Hwy 641 North
Holladay, TN
731-847-2278

Days Inn Hurricane Mills
15415 Hwy. 13 South
Hurricane Mills, TN
931-296-7647

America's Best Value Inn And
Suites - Jackson
220 Vann Drive
Jackson, TN
731-668-0808

Days Inn Jackson
1919 Hwy 45 Bypass
Jackson, TN

731-668-3444

Knights Inn Jackson
2659 North Highland
Jackson, TN

731-664-8600

Rodeway Inn Jackson
2239 N Hollywood Dr
Jackson, TN

731-668-4840

Days Inn Jellico - Tennessee State
Line
1417 5th Street
Jellico, TN
423-784-7281

Days Inn Joelton/Nashville
201 Gifford Place
Joelton, TN
615-876-3261

Best Western Johnson City Hotel &
Conference Center
2406 N Roan Street
Johnson City, TN
423-282-2161

Holiday Inn Johnson City
101 West Springbrook Drive
Johnson City, TN

423-282-4611

Quality Inn Johnson City
1900 S. Roan St.
Johnson City, TN

423-928-9600

Red Roof Inn Johnson City
210 Broyles Drive
Johnson City, TN

423-282-3040

Super 8 Kimball
395 Main Street
Kimball, TN
423-837-7185

Red Roof Inn Kingsport
100 Indian Center Court
Kingsport, TN
423-378-4418

Super 8 Kingsport
700 Lynn Garden Drive
Kingsport, TN

423-246-5515

Lakeview Inn - Kingston
1200 North Kentucky Street
Kingston, TN
865-376-3477

Quality Inn Kingston Springs
116 Luyben Hills Rd
Kingston Springs, TN
615-952-3961

Americas Best Value Inn-Knoxville
East/Strawberry Plains
722 Brakebill Road
Knoxville, TN

Best Western Knoxville Suites
5317 Pratt Road
Knoxville, TN

865-687-9922

Candlewood Suites Knoxville
10206 Parkside Drive
Knoxville, TN

865-777-0400

Clarion Inn Knoxville
5634 Merchant Center Blvd
Knoxville, TN

865-687-8989

Crowne Plaza Knoxville
401 West Summit Hill Drive
Knoxville, TN

865-522-2600

Days Inn Knoxville East
5423 Asheville Highway
Knoxville, TN

865-637-3511

Days Inn Knoxville North
5335 Central Avenue Pike
Knoxville, TN

865-687-5800

Days Inn West Knoxville
9240 Park West Boulevard
Knoxville, TN

865-693-6061

Econo Lodge Inn And Suites East
7424 Strawberry Plains Pike
Knoxville, TN

865-932-1217

Extended Stay America - Knoxville -
Cedar Bluff
214 Langley Place
Knoxville, TN

865-769-0822

Extended Stay America - Knoxville -
West Hills
1700 Winston Rd.
Knoxville, TN

865-694-4178

Hilton Knoxville
501 West Church Street
Knoxville, TN

865-523-2300

Holiday Inn Express Knoxville-
Strawberry Plains
730 Rufus Graham Road
Knoxville, TN

865-525-5100

Homewood Suites Knoxville West
10935 Turkey Drive
Knoxville, TN

865-777-0375

Quality Inn East Knoxville
7471 Crosswood Blvd
Knoxville, TN

865-342-0003

Quality Inn Merchants Drive
117 Cedar Lane
Knoxville, TN

865-342-3701

Red Roof Inn Knoxville - Merchants
Drive
5334 Central Avenue Pike
Knoxville, TN

865-688-1010

Residence Inn By Marriott Knoxville
Cedar Bluff
215 Langley Place
Knoxville, TN

865-539-5339

Sleep Inn Knoxville

214 Prosperity Dr
Knoxville, TN

865-531-5900

Super 8 Knoxville
341 Merchants Drive
Knoxville, TN

865-689-7666

Super 8 Knoxville East
7585 Crosswood Boulevard  ;
Knoxville, TN

865-524-0855

Super 8 Knoxville/West
11748 Snyder Road
Knoxville, TN

865-675-5566

Towneplace Suites By Marriott
Knoxville Cedar Bluff
205 Langley Place
Knoxville, TN

865-693-5216

Travelodge Knoxville West
6200 Paper Mill Rd, I-40/I-75 Exit
383
Knoxville, TN

865-584-8511

Baymont Inn And Suites Kodak
2863 Winfield Dunn Parkway
Kodak, TN
865-933-9448

Days Inn Sevierville Interstate
Smokey Mountains
3402 Winfield Dunn Parkway
Kodak, TN

865-933-4500

Econo Lodge Rocky Top
221 Colonial Lane
Lake City, TN
865-426-2816

Super 8 Lakeland
9779 Huff And Puff Road
Lakeland, TN
901-372-4575

Econo Lodge Lebanon
829 South Cumberland Street
Lebanon, TN
615-444-1001

Quality Inn Lebanon
641 S Cumberland St
Lebanon, TN

615-444-7020

Ramada Inn And Suites Lebanon
704 S Cumberland St

Lebanon, TN

615-444-7400

Days Inn Lenoir City
1110 Highway 321 North
Lenoir City, TN
865-986-2011

Econo Lodge Lexington
732 West Church Street
Lexington, TN
731-968-0171

Rodeway Inn & Suites Manchester
2259 Hillsboro Boulevard
Manchester, TN
931-728-9530

Sleep Inn & Suites Manchester
84 Relco Drive
Manchester, TN

931-954-0580

Days Inn Martin
800 University Street
Martin, TN
731-587-9577

Best Western Mckenzie
16180 Highland Drive
Mc Kenzie, TN
731-352-1083

Best Western Tree City Inn
809 Sparta Street
Mc Minnville, TN
931-473-2159

Baymont Inn And Suites - Memphis
6020 Shelby Oaks Drive
Memphis, TN
901-377-2233

Candlewood Suites Memphis
7950 Centennial Drive
Memphis, TN

901-755-0877

Comfort Inn & Suites Memphis
1556 Sycamore View Road
Memphis, TN

901-373-8200

Country Hearth Inn And Suites
Memphis
3005 Millbranch Road
Memphis, TN

901-396-5411

Crosslands Memphis - Sycamore
View
5885 Shelby Oaks Drive
Memphis, TN

901-386-0026

Dog-Friendly Lodging - Please always call ahead to make sure an establishment is still dog-friendly.

Days Inn Memphis At Graceland
3839 Elvis Presley Blvd
Memphis, TN
901-346-5500

Extended Stay America - Memphis -
Airport
2541 Corporate Avenue East
Memphis, TN
901-344-0010

Extended Stay America - Memphis -
Apple Tree
6085 Apple Tree Drive
Memphis, TN
901-360-1114

Extended Stay America - Memphis -
Germantown
6500 Poplar Avenue
Memphis, TN
901-767-5522

Extended Stay America - Memphis -
Germantown West
6325 Quail Hollow
Memphis, TN
901-685-7575

Extended Stay America - Memphis -
Mt. Moriah
6520 Mt. Moriah Road
Memphis, TN
901-362-0338

Hilton Memphis
939 Ridge Lake Boulevard
Memphis, TN
901-684-6664

Homewood Suites By Hilton®
Memphis-Hacks Cross
3583 Hacks Cross Road
Memphis, TN
901-758-5018

Motel 6 Memphis
2889 Old Austin Peay Highway
Memphis, TN
901-386-0033

Motel 6 Memphis - Graceland
1581 East Brooks Road
Memphis, TN
901-345-3344

Quality Suites I-240 East-Airport
2575 Thousand Oaks Cove
Memphis, TN
901-365-2575

Red Roof Inn - Memphis East

6055 Shelby Oaks Drive
Memphis, TN
901-388-6111

Residence Inn By Marriott Memphis
Downtown
110 Monroe Avenue
Memphis, TN
901-578-3700

Residence Inn By Marriott Memphis
East
6141 Old Poplar Pike
Memphis, TN
901-685-9595

Rodeway Inn Memphis
1321 Sycamore View Road
Memphis, TN
901-726-4171

Sheraton Memphis Downtown Hotel
250 North Main Street
Memphis, TN
901-527-7300

Sleep Inn Memphis
2855 Old Austin Peay Highway
Memphis, TN
901-312-7777

Staybridge Suites Memphis-Poplar
Ave East
1070 Ridgelake Blvd
Memphis, TN
901-682-1722

Motel 6 Monteagle
742 Dixie Lee Avenue
Monteagle, TN
931-924-2900

Bethel Inn and Suites
522 East Stratton Avenue
Monterey, TN
931-584-0070

Days Inn Morristown
2512 East Andrew Johnson Highway
Morristown, TN
423-587-2200

Morristown Hotel and Suites
3304 West Andrew Johnson
Highway
Morristown, TN
423-581-8700

Super 8 Morristown
5400 South Davy Crockett Parkway
Morristown, TN
423-318-8888

Baymont Inn And Suites
Murfreesboro
2230 Armory Drive
Murfreesboro, TN
615-896-1172

Best Western Chaffin Inn
168 Chaffin Place
Murfreesboro, TN
615-895-3818

Candlewood Suites Murfreesboro
850 North Thompson Lane
Murfreesboro, TN
615-617-3075

Clarion Inn Murfreesboro
2227 Old Fort Parkway
Murfreesboro, TN
615-896-2420

Doubletree Hotel Murfreesboro
1850 Old Fort Parkway
Murfreesboro, TN
615-895-5555

Econo Lodge Inn & Suites
Murfreesboro
110 North Thompson Lane
Murfreesboro, TN
615-890-2811

Hampton Inn Murfreesboro
325 North Thompson Lane
Murfreesboro, TN
615-890-2424

Quality Inn Murfreesboro
2135 South Church Street
Murfreesboro, TN
615-890-1006

Ramada Murfreesboro
1855 South Church Street
Murfreesboro, TN
615-896-5080

Red Roof Inn Murfreesboro
2282 Armory Drive
Murfreesboro, TN
615-893-0104

Aloft Nashville West End
1719 West End Avenue
Nashville, TN
615-329-4200

Comfort Inn Downtown
1501 Demonbreun Street
Nashville, TN
615-255-9977

Days Inn Nashville At Opryland/Music Valley Dr
2460 Music Valley Drive
Nashville, TN
615-889-0090

Drury Inn & Suites Nashville Airport
555 Donelson Pike
Nashville, TN
615-902-0400

East Park Inn
822 Boscobel Street
Nashville, TN
615-226-8691

Embassy Suites Hotel Nashville-Airport
10 Century Blvd
Nashville, TN
615-871-0033

Extended Stay America - Nashville - Airport
2525 Elm Hill Pike
Nashville, TN
615-883-7667

Extended Stay America - Nashville - Airport - Music City
727 Mcgavock Pike
Nashville, TN
615-316-9020

Extended Stay America - Nashville - Vanderbilt
3311 West End Avenue
Nashville, TN
615-383-7490

Hilton Nashville Downtown
121 4th Avenue South
Nashville, TN
615-620-1000

Homewood Suites By Hilton Nashville-Downtown
706 Church Street
Nashville, TN
615-742-5550

Hotel Preston Nashville Airport, A Provenance Hotel
733 Briley Parkway
Nashville, TN
615-361-5900

Hutton Hotel
1808 West End Ave
Nashville, TN
615-340-9333

Kimpton Aertson Hotel
2021 Broadway
Nashville, TN
615-340-6376

Loews Vanderbilt Hotel
2100 West End Avenue
Nashville, TN
615-320-1700

Microtel Inn & Suites By Wyndham Nashville
100 Coley Davis Court
Nashville, TN
615-662-0004

Motel 6 Nashville
1412 Brick Church Pike
Nashville, TN
615-226-3230

Quality Inn Nashville
2401 Brick Church Pike
Nashville, TN
615-226-4600

Red Roof Inn Nashville - Music City
2407 Brick Church Pike
Nashville, TN
615-226-3300

Red Roof Inn Nashville Fairgrounds
4271 Sidco Drive
Nashville, TN
615-832-0093

Red Roof PLUS+ Nashville Airport
510 Claridge Drive
Nashville, TN
615-872-0735

Residence Inn Nashville Airport
2300 Elm Hill Pike
Nashville, TN
615-889-8600

Rodeway Inn Nashville
893 Murfreesboro Road
Nashville, TN
615-361-6830

Sheraton Grand Nashville Downtown
623 Union Street
Nashville, TN
615-259-2000

Sheraton Grand Nashville Downtown
623 Union Street
Nashville, TN

615-259-2000

Sheraton Music City Hotel
777 Mcgavock Pike
Nashville, TN
615-885-2200

Super 8 Nashville West
6924 Charlotte Pike
Nashville, TN
615-356-6005

Comfort Inn Newport Tn
1149 Smokey Mountain Lane
Newport, TN
423-623-5355

Staybridge Suites-Knoxville Oak Ridge
420 South Illinois Avenue
Oak Ridge, TN
865-298-0050

Best Western Heritage Inn
7641 Lee Highway
Ooltewah, TN
423-899-3311

Great Outdoor Rentals
Call to Arrange
Pigeon Forge, TN
865-712-5669

Hampton Inn & Suites Pigeon Forge On The Parkway
2025 Parkway
Pigeon Forge, TN
865-428-1600

La Quinta Inn & Suites Pigeon Forge
2510 Parkway
Pigeon Forge, TN
865-908-6633

National Parks Resort Lodge
2385 Parkway (US 441)
Pigeon Forge, TN
865-453-4106

Sunset Cottage Rentals and Realtly
3603 S River Road
Pigeon Forge, TN
865-429-8478

Super 8 Pigeon Forge-Emert St
215 Emert Street
Pigeon Forge, TN
865-428-2300

Terry Kay Cabin Rentals
Call to Arrange
Pigeon Forge, TN
865-908-2700

Fall Creek Falls Inn
2536 Lakeside Drive
Pikeville, TN
423-881-5298

Super 8 Powell
323 East Emory Road
Powell, TN
865-938-5501

Motel 6 Pulaski
2400 Us-64 East
Pulaski, TN
931-363-4501

Baymont Inn & Suites Sevierville
Pigeon Forge
711 Parkway
Sevierville, TN
865-428-1000

Quality Inn & Suites River Suites
860 Winfield Dunn Parkway
Sevierville, TN
865-428-5519

Sleep Inn Sevierville
1020 Parkway
Sevierville, TN
865-429-0484

Best Western Celebration Inn &
Suites
724 Madison Street
Shelbyville, TN
931-684-2378

Rodeway Inn & Suites Smyrna
1300 Plaza Drive
Smyrna, TN
615-355-6161

Days Inn Sweetwater
229 Highway 68
Sweetwater, TN
423-337-4200

Quality Inn West
249 Hwy 68 I-75 Exit 60
Sweetwater, TN
423-337-3353

Best Western Cades Cove Inn
7824 East Lamar Alexander Parkway
Townsend, TN
865-448-9000

Motel 6 White House
340 Hester Drive
White House, TN
615-672-8850

Econo Lodge White Pine
3670 Roy Messer Highway
White Pine, TN
865-674-2573

Super 8 Whites Creek/Nashville Nw
Area
7551 Old Hickory Boulevard
Whites Creek, TN
615-876-3971

Super 8 Whiteville
2040 Highway 64
Whiteville, TN
731-254-8884

Best Western Inn
1602 Dinah Shore Boulevard
Winchester, TN
931-967-9444

# Texas Listings

Quality Inn Abilene
1758 East Interstate 20
Abilene, TX
325-676-0203

Residence Inn By Marriott Abilene
1641 Musgraves Blvd
Abilene, TX
325-677-8700

Ridgemont Animal Clinic
3981 RIDGEMONT DR
Abilene, TX
325-692-8412

Super 8 Abilene South
4397 Sayles Boulevard
Abilene, TX
325-701-4779

Super 8 Motel Abilene
1525 East Stamford Road
Abilene, TX
325-673-5251

Motel 6 Dallas - Addison
4325 Beltline Road
Addison, TX

Super 8 By The Galleria / North
Dallas
4150 Beltway Drive
Addison, TX
972-233-2525

Texas Inn Alamo
714 North Alamo Road
Alamo, TX
956-787-9444

Days Inn Alice
555 North Johnson Street
Alice, TX
361-664-6616

Courtyard By Marriott Dallas Allen At
The John Q. Hammons Center
210 East Stacy Road
Allen, TX
214-383-1151

Holiday Inn Express And Suites
Alvarado
325 Village Park Drive
Alvarado, TX
817-783-7573

Big Texan Steak Ranch Motel
7701 E I 40
Amarillo, TX
800-657-7177

Days Inn Medical Center Amarillo
2102 South Coulter Drive
Amarillo, TX
806-359-9393

Drury Inn & Suites Amarillo
8540 West Interstate 40
Amarillo, TX
806-351-1111

Extended Stay America - Amarillo -
West
2100 Cinema Dr.
Amarillo, TX
806-351-0117

Holiday Inn Express Hotel & Suites
Amarillo South
6701 Hollywood Road
Amarillo, TX
806-352-1900

Motel 6 Amarillo
8601 Canyon Drive
Amarillo, TX
806-468-7100

Motel 6 Amarillo - Airport
4301 I-40 East
Amarillo, TX

Motel 6 West Amarillo
2032 Paramount Boulevard
Amarillo, TX

Red Roof Inn Amarillo West
6800 I-40 West
Amarillo, TX
806-358-7943

Residence Inn By Marriott Amarillo
6700 Interstate 40 West
Amarillo, TX
806-354-2978

Super 8 Amarillo
8701 I-40 East
Amarillo, TX

806-335-2836

Super 8 Amarillo Central
2909 I-40 East
Amarillo, TX

806-373-3888

Travelodge Amarillo West
2035 Paramount Blvd
Amarillo, TX

806-353-3541

BEST WESTERN Angleton Inn
1809 North Velasco Street
Angleton, TX
979-849-5822

Americas Best Value Inn Anthony/El Paso Area
100 Park North Drive
Anthony, TX
915-886-2888

Americas Best Inn - Arlington
1175 North Watson Road
Arlington, TX
817-652-3100

Candlewood Suites Arlington
2221 Brookhollow Plaza Dr
Arlington, TX

817-649-3336

Extended Stay America - Arlington
1221 North Watson Road
Arlington, TX

817-633-7588

Hawthorn Suites By Wyndham Arlington/Dfw South
2401 Brookhollow Plaza Drive
Arlington, TX

817-640-1188

Homewood Suites By HiltonÂ® Dallas/Arlington
2401 East Road To Six Flags
Arlington, TX

817-633-1594

Residence Inn Arlington
1050 Brookhollow Plaza Drive
Arlington, TX

817-649-7300

Residence Inn Dallas Arlington South
801 Highlander Blvd
Arlington, TX

817-465-2244

Studio 6 Arlington
1607 North Watson Road
Arlington, TX

817-640-4444

Super 8 Athens Tx
205 Us Hwy 175 West
Athens, TX
903-675-7511

BEST WESTERN PLUS Austin Airport Inn & Suites
1805 Airport Commerce Drive
Austin, TX
512-386-5455

BEST WESTERN PLUS Austin City Hotel
2200 S Interstate 35
Austin, TX

512-444-0561

Brava House
1108 Blanco Street
Austin, TX

512-478-5034

Candlewood Suites Austin Arboretum - Northwest
9701 Stonelake Boulevard
Austin, TX

512-338-1611

Candlewood Suites Austin South
4320 Ih 35 South
Austin, TX

512-444-8882

Days Inn Austin South
4220 South Ih-35
Austin, TX

512-441-9242

Extended Stay America - Austin - Arboretum - South
9100 Waterford Centre Blvd.
Austin, TX

512-837-6677

Extended Stay America - Austin - Arboretum-Capital Of Texas Hwy
10100 N. Capital Of Texas Hwy.
Austin, TX

512-231-1520

Extended Stay America - Austin - Downtown - Town Lake
507 South First Street
Austin, TX

512-476-1818

Extended Stay America - Austin - Northwest - Lakeline Mall
13858 N Us Hwy. 183
Austin, TX

512-258-3365

Extended Stay America - Austin - Round Rock - South
16950 N I-35
Austin, TX

512-255-1400

Extended Stay America - Austin - Southwest
5100 Us Hwy. 290 W
Austin, TX

512-892-4272

Extended Stay America Austin - Downtown - 6th St.
600 Gaudalupe Street
Austin, TX

512-457-9994

Hilton Austin
500 East Fourth Street
Austin, TX

512-482-8000

Hilton Austin Airport
9515 Hotel Drive
Austin, TX

512-385-6767

Lost Parrot Cabins
15116 Storm Drive
Austin, TX

512-266-8916

Motel 6 Austin Central - North
8010 I-35 North
Austin, TX

Motel 6 Austin Central - South/University of Texas
5330 North Interregional Highway
Austin, TX

Motel 6 Austin South - Airport
2707 Interregional Hwy South
Austin, TX

RENAISSANCE AUSTIN HOTEL, A Marriott Luxury & Lifestyle Hotel
9721 Arboretum Boulevard
Austin, TX

512-343-2626

Red Roof Inn Austin North
8210 North Interstate 35
Austin, TX

512-835-2200

Red Roof Plus Austin South
4701 South Interstate Highway 35
Austin, TX

512-448-0091

Dog-Friendly Lodging - Please always call ahead to make sure an establishment is still dog-friendly.

Residence Inn Austin Northwest
3713 Tudor Blvd
Austin, TX
512-502-8200

Residence Inn By Marriott Austin
North/Parmer Lane
12401 N Lamar Blvd
Austin, TX
512-977-0544

Rodeway Inn University/Downtown
Austin
2900 N. I-35
Austin, TX
512-477-6395

Staybridge Suites Austin Arboretum
10201 Stonelake Blvd
Austin, TX
512-349-0888

Staybridge Suites Austin Northwest
13087 Us Hwy 183 North
Austin, TX
512-336-7829

The Westin Austin At The Domain
11301 Domain Drive
Austin, TX
512-832-4197

Towneplace Suites By Marriott Austin
Nw
10024 Capital Of Texas Hwy
Austin, TX
512-231-9360

W Austin
200 Lavaca Street
Austin, TX
512-542-3600

Comfort Suites Bastrop
505 Agnes Street
Bastrop, TX
512-321-3377

Candlewood Suites Baytown
6126 Garth Road
Baytown, TX
281-421-2300

Motel 6 Baytown West - Garth Road
4911 Interstate 10 East
Baytown, TX

Days Inn Beaumont
2155 North 11th Street
Beaumont, TX
409-898-8150

Holiday Inn Hotel & Suites Beaumont-
Plaza (I-10 & Walden)

3950 I-10 South &; Walden Rd
Beaumont, TX
409-842-5995

Howard Johnson Beaumont
1610 I-10 South
Beaumont, TX
409-842-0037

Residence Inn By Marriott Beaumont
5380 Clearwater Court
Beaumont, TX
409-434-0600

Motel 6 Ft Worth - Bedford
2904 Crystal Springs
Bedford, TX

Holiday Inn Express Hotel & Suites
Beeville
2199 Hwy 59 East
Beeville, TX
361-358-7300

Motel 6 Fort Worth - Benbrook
8601 Benbrook Boulevard
Benbrook, TX

BEST WESTERN Borger Inn
206 South Cedar Street
Borger, TX
806-274-7050

BEST WESTERN Bowie Inn &
Suites
900 Us Highway 287 South
Bowie, TX
940-872-9595

BEST WESTERN Brady Inn
2200 South Bridge Street
Brady, TX
325-597-3997

Holiday Inn Express Hotel & Suites
Brady
2320 S Bridge St
Brady, TX
325-597-1800

BEST WESTERN Inn Of Brenham
1503 Highway 290 East
Brenham, TX
979-251-7791

Knights Inn Brenham
201 Highway 290 East
Brenham, TX
979-830-1110

BEST WESTERN Caprock Inn
321 Lubbock Road
Brownfield, TX
806-637-9471

Motel 6 Brownsville North

2377 North Expressway 83
Brownsville, TX

Motel 6 Brownsville North
2377 North Expressway 83
Brownsville, TX
956-504-2300

Residence Inn By Marriott Brownsville
3975 North Expressway 83
Brownsville, TX
956-350-8100

Staybridge Suites Brownsville
2900 Pablo Kisel Boulevard
Brownsville, TX
956-504-9500

BEST WESTERN PREMIER Old
Town Center
1920 Austins Colony Parkway
Bryan, TX
979-731-5300

Red River Inn Near Wichita Falls
1008 Sheppard Road
Burkburnett, TX
940-569-8109

Canyon of the Eagles
16942 Ranch Road
Burnett, TX
512-334-2070

BEST WESTERN Canton Inn
2251 N. Trade Days Blvd.
Canton, TX
903-567-6591

Days Inn Canton
17299 S. I-20
Canton, TX
903-567-6588

Motel 6 Canton
3001 North Trade Days Boulevard
Canton, TX

Candlewood Suites Austin N-Cedar
Park
1100 Cottonwood Creek Trail
Cedar Park, TX
512-986-4825

Holiday Inn Express Hotel & Suites
Center
143 Express Boulevard
Center, TX
936-591-8101

Texas Inn Channelview
16939 East Freeway
Channelview, TX
281-457-1640

Econo Lodge Childress
1804 Avenue F Northwest

Childress, TX
940-937-6363

Holiday Inn Express Hotel & Suites
Childress
3001 Avenue F Northwest
Childress, TX

940-937-0900

Red Roof Inn Childress
1801 Avenue F Northwest
Childress, TX

940-937-6353

BEST WESTERN PLUS Red River
Inn
902 West 2nd Street
Clarendon, TX
806-874-0160

Bar H Working Dude Ranch
12064 Bar H Ranch Road
Clarendon, TX

806-874-2634

Days Inn & Suites Cleburne Tx
2005 North Main Street
Cleburne, TX
817-645-8953

Holiday Inn Express Hotel & Suites
Cleburne
1800 West Henderson Street
Cleburne, TX

817-641-5300

Motel 6 Cleburne
1720 West Henderson Street
Cleburne, TX

Quality Inn & Suites Near Cleburne
Conference Center
2117 N. Main
Cleburne, TX

817-641-4702

Econo Lodge College Station
104 Texas Avenue South
College Station, TX
979-691-6300

Hilton College Station And
Conference Center
801 University Drive East
College Station, TX

979-693-7500

Towneplace Suites By Marriott Bryan
College Station
1300 University Drive East
College Station, TX

979-260-8500

River Oaks Resort
210 Encino Drive

Concan, TX
800-800-5773

Baymont Inn & Suites Conroe
1506 Interstate 45 South
Conroe, TX
936-539-5100

Motel 6 Conroe
820 Interstate 45 South
Conroe, TX

BEST WESTERN On The Island
14050 South Padre Island Drive
Corpus Christi, TX
361-949-2300

Bayfront Inn
601 North Shoreline Blvd.
Corpus Christi, TX

361-883-7271

Candlewood Suites Corpus Christi -
Spid
5014 Crosstown Expressway
Corpus Christi, TX

361-853-3413

Emerald Beach Hotel
1102 South Shoreline Boulevard
Corpus Christi, TX

361-883-5731

Homewood Suites By Hilton®
Corpus Christi
5201 Crosstown Expressway
Corpus Christi, TX

361-854-1331

Motel 6 Corpus Christi East - N.
Padre Island
8202 South Padre Island Drive
Corpus Christi, TX

Motel 6 Corpus Christi Northwest
845 Lantana Street
Corpus Christi, TX

Red Roof Inn & Suites Corpus
Christi
3030 Buffalo Street
Corpus Christi, TX

361-888-7683

Staybridge Suites Corpus Christi
5201 Oakhurst Dr
Corpus Christi, TX

361-857-7766

Surfside Condominiums
15005 Windward Drive
Corpus Christi, TX

361-949-8128

Days Inn And Suites Corsicana, Tx
2008 South Us Highway 287
Corsicana, TX
903-872-4645

Days Inn Dalhart
701 Liberal Street
Dalhart, TX
806-244-5246

Econo Lodge Dalhart
123 Liberal St.
Dalhart, TX

806-244-6464

Candlewood Suite Dallas Park
Central
12525 Greenville
Dallas, TX
972-669-9606

Candlewood Suites Dallas Market
Center
7930 North Stemmons
Dallas, TX

214-631-3333

Comfort Inn & Suites Market Center
7138 N. Stemmons Fwy
Dallas, TX

214-461-2677

Econo Lodge Airport I-35 North
2275 Valley View Lane
Dallas, TX

972-243-5500

Embassy Suites Hotel Dallas - Love
Field
3880 West Northwest Hwy
Dallas, TX

214-357-4500

Extended Stay America - Dallas - Coit
Road
12121 Coit Rd
Dallas, TX

972-663-1800

Extended Stay America - Dallas -
Frankford Road
18470 N. Dallas Pkwy
Dallas, TX

972-248-2233

Extended Stay America - Dallas -
Greenville Avenue
12270 Greenville Ave.
Dallas, TX

972-238-1133

Fairmont Dallas
1717 North Akard Street
Dallas, TX

214-720-2020

Hawthorn Suites By Wyndham Dallas
Park Central
7880 Alpha Road
Dallas, TX

972-391-0000

Holiday Inn Express Hotel & Suites
Dallas East
8703 East Rl Thornton Freeway
Dallas, TX

214-660-0006

Holiday Inn Market Center
4500 Harry Hines Blvd
Dallas, TX

214-219-3333

Hotel Indigo Dallas Downtown
1933 Main Street
Dallas, TX

214-741-7700

Hotel ZaZa Dallas
2332 Leonard Street
Dallas, TX

214-468-8399

Knights Inn Market Center
1550 Empire Central
Dallas, TX

214-638-5151

Le Meridien Dallas By The Galleria
13402 Noel Road
Dallas, TX

972-503-8700

Motel 6 Dallas - Galleria
2660 Forest Lane
Dallas, TX

Motel 6 Dallas - North
13185 North Central Express Way
Dallas, TX

Motel 6 Dallas Market Center
1625 Regal Row
Dallas, TX

Motel 6 Dallas Northwest
2380 West Northwest Highway
Dallas, TX

Residence Inn Dallas
Addison/Quorum Drive
14975 Quorum Drive
Dallas, TX

972-866-9933

Staybridge Suites Dallas-Addison
16060 Dallas Parkway

Dallas, TX
972-726-9990

The Highland Dallas, Curio
Collection By Hilton
5300 East Mockingbird Lane
Dallas, TX

214-520-7969

The Joule Dallas
1530 Main Street
Dallas, TX

214-748-1300

The Lumen, A Kimpton Hotel
6101 Hillcrest Avenue
Dallas, TX

214-219-2400

The Mansion On Turtle Creek, a
Rosewood Hotel
2821 Turtle Creek Dr
Dallas, TX

214-559-2100

Days Inn And Suites Desoto
1401 North I-35e
DeSoto, TX
972-224-7100

Americas Best Value Inn Decatur
1600 South Highway 287
Decatur, TX
940-627-0250

Candlewood Suites Decatur Medical
Center
601 W Thompson Rd
Decatur, TX

940-627-5480

Econo Lodge Decatur
1709 South Highway 287
Decatur, TX

940-627-6919

Holiday Inn Express Hotel & Suites
Decatur
1051 North Highway 81/287
Decatur, TX

940-627-0776

Ramada - Decatur Texas
1507 Hwy 287 South
Decatur, TX

940-627-6262

Candlewood Suites Deer Park Tx
1300 East Blvd
Deer Park, TX
281-478-0200

Motel 6 Del Rio

2115 Veterans Boulevard
Del Rio, TX

Ramada Del Rio
2101 Veterans Boulevard
Del Rio, TX

830-775-1511

Studio 6 Del Rio
3808 Veterans Boulevard
Del Rio, TX

830-775-0585

BEST WESTERN PLUS Texoma
Hotel & Suites
810 North Us Highway 75
Denison, TX
903-327-8883

Howard Johnson Inn Denton
3116 Bandera Street
Denton, TX
940-383-1681

Motel 6 Denton
700 Fort Worth Drive
Denton, TX

Motel 6 Denton
4125 Interstate 35 North
Denton, TX

Super 8 Denton
620 South I-35 East
Denton, TX

940-380-8888

Red Roof Inn Dumas
1525 South Dumas Avenue
Dumas, TX
806-935-4000

Motel 6 Eagle Pass Lakeside
2338 East Main Street
Eagle Pass, TX

Days Inn Eastland
2501 I-20 East
Eastland, TX
254-629-2655

Super 8 Eastland
3900 Interstate 20 East
Eastland, TX

254-629-3336

BEST WESTERN PLUS Edinburg
Inn And Suites
2708 S Business Hwy 281 (Closner
Blvd)
Edinburg, TX
956-318-0442

Comfort Inn Edinburg
4001 Closner
Edinburg, TX

956-318-1117

Knights Inn & Suites - City Center
Edinburg/Mcallen
202 North 25th Avenue
Edinburg, TX
956-381-1688

Motel 6 Edinburg
1806 South Closner Boulevard
Edinburg, TX

Texas Inn and Suites - Rio Grande
Valley
1210 East Canton Road
Edinburg, TX
956-381-8888

Americas Best Value Inn - Medical
Center/Airport
450 Raynolds
El Paso, TX
915-771-8388

Americas Best Value Inn And Suites
El Paso
500 Executive Center Boulevard
El Paso, TX

BEST WESTERN Sunland Park Inn
1045 Sunland Park Drive
El Paso, TX
915-587-4900

Chase Suite Hotel by Woodfin
6791 Montana Ave
El Paso, TX
915-772-8000

Country Inn & Suites By Carlson, El
Paso Sunland Park
900 Sunland Park Drive
El Paso, TX
915-833-2900

Days Inn El Paso West
5035 South Desert Boulevard
El Paso, TX
915-845-3500

Extended Stay America - El Paso -
Airport
6580 Montana Ave.
El Paso, TX
915-772-5754

Holiday Inn Express El Paso-Central
409 East Missouri Avenue
El Paso, TX
915-544-3333

Motel 6 El Paso East
1330 Lomaland Drive

El Paso, TX

Motel 6 El Paso West
7840 North Mesa
El Paso, TX

Motel 6 El Paso-Airport-Fort Bliss
6363 Montana Avenue
El Paso, TX

Quality Inn Airport East
900 Yarbrough Drive
El Paso, TX
915-594-9111

Ramada Suites El Paso Tx
8250 Gateway East Boulevard
El Paso, TX
915-591-9600

Red Roof Inn - El Paso West
7530 Remcon Circle
El Paso, TX
915-587-9977

Red Roof Inn El Paso East
11400 Chito Samaniego Drive
El Paso, TX
915-599-8877

Motel 6 Fort Worth Northlake
Speedway
13601 Raceway Drive
Elizabethtown, TX

Holiday Inn Express Hotel & Suites
Ennis
601 N. Sonoma Trails
Ennis, TX
972-872-2829

Motel 6 Ennis TX
100 South Interstate Highway 45
Ennis, TX
972-875-3390

Motel 6 Dallas - Euless
110 West Airport Freeway
Euless, TX

Motel 6 Euless - DFW West
1001 West Airport Freeway
Euless, TX
817-445-5000

Motel 6 Farmers Branch
13235 Stemmons Freeway
Farmers Branch, TX

BEST WESTERN Floresville Inn
1720 10th Street
Floresville, TX
830-393-0443

Super 8 Forney

103 West Highway 80
Forney, TX
972-552-3888

Hotel Limpia
P.O. Box 1341
Fort Davis, TX
800-662-5517

Candlewood Suites Fort Stockton
2469 W Ih-10
Fort Stockton, TX
432-336-7700

Motel 6 Fort Stockton
3001 West Dickinson Boulevard
Fort Stockton, TX

Quality Inn Fort Stockton
1308 North Us Hwy 285
Fort Stockton, TX
432-336-5955

Candlewood Suites Dallas, Fort
Worth/Fossil Creek
5201 Endicott Avenue
Fort Worth, TX
817-838-8229

Candlewood Suites Dfw South
4200 Reggis Drive
Fort Worth, TX
817-868-1900

Candlewood Suites Fort Worth/West
402 N Jim Wright Freeway
Fort Worth, TX
817-246-6800

Courtyard By Marriott Fort Worth
Downtown/Blackstone
601 Main Street
Fort Worth, TX
817-885-8700

Dallas/Fort Worth Marriott Hotel &
Golf Club At Champions Circle
3300 Championship Parkway
Fort Worth, TX
817-961-0800

Days Inn Fort Worth West
8500 West Freeway
Fort Worth, TX
817-246-4961

Days Inn South Fort Worth
4213 I-35 W South Freeway
Fort Worth, TX
817-923-1987

Extended Stay America - Fort Worth -
City View
5831 Overton Ridge Blvd.
Fort Worth, TX

817-263-9006

Extended Stay America - Fort Worth -
Medical Center
1601 River Run
Fort Worth, TX
817-338-4808

Motel 6 - Fort Worth - White
Settlement
7960 West Freeway
Fort Worth, TX

Motel 6 Fort Worth
3861 Tanacross Drive
Fort Worth, TX

Motel 6 Fort Worth - Downtown East
2425 Scott Avenue
Fort Worth, TX

817-535-2591

Motel 6 Fort Worth East
1236 Oakland Boulevard
Fort Worth, TX

Motel 6 Fort Worth North
3271 I-35 West
Fort Worth, TX

Motel 6 Fort Worth South
6600 South Freeway
Fort Worth, TX

Quality Inn & Suites
2700 S. Cherry Lane
Fort Worth, TX

817-560-4180

Residence Inn By Marriott Fort Worth
Cultural District
2500 Museum Way
Fort Worth, TX

817-885-8250

Residence Inn Fort Worth
Alliance/Airport
13400 North Freeway
Fort Worth, TX

817-750-7000

Residence Inn Fossil Creek
5801 Sandshell
Fort Worth, TX

817-439-1300

Sheraton Fort Worth Downtown Hotel
1701 Commerce Street
Fort Worth, TX

817-335-7000

Staybridge Suites West Fort Worth
229 Clifford Center Drive
Fort Worth, TX

817-935-6500

THE WORTHINGTON
RENAISSANCE FORT WORTH
HOTEL, A Marriott Luxury &
Lifestyle Hotel
200 Main Street
Fort Worth, TX

817-870-1000

Towneplace Suites By Marriott Fort
Worth Downtown
805 East Belknap
Fort Worth, TX

817-332-6300

Towneplace Suites Fort Worth
Southwest
4200 International Plaza Drive
Fort Worth, TX

817-732-2224

BEST WESTERN PLUS
Fredericksburg
314 East Highway Street
Fredericksburg, TX

830-992-2929

Econo Lodge Fredericksburg
810 S Adams St
Fredericksburg, TX

830-997-3437

Motel 6 Fredericksburg - Texas
705 South Washington Street
Fredericksburg, TX

Super 8 Fredericksburg
514 East Main Street
Fredericksburg, TX

830-997-6568

Embassy Suites Dallas
-Frisco/Hotel, Convention Center &
Spa
7600 John Q. Hammons Drive
Frisco, TX

972-712-7200

Avenue O
2323 Avenue O
Galveston, TX

409-762-2868

Candlewood Suites Galveston
808 61st Street
Galveston, TX

409-744-4440

Motel 6 Ganado
203 West York Street
Ganado, TX

Motel 6 Garland Northwest Highway
12721 Interstate 635

Garland, TX

Ramada Gatesville
111 North Highway 36
Gatesville, TX

254-865-1207

Candlewood Suites Georgetown
451 North Ih-35
Georgetown, TX

512-591-7888

Econo Lodge Georgetown
1005 Leander Rd.
Georgetown, TX

512-863-7504

Ramada Giddings
4002 E Austin St
Giddings, TX

979-542-9666

BEST WESTERN Dinosaur Valley
Inn & Suites
1311 North East Big Bend Trail
Glen Rose, TX

254-897-4818

Country Woods Inn
420 Grand Avenue
Glen Rose, TX

817-279-3002

Wildcatter Ranch and Resort
6062 Highway 16 South
Graham, TX

940-549-3555

Super 8 Grand Prairie North
402 East Palace Parkway
Grand Prairie, TX

972-263-4421

Embassy Suites Dallas - Dfw Airport
North At Outdoor World
2401 Bass Pro Drive
Grapevine, TX

972-724-2600

Residence Inn Dfw Airport
North/Grapevine
2020 State Highway 26
Grapevine, TX

972-539-8989

Super 8 Grapevine/Dfw Airport
Northwest
250 E. Highway 114
Grapevine, TX

817-329-7222

Express Inn & Suites
1215 East Interstate 30
Greenville, TX

903-454-7000

Knights Inn Greenville

5000 Interstate 30
Greenville, TX

903-455-9600

Motel 6 Greenville
5109 Interstate 30
Greenville, TX

Super 8 Greenville
5010 Highway 69 South
Greenville, TX

903-454-3736

Country Inn And Suites By Carlson
Harlingen
3825 South Expressway 83
Harlingen, TX
956-428-0043

Motel 6 Harlingen
205 North Expressway 77
Harlingen, TX

Super 8 Motel Harlingen
1115 South Expressway 77/83
Harlingen, TX

956-412-8873

Inn of Henderson
1500 Us Highway 259 South
Henderson, TX
903-657-9561

BEST WESTERN Red Carpet Inn
830 W. 1st Street
Hereford, TX
806-364-0540

Holiday Inn Express Hereford
1400 West First Street
Hereford, TX

806-364-3322

Super 8 Hillsboro, Tx
1512 Hillview Drive
Hillsboro, TX
254-580-0404

BEST WESTERN Inn Hondo
301 Us Highway 90 E
Hondo, TX
830-426-4466

Candlewood Suites Beltway
8/Westheimer
11280 Westheimer Road
Houston, TX
713-244-0400

Candlewood Suites Houston By The
Galleria
4900 Loop Central Drive
Houston, TX

713-839-9411

Candlewood Suites Houston I-10

East
1020 Maxey Road
Houston, TX

713-453-3337

Candlewood Suites Houston Iah /
Beltway 8
1500 North Sam Houston Parkway
East
Houston, TX

281-987-3900

Candlewood Suites Houston
Medical Center
10025 South Main Street
Houston, TX

713-665-3300

Candlewood Suites Houston Nw -
Willowbrook
8719 Fm 1960 West
Houston, TX

832-237-7300

Candlewood Suites Houston-
Westchase
4033 W Sam Houston Pkwy South
Houston, TX

713-780-7881

Doubletree Houston Downtown
400 Dallas Street
Houston, TX

713-759-0202

Drury Inn & Suites Houston Galleria
1615 West Loop South
Houston, TX

713-963-0700

Drury Inn & Suites Houston Hobby
Airport
7902 Mosley Road
Houston, TX

713-941-4300

Drury Inn & Suites Houston
West/Energy Corridor
1000 North Highway 6
Houston, TX

281-558-7007

Extended Stay America - Houston -
Katy Frwy - Beltway 8
11175 Katy Freeway
Houston, TX

713-461-6696

Extended Stay America - Houston -
Med Ctr-NRG Park-Fannin St
7979 Fannin Street
Houston, TX

713-797-0000

Extended Stay America - Houston -
Med. Ctr. - Greenway Plaza
2330 Southwest Freeway
Houston, TX

713-521-0060

Extended Stay America Houston -
Galleria - Uptown
2300 West Loop South
Houston, TX

713-960-9660

Extended Stay America Houston -
Galleria - Westheimer
4701 Westheimer Road
Houston, TX

713-355-8500

Extended Stay America Houston -
Nasa - Johnson Space Center
1410 Nasa Rd. 1
Houston, TX

281-333-9494

Extended Stay America Houston -
Westchase - Richmond
3200 West Sam Houston Parkway
Houston, TX

713-952-4644

Extended Stay America Houston -
Willowbrook
13223 Champions Centre Drive
Houston, TX

281-397-9922

Extended Stay America Houston -
Willowbrook - Hwy 249
16939 Tomball Parkway
Houston, TX

281-970-2403

Four Points By Sheraton Houston -
Citycentre
10655 Katy Freeway
Houston, TX

281-501-4600

Frontier Hotel
11230 South West Fwy
Houston, TX

281-498-9000

Hilton Houston Nasa Clear Lake
3000 Nasa Road One
Houston, TX

281-333-9300

Hilton Houston North
12400 Greenspoint Drive

Houston, TX

281-875-2222

Hilton Houston Post Oak
2001 Post Oak Boulevard
Houston, TX

713-961-9300

Hilton Houston Westchase
9999 Westheimer Road
Houston, TX

713-974-1000

Homewood Houston Northwest
13110 Wortham Center Drive
Houston, TX

832-237-2000

Homewood Suites Houston Near The
Galleria
2950 Sage Road
Houston, TX

713-439-1305

Hotel Indigo Houston At The Galleria
5160 Hidalgo Street
Houston, TX

713-621-8988

Hotel Zaza Houston
5701 Main Street
Houston, TX

713-526-1991

Motel 6 Houston Hobby
9005 Airport Boulevard
Houston, TX

Motel 6 Houston Hobby
9005 Airport Boulevard
Houston, TX

713-943-3300

Motel 6 Houston Westchase
2900 West Sam Houston Parkway
South
Houston, TX

Quality Inn & Suites Reliant
Park/Medical Center
2364 South Loop West
Houston, TX

713-799-2436

Quality Inn & Suites West - Energy
Corridor
715 Highway 6 South
Houston, TX

281-493-0444

Red Roof Inn - Houston Westchase
2960 W Sam Houston Pkwy South

Houston, TX

713-785-9909

Red Roof Inn Houston Brookhollow
12929 Northwest Freeway
Houston, TX

713-939-0800

Red Roof Plus+ Houston - Energy
Corridor
15701 Park Ten Place
Houston, TX

281-579-7200

Residence Inn By Marriott Houston
Clear Lake
525 Bay Area Blvd
Houston, TX

281-486-2424

Residence Inn By Marriott Houston
Westchase On Westheimer
9965 Westheimer At Elmside
Houston, TX

713-974-5454

Residence Inn Houston
Intercontinental Airport At
Greenspoint
655 North Sam Houston Parkway
East
Houston, TX

281-820-4563

Residence Inn Houston
Northwest/Willowbrook
7311 W. Greens Road
Houston, TX

832-237-2002

Residence Inn Houston West -
Energy Corridor
1150 Eldridge Parkway
Houston, TX

281-293-8787

Robin's Nest Bed And Breakfast
4104 Greeley Street
Houston, TX

713-528-5821

Sheraton Suites Houston Near The
Galleria
2400 West Loop South
Houston, TX

713-586-2444

Sonesta Es Suites Houston Galleria
5190 Hidalgo Street
Houston, TX

713-355-8888

Staybridge Suites Houston
West/Energy Corridor
1225 Eldridge Parkway
Houston, TX

281-759-7829

The St. Regis Houston
1919 Briar Oaks Street
Houston, TX

713-840-7600

Towneplace Suites By Marriott
Houston Central/Northwest Freeway
12820 Nw Freeway
Houston, TX

713-690-4035

Towneplace Suites By Marriott
Houston Intercontinental Airport
4015 Interwood North Parkway
Houston, TX

281-227-2464

Towneplace Suites By Marriott
Houston West
15155 Katy Freeway
Houston, TX

281-646-0058

BEST WESTERN PLUS Atascocita
Inn & Suites
7730 Fm 1960 Road East
Humble, TX
281-852-5665

Motel 6 Humble
20145 Eastway Village Drive
Humble, TX

BEST WESTERN Huntsville Inn &
Suites
201 W Hill Park Circle
Huntsville, TX
936-295-9000

Motel 6 Hutchins
110 Interstate 45 South
Hutchins, TX

Holiday Inn Express Hotel & Suites
Hutto
323 Ed Schmidt Blvd
Hutto, TX
512-846-1168

BEST WESTERN Naval Station Inn
2025 State Highway 361
Ingleside, TX
361-776-2767

Candlewood Suites Dallas - Las
Colinas
5300 Green Park Drive
Irving, TX
972-714-9990

Days Inn Irving Grapevine Dfw Airport North
4325 West John Carpenter Fwy
Irving, TX

972-621-8277

Extended Stay America - Dallas - Dfw Airport N.
7825 Heathrow Dr
Irving, TX

972-929-3333

Extended Stay America - Dallas - Las Colinas - Carnaby Street
5315 Carnaby St.
Irving, TX

972-756-0458

Motel 6 Dallas - DFW Airport South
2531 West Airport Freeway
Irving, TX

Motel 6 Dallas - Irving
510 South Loop 12
Irving, TX

Motel 6 Irving - Dallas Fort Worth International Airport North
7800 Heathrow Drive
Irving, TX

NYLO Dallas Las Colinas Hotel
1001 W Royal Lane
Irving, TX

972-373-8900

Red Roof Inn - Dallas Dfw North Airport
8150 Esters Boulevard
Irving, TX

972-929-0020

Residence Inn By Marriott Dallas Dfw Airport North/Irving
8600 Esters Blvd
Irving, TX

972-871-1331

Residence Inn Las Colinas
950 Walnut Hill Lane
Irving, TX

972-580-7773

Sheraton Dfw Airport Hotel
4440 W. John Carpenter Freeway
Irving, TX

972-929-8400

Staybridge Suites Dallas Las Colinas
1201 Executive Circle
Irving, TX

972-465-9400

Staybridge Suites Dfw Airport North
2220 Market Place Boulevard
Irving, TX

972-401-4700

Towneplace Suites By Marriott Las Colinas
900 West Walnut Hill Lane
Irving, TX

972-550-8807

BEST WESTERN Johnson City Inn
107 Highway 281 And 290
Johnson City, TX
830-868-4044

The Exotic Resort Zoo
235 Zoo Trail
Johnson City, TX

830-868-4357

Motel 6 Katy
22105 Katy Freeway
Katy, TX

BEST WESTERN La Hacienda Inn
200 East Highway 175
Kaufman, TX
972-962-6272

BEST WESTERN Sunday House Inn
2124 Sidney Baker Street
Kerrville, TX
830-896-1313

Days Inn Kerrville
2000 Sidney Baker Street
Kerrville, TX

830-896-1000

Motel 6 Kerrville
1810 Sidney Baker Street
Kerrville, TX

BEST WESTERN Inn Of Kilgore
1411 Us Highway 259 N
Kilgore, TX
903-986-1195

Days Inn Kilgore
4312 State Highway 42 N
Kilgore, TX

903-983-2975

Manor Inn Kilgore
3501 Highway 259 North
Kilgore, TX

903-983-3456

Motel 6 Killeen
800 East Central Texas Expressway
Killeen, TX

BEST WESTERN Kingsville Inn

2402 East King Avenue
Kingsville, TX
361-595-5656

Candlewood Suites Houston - Kingwood
291 Kingwood Medical Drive
Kingwood, TX
281-713-8989

Texas Inn La Feria
1202 North Main Street
La Feria, TX
956-797-0200

Candlewood Suites Lake Jackson Clute
506 E. Hwy 332
Lake Jackson, TX
979-297-0011

Motel 6 Dallas DeSoto Lancaster
1750 North Interstate 35 East
Lancaster, TX

Days Inn & Suites - Laredo Tx
7060 San Bernardo
Laredo, TX
956-724-8221

Extended Stay America - Laredo - Del Mar
106 W. Village Blvd
Laredo, TX

956-724-1920

Family Garden Inn
5830 San Bernardo
Laredo, TX

956-723-5300

Motel 6 Laredo Airport
7124 Rosson Lane
Laredo, TX

Motel 6 Laredo North
5920 San Bernardo Avenue
Laredo, TX

Motel 6 Laredo South
5310 San Bernardo Avenue
Laredo, TX

Red Roof Inn - Laredo
1006 West Calton Road
Laredo, TX

956-712-0733

Red Roof Inn Laredo - I-83 South
2010 Lomas Del Sur
Laredo, TX

956-724-7300

Residence Inn Laredo Del Mar
310 Lost Oaks Road
Laredo, TX

956-753-9700

Staybridge Suites Laredo
7010 Bob Bullock Loop
Laredo, TX
956-722-0444

Candlewood Suites League City
2350 Gulf Freeway South
League City, TX
281-534-9848

Holiday Inn Express Hotel & Suites
Levelland
703 E State Road 114
Levelland, TX
806-894-8555

Country Inn and Suites Lewisville
755 B East Vista Ridge Mall Drive
Lewisville, TX
972-315-6565

Extended Stay America Dallas -
Lewisville
1900 Lake Pointe Drive
Lewisville, TX

972-315-7455

Homewood Suites By Hilton®
Dallas/Lewisville
700 Hebron Parkway
Lewisville, TX

972-315-6123

Motel 6 Dallas - Lewisville
1705 Lakepointe Drive
Lewisville, TX

Towneplace Suites By Marriott Dallas
Lewisville
731 East Vista Ridge Mall Drive
Lewisville, TX

972-459-1275

Motel 6 Livingston Texas
117 Highway 59 Loop South
Livingston, TX
936-327-2451

BEST WESTERN Llano
901 West Young Street
Llano, TX
915-247-4101

Baymont Inn And Suites Longview
502 South Access Road
Longview, TX
903-757-3663

Candlewood Suites Longview
2904 Tuttle Blvd
Longview, TX

903-663-9751

Motel 6 Longview
110 South Access Road
Longview, TX

Motel 6 Longview North
419 North Spur 63
Longview, TX

Motel 6 Longview North
419 North Spur 63
Longview, TX

Hyatt Regency Lost Pines Resort
and Spa
575 Hyatt Lost Pines Road
Lost Pines, TX
512-308-1234

4115 Marsha Sharp Loop
4115 Marsha Sharp Fwy.
Lubbock, TX

BEST WESTERN PLUS Lubbock
Windsor Inn
5410 Interstate 27
Lubbock, TX

806-762-8400

Days Inn Lubbock Texas Tech
University
2401 Marsha Sharp Freeway
Lubbock, TX

806-747-7111

Extended Stay America - Lubbock -
Southwest
4802 S Loop 289
Lubbock, TX

806-785-9881

Motel 6 Lubbock
909 66th Street
Lubbock, TX

Red Roof Inn And Conference
Center Lubbock
6624 Interstate 27
Lubbock, TX

806-745-2208

Staybridge Suites Lubbock
2515 19th Street
Lubbock, TX

806-765-8900

Super 8 Motel - Lubbock/Civic
Ctr/North
501 Avenue Q
Lubbock, TX

806-762-8726

BEST WESTERN PLUS Crown
Colony Inn And Suites
3211 South 1st Street
Lufkin, TX

936-634-3481

Quality Inn & Suites Lufkin
4306 S. 1st St.
Lufkin, TX

936-639-3333

Days Inn San Antonio Lytle
19525 Mcdonald Street
Lytle, TX
830-772-4777

Texas Inn Downtown McAllen
1420 E Jackson Ave
MCALLEN, TX
956-682-1190

Americas Best Value Inn And Suites
11301 Highway 290 East
Manor, TX
512-272-9373

BEST WESTERN PLUS Manvel Inn
& Suites
19301 Highway 6
Manvel, TX
281-489-2266

Motel 6 Marble Falls
1400 Ollie Lane
Marble Falls, TX

Chinati Hot Springs
1 Hot Springs Road
Marfa, TX
432-229-4165

BEST WESTERN Executive Inn
5201 East End Boulevard South
Marshall, TX
903-935-0707

Days Inn And Suites Marshall
5555 East End Boulevard South
Marshall, TX

903-935-1941

Motel 6 - McAllen
700 West Expressway 83
McAllen, TX

Residence Inn Mcallen
220 West Expressway 83
McAllen, TX

956-994-8626

Studio 6 Mcallen
700 Savannah Avenue
McAllen, TX

Super 8 - Mcallen/Downtown
1505 South 9th Street
McAllen, TX

956-686-4401

Texas Inn & Suites McAllen
6420 South 23rd Street

Dog-Friendly Lodging - Please always call ahead to make sure an establishment is still dog-friendly.

McAllen, TX
956-688-6666

Days Inn Mckinney
2104 North Central Expressway
McKinney, TX
972-548-8888

Drury Inn Mcallen
612 West Expressway 83
Mcallen, TX
956-687-5100

Drury Suites Mcallen
300 West Expressway 83
Mcallen, TX
956-682-4900

Drury Suites Mcallen
300 West Expressway 83
Mcallen, TX
956-682-3222

Staybridge Suites Mcallen
620 Wichita Avenue
Mcallen, TX
956-213-7829

BEST WESTERN Clubhouse Inn &
Suites
4410 Hwy 180 East
Mineral Wells, TX
940-325-2270

Motel 6 Mission
1813 East Expressway 83
Mission, TX

BEST WESTERN Lake Conroe Inn
14643 Highway 105 W
Montgomery, TX
936-588-3030

Candlewood Suites Mount Pleasant
2407 S Jefferson Avenue &; Hwy Us
271
Mount Pleasant, TX
903-572-4600

Quality Inn Mt. Pleasant
2515 W. Ferguson Rd.
Mount Pleasant, TX
903-577-7553

Super 8 Mount Vernon
401 West Interstate 30
Mount Vernon, TX
903-588-2882

Super 8 Nacogdoches
3909 South Street
Nacogdoches, TX
936-560-2888

Comfort Inn & Suites Navasota
9345 State Highway 6

Navasota, TX
936-825-9464

Candlewood Suites Nederland
2125 Highway 69
Nederland, TX
409-729-9543

Motel 6 New Braunfels
1275 North I-35
New Braunfels, TX

Red Roof Inn New Braunfels
815 I-35 South
New Braunfels, TX

830-626-7000

Super 8 New Braunfels
510 Highway 46 South
New Braunfels, TX
830-629-1155

Motel 6 North Richland Hills
5151 Thaxton Parkway
North Richland Hills, TX

Travelodge North Richland
Hills/Dallas/Fort Worth
7920 Bedford Euless Road
North Richland Hills, TX
817-485-2750

Comfort Suites Odessa
4801 East 50th Street
Odessa, TX
432-362-1500

Motel 6 Odessa
200 East I-20 Service Road
Odessa, TX

Super 8 Ozona
3331 I 10 East
Ozona, TX
325-392-2611

Travelodge Ozona
8 11th Street
Ozona, TX

325-392-2656

BEST WESTERN Palestine Inn
1601 West Palestine Avenue
Palestine, TX
903-723-4655

Motel 6 Pasadena
3010 Pasadena Freeway
Pasadena, TX

BEST WESTERN Pearland Inn
1855 N Main Street (Hwy 35)
Pearland, TX
281-997-2000

Candlewood Suites Pearland
9015 Broadway

Pearland, TX
281-412-7400

Knights Inn Laura Lodge Pecos Tx
1000 East 3rd Street
Pecos, TX
432-445-4924

BEST WESTERN Perryton Inn
3505 South Main Street (Highway 83)
Perryton, TX
806-434-2850

Comfort Inn & Suites Pharr
2706 North Cage Boulevard
Pharr, TX
956-783-7777

Motel 6 Pharr
4701 North Cage Boulevard
Pharr, TX

Red Roof Inn Pharr
4401 North Cage Boulevard
Pharr, TX
956-782-8880

Candlewood Suites Dallas - Plano -
East Richardson
2401 East George Bush Turnpike
Plano, TX
214-474-2770

Candlewood Suites Dallas-Plano
4701 Legacy Drive
Plano, TX
972-618-5446

Extended Stay America - Dallas -
Plano Parkway
4709 W. Plano Pkwy
Plano, TX
972-596-9966

Motel 6 Dallas - Plano Northeast
2550 North Central Expressway
Plano, TX

Motel 6 Dallas Plano Southeast
1820 North Central Expressway
Plano, TX

Motel 6 Plano - Preston Point
4801 W Plano Parkway
Plano, TX

Plano Inn & Suites
301 Ruisseau Drive
Plano, TX
972-881-8191

Residence Inn Plano
5001 Whitestone Lane
Plano, TX
972-473-6761

Towneplace Suites By Marriott Dallas Plano
5005 Whitestone Lane
Plano, TX

972-943-8200

Baymont Inn And Suites Port Arthur
3801 Highway 73
Port Arthur, TX

Studio 6 Port Arthur
3000 Jimmy Johnson Boulevard Us 69/287 At Jimmy Johnson Boulevard
Port Arthur, TX

Americas Best Value Inn Port Lavaca
2100 Highway 35
Port Lavaca, TX
361-552-4511

BEST WESTERN Port Lavaca Inn
2202 State Highway 35 North
Port Lavaca, TX

361-553-6800

Palace Inn Porter
24085 Us Highway 59 North
Porter, TX
281-354-7227

Motel 6 Red Oak
202 South Interstate 35 Service Road
Red Oak, TX

Extended Stay America - Dallas - Richardson
901 E. Campbell
Richardson, TX
972-479-0500

RENAISSANCE DALLAS RICHARDSON, A Marriott Luxury & Lifestyle Hotel
900 E Lookout Drive
Richardson, TX

972-367-2000

Red Roof Inn Dallas/Richardson
13685 North Central Expressway
Richardson, TX

972-234-1016

Residence Inn Dallas Richardson
1040 Waterwood Drive
Richardson, TX

972-669-5888

Denton Creek Inn
13471 Raceway Drive
Roanoke, TX
817-491-3120

BEST WESTERN PLUS Rockwall Inn & Suites
996 East Interstate 30

Rockwall, TX
972-722-3265

Motel 6 Rosenberg
27927 Southwest Freeway
Rosenberg, TX

BEST WESTERN Executive Inn
1851 North I-35
Round Rock, TX
512-255-3222

Extended Stay America - Austin - Round Rock - North
555 S I-35
Round Rock, TX

512-671-7872

Red Roof Inn Austin Round Rock
1990 North Interstate 35
Round Rock, TX

512-310-1111

Residence Inn By Marriott Austin Round Rock
2505 South Ih 35
Round Rock, TX

512-733-2400

Staybridge Suites Round Rock
520 I 35 South Round Rock
Round Rock, TX

512-733-0942

Motel 6 San Angelo
311 North Bryant Boulevard
San Angelo, TX

Motel 6 San Angelo South
4205 South Bryant Boulevard
San Angelo, TX

Ramada Limited San Angelo
2201 North Bryant Boulevard
San Angelo, TX

325-653-8442

Staybridge Suites San Angelo
1355 Knickerbocker Road
San Angelo, TX

325-653-1500

Candlewood Suites Nw Medical Center
9350 Ih 10 West
San Antonio, TX
210-615-0550

Candlewood Suites San Antonio Downtown
1024 South Laredo Street
San Antonio, TX

210-226-7700

Candlewood Suites San Antonio Nw Near Seaworld
9502 Amelia Pass
San Antonio, TX

210-523-7666

Drury Inn & Suites San Antonio Near La Cantera
15806 Interstate 10 West
San Antonio, TX

210-696-0800

Drury Inn & Suites San Antonio North Stone Oak
801 North Loop 1604 East
San Antonio, TX

210-404-1600

Drury Plaza Hotel San Antonio Riverwalk
105 South St Mary`s Street
San Antonio, TX

210-270-7799

Econo Lodge Downtown South
606 Division Avenue
San Antonio, TX

210-927-4800

Econo Lodge Inn & Suites Downtown Northeast
2755 North Panam Expressway
San Antonio, TX

Extended Stay America - San Antonio - Airport
1015 Central Parkway South
San Antonio, TX

210-491-9009

Holiday Inn San Antonio International Airport
77 Northeast Loop 410
San Antonio, TX

210-349-9900

Hotel Indigo San Antonio At The Alamo
105 N. Alamo
San Antonio, TX

210-933-2000

Hotel Indigo San Antonio-Riverwalk
830 N. St. Marys Street
San Antonio, TX

210-527-1900

Knights Inn San Antonio Near At&T Center
4039 East Houston Street
San Antonio, TX

210-333-9100

Motel 6 - South W.W. White Road
218 South W.W. White Road
San Antonio, TX

210-333-3346

Motel 6 San Antonio - Fiesta
16500 I-10 West
San Antonio, TX

Motel 6 San Antonio - Fiesta Trails
9447 Interstate Highway 10 West
San Antonio, TX

Motel 6 San Antonio Downtown -
Market Square
211 North Pecos La Trinidad
San Antonio, TX

Motel 6 San Antonio Downtown -
Riverwalk
900 North Main Ave
San Antonio, TX

210-223-2951

Motel 6 San Antonio East
138 North WW White Road
San Antonio, TX

Motel 6 San Antonio I-10 West
6015 Ih-10 West
San Antonio, TX

210-737-1855

Motel 6 San Antonio Medical Center
South
7500 Louis Pasteur Drive
San Antonio, TX

Motel 6 San Antonio West - Seaworld
2185 Southwest Loop 410
San Antonio, TX

Red Roof Inn & Suites San Antonio -
Fiesta Park
13279 I H 10 West
San Antonio, TX

Red Roof Inn San Antonio - Ft. Sam
Houston
4403 I-10 East
San Antonio, TX

210-333-9430

Red Roof Inn San Antonio - Lackland
Southwest
6861 Highway 90 West
San Antonio, TX

210-675-4120

Red Roof Inn San Antonio Seaworld /
Nw
6880 Northwest Loop 410
San Antonio, TX

210-509-3434

Red Roof Plus San Antonio
Downtown
1011 East Houston Street
San Antonio, TX

210-229-9973

Residence Inn By Marriott San
Antonio Downtown/Alamo Plaza
425 Bonham
San Antonio, TX

210-212-5555

Residence Inn By Marriott San
Antonio North-Stone Oak
1115 North 1604 East
San Antonio, TX

210-490-1333

Residence Inn San Antonio
Seaworld/Lackland
2838 Cinema Ridge
San Antonio, TX

210-509-3100

Residence Inn San Antonio Six
Flags At The Rim
5707 Rim Pass Drive
San Antonio, TX

210-561-0200

Residence Inn by Marriott San
Antonio Airport/Alamo Heights
1014 Ne Loop 410
San Antonio, TX

210-805-8118

Staybridge Suites Nw Near Six
Flags Fiesta
6919 North Loop 1604 West
San Antonio, TX

210-691-3443

Staybridge Suites San Antonio -
Stone Oak
808 North Loop 1604 East
San Antonio, TX

210-497-0100

Staybridge Suites San Antonio Nw
Medical Center
4320 Spectrum One
San Antonio, TX

210-558-9009

Staybridge Suites San Antonio,
Downtown Convention Center
123 Hoefgen
San Antonio, TX

210-444-2700

Staybridge Suites San Antonio-
Airport
66 North East Loop 410

San Antonio, TX

210-341-3220

Super 8 San Antonio/Riverwalk Area
302 Roland Avenue
San Antonio, TX

210-798-5500

The Inn at Market Square Downtown
1500 Interstate 35 South Laredo
Street
San Antonio, TX

210-271-3334

Towneplace Suites By Marriott San
Antonio Downtown
409 East Houston Street
San Antonio, TX

210-271-3444

Towneplace Suites By Marriott San
Antonio Northwest
5014 Prue Road
San Antonio, TX

210-694-5100

Travelodge San Antonio At&T Center
/ I-10 East
3939 E. Houston St.
San Antonio, TX

210-359-1111

Travelodge San Antonio Downtown
1122 S Laredo St
San Antonio, TX

210-229-1133

San Juan Inn
112 West Expressway 83
San Juan, TX
956-782-1510

Crystal River Inn
326 West Hopkins Street
San Marcos, TX
512-396-3739

Motel 6 San Marcos
1321 North I-35
San Marcos, TX

Red Roof Inn San Marcos
817 Interstate Highway 35 North
San Marcos, TX

512-754-8899

BEST WESTERN PLUS
Schulenburg Inn & Suites
101 Huser Boulevard
Schulenburg, TX
979-743-2030

BEST WESTERN PLUS Seabrook
Suites

5755 Bayport Boulevard
Seabrook, TX
281-291-9090

BEST WESTERN PLUS Shamrock
Inn & Suites
1802 North Main Street
Shamrock, TX
806-256-1001

Econo Lodge Shamrock
1006 E. 12th St.
Shamrock, TX

806-256-2111

Towneplace Suites By Marriott
Houston The Woodlands
107 Vision Park Blvd
Shenandoah, TX
936-273-7772

Super 8 Sherman
111 East Fm 1417
Sherman, TX
903-868-9325

Knights Inn Slaton
902 N Highway 84
Slaton, TX
806-828-5831

Katy House
201 Ramona Street
Smithville, TX
512-237-4262

DCH Condo Rentals
111 E Hybiscus
South Padre Island, TX
956-459-7499

Motel 6 South Padre Island
4013 Padre Boulevard
South Padre Island, TX

The Inn at South Padre
1709 Padre Boulevard
South Padre Island, TX

956-761-5658

Wanna Wanna Inn
5100 Gulf Blvd.
South Padre Island, TX

956-761-7677

Hilton Dallas/Southlake Town Square
1400 Plaza Place
Southlake, TX
817-442-9900

Drury Inn & Suites The Woodlands
28099 I-45 North
Spring, TX
281-362-7222

Extended Stay America Houston -
The Woodlands

150 Valley Wood Rd.
Spring, TX

281-296-2799

Motel 6 Houston North-Spring
19606 Cypresswood Court
Spring, TX

Extended Stay America Houston -
Stafford
4726 Sugar Grove Boulevard
Stafford, TX
281-240-0025

Staybridge Suites Houston Stafford -
Sugar Land
11101 Fountain Lake Drive
Stafford, TX

281-302-6535

Motel 6 Stephenville
701 East South Loop
Stephenville, TX
254-968-3392

Motel 6 Stephenville
701 East South Loop
Stephenville, TX

Super 8 Stephenville
921 S Second Street
Stephenville, TX

254-965-0888

Easter Egg Valley Motel
H 170 1/2 mile W of H 118
Study Butte, TX
432-371-2254

Drury Inn & Suites Houston Sugar
Land
13770 Southwest Freeway
Sugar Land, TX
281-277-9700

Motel 6 Sulphur Springs
1529 East Industrial Drive
Sulphur Springs, TX

BEST WESTERN PLUS
Sweetwater Inn & Suites
300 Nw Georgia Ave
Sweetwater, TX
325-236-6512

Motel 6 Temple South
1100 North General Bruce Drive
Temple, TX

Motel 6 Temple-North
1610 West Nugent Avenue
Temple, TX

Days Inn Terrell
1618 Highway 34 South
Terrell, TX
972-551-1170

Motel 6 Terrell
101 Mira Place
Terrell, TX

Super 8 Terrell
1705 Highway 34 South
Terrell, TX

972-563-1511

Candlewood Suites Texarkana
2901 South Cowhorn Creek Loop
Texarkana, TX
903-334-7418

Rodeway Inn Texarkana
5105 North Stateline Avenue
Texarkana, TX

903-792-6688

Candlewood Suites Texas City
1700 Hwy 146 North
Texas City, TX
409-945-6500

Motel 6 Texas City
1121 Highway 146 North
Texas City, TX

Candlewood Suites Houston (The
Woodlands)
17525 Saint Lukes Way
The Woodlands, TX
936-271-2100

Homewood Suites By HiltonÂ®
Houston-Woodlands
29813 I-45 North
The Woodlands, TX

281-681-9199

Residence Inn Houston The
Woodlands/Lake Front Circle
1040 Lake Front Circle
The Woodlands, TX

281-292-3252

Residence Inn Houston The
Woodlands/Market Street
9333 Six Pines Drive
The Woodlands, TX

281-419-1542

Baymont Inn And Suites Tyler
3913 Frankston Highway
Tyler, TX
903-939-0100

Candlewood Suites Tyler
315 East Rieck Road
Tyler, TX

903-509-4131

Holiday Inn South Broadway
5701 South Broadway

Tyler, TX
903-561-5800

Motel 6 Tyler Northwest
3300 Mineola Highway
Tyler, TX
903-597-6300

Staybridge Suites Tyler University
Area
2759 Mcdonald Road
Tyler, TX
903-566-1100

Motel 6 Uvalde
924 East Main Street
Uvalde, TX

Days Inn Van Horn
600 East Broadway
Van Horn, TX
432-283-1007

Knights Inn Van Horn
1309 West Broadway
Van Horn, TX

432-283-2030

Motel 6 Van Horn
1805 West Broadway
Van Horn, TX

Red Roof Inn Van Horn
200 Golf Course Drive
Van Horn, TX

432-283-2800

Super 8 Van Horn
1807 East Frontage Road
Van Horn, TX

432-283-2282

Hotel Vernon
1615 Expressway- 287 East
Vernon, TX
940-552-5417

Super 8 Vernon
1829 Hwy 287
Vernon, TX
940-552-9321

BEST WESTERN PLUS Victoria Inn
& Suites
8106 Ne Zac Lentz Pkwy
Victoria, TX
361-485-2300

Candlewood Suites Victoria
7103 N. Navarro Street
Victoria, TX

361-578-0236

Motel 6 Victoria

3716 Houston Highway
Victoria, TX

Days Inn Waco
1504 I-35 North
Waco, TX
254-799-8585

Extended Stay America - Waco -
Woodway
5903 Woodway Dr.
Waco, TX

254-399-8836

Hilton Waco
113 South University Parks Drive
Waco, TX

254-754-8484

Knights Inn Waco
1510 I-35 North
Waco, TX

254-799-0244

Knights Inn Waco South
3829 Franklin Avenue
Waco, TX

254-754-0363

Motel 6 Waco
7007 Woodway Drive
Waco, TX

254-751-7400

Residence Inn By Marriott Waco
501 University Parks Drive
Waco, TX

254-714-1386

Super 8 Waco/Mall Area
6624 Hwy 84 West/Woodway Dr
Waco, TX

254-776-3194

Motel 6 Waxahachie
200 North I-35 East
Waxahachie, TX

BEST WESTERN PLUS Cutting
Horse Inn & Suites
210 Alford Drive
Weatherford, TX
817-599-3300

BEST WESTERN PLUS Cutting
Horse Inn & Suites
210 Alford Drive
Weatherford, TX

817-599-3300

Candlewood Suites Weatherford
215 Alford Drive
Weatherford, TX

817-599-9999

Motel 6 Weatherford
150 Alford Drive
Weatherford, TX

Super 8 Weatherford
720 Adams Drive
Weatherford, TX

817-598-0852

Motel 6 Houston - Nasa
1001 West Nasa Road 1
Webster, TX

Staybridge Suites Houston-Clear
Lake
501 W. Texas Ave
Webster, TX

281-338-0900

Scottish Inn Weimar
102 Townsend Drive
Weimar, TX
979-725-9700

Studio 6 Fort Worth West Medical
Center
7888 Interstate 30 West
White Settlement, TX

Baymont Inn & Suites Wichita Falls
4510 Kell Boulevard
Wichita Falls, TX
940-691-7500

Candlewood Suites At Maurine
1320 Central Freeway
Wichita Falls, TX

940-322-4400

Econo Lodge Wichita Falls
1700 Fifth St.
Wichita Falls, TX

940-761-1889

Howard Johnson Wichita Falls
3209 Northwest Freeway
Wichita Falls, TX

940-855-0085

Motel 6 Wichita Falls
1212 Broad Street
Wichita Falls, TX

Motel 6 Wichita Falls - North
1211 Central Expressway
Wichita Falls, TX

Quality Inn & Suites Wichita Falls
1740 Maurine Street
Wichita Falls, TX

940-767-2100

Days Inn And Suites Winnie
14932 Fm 1663 Rd
Winnie, TX
409-296-2866

BEST WESTERN PLUS Wylie Inn
2011 N Highway 78
Wylie, TX
972-429-1771

# Utah Listings

Holiday Inn American Fork - North
Provo
712 South Utah Valley Drive
American Fork, UT
801-763-8500

Four Corners Inn
131 East Center Street
Blanding, UT
435-678-3257

Best Western Plus Ruby's Inn
26 South Main Street
Bryce Canyon, UT
435-834-5341

Cedar City Days Inn
1204 South Main Street
Cedar City, UT
435-867-8877

Cedar City Travelodge
2555 North Freeway Drive
Cedar City, UT

Comfort Inn And Suites Cedar City
1288 South Main Street
Cedar City, UT

435-865-0003

Holiday Inn Express Hotel & Suites
Cedar City
1555 South Old Highway 91
Cedar City, UT

435-865-7799

Super 8 Cedar City
145 North 1550 West
Cedar City, UT

435-586-8880

Days Inn Clearfield
572 North Main Street
Clearfield, UT
801-825-8000

Days Inn Delta
527 E. Topaz Blvd
Delta, UT
435-864-3882

Ramada Inn Draper
12605 South Minuteman Drive
Draper, UT

801-571-1122

Americas Best Value Inn Green
River
2125 East Main Street
Green River, UT
435-564-8441

Holiday Inn Express Green River
1845 East Main Streeet
Green River, UT
435-564-4439

Super 8 Green River
1248 E Main St
Green River, UT

435-564-8888

Holiday Inn Express Springdale -
Zion National Park Area
1215 Zion Park Blvd
Hurricane, UT
435-772-3200

Red Mountain Resort
1275 East Red Mountain Circle
Ivins, UT
435-673-4905

Red Mountain Resort
1275 East Red Mountain Circle
Ivins, UT

435-673-4905

Red Mountain Resort
1275 East Red Mountain Circle
Ivins, UT

435-673-4905

Days Inn And Suites Kanab
296 West 100 North
Kanab, UT
435-644-2562

Parry Lodge
89 East Center Street
Kanab, UT

435-644-2601

Quail Park Lodge
125 N 300 W/H 89
Kanab, UT

435-644-8700

Quality Inn Kanab
815 East Highway 89
Kanab, UT

435-644-8888

Rodeway Inn Kanab
70 South 200 West
Kanab, UT

435-644-5500

Ticaboo Lodge - Lake Powell
Mm 28 Hwy 276
Lake Powell, UT
800-528-6154

Hampton Inn Salt Lake City/Layton
1700 N Woodland Park Dr
Layton, UT
801-775-8800

Towneplace Suites Salt Lake City
Layton
1743 Woodland Park Blvd
Layton, UT

801-779-2422

Super 8 Lehi
125 South 850 East
Lehi, UT
801-766-8800

Best Western Plus Weston Inn
250 North Main Street
Logan, UT
435-752-5700

Comfort Inn Logan
2002 South Highway 89/91
Logan, UT

435-787-2060

Holiday Inn Express Hotel & Suites
Logan
2235 North Main Street
Logan, UT

435-752-3444

Super 8 Logan
865 South Main Street
Logan, UT

435-753-8883

Extended Stay America - Salt Lake
City - Union Park
7555 South Union Park Avenue
Midvale, UT
801-567-0404

Super 8 Motel Midvalley/Salt Lake
City Area
7048 S 900 E
Midvale, UT

801-255-5559

Apache Hotel
166 S 400 East
Moab, UT
435-259-5727

Gonzo Inn
100 W 200 South
Moab, UT

435-259-2515

Kokopelli Lodge and Suites

72 S 100 E
Moab, UT

435-259-7615

Quality Suites Moab
800 S Main St
Moab, UT

435-259-5252

River Canyon Lodge
71 West 200 North
Moab, UT

435-259-8838

Sleep Inn Moab
1051 South Main Street
Moab, UT

435-259-4655

Rodeway Inn And Suites
649 North Main Street
Monticello, UT
435-587-2489

Goulding's Lodge
1000 Main Street
Monument Valley, UT
435-727-3231

Best Western Paradise Inn Of Nephi
1025 S Main Street
Nephi, UT
435-623-0624

Super 8 Nephi
1901 South Main Street ·
Nephi, UT

435-623-0888

Best Western Plus Cottontree Inn
North Salt Lake City
1030 North 400 East
North Salt Lake, UT
801-292-7666

Comfort Suites Ogden
2250 South 1200 West
Ogden, UT
801-621-2545

Days Inn Ogden
3306 Washington Blvd
Ogden, UT

801-399-5671

Holiday Inn Express Hotel And Suites
Ogden
2245 South 1200 West
Ogden, UT

801-392-5000

Sleep Inn Ogden
1155 South 1700 West
Ogden, UT

801-731-6500

Comfort Inn And Suites Orem
427 West University Parkway
Orem, UT
801-431-0405

Holiday Inn Express Hotel & Suites
Orem, Ut
1290 West University Parkway
Orem, UT

801-655-1515

Towneplace Suites By Marriott
Provo Orem
873 North 1200 West
Orem, UT

801-225-4477

Bryce Way Motel
429 North Main Street
Panguitch, UT
435-676-2400

Marianna Inn
699 North Main Street
Panguitch, UT

435-676-8844

Best Western Plus Landmark Inn &
Pancake House
6560 North Landmark Drive
Park City, UT
435-649-7300

Holiday Inn Express Hotel & Suites
Park City
1501 West Ute Boulevard
Park City, UT

435-658-1600

The Gables Hotel
1335 Lowell Avenue, PO Box 905
Park City, UT

435-655-3315

Quality Inn Payson
830 N Main St
Payson, UT
801-465-4861

National 9 Inn Price
641 West Price River Drive
Price, UT
435-637-7000

Baymont Inn & Suites Provo River
2230 North University Parkway
Provo, UT
801-373-7044

Days Inn Provo
1675 North Freedom Blvd
Provo, UT

801-375-8600

Econo Lodge Provo
1625 West Center Street
Provo, UT

801-373-0099

Hampton Inn Provo
1511 South 40 East
Provo, UT

801-377-6396

Sleep Inn Provo
1505 South 4o East
Provo, UT

801-377-6597

Super 8 Motel Provo Byu Orem
1555 North Canyon Road
Provo, UT

801-374-6020

Days Inn Richfield
333 North Main Street
Richfield, UT
435-896-6476

Holiday Inn Express Hotel & Suites
Richfield
20 West 1400 North
Richfield, UT

435-896-8552

Motel 6 Richfield
647 South Main Street
Richfield, UT

Super 8 Richfield Ut
1377 North Main Street
Richfield, UT

435-896-9204

Frontier Motel
75 S 200 E
Roosevelt, UT
435-722-2201

Scenic Hills Super 8
375 East 1620 South
Salina, UT
435-529-7483

Baymont Inn & Suites Murray
4465 Century Drive
Salt Lake City, UT
801-268-2533

Candlewood Suites Salt Lake City
Airport
2170 West North Temple
Salt Lake City, UT

801-359-7500

Comfort Inn Downtown Salt Lake City
171 West 500 Street

Dog-Friendly Lodging - Please always call ahead to make sure an establishment is still dog-friendly.

Salt Lake City, UT
801-325-5300

Crosslands Salt Lake City - Mid Valley
5683 South Redwood Road
Salt Lake City, UT
801-269-9292

Doubletree By Hilton Hotel Salt Lake City Airport
5151 Wiley Post Way
Salt Lake City, UT
801-539-1515

Econo Lodge Downtown
715 West North Temple
Salt Lake City, UT
801-363-0062

Extended Stay America - Salt Lake City - Sugar House
1220 East 2100 South
Salt Lake City, UT
801-474-0771

Hilton Salt Lake City Center
255 South West Temple
Salt Lake City, UT
801-328-2000

Holiday Inn Express Hotel & Suites Salt Lake City-Airport East
200 North 2100 West
Salt Lake City, UT
801-741-1500

Holiday Inn Hotel & Suites Salt Lake City-Airport West
5001 West Wiley Post Way
Salt Lake City, UT
801-741-1800

Microtel Inn & Suites By Wyndham Salt Lake City Airport
61 North Tommy Thompson Road
Salt Lake City, UT
801-236-2800

Monaco Salt Lake City, A Kimpton Hotel
15 West 200 South
Salt Lake City, UT
877-294-9710

Motel 6 Salt Lake City - Central
315 West 3300 South
Salt Lake City, UT
801-486-8780

Quality Inn & Suites Airport West Salt Lake City

315 Admiral Byrd Boulevard
Salt Lake City, UT
801-539-5005

Ramada Salt Lake City
2455 South State Street
Salt Lake City, UT
801-486-2400

Ramada Salt Lake City Airport Hotel
5575 West Amelia Earhart Drive
Salt Lake City, UT
801-537-7020

Ramada Salt Lake City North Temple
1659 West North Temple
Salt Lake City, UT
801-533-9000

Red Lion Hotel Salt Lake City Downtown
161 West 600 South
Salt Lake City, UT
801-521-7373

Residence Inn By Marriott Salt Lake City Airport
4883 West Douglas Corrigan Way
Salt Lake City, UT
801-532-4101

Residence Inn By Marriott Salt Lake City Cottonwood
6425 South 3000 East
Salt Lake City, UT
801-453-0430

Residence Inn by Marriott Salt Lake City Downtown
285 W. Broadway, 300 South
Salt Lake City, UT
801-355-3300

Rodeway Inn Salt Lake City
616 S. 200 West
Salt Lake City, UT
801-534-0808

Sheraton Salt Lake City Hotel
150 West 500 South
Salt Lake City, UT
801-401-2000

Sleep Inn Salt Lake City
3440 South Decker Lake Drive
Salt Lake City, UT
801-975-1888

Super 8 Motel - Salt Lake City/Airport
223 N. Jimmy Doolittle Rd.

Salt Lake City, UT
801-533-8878

Extended Stay America - Salt Lake City - Sandy
10715 Auto Mall Drive
Sandy, UT
801-523-1331

Holiday Inn Express Hotel & Suites Sandy - South Salt Lake City
10680 South Automall Drive
Sandy, UT
801-495-1317

Residence Inn Salt Lake City - Sandy
270 West 10000 South
Sandy, UT
801-561-5005

Scipio Hotel
230 West 400 North
Scipio, UT
435-758-9188

Sleep Inn South Jordan
10676 S 300 W
South Jordan, UT
801-572-2020

Canyon Ranch Motel
668 Zion Park Blvd
Springdale, UT
435-772-3357

Driftwood Lodge
1515 Zion Park Boulevard
Springdale, UT
435-772-3262

Best Western Mountain View Inn
1455 N 1750 W
Springville, UT
8014893641

Howard Johnson Inn-Saint George
1040 South Main Street
St George, UT
435-628-8000

Super 8 St. George Ut
260 East Saint George Blvd
St George, UT
435-673-6161

Towneplace Suites By Marriott St. George
251 South 1470 East
St George, UT
455-986-9955

Holiday Inn Express Hotel & Suites Tooele
1531 North Main Street
Tooele, UT

Dog-Friendly Lodging - Please always call ahead to make sure an establishment is still dog-friendly.

435-833-0500

Hampton Inn Tremonton
2145 West Main Street
Tremonton, UT
435-257-6000

Econo Lodge Downtown Vernal
311 East Main Street
Vernal, UT
435-789-2000

Motel 6 Vernal
590 West Main Street
Vernal, UT

435-789-8172

Sage Motel
54 West Main Street
Vernal, UT

435-789-1442

Holiday Inn Express Hotel & Suites
Washington-North St. George
2450 N Town Center Drive
Washington, UT
435-986-1313

Best Western Plus Wendover Inn
685 East Wendover Boulevard
Wendover, UT
435-665-2215

Knights Inn Wendover
505 East Wendover Boulevard
Wendover, UT

435-665-7744

Comfort Inn West Valley - Salt Lake
City South
2229 West City Center Court
West Valley City, UT
801-886-1300

Extended Stay America - Salt Lake
City - West Valley Center
2310 West City Center Court
West Valley, UT
801-886-2400

Holiday Inn Express Hotel And Suites
3036 S Decker Lake Drive
West Valley City, UT
801-517-4000

Staybridge Suites Salt Lake-West
Valley City
3038 South Decker Drive
West Valley City, UT

801-746-8400

Hampton Inn Salt Lake City-North
2393 South 800 West
Woods Cross, UT
801-296-1211

# Virgin Is. Listings

Emerald Beach Resort
8070 Lindbergh Bay
Saint Thomas, VI
340-777-8800

# Vermont Listings

Whitford House Inn
912 Grandey Road
Addison, VT
802-758-2704

Inn at Maplemont
2742 H 5S
Barnet, VT
802-633-4880

Rodeway Inn - Bellows Falls
593 Rockingham Road
Bellows Falls, VT
802-463-4536

Knotty Pine Motel
130 Northside Drive
Bennington, VT
802-442-5487

South Gate Motel
US 7S
Bennington, VT

802-447-7525

Greenhurst Inn
88 North Road
Bethel, VT
802-234-9474

The Black Bear Inn
4010 Bolton Access Road
Bolton Valley, VT
802-434-2126

Lilac Inn
53 Parks Street
Brandon, VT
802-247-5463

Forty Putney Road
192 Putney Road/H 5
Brattleboro, VT
802-254-6268

Molly Stark Motel
829 Marlboro Road
Brattleboro, VT

802-254-2440

Quality Inn & Conference Center
1380 Putney Road
Brattleboro, VT

Super 8 Motel - Brattleboro
1043 Putney Road
Brattleboro, VT

802-254-8889

Doubletree Burlington
1117 Williston Road
Burlington, VT
802-658-0250

Hilton Burlington
60 Battery Street
Burlington, VT

802-658-6500

Hilton Burlington
60 Battery Street
Burlington, VT

802-658-6500

Sheraton Burlington Hotel
870 Williston Road
Burlington, VT

802-865-6600

Suzanne's B&B - Your Pet-Friendly
Home Away From Home
218 N. Main St.
Cambridge, VT
802-644-6325

Woodlands At Mountain Top
195 Mountain Top Road
Chittenden, VT
802-483-2311

Woodlands At Mountain Top
195 Mountain Top Road
Chittenden, VT

802-483-4152

Days Inn Burlington Colchester
124 College Parkway
Colchester, VT
802-655-0900

Hampton Inn Burlington
42 Lower Mountain View Drive
Colchester, VT

802-655-6177

Sonesta Es Suites Burlington Vt
35 Hurricane Lane
Colchester, VT

802-878-2001

Craftsburg Outdoor Center
535 Lost Nation Road
Craftsbury Common, VT
802-586-7767

Inn at Mountain View Farm
3383 Darling Hill Road
East Burke, VT
802-626-9924

The Inn at Essex

94 Poker Hill Road
Essex, VT
802-878-1100

Inn At Buck Hollow Farm
2150 Buck Hollow Rd
Fairfax, VT
802-849-2400

Silver Maple Lodge
520H 5 S
Fairlee, VT
802-333-4326

Blueberry Hill Inn
1307 Goshen Ripton Road
Goshen, VT
802-247-6735

Happy Bear Motel
1784 Killington Road
Killington, VT
802-422-3305

The Cascades Lodge
Killington Village, 58 Old Mill Rd
Killington, VT

802-422-3731

The Paw House
1376 Clarendon Avenue
Killington, VT

802-558-2661

Wise Vacations
P. O. Box 231
Killington, VT

802-422-3139

The Combs Family Inn
953 E Lake Road
Ludlow, VT
802-228-8799

Inns at Equinox
3567 Main Street Route 7a
Manchester Village, VT
802-362-4700

Red Clover Inn
7 Woodward Road
Mendon, VT
802-775-2290

Fairhill
724 E Munger Street
Middlebury, VT
802-388-3044

Middlebury Inn
14 Courthouse Square
Middlebury, VT

802-388-4961

Phineas Swann Bed & Breakfast Inn
195 Main Street
Montgomery Center, VT

802-326-4306

Four Columns
21 West Street
Newfane, VT
802-365-7713

Quality Inn At Quechee Gorge
5817 Woodstock Rd., Rt. 4
Quechee, VT
802-295-7600

The Parker House Inn and
Restaurant
1792 Main Street
Quechee, VT

802-295-6077

Holiday Inn Rutland Killington
476 Us Route 7 South
Rutland, VT
802-775-1911

Rodeway Inn Rutland
138 North Main Street
Rutland, VT

802-775-2575

Rodeway Inn Rutland
115 Woodstock Avenue
Rutland, VT

802-773-9176

Econo Lodge Inn & Suites
Shelburne
3164 Shelburne Rd.
Shelburne, VT
802-985-3377

Quality Inn Shelburne
2572 Shelburne Rd
Shelburne, VT

802-985-8037

Quality Inn Shelburne
2572 Shelburne Rd
Shelburne, VT

802-985-8037

Best Western Plus Windjammer Inn
& Conference Center
1076 Williston Road
South Burlington, VT
802-863-1125

Travelodge South Burlington
1016 Shelburne Road
South Burlington, VT

802-862-6421

Paradise Bay
50 Light House Road
South Hero, VT
802-372-5393

Kedron Valley Inn
10671 South Road
South Woodstock, VT
802-457-1473

Holiday Inn Express Springfield
818 Charlestown Road
Springfield, VT
802-885-4516

Fairbanks Inn
401 Western Avenue
St Johnsbury, VT
802-748-5666

Commodores Inn
823 South Main Street
Stowe, VT
802-253-7131

LJ's Lodge
2526 Waterbury Rd
Stowe, VT

802-253-7768

Mountain Road Resort
1007 Mountain Road
Stowe, VT

802-253-4566

Stowe Motel
2043 Mountain Road
Stowe, VT

802-253-7629

Stowe Mountain Lodge
7412 Mountain Road
Stowe, VT

802-253-3560

Ten Acres Lodge
14 Barrows Rd
Stowe, VT

802-253-7638

The Riverside Inn
1965 Mountain Road
Stowe, VT

802-253-4217

Topnotch at Stowe Resort and Spa
4000 Mountain Road
Stowe, VT

802-253-8585

Basin Harbor Club
4800 Basin Harbor Road
Vergennes, VT
802-475-2311

Grunberg Haus
94 Pine Street/3 miles S of Waterbury
on H 100
Waterbury, VT
802-244-7726

Snow Goose Inn
259 H 100, Box 366
West Dover, VT
802-464-3984

Super 8 White River Junction
442 North Hartland Road
White River Jct, VT
802-295-7577

Comfort Inn White River Junction
56 Ralph Lehman Dr.
White River Junction, VT
802-295-3051

Towneplace Suites By Marriott
Burlington Williston
66 Zephyr Road
Williston, VT
802-872-5900

# Virginia Listings

Americas Best Value Inn Abingdon
887 Empire Drive
Abingdon, VA
276-628-7131

Super 8 Abingdon
298 Towne Center Drive
Abingdon, VA

276-676-3329

Comfort Inn & Suites Alexandria
5716 South Van Dorn Street
Alexandria, VA
703-922-9200

Extended Stay America - Washington
D.C-Alexandria-Eisenhow Ave
200 Blue Stone Road
Alexandria, VA

703-329-3399

Extended Stay America - Washington
D.C. - Alexandria - Landmark
205 North Breckinridge Place
Alexandria, VA

703-941-9440

Hilton Alexandria Mark Center
5000 Seminary Road
Alexandria, VA

703-845-1010

Kimpton Morrison House
116 South Alfred Street
Alexandria, VA

703-838-8000

Lorien Hotel & Spa, A Kimpton Hotel
1600 King Street
Alexandria, VA

703-894-3434

Monaco Alexandria, A Kimpton
Hotel
480 King Street
Alexandria, VA

703-549-6080

Quality Inn Mount Vernon
7212 Richmond Highway
Alexandria, VA

703-765-9000

Red Roof Plus+ Washington DC
Alexandria
5975 Richmond Hwy
Alexandria, VA

703-960-5200

Residence Inn Alexandria Old Town
1456 Duke Street
Alexandria, VA

703-548-5474

Residence Inn By Marriott
Alexandria Old Town South At
Carlyle
2345 Mill Road
Alexandria, VA

703-549-1155

Sheraton Suites Old Town
Alexandria
801 N Saint Asaph Street
Alexandria, VA

703-836-4700

Travelodge - Alexandria
700 North Washington Street
Alexandria, VA

703-836-5100

Washington Suites
100 South Reynolds Street
Alexandria, VA

703-370-9600

Comfort Inn Lynchburg South
1558 Main Street
Altavista, VA
434-369-4000

Clarion Collection Arlington Court
Suites Hotel
1200 North Courthouse Road
Arlington, VA
703-524-4000

Residence Inn Arlington Courthouse
1401 North Adams Street
Arlington, VA

703-312-2100

Residence Inn Pentagon City
550 Army Navy Drive
Arlington, VA

703-413-6630

Sheraton Pentagon City
900 S. Orme Street
Arlington, VA

703-521-1900

The Westin Crystal City
1800 Jefferson Davis Highway
Arlington, VA

703-486-1111

Homewood Suites By Hilton Dulles-
North/Loudoun, Va
44620 Waxpool Road
Ashburn, VA
703-723-7500

Days Inn Ashland
806 England Street
Ashland, VA
804-798-4262

Days Inn Ashland
806 England Street
Ashland, VA

804-752-7000

Quality Inn and Suites Ashland
107 N. Carter Road
Ashland, VA

804-521-2377

Days Inn Bedford
921 Blue Ridge Ave
Bedford, VA
540-586-8286

The Lost Dog
211 S Church Street
Berryville, VA
540-955-1181

Clay Corner Inn - Bed And Breakfast
401 Clay Street Sw
Blacksburg, VA
540-552-4030

Comfort Inn Blacksburg
3705 S. Main St.
Blacksburg, VA

540-951-1500

Days Inn Blacksburg Conference
Center
3503 Holiday Lane
Blacksburg, VA

540-951-1330

Econo Lodge Near Motor Speedway

912 Commonwealth Avenue
Bristol, VA
276-466-2112

Extended Stay America Washington,
D.C. - Centreville - Manassas
5920 Fort Drive
Centreville, VA
703-988-9955

Extended Stay America - Washington
D.C. Chantilly - Dulles South
14420 Chantilly Crossing Lane
Chantilly, VA
703-263-7173

Extended Stay America -
Washington, D.C. - Chantilly
4504 Brookfield Corporate Drive
Chantilly, VA

703-263-3361

Hampton Inn Washington-Dulles Int'L
Airport South
4050 Westfax Drive
Chantilly, VA

703-818-8200

Holiday Inn Chantilly-Dulles Expo
4335 Chantilly Shopping Center
Chantilly, VA

703-815-6060

Residence Inn Fairfax Merrifield
8125 Gatehouse Road
Chantilly, VA

703-573-5200

Staybridge Suites Chantilly - Dulles
Airport
3860 Centerview Drive
Chantilly, VA

703-435-8090

Towneplace Suites By Marriott
Chantilly Dulles South
14036 Thunderbolt Place
Chantilly, VA

703-709-0453

Days Inn Charlottesville/University
Area
1610 Emmet Street
Charlottesville, VA
434-971-3746

Days Inn Charlottesville/University
Area
1610 Emmet Street
Charlottesville, VA

434-293-9111

Doubletree Hotel Charlottesville
990 Hilton Heights Road
Charlottesville, VA

434-973-2121

Holiday Inn Charlottesville-
Monticello
1200 5th Street Ext.,(I-64 And Route
631)
Charlottesville, VA

434-977-5100

La Quinta Inn & Suites
Charlottesville
1803 Emmet Street North
Charlottesville, VA

434-293-6188

Super 8 Charlottesville
390 Greenbrier Drive
Charlottesville, VA

434-973-0888

Candlewood Suites
Chesapeake/Suffolk
4809 Market Place
Chesapeake, VA
757-405-3030

Comfort Inn & Suites Chesapeake
3355 S. Military Highway
Chesapeake, VA

757-673-8585

Extended Stay America -
Chesapeake - Churchland Blvd.
3214 Churchland Blvd
Chesapeake, VA

757-483-9200

Extended Stay America -
Chesapeake - Crossways Blvd.
1540 Crossways Blvd
Chesapeake, VA

757-424-8600

Extended Stayamerica -
Chesapeake - Greenbrier Circle
809 Greenbrier Circle
Chesapeake, VA

757-523-7377

Hampton Inn And Suites
Chesapeake-Battlefield Blvd
1421 North Battlefield Boulevard
Chesapeake, VA

757-819-5230

Hampton Inn Norfolk/Chesapeake
701a Woodlake Drive
Chesapeake, VA

757-420-1550

Quality Inn Chesapeake
100 Red Cedar Court
Chesapeake, VA

757-547-8880

Red Roof Inn Chesapeake
Conference Center
724 Woodlake Drive
Chesapeake, VA

757-523-0123

Residence Inn Chesapeake
Greenbrier
1500 Crossways Boulevard
Chesapeake, VA

757-502-7300

Staybridge Suites Chesapeake
709 Woodlake Drive
Chesapeake, VA

757-420-2525

Days Inn Chester
2410 West Hundred Road
Chester, VA
804-748-5871

Channel Bass Inn
6228 Church Street
Chincoteague, VA
757-336-6148

Rodeway Inn Chincoteague
6273 Maddox Boulevard
Chincoteague, VA

757-336-6565

Chincoteague Island
6378 Church Street
Chincoteague Island, VA
757-336-3100

VIP Island Vacation Rentals
6353 Maddox Blvd
Chincoteague Island, VA

757-336-7288

Days Inn Christiansburg
2635 Roanoke Street
Christiansburg, VA
540-382-0261

Econo Lodge Christiansburg
2430 Roanoke Street
Christiansburg, VA

540-382-6161

Hampton Inn
Christiansburg/Blacksburg
380 Arbor Drive
Christiansburg, VA

540-381-5874

Quality Inn Christiansburg
50 Hampton Boulevard
Christiansburg, VA

Dog-Friendly Lodging - Please always call ahead to make sure an establishment is still dog-friendly.

540-382-2055

Super 8 Christiansburg
55 Laurel Street Northeast
Christiansburg, VA

540-382-5813

Super 8 Christiansburg
2780 Roanoke Street
Christiansburg, VA

540-382-7421

Knights Inn Collinsville
2357 Virginia Ave.
Collinsville, VA
276-647-3716

Quality Inn Dutch Inn
2360 Virginia Avenue
Collinsville, VA

276-647-3721

Candlewood Suites Colonial Heights
15820 Woods Edge Road
Colonial Heights, VA
804-526-0111

Microtel Inn & Suites By Wyndham
Culpeper
885 Willis Lane
Culpeper, VA
540-829-0330

Quality Inn Culpeper
890 Willis Lane
Culpeper, VA

540-825-4900

Quality Inn King George
4661 James Madison Pkwy.
Dahlgren, VA
540-663-3060

Howard Johnson Inn
Daleville/Roanoke North
437 Roanoke Road
Daleville, VA
540-992-1234

Courtyard Danville
2136 Riverside Drive
Danville, VA
434-791-2661

La Quinta Inn & Suites Richmond -
Kings Dominion
16280 International Street
Doswell, VA
804-876-6900

Residence Inn Dulles Airport At
Dulles 28 Centre
45250 Monterey Place
Dulles, VA
703-421-2000

Knights Inn Williamsburg Busch
Gardens Area
620 York Street
East Williamsburg, VA
757-220-0960

Days Inn Emporia
921 West Atlantic Street
Emporia, VA
434-634-9481

Hampton Inn Emporia
898 Wiggins Road
Emporia, VA

434-634-9200

Knights Inn Emporia
3173 Susset Drive
Emporia, VA

434-535-8535

Red Roof Inn Emporia
1207 West Atlantic Street I-95 At
Exit 11b
Emporia, VA

434-348-8888

Sleep Inn Emporia
899 Wiggins Road
Emporia, VA

434-348-3900

Candlewood Suites Fairfax
11400 Random Hills Road
Fairfax, VA
703-359-4490

Comfort Inn University Center
11180 Fairfax Blvd
Fairfax, VA

703-591-5900

Extended Stay America -
Washington D.C - Fairfax-Fair Oaks
Mall
12055 Lee Jackson Memorial Hwy
Fairfax, VA

703-267-6770

Extended Stay America -
Washington, D.C. - Fairfax - Fair
Oaks
12104 Monument Drive
Fairfax, VA

703-273-3444

Extended Stay America
-Washington, D.C.-Falls Church-
Merrifield
8281 Willow Oaks Corp Dr
Fairfax, VA

703-204-0088

Residence Inn Fair Lakes

12815 Fair Lakes Parkway
Fairfax, VA

703-266-4900

Fox Hill Bed & Breakfast Suites
4383 Borden Grant Trail
Fairfield, VA
540-377-9922

Homewood Suites By Hilton® Falls
Church - I-495 At Rt. 50
8130 Porter Rd
Falls Church, VA
703-560-6644

Residence Inn Charlottesville
1111 Millmont Street
Falls Church, VA

434-923-0300

Towneplace Suites By Marriott Falls
Church
205 Hillwood Ave
Falls Church, VA

703-237-6172

Westin Tysons Corner
7801 Leesburg Pike
Falls Church, VA

703-893-1340

Doe Run Lodging
Milepost 189 Blue Ridge Parkway
Fancy Gap, VA
276-398-4099

Grasssy Creek Cabooses
278 Caboose Lane
Fancy Gap, VA
276-398-1100

Days Inn Farmville
2015 South Main Street
Farmville, VA
434-392-6611

Flint Hill Public House & Country Inn
675 Zachary Taylor H/H 522
Flint Hill, VA
540-675-1700

Miracle Farm Spa and Resort
179 Ida Rose Lane
Floyd, VA
540-789-2214

Days Inn Franklin
1660 Armory Drive
Franklin, VA
757-562-2225

Quality Inn & Suites Franklin
1620 Armory Dr
Franklin, VA

757-569-0018

Dog-Friendly Lodging - Please always call ahead to make sure an establishment is still dog-friendly.

Super 8 Franklin
1599 Armory Dr
Franklin, VA
757-562-2888

Clarion Inn Fredericksburg
564 Warrenton Road
Fredericksburg, VA
540-371-5550

Days Inn Fredericksburg North
14 Simpson Road
Fredericksburg, VA
540-373-5340

Homewood Suites By Hilton
Fredericksburg
1040 Hospitality Lane
Fredericksburg, VA
540-786-9700

Quality Inn Fredericksburg
543 Warrenton Road
Fredericksburg, VA
540-373-0000

Residence Inn Fredericksburg
60 Towne Centre Boulevard
Fredericksburg, VA
540-786-9222

Super 8 Motel -
Fredericksburg/Central Plz Area
3002 Mall Court
Fredericksburg, VA
540-786-8881

Towneplace Suites Fredericksburg
4700 Market Street (Route 1489)
Fredericksburg, VA
540-891-0775

Travelodge Fredericksburg
5316 Jefferson Davis Highway
Fredericksburg, VA
540-898-6800

Bluemont Inn
1525 N. Shenandoah Ave.
Front Royal, VA
540-635-9447

Hot Tub Heaven
Off I 66 (address given with
reservation)
Front Royal, VA
540-636-1522

Hot Tub Heaven Vacation Cabins
Call to Arrange
Front Royal, VA

540-636-1522

Quality Inn Skyline Drive
10 South Commerce Ave.
Front Royal, VA
540-635-3161

Super 8 Front Royal
111 South Street
Front Royal, VA
540-636-4888

Aloft Richmond West
3939 Duckling Drive
Glen Allen, VA

Candlewood Suites Glen Allen - Va
Center Commons
10609 Telegraph Road
Glen Allen, VA
804-262-2240

Candlewood Suites Richmond West
End Short Pump
4120 Brookriver Drive
Glen Allen, VA
804-364-2000

Extended Stay America - Richmond
- West End - I-64
10961 W. Broad St.
Glen Allen, VA
804-747-8898

Towneplace Suites Richmond
4231 Park Place Court
Glen Allen, VA
804-747-5253

Comfort Inn Gloucester
6639 Forest Hill Avenue
Gloucester, VA
804-695-1900

Best Western Plus Crossroads Inn
& Suites
135 Wood Ridge Terrace
Gordonsville, VA
540-832-1700

Arrow Inn
3361 Commander Shepard
Boulevard
Hampton, VA
757-865-0300

Candlewood Suites Hampton
401 Butler Farm Road
Hampton, VA
757-766-8976

Extended Stay America - Hampton -
Coliseum
1915 Commerce Dr

Hampton, VA
757-896-3600

Red Roof Inn Hampton Coliseum
1925 Coliseum Drive
Hampton, VA
757-838-1870

Candlewood Suites Harrisonburg
1560 Country Club Road
Harrisonburg, VA
540-437-1400

Comfort Inn Harrisonburg
1440 East ;Market Street
Harrisonburg, VA
540-433-6066

Days Inn Harrisonburg
1131 Forest Hill Road
Harrisonburg, VA
540-433-9353

Ramada Harrisonburg
91 Pleasant Valley Road
Harrisonburg, VA
540-434-9981

Residence Inn Chantilly Dulles South
14440 Chantilly Crossing Lane
Harrisonburg, VA
703-263-7900

Residence Inn by Marriott
Harrisonburg
1945 Deyerle Avenue
Harrisonburg, VA
540-437-7426

Sleep Inn & Suites Harrisonburg
1891 Evelyn Byrd Avenue
Harrisonburg, VA
540-433-7100

Super 8 Harrisonburg
3330 South Main Street
Harrisonburg, VA
540-433-8888

Candlewood Suites Herndon
13845 Sunrse Valley Dr
Herndon, VA
703-793-7100

Extended Stay America - Washington
D.C. - Herndon - Dulles
1021 Elden Street
Herndon, VA
703-481-5363

Residence Inn by Marriott Herndon
Reston

315 Elden Street
Herndon, VA

703-435-0044

Sheraton Herndon Dulles Airport
Hotel
13715 Sayward Boulevard
Herndon, VA

571-643-0950

Staybridge Suites Herndon
13700 Coppermine Road
Herndon, VA

703-713-6800

Quality Inn Hillsville
85 Airport Road
Hillsville, VA
276-728-2120

Candlewood Suites Hopewell
5113 Plaza Drive
Hopewell, VA
804-541-0200

Hope and Glory Inn
65 Tavern Road
Irvington, VA
804-438-6053

Super 8 Lebanon
711 Townview Drive
Lebanon, VA
276-889-1800

Best Western Leesburg Hotel &
Conference Center
726 E Market Street
Leesburg, VA
703-777-9400

Clarion Inn Historic Leesburg
1500 East Market Street
Leesburg, VA

703-771-9200

Days Inn Leesburg
721 E. Market Street
Leesburg, VA

703-777-6622

Lansdowne Resort
44050 Woodridge Parkway
Leesburg, VA

877-419-8400

1780 Stone House, rental #1350
218 S Main Street/H 11
Lexington, VA
540-463-2521

Applewood Inn
242 Tarn Beck Lane
Lexington, VA

540-463-1962

Best Western Lexington Inn
850 N Lee Highway
Lexington, VA

540-458-3020

Comfort Inn Virginia Horse Center
62 Comfort Way
Lexington, VA

540-463-7311

Days Inn Lexington
2809 North Lee Highway
Lexington, VA

540-463-9131

Howard Johnson Hotel Lexington
2836 North Lee Highway
Lexington, VA

540-463-9181

Sleep Inn & Suites Lexington
95 Maury River Road
Lexington, VA

540-463-6000

Super 8 Lexington
1139 North Lee Highway
Lexington, VA

540-463-7858

Comfort Inn Gunston Corner Near
Ft. Belvoir
8180 Silverbrook Road
Lorton, VA
703-643-3100

Inn At Meander Plantation
2333 North James Madison Hwy
Lotus Dale, VA
540-672-4912

Accokeek Farm
170 Kibler Drive
Luray, VA
540-743-2305

Adventures Await

Luray, VA

540-743-5766

Avalon Escape
21 Wallace Avenue
Luray, VA

540-843-0606

Days Inn Luray Shenandoah
138 Whispering Hill Road
Luray, VA

540-743-4521

Best Western Lynchburg

2815 Candlers Mountain Road
Lynchburg, VA
434-237-2986

Extended Stay America - Lynchburg -
University Blvd.
1910 University Blvd.
Lynchburg, VA

434-239-8863

Hill City Inn
1500 Main Street
Lynchburg, VA

434-845-5975

Super 8 Lynchburg VA
3736 Candlers Mountain Road
Lynchburg, VA

434-846-1668

Knights Inn Madison Heights
3642 S. Amherst Highway
Madison Heights, VA
434-929-6506

Best Western Battlefield Inn
10820 Balls Ford Road
Manassas, VA
703-361-8000

Candlewood Suites Manassas
11220 Balls Ford Road
Manassas, VA

703-530-0550

Comfort Suites Manassas Battlefield
Park
7350 Williamson Blvd
Manassas, VA

703-686-1100

Red Roof Inn Washington DC
Manassas
10610 Automotive Drive
Manassas, VA

703-335-9333

Residence Inn Manassas Battlefield
Park
7345 Williamson Boulevard
Manassas, VA

703-330-8808

Econo Lodge Marion
1420 N. Main Street
Marion, VA
276-783-6031

Econo Lodge Martinsville
1755 Virginia Avenue
Martinsville, VA
276-632-5611

Super 8 Chiswell/Max Meadows Area
194 Ft. Chiswell Rd.

Dog-Friendly Lodging - Please always call ahead to make sure an establishment is still dog-friendly.

Max Meadows, VA
276-637-4141

Staybridge Suites Mclean-Tysons Corner
6845 Old Dominion Drive
Mclean, VA
703-448-5400

Econo Lodge Inn & Suites Middletown
91 Reliance Road
Middletown, VA
540-868-1800

Highland Inn
68 West Main Street/H 250
Monterey, VA
540-468-2143

Super 8 - Mount Jackson
250 Conicville Blvd
Mount Jackson, VA
540-477-2911

The Widow Kip's Country Inn
355 Orchard Drive
Mount Jackson, VA

540-477-2400

Rugby Creek Cabins and Equestrian Resort
1228 Rugby Road
Mouth of Wilson, VA
276-579-4215

1926 Caboose Vacation Rental
218 S Main Street/H 11
Natural Bridge, VA
540-463-2521

Natural Bridge Historic Hotel and Conference Center
15 Appledore Lane
Natural Bridge, VA

540-291-2121

Garden And The Sea B&b Inn
4188 Nelson Road
New Church, VA
800-824-0672

Days Inn New Market Battlefield
9360 George Collins Parkway
New Market, VA
540-740-4100

Comfort Inn Newport News
12330 Jefferson Ave.
Newport News, VA
757-249-0200

Days Inn Newport News
14747 Warwick Blvd
Newport News, VA

757-874-0201

Days Inn Newport News/Oyster Point At City Center
11829 Fishing Point
Newport News, VA

757-873-6700

Extended Stay America - Newport News - Oyster Point
11708 Jefferson Ave.
Newport News, VA

757-873-2266

Microtel Inn & Suites by Wyndham Newport News Airport
501 Operations Drive
Newport News, VA

757-249-8355

Residence Inn Newport News Airport
531 St. Johns Road
Newport News, VA

757-842-6214

Super 8 Newport News
6105 Jefferson Avenue
Newport News, VA

757-825-1422

Candlewood Suites Norfolk Airport
5600 Lowery Road
Norfolk, VA
757-605-4001

Doubletree By Hilton Hotel Norfolk Airport
1500 North Military Highway
Norfolk, VA

757-466-8000

Econo Lodge Near Norfolk State University
865 North Military Highway
Norfolk, VA

757-461-4865

Page House Inn
323 Fairfax Avenue
Norfolk, VA

757-625-5033

Quality Suites Lake Wright - Norfolk Airport
6280 Northampton Boulevard
Norfolk, VA

757-461-6251

Quality Suites Lake Wright - Norfolk Airport
6280 Northampton Boulevard
Norfolk, VA

757-461-1133

Residence Inn By Marriott Norfolk Airport
1590 North Military Highway
Norfolk, VA

757-333-3000

Residence Inn Norfolk Downtown
227 West Brambleton Avenue
Norfolk, VA

757-842-6216

Holiday Inn Norton
1051 Park Avenue South West
Norton, VA
276-679-6655

Super 8 Norton Va
425 Wharton Lane
Norton, VA

276-679-0893

Holladay House Bed And Breakfast
155 W Main Street
Orange, VA
540-672-4893

Days Inn Petersburg-South
12208 South Crater Road
Petersburg, VA
804-733-4400

Econo Lodge Petersburg
900 Winfield Road
Petersburg, VA

804-861-8400

Econo Lodge South
16905 Parkdale Rd
Petersburg, VA

804-862-2717

Quality Inn Petersburg
11974 S Crater Rd
Petersburg, VA

804-732-2900

Rodeway Inn Petersburg
12205 South Crater Road
Petersburg, VA

804-733-0600

Travel Inn Petersburg Fort Lee
530 East Washington Street
Petersburg, VA

Gov Dinwiddie Hotel Old Towne, An Ascend Hotel Collection Member
506 Dinwiddie Street
Portsmouth, VA
757-392-1330

Holiday Inn Express Hotel & Suites Claypool Hill -Richlands Area
180 Clay Drive
Pounding Mill, VA

276-596-9880

Super 8 Richlands/Claypool Hill Area
12367 Gov. G.C. Peery Hwy
Pounding Mill, VA

276-964-9888

Best Western Radford Inn
1501 Tyler Avenue
Radford, VA
540-639-3000

Super 8 Radford Va
1600 Tyler Ave
Radford, VA

540-731-9355

Comfort Inn & Suites Raphine
584 Oakland Circle
Raphine, VA
540-377-2604

Fleeton Fields
2783 Fleeton Road
Reedville, VA
804-453-7016

Extended Stay America -
Washington, D.C. - Reston
12190 Sunset Hills Rd
Reston, VA
703-707-9700

Sheraton Reston Hotel
11810 Sunrise Valley Drive
Reston, VA

703-620-9000

Candlewood Suites RICHMOND -
WEST BROAD
2100 Dickens Road
Richmond, VA
804-282-3300

Candlewood Suites Richmond Airport
5400 Audubon Drive
Richmond, VA

804-652-1888

Candlewood Suites Richmond South
4301 Commerce Road
Richmond, VA

804-271-0016

Days Inn Richmond
6910 Midlothian Turnpike
Richmond, VA

804-745-7100

Extended Stay America - North
Chesterfield - Arboretum
241 Arboretum Place
Richmond, VA

804-272-1800

Extended Stay America-Richmon
-W. Broad Street-Glenside-South
6811 Paragon Pl.
Richmond, VA

804-285-2065

Four Points By Sheraton Richmond
9901 Midlothian Turnpike
Richmond, VA

804-323-1144

Hilton Richmond Hotel & Spa/Short
Pump
12042 West Broad Street
Richmond, VA

804-364-3600

Holiday Inn Richmond South-Bells
Road
4303 Commerce Road
Richmond, VA

804-592-2900

Quality Inn & Suites Richmond
3200 West Broad Street
Richmond, VA

804-359-4061

Red Roof Inn Richmond South
4350 Commerce Road
Richmond, VA

804-271-7240

Residence Inn By Marriott Richmond
Northwest
3940 Westerre Parkway
Richmond, VA

804-762-9852

Residence Inn Richmond West End
2121 Dickens Road
Richmond, VA

804-285-8200

Super 8 Richmond/Chamberlayne
Rd
5615 Chamberlayne Rd.
Richmond, VA

804-262-8880

The Jefferson Hotel
101 West Franklin Street
Richmond, VA

804-788-8000

Travelodge Ridgeway Martinsville
Area
3841 Greensboro Road
Ridgeway, VA
276-638-3914

Best Western Plus Inn At Valley View
5050 Valley View Boulevard North
West
Roanoke, VA
540-362-2400

Days Inn Roanoke Airport I-81
8118 Plantation Road
Roanoke, VA

540-366-0341

Extended Stay America - Roanoke -
Airport
2705 Frontage Rd.
Roanoke, VA

540-366-3216

Holiday Inn Roanoke Valley View
3315 Ordway Drive
Roanoke, VA

540-362-4500

Howard Johnson Inn Roanoke/Airport
6520 Thirlane Road Nw
Roanoke, VA

540-265-7600

Quality Inn Roanoke-Tanglewood
3816 Franklin Road Southwest
Roanoke, VA

540-989-4000

Residence Inn Roanoke Airport
3305 Ordway Drive
Roanoke, VA

540-265-1119

Rodeway Inn Civic Center
526 Orange Ave Ne
Roanoke, VA

540-981-9341

Sheraton Roanoke Hotel And
Conference Center
2801 Hershberger Road
Roanoke, VA

540-563-9300

Super 8 Roanoke
6616 Thirlane Road
Roanoke, VA

540-563-8888

Comfort Inn Smith Mt. Lake
1730 N. Main St.
Rocky Mount, VA
540-489-4000

Holiday Inn Express Hotel & Suites
Rocky Mount
395 Old Franklin Turnpike
Rocky Mount, VA

540-489-5001

Dog-Friendly Lodging - Please always call ahead to make sure an establishment is still dog-friendly.

Econo Lodge Ruther Glen
24368 Rogers Clark Blvd
Ruther Glen, VA
804-448-9694

Super 8 Motel Ruther Glen Kings
Dominion Area
24011 Ruther Glen Road
Ruther Glen, VA

804-448-2608

Baymont Inn & Suites Salem
Roanoke Area
179 Sheraton Drive
Salem, VA
540-562-1912

Days Inn Salem
1535 East Main Street
Salem, VA

540-986-1000

Howard Johnson Inn & Conference
Center Salem
1671 Skyview Road
Salem, VA

540-389-7061

Quality Inn Salem
151 Wildwood Road
Salem, VA

540-387-1600

Stay at Inn
301 Wildwood Road
Salem, VA

540-389-0280

Super 8 Salem Va
300 Wildwood Road
Salem, VA

540-389-0297

Microtel Inn & Suites By Wyndham
Richmond Airport
6000 Audubon Drive
Sandston, VA
804-737-3322

Days Inn & Suites South Boston
1074 Bill Tuck Hwy
South Boston, VA
434-575-4000

Super 8 South Boston VA
1040 Bill Tuck Highway
South Boston, VA

434-572-8868

Days Inn South Hill
911 East Atlantic Street
South Hill, VA
434-447-3123

Quality Inn South Hill
918 E. Atlantic St.
South Hill, VA

434-447-2600

Hopkins Ordinary
47 Main Street
Sperryville, VA
540-987-3383

Extended Stay America -
Washington, D.C. - Springfield
6800 Metropolitan Center Dr
Springfield, VA
703-822-0992

Residence Inn Springfield Old
Keene Mill
6412 Backlick Road
Springfield, VA

703-644-0020

Towneplace Suites By Marriott
Springfield
6245 Brandon Avenue
Springfield, VA

703-569-8060

Best Western Aquia/Quantico Inn
2868 Jefferson Davis Highway
Stafford, VA
540-659-0022

Staybridge Suites Stafford
2996 Jefferson Davis Highway
Stafford, VA

540-720-2111

Towneplace Suites Stafford
2772 Jefferson Davis Highway
Stafford, VA

540-657-1990

Best Western Staunton Inn
92 Rowe Rd
Staunton, VA
540-885-1112

Comfort Inn Staunton
1302 Richmond Avenue
Staunton, VA

540-886-5000

Days Inn Staunton Mint Springs
372 Whitehill Road
Staunton, VA

540-337-3031

Days Inn Staunton North
273-D Bells Lane
Staunton, VA

540-248-0888

Howard Johnson Express Inn
Staunton
268 N. Central Avenue
Staunton, VA

540-886-5330

Sleep Inn Staunton
222 Jefferson Highway
Staunton, VA

540-887-6500

Comfort Inn Stephens City
167 Town Run Lane
Stephens City, VA
540-869-6500

Best Western Dulles Airport Inn
45440 Holiday Drive
Sterling, VA
703-471-8300

Candlewood Suites Sterling
45520 East Severn Way
Sterling, VA

703-674-2288

Extended Stay America -
Washington, D.C. - Sterling
46001 Waterview Plaza
Sterling, VA

703-444-7240

Extended Stay America -
Washington, D.C. - Sterling - Dulles
45350 Catalina Court
Sterling, VA

703-904-7575

Hampton Inn Dulles/Cascades
46331 Mcclellan Way
Sterling, VA

703-450-9595

Hawthorn Suites By Wyndham
Sterling Dulles
21123 Whitfield Place
Sterling, VA

703-521-1090

Towneplace Suites Dulles Airport
22744 Holiday Park Drive
Sterling, VA

703-707-2017

Sleep Inn & Suites Stony Creek -
Petersburg South
11019 Blue Star Hwy.
Stony Creek, VA
434-246-5100

Days Inn - Suffolk
1526 Holland Road
Suffolk, VA
757-539-5111

Towneplace Suites By Marriott
Suffolk Chesapeake
8050 Harbour View Boulevard
Suffolk, VA

757-483-5177

Days Inn Tappahannock
1414 Tappahannock Boulevard
Tappahannock, VA
804-443-9200

Comfort Inn Troutville
2545 Lee Highway
Troutville, VA
540-992-5600

Red Roof Inn Roanoke - Troutville
3231 Lee Highway South
Troutville, VA

540-992-5055

Knights Inn Staunton/Verona
70 Lodge Lane
Verona, VA
540-248-8981

Extended Stay America Washington
D.C. - Tysons Corner
8201 Old Courthouse Road
Vienna, VA
703-356-6300

Residence Inn By Marriott Tysons
Corner
8616 Westwood Center Drive
Vienna, VA

703-893-0120

Residence Inn By Marriott Tysons
Corner Mall
8400 Old Courthouse Road
Vienna, VA

703-917-0800

Sheraton Tysons Hotel
8661 Leesburg Pike
Vienna, VA

703-448-1234

Candlewood Suites Virginia
Beach/Norfolk
4437 Bonney Road
Virginia Beach, VA
757-213-1500

Clarion Inn & Suites Virginia Beach
2604 Atlantic Avenue
Virginia Beach, VA

757-425-5971

Doubletree Hotel Virginia Beach
1900 Pavilion Drive
Virginia Beach, VA

757-422-8900

Econo Lodge Town Center
3637 Bonney Rd.
Virginia Beach, VA

757-486-5711

Extended Stay America - Virginia
Beach - Independence Blvd.
4548 Bonney Rd.
Virginia Beach, VA

757-473-9200

Homewood Virginia Beach
5733 Cleveland Street
Virginia Beach, VA

757-552-0080

North Landing Beach Campground
& RV Resort
161 Princess Anne Road
Virginia Beach, VA

757-426-6241

Red Roof Inn Virginia Beach
196 Ballard Court
Virginia Beach, VA

757-490-0225

Red Roof Inn Virginia Beach Norfolk
Airport
5745 Northhampton Boulevard
Virginia Beach, VA

757-460-3414

Residence Inn Virginia Beach
Oceanfront
3217 Atlantic Avenue
Virginia Beach, VA

757-425-1141

Sandbridge Realty Dog Friendly
Beach Vacation Rentals
Call to Arrange
Virginia Beach, VA

757-426-6262

Sandswept
Northend at 83rd Street; Call to
arrange
Virginia Beach, VA

757-513-7555

Sheraton Virginia Beach Oceanfront
Hotel
3501 Atlantic Avenue
Virginia Beach, VA

757-425-9000

Siebert Realty
Call to Arrange
Virginia Beach, VA

757-426-6200

Towneplace Suites By Marriott
Virginia Beach/Newtown Road
5757 Cleveland St
Virginia Beach, VA

757-490-9367

Holiday Inn Express Hotel & Suites
Warrenton
410 Holiday Court
Warrenton, VA
540-341-3461

Howard Johnson Inn - Warrenton
6 Broadview Ave
Warrenton, VA

540-347-4141

Quality Inn Warsaw
4522 Richmond Road
Warsaw, VA
804-333-1700

Best Western Plus Waynesboro Inn
& Suites Conference Center
109 Apple Tree Lane
Waynesboro, VA
540-942-1100

Days Inn Waynesboro
2060 Rosser Avenue/I-64
Waynesboro, VA

540-943-1101

Residence Inn Waynesboro
44 Windigrove Drive
Waynesboro, VA

540-943-7426

Super 8 Waynesboro
2045 Rosser Ave.
Waynesboro, VA

540-943-3888

Clarion Hotel Historic District
351 York Street
Williamsburg, VA
757-229-4100

Days Inn Williamsburg Colonial Area
902 Richmond Road
Williamsburg, VA

757-229-5060

Quality Inn & Suites Williamsburg
Central
5351 Richmond Road
Williamsburg, VA

757-645-3636

Quality Inn Historic East - Busch
Gardens Area
505 York St., Building A
Williamsburg, VA

Residence Inn Williamsburg
1648 Richmond Road
Williamsburg, VA

757-941-2000

Woodlands Cascades Motel
105 Visitor Center Drive
Williamsburg, VA

757-229-1000

Aloft Winchester
1055 Millwood Pike
Winchester, VA
540-678-8899

Americas Best Value Inn Hotel
2649 Valley Avenue
Winchester, VA

540-662-2521

Candlewood Suites Winchester
1135 Millwood Pike And Route 50
Winchester, VA

540-667-8323

Comfort Inn Winchester
1601 Martinsburg Pike
Winchester, VA

540-667-8894

Econo Lodge North Winchester
1593 Martinsburg Pike
Winchester, VA

540-662-4700

Red Roof Inn Winchester
991 Millwood Pike
Winchester, VA

540-667-5000

Super 8 Winchester
1077 Millwood Pike
Winchester, VA

540-665-4450

Towneplace Suites Winchester
170 Getty Lane
Winchester, VA

540-722-2722

Quality Inn Near Potomac Mills
1109 Horner Rd
Woodbridge, VA
703-494-0300

Residence Inn By Marriott Potomac
Mills
14301 Crossing Place
Woodbridge, VA

703-490-4020

Comfort Inn Woodstock
1011 Motel Drive
Woodstock, VA
540-459-7600

Best Western Wytheville Inn
355 Nye Road
Wytheville, VA
276-228-7300

Comfort Inn Wytheville
2594 East Lee Highway
Wytheville, VA

276-637-4281

Days Inn - Wytheville
150 Malin Drive
Wytheville, VA

276-228-5500

Econo Lodge Wytheville
280 Lithia Road
Wytheville, VA

276-228-5525

Ramada Wytheville
955 Peppers Ferry Road
Wytheville, VA

276-228-6000

Red Roof Inn And Suites Wytheville
1900 East Main Street
Wytheville, VA

276-223-1700

Super 8 Wytheville
130 Nye Circle
Wytheville, VA

276-228-6620

Candlewood Suites Newport News
Yorktown
329 Commonwealth Drive
Yorktown, VA
757-952-1120

Marl Inn
220 Church Street
Yorktown, VA

757-898-3859

Red Roof Inn Yorktown
4531 George Washington Memorial
Highway
Yorktown, VA

757-283-1111

Staybridge Suites Yorktown
401 Commonwealth Drive
Yorktown, VA

757-251-6644

Towneplace Suites Newport News

Yorktown
200 A B Cybernetics Way
Yorktown, VA

757-874-8884

# Washington Listings

Travelodge Aberdeen
521 W Wishkah Street
Aberdeen, WA
360-532-5210

Days Inn And Suites Airway
Heights/Spokane Airport
1215 South Garfield
Airway Heights, WA
509-244-0222

Anacortes Inn
3006 Commercial Avenue
Anacortes, WA
360-293-3153

Fidalgo Country Inn
7645 State Route 20
Anacortes, WA

360-293-3494

Quality Inn Near Seattle Premium
Outlets
5200 172nd Street N.E.
Arlington, WA
360-403-7222

Best Western Plus Peppertree
Auburn Inn
401 8th Street Sw
Auburn, WA
253-887-7600

Best Western Plus Bainbridge Island
Suites
350 Ne High School Road
Bainbridge Island, WA
206-855-9666

Extended Stay America - Seattle -
Bellevue - Downtown
11400 Main Street
Bellevue, WA
425-453-8186

Extended Stay America - Seattle -
Redmond
15805 Ne 28th Street
Bellevue, WA

425-885-6675

Extended Stay America Seattle -
Bellevue - Factoria
3700 132nd Ave Se
Bellevue, WA

425-865-8680

Red Lion Hotel Bellevue
11211 Main Street
Bellevue, WA

425-455-5240

Residence Inn By Marriott Seattle
Bellevue
605 114th Ave Se
Bellevue, WA

425-637-8500

Sheraton Bellevue Hotel
100 112th Avenue Northeast
Bellevue, WA

425-455-3330

Aloha Motel
315 N Samish Way
Bellingham, WA
360-733-4900

Four Points by Sheraton Bellingham
Hotel & Conference Center
714 Lakeway Drive
Bellingham, WA

360-671-1011

Four Points by Sheraton Bellingham
Hotel & Conference Center
714 Lakeway Drive
Bellingham, WA

360-671-1011

Quality Inn Grand Suites
100 E. Kellogg Rd.
Bellingham, WA

360-647-8000

Rodeway Inn Bellingham
3710 Meridian St.
Bellingham, WA

360-738-6000

Semiahmoo Resort And Spa
9565 Semiahmoo Parkway
Blaine, WA
360-371-2000

Extended Stay America Seattle -
Bothell - West
923 228th Street Se
Bothell, WA
425-402-4252

Residence Inn Seattle North
Lynnwood
18200 Alderwood Mall Parkway
Bothell, WA

425-771-1100

Super 8 Bremerton
5068 Kitsap Way
Bremerton, WA
360-377-8881

Econo Lodge Buckley
29405 State Route 410 East
Buckley, WA
360-829-1100

Travelodge Centralia
702 Harrison Avenue
Centralia, WA

Holiday Inn Express Hotel & Suites
Chehalis-Centralia
730 Nw Liberty Plaza
Chehalis, WA
360-740-1800

Quality Inn & Suites Conference
Center Clarkston
700 Port Drive
Clarkston, WA
509-758-9500

Best Western Wheatland Inn
701 North Main Street
Colfax, WA
509-397-0397

Iron Springs Ocean Beach Resort
P. O. Box 207
Copalis Beach, WA
360-276-4230

Blue Heron Bed and Breakfast
982 Deer Harbor Rd
Eastsound, WA
360-376-4198

Best Western Plus Edmonds Harbor
Inn
130 West Dayton Street
Edmonds, WA
425-771-5021

Best Western Plus Lincoln Inn And
Suites
211 West Umptanum Road
Ellensburg, WA
509-925-4244

Comfort Inn Ellensburg
1722 Canyon Road
Ellensburg, WA

509-925-7037

Holiday Inn Express Ellensburg
1620 Canyon Road
Ellensburg, WA

509-962-9400

Quality Inn & Conference Center
Ellensburg
1700 S. Canyon Road
Ellensburg, WA

509-925-9800

Super 8 Ellensburg
1500 Canyon Road

Ellensburg, WA

509-962-6888

Best Western Rama Inn
1818 Basin Street Southwest
Ephrata, WA
509-754-7111

Best Western Cascadia Inn
2800 Pacific Ave
Everett, WA
425-258-4141

Best Western Plus Navigator Inn &
Suites
10210 Evergreen Way
Everett, WA

425-347-2555

Days Inn Everett
1602 Southeast Everett Mall Way
Everett, WA

425-355-1570

Extended Stay America Seattle -
Everett - North
8410 Broadway
Everett, WA

425-355-1923

Holiday Inn Downtown Everett
3105 Pine Street
Everett, WA

425-339-2000

Best Western Plus Evergreen Inn
And Suites
32124 25th Avenue South
Federal Way, WA
253-529-4000

Clarion Hotel
31611 20th Avenue South
Federal Way, WA

253-941-6000

Comfort Inn Federal Way
31622 Pacific Highway South
Federal Way, WA
253-529-0101

Extended Stay America - Seattle -
Federal Way
1400 South 320th Street
Federal Way, WA

253-946-0553

Quality Inn & Suites Federal Way
1400 South 348th Street
Federal Way, WA

253-835-4141

Red Lion Inn & Suites Federal Way

1688 S. 348th Street
Federal Way, WA
253-838-8808

Super 8 Bellingham Airport/Ferndale
Interstate 5 Exit 262, 5788 Barrette Road
Ferndale, WA
360-384-8881

Econo Lodge Fife
3501 Pacific Highway East
Fife, WA
253-926-1000

Extended Stay America - Tacoma - Fife
2820 Pacific Hwy East
Fife, WA
253-926-6316

Quality Inn And Suites Fife/Tacoma
5805 Pacific Highway East
Fife, WA
253-922-2500

Rodeway Inn & Suites Fife
3100 Pacific Highway East
Fife, WA
253-922-9520

Kalaloch Lodge
157151 Highway 101
Forks, WA
360-962-2271

Earthbox Motel And Spa
410 Spring Street P.O. Box 1729
Friday Harbor, WA
360-378-4000

Friday Harbor Suites
680 Spring Street
Friday Harbor, WA
360-378-3031

Best Western Plus Wesley Inn & Suites
6575 Kimball Drive
Gig Harbor, WA
206-858-9690

Mt. Baker Lodging
7463 Mt. Baker Highway
Glacier, WA
360-599-2453

Best Western Plus Peppertree Liberty Lake Inn
1816 N Pepper Ln
Greenacres, WA
509-755-1111

Econo Lodge Inn & Suites Hoquiam
910 Simpson Avenue
Hoquiam, WA

360-532-8161

Best Western Aladdin Inn
310 Long Avenue
Kelso, WA
360-425-9660

Red Lion Hotel Kelso
510 Kelso Drive
Kelso, WA
360-636-4400

Super 8 Kelso Longview Area
250 Kelso Drive
Kelso, WA
360-423-8880

Baymont Inn & Suites Kennewick
4220 West 27th Place
Kennewick, WA
509-736-3326

Best Western Plus Kennewick Inn
4001 West 27th Avenue
Kennewick, WA
509-586-1332

Comfort Inn Kennewick
7801 W. Quinault Ave
Kennewick, WA
509-783-8396

Days Inn Kennewick
2811 West 2nd Avenue
Kennewick, WA
509-735-9511

Red Lion Hotel Columbia Center
1101 N Columbia Center Blvd
Kennewick, WA
509-738-0611

Super 8 - Kennewick
626 North Columbia Center Boulevard
Kennewick, WA
509-736-6888

Extended Stay America Seattle - Kent
22520 83th Avenue South
Kent, WA
253-872-6514

Howard Johnson Inn - Kent
1233 North Central Avenue
Kent, WA
253-852-7224

Towneplace Suites By Marriott Seattle South Center
18123-72nd Avenue South
Kent, WA

253-796-6000

China Bend Bed and Breakfast and Winery
3751 Vineyard Way
Kettle Falls, WA
509-732-6123

Candlewood Suites Olympia - Lacey
4440 3rd Avenue Southeast
Lacey, WA
360-491-1698

Candlewood Suites Lakewood
10720 Pacific Highway Southwest
Lakewood, WA
253-584-0868

Evergreen Inn
1117 Front Street
Leavenworth, WA
509-548-5515

Howard Johnson Express Inn - Leavenworth
405 Highway 2
Leavenworth, WA
509-548-4326

Quality Inn & Suites Longview
723 7th Avenue
Longview, WA
360-414-1000

Island Vacation Rentals
1695 Seacrest Drive
Lummi Island, WA
360-758-7064

Extended Stay America Seattle - Lynnwood
3021 196th Street Sw
Lynnwood, WA
425-670-2520

Residence Inn Bellevue
14455 Ne 29th Place
Lynnwood, WA
425-882-1222

Holiday Inn Express Hotel & Suites Marysville
8606 36th Ave Ne
Marysville, WA
360-530-1234

Hi-Tide Ocean Beach Resort
4890 Railroad Avenue
Moclips, WA
360-276-4142

Ocean Crest Resort
4651 Sr 109
Moclips, WA
360-276-4465

Best Western Plus Lake Front Hotel

3000 Marina Drive
Moses Lake, WA
509-765-9211

Quality Inn Moses Lake
449 Melva Lane
Moses Lake, WA

509-765-8886

Ramada Moses Lake
1745 Kittleson Road
Moses Lake, WA

509-766-1000

Best Western College Way Inn
300 West College Way
Mount Vernon, WA
360-424-4287

Days Inn Mt. Vernon
2009 Riverside Drive
Mount Vernon, WA

360-424-4141

Quality Inn Mount Vernon
1910 Freeway Drive
Mount Vernon, WA

360-428-7020

Extended Stay America Seattle -
Mukilteo
3917 Harbour Pointe Blvd Sw
Mukilteo, WA
425-493-1561

Staybridge Suites Mukilteo Everett
9600 Harbour Place
Mukilteo, WA

425-493-9500

Towneplace Suites By Marriott
Seattle Everett/Mukilteo
8521 Mukilteo Speedway
Mukilteo, WA

425-551-5900

Candlewood Suites Oak Harbor
33221 Sr 20
Oak Harbor, WA
360-279-2222

Coastal Cottages of Ocean Park
1511 264th Place
Ocean Park, WA
360-665-4658

Canterbury Inn
643 Ocean Shores Blvd. NW
Ocean Shores, WA
360-289-3317

The Polynesian Resort
615 Ocean Shores Boulevard
Northwest
Ocean Shores, WA

360-289-3361

Best Western Tumwater Inn
5188 Capitol Blvd Se
Olympia, WA
360-956-1235

Quality Inn Olympia
1211 Quince Street Southeast
Olympia, WA

360-943-4710

Red Lion Hotel Olympia
2300 Evergreen Park Drive
Olympia, WA

360-943-4000

Best Western Plus Peppertree Inn
At Omak
820 Koala Drive
Omak, WA
509-422-2088

Quality Inn Othello
1020 E Cedar Street
Othello, WA
509-488-5671

Sand Dollar Inn & Cottages
56 Central Avenue
Pacific Beach, WA
360-276-4525

Sandpiper Beach Resort
4159 State Route 109
Pacific Beach, WA

360-276-4580

Best Western Plus Pasco Inn &
Suites
2811 N 20th Ave
Pasco, WA
509-543-7722

King City Knights Inn/Pasco Wa
2100 East Hillsboro Street
Pasco, WA

509-547-3475

Red Lion Hotel Pasco
2525 North 20th Avenue
Pasco, WA

509-547-0701

Sleep Inn Pasco
9930 Bedford Street
Pasco, WA

509-545-9554

Days Inn Port Angeles
1510 E Front St
Port Angeles, WA
360-452-4015

Red Lion Hotel Port Angeles
221 North Lincoln Street
Port Angeles, WA

360-452-9215

Sol Duc Hot Springs Resort
12076 Sol Duc Hot Springs Road
Port Angeles, WA

360-327-3593

Days Inn - Port Orchard
220 Bravo Terrace
Port Orchard, WA
360-895-7818

Best Western Plus The Inn At Horse
Heaven
259 Merlot Drive
Prosser, WA
509-786-7977

Holiday Inn Express Hotel And Suites
Pullman
1190 Southeast Bishop Boulevard
Pullman, WA
509-334-4437

Quality Inn Paradise Creek
S.E. 1400 Bishop Blvd.
Pullman, WA

509-332-0500

Best Western PREMIER Plaza Hotel
& Conference Center
620 South Hill Park Dr.
Puyallup, WA
253-848-1500

Holiday Inn Express Hotel & Suites
Puyallup (Tacoma Area)
812 South Hill Park Drive
Puyallup, WA

253-848-4900

Residence Inn Seattle South/Tukwila
16201 West Valley Highway
Redmond, WA
425-226-5500

Towneplace Suites Seattle
South/Renton
300 Sw 19th Street
Renton, WA
525-917-2000

Days Inn Richland
615 Jadwin Avenue
Richland, WA
509-943-4611

Holiday Inn Express Hotel & Suites
Richland
1970 Center Parkway
Richland, WA

509-737-8000

M Hotel & Conference Center
1515 George Washington Way
Richland, WA
509-946-4121

Red Lion Hotel Richland Hanford
House
802 George Washington Way
Richland, WA
509-946-7611

Holiday Inn Express Suites Seattle
Airport
19621 International Blvd
Seatac, WA
206-824-3200

Alexis Seattle, A Kimpton Hotel
1007 First Avenue
Seattle, WA
206-624-4844

Country Inn & Suites By Carlson,
Seattle-Tacoma International Airport,
Wa
3100 S 192nd Street
Seattle, WA
206-433-8188

Doubletree Hotel Seattle Airport
18740 International Boulevard
Seattle, WA
206-246-8600

Econo Lodge Seatac Airport North
Seattle
13910 International Boulevard
Seattle, WA
206-244-0810

Extended Stay America Seattle -
Northgate
13300 Stone Avenue North
Seattle, WA
206-365-8100

Fairmont Olympic Hotel
411 University Street
Seattle, WA
206-621-1700

Hilton Seattle Airport And Conference
Center
17620 International Boulevard
Seattle, WA
206-244-4800

Homewood Suites By Hilton Seattle
Conv Center Pike Street
1011 Pike Street
Seattle, WA
206-682-8282

Homewood Suites By HiltonÂ®
Seattle-Downtown
206 Western Avenue West
Seattle, WA
206-281-9393

Hotel Vintage Seattle, A Kimpton
Hotel
1100 Fifth Avenue
Seattle, WA
206-624-8000

Kimpton Palladian Hotel
2000 Second Avenue
Seattle, WA
206-448-1111

Monaco Seattle, A Kimpton Hotel
1101 Fourth Avenue
Seattle, WA
206-621-1770

Motif Seattle
1415 Fifth Avenue
Seattle, WA
206-971-8000

Pan Pacific Seattle
2125 Terry Avenue
Seattle, WA
206-264-8111

Pensione Nichols Bed and Breakfast
1923 1st Avenue
Seattle, WA
206-441-7125

RENAISSANCE SEATTLE HOTEL,
A Marriott Luxury & Lifestyle Hotel
515 Madison Street
Seattle, WA
206-583-0300

Red Lion Hotel Seattle Airport
18220 International Boulevard
Seattle, WA
206-246-5535

Red Roof Inn Seattle Airport -
Seatac
16838 International Boulevard
Seattle, WA
206-248-0901

Residence Inn By Marriott Spokane
East Valley
15915 East Indiana Avenue
Seattle, WA
509-892-9300

Residence Inn Portland North
Vancouver

8005 Northeast Parkway Drive
Seattle, WA
360-253-4800

Seattle Pacific Hotel
325 Aurora Ave. North
Seattle, WA
206-441-0400

Seattle Pacific Hotel
325 Aurora Ave. North
Seattle, WA
206-441-0400

Sheraton Seattle
1400 Sixth Avenue
Seattle, WA
206-621-9000

The Westin Seattle
1900 Fifth Ave
Seattle, WA
206-728-1000

University Inn
4140 Roosevelt Way Northeast
Seattle, WA
206-632-5055

W Seattle Hotel
1112 Fourth Ave
Seattle, WA
206-264-6000

Super 8 Shelton
2943 Northview Circle
Shelton, WA
360-426-1654

Best Western Plus Silverdale Beach
Hotel
3073 Northwest Bucklin Hill Road
Silverdale, WA
360-698-1000

The Summit Inn
603 State Route 906
Snoqualmie Pass, WA

Pacific Beach Inn
12 First Street
South Pacific Beach, WA
360-276-4433

Best Western Plus Peppertree Airport
Inn
3711 S. Geiger Blvd.
Spokane, WA
509-624-4655

Comfort Inn University District
Downtown
923 East Third Avenue
Spokane, WA

509-535-9000

Days Inn Spokane
120 West 3rd Avenue
Spokane, WA
509-747-2011

Doubletree By Hilton Spokane City Center
322 North Spokane Falls Court
Spokane, WA
509-455-9600

La Quinta Inn & Suites Spokane North
9601 North Newport Highway
Spokane, WA
509-468-4201

Motel 6 Spokane WA
3033 N Division
Spokane, WA
509-326-5500

Quality Inn Valley Suites Spokane
E. 8923 Mission Ave.
Spokane, WA
509-928-5218

Ramada At Spokane Airport
8909 West Airport Drive
Spokane, WA
509-838-5211

Ramada Spokane
7111 North Division Street
Spokane, WA
509-467-7111

Red Lion Hotel Spokane At The Park
303 W North River Drive
Spokane, WA
509-326-8000

Red Lion River Inn
700 North Division Street
Spokane, WA
509-326-5577

Red Lion River Inn
700 North Division Street
Spokane, WA
509-326-5577

Residence Inn Redmond
7575 164th Ave Ne
Spokane, WA
425-497-9226

Rodeway Inn & Suites
6309 East Broadway

Spokane, WA
509-535-7185

Ruby2
123 South Post Street
Spokane, WA
509-838-8504

Super 8 Spokane Airport West
11102 West Westbow Lane
Spokane, WA
509-838-8800

Super 8 Spokane Valley
2020 North Argonne Road
Spokane, WA
509-928-4888

THE HISTORIC DAVENPORT, AUTOGRAPH COLLECTION, A Marriott Luxury & Lifestyle Hotel
10 South Post Street
Spokane, WA
509-455-8888

Ramada Spokane Valley
905 N Sullivan Rd
Spokane Valley, WA
509-924-3838

Mysty Mountain Properties
Call to arrange
Stevens Pass, WA
206-219-6427

Quality Inn Sunnyside
3209 Picard Place
Sunnyside, WA
509-837-5781

Best Western Plus Tacoma Dome Hotel
2611 East E Street
Tacoma, WA
253-272-7737

Days Inn Tacoma - Tacoma Mall
6802 Tacoma Mall Boulevard
Tacoma, WA
253-475-5900

Extended Stay America - Tacoma - South
2120 S. 48th St.
Tacoma, WA
253-475-6565

Quality Inn & Suites Toppenish - Yakima Valley
511 South Elm Street
Toppenish, WA
509-865-5800

Extended Stay America Seattle - Southcenter

15635 West Valley Highway
Tukwila, WA
425-235-7160

Extended Stay America Seattle - Tukwila
15451 53rd Avenue South
Tukwila, WA
206-244-2537

Homewood Suites By Hilton Seattle Tacoma Airport/Tukwila
6955 Fort Dent Way
Tukwila, WA
206-433-8000

Comfort Inn Conference Center Tumwater - Olympia
1620 74th Ave. Sw
Tumwater, WA
360-352-0691

Extended Stay America - Olympia - Tumwater
1675 Mottman Road Sw
Tumwater, WA
360-754-6063

Super 8 Union Gap Yakima Area
2605 South Rudkin Rd
Union Gap, WA
509-248-8880

Comfort Suites Vancouver
4714 N E 94th Ave
Vancouver, WA
360-253-3100

Days Inn & Suites Vancouver
9107 Ne Vancouver Mall Drive
Vancouver, WA
360-253-5000

Econo Lodge Vancouver
601 Broadway
Vancouver, WA
360-693-3668

Extended Stay America - Portland - Vancouver
300 Ne 115th Avenue
Vancouver, WA
360-604-8530

Hilton Vancouver Washington
301 W 6th Street
Vancouver, WA
360-993-4500

Homewood Suites By HiltonÂ®
Vancouver-Portland
701 Se Columbia Shores
Vancouver, WA
360-750-1100

Howard Johnson Vancouver Wa
9201 Ne Vancouvermall Dr
Vancouver, WA

360-254-0900

La Quinta Inn & Suites Vancouver
1500 Northeast 134th Street
Vancouver, WA

360-566-1100

Quality Inn & Suites Vancouver
7001 N.E. Highway 99
Vancouver, WA

360-696-0516

Quality Inn Vancouver
13207 North East 20th Avenue
Vancouver, WA

360-574-6000

Red Lion Hotel Vancouver At The
Quay
100 Columbia Street
Vancouver, WA

360-694-8341

Residence Inn By Marriott Seattle
Northeast-Bothell
11920 Ne 195th Street
Vancouver, WA

425-485-3030

Staybridge Suites Vancouver
Portland
7301 Northeast 41st Street
Vancouver, WA

360-891-8282

Best Western Plus Walla Walla
Suites Inn
7 East Oak Street
Walla Walla, WA
509-525-4700

Comfort Inn & Suites Walla Walla
1419 West Pine Street
Walla Walla, WA

509-522-3500

Holiday Inn Express Walla Walla
1433 West Pine Street
Walla Walla, WA

509-525-6200

Super 8 Walla Walla
2315 Eastgate Street North
Walla Walla, WA

509-525-8800

Econo Lodge Wenatchee
232 North Wenatchee Avenue

Wenatchee, WA
509-663-7121

Red Lion Hotel Wenatchee
1225 North Wenatchee Avenue
Wenatchee, WA

509-663-0711

Super 8 Wenatchee
1401 North Miller Street
Wenatchee, WA

509-662-3443

Winthrop Inn
960 Highway 20
Winthrop, WA
509-996-2217

Willows Lodge
14580 North East 145th Street
Woodinville, WA
425-424-3900

Rodeway Inn - Woodland
1500 Atlantic Avenue
Woodland, WA
360-225-6548

Best Western Plus Ahtanum Inn
2408 Rudkin Road
Yakima, WA
509-248-9700

Best Western Plus Lincoln Inn
1614 North 1st Street
Yakima, WA

509-453-8898

Days Inn Yakima
1504 North 1st Street
Yakima, WA

509-248-3393

Holiday Inn Yakima
802 East Yakima Avenue
Yakima, WA

509-494-7000

Howard Johnson Plaza
Yakima/Near Convention Center
9 North 9th Street
Yakima, WA

509-452-6511

Quality Inn Yakima
12 East Valley Mall Boulevard
Yakima, WA

509-248-6924

Red Lion Hotel Yakima Center
607 East Yakima Avenue
Yakima, WA

509-248-5900

Yakima Valley Inn
818 North 1st Street
Yakima, WA

509-453-0391

# West Virginia Listings

Best Western Huntington Mall Inn
3441 Us Route 60 East
Barboursville, WV
304-736-9772

Comfort Inn Barboursville
249 Mall Rd
Barboursville, WV

304-733-2122

Econo Lodge Beckley
1909 Harper Rd
Beckley, WV
304-255-2161

Howard Johnson Express Inn
1907 Harper Road
Beckley, WV

304-255-5900

Berkeley Springs Motel
468 Wilkes Street
Berkeley Springs, WV
304-258-1776

Hannah's House
867 Libby's Ridge Road
Berkeley Springs, WV

304-258-1718

Sleepy Creek Tree Farm
37 Shades Lane
Berkeley Springs, WV

304-258-4324

Sunset Mountain Farm
Stickey Kline Road
Berkeley Springs, WV

304-258-4239

Econo Lodge Near Bluefield College
3400 East Cumberland Rd.
Bluefield, WV
304-327-8171

Knights Inn Bluefield
3144 East Cumberland Road
Bluefield, WV

304-325-9131

Quality Hotel And Conference Center
3350 Big Laurel Highway
Bluefield, WV

304-325-6170

Dog-Friendly Lodging - Please always call ahead to make sure an establishment is still dog-friendly.

Super 8 Bridgeport
168 Barnett Run Road
Bridgeport, WV
304-842-7381

Centennial Motel
22 North Locust Street
Buckhannon, WV
304-472-4100

North Fork Mountain Inn
Smoke Hole Road
Cabins, WV
304-257-1108

A Room with A View
Black Bear Woods Resort-Northside
Cortland Rd
Canaan Valley, WV
301-767-6853

Country Inn & Suites By Carlson,
Charleston South, Wv
105 Alex Lane
Charleston, WV
304-925-4300

Holiday Inn Hotel & Suites Charleston
West
400 2nd Avenue Sw
Charleston, WV

304-744-4641

Residence Inn Charleston
200 Hotel Circle
Charleston, WV

304-345-4200

The Resort At Glade Springs
255 Resort Drive
Daniels, WV
866-562-8054

Super 8 Dunbar
911 Dunbar Avenue
Dunbar, WV
304-768-6888

Cheat River Lodge
Route 1, Box 115
Elkins, WV
304-636-2301

Super 8 Fairmont
2208 Pleasant Valley Road
Fairmont, WV
304-363-1488

Quality Inn New River Gorge
103 Elliotts Way
Fayetteville, WV
304-574-3443

Econo Lodge Huntington
3325 Us Route 60
Huntington, WV
304-525-7001

Red Roof Inn - Huntington
5190 Us Rt 60 East
Huntington, WV

304-733-3737

Towneplace Suites By Marriott
Huntington
157 Kenitic Drive
Huntington, WV

304-525-4877

Red Roof Charleston West
Hurricane Wv
500 Putnam Village Drive
Hurricane, WV
304-757-6392

Red Roof Inn Charleston-Kanawha
City
6305 Maccorkle Avenue South East
Kanawha City, WV
304-925-6953

Quality Inn Lewisburg
540 North Jefferson Street
Lewisburg, WV
304-645-7722

Super 8 Lewisburg
550 N Jefferson St
Lewisburg, WV

304-647-3188

Days Inn Martinsburg
209 Viking Way
Martinsburg, WV
304-263-1800

Holiday Inn Martinsburg
301 Foxcroft Avenue
Martinsburg, WV

304-267-5500

Knights Inn Martinsburg
1997 Edwin Miller Blvd
Martinsburg, WV

304-267-2211

Rodeway Inn
94 Mcmillan Court
Martinsburg, WV

304-263-8811

Super 8 Martinsburg
2048 Edwin Miller Blvd
Martinsburg, WV

304-263-0801

Comfort Suites Parkersburg South
167 Elizabeth Pike
Mineral Wells, WV
304-489-9600

Alpine Lake Resort
700 West Alpine Drive
Morgantown, WV
304-789-2481

Econo Lodge Coliseum
3506 Monongahela Blvd.
Morgantown, WV

304-599-8181

Quality Inn Morgantown
225 Comfort Inn Drive
Morgantown, WV

304-296-9364

Ramada Conference Center
Morgantown
20 Scott Avenue
Morgantown, WV

304-296-3431

Residence Inn By Marriott
Morgantown
1046 Willowdale Road
Morgantown, WV

304-599-0237

Super 8 Morgantown
603 Venture Dr
Morgantown, WV

304-296-4000

Blennerhassett Hotel
320 Market Street
Parkersburg, WV
304-422-3131

Red Carpet Inn Parkersburg
6333 Emerson Avenue
Parkersburg, WV

304-485-1851

Red Roof Parkersburg
3714 East 7th St
Parkersburg, WV

304-485-1741

Days Inn Princeton
347 Meadow Field Lane
Princeton, WV
304-425-8100

Quality Inn Princeton
136 Ambrose Lane
Princeton, WV

304-487-6101

Sleep Inn & Suites Princeton
1015 Oakvale Road
Princeton, WV

304-431-2800

Holiday Inn Express Hotel & Suites

# Wisconsin Listings

Ripley
110 Memorial Drive
Ripley, WV
304-372-4444

Quality Inn Ripley
1 Hospitality Dr.
Ripley, WV
304-372-5000

Super 8 Ripley
102 Duke Dr
Ripley, WV
304-372-8880

Quality Inn Shepherdstown
70 Maddex Square Drive
Shepherdstown, WV
304-876-3160

Morning Glory Inn
H 219
Snowshoe, WV
304-572-5000

Baymont Inn & Suites Summersville
903 Industrial Drive North
Summersville, WV
304-872-6500

Econo Lodge Summersville
1203 Broad Street
Summersville, WV

304-872-6900

Super 8 Summersville
306 Merchants Walk
Summersville, WV

304-872-4888

Comfort Inn & Suites Triadelphia
675 Fort Henry Road
Triadelphia, WV
304-547-0610

Super 8 Weston Wv
100 Market Place Mall Ste 12
Weston, WV
304-269-1086

Oglebay's Wilson Lodge
Route 88 North
Wheeling, WV
304-243-4000

Super 8 Wheeling
2400 National Road
Wheeling, WV

304-243-9400

Rodeway Inn Williamstown
1339 Highland Avenue Building A
Williamstown, WV
304-375-3730

Rodeway Inn Abbotsford
300 East Elderberry Road
Abbotsford, WI
715-223-3337

Algoma Beach Motel
1500 Lake Street
Algoma, WI
920-487-2828

America's Best Inn Antigo
525 Memory Lane
Antigo, WI
715-623-0506

Holiday Inn Express Hotel & Suites
Antigo
2407 Neva Road
Antigo, WI
715-627-7500

Best Western Fox Valley Inn
3033 West College Avenue
Appleton, WI
920-731-4141

Candlewood Suites Appleton
4525 West College Avenue
Appleton, WI
920-739-8000

Comfort Suites Appleton Airport
3809 West Wisconsin Avenue
Appleton, WI
920-730-3800

Extended Stay America - Appleton -
Fox Cities
4141 Boardwalk Court
Appleton, WI
920-830-9596

Motel 6 Appleton
210 Westhill Boulevard
Appleton, WI
920-733-5551

Residence Inn Appleton
310 Metro Drive
Appleton, WI
920-954-0570

Americinn Ashland
3009 Lakeshore Drive East
Ashland, WI
715-682-9950

Lake Aire Inn
101 E. Lake Shore Dr.
Ashland, WI
715-682-4551

Isaac Wing House
17 South First Street/H 13
Bayfield, WI
715-779-3363

Super 8 Beaver Dam
711 Park Avenue
Beaver Dam, WI
920-887-8880

Quality Inn Beloit
2786 Milwaukee Rd
Beloit, WI
608-362-2666

Rodeway Inn Beloit
2956 Milwaukee Road
Beloit, WI
608-364-4000

The Cobblestone
319 S Main Street
Birchwood, WI
715-354-3494

Best Western Arrowhead Lodge &
Suites
600 Oasis Road
Black River Falls, WI
715-284-9471

Days Inn Black River Falls
919 Highway 54 East
Black River Falls, WI

715-284-4333

Extended Stay America - Milwaukee -
Brookfield
325 N Brookfield Rd
Brookfield, WI
262-782-9300

Midway Hotel & Suites Brookfield
1005 South Moorland Road
Brookfield, WI

262-786-9540

Residence Inn By Marriott
Milwaukee/Brookfield
950 South Pinehurst Court
Brookfield, WI

262-782-5990

Sheraton Milwaukee Brookfield
375 South Moorland Rd
Brookfield, WI

262-364-1100

Towneplace Suites By Marriott
Brookfield
600 North Calhoun
Brookfield, WI

262-784-8450

Candlewood Suites Milwaukee Brown

Deer
4483 West Schroeder Drive
Brown Deer, WI
414-355-3939

Telemark Resort
4225 Telemark Road
Cable, WI
715-798-3999

Americas Best Value Inn Chetek
115 2nd Street
Chetek, WI
715-924-4888

Americinn Of Chippewa Falls, Wi
11 West South Avenue
Chippewa Falls, WI
715-723-5711

Indianhead Motel
501 Summit Avenue
Chippewa Falls, WI

715-723-9171

Super 8 Columbus
219 Industrial Drive
Columbus, WI
920-623-8800

Best Western Crandon Inn & Suites
9075 E Pioneer Street, Crandon,
Wisconsin, United State
Crandon, WI
715-478-4000

Kress Inn, An Ascend Hotel
Collection Member
300 Grant Street
De Pere, WI
920-403-5100

Comfort Inn And Suites
5025 County Hwy. V
DeForest, WI
608-846-9100

Super 8 Dodgeville
1308 Johns Street
Dodgeville, WI
608-935-3888

Days Inn Eagle River
844 Railroad Street North
Eagle River, WI
715-479-5151

Gypsy Villa Resort
950 Circle Drive
Eagle River, WI

715-479-8644

Best Western Plus Trail Lodge Hotel
& Suites
3340 Mondovi Road
Eau Claire, WI
715-838-9989

Clarion Hotel Campus Area
2703 Craig Road
Eau Claire, WI

715-835-2211

Econo Lodge Inn & Suites Eau
Claire
4608 Royal Drive
Eau Claire, WI

715-833-8818

Motel 6 Eau Claire, WI
2305 Craig Road
Eau Claire, WI

715-834-3193

Rodeway Inn & Suites Eau Claire
1828 South Hasting Way
Eau Claire, WI

715-835-3600

Sleep Inn & Suites Conference
Center Eau Claire
5872 33rd Avenue
Eau Claire, WI

715-874-2900

Comfort Inn Edgerton
11102 Goede Road
Edgerton, WI
608-884-2118

Door County Cottages
Highway T
Egg Harbor, WI
920-868-2300

The Feathered Star
6202 H 42
Egg Harbor, WI

920-743-4066

Comfort Inn Fond Du Lac
77 Holiday Lane
Fond Du Lac, WI
920-921-4000

Days Inn Fond Du Lac
107 North Pioneer Road
Fond Du Lac, WI

920-923-6790

Holiday Inn Fond Du Lac
625 W Rolling Meadows Drive
Fond Du Lac, WI

920-923-1440

Super 8 Fond Du Lac
391 North Pioneer Road
Fond Du Lac, WI

920-922-1088

Staybridge Suites Franklin

9575 South 27th Street
Franklin, WI
414-761-3800

Super 8 Germantown/Milwaukee
N 96 W 17490 County Line Rd
Germantown, WI
262-255-0880

Harbor House Inn
12666 H 42
Gills Rock, WI
920-854-5196

Comfort Inn & Suites Grafton
1415 Port Washington Road
Grafton, WI
262-387-1180

Americinn Green Bay West
2032 Velp Avenue
Green Bay, WI
920-434-9790

Hawthorn Suites By Wyndham Green
Bay
335 W. St. Joseph St.
Green Bay, WI

920-435-2222

Quality Inn & Suites Downtown
321 South Washington Street
Green Bay, WI

920-437-8771

Quality Inn Stadium Area
1978 Holmgren Way
Green Bay, WI

920-498-8088

Super 8 Green Bay
2868 S. Oneida Street
Green Bay, WI

920-494-2042

Super 8 Green Bay I-43 Business
Park
2911 Voyager Drive
Green Bay, WI

920-406-8200

Super 8 Hartford Wi
1539 E Sumner St
Hartford, WI
262-673-7431

Americas Best Value Inn
10444 North State Highway 27 South
Hayward, WI
715-634-2646

Comfort Suites Hayward
15586 County Road B
Hayward, WI

715-634-0700

Ross' Teal Lake Lodge
12425 N Ross Rd
Hayward, WI

715-462-3631

Super 8 Hudson
808 Dominion Drive
Hudson, WI
715-386-8800

Comfort Inn & Suites Jackson
W227 North 16890 Tillie Lake Court
Jackson, WI
262-677-1133

Baymont Inn & Suites Janesville
616 Midland Road
Janesville, WI
608-758-4545

Econo Lodge Janesville
3520 Milton Avenue
Janesville, WI

608-754-0251

Days Inn Johnson Creek
West 4545 Linmar Lane
Johnson Creek, WI
920-699-8000

Candlewood Suites Kenosha
10200 74th Street
Kenosha, WI
262-842-5000

Quality Inn & Suites Kimberly
761 Truman Street
Kimberly, WI
920-788-4400

Best Western Riverfront Hotel
1835 Rose St.
La Crosse, WI
608-781-7000

Candlewood Suites La Crosse
56 Copeland Avenue
La Crosse, WI

608-785-1110

Bog Lake
2848 School House Road
La Pointe, WI
715-747-2685

Brittany Cottages at Coole Park
351 Old Fort Road
La Pointe, WI

715-747-5023

Woods Manor
RR 1, Box 7
La Pointe, WI

715-747-3102

Holiday Inn Hotel And Suites La Crosse
200 Pearl Street
Lacrosse, WI
608-784-4444

Eleven Gables Inn on Lake Geneva
493 Wrigley Drive
Lake Geneva, WI
262-248-8393

Maria's Bed & Breakfast
512 S Wells Street
Lake Geneva, WI

262-249-0632

T. C. Smith Historic Inn
834 Dodge Street
Lake Geneva, WI

262-248-1097

Loon Call Cottage

Lake Tomahawk, WI
760-399-6308

Quality Inn & Suites Lodi
W9250 Prospect Dr
Lodi, WI
608-592-1450

Baymont Inn & Suites Madison West/ Middleton Wi West
8102 Excelsior Drive
Madison, WI
608-831-7711

Best Western East Towne Suites
4801 Annamark Drive
Madison, WI
608-244-2020

Best Western West Towne Suites
650 Grand Canyon Drive
Madison, WI
608-833-4200

Candlewood Suites Fitchburg
5421 Caddis Bend
Madison, WI
608-271-3400

Clarion Suites At The Alliant Energy Center
2110 Rimrock Rd
Madison, WI
608-284-1234

Comfort Inn & Suites Madison - Airport
4822 East Washington Avenue
Madison, WI
608-244-6265

Comfort Suites Madison

1253 John Q Hammons Drive
Madison, WI
608-836-3033

Days Inn & Suites Madison
4402 East Broadway Service Road
Madison, WI
608-223-1800

Econo Lodge Madison
4726 E Washington Ave
Madison, WI
608-241-4171

Extended Stay America - Madison - Junction Court
55 Junction Court
Madison, WI
608-833-1400

Hilton Madison Monona Terrace
9 East Wilson Street
Madison, WI
608-255-5100

Homewood Suites By Hilton Madison
479 Commerce Drive
Madison, WI
608-271-0600

Howard Johnson Plaza Hotel Madison
3841 East Washington Avenue
Madison, WI
608-244-2481

Red Roof Inn - Madison
4830 Hayes Road
Madison, WI
608-241-1787

Residence Inn Madison East
4862 Hayes Road
Madison, WI
608-244-5047

Rodeway Inn & Suites Wi Madison-Northeast
4845 Hayes Road
Madison, WI
608-249-1815

Sheraton Hotel Madison
706 John Nolen Drive
Madison, WI
608-251-2300

Sleep Inn & Suites
4802 Tradewinds Parkway
Madison, WI
608-221-8100

Staybridge Suites Madison East
3301 City View Drive
Madison, WI

608-241-2300

Super 8 Madison East
4765 Hayes Road
Madison, WI

608-249-5300

Super 8 Madison South
1602 West Beltline Highway
Madison, WI

608-258-8882

Wyndham Garden Madison Fitchburg
2969 Cahill Main
Madison, WI

608-274-7200

Baymont Inn & Suites Manitowoc
Lakefront
101 Maritime Drive
Manitowoc, WI
920-682-7000

Econo Lodge Manitowoc
908 Washington St
Manitowoc, WI

920-682-8271

Holiday Inn Manitowoc
4601 Calumet Ave.
Manitowoc, WI

920-682-.600

Quality Inn Manitowoc
2200 South 44th Street
Manitowoc, WI

920-683-0220

Super 8 Manitowoc
4004 Calumet Avenue
Manitowoc, WI

920-684-7841

Budget Inn Marinette
1301 Marinette Avenue
Marinette, WI
715-735-6687

Quality Inn & Suites Marinette
1508 Marinette Avenue
Marinette, WI

715-735-7887

Quality Inn Marshfield
114 East Upham Street
Marshfield, WI
715-387-8691

Super 8 Mauston

1001 A Hwy 82e
Mauston, WI
608-847-2300

Super 8 Menomonie
1622 North Broadway
Menomonie, WI
715-235-8889

Badger Hotel
3209 East Main Street
Merrill, WI
715-536-6880

Econo Lodge Merrill
200 South Pine Ridge Avenue
Merrill, WI

715-536-9526

Residence Inn Middleton
8400 Market Street
Middleton, WI
608-662-1100

Staybridge Suites
Middleton/Madison-West
7790 Elmwood Avenue
Middleton, WI

608-664-5888

Acanthus Inn
3009 W Highland Blvd/H 18
Milwaukee, WI
414-342-9788

Hilton Milwaukee City Center
509 W Wisconsin Ave
Milwaukee, WI

414-271-7250

Kimpton Journeyman Hotel
310 E Chicago Street
Milwaukee, WI

414-291-3970

Sleep Inn & Suites Milwaukee
4600 South 6th Street
Milwaukee, WI

414-831-2000

The Iron Horse Hotel
500 West Florida Street
Milwaukee, WI

414-374-4766

The Westin Milwaukee
550 N Van Buren Street
Milwaukee, WI

800-675-2671

Quality Inn Minocqua
8729 Us 51 North
Minocqua, WI
715-358-2588

Super 8 Monroe Wi
500 6th St And Hwy 69
Monroe, WI
608-325-1500

Super 8 Neillsville Wi
1000 East Division Street
Neillsville, WI
715-743-8080

Asteria Inn and Suites
1561 Dorset Lane
New Richmond, WI
715-246-7829

Candlewood Suites Milwaukee
Airport - Oak Creek
6440 S. 13th Street
Oak Creek, WI
414-570-9999

Comfort Suites Milwaukee Airport
6362 South 13th Street
Oak Creek, WI

414-570-1111

Red Roof Inn - Milwaukee Airport
6360 South 13th Street
Oak Creek, WI

414-764-3500

Staybridge Suites Milwaukee West-
Oconomowoc
1141 Blue Ribbon Drive
Oconomowoc, WI
262-200-2900

Comfort Inn Onalaska
1223 Crossing Meadows Drive
Onalaska, WI
608-781-7500

Holiday Inn Express Onalaska
9409 Highway 16
Onalaska, WI

608-783-6555

Holiday Inn Express Hotel & Suites
Oshkosh-Sr41
2251 Westowne Avenue
Oshkosh, WI
920-303-1300

Super 8 Oshkosh Airport
1581 W. South Park Ave.
Oshkosh, WI

920-426-2885

Americas Best Value Inn - Park Falls
1212 Highway 13 South
Park Falls, WI
715-762-3383

Best Western Waukesha Grand
2840 North Grandview Boulevard
Pewaukee, WI

Dog-Friendly Lodging - Please always call ahead to make sure an establishment is still dog-friendly.

262-524-9300

Super 8 Phillips
726 South Lake Avenue
Phillips, WI
715-339-2898

Governer Dodge Hotel and
Convention Center
300 Bus H 151
Platteville, WI
608-348-2301

Super 8 Pleasant Prairie
7601 118th Ave
Pleasant Prairie, WI
262-857-7963

Comfort Inn Plover
1560 American Drive
Plover, WI
715-342-0400

52 Stafford Inn
52 Stafford Street
Plymouth, WI
920-893-0552

Comfort Suites Portage
North 5780 Kinney Road
Portage, WI
608-745-4717

Days Inn Portage
N5781 Kinney Rd
Portage, WI

608-742-1554

Super 8 Portage
3000 New Pinery Road
Portage, WI

608-742-8330

Super 8 Prairie Du Chien
1930 South Marquette Road
Prairie Du Chien, WI
608-326-8777

Racine Architect Hotel & Conference
Center
7111 Washington Avenue
Racine, WI
262-886-6100

Quality Inn Reedsburg
2115 East Main Street
Reedsburg, WI
608-524-8535

Days Inn & Suites Rhinelander
70 North Stevens Street
Rhinelander, WI
715-362-7100

Holiday Acres Resort on Lake
Thompson
4060 S Shore Road
Rhinelander, WI

715-369-1500

Quality Inn Rhinelander
668 West Kemp Street - Hwy 8 &;
47
Rhinelander, WI

715-369-3600

Currier's Lakeview Lodge
2010 E. Sawyer Street
Rice Lake, WI
715-234-7474

Super 8 Rice Lake
2401 South Main
Rice Lake, WI

715-234-6956

Comfort Suites At Royal Ridges
2 Westgate Drive
Ripon, WI
920-748-5500

Best Western Plus
Wausau/Rothschild Hotel
803 W Industrial Park Avenue
Rothschild, WI
715-355-8900

Econo Lodge Rothschild
1510 County Road Xx
Rothschild, WI

715-355-4449

Holiday Inn Hotel And Suites
Wausau-Rothschild
1000 Imperial Avenue
Rothschild, WI

715-355-1111

Motel 6 Saukville
180 South Foster Street
Saukville, WI
262-284-9399

Boarders Inn & Suites - Shawano
West 7393 River Bend Road
Shawano, WI
715-524-9090

Super 8 Shawano
211 Waukechon Street
Shawano, WI

715-526-6688

Quality Inn Sheboygan
4332 North 40th Street
Sheboygan, WI
920-457-7724

Sleep Inn & Suites Sheboygan
3912 Motel Road
Sheboygan, WI

920-694-0099

Days Inn Sheboygan/The Falls
600 Main St. North Hwy 32
Sheboygan Falls, WI
920-467-4314

Country House Resort
2468 Sunnyside Road
Sister Bay, WI
920-854-4551

Patio Motel and Restaurant
10440 Orchard Drive
Sister Bay, WI

920-854-1978

Country Inn & Suites By Carlson,
Sparta, WI
737 Avon Road
Sparta, WI
608-269-3110

Grapevine Log Cabins
19149 Jade Road
Sparta, WI

608-269-3619

Justin Trails Resort
7452 Kathryn Avenue
Sparta, WI

608-269-4522

Super 8 Sparta
716 Avon Road
Sparta, WI

608-269-8489

Best Western American Heritage Inn
101 W Maple Street
Spooner, WI
715-635-9770

Beach Harbor Resort
3662 North Duluth Avenue
Sturgeon Bay, WI
920-743-3191

Best Western Maritime Inn
1001 North 14th Avenue
Sturgeon Bay, WI

920-743-7231

Holiday Motel - Bed And Breakfast
30 N 1st Avenue
Sturgeon Bay, WI

920-743-5571

Super 8 Sturgeon Bay
409 Green Bay Road
Sturgeon Bay, WI

920-743-9211

Quality Inn & Suites Sun Prairie
105 Business Park Drive

Sun Prairie, WI
608-834-9889

Super 8 Sun Prairie
1033 Emerald Terrace
Sun Prairie, WI
608-837-8889

Best Western Bridgeview Motor Inn
415 Hammond Ave.
Superior, WI
715-392-8174

Americinn Tomah
750 Vandervort Street
Tomah, WI
608-372-4100

Cranberry Country Lodge
319 Wittig Road
Tomah, WI
608-374-2801

Econo Lodge Tomah
2005 North Superior
Tomah, WI
608-372-9100

Lark Inn
229 N Superior Ave
Tomah, WI
608-372-5981

Quality Inn Tomah
305 Wittig Road
Tomah, WI
608-372-6600

Super 8 Tomah
1008 E Mccoy Blvd
Tomah, WI
608-372-3901

Rodeway Inn & Suites
1738 Comfort Drive
Tomahawk, WI
715-453-8900

Viking Village Motel
Main Road at Detroit Harbor, P.O.
Box 188.
Washington Island, WI
920-847-2551

Baymont Inn & Suites
Waterford/Burlington
750 Fox Lane
Waterford, WI
262-534-4100

Baymont Inn & Suites Waukesha
2111 East Moreland Boulevard,
Waukesha, WI
262-547-7770

Extended Stay America - Waukesha
2520 Plaza Court
Waukesha, WI

262-798-0217

Super 8 Waukesha
2510 Plaza Court
Waukesha, WI

262-786-6015

Quality Inn Wausau
2901 Hummingbird Road
Wausau, WI
715-842-1616

Stewart Inn
521 Grant Street
Wausau, WI

715-849-5858

Super 8 Wausau
2006 West Stewart Avenue
Wausau, WI

715-848-2888

Super 8 Motel - Wautoma
W 7607 State Road 21 73
Wautoma, WI
920-787-4811

Extended Stay America - Milwaukee
- Wauwatosa
11121 W North Ave
Wauwatosa, WI
414-443-1909

Holiday Inn Express Milwaukee
West Medical Center
11111 West North Avenue
Wauwatosa, WI

414-778-0333

Super 8 Windsor/Madison North
4506 Lake Circle
Windsor, WI
608-846-3971

Bakers Sunset Bay Resort
921 Canyon Road
Wisconsin Dells, WI
608-254-8406

Econo Lodge Wisconsin Dells
2504 Wisconsin Dells Parkway
Wisconsin Dells, WI

608-254-6444

Kings Inn Motel
31 Whitlock Street
Wisconsin Dells, WI

608-254-2043

Paradise Motel
1700 Wisconsin Dells Parkway/H
12/23

Wisconsin Dells, WI

608-254-7333

Pine-Aire Motel
511 Wisconsin Dells Parkway/H
12/23
Wisconsin Dells, WI

608-254-2131

Spring Brook Wisconsin Dells
242 Lake Shore Dr
Wisconsin Dells, WI

877-228-8686

Thunder Valley Inn
W15344 Waubeek Road
Wisconsin Dells, WI

608-254-4145

Rapids Inn And Suites
3300 8th Street South
Wisconsin Rapids, WI
715-423-7000

Sleep Inn & Suites
4221 8th Street South
Wisconsin Rapids, WI

715-424-6800

Best Western Wittenberg Inn
W17267 Red Oak Lane
Wittenberg, WI
715-253-3755

# Wyoming Listings

Drifter's Inn Motel
210 Penland Street/H 789
Baggs, WY
307-383-2015

Canyon Ranch Guest Ranch
22 Johnson Street
Big Horn, WY
307-674-6239

Comfort Inn Buffalo
65 Us Highway 16 East
Buffalo, WY
307-684-9564

Days Inn Buffalo Wy
333 East Hart Street
Buffalo, WY

307-684-2219

Quality Inn
75 North Bypass Road
Buffalo, WY

307-684-2256

Super 8 Buffalo
655 East Hart Street Highway 16 &; I-

25
Buffalo, WY

307-684-2531

Days Inn Casper
301 East E Street
Casper, WY
307-234-1159

Quality Inn & Suites Casper
821 North Poplar
Casper, WY

307-266-2400

Ramada Plaza Riverside Casper
300 West F Street
Casper, WY

307-235-2531

Ramkota Hotel
800 North Poplar Street
Casper, WY

307-266-6000

Super 8 Casper West
3838 Cy Avenue
Casper, WY

307-266-3480

Best Western Plus Frontier Inn
8101 Hutchins Drive
Cheyenne, WY
307-638-8891

Candlewood Suites Cheyenne
2335 Tura Parkway
Cheyenne, WY

307-634-6622

Days Inn Cheyenne Wy
2360 W Lincoln Way Po Box 1286
Cheyenne, WY

307-778-8877

Historic Plains Hotel
1600 Central Avenue
Cheyenne, WY

307-638-3311

Nagle Warren Mansion Bed And
Breakfast
222 East 17th Street
Cheyenne, WY

307-637-3333

Oak Tree Inn Cheyenne
1625 Stillwater Avenue
Cheyenne, WY

307-778-6620

Quality Inn Cheyenne
2245 Etchepare Dr

Cheyenne, WY

307-638-7202

Rodeway Inn Cheyenne
5401 Walker Road
Cheyenne, WY

307-632-8901

Super 8 Cheyenne Wy
1900 W Lincolnway
Cheyenne, WY

307-635-8741

Windy Hills Guest House
393 Happy Jack Rd
Cheyenne, WY

307-632-6423

Cody Lodging Company
1102 Beck Avenue
Cody, WY
307-587-6000

Hunter Peak Ranch
4027 Crandall Road/H 296
Cody, WY

307-587-3711

Super 8 Cody
730 Yellowstone Rd
Cody, WY

307-527-6214

Holiday Inn Express Hotel & Suites
Douglas, Wy
900 West Yellowstone Highway
Douglas, WY
307-358-4500

Super 8 Douglas
314 Russell Ave
Douglas, WY

307-358-6800

Branding Iron Inn
401 W Ramshorn
Dubois, WY
307-455-2893

Chinook Winds Mountain Lodge
640 S 1st St
Dubois, WY

307-455-2987

Pinnacle Buttes Lodge and
Campground
3577 US Hwy 26W
Dubois, WY

307-455-2506

Super 8 Dubois
1412 Warm Springs Drive
Dubois, WY

307-455-3694

Comfort Inn Evanston
1931 Harrison Dr.
Evanston, WY
307-789-7799

Days Inn Evanston Wy
1983 Harrison Drive
Evanston, WY

307-789-0783

Knights Inn Evanston
339 Wasatch Road
Evanston, WY

307-789-2220

Super 8 Evanston
1710 Harrison Drive
Evanston, WY

307-789-2777

Baymont Inn And Suites - Casper
East
480 Lathrop Road
Evansville, WY
307-235-3038

Comfort Inn Evansville
269 Miracle Street
Evansville, WY

307-237-8100

Sleep Inn & Suites Evansville
6733 Bonanza Road
Evansville, WY

307-235-3100

Best Western Tower West Lodge
109 N Us Highway 14-16
Gillette, WY
307-686-2210

Candlewood Suites Gillette
904 Country Club Road
Gillette, WY

307-682-6100

Days Inn Gillette
910 East Boxelder Road
Gillette, WY

307-682-3999

Holiday Inn Express Hotel & Suites
Gillette
1908 Cliff Davis Drive
Gillette, WY

307-686-9576

Ramada Plaza Gillette
2009 South Douglas Hwy
Gillette, WY

307-686-3000

Super 8 Gillette
208 S Decker Court
Gillette, WY

307-682-8078

Jackson Lake Lodge
100 Jackson Lake Lodge Road,
Highway 89
Grand Teton National Park, WY
800-628-9988

Jackson Lake Lodge
100 Jackson Lake Lodge Road,
Highway 89
Grand Teton National Park, WY

800-628-9988

Oak Tree Inn Green River
1170 West Flaming Gorge Way
Green River, WY
307-875-3500

Elk Country Inn
480 W Pearl Avenue
Jackson, WY
307-733-2364

Flat Creek Inn
1935 N H 89/26
Jackson, WY

307-733-5276

Homewood Suites By Hilton®
Jackson, Wy
260 N. Millward
Jackson, WY

307-739-0808

Homewood Suites By Hilton®
Jackson, Wy
260 N. Millward
Jackson, WY

307-739-0808

Pony Express Motel
1075 W Broadway/H 26/89/189/191
Jackson, WY

307-733-3835

Jackson Hole Lodge
420 West Broadway
Jackson Hole, WY
307-733-2992

Painted Buffalo Inn
400 West Broadway
Jackson Hole, WY

307-733-4340

Snow King Resort Hotel
400 East Snow King Avenue
Jackson Hole, WY

307-733-5200

Best Western Plus Fossil Country
Inn & Suites
760 Highway 189/30
Kemmerer, WY
307-877-3388

Holiday Inn Express Hotel & Suites
Lander
1002 11th Street
Lander, WY
307-332-4005

Best Western Laramie Inn & Suites
1767 N Banner Road
Laramie, WY
307-745-5700

Holiday Inn Laramie
204 S 30th Street
Laramie, WY

307-721-9000

Quality Inn & Suites Laramie
1655 Centennial Drive
Laramie, WY

307-742-6665

Ramada Center
2313 Soldier Springs Road
Laramie, WY

307-742-6611

Wyoming High Country Guest
Ranch
H 14A, Bighorn National Forest
Lovell, WY
307-548-7820

Rawhide Motel
805 S Main Street/H 85
Lusk, WY
307-334-2440

Best Western Pinedale Inn
864 West Pine Street
Pinedale, WY
307-367-6869

Lodge At Pinedale
1054 W Pine Ste 191
Pinedale, WY

307-367-8800

Super 8 Powell
845 East Coulter Avenue
Powell, WY
307-754-7231

Days Inn Rawlins
2222 East Cedar Street
Rawlins, WY
307-324-6615

Econo Lodge Rawlins

1500 West Spruce Street
Rawlins, WY

307-324-2905

Hampton Inn Rawlins
406 Airport Road
Rawlins, WY

307-324-2320

Holiday Inn Express Rawlins
201 Airport Road
Rawlins, WY

307-324-3760

Lazy Acres Motel and Campground
110 Fields Avenue
Riverside, WY
307-327-5968

Comfort Inn & Suites Riverton
2020 N. Federal Blvd
Riverton, WY
307-856-8900

Comfort Inn & Suites Riverton
2020 North Federal Boulevard
Riverton, WY

307-856-8900

Days Inn Riverton
909 West Main Street
Riverton, WY

307-856-9677

Hampton Inn And Suites Riverton,
Wy
2500 North Federal Blvd
Riverton, WY

307-856-3500

Rodeway Inn & Suites Riverton
611 West Main Street
Riverton, WY

307-856-2900

Sundowner Station
1616 N Federal Blvd
Riverton, WY

307-856-6503

Super 8 Riverton
1040 North Federal Boulevard
Riverton, WY

307-857-2400

Econo Lodge Rock Springs
1635 North Elk
Rock Springs, WY
307-382-4217

Hampton Inn Rock Springs
1901 Dewar Drive
Rock Springs, WY

307-382-9222

Quality Inn Rock Springs
1670 Sunset Dr.
Rock Springs, WY

307-382-9490

Budget Host Sheridan
2007 North Main Street
Sheridan, WY
307-674-7496

Candlewood Suites Sheridan
1709 Sugarland Drive
Sheridan, WY

307-675-2100

Days Inn Sheridan
1104 East Brundage Lane
Sheridan, WY

307-672-2888

Holiday Inn Sheridan - Convention
Center
1809 Sugarland Drive
Sheridan, WY

307-672-8931

Quality Inn Sheridan
1450 E. Brundage Ln.
Sheridan, WY

307-672-5098

Super 8 Sheridan
2435 North Main Street
Sheridan, WY

307-672-9725

Days Inn Thermopolis
115 E Park Street
Thermopolis, WY
307-864-3131

Quality Inn Thermopolis
166 Us Highway 20 South
Thermopolis, WY

307-864-5515

Holiday Inn Express Hotel & Suites
Torrington
1700 East Valley Road
Torrington, WY
307-532-7600

Green Creek Inn
2908 Yellowstone Hwy
Wapiti, WY
307-587-5004

Best Western Torchlite Motor Inn
1809 North 16th Street
Wheatland, WY
307-322-4070

Vimbo's Motel
203 16th St
Wheatland, WY

307-322-3842

Sunset Inn
2500 Big Horn Ave
Worland, WY
307-347-9236

Headwaters Lodge & Cabins at
Flagg Ranch
100 Grassy Lake Road, Highway 89,
2 Miles South Of The South
Entrance Of Yellowstone National
Park
Yellowstone National Park, WY
307-543-2861

Headwaters Lodge & Cabins at
Flagg Ranch
100 Grassy Lake Road, Highway 89,
2 Miles South Of The South
Entrance Of Yellowstone National
Park
Yellowstone National Park, WY

307-344-7311

Jackson Lake Lodge
100 Jackson Lake Lodge Road,
Highway 89
Yellowstone National Park, WY

307-344-7311

Mammoth Hot Springs Cabins
Mammoth Hot Springs
Yellowstone National Park, WY

307-344-7311

Old Faithful Lodge Cabins
Old Faithful
Yellowstone National Park, WY

307-344-7311

Wyoming Motel Wheatland

Yellowstone National Park, WY

307-344-7311

Wyoming Motel Wheatland

Yellowstone National Park, WY

307-344-7311

# Alberta Listings

Holiday Inn Express & Suites Airdrie-
Calgary North
64 East Lake Avenue Ne
Airdrie, AB
403-912-1952

Ramada Airdrie Hotel And Suites
191 East Lake Crescent
Airdrie, AB

403-945-1288

Super 8 Motel - Airdrie
815 East Lake Boulevard
Airdrie, AB

403-948-4188

Vantage Inn & Suites
200 Parent Way Fort McMurray
Alberta, AB
866-650-FORT (3678)

Days Inn Athabasca
2805 48th Ave
Athabasca, AB
780-675-7020

Super 8 Athabasca Ab
4820b Wood Heights Road
Athabasca, AB

780-675-8888

Banff Ptarmigan Inn
337 Banff Avenue
Banff, AB
403-762-4496

Best Western Plus Siding 29 Lodge
453 Marten St Box 1387
Banff, AB

403-762-5575

Beaverlodge Motor Inn
116 6A St
Beaverlodge, AB
780-354-2291

Days Inn Bonnyville
5810 50th Avenue
Bonnyville, AB
780-815-4843

Canalta Brooks
115 15th Avenue
Brooks, AB
403-363-0080

Ramada Brooks
1319 2nd Street West
Brooks, AB

403-362-6440

Travelodge Brooks Ab
1240 Cassils Place E
Brooks, AB
403-362-8000

5 Calgary Downtown Suites
618 - 5th Ave SW
Calgary, AB
403-451-5551

Calgary Marriott Downtown Hotel
110 9th Avenue Southeast
Calgary, AB

403-266-7331

Coast Plaza Hotel & Conference
Centre
1316 33 Street Ne
Calgary, AB

403-248-8888

Days Inn And Suites Calgary South
Cn
3828 Macleod Trail South
Calgary, AB

403-243-5531

Econo Lodge South
7505 Macleod Trail South
Calgary, AB

403-252-4401

Holiday Inn Calgary Airport
1250 Mckinnon Drive Northeast
Calgary, AB

403-230-1999

Holiday Inn Calgary-Macleod Trail
South
4206 Macleod Trail
Calgary, AB

403-287-2700

Ramada Limited Calgary
2363 Banff Trail Nw
Calgary, AB

403-289-5571

Sheraton Cavalier Calgary Hotel
2620 32nd Avenue Ne
Calgary, AB

403-291-0107

Sheraton Suites Calgary Eau Claire
255 Barclay Parade S W
Calgary, AB

403-266-7200

Sheraton Suites Calgary Eau Claire
255 Barclay Parade S W
Calgary, AB

403-266-7200

Super 8 Calgary Motel Village
1904 Crowchild Trail Northwest
Calgary, AB

403-289-9211

Super 8 Motel - Calgary Shawnessy
Area
60 Shawville Road Southeast
Calgary, AB

403-254-8878

The Fairmont Palliser
133 9th Avenue Southwest
Calgary, AB

403-262-1234

The Westin Calgary
320 Fourth Ave Sw
Calgary, AB

403-266-1611

The Westin Calgary
320 Fourth Ave Sw
Calgary, AB

403-266-1611

Travelodge Calgary International
Airport
2750 Sunridge Blvd N E
Calgary, AB

403-291-1260

Travelodge Calgary University North
2227 Banff Trail Nw
Calgary, AB

403-289-6600

Travelodge Hotel Calgary Macleod
Trail
9206 Macleod Trail South
Calgary, AB

403-253-7070

Westways Bed and Breakfast
216 - 25 Avenue SW
Calgary, AB

403-229-1758

Wingate By Wyndham Calgary
400 Midpark Way Southeast
Calgary, AB

403-514-0099

Canalta Camrose
4710 73rd Street
Camrose, AB
780-672-7303

Ramada Inn Camrose
4702 73rd Street

Camrose, AB

780-672-5220

Best Western Plus Pocaterra Inn
1725 Mountain Avenue
Canmore, AB
780-678-4334

Econo Lodge Canmore
1602 2nd Avenue
Canmore, AB

403-678-5488

Quality Resort Chateau Canmore
1718 Bow Valley Trail
Canmore, AB

403-678-6699

Westridge Country Inn/Canmore
Rocky Mountain Inn
1719 Bow Valley Trail
Canmore, AB

403-678-5221

Ramada Grande Prairie
7201 99th St.
Clairmont, AB
780-814-7448

Lazy J Motel
5225 1st Street/H 2
Claresholm, AB
403-625-4949

Days Inn & Suites Cochrane
5 Westside Drive
Cochrane, AB
403-932-5588

Ramada Cochrane
10 Westside Drive
Cochrane, AB

403-932-6355

Ramada Drayton Valley
2051 50th Street
Drayton Valley, AB
780-514-7861

Super 8 Drayton Valley
3727 50th Street
Drayton Valley, AB

780-542-9122

Econo Lodge Inn & Suites
392 Centre Street &; Railway
Drumheller, AB
403-823-3322

Ramada Inn And Suites Drumheller
680 2nd Street Southeast
Drumheller, AB

403-823-2028

Super 8 Drumheller
600-680 2nd Street Se
Drumheller, AB

403-823-8887

Best Western Plus Westwood Inn
18035 Stony Plain Road
Edmonton, AB
780-483-7770

Chateau Nova Kingsway
159 Airport Road
Edmonton, AB

888-919-NOVA (6682)

Coast Edmonton Plaza Hotel
10155 105th Street
Edmonton, AB

780-423-4811

Comfort Inn West
17610 100th Avenue
Edmonton, AB

780-484-4415

Four Points By Sheraton Edmonton
South
7230 Argyll Road
Edmonton, AB

780-465-7931

Holiday Inn Express Edmonton
Downtown
10010 104th Street
Edmonton, AB

780-423-2450

Holiday Inn Express Hotel & Suites
Edmonton South
2440 Calgary Trail
Edmonton, AB

780-440-5000

Quality Inn West Edmonton
17803 Stony Plain Road
Edmonton, AB

780-484-8000

Ramada Hotel And Conference
Centre
11834 Kingsway
Edmonton, AB

780-454-5454

Super 8 Hotel - Edmonton South
3610 Gateway Blvd. Nw
Edmonton, AB

780-433-8688

The Westin Edmonton
10135 100th Street
Edmonton, AB

780-426-3636

Travelodge Edmonton East
3414 118th Avenue
Edmonton, AB

780-474-0456

Travelodge Edmonton South
10320 45th Avenue
Edmonton, AB

780-436-9770

Best Western High Road Inn
300 52nd Street
Edson, AB
780-712-2378

Super 8 Edson
5220 2nd Avenue
Edson, AB

780-723-7373

D.J. Motel
416 Main Street
Fort MacLeod, AB
403-553-4011

Sunset Motel
104 Highway 3 West
Fort MacLeod, AB

403-553-4448

Quality Hotel And Conference Centre
424 Gregoire Drive
Fort McMurray, AB
780-791-7200

Foxwood Inn and Suites
210 Highway Avenue, Po Box 330
Fox Creek, AB
780-622-2280

Best Western Grande Prairie Hotel
And Suites
10745 117th Avenue
Grande Prairie, AB
780-402-2378

Holiday Inn Express Grande Prairie
10226 117 Avenue
Grande Prairie, AB

780-814-9446

Stanford Inn - Grande Prairie
11401-100 Avenue
Grande Prairie, AB

780-539-5678

Best Western Plus Mirage Hotel &
Resort
9616 Highway 58
High Level, AB
780-821-1000

Super 8 High Level Ab
9502-114 Avenue
High Level, AB

780-841-3448

Ramada High River
1512 13th Avenue South East
High River, AB
403-603-3183

Super 8 High River
1601 13th Avenue
High River, AB

403-652-4448

Old Entrance Cabins
P.O. Box 6054
Hinton, AB
780-865-4760

Super 8 Hinton
284 Smith Street
Hinton, AB

Econo Lodge Inn & Suites Innisfail
5004 42nd Avenue
Innisfail, AB
403-227-5199

Chateau Jasper
96 Geikie Street Box 1200
Jasper, AB
780-852-5644

Glacier View Inn
Icefields Parkway/H 93 N
Jasper, AB
780-852-6550/April - October and

403-762-7431/November - March

Maligne Lodge
900 Connaught Drive
Jasper, AB

780-852-3143

Marmot Lodge
86 Connaught Drive
Jasper, AB

780-852-4471

The Fairmont Jasper Park Lodge
Old Lodge Road
Jasper, AB

780-852-3301

Tonquin Inn
100 Juniper Street
Jasper, AB

780-852-4987

Fairmont Château Lake Louise
111 Lake Louise Drive
Lake Louise, AB
403-522-3511

Comfort Inn Lethbridge
3226 Fairway Plaza Road S
Lethbridge, AB
403-320-8874

Days Inn Lethbridge
100 3rd Avenue South
Lethbridge, AB

403-327-6000

Econo Lodge And Suites
1124 Mayor Magrath Dr. S.
Lethbridge, AB

403-328-5591

Holiday Inn Express Hotel & Suites
Lehtbridge
120 Stafford Drive South
Lethbridge, AB

403-394-9292

Holiday Inn Lethbridge
2375 Mayor Magrath Drive South
Lethbridge, AB

403-380-5050

Holiday Inn Lethbridge
2375 Mayor Magrath Drive South
Lethbridge, AB

403-380-5050

Howard Johnson Express Inn
Lethbridge
1026 Mayor Magrath Drive South
Lethbridge, AB

403-327-4576

Lethbridge Lodge Hotel
320 Scenic Drive
Lethbridge, AB

403-328-1123

Quality Inn & Suites Lethbridge
4070 2nd Avenue South
Lethbridge, AB

403-331-6440

Days Hotel & Suites - Lloydminster
5411 44th Street
Lloydminster, AB
780-875-4404

Holiday Inn Express & Suites
MEDICINE HAT TRANSCANADA
HWY 1
9 Strachan Bay Se
Medicine Hat, AB
403-504-5151

Super 8 Medicine Hat
1280 Transcanada Way Southeast
Medicine Hat, AB

403-528-8888

Travelodge Hotel Medicine Hat
1100 Redcliff Dr Sw
Medicine Hat, AB

403-527-2275

Canalta Oyen
Junction Highway 9 and 41
Oyen, AB
403-664-3010

Ramada Pincher Creek
1132 Table Mountain Street
Pincher Creek, AB
403-627-3777

Canalta Ponoka
#1 6707 Highway 53 West
Ponoka, AB
403-704-1177

Best Western Plus Red Deer Inn &
Suites
6839 66th Street
Red Deer, AB
403-346-3555

Best Western Plus Red Deer Inn &
Suites
6839 66th Street
Red Deer, AB

403-346-3555

Howard Johnson Red Deer
71 Gasoline Alley East
Red Deer, AB

403-343-8444

Quality Inn North Hill
7150 - 50th Avenue
Red Deer, AB

403-343-8800

Ramada Inn And Suites Red Deer
6853 66 Street
Red Deer, AB

403-342-4445

Sandman Hotel Red Deer
2818 Gaetz Avenue
Red Deer, AB

403-343-7400

Super 8 Red Deer
7474 Gaetz Ave
Red Deer, AB

403-343-1102

Travelodge Red Deer
2807 50th Avenue
Red Deer, AB

403-346-2011

Best Western Rimstone Ridge
Box 1546 5501 50th Avenue
Rimbey, AB
403-843-2999

Super 8 Rimbey
5702 43rd Street
Rimbey, AB

403-843-3808

Best Western Rocky Mountain House
Inn & Suites
4407 41st Avenue
Rocky Mountain House, AB
403-844-3100

Canalta Rocky Mountain House
4406 41st Avenue
Rocky Mountain House, AB

403-846-0088

Best Western Plus The Inn At St.
Albert
460 Street Albert Trail
Saint Albert, AB
780-470-3800

Ramada Sherwood Park
30 Broadway Blvd
Sherwood Park, AB
780-467-6727

Super 8 Slave Lake
101 14th Avenue Southwest
Slave Lake, AB
780-805-3100

High Rigg Retreat
#3-51119 RR 255
Spruce Grove, AB
780-470-0462

Super 8 St Paul Ab
5008 43rd Street
St Paul, AB
780-645-5581

Ramada Stettler
6711 49th Avenue
Stettler, AB
403-742-6555

Super 8 Stettler
5720 44th Avenue
Stettler, AB

403-742-3391

Travelodge Stony Plain
74 Boulder Boulevard
Stony Plain, AB
780-963-1161

Best Western Strathmore Inn
550 Highway 1
Strathmore, AB
403-934-5777

Super 8 Strathmore
450 Westlake Road
Strathmore, AB

403-934-1808

Travelodge Strathmore
350 Ridge Road
Strathmore, AB

403-901-0000

Best Western Plus Chateau Inn
Sylvan Lake
5027 Lakeshore Drive
Sylvan Lake, AB
403-887-7788

Best Western Diamond Inn
351 7th Avenue Ne
Three Hills, AB
403-443-7889

Super 8 Three Hills
208 18th Ave North
Three Hills, AB

403-443-8888

Hi Valley Motor Inn
4001 Highway Street
Valleyview, AB
780-524-3324

Horizon Motel & Steakhouse
5204 Highway Street
Valleyview, AB

780-524-3904

Best Western Wainwright Inn &
Suites
1209 27th Street
Wainwright, AB
780-845-9934

Ramada Wainwright
1510 27th Street
Wainwright, AB

780-842-5010

Ramada Westlock
11311 - 100 Street
Westlock, AB
780-349-2245

Best Western Wayside Inn
4103 56th Street
Wetaskiwin County, AB
780-312-7300

Alaska Highway Motel
3511 Highway St
Whitecourt, AB
780-778-4156

Holiday Inn Express & Suites
Whitecourt Southeast
4721 49th Street

Whitecourt, AB

780-778-2512

Quality Inn Whitecourt
5420 49th Ave.
Whitecourt, AB
780-778-5477

Super 8 Motel - Whitecourt
4121 Kepler Street
Whitecourt, AB
780-778-8908

Whitecourt Conference Centre &
Suites
5003 50th Street
Whitecourt, AB
780-778-2216

# British Columbia Listings

Ramada Limited 100 Mile House
917 Alder Avenue
100 Mile House, BC
250-395-2777

Abbotsford Hotel
2073 Clearbrook Road
Abbotsford, BC
604-859-6211

Best Western Bakerview Inn
1821 Sumas Way
Abbotsford, BC

604-859-1341

Coast Abbotsford Hotel & Suites
2020 Sumas Way
Abbotsford, BC
604-853-1880

Ramada Plaza & Conference Centre
36035 N Parallel Rd
Abbotsford, BC

604-870-1050

Super 8 Abbotsford Bc
1881 Sumas Way
Abbotsford, BC

604-853-1141

Nimpkish Hotel
318 Fir Street
Alert Bay, BC
250-974-2324

Best Western Plus Kings Inn And
Conference Center
5411 Kingsway
Burnaby, BC
604-438-1383

Hilton Vancouver Metrotown
6083 Mckay Avenue
Burnaby, BC

604-438-1200

Canadas Best Value Inn
1069 South Trans-Canada Highway
Cache Creek, BC
250-457-6226

Robbie's Motel
1067 Todd Road
Cache Creek, BC

250-457-6221

Tumbleweed Motel
1221 Quartz Road
Cache Creek, BC

250-457-6522

Best Western Plus Austrian Chalet
462 South Island Highway
Campbell River, BC
250-923-4231

Campbell River Travelodge
340 S. Island Hwy
Campbell River, BC

250-286-6622

Coast Discovery Inn
975 Shoppers Row
Campbell River, BC

250-287-7155

Canadas Best Value Inn And Suites
Castlegar
1935 Columbia Avenue
Castlegar, BC
250-365-2177

Super 8 Castlegar
651-18 Street
Castlegar, BC

250-365-2700

Best Western Plus Wine Country
Hotel & Suites
3460 Carrington Road
Central Okanagan, BC
250-707-1637

Chetwynd Court Motel
5104 North Access Road
Chetwynd, BC
250-788-2271

Pine Cone Motor Inn
5224 53rd Ave
Chetwynd, BC

250-788-3311

Stagecoach Inn

5413 South Access Road
Chetwynd, BC

250-788-9666

Best Western Rainbow Country Inn
43971 Industrial Way
Chilliwack, BC
604-795-3828

Comfort Inn Chilliwack
45405 Luckakuck Way
Chilliwack, BC

604-858-0636

Ranch Park Rentals
Off H 1
Chilliwack, BC

480-600-5114

Travelodge Chilliwack
45466 Yale Road West
Chilliwack, BC

604-792-4240

Best Western The Westerly Hotel &
Convention Centre
1590 Cliffe Avenue
Courtenay, BC
250-338-7741

Holiday Inn Express & Suites
Courtenay Comox Valley Sw
2200 Cliffe Avenue
Courtenay, BC

778-225-0010

Kingfisher Oceanside Resort and
Spa
4330 Island H S/H 19A
Courtenay, BC

250-338-1323

Travelodge Courtenay Bc
2605 Cliffe Avenue
Courtenay, BC

250-334-4491

Days Inn Cranbrook
600 Cranbrook Street North
Cranbrook, BC
250-426-6683

Super 8 Cranbrook
2370 Cranbrook Street North
Cranbrook, BC

250-489-8028

Airport Inn - Dawson Creek
800 - 120 Avenue
Dawson Creek, BC
250-782-9404

Comfort Inn Dawson Creek
1200 Alaska Avenue

Dawson Creek, BC

250-782-1222

Inn On The Creek
10600 8 Street
Dawson Creek, BC

250-782-8136

Stonebridge Hotel Dawson Creek
500 Highway 2
Dawson Creek, BC

250-782-6226

Travelodge Silver Bridge Inn
140 Trans Canada Highway
Duncan, BC
250-748-4311

Howard Johnson Inn Enderby
1510 George Street
Enderby, BC
250-838-6825

Best Western Plus Fernie Mountain
Lodge
1622 7th Avenue
Fernie, BC
250-423-5500

Travelodge Three Sisters
401 Highway #3
Fernie, BC

250-423-4438

Blue Bell Inn
4720 50 Ave
Fort Nelson, BC
250-774-6961

Pioneer Motel
5207-50 Ave S
Fort Nelson, BC

250-774-5800

Super 8 Fort Nelson
4503 50th Ave South
Fort Nelson, BC

250-233-5025

Econo Lodge Fort St. John
10419 Alaska Road
Fort St John, BC
250-787-8475

Lakeview Inn & Suites - Fort St. John
10103 98 Avenue
Fort St John, BC

250-787-0779

Northern Grand Hotel
9830 - 100th Ave
Fort St John, BC

250-787-0521

Super 8 Motel Fort St. John, Bc
9500 West Alaska Rd
Fort St John, BC

250-785-7588

The Shepherd's Inn
Mile 72 Alaska Highway
Fort St John, BC

250-827-3676

Best Western Plus Valemount Inn &
Suites
1950 Highway 5 South
Fraser Fort George, Subd b, BC
250-566-0086

Best Western Mountainview Inn
1024 11th Street North
Golden, BC
250-344-2333

Harrison Beach Hotel
160 Esplanade Avenue
Harrison Hot Springs, BC
604-796-1111

Harrison Hot Springs Resort & Spa
100 Esplanade
Harrison Hot Springs, BC

604-796-2244

Inn Towne Motel
510 Trans-Canada Hwy
Hope, BC
604-869-7276

Maple Leaf Motor Inn
377 Old Hope Princeton Way
Hope, BC

604-869-7107

Travelodge Hope
350 Old Hope Princeton Way
Hope, BC

604-869-9951

Windsor Motel
778 3rd Avenue
Hope, BC

604-869-9944

Houston Motor Inn
2940 H 16W
Houston, BC
250-845-7112

Accent Inn Kamloops
1325 Columbia Street West
Kamloops, BC
250-374-8877

Best Western Plus Kamloops Hotel
660 West Columbia Street
Kamloops, BC

250-374-7878

Doubletree By Hilton - Kamloops
339 St. Paul Street
Kamloops, BC

250-372-5201

Econo Lodge Inn & Suites
Kamloops
1773 East Trans Canada Hwy
Kamloops, BC

250-372-8533

Hampton Inn Kamloops
1245 Rogers Way
Kamloops, BC

250-571-7897

Holiday Inn Express Kamloops
1550 Versatile Drive
Kamloops, BC

250-372-3474

Holiday Inn Hotel & Suites
Kamloops
675 Tranquille Road
Kamloops, BC

250-376-8288

Panorama City Centre Inn
610 Columbia Street West
Kamloops, BC

Super 8 Kamloops Bc
1521 Hugh Allan Drive
Kamloops, BC

250-374-8688

Accent Inn Kelowna
1140 Harvey Avenue
Kelowna, BC
250-862-8888

Best Western Plus Kelowna Hotel &
Suites
2402 Highway 97 North
Kelowna, BC

250-860-1212

Coast Capri Hotel
1171 Harvey Avenue
Kelowna, BC

250-860-6060

Days Inn Kelowna
2649 Hwy 97 North
Kelowna, BC

250-868-3297

Fairfield Inn & Suites By Marriott
Kelowna
1655 Powick Rd
Kelowna, BC

250-763-2800

Four Points By Sheraton Kelowna
Airport
5505 Airport Way
Kelowna, BC

855-900-5505

Kelowna Ramada Hotel And
Conference Centre
2170 Harvey Avenue
Kelowna, BC

250-860-9711

Super 8 West Kelowna
1655 Westgate Road
Kelowna, BC

250-769-2355

Best Western Plus Langley Inn
5978 Glover Road
Langley, BC
604-530-9311

Langley Hwy Hotel
20470 88th Avenue
Langley, BC

604-888-4891

Super 8 Langley
26574 Gloucester Way
Langley, BC

604-856-8288

Liard Hot Springs Lodge
Mile 497 Alaska H
Liard River, BC
250-776-7349

Best Western Maple Ridge Hotel
21650 Lougheed Highway
Maple Ridge, BC
604-467-1511

Quality Inn Maple Ridge
21735 Lougheed Highway
Maple Ridge, BC

604-463-5111

Knights Inn Merritt
2702 Nicola Avenue
Merritt, BC
250-378-9244

Quality Inn Merritt
4025 Walters Street
Merritt, BC

250-378-4253

Ramada Limited Merritt
3571 Voght Street
Merritt, BC

250-378-3567

Super 8 Merritt
3561 Voght Street
Merritt, BC

250-378-9422

Northern Rockies Lodge
Mile 462 Alaska Highway, Box 8
Muncho Lake, BC
250-776-3481

Best Western Northgate
6450 Metral Drive
Nanaimo, BC
250-390-2222

Coast Bastion Hotel
11 Bastion Street
Nanaimo, BC

250-753-6601

Days Inn Nanaimo
809 Island Highway South
Nanaimo, BC

250-754-8171

Howard Johnson Hotel - Nanaimo
Harbourside
1 Terminal Avenue
Nanaimo, BC

250-753-2241

Nanaimo Vancouver Island
Travelodge
96 Terminal Avenue North
Nanaimo, BC

250-754-6355

Best Western Plus Baker Street Inn &
Convention Centre
153 Baker Street
Nelson, BC
250-352-3525

Best Western Cowichan Valley Inn
6474 Trans Canada Highway
North Cowichan, BC
250-748-2722

Best Western Plus Chemainus Inn
9573 Chemainus Road
North Cowichan, BC

250-246-4181

Holiday Inn And Suites North
Vancouver
700 Old Lillooet Road
North Vancouver, BC
604-985-3111

Vancouver Lions Gate Travelodge
2060 Marine Drive
North Vancouver, BC

604-985-5311

Best Western Plus Sunrise Inn
5506 Main Street
Osoyoos, BC
250-495-4000

Quality Resort Bayside Parksville
240 Dogwood Street
Parksville, BC
250-248-8333

Tigh-Na-Mara Resort & Conference
Centre
1155 Resort Drive
Parksville, BC

250-248-2072

Travelodge Parksville
424 West Island Highway
Parksville, BC

250-248-2232

Days Inn And Conference Centre -
Penticton
152 Riverside Drive
Penticton, BC
250-493-6616

Super 8 Penticton Bc
1706 Main Street
Penticton, BC

250-492-3829

Buckinghorse River Lodge
Mile 175 Alaska Highway
Pinkmountain, BC
250-772-4999

Ramada Inn Pitt Meadows
19267 Lougheed Highway
Pitt Meadows, BC
604-460-9859

Howard Johnson Hotel Port Alberni
4850 Beaver Creek Road
Port Alberni, BC
250-724-2900

The Hospitality Inn
3835 Redford Street
Port Alberni, BC

250-723-8111

Pioneer Inn
8405 Byng Road
Port Hardy, BC
250-949-7271

The Quarterdeck Inn & Marina
Resort
6555 Hardy Bay Road
Port Hardy, BC

250-902-0455

Haida-Way Motor Inn Hotel
1817 Campbell Way

Port McNeill, BC
250-956-3373

Powell River Town Centre Hotel
4660 Joyce Avenue
Powell River, BC
604-485-3000

Bon Voyage Inn
4222 Highway 16 West
Prince George, BC
250-964-2333

Coast Inn Of The North Prince
George
770 Brunswick Street
Prince George, BC

250-563-0121

Sandman Inn Prince George
1650 Central Street
Prince George, BC

250-563-8131

Anchor Inn Hotel Prince Rupert
1600 Park Avenue
Prince Rupert, BC
250-627-8522

Andree's Bed and Breakfast
315 4th Avenue E
Prince Rupert, BC

250-624-3666

Crest Hotel
221 1 Avenue West
Prince Rupert, BC

250-624-6771

Prestige Prince Rupert
118 6th Street
Prince Rupert, BC

250-624-6711

The Pacific Inn
909 3rd Avenue West
Prince Rupert, BC

250-627-1711

Ramada Limited Quesnel
383 Saint Laurent Avenue
Quesnel, BC
250-992-5575

Super 8 Quesnel BC
2010 Valhalla Rd
Quesnel, BC

250-747-1111

Travelodge Quesnel
524 Front Street
Quesnel, BC

250-992-7071

Dog-Friendly Lodging - Please always call ahead to make sure an establishment is still dog-friendly.

Best Western Plus Revelstoke
1925 Laforme Boulevard
Revelstoke, BC
250-837-2043

Coast Hillcrest Hotel
2100 Oak Drive
Revelstoke, BC

250-837-3322

Days Inn & Suites-Revelstoke
301 Wright Street
Revelstoke, BC

250-837-2191

Sutton Place Hotel Revelstoke
Mountain Resort
2950 Camozzi Road
Revelstoke, BC

250-814-5000

Accent Inn Vancouver Airport
10551 Saint Edwards Drive
Richmond, BC
604-273-3311

River Rock Casino Resort
8811 River Road
Richmond, BC

604-247-8900

Sheraton Vancouver Airport Hotel
7551 Westminster Highway
Richmond, BC

604-273-7878

The Fairmont Vancouver Airport
3111 Grant Mcconachie Way
Richmond, BC

604-207-5200

The Westin Wall Centre Vancouver
Airport
3099 Corvette Way
Richmond, BC

604-303-6565

Quality Inn Waddling Dog
2476 Mt. Newton Cross Roads
Saanichton, BC
250-652-1146

Super 8 Saanichton Victoria Airport
2477 Mount Newton Cross Road
Saanichton, BC

250-652-6888

Wintercott Country House
1950 Nicholas Rd.
Saanichton, BC

250-652-2117

Best Western Salmon Arm Inn

61 10th Street Sw
Salmon Arm, BC
250-832-9793

Travelodge Salmon Arm
2401 Trans-Canada Highway West
Salmon Arm, BC

250-832-9721

Best Western Sicamous Inn
806 Trans Canada Highway East
Sicamous, BC
250-836-4117

Super 8 Sicamous
1120 Riverside Avenue
Sicamous, BC

250-836-4988

Best Western Plus Emerald Isle
Motor Inn
2306 Beacon Ave
Sidney, BC
250-656-4441

The Cedarwood Inn & Suites
9522 Lochside Drive
Sidney, BC

250-656-5551

Victoria Airport/Sidney Travelodge
2280 Beacon St
Sidney, BC

250-656-1176

Gordon's Beach Farm Stay B&B
4530 Otter Point Road
Sooke, BC
250-642-5291

Ocean Wilderness Inn - Bed And
Breakfast
9171 West Coast Road
Sooke, BC

250-646-2116

Sooke Harbour House
1528 Whiffen Spit Road
Sooke, BC

250-642-3421

Mountain Retreat Hotel & Suites
38922 Progress Way
Squamish, BC
604-815-0883

King Edward Hotel and Motel
5th Avenue/P. O. Box 86
Stewwart, BC
250-636-2244

Comfort Inn & Suites
8255-166 Street
Surrey, BC
604-576-8888

Sheraton Vancouver Guildford Hotel
15269 104th Avenue
Surrey, BC

604-582-9288

Sheraton Vancouver Guildford Hotel
15269 104th Avenue
Surrey, BC

604-582-9288

Toad River Lodge
Mile 422 Alaska H
Toad River, BC
250-232-5401

Long Beach Lodge Resort
1441 Pacific Rim Highway/H 4
Tofino, BC
250725-2442

The Inn at Tough City
350 Main Street
Tofino, BC

250-725-2021

Best Western Plus Sands
1755 Davie Street
Vancouver, BC
604-682-1831

Coast Plaza Suite Hotel
1763 Comox Street
Vancouver, BC

604-688-7711

Comfort Inn Downtown Vancouver
654 Nelson Street
Vancouver, BC

604-605-4333

Granville Island Hotel
1253 Johnston Street
Vancouver, BC

604-683-7373

Metropolitan Hotel Vancouver
645 Howe Street
Vancouver, BC

604-687-1122

Pinnacle Hotel Vancouver
Harbourfront
1133 West Hastings Street
Vancouver, BC

604-689-9211

Ramada Inn & Suites Downtown
Vancouver
1221 Granville Street
Vancouver, BC

604-685-1111

Sheraton Vancouver Wall Centre
1088 Burrard Street
Vancouver, BC

604-331-1000

Sheraton Vancouver Wall Centre
1088 Burrard Street
Vancouver, BC

604-331-1000

The Fairmont Hotel Vancouver
900 W. Georgia Street
Vancouver, BC

604-684-3131

The Fairmont Waterfront
900 Canada Place Way
Vancouver, BC

604-691-1991

The Sylvia Hotel
1154 Gilford Street
Vancouver, BC

604-681-9321

The Westin Grand Vancouver
433 Robson Street And Homer
Vancouver, BC

604-602-1999

Vancouver Marriott Pinnacle
Downtown Hotel
1128 West Hastings Street
Vancouver, BC

604-684-1128

Canadas Best Value Inn & Suites
4006 32nd Street
Vernon, BC
250-549-1241

Holiday Inn Express Hotel & Suites
Vernon
4716 34th Street
Vernon, BC

250-550-7777

Accent Inn Victoria
3233 Maple Street
Victoria, BC
250-475-7500

Coast Victoria Harbourside Hotel
146 Kingston Street
Victoria, BC

250-360-1211

Days Inn - Victoria On The Harbour
427 Belleville Street
Victoria, BC

250-386-3451

Econo Lodge Inn & Suites
101 Island Hwy.
Victoria, BC

250-388-7861

Fairmont Empress Hotel
721 Government Street
Victoria, BC

250-384-8111

Harbour Towers Hotel & Suites
345 Quebec Street
Victoria, BC

250-385-2405

Hotel Zed
3110 Douglas Street
Victoria, BC

250-388-4345

Howard Johnson Hotel And Suites
Victoria Elk Lake
4670 Elk Lake Drive
Victoria, BC

250-704-4656

Inn At Laurel Point
680 Montreal St
Victoria, BC

250-386-8721

Malahat Bungalows Motel
300 Trans Canada Highway
Victoria, BC

800-665-8066

Ramada Victoria
123 Gorge Road East
Victoria, BC

250-386-1422

Ryan's Bed and Breakfast
224 Superior St
Victoria, BC

250-389-0012

Spinnakers Gastro Brewpub &
GuestHouses
308 Catherine Street
Victoria, BC

250-386-2739

Tally Ho Hotel
3020 Douglas Street
Victoria, BC

250-386-6141

Victoria Travelodge
229 Gorge Road East
Victoria, BC

250-388-6611

Delta Whistler Village Suites
4308 Main Street
Whistler, BC
604-905-3987

Fairmont Chateau Whistler
4599 Chateau Boulevard
Whistler, BC

604-938-8000

Fairmont Chateau Whistler
4599 Chateau Boulevard
Whistler, BC

604-938-8000

Hilton Whistler Resort And Spa
4050 Whistler Way
Whistler, BC

604-932-1982

The Westin Resort & Spa At Whistler
4090 Whistler Way
Whistler, BC

604-905-5000

Coast Fraser Inn
285 Donald Road
Williams Lake, BC
250-398-7055

Drummond Lodge
1405 Cariboo Highway South
Williams Lake, BC

250-392-5334

Sandman Hotel & Suites Williams
Lake
664 Oliver Street
Williams Lake, BC

250-392-6557

Springhouse Trails Ranch
3061 Dog Creek Road
Williams Lake, BC

250-392-4780

# Manitoba Listings

Comfort Inn Brandon
925 Middleton Ave
Brandon, MB
204-727-6232

Days Inn - Brandon
2130 Currie Boulevard
Brandon, MB

204-727-3600

Keystone Motor Inn
1050 18th Street
Brandon, MB

204-728-6620

Victoria Inn Brandon
3550 Victoria Avenue
Brandon, MB
204-725-1532

Super 8 Dauphin
1457 Main Street South
Dauphin, MB
204-638-0800

Victoria Inn North
160 Hwy 10A N
Flin Flon, MB
204-687-7555

Solmundson Gesta Hus B&B
Hwy 8 in Hecla
Hecla, MB
204-279-2088

Super 8 Morden
3010 Thornhill Street
Morden, MB
204-822-2003

Days Inn Portage La Prairie
Highway 1 &; Yellowquill Trail
Portage La Prairie, MB
204-857-9791

Super 8 Portage La Prairie MB
Hwy 1a And Saskatchewan
Portage La Prairie, MB
204-857-8883

Super 8 Swan River
115 Kelsey Trail,
Swan River, MB
204-734-7888

Best Western Plus Pembina Inn &
Suites
1714 Pembina Highway
Winnipeg, MB
204-269-8888

Clarion Hotel & Suites
1445 Portage Avenue
Winnipeg, MB
204-774-5110

Comfort Inn South
3109 Pembina Hwy
Winnipeg, MB
204-269-7390

Comfort Inn Winnipeg Airport
1770 Sargent Avenue
Winnipeg, MB
204-783-5627

Country Inn & Suites By Carlson,
Winnipeg, Mb

730 King Edward Street
Winnipeg, MB
204-783-6900

Delta Winnipeg Hotel
350 St Mary Avenue
Winnipeg, MB
204-942-0551

Four Points by Sheraton Winnipeg
International Airport
1999 Wellington Avenue
Winnipeg, MB
204-775-5222

Hilton Suites Winnipeg Airport
1800 Wellington Avenue
Winnipeg, MB
204-783-1700

Holiday Inn Winnipeg-South
1330 Pembina Highway
Winnipeg, MB
204-452-4747

Place Louis Riel Suite Hotel
190 Smith Street
Winnipeg, MB
204-947-6961

Quality Inn And Suites Winnipeg
635 Pembina Hwy.
Winnipeg, MB
204-453-8247

Radisson Hotel Winnipeg
288 Portage Avenue
Winnipeg, MB
204-956-0410

The Fairmont Winnipeg
2 Lombard Place
Winnipeg, MB
204-957-1350

# New Brunswick Listings

Comfort Inn Bathurst
1170 St. Peter Avenue
Bathurst, NB
506-547-8000

Comfort Inn Campbellton
111 Val D Amour Rd
Campbellton, NB
506-753-4121

Quality Hotel & Conference Centre
157 Water Street
Campbellton, NB

506-753-4133

Days Inn Dalhousie
385 Adelaide Street
Dalhousie, NB
506-684-5681

Quality Inn Airport
370 Boulevard Dieppe
Dieppe, NB
506-858-8880

Best Western Plus Edmundston
Hotel
280 Boulevard Hebert
Edmundston, NB
506-739-0000

Days Inn Edmundston
10 Rue Mathieu
Edmundston, NB
506-263-0000

Four Points By Sheraton Edmundston
100 Rice Street
Edmundston, NB
506-739-7321

Quality Inn Edmundston
919 Canada Road
Edmundston, NB
506-735-5525

Best Western Plus Fredericton Hotel
& Suites
333 Bishop Drive
Fredericton, NB
506-455-8448

Comfort Inn Fredericton
797 Prospect Street
Fredericton, NB
506-453-0800

Crowne Plaza Hotel Fredericton-Lord
Beaverbrook
659 Queen Street
Fredericton, NB
506-455-3371

Fort Nashwaak Motel
15 Riverside Drive/H 105
Fredericton, NB
506-472-4411

Howard Johnson Plaza Hotel
Fredericton
958 Prospect Street
Fredericton, NB
506-462-4444

Ramada Fredericton
480 Riverside Drive
Fredericton, NB

506-460-5500

Comfort Inn East
20 Maplewood Drive
Moncton, NB
506-859-6868

Comfort Inn Magnetic Hill
2495 Mountain Rd
Moncton, NB

506-384-3175

Econo Lodge Inn & Suites
1905 W Main Street
Moncton, NB

506-382-2587

Four Points By Sheraton Moncton
40 Lady Ada Boulevard
Moncton, NB

506-852-9600

Hampton Inn & Suites Moncton
700 Mapleton Road
Moncton, NB

506-855-4819

Residence Inn By Marriott Moncton
600 Main Street
Moncton, NB

506 854 7100

Travelodge Suites Moncton
2475 Mountain Road
Moncton, NB

506-852-7000

Days Inn Oromocto
60 Brayson Blvd.
Oromocto, NB
506-357-5657

Double Barn Ranch
566 West Galloway Road
Rexton, NB
506-523-9217

Best Western Plus Saint John Hotel
& Suites
55 Majors Brook Drive
Saint John, NB
506-657-9966

Comfort Inn Saint John
1155 Fairville Blvd
Saint John, NB

506-674-1873

Holiday Inn Express Hotel & Suites
Saint John Harbour Side
400 Main Street
Saint John, NB

506-642-2622

Quality Inn Grand Falls
10039 Route 144
St Andre, NB
506-473-1300

Kingsbrae Cottage
219 King Street
St Andrews, NB
506-529-1897

ALGONQUIN RESORT ST.
ANDREWS BY THE SEA,
AUTOGRAPH COLLECTION, A
Marriott Luxury & Lifestyle Hotel
184 Adolphus Street
St Andrews by the Sea, NB
506-529-8823

Hampton Inn & Suites Saint John-
New Brunswick
51 Fashion Drive
St John, NB
506-657-4600

Hilton Saint John
One Market Square
St John, NB

506-693-8484

Canadas Best Value Inn & Suites
168 Route 555
Woodstock, NB
506-328-8876

Howard Johnson Inn Woodstock Nb
159 Route 555
Woodstock, NB

506-328-3315

# Newfoundland Listings

The Valhalla Lodge
Address with reservation
L'Anse aux Meadows, NF
709-754-3105

Gros Morne Cabins
P.O. Box 151
Rocky Harbour, NF
709-458-2020

Sheraton Hotel Newfoundland
115 Cavendish Square
St John's, Newfoundland and
Labrador, NF
709-726-4980

Holiday Inn St. Johns-Govt Center
180 Portugal Cove Road
St Johns, NF
709-722-0506

Sheraton Hotel Newfoundland
115 Cavendish Square

St Johns, NF

709-726-4980

Super 8 Motel St Johns Nl
175 Higgins Line
St Johns, NF

709-739-8888

Days Inn Stephenville
44 Queen Street
Stephenville, NF
709-643-6666

The Village Inn
Cavenor Street
Trinity, NF
709-464-3269

# Northwest Territories Listings

Coast Fraser Tower
5303 52nd Street
Yellowknife, NT
867-873-8700

Super 8 Yellowknife
308 Old Airport Road
Yellowknife, NT

867-669-8888

# Nova Scotia Listings

Comfort Inn Amherst
143 South Albion St
Amherst, NS
902-667-0404

Super 8 Amherst
40 Lord Amherst Drive
Amherst, NS

902-660-8888

Best Western Plus Bridgewater Hotel
& Convention Centre
527 Highway 10 Exit 12
Bridgewater, NS
902-530-0101

Comfort Inn Bridgewater
49 North St
Bridgewater, NS

902-543-1498

Days Inn And Conference Center -
Bridgewater
50 North Street
Bridgewater, NS

902-543-7131

Hampton Inn & Suites By Hilton
Halifax - Dartmouth
65 Cromarty Drive
Dartmouth, NS
902-406-7700

Come from Away B&"";B
98 Montague Row
Digby, NS
902-245-4490

Holiday Inn Express Hotel & Suites
Halifax Airport
180 Pratt &; Whitney Drive
Enfield, NS
902-576-7600

Quality Inn Halifax Airport
60 Sky Blvd.
Goffs, NS
902-873-3000

Best Western Plus Chocolate Lake
Hotel
20 St. Margarets Bay Rd.
Halifax, NS
902-477-5611

Chateau Bedford, an Ascend Hotel
Collection Member
133 Kearney Lake Road
Halifax, NS

902-445-1100

Comfort Inn Halifax
560 Bedford Hwy
Halifax, NS

902-443-0303

Delta Halifax
1990 Barrington Street/H 2
Halifax, NS

902-474-5150

Four Points By Sheraton Halifax
1496 Hollis St
Halifax, NS

902-423-4444

Halifax Marriott Harbourfront Hotel
1919 Upper Water Street
Halifax, NS

902-421-1700

Residence Inn By Marriott Halifax
Downtown
1599 Grafton Street
Halifax, NS

902 422 0493

The Lord Nelson Hotel & Suites
1515 South Park Street
Halifax, NS

902-423-6331

The Westin Nova Scotian
1181 Hollis Street
Halifax, NS

902-421-1000

Best Western Aurora Inn
831 Main Street
Kingston, NS
902-765-3306

Best Western Plus Liverpool Hotel &
Conference Centre
63 Queens Place Dr
Liverpool, NS
902-354-2377

Comfort Inn New Glasgow
740 Westville Rd
New Glasgow, NS
902-755-6450

Travelodge Suites New Glasgow
700 Westville Road
New Glasgow, NS

902-928-1333

Caribou River Cottage Lodge
1308 Shore Road, RR# 3
Pictou, NS
902-485-6352

Canadas Best Value Inn
373 Highway 4
Port Hastings, NS
902-625-0621

Holiday Inn Express Stellarton-New
Glasgow
86 Lawrence Boulevard
Stellarton, NS
902-755-1020

Comfort Inn Sydney
368 Kings Rd
Sydney, NS
902-562-0200

Hearthstone Inn Sydney
560 Kings Road
Sydney, NS

902-539-8101

Travelodge Sydney Nova Scotia
480 Kings Road
Sydney, NS

902-539-6750

Comfort Inn Truro
12 Meadow Dr
Truro, NS
902-893-0330

Holiday Inn Truro
437 Prince Street
Truro, NS

902-895-1651

Super 8 Truro Ns
85 Treaty Trail
Truro, NS

902-895-8884

Super 8 Windsor
63 Cole Drive
Windsor, NS
902-792-8888

Best Western Mermaid
545 Main Street
Yarmouth, NS
902-742-7821

Comfort Inn Yarmouth
96 Starrs Rd
Yarmouth, NS

902-742-1119

# Ontario Listings

Super 8 Ajax/Toronto On
210 Westney Road South
Ajax, ON
905-428-6884

Quality Inn Arnprior
70 Madawaska Boulevard
Arnprior, ON
613-623-7991

Sword Inn Bancroft
146 Hastings Street North
Bancroft, ON
613-332-2474

Comfort Inn Barrie
210 Essa Road
Barrie, ON
705-721-1122

Comfort Inn Barrie
75 Hart Dr.
Barrie, ON
705-722-3600

Holiday Inn Barrie
20 Fairview Road
Barrie, ON
705-728-6191

Knights Inn Barrie
150 Dunlop Street West
Barrie, ON
705-728-1312

Quality Inn Barrie
55 Hart Drive
Barrie, ON
705-734-9500

Super 8 Barrie

Dog-Friendly Lodging - Please always call ahead to make sure an establishment is still dog-friendly.

441 Bryne Drive
Barrie, ON

705-814-8888

Travelodge Barrie On Bayfield
300 Bayfield Street
Barrie, ON

705-722-4466

Best Western Belleville
387 N. Front Street
Belleville, ON
613-969-1112

Comfort Inn Belleville
200 North Park St
Belleville, ON

613-966-7703

Travelodge Hotel Belleville
11 Bay Bridge Road
Belleville, ON

613-968-3411

Blue Mountain Rentals - Furnished
Loft
796455 Grey Road 19
Blue Mountains, ON
705-445-1467

Holiday Inn Express & Suites
Clarington - Bowmanville
37 Spicer Square
Bowmanville, ON
905-697-8089

Sleep Inn Bracebridge
510 Muskoka Road 118 West
Bracebridge, ON
705-645-2519

Travelodge Bracebridge
320 Taylor Road
Bracebridge, ON

The Marigold Hotel
226 Queen Street East
Brampton, ON
905-451-6000

Comfort Inn Brantford
58 King George Rd
Brantford, ON
519-753-3100

Brockville Travelodge
7789 Kent Boulevard
Brockville, ON
613-345-3900

Comfort Inn Brockville
7777 Kent Blvd.
Brockville, ON

613-345-0042

Super 8 Brockville

1843 Highway 2 East
Brockville, ON

613-345-1622

Comfort Inn Burlington
3290 South Service Road
Burlington, ON
905-639-1700

Comfort Inn Cambridge
220 Holiday Inn Drive
Cambridge, ON
519-658-1100

Homewood Suites By Hilton
Cambridge-Waterloo, Ontario
800 Jamieson Parkway
Cambridge, ON

519-651-2888

Langdon Hall Country House Hotel
& Spa
1 Langdon Drive
Cambridge, ON

519-740-2100

Comfort Inn Chatham
1100 Richmond St
Chatham, ON
519-352-5500

Super 8 Motel - Chatham
25 Michener Road
Chatham, ON

519-354-3366

Travelodge Chatham
555 Bloomfield Road
Chatham, ON

519-436-1200

Comfort Inn Cobourg
121 Densmore Rd
Cobourg, ON
905-372-7007

Comfort Inn Cornwall
1625 Vincent Massey Drive
Cornwall, ON
613-937-0111

Howard Johnson Cornwall
1142 Brookdale Avenue
Cornwall, ON

613-936-1996

Best Western Plus Dryden Hotel &
Conference Centre
349 Government Street
Dryden, ON
807-223-3201

Comfort Inn Dryden
522 Government St.
Dryden, ON

807-223-3893

Comfort Inn Fort Erie
1 Hospitality Drive
Fort Erie, ON
905-871-8500

Super 8 Fort Frances
810 Kings Hwy
Fort Frances, ON
807-274-4945

Country Squire Resort & Spa
715 King Street East
Gananoque, ON
613-382-3511

Holiday Inn Express Hotel & Suites
1000 Islands - Gananoque
777 East King Street
Gananoque, ON
613-382-8338

Howard Johnson Inn Gananoque
550 King St East
Gananoque, ON
613-382-3911

Quality Inn And Suites 1000 Islands
650 King Street East
Gananoque, ON
613-382-1453

Travelodge Gananoque
785 King Street East
Gananoque, ON
613-382-4728

Value Inn Ottawa
2098 Montreal Road
Gloucester, ON
613-745-1531

Howard Johnson Inn Gravenhurst
1165 Muskoka Rd South
Gravenhurst, ON
705-687-7707

Residence Inn Gravenhurst Muskoka
Wharf
285 Steamship Bay Road
Gravenhurst, ON

705 687 6600

Super 8 Motel Grimsby, On
11 Windward Drive
Grimsby, ON
905-309-8800

Comfort Inn Guelph
480 Silvercreek Parkway
Guelph, ON
519-763-1900

Days Inn - Guelph

275

785 Gordon Street
Guelph, ON
519-822-9112

Holiday Inn Guelph Hotel And
Conference Centre
601 Scottsdale Drive
Guelph, ON
519-836-0231

Staybridge Suites Guelph
11 Corporate Court
Guelph, ON
519-767-3300

Sheraton Hamilton Hotel
116 King Street West
Hamilton, ON
905-529-5515

Comfort Inn Huntsville
86 King William St
Huntsville, ON
705-789-1701

Econo Lodge Huntsville
117 Main Street West
Huntsville, ON
705-788-5051

Holiday Inn Express & Suites
Huntsville
100 Howland Drive
Huntsville, ON
705-788-9500

Super 8 Huntsville
225 Main Street West
Huntsville, ON
705-789-5504

Comfort Inn & Suites
20 Samnah Crescent
Ingersoll, ON
519-425-1100

Super 8 Kenora
240 Lakeview Drive
KENORA, ON
807-468-8016

Viva Villa Vacation Rentals
497 Lakeshore Road
Kagawong, ON
705-282-2896

Comfort Inn West
222 Hearst Way
Kanata, ON
613-592-2200

Comfort Inn Kapuskasing
172 Government Rd. E.
Kapuskasing, ON
705-335-8583

Super 8 Kapuskasing
430 Government Road
Kapuskasing, ON

705-335-8887

Knights Inn Kemptville
4022 County Road 43 East
Kemptville, ON
613-258-5939

Clarion Inn Lakeside and
Conference Centre
470 1st Avenue South
Kenora, ON
807-468-5521

Comfort Inn Kenora
1230 Hwy 17 E
Kenora, ON
807-468-8845

Days Inn Kenora
920 Highway 17 East
Kenora, ON
807-468-2003

Holiday Inn Express Hotel & Suites
Kincardine - Downtown
2 Millenium Way
Kincardine, ON
519-395-3545

Best Western Fireside Inn
1217 Princess St
Kingston, ON
613-549-2211

Comfort Inn Hwy. 401
55 Warne Crescent
Kingston, ON
613-546-9500

Comfort Inn Midtown
1454 Princess St. -- Hwy. 2
Kingston, ON
613-549-5550

Confederation Place Hotel
237 Ontario Street
Kingston, ON
613-549-6300

Four Points By Sheraton Hotel And
Suites Kingston
285 King Street East
Kingston, ON
613-544-4434

Holiday Inn Kingston Waterfront
2 Princess St
Kingston, ON
613-549-8400

Ramada Kingston Hotel, and
Conference Center
33 Benson Street
Kingston, ON
613-546-3661

Residence Inn By Marriott Kingston
Water's Edge
7 Earl Street
Kingston, ON
613 544 4888

Comfort Inn Kirkland Lake
455 Government Road West
Kirkland Lake, ON
705-567-4909

Howard Johnson Hotel - Kitchener
Conestoga
1333 Weber Street East
Kitchener, ON
519-893-1234

Ramada Jordan/Beacon Harbourside
Resort
2793 Beacon Boulevard
Lincoln, ON
905-562-4155

Best Western Plus Lamplighter Inn &
Conference Centre
591 Wellington Road South
London, ON
519-681-7151

Comfort Inn London
1156 Wellington Road
London, ON

519-685-9300

Hilton London Ontario Hotel
300 King Street
London, ON

519-439-1661

Homewood Suites By Hilton London
Ontario
45 Bessemer Road
London, ON

519-686-7700

Residence Inn London Ontario
383 Colborne Street
London, ON

519 433 7222

Staybridge Suites London
824 Exeter Road
London, ON

519-649-4500

Super 8 London
1170 Wellington Road
London, ON

519-681-1550

Hilton Suites Toronto/Markham
Conference Center And Spa
8500 Warden Avenue
Markham, ON
905-470-8500

Homewood Suites By Hilton Toronto-
Markham
50 Bodrington Crt.
Markham, ON
905-477-4663

Residence Inn By Marriott Toronto
Markham
55 Minthorn Boulevard
Markham, ON
905 707 7933

Staybridge Suites Toronto Markham
355 South Park Road
Markham, ON
905-771-9333

Towneplace Suites By Marriott
Toronto Northeast/Markham
7095 Woodbine Avenue
Markham, ON
905-474-0444

Mohawk Motel
335 Sable Street
Massey, ON
705-865-2722

Comfort Inn Midland
980 King St.
Midland, ON
705-526-2090

Knights Inn Midland
751 Yonge Street
Midland, ON
705-526-2219

Super 8 Midland
1144 Hugel Avenue
Midland, ON
705-526-8288

Best Western Plus Milton
161 Chisholm Drive
Milton, ON
905-875-3818

Comfort Inn Meadowvale
2420 Surveyor Road
Mississauga, ON
905-858-8600

Comfort Inn Toronto Airport
6355 Airport Rd.
Mississauga, ON

905-677-7331

Four Points By Sheraton
Mississauga Meadowvale
2501 Argentia Road
Mississauga, ON
905-858-2424

Holiday Inn Toronto-Mississauga
2125 N Sheridan Way
Mississauga, ON
905-855-2000

Homewood Suites By HiltonÂ®
Toronto-Mississauga
6430 Edwards Boulevard
Mississauga, ON
905-564-5529

Residence Inn Marriott Mississauga-
Airport Corporate Ctr West
5070 Creekbank Road
Mississauga, ON
905 602 7777

Residence Inn Toronto
Mississauga/Meadowvale
7005 Century Avenue
Mississauga, ON
905 567 2577

Star Express Inn And Suites
5599 Ambler Drive
Mississauga, ON
905-624-9500

Staybridge Suites Toronto
Mississauga
6791 Hurontario Street
Mississauga, ON
905-564-6892

Days Inn - Ottawa West
350 Moodie Drive
Nepean, ON
613-726-1717

Algonquin Motel
81 N Highway 11
New Liskeard, ON
705-647-6705

Algonquin Motel
81 N Highway 11
New Liskeard, ON
705-647-7357

Comfort Inn Newmarket
1230 Journey S End Cir
Newmarket, ON
905-895-3355

Howard Johnson Express Inn -

Niagara Falls
8100 Lundys Lane
Niagara Falls, ON
905-358-9777

Niagara Parkway Court Motel
3708 Main Street
Niagara Falls, ON
905-295-3331

Best Western North Bay Hotel &
Conference Centre
700 Lakeshore Drive
North Bay, ON
705-474-5800

Clarion Resort Pinewood Park
201 Pinewood Park Drive
North Bay, ON
705-472-0810

Comfort Inn Airport
1200 O Brien St
North Bay, ON
705-476-5400

Comfort Inn North Bay
676 Lakeshore Dr
North Bay, ON
705-494-9444

Holiday Inn Express Hotel & Suites
North Bay
1325 Seymour Street
North Bay, ON
705-476-7700

Super 8 North Bay
570 Lakeshore Drive
North Bay, ON
705-495-4551

Travelodge Airport North Bay
1525 Seymour Street
North Bay, ON
705-495-1133

Travelodge North Bay Lakeshore
718 Lakeshore Drive
North Bay, ON
705-472-7171

Comfort Inn Toronto North
66 Norfinch Drive
North York, ON
416-736-4700

Holiday Inn Express Toronto North
York
30 Norfinch Drive
North York, ON
416-665-3500

Hilton Mississauga/Meadowvale
6750 Mississauga Road
ON, ON

Holiday Inn Oakville
590 Argus Road
Oakville, ON
905-842-5000

Staybridge Suites Oakville-Burlington
2511 Wyecroft Road
Oakville, ON

905-847-2600

Best Western Plus Couchiching Inn
440 Couchiching Point Road
Orillia, ON
705-325-6505

Best Western Plus Mariposa Inn &
Conference Centre
400 Memorial Avenue
Orillia, ON

705-325-9511

Econo Lodge Orillia
265 Memorial Ave
Orillia, ON

705-326-3554

Rodeway Inn Champlain Waterfront
2 Front Street North
Orillia, ON

705-325-0770

Travelodge Oshawa Whitby
940 Champlain Avenue
Oshawa, ON
905-436-9500

Bostonian Executive Suites
341 Maclaren
Ottawa, ON
613-594-5757

Cartier Place Suite Hotel
180 Cooper Street
Ottawa, ON

613-236-5000

Comfort Inn Ottawa East
1252 Michael St
Ottawa, ON

613-744-2900

Days Inn - Ottawa
319 Rideau Street
Ottawa, ON

613-789-5555

Downtown Bed and Breakfast
263 Mcleod Street
Ottawa, ON

613-563-4399

Fairmont Chateau Laurier
1 Rideau Street
Ottawa, ON

613-241-1414

Hotel Indigo Ottawa Downtown City
Centre
123 Metcalfe Street
Ottawa, ON
613-231-6555

Les Suites Hotel, Ottawa
130 Besserer Street
Ottawa, ON

613-232-2000

Ottawa Marriott Hotel
100 Kent Street
Ottawa, ON

613-238-1122

Residence Inn Ottawa Downtown
161 Laurier Avenue West
Ottawa, ON

613 231 2020

Sammy's Retreat
2013 Alta Vist Dr. , Ottawa, Ontario
Ottawa, ON

Sheraton Ottawa Hotel
150 Albert Street
Ottawa, ON

613-238-1500

Southway Hotel
2431 Bank Street
Ottawa, ON

613-737-0811

The National Hotel & Suites, An
Ascend Collection Hotel
361 Queen Street
Ottawa, ON

613-238-6000

The Westin Ottawa
11 Colonel By Drive
Ottawa, ON

613-560-7000

Travelodge Ottawa East Gloucester
1486 Innes Road
Ottawa, ON

613-745-1133

Travelodge Ottawa West
1376 Carling Avenue
Ottawa, ON

613-722-7600

Comfort Inn Owen Sound
955 9th Ave E
Owen Sound, ON
519-371-5500

Days Inn and Conference Centre -
Owen Sound
950 Sixth Street East
Owen Sound, ON

519-376-1551

Comfort Inn Parry Sound
120 Bowes Street
Parry Sound, ON
705-746-6221

Parry Sound Inn and Suites
292 Louisa Street
Parry Sound, ON

705-746-2700

Quality Inn & Conference Center
Parry Sound
1 J.R. Drive, R.R. #2
Parry Sound, ON

705-378-2461

Comfort Inn Pembroke
959 Pembroke St E
Pembroke, ON
613-735-1057

Econo Lodge Inn & Suites -
Pembroke
1218 Pembroke Street East
Pembroke, ON

613-732-4222

Comfort Hotel & Suites Peterborough
1209 Lansdowne St West
Peterborough, ON
705-740-7000

King Bethune Guest House and Spa
270 King Street
Peterborough, ON

705-743-4101

Quality Inn Peterborough
1074 Lansdowne Street West
Peterborough, ON

705-748-6801

Super 8 Peterborough
1257 Lansdowne St
Peterborough, ON

705-876-8898

Comfort Inn Pickering
533 Kingston Rd
Pickering, ON
905-831-6200

Best Western Plus Guildwood Inn
1400 Venetian Blvd

Point Edward, ON
519-337-7577

Comfort Inn Port Hope
Route 2211 County Road 28
Port Hope, ON
905-885-7000

Days Inn & Conference Centre -
Renfrew
760 Gibbons Road
Renfrew, ON
613-432-8109

Holiday Inn Express Hotel & Suites
Toronto - Markham
10 East Pearce Street
Richmond Hill, ON
905-695-5990

Sheraton Parkway Hotel Toronto
North
600 Highway 7 East
Richmond Hill, ON

905-881-2600

Sheraton Parkway Hotel Toronto
North
9005 Leslie Street
Richmond Hill, ON

905-881-2121

Travelodge Richmond Hill
10711 Yonge Street
Richmond Hill, ON

905-884-1007

Howard Johnson Ridgetown
21198 Victoria Road
Ridgetown, ON
519-674-5454

Best Western St. Catharines Hotel &
Conference Centre
2 North Service Road
Saint Catharines, ON
905-934-8000

Comfort Inn Sarnia
815 Mara Street
Sarnia, ON
519-383-6767

Super 8 Sarnia On
420 North Christina Street
Sarnia, ON

519-337-3767

Howard Johnson Inn Sault Ste Marie
On
503 Trunk Road
Sault Ste Marie, ON
705-253-2327

Super 8 Sault Ste Marie On
184 Great Northern Rd
Sault Ste Marie, ON

705-254-6441

Comfort Inn Sault Ste. Marie
333 Great Northern Rd
Sault Ste. Marie, ON
705-759-8000

Sleep Inn Sault Ste. Marie
727 Bay St
Sault Ste. Marie, ON
705-253-7533

Best Western Little River Inn
203 Queens Way West
Simcoe, ON
519-426-2125

Comfort Inn Simcoe
85 Queensway E.
Simcoe, ON
519-426-2611

Canadas Best Value Inn
420 Ontario Street
St Catharines, ON
905-688-1646

Days Inn St Catharines Niagara
89 Meadowvale Drive
St Catharines, ON
905-934-5400

Holiday Inn Hotel & Suites St.
Catharines Conf Ctr
327 Ontario Street
St Catharines, ON
905-688-2324

Holiday Inn Hotel & Suites St.
Catharines Conf Ctr
327 Ontario Street
St Catharines, ON
905-688-2324

Comfort Inn St. Thomas
100 Centennial Ave.
St Thomas, ON
519-633-4082

Comfort Inn Sturgeon Falls
11 Front Street
Sturgeon Falls, ON
705-753-5665

Best Western Downtown Sudbury
Centreville
151 Larch Street
Sudbury, ON
705-673-7801

Clarion Hotel Sudbury
117 Elm Street
Sudbury, ON
705-674-7517

Comfort Inn East Sudbury
440 Second Avenue North
Sudbury, ON

705-560-4502

Comfort Inn Sudbury
2171 Regent St S
Sudbury, ON

705-522-1101

Holiday Inn Sudbury
1696 Regent Street
Sudbury, ON

705-522-3000

Homewood Suites By Hilton Sudbury
2270 Regent St.
Sudbury, ON

705-523-8100

Quality Inn & Conference Centre
Downtown
390 Elgin Street South
Sudbury, ON

705-675-1273

Sudbury Travelodge Hotel
1401 Paris Street
Sudbury, ON

705-522-1100

Super 8 Motel - Sudbury
1956 Regent Street
Sudbury, ON

Towneplace Suites By Marriott
Sudbury
1710 The Kingsway
Sudbury, ON

705-525-7700

Kicking Mule Ranch
Gauthier Road
Tehkummah, ON
705-859-1234

Four Points By Sheraton St.
Catharines Niagara Suites
3530 Schmon Parkway
Thorold, ON
905-984-8484

Airlane Hotel and Conference Centre
698 West Arthur Street
Thunder Bay, ON
807-473-1600

Best Western Crossroads Motor Inn
655 West Arthur St
Thunder Bay, ON

807-577-4241

Best Western Plus Nor'Wester Hotel

& Conference Centre
2080 Highway 61
Thunder Bay, ON

807-473-9123

Comfort Inn Thunder Bay
660 W Arthur St
Thunder Bay, ON

807-475-3155

Econo Lodge Thunder Bay
686 Memorial Avenue
Thunder Bay, ON

807-344-6688

Super 8 Thunder Bay
439 Memorial Ave
Thunder Bay, ON

807-344-2612

Travelodge Thunder Bay
450 Memorial Avenue
Thunder Bay, ON

807-345-2343

Valhalla Inn
1 Valhalla Inn Road
Thunder Bay, ON

807-577-1121

Howard Johnson Tillsonburg On
92 Simcoe Street
Tillsonburg, ON
519-842-7366

Comfort Inn Timmins
939 Algonquin Blvd E
Timmins, ON
705-264-9474

Days Inn And Conference Centre -
Timmins
14 Mountjoy Street South
Timmins, ON

705-267-6211

Travelodge Timmins
1136 Riverside Drive
Timmins, ON

705-360-1122

Beaches Bed and Breakfast Inn
174 Waverley Road
Toronto, ON
416-699-0818

Best Western PREMIER Toronto
Airport Carlingview Hotel
135 Carlingview Drive
Toronto, ON

416-637-7000

Holiday Inn Toronto-Airport East

600 Dixon Road
Toronto, ON

416-240-7511

Howard Johnson Toronto West
Lakeshore
14 Roncesvalles Avenue
Toronto, ON

416-532-9900

Intercontinental Toronto Center
225 Front Street West
Toronto, ON

416-597-1400

Intercontinental Toronto Yorkville
220 Bloor Street West
Toronto, ON

416-960-5200

Quality Suites Toronto Airport
262 Carlingview Drive
Toronto, ON

416-674-8442

Residence Inn By Marriott Toronto
Airport
17 Reading Court
Toronto, ON

416 798 2900

Residence Inn By Marriott Toronto
Downtown/Entertainment Dist.
255 Wellington Street West
Toronto, ON

416 581 1800

Sheraton Gateway Toronto Intl
Airport
Terminal 3 Toronto Amf P.O. Box
3000
Toronto, ON

905-672-7000

Sheraton Toronto Airport Hotel &
Conference Centre
801 Dixon Road
Toronto, ON

416-675-6100

Super 8 Toronto
222 Spadina Ave.
Toronto, ON

647-426-8118

The Fairmont Royal York
100 Front Street West
Toronto, ON

416-368-2511

The Omni King Edward Hotel
37 King Street East

Toronto, ON

416-863-9700

Toronto Marriott Bloor Yorkville Hotel
90 Bloor Street East
Toronto, ON

416-961-8000

Travelodge Toronto Airport
925 Dixon Road
Toronto, ON

416-674-2222

Comfort Inn Trenton
68 Monogram Pl
Trenton, ON
613-965-6660

Ramada Trenton Hotel
99 Glen Miller Road
Trenton, ON

613-394-4855

Travelodge Trenton
598 Old Hwy 2
Trenton, ON

613-965-6789

Holiday Inn Express Hotel & Suites
Vaughan-Southwest
6100 Highway 7
Vaughan, ON
905-851-1510

Residence Inn By Marriott Toronto
Vaughan
11 Interchange Way
Vaughan, ON

905 695 4002

Days Inn Wallaceburg
76 Mcnaughton Avenue
Wallaceburg, ON
519-627-0781

Comfort Inn Waterloo
190 Weber St N
Waterloo, ON
519-747-9400

Comfort Inn Welland
870 Niagara Street
Welland, ON
905-732-4811

Massey Motel
295 Sable Street West
West Massey, ON
705-865-2500

Quality Suites East Whitby
1700 Champlain Ave
Whitby, ON
905-432-8800

Residence Inn By Marriott Whitby
160 Consumers Drive
Whitby, ON
905 444 9756

Best Western Plus Waterfront Hotel
277 Riverside Drive West
Windsor, ON
519-973-5555

Comfort Inn & Suites Ambassador
Bridge
2330 Huron Church Road
Windsor, ON

519-972-1100

Comfort Inn Windsor
2955 Dougall Avenue
Windsor, ON

519-966-7800

Comfort Suites Downtown
500 Tuscarora Rd. East
Windsor, ON

519-971-0505

Hampton Inn & Suites Windsor, On
1840 Huron Church Road
Windsor, ON

519-972-0770

Quality Suites Downtown
250 Dougall Ave
Windsor, ON

519-977-9707

Travelodge Hotel Downtown/Windsor
33 Riverside Drive East
Windsor, ON

519-258-7774

Element Vaughan Southwest
6170 Highway 7
Woodbridge, ON
905-264-6474

Days Inn Woodstock
560 Norwich Avenue
Woodstock, ON
519-421-4588

Quality Hotel & Suites Woodstock
580 Bruin Blvd.
Woodstock, ON

519-537-5586

## Prince Edward Island Listings

Caernarvon Cottages and Gardens
4697 H 12
Bayside, PE

902-854-3418

Shaw's Hotel
99 Apple Tree Road
Brackley Beach, PE
902-672-2022

Best Western Charlottetown
238 Grafton St
Charlottetown, PE
902-892-2461

Comfort Inn Charlottetown
112 Capital Drive
Charlottetown, PE

902-566-4424

Delta Prince Edward
18 Queen Street
Charlottetown, PE

902-566-2222

Econo Lodge Charlottetown
20 Lower Malpeque Road
Charlottetown, PE

902-368-1110

Holiday Inn Express Hotel & Suites
Charlottetown
200 Capital Drive
Charlottetown, PE

902-892-1201

Quality Inn & Suites Downtown
Charlottetown
150 Euston St.
Charlottetown, PE

902-894-8572

Super 8 Charlottetown Pe
15 York Point Road
Charlottetown, PE

902-892-7900

Cavendish Gateway Resort
6596 Route 13
Mayfield, PE
902-963-2213

Quality Inn & Suites Garden Of The
Gulf
618 Water St. E.
Summerside, PE
902-436-2295

Traveller's Inn Prince Edward Island
80 All Weather Highway
Summerside, PE

902-436-9100

Doctor's Inn
32 Allen Road
Tyne Valley, PE
902-831-3057

## Quebec Listings

Chalet Le Bruant
410 Chemin du Cap-aux-rets
Baie-Saint-Paul, PQ
418-801-9153

Hotel Baie-Saint-Paul
911 boul Mgr Laval
Baie-Saint-Paul, PQ

418-435-3683

Days Inn - Berthierville
760 Rue Gadoury
Berthierville, PQ
450-836-1621

Hampton Inn & Suites By Hilton
Montreal-Dorval
1900 Trans-Canada Highway
Dorval, PQ
514-633-8243

Crowne Plaza Gatineau-Ottawa
2 Montcalm Street
Gatineau, PQ
819-778-3880

Four Points By Sheraton Hotel And
Conference Centre Gatineau
35 Rue Laurier
Gatineau, PQ

819-778-6111

Hotel du Lac Carling
2255 Route #327 Nord
Grenville-sur-la-Rouge, PQ
450-533-9211

Hilton Lac-Leamy
3 Boulevard du Casino
Hull, PQ
819-790-6444

Fairmont Le Manoir Richelieu
181 Rue Richelieu
La Malbaie, PQ
418-665-3703

Mont-Tremblant Cottage Rental
Call to Arrange
Labelle, PQ
514-923-5787

La Paysanne Motel
42 rue Queen
Lennoxville, PQ
819-569-5585

Gite du Carrefour
11 ave St-Laurent ouest
Louiseville, PQ
819-228-4932

Auberge Du Vieux-Port
97, De La Commune Street East

Montreal, PQ
514-876-0081

Candlewood Suites Montreal Centre-Ville
191 Rene Levesque Boulevard East
Montreal, PQ

514-667-5002

Delta Montreal
475 President Kennedy Avenue
Montreal, PQ

514-286-1986

Hotel 10 Montreal
10 Sherbrooke West
Montreal, PQ

514-843-6000

Hotel Bonaventure Montreal
900 de la Gauchetiere West
Montreal, PQ

514-878-2332

Hotel Le Germain
2050 Mansfield Street
Montreal, PQ

514-849-2050

Hotel St Paul
355 Mcgill Street
Montreal, PQ

514-380-2222

Intercontinental Montreal
360 Rue Saint Antoine Ouest
Montreal, PQ

514-987-9900

Intercontinental Montreal
360 Saint-Antoine Street W
Montreal, PQ

514-847-8525

Le Centre Sheraton Montreal Hotel
1201 Rene Levesque Blvd West
Montreal, PQ

514-878-2000

Le Meridien Versailles
1808 Sherbrooke Street West
Montreal, PQ

514-933-8111

Le Meridien Versailles
1808 Sherbrooke Street West
Montreal, PQ

514-933-8111

Le Saint-Sulpice Hotel Montreal
414 Rue St Sulpice
Montreal, PQ

514-288-1000

Loews Hotel Vogue
1425 Rue de la Montagne
Montreal, PQ

514-285-5555

Residence Inn By Marriott Montreal Airport
6500 Place Robert-Joncas
Montreal, PQ

514 336 9333

Residence Inn By Marriott Montreal Downtown
2045 Peel Street
Montreal, PQ

514 982 6064

Residence Inn Montreal Westmount
2170 Lincoln Avenue
Montreal, PQ

514 935 9224

The Ritz-Carlton, Montreal
1228 Sherbrooke Street West
Montreal, PQ

514-842-4212

Hotel Motel Manoir de Perce
212 Route 132
Perce, PQ
418-782-2022

Delta Quebec Hotel
690 Boulevard Rene-Ylevesque East
Quebec, PQ
418-647-1717

Dominion 1912, Hotel
126 Rue Saint Pierre
Quebec, PQ
418-692-2224

Hilton Quebec
1100 Rene Levesque East
Quebec, PQ
418-647-2411

L`hotel Du Vieux Quebec
1190 St. Jean Street
Quebec, PQ
418-692-1850

Days Inn Riviere-De-Loup
182 Rue Fraser
Riviere-du-loup, PQ
418-862-6354

Holiday Inn Express Hotel & Suites
Saint - Hyacinthe
1500 Johnson Street East

Saint - Hyacinthe, PQ
450-251-1111

Super 8 St-Jerome
3 J F Kennedy
Saint-Jerome, PQ
450-438-4388

Super 8 St. Agathe Des Monts
Jct Of Expressway15 At Hwy 117
Sainte-Agathe-des-Monts, PQ
819-324-8880

Holiday Inn Express St. Jean Sur Richelieu
700 Rue Gadbois
St Jean Sur Richelieu, PQ
450-359-4466

Auberge du Faubourg
280 ave de Gaspe ouest
St-Jean-Port-Joli, PQ
418-598-6455

Days Inn - Ste. Helene-De-Bagot
410 Rue Couture
Ste. Helene-de-Bagot, PQ
450-791-2580

Super 8 Lachenaie/Terrebonne
1155 Yves Blais
Terrebonne, PQ
450-582-8288

Days Inn - Trois-Rivieres
3155 Boulevard Saint Jean
Trois-Rivieres, PQ
819-377-4444

Delta Trois-Rivieres
1620 Rue Notre-Dame Centre
Trois-Rivieres, PQ
819-376-1991

Super 8 Trois-Rivieres
3185 Boulevard Saint-Jean
Trois-Rivieres, PQ
819-377-5881

# Saskatchewan Listings

The Pilgrim Inn
510 College Dr (Hwy 1 W)
Caronport, SK
306-756-5002

Best Western Plus Blairmore
306 Shillington Cres
Corman Park, SK
306-242-2299

Super 8 Kindersley
508 12th Avenue East
Kindersley, SK
306-463-8218

Maple Creek Motor Inn
410 Hwy 21 North
Maple Creek, SK
306-662-4477

Super 8 Meadow Lake
702 9th Street West
Meadow Lake, SK
306-236-1188

Blue Bird Hotel
101 Spruce Haven Road
Melfort, SK
306-752-5961

Comfort Inn & Suites Moose Jaw
155 Thatcher Drive W.
Moose Jaw, SK
306-692-2100

Days Inn - Moose Jaw
1720 Main Street North
Moose Jaw, SK

306-691-5777

Super 8 North Battleford
1006 Highway 16 Bypass
North Battleford, SK
306-446-8888

Comfort Inn Prince Albert
3863 2nd Ave W
Prince Albert, SK
306-763-4466

Ramada Prince Albert
3245 2nd Avenue West
Prince Albert, SK

306-922-1333

Super 8 Prince Albert
4444 2nd Ave West
Prince Albert, SK

306-953-0088

Travelodge Prince Albert
3551 2nd Avenue West
Prince Albert, SK

306-764-6441

Best Western Seven Oaks Inn
777 Albert Street
Regina, SK
306-757-0121

Comfort Inn Regina
3221 E Eastgate Dr
Regina, SK

306-789-5522

Delta Regina
1919 Saskatchewan Drive
Regina, SK

306-525-5255

Quality Hotel Regina
1717 Victoria Ave
Regina, SK

306-569-4656

Super 8 Regina
2730 Victoria Avenue East
Regina, SK

306-789-8833

THE HOTEL SASKATCHEWAN, A
Marriott Luxury & Lifestyle Hotel
2125 Victoria Avenue
Regina, SK

306-522-7691

Wingate By Wyndham Regina
1700 Broad Street
Regina, SK

306-584-7400

Wingate By Wyndham Regina
1700 Broad Street
Regina, SK

306-584-7400

Best Western Royal Hotel
1715 Idylwyld Drive North
Saskatoon, SK
306-244-5552

Comfort Inn Saskatoon
2155 Northridge Dr
Saskatoon, SK

306-934-1122

Country Inn & Suites By Carlson,
Saskatoon, SK
617 Cynthia St
Saskatoon, SK

306-934-3900

Delta Bessborough
601 Spadina Crescent East
Saskatoon, SK

306-244-5521

Radisson Hotel Saskatoon
405 Twentieth Street East
Saskatoon, SK

306-665-3322

Ramada Hotel And Golf Dome -
Saskatoon
806 Idylwyld Drive North
Saskatoon, SK

306-665-6500

Sheraton Cavalier Hotel Saskatoon
612 Spadina Crescent East
Saskatoon, SK

306-652-6770

Super 8 Saskatoon
706 Circle Drive East
Saskatoon, SK

306-384-8989

Travelodge Hotel Saskatoon
106 Circle Drive West
Saskatoon, SK

306-242-8881

Westgate Inn Motel
2501 22nd Street W/H 14
Saskatoon, SK

306-382-3722

Comfort Inn Swift Current
1510 South Service Rd E
Swift Current, SK
306-778-3994

Travelodge Swift Current
1150 South Service Road East
Swift Current, SK

306-778-7730

Ramada Weyburn
1420 Sims Avenue
Weyburn, SK
306-842-4994

Comfort Inn And Suites
22 Dracup Avenue
Yorkton, SK
306-783-0333

# Yukon Listings

1202 Motor Inn and RV Park
Mile 1202 Alaska H
Beaver Creek, YU
867-862-7600

Buckshot Betty's Restaurant and
Rooms
1202 Alaska H
Beaver Creek, YU

867-862-7111

Westmark Inn Beaver Creek
Mile 1202 Alaska Hwy
Beaver Creek, YU

867-862-7501

Spirit Lake Wilderness Resort
Km 115.4 South Klondike Hwy Box
155
Carcross, YU
866-739-8566

Hotel Carmacks
On Free Gold Road

Carmacks, YU
867-863-5221

Bonanza Gold Motel
715.2 N Klondike H
Dawson City, YU
867-993-6789

Canadas Best Value Inn - Downtown Hotel
1026 2nd Avenue Po Box 780
Dawson City, YU

867-993-5346

Klondike Kate's Cabins and Restaurant
3rd Avenue and King Street
Dawson City, YU

867-993-6527

Whitehouse Cabins
1626 Front Street/H 2
Dawson City, YU

867-993-5576

Destruction Bay Lodge
Mile 1083 Alaska Hwy
Destruction Bay, YU
867-841-5332

Talbot Arm Motel
Mile 1083 Alaska Hwy
Destruction Bay, YU

867-841-4461

Eagle Plains Hotel
On the Dempster H
Eagle Plains, YU
867-993-2453

Alcan Motor Inn
Box 5460
Haines Junction, YU
867-634-2371

Kluane Park Inn
1635 Alaska Highway
Haines Junction, YU

867-634-2261

Stewart Valley Bedrock Motel
Lot 99 H 11
Mayo, YU
867-996-2290

Continental Divide Lodge and RV Park
Mile 721 Alaska H
Swift River, YU
867-851-6451

Dawson Peaks Resort and RV Park
KM 1232 Alaska H
Teslin, YU
867-390-2244

Mukluk Annie's Salmon Bake and Motel
Mile 784 Alaska Hwy
Teslin, YU

867-390-2600

Nisultin Trading Post Motel
Mile 804 Alaska Hwy
Teslin, YU

867-390-2521

Yukon Motel
Mile 804 Alaska Hwy
Teslin, YU

867-390-2575

Belvedere Motor Hotel
Box 370
Watson Lake, YU
867-536-7712

Big Horn Hotel
Frank Trail just S of Alaska Hwy
Watson Lake, YU

867-536-2020

Big Horn Hotel
Alaska H/H 1
Watson Lake, YU

867-536-2020

Gateway Motor Inn
Box 370
Watson Lake, YU

867-536-7744

Northern Beaver Post Cottages
H 1 Historic Mile 650
Watson Lake, YU

867-536-2307

Northern Beaver Post Lodge
KM 1003 Alaska H
Watson Lake, YU

867-536-2307

Racheria Lodge
MM 710 Alaska H
Watson Lake, YU

867-851-6456

Airport Chalet
91634 Alaska Hwy
Whitehorse, YU
867-668-2166

Canada`s Best Value Inn
102 Wood Street
Whitehorse, YU

867-667-7801

Hi Country Inn

4051 4th Avenue
Whitehorse, YU

867-667-4471

Inn on the Lake
Strictland Street
Whitehorse, YU

867-660-5253

Inn on the River Wilderness Resort
PO Box 10420
Whitehorse, YU

867-660-5253

Sundog Retreat
Lot 1160, Policeman's Point Road
Whitehorse, YU

867-633-4183

The Yukon Inn
4220 4th Avenue
Whitehorse, YU

867-667-2527

Chapter 2

# Dog-Friendly Beaches

# Alabama Listings

The Dauphin Island Beaches
at the end of H 193
Dauphin Island, AL
251-861-3607
dauphinisland.org/public-beach/
Considered one of the most pet-friendly beach areas on the Gulf
Coast, the white sandy beaches of
Dauphin Island offers several play
areas for fun-loving pooches. There
are large beach play areas by the
Red School House and the old fishing
pier; plus a few miles of undeveloped
barrier beach and a campground with
a beach where pets are welcome.
Dogs are not allowed at the West
End Beach Park on the island's far
west end. Dogs must be kept
leashed, cleaned up after promptly,
and be hound and human friendly.

# Alaska Listings

Homer Beaches

Homer, AK
907-235-7740
Leashed dogs are allowed on the
beaches of Homer Alaska. The tide in
Homer varies significantly during the
day and a lot of land is covered up
and uncovered at various times. So
keep a close eye on the tides while in
Homer.

# Arizona Listings

Tempe Beach Park
54 W Rio Salado Pkwy
Tempe, AZ

Dogs are allowed in the water of
Tempe City Lake at Tempe Beach
Park. Dogs must be leashed in the
park.

# California Listings

Rio Del Mar Beach
Rio Del Mar
Aptos, CA
831-685-6500
Dogs on leash are allowed at this
beach which offers a wide strip of
sand. From Highway 1, take the Rio
Del Mar exit.

Mad River Beach County Park
Mad River Road
Arcata, CA
707-445-7651
Enjoy walking or jogging for several
miles on this beach. Dogs on leash
are allowed. The park is located

about 4-5 miles north of Arcata. To
get there, take Highway 101 and exit
Giuntoli Lane. Then go north onto
Heindon Rd. Turn left onto Miller Rd.
Turn right on Mad River Road and
follow it to the park.

Avila Beach
off Avila Beach Drive
Avila Beach, CA
805-595-5400
This beach is about a 1/2 mile long.
Dogs are not allowed between 10am
and 5pm and must be leashed.

Olde Port Beach
off Avila Beach Drive
Avila Beach, CA
805-595-5400
This beach is about a 1/4 mile long.
Dogs are not allowed between 10am
and 5pm and must be leashed.

Big Bear Lake Beaches
Hwy 38
Big Bear Lake, CA

There are various beaches along the
lake on Hwy 38. You can get to any
of the beaches via the Alpine Pedal
Path. To get there, (going away from
the village), take the Stanfield Cutoff
to the other side of the lake and turn
left onto Hwy 38. In about 1/4 - 1/2
mile, parking will be on the left.

Pfieffer Beach
Sycamore Road
Big Sur, CA
805-968-6640
Dogs on leash are allowed at this
day use beach which is located in
the Los Padres National Forest. The
beach is located in Big Sur, south of
the Big Sur Ranger Station. From
Big Sur, start heading south on
Highway 1 and look carefully for
Sycamore Road. Take Sycamore
Road just over 2 miles to the beach.
There is a $5 entrance fee per car.

Doran Regional Park
201 Doran Beach Road
Bodega Bay, CA
707-875-3540
This park offers 2 miles of sandy
beach. It is a popular place to picnic,
walk, surf, fish and fly kites. Dogs
are allowed but must be on a 6 foot
or less leash and proof of a rabies
vaccination is required. There is a
minimal parking fee. The park is
located south of Bodega Bay.

Agate Beach
Elm Road
Bolinas, CA
415-499-6387
During low tide, this 6 acre park
provides access to almost 2 miles of

shoreline. Leashed dogs are allowed.

Cardiff State Beach
Old Highway 101
Cardiff, CA
760-753-5091
This is a gently sloping sandy beach
with warm water. Popular activities
include swimming, surfing and
beachcombing. Dogs on leash are
allowed and please clean up after
your pets. The beach is located on
Old Highway 101, one mile south of
Cardiff.

Carmel City Beach
Ocean Avenue
Carmel, CA
831-624-9423
This beach is within walking distance
(about 7 blocks) from the quaint
village of Carmel. There are a couple
of hotels and several restaurants that
are within walking distance of the
beach. Your pooch is allowed to run
off-leash as long as he or she is
under voice control. To get there,
take the Ocean Avenue exit from Hwy
1 and follow Ocean Ave to the end.

Carmel River State Beach
Carmelo Street
Carmel, CA
831-624-9423
This beach is just south of Carmel. It
has approximately a mile of beach
and leashes are required. It's located
on Carmelo Street.

Garrapata State Park
Highway 1
Carmel, CA
831-649-2836
There are two miles of beach front at
this park. Dogs are allowed but must
be on a 6 foot or less leash and
people need to clean up after their
pets. The beach is on Highway 1,
about 6 1/2 miles south of Rio Road
in Carmel. It is about 18 miles north
of Big Sur.

Caspar Beach
14441 Point Cabrillo Drive
Caspar, CA
707-937-5804
Dogs on leash are allowed at this
sandy beach across from the Caspar
Beach RV Park. The beach is located
about 4 miles north of Mendocino.
Please clean up after your dog.

Cayucos State Beach
Cayucos Drive
Cayucos, CA
805-781-5200
This state beach allows leashed
dogs. The beach is located in the
small town of Cayucos. To get to the

beach from Hwy 1, exit Cayucos Drive and head west. There is a parking lot and parking along the street.

Cloverdale River Park
31820 McCray Road
Cloverdale, CA
707-565-2041
This park is located along the Russian River and offers seasonal fishing and river access for kayaks and canoes. There are no lifeguards at the beach area. Dogs are allowed, but must be on a 6 foot or less leash. They can wade into the water, but cannot really swim because pets must remain on leash. There is a $3 per car parking fee.

Corona Del Mar State Beach
Iris Street and Ocean Blvd.
Corona Del Mar, CA
949-644-3151
This is a popular beach for swimming, surfing and diving. The sandy beach is about a half mile long. Dogs are allowed on this beach during certain hours. They are allowed before 9am and after 5pm, year round. Pets must be on a 6 foot or less leash. Tickets will be issued if your dog is off leash.

Coronado Dog Beach
100 Ocean Blvd
Coronado, CA
619-522-7342
Coronado's Dog Beach is at the north end of Ocean Blvd. Just north of the famous Hotel del Coronado (unfortunately dogs are not allowed at the hotel)the area that is designated off leash is marked by signs. The off-leash beach is open 24 hours. Dogs must be supervised and cleaned up after. Dogs must be leashed outside of the off-leash area and fines are very steep for any violations. There are also fines for not cleaning after your dog at the dog beach. Food and Pet Treats are not allowed at the beach.

Crescent Beach - Del Norte SP
Enderts Beach Rd
Crescent Beach, CA
707-464-6101
Dogs are allowed on the ocean beach at Crescent Beach in the Del Norte Coast Redwoods State Park. They are not allowed on any trails within the Redwood National or State Parks. Pets are also allowed at road accessible picnic areas and campgrounds. Dogs must be on a 6 foot or less leash and people need to pick up after their pets. To get to the beach take Enderts Beach Road South from Highway 101 just south of Crescent City.

Beachfront Park
Front Street
Crescent City, CA
707-464-9507
Dogs are allowed at park and the beach, but must be leashed. Please clean up after your pets. To get there, take Highway 101 to Front Street. Follow Front Street to the park.

Crescent Beach
Enderts Beach Road
Crescent City, CA
707-464-6101
While dogs are not allowed on any trails in Redwood National Park, they are allowed on a couple of beaches, including Crescent Beach. Enjoy beachcombing or bird watching at this beach. Pets are also allowed at road accessible picnic areas and campgrounds. Dogs must be on a 6 foot or less leash and people need to pick up after their pets. The beach is located off Highway 101, about 3 to 4 miles south of Crescent City. Exit Enderts Beach Road and head south.

Davenport Landing Beach
Hwy 1
Davenport, CA
831-462-8333
This beautiful beach is surrounded by high bluffs and cliff trails. Leashes are required. To get to the beach from Santa Cruz, head north on Hwy 1 for about 10 miles.

Del Mar Beach
Seventeenth Street
Del Mar, CA
858-755-1556
Dogs are allowed on the beach as follows. South of 17th Street, dogs are allowed on a 6 foot leash year-round. Between 17th Street and 29th Street, dogs are allowed on a 6 foot leash from October through May (from June through September, dogs are not allowed at all). Between 29th Street and northern city limits, dogs are allowed without a leash, but must be under voice control from October through May (from June through September, dogs must be on a 6 foot leash). Owners must clean up after their dogs.

Dog Beach Del Mar
3006 Sandy Ln
Del Mar, CA
858-755-9313
The Dog Beach in Del Mar is a off-leash dog beach September through May. During the summer your pooch must be on a leash. Dogs must be

well behaved and multiple poop bag stations and trash cans are located on the beach for your convenience.

Rivermouth Beach
Highway 101
Del Mar, CA

This beach allows voice controlled dogs to run leash free from September 15 through June 15 (no specified hours). Leashes are required during mid-summer tourist season from mid June to mid Sept. Fans of this beach are trying to convince the Del Mar City council to extend the leash-free period to year round. The beach is located on Highway 101 just south of Border Avenue at the north end of the City of Del Mar. Thanks to one of our readers for recommending this beach.

MacKerricher State Park
Highway 1
Fort Bragg, CA
707-964-9112
Dogs are allowed on the beach, but not on any park trails. Pets must be leashed and people need to clean up after their pets. Picnic areas, restrooms and campsites (including an ADA restroom and campsites), are available at this park. The park is located three miles north of Fort Bragg on Highway 1, near the town of Cleone.

Noyo Beach Off-Leash Dog Beach
North Harbor Drive
Fort Bragg, CA

The dog beach is located at the north side of where the Noyo River enters the Pacific Ocean. To get to the dog beach, turn EAST (away from the ocean) on N. Harbor Drive from Highway 1. N. Harbor will go down to the river and circle under Highway 1 to the beach. The beach was organized by MCDOG (Mendocino Coast Dog Owners Group) which is now working on an off-leash dog park for the Mendocino area.

Goleta Beach County Park
5990 Sandspit Road
Goleta, CA
805-568-2460
Leashed dogs are allowed at this county beach. The beach and park are about 1/2 mile long. There are picnic tables and a children's playground at the park. It's located near the Santa Barbara Municipal Airport in Goleta, just north of Santa Barbara. To get there, take Hwy 101 to Hwy 217 and head west. Before

you reach UC Santa Barbara, there will be an exit for Goleta Beach.

Kirk Creek Beach and Trailhead
Highway 1
Gorda, CA
831-385-5434
Both the Kirk Creek Beach and hiking trails allow dogs. Pets must be leashed. You can park next to the Kirk Creek Campground and either hike down to the beach or start hiking at the Kirk Creek Trailhead which leads to the Vicente Flat Trail where you can hike for miles with your dog. The beach and trailhead is part of the Los Padres National Forest and is located about 25 miles south of Big Sur.

Sand Dollar Beach
Highway 1
Gorda, CA
805-434-1996
Walk down a path to one of the longest sandy beaches on the Big Sur Coast. This national forest managed beach is popular for surfing, fishing and walking. Dogs must be on leash and people need to clean up after their pets. There is a minimal day use fee. The dog-friendly Plaskett Creek Campground is within walking distance. This beach is part of the Los Padres National Forest and is located about 5 miles south of Kirk Creek and about 30 miles south of Big Sur.

Willow Creek Beach
Highway 1
Gorda, CA
831-385-5434
Dogs on leash are allowed at this day use beach and picnic area. The beach is part of the Los Padres National Forest and is located about 35 miles south of Big Sur.

Gualala Point Regional Park Beach
42401 Coast Highway 1
Gualala, CA
707-565-2041
This county park offers sandy beaches, hiking trails, campsites, picnic tables and restrooms. Dogs are allowed on the beach, on the trails, and in the campground, but they must be on a 6 foot or less leash. People also need to clean up after their pets. There is a $3 day use fee.

Blufftop Coastal Park
Poplar Street
Half Moon Bay, CA
650-726-8297
Leashed dogs are allowed at this beach. The beach is located on the west end of Poplar Street, off Highway 1.

Montara State Beach
Highway 1
Half Moon Bay, CA
650-726-8819
Dogs on leash are allowed at this beach. Please clean up after your pets. The beach is located 8 miles north of Half Moon Bay on Highway 1. There are two beach access points. The first access point is across from Second Street, immediately south of the Outrigger Restaurant. The second access point is about a 1/2 mile north on the ocean side of Highway 1. Both access points have steep paths down to the beach.

Surfer's Beach
Highway 1
Half Moon Bay, CA
650-726-8297
Dogs on leash are allowed on the beach. It is located at Highway 1 and Coronado Street.

Healdsburg Veterans Memorial Beach
13839 Old Redwood Highway
Healdsburg, CA
707-565-2041
This man-made swimming beach is located on the Russian River. Dogs are allowed at this park, but must be on a 6 foot or less leash. They can wade into the water, but cannot really swim because pets must remain on leash. People are urged to swim only when lifeguards are present, which is usually between Memorial Day and Labor Day. The beach area also offers picnic tables and a restroom. There is a $3 to $4 parking fee per day, depending on the season.

Huntington Dog Beach
Pacific Coast Hwy (Hwy 1)
Huntington Beach, CA
714-841-8644
dogbeach.org
This beautiful beach is about a mile long and allows dogs from 5 am to 10 pm. Dogs must be under control but may be off leash and owners must pick up after them. Dogs are only allowed on the beach between Golden West Street and Seapoint Ave. Please adhere to these rules as there are only a couple of dog-friendly beaches left in the entire Los Angeles area. The beach is located off the Pacific Coast Hwy (Hwy 1) at Golden West Street. Please remember to pick up after your dog... the city wanted to prohibit dogs in 1997 because of the dog

waste left on the beach. But thanks to The Preservation Society of Huntington Dog Beach (http://www.dogbeach.org), it continues to be dog-friendly. City ordinances require owners to pick up after their dogs. It is suggested that you bring plenty of quarters in order to feed the parking meters near the beach.

Imperial Beach
Seacoast Drive at Imperial Beach Blvd
Imperial Beach, CA
619-424-3151
Dogs on leash are allowed on the portions of the beach that are north of Palm Avenue and south of Imperial Beach Blvd. They are not allowed on the beach between Palm Avenue and Imperial Beach Blvd.

Stillwater Cove Regional Park
22455 Highway 1
Jenner, CA
707-565-2041
This 210 acre park includes a small beach, campground, picnic tables, and restrooms. The park offers a great view of the Pacific Ocean from Stillwater Cove. Dogs are allowed on the beach, and in the campground, but they must be on a 6 foot or less leash. People also need to clean up after their pets. There is a $3 day use fee. The park is located off Highway 1, about 16 miles north of Jenner.

Coon Street Beach
Coon Street
Kings Beach, CA

northtahoeparks.com/beaches
Located at the end of Coon Street, on the east side of Kings Beach is a small but popular dog beach. There are also picnic tables, BBQs and restrooms at this beach.

La Jolla Shores Beach
Camino Del Oro
La Jolla, CA
619-221-8900
Leashed dogs are allowed on this beach and the adjacent Kellogg Park from 6pm to 9am. The beach is about 1/2 mile long. To get there, take Hwy 5 to the La Jolla Village Drive exit heading west. Turn left onto Torrey Pines Rd. Then turn right onto La Jolla Shores Drive. Go 4-5 blocks and turn left onto Vallecitos. Go straight until you reach the beach and Kellogg Park.

Point La Jolla Beaches
Coast Blvd.
La Jolla, CA
619-221-8900
Leashed dogs are allowed on this

beach and the walkway (paved and dirt trails) from 6pm to 9am. The beaches and walkway are at least a 1/2 mile long and might continue further. To get there, exit La Jolla Village Drive West from Hwy 5. Turn left onto Torrey Pines Rd. Turn right on Prospect and then park or turn right onto Coast Blvd. Parking is limited around the village area.

Main Beach
Pacific Hwy (Hwy 1)
Laguna Beach, CA
949-497-3311
Dogs are allowed on this beach between 6pm and 8am, June 1 to September 16. The rest of the year, they are allowed on the beach from dawn until dusk. Dogs must be on a leash at all times.

Rosie's Dog Beach
between Roycroft and Argonne Avenues
Long Beach, CA
562-570-3100
hautedogs.org/beach.html
This 3 acre off-leash unfenced dog beach is the only off-leash dog beach in Los Angeles County. It is open daily from 6am until 8pm. It opened on August 1, 2003. The "zone" is 235 yards along the water and 60 yards deep. There is a fresh water fountain called the "Fountain of Woof" which is located near the restrooms at the end of Granada Avenue, near the Dog Zone. Only one dog is allowed per adult and dog owners are entirely responsible for their dog's actions. The beach is located between Roycroft and Argonne avenues in Belmont Shore, Long Beach. It is a few blocks east of the Belmont Pier and Olympic pool. From Ocean Blvd, enter at Bennett Avenue for the beachfront metered parking lot. The cost is 25 cents for each 15 minutes from 8am until 6pm daily. Parking is free after 5pm in the beachfront lot at the end of Granada Avenue. You can check with the website http://www.hautedogs.org for updates and additional rules about the Long Beach Dog Beach Zone.

Leo Carrillo State Beach
Hwy 1
Malibu, CA
818-880-0350
This beach is one of the very few dog-friendly beaches in the Los Angeles area. In a press release dated November 27, 2002, the California State Parks clarified the rules for dogs at Leo Carrillo State Beach. We thank the State Parks for this clear announcement of the regulations. Dogs are allowed on a

maximum 6 foot leash when accompanied by a person capable of controlling the dog on all beach WEST (up coast) of lifeguard tower 3 at Leo Carrillo State Park, Staircase Beach, County Line Beach, and all Beaches within Point Mugu State Park. Dogs are NOT allowed EAST of lifeguard tower 3 at Leo Carrillo State Beach at any time. And please note that dogs are not allowed in the tide pools at Leo Carrillo. There should be signs posted. A small general store is located on the mountain side of the freeway. Here you can grab some snacks and other items. The park is located on Hwy 1, approximately 30 miles northwest of Santa Monica. We ask that all dog people closely obey these regulations so that the beach continues to be dog-friendly.

Manresa State Beach
San Andreas Road
Manresa, CA
831-761-1795
Surfing and surf fishing are both popular activities at this beach. Dogs are allowed on the beach, but must be leashed. To get there from Aptos, head south on Highway 1. Take San Andreas Road southwest for several miles until you reach Manresa. Upon reaching the coast, you will find the first beach access point.

Clam Beach County Park
Highway 101
McKinleyville, CA
707-445-7651
This beach is popular for fishing, swimming, picnicking and beachcombing. Of course, there are also plenty of clams. Dogs on leash are allowed on the beach and at the campgrounds. There are no day use fees. The park is located off Highway 101, about eight miles north of Arcata.

Big River Beach
N. Big River Road
Mendocino, CA
707-937-5804
This small beach is located just south of downtown Mendocino. There are two ways to get there. One way is to head south of town on Hwy 1 and turn left on N. Big River Rd. The beach will be on the right. The second way is to take Hwy 1 and exit Main Street/Jackson heading towards the coastline. In about 1/4-1/2 mile there will be a Chevron Gas Station and a historic church on the left. Park and then walk behind the church to the trailhead. Follow the trail, bearing left when appropriate, and there will

be a wooden staircase that goes down to Big River Beach. Dogs must be on leash.

Van Damme State Beach
Highway 1
Mendocino, CA

This small beach is located in the town of Little River which is approximately 2 miles south of Mendocino. It is part of Van Damme State Park which is located across Highway 1. Most California State Parks, including this one, do not allow dogs on the hiking trails. Fortunately this one allows dogs on the beach. There is no parking fee at the beach and dogs must be on leash.

Monterey Recreation Trail
various (see comments)
Monterey, CA

Take a walk on the Monterey Recreation Trail and experience the beautiful scenery that makes Monterey so famous. This paved trail extends for miles, starting at Fisherman's Wharf and ending in the city of Pacific Grove. Dogs must be leashed. Along the path there are a few small beaches that allow dogs such as the one south of Fisherman's Wharf and another beach behind Ghirardelli Ice Cream on Cannery Row. Along the path you'll find a few more outdoor places to eat near Cannery Row and by the Monterey Bay Aquarium. Look at the Restaurants section for more info.

Monterey State Beach
various (see comments)
Monterey, CA
831-649-2836
Take your water loving and beach loving dog to this awesome beach in Monterey. There are various starting points, but it basically stretches from Hwy 1 and the Del Rey Oaks Exit down to Fisherman's Wharf. Various beaches make up this 2 mile (each way) stretch of beach, but leashed dogs are allowed on all of them . If you want to extend your walk, you can continue on the paved Monterey Recreation Trail which goes all the way to Pacific Grove. There are a few smaller dog-friendly beaches along the paved trail.

Muir Beach
Hwy 1
Muir Beach, CA

Dogs on leash are allowed on Muir Beach with you. Please clean up after your dog on the beach. To get to Muir

Beach from Hwy 101 take Hwy 1 North from the north side of the Golden Gate Bridge.

Newport and Balboa Beaches
Balboa Blvd.
Newport Beach, CA
949-644-3211
There are several smaller beaches which run along Balboa Blvd. Dogs are only allowed before 9am and after 5pm, year round. Pets must be on a 6 foot or less leash and people are required to clean up after their pets. Tickets will be issued if your dog is off leash. The beaches are located along Balboa Blvd and ample parking is located near the Balboa and Newport Piers.

Ocean Beach
Point Loma Blvd.
Ocean Beach, CA
619-221-8900
Leashed dogs are allowed on this beach from 6pm to 9am. The beach is about 1/2 mile long. To get there, take Hwy 8 West until it ends and then it becomes Sunset Cliffs Blvd. Then make a right turn onto Point Loma Blvd and follow the signs to Ocean Beach Park. A separate beach called Dog Beach is at the north end of this beach which allows dogs to run off-leash.

San Diego Dog Beach
Point Loma Blvd.
Ocean Beach, CA
619-221-8900
Dogs are allowed to run off leash at this beach anytime during the day. This is a very popular dog beach which attracts lots and lots of dogs on warm days. To get there, take Hwy 8 West until it ends and then it becomes Sunset Cliffs Blvd. Then make a right turn onto Point Loma Blvd and follow the signs to Ocean Beach's Dog Beach.

Oceano Dunes State Vehicular Recreation Area
Highway 1
Oceano, CA
805-473-7220
This 3,600 acre off road area offers 5 1/2 miles of beach which is open for vehicle use. Pets on leash are allowed too. Swimming, surfing, horseback riding and bird watching are all popular activities at the beach. The park is located three miles south of Pismo Beach off Highway 1.

Point Reyes National Seashore

Olema, CA
415-464-5100
nps.gov/pore/

Leashed dogs (on a 6 foot or less leash) are allowed on four beaches. The dog-friendly beaches are the Limantour Beach, Kehoe Beach, North Beach and South Beach. Dogs are not allowed on the hiking trails. However, they are allowed on some hiking trails that are adjacent to Point Reyes. For a map of dog-friendly hiking trails, please stop by the Visitor Center. Point Reyes is located about an hour north of San Francisco. From Highway 101, exit at Sir Francis Drake Highway, and continue west on Sir Francis Drake to Olema. To find the Visitor Center, turn right in Olema onto Route 1 and then make a left onto Bear Valley Road. The Visitor Center will be on the left.

Freshwater Lagoon Beach - Redwood NP
Highway 101 south end of Redwood National Park
Orick, CA
707-464-6101
nps.gov/redw
Dogs are allowed on the ocean beaches around Freshwater Lagoon, but not on any trails within Redwood National Park. Picnic tables are available at the beach. Pets are also allowed at road accessible picnic areas and campgrounds. Dogs must be on a 6 foot or less leash and people need to pick up after their pets. The beach is located off Highway 101 behind the Redwood Information Center at the south end of the Redwood National Park. The parking area for the beach is about 2 miles south of Orick. Some portions of this beach are rather rocky but there are also sandy portions as well.

Gold Bluffs Beach - Redwood NP
Davison Road
Orick, CA
707-464-6101
nps.gov/redw
Dogs are allowed on this beach, but not on any trails within this park. Picnic tables and campgrounds are available at the beach. Pets are also allowed at road accessible picnic areas and campgrounds. Dogs must be on a 6 foot or less leash and people need to pick up after their pets. The beach is located off Highway 101. Take Highway 101 heading north. Pass Orick and drive about 3-4 miles, then exit Davison Rd. Head towards the coast on an unpaved road (trailers are not allowed on the unpaved road).

Hollywood Beach
4199 Ocean Drive

Oxnard, CA

This beach is located on the west side of the Channel Islands Harbor. The beach is 4 miles southwest of Oxnard. Dogs must be on leash and owners must clean up after their pets. Dogs are allowed on Hollywood Beach before 9 am and after 5 pm.

Oxnard Beach Park
Harbor Blvd.
Oxnard, CA
805-385-7946
North of 5th street is Mandalay State Beach and dogs are not allowed at all. This beach is nesting habitat for the endangered western snowy plover. Dog owners entering the beach from 5th street must go south towards the houses.

Silver Strand Beach
various addresses
Oxnard, CA

This beach is located between the Channel Islands Harbor and the U.S. Naval Construction Battalion Center. Dogs are now only allowed on the beach after 5 pm and before 8 am. The beach is 4 miles southwest of Oxnard. Dogs must be on leash and owners must clean up after their pets.

Asilomar State Beach
Along Sunset Drive
Pacific Grove, CA
831-372-4076
Dogs are permitted on leash on the beach and the scenic walking trails. If you walk south along the beach and go across the stream that leads into the ocean, you can take your dog off-leash, but he or she must be under strict voice control and within your sight at all times.

Esplanade Beach
Esplanade
Pacifica, CA
650-738-7381
This beach offers an off-leash area for dogs. To get to the beach, take the stairs at the end of Esplanade. Esplanade is just north of Manor Drive, off Highway 1.

Lake Nacimento Resort Day Use Area
10625 Nacimiento Lake Drive
Paso Robles, CA
805-238-3256
In addition to the campgrounds and RV area, this resort also offers day use of the lake. Dogs can swim in the water, but be very careful of boats, as this is a popular lake for water-skiing. Day use fees vary by season and

location, but in general rates are about $5 to $8 per person. Senior discounts are available. Dogs are an extra $5 per day. Proof of your dog's rabies vaccination is required.

Bean Hollow State Beach
Highway 1
Pescadero, CA
650-879-2170
This is a very rocky beach with not much sand. Dogs are allowed but must be on a 6 foot or less leash. Please clean up after your pets. The beach is located 3 miles south of Pescadero on Highway 1.

Pismo State Beach
Grand Ave.
Pismo Beach, CA
805-489-2684
Leashed dogs are allowed on this state beach. This beach is popular for walking, sunbathing, swimming and the annual winter migration of millions of monarch butterflies (the park has the largest over-wintering colony of monarch butterflies in the U.S.). To get there from Hwy 101, exit 4th Street and head south. In about a mile, turn right onto Grand Ave. You can park along the road.

Sonoma Coast State Beach
Highway 1
Salmon Creek, CA
707-875-3483
Dogs on leash are allowed at some of the beaches in this state park. Dogs are allowed at Shell Beach, Portuguese Beach and Schoolhouse Beach. They are not allowed at Goat Rock or Salmon Creek Beach due to the protected seals and snowy plovers. Please clean up after your pets. While dogs are allowed on some of the beaches and campgrounds, they are not allowed on any hiking trails at this park.

Samoa Dunes Recreation Area
New Navy Base Road
Samoa, CA
707-825-2300
The Bureau of Land Management oversees this 300 acre sand dune park. It is a popular spot for off-highway vehicles which can use about 140 of the park's acres. Dogs are allowed on leash or off-leash but under voice control. Even if your dog runs off-leash, the park service requests that you still bring a leash just in case. To get there, take Highway 255 and turn south on New Navy Base Road. Go about four miles to the parking area.

Fiesta Island
Fiesta Island Road
San Diego, CA

619-221-8900
On this island, dogs are allowed to run off-leash anywhere outside the fenced areas, anytime during the day. It is mostly sand which is perfect for those beach loving hounds. You might, however, want to stay on the north end of the island. The south end was used as the city's sludge area (mud and sediment, and possibly smelly) processing facility. The island is often used to launch jet-skis and motorboats. There is a one-way road that goes around the island and there are no fences, so please make sure your dog stays away from the road. About half way around the island, there is a completely fenced area on the beach. Please note that the fully enclosed area is not a dog park. The city of San Diego informed us that is supposed to be locked and is not intended to be used as a dog park even though there may occasionally be dogs running in this off-limits area.

Mission Beach & Promenade
Mission Blvd.
San Diego, CA
619-221-8900
Leashed dogs are allowed on this beach and promenade walkway from 6pm to 9am. It is about 3 miles long and located west of Mission Bay Park.

Baker Beach
Lincoln Blvd and Bowley St/Golden Gate Nat'l Rec Area
San Francisco, CA
415-561-4700
This dog-friendly beach in the Golden Gate National Recreation Area has a great view of the Golden Gate Bridge. Dogs are permitted off leash under voice control on Baker Beach North of Lobos Creek; they must be leashed South of Lobos Creek. The beach is located approx. 1.5 to 2 miles south of the Golden Gate Bridge. From Lincoln Avenue, turn onto Bowley Street and head towards the ocean. There is a parking lot next to the beach. This is a clothing optional beach, so there may be the occasional sunbather.

Fort Funston/Burton Beach
Skyline Blvd./Hwy 35
San Francisco, CA

This is a very popular dog-friendly park and beach. Dogs are allowed off leash here with the exception of the 12 acre enclosure in the northwest section. In the past, dogs have been allowed off-leash. However, currently all dogs must be

on leash. Fort Funston is part of the Golden Gate National Recreation Area. There are trails that run through the dunes & ice plant from the parking lot above with good access to the beach below. It overlooks the southern end of Ocean Beach, with a large parking area accessible from Skyline Boulevard. There is also a water faucet and trough at the parking lot for thirsty pups. It's located off Skyline Blvd. (also known Hwy 35) by John Muir Drive. It is south of Ocean Beach. Thanks to one of our readers for this info. Expect to see lots and lots of dogs having a great time. But not to worry, there is plenty of room for everyone.

Lands End Off Leash Dog Area
El Camino Del Mar
San Francisco, CA
415-561-4700
Owned and operated by the Golden Gate National Recreation Area, Lands End is everything west of and including the Coast Trail, and is an extraordinary combination of parkland, natural areas, and dramatic coastal cliffs. It offers great hiking, ocean and city views, a museum, the ruins of the Sutro Baths, and includes the Sutro Heights Park (dogs must be on lead in this area). This area can be accessed at Merrie Way for the cliffside paths, and at this entrance or the large lot at the end of El Camino Del Mar off Point Lobos for the Coast Trail and beaches. Dogs must be on leash on the Coast Trail, under firm voice control when in off leash areas, and they must be cleaned up after.

Ocean Beach
Great Hwy
San Francisco, CA
415-556-8642
You'll get a chance to stretch your legs at this beach which has about 4 miles of sand. The beach runs parallel to the Great Highway (north of Fort Funston). There are several access points including Sloat Blvd., Fulton Street or Lincoln Way. This beach has a mix of off-leash and leash required areas. Thanks to the San Francisco Dog Owners Group (SFDOG) for providing the following information: Dogs must be on leash on Ocean Beach between Sloat Blvd and Stairwell #21 (roughly at Fulton). North of Fulton to the Cliff House and South of Sloat for several miles are still okay for off-leash dogs, however parts of these areas may be impassible at high tide. The Golden Gate National Rec Area (GGNRA) strictly enforces the on-leash area between Sloat and Fulton. They usually give no warning tickets ($50

fine). As with all other leash required areas, we encourage dog owners to comply with the rules.

Coastal Access
off Hearst Drive
San Simeon, CA

There is parking just north of the Best Western Hotel, next to the "Coastal Access" sign. Dogs must be on leash.

Arroyo Burro Beach County Park
2981 Cliff Drive
Santa Barbara, CA
805-967-1300
Leashed dogs are allowed at this county beach and park. The beach is about 1/2 mile long and it is adjacent to a palm-lined grassy area with picnic tables. To get to the beach from Hwy 101, exit Las Positas Rd/Hwy 225. Head south (towards the ocean). When the street ends, turn right onto Cliff Drive. The beach will be on the left.

Arroyo Burro Off-Leash Beach
Cliff Drive
Santa Barbara, CA

countyofsb.org/parks/dog.sbc
While dogs are not allowed off-leash at the Arroyo Burro Beach County Park (both the beach and grass area), they are allowed to run leash free on the adjacent beach. The dog beach starts east of the slough at Arroyo Burro and stretches almost to the stairs at Mesa Lane. To get to the off-leash area, walk your leashed dog from the parking lot to the beach, turn left and cross the slough. At this point you can remove your dog's leash.

Rincon Park and Beach
Bates Road
Santa Barbara, CA

This beach is at Rincon Point which has some of the best surfing waves in the world. In the winter, it is very popular with surfers. In the summer, it is a popular swimming beach. Year-round, leashed dogs are welcome. The beach is about 1/2-1 mile long. Next to the parking lot there are picnic tables, phones and restrooms. The beach is in Santa Barbara County, about 15-20 minutes south of Santa Barbara. To get there from Santa Barbara, take Hwy 101 south and go past Carpinteria. Take the Bates Rd exit towards the ocean. When the road ends, turn right into the Rincon Park and Beach parking lot.

East Cliff Coast Access Points

East Cliff Drive
Santa Cruz, CA
831-454-7900
There are many small dog-friendly beaches and coastal access points that stretch along East Cliff Drive between 12th Avenue to 41st Avenue. This is not one long beach because the water comes up to cliffs in certain areas and breaks it up into many smaller beaches. Dogs are allowed on leash. Parking is on city streets along East Cliff or the numbered avenues. To get there from Hwy 17 south, take the Hwy 1 exit south towards Watsonville. Take the exit towards Soquel Drive. Turn left onto Soquel Avenue. Turn right onto 17th Avenue. Continue straight until you reach East Cliff Drive. From here, you can head north or south on East Cliff Drive and park anywhere between 12th and 41st street to access the beaches.

Its Beach
West Cliff Drive
Santa Cruz, CA
831-429-3777
This is not a large beach, but it is big enough for your water loving dog to take a dip in the water and get lots of sand between his or her paws. Dogs must be on leash at all times. The beach is located on West Cliff Drive, just north of the Lighthouse, and south of Columbia Street.

Mitchell's Cove Beach
West Cliff Drive at Almar
Santa Cruz, CA
831-420-5270
Dogs are allowed off-leash on Mitchell's Cove Beach between sunrise and 10 am and from 4 pm to sunset. They must be on-leash during other hours. The beach is along West Cliff Drive between Woodward and Almar. While off-leash dogs must be under voice control.

Seabright Beach
Seabright Ave
Santa Cruz, CA
831-429-2850
This beach is located south of the Santa Cruz Beach Boardwalk and north of the Santa Cruz Harbor. Dogs are allowed on leash. Fire rings are available for beach bonfires. It is open from sunrise to sunset. To get there from Hwy 17 south, exit Ocean Street on the left towards the beaches. Merge onto Ocean Street. Turn left onto East Cliff Drive and stay straight to go onto Murray Street. Then turn right onto Seabright Ave. Seabright Ave

will take you to the beach (near the corner of East Cliff Drive and Seabright).

Twin Lakes State Beach
East Cliff Drive
Santa Cruz, CA
831-429-2850
This beach is one of the area's warmest beaches, due to its location at the entrance of Schwann Lagoon. Dogs are allowed on leash. The beach is located just south of the Santa Cruz Harbor where Aldo's Restaurant is located. Fire rings for beach bonfires, outdoor showers and restrooms are available. It is open from sunrise to sunset. To get there from Hwy 17 south, exit Ocean Street on the left towards the beaches. Merge onto Ocean Street. Turn left onto East Cliff Drive and stay straight to go onto Murray Street. Murray Street becomes Eaton Street. Turn right onto 7th Avenue.

Sea Ranch Coastal Access Trails
Highway 1
Sea Ranch, CA
707-785-2377
Walk along coastal headlands or the beach in Sea Ranch. There are six trailhead parking areas which are located along Highway 1, south of the Sonoma Mendocino County Line. Access points include Black Point, Bluff Top Trail, Pebble Beach, Stengal Beach, Shell Beach and Walk on Beach. Dogs must be on a 6 foot or less leash. There is a $3 per car parking fee. RVs and vehicles with trailers are not allowed to use the parking areas.

Kiva Beach
Hwy 89
South Lake Tahoe, CA
530-573-2600
tahoeactivities.com/kiva-beach/
This small but lovely beach is a perfect place for your pup to take a dip in Lake Tahoe. Dogs must be on leash. To get there from the intersection of Hwys 89 and 50, take Hwy 89 north approx 2-3 miles to the entrance on your right. Follow the road and towards the end, bear left to the parking lot. Then follow the path to the beach.

Upton Beach
Highway 1
Stinson Beach, CA
415-499-6387
Dogs not allowed on the National Park section of Stinson Beach but are allowed at Upton Beach which is under Marin County's jurisdiction. This beach is located north of the

National Park. Dogs must be leashed on the beach.

Summerland Beach
Evans Avenue
Summerland, CA
805-568-2461
This conveniently located beach sits only a block off Highway 101, features an easy paved path to the water, and offers a mile of beach to explore. The beach also sits below Lookout Park complete with picnic tables, BBQs, and a playground. Dogs are welcome to frolic on the beach, but they must be kept leashed and cleaned up after promptly.

Pebble Beach/Dog Beach
Hwy 89
Tahoe City, CA

This beach is not officially called "pebble beach" but it is an accurate description. It is actually Elizabech Williams Beach. No sand at this beach, but your water-loving dog won't mind. The water is crisp and clear and perfect for a little swimming. It's not a large area, but it is very popular with many dogs. There is also a paved bike trail that is parallel to the beach. There was no official name posted for this beach, but it's located about 1-2 miles south of Tahoe City on Hwy 89. From Tahoe City, the beach and parking will be on your left. Dogs should be on leash on the beach.

Harbor Cove Beach
West end of Spinnaker Drive
Ventura, CA
805-652-4550
This beach is considered the safest swimming area in Ventura because of the protection of the cove. Dogs of all sizes are allowed at this beach as well as on the 6 miles of Ventura City Beaches and on the long wooden pier, but they are not allowed on any of the beaches south of the Ventura Pier or on any of the State beaches. Dogs must be leashed and cleaned up after at all times.

Promenade Park
Figueroa Street at the Promenade
Ventura, CA
805-652-4550
This park is a one acre oceanfront park on the site of an old Indian village near Seaside Park. Dogs of all sizes are are allowed at this beach as well as on the 6 miles of Ventura City Beaches and on the long wooden pier, but they are not allowed on any of the beaches south of the Ventura Pier or on any of the State beaches. Dogs must be leashed and cleaned

up after at all times.

Surfers Point at Seaside Park
Figueroa Street at the Promenade
Ventura, CA
800-483-6215
This park is one of the area's most popular surfing and windsurfing beaches, and it offers showers, picnic facilities and restrooms, and is connected with the Ventura Pier by a scenic landscaped Promenade walkway and the Omer Rains Bike Trail. Dogs are allowed on the 6 miles of Ventura City Beaches and on the long wooden pier, but they are not allowed on any of the beaches south of the Ventura Pier or on any of the State beaches. Dogs must be leashed and cleaned up after at all times.

Westport-Union Landing State Beach
Highway 1
Westport, CA
707-937-5804
This park offers about 2 miles of sandy beach. Dogs must be on a 6 foot or less leash at all times and people need to clean up after their pets. Picnic tables, restrooms (including an ADA restroom) and campsites are available at this park. Dogs are also allowed at the campsites, but not on any park trails. The park is located off Highway 1, about 2 miles north of Westport or 19 miles north of Fort Bragg.

# Colorado Listings

Union Reservoir Dog Beach
County Line Rd at E 9th Ave
Longmont, CO
303-651-8447
This is an unfenced off-leash area where dogs may swim in the Union Reservoir. Dogs may only be off-leash in the designated area and must be leashed when in the rest of the rec area. Dogs are not allowed on beaches outside of the dog beach. To get to Union Reservoir Rec Area from I-25 take Ute Hwy west to E County Line Rd and turn left (south). Turn left onto Highway 26 into the park in just over one mile.

# Connecticut Listings

Town of Fairfield Beaches
off Highway 1
Fairfield, CT

203-256-3010
Dogs are only allowed on the town beaches during the off-season. Pets are not allowed on the beaches from April 1 through October 1. Dogs must be on leash and people need to clean up after their pets.

# Delaware Listings

Bethany Beach
off Route 1
Bethany Beach, DE
302-539-8011
From May 15 to September 30, pets are not allowed on the beach or boardwalk at any time. But during the off-season, dogs are allowed but need to be leashed and cleaned up after.

Dewey Beach
Coastal Highway/Route 1
Dewey Beach, DE
302-227-1110
Dogs are allowed on the beach year-round only with a special license and with certain hour restrictions during the summer season. A special license is required for your dog to go on the beach. You do not have to be a resident of Dewey Beach to get the license. You can obtain one from the Town of Dewey Beach during regular business hours at 105 Rodney Avenue in Dewey Beach. The cost is $15 per dog and is good for the lifetime of your dog. During the summer, from May 15 to September 15, dogs are only allowed before 9:30am and after 5:30pm. During the off-season there are no hourly restrictions. Year-round, dogs can be off-leash but need to be under your control at all times and cleaned up after.

Fenwick Island Beach
off Route 1
Fenwick Island, DE
302-539-2000
From May 1 to September 30, dogs are not allowed on the beach at any time. The rest of the year, pets are allowed on the beach but must be leashed and cleaned up after. The beach is located of Route 1, south of Dewey Beach.

Cape Henlopen State Park
42 Cape Henlopen Drive
Lewes, DE
302-645-8983
This park draws thousands of visitors who enjoy sunbathing and ocean swimming. Dogs on a 6 foot or less leash are allowed on the beach, with some exceptions. Dogs are not allowed on the two swimming

beaches during the summer, but they are allowed on surfing and fishing beaches, bike paths and some of the trails. Pets are not allowed on the fishing pier. During the off-season, dogs are allowed on any of the beaches, but still need to be leashed. People are required to clean up after their pets. The park is located one mile east of Lewes, 1/2 mile past the Cape May-Lewes Ferry Terminal.

Delaware Seashore State Park
Inlet 850
Rehoboth Beach, DE
302-227-2800
This park offers six miles of ocean and bay shoreline. Dogs on a 6 foot or less leash are allowed on the beach, with a couple of exceptions. Dogs are not allowed at the lifeguarded swimming areas. However, there are plenty of non-guarded beaches where people with dogs can walk or sunbathe. During the off-season, dogs are allowed on any of the beaches, but still need to be leashed. People are required to clean up after their pets. The park is located south of Dewey Beach, along Route 1.

Rehoboth Beach
off Route 1
Rehoboth Beach, DE
302-227-6181
From April 1 to October 31, pets are not allowed on the beach or boardwalk at any time. However, during the off-season, dogs are allowed but need to be leashed and cleaned up after. The beach is located off Route 1, north of Dewey Beach.

South Bethany Beach
off Route 1
South Bethany, DE
302-539-3653
From May 15 to October 15, dogs are not allowed on the beach at any time. The rest of the year, during the off-season, dogs are allowed on the beach. Pets must be leashed and cleaned up after. The beach is located of Route 1, south of Dewey Beach.

# Florida Listings

De Soto National Memorial Beach Area
PO Box 15390
Bradenton, FL
941-792-0458
nps.gov/deso/index.htm
Dogs must be on leash and must be cleaned up after in this park. Leashed dogs are allowed in the beach area,

which is past a hut following a shell path.

Cape San Blas Barrier Dunes

Cape San Blas, FL

This is one of the nicer pet-friendly beaches in Florida. Leashed dogs are allowed year round on the beach which has a number of stations with clean up bags. Please clean up after your dog.

Carrabelle Beach
Carrabelle Beach Rd
Carrabelle, FL
850-697-2585
Dogs are allowed on this beach, but the following rules apply. Dogs must be on leash when near sunbathers. In areas where there are no sunbathers, dogs can be off-leash, but must be under direct voice control. Picnic areas and restrooms are available. The beach is located 1.5 miles west of town.

Clearwater Beach
Mandalay Avenue and Somerset St
Clearwater Beach, FL

Leashed dogs are welcomed in the pet-friendly areas of Clearwater Beach. Dogs are allowed year round on the portion of the beach north of Somerset Street. They are not allowed south of Somerset Street. Dogs must be cleaned up after and you will need to bring your own cleanup bags. The dog-friendly part of this beach is quite big.

Dog Island Beaches

Dog Island, FL
850-697-2585
This island is a small remote island that is accessible only by boat, ferry or airplane. Dogs are allowed on the beach, but must be on leash. There are some areas of Dog Island that are within a nature conservancy and dogs are not allowed in these areas. Dog owners will be fined in the nature conservatory. This island is south of Carrabelle.

Veterans Memorial Park
Highway 1
Duck Key, FL
305-872-2411
Dogs on leash are allowed at this park and on the beach. People need to clean up after their pets. The park is located near mile marker 40, off Highway 1.

Honeymoon Island State Park
1 Causeway Blvd
Dunedin, FL

727-469-5942
The Honeymoon Island State Park not only offers gulf beaches, mangrove swamps, tidal flats, and much more, but there is a designated doggy beach/park on the island, as well as a hiking trail to the popular dog beach.

Honeymoon Island State Park
1 Causeway Blvd.
Dunedin, FL
727-469-5942
Dogs on a 6 foot or less leash are allowed on part of the beach. Please ask the rangers for details when you arrive at the park. The park is located at the extreme west end of SR 586, north of Dunedin.

Fernandina City Beach
14th St at the Atlantic Ocean
Fernandina Beach, FL
904-277-7305
The Fernandina City Beaches allow dogs on leash. The beach is about 2 miles long. Please make sure that you pick up after your dog.

Flagler Beach
1A at N. 10th Street
Flagler Beach, FL
386-517-2000
Dogs are allowed north of N. 10th Street and south of S. 10th Street. They are not allowed on or near the pier at 10th Street. Dogs must be on leash and people need to clean up after their dogs.

Canine Beach
East End of Sunrise Blvd
Fort Lauderdale, FL
954-761-5346
There is a 100 yard stretch of beach which dogs can use. Dogs must be on leash when they are not in the water. The beach is open to dogs only on Friday, Saturday and Sundays. In winter, the hours are 3 pm - 7 pm and the summer hours are 5 pm - 9 pm. A permit is required to use the Canine Beach. There are annual permits available for $25 for residents of the city or $40 for non-residents or you can get a one weekend permit for $5.65. Permits can be purchased at Parks and Recreation Department, 1350 W. Broward Boulevard. Call (954) 761-5346 for permit information.

Dog Swim at Snyder Park
3299 SW 4th Avenue
Fort Lauderdale, FL
954-828-4343
There is a $1 park admission fee for entering the park for the doggy swim area; it is available on Saturdays and Sundays from 10AM to 5PM (closed

Christmas/New Years). Dogs must be sociable, current on all vaccinations and license, and under their owner's control at all times. Dogs must be leashed when not in designated off-lead areas.

Dog Beach
Estero Blvd/H 865
Fort Myers Beach, FL
239-461-7400
Located just north of the New Pass Bridge, this barrier island beach offers a perfect off-leash area for beach-lov'in pups.This beach is actually in Bonita Beach on the city line with Fort Myers Beach. Dogs are allowed in designated areas only, and they must be licensed, immunized, and non-aggressive to people, other pets, or wildlife. Dogs may not be left unattended at any time, and they must be under their owner's control at all times; clean-up stations are provided. Two healthy dogs are allowed per person over 15 years old. Dogs on Fort Myers Beach must be leashed at all times.

Fort Myers Dog Beach
3410 Palm Beach Blvd
Fort Myers Beach, FL
239-461-7400
Dogs are allowed off leash on this section of the beach. Cleanup stations are provided. Must have a copy of health records with you at all times. The beach is run by Lees County Parks and Recreation.

Lee County Off-Leash Dog Beach Park
Route 865
Fort Myers Beach, FL

Dogs are allowed off-leash at this beach. Please clean up after your dog and stay within the dog park boundaries. Dog Beach is located south of Ft. Myers Beach and north of Bonita Beach on Route 865. Parking is available near New Pass Bridge.

Walton Rocks Beach
S H A1A
Fort Pierce, FL
772-462-1517
This dog friendly beach offers 24 acres of untouched beach, covered picnic tables, bathrooms with showers, a natural reef that is exposed at low tide, and plenty of parking. Dogs must be under their owner's control at all times.

Hollywood Dog Beach
North Broadwalk at Pershing St
Hollywood, FL

hollywoodfl.org/318/Dog-Parks
This dog beach with limited hours was approved and opened in 2008. The beach is located between Pershing Street and Custer Street along N. Broadwalk and one block from A1A. Dogs are allowed on the beach only on Fridays, Saturdays and Sundays. Please do not bring a dog to the beach on any other day. In addition during the Summer dogs are allowed on the beach only from 5 pm to 9 pm and in the Winter months they are allowed from 3 pm to 7 pm. Summer months begin when Daylight Savings time begins in March and end when Eastern Standard time is resumed in the fall. The permission to use the beach will be reviewed every six months or so so it is very important that all dog owners clean up and follow the hours and other rules of the beach. For more information see the website at http://www.dboh.org. The beach is sponsored and maintained by the "Dog Beach of Hollywood" organization.

Anne's Beach
Highway 1
Islamorada, FL

annesbeach.com/
Dog on leash are allowed at this beach. Please clean up after your dog. The beach is located around mile markers 72 to 74. There should be a sign.

Dogwood Park Lake Bow Wow
7407 Salisbury Rd South
Jacksonville, FL
904-296-3636
jaxdogs.com
This dog park is great for any size canine. It has 25 fenced acres in a 42 acre park. Dogs can be off leash in any part of the park. The park offers picnic tables, a pond for small dogs, a pond for large dogs (Lake Bow Wow), shower for dogs, warm water for dog baths, tennis balls and toys for play, a playground with games for your dogs, trails to walk on, and bag stations for cleanup. Locals can become members for a year for about $24.00 per month or out-of-town visitors can pay about $11 for a one time visit. There may be some non-member hours available as well.

Kathryn Abby Hanna Park Beach
500 Wonderwood Dr
Jacksonville, FL
904-249-4700
Dogs are allowed in this park for camping, hiking, picnics and on the

dog friendly beach.

Jupiter Beach
A1A at Xanadu Road
Jupiter, FL

This is a wide, nice, white sandy beach that stretches 2 miles along the Atlantic Coast. It is one of the nicer beaches that allow dogs in South Florida. Please follow the dog rules requiring leashes and cleaning up after your dog.

Jupiter Off-leash Dog Beach
A1A/Ocean Blvd
Jupiter, FL
561-746-5134
Although dogs are not allowed at any of the city parks, they are allowed at this beach off-leash site. According to the parks department, take Highway 1 to Highway 706/E Indiantown Road East to old A1A (the beach road) and go South; dogs are allowed on the beach after passing Carlin Park and the lifeguards. Dogs must be under their owner's control at all times and cleaned up after promptly.

Hobie Beach (Rickenbacker Causeway)
Rickenbacker Causeway (South end)
Key Biscayne, FL
305-361-2833
Hobie Beach, also known as Windsurfer Beach, is located just off the Rickenbacker Causeway. You can take windsurfing lessons here. You dog can run off-leash here as well. It is a relatively shallow and safe beach for dog play. The beach is located between Brickell, Downtown and Key Biscayne and offers great views in each direction.

Dog Beach
Vernon Ave and Waddell Ave
Key West, FL

This tiny stretch of beach is the only beach we found in Key West that a dog can go to.

Bicentennial Park
591 Tom Stuart Cswy
Madeira Beach, FL
727-391-9951
The Bicentenial Park is located on State Road 699 (Tom Stuart/Welch/Madeira Beach Causeway) on the waterfront. The small park is just southwest of Madeira Middle School. The park features a small beach, which is dog friendly.

Bicentennial Park
591 Tom Stuart Cswy.
Madeira Beach, FL
727-391-9951

The Bi Centennial Park, located on the waterfront of Boca Ciega Bay in Madeira Beach, is a small dog park that features a small beach. No facilities are available.

Rickenbacker Causeway Beach
Hobie Beach (Rickenbacker Causeway)
Miami, FL

This beach extends the length of the Rickenbacker Causeway from Downtown Miami to Key Biscayne. Dogs are allowed on the entire stretch. There are two types of beach, a Tree lined Dirt beach and a standard type of sandy beach further towards Key Biscayne. Dogs should be leashed on the beach.

Smyrna Dunes Park
2995 N. Peninsula Drive
New Smyrna Beach, FL
386-424-2935
The Smyrna Dunes Park in New Smyrna Beach, Florida, is a state park with a dog-friendly beach. Admission is $5.00 per vehicle, and the park provides an outdoor shower, drinking water and doggie bags for cleaning up after your pet. There is also a dog-friendly trail along the beach.

Smyrna Dunes Park
Highway 1
New Smyrna Beach, FL
386-424-2935
Dogs are not allowed on the ocean beach, but are allowed almost everywhere else, including on the inlet beach and river. Bottlenosed dolphins are typically seen in the inlet as well as the ocean. Dogs must be leashed and people need to clean up after their pets. The park is located on the north end of New Smyrna Beach.

Bayview Dog Beach
In Bayou Texar off E Lloyd Street
Pensacola, FL
850-436-5511
This water park for dogs offers pets beach and water fun, and there are benches, picnic tables, trash cans, pooper scooper stations, and a washing station on site. Dogs must be sociable, current on all vaccinations, licensed, and under their owner's control at all times. Dogs must be leashed when not in designated off-lead areas.

Lighthouse Point Park
A1A
Ponce Inlet, FL
386-239-7873
You might see some dolphins along

the shoreline at this park. The park is also frequented by people watching a space shuttle launch out of Cape Canaveral. If you go during a shuttle launch, be sure to hold on tight to your pooch, as the shuttles can become very, very noisy and loud. Dogs on leash are allowed at the park and on the beach. Please clean up after your dog. This park is located at the southern point of Ponce Inlet.

Bowman's Beach
Bowman Beach Road
Sanibel, FL
239-472-6477
Walk over a bridge to get to the beach. Dogs on leash are allowed and people need to clean up after their pets. Picnic tables are available. This beach is located on the west side of the island, near Captiva. From the Sanibel causeway, turn right on Periwinkle Way. Turn right on Palm Ridge Rd and then continue on Sanibel-Captiva Road. Turn left onto Bowman's Beach Rd.

Gulfside City Beach (Algiers Beach)
Algiers Lane
Sanibel, FL
239-472-6477
This beach is located in Gulfside City Park. Dogs on leash are allowed and people need to clean up after their pets. Picnic tables and restrooms are available. There is an hourly parking fee. This beach is located about mid-way on the island. From the Sanibel causeway, turn right onto Periwinkle Way. Turn left onto Casa Ybel Rd and then left on Algiers Lane.

Lighthouse Park Beach
Periwinkle Way
Sanibel, FL
239-472-6477
This park offers a long thin stretch of beach. Dogs on leash are allowed and people need to clean up after their pets. Picnic tables are available. This park is located on the east end of the island. From Causeway Road, turn onto Periwinkle Way.

Sanibel Causeway Beach
Sanibel Causeway
Sanibel, FL
239-472-6477
This stretch of beach runs along both sides of the causeway. Dogs on leash are allowed and people need to clean up after their pets. Picnic tables and restrooms are available. There are no parking fees.

Tarpon Bay Road Beach
Tarpon Bay Road
Sanibel, FL
239-472-6477
sanibeltrails.com/tarponbay.aspx
Take a short walk from the parking lot to the beach. Dogs on leash are allowed and people need to clean up after their pets. Picnic tables and restrooms are available. There is an hourly parking fee. This beach is located mid-way on the island. From the Sanibel causeway, turn right onto Periwinkle Way. Then turn left onto Tarpon Bay Road.

Fort Matanzas National Monument
8635 A1A South
St Augustine, FL
904-471-0116
nps.gov/foma/index.htm
Dogs on 6 ft leash are allowed in this National monument. Dogs are allowed in the park, on the beach, and on the trails. They are not allowed in the visitor center, boats, or fort.

St Augustine Lighthouse and Museum
81 Lighthouse Avenue
St Augustine, FL
904-829-0745
Dogs on leash are allowed on the grounds of the lighthouse and beach area. There are some tables for picnics or bring a blanket. There is a fee to enter the lighthouse grounds.

St Augustine Beach
Most Beaches
St Augustine Beach, FL
904-209-0655
sabpd.org/beach-rules/
The St. Augustine Beach allows leashed people. Owners must clean up after their pets. This policy extends to most of the beaches in St John's County but other rules will apply to beaches in State Parks, many of which don't allow dogs.

Public Access Beaches
Gulf Beach Drive
St George Island, FL

St. George Island beaches have been consistently ranked as one of the top 10 beaches in America. One third of the island is Florida state park land which does not allow dogs. But the rest of the island offers Franklin County public beaches, which do allow dogs on a 6 foot leash or off-leash and under direct voice control.

St George Island Beaches

St George Island, FL
850-927-2111
Dogs on leash are allowed on the beaches of St George Island. However, they are not allowed on the beaches, trails, or boardwalks in St. George State Park. Dog Owners can be fined in the state park.

Fort de Soto Park
3500 Pinellas Bayway S
St Petersburg, FL
727-552-1862
The Fort de Soto park offers a dog park where dogs are allowed on the beach in a designated area. There are also 2 fenced in areas near the beach for large and small dogs, complete with water stations.

Gandy Bridge Causeway
Gandy Bridge east end
St Petersburg, FL

This stretch of beach allows dogs to run and go swimming. We even saw a horse here. Dogs should be leashed on the beach.

Pinellas Causeway Beach
Pinellas Bayway
St Petersburg, FL

This stretch of beach is open to humans and dogs. Dogs should be on leash on the beach.

Haulover Beach
10800 Collins Avenue
Sunny Isles Beach, FL
305-947-3525
One of the few beaches in Miami where you can take your dog, Haulover Park north of Bal Harbour is also home to a 3 1/2 acre dog park. Dogs have limited access to the beach. On Saturday and Sunday from 8 am to 3 pm, dogs are allowed on the beach near lifeguard tower 3. Park in lots 3 and 4. There is a $2 fee to use the beach here. The dog park is open from 8 am to sunset seven days a week and offers two fenced areas for small dogs and large dogs.

Davis Island Dog Park
Severn Ave and Martinique Ave
Tampa, FL

This dog beach is fenced and offers a large parking area and even a doggie shower. To get there go towards Davis Island and head for the Peter Knight Airport. Loop around until you reach the water (the airport should be on the left). Thanks to one of our readers for the updated information.

# Georgia Listings

Jekyll Island Beaches and Trails
off SR 520
Jekyll Island, GA
877-453-5955
These beaches look like a Carribean island setting. It is hard to believe that you just drove here over a causeway. Dogs on leash are welcome year round on the beach and the paved and dirt trails. There are about 10 miles of beaches and 20 miles of inland paved and dirt trails. It is recommended that your pooch stay on the paved trails instead of the dirt trails during the warm summer months because there are too many ticks along the dirt trails. On warmer days you might choose a beach walk rather than the inland trails anyway because of the cooler ocean breezes.

Little St. Simons Island Beaches
off U.S. 17
St Simons Island, GA
912-554-7566
Dogs are allowed, but only during certain hours in the summer. From Memorial Day through Labor Day, dogs are allowed on the beach before 9:30am and after 4pm. During the rest of the year, dogs are allowed anytime during park hours. Dogs must be on leash and people need to clean up after their pets.

St. Simons Island Beaches
off U.S. 17
St Simons Island, GA
912-554-7566
Dogs are allowed, but only during certain hours in the summer. From Memorial Day through Labor Day, dogs are allowed on the beach before 9:30am and after 4pm. During the rest of the year, dogs are allowed anytime during park hours. Dogs must be on leash and people need to clean up after their pets.

# Hawaii Listings

Oahu Dog-Friendly Beaches
(Leashes required)
Various
Honolulu, HI
808-946-2187
According to the Hawaiian Humane Society website the following beaches on Oahu allow dogs on leash. Please check with them at: https://www.hawaiianhumane.org/dog-friendly-beaches/ for updates. The beaches that allow well-behaved, leashed dogs are:
Aukai Beach, Jauula

Gray's Beach (Halekulani Beach), Waikiki
Haleaha Beach, Punaluu
Hanakailio Beach, Kahuku
Kaalawai Beach, Diamond Head
Kahala Beach, Kahala
Kahuku Golf Course Beach, Kahuka
Kailua Beach, Kahuku
Kaipapau Beach, Hauula
Kakela Beach, Hauula
Kaloko Beach,Kokohead
Kaluahole Beach, Diamond Head
Kanenelu Beach, Kaaawa
Kapaeloa Beach, North Shore
Kawela Bay Beach, North Shore
Kealia Beach, Mokuleia
,Kualoa Sugar Mill Beach,Kualoa
Kuilima Cove Beach, Kahuku
Laie Beach, Laie
Lanikai Beach, Kailua
Laniloa Beach, Laie
Mahakea Beach, Laie
Makao Beach, Hauula
Makua Beach, Makua
Manner's Beach, Kahe
Mokuleia Army Beach, Mokuleia
Moluleia Beach, Mokuleia
Niu Beach, Niu Valley
Oneawa Beach, Kailua
Outrigger Canoe Club Beach, Waikiki
Pahipahialua Beach, North Shore
Paiko Beach,Kuliouou
Punaluu Beach, Punaluu
Puuiki Beach, Mokuleia
Royal-Moana Beach, Waikiki
Turtle Bay Beach, North Shore.

# Illinois Listings

Belmont Harbor Dog Beach
located on Belmont Ave off Lake Shore Dr
Chicago, IL

Dogs are allowed in this small fenced beach area on-leash. The city may ticket dog owners whose dogs are off-leash even though it is often used as an off-leash area by some people.

Montrose Harbor Dog Beach
Lake Shore Drive
Chicago, IL
312-742-7529
mondog.org/index.php/faq/faq-2
Dogs are allowed on part of the beach near Montrose. Dogs can run leash-free on the beach. Please note that people who violate the leash law by not having their dog on a leash between the parking lot and the beach are being fined with $75 tickets, so be sure to bring your dog's leash. Beginning in September, 2005 all dogs that use the dog parks are required to have an annual permit. The permits currently cost $5 per dog. You will have to visit an approved location to get a permit. Proof of certain vaccinations are also

required.

Evanston Dog Beach
Church Street
Evanston, IL
847-866-2900
Dogs are not allowed on this beach unless you first purchase a token from the city of Evanston. The cost per dog for one season is $88 for non-residents of Evanston and $44 for residents. Prices are subject to change. To purchase a token, you must have proof of your dog's current rabies vaccination and a current dog license. Dog beach is a large strip of sand located just north of the Church Street launch facility, where Church Street meets the beach. Beach hours are 7am to 8pm, May through October, weather permitting. Dog beach tokens can be purchased at the Dempster Street Beach Office from 10am to 5pm weekends only in May and after memorial day the office is open seven days a week. Tokens can also be purchased at the City Collectors Office in the Civic Center at 2100 Ridge Avenue, 8:30am to 5pm, Monday through Friday. Dog beach rules and regulations are available at the Dempster Street Beach Office.

# Indiana Listings

Indiana Dunes National Lakeshore
off Highway I-94
Porter, IN
219-926-7561x225
nps.gov/indu/
Dogs are not allowed on all of the beaches, but are allowed on two beaches which are located at the far east side of the park. One of the beaches is near Mt. Baldy and the other is near Central Avenue. Check with the visitor center when you arrive for exact locations. Pets are also allowed on some of the trails, campground and picnic area but must be leashed and cleaned up after. The park is located on Lake Michigan. To get there, take Highway 94 east and take Exit 26 Chesterton/49 North and head north.

# Louisiana Listings

Cameron Parish Beaches
433 Marshall Street (Chamber of Commerce)
Cameron, LA
337-775-5222
Located in the southwestern part of the state bordering Texas, this parish offers over 25 miles of beaches on

the Gulf of Mexico to be enjoyed by people and pooches. Dogs must be kept leashed and picked up after at all times.

Grand Isle State Park
Admiral Craik Drive
Grand Isle, LA
985-797-2559
Dogs on leash are allowed at the beaches, except for some designated swimming areas. This park offers many recreational opportunities like fishing, crabbing, sunbathing, nature watching and camping. Leashed pets are also allowed at the campsites. The park is located on the east end of Grand Isle, off Highway 1 on Admiral Craik Drive. It is about 2 hours outside of New Orleans.

# Maine Listings

Hadley Point Beach
Highway 3
Bar Harbor, ME

Dogs are allowed on the beach, but must be leashed. The beach is located about 10 minutes northwest of downtown Bar Harbor, near Eden.

Kennebunk Beaches
Beach Avenue
Kennebunk, ME

Dogs are allowed with certain restrictions year round. Leashed and off-leash dogs are allowed on the beach before 9am and after 5pm. Dogs are not allowed on the beach during the hours of 9 am to 5 pm. There are a string of beaches, including Kennebunk, Gooch's and Mother's, that make up a nice stretch of wide sandy beaches. People need to clean up after their pets. The beaches are located on Beach Avenue, off Routes 9 and 35.

Goose Rocks Beach
Dyke Street
Kennebunkport, ME

Leashed dogs are allowed, with certain restrictions. From June 15 through September 15, dogs are only allowed on the beach before 8am and after 6pm. During the rest of the year, dogs are allowed on the beach during park hours. People need to clean up after their pets. The beach is located about 3 miles east of Cape Porpoise. From Route 9, exit onto Dyke Street.

Old Orchard Beach City Beach

Old Orchard Beach, ME
207-934-0860
Leashed dogs are allowed on this beach only before 10 am and after 5 pm daily year round. People need to make sure they pick up their dog's waste with a plastic bag and throw it away in a trash can.

East End Beach
Cutter Street
Portland, ME
207-874-8793
Dogs are only allowed on this beach from the day after Labor Day to the day before Memorial Day. Dogs are not allowed on the beach from Memorial Day through Labor Day. During the months that dogs are allowed, they can be off-leash but need to be under direct voice control. People need to make sure they pick up their dog's waste with a plastic bag and throw it away in a trash can.

Old Orchard
Cutter Street
Portland, ME
207-874-8793
Dogs are only allowed on this beach from the day after Labor Day to the day before Memorial Day. Dogs are not allowed on the beach from Memorial Day through Labor Day. During the months that dogs are allowed, they can be off-leash but need to be under direct voice control. People need to make sure they pick up their dog's waste with a plastic bag and throw it away in a trash can.

Willard Beach

South Portland, ME
207-767-7601
At Willard Beach there are restrooms, lifeguards, and parking for 75 cars. Dogs are only allowed on the beach from 6:00 a.m. to 9:00 a.m. year round. Dogs must be kept away from bird eggs and out of the dunes. There are dog bag stations at many entrances to the mile long beach. Dogs must be cleaned up after at all times. Dogs must be leashed at all times or off-leash and under excellent voice control within a limited distance of the owner.

Wells Beach
Route 1
Wells, ME
207-646-2451
Leashed dogs are allowed, with certain restrictions. During the summer, from June 16 through September 15, dogs are only allowed on the beach before 8am and after 6pm. The rest of the year, dogs are allowed on the beach during all park

hours. There are seven miles of sandy beaches in Wells. People are required to clean up after their pets.

Long Sands Beach
Route 1A
York, ME
207-363-4422
Leashed dogs are allowed, with certain restrictions. During the summertime, from about Memorial Day weekend through Labor Day weekend, dogs are only allowed on the beach before 8am and after 6pm. During the off-season, dogs are allowed during all park hours. This beach offers a 1.5 mile sandy beach. Metered parking and private lots are available. The beach and bathhouse are also handicap accessible. People are required to clean up after their pets.

Short Sands Beach
Route 1A
York, ME
207-363-4422
Leashed dogs are allowed, with certain restrictions. During the summertime, from about Memorial Day weekend through Labor Day weekend, dogs are only allowed on the beach before 8am and after 6pm. During the off-season, dogs are allowed during all park hours. At the beach, there is a large parking area and a playground. People are required to clean up after their pets.

York Harbor Beach
Route 1A
York, ME
207-363-4422
Leashed dogs are allowed, with certain restrictions. During the summertime, from about Memorial Day weekend through Labor Day weekend, dogs are only allowed on the beach before 8am and after 6pm. During the off-season, dogs are allowed during all park hours. This park offers a sandy beach nestled against a rocky shoreline. There is limited parking. People are required to clean up after their pets.

# Maryland Listings

Quiet Waters Park Dog Beach
600 Quiet Waters Park Road
Annapolis, MD
410-222-1777
This park is located on Chesapeake Bay, not on the ocean. Dogs are welcome to run off-leash at this dog beach and dog park. The dog park is closed every Tuesday. Leashed dogs are also allowed at Quiet Waters

Park. The park offers over 6 miles of scenic paved trails, and a large multi-level children's playground. People need to clean up after their pets. To get there, take Route 665 until it ends and merges with Forrest Drive. Take Forrest Drive for 2 miles and then turn right onto Hillsmere Drive. The park entrance is about 100 yards on the right. The dog beach is located to the left of the South River overlook. Park in Lot N.

Assateague Island National Seashore
Route 611
Assateague Island, MD
410-641-1441
nps.gov/asis/
Dogs on leash are allowed on beaches, except for any lifeguarded swimming beaches (will be marked off with flags). There are plenty of beaches to enjoy at this park that are not lifeguarded swimming beaches. Dogs are not allowed on trails in the park. The park is located eight miles south of Ocean City, at the end of Route 611.

Elm's Beach Park
Bay Forest Road
Hermanville, MD
301-475-4572
The park is located on Chesapeake Bay, not on the ocean. Enjoy great views of the bay or swim at the beach. Dogs on leash are allowed at the beach. People need to clean up after their pets. Take Route 235 to Bay Forest Road and then go 3 miles. The park will be on the left.

Ocean City Beaches
Route 528
Ocean City, MD
1-800-OC-OCEAN
Dogs are only allowed during certain times of the year on this city beach. Pets are not allowed on the beach or boardwalk at any time from May 1 through September 30. The rest of the year, dogs are allowed on the beach and boardwalk, but must be on leash and people must clean up after them.

Downs Park Dog Beach
8311 John Downs Loop
Pasadena, MD
410-222-6230
This dog beach is located on Chesapeake Bay, not on the ocean. People are not permitted to go swimming, but dogs can run off-leash at this beach. The dog beach is closed every Tuesday. Dogs on leash are also allowed in Downs Park. People need to clean up after their pets. Take Route 100 until it merges with Mountain Road (Rt. 177

East). Follow Mt. Road for about 3.5 miles and the park entrance will be on your right. The dog beach is located in the northeast corner of the park.

# Massachusetts Listings

Barnstable Town Beaches
off Route 6A
Barnstable, MA
508-790-6345
Dogs are allowed only during the off-season, from September 15 to May 15. Dogs must be on leash or under voice control. People need to clean up after their pets. The town of Barnstable oversees Hyannis beaches and the following beaches: Craigville, Kalmus, and Sandy Neck. Before you go, always verify the seasonal dates and times when dogs are allowed on the beach.

Carson Beach
I-93 and William Day Blvd
Boston, MA
617-727-5114
Dogs are only allowed on the beach during the off-season. Pets are not allowed from Memorial Day weekend through Labor Day weekend. Dogs must be leashed and people are required to clean up after their pets.

Chatham Town Beaches
off Route 28
Chatham, MA
508-945-5100
chathaminfo.com/beaches
Dogs are allowed only during the off-season, from mid September to end the end of May. Dogs must be leashed and people need to clean up after their pets. The town of Chatham oversees the following beaches: Hardings, Light, and Ridgevale. Before you go, always verify the seasonal dates and times when dogs are allowed on the beach.

Dennis Town Beaches
Route 6A
Dennis, MA
508-394-8300
Dogs are allowed only during the off-season, from after Labor Day up to Memorial Day. Dogs must be leashed on all town beaches, and people need to clean up after their pets. The town of Dennis oversees the following beaches: Chapin, Mayflower, Howes Street and Sea Street. Before you go, always verify the seasonal dates and times when dogs are allowed on the beach.

Duxbury Beach
150 Gurnet Road

Duxbury, MA

This 6 mile long barrier beach reaches from Marshfield in the north to Gurnet Point and Saquish in the south. From April 1st until September 15th dogs are allowed on the beach; they must be leashed, registered at the Duxbury Town Hall if they are to be taken on the beach, and the permit acquired must be carried by the handler of the dog at all times while on beach properties. Dogs are allowed on Duxbury Beach properties from 8 am until sunset only. Dogs are not allowed on dunes, wildlife areas, or any fenced areas, and they must be cleaned up after promptly. Dogs may not be on the front beach (Resident Beach) south to the poles defining the beginning of the 4 X 4 beach or on the back beach north of the Powder Point Bridge adjacent to the resident parking lot from April 1st until September 15th. Dogs must be under their owner's control at all times.

Joseph Sylvia State Beach
Beach Road
Edgartown, MA
508-696-3840
Dogs are allowed during the summer, only before 9am and after 5pm. You will need to keep your dog away from any bird nesting areas, which should have signs posted. During the off-season, from mid-September to mid-April, dogs are allowed all day. This beach is about 2 miles long. Dogs must be leashed and people need to clean up after their pets. Before you go, always verify the seasonal dates and times when dogs are allowed on the beach.

Norton Point Beach
end of Katama Road
Edgartown, MA
508-696-3840
Dogs are allowed during the summer, only before 9am and after 5pm. You will need to keep your dog away from any bird nesting areas, which should have signs posted. During the off-season, from mid-September to mid-April, dogs are allowed all day. This beach is about 2.5 miles long. Dogs must be leashed and people need to clean up after their pets. Before you go, always verify the seasonal dates and times when dogs are allowed on the beach.

South Beach State Park
Katama Road
Edgartown, MA
508-693-0085
Dogs are allowed during the summer, only after 5pm. During the off-season,

from mid-September to mid-April, dogs are allowed all day. This 3 mile beach is located on the South Shore. Dogs must be leashed and people need to clean up after their pets. Before you go, always verify the seasonal dates and times when dogs are allowed on the beach.

Falmouth Town Beaches
off Route 28
Falmouth, MA
508-457-2567
Dogs are not allowed during the summer from May 1 through October 1. During the off-season, dogs are allowed all day. Dogs must be leashed and people need to clean up after their pets. The town of Falmouth oversees the following beaches: Menauhant, Surf Drive, and Old Silver. Before you go, always verify the seasonal dates and times when dogs are allowed on the beach.

Harwich Town Beach
off Route 28
Harwich, MA
508-430-7514
harwich-ma.gov/beaches
Dogs are allowed only during the off-season, from October to mid-May. Dogs must be on leash or under voice control. People need to clean up after their pets. The town of Harwich oversees Red River Beach. Before you go, always verify the seasonal dates and times when dogs are allowed on the beach.

Singing Beach
Beach Street
Manchester, MA
978-526-2040
Dogs under excellent voice control are allowed off-leash from October 1 through May 1 on the pristine Singing Beach. Dogs are not allowed on the beach during the other months. From Manchester, take Beach Street to the water. Parking can be difficult in this area.

Brant Rock Beach
Ocean Street/H 139
Marshfield, MA
781-834-0268
Leashed dogs are allowed on the Brant Rock Beach all through the year; they must be cleaned up after promptly. Sometimes there are waste dispenser bags at the entrances.

Nantucket Island Beaches
various locations
Nantucket, MA
508-228-1700
nantucket.net/beaches/north.php

Dogs are allowed during the summer on beaches with lifeguards only before 9am and after 5pm. On beaches that have no lifeguards, or during the winter months, dogs are allowed all day on the beach. Dogs must always be leashed. Before you go, always verify the seasonal dates and times when dogs are allowed on the beach.

Eastville Point Beach
At bridge near Vineyard Haven
Oak Bluffs, MA
508-696-3840
Dogs are allowed during the summer, only before 9am and after 5pm. You will need to keep your dog away from any bird nesting areas, which should have signs posted. During the off-season, from mid-September to mid-April, dogs are allowed all day. Dogs must be leashed and people need to clean up after their pets. Before you go, always verify the seasonal dates and times when dogs are allowed on the beach.

Orleans Town Beaches
off Route 28
Orleans, MA
508-240-3775
town.orleans.ma.us/beaches
Dogs are allowed only during the off-season, from after Columbus Day to the Friday before Memorial Day. Dogs are allowed off leash, but must be under voice control. People need to clean up after their pets. The town of Orleans oversees Nauset and Skaket beaches. Before you go, always verify the seasonal dates and times when dogs are allowed on the beach.

Plymouth City Beach
Route 3A
Plymouth, MA
508-747-1620
The beach in Plymouth allows dogs year round on the beach and in the water. Dogs must be leashed and cleaned up after.

Provincetown Town Beaches
off Route 6
Provincetown, MA
508-487-7000
Dogs on leash are allowed year-round. During the summer, from 6am to 9am, dogs are allowed off-leash. Before you go, always verify the seasonal dates and times when dogs are allowed on the beach.

Sandwich Town Beaches
off Route 6A
Sandwich, MA
508-888-4361
Dogs are allowed only during the off-season, from October through March.

Dogs must be leashed and people need to clean up after their pets. The town of Sandwich oversees the following beaches: East Sandwich and Town Neck. Before you go, always verify the seasonal dates and times when dogs are allowed on the beach.

Truro Town Beaches
off Route 6
Truro, MA
508-487-2702
Dogs are allowed during the summer, only before 9am and after 6pm. This policy is in effect from about the third weekend in June through Labor Day. During the off-season, dogs are allowed all day. Dogs must be leashed and people need to clean up after their pets. The town of Truro oversees the following beaches: Ballston, Corn Hill, Fisher, Great Hollow, Head of the Meadow, Longnook and Ryder. Before you go, always verify the seasonal dates and times when dogs are allowed on the beach.

Cape Cod National Seashore
Route 6
Wellfleet, MA
508-349-3785
nps.gov/caco
The park offers a 40 mile stretch of pristine sandy beaches. Dogs on leash are allowed year-round on all of the seashore beaches, except for seasonally posted nesting or lifeguarded beaches. Leashed pets are also allowed on fire roads, and the Head of the Meadow bicycle trail in Truro. Check with the visitor center or rangers for details about fire road locations. To get there from Boston, take Route 3 south to the Sagamore Bridge. Take Route 6 east towards Eastham.

Wellfleet Town Beaches
off Route 6
Wellfleet, MA
508-349-9818
wellfleet-ma.gov/beaches
Dogs are allowed during the summer, only before 9am and after 6pm. During the off-season, from after Labor Day to the end of June, dogs are allowed all day. Dogs must be leashed and people need to clean up after their pets. The town of Wellfleet oversees the following beaches: Marconi, Cahoon Hollow, and White Crest. Before you go, always verify the seasonal dates and times when

dogs are allowed on the beach.

Sandy Neck Beach
425 Sandy Neck Road
West Barnstable, MA

508-362-8300
In addition to being a haven for endangered bird and wildlife, this 6 mile long coastal barrier beach also shares a unique ecology and rich cultural history. There is an off-road beach, a public beach and miles of trails here. Dogs are allowed on the trails and on the Off-Road beach area anytime (but stay on water side) throughout the year, but they are not allowed on the public beach from May 15 to September 15. Dogs are not allowed in the primitive camp area. Visitors and their pets must remain on designated trails, off the dunes, and off the few areas of private property. Please consult trail maps. Dogs must be leashed and cleaned up after at all times.

# Michigan Listings

Young State Park Beach
C56 off 131
Boyne City, MI
231-582-7523
While dogs are not allowed on the beach, they can go into the water past the boat launch. There is a sandy and rocky area that leads to the water. Pets must be leashed and attended at all times and cleaned up after.

Burt Lake State Park Beach
Old 27 Highway
Burt Lake, MI
231-238-9392
This is not a Great Lakes beach, but is conveniently located off of I-75. While dogs are not allowed on the swimming beach, there is a special designated spot where dogs can go into the water. It is near campsite lot number 42, off Road 1, at the west end of the park. The road leads to the beach and dog run. Pets must be on a 6 foot or less leash and attended at all times.

Aloha State Park Beach
off I-75
Cheboygan, MI
231-625-2522
This is not a Great Lakes beach, but is conveniently located off of I-75. The park has a special pet swimming area which is located by the playground. Pets need to be leashed and cleaned up after. The park is located 7 miles south of Cheboygan and 25 miles from the Mackinac Bridge.

Sleeping Bear Dunes National Lakeshore Beaches
off M-72
Empire, MI

231-326-5134
nps.gov/slbe/
While pets are not allowed in certain areas of the park like the islands, Dune Climb, backcountry campsites, or inside buildings, they are allowed on some trails, campgrounds and on the following beaches. Pets are welcome on the beach at Esch Road (south of Empire), on the south side of Peterson Beach and on Empire Beach. Dogs must be leashed at all times and cleaned up after. To get there from Traverse City, take M-72 west to Empire.

Wilderness State Park Beach
Wilderness Park Drive
Mackinaw City, MI
231-436-5381
Dogs are not allowed at the beach but they can swim in the water on the other side of the boat launch. Pets must be a on a 6 foot or less leash and cleaned up after. The park is located 11 miles west of Mackinaw City.

Norman F. Kruse Park - Dog Beach
W Sherman Blvd and Beach Street
Muskegon, MI
231-724-6704
Although dogs are not allowed in the park area here, they are allowed at their own piece of the beach at the end of Sherman Road. Dogs must be on leash unless in the water and cleaned up after at all times. The site is open from 7 am until 11 pm.

Grand Mere State Park Beach
Thornton Drive
Stevensville, MI
269-426-4013
Dogs on leash are allowed at the beach and on the hiking trails. The one mile beach is located along the shoreline of Lake Michigan. Remember to clean up after your pet. To get there, take I-94 south of St. Joseph and take Exit 22. Go west .25 miles to Thornton Drive and head south on Thornton for .5 miles.

# Mississippi Listings

Hancock County Beaches
Beach Blvd.
Bay St Louis, MS
228-463-9222 (800-466-9048)
Dogs on leash are allowed on Hancock County beaches. People need to clean up after their pets. The county beaches are located along the coast, between the cities of Waveland and Bay St. Louis.

# Montana Listings

Canine Beach at Bozeman Ponds
700 - 550 N. Fowler Lane
Bozeman, MT
406-582-3200
The Canine Beach is an off-leash dog beach on the west side of the Bozeman Pond. The park is open from 8 am to 10 pm daily. Pets must be picked up after at the beach and leashed outside of the leash-free area.

# Nevada Listings

Sparks Marina Dog Park and Beach
300 Howard Drive
Reno, NV
775-353-2376
This city park surrounding a 77 acre lake offers a wide variety of land and water activities and recreational pursuits. They also have the only fenced, off-lead dog park in the Reno area where dogs can play in the water. The off lead area is almost an acre in size on the south side of the marina and features lots of grass, 150 feet of shoreline, clean-up stations, a fire hydrant, and a doggie drinking fountain. The marina is surrounded by a walking trail almost 2 miles long that is lighted for nighttime walks with your pet. Dogs must be on leash when not in the fenced, off-lead area, and they must be cleaned up after at all times. Dogs are not allowed on any of the beaches except for the dog beach in the dog park.

Sparks Marina Park
300 Howard Drive
Reno, NV
775-353-2376
This city park surrounding a 77 acre lake offers a wide variety of land and water activities and recreational pursuits. They also have the only fenced, off-lead dog park in the Reno area where dogs can play in the water. The off lead area is almost an acre in size on the south side of the marina and features lots of grass, 150 feet of shoreline, clean-up stations, a fire hydrant, and a doggie drinking fountain. The marina is surrounded by a walking trail almost 2 miles long that is lighted for nighttime walks with your pet. Dogs must be on leash when not in the fenced, off-lead area, and they must be cleaned up after at all times. Dogs are not allowed on any of the beaches except for the dog beach in the dog park.

North Beach at Zephyr Cove Resort
460 Highway 50

Zephyr Cove, NV
775-588-6644
Dogs are not allowed at the main beach at the Zephyr Cove Resort. They are allowed on leash, however, at the north beach at the resort. There is a $5.00 parking fee for day use. When you enter Zephyr Cover Resort head to the beach (North) to the last parking area and walk the few hundred feet to the beach. The North Beach is located just into the National Forest. There usually are cleanup bags on the walkway to the beach but bring your own in case they run out. This is a nice beach that is used by a lot of people in the summer. The cabins at Zephyr Cove Resort also allow dogs.

# New Jersey Listings

Barnegat Lighthouse State Park Beaches
At Broadway and the Bay
Barnegat Light, NJ
609-494-2016
Although dogs are not allowed in the lighthouse or on the beaches from April 15th to August 15, and never on the trails here, they are allowed in the park and picnic areas which provide visitors with great views of the ocean and waterway activities. Dogs are allowed on the park beaches from October 1 through April 14 each year. Dogs are welcome for no additional fee. Dogs must be under their owner's control, leashed, and cleaned up after at all times.

Cape May City Beaches (Restricted)

Cape May, NJ
609-884-9525
Dogs are only permitted on the Cape May City Beaches from Madison Avenue to Third Avenue. They are only permitted on this section of beach from November 1 to March 31.

Higbee Beach Wildlife Management Area
County Road 641
Cape May, NJ
609-628-2103
This park offers a 1 1/2 mile stretch of beach. The beach is managed specifically to provide habitat for migratory wildlife. Dogs on leash and under control are allowed at the beach from September through April. To get there, take SR 109 west to US9. Turn left onto US9 and go to the first traffic light. Turn left onto County Road 162 (Seashore

Rd.). Then turn right onto Country Road 641 (New England Rd.). Take CR641 for 2 miles to the end and the beach access parking area. Parking areas near the beach may be closed during the summer. The park is open daily from dawn to dusk.

Lower Township Beaches (Delaware Bay)
Lower Township
Cape May, NJ

Dogs on leash are permitted on Lower Township Beaches year round. This is the only year round dog-friendly beach currently in the Cape May area.

Cape May Point State Park
Lighthouse Avenue
Cape May Point, NJ
609-884-2159
Dogs are only allowed on the beach during the off-season. Pets are not allowed from April 15 through September 15. Pets must be on a 6 foot or less leash and people need to clean up after their pets. The park is located off the southern end of the Garden State Parkway. Go over the Cape May Bridge to Lafayette Street. At the intersection, go right onto Route 606 (Sunset Blvd.), then turn left onto Lighthouse Ave.

Gateway National Recreation Area (Sandy Hook)
off Route 36
Highlands, NJ
732-872-5970
nps.gov/gate/
Dogs are allowed at the Sandy Hook unit of this park, located in northern New Jersey. There are certain restrictions for pets on the beach. Leashed dogs are allowed on the bayside beaches, year-round. Leashed dogs are only allowed on the oceanside beaches during the off-season (pets are not allowed on the oceanside beaches from March 15 through Labor Day weekend).

Brant Beach
Off Long Beach Blvd
Long Beach, NJ
609-361-1000
This seasonal dog-friendly beach is located between Ship Bottom and Beach Haven Crest from 31st Street to 74th. Dogs are only allowed here from October 1st to April or May 30th of any given year. Dogs must be under their owner's control at all times and cleaned up after promptly.

Brant Beach
6805 S Long Beach Blvd

Long Beach Township, NJ
609-361-1000
longbeachisland.com/beach.html
Visitors will find dune fencing here giving easy access for the dogs from the beach to the water. Dogs are not allowed on the beaches from May 1st until October 1st. Owners must pick up after their pets

Fisherman's Cove Conservation Area
391 Third Avenue
Manasquan, NJ
732-922-4080
This is a 52 acre tract on the Manasquan Inlet. It is used for fishing, walking on the beach and sunbathing. Dogs must be on-leash everywhere in the park. To get to the beach take exit 98 from the Garden State Parkway and head south on Rt 34 which becomes Rt 35. Turn right on Higgins Avenue, then left onto Union Avenue (Rt 71), right on Fisk Avenue and right onto 3rd Ave.

Bayshore Waterfront Park Beach
Port Monmouth Road
Port Monmouth, NJ
732-842-4000
Located near the Monmouth Cove Marina, this 227 acre park offers a fishing pier, views of the New York City skyline, miles of beach, and access to Raritan Bay. Leashed dogs are allowed at the park; they must be leashed and cleaned up after promptly at all times.

Island Beach State Park
off Route 35
Seaside Park, NJ
732-793-0506
One of the states last significant remnants of a barrier island ecosystem, it is home to diverse wildlife and maritime plant life, and with a variety of land and water activities and 8 interesting trails. During the winter months, dogs are allowed on all of the beaches, but must be on a 6 foot or less leash. People are required to clean up after their pets. To get to the park, take Route 37 east. Then take Route 35 south to the park entrance. Dogs are not allowed on the lifeguarded swimming beaches during the summer. Dogs are not allowed on the Spizzle Creek Bird Blind Trail at any time of year.

Stone Harbor Beach
1st Avenue
Stone Harbor, NJ
609-368-6101
stoneharbornj.org/general-info/
Stone Harbor has 'unleashed' its summer ban of dogs on the beach to allow them on the beach between 80th and 83rd Streets from dawn to 9

am and from 6 pm until dusk. Dogs must be leashed and owners must clean up after their pets.

# New Mexico Listings

Tingley Beach
1800 Tingley Drive SW
Albuquerque, NM
505-768-2000
Open from dawn to dusk daily, year around, this site offers 3 fishing lakes, a train station with a gift shop, a model boating pond, bike and watercraft rentals, walking paths, and concessionaires. This site is also home to the world's largest caught Trout; fishing licenses are available at the gift shop - open daily from 9 am until 5 pm. Dogs are allowed at Tingley; they must be leashed at all times and cleaned up after promptly; they are not allowed at the Zoo, Botanic Garden grounds, or inside the aquarium.

# New York Listings

Gardiner County Park Beach
Montauk Highway & West Bay Shore
Bay Shore, NY
631-854-4949
This large 231 acre park was once part of the historic Sagtikos Manor Estate. It has a number of nature trails, fitness trails, hiking and facilities. Leashed dogs are allowed in the outdoor areas of the park. There is a dog water fountain in the park as well. There is a trail in Gardiner Park that leads down to the beach where your leashed dog may go as well.

Gateway National Recreation Area
Cross Bay Blvd.
Brooklyn, NY
718-338-3799
nps.gov/gate/
Dogs are allowed in the park and on the beach at the Jamaica Bay Unit. Stop at the visitor's center located off Cross Bay Blvd. for information about beach locations. The park is located near the JFK airport. To get there from the Shore (Belt) Parkway, exit 17 south (Crossbay Blvd.) and go over the bridge. Continue about 1 to 2 miles to the park entrance on the right. Dogs are not allowed during plover seasons.

New York City Beaches and Boardwalks
Various

Brooklyn, NY
212-NEW-YORK
From October 1 through April 30 each year, leashed dogs are allowed on the sand and the boardwalk at certain beaches. Currently, these beaches are Rockaway Beach, Coney Island, Brighton Beach, Manhattan Beach, Midland Beach and South Beach. Dogs are not allowed on the sand at any New York City beaches between May 1 and September 30. Leashed dogs are allowed year-round on the boardwalks and promenade at Coney Island, Brighton, Midland, South and Manhattan Beaches. Please check the website at http://www.nycgovparks.org for updated information and changes.

Dog Beach
Beach Road
Lake George Village, NY

The Dog Beach in Lake George Village, NY is exclusively for dogs and their owners to enjoy the lake & sandy beach during the summer months, from Memorial Day weekend through Labor Day weekend.

Dog Beach
End of Beach Avenue
Larchmont, NY

animal-link.org/parks.shtml
This is an un-official off-leash beach area. It is located at the end of Beach Avenue (where it becomes Park Avenue) in Larchmont. The beach is located between the Larchmont Shore Club and Manor Park.

Camp Hero State Park
50 South Fairview Avenue
Montauk, NY
631-668-3781
The park boasts some of the best surf fishing spots in the world. Dogs on a 6 foot or less leash are allowed on the beach year-round, but not in the picnic areas. To get to the park, take Route 27 (Sunrise Highway) east to the end. The park is about 130 miles from New York City.

Hither Hills State Park
50 South Fairview Avenue
Montauk, NY
631-668-2554
This park offers visitors a sandy ocean beach. Dogs are allowed with certain restrictions. During the off-season, dogs are allowed on the beach. During the summer, dogs are not allowed on the beach, except for the undeveloped area on the other side of the freeway. Dogs must be on a 6 foot or less leash and people need to clean up after their pets.

Dogs are not allowed in buildings or on walkways and they are not allowed in the camping, bathing and picnic areas.

Montauk Point State Park
50 South Fairview Avenue
Montauk, NY
631-668-3781
This park is located on the eastern tip of Long Island. Dogs are allowed on the beach, but not near the food area. Dogs must be on a 6 foot or less leash and people need to clean up after their pets. Dogs are not allowed in buildings or on walkways and they are not allowed in the camping, bathing and picnic areas. Please note that dogs are not allowed in the adjacent Montauk Downs State Park. The park is located 132 miles from Manhattan, off Sunrise Highway

(Route 27).

New York City Beaches and Boardwalks
Various
New York, NY
212-NEW-YORK
From October 1 through April 30 each year, leashed dogs are allowed on the sand and the boardwalk at certain beaches. These beaches are Rockaway Beach, Coney Island, Brighton Beach, Manhattan Beach, Midland Beach and South Beach. Dogs are not allowed on the sand at any New York City beaches between May 1 and September 30. Leashed dogs are allowed year-round on the boardwalks and promenade at Coney Island, Brighton, Midland, South and Manhattan Beaches. Please check the website at http://www.nycgovparks.org for updated information and changes.

Prospect Park Dog Beach
Prospect Park - Brooklyn
New York, NY
212-NEW-YORK
This man made, concrete beach was designed for our canine friends. It is located in Prospect Park, off 9th Street on the path leading down from the Tennis House. Dogs may only be off-leash before 9 am and after 9 pm in the summer and after 5 pm in the winter. People are not permitted to swim in the dog pool. There is a fence to keep the dogs in so you don't have to chase them across the pond.

Fire Island National Seashore
120 Laurel Street
Patchogue, NY
631-281-3010
nps.gov/fiis/
Dogs on a 6 foot or less leash are allowed on the beach, but only from Labor Day until March 15. They are not allowed on the beaches during the summer season. People will be fined if they let their dogs run off-leash. Please note that the park has had many bad experiences with dogs off leash and they may stop allowing dogs completely if they have more problems. Dogs are also allowed on the trails at this park, but it is not advised, since about 50% of the ticks here carry Lyme disease. People are required to clean up after their pets. The park is located on Long Island. There are only two bridges to the park. The Robert Moses Causeway on the western end of Fire Island leads to parking lots at Robert Moses State Park. The William Floyd Parkway leads to Smith Point County Park on the eastern end of Fire Island, where there are also parking lots. Parking fees are charged at both lots. There are no public roads on the island itself.

# North Carolina Listings

Fort Macon State Park
Highway 58
Atlantic Beach, NC
252-726-3775
This park offers beach access. Dogs on a 6 foot leash or less are allowed on the beach, but not inside the Civil War fort located in the park. People need to clean up after their pets. The park is located on the eastern end of Bogue Banks, south of Morehead City.

Corolla Beaches
Ocean Trail
Corolla, NC
252-232-0719
Dogs are allowed on the beaches in and around the Corolla area year round; they must be leashed and cleaned up after at all times.

Duck Beach
H 12
Duck, NC
252-255-1234
townofduck.com/our-beach/
Dogs are welcome to romp on the beach here, and they may be off leash if they are under good voice control. Dogs must be licensed, have current rabies tags, be under their owner's control, and cleaned up after at all times. Dogs must be on no more than a 10 foot leash when off the beach.

Kill Devil Hills Beaches
N Virginia Dare Trail
Kill Devil Hills, NC
252-449-5300
killdevilhills.com/beaches.html
From May 15th to September 15th dogs are not allowed on the beaches between 9 AM and 6 PM. When dogs are allowed on the beach, they must be licensed, have current rabies tags, be under their owner's control, on no more than a 10 foot leash, and cleaned up after at all times.

Kitty Hawk Beaches
Virginai Dare Trail/H 12
Kitty Hawk, NC
252-261-3552
Between 10 am and 6 pm from the Friday before Memorial Day until the day after Labor Day, dogs may be on the beach on a maximum 6 foot leash; for all other times they may be on a retractable leash up to 12 feet. Well trained dogs may be off-leash from Labor Day to the Friday before Memorial Day if they are under strict voice control and never more than 30 feet from the owner. Resident dogs must display a county registration tag plus a valid rabies tags, and non-resident dogs must have a valid rabies tag. Dogs must be under their owner's control and cleaned up after at all times.

Ft. Fisher State Recreation Area
Highway 421
Kure Beach, NC
910-458-5798
Enjoy miles of beachcombing, sunbathing or hunting for shells at this beach. Dogs on leash are allowed everywhere on the beach, except for swimming areas that have lifeguards on duty. People need to clean up after their pets. The park is located on the southern tip of Pleasure Island, near Wilmington.

Cape Hatteras National Seashore
Highway 12
Manteo, NC
252-473-2111
nps.gov/caha/
This park offers long stretches of pristine beach. Dogs on a 6 foot or less leash are allowed year-round, except on any designated swimming beaches. Most of the beaches are non-designated swim beaches. People are required to clean up after their pets.

Nags Head Beaches
N Vriginia Dare Trail/H 12
Nags Head, NC
252-441-5508
nags-head.com/beaches.html
The beaches here consist mostly of open spaces and low-density building. Dogs are allowed on the

beaches year round; they must be licensed, have current rabies tags, be under their owner's control, on no more than a 10 foot leash, and cleaned up after at all times.

Oak Island Beaches
Beach Drive
Oak Island, NC
910-278-5011
Dogs are allowed on city beaches year round, but from mid November to about the 1st of April dogs may be off lead if they are under strict voice control. Dogs must be under their owner's control, leashed April to November, and cleaned up after at all times.

Southern Shores Beaches
H 12
Southern Shores, NC
252-261-2394
From May 15th to September 15th dogs are not allowed on the beaches. Dogs must be licensed, have current rabies tags, be under their owner's control, on no more than a 10 foot leash, and cleaned up after at all times. A parking permit is required for parking in town and can be obtained at the Town Hall, 5375 N. Virginia Dare Trail.

Topsail Beach
Ocean Blvd
Topsail Beach, NC
910-328-5841
There are about 20 public assesses to the beaches in this town. From May 15th to September 30th dogs must be leashed when on the beach; otherwise dogs may be off lead if they are under strict adult voice control. Dogs must be cleaned up after at all times and always be leashed when not on the beach.

# Ohio Listings

Berlin Lake
7400 Bedell Rd
Berlin Center, OH
330-547-3781
wildlife.ohiodnr.gov/berlinlake
Berlin Lake is located on the Mahoning River, where it covers 3,590 acres and 70 miles of shoreline. A large variety of wildlife lives around the lake. The lake is a popular destination for boating, fishing, and swimming. The main swimming and bathing areas are off limits to dogs, but dogs are allowed in the dog friendly areas on the north-west side of the lake.

Fairport Harbor Lakefront Park Dog Swim Area

301 Huntington Beach Drive
Fairport Harbor, OH
440-639-9972
Open May to September, this 21 acre lakefront park offers family fun recreation for all ages - even the family pooch. It has a doggy swim area where dogs can play while the park is open from dawn to dusk. Dogs must be kept leashed and are only allowed in the paved parking area and the designated dog swim area of the park.

Geneva State Park
4499 Padanarum Road
Geneva, OH
440-466-8400
parks.ohiodnr.gov/geneva
While dogs are cannot go on the swim beach, they can go in the water outside of the designated swim beach. Pets must be leashed and cleaned up after. To get there from Cleveland, take Interstate 90 east to Route 534 north. The park entrance is six miles north on Route 534, on the left.

Geneva State Park
4499 Padanarum Road
Geneva, OH
440-466-8400
parks.ohiodnr.gov/geneva
Dogs are allowed at this park including on the 3 miles of hiking trails and in the campgrounds. While dogs are cannot go on the swim beach, they can go in the water outside of the designated swim beach. Pets must be leashed, cleaned up after and are not allowed inside any buildings. This park allows hunting in certain areas. To get there from Cleveland, take Interstate 90 east to Route 534 north. The park entrance is six miles north on Route 534, on the left.

Kelleys Island State Park Beach
Division Street
Kelleys Island, OH
419-746-2546
parks.ohiodnr.gov/kelleysisland
While pets are not allowed at the small 100 foot swimming beach, they are welcome to join you at the "long beach" but you will need to keep them away from other beachgoers. Pets must be leashed and cleaned up after. To get there you will need to take a ferry to the island. Kelleys Island Ferry Boat Line operates year round, weather permitting, and offers passenger and limited vehicle service from Marblehead, Ohio to the island. Leashed pets are welcome on the ferry. Once on Kelleys Island, go west on E. Lakeshore Drive and turn

right on Division Street. The park is at the end of Division Street on the right.

Lake Hope State Park
27331 State Route 278
McArthur, OH

parks.ohiodnr.gov/lakehope
This 2,900 acre park offers hiking trails, swimming, fishing, boating, camping and picnicking. Dogs are allowed at this park including on the 17 mile of hiking trails and in the campgrounds. While dogs are not allowed on the designated swim beach, they can go on leash into the water outside of the swim beach area. Pets must be leashed, cleaned up after and are not allowed inside any buildings. Hunting is permitted in the adjacent state forest.

Maumee Bay State Park Beach
1400 State Park Road
Oregon, OH
419-836-7758
parks.ohiodnr.gov/maumeebay
While dogs are not allowed at any beaches at this park, either on the Lake Erie shore or at the park's inland lake, dogs are permitted to take a dip in the water at the end of the inland lake which is on the south side of the road. Pets must be leashed even when in the water, and cleaned up after.

Catawba Island State Park
4049 East Moores Dock Rd.
Port Clinton, OH
419-797-4530
parks.ohiodnr.gov/catawbaisland
This day use park offers a small beach, launch ramps, fishing pier and picnic areas. Swimming is permitted but there are no lifeguards. Dogs are not allowed on the swim beach or anywhere on the north beaches; however, they are allowed at what they call the South Beach, aka The Boater's Beach. Directions: Toward the lake on Park Road 1; stay left in the lane and when the lake comes into view turn right; parking is available by the Pavilion. The gravel path to the right will lead to the beach. Dogs may be off leash in this area and while in the water; otherwise they must be kept leashed. Maps are available at the Main Offices, the Camp Store, or at the Check Window. The park is off of State Route 53.

Catawba Island State Park Beach
4049 East Moores Dock Rd.
Port Clinton, OH
419-797-4530
parks.ohiodnr.gov/catawbaisland
Swimming is permitted on this small beach but there are no lifeguards.

Dogs are welcome at the beach but need to be leashed when not in the water. The park is off of State Route 53.

East Harbor State Park Beach
Route 269
Port Clinton, OH
419-734-4424
parks.ohiodnr.gov/eastharbor
While dogs are not allowed on any sandy beach at this park, they can take a dip in the pond which is located off the exit road, next to the shelter road. Pets must be leashed and cleaned up after. To get there from Cleveland, take State Route 2 West to State Route 269 North. The park is located on State Route 269. To get there from Port Clinton, go east on Route 163 to Route 269 north.

Bow Wow Beach Dog Park
5027 Stow Rd
Stow, OH
330-689-5100
This off-leash dog park and beach is located in Silver Springs Park in Stow. It includes a 3 acre lake with a beach and a separate area for small dogs. Dogs can swim in the lake. The beach is closed in Winter while the lake is frozen and it is also closed on Thursday mornings for maintenance.

Main Street Beach
Main Street off OH-60
Vermilion, OH
440-204-2490
The Main Street Beach in Ohio is a small, popular Lake Erie swimming beach in downtown Vermilion. A replica of the Vermilion lighthouse, the pleasure boats entering and exiting the mouth of the Vermilion River, and Lake Erie can be seen from the beach. Well-behaved, leashed dogs are allowed.

Lake Alma State Park
422 Lake Alma Road
Wellston, OH
740-384-4474
parks.ohiodnr.gov/lakealma
This 292 acre park is home to 60 acre Lake Alma Lake. The majority of the park is wooded. Leashed dogs are allowed throughout the park. The park is notable as it has an off-leash dog park with lake access for canine swimming.

# Oregon Listings

Bullards Beach State Park
Highway 101
Bandon, OR
541-347-2209
Enjoy a walk along the beach at this park. Picnic tables, restrooms, hiking and campgrounds are available at the park. There is a minimal day use fees. Leashed dogs are allowed on the beach. Dogs are also allowed on hiking trails and campgrounds. They must be on a six foot or less leash at all times and people are required to clean up after their pets. On beaches located outside of Oregon State Park boundaries, dogs might be allowed off-leash and under direct voice control, please look for signs or postings. This park is located off U.S. Highway 101, 2 miles north of Bandon.

Seven Devils State Recreation Site
Highway 101
Bandon, OR
800-551-6949
Enjoy several miles of beach at this park. Picnic tables are available at this park. There are no day use fees. Dogs are allowed on the beach. They must be on a six foot or less leash at all times and people are required to clean up after their pets. On beaches located outside of Oregon State Park boundaries, dogs might be allowed off-leash and under direct voice control, please look for signs or postings. This park is located off U.S. Highway 101, 10 miles north of Bandon.

Harris Beach State Park
Highway 101
Brookings, OR
541-469-2021
oregonstateparks.org/park_79.php
The park offers sandy beaches for beachcombing, whale watching, and sunset viewing. Picnic tables, restrooms (including an ADA restroom) and shaded campsites are available at this park. There is a minimal day use fee. Leashed dogs are allowed on the beach. Dogs are also allowed at the campgrounds. They must be on a six foot or less leash at all times and people are required to clean up after their pets. On beaches located outside of Oregon State Park boundaries, dogs might be allowed off-leash and under direct voice control, please look for signs or postings. This park is located off U.S. Highway 101, just north of Brookings.

McVay Rock State Recreation Site
Highway 101
Brookings, OR
800-551-6949
This beach is a popular spot for clamming, whale watching and walking. Picnic tables and restrooms are available at this park. There are no day use fees. Dogs are allowed on the beach. They must be on a six foot or less leash at all times and people are required to clean up after their pets. On beaches located outside of Oregon State Park boundries, dogs might be allowed off-leash and under direct voice control, please look for signs or postings. This park is located off U.S. Highway 101, just south of Brookings.

Samuel H. Boardman State Scenic Corridor
Highway 101
Brookings, OR
800-551-6949
Steep coastline at this 12 mile long corridor is interrupted by small sandy beaches. Picnic tables, restrooms (including an ADA restroom), and a hiking trail are available at this park. There are no day use fees. Leashed dogs are allowed on the beach. Dogs are also allowed on the hiking trail. They must be on a six foot or less leash at all times and people are required to clean up after their pets. On beaches located outside of Oregon State Park boundaries, dogs might be allowed off-leash and under direct voice control, please look for signs or postings. This park is located off U.S. Highway 101, 4 miles north of Brookings.

Arcadia Beach State Recreation Site
Highway 101
Cannon Beach, OR
800-551-6949
This sandy ocean beach is just a few feet from where you can park your car. Picnic tables and restrooms are available at this park. There are no day use fees. Dogs are allowed on the beach. They must be on a six foot or less leash at all times and people are required to clean up after their pets. On beaches located outside of Oregon State Park boundaries, dogs might be allowed off-leash and under direct voice control, please look for signs or postings. This park is located off U.S. Highway 101, 3 miles south of Cannon Beach.

Ecola State Park
Highway 101
Cannon Beach, OR
503-436-2844
According to the Oregon State Parks Division, this park is one of the most photographed locations in Oregon. To reach the beach, you will need to walk down a trail. Restrooms, hiking and primitive campgrounds are available at this park. There is a $3 day use fee. Leashed dogs are

allowed on the beach. Dogs are also allowed on hiking trails and campgrounds. They must be on a six foot or less leash at all times and people are required to clean up after their pets. On beaches located outside of Oregon State Park boundaries, dogs might be allowed off-leash and under direct voice control, please look for signs or postings. This park is located off U.S. Highway 101, 2 miles north of

Cannon Beach.

Hug Point State Recreation Site
Highway 101
Cannon Beach, OR
800-551-6949
According to the Oregon State Parks Division, people used to travel via stagecoach along this beach before the highway was built. Today you can walk along the original trail which was carved into the point by stagecoaches. The trail is located north of the parking area. Visitors can also explore two caves around the point, but be aware of high tide. Some people have become stranded at high tide when exploring the point! This beach is easily accessible from the parking area. Picnic tables and restrooms are available at this park. There are no day use fees. Dogs are allowed on the beach. They must be on a six foot or less leash at all times and people are required to clean up after their pets. On beaches located outside of Oregon State Park boundaries, dogs might be allowed off-leash and under direct voice control, please look for signs or postings. This park is located off U.S. Highway 101, 5 miles south of

Cannon Beach.

Tolovana Beach State Recreation Site
Highway 101
Cannon Beach, OR
800-551-6949
Indian Beach is popular with surfers. There is a short walk down to the beach. Picnic tables are available at this park. There are no day fees. Dogs are allowed on the beach. They must be on a six foot or less leash at all times and people are required to clean up after their pets. On beaches located outside of Oregon State Park boundaries, dogs might be allowed off-leash and under direct voice control, please look for signs or postings. This park is located off U.S. Highway 101, 1 mile south of Cannon

Beach.

Sunset Bay State Park
89814 Cape Arrago H

Coos Bay, OR
541-888-4902
This scenic park's beautiful sandy beaches are protected by the towering sea cliffs surrounding them, and the day-use and picnic facilities are only a short walk from the beach allowing for easy access for beachcombing, fishing, swimming, and boating. There is a network of hiking trails that connect Sunset Bay with nearby Shore Acres and Cape Arago State Parks. These trails give the hiker opportunities to experience the pristine coastal forests, seasonal wildflowers, and the spectacular ocean vistas of the area. There is a fully enclosed observation building that has interpretive panels describing the history of the Simpson estate along the way. From points along the trail you can see views of Gregory Point and the Cape Arago lighthouse. The park is open year round from 8 a.m. until sunset. Dogs on lead at all times are allowed, and pets must be cleaned up after. Dogs may not be left unattended at any time. There is a campground here that offer a variety of activities and recreation.

Fogarty Creek State Recreation Area
Highway 101
Depoe Bay, OR
800-551-6949
This beach and park offer some of the best birdwatching and tidepooling. Picnic tables and hiking are available at this park. There is a $3 day use fees. Leashed dogs are allowed on the beach. Dogs are also allowed on hiking trails. They must be on a six foot or less leash at all times and people are required to clean up after their pets. On beaches located outside of Oregon State Park boundaries, dogs might be allowed off-leash and under direct voice control, please look for signs or postings. This park is located off U.S. Highway 101, 2 miles north of Depoe Bay.

Carl G. Washburne Memorial State Park
Highway 101
Florence, OR
541-547-3416
This park offers five miles of sandy beach. Picnic tables, restrooms, hiking and campgrounds are available at this park. There is a day use fee. Leashed dogs are allowed on the beach. Dogs are also allowed on hiking trails and campgrounds. They must be on a six foot or less leash at all times and people are required to clean up after their pets. On beaches located outside of

Oregon State Park boundaries, dogs might be allowed off-leash and under direct voice control, please look for signs or postings. This park is located off U.S. Highway 101, 14 miles north of Florence.

Heceta Head Lighthouse State Scenic Viewpoint
Highway 101
Florence, OR
800-551-6949
Go for a walk above the beach or explore the natural caves and tidepools along the beach. This is a great spot for whale watching. According to the Oregon State Parks Division, the lighthouse located on the west side of 1,000-foot-high Heceta Head (205 feet above ocean) is one of the most photographed on the Oregon coast. Picnic tables, restrooms and hiking are available at this park. There is a $3 day use fee. Leashed dogs are allowed on the beach. Dogs are also allowed on hiking trails. They must be on a six foot or less leash at all times and people are required to clean up after their pets. On beaches located outside of Oregon State Park boundaries, dogs might be allowed off-leash and under direct voice control, please look for signs or postings. This park is located off U.S. Highway 101, 13 miles north of Florence.

Pistol River State Scenic Viewpoint
Highway 101
Gold Beach, OR
800-551-6949
This beach is popular for ocean windsurfing. There has even been windsurfing national championships held at this beach. Picnic tables and restrooms are available here. There are no day use fees. Dogs are allowed on the beach. They must be on a six foot or less leash at all times and people are required to clean up after their pets. On beaches located outside of Oregon State Park boundaries, dogs might be allowed off-leash and under direct voice control, please look for signs or postings. This park is located off U.S. Highway 101, 11 miles south of Gold Beach.

D River State Recreation Site
Highway 101
Lincoln City, OR
800-551-6949
This beach, located right off the highway, is a popular and typically windy beach. According to the Oregon State Parks Division, this park is home to a pair of the world's largest kite festivals every spring and

fall which gives Lincoln City the name Kite Capital of the World. Restrooms are available at the park. Dogs are allowed on the beach. They must be on a six foot or less leash at all times and people are required to clean up after their pets. On beaches located outside of Oregon State Park boundaries, dogs might be allowed off-leash and under direct voice control, please look for signs or postings. This park is located off U.S. Highway 101 in Lincoln City.

Roads End State Recreation Site
Highway 101
Lincoln City, OR
800-551-6949
There is a short trail here that leads down to the beach. Picnic tables are available at this park. There are no day use fees. Dogs are allowed on the beach. They must be on a six foot or less leash at all times and people are required to clean up after their pets. On beaches located outside of Oregon State Park boundaries, dogs might be allowed off-leash and under direct voice control, please look for signs or postings. This park is located off U.S. Highway 101, 1 mile north of Lincoln City.

Nehalem Bay State Park
Highway 101
Manzanita, OR
503-368-5154
The beach can be reached by a short walk over the dunes. This park is a popular place for fishing and crabbing. Picnic tables, restrooms (including an ADA restroom), hiking and camping are available at this park. There is a $3 day use fee. Leashed dogs are allowed on the beach. Dogs are also allowed on hiking trails and campgrounds. They must be on a six foot or less leash at all times and people are required to clean up after their pets. On beaches located outside of Oregon State Park boundaries, dogs might be allowed off-leash and under direct voice control, please look for signs or postings. This park is located off U.S. Highway 101, 3 miles south of Manzanita Junction.

Oswald West State Park
Highway 101
Manzanita, OR
800-551-6949
The beach is located just a quarter of a mile from the parking areas. It is a popular beach that is frequented by windsurfers and boogie boarders. Picnic tables, restrooms, hiking and campgrounds are available at this park. There are no day use fees. Leashed dogs are allowed on the

beach. Dogs are also allowed on hiking trails and campgrounds. They must be on a six foot or less leash at all times and people are required to clean up after their pets. On beaches located outside of Oregon State Park boundaries, dogs might be allowed off-leash and under direct voice control, please look for signs or postings. This park is located off U.S. Highway 101, 10 miles south of Cannon Beach.

Neskowin Beach State Recreation Site
Highway 101
Neskowin, OR
800-551-6949
Not really any facilities (picnic tables, etc.) here, but a good place to enjoy the beach. Dogs are allowed on the beach. They must be on a six foot or less leash at all times and people are required to clean up after their pets. On beaches located outside of Oregon State Park boundaries, dogs might be allowed off-leash and under direct voice control, please look for signs or postings. This park is located off U.S. Highway 101 in Neskowin.

Agate Beach State Recreation Site
Highway 101
Newport, OR
800-551-6949
This beach is popular with surfers. Walk through a tunnel to get to the beach. According to the Oregon State Parks Division, many years ago Newport farmers led cattle westward through the tunnel to the ocean salt. Picnic tables and restrooms are available at this park. There is no day use fees. Dogs are allowed on the beach. They must be on a six foot or less leash at all times and people are required to clean up after their pets. On beaches located outside of Oregon State Park boundaries, dogs might be allowed off-leash and under direct voice control, please look for signs or postings. This park is located off U.S. Highway 101, 1 mile north of Newport.

Beverly Beach State Park
Highway 101
Newport, OR
541-265-9278
To get to the beach, there is a walkway underneath the highway that leads to the ocean. Picnic tables, restrooms (including an ADA restroom), a walking trail and campgrounds are available at this park. There is a day use fee. Leashed dogs are allowed on the

beach. Dogs are also allowed on the walking trail and campgrounds. They must be on a six foot or less leash at all times and people are required to clean up after their pets. On beaches located outside of Oregon State Park boundaries, dogs might be allowed off-leash and under direct voice control, please look for signs or postings. This park is located off U.S. Highway 101, 7 miles north of Newport.

Devils Punchbowl State Natural Area
Highway 101
Newport, OR
800-551-6949
This is a popular beach for surfing. Picnic tables, restrooms and hiking are available at this park. There are no day use fees. Leashed dogs are allowed on the beach. Dogs are also allowed on hiking trails. They must be on a six foot or less leash at all times and people are required to clean up after their pets. On beaches located outside of Oregon State Park boundaries, dogs might be allowed off-leash and under direct voice control, please look for signs or postings. This park is located off U.S. Highway 101, 8 miles north of Newport.

South Beach State Park
Highway 101
Newport, OR
541-867-4715
This park offers many recreational opportunities like beachcombing, fishing, windsurfing and crabbing. Picnic tables, restrooms (including an ADA restroom), hiking (including an ADA hiking trail), and campgrounds are available at this park. There is a day use fee. Leashed dogs are allowed on the beach. Dogs are also allowed on hiking trails and campgrounds. They must be on a six foot or less leash at all times and people are required to clean up after their pets. On beaches located outside of Oregon State Park boundaries, dogs might be allowed off-leash and under direct voice control, please look for signs or postings. This park is located off U.S. Highway 101, 2 miles south of Newport.

Bob Straub State Park
Highway 101
Pacific City, OR
800-551-6949
This is a nice stretch of beach to walk along. Picnic tables and restrooms (including an ADA restroom) are available at this park. There are no day use fees. Dogs are allowed on

the beach. They must be on a six foot or less leash at all times and people are required to clean up after their pets. On beaches located outside of Oregon State Park boundaries, dogs might be allowed off-leash and under direct voice control, please look for signs or postings. This park is located off U.S. Highway 101 in Pacific City.

Cape Kiwanda State Natural Area
Highway 101
Pacific City, OR
800-551-6949
This beach and park is a good spot for marine mammal watching, hang gliding and kite flying. Picnic tables are available at this park. There are no day use fees. Dogs are allowed on the beach. They must be on a six foot or less leash at all times and people are required to clean up after their pets. On beaches located outside of Oregon State Park boundaries, dogs might be allowed off-leash and under direct voice control, please look for signs or postings. This park is located off U.S. Highway 101, 1 mile north of Pacific City.

Cape Blanco State Park
Highway 101
Port Orford, OR
541-332-6774
Take a stroll on the beach or hike on over eight miles of trails which offer spectacular ocean vistas. Picnic tables, restrooms, hiking and campgrounds are available at this park. There is a minimal day use fee. Leashed dogs are allowed on the beach. Dogs are also allowed on hiking trails and campgrounds. They must be on a six foot or less leash at all times and people are required to clean up after their pets. On beaches located outside of Oregon State Park boundaries, dogs might be allowed off-leash and under direct voice control, please look for signs or postings. This park is located off U.S. Highway 101, 9 miles north of Port Orford.

Humbug Mountain State Park
Highway 101
Port Orford, OR
541-332-6774
This beach is frequented by windsurfers and scuba divers. A popular activity at this park is hiking to the top of Humbug Mountain (elevation 1,756 feet) . Picnic tables, restrooms, hiking and campgrounds are available at this park. There is a minimal day use fee. Leashed dogs are allowed on the beach. Dogs are also allowed on hiking trails and campgrounds. They must be on a six foot or less leash at all times and

people are required to clean up after their pets. On beaches located outside of Oregon State Park boundaries, dogs might be allowed off-leash and under direct voice control, please look for signs or postings. This park is located off U.S. Highway 101, 6 miles south of Port Orford.

Manhattan Beach State Recreation Site
Highway 101
Rockaway Beach, OR
800-551-6949
The beach is a short walk from the parking area. Picnic tables are available at this park. There are no day use fees. Dogs are allowed on the beach. They must be on a six foot or less leash at all times and people are required to clean up after their pets. On beaches located outside of Oregon State Park boundaries, dogs might be allowed off-leash and under direct voice control, please look for signs or postings. This park is located off U.S. Highway 101, 2 miles north of Rockaway Beach.

Del Rey Beach State Recreation Site
Highway 101
Seaside, OR
800-551-6949
There is a short trail to the beach. There is no day use fee. Dogs are allowed on the beach. They must be on a six foot or less leash at all times and people are required to clean up after their pets. On beaches located outside of Oregon State Park boundaries, dogs might be allowed off-leash and under direct voice control, please look for signs or postings. This park is located off U.S. Highway 101, 2 miles north of Gearhart.

Cape Lookout State Park
Highway 101
Tillamook, OR
503-842-4981
This is a popular beach during the summer. The beach is a short distance from the parking area. It is located about an hour and half west of Portland. Picnic tables, restrooms (including an ADA restroom), hiking trails and campgrounds are available at this park. There is a $3 day use fee. Leashed dogs are allowed on the beach. Dogs are also allowed on hiking trails and campgrounds. They must be on a six foot or less leash at all times and people are required to clean up after their pets. On beaches located outside of Oregon State Park

boundaries, dogs might be allowed off-leash and under direct voice control, please look for signs or postings. This park is located off U.S. Highway 101, 12 miles southwest of Tillamook.

Cape Meares State Scenic Viewpoint
Highway 101
Tillamook, OR
800-551-6949
The beach is located south of the scenic viewpoint. The viewpoint is situated on a headland, about 200 feet above the ocean. According to the Oregon State Parks Division, bird watchers can view the largest colony of nesting common murres (this site is one of the most populous colonies of nesting sea birds on the continent). Bald eagles and a peregrine falcon have also been known to nest near here. In winter and spring, this park is an excellent location for viewing whale migrations. Picnic tables, restrooms and hiking are available at this park. There are no day use fees. Leashed dogs are allowed on the beach. Dogs are also allowed on hiking trails. They must be on a six foot or less leash at all times and people are required to clean up after their pets. On beaches located outside of Oregon State Park boundaries, dogs might be allowed off-leash and under direct voice control, please look for signs or postings. This park is located off U.S. Highway 101, 10 miles west of Tillamook.

Beachside State Recreation Site
Highway 101
Waldport, OR
541-563-3220
Enjoy miles of broad sandy beach at this park or stay at one of the campground sites that are located just seconds from the beach. Picnic tables, restrooms (including an ADA restroom), and hiking are also available at this park. There is a day use fees. Leashed dogs are allowed on the beach. Dogs are also allowed on hiking trails and campgrounds. They must be on a six foot or less leash at all times and people are required to clean up after their pets. On beaches located outside of Oregon State Park boundaries, dogs might be allowed off-leash and under direct voice control, please look for signs or postings. This park is located off U.S. Highway 101, 4 miles south of Waldport.

Governor Patterson Memorial State Recreation Site
Highway 101
Waldport, OR

800-551-6949
This park offers miles of flat, sandy beach. It is also an excellent location for whale watching. Picnic tables and restrooms are available at this park. There are no day use fees. Dogs are allowed on the beach. They must be on a six foot or less leash at all times and people are required to clean up after their pets. On beaches located outside of Oregon State Park boundaries, dogs might be allowed off-leash and under direct voice control, please look for signs or postings. This park is located off U.S. Highway 101, 1 mile south of Waldport.

Fort Stevens State Park
Highway 101
Warrenton, OR
503-861-1671
visitftstevens.com/
There are miles of ocean beach. Picnic tables, restrooms (including an ADA restroom), hiking and campgrounds are available at this park. There is a $3 day use fee. Leashed dogs are allowed on the beach. Dogs are also allowed on hiking trails and campgrounds. They must be on a six foot or less leash at all times and people are required to clean up after their pets. On beaches located outside of Oregon State Park boundaries, dogs might be allowed off-leash and under direct voice control, please look for signs or postings. This park is located off U.S. Highway 101, 10 miles west of Astoria.

Neptune State Scenic Viewpoint
Highway 101
Yachats, OR
800-551-6949
During low tide at this beach you can walk south and visit a natural cave and tidepools. Or sit and relax at one of the picnic tables that overlooks the beach below. Restrooms (including an ADA restroom) are available at this park. There are no day use fees. Dogs are allowed on the beach. They must be on a six foot or less leash at all times and people are required to clean up after their pets. On beaches located outside of Oregon State Park boundaries, dogs might be allowed off-leash and under direct voice control, please look for signs or postings. This park is located off U.S. Highway 101,

Yachats State Recreation Area
Highway 101
Yachats, OR
800-551-6949
This beach is a popular spot for whale watching, salmon fishing, and

exploring tidepools. Picnic tables and restrooms are available at this park. There are no day use fees. Dogs are allowed on the beach. They must be on a six foot or less leash at all times and people are required to clean up after their pets. On beaches located outside of Oregon State Park boundaries, dogs might be allowed off-leash and under direct voice control, please look for signs or postings. This park is located off U.S. Highway 101 in Yachats.

# Puerto Rico Listings

El Combate Beach
Beach Road
Cabo Rojo, PR
800-866-7827
White soft sandy beaches, shade trees/palms, exquisite ocean scenery, a long dock into the water, and food close by are just some of the attractions of this popular family recreation area. Dogs are allowed throughout the park and on the beach; they must be leashed and cleaned up after promptly.

# Pennsylvania Listings

Presque Isle State Park Beach
PA Route 832
Erie, PA
814-833-7424
This state park offers beaches and almost 11 miles of hiking trails. Popular activities at the park include surfing, swimming, boating, hiking, in-line skating and bicycling. Dogs are allowed on a 6 foot or less leash at the park including on the hiking trails and only on beaches that are not guarded by lifeguard staff. Dogs can go into the water, still on leash, but people can only wade in up to their knees since there are no lifeguards in those areas. The unguarded beaches are located throughout the park, but if you want to know exact locations, please stop at the park office for details. The park is located four miles west of downtown Erie, off Route 832.

# Rhode Island Listings

Block Island Beaches
Corn Neck Road

Block Island, RI
401-466-2982
Dogs are allowed year-round on the island beaches, but they must be leashed and people are required to clean up after their pets. To get to the beaches, take a right out of town and follow Corn Neck Road. To get to the island, you will need to take the Block Island Ferry which allows leashed dogs. The ferry from Port Judith, RI to Block Island operates daily. If you are taking the ferry from Newport, RI or New London, CT to the island, please note these ferries only operate during the summer. If you are bringing a vehicle on the ferry, reservations are required. Call the Block Island Ferry at 401-783-4613 for auto reservations.

East Beach State Beach
East Beach Road
Charlestown, RI
401-322-0450
Dogs are only allowed on the beach during the off-season, from October 1 through March 31. Pets must be on leash and people are required to clean up after their pets. However, according to a representative at the Rhode Island State Parks Department, in a conversation with them July 2004, the rules may change in the future to have no dogs on the beach year round. To get there, take I-95 to Route 4 South. Then take Route 1 South to East Beach exit in Charlestown.

East Ferry
Conanicus Avenue
Jamestown, RI
401-849-2822
There is a nice green area with a memorial here, and benches placed to watch out over the busy harbor life. Leashed dogs are allowed on the wharf; they must be leashed and under their owner's control at all times. There is also dog friendly dining on the wharf.

Salty Brine State Beach
254 Great Road
Narragansett, RI
401-789-3563
Dogs are only allowed on the beach during the off-season, from October 1 through March 31. Pets must be on leash and people are required to clean up after their pets. However, according to a representative at the Rhode Island State Parks Department, in a conversation with them July 2004, the rules may change in the future to have no dogs on the beach year round. To get there, take I-95 to Route 4 South. Then take Route 1 South to Route 108 South to Point Judith. If you are

there during the summer, take the dog-friendly ferry at Pt. Judith in Block Island where leashed dogs are allowed year-round on the island beaches.

Easton's Beach
Memorial Blvd.
Newport, RI
401-847-6875
Dogs are only allowed on the beach during the off-season. They are not allowed on the beach from Memorial Day weekend through Labor Day weekend. Pets must be on leash and people need to clean up after their pets. The beach is located off Route 138A (Memorial Blvd.). There is a parking fee.

Teddy's Beach
Park Avenue
Portsmouth, RI
401-683-7899
Although located in Island Park, this is not a staffed town beach. There are no restrooms and it is a carry in/carries out facility. Dogs are allowed; they must be leashed and cleaned up after at all times.

East Matunuck State Beach
950 Succotash Road
South Kingston, RI
401-789-8585
Dogs are only allowed on the beach during the off-season, from October 1 through March 31. Pets must be on leash and people are required to clean up after their pets. However, according to a representative at the Rhode Island State Parks Department, in a conversation with them July 2004, the rules may change in the future to have no dogs on the beach year round. To get there, take I-95 to Route 4 South. Then take Route 1 South to East Matunuck Exit and follow the signs to the state beach.

Misquamicut State Beach
257 Atlantic Avenue
Westerly, RI
401-596-9097
Dogs are only allowed on the beach during the off-season, from October 1 through March 31. Pets must be on leash and people are required to clean up after their pets. However, according to a representative at the Rhode Island State Parks Department, in a conversation to them July 2004, the rules may change in the future to have no dogs on the beach year round. To get there, take I-95 to Route 4 South. Then take Route 1 South to Westerly. Follow the signs to the state beach.

# South Carolina Listings

Edisto Beach State Park
8377 State Cabin Road
Edisto Island, SC
843-869-2756
Sunbathe, beachcomb or hunt for seashells on this 1.5 mile long beach. This park also has a 4 mile nature trail that winds through a maritime forest with great vistas that overlook the salt marsh. Dogs on a 6 foot or less leash are allowed on the beach and on the trails. People need to clean up after their pets.

Folly Beach County Park
Ashley Avenue
Folly Beach, SC
843-588-2426
Dogs are only allowed during the off-season at this beach. They are not allowed from May 1 through September 30. But the rest of the year, dogs on leash are allowed on the beach during park hours. People are required to clean up after their pets. The park is located on the west end of Folly Island. On the island, turn right at Ashley Avenue stoplight and go to the end of the road.

Alder Lane Beach Access
S. Forest Beach Drive
Hilton Head Island, SC
843-341-4600
This beach has restricted seasons and hours for dogs. During the summertime, from the Friday before Memorial Day through the Tuesday after Labor Day, dogs can only be on the beach before 10am and then after 5pm (they are not allowed from 10am to 5pm). Pets must be leashed. During the off-season and winter months, from April 1 through the Thursday before Memorial Day, dogs must be on a leash between 10am and 5pm. From the Tuesday after Labor Day through September 30, dogs again must be on a leash between 10am and 5pm. At all other times, dogs may be off-leash, but must be under direct, positive voice control. People are required to clean up after their pets. There are 22 metered spaces for beach parking. The cost is a quarter for each 15 minutes.

Coligny Beach Park
Coligny Circle
Hilton Head Island, SC
843-341-4600
This beach has restricted seasons and hours for dogs. During the summertime, from the Friday before

Memorial Day through the Tuesday after Labor Day, dogs can only be on the beach before 10am and then after 5pm (they are not allowed from 10am to 5pm). Pets must be leashed. During the off-season and winter months, from April 1 through the Thursday before Memorial Day, dogs must be on a leash between 10am and 5pm. From the Tuesday after Labor Day through September 30, dogs again must be on a leash between 10am and 5pm. At all other times, dogs may be off-leash, but must be under direct, positive voice control. People are required to clean up after their pets. There are 30 metered spaces for beach parking. The cost is a quarter for each 15 minutes. A flat fee of $4 is charged at the parking lot on Fridays through Sundays and holidays.

Folly Field Beach Park
Folly Field Road
Hilton Head Island, SC
843-341-4600
This beach has restricted seasons and hours for dogs. During the summertime, from the Friday before Memorial Day through the Tuesday after Labor Day, dogs can only be on the beach before 10am and then after 5pm (they are not allowed from 10am to 5pm). Pets must be leashed. During the off-season and winter months, from April 1 through the Thursday before Memorial Day, dogs must be on a leash between 10am and 5pm. From the Tuesday after Labor Day through September 30, dogs again must be on a leash between 10am and 5pm. At all other times, dogs may be off-leash, but must be under direct, positive voice control. People are required to clean up after their pets. There are 52 metered spaces for beach parking. The cost is a quarter for each 15 minutes.

Hilton Head Island Beaches

Hilton Head Island, SC
800-523-3373
Dogs are welcome on the beaches of the island during certain times/days: They are not permitted on the beach between 10 AM and 5 PM from the Friday before Memorial Day through Labor Day; they may be on the beach between 10 AM and 5 PM from April 1st to the Thursday before Memorial Day, and between 10 AM and 5 PM the Tuesday after Labor Day through September 30th. Dogs must be leashed and picked up after at all times.

311

Hunting Island State Park
2555 Sea Island Parkway
Hunting Island, SC
843-838-2011
huntingisland.com/
This park offers over 4 miles of beach. Dogs on a 6 foot or less leash are allowed on the beach and on the trails at this state park. People need to clean up after their pets.

Isle of Palms County Park Beach
14th Avenue
Isle of Palms, SC
843-886-3863
Dogs on leash are allowed year-round at this beach. People are required to clean up after their pets. The park is located on the Isle of Palms, on 14th Ave., between Palm Blvd. and Ocean Blvd. Then coming to Isle of Palms from 517, continue straight at the Palm Blvd intersection and then take the next left at the park gate.

Beachwalker County Park
Beachwalker Drive
Kiawah, SC
843-768-2395
Dogs on leash are allowed year-round at this beach. People are required to clean up after their pets. The park is located on the west end of Kiawah Island. Take Bohicket Road to the island. Just before the island security gate, turn right on Beachwalker Drive. Follow the road to the park.

Huntington Beach State Park
16148 Ocean Highway
Murrells Inlet, SC
843-234-4440
This beach is the best preserved beach on the Grand Strand. Dogs on a 6 foot or less leash are allowed on the beach. People need to clean up after their pets.

Myrtle Beach City Beaches
off Interstate 73
Myrtle Beach, SC
843-281-2662
There are certain restrictions for pets on the beach. Dogs are not allowed on the right of way of Ocean Blvd. (part of I-73), between 21st Avenue North and 13th Avenue South during March 1 through September 30. From Memorial Day weekend through Labor Day weekend, leashed dogs are allowed on Myrtle Beach city beaches before 9am and after 5pm. During off-season, leashed dogs are allowed on the city beaches anytime during park hours. People need to clean up after their pets.

Myrtle Beach State Park
4401 South Kings Highway

Myrtle Beach, SC
843-238-5325
This is one of the most popular public beaches on the South Carolina coast. It is located in the heart of the Grand Strand. During the summer time, dogs are only allowed during certain hours. From May `15 through Sept 15, dogs are only allowed on the beach after 5 pm and before 8 am. For all other months of the year, dogs are allowed on the beach anytime during park hours. Dogs must be on leash at all times. People are required to clean up after their pets.

Sullivan Island Beach
Atlantic Avenue
Sullivan's Island, SC
843-883-3198
Dogs are allowed off leash on this barrier island beach from 5 AM to 10 AM April through October, and from 5 AM to 12 Noon November 1st to March 31st; this does not include walkways or access paths to the area where they must be leashed (no longer than 10 feet). A pet permit is required that can be obtained at the Town Hall at 1610 Middle Street-proof of vaccinations and rabies required. Dogs are NOT allowed on the beach, paths, or the adjacent waters at any time from 10 AM to 6 PM from April 1st to October 31st; however they are allowed at these areas on a leash from 6 PM to 5 AM, April 1st to October 31st, and from 12 Noon to 5 AM from November 1st to March 31st. Dogs must be under their owner's control at all times. Dogs must be leashed when not in designated off-lead areas.

# Texas Listings

Cole Park
Ocean Drive
Corpus Christi, TX
800-766-2322
Dogs on leash are allowed on the beach. People need to clean up after their pets.

Bryan Beach
Road 1495
Freeport, TX
979-233-3526
Pooches are allowed to come and frolic on this 3.5 mile long city beach or even primitive camp overnight; there are no facilities here. Dogs must be leashed and under their owner's immediate control at all times.

Big Reef Nature Park

Boddeker Drive
Galveston, TX
409-765-5023
Take a walkway to the beach which runs parallel to Bolivar Rd. Dogs on leash are allowed on the beach. People need to clean up after their pets. There are no day use fees. This park is part of East Beach which does not allow dogs on the pavilion. The beach is located on the east end of Galveston Isle, off Boddeker Drive.

Dellanera RV Park
FM 3005 at 7 Mile Rd.
Galveston, TX
409-740-0390
This RV park offers 1,000 feet of sandy beach. Dogs on leash are allowed on the beach and at the RV spaces. People need to clean up after their pets. There are over 60 full RV hookups, over 20 partial hookups and day parking. Picnic tables and restrooms are available at this park. There is a $5 day parking fee. RV spaces are about $25 and up.

Galveston Island State Park
14901 FM 3005
Galveston, TX
409-737-1222
Leashed dogs are allowed on the beach and at the campsites. There is a $3 per person (over 13 years old) day use fee. There is no charge for children 12 and under. The park can be reached from Interstate 45 by exiting right onto 61st Street and traveling south on 61st Street to its intersection with Seawall Boulevard and then right (west) on Seawall (FM 3005) 10 miles to the park entrance.

Stewart Beach
6th and Seawall Boulevard
Galveston, TX
409-765-5023
This is one of the best family beaches in Galveston. Many family-oriented events including a sandcastle competition are held at this beach. Restrooms, umbrella and chair rentals, and volleyball courts are available. There is a $7 per car admission fee. Dogs on leash are allowed on the beach. People need to clean up after their pets. The beach is located at 6th Street and Seawall Blvd.

Padre Island National Seashore
Highway 22
Padre Island, TX
361-949-8068
nps.gov/pais/
Visitors to this beach can swim, sunbathe, hunt for shells or just enjoy a walk. About 800,000 visitors per

year come to this park. Dogs on leash are allowed on the beach. People need to clean up after their pets. There is a minimal day use fee. The park is located on Padre Island, southeast of Corpus Christi.

Andy Bowie Park
Park Road 100
South Padre Island, TX
956-761-3704
Dogs on leash are allowed on the beach. People need to clean up after their pets. There is a minimal day use fee. This park is located on the northern end of South Padre Island.

Edwin K. Atwood Park
Park Road 100
South Padre Island, TX
956-761-3704
This beach offers 20 miles of beach driving. Dogs on leash are allowed on the beach. People need to clean up after their pets. There is a minimal day use fee. This park is located almost 1.5 miles north of Andy Bowie Park.

Isla Blanca Park
Park Road 100
South Padre Island, TX
956-761-5493
This popular beach offers about a mile of clean, white beach. Picnic tables, restrooms, and RV spaces are available at this park. Dogs on leash are allowed on the beach. People need to clean up after their pets. There is a minimal day use fee. The park is located on the southern tip of South Padre Island.

# Virginia Listings

First Landing State Park
2500 Shore Drive
Virginia Beach, VA
757-412-2300
first-landing-state-park.org/
Dogs on a 6 foot or less leash are allowed year-round on the beach. People need to clean up after their pet. All pets must have a rabies tag on their collar or proof of a rabies vaccine. To get there, take I-64. Then take the Northampton Blvd/US 13 North (Exit 282). You will pass eight lights and then turn right at the Shore Drive/US 60 exit. Turn right onto Shore Drive and go about 4.5 miles to the park entrance.

Virginia Beach Public Beaches
off Highway 60
Virginia Beach, VA
757-437-4919
Dogs are only allowed during off-season on Virginia Beach public beaches. From the Friday before Memorial Day through Labor Day weekend, pets are not allowed on public sand beaches, the boardwalk or the grassy area west of the boardwalk, from Rudee Inlet to 42nd Street. People are required to clean up after their pets and dogs must be leashed.

# Washington Listings

Fay Bainbridge State Park
Sunset Drive NE
Bainbridge Island, WA
360-902-8844
This park is located on the northeast side of Bainbridge Island on Puget Sound. On a clear day, you can see Mt. Rainer and Mt. Baker from the beach. Picnic tables, restrooms and campgrounds are available at this park. Leashed dogs are allowed on the beach. Pets are not permitted on designated swimming beaches. However, there is usually a non-designated swimming beach area as well. Dogs are also allowed at the campgrounds. They must be on a eight foot or less leash at all times and people are required to clean up after their pets. To get there from From Poulsbo, take Hwy. 305 toward Bainbridge Island. Cross the Agate Pass Bridge. After three miles, come to stoplight and big brown sign with directions to park. Turn left at traffic light onto Day Rd. NE. Travel approximately two miles to a T-intersection. Turn left onto Sunrise Drive NE, and continue to park entrance, about two miles away.

Birch Bay State Park
Grandview
Blaine, WA
360-902-8844
parks.state.wa.us/170/Birch-Bay
This beach, located near the Canadian border, offers panoramic coastal views. Picnic tables, restrooms (including an ADA restroom), and campgrounds (including ADA campsites) are available at this park. Leashed dogs are allowed on the beach. Pets are not permitted on designated swimming beaches. However, there is usually a non-designated swimming beach area as well. Dogs are also allowed in the campgrounds. They must be on a eight foot or less leash at all times and people are required to clean up after their pets. This park is located

20 miles north of Bellingham and ten miles south of Blaine. From the south take exit #266 off of I-5. Go left on Grandview for seven miles, then right on Jackson for one mile, then turn left onto Helweg. From the north take exit #266 off of I-5, and turn right onto Grandview.

Griffith-Priday State Park
State Route 109
Copalis Beach, WA
360-902-8844
This beach extends from the beach through low dunes to a river and then north to the river's mouth. Picnic tables and restrooms are available at this park. Dogs are allowed on the beach. They must be on a eight foot or less leash and people are required to clean up after their pets. This park is located 21 miles northwest of Hoquiam. From Hoquiam, go north on SR 109 for 21 miles. At Copalis Beach, at the sign for Benner Rd., turn left (west).

Saltwater State Park
Marine View Drive
Des Moines, WA
360-902-8844
parks.state.wa.us/578/Saltwater
This state beach is located on Puget Sound, halfway between the cities of Tacoma and Seattle (near the Sea-Tac international airport). Picnic tables, restrooms and campgrounds are available at this park. Leashed dogs are allowed on the beach. Pets are not permitted on designated swimming beaches. However, there is usually a non-designated swimming beach area as well. Dogs are also allowed at the campgrounds. They must be on a eight foot or less leash at all times and people are required to clean up after their pets. To get there from the north, take exit #149 off of I-5. Go west, then turn south on Hwy. 99 (sign missing). Follow the signs into the park. Turn right on 240th at the Midway Drive-in. Turn left on Marine View Dr. and turn right into the park.

Off-Leash Area and Beach
498 Admiral Way
Edmonds, WA
425-771-0230
olae.org
The Off-leash area and beach in Edmonds gives dogs a place to run free, swim and meet other dogs. The area is maintained and supported by O.L.A.E. and overseen by the City of Edmonds Parks and Rec Dept. From I-5 follow signs to the Edmonds Ferry until Dayton Street. Turn west on Dayton Street and then south on Admiral Way. The off-leash area is south of Marina Beach.

Howarth Park Dog Beach
1127 Olympic Blvd.
Everett, WA
425-257-8300
Most of the park and beach areas require that dogs are on-leash and there are fines for violations. There is an off-leash beach area north of the pedestrian bridge that crosses the railroad tracks. Your dog should be under excellent voice control at this beach if it is off-leash due to the nearby train tracks. In addition, the train may spook a dog. There are also some trails for leashed dogs. The park is open from 6 am to 10 pm.

Dash Point State Park
Dash Point Rd.
Federal Way, WA
360-902-8844
parks.state.wa.us/496/Dash-Point
This beach offers great views of Puget Sound. Picnic tables, restrooms, 11 miles of hiking trails and campgrounds are available at this park. Leashed dogs are allowed on the beach. Pets are not permitted on designated swimming beaches. However, there is usually a non-designated swimming beach area as well. Dogs are also allowed on hiking trails and campgrounds. They must be on a eight foot or less leash at all times and people are required to clean up after their pets. This park is located on the west side of Federal Way in the vicinity of Seattle. From Highway 5, exit at the 320th St. exit (exit #143). Take 320th St. west approximately four miles. When 320th St. ends at a T-intersection, make a right onto 47th St. When 47th St. ends at a T-intersection, turn left onto Hwy. 509/ Dash Point Rd. Drive about two miles to the park. (West side of street is the campground side, and east side is the day-use area.)

Double Bluff Beach
6400 Double Bluff Road
Freeland, WA
360-321-4049
fetchparks.org/doublebluff.html
South of Freeland and on Whidbey Island, this unfenced off-leash area also includes a dog beach. This is one of the largest off-leash beaches in the U.S. The off-leash beach is about 2 miles long. On clear days you can see Mt Rainier, the Seattle skyline and many ships. The beach nearest the parking lot is an on-leash area and the off-leash beach starts about 500 feet from the lot. There will be steep fines for dogs that are unleashed in an inappropriate area. From WA-525 watch for a sign for Double Bluff Road and it south. The road ends at the beach.

South Beach
125 Spring Street
Friday Harbor, WA
360-378-2902
Dogs on leash are allowed at South Beach, which is located at the American Camp in the San Juan Island National Historic Park.

Grayland Beach State Park
Highway 105
Grayland, WA
360-902-8844
This 412 acre park offers beautiful ocean frontage and full hookup campsites (including ADA campsites). Leashed dogs are allowed on the beach. Dogs are also allowed at the campgrounds. They must be on a eight foot or less leash at all times and people are required to clean up after their pets. This park is located five miles south of Westport. From Aberdeen, drive 22 miles on Highway 105 south to Grayland. Traveling through the town, watch for park signs.

Cape Disappointment State Park
Highway 101
Ilwaco, WA
360-902-8844
This park offers 27 miles of ocean beach and 7 miles of hiking trails. Enjoy excellent views of the ocean, Columbia River and two lighthouses. Picnic tables, restrooms (including an ADA restroom), hiking and campgrounds (includes ADA campsites) are available at this park. Leashed dogs are allowed on the beach. Dogs are also allowed on hiking trails and campgrounds. They must be on a eight foot or less leash at all times and people are required to clean up after their pets. This park is located two miles southwest of Ilwaco.From Seattle, Take I-5 south to Olympia, SR 8 west to Montesano. From there, take U.S. Hwy. 101 south to Long Beach Peninsula.

Spencer Spit State Park
Bakerview Road
Lopez Island, WA
360-902-8844
Located in the San Juan Islands, this lagoon beach offers great crabbing, clamming and beachcombing. Picnic tables, restrooms, campgrounds and 2 miles of hiking trails are available at this park. Leashed dogs are allowed on the beach. Pets are not permitted on designated swimming beaches. However, there is usually a non-designated swimming beach area as well. Dogs are also allowed on hiking trails and campgrounds. They

must be on a eight foot or less leash at all times and people are required to clean up after their pets. This park is located on Lopez Island in the San Juan Islands. It is a 45-minute Washington State Ferry ride from Anacortes. Dogs are allowed on the ferry. Once on Lopez Island, follow Ferry Rd. Go left at Center Rd., then left at Cross Rd. Turn right at Port Stanley and left at Bakerview Rd. Follow Bakerview Rd. straight into park. For ferry rates and schedules, call 206-464-6400.

Fort Ebey State Park
Hill Valley Drive
Oak Harbor, WA
360-902-8844
parks.state.wa.us/507/Fort-Ebey
This 600+ acre park is popular for hiking and camping, but also offers a saltwater beach. Picnic tables and restrooms (including an ADA restroom) are available at this park. Leashed dogs are allowed on the saltwater beach. Dogs are also allowed on hiking trails and campgrounds. They must be on a eight foot or less leash at all times and people are required to clean up after their pets. To get to the park from Seattle, take exit #189 off of I-5, just south of Everett. Follow signs for the Mukilteo/ Clinton ferry. Take the ferry to Clinton on Whidbey Island. Dogs are allowed on the ferry. Once on Whidbey Island, follow Hwy. 525 north, which becomes Hwy. 20. Two miles north of Coupeville, turn left on Libbey Rd. and follow it 1.5 miles to Hill Valley Dr. Turn left and enter park.

Joseph Whidbey State Park
Swantown Rd
Oak Harbor, WA
360-902-8844
This 112 acre park offers one of the best beaches on Whidbey Island. Picnic tables, restrooms, and several miles of hiking trails (including a half mile ADA hiking trail) are available at this park. Leashed dogs are allowed on the beach. Pets are not permitted on designated swimming beaches. However, there is usually a non-designated swimming beach area as well. Dogs are also allowed on hiking trails. They must be on a eight foot or less leash at all times and people are required to clean up after their pets. To get there from the south, drive north on Hwy. 20. Just before Oak Harbor, turn left on Swantown Rd. and follow it about three miles.

Pacific Pines State Park
Highway 101
Ocean Park, WA

360-902-8844
Fishing, crabbing, clamming and beachcombing are popular activities at this beach. Picnic tables and a restroom are available at this park. Dogs are allowed on the beach. They must be on a eight foot or less leash at all times and people are required to clean up after their pets. This park is located approximately one mile north of Ocean Park. From north or south, take Hwy. 101 until you reach Ocean Park. Continue on Vernon St. until you reach 271st St.

Ocean City State Park
State Route 115
Ocean Shores, WA
360-902-8844
parks.state.wa.us/554/Ocean-City
Beachcombing, clamming, surfing, bird watching, kite flying and winter storm watching are all popular activites at this beach. Picnic tables, restrooms, and campgrounds (including ADA campgrounds) are available at this park. Leashed dogs are allowed on the beach. Dogs are also allowed at the campgrounds. They must be on a eight foot or less leash at all times and people are required to clean up after their pets. This park is located on the coast one-and-a-half miles north of Ocean Shores on Hwy. 115. From Hoquiam, drive 16 miles west on SR 109, then turn south on SR 115 and drive 1.2 miles to the park.

Pacific Beach State Park
State Route 109
Pacific Beach, WA
360-902-8844
The beach is the focal point at this 10 acre state park. This sandy ocean beach is great for beachcombing, wildlife watching, windy walks and kite flying. Picnic tables, restrooms (including an ADA restroom), and campgrounds (some are ADA accessible) are available at this park. Leashed dogs are allowed on the beach. Dogs are also allowed in the campgrounds. They must be on a eight foot or less leash at all times and people are required to clean up after their pets. This park is located 15 miles north of Ocean Shores, off SR 109. From Hoquiam, follow SR 109, 30 miles northwest to the town of Pacific Beach. The park is located in town.

Kalaloch Beach
Olympic National Park
Port Angeles, WA
360-962-2283
nps.gov/olym/
Dogs are allowed on leash that is no longer than 6 feet, during daytime hours only, on Kalaloch Beach along the Pacific Ocean and from Rialto Beach north to Ellen Creek. These beaches are in Olympic National Park, but please note that pets are not permitted on this national park's trails, meadows, beaches (except Kalaloch and Rialto beaches) or in any undeveloped area of the park. For those folks and dogs who want to hike on a trail, try the adjacent dog-friendly Olympic National Forest. Kalaloch Beach is located off Highway 101 in Olympic National Park.

Alki Beach
1702 Alki Avenue SW
Seattle, WA

This is a really nice place to take your pup for a good jaunt along the beach in an area known to be strict about dogs being on the beach. A 2.5 mile boardwalk runs along the length of the beach giving an easy place for your canine companion to run/walk alongside. Dogs must be leashed and cleaned up after promptly.

Sand Point Magnuson Park Dog Off-Leash Beach and Area
7400 Sand Point Way NE
Seattle, WA
206-684-4075
This leash free dog park covers about 9 acres and is the biggest fully fenced off-leash park in Seattle. It also offers an access point to the lake where your pooch is welcome to take a dip in the fresh lake water. To find the dog park, take Sand Point Way Northeast and enter the park at Northeast 74th Street. Go straight and park near the playground and sports fields. The main gate to the off-leash area is located at the southeast corner of the main parking lot. Dogs must be leashed until you enter the off-leash area.

Twin Harbors State Park
Highway 105
Westport, WA
360-902-8844
This beach is popular for beachcombing, bird watching, and fishing. Picnic tables, restrooms (including an ADA restroom), and campgrounds (includes ADA campgrounds) are available at this park. Leashed dogs are allowed on the beach. Dogs are also allowed at the campgrounds. They must be on a eight foot or less leash at all times and people are required to clean up after their pets. This park is located three miles south of Westport on Highway 105. From Aberdeen,

Westport Light State Park
Ocean Avenue
Westport, WA
360-902-8844
Enjoy the panoramic view at this park or take the easy access trail to the beach. Swimming in the ocean here is not advised because of variable currents or rip tides. Picnic tables, restrooms (including an ADA restroom), and a 1.3 mile paved trail (also an ADA trail) are available at this park. Leashed dogs are allowed on the beach. Dogs are also allowed on the paved trail. They must be on a eight foot or less leash at all times and people are required to clean up after their pets. This park is located on the Pacific Ocean at Westport, 22 miles southwest of Aberdeen. To get there from Westport, drive west on Ocean Ave. about one mile to park entrance.

# Wisconsin Listings

Apostle Islands National Lakeshore
Route 1
Bayfield, WI
715-779-3398
nps.gov/apis/index.htm
You will pretty much need your own boat to access this park and beach as the boat cruise tours do not allow pets. If you do have a boat and can reach the islands, dogs are allowed on the trails, in the backcountry campgrounds and on the beaches but must be on a 6 foot or less leash at all times. People need to clean up after their pets.

Harrington Beach State Park
531 Highway D
Belgium, WI
262-285-3015
Pets are allowed only on part of South Beach. They must be leashed except while swimming in the water. But once out of the water, they need to be leashed. Pets are also allowed at one of the picnic areas and on all trails except for the nature trail. Please remember to clean up after your pet.

Kohler-Andrae State Park Beach
1020 Beach Park Lane
Sheboygan, WI
920-451-4080
Pets are not allowed on the swimming beaches but they are allowed only on the beach area north of the nature center. Pets must be on an 8 foot or less leash and cleaned up after. Pets can be off leash only in the water but if one paw hits the sand, he or she must be back on leash or

you may get a citation from a park ranger. Dogs are also allowed at certain campsites and on the regular hiking trails but not on nature trails, in the picnic areas or the playground.

Potawatomi State Park Beach
3740 Park Drive
Sturgeon Bay, WI
920-746-2890
Dogs are allowed on the beach but must be leashed except when in the water. To get there from Green Bay, take Highway 57 north. Go about 37 miles to County Highway PD. Turn north onto Highway PD and go 2.4 miles to the park entrance.

Point Beach State Forest
9400 County Highway O
Two Rivers, WI
920-794-7480
Pets are allowed only on a certain part of the beach, located south of the lighthouse. Dogs must be leashed at all times including on the beach and are not allowed in the picnic areas except for the one near the beach that allows dogs. Pets are also allowed on some of the park trails. Please remember to clean up after your pet.

# Canada

## British Columbia Listings

CRAB Park at Portside Off-Leash Dog Water Access and Dog Park
101 E Waterfront Road
Vancouver, BC
604-257-8400
The CRAB Park unfenced dog off-leash area and dog beach is available for off-leash play from 6 am to 10 am and 5 pm to 10 pm. The off-leash area is the east side of the park. Dogs are not allowed in the area of the playground. Dogs must be well-behaved, have a current license, leashed outside of the off-leash areas and cleaned up after.

Fraser River Park Off-Leash Dog Water Access and Dog Park
8705 Angus Drive
Vancouver, BC
604-257-8689
The Fraser River Park unfenced dog off-leash area and dog beach is available for off-leash play from 6 am to 10 am and 5 pm to 10 pm. Please see the signs outlining the off-leash area. Dogs must be well-behaved, have a current license, leashed outside of the off-leash areas and cleaned up after. The park is located at W 75th Avenue at Angus Drive.

John Hendry Park Off-Leash Dog Water Access and Dog Park
3300 Victoria Drive
Vancouver, BC
604-257-8613
The John Hendry Park unfenced dog off-leash area and dog beach is available for off-leash play from 5 am to 10 pm. Please see the signs outlining the off-leash area. Dogs must be well-behaved, have a current license, leashed outside of the off-leash areas and cleaned up after.

New Brighton Park Off-Leash Dog Water Access and Dog Park
8705 Angus Drive
Vancouver, BC
604-257-8613
The Fraser River Park unfenced dog off-leash area and dog beach is available for off-leash play from 5 am to 10 am from May 1 to September 30 and 5 am to 10 pm during the rest of the year. Please see the signs outlining the off-leash area. Dogs must be well-behaved, have a current

license, leashed outside of the off-leash areas and cleaned up after.

Spanish Bank Beach Park Off-Leash Dog Water Access and Dog Park
4801 NW Marine Drive
Vancouver, BC
604-257-8689
The Spanish Bank Beach Park unfenced dog off-leash area and dog beach is available for off-leash play from 6 am to 10 pm. Please see the signs outlining the off-leash area. Dogs must be well-behaved, have a current license, leashed outside of the off-leash areas and cleaned up after. The park is located on NW Marine Drive at the entrance to Pacific Spirit Park.

Sunset Beach Park Off-Leash Dog Water Access and Dog Park
1204 Beach Avenue
Vancouver, BC
604-257-8400
The Sunset Beach Park unfenced dog off-leash area and dog beach is available for off-leash play from 6 am to 10 pm. Please see the signs outlining the off-leash area. Dogs must be well-behaved, have a current license, leashed outside of the off-leash areas and cleaned up after.

Vanier Park Off-Leash Dog Water Access and Dog Park
1000 Chestnut Street
Vancouver, BC
604-257-8689
The Vanier Park unfenced dog off-leash area and dog beach is available for off-leash play from 6 am to 10 am and 5 pm to 10 pm from May 1 to September 30 and from 6 am to 10 pm during the rest of the year. Please see the signs outlining the off-leash area. Dogs must be well-behaved, have a current license, leashed outside of the off-leash areas and cleaned up after. The park is located at Chestnut Street at English Bay.

Dallas Road Off-Leash Beach
Dallas Road at Douglass St
Victoria, BC
250-385-5711
Dogs are allowed off-leash year round at the gravel beach in Beacon Hill Park. People are required to clean up after their dogs. The beach is located in downtown Victoria, along Dallas Road, between Douglas Street and Cook Street.

Gonzales Beach Off-Leash Area

South end of Foul Bay Rd
Victoria, BC
250-361-0600
Gonzales Beach is a large beach that circles Gonzales Bay in the south-eastern section of Victoria. Dogs are allowed on Gonzales Beach 24 hours a day except from June 1 to August 31 when they are not allowed on the beach at all. Dogs must be under control at all times, must be cleaned up after and must be on-leash whenever they are outside of the off-leash area.

## Ontario Listings

Kincardine Beaches
H 21, N of H 9 beside KFC (visitor center)
Kincardine, ON
519-396-3491
There are more than 30 km of sandy beaches here and dogs are allowed on the beaches (unless otherwise indicated) except at Station Beach. Dogs are allowed on no more than a 6 foot leash, and they must be cleaned up after promptly at all times.

Awenda Provincial Park
670 Concession 18 E
Penetanguishene, ON
705-549-2231
ontarioparks.com/park/awenda
At this park that sits overlooking the Georgian Bay is a pet beach area where dogs are allowed; it is at the 2nd beach site and there is signage once in the park. It is a seasonal park and the gates are locked during the off season; it is a 45 minute walk to the beach from this outer parking lot. Dogs are allowed on no more than a 6 foot leash, and they must be cleaned up after promptly at all times.

Port Burwell Provincial Park Beach
Box 9
Port Burwell, ON
519-874-4691
This park provides a beach for dog frolicking fun; there is signage directing pet owners to the section of beach where they are allowed. Dogs must be on no more than a 6 foot leash and cleaned up after promptly at all times.

Neys Provincial Park
H 17
Thunder Bay District, ON
807-229-1624
ontarioparks.com/park/neys
This park provides a beach for dog frolicking fun; there is signage directing pet owners to the section of beach where they are allowed. Dogs must be on no more than a 6 foot

leash and cleaned up after promptly at all times.

Wasaga Beach Provincial Park
Beach Drive
Wasaga Beach, ON
705-429-0412
This beach is home to the world's longest freshwater beach and is a prime tourist attraction. Dogs are allowed on one designated section - beach area #3. Otherwise dogs must stay on the grassy area that follows along the beach. This park closes in winter and there are no restrooms available; however, gate #1 is still left open for visitors. Dogs are allowed on no more than a 6 foot leash, and they must be cleaned up after promptly at all times.

Chapter 3

# Transportation

# Alaska Listings

The Stage Line
P.O. Box 353
Anchor Point, AK
907-868-3914
thestageline.net
This transportation bus services connects Anchorage, Homer, Kenai, Soldotna, and Seward. Dogs are also allowed for transport; their tickets are 1/2 price and they must be kenneled and ride in the back. With prior arrangements a larger dog may be permitted to go and the back seat would be removed for more space.

The Stage Line
P.O. Box 353
Anchor Point, AK
907-868-3914
thestageline.net
This transportation bus services connects Anchorage, Homer, Kenai, Soldotna, and Seward. Dogs are also allowed for transport; their tickets are 1/2 price and they must be kenneled and ride in the back. With prior arrangements a larger dog may be permitted to go and the back seat would be removed for more space.

The Stage Line
P.O. Box 353
Anchor Point, AK
907-868-3914
thestageline.net
This transportation bus services connects Anchorage, Homer, Kenai, Soldotna, and Seward. Dogs are also allowed for transport; their tickets are 1/2 price and they must be kenneled and ride in the back. With prior arrangements a larger dog may be permitted to go and the back seat would be removed for more space.

The Stage Line
P.O. Box 353
Anchor Point, AK
907-868-3914
thestageline.net
This transportation bus services connects Anchorage, Homer, Kenai, Soldotna, and Seward. Dogs are also allowed for transport; their tickets are 1/2 price and they must be kenneled and ride in the back. With prior arrangements a larger dog may be permitted to go and the back seat would be removed for more space.

The Stage Line
P.O. Box 353
Anchor Point, AK
907-868-3914
thestageline.net
This transportation bus services

connects Anchorage, Homer, Kenai, Soldotna, and Seward. Dogs are also allowed for transport; their tickets are 1/2 price and they must be kenneled and ride in the back. With prior arrangements a larger dog may be permitted to go and the back seat would be removed for more space.

Alaska Air Transit
2331 Merrill Field Drive #A
Anchorage, AK
907-276-5422
alaskaairtransit.com/
This air service company provides flightseeing and taxi service for the state of Alaska. Dogs are not allowed on tours; however, they are allowed for taxi service by charter. If the pet is well behaved and leashed, a kennel is not needed. Charter rates run from $700 per hour plus 7.5% tax and fuel surcharge, and up to 8 people can be transported.

Birchwood Air Services
1000 Merrill Field Drive
Anchorage, AK
907-276-0402
This air service company will transport canine companions also. The fee is $40 for a small dog, $65 for a medium dog, and $95 for a large dog each way. Dogs can ride up front with owners, and they must be under their owner's control and leashed or crated at all times.

Era Aviation
6160 Carl Brady Drive (HQ)
Anchorage, AK
800-866-8394
flyera.com/
Offering air service to a number of Alaskan areas, this company will transport dogs for an additional fee of $50 per pet each way. Kennels must be provided by owners and they may not be over a 500 series.

Grant Aviation
4451 Aircraft Drive
Anchorage, AK
888-Fly-Grant (359-4726)
flygrant.com
This air transport company has 7 bases throughout the state and services over 100 communities. Their services include daily and weekly schedules, charter services, and cargo runs. Dogs of all sizes are also allowed for air transport for an additional fee of $30 one way or round trip passage. Dogs must be kenneled during flight; there is usually an extra kennel on-site if needed.

Rust's Flying Service
P.O. Box 190867
Anchorage, AK
907-243-1595
flyrusts.com/
This air service company provides flightseeing and taxi service for the state of Alaska. Dogs are not allowed on tours; however, they are allowed for taxi service by charter. If the pet is well behaved and leashed, a kennel is not needed. Charter rates run from about $375 to $500 per hour.

Alaska Ferry
14 miles north of downtown Juneau
Auke Bay, AK
360-676-8445 (800-642-0066)
dot.state.ak.us/amhs
The Alaska Ferry, or Alaska Maritime Highway System connects Bellingham, Washington and Prince Rupert, BC with many Alaskan ports and also serves these Alaskan ports with Car, RV and passenger service. The ferry is essential, as many of the ports served are not accessible from the mainland by car, only by ferry or air. Dogs are allowed, but with significant restrictions. They must remain on the car deck at all times. If you have an RV or a car, this means that the dog must remain in the vehicle. If you are a foot passenger, you will have to leave your pet on the car deck in a closed kennel. You may not visit the car deck while the ferry is not in port. An exception is made for ferry segments greater than 8 hours, where they will hold occasional pet visits to the car deck to allow the dogs to relieve themselves. This is not much fun for the dogs, so we recommend that you stop often at intermediate ports with pets. In port, you may take your dog off of the ferry usually for about 20 minutes to 45 minutes. The ferry serves the Southeast area of Alaska, the Prince William Sound area, and Kodiak and points in the Aleutian Islands. The pet information is listed at http://www.dot.state.ak.us/amhs/pets.shtml.

Coyote Air
Po Box 9053/City Airport
Coldfoot, AK
907-678-5995
flycoyote.com/
In addition to providing sightseeing flights, this air service company will also help travelers with trip planning- including everything from weather conditions to the contacts needed for each leg of the journey. Customers with pets may charter the plane individually; the fee is $725 per hour with room for 4 to 6 people depending

on size of adults and pooches. Dogs must be under their owner's control and leashed or crated at all times.

**Alaska Ferry**
4 Blocks NE of downtown
Cordova, AK
907-424-7333 (800-642-0066)
dot.state.ak.us/amhs
The Alaska Ferry, or Alaska Maritime Highway System connects Bellingham, Washington and Prince Rupert, BC with many Alaskan ports and also serves these Alaskan ports with Car, RV and passenger service. The ferry is essential, as many of the ports served are not accessible from the mainland by car, only by ferry or air. Dogs are allowed, but with significant restrictions. They must remain on the car deck at all times. If you have an RV or a car, this means that the dog must remain in the vehicle. If you are a foot passenger, you will have to leave your pet on the car deck in a closed kennel. You may not visit the car deck while the ferry is not in port. An exception is made for ferry segments greater than 8 hours, where they will hold occasional pet visits to the car deck to allow the dogs to relieve themselves. This is not much fun for the dogs, so we recommend that you stop often at intermediate ports with pets. In port, you may take your dog off of the ferry usually for about 20 minutes to 45 minutes. The ferry serves the Southeast area of Alaska, the Prince William Sound area, and Kodiak and points in the Aleutian Islands. The pet information is listed at http://www.dot.state.ak.us/amhs/pets.shtml.

**Alaska Inter-Island Ferry**
P. O. Box 495
Craig, AK
866-308-4848
interislandferry.com/
This ferry provides service between Ketchikan and Hollis, and between Coffman Cove and Wrangell. Dogs are allowed on board for no additional fee on the auto deck, either in the car or in an owner provided container.

**Frontier Flying Service Inc**
5245 Airport Industrial Road
Fairbanks, AK
907-450-7200
frontierflying.com/
Flying the frontiers of Alaska, this passenger and freight company will also transport dogs. The fee is $50 each way for a series 300 kennel or less, and $100 each way for a series 400 kennel or larger. Owners must supply the kennel.

**Larry's Flying Service/ East Ramp**

International Airport
3822 University Avenue S
Fairbanks, AK
907-474-9169
larrysflying.com/
This air service company will transport dogs when the plane is chartered solely by the pet owner; the fee is $350 per hour and they can hold up to 5 to 8 passengers/pets depending on the plane. Kennels must be provided by the owner's and 400 series kennels are the largest allowed.

**Alaska Ferry**
5 miles north of downtown
Haines, AK
907-766-2113 (800-642-0066)
dot.state.ak.us/amhs
The Alaska Ferry, or Alaska Maritime Highway System connects Bellingham, Washington and Prince Rupert, BC with many Alaskan ports and also serves these Alaskan ports with Car, RV and passenger service. The ferry is essential, as many of the ports served are not accessible from the mainland by car, only by ferry or air. Dogs are allowed, but with significant restrictions. They must remain on the car deck at all times. If you have an RV or a car, this means that the dog must remain in the vehicle. If you are a foot passenger, you will have to leave your pet on the car deck in a closed kennel. You may not visit the car deck while the ferry is not in port. An exception is made for ferry segments greater than 8 hours, where they will hold occasional pet visits to the car deck to allow the dogs to relieve themselves. This is not much fun for the dogs, so we recommend that you stop often at intermediate ports with pets. In port, you may take your dog off of the ferry usually for about 20 minutes to 45 minutes. The ferry serves the Southeast area of Alaska, the Prince William Sound area, and Kodiak and points in the Aleutian Islands. The pet information is listed at http://www.dot.state.ak.us/amhs/pets.shtml.

**Haines-Skagway Fast Ferry**
121 Beach Road
Haines, AK
907-766-2100
hainesskagwayfastferry.com
Dogs are allowed on the ferry for an additional fee of $5 per pet per trip. They are only allowed for water taxi service and not allowed on tours or cruises. Dogs must be under their owner's control, leashed, and cleaned up after at all times.

**LAB Flying Services**
Main and 4th
Haines, AK
907-766-2222
labflying.com/
Dogs are allowed on regular scheduled flights; a fee for a small kennel is $30; a medium is $40; a large is $60, and an extra-large is $150. There is no additional pet fee when the plane is chartered.

**Alaska Ferry**
4558 Homer Spit Rd
Homer, AK
907-235-8449 (800-642-0066)
dot.state.ak.us/amhs
The Alaska Ferry, or Alaska Maritime Highway System connects Bellingham, Washington and Prince Rupert, BC with many Alaskan ports and also serves these Alaskan ports with Car, RV and passenger service. The ferry is essential, as many of the ports served are not accessible from the mainland by car, only by ferry or air. Dogs are allowed, but with significant restrictions. They must remain on the car deck at all times. If you have an RV or a car, this means that the dog must remain in the vehicle. If you are a foot passenger, you will have to leave your pet on the car deck in a closed kennel. You may not visit the car deck while the ferry is not in port. An exception is made for ferry segments greater than 8 hours, where they will hold occasional pet visits to the car deck to allow the dogs to relieve themselves. This is not much fun for the dogs, so we recommend that you stop often at intermediate ports with pets. In port, you may take your dog off of the ferry usually for about 20 minutes to 45 minutes. The ferry serves the Southeast area of Alaska, the Prince William Sound area, and Kodiak and points in the Aleutian Islands. The pet information is listed at http://www.dot.state.ak.us/amhs/pets.shtml.

**Grant Aviation**
3720 FAA Road # 110
Homer, AK
907-235-2757 (888-359-4726)
flygrant.com
This commuter airline flys between Homer and Anchorage many times a day. The flight takes under one hour. They fly 9 seat airplanes and a dog may travel with you. The dog must be in a crate and will be behind the last seats. There is a charge of about $1 per pound for the dog and crate, so a 50 pound dog with a 10 pound kennel would cost an extra $60.

**Kachemak Bay Flying Services**

1158 Lakeshore Drive
Homer, AK
907-235-8924
alaskaseaplanes.com/
Offering flight service in Kachemak Bay area, this float plane will also take canine companions for no additional fee. The plane can be chartered for a fee of $150 per adult per hour with a 2 person minimum. They request to first meet the dog, and they must be friendly, well behaved, leashed (or kenneled), and cleaned up after at all times.

Wings of Alaska
8421 Livingston Way
Juneau, AK
907-789-0790
Serving Southeast Alaska, this air service provider offers fast freight and charter service in addition to scheduled passenger service. Dogs are allowed for transport for 1½ times normal freight rate or there can be a slightly higher fee if going as passenger luggage. Dogs must be leashed or crated when in cargo. The cargo office number is 907-790-3100.

Wings of Alaska
8421 Livingston Way
Juneau, AK
907-697-2201
Serving Southeast Alaska, this air service provider offers fast freight and charter service in addition to scheduled passenger service. Dogs are allowed for transport for 1½ times normal freight rate or there can be a slightly higher fee if going as passenger luggage. Dogs must be leashed or crated when in cargo. The cargo office number is 907-790-3100.

Wings of Alaska
8421 Livingston Way
Juneau, AK
907-766-2030
Serving Southeast Alaska, this air service provider offers fast freight and charter service in addition to scheduled passenger service. Dogs are allowed for transport for 1½ times normal freight rate or there can be a slightly higher fee if going as passenger luggage. Dogs must be leashed or crated when in cargo. The cargo office number is 907-790-3100.

Wings of Alaska
8421 Livingston Way
Juneau, AK
907-983-2442
Serving Southeast Alaska, this air service provider offers fast freight and charter service in addition to scheduled passenger service. Dogs are allowed for transport for 1½ times

normal freight rate or there can be a slightly higher fee if going as passenger luggage. Dogs must be leashed or crated when in cargo. The cargo office number is 907-790-3100.

Grant Aviation
305 N Willow St
Kenai, AK
907-283-6012 (888-359-4726)
flygrant.com
This commuter airline flys between Kenai and Anchorage many times a day. The flight takes under one hour. They fly 9 seat airplanes and a dog may travel with you. The dog must be in a crate and will be behind the last seats. There is a charge of about $1 per pound for the dog and crate, so a 50 pound dog with a 10 pound kennel would cost an extra $60.

Alaska Ferry
2.5 north of Downtown
Ketchikan, AK
907-225-6181 (800-642-0066)
dot.state.ak.us/amhs
The Alaska Ferry, or Alaska Maritime Highway System connects Bellingham, Washington and Prince Rupert, BC with many Alaskan ports and also serves these Alaskan ports with Car, RV and passenger service. The ferry is essential, as many of the ports served are not accessible from the mainland by car, only by ferry or air. Dogs are allowed, but with significant restrictions. They must remain on the car deck at all times. If you have an RV or a car, this means that the dog must remain in the vehicle. If you are a foot passenger, you will have to leave your pet on the car deck in a closed kennel. You may not visit the car deck while the ferry is not in port. An exception is made for ferry segments greater than 8 hours, where they will hold occasional pet visits to the car deck to allow the dogs to relieve themselves. This is not much fun for the dogs, so we recommend that you stop often at intermediate ports with pets. In port, you may take your dog off of the ferry usually for about 20 minutes to 45 minutes. The ferry serves the Southeast area of Alaska, the Prince William Sound area, and Kodiak and points in the Aleutian Islands. The pet information is listed at http://www.dot.state.ak.us/amhs/pet s.shtml.

Island Wings Air Service
1935Tongass Avenue/H 7
Ketchikan, AK
907-225-2444

islandwings.com/
This air service offers a variety of tour and recreational options. Dogs are allowed on board if the plane is chartered by their owner for a sum of $575 per hour; the dog fee is inclusive. They are not allowed on board with other travelers. Dogs must be well behaved, under their owner's control, and leashed or kenneled at all times.

Alaska Ferry
100 Marine Way
Kodiak, AK
907-486-3800 (800-642-0066)
dot.state.ak.us/amhs
The Alaska Ferry, or Alaska Maritime Highway System connects Bellingham, Washington and Prince Rupert, BC with many Alaskan ports and also serves these Alaskan ports with Car, RV and passenger service. The ferry is essential, as many of the ports served are not accessible from the mainland by car, only by ferry or air. Dogs are allowed, but with significant restrictions. They must remain on the car deck at all times. If you have an RV or a car, this means that the dog must remain in the vehicle. If you are a foot passenger, you will have to leave your pet on the car deck in a closed kennel. You may not visit the car deck while the ferry is not in port. An exception is made for ferry segments greater than 8 hours, where they will hold occasional pet visits to the car deck to allow the dogs to relieve themselves. This is not much fun for the dogs, so we recommend that you stop often at intermediate ports with pets. In port, you may take your dog off of the ferry usually for about 20 minutes to 45 minutes. The ferry serves the Southeast area of Alaska, the Prince William Sound area, and Kodiak and points in the Aleutian Islands. The pet information is listed at http://www.dot.state.ak.us/amhs/pets. shtml.

Sea Hawk Air
506 Trident Way
Kodiak, AK
907-486-8282
seahawkair.com
Flying from their base in Kodiak, this seaplane company services the Kodiak Island and the Alaska Peninsula. They suggest allowing for a few extra days on your trip in case of inclement weather. Dogs of all sizes are also allowed for air transport for no additional fee; they are just included in the weight. Dogs must be crated and under their owner's control at all times; there may be times where only a leash is required.

Sea Hawk Air Inc
505 Trident Way
Kodiak, AK
907-486-8282
seahawkair.com/
This air service company provides recreational, business, and personal flights throughout the year for Kodiak Island and the Alaskan Peninsula. Dogs are not allowed for tours, but they will provide taxi services. The fee is determined by combined weight which includes the dog. The only request the company makes is that dogs must be dry for transport. Dogs must be well behaved, under their owner's control, and leashed or crated at all times.

Bering Air
1470 Sepalla Drive
Nome, AK
907-443-5464
beringair.com/
With an exception of a couple of holiday days, this air service company is providing private charters and a number of services for visitors and 32 Western Alaska cities, with hubs in Nome, Kotzebue, and Unalakleet. They will also transport pets for a fee based on a percentage of size, weight, and destination. Owners supply the transport kennel.

Alaska Ferry
0.9 Miles South of Downtown
Petersburg, AK
907-772-3855 (800-642-0066)
dot.state.ak.us/amhs
The Alaska Ferry, or Alaska Maritime Highway System connects Bellingham, Washington and Prince Rupert, BC with many Alaskan ports and also serves these Alaskan ports with Car, RV and passenger service. The ferry is essential, as many of the ports served are not accessible from the mainland by car, only by ferry or air. Dogs are allowed, but with significant restrictions. They must remain on the car deck at all times. If you have an RV or a car, this means that the dog must remain in the vehicle. If you are a foot passenger, you will have to leave your pet on the car deck in a closed kennel. You may not visit the car deck while the ferry is not in port. An exception is made for ferry segments greater than 8 hours, where they will hold occasional pet visits to the car deck to allow the dogs to relieve themselves. This is not much fun for the dogs, so we recommend that you stop often at intermediate ports with pets. In port, you may take your dog off of the ferry usually for about 20 minutes to 45 minutes. The ferry serves the

Southeast area of Alaska, the Prince William Sound area, and Kodiak and points in the Aleutian Islands. The pet information is listed at http://www.dot.state.ak.us/amhs/pets.shtml.

Alaska Ferry
downtown
Seldovia, AK
907-234-7868 (800-642-0066)
dot.state.ak.us/amhs
The Alaska Ferry, or Alaska Maritime Highway System connects Bellingham, Washington and Prince Rupert, BC with many Alaskan ports and also serves these Alaskan ports with Car, RV and passenger service. The ferry is essential, as many of the ports served are not accessible from the mainland by car, only by ferry or air. Dogs are allowed, but with significant restrictions. They must remain on the car deck at all times. If you have an RV or a car, this means that the dog must remain in the vehicle. If you are a foot passenger, you will have to leave your pet on the car deck in a closed kennel. You may not visit the car deck while the ferry is not in port. An exception is made for ferry segments greater than 8 hours, where they will hold occasional pet visits to the car deck to allow the dogs to relieve themselves. This is not much fun for the dogs, so we recommend that you stop often at intermediate ports with pets. In port, you may take your dog off of the ferry usually for about 20 minutes to 45 minutes. The ferry serves the Southeast area of Alaska, the Prince William Sound area, and Kodiak and points in the Aleutian Islands. The pet information is listed at http://www.dot.state.ak.us/amhs/pets.shtml.

Alaska Ferry
7.1 Miles North of Downtown
Sitka, AK
907-747-3300 (800-642-0066)
dot.state.ak.us/amhs
The Alaska Ferry, or Alaska Maritime Highway System connects Bellingham, Washington and Prince Rupert, BC with many Alaskan ports and also serves these Alaskan ports with Car, RV and passenger service. The ferry is essential, as many of the ports served are not accessible from the mainland by car, only by ferry or air. Dogs are allowed, but with significant restrictions. They must remain on the car deck at all times. If you have an RV or a car, this means that the dog must remain in the vehicle. If you are a foot passenger, you will have to leave your pet on the car deck in a closed

kennel. You may not visit the car deck while the ferry is not in port. An exception is made for ferry segments greater than 8 hours, where they will hold occasional pet visits to the car deck to allow the dogs to relieve themselves. This is not much fun for the dogs, so we recommend that you stop often at intermediate ports with pets. In port, you may take your dog off of the ferry usually for about 20 minutes to 45 minutes. The ferry serves the Southeast area of Alaska, the Prince William Sound area, and Kodiak and points in the Aleutian Islands. The pet information is listed at http://www.dot.state.ak.us/amhs/pets.shtml.

Alaska Ferry
3 Blocks South of Downtown
Skagway, AK
907-983-2229 (800-642-0066)
dot.state.ak.us/amhs
The Alaska Ferry, or Alaska Maritime Highway System connects Bellingham, Washington and Prince Rupert, BC with many Alaskan ports and also serves these Alaskan ports with Car, RV and passenger service. The ferry is essential, as many of the ports served are not accessible from the mainland by car, only by ferry or air. Dogs are allowed, but with significant restrictions. They must remain on the car deck at all times. If you have an RV or a car, this means that the dog must remain in the vehicle. If you are a foot passenger, you will have to leave your pet on the car deck in a closed kennel. You may not visit the car deck while the ferry is not in port. An exception is made for ferry segments greater than 8 hours, where they will hold occasional pet visits to the car deck to allow the dogs to relieve themselves. This is not much fun for the dogs, so we recommend that you stop often at intermediate ports with pets. In port, you may take your dog off of the ferry usually for about 20 minutes to 45 minutes. The ferry serves the Southeast area of Alaska, the Prince William Sound area, and Kodiak and points in the Aleutian Islands. The pet information is listed at http://www.dot.state.ak.us/amhs/pets.shtml.

Haines-Skagway Fast Ferry
121 Beach Road
Skagway, AK
907-766-2100
hainesskagwayfastferry.com
Dogs are allowed on the ferry for an additional fee of $5 per pet per trip. They are only allowed for water taxi service and not allowed on tours or cruises. Dogs must be under their

owner's control, leashed, and cleaned up after at all times.

Alaska Ferry
West End of City Dock
Valdez, AK
907-835-4436 (800-642-0066)
dot.state.ak.us/amhs
The Alaska Ferry, or Alaska Maritime Highway System connects Bellingham, Washington and Prince Rupert, BC with many Alaskan ports and also serves these Alaskan ports with Car, RV and passenger service. The ferry is essential, as many of the ports served are not accessible from the mainland by car, only by ferry or air. Dogs are allowed, but with significant restrictions. They must remain on the car deck at all times. If you have an RV or a car, this means that the dog must remain in the vehicle. If you are a foot passenger, you will have to leave your pet on the car deck in a closed kennel. You may not visit the car deck while the ferry is not in port. An exception is made for ferry segments greater than 8 hours, where they will hold occasional pet visits to the car deck to allow the dogs to relieve themselves. This is not much fun for the dogs, so we recommend that you stop often at intermediate ports with pets. In port, you may take your dog off of the ferry usually for about 20 minutes to 45 minutes. The ferry serves the Southeast area of Alaska, the Prince William Sound area, and Kodiak and points in the Aleutian Islands. The pet information is listed at http://www.dot.state.ak.us/amhs/pets.shtml.

Alaska Ferry
In Town
Whittier, AK
907-472-2378 (800-642-0066)
dot.state.ak.us/amhs
The Alaska Ferry, or Alaska Maritime Highway System connects Bellingham, Washington and Prince Rupert, BC with many Alaskan ports and also serves these Alaskan ports with Car, RV and passenger service. The ferry is essential, as many of the ports served are not accessible from the mainland by car, only by ferry or air. Dogs are allowed, but with significant restrictions. They must remain on the car deck at all times. If you have an RV or a car, this means that the dog must remain in the vehicle. If you are a foot passenger, you will have to leave your pet on the car deck in a closed kennel. You may not visit the car deck while the ferry is not in port. An exception is made for ferry segments greater than 8 hours, where they will hold occasional pet

visits to the car deck to allow the dogs to relieve themselves. This is not much fun for the dogs, so we recommend that you stop often at intermediate ports with pets. In port, you may take your dog off of the ferry usually for about 20 minutes to 45 minutes. The ferry serves the Southeast area of Alaska, the Prince William Sound area, and Kodiak and points in the Aleutian Islands. The pet information is listed at http://www.dot.state.ak.us/amhs.shtml.

Alaska Ferry
2 Blocks North of Downtown
Wrangell, AK
907-874-3711 (800-642-0066)
dot.state.ak.us/amhs
The Alaska Ferry, or Alaska Maritime Highway System connects Bellingham, Washington and Prince Rupert, BC with many Alaskan ports and also serves these Alaskan ports with Car, RV and passenger service. The ferry is essential, as many of the ports served are not accessible from the mainland by car, only by ferry or air. Dogs are allowed, but with significant restrictions. They must remain on the car deck at all times. If you have an RV or a car, this means that the dog must remain in the vehicle. If you are a foot passenger, you will have to leave your pet on the car deck in a closed kennel. You may not visit the car deck while the ferry is not in port. An exception is made for ferry segments greater than 8 hours, where they will hold occasional pet visits to the car deck to allow the dogs to relieve themselves. This is not much fun for the dogs, so we recommend that you stop often at intermediate ports with pets. In port, you may take your dog off of the ferry usually for about 20 minutes to 45 minutes. The ferry serves the Southeast area of Alaska, the Prince William Sound area, and Kodiak and points in the Aleutian Islands. The pet information is listed at http://www.dot.state.ak.us/amhs.shtml.

## Arizona Listings

Arizona Valley Metro Bus
302 N 1st Avenue, Suite 700
Phoenix, AZ
602-262-7433
valleymetro.org/valley_metro/
Although service animals are allowed on busses without size restriction; non-service animals may only be brought on board if they can comfortably fit in a hand held carrier and do not take up a seat. Dogs

must be well mannered and under owner's control at all times.

## California Listings

San Diego Pet Driver
7514 Girard Avenue
La Jolla, CA
619-252-5244
sandiegopetdriver.com/
Professionals trained in pet handling and safety offer VIP transportation in pet safe vehicles throughout the local San Diego area. Additional services offered include walking or sitting with your pet, taking them to the beach or park, or to pick up and deliver pet food, medicine, or supplies.

Metro Transit Authority
1 Gateway Plaza
Los Angeles, CA
213-580-7500
metro.net
Small dogs in an enclosed carrier are allowed on the light rail and buses for no additional fee.

BART (Bay Area Rapid Transit)
Regional
Oakland, CA
888-968-7282
bart.gov
A small dog in an enclosed carrier is allowed on BART trains.

RT (Rapid Transit)
Regional
Sacramento, CA
916-321-2877
sacrt.com
Small dogs in carriers are allowed on the buses and light rail. The carrier must fit on the person's lap.

Metropolitan Transit System
Regional
San Diego, CA
619-233-3004
Small dogs in enclosed carriers are allowed on the buses and light rail. You must be able to transport your dog and the carrier by yourself, and you need to hold the carrier on your lap. Noise or odor may give cause for refusal to transport the animal.

BART (Bay Area Rapid Transit)
Regional
San Francisco, CA
888-968-7282
bart.gov
A small dog in an enclosed carrier is allowed on BART trains.

SF Municipal Railway (MUNI)
Throughout City
San Francisco, CA
415-673-6864

sfmuni.com
Both small and large dogs are allowed on cable cars, historic streetcars and trolley buses. People must pay the same fare for their dog that they do for themselves. Dogs are allowed to ride on Muni vehicles from 9 a.m. to 3 p.m. and from 7 p.m. to 5 a.m. on weekdays, and all day on Saturdays, Sundays, and holidays. Only one of dog may ride per vehicle. Dogs must be muzzled and on a short leash or in a small closed container.

# Colorado Listings

RTD
Regional
Denver, CO
303-299-6000
rtd-denver.com
Small dogs in hard-sided carriers are allowed on the buses and light rail.

# Connecticut Listings

The Chester - Hadlyme Ferry
Ferry Landing
Chester, CT
860-526-2743
This ferry runs between April 1st and November 30th providing a convenient link across the Connecticut River between Chester and Hadlyme. Well behaved dogs on leash are allowed on the ferry for no additional fee.

Cross Sound Ferry Services
2 Ferry Street, PO Box 33
New London, CT
860-443-5281
longislandferry.com/Default.asp
This auto ferry service provides transportation between New London, CT and Orient Point on Long Island, NY. Dogs are allowed on the car ferry in dog designated areas only for no additional fee. Dogs must be well behaved, leashed or in an approved pet carrier, and cleaned up after at all times.

Cross Sound Ferry Services
2 Ferry Street, PO Box 33
New London, CT
860-443-5281
longislandferry.com/Default.asp
This auto ferry service provides transportation between New London, CT and Orient Point on Long Island, NY. Dogs are allowed on the car ferry in dog designated areas only for no additional fee. Dogs must be well

behaved, leashed or in an approved pet carrier, and cleaned up after at all times.

Fishers Island Ferry
5 Waterfront Park
New London, CT
860-442-0165
fiferry.com/
This is the connector ferry between New London, Connecticut and Fisher's Island, New York. Dogs of all sizes are allowed for no addition fee. Dogs must be well behaved, leashed, and cleaned up after at all times.

Thimble Islands Cruise & Charters
P.O. Box 3138
Stony Creek, CT
203-488-8905
thimbleislandcruise.com/
Well behaved pooches are welcome aboard the ferry for transport to the islands for no additional fee; they are not allowed on tours. Dogs must be crated or leashed, cleaned up after, and under their owner's control at all times.

# D.C. Listings

WMATA
Regional
Washington, DC
202-962-1234
wmata.com
Small dogs in carriers are allowed on the buses and trains. Pets must remain in the carrier, with no possibility that the pet can get out.

# Florida Listings

Executive Jet Charters
240 SW 34th Street
Fort Lauderdale, FL
954-359-9991 (888-355-5387)
jetscapefbo.com
This airline charter company offers charter flights from Florida to points in the Caribbean. Dogs are allowed for no additional fee unless extra cleaning is required. They are allowed in the cabin, leashed or crated, and they must be of a calm nature.

Island Air Charters
1050 Lee Wagener Boulevard Suite 102
Fort Lauderdale, FL
954-359-9942 (800-444-9904)
islandaircharters.com
Dogs are allowed on chartered aircraft for no additional fee; they are

allowed in the cabin on lap or leashed on the floor. Charters run from about $650 up depending on the destination.

Queen Mary II
Port of Ft Lauderdale
Fort Lauderdale, FL
800-728-6273
cunard.com/Ships/Queen-Mary-2/
Considered to be the grandest ship ever built to date, this luxury ocean liner features indulgences from bow to stern. Travelers can enjoy all the modern amenities as well as it's striking opulent decor, world class dining and entertainment, lounges, theaters, personalized services, and a Planetariu - the only one at sea. Travelers may embark from a dozen ports around the world; the US ports are Ft Lauderdale, Los Angeles, and New York. Dogs are allowed on board and preplanning is highly recommended as there are only a limited number of kennels. Depending on the destination, certain preparations must be made for the dogs that usually take up to about 6 months prior to the trip: example - blood work, shots, destination requirements, etc. One kennel will accommodate dogs 25 pounds and under; dogs over 25 pounds will need 2 kennels. A Kennel Master is always on duty to see to the walking, feeding, and cleaning of their canine guests.

Each kennel costs $700 per trip.

Miami/Dade Transit
South of SW 216 Street
Miami, FL
305-770-3131
co.miami-dade.fl.us/transit/
A small dog in an enclosed, escape proof carrier are allowed on Metro-rail and Metro buses at no additional fee.

LYNX
Regional
Orlando, FL
407-841-5969
golynx.com
Small dogs in carriers that fit on your lap are allowed on the buses.

Broward County Transit (BCT)
3201 W Cobans Road
Pompano Beach, FL
954-357-8400
broward.org/bct
A small dog in a carrier is allowed on the trains or buses at no additional fee.

Fair Wind Air Charter
2555 S.E. Witham Field
Stuart, FL
772-288-4130 (800-989-9665)

flyfairwind.com
This airline charter company offers charter flights from Florida to points in the Caribbean. Dogs are allowed on some of their aircraft for no additional fee unless extra cleaning is required. They are allowed in the cabin crated or leashed. These charter flights use jet airplanes of various sizes.

Karl Klopman Transportation
Throughout Palm Beach and Broward Counties
West Palm Beach, FL
561-312-6117
This limo/car transportation service serves the region from Palm Beach to Ft Lauderdale with airport and port service and car services to other destinations. You may bring small or medium sized dogs up to around 30 pounds.

# Georgia Listings

MARTA
Regional
Atlanta, GA
404-848-4900
itsmarta.com
Small dogs carried in a closed pet carrier that fits on your lap are allowed on the buses and trains.

# Hawaii Listings

Island Air
550 Paiea St. Ste. 236
Honolulu, HI
1-800-652-6541
Island Air is a airline based in Honolulu, Hawaii. It operates scheduled inter-island passenger services in Hawaii. Pets are allowed on Island Air's flights. Call their reservations department at 1-800-652-6541 to list your pet on any Island Air flight. There are only 4 pets allowed per flight - 2 in the cabin and 2 in the cargo hold. Approved animals are subject to an additional fare (AFC) of $35.00, and your pet must remain in the carrier at all times at airport facilities and during the flight. The pet carrier will be accepted as a carry-on baggage in addition to the passenger's carry-on baggage allowance. The pet carrier must fit under the passenger seat. All other pets must be shipped in the cargo compartment on a space-available basis. The total weight of kennel and pet must be 70 lbs. (32 kg.) or less. There is an additional fee to check in a pet for cargo transportation: Charge is $35.00 for a total weight of 0-50lbs and $60.00 for a total weight of 51-70lbs. For more information and

important information about bringing your pet, visit
http://www.islandair.com/traveling-with-pets

Mokulele Airlines
73-350 U'u Street
Kailua-Kona, HI
866-260-7070
mokuleleairlines.com/
Mokulele Airlines is an inter-island airline serving 9 airports on 5 islands. Prices start at $39 one way including tax and fees. Pets such as dogs and cats may travel with you in the passenger cabin if they are in a kennel small enough to fit under the seat (Size must not exceed 15"W X 14"D X 10"H.) For this, there is a $25/one way charge. If you are booking with your pet, please call their reservation center.

Expeditions
658 Front St
Lahaina, HI
808-661-3756
go-lanai.com/index.html
Expeditions operates between the islands of Maui and Lana`i across the Auau Channel. Their vessels are fast and United States Coast Guard certified. Expeditions also advertises spectacular views of Maui County, including the islands of Maui, Lana`i, Moloka`i and Kaho`olawe, and on a clear day you may even see the Big Island of Hawai`i. Dogs are allowed on the ferry, but may be charged an extra fee.

Molokai Ferry
675 Wharf St
Lahaina, HI
877-500-6284
The Molokai Ferry offers trips from Molokai to Maui as well as day tours and other programs. Dogs are allowed, but they must be in kennels and there is a $15 per way charge.

# Illinois Listings

Chicago Transit Authority (CTA)
567 W Lake Street
Chicago, IL
888-968-7282
transitchicago.com/
A small dog in an enclosed carrier is allowed on the CTA buses and on the CTA "L" trains at no additional fee.

Paws Around Chicago

Chicago, IL
773-278-1937
pawsaroundchicago.com/
Taxi service, emergency service,

long distance and airport transport, or any other special destination - this company is here to provide all your pet's transportation needs. The pet taxi is available Monday thru Friday from 7 am until 7 pm; Saturday from 7 am until 5 pm, and on Sunday for emergency service only or for appointments that have been scheduled 3 days in advance. Emergency transport hours are Monday thru Friday from 7 pm until 7 am the following morning; Saturday and Sunday from 5 pm until 7 am Monday morning, and they are open all day only for emergency service on major holidays.

Brussels Free Ferry
H 100
Grafton, IL
618-786-3636
Run by the state for vehicles and passengers, this free ferry links Highway 100 in Grafton to the village of Brussels in Calhoun County, and it has become a prime bald eagle viewing route as they feed on the stunned fish from the propellers churning up the ice in winter. Dogs are allowed on the ferry for no additional fee. Dogs must be leashed, crated, or in the vehicle, and under their owner's care at all times.

Kampsville Free Ferry
H 108
Kampsville, IL
618-653-4518
Run by the state for vehicles and passengers, this free ferry crosses the Illinois River to connect Kampsville with northern Jersey County. Dogs are allowed on the ferry for no additional fee. Dogs must be leashed, crated, or in the vehicle, and under their owner's care at all times.

# Indiana Listings

Indigo Transit
209 N Delaware
Indianapolis, IN
317-635-3344
indigo.net
Small dogs in an enclosed carrier are allowed on the buses at no additional charge.

# Maine Listings

Island Explorer Buses
Bar Harbor and Acadia
Bar Harbor, ME
207-667-5796
exploreacadia.com/
Leashed dogs are allowed on the

Island Explorer buses that take people between Bar Harbor, Campgrounds and hotels and Acadia National Park.

The Cat Ferry, Bar Harbor Terminal
121 Eden Street
Bar Harbor, ME
207-288-3395
catferry.com/
Quickly gaining recognition for its speed and agility on the water, this CAT carries up to 775 passengers and 240 cars (not to mention a few furry friends also) across the Gulf of Maine between Yarmouth Nova Scotia and Bar Harbor and Portland Maine from June to mid-October. Dogs of all sizes are allowed for no additional pet fee. Dogs must be well behaved, and remain in a vehicle on the auto deck or in a kennel during passage. Kennels are available on a 1st come 1st served basis.

Mohegan Boat Line
End of Port Clyde Road/H 131
Port Clyde, ME
207-372-8848
monheganboat.com/
Nature and art lovers from all over come to experience this wonderfully scenic island that provides about 17 miles of trails to explore it plus a number of shops and artists' studios. This ferry will transport dogs to the island for an additional pet fee of $5 per dog. Dogs must be well mannered, under their owner's control, leashed, and cleaned up after at all times.

Casco Bay Lines
56 Commercial Street
Portland, ME
207-774-7871
Casco Bay Lines
This year round ferry service carries vehicles, passengers, and freight from Portland to a number of off-shore islands. Dogs are allowed for an additional fee of $3.25. Dogs must be well behaved, under their owner's control, leashed, and cleaned up after at all times.

The Cat Ferry, Portland Terminal
14 Ocean Gateway Pier
Portland, ME
207-761-4228
catferry.com/
Quickly gaining recognition for its speed and agility on the water, this CAT carries up to 775 passengers and 240 cars (not to mention a few furry friends also) across the Gulf of Maine between Yarmouth Nova Scotia and Bar Harbor and Portland Maine from June to mid-October. Dogs of all sizes are allowed for no

additional pet fee. Dogs must be well behaved, and remain in a vehicle on the auto deck or in a kennel during passage. Kennels are available on a 1st come 1st served basis.

Maine State Ferry Service (Maine D.O.T.)
517A Main Street
Rockland, ME
207-596-2202
This state owned/operated year round ferry service provides a fixed route from Bass Harbor to Swans Island and Frenchboro ports. Dogs of all sizes are allowed for no additional pet fee. Dogs must be well behaved, under their owner's immediate control, securely leashed, crated, or caged, and cleaned up after at all times. There is a separate room for passengers with pets.

Maine State Ferry Service
Bass Harbor
Southwest Harbor, ME
207-596-2202
Dogs are allowed on the ferries if they are leashed, crated or caged. The ferries closest to Bar Harbor depart at the nearby Southwest Harbor and go to Swans Island. Cars can also be transported on the ferry.

# Maryland Listings

Maryland Transit Administration
Baltimore and Suburbs
Baltimore, MD
866-RIDE-MTA (743-3682)
mtamaryland.com/
MTA provides a variety of transportation options throughout Baltimore and surrounding areas with numerous pick-up and drop-off sites. A small dog is allowed to be transported in hand-held carriers for no extra fee.

# Massachusetts Listings

Boston T

Boston, MA
617-222-3200
mbta.com/
Both small and large dogs are allowed on the Boston T (subway) and the commuter trains run by the T from Boston. Small dogs may be transported in a carrier. Larger dogs may be taken on the T during off-peak hours and must be leashed

and controlled at all times. At no time should a pet compromise safety, get in a passenger's way or occupy a seat.

Salem Ferry
New England Aquarium Dock
Boston, MA
978-741-0220
salemferry.com/
This high speed catamaran offers 45 minute service between downtown Boston and Salem. Dogs on leash are allowed. The service is open seasonally from late May through October.

Island Queen Ferry
Falmouth Heights Road
Falmouth, MA
508-548-4800
islandqueen.com/
This ferry carries passengers, bicycles and leashed dogs. It does not transport vehicles. The ferry runs between Falmouth in Cape Cod and Oak Bluffs in Martha's Vineyard (about 35 to 45 minutes).

Hy-Line Cruises Ferry Service
Ocean Street Dock
Hyannis, MA
508-778-2600
hy-linecruises.com/
This ferry service runs from Cape Cod to Nantucket Island (1 hour on the high speed ferry) or Martha's Vineyard (1.5 hours). They also offer the only Inter-Island Ferry between Nantucket and Martha's Vineyard (2.25 hours). Pets are allowed on the ferries, but not in the first class lounge. Pets need to be leashed. This ferry company provides year-round service to Nantucket and seasonal service to Martha's Vineyard. The Inter-Island Ferry is also seasonal. No vehicles are transported on these ferries. Call ahead to make reservations.

Hy-Line Cruises Ferry Service
Ocean Street Dock
Hyannis, MA
508-778-2600
hy-linecruises.com/
This ferry service runs from Cape Cod to Nantucket Island (1 hour on the high speed ferry) or Martha's Vineyard (1.5 hours). They also offer the only Inter-Island Ferry between Nantucket and Martha's Vineyard (2.25 hours). Pets are allowed on the ferries, but not in the first class lounge. Pets need to be leashed. This ferry company provides year-round service to Nantucket and seasonal service to Martha's Vineyard. The Inter-Island Ferry is also seasonal. No vehicles are transported on these

ferries. Call ahead to make reservations.

Hy-Line Cruises Ferry Service
Ocean Street Dock
Hyannis, MA
508-778-2600
hy-linecruises.com/
This ferry service runs from Cape Cod to Nantucket Island (1 hour on the high speed ferry) or Martha's Vineyard (1.5 hours). They also offer the only Inter-Island Ferry between Nantucket and Martha's Vineyard (2.25 hours). Pets are allowed on the ferries, but not in the first class lounge. Pets need to be leashed. This ferry company provides year-round service to Nantucket and seasonal service to Martha's Vineyard. The Inter-Island Ferry is also seasonal. No vehicles are transported on these ferries. Call ahead to make reservations.

Nantucket Airlines
660 Barnstable Road/North Ramp
Hyannis, MA
508-790-0300 (800-635-8787)
nantucketairlines.com
This airline offers daily flights between Hyannis and Nantucket (20 minute flight). Dogs are allowed in the cabin with you on this airline! Dogs under 35 pounds can be carried on your lap and no kennel is required. For dogs over 35 pounds, there is a "shelf" which is just a few inches off the floor, in the back of the plane where your dog can sit or lay. While you cannot sit next to your dog, you can try to get the seat directly in front of him or her. There is no reserved seating, so you'll need to arrive early to try and make special arrangements to sit in front of your pooch. Large dogs must be properly restrained with a leash, harness or similar device. No kennel is required. You will need to reserve a space for your pet in advance as the airline usually only allows one dog per flight. Their sister airline, Cape Air also allows dogs in the cabin, but most flights require your dog to be in a kennel, and they have a size limit for dogs.

Nantucket Airlines
660 Barnstable Road/North Ramp
Hyannis, MA
508-790-0300 (800-635-8787)
nantucketairlines.com
This airline offers daily flights between Hyannis and Nantucket (20 minute flight). Dogs are allowed in the cabin with you on this airline! Dogs under 35 pounds can be carried on your lap and no kennel is required. For dogs over 35 pounds, there is a

"shelf" which is just a few inches off the floor, in the back of the plane where your dog can sit or lay. While you cannot sit next to your dog, you can try to get the seat directly in front of him or her. There is no reserved seating, so you'll need to arrive early to try and make special arrangements to sit in front of your pooch. Large dogs must be properly restrained with a leash, harness or similar device. No kennel is required. You will need to reserve a space for your pet in advance as the airline usually only allows one dog per flight. Their sister airline, Cape Air also allows dogs in the cabin, but most flights require your dog to be in a kennel, and they have a size limit for dogs.

Steamship Authority Ferry Service
South Street Dock
Hyannis, MA
508-477-8600
steamshipauthority.com
This ferry services runs from Cape Cod to Nantucket Island (2.25 hours) or Martha's Vineyard (1.5 hours). Pets are allowed on all ferries except for the M/V Flying Cloud fast ferry. Pets must be leashed or in a crate at all times. Pets are not allowed on the seats, tables, or in the concession areas. The ferries transport both passengers and cars. They provide year-round service to Nantucket and Martha's Vineyard. Call ahead to make reservations.

Steamship Authority Ferry Service
South Street Dock
Hyannis, MA
508-477-8600
steamshipauthority.com
This ferry services runs from Cape Cod to Nantucket Island (2.25 hours) or Martha's Vineyard (1.5 hours). Pets are allowed on all ferries except for the M/V Flying Cloud fast ferry. Pets must be leashed or in a crate at all times. Pets are not allowed on the seats, tables, or in the concession areas. The ferries transport both passengers and cars. They provide year-round service to Nantucket and Martha's Vineyard. Call ahead to make reservations.

Steamship Authority Ferry Service
South Street Dock
Hyannis, MA
508-477-8600
steamshipauthority.com
This ferry services runs from Cape Cod to Nantucket Island (2.25 hours) or Martha's Vineyard (1.5

hours). Pets are allowed on all ferries except for the M/V Flying Cloud fast ferry. Pets must be leashed or in a crate at all times. Pets are not allowed on the seats, tables, or in the concession areas. The ferries transport both passengers and cars. They provide year-round service to Nantucket and Martha's Vineyard.

Call ahead to make reservations.

Salem Ferry
Derby Street at Blaney Street
Salem, MA
978-741-0220
salemferry.com/
This high speed catamaran offers 45 minute service between downtown Boston and Salem. Dogs on leash are allowed. The service is open seasonally from late May through October.

# Michigan Listings

Arbor Limousine
2050 Commerce
Ann Arbor, MI
734-663-8898
This transport company services Washtenaw County and further with the area's largest variety of fleet vehicles. Well mannered dogs are allowed in some of the vehicles; they must be leashed or crated and under their owner's control at all times.

A Dream Limousine

Canton, MI
734-542-6800
adreamlimo.com/
Serving southeastern Michigan and the Detroit metro area, this limousine services offers a variety of vehicles and special pricings; they are available for simple pick-ups to a night on the town. Well mannered dogs up to 60 pounds are welcome for transport for no additional fee; they must be under their owner's control at all times.

Beaver Island Boat Co.
103 Bridge Park Drive
Charlevoix, MI
231-547-2311
bibco.com
This ferry line provides passenger and vehicle service between Charlevoix and St. James Harbor on Beaver Island. All trips are weather permitting and additional trips may be possible in December. Rates during non-peak travel times start at $22 per person one way ($44 round trip) and $11.00 per child one way ($22 round trip). Vehicles cost $75 and up one way ($150) round trip. During Peak

Travel times rates start at $24 per person one way ($48 round trip) and $13.00 per child one way ($26 round trip). Vehicles cost $80 and up one way ($160) round trip. Pets are allowed but the following rules apply. Pets less than 10 pounds are free with the purchase of a passenger ticket. Pets over ten pounds travel for $10 each way. Leashed pets are allowed on the top deck but

Ironton Ferry
Ferry Road
Ironton, MI
231-547-7200
This 4 car cable ferry operates from mid-April through mid-November and crosses a narrow point on the south arm of Lake Charlevoix. Dogs are allowed on the ferry for no extra fee.

Lake Michigan Car Ferry Company
701 Maritime Drive
Ludington, MI
800-841-4243
ssbadger.com
The S.S. Badger offers the largest cross-lake passenger service on the Great Lakes. The relaxing four-hour, 60-mile cruise takes passengers, and vehicles across Lake Michigan between Ludington, Michigan and Manitowoc, Wisconsin from mid-May through mid-October. Dogs may be transported in the owner's vehicle or kept in a well ventilated portable kennel on the car deck. A limited number of kennels are available free of charge on a first-come, first served basis. Owners may also bring their own kennels. (If animals are left in the vehicle, windshield sunscreens are strongly recommended during warm weather.) No pets of any kind are allowed in any passenger areas, and pets are not accessible during the cruise.

Lake Michigan Car Ferry Company
701 Maritime Drive
Ludington, MI
800-841-4243
ssbadger.com
The S.S. Badger offers the largest cross-lake passenger service on the Great Lakes. The relaxing four-hour, 60-mile cruise takes passengers, and vehicles across Lake Michigan between Ludington, Michigan and Manitowoc, Wisconsin from mid-May through mid-October. Dogs may be transported in the owner's vehicle or kept in a well ventilated portable kennel on the car deck. A limited number of kennels are available free of charge on a first-come, first served basis. Owners may also bring their own kennels. (If animals are left in the vehicle, windshield sunscreens are strongly recommended during warm

weather.) No pets of any kind are allowed in any passenger areas, and pets are not accessible during the cruise.

Horse Taxis
Main Street
Mackinac Island, MI
906-847-3307
mict.com/
Mackinac Island horse taxis are provided by Mackinac Island Carriage Tours Co. Rates range from $3.75 to $6.25 per person depending on the distance traveled. Baggage is allowed at no extra charge but they reserve the right to charge for excess baggage. No bicycles are allowed on the taxis, including on the luggage racks. Call about 45 minutes prior to your requested travel time and a horse taxi will be radio dispatched to your location. If arriving by ferry, also call ahead or you can also sometimes ask the ferry personnel to contact a horse taxi in advance.

Arnold Mackinac Island Ferry
various docks-see comments
Mackinaw City, MI
906-847-3351
arnoldline.com/
This passenger ferry line offers the largest ferries to Mackinac Island. They have a fleet of three triple-decked Catamaran ferries. The ride takes less than 20 minutes. Ferries depart about every hour. Round trip rates are $17 per adult, $8 per child ages 5 to 12 and free for children under 5. Bikes cost an extra $6.50. Leashed pets are allowed but you will need to show proof of current rabies vaccine (dog tag) and current license (dog tag). These large ferries offer the most room for pets versus the other ferries. Restroom and handicap facilities are available on all ferries. Parking at the dock is free for one day but overnight costs $1 to $15 per night. To get to the docks, follow the red, green and white signs to the Arnold Line Docks in Mackinaw City or St. Ignace.

Shepler's Mackinac Island Ferry
various docks-see comments
Mackinaw City, MI
231-436-5023
This ferry line provides passenger service from Mackinaw City or St. Ignace to Mackinaw Island. The ride takes less than 20 minutes. During peak times, ferries depart every 15 minutes. Round trip rates for adults are $16 per person, $7.50 for children 5 to 12 and free for children under 5. Family pets are welcome but need to be leashed and you will

need to show proof of current rabies vaccine (dog tag) and current license (dog tag). Bikes are an extra $6.50. Rates are subject to change. The ferries also have wheelchair accessible facilities. To get to the Mackinaw City dock, take exit 339 off I-75. Turn left at the stop sign and continue to Central Avenue. Turn left and into the Gateway. To get to the St. Ignace dock, take exit 344-A off I-75. Follow US 2 east through downtown to the north end of town. Free daily and overnight onsite parking are guaranteed.

Star Line Mackinac Island Ferry
various docks-see comments
Mackinaw City, MI
906-643-7635
mackinacferry.com/
This ferry line offers passenger service from St. Ignace and Mackinaw City to Mackinac Island. The ride takes less than 20 minutes. Ferries depart about every half hour during the peak season. Round trip rates are $17 per adult, $8 per child ages 5 to 12 and free for children under 5. Bikes cost an extra $6.50. Leashed dogs are allowed and you will need to show proof of current rabies vaccine (dog tag) and current license (dog tag). Secure overnight parking is available for $2 per night. The St. Ignace docks are located at 587 N. State Street in St. Ignace and the Mackinaw City Dock is located at 711 South Huron in Mackinaw City.

Tecumseh Trolley and Limousine Service
223 East Patterson Street
Tecumseh, MI
866-423-3335
michigantrolleys.com/
This transport company will allow well mannered dogs in some of the vehicles; they must be crated and under their owner's control at all times.

Crown Limousine
3161 E 9 Mile Road
Warren, MI
313-864-3651
crownlimousine4u.com/
Serving southeastern Michigan, this limousine services offers a variety of vehicles and special pricings; they are available for simple pick-ups to a night on the town. Well mannered dogs are welcome for transport for no additional fee; they must be under their owner's control at all times.

# Minnesota Listings

Island Passenger Service
2379 Flag Island
Angle Inlet, MN
218-223-5015
This passenger only ferry will transport dogs for no additional fees. Dogs must be leashed or crated and under their owner's control at all times. Directions for visitors coming from the west or south are to go north on H 310 from Roseau to Canadian Customs to clear entry; about 1½ miles from there turn onto Canada H 12 toward Sprague; in about 32 miles take a right on H 525 at the "T" junction; go about 14 miles to the customs phone booth to reenter the US, and continue on from there to the Northwest Angle. The reporting custom's booth is located at Jim's Corner.

Metro Transit
560 N Sixth Avenue (office)
Minneapolis, MN
612-373-3333
metrotransit.org/
Metro Transit will allow a small dog that can be held in a carrier for no additional fee. Dogs must be well mannered and under their owner's control and care at all times.

# New Jersey Listings

NJ Transit
Regional
Hoboken, NJ
973-762-5100
njtransit.com
Small dogs in carriers are allowed on the trains.

Cape May-Lewes Ferry
Sandman Blvd. & Lincoln Drive
N Cape May, NJ
609-889-7200
capemaylewesferry.com/
This ferry service provides transportation for vehicles and passengers between Cape May, New Jersey and Lewes, Delaware. The ferry cuts miles off of driving along the Atlantic coast. Pets are welcome but the following rules apply. For the M.V. Cape May, M.V. Delaware and M.V. Twin Cape ferries, pets are welcome on the ferry on exterior decks and any lounge areas where food is not being made, served or eaten. Pets are not allowed in the lounge area whenever there is a private party being hosted. For the M.V. Cape Henlopen and M.V. New Jersey ferries, pets are not allowed in any interior space but are allowed on all exterior decks. For all ferries, dogs of all sizes are allowed but need to be kept under control at all times and leashed or in a carrier. People need

to clean up after their pets. Pets are not allowed in the shuttles. Rates start at $20 to $25 for a vehicle and driver. For a foot passenger with no car, rates start at $6 to $8 per person. Larger vehicles can be accommodated but there is an extra charge. The Cape May Terminal is located at Sandman Blvd. and Lincoln Drive in North Cape May, New Jersey. The Lewes Terminal is located at 43 Henlopen Drive in Lewes, Delaware. Rates are subject to change. For reservations or to check rates, call the ferry line toll free at 1-800-643-3779.

Cape May-Lewes Ferry
Sandman Blvd. & Lincoln Drive
North Cape May, NJ
609-889-7200
capemaylewesferry.com/
This ferry service provides transportation for vehicles and passengers between Cape May, New Jersey and Lewes, Delaware. The ferry cuts miles off of driving along the Atlantic coast. Pets are welcome but the following rules apply. For the M.V. Cape May, M.V. Delaware and M.V. Twin Cape ferries, pets are allowed on the ferry on exterior decks and any lounge areas where food is not being made, served or eaten. Pets are not allowed in the lounge area whenever there is a private party being hosted. For the M.V. Cape Henlopen and M.V. New Jersey ferries, pets are not allowed in any interior space but are allowed on all exterior decks. For all ferries, dogs of all sizes are allowed but need to be kept under control at all times and leashed or in a carrier. People need to clean up after their pets. Pets are not allowed in the shuttles. Rates start at $20 to $25 for a vehicle and driver. For a foot passenger with no car, rates start at $6 to $8 per person. Larger vehicles can be accommodated but there is an extra charge. The Cape May Terminal is located at Sandman Blvd. and Lincoln Drive in North Cape May, New Jersey. The Lewes Terminal is located at 43 Henlopen Drive in Lewes, Delaware. Rates subject to change. For reservations or to check rates, call the ferry line toll free at 1-800-643-3779.

# New York Listings

Fire Island Ferry
99 Maple Avenue
Bay Shore, NY
631-665-3600
fireislandferries.com/
After 4th avenue becomes Maple

Avenue, the main terminal for Ocean Beach is on the left, and the Seaview/Ocean Bay Park terminal is on the right. Dogs may not go on the trips to Ocean Beach as dogs are not allowed there. Well behaved dogs are allowed on the ferry to Seaview/Ocean Bay for an additional fee of $4 each way. Dogs must be well mannered, and leashed and cleaned up after at all times.

Long Island Railroad and Buses
Regional
Long Island, NY
718-330-1234
mta.nyc.us
Small dogs in carriers are allowed on the Long Island Railroad, Long Island Bus and New York City Transit buses and subways. Small dogs in carriers or on a secure leash are allowed on the Metro-North Railroad. The pet carrier should be able to fit on your lap and should not occupy a seat. Dogs should not bother other passengers.

Long Island Railroad and Buses
Regional
Long Island, NY
718-330-1234
mta.nyc.ny.us
Small dogs in carriers are allowed on the Long Island Railroad, Long Island Bus and New York City Transit buses and subways. Small dogs in carriers or on a secure leash are allowed on the Metro-North Railroad. The pet carrier should be able to fit on your lap and should not occupy a seat. Dogs should not bother other passengers.

Viking Fleet
462 W Lake Drive
Montauk, NY
631-668-5700
This ferry features a triple decker, 120 foot vessel with comfort amenities on board, and service is provided between Montauk Long Island and Block Island RI, New London CT, and Martha's Vineyard, MA. Well behaved dogs are allowed on board for no additional fee. Dogs must be under their owner's control and leashed at all times. The ferry docks at Montauk at the Viking Dock at 462 Westlake Drive.

Viking Fleet
462 W Lake Drive
Montauk, NY
631-668-5700
This ferry features a triple decker, 120 foot vessel with comfort amenities on board, and service is provided between Montauk Long Island and Block Island RI, New

London CT, and Martha's Vineyard, MA. Well behaved dogs are allowed on board for no additional fee. Dogs must be under their owner's control and leashed at all times. The ferry docks on Block Island at Champlin's Marina.

Viking Fleet
462 W Lake Drive
Montauk, NY
631-668-5700
This ferry features a triple decker, 120 foot vessel with comfort amenities on board, and service is provided between Montauk Long Island and Block Island RI, New London CT, and Martha's Vineyard, MA. Well behaved dogs are allowed on board for no additional fee. Dogs must be under their owner's control and leashed at all times. The ferries leave from the Cross Sound Ferry Dock.

Viking Fleet
462 W Lake Drive
Montauk, NY
631-668-5700
This ferry features a triple decker, 120 foot vessel with comfort amenities on board, and service is provided between Montauk Long Island and Block Island RI, New London CT, and Martha's Vineyard, MA. Well behaved dogs are allowed on board for no additional fee. Dogs must be under their owner's control and leashed at all times.

HoundXpress.com
Call to arrange
New York, NY
917-693-5652
houndXpress.com
This service in Manhattan provides dog walking, dog daycare in your place and a dog taxi service.

MTA
Regional
New York, NY
718-330-1234
mta.nyc.ny.us
Small dogs in carriers are allowed on the Long Island Railroad, Long Island Bus and New York City Transit buses and subways. Small dogs may also be carried in your lap on the New York City buses and subways. Small dogs in carriers or on a secure leash are allowed on the Metro-North Railroad. The pet carrier should be able to fit on your lap and should not occupy a seat. Dogs should not bother other passengers.

Madison Avenue Limousine Inc.

348 East 15th Street, Suite 16
New York, NY
212-674-0060
madisonavenuelimo.com/
This Limousine company will pick you and your pup up at your front door, and there is no additional pet fee if there is no extra cleaning. They suggest bringing a large sheet or cover depending on how large or hairy the dog is. There is a 2 hour rental minimum and they suggest calling 48-72 hours in advance. Dogs must be under their owner's care/control at all times.

Metro-North Railroad
42nd Street and Park Avenue
New York, NY
212-532-4900
mta.info/mnr/index.html
Dogs up to 65 pounds are allowed on the train for no additional pet fee. Dogs are not allowed on the train when it is crowed or during peak hours and they may not take up a seat. Dogs must be well behaved, under their owner's control at all times, and they must be securely leashed or in a carrier and cleaned up after at all times.

Pet Chauffeur

New York, NY
718-752-1767 (866-PETRIDE)
petride.com
This pet transportation service will take you and your pet (or your pet alone) just about anywhere you need or want to go. They recommend calling well in advance but you can try last minute bookings.

Pet Taxi
227 E 56th St
New York, NY
212-755-1757
When want to get around town without driving, there are numerous taxi cabs. A typical New York yellow taxi cab is supposed to pick up people with pets, however, they don't always stop if you have a pooch. Don't feel too bad, many NY cabs don't stop even for people without pets! However, with a little advance planning, you can reserve the Pet Taxi. The Pet Taxi makes runs to the vet, groomer and other pet related stuff. But they are also rented to transport you and your pooch to a park, outdoor restaurant, across town, etc. For example, if you are at a hotel near Central Park but would like to go to Little Italy and Chinatown for half a day, they will take you to your destination and then several hours later, they will

pick you up and take you back to your hotel. Just be sure to reserve the Pet Taxi at least one day in advance during the weekdays. If you need the taxi on Saturday or Sunday, book your reservation by Thursday or Friday. They are open from 8am-7pm during the weekday and by reservation on the weekends. They can be reserved for $35 per hour or $25 each way for a pick up or drop off. Pet Taxi serves the Manhattan area.

Queen Mary II
92 North River Piers (NY Terminal)
New York, NY
800-728-6273
cunard.com/Ships/Queen-Mary-2/
Considered to be the grandest ship ever built to date, this luxury ocean liner features indulgences from bow to stern. Travelers can enjoy all the modern amenities as well as it's striking opulent decor, world class dining and entertainment, lounges, theaters, personalized services, and a Planetariu - the only one at sea. Travelers may embark from a dozen ports around the world; the US ports are Ft Lauderdale, Los Angeles, and New York. Dogs are allowed on board and preplanning is highly recommended as there are only a limited number of kennels. Depending on the destination, certain preparations must be made for the dogs that usually take up to about 6 months prior to the trip: example - blood work, shots, destination requirements, etc. One kennel will accommodate dogs 25 pounds and under; dogs over 25 pounds will need 2 kennels. A Kennel Master is always on duty to see to the walking, feeding, and cleaning of their canine guests.

Each kennel costs $700 per trip.

Seastreak Ferry Rides
various (see below)
New York, NY
800-BOAT-RIDE
seastreakusa.com
Want to enjoy the sights of New York City from the water, including the Manhattan Skyline and the Statue of Liberty? Or maybe you want to stay at a hotel in New Jersey and visit New York City during the day. Well, the nice folks at Seastreak allow dogs onboard their commuter ferries. Here are the rules: Dogs of all sizes must stay on the outside portion of the ferry and they need to be on a short leash. Dogs are not allowed on the inside area regardless of the weather unless you have a small dog and he or she is in a carrier. The ferries operate between Manhattan and New Jersey on a daily basis with up to 11 ferry

rides during the weekday and about 4 ferry rides on the weekend. The ride lasts about 45 minutes each way and costs approximately $20 per round trip, half price for children and free for dogs! The ferries depart from Pier 11 (Wall Street) and East 34th Street in Manhattan and Atlantic Highlands and Highlands in New Jersey. Please visit their website for current ferry schedules, times and fares.

Staten Island Ferry
Whitehall Street
New York, NY
718-876-8441
siferry.com/
Small dogs in a cage or carrier are allowed on these ferries. The ferry service provides passenger transportation between St. George, Staten Island and Whitehall Street in Manhattan. The 25 minute ride provides a great view of New York Harbor, the Statue of Liberty and Ellis Island.

Lake Champlain Ferries
838-842 Cumberland Head Road
Plattsburgh, NY
802-864-9804
ferries.com/
Leashed dogs of all sizes are allowed on the Lake Champlain Ferry crossing that travels between New York and Vermont. Ferry schedules changes constantly so please confirm the time of your voyage.

Sayville Ferry Service
41 River Road
Sayville, NY
631-589-0810
sayvilleferry.com/
This ferry service offers daily schedules to a variety of stops in the South Bay area, and dogs are allowed for an additional $4 per round trip. Dogs must be under their owner's control at all times, and they must be leashed and cleaned up after.

North Ferry Company
12 Summerfield Place
Shelter Island Heights, NY
631-749-0139
northferry.com/
This ferry provides transportation service between Long Island and Shelter Island. Dogs of all sizes are allowed for no additional fee. Dogs must be under their owner's control, leashed, and cleaned up after at all times.

# North Carolina

# Listings

North Carolina Ferry-Bayview
229 H 306N
Bath, NC
800-BY FERRY (293-3779)
These vehicle and passenger transport ferries are run by the state and provide service every day of the year on all routes; however weather conditions can influence travel. Dogs are allowed on all ferries for no additional fee; they must be kept in the vehicle or leashed when out of the vehicle. Dogs must be under their owner's control at all times.

North Carolina Ferry-Cedar Island
H 12
Cedar Island, NC
800-BY FERRY (293-3779)
These vehicle and passenger transport ferries are run by the state and provide service every day of the year on all routes; however weather conditions can influence travel. Dogs are allowed on all ferries for no additional fee; they must be kept in the vehicle or leashed when out of the vehicle. Dogs must be under their owner's control at all times.

North Carolina Ferry-Currituck
Courthouse Road
Currituck, NC
800-BY FERRY (293-3779)
These vehicle and passenger transport ferries are run by the state and provide service every day of the year on all routes; however weather conditions can influence travel. Dogs are allowed on all ferries for no additional fee; they must be kept in the vehicle or leashed when out of the vehicle. Dogs must be under their owner's control at all times.

North Carolina Ferry-Knotts Island
S end of H 615 (on the island)
Ferry Dock Road, NC
800-BY FERRY (293-3779)
These vehicle and passenger transport ferries are run by the state and provide service every day of the year on all routes; however weather conditions can influence travel. Dogs are allowed on all ferries for no additional fee; they must be kept in the vehicle or leashed when out of the vehicle. Dogs must be under their owner's control at all times.

Fort Fisher Ferry
Fort Fisher Blvd S
Fort Fisher, NC
800-BY FERRY (293-3779)
ncdot.org/transit/ferry/
This water taxi provides services between the outer islands and the mainland. Dogs are allowed on

board for no additional fee; they must be leashed, crated, or in a vehicle for the duration of the trip. Dogs must be under their owner's control at all times.

North Carolina Ferry-Fort Fisher
Fort Fisher Road S/H 421
Fort Fisher, NC
800-BY FERRY (293-3779)
These vehicle and passenger transport ferries are run by the state and provide service every day of the year on all routes; however weather conditions can influence travel. Dogs are allowed on all ferries for no additional fee; they must be kept in the vehicle or leashed when out of the vehicle. Dogs must be under their owner's control at all times.

North Carolina Ferry-Hatteras
H 12
Hatteras, NC
800-BY FERRY (293-3779)
These vehicle and passenger transport ferries are run by the state and provide service every day of the year on all routes; however weather conditions can influence travel. Dogs are allowed on all ferries for no additional fee; they must be kept in the vehicle or leashed when out of the vehicle. Dogs must be under their owner's control at all times.

North Carolina Ferry-Cherry Branch
Ferry Road
Havelock, NC
800-BY FERRY (293-3779)
These vehicle and passenger transport ferries are run by the state and provide service every day of the year on all routes; however weather conditions can influence travel. Dogs are allowed on all ferries for no additional fee; they must be kept in the vehicle or leashed when out of the vehicle. Dogs must be under their owner's control at all times.

North Carolina Ferry-Minnesott Beach
Point Road/H 306
Minnesott Beach, NC
800-BY FERRY (293-3779)
These vehicle and passenger transport ferries are run by the state and provide service every day of the year on all routes; however weather conditions can influence travel. Dogs are allowed on all ferries for no additional fee; they must be kept in the vehicle or leashed when out of the vehicle. Dogs must be under their owner's control at all times.

North Carolina Ferry-Ocracoke #1
H 12 N end of Island (to Hatteras)
Ocracoke, NC
800-BY FERRY (293-3779)

These vehicle and passenger transport ferries are run by the state and provide service every day of the year on all routes; however weather conditions can influence travel. Dogs are allowed on all ferries for no additional fee; they must be kept in the vehicle or leashed when out of the vehicle. Dogs must be under their owner's control at all times.

North Carolina Ferry-Ocracoke #2
H 12 S end of Island (to Cedar Island and Swan Quarter)
Ocracoke, NC
800-BY FERRY (293-3779)
These vehicle and passenger transport ferries are run by the state and provide service every day of the year on all routes; however weather conditions can influence travel. Dogs are allowed on all ferries for no additional fee; they must be kept in the vehicle or leashed when out of the vehicle. Dogs must be under their

owner's control at all times.

North Carolina Ferry-Southport
Southport Ferry Road
Southport, NC
800-BY FERRY (293-3779)
These vehicle and passenger transport ferries are run by the state and provide service every day of the year on all routes; however weather conditions can influence travel. Dogs are allowed on all ferries for no additional fee; they must be kept in the vehicle or leashed when out of the vehicle. Dogs must be under their owner's control at all times.

North Carolina Ferry-Swan Quarter
Swan Quarter Ferry Road
Swan Quarter, NC
800-BY FERRY (293-3779)
These vehicle and passenger transport ferries are run by the state and provide service every day of the year on all routes; however weather conditions can influence travel. Dogs are allowed on all ferries for no additional fee; they must be kept in the vehicle or leashed when out of the vehicle. Dogs must be under their owner's control at all times.

# Ohio Listings

Miller Boat Line
Catawba Dock
Catawba Island, OH
800-500-2421
millerferry.com/
This ferry line offers service from the town of Catawba on the Ohio mainland to the Lilm Kiln Dock on South Bay Island which is home to the town of Put-in-Bay. Travel time

from dock to dock is about 18 minutes. The ferries runs year round, weather permitting, with ferries leaving every half hour during the day. Rates start at about $5 to $6 per person one way and $1 per child. The fare is free for children under 6 years old and for dogs. Leashed dogs are welcome on the ferries. Once on the island, there is a 2.5 mile walk from the ferry dock to Put-in-Bay. If you do not want to walk, you can opt to take the public Lilm Kiln Bus, a taxi or rent a golf cart. Dogs of all sizes are allowed in all of the above mentioned methods of transportation as long as they are well-behaved and leashed. The Miller Boat Line transports mainly passengers but also offers limited vehicle service. Vehicles leaving Catawba cannot be transported round trip on Saturdays, Sundays or Holiday Mondays. Drivers must show written proof of an accommodation in order to bring a vehicle to the island on the weekends. For full vehicle requirements please contact the ferry line directly by phone or check their web site at http://www.millerferry.com. This ferry line also offers passenger and vehicle service from Catawba to Middle Bass Island. To get to the Catawba Dock, take Route 2 to Route 53 which will bring you right to the dock. Free parking is provided.

SORTA Metro
1014 Vine Street, Suite 2000
Cincinnati, OH
513-632-7575
sorta.com
The Southwest Ohio Regional Transit Authority (SORTA) allows small dogs in carriers that you can hold on your lap on their buses.

Greater Cleveland RTA
1240 West 6th Street
Cleveland, OH
216-566-5227
gcrta.org
The Greater Cleveland Regional Transit Authority (RTA) allows people to bring dogs less than 25 pounds in a carrier on their buses.

Kelleys Island Ferry Boat Line
510 West Main St. (Route 163)
Marblehead, OH
419-798-9763
kelleysislandferry.com/
This ferry line transports passengers from Marblehead to Kelleys Island which is about a 20 minute ride. It operates year round, weather permitting. They offer limited vehicle transportation. Dogs are welcome but need to be leashed.

Jet Express
off exit 163
Port Clinton, OH
800-245-1538
jet-express.com
This ferry company offers passenger service from Port Clinton on the Ohio mainland directly to downtown Put-in-Bay on South Bass Island. This catamaran boat can travel up to 40 miles per hour making it a fast ride across the lake. Fares start at about $12 per person one way. Children 12 and under, as well as pets of all ages, ride free. Dogs are welcome but need to be leashed and well-behaved. Pets must stay on the outside deck of the ferry. To get to the Port Clinton dock, take Route 2 and take exit 163 North Port Clinton.

Commodore Perry Cab Company
various locations
Put-in-Bay, OH

This taxi cab company provides seasonal service during the summer months. They can transport you and your dog from the Lilm Kiln Dock to downtown Put-in-Bay for about $3 per person each way. There is not usually any extra charge for pets. Well-mannered leashed dogs are welcome.

Lilm Kiln Bus
Box 190
Put-in-Bay, OH
419-285-4855
put-in-bay-trans.com/lkbus.htm
Well-behaved dogs on leash are allowed on the island shuttle bus as long as there is room for them. The bus transports passengers between the Miller Ferry Dock (Lilm Kiln Dock) and downtown Put-in-Bay. The fare is $2 per person one way.

Island Bike Rental
various island docks
South Bass Island, OH
419-285-2016
put-in-bay-trans.com/bikmini.htm
You and your pooch can rent a mini golf cart to drive from the ferry docks to the town of Put-in-Bay or around the rest of the island. Golf carts vary in size and can carry from 2 to 6 passengers. Leashed dogs are welcome on the cart rentals. The rentals are located both at the Jet Express dock in downtown Put-in-Bay and at the Miller Boat Line Ferry at the Lilm Kiln dock. Rates run about $10 to $16 per hour or $50 to $70 per day depending on the size of the golf cart.

# Oregon Listings

Tri-Met
4012 SE Center
Portland, OR
503-238-RIDE (7433)
trimet.org
A small dog in a carrier is allowed on the rail and bus lines at no additional fee.

# Pennsylvania Listings

Port Authority of Allegheny County
534 Smithfield Street
Pittsburgh, PA
412-442-2000
ridegold.com
A small dog in an enclosed carrier is allowed on both light rail and the buses at no additional fee.

the Centre Area Transportation Authority
2081 W. Whitehall Road (Main Office)
State College, PA
888-738-CATA
catabus.com/acoffice.htm
This city bus line will allow pooches to ride with their human companions for no additional fee. They may not be allowed if they are very large or aggressive. Dogs must be in a secure pet carrier, or leashed and muzzled, and they must be under their owner's control at all times.

# Rhode Island Listings

Block Island Ferry
two location-see comments
Block Island, RI
401-783-4613
This ferry line provides passenger and vehicle service from Point Judith to Block Island (one hour trip) and from Fort Adams in Newport to Block Island (two hour trip). Pets on a leash or in a carrier are allowed on the ferry. One way fares start at just under $10 per person and about $5 per child. Vehicles are transported on the ferry that leaves from Point Judith. Rates for vehicles range from about $40 to $95 or more depending on the size and type of vehicle. Call ahead to make reservations for vehicles. Only cash or travelers checks are accepted at the Newport location. At Point Judith, credit cards are also accepted. Rates are subject to change. Parking for the Point Judith ferry is located across the street from the ferry. Prices range from $5 to $10 per day. Parking for the Newport ferry is located at Fort Adams State Park at no charge.

Interstate Navigation/Block Island Ferry
304 Grey Island Road
Narragansett, RI
401-783-4613
blockislandferry.com/
The ferry rides are about 1 hour, and they are open all year. Ther ferries leave from Newport at Fort Adams State Park and Point Judith (Galilee) just south of Narragansett. The ferries sail from Old Harbor on Block Island. Dogs are allowed, but they must be friendly, well behaved, and leashed. They request to have dogs relieve themselves before boarding, and doggie bags are required.

Interstate Navigation/Block Island Ferry
304 Grey Island Road
Narragansett, RI
401-783-4613
blockislandferry.com/
The ferry rides are about 1 hour, and they are open all year. Ther ferries leave from Newport at Fort Adams State Park and Point Judith (Galilee) just south of Narragansett. The ferries sail from Old Harbor on Block Island. Dogs are allowed, but they must be friendly, well behaved, and leashed. They request to have dogs relieve themselves before boarding, and doggie bags are required.

# Texas Listings

DART
Regional
Dallas, TX
214-979-1111
dart.org
Small dogs in carriers are allowed on the light rail and buses.

Galveston Ferry - Car Only
At End of H 87
Galveston, TX
409-795-2230
galveston.com/galvestonferry/
This ferry goes from Galveston to Bolivar and back. The trips take about 15 minutes each way. Dogs are allowed to go on the ferry if they are in your car only. They may not go as a "walk on". The ferry runs 24 hours a day.

Metropolitan Transit Authority
1900 Main
Houston, TX
713-635-4000
ridemetro.org

Small dogs in an enclosed carrier are allowed on the bus or light rail at no additional charge.

VIA
Regional
San Antonio, TX
210-362-2020
viainfo.net
Small dogs in carriers or on your lap are allowed on the buses.

# Utah Listings

Utah Transit Authority (UTA)

Salt Lake City, UT
801-RIDEUTA (743-3882)
rideuta.com/
This multi-modal transportation provider offers service throughout Salt Lake City and surrounding areas. At the driver's discretion, small dogs can be brought on board in a secure hand-held carrier. No aggressive breeds are allowed; and dogs may not take up an additional seat or be in the isles.

# Vermont Listings

Lake Champlain Ferries
King Street Dock
Burlington, VT
802-864-9804
ferries.com/
Leashed dogs of all sizes are allowed on the Lake Champlain Ferry crossing that travels between New York and Vermont. Ferry schedules changes constantly so please confirm the time of your voyage.

# Virginia Listings

Elizabeth River Ferry
6 Crawford Parkway
Portsmouth, VA
757-393-5111
Famous for being the oldest continually operating public transport in America, this ferry system can be boarded at #1 High Street or at the Parkway address, and it connects pedestrians from Olde Towne Portsmouth to Norfolk's Waterside Festival Marketplace. Dogs are allowed on board for no additional fee. Dogs must be well behaved, under their owner's control, and leashed at all times.

GRTC
Regional
Richmond, VA
804-358-GRTC

ridegrtc.com
Small dogs in carriers are allowed on the buses.

# Washington Listings

Alaska Ferry
I-5 Exit #250
Bellingham, WA
360-676-8445 (800-642-0066)
dot.state.ak.us/amhs
The Alaska Ferry, or Alaska Maritime Highway System connects Bellingham, Washington and Prince Rupert, BC with many Alaskan ports and also serves these Alaskan ports with Car, RV and passenger service. The ferry is essential, as many of the ports served are not accessible from the mainland by car, only by ferry or air. Dogs are allowed, but with significant restrictions. They must remain on the car deck at all times. If you have an RV or a car, this means that the dog must remain in the vehicle. If you are a foot passenger, you will have to leave your pet on the car deck in a closed kennel. You may not visit the car deck while the ferry is not in port. An exception is made for ferry segments greater than 8 hours, where they will hold occasional pet visits to the car deck to allow the dogs to relieve themselves. This is not much fun for the dogs, so we recommend that you stop often at intermediate ports with pets. In port, you may take your dog off of the ferry usually for about 20 minutes to 45 minutes. The ferry serves the Southeast area of Alaska, the Prince William Sound area, and Kodiak and points in the Aleutian Islands. The pet information is listed at http://www.dot.state.ak.us/amhs/pets.shtml.

Lake Chelan Boat Company
1418 W Woodin Ave
Chelan, WA
509-682-4584
ladyofthelake.com/
Daily service passenger boats provide round-trip service between Chelan and Stehekin, with a few scheduled stops in between, from about mid-March through October 31st, and then reduced service during the winter. Dogs up to 100 pounds are allowed. Dogs must remain in a crate in the luggage area on the outside deck with the owner present at all times while underway. There is an additional fee of $13.00 round-trip in the owner's cage or $24.00 round-tip in a boat company cage.

Alaska Ferry

I-5 Exit #250
From Bellingham, WA
360-676-8445 (800-642-0066)
dot.state.ak.us/amhs
The Alaska Ferry, or Alaska Maritime Highway System connects Bellingham, Washington and Prince Rupert, BC with many Alaskan ports and also serves these Alaskan ports with Car, RV and passenger service. The ferry is essential, as many of the ports served are not accessible from the mainland by car, only by ferry or air. Dogs are allowed, but with significant restrictions. They must remain on the car deck at all times. If you have an RV or a car, this means that the dog must remain in the vehicle. If you are a foot passenger, you will have to leave your pet on the car deck in a closed kennel. You may not visit the car deck while the ferry is not in port. An exception is made for ferry segments greater than 8 hours, where they will hold occasional pet visits to the car deck to allow the dogs to relieve themselves. This is not much fun for the dogs, so we recommend that you stop often at intermediate ports with pets. In port, you may take your dog off the ferry usually for about 20 minutes to 45 minutes. The ferry serves the Southeast area of Alaska, the Prince William Sound area, and Kodiak and points in the Aleutian Islands. The pet information is listed at http://www.dot.state.ak.us/amhs/pets.shtml.

Leavenworth Shuttle
188 H 2
Leavenworth, WA
509-548-RIDE (7433)
leavenworthshuttle.com/
This shuttle and on-call taxi service will allow well behaved dogs transportation. Dogs must be in a carrier or leashed and under their owner's control at all times.

Black Ball Ferry Line
101 E Railroad Avenue
Port Angeles, WA
360-457-4491
cohoferry.com/main/
Offering breathtaking scenic passage for vehicles and passengers between Vancouver Island and the Olympic Peninsula is this ferry service's specialty. Dogs are also allowed for passage for no additional fee. They must have a current rabies certificate from a veterinarian, and they are allowed on the outer decks or in the vehicle only.

Victoria Express
115 Railroad Avenue

Port Angeles, WA
360-452-8088
victoriaexpress.com/welcome.html
This fast passenger ferry offers several stops between Port Angeles, Washington and Victoria, British Columbia. They have a galley on board, a currency exchange office, and duty free shopping on board. Dogs are allowed on board for no additional fee; there is a pet waiver to sign. Dogs must be leashed or in a carrier.

Sound Flight
300 Airport Way
Renton, WA
866-921-3474
soundflight.net/
This air charter offers a variety of seaplane and landplane flights throughout the northwest and beyond. Dogs are allowed in the cabin seating area for no additional fee unless clean up is required. Dogs must be well mannered and under their owner's control at all times.

King County Metro
Regional
Seattle, WA
206-553-3000
transit.metrokc.gov
Both small and large dogs are allowed on the street cars and buses. Small dogs that fit in their owner's lap ride for free. Large dogs are charged the same fare as their owner and should not occupy a seat. One large dog per bus is allowed. Large dogs should ride on the floor of the bus, preferably under the seat. It is up to the driver as to whether or not your dog will be allowed if you have a very large dog, if there is another animal already onboard or if the bus or street car is excessively crowded. Dogs must be leashed.

Washington State Ferries
Pier 52
Seattle, WA
206-464-6400
wsdot.wa.gov/ferries/
The Washington State Ferries is the nation's largest ferry system and the state's number one tourist attraction. This ferry service offers many ferry routes, including Seattle to Bainbridge Island, Seattle to Bremerton, Edmonds to Kingston, Anacortes to Friday Harbor (San Juan Islands), and Anacortes to Sidney in British Columbia, Canada. Please see our Washington State Ferry listing in our Victoria, British Columbia, Canada City Guide for customs requirements for both people and dogs. While leashed dogs are allowed on the ferry routes mentioned

above, the following pet regulations apply. On the newer ferries that have outside stairwells, dogs are allowed on the car deck and on the outdoor decks above the car deck. If the ferry has indoor stairwells, dogs are only allowed on the deck where they boarded the ferry. For example, if your dog comes onto the ferry in your car, he or she has to remain on the car deck. If you walk onto the ferry with your dog, your pooch is allowed on the outside deck where you boarded but cannot go onto other decks. In cases where your pet has to remain on the car deck, you can venture to the above decks without your pet to get food at the snack bars. However, the ferry system recommends in general that you stay with your pooch in the car. For any of the ferries, dogs are not allowed inside the ferry terminals. Ferry prices for people and autos are determined by the route and peak times, but in general tickets for people can start under $10 round trip, and more for autos. Dogs ride free!

and vehicle service between Milwaukee, Wisconsin and Muskegon, Michigan. The high speed crossing takes only 2.5 hours saving a long drive through Chicago. Pets are allowed but the following rules apply. Pets need to stay in your vehicle or in a kennel which is kept on the car deck. You cannot visit your pet during the ferry ride, but a crew person is stationed on the car deck throughout the trip. A limited supply of kennels are available to rent. Rates are $7.50 per kennel one way and $15 round trip. Reservations are required for a kennel. You can also use your own portable kennel on the car deck. Rates start at $50 per person one way ($85 round trip) and less for children and seniors. Transporting a vehicle starts a rate of $50 one way ($118 round trip). Vehicle rates do not include fares for a driver or passengers. Trailers can be accommodated for an extra fee. Rates are subject to change.

# Wisconsin Listings

Washington Island Ferry
Northpoint Pier
Ellison Bay, WI
920-847-2546
wisferry.com
This ferry is at the north end of Highway 42 and is a 30 minute crossing to Washington Island where some of the attractions include an art and nature center, a farm museum, a park and lookout tower, shops, and ample food. The ferry runs year round. Dogs on leash are allowed on the ferry.

Madeline Island Ferry Line
Bayfield or La Pointe docks
La Pointe, WI
715-474-2051
madferry.com/
Leashed dogs are allowed on this ferry line that provides both passenger and vehicle service to Madeline Island. Round trip rates are about $8.50 per person 12 and up, $4 for children 6 to 11 and free for children 5 and under. Vehicles cost about $28 and up. They can accommodate large motorhomes. The docks are located at Bayfield and on the island at La Pointe.

Lake Express Ferry Service
2330 S. Lincoln Memorial Drive
Milwaukee, WI
866-914-1010
lake-express.com
This ferry line provides passenger

# Canada

## Alberta Listings

Calgary Transit

Calgary, AB
403-262-1000
Dogs are allowed on Calgary city buses and LRT for a fee of $2.50 each way. Dogs must be well behaved, kept leashed, and under their owner's control at all times.

VIA Rail Canada

Edmonton, AB
888-VIA-RAIL (888-842-7245)
viarail.ca/en
This train system serves more than 450 destinations throughout Canada; Dogs are allowed for transport in the baggage area for an additional fee, and they may be fed and walked during stops. Pets must be crated and crates are available at the station if needed. The fee for small dogs is $15 per train each way; a small crate is 22X13X16 inches and rents for $50. The fee for medium sized dogs is $25 per train each way; a medium crate is 24X18X21 inches and rents for $75. The fee for a large dog is $40 per train each way; a large crate is 36X24X27 inches and rents for $120. The fee for an extra large dog is $50 per train each way; an extra large crate is 48X30X33 inches and rents for $150. Most stations are no longer than 1 to 2 hours apart, with longer stops each 6 - 10 hours even on cross country trips. The Train goes coast to coast in Canada from Vancouver to Toronto to Halifax, from Prince Rupert to Jasper, and other routes covering most of Canada.

VIA Rail Canada

Jasper, AB
888-VIA-RAIL (888-842-7245)
viarail.ca/en
This train system serves more than 450 destinations throughout Canada; Dogs are allowed for transport in the baggage area for an additional fee, and they may be fed and walked during stops. Pets must be crated and crates are available at the station if needed. The fee for small dogs is $15 per train each way; a small crate is 22X13X16 inches and rents for $50. The fee for medium sized dogs is $25 per train each way; a medium crate is 24X18X21 inches and rents for $75. The fee for a large dog is $40 per train each way; a large crate is 36X24X27 inches and rents for $120. The fee for an extra large dog is $50

per train each way; an extra large crate is 48X30X33 inches and rents for $150. Most stations are no longer than 1 to 2 hours apart, with longer stops each 6 - 10 hours even on cross country trips. The Train goes coast to coast in Canada from Vancouver to Toronto to Halifax, from Prince Rupert to Jasper, and other routes covering most of Canada.

## British Columbia Listings

BC Ferries Inside Passage Route

Bella Bella, BC
888-223-3779
bcferries.com
This ferry takes cars, RVs and passengers between Port Hardy and Prince Rupert and also to the Queen Charlotte Islands, Bella Bella and some other destinations. The principal route is between Port Hardy and Prince Rupert. This ferry is a new, large ship which appears as a small scale cruise ship. It has a number of restaurants, a bar and movies. Cabins are available for the 15 hour Inside Passage route. Dogs must remain on the car deck the entire time. They must stay in your car, RV or in a kennel. There is a separate, closed room for kenneled dogs on the car deck. There is a schedule of pet visits where people with pets are allowed to visit the car deck to walk their dogs. Each visit is about 3 hours apart. The dog will have to go on the car deck as there is a 15 hour sailing time. You can probably visit with your pet about 5 times during the 15 hour crossing. For people wanting to take the ferries to Alaska from Victoria, Vancouver or Washington we recommend this ferry from Port Hardy to Prince Rupert, then the Alaska Ferry to Juneau or Haines with intermediate stops possible on the Alaska Ferry.

VIA Rail Canada

Courtenay, BC
888-VIA-RAIL (888-842-7245)
viarail.ca/en
This train system serves more than 450 destinations throughout Canada; Dogs are allowed for transport in the baggage area for an additional fee, and they may be fed and walked during stops. Pets must be crated and crates are available at the station if needed. The fee for small dogs is $15 per train each way; a small crate is 22X13X16

inches and rents for $50. The fee for medium sized dogs is $25 per train each way; a medium crate is 24X18X21 inches and rents for $75. The fee for a large dog is $40 per train each way; a large crate is 36X24X27 inches and rents for $120. The fee for an extra large dog is $50 per train each way; an extra large crate is 48X30X33 inches and rents for $150. Most stations are no longer than 1 to 2 hours apart, with longer stops each 6 - 10 hours even on cross country trips. The Train goes coast to coast in Canada from Vancouver to Toronto to Halifax, from Prince Rupert to Jasper, and other routes covering most of Canada.

BC Ferries Inside Passage Route

Port Hardy, BC
888-223-3779
bcferries.com
This ferry takes cars, RVs and passengers between Port Hardy and Prince Rupert and also to the Queen Charlotte Islands, Bella Bella and some other destinations. The principal route is between Port Hardy and Prince Rupert. This ferry is a new, large ship which appears as a small scale cruise ship. It has a number of restaurants, a bar and movies. Cabins are available for the 15 hour Inside Passage route. Dogs must remain on the car deck the entire time. They must stay in your car, RV or in a kennel. There is a separate, closed room for kenneled dogs on the car deck. There is a schedule of pet visits where people with pets are allowed to visit the car deck to walk their dogs. Each visit is about 3 hours apart. The dog will have to go on the car deck as there is a 15 hour sailing time. You can probably visit with your pet about 5 times during the 15 hour crossing. For people wanting to take the ferries to Alaska from Victoria, Vancouver or Washington we recommend this ferry from Port Hardy to Prince Rupert, then the Alaska Ferry to Juneau or Haines with intermediate stops possible on the Alaska Ferry.

VIA Rail Canada

Prince George, BC
888-VIA-RAIL (888-842-7245)
viarail.ca/en
This train system serves more than 450 destinations throughout Canada; Dogs are allowed for transport in the baggage area for an additional fee, and they may be fed and walked during stops. Pets must be crated and crates are available at the station if needed. The fee for small dogs is $15 per train each way; a small crate

is 22X13X16 inches and rents for $50. The fee for medium sized dogs is $25 per train each way; a medium crate is 24X18X21 inches and rents for $75. The fee for a large dog is $40 per train each way; a large crate is 36X24X27 inches and rents for $120. The fee for an extra large dog is $50 per train each way; an extra large crate is 48X30X33 inches and rents for $150. Most stations are no longer than 1 to 2 hours apart, with longer stops each 6 - 10 hours even on cross country trips. The Train goes coast to coast in Canada from Vancouver to Toronto to Halifax, from Prince Rupert to Jasper, and other routes covering most of Canada.

Alaska Ferry
Yellowhead Hwy # 16
Prince Rupert, BC
250-627-1744 (800-642-0066)
dot.state.ak/amhs
The Alaska Ferry, or Alaska Maritime Highway System connects Bellingham, Washington and Prince Rupert, BC with many Alaskan ports and also serves these Alaskan ports with Car, RV and passenger service. The ferry is essential, as many of the ports served are not accessible from the mainland by car, only by ferry or air. Dogs are allowed, but with significant restrictions. They must remain on the car deck at all times. If you have an RV or a car, this means that the dog must remain in the vehicle. If you are a foot passenger, you will have to leave your pet on the car deck in a closed kennel. You may not visit the car deck while the ferry is not in port. An exception is made for ferry segments greater than 8 hours, where they will hold occasional pet visits to the car deck to allow the dogs to relieve themselves. This is not much fun for the dogs, so we recommend that you stop often at intermediate ports with pets. In port, you may take your dog off of the ferry usually for about 20 minutes to 45 minutes. The ferry serves the Southeast area of Alaska, the Prince William Sound area, and Kodiak and points in the Aleutian Islands. The pet information is listed at http://www.dot.state.ak.us/amhs/pets.shtml.

BC Ferries Inside Passage Route

Prince Rupert, BC
888-223-3779
bcferries.com
This ferry takes cars, RVs and passengers between Port Hardy and Prince Rupert and also to the Queen Charlotte Islands, Bella Bella and some other destinations. The principal route is between Port Hardy

and Prince Rupert. This ferry is a new, large ship which appears as a small scale cruise ship. It has a number of restaurants, a bar and movies. Cabins are available for the 15 hour Inside Passage route. Dogs must remain on the car deck the entire time. They must stay in your car, RV or in a kennel. There is a separate, closed room for kenneled dogs on the car deck. There is a schedule of pet visits where people with pets are allowed to visit the car deck to walk their dogs. Each visit is about 3 hours apart. The dog will have to go on the car deck as there is a 15 hour sailing time. You can probably visit with your pet about 5 times during the 15 hour crossing. For people wanting to take the ferries to Alaska from Victoria, Vancouver or Washington we recommend this ferry from Port Hardy to Prince Rupert, then the Alaska Ferry to Juneau or Haines with intermediate stops possible on the Alaska Ferry.

Inland Air Charters Ltd.
1 Bellas Road/Seal Cove
Prince Rupert, BC
250-624-2577
inlandair.bc.ca
Headquartered in Prince Rupert with a summer base in the Queen Charlotte Islands/Haida Gwaii, this private charter company offers a number of different services and tours. One dog up to about 50 pounds is allowed on board for no additional fee; they must be quiet, very well mannered, and under their owner's control at all times.

North Pacific Seaplanes
Seal Cove
Prince Rupert, BC
250-627-1341
northpacificseaplanes.com
Dogs are allowed on the regularly scheduled flights for an addition fee of $28 for small dogs, $45 for medium sized dogs, and up to $140 for large dogs; there is no addition pet fee if the whole plane is chartered. Dogs must be well behaved, under their owner's control, and leashed or kenneled at all times.

VIA Rail Canada

Prince Rupert, BC
888-VIA-RAIL (888-842-7245)
viarail.ca/en
This train system serves more than 450 destinations throughout Canada; Dogs are allowed for transport in the baggage area for an

additional fee, and they may be fed and walked during stops. Pets must be crated and crates are available at the station if needed. The fee for small dogs is $15 per train each way; a small crate is 22X13X16 inches and rents for $50. The fee for medium sized dogs is $25 per train each way; a medium crate is 24X18X21 inches and rents for $75. The fee for a large dog is $40 per train each way; a large crate is 36X24X27 inches and rents for $120. The fee for an extra large dog is $50 per train each way; an extra large crate is 48X30X33 inches and rents for $150. Most stations are no longer than 1 to 2 hours apart, with longer stops each 6 - 10 hours even on cross country trips. The Train goes coast to coast in Canada from Vancouver to Toronto to Halifax, from Prince Rupert to Jasper, and other routes covering most of Canada.

Translink (Ferry, Train, and Bus) Regional
Vancouver, BC
604-953-3333
translink.bc.ca
Small dogs in hard-sided carriers are allowed on the SeaBus (ferry), SkyTrain (train) and buses.

VIA Rail Canada

Vancouver, BC
888-VIA-RAIL (888-842-7245)
viarail.ca/en
This train system serves more than 450 destinations throughout Canada; Dogs are allowed for transport in the baggage area for an additional fee, and they may be fed and walked during stops. Pets must be crated and crates are available at the station if needed. The fee for small dogs is $15 per train each way; a small crate is 22X13X16 inches and rents for $50. The fee for medium sized dogs is $25 per train each way; a medium crate is 24X18X21 inches and rents for $75. The fee for a large dog is $40 per train each way; a large crate is 36X24X27 inches and rents for $120. The fee for an extra large dog is $50 per train each way; an extra large crate is 48X30X33 inches and rents for $150. Most stations are no longer than 1 to 2 hours apart, with longer stops each 6 - 10 hours even on cross country trips. The Train goes coast to coast in Canada from Vancouver to Toronto to Halifax, from Prince Rupert to Jasper, and other routes covering most of Canada.

BC Ferries
1112 Fort Street
Victoria, BC
250-386-3431

bcferries.bc.ca
Pets are allowed on most of the BC ferries, including the route from Vancouver to Victoria. This route departs from Tsawwassen which is south of Vancouver and arrives at Swartz Bay, which is north of Victoria. You will need to bring your car on the ferry in order to visit most of the dog-friendly places in Victoria. Dogs are only allowed on the open air car deck and must stay in the car or tied in a designated pet area. Owners must stay with their pets. The travel time for this route is approximately 1 hour and 35 minutes. Guide dogs and certified assistance dogs are not required to stay on the car decks.

BC Ferries
1112 Fort Street
Victoria, BC
250-386-3431
bcferries.bc.ca
Pets are allowed on most of the BC ferries, including the route from Vancouver to Victoria. These ferries depart from Tsawwassen which is south of Vancouver and arrives at Swartz Bay, which is north of Victoria. Dogs are only allowed on the open air car deck and must stay in your car or tied in a designated pet area on the car deck. Owners must stay with their pets. The travel time for this route is approximately 1 hour and 35 minutes. Guide dogs and certified assistance dogs are not required to stay on the car decks.

Black Ball Ferry Line
430 Belleville St
Victoria, BC
250-386-2202
cohoferry.com/main/
Offering breathtaking scenic passage for vehicles and passengers between Vancouver Island and the Olympic Peninsula is this ferry service's specialty. Dogs are also allowed for passage for no additional fee. They must have a current rabies certificate from a veterinarian, and they are allowed on the outer decks or in the vehicle only.

Blue Bird Cab
2659 Douglas StreetH 1
Victoria, BC
800-665-7055
taxicab.com/
In addition to providing taxi service throughout the greater Victoria area, this cab company also offers a number of customer service amenities. Dogs are allowed for transport with prior notice for no additional fee. They must be well mannered, in a carrier or leashed, and under their owner's control at all times.

VIA Rail Canada

Victoria, BC
888-VIA-RAIL (888-842-7245)
viarail.ca/en
This train system serves more than 450 destinations throughout Canada; Dogs are allowed for transport in the baggage area for an additional fee, and they may be fed and walked during stops. Pets must be crated and crates are available at the station if needed. The fee for small dogs is $15 per train each way; a small crate is 22X13X16 inches and rents for $50. The fee for medium sized dogs is $25 per train each way; a medium crate is 24X18X21 inches and rents for $75. The fee for a large dog is $40 per train each way; a large crate is 36X24X27 inches and rents for $120. The fee for an extra large dog is $50 per train each way; an extra large crate is 48X30X33 inches and rents for $150. Most stations are no longer than 1 to 2 hours apart, with longer stops each 6 - 10 hours even on cross country trips. The Train goes coast to coast in Canada from Vancouver to Toronto to Halifax, from Prince Rupert to Jasper, and other routes covering most of Canada.

Vancouver to Alaska Ferries
1112 Fort Street
Victoria, BC
250-386-3431
bcferries.bc.ca
While we do not recommend this route for pet owners because you cannot always be with your pet, here is some information about taking a ferry with your dog from Vancouver to Alaska. First take a BC Ferry from Port Hardy to Prince Ruppert via the Inside Passage. The ferry ride is about 15 hours. Dogs are allowed on the car decks and pet owners are not allowed to stay with their pets. You can still visit your pet about 4 to 5 times during the day only when crew members designate certain visiting times. From Prince Rupert in Canada to Seward in Alaska, you will need to take an Alaska State Ferry. This route takes about 4 days. Pets are required to have current health certificates within 30 days of travel. Pets must remain in your car or in your carrier, on the car decks only. People are not allowed to stay with their pets. The captain will announce "pet calls" so pet owners can take their pets out for a short walk onboard in the designated pet area. While there are usually three pet visitation times per day, it is entirely up to the captain. The captain's decision is based on the weather and other factors. On both ferries, there is a designated pet area where your pets can relieve themselves. Owners must clean up after their pets. Guide dogs and certified assistance dogs are not required to stay on the car decks.

Victoria Express
Belleville Street
Victoria, BC
250-361-9144
victoriaexpress.com/
This passenger ferry service runs between Port Angeles in Washington and Victoria. Crossing time is about one hour. Dogs are allowed and must be leashed. The ferries in Port Angeles leave from the Landing Mall on Railroad Avenue. The ferries in Victoria leave from the port on Belleville Street. Currency exchange is available at the Port Angeles Reservation Office. Their toll free number in the U.S. is 1-800-633-1589. Reservations are recommended. Because you will be crossing over an international border, identification for Customs and Immigration is required. U.S. and Canadian citizens traveling across the border will need proof of citizenship such as your passport or a certified copy of your birth certificate issued by the city, county or state/province where you were born. You will also need photo identification such as a current valid driver's license. People with children need to bring their child's birth certificate. Single parents, grandparents or guardians traveling with children often need proof or notarized letters from the other parent authorizing travel. Dogs traveling to Canada or returning to Canada need a certificate from their vet showing a rabies vaccination within the past 3 years. Dogs traveling to the U.S. or returning to the U.S. need to have a valid rabies vaccination certificate (including an expiration date and vet signature). The certificate must show that your dog has had the rabies vaccine at least 30 days prior to entry and within the past 36 months.

Victoria Regional Transit System
250 Gorge Road E
Victoria, BC
250-385-2551
bctransit.com/
This regional transit system links over 50 communities throughout the province. Dogs that can be transported in a hard-case carrier and held on the lap are allowed for no

additional fee.

# Manitoba Listings

VIA Rail Canada

Churchill, MB
888-VIA-RAIL (888-842-7245)
viarail.ca/en
This train system serves more than 450 destinations throughout Canada; Dogs are allowed for transport in the baggage area for an additional fee, and they may be fed and walked during stops. Pets must be crated and crates are available at the station if needed. The fee for small dogs is $15 per train each way; a small crate is 22X13X16 inches and rents for $50. The fee for medium sized dogs is $25 per train each way; a medium crate is 24X18X21 inches and rents for $75. The fee for a large dog is $40 per train each way; a large crate is 36X24X27 inches and rents for $120. The fee for an extra large dog is $50 per train each way; an extra large crate is 48X30X33 inches and rents for $150. Most stations are no longer than 1 to 2 hours apart, with longer stops each 6 - 10 hours even on cross country trips. The Train goes coast to coast in Canada from Vancouver to Toronto to Halifax, from Prince Rupert to Jasper, and other routes covering most of Canada.

VIA Rail Canada

Winnipeg, MB
888-VIA-RAIL (888-842-7245)
viarail.ca/en
This train system serves more than 450 destinations throughout Canada; Dogs are allowed for transport in the baggage area for an additional fee, and they may be fed and walked during stops. Pets must be crated and crates are available at the station if needed. The fee for small dogs is $15 per train each way; a small crate is 22X13X16 inches and rents for $50. The fee for medium sized dogs is $25 per train each way; a medium crate is 24X18X21 inches and rents for $75. The fee for a large dog is $40 per train each way; a large crate is 36X24X27 inches and rents for $120. The fee for an extra large dog is $50 per train each way; an extra large crate is 48X30X33 inches and rents for $150. Most stations are no longer than 1 to 2 hours apart, with longer stops each 6 - 10 hours even on cross country trips. The Train goes coast to coast in Canada from Vancouver to Toronto to Halifax, from Prince Rupert to Jasper, and other routes covering most of Canada.

# New Brunswick Listings

VIA Rail Canada

Moncton, NB
888-VIA-RAIL (888-842-7245)
viarail.ca/en
This train system serves more than 450 destinations throughout Canada; Dogs are allowed for transport in the baggage area for an additional fee, and they may be fed and walked during stops. Pets must be crated and crates are available at the station if needed. The fee for small dogs is $15 per train each way; a small crate is 22X13X16 inches and rents for $50. The fee for medium sized dogs is $25 per train each way; a medium crate is 24X18X21 inches and rents for $75. The fee for a large dog is $40 per train each way; a large crate is 36X24X27 inches and rents for $120. The fee for an extra large dog is $50 per train each way; an extra large crate is 48X30X33 inches and rents for $150. Most stations are no longer than 1 to 2 hours apart, with longer stops each 6 - 10 hours even on cross country trips. The Train goes coast to coast in Canada from Vancouver to Toronto to Halifax, from Prince Rupert to Jasper, and other routes covering most of Canada.

# Nova Scotia Listings

VIA Rail Canada

Halifax, NS
888-VIA-RAIL (888-842-7245)
viarail.ca/en
This train system serves more than 450 destinations throughout Canada; Dogs are allowed for transport in the baggage area for an additional fee, and they may be fed and walked during stops. Pets must be crated and crates are available at the station if needed. The fee for small dogs is $15 per train each way; a small crate is 22X13X16 inches and rents for $50. The fee for medium sized dogs is $25 per train each way; a medium crate is 24X18X21 inches and rents for $75. The fee for a large dog is $40 per train each way; a large crate is 36X24X27 inches and rents for $120. The fee for an extra large dog is $50 per train each way; an extra large crate is 48X30X33 inches and

rents for $150. Most stations are no longer than 1 to 2 hours apart, with longer stops each 6 - 10 hours even on cross country trips. The Train goes coast to coast in Canada from Vancouver to Toronto to Halifax, from Prince Rupert to Jasper, and other routes covering most of Canada.

East Coast Ferries/ North Sydney Terminal
355 Purves Street
N Sydney, NS
800-341-7981
marineatlantic.ca/
This ferry provides year around passenger and vehicle transport between the Island of Newfoundland and Nova Scotia. Dogs are allowed on board for no additional fee; they are allowed in the vehicle or in a kennel only. Kennels are provided on a 1st come, 1st served basis.

The Cat Ferry, Yarmouth Terminal
58 Water Street
Yarmouth, NS
902-742-6800
catferry.com/
Quickly gaining recognition for its speed and agility on the water, this CAT carries up to 775 passengers and 240 cars (not to mention a few furry friends also) across the Gulf of Maine between Yarmouth Nova Scotia and Bar Harbor and Portland Maine from June to mid-October. Dogs of all sizes are allowed for no additional pet fee. Dogs must be well behaved, and remain in a vehicle on the auto deck or in a kennel during passage. Kennels are available on a 1st come 1st served basis.

# Ontario Listings

VIA Rail Canada

Niagara Falls, ON
888-VIA-RAIL (888-842-7245)
viarail.ca/en
This train system serves more than 450 destinations throughout Canada; Dogs are allowed for transport in the baggage area for an additional fee, and they may be fed and walked during stops. Pets must be crated and crates are available at the station if needed. The fee for small dogs is $15 per train each way; a small crate is 22X13X16 inches and rents for $50. The fee for medium sized dogs is $25 per train each way; a medium crate is 24X18X21 inches and rents for $75. The fee for a large dog is $40 per train each way; a large crate is 36X24X27 inches and rents for $120. The fee for an extra large dog is $50 per train each way; an extra large crate is 48X30X33 inches and rents

340

for $150. Most stations are no longer than 1 to 2 hours apart, with longer stops each 6 - 10 hours even on cross country trips. The Train goes coast to coast in Canada from Vancouver to Toronto to Halifax, from Prince Rupert to Jasper, and other routes covering most of Canada.

VIA Rail Canada

Ottawa, ON
888-VIA-RAIL (888-842-7245)
viarail.ca/en
This train system serves more than 450 destinations throughout Canada; Dogs are allowed for transport in the baggage area for an additional fee, and they may be fed and walked during stops. Pets must be crated and crates are available at the station if needed. The fee for small dogs is $15 per train each way; a small crate is 22X13X16 inches and rents for $50. The fee for medium sized dogs is $25 per train each way; a medium crate is 24X18X21 inches and rents for $75. The fee for a large dog is $40 per train each way; a large crate is 36X24X27 inches and rents for $120. The fee for an extra large dog is $50 per train each way; an extra large crate is 48X30X33 inches and rents for $150. Most stations are no longer than 1 to 2 hours apart, with longer stops each 6 - 10 hours even on cross country trips. The Train goes coast to coast in Canada from Vancouver to Toronto to Halifax, from Prince Rupert to Jasper, and other routes covering most of Canada.

AutoShare - Car Sharing Network Inc.
26 Soho Street, Suite 203
Toronto, ON
416-340-7888
autoshare.com
A unique mode of transportation, this AutoShare program offers the largest fleet of shared cars and cargo vans in Toronto with more than 100 pick-up/drop-off locations in the city. Cars can be reserved in less than an hour and delivered to their customers location of choice 24/7; cars are insured and gas is included. Well behaved dogs are allowed in most of the autos, and there is no additional pet fee; they need to be declared at the time of reserving the vehicle.

TTC
Regional
Toronto, ON
416-393-INFO
city.toronto.on.ca/ttc
Both small and large dogs are allowed on the subway, buses, and streetcars. The driver has the discretion to decide whether or not pets are allowed if it is too crowded,

there are too many pets onboard or if you have a very large dog. Pets must be on a leash or in a carrier.

VIA Rail Canada

Toronto, ON
888-VIA-RAIL (888-842-7245)
viarail.ca/en
This train system serves more than 450 destinations throughout Canada; Dogs are allowed for transport in the baggage area for an additional fee, and they may be fed and walked during stops. Pets must be crated and crates are available at the station if needed. The fee for small dogs is $15 per train each way; a small crate is 22X13X16 inches and rents for $50. The fee for medium sized dogs is $25 per train each way; a medium crate is 24X18X21 inches and rents for $75. The fee for a large dog is $40 per train each way; a large crate is 36X24X27 inches and rents for $120. The fee for an extra large dog is $50 per train each way; an extra large crate is 48X30X33 inches and rents for $150. Most stations are no longer than 1 to 2 hours apart, with longer stops each 6 - 10 hours even on cross country trips. The Train goes coast to coast in Canada from Vancouver to Toronto to Halifax, from Prince Rupert to Jasper, and other routes covering most of Canada.

VIA Rail Canada

Windsor, ON
888-VIA-RAIL (888-842-7245)
viarail.ca/en
This train system serves more than 450 destinations throughout Canada; Dogs are allowed for transport in the baggage area for an additional fee, and they may be fed and walked during stops. Pets must be crated and crates are available at the station if needed. The fee for small dogs is $15 per train each way; a small crate is 22X13X16 inches and rents for $50. The fee for medium sized dogs is $25 per train each way; a medium crate is 24X18X21 inches and rents for $75. The fee for a large dog is $40 per train each way; a large crate is 36X24X27 inches and rents for $120. The fee for an extra large dog is $50 per train each way; an extra large crate is 48X30X33 inches and rents for $150. Most stations are no longer than 1 to 2 hours apart, with longer stops each 6 - 10 hours even on cross country trips. The Train goes coast to coast in Canada from Vancouver to Toronto to Halifax,

from Prince Rupert to Jasper, and other routes covering most of Canada.

# Prince Edward Island Listings

Bay Ferries Ltd
94 Water Street, Box 634
Charlottetown, PE
888-249-SAIL (7245)
nfl-bay.com/
These passenger/vehicle ships offer more than just high speed transport with amenities like onboard cafes, casinos, and movie theaters; routes cover from Maine, Nova Scotia, New Brunswick, and Prince Edward Island. Dogs are allowed on board all the ships in the vehicle or in a kennel only. The kennels are free upon request, but they are on a 1st come, 1st served basis and prior arrangements should be made or requested at the terminals. Dogs must be licensed and have proof of vaccinations.

# Quebec Listings

Atlas Taxi

Montreal, PQ
514-485-8585
Well-behaved, leashed dogs may ride in Montreal taxis with you. However, in winter you must provide a cover for the seats and you must report that you have a dog when calling for a taxi to avoid additional fees.

Metro (Subway)
Throughout the Region
Montreal, PQ
514-786-4636
stm.info
Small dogs in carriers are allowed. There is no fee for the dog but they may not take up a seat.

Unitaxi

Montreal, PQ
514-482-3000
Well-behaved, leashed dogs may ride in Montreal taxis with you. However, in winter you must provide a cover for the seats and you must report that you have a dog when calling for a taxi to avoid additional fees.

VIA Rail Canada

Montreal, PQ
888-VIA-RAIL (888-842-7245)
viarail.ca/en

This train system serves more than 450 destinations throughout Canada; Dogs are allowed for transport in the baggage area for an additional fee, and they may be fed and walked during stops. Pets must be crated and crates are available at the station if needed. The fee for small dogs is $15 per train each way; a small crate is 22X13X16 inches and rents for $50. The fee for medium sized dogs is $25 per train each way; a medium crate is 24X18X21 inches and rents for $75. The fee for a large dog is $40 per train each way; a large crate is 36X24X27 inches and rents for $120. The fee for an extra large dog is $50 per train each way; an extra large crate is 48X30X33 inches and rents for $150. Most stations are no longer than 1 to 2 hours apart, with longer stops each 6 - 10 hours even on cross country trips. The Train goes coast to coast in Canada from Vancouver to Toronto to Halifax, from Prince Rupert to Jasper, and other routes covering most of Canada.

Quebec - Levis Ferry
Rue Dalhousie, Lower Town
Quebec, PQ
418-644-3704
For a fabulous view of Quebec from the river take the ferry from the Lower Town to Levis. The ferry ride takes about ten minutes each way and they leave about every 30 minutes throughout the day and evening. Well-behaved, leashed dogs are allowed for no additional fee. You can take the ferry for the views or if you need transportation to Levis.

Taxi Coop de Quebec
Throughout the city
Quebec, PQ
418-525-5191
Pets are allowed on these taxis in Quebec. They must be leashed or in a carrier at all times. People planning to take a pet on a taxi need to call ahead to get a pet-friendly cab driver.

Taxi Quebec
Throughout the city
Quebec, PQ
418-522-2001
Pets are allowed on these taxis in Quebec. They must be leashed or in a carrier at all times. People planning to take a pet on a taxi need to call ahead to get a pet-friendly cab driver.

VIA Rail Canada

Quebec, PQ
888-VIA-RAIL (888-842-7245)
viarail.ca/en
This train system serves more than

450 destinations throughout Canada; Dogs are allowed for transport in the baggage area for an additional fee, and they may be fed and walked during stops. Pets must be crated and crates are available at the station if needed. The fee for small dogs is $15 per train each way; a small crate is 22X13X16 inches and rents for $50. The fee for medium sized dogs is $25 per train each way; a medium crate is 24X18X21 inches and rents for $75. The fee for a large dog is $40 per train each way; a large crate is 36X24X27 inches and rents for $120. The fee for an extra large dog is $50 per train each way; an extra large crate is 48X30X33 inches and rents for $150. Most stations are no longer than 1 to 2 hours apart, with longer stops each 6 - 10 hours even on cross country trips. The Train goes coast to coast in Canada from Vancouver to Toronto to Halifax, from Prince Rupert to Jasper, and other routes covering most of Canada.

# Saskatchewan Listings

VIA Rail Canada

Saskatoon, SK
888-VIA-RAIL (888-842-7245)
viarail.ca/en
This train system serves more than 450 destinations throughout Canada; Dogs are allowed for transport in the baggage area for an additional fee, and they may be fed and walked during stops. Pets must be crated and crates are available at the station if needed. The fee for small dogs is $15 per train each way; a small crate is 22X13X16 inches and rents for $50. The fee for medium sized dogs is $25 per train each way; a medium crate is 24X18X21 inches and rents for $75. The fee for a large dog is $40 per train each way; a large crate is 36X24X27 inches and rents for $120. The fee for an extra large dog is $50 per train each way; an extra large crate is 48X30X33 inches and rents for $150. Most stations are no longer than 1 to 2 hours apart, with longer stops each 6 - 10 hours even on cross country trips. The Train goes coast to coast in Canada from Vancouver to Toronto to Halifax, from Prince Rupert to Jasper, and other routes covering most of Canada.

# Washington Listings

Washington State Ferries
2100 Ferry Terminal Rd
Anacortes, WA
206-464-6400
wsdot.wa.gov/ferries/
This ferry service offers many routes in Washington State, as well as a route from Sidney, near Victoria, to Anacortes in Washington. The ferry ride is about 3 hours long and the ferry carries both passengers and vehicles. You can also catch a ferry to Sidney from Friday Harbor, Washington, in the San Juan Islands. This ferry ride is about 1 hour and 15 minutes. While leashed dogs are allowed on the ferry routes mentioned above, the following pet regulations apply. On the newer ferries that have outside stairwells, dogs are allowed on the car deck and the outdoor decks above the car deck. If the ferry has indoor stairwells, dogs are only allowed on the deck where they boarded the ferry. For example, if your dog comes onto the ferry in your car, he or she has to remain on the car deck. If you walk onto the ferry with your dog, your pooch is allowed on the outside deck where you boarded but cannot go onto other decks. In cases where your pet has to remain on the car deck, you can venture to the above decks without your pet to get food at the snack bars. However, the ferry system recommends in general that you stay with your pooch in the car. For any of the ferries, dogs are not allowed inside the ferry terminals. The ferries in Anacortes leave from 2100 Ferry Terminal Road. The ferries in Friday Harbor leave from 91 Front Street and the ferries in Sidney leave from 2499 Ocean Avenue. Reservations are recommended 48 hours or more in advance if you are bringing a vehicle. Because you will be crossing over an international border, identification for Customs and Immigration is required. U.S. and Canadian citizens traveling across the border will need proof of citizenship such as your passport or a certified copy of your birth certificate issued by the city, county or state/province where you were born. You will also need photo identification such as a current valid driver's license. People with children need to bring their child's birth certificate. Single parents, grandparents or guardians traveling with children often need proof or notarized letters from the other parent authorizing travel. Dogs traveling to Canada or returning to Canada need a certificate from

their vet showing a rabies vaccination within the past 3 years. Dogs traveling to the U.S. or returning to the U.S. need to have a valid rabies vaccination certificate (including an expiration date and vet signature). The certificate must show that the dog had the rabies vaccine at least 30 days prior to entry and within the past 36 months.

# Yukon Listings

Dawson City Ferry
H 2/Front Street
Dawson City, YU
867-993-5441
This small vehicle and passenger ferry offers free ferry rides across the Yukon River. With the exception of being closed on Wednesday mornings between 5 am and 7 am for servicing, the ferry runs 24 hours a day (there is other traffic that gets priority so check ahead for schedules). The trip is fairly short so dogs may be either stay in the vehicle or be on leash on deck.

Chapter 4

# United States National Parks

# Alaska Listings

Wrangell-St Elias National Park and Preserve
PO Box 439
Copper Center, AK
907-822-5234
nps.gov/wrst/index.htm
Dogs on leash are allowed in the park. They are not allowed in buildings. The park features camping, hiking, auto touring, and more.

Denali National Park and Preserve
PO Box 9
Denali Park, AK
907-683-2294
nps.gov/dena/index.htm
Dogs must be on leash and must be cleaned up after in Denali National Park. Dogs are only allowed on the paved roads and dirt roads. One place to walk is on the road to Savage after mile 15, which is a dirt road and only the park buses are allowed. Access is by car depending on weather. Dogs on leash are allowed in the Denali National Park campgrounds, but they may not be left unattended in the campgrounds. The park features auto touring, camping, and scenery.

Gates of the Arctic National Park and Preserve
201 First Avenue
Fairbanks, AK
907-692-5494
nps.gov/gaar/index.htm
Dogs must be on leash and must be cleaned up after in the park. The park is accessed by plane, foot and car depending on weather. Dogs are allowed in the backcountry of the park but there are no man-made trails. It is a wilderness park. The nearest places to stay when visiting the park is the town of Bettles Field or Wiseman. There are no campgrounds in the park and there are no facilities in the park.

Glacier Bay National Park
1 Park Road
Gustavus, AK
907-697-2230
nps.gov/glba
This national park offers coastal beaches and high mountains. The way to arrive at this park is by plane, boat, or ferry, usually from Juneau. The Glacier Bay Visitor Center is open daily from May 27 to September 11, from noon to 8:45 p.m. Dogs are not allowed to be off the road more than 100 feet, and they are not allowed on any of the trails into the back country. They are also not allowed on the Barlett Trail or on the Forest Loop Trail, or in any of the

camp buildings. The Visitor Information Station for boaters and campers, is open May through June from 8 to 5 p.m.; June, July, and August from 7 to 9 p.m., and September 8 to 5 p.m. Dogs are allowed at no additional fee, and they can be in the developed Barlett Cove area, or on any of the marked trails. Dogs may not be left unattended at any time, and they must be leashed at all times, and cleaned up after.

Katmai National Park and Preserve
PO Box 7
King Salmon, AK
907-246-3305
nps.gov/katm/index.htm
Dogs on leash are allowed only in developed areas. They are not allowed in the Brooks camping area. The park is accessed by plane or dogsled only.

Kobuk Valley National Park
PO Box 1029
Kotzebue, AK
907-442-3760
nps.gov/kova/index.htm
Dogs on leash are allowed in the park. The park is accessed by plane, foot, or dogsled only.

Western Arctic National Parklands
PO Box 1029
Kotzebue, AK
907-442-3760
nps.gov/nwak/index.htm
Pets are allowed. There is not an official pet policy. The park is accessed by plane and dogsledding.

Lake Clark National Park and Preserve
1 Park Place
Port Alsworth, AK
907-781-2218
nps.gov/lacl/index.htm
Dogs on leash are allowed in the park area. The park is accessed by plane or dogsled only. The park features boating, camping, fishing, hiking, and more.

Kenai Fjords National Park
PO Box 1727
Seward, AK
907-224-2132
nps.gov/klgo/index.htm
Dogs on leash are only allowed in the parking lot area and along roads. They are not allowed in buildings, on trails, or in the back country.

# Arizona Listings

Grand Canyon National Park

Hwy 64
Grand Canyon, AZ
928-638-7888
nps.gov/grca/
The Grand Canyon, located in the northwest corner of Arizona, is considered to be one of the most impressive natural splendors in the world. It is 277 miles long, 18 miles wide, and at its deepest point, is 6000 vertical feet (more than 1 mile) from rim to river. The Grand Canyon has several entrance areas, but the most popular is the South Rim. Dogs are not allowed in most areas of the North Rim of the Park. On the North Rim, the only trail that dogs are allowed on is the bridle trail from the lodge to the North Kaibab Trail (but not on the North Kaibab Trail). Dogs are not allowed on any trails below the rim, but leashed dogs are allowed on the paved rim trail. This dog-friendly trail is about 2.7 miles each way and offers excellent views of the Grand Canyon. Remember that the elevation at the rim is 7,000 feet, so you or your pup may need to rest more often than usual. Also, the weather can be very hot during the summer and can be snowing during the winter, so plan accordingly. And be sure you or your pup do not get too close to the edge! Feel like taking a tour? Well-behaved dogs are allowed on the Geology Walk. This is a one hour park ranger guided tour and consists of a leisurely walk along a 3/4 mile paved rim trail. They discuss how the Grand Canyon was created and more. The tour departs at 11am daily (weather permitting) from the Yavapai Observation Station. Pets are allowed in the Grand Canyon's Mather Campground in Grand Canyon Village, the Desert View Campground 26 miles east of the village, and, for RVs, the Trailer Village in Grand Canyon Village. Dogs must be leashed at all times in the campgrounds and may not be left unattended. There are kennels available at the South Rim. Its hours are 7:30 am to 5 pm. To make kennel reservations or for other kennel information call 928-638-0534. The Grand Canyon park entrance fee is currently $25.00 per private vehicle, payable upon entry to the park. Admission tickets are for 7 days.

Petrified Forest National Park
Entrances on Hwy 40 and Hwy 180
Petrified Forest National Park, AZ
928-524-6228
nps.gov/pefo/
The Petrified Forest is located in northeastern Arizona and features one of the world's largest and most colorful concentrations of petrified wood. Also included in the park's

345

93,533 acres are the multi-hued badlands of the Painted Desert, archeological sites and displays of 225 million year old fossils. Your leashed dog is welcome on all of the paved trails and scenic overlooks. Take a walk on the self-guided Giant Logs trail or view ancient petroglyphs from an overlook. The entrance fee is $10 per private vehicle.

Saguaro National Park
3693 South Old Spanish Trail
Tucson, AZ
520-733-5100
nps.gov/sagu/index.htm
Dogs must be on leash and must be cleaned up after on roadways and picnic areas. They are not allowed on any trails or buildings.

# Arkansas Listings

Hot Springs National Park
369 Central Avenue
Hot Springs, AR
501-624-2701
nps.gov/hosp
There are 47 hot springs here, and this reserve was established in 1832 to protect them. That makes this park our oldest national park. The park is open daily from 9:00 a.m. to 5:00 p.m., except in the summer from May 28 to August 12, when they stay open until 6:00 p.m. Dogs are allowed at no additional fee at the park and in the campground, which does not have hookups. Dogs may not be left unattended, they must be leashed, and cleaned up after. Dogs are allowed throughout the park, trails and in the camp area.

# California Listings

Death Valley National Park
Highway 190
Death Valley, CA
760-786-2331
nps.gov/deva
Death Valley is one of the hottest places on Earth, with summer temperatures averaging well over 100 degrees Fahrenheit. It is also the lowest point on the Western Hemisphere at 282 feet below sea level. Average rainfall here sets yet another record. With an average of only 1.96 inches per year, this valley is the driest place in North America. Because of the high summer heat, the best time to visit the park is during the winter. Even though dogs are not allowed on any trails, you will still be able to see the majority of the sights and attractions from your car. There are several scenic drives that

are popular with all visitors, with or without dogs. Dante's View is a 52 mile round trip drive that takes about 2 hours or longer. Some parts of the road are graded dirt roads and no trailers or RVs are allowed. On this drive you will view scenic mudstone hills which are made of 7 to 9 million year old lakebed sediments. You will also get a great view from the top of Dantes View. Another scenic drive is called Badwater. It is located about 18 miles from the Visitor Center and can take about 1.5 to 2 hours or longer. On this drive you will view the Devil's Golf Course where there are almost pure table salt crystals from an ancient lake. You will also drive to Badwater which is the lowest point in the Western Hemisphere at 282 feet below sea level. Dogs are allowed at view points which are about 200 yards or less from roads or parking lots. Pets must be leashed and attended at all times. Please clean up after your pets. While dogs are not allowed on any trails in the park, they can walk along roads. Pets are allowed up to a few hundred yards from the paved and dirt roads. Stop at the Furnance Creek Visitor Center to pick up a brochure and more information. The visitor center is located on Highway 190, north of the lowest point.

Lassen Volcanic National Park
Highway36
Mineral, CA
530-595-4480 (877-444-6777)
nps.gov/lavo/index.htm
This park has the distinction of being home to all 4 types of volcanoes found in the world. It is also home to the Lassen Smelowskia Flower that blooms no where else on earth. Much can be seen from their seasonal 29 mile auto-tour (Highway89) that offers turn-outs for some great views of the park including Lassen Peak, Brokeoff Mountain, the Devastated Area, and more. Dogs are allowed in the park in developed areas, campgrounds, picnic areas, established roadways, and scenic pull-outs. There are no additional pet fees for camping, and they must be kept on a leash no longer than 6 feet, be cleaned up after promptly, and be current on vaccinations. Dogs may not be left unattended outside or left in a vehicle that may be a hazard to the pet without proper cooling, food, and water. Dogs are not allowed in buildings, in any body of water, in the backcountry, or on any trails or boardwalks. For those who would like to hike with their pets, this park is surrounded by great hiking places such as the Caribou Wilderness to

the East, the Thousand Lakes Wilderness to the North, or the Spencer Meadows and Mill Creek Trails just outside the park off of Highway 36. Multiple dogs may be allowed.

Lassen Volcanic National Park
PO Box 100
Mineral, CA
530-595-4444
nps.gov/lavo/
This national park does not really have much to see or do if you bring your pooch, except for staying overnight at the campgrounds. However, the dog-friendly Lassen National Forest surrounds the national park. At the national forest you will be able to find dog-friendly hiking, sightseeing and camping. Pets must be leashed and attended at all times. Please clean up after your pet.

Sequoia and Kings Canyon National Park
47050 General Highway
Three Rivers, CA
559-565-3341
nps.gov/seki/
This national park does not really have much to see or do if you bring your pooch, except for driving through a giant redwood forest in your car and staying overnight at the campgrounds. However, located to the west and south of this national park is the dog-friendly Giant National Sequoia Monument. There you will be able to find dog-friendly hiking, sightseeing and camping. Pets must be leashed and attended at all times. Please clean up after your pet.

Joshua Tree National Park
74485 National Park Drive
Twentynine Palms, CA
760-367-5500
nps.gov/jotr
Dogs are not allowed on the trails, cannot be left unattended, and must be on leash. However, they are allowed on dirt and paved roads including the Geology Tour Road. This is actually a driving tour, but you'll be able to see the park's most fascinating landscapes from this road. It is an 18 mile tour with 16 stops. The park recommends taking about 2 hours for the round trip. At stop #9, about 5 miles out, there is room to turnaround if you do not want to complete the whole tour.

Channel Islands National Park
1901 Spinnaker Drive
Ventura, CA
805-658-5730
nps.gov/chis/index.htm

Pets are not allowed on the islands.

Yosemite National Park
PO Box 577
Yosemite National Park, CA
209-372-0200
nps.gov/yose
This 750,000 acre park is one of the most popular national parks in the country. Yosemite's geology is world famous for its granite cliffs, tall waterfalls and giant sequoia groves. As with most national parks, pets have limited access within the park. Pets are not allowed on unpaved or poorly paved trails, in wilderness areas including hiking trails, in park lodging (except for some campgrounds) and on shuttle buses. However, there are still several nice areas to walk with your pooch and you will be able to see the majority of sights and points of interest that most visitors see. Dogs are allowed in developed areas and on fully paved trails, include Yosemite Valley which offers about 2 miles of paved trails. From these trails you can view El Capitan, Half Dome and Yosemite Falls. You can also take the .5 mile paved trail right up to the base of Bridalveil Fall which is a 620 foot year round waterfall. The best time to view this waterfall is in the spring or early summer. The water thunders down and almost creates a nice rain at the base. Water-loving dogs will be sure to like this attraction. In general dogs are not allowed on unpaved trails, but this park does make the following exceptions. Dogs are allowed on the Meadow Loop and Four Mile fire roads in Wawona. They are also allowed on the Carlon Road and on the Old Big Oak Flat Road between Hodgdon Meadow and Hazel Green Creek. Dogs must be on a 6 foot or less leash and attended at all times. People must also clean up after their pets. For a detailed map of Yosemite, visit their web site at http://www.nps.gov/yose/pphtml/maps .html. The green dots show the paved trails. There are four main entrances to the park and all four lead to the Yosemite Valley. The park entrance fees are as follows: $20 per vehicle, $40 annual pass or $10 per individual on foot. The pass is good for 7 days. Prices are subject to change. Yosemite Valley is open year round and may be reached via Highway 41 from Fresno, Highway 140 from Merced, Highway 120 from Manteca and in late spring through late fall via the Tioga Road (Highway 120 East) from Lee Vining. From November through March, all park roads are subject to snow chain control (including 4x4s) or temporary closure at any time due to hazardous winter

driving conditions. For updated 24 hour road and weather conditions call (209) 372-0200.

# Colorado Listings

Rocky Mountain National Park
1000 Highway 36
Estes Park, CO
970-586-1206
nps.gov/romo/
Dogs cannot really do much in this park, but as you drive through the park, you will find some spectacular scenery and possibly some sightings of wildlife. Pets are not allowed on trails, or in the backcountry. Pets are allowed in your car, along the road, in parking lots, at picnic areas and campgrounds. Dogs must be on a 6 foot or less leash. You can still take your dog for a hike, not in the national park, but in the adjacent Arapaho-Roosevelt National Forest.

Black Canyon of the Gunnison National Park
102 Elk Creek
Gunnison, CO
970-641-2337
nps.gov/blca/index.htm
This unique canyon in the Rockies is narrow and deep. Dogs may view the Canyon with you from the Rim Rock Trail. Dogs on leash are allowed on roads, campgrounds, overlooks, the Rim Rock trail, Cedar Point Nature trail, and North Rim Chasm View Nature trail. They are not allowed on other hiking trails, inner canyon routes, or in the wilderness area within the park. Dogs on leash are permitted throughout the Curecanti National Recreation Area nearby.

Mesa Verde National Park
PO Box 8
Mesa Verde, CO
970-529-4465
nps.gov/meve/index.htm
Dogs on leash are allowed in the campgrounds and parking lots only. Dogs are not allowed on hiking trails or archaeological sites. Pets cannot be left alone or in vehicles.

Great Sand Dunes National Park and Preserve
11999 Highway 150
Mosca, CO
719-378-6300
nps.gov/grsa/index.htm
The dunes of Great Sand Dunes National Park rise over 750 feet high. Dogs are allowed throughout the park and must be on leash. You must clean up after your dog and dogs may not be left unattended in

the park. Leashed dogs are also welcome in the campgrounds. The park features auto touring, camping fishing, hiking, and more.

# Florida Listings

Biscayne National Park
9700 SW 328 Street
Homestead, FL
305-230-7275
nps.gov/bisc/
In addition to providing protection for and educating visitors of the 4 primary ecosystems that this park maintains, it also shares a long cultural history with evidence of human occupation of more than 10,000 years. Guests will also find a wide variety of planned Ranger activities and plenty of land and water recreation. Dogs are allowed for no additional fee; they must be leashed and cleaned up after at all times. They are only allowed at the Elliot campground, and they are allowed on the trails unless otherwise marked. Multiple dogs may be allowed.

Everglades National Park
40001 H 9336/Main Park Road
Homestead, FL
305-242-7700 (800/365-CAMP (2267))
nps.gov/ever/
Home to many rare and endangered species, this park is also the country's largest subtropical wilderness - now designated a World Heritage Site, a Wetland of International Importance site, and an International Biosphere Reserve. Dogs are allowed for no additional fee; they may only be in the campground, picnic areas, in the parking lots and on paved roads. Dogs may not be left unattended at any time, and they must be leashed and cleaned up after. Multiple dogs may be allowed.

Dry Tortugas National Park
PO Box 6208
Key West, FL
305-242-7100
nps.gov/drto/index.htm
This set of Islands is 70 miles west of Key West in the Gulf of Mexico. Dogs must be on leash and must be cleaned up after on this island. Dogs are not allowed on the ferry but they can come over by private boat or charter from Key West. The park features picnicking, camping, fishing, swimming and more. It is open year round.

# Hawaii Listings

Haleakala National Park
It is located off Hana Highway
Hawaii, HI
808-572-4400
nps.gov/hale
Dogs are not allowed on the trails or in any wilderness area. They are allowed in the campgrounds. There are no water or bathroom facilities at this park, so be sure to bring enough for you and your pet.

Hawaii Volcanoes National Park
MM 31.5 H 11
Hawaii National Park, HI
808-985-6000
nps.gov/havo
This park covers the top of earth's most massive volcano the Mauna Loa at almost 14,000 feet. The park is open 7 days a week year round. Dogs are allowed at no additional fee, but they may only be on paved roads, the developed areas, and the campgrounds. They are not allowed on any of the trails or off the roads. Dogs may not be left unattended at any time, and they must be leashed and cleaned up after.

# Kentucky Listings

Mammoth Cave National Park
off Interstate 65
Mammoth Cave, KY
270-758-2251
nps.gov/maca/
At this national park, leashed dogs are allowed on hiking trails and in campgrounds. There are over 70 miles of hiking trails which go through valleys, up into hills, and next to rivers, lakes and waterfalls. However, dogs are not allowed in the cave, which is the main attraction at this park. The park does offer kennels that are located near the Mammoth Cave Hotel. The kennels are outdoor and not heated or air-conditioned. If you want to try the kennels at Mammoth Cave, be sure to check them out first. You will need to make a reservation for the kennels and there is a $5 key deposit fee for the cage lock and a $2.50 fee for half a day or a $5.00 fee for the entire day. To make kennel reservations, call the Mammoth Cave Hotel directly at 270-758-2225.

# Maine Listings

Acadia National Park
Eagle Lake Road
Bar Harbor, ME
207-288-3338
nps.gov/acad/
This National Park ranks high on the

tail wagging meter. Dogs are allowed on most of the hiking trails, which is unusual for a national park. There are miles and miles of both hiking trails and carriage roads. Pets are also allowed at the campgrounds, but must be attended at all times. They are not allowed on sand beaches during the summer or on the steeper hiking trails year-round. Pets must be on a 6 foot or less leash at all times. There is one exception to the leash rule. There is an area in the park that is privately owned where dogs are allowed to run leash-free. It is called Little Long Pond and is located near Seal Harbor. Don't miss the awe-inspiring view from the top of Cadillac Mountain in the park. Overall, this is a pretty popular national park for dogs and their dog-loving owners. There is a $10 entrance fee into the park, which is good for 7 days. You can also purchase an audio tape tour of the Park Loop Road which is a self-guided auto tour. The driving tour is about 27 miles and takes 3 to 4 hours including stops. Audio tapes are available at the Hulls Cove Visitor Center.

# Maryland Listings

Chesapeake Bay Gateways Network
National Park
410 Severn Avenue Ste 109
Annapolis, MD
888-BAYWAYS
nps.gov/cbpo/index.htm
Dogs must be on leash and must be cleaned up after in most of the park areas. The park is located in Washinton D.C., Maryland, New York, Pennsylvania, Virginia, and West Virginia. You must follow all local and state park rules pertaining to pets. The park features in most states camping, auto touring, hiking, swimming, fishing, boating, and more.

# Michigan Listings

Isle Royale National Park
800 East Lakeshore Drive
Houghton, MI
906) 482-0984
nps.gov/isro
No dogs are allowed within the park.

# Minnesota Listings

Voyageurs National Park
3131 H 53S

International Falls, MN
218-283-9821
nps.gov/voya
Voyageurs is a water based park located on the northern edge of Minnesota, and has some of the oldest exposed rock formations in the world. The park can also be accessed on Highway 11 from the west. There is camping, but a boat is required to access the trailheads to get there. There is another camping area just outside of the park as well. Dogs are allowed in developed areas of the park, outside visitor centers, at boat ramps, picnic areas, at tent camping areas, houseboats, and day use sites on the four main lakes. There are no additional pet fees. Dogs may not be left unattended at any time, they must be on no more than a 6 foot leash, and be cleaned up after. Pets are not allowed on park trails or in the backcountry.

# Montana Listings

Glacier National Park
On Highway 2
West Glacier, MT
406-888-7800
nps.gov/glac
This national park features more than a million acres of spectacular scenery, hundreds of miles of trails, a rich and diverse cultural history, and diverse ecosystems that support a large variety of flora, fauna, recreation, and educational opportunities. Dogs are allowed for no additional fee; they may not be left unattended; must be kept on no more than a 6 foot leash, and cleaned up after promptly. Dogs are allowed in campgrounds, developed areas, and on main roads when they are not closed off; they are not allowed in the back country, on any of the regular trails, or on lake shores. There is one 2-mile bike trail that allows dogs spanning from W. Glacier (end of main road in town) to Apgar (on Apgar Loop - there is signage on both sides). Multiple dogs may be allowed.

# Nevada Listings

Great Basin National Park
100 Great Basin
Baker, NV
775-234-7331
nps.gov/grba
The Great Basin Park rises to over 13,000 feet and hosts the Lehman Caves and an abundant variety of wildlife, plants, and waterways. They are open year round for tent and RV

camping with no hook ups. There is no additional fee for dogs, but they may not be left unattended, they must be on no more than a 6 foot leash, and be cleaned up after. Dogs are not allowed on any of the trails.

# New Jersey Listings

New Jersey Coastal Heritage Trail Route National Park
389 Fortescue Road
Newport, NJ
856-447-0103
nps.gov/neje/index.htm
Dogs must be on leash and must be cleaned up after on most trails and stops on the route. You must follow local and state parks rules and pet policies along the route. Mainly auto touring, but also features hiking, boating, swimming, and more.

# New Mexico Listings

Carlsbad Canyon National Park
727 Carlsbad Canyon H 62/180
Carlsbad, NM
505-785-2232
nps.gov/cave/
This national park was established to preserve the Carlsbad Caverns, and over 100 other caves housed within a fossil reef. It is also home to America's deepest and 4th longest limestone cave. Dogs are not allowed at the park, except in the parking lot and at the kennel that is on site, and they must be on leash and cleaned up after.

# New York Listings

Manhattan Sites National Park Service
26 Wall Street
New York, NY
212-825-6888
nps.gov/masi/index.htm
Dogs must be on leash and must be cleaned up after on the pathways in this city park on Wall Street. There are six separate sites representing the 1600's to the present.

# North Carolina Listings

Great Smoky Mountains National Park
107 Park Headquarters Road
Cherokee, NC
865-436-1200

(http://www.nps.gov/grsm/)
Great Smoky Mountains National Park is located both in Tennessee and North Carolina and is one of the most popular of the National Parks. Pets must be leashed or restrained at all times within the park and are not allowed on most of the hiking trails. They can accompany you in your car and at lookouts and stops near the road. However, there are two trails in Great Smoky Mountains National Park that will allow leashed dogs. The Gatlinburg Trail is a 1.9 mile trail from the Sugarland's Visitor Center to the outskirts of Gatlinburg; it runs along the forest with beautiful river views and it passes old homesteads along the way. It follows a creek a good portion of the way. The Oconaluftee River Trail follows along the river for a 1.5 mile

# North Dakota Listings

Theodore Roosevelt National Park
On I 94 at Exits 25 or 27 (South Unit)
Medora, ND
701-623-4466
nps.gov/thro
This Park is located in the North Dakota Badlands. It is named after the 26th president, Theodore Roosevelt. He was a great conservationist, who, out of concern for the future of our lands, established the National Forest Service in 1906. The park is open all year although some roads close at times due to snow. The campgrounds are also open all year (no hookups). Dogs are allowed in the park and the campgrounds at no additional fee, but dogs may not be left unattended at any time, and they are not allowed in any of the buildings, or on any of the trails. However, there are trails just outside the park where dogs are allowed. One of the trails is the Maahdaahhey Trail.

# Ohio Listings

Cuyahoga Valley National Park
Canal Road
Brecksville, OH
216-524-1497
nps.gov/cuva/
This national park consists of 33,000 acres along the banks of the Cuyahoga River. Scenery and terrain varies from a rolling floodplain to steep valley walls,

ravines and lush upland forests. Popular activities at this park include hiking, bicycling, birdwatching and picnicking. Dogs are allowed at the park including the hiking trails. Pets must be leashed and cleaned up after. Pets are not allowed inside any buildings. The park is open daily and can be accessed by many different highways, including I-77, I-271, I-80/Ohio Turnpike, and State Route 8. To get to Canal Visitor Center, exit I-77 at Rockside Road. Go approximately 1 mile east to Canal Road and turn right. The visitor center is about 1.5 miles on the right. To get to Happy Days Visitor Center, take State Route 8 to west State Route 303. The visitor center is about 1 mile on the left. There is no park entrance fee.

Hopewell Mounds National Park
16062 H 104
Chillicothe, OH
740-774-1126
nps.gov/hocu/index.htm
It is believed that the earthworks here date back to between 200 BC to 50 AD, and that they hold significance to the social and ceremonial activities of that time. In addition to their visitor's center, there is a 1 mile paved trail and interpretive trails. Dogs are allowed in the park and on the trails; they are not allowed in park buildings. Dogs must be leashed and cleaned up after promptly.

# Oregon Listings

Crater Lake National Park
PO Box 7
Crater Lake, OR
541-594-3100
nps.gov/crla/index.htm
Dogs must be on leash and must be cleaned up after in park. Dogs must remain in the developed portions of the park and are not allowed on the dirt trails or in the backcountry. They are allowed on the roads and the sidewalks. There is a road and sidewalk surrounding Crater Lake so you and your dog may view the lake and walk quite a ways around it. Dogs are not allowed in any buildings. Dogs are allowed in the campgrounds on leash in the park.

# Pennsylvania Listings

Upper Delaware Scenic and Recreational River National Park
274 River Road
Beach Lake, PA

570-685-4871
nps.gov/upde/index.htm
Dogs must be on leash and must be cleaned up after in most of the national park areas. You must follow state and local park rules. The park features auto touring, camping, boating, fishing, and more.

Deshler-Morris House National Park
5442 Germantown Avenue
Philadelphia, PA
215-596-1748
nps.gov/demo/index.htm
Dogs must be on leash and must be cleaned up after in the park. Dogs are not allowed in the house.

# South Carolina Listings

Congaree National Park
48 Old Bluff Road
Columbia, SC
803-776-4396
nps.gov/cosw
This 22,200-acre park protects the largest contiguous tract of old-growth bottomland hardwood forest still in the US. The park's floodplain forest has one of the highest canopies and some of the tallest trees in the eastern US. Enjoy hiking, primitive camping, birdwatching, picnicking, canoeing, kayaking, Ranger guided interpretive walks, canoe tours, nature study, and environmental education programs. Open all year; Monday to Thursday from 8:30 am to 5 pm, and Friday to Sunday from 8 am to 7 pm. To walk the trails after hours park outside the gate. Well behaved dogs on leash are allowed on the trails and the outside guided tours, but they are not allowed on the Boardwalk or in the buildings.

# South Dakota Listings

Wind Cave National Park
26611 H 385
Hot Springs, SD
605-745-4600
nps.gov/wica
This park is home to one of the world's longest and most complex caves. The park is open year round from 8 to 5 pm during summer hours and until 4:30 pm winter hours. Dogs are allowed at the park and at the campground (no hookups) for no additional fee, but basically they can only go where your car can go. The campground is open year round except when it snows and they have to close the roads to the camping

areas. Dogs are not allowed on the trails, they may not be left unattended, they must be leashed at all times, and cleaned up after.

Badlands National Park
25216 Ben Reifel Rd
Interior, SD
605-433-5361
nps.gov/badl/
This park covers 160 square acres, has America's largest mixed grass prairies, and is home to the Badlands National Monument. Highway 240 is the Badlands Loop Scenic Byway and is 31 1/2 miles long with 14 lookouts. Dogs are not allowed on any of the trails in the park. They are allowed only at the campground or the parking lots. The contact station for the Cedar Pass Campground is on Highway 240, and this campground has an amphitheater. The other campground, White River, has a visitor's center on Highway 27. The campgrounds are open year round, and there are no hook-ups at either camp. Dogs of all sizes are allowed in the campgrounds. There are no additional fees. Dogs may not be left unattended outside, and only inside if it creates no danger to the pet. Dog must be leashed and cleaned up after.

# Tennessee Listings

Great Smoky Mountains National Park
107 Park Headquarters Road
Gatlinburg, TN
865-436-1200
(http://www.nps.gov/grsm/)
Great Smoky Mountains National Park is located both in Tennessee and North Carolina and is one of the most popular of the National Parks. Pets must be leashed or restrained at all times within the park and are not allowed on most of the hiking trails. They can accompany you in your car and at lookouts and stops near the road. However, there are two trails in Great Smoky Mountains National Park that will allow leashed dogs. The Gatlinburg Trail is a 1.9 mile trail from the Sugarland's Visitor Center to the outskirts of Gatlinburg; it runs along the forest with beautiful river views and it passes old homesteads along the way. It follows a creek a good portion of the way. The Oconaluftee River Trail follows along the river for a 1.5 mile relatively easy hike from the visitor center to the outskirts of Cherokee, NC and is an exceptionally pretty walk in spring. If

you want to hike the backcountry with your dog you will need to try the nearby dog-friendly Pisgah National Forest or the Nantahala National Forest. Both are in North Carolina, and they are located about a two hour drive from the national park.

# Texas Listings

Big Bend National Park
P.O. Box 129
Big Bend National Park, TX
432-477-2251
nps.gov/bibe/
This park is at the big bend of the Rio Grande, and there are 2 entrances; in the North on Highway 118, and in the West on Highway 385. Dogs are not allowed anywhere in the back country, on any of the trails, at the river, or off any of the roads. There are 3 campgrounds, and an RV park. The RV park is the only camp area with full hookups. It is concession operated, sites are on a first come/ first served basis, and full hookup capability is required. Dogs may not be left unattended at any time, they must be leashed or crated at all times, and be cleaned up after.

Guadalupe Mountains National Park
H 62/180
Pine Springs, TX
915-828-3251
nps.gov/gumo
This parks hosts an extensive Permisan Limestone fossil reef. The park is open year-round; visitor center hours are from 8:00 a.m. to 4:30 p.m., and a bit longer in summer. Dogs on lead are allowed to go to the Sitting Bull Falls and the Last Chance Canyon. Dogs are not allowed on any of the other trails, but they are allowed on the trails in the neighboring Lincoln National Forest. This forest is very rugged, and pets must be watched very closely that they do not step on the plant called Letchigia Cactus. It may even go through tires and must be removed only by surgical means. Dogs are allowed at no additional fee at either of the campgrounds, and the campsites do not have hookups. Dogs may not be left unattended, they must be leashed, and cleaned up after. This park can also be accessed from the New Mexico side on Highway 137.

# Utah Listings

Bryce Canyon National Park
PO Box 640201/ On H 63
Bryce, UT

435-834-5322
nps.gov/brca/
This park is famous for it's unique geology, creating vast and unusual limestone formations throughout the region. Dogs are not allowed on any of the trails, the shuttle, the viewpoints, or the visitor's center. The park is open 24 hours a day year round. There are 2 campgrounds; Loop A, the north campground, is open all year, and the Sunset campground is only open for the season. There are no hookups at either campground. Dogs can walk along the road in the campground. There are no additional fees for the dogs. Dogs may not be left unattended, they must be leashed at all times, and cleaned up after.

Arches National Park
PO Box 907
Moab, UT
435-719-2299
nps.gov/arch/index.htm
Pets on leash with cleanup are allowed in the campsites and paved areas of the parks. Dogs are not allowed on any trails or backcountry. They are allowed unattended if well-behaved in the Devil's Garden campground.

Canyonlands National Park
2282 SW Resource Blvd
Moab, UT
435-719-2313
nps.gov/cany/index.htm
Pets on leash are allowed in developed areas, such as campgrounds, paved roads, and the Potash/Shafer Canyon road between Moab and the Island in the Sky. They are not allowed on hiking trails or in the backcountry.

Zion National Park
State Route 9
Springdale, UT
435-772-3256
nps.gov/zion/
Dogs are allowed on one walking trail at this national park. Dogs on a 6 foot or less leash are allowed on the Pa'rus Trail which is a 1.5 mile long trail that runs from the South Campground to Canyon Junction. You and your pooch can also enjoy a 10-12 mile scenic drive on the Zion-Mount Carmel Highway which goes through the park. If you are there from November through March, you can also take your car on the Zion Canyon Scenic Drive. If you arrive during the summer months, the Zion Canyon Scenic Drive is closed and only allows park shuttle buses. Other pet rules include no pets on shuttle buses, in the backcountry, or in public

buildings. Pets are allowed in the campgrounds and along roadways.

Capitol Reef National Park
HC 70 Box 15
Torrey, UT
435-425-3791
nps.gov/care/index.htm
Dogs on leash are allowed in campsites and on paved road areas. Dogs are not allowed on hiking trails or in the backcountry.

# Virgin Islands Listings

Virgin Islands National Park
1300 Cruz Bay Creek
St John, VI
340-776-6201
nps.gov/viis
The Virgin Islands National Park is one of breathtaking beauty offering white sandy beaches, tropical forests, and coral reefs. The visitor center is open daily from 8 to 4:30pm. Park areas are open 24 hours a day year-round. Dogs are allowed in the park and on the trails. They are not allowed at the campground, or at Trunk Bay. Dogs must be leashed, cleaned up after, and under owners control at all times.

# Virginia Listings

Shenandoah National Park
3655 U.S. Highway 211 East
Luray, VA
540-999-3500
nps.gov/shen/
Shenandoah National Park is one of the most dog-friendly National Parks, with dogs allowed on most of the trails. Covering 300 mostly forested square miles of the Blue Ridge Mountains the park provides many diverse habitats for thousands of birds and wildlife. The park also provides a wide range of recreational opportunities. There are more than 500 miles of trails, including 101 miles of the Appalachian Trail, summer and fall festivals/reenactments, a rich cultural history to share, interpretive programs, and breathtaking natural beauty. There are several highlights along the 105 mile long, 35 MPH, Skyline Drive (the only public road through the park), such as 75 scenic overlooks and Mary's Rock Tunnel at milepost 32. The 610 foot-long tunnel was considered an engineering feet in 1932; just note that the clearance for the tunnel is

12'8". Dogs of all sizes are allowed for no additional fee. Dogs must be under their owner's control, on no more than a 6 foot leash or securely crated, cleaned up after at all times, and are not to be left unattended. Dogs are not allowed in buildings or on about 14 miles of the trails; please ask the attendant at the gate for a list of the trails.

Wolf Trap National Park for the Performing Arts
1551 Trap Road
Vienna, VA
703-255-1800
nps.gov/wotr/
This park is the first national park for the performing arts, and it offers a wealth of natural and cultural resources, interpretive programs, and "Theater in the Woods". The park is open daily from dawn to dusk, however there are some exceptions; during park festivals and Filene Center performances. Dogs are allowed throughout the park, except they are not allowed in the concert area during performances. Dogs of all sizes are allowed at no additional fee. Dogs may not be left unattended, and they must be leashed and cleaned up after.

# Washington Listings

Mount Rainer National Park
Tahoma Woods State Route
Ashford, WA
360-569-2211
nps.gov/mora/index.htm
Dogs must be on leash where they are allowed. Dogs are only allowed on roads, parking lots, and campgrounds. They are not allowed on trails, snow, in buildings, or any wilderness areas. There is a small portion of Pacific Crest Trail near the park's eastern boundary that allows pets on leash.

North Cascades National Park
State Route 20
Newhalem, WA
360-856-5700
nps.gov/noca
Dogs are allowed on one of the hiking trails, the Pacific Crest Trail. This scenic hiking trail runs through the park and is rated moderate to difficult. The trail is located off Highway 20, about one mile east of Rainy Pass. At the Bridge Creek Trailhead, park on the north side of the highway and then hike north (uphill) or south (downhill). A Northwest Forest Pass is required to park at the trailhead. The cost is about $5 and can be

purchased at the Visitor's Center in Newhalem. For a larger variety of trails, including a less strenuous hike, dogs are also allowed on trails at the adjacent Ross Lake National Recreation Area and the Lake Chelan National Recreation Area. Both recreation areas are managed by the national park.

Olympic National Park
600 East Park Avenue
Port Angeles, WA
360-565-3130
nps.gov/olym/
Pets are not permitted on park trails, meadows, beaches or in any undeveloped area of the park. There is one exception. Dogs are allowed on leash, during daytime hours only, on Kalaloch Beach along the Pacific Ocean and from Rialto Beach north to Ellen Creek. For those folks and dogs who want to hike on a trail, try the adjacent dog-friendly Olympic National Forest. Dogs must be cleaned up after.

# Wyoming Listings

Grand Teton National Park

Moose, WY
307-739-3300
nps.gov/grte/
Grand Teton National Park offers spectacular views of the jagged Teton Range, meadows, pine trees and beautiful blue lakes. This national park limits pets mostly to where cars can go. Pets are allowed in your car, on roads and within 50 feet of any road, campgrounds, picnic areas and parking lots. Pets are not allowed on any hiking trails, in the backcountry, on swimming beaches, or in any visitor centers. However, dogs are allowed on paths in the campgrounds, and can ride in a boat on Jackson Lake only. Dogs must be on a 6 foot leash or less, caged, crated, or in your car at all times. Pets cannot be left unattended or tied to an object. An activity you can do with your pet is to take a scenic drive. There are three scenic drives in the park. Many turnouts along the road offer exhibits on park geology, wildlife and plants. The Teton Park Road follows along the base of the Teton Range from Moose to Jackson Lake Junction. The Jenny Lake Scenic Drive skirts along Jenny Lake and offers great views of the Grand Teton peaks. This drive is one-way and starts just south of String Lake. You can reach this scenic drive by driving south at the North Jenny Lake Junction. Another scenic drive is the Signal Mountain Summit Road which

climbs 800 feet to offer panoramic views of the Teton Range, Jackson Hole valley and Jackson Lake. For accommodations within the park, dogs are welcome in some of the Colter Bay Cabins and in some rooms at the Jackson Lake Lodge. For hiking trails that are dog-friendly, try the nearby Bridger-Teton National Forest.

John D Rockefeller Jr Memorial Parkway National Park
PO Box 170
Moose, WY
307-739-3300
nps.gov/jodr/index.htm
Pets on leash with cleanup are allowed on roads, road shoulders, campgrounds, and picnic areas. Dogs are not allowed on hiking trails or in the park backcountry.

Yellowstone National Park
various
Yellowstone National Park, WY
307-344-7381
nps.gov/yell
Yellowstone National Park was established in 1872 and is America's first national park. Most of the park is at a high altitude of 7,500 feet or greater. The park is home to a wide variety of wildlife including grizzly bears, wolves, bison, elk, deer, coyotes and more. Yellowstone is also host to many natural scenic attractions including the popular Old Faithful geyser. There are numerous other geysers, hot springs, mudpots, and fumaroles which are all evidence of ongoing volcanic activity. Included in this park is Yellowstone Lake, which is the largest high-altitude lake in North America. While the lake looks stunning with its brilliantly blue water, it does have many hot hydrothermal spots, so people are advised not to swim in most of the lake areas and pets are prohibited from swimming. Traveling to Yellowstone Park with a pet can be pretty restrictive, but you will still be able to view most of the popular sights that tourists without pets usually come to see. While pets are not allowed on the trails, in the backcountry, in thermal areas, or on the boardwalks, you will still be able to view Old Faithful from about 200 feet back. Even at that distance, Old Faithful can look pretty spectacular. And if you drive the Grand Loop Road, you will be able to view some points of interest and perhaps see some wildlife including black bears, grizzly bears, bison and elk. Dogs are allowed in parking areas, campgrounds and within 100 feet of

roads. Pets must be on a 6 foot or less leash or crated or caged at all times. Pets are not allowed to be left unattended and tied to an object. However, they can remain in your car while you view attractions near roads and parking areas. The park officials do require that you provide sufficient ventilation in the car for your pet's comfort and survival. For accommodations within the park, dogs are welcome in some of the park's cabins. There are some dog-friendly cabins within easy walking distance of Old Faithful. If you are looking for some dog-friendly hiking trails, there are numerous dog-friendly trails in the nearby Shoshone National Forest, located between the town of Cody and Yellowstone National Park.

Chapter 5

# Dog-Friendly Attractions

## Alabama Listings

| | | | |
|---|---|---|---|
| Axis AL | Kirk House and Gardens | 251-861-4605 | 11525 H 43 N |
| Bessemer AL | WaterMark Place Outlets | 205-425-4554 | 4500 Katies Way |
| Birmingham AL | Arlington Antebellum Home and Gardens | 205-780-5656 | 331 Cotton Avenue SW |
| Birmingham AL | Kelly Ingram Park (Also known as West Park) | 205-254-1291 | 500 17th Street N |
| Birmingham AL | Ruffner Mountain Nature Center | 205-833-8264 | 1214 81st Street S |
| Birmingham AL | Sloss Furnaces | 205-324-1911 | 20 32nd Street North |
| Birmingham AL | Southern Museum of Flight | 205-833-8226 | 4343 73rd Street N |
| Birmingham AL | Vulcan Park and Museum | 205-739-7141 | 1701 Valley View Drive |
| Birmingham AL | Vulcan Trail | 205-254-2699 | 21st Street S/Richard Arrington Jr Blvd S |
| Boaz AL | Tanger Outlet Center | 256-593-9255 | 214 S McCleskey Street |
| Bridgeport AL | Russell Cave | 256-495-2672 | 3729 County Road 98 |
| Cullman AL | Ave Maria Grotto | 256-734-4110 | 1600 St. Bernard Drive SE |
| Dauphin Island AL | Estuarium at the Dauphin Island Sea Lab | 251-861-7500 | 101 Bienville Blvd |
| Dauphin Island AL | Fort Gaines Historic Site | 251-861-6992 | 51 Bienville Blvd |
| Dauphin Island AL | Mobile Bay Ferry | 251-861-3000 | 918-B Bienville Blvd |
| Daviston AL | Horseshoe Bend National Military Park | 256-234-7111 | 11288 Horseshoe Bend Road |
| Decatur AL | Civil War Self-Guided Walking Tour | 256-350-2028 | Church Street |
| Delta AL | Chinnabee Silent Trail | 256-362-2909 | H 281 |
| Dothan AL | George Washington Carver Monument | 334-793-4323 | 5622 H 231 S |
| Dothan AL | Maria's Vineyard | 334-702-0679 | 3940 Fortner Street |
| Fairhope AL | Downtown Fairhope | 251-928-2136 | Fairhope Avenue and side streets |
| Fairhope AL | Fairhope Municipal Pier | 251-928-2136 | West end of Fairhope Avenue |
| Foley AL | Tanger Outlet Center | 251-943-8888 | 2601 S McKenzie Street/H 59 |
| Fort Payne AL | Little River Canyon National Preserve | 256-845-9605 | 2141 Gault/H 35 |
| Gulf Shores AL | AAA Charters | 251-948-2525 | 317 W Canal Drive |
| Gulf Shores AL | Fort Morgan State Historic Park | 251-540-7202 | 51 H 180 |
| Haynesville AL | Selma to Montgomery National Historic Trail | 334-877-1983 | 7001 US Highway 80 |
| Haynesville AL | Selma to Montgomery National Historic Trail | 334-877-1983 | 7001 US Highway 80 |
| Helena AL | When it Rains, Inc. | 205-874-5623 | PO Box 757 |
| Hoover AL | Moss Rock Preserve | 205-739-7141 | Preserve Parkway |
| Huntsville AL | Huntsville Botanical Garden | 256-830-4447 | 4747 Bob Wallace Avenue SW |
| Huntsville AL | US Space and Rocket Center | 256-837-3400 | One Tranquility Base |
| Mobile AL | Battleship Memorial Park | 251-433-2703 | 2703 Battleship ParkwayH 90/9998 |
| Mobile AL | Civil War Trail - Battle for Mobile Bay | 800-566-2453 | Mobile Bay Visitors Bureau/P. O. Box 204 |
| Mobile AL | Mobile Botanical Gardens | 251-342-0555 | 5151 Museum Drive |
| Montgomery AL | Alabama State Capitol and Grounds | 334-242-3935 | 600 Dexter Avenue |
| Moundville AL | Mound State Monument Museum | 205-371-2572 | 1499 Mound State Parkway |
| Orange Beach AL | Fishing and Cruises on America II | 251-981-4127 | 4575 Wilson Blvd |
| Orange Beach AL | Sailaway Charters | 251-974-5055 | 24231 Gulf Bay Road |
| Orange Beach AL | Sanroc Cay Marina | 251-981-5423 | 27267 Perdido Beach Blvd |
| Payneville AL | The Selma to Montgomery National Voting Rights Trail | 334-877-1983 | 7002 H 80 |
| Troy AL | Pike Pioneer Village | 334-566-2830 | 138 E H 6 |
| Troy AL | Pioneer Museum of Alabama | 334-566-3597 | 248 H 231 N |
| Tuscumbia AL | Ivy Green (Helen Keller Birthplace) | 256-383-4066 | 300 West North Commons |
| Tuskegee AL | Tuskegee Airman National Historic Site | 334-724-0922 | 1616 Chappie James Avenue |
| Tuskegee AL | Tuskegee Institute National Historic Site | 334-727-3200 | 1212 West Montgomery Rd |

## Alaska Listings

| | | | |
|---|---|---|---|
| Anchorage AK | Anchorage Market & Festival | 907-272-5634 | 3rd & E Street |
| Anchorage AK | Anchorage Trolley Tours | 907-276-5603 | 612 W 4th Ave |
| Anchorage AK | Balto Statue | | 4th Street and D Street |

| | | | |
|---|---|---|---|
| Anchorage AK | Northway Mall Wednesday Market | 907-272-5634 | 3101 Penland Blvd |
| Anchorage AK | Planet Walk | 907-258-0415 | 621 W 6th Ave |
| Anchorage AK | Tony Knowles Coastal Trail | 907 343-4355 | W 2nd Avenue |
| Cordova AK | Childs Glacier | 907-743-9500 | Cordova River Road H/ H10 |
| Cordova AK | Historical Walking Tour | 907-424-6665 | 622 1st Street |
| Dalton Highway AK | Dalton Highway and the Arctic Circle | 907-474-2200 | |
| Eklutna AK | Eklutna Historical Park | 907-688-6026 | Mile 26 Glenn H |
| Fairbanks AK | Alaska Outdoor Rental and Guides | 907-457-2453 | Peger Road/P.O. Box 82388 |
| Fairbanks AK | Creamer's Field | 907-474-1744 | 1300 College Road |
| Fairbanks AK | Pioneer Park | 907-459-1059 | 2300 Airport Way |
| Girdwood AK | Alyeska Aerial Tram | 907-754-2275 | 1000 Arlberg Avenue |
| Girdwood AK | Portage Glacier | 907-783-2326 | Portage Valley Road |
| Haines AK | Chilkat Cruises and Tours | 907-766-2100 | 142 Beach Road |
| Haines AK | Haines Self-Guided Tours | 800-458-3579 | 122 2nd Avenue |
| Haines AK | Mt Riley Hike | 800-458-3579 | 122 2nd Avenue |
| Homer AK | Bay Excursions | 907-235-7525 | Homer Spit Road, Ramp 3 (H 1) |
| Homer AK | Central Charters Booking Agency | 907-235-7847 | 4241 Homer Spit Road |
| Homer AK | Mako's Water Taxi and Charters | 907-235-9055 | Home Spit Road (at end) |
| Homer AK | Nomad Shelter Yurts | 907-235-0132 | Sterling Highway |
| Homer AK | Pratt Museum | 907-235-8635 | 3779 Bartlett St |
| Homer AK | Rainbow Tours and Taxi | 907-235-7272 | P. O. Box 1526/Homer Spit Road |
| Homer AK | Seldovia Bay Ferry LLC | 907-435-3299 | Lot 21 - Freight Dock Road - System 6 Dock JJ Small Boat Harbor |
| Homer AK | Seldovia Tours | 907-235-7847 | 4241 Homer Spit Road/H 1 |
| Homer AK | Smokey Bay Air | 907-235-1511 | 2100 Kachemak Drive |
| Homer AK | The Homer Spit | 907-235-7740 | Homer Spit Road |
| Homer AK | The Kachemak Bay Ferry to Halibut Cove | 907-399-2683 | Homer Spit Road/H 1 |
| Hope AK | Hope and Sunrise Historical and Mining Museum | 907-782-3740 | P. O. Box 88/2nd Avenue |
| Juneau AK | Mendenhall Glacier and Visitor Center | 907-789-0097 | Glacier Spur Road |
| Juneau AK | Orca Eco Tours | 888-SEE-ORCA (733-6722) | PO Box 35431/Franklin Street |
| Juneau AK | Whale Watch Company | 907-463-3422 | 11517 Glacier Way |
| Ketchikan AK | Creek Street Boardwalk Shopping Area | 800-770-3300 | Creek Street |
| Ketchikan AK | Ketchikan Walking Tour | 907-225-6166 | 131 Front Street |
| Ketchikan AK | Tongass Water Taxi | 907-225-8294 | PO Box 23143 |
| Ketchikan AK | Totem Bright State Historical Park | 907-247-8574 | 9883 N Tongass H/H 7 |
| Kodiak AK | Possibilities Unlimited Alaska | 907-486-4093 | P. O. Box 1426 |
| Matanuska Glacier AK | Matanuska Glacier | 888-253-4480 | Mile 102 Glenn Hwy |
| Metlakatla AK | Metlakatla Indian Community | 907-886-4441 | Off 5 Mile Airport Road |
| Nome AK | Nome Discovery Tours | 907-443-2814 | 1st and D Street |
| Portage Glacier AK | Alaska Wildlife Drive-Thru Preserve: | 907-783-2025 | Mile 79 Seward H |
| Seward AK | Miller's Landing Water Taxi | 866-541-5739 | 1820 Beach Drive |
| Sitka AK | Sitka Charters | 907-747-0616 | P. O. Box 556 |
| Skagway AK | Dyea Townsite Walking Tour | 907-983-2921 | Broadway and 2nd Avenue |
| Skagway AK | White Pass and Yukon Railroad | 800-343-7373 | 231 Second Avenue |
| Spenard AK | Spenard Farmers Market | 907-561-5314 | Spenard Road and 26th Avenue |
| Sutton AK | Matanuska Glacier | 888-253-4480 | Mile 102 Glenn H |
| Valdez AK | Salmon Fishing Area | | |
| Valdez AK | Valdez Overlook | | |
| Valdez AK | Worthington Glacier State Rec Site | 907-269-8400 | Mile 28.7 Richardson Highway |
| Whittier AK | Aquetex Water Taxi | 907-362-1290 | P.O. Box 643 |
| Whittier AK | Bread N Butter Charters | 907-472-2396 | Harbor View Drive #7 |
| Whittier AK | Honey Charters | 907-278-2493 | Harbor Traiangle #4, Port of Whittier |
| Whittier AK | Prince William Sound Kayak Center | 907-472-2452 | PO Box 622 |
| Whittier AK | Whittier Town Center | | Downtown |
| Wrangell AK | Mount Dewey Hiking Trails | 907-874-2829 | 296 Campbell Drive |
| Wrangell AK | Rainbow Falls Hiking Trail | 800-367-9745 | MM 4.6 Zimovia H |
| Wrangell AK | Rainwalker Expeditions | 907-874-2549 | P.O. Box 2074 |

**Arizona Listings**

| | | | |
|---|---|---|---|
| Bisbee AZ | Bisbee Farmers' Market | 520-236-8409 | Vista Street |
| Bisbee AZ | Historic Walking Tours | 520-432-3554 | #2 Copper Queen Plaza/Visitor Center |
| Bisbee AZ | Lavender Jeep Tours | 520-432-5369 | #1 Copper Queen Plaza |
| Bisbee AZ | The Old Bisbee Ghost Tour | 520-432-3308 | |

| | | | |
|---|---|---|---|
| Bowie AZ | Fort Bowie National Historic Site | 520-847-2500 | 3203 South Old Fort Bowie Road |
| Camp Verde AZ | Montezuma Castle National Monument | 928-567-3322 | PO Box 219 |
| Concho AZ | Concho Farmers Market | | Corner of H 61 and H 180A |
| Coolidge AZ | Casa Grand Ruins National Monument | 520-723-3172 | 1100 W Ruins Drive |
| Cornville AZ | Oak Creek Vineyards and Winery | 928-649-0290 | 1555 N Page Springs Road |
| Ganado AZ | Hubbell Trading Post National Historic Site | 928-755-3475 | PO Box 150 |
| Gilbert AZ | Santan Village Shopping Center | 480-282-9500 | 2290 S. SanTan Village Parkway |
| Glendale AZ | Twilight Farmers' Market | 623-848-1234 | 59th Avenue and Utopia (Arrowhead Ranch) |
| Goldfield AZ | Goldfield Ghost Town | 480-983-0333 | 4650 N Mammoth Mine Road |
| Kingman AZ | Powerhouse Visitor Center & Route 66 Museum | 866-427-RT66 | 120 W. Route 66 |
| Lake Havasu City AZ | A-1 Watercraft Rentals | 928-855-8088 | 1435 Countryshire Ave #103 |
| Lake Havasu City AZ | The London Bridge | 928-453-8883 | 314 London Bridge Road (Lake Havasu City Visitor's Center) |
| Oatman AZ | Town of Oatman | | Route 66 |
| Page AZ | Antelope Canyon Adventures | 928-645-5501 | 104 Lake Powell Blvd |
| Page AZ | Lake Powell - Glen Canyon Recreation Area | 435-684-7400 | |
| Page AZ | Navajo Village | 928-660-0304 | 1235 Copper Mine Road |
| Page AZ | Wahweap Lodge and Marina Boat Rentals | 928-645-2433 | 100 Lakeshore Drive |
| Phoenix AZ | Biltmore Fashion Park | 602-955-8400 | 2502 E. Camelback Rd. |
| Phoenix AZ | Downtown Phoenix Public Market | 602-430-8345 | 721 N Central at McKinley Street |
| Phoenix AZ | Pioneer Living History Village | 623-465-1052 | 3901 West Pioneer Road |
| Phoenix AZ | Roadrunner Park Farmers Market | 623-848-1234 | 3502 E Cactus Road |
| Scottsdale AZ | Bartlett Lake Marina & Boat Club | 602-316-3378 | 20808 E Bartlett Dam Road |
| Scottsdale AZ | Scottsdale Downtown's Old Town Farmers' Market | 623-848-1234 | N Brown Avenue and 1st Street In the Old Town area |
| Sedona AZ | Adventure Company Jeep Tours | 928-204-1973 | 336 H 179 |
| Sedona AZ | Red Rock Country - Coconino National Forest | 928-527-3600 | various |
| Superior AZ | Boyce Thompson Arboretum | 520-689-2723 | 37615 U.S. Highway 60 |
| Tombstone AZ | 1880 Historic Tombstone | 800-457-3423 | 70 miles from Tucson |
| Tombstone AZ | Charleston Ghost Town | 866-275-5816 | Old Charleston Road |
| Tombstone AZ | Gleeson Ghost Town | 866-275-5816 | Gleeson Road |
| Tombstone AZ | Old Tombstone Stagecoach Tours | 520-457-3018 | Allen Street (between 4th and 5th Streets) |
| Tombstone AZ | WF Trading Company | 520-457-3664 | 418 Allen St |
| Tucson AZ | Fort Lowell Museum | 520-885-3832 | 2900 North Craycroft Road |
| Tucson AZ | Pima Air and Space Museum | 520-574-0462 | 6000 East Valencia Road |
| Tucson AZ | Trail Dust Town | 520-296-4551 | 6541 E Tanque Verde Road |
| Tumacacori AZ | Tumacacori National Historical Park | 520-398-2341 | 1891 E Frontage Rd |
| Vail AZ | Charron Vineyards & Winery | 520-489-6033 | 18585 S Sonoita H |
| Valle AZ | The Planes of Fame Air Museum | 928-635-1000 | 755 Mustang Way |
| Wickenburg AZ | Robson's Mining World | 928-685-2609 | P. O. Box 3465 (On H 71) |
| Williams AZ | Historic Route 66 Driving Tour | | Bill Williams Avenue |
| Winslow AZ | Homolovi Ruins State Park | 928-289-4106 | State Route 87 |

**Arkansas Listings**

| | | | |
|---|---|---|---|
| Altus AR | Chateau aux Arc | 800-558-WINE | 8045 Highway 186 |
| Altus AR | Post Familie Vineyards | 479-468-2741 | 1700 St Mary's Mountain Road |
| Bull Shoals AR | Mountain Village 1890 and the Bull Shoals Caverns | 870-445-7177 | 1011 C.S. Woods Blvd |
| Bull Shoals AR | Top O' The Ozarks | 870-445-4302 | Tower Road |
| El Dorado AR | South Arkansas Arboretum | 888-AT-PARKS (287-2757) | Timberland |
| Eureka Springs AR | Christ of the Ozarks | 800-882-7529 | Passion Play Road |
| Eureka Springs AR | Eureka Springs Self Guided Tours | 800-638-7352 | 516 Village Circle/H 62E |
| Eureka Springs AR | Eureka Springs-North Railway | 479-253-6200 | 299 N Main Street/H 23 |
| Eureka Springs AR | Pine Mountain Village | 479-253-9156 | 2075 East Van Buren Street/H 62 |
| Eureka Springs AR | Pivot Rock | 479-253-8860 | 1708 Pivot Rock Road |
| Fort Smith AR | Fort Smith National Historic Site | 479-783-3961 | 301 Parker Avenue |
| Gamaliel AR | Raimondo Winery | 870-421-2076 | 149 Country Road 820 |
| Garfield AR | Pea Ridge National Military Park | 479-451-8122 | 15930 H 62E |

| | | | |
|---|---|---|---|
| Hope AR | President Bill Clinton Birthplace | 870-777-4455 | 117 S Hervey Street |
| Hot Springs AR | Belle of Hot Springs Riverboat | 501-525-4438 | 5200 Central Avenue/H 7 |
| Hot Springs AR | Garvan Woodland Gardens | 501-262-9300 | 550 Arkridge Road |
| Little Rock AR | Big Dam Bridge | 501-340-6800 | 7600 Rebsamen Park Road |
| Little Rock AR | Clinton Presidential Center and Park | 501-374-4242 | 1200 President Clinton Ave. |
| Little Rock AR | MacArthur Museum of Arkansas Military History | 501-376-4602 | 503 E. Ninth Street/MacArthur Park |
| Little Rock AR | River Market | 501-375-2552 | 400 President Clinton Avenue |
| N Little Rock AR | Argenta Farmers Market | 501-231-0094 | 6th and Main Streets |
| North Little Rock AR | Arkansas Inland Maritime Museum | 501-371-8320 | 120 Riverfront Drive |
| Paris AR | Cowie Wine Cellars | 479-963-3990 | 101 N Carbon City Rd |
| Pine Bluff AR | Arkansas Railroad Museum | 870-535-8819 | 1700 Port Road |
| Prairie Grove AR | Prairie Grove Battlefield State Park | 479-846-2990 | 506 E Douglas Street/H 45/62 |
| Rogers AR | War Eagle Cavern | 479-789-2909 | 21494 Cavern Road |
| Scott AR | Plantation Agriculture Museum | 501-961-1409 | 4815 H 161S |
| Scott AR | Toltec Mounds Archeological State Park | 501-961-1409 | 490 Toltec Mounds Road |
| Washington AR | Historic Washington State Park | 870-983-2684 | 100 SW Morrison |
| Wiederkehr Village AR | Wiederkehr Wine Cellars | 479-468-9463 | 3324 Swiss Family Drive |

**California Listings**

| | | | |
|---|---|---|---|
| Agoura Hills CA | Paramount Ranch | 805-370-2301 | Cornell Road |
| Alameda CA | Rosenblum Cellars | 510-865-7007 | 2900 Main Street |
| Anaheim CA | Disneyland Kennel | 714-781-4565 | 1313 Harbor Blvd |
| Arroyo Grande CA | Lake Lopez Boat Rentals | 805-489-1006 | 6820 Lopez Drive |
| Barstow CA | Calico Early Man Site | 760-252-6000 | Minneola Road |
| Barstow CA | Route 66 Mother Road Museum | 760-255-1890 | 681 North First Ave |
| Berkeley CA | Redwood Valley Railway | 510-548-6100 | Tilden Park |
| Berkeley CA | Telegraph Ave | | Telegraph Ave |
| Beverly Hills CA | Beverly Hills Rodeo Drive Shopping District | | Rodeo Drive |
| Beverly Hills CA | Hollywood Star's Homes | | Self-Guided Walking Tour |
| Big Bear Lake CA | Bear Valley Stage Lines | 909-584-2277 | Village Drive and Pine Knot Avenue |
| Big Bear Lake CA | Belleville Ghost Town | | Holcomb Valley Road |
| Big Bear Lake CA | Big Bear Marina | 909-866-3218 | 500 Paine Road |
| Big Bear Lake CA | Holloway's Marina | 909-866-5706 | 398 Edgemoor Road |
| Big Bear Lake CA | Pine Knot Landing-Boat Rentals & Paddleboat | 909-866-7766 | 400 Pine Knot Ave. |
| Big Bear Lake CA | Pleasure Point Landing | 909-866-2455 | 603 Landlock Landing Rd |
| Bishop CA | Bristlecone Pine Forest | 760-873-2500 | White Mountain Rd |
| Boonville CA | Anderson Valley Brewing Company | 707-895-BEER (895-2337) | 17700 H 253 |
| Boonville CA | Boont Berry Farm | 707-895-3441 | 13980 H 128 |
| Boonville CA | Foursight Wines | 707-895-2889 | 14475 H 128 |
| Boonville CA | Zina Hyde Cunningham Winery | 707-895-9462 | 14077 H 128 |
| Bridgeport CA | Bodie State Historic Park | 760-647-6445 | State Route 270 |
| Burbank CA | Los Angeles Equestrian Center | 818-840-9066 | 480 Riverside Drive |
| Calistoga CA | Chateau Montelena | 707-942-5105 | 1429 Tubbs Lane |
| Calistoga CA | Cuvaison Winery | 707-942-6266 | 4550 Silverado Trail |
| Calistoga CA | Dutch Henry Winery | 707-942-5771 | 4300 Silverado Trail |
| Calistoga CA | Graeser Winery | 707-942-4437 | 255 Petrified Forest Road |
| Calistoga CA | Old Faithful Geyser | 707-942-6463 | 1299 Tubbs Lane |
| Calistoga CA | Petrified Forest | 707-942-6667 | 4100 Petrified Forest Rd. |
| Camarillo CA | Camarillo Outlet Stores | 805-445-8520 | 740 E. Ventura Blvd, Camarillo, CA 93010 |
| Cambria CA | Cambria Historic Downtown | | 1880-2580 Main Street |
| Camino CA | Argyres Orchard | 530-644-3862 | 4220 N. Canyon Rd. |
| Camino CA | Bodhaine Ranch | 530-644-1686 | 2315 Cable Road |
| Camino CA | Bolster's Hilltop Ranch | 530-644-2230 | 2000 Larsen Drive |
| Camino CA | Celtic Gardens Organic Farm | 530-647-0689 | 4221 North Canyon Road |
| Camino CA | Crystal Basin Cellars | 530 647-1767 | 3550 Carson Road |
| Camino CA | Denver Dan's | 530-644-6881 | 4344 Bumblebee Ln. |
| Camino CA | Grandpa's Cellar | 530-644-2153 | 2360 Cable Rd. |
| Camino CA | Honey Bear Ranch | 530-644-3934 | 2826 Barkley Rd. |
| Camino CA | Kids, Inc. | 530-622-0084 | 3245 N. Canyon Rd. |
| Camino CA | Mother Lode Orchards | 530-644-5101 | 4341 N. Canyon Rd. |
| Camino CA | O'Hallorans Apple Trail Ranch | 530-644-3389 | 2261 Cable Rd. |

|  |  |  |  |
|---|---|---|---|
| Camino CA | Plubell's Family Orchard | 530-647-0613 | 1800 Larsen Dr. |
| Camino CA | Stone's Throw Vineyard & Winery | 530-622-5100 | 3541 North Canyon Rd. |
| Camino CA | Summerfield Berry Farm | 530-647-2833 | 4455 Pony Express Trail |
| Carlsbad CA | Carlsbad Village | | Carlsbad Village Drive |
| Carlsbad CA | Legoland Kennel | 760-918-5346 | One Legoland Drive |
| Carlsbad CA | Witch Creek Winery | 760-720-7499 | 2906 Carlsbad Blvd/H 101 |
| Carmel CA | Carmel Village Shopping Area | | Ocean Ave |
| Carmel CA | Carmel Walks-Walking Tours | 831-642-2700 | Lincoln and Ocean Streets |
| Carmel CA | Seventeen Mile Drive | | Seventeen Mile Drive |
| Carmel CA | Taste Mogan | 831-626-3700 | 204 Crossroads Blvd |
| Carmel Valley CA | Crossroads Shopping Center | | Cabrillo Hwy (Hwy 1) |
| Carmel-by-the-Sea CA | Carmel Plaza | 831-624-1385 | Ocean Avenue and Mission Street |
| Cedarville CA | Surprise Valley Back Country Byway | 530-279-6101 | Highway 299 |
| Chula Vista CA | Otay Ranch Town Center | 619-656-9100 | Eastlake Pkwy At Olympic Pkwy |
| Coloma CA | Gold Country Carriages | 530-622-6111 | Hwy 49 |
| Coloma CA | Marshall Gold Discovery State Park | 530-622-3470 | Hwy 49 |
| Coloma CA | Venezio Winery & Vineyard | 530-885-WINE | 5821 Highway 49 |
| Columbia CA | Columbia State Historic Park | 209-532-0150 | Parrotts Ferry Rd. |
| Corona CA | The Promenade Shops at Dos Lagos | 921-277-7601 | 2780 Cabot Drive |
| Corte Madera CA | The Village at Corte Madera | 415-924-8557 | 1618 Redwood H |
| Dana Point CA | Catalina Express | 800-360-1212 | 34675 Golden Lantern |
| Danville CA | Eugene O'Neill National Historic Site | 925-838-0249 | PO Box 280 |
| Drytown CA | Drytown Cellars | 209-245-3500 | 16030 Highway 49 |
| East Sonoma CA | Sebastiani Vineyards and Winery | 800-888-5532 | 389 Fourth Street |
| El Centro CA | Tumco Historic Townsite | 760-337-4400 | Ogilby Road |
| Encino CA | Los Encinos State Historic Park | 818-784-4849 | 16756 Moorpark Street |
| Escondido CA | Belle Marie Winery and Chateau Dragoo | 760-796-7557 | 26312 Mesa Rock Road |
| Escondido CA | Orfila Vineyards | 760-738-6500 | 13455 San Pasqual Road |
| Fair Play CA | Charles B. Mitchell Vineyards | 800-704-WINE | 8221 Stoney Creek Road |
| Fair Play CA | Oakstone Winery | 530-620-5303 | 6440 Slug Gulch Rd. |
| Fair Play CA | Perry Creek Vineyards | 530-620-5175 | 7400 Perry Creek Rd. |
| Fawnskin CA | Captain John's Fawn Harbor and Marina | 909-866-6478 | 39368 North Shore Drive |
| Felton CA | Roaring Camp & Big Trees RR | 831-335-4484 | P.O.Box G-1 |
| Fish Camp CA | Yosemite Mountain Sugar Pine Railroad | 559-683-7273 | 56001 Highway 41 |
| Folsom CA | Old Towne Folsom | | Sutter St & Riley St |
| Folsom CA | Palladio | 916-983-9793 | East Bidwell Rd & Iron Point Rd |
| Forestville CA | Joseph Swan Vineyards | 707-573-3747 | 2916 Laguna Road |
| Forestville CA | Topolos Vineyards | 707-887-1575 | 5700 Gravenstein Hwy N. |
| Fort Bragg CA | All Aboard Adventures | 707-964-1881 | 32400 N Harbor Drive, Noyo Harbor |
| Fort Bragg CA | Anchor Charter Boats and the Lady Irma II | 707-964-4550 | 780 N Harbor Drive |
| Fort Bragg CA | Mendocino Coast Botanical Gardens | 707-964-4352 | 18220 N. Highway 1 |
| Fortuna CA | Fortuna Depot Museum | 707-725-7645 | 3 Park St |
| Garberville CA | One Log House | 707-247-3717 | 705 US Hwy 101 |
| Gilroy CA | Bonfante Gardens Family Theme Park Kennel | 408-840-7100 | 3050 Hecker Pass H/H 152 |
| Gilroy CA | Kirigin Cellars | 408-847-8827 | 11550 Watsonville Road |
| Glen Ellen CA | Benziger Family Winery | 707-935-3000 | 1883 London Ranch Road |
| Glen Ellen CA | Jack London State Historic Park | 707-938-5216 | 2400 London Ranch Road |
| Glendale CA | The Americana at Brand | 877-897-2097 | 889 Americana Way |
| Goleta CA | Chumash Painted Cave State Historic Park | 805-733-3713 | Painted Caves Road |
| Grass Valley CA | Empire Mine State Historic Park | 530-273-8522 | 10791 East Empire Street |
| Guerneville CA | F. Korbel and Brothers Champagne Cellars | 707-824-7000 | 13250 River Road |
| Half Moon Bay CA | Santa's Tree Farm | 650-726-2246 | 78 Pilarcitos Creek Road |
| Harmony CA | Harmony Cellars Winery | 805-927-1625 | 3255 Harmony Valley Road |
| Healdsburg CA | Dry Creek Vineyard | 707-433-1000 | 3770 Lambert Bridge Road |
| Healdsburg CA | Foppiano Vineyards | 707-433-7272 | 12707 Old Redwood Highway |
| Healdsburg CA | Lambert Bridge Winery | 800-975-0555 | 4085 W. Dry Creek Rd |
| Healdsburg CA | Porter Creek Vineyard and Winery | 707-433-6321 | 8735 Westside Road |
| Healdsburg CA | Porter Creek Vineyard and Winery | 707-433-6321 | 8735 Westside Road |
| Healdsburg CA | Quivira Vineyards | 707-431-8333 | 4900 W Dry Creek Road |
| Healdsburg CA | Rodney Strong Vineyards | 707-433-6511 | 11455 Old Redwood H |
| Herald CA | Blue Gum Winery | 209-748-5669 | 13637 Borden Road |
| Homewood CA | Mountain High Weddings | 530-525-9320 | PO Box 294 |
| Hope Valley CA | Hope Valley Outdoor Center | 530-694-2266 | Intersection of H 88 and H 89 |
| Hopland CA | Brutocao Cellars and Vineyards | 707-744-1664 | 13500 H 101 |

Dog-Friendly Attractions - Please always call ahead to make sure an establishment is still dog-friendly

| Idyllwild CA | Annual Plein Air Festival | 866-439-5278 | North Circle Drive |
| Indio CA | Oasis Date Gardens | 800-827-8017 | 59111 Hwy 111 |
| Irvine CA | Irvine Spectrum Center | 877-ISC-4FUN | 71 Fortune Drive |
| Irvine CA | Orange County Great Park | 866-829-3829 | 6990 Marine Way |
| Jamestown CA | Railtown 1897 State Historic Park | 209-984-3953 | Highway 49 |
| Julian CA | Blue Door Winery | 858-278-1640 | 1255 Julian Orchards Drive |
| Julian CA | Country Carriages | 760-765-1471 | Washington and Main St |
| Julian CA | J. Jenkins Winery | 760-765-3267 | 12555 Julian Orchards Drive |
| Julian CA | Julian Downtown and Walking Tour | 760-765-1857 | Main Street |
| Julian CA | Menghini Winery | 760-765-2072 | 1150 Julian Orchards Drive |
| Kenwood CA | Deerfield Ranch Winery and Tasting Room | 707-833-5215 | 10200 Sonoma H/H 12 |
| Klamath CA | Trees of Mystery | 800-638-3389 | 15500 Highway 101 N. |
| Lake Arrowhead CA | Arrowhead Queen Boat Tours | 909-336-6992 | 28200 H 189 Building C100 |
| Lake Arrowhead CA | Lake Arrowhead Village | 909-337-2533 | 28200 Highway 189 |
| Lake Shasta CA | Self Guided Audio Cassette Tour | 530-926-4511 | 204 West Alma St |
| Lee Vining CA | Mono Basin National Forest Scenic Area | 760-647-3044 | Hwy 395, 1/2 mile North of Lee Vining |
| Leggett CA | Leggett Drive Thru Tree | | Hwy 1 and Hwy 101 |
| Lewiston CA | Trinity Alps Marina | 530-286-2282 | Fairview Marina Rd. |
| Livermore CA | Marina Boat Rentals | 925-373-0332 | Del Valle Road |
| Lodi CA | Jessie's Grove Winery | 209-368-0880 | 1973 W Turner Road |
| Lodi CA | Phillips Farm/ Michael-David Vineyards | 209-368-7384 | 4580 H 12 |
| Lodi CA | The Downtown Lodi Certified Farmers Market | 209-369-8052 | School Street between Lodi Avenue and Elm Street |
| Lompoc CA | Foley Estates Vineyard & Winery | 805-737-6222 | 6121 E H 246 |
| Lompoc CA | La Purisima Mission State Historic Park | 805-733-3713 | 2295 Purisima Road |
| Lone Pine CA | Alabama Hills | 760-876-6222 | Movie Road |
| Long Beach CA | Catalina Explorer Ferry | 877-432-6276 | 100 Aquarium Way, Pine Avenue Pier |
| Long Beach CA | Catalina Express | 800-360-1212 | 320 Golden Shore |
| Los Angeles CA | Century City Shopping Center | 310-277-3898 | 10250 Santa Monica Blvd |
| Los Angeles CA | Griffith Observatory | 323-664-1181 | 2800 East Observatory Road |
| Los Angeles CA | Hollywood Walk of Fame | 323-469-8311 | 6100-6900 Hollywood Blvd. |
| Los Angeles CA | The Grove Shopping Center | 323-900-8080 | 189 The Grove Drive |
| Los Angeles CA | Travel Town Museum | 323-662-5874 | 5200 Zoo Drive |
| Los Angeles CA | Westfield Century City | 310-277-3898 | 10250 Santa Monica Blvd/H 2 |
| Madera CA | Mariposa Wine Company | 559-673-6372 | 20146 Road 21 |
| Mammoth Lakes CA | Hot Creek Geologic Site | 760-924-5500 | Hot Creek Hatchery Road |
| Mammoth Lakes CA | Mammoth Mountain-Gondola | 760-934-0745 | #1 Minaret Road |
| Mammoth Lakes CA | The Village at Mammoth | | |
| Manteca CA | Manteca Farmers Market | 209-823-7229 | Yosemite and Manteca Avenues |
| Manton CA | Alger Vineyards | 530-474-WINE (9463) | 31636 Forward Road |
| Manton CA | Ringtail Vineyards | 530-474-5350 | 32055 Forward Road |
| Marina del Rey CA | Catalina Ferries | 310-305-7250 | 13763 Fiji Way , C2 Terminal Building |
| Mariposa CA | Mount Bullion Vineyard | 209-377-8450 | 6947 H 49N |
| Mendocino CA | Catch a Canoe Rentals | 707-937-5615 | 44850 Comptche-Ukiah Rd |
| Mendocino CA | Mendocino Village | | Main Street at Lansing Street |
| Mokelumne Hill CA | French Hill Winery | 209-728-0638 | 8032 S Main Street |
| Monterey CA | Ag Venture Tours & Consulting | 831-761-8463 | P. O. Box 2634 |
| Monterey CA | Del Monte Center | | 1410 Del Monte Center |
| Monterey CA | La Mirada House and Gardens | 831-372-3689 | 720 Via Mirada |
| Monterey CA | Monterey Bay Whale Watch Boat Tours | 831-375-4658 | Fisherman's Wharf |
| Monterey CA | Princess Monterey Whale Watch | 800-200-2203 | 96 Fishermans Wharf |
| Monterey CA | Randy's Fishing Trips | 800-251-7440 | 66 Old Fisherman's Wharf #1 |
| Monterey CA | Sea Life Tours | 831-372-7150 | 90 Fishermans Wharf |
| Monterey CA | Ventana Vineyards | 831-372-7415 | 2999 Monterey-Salinas Highway, #10 |
| Mount Shasta CA | Volcanic Legacy Byway | 866-722-9929 | P. O. Box 832 |
| Mount Aukum CA | Latcham Vineyards | 530-620-6642 | 2860 Omo Ranch Road |
| Mount Shasta CA | Volcanic Legacy Byway | 866-722-9929 | P. O. Box 832 |
| Murphys CA | Black Sheep Winery | 209-728-2157 | West end of Main Street |
| Murphys CA | Rocco's Com'e Bella Winery | 209-728-9030 | 457-C Algiers |
| Murphys CA | Stevenot Winery | 209-728-0638 | 2690 San Domingo Road |
| Murphys CA | Twisted Oak Winery | 209-736-9080 | 350 Main Street |
| Napa CA | Clos Du Val Winery | 800-993-9463 | 5330 Silverado Trail |
| Napa CA | Hess Collection Winery | 707-255-1144 | 4411 Redwood Road |
| Napa CA | Pine Ridge Winery | 707-252-9777 | 5901 Silverado Trail |
| Napa CA | Small Lot Wine Tours | 707-294-2232 | Various |

| | | | |
|---|---|---|---|
| Napa CA | Starmont Winery | 707-252-8001 | 1451 Stanly Ln |
| Nevada City CA | Nevada City Horse & Carriage | 530-265-9646 | downtown Nevada City |
| Newport Beach CA | Boat Rentals of America | 949-673-7200 | 510 E Edgewater |
| Newport Beach CA | Fashion Island Mall | 800-495-4753 | 1133 Newport Center Dr |
| Newport Beach CA | Fun Zone Boat Tours | 949-673-0240 | 6000 Edgewater Place |
| Newport Beach CA | Fun Zone Boat-Whale Watching Tours | 949-673-0240 | 600 Edgewater Place |
| Newport Beach CA | Marina Water Sports-Boat Rentals | 949-673-3372 | 600 E Bay Ave |
| Oak View CA | Casitas Boat Rentals | 805-649-2043 | 11311 Santa Ana Road |
| Oakland CA | BART: Bay Area Regional Transit | 510-465-2278 | P.O. Box 12688 |
| Oakland CA | Jack London Square | 510-814-6000 | Broadway & Embarcadero |
| Oakland CA | Juan Bautista de Anza National Historic Trail | 510-817-1438 | 1111 Jackson Street #700 |
| Oceanside CA | California Surf Museum | 760-721-6876 | 223 N Coast H |
| Ojai CA | Downtown Ojai | 805-646-8126 | E Ojai Ave at S Montgomery St |
| Old Station CA | Spatter Cones Trail | 530-257-2151 | Highway89 |
| Olympic Valley CA | Ann Poole Weddings, Nature's Chapel | 530-412-5436 | P.O. Box 3768 |
| Olympic Valley CA | Squaw Valley USA-Gondola | 530-583-5585 | 1910 Squaw Valley Rd |
| Olympic Valley CA | The Village At Squaw Valley | 530-584-6267 | Squaw Valley |
| Orleans CA | Coates Family Vineyards | 530-627-3369 | 3255 Red Cap Road |
| Oxnard CA | Hopper Boat Rentals | 805-382-1100 | 3600 Harbor Blvd # 368 |
| Pacific Palisades CA | Will Rogers State Hist. Park | 310-454-8212 | 1501 Will Rogers State Park Rd. |
| Palm Desert CA | El Paseo Shopping District | | El Paseo Drive |
| Palm Springs CA | Moorten Botanical Garden | 760-327-6555 | 1701 S Palm Drive |
| Palm Springs CA | Palm Canyon Drive/Star Walk | | Palm Canyon Drive |
| Palm Springs CA | Palm Canyon Shopping District | | Palm Canyon Drive/H 111 |
| Palo Alto CA | Downtown Palo Alto | | University Ave |
| Palo Alto CA | Hewlett-Packard Garage | | 367 Addison Ave |
| Palo Alto CA | Stanford Shopping Center | 650-617-8585 | 680 Stanford Shopping Center |
| Palomar Mountain CA | Palomar Observatory | 760-742-2100 | County Road S-6 |
| Pasadena CA | Frisbee Golf Course | | Oak Grove Drive |
| Pasadena CA | Old Town Pasadena | | 100W-100E Colorado Blvd. |
| Paso Robles CA | Canterbury Tails Dog Resort | 805-467-0021 | 6970 Benton Rd |
| Paso Robles CA | Changala Winery | 805-226-9060 | 3770 Willow Creek Road |
| Paso Robles CA | Chumeia Vineyards | 805-226-0102 | 8331 H 46E |
| Paso Robles CA | Paso Robles Pet Boarding | 805-238-4340 | 2940 Union Rd |
| Paso Robles CA | Tablas Creek Vineyard | 805-237-1231 | 9339 Adelaida Rd |
| Perris CA | Orange Empire Railway Museum | 951-657-2605 | 2201 South A Street |
| Petaluma CA | Petaluma Adobe State Historic Park | 707-762-4871 | 3325 Adobe Road |
| Petaluma CA | Petaluma Self-Guided Film Walking Tour | 707-769-0429 | Keller St. and Western Ave. |
| Petaluma CA | Petaluma Village Premium Outlets | 707-778-9300 | 2200 Petaluma Blvd N. |
| Petaluma CA | River Walk | 707-769-0429 | Near D St. bridge and Washington St. |
| Phillipsville CA | Avenue of the Giants | 707-722-4291 | Highway 101 |
| Philo CA | Christine Woods Vineyards | 707-895-2115 | 3155 H 128 |
| Philo CA | Esterlina Vineyards | 707-895-2920 | 1200 Holmes Ranch Road |
| Philo CA | Handley Cellars | 707-895-3876 | 3151 H 128 |
| Philo CA | Husch Vineyards | 1-800-55-HUSCH (555-8724) | 4400 H 128 |
| Philo CA | Navarro Vineyards | 800-537-9463 | 5601 H 128 |
| Philo CA | Toulouse Vineyards | 707-895-2828 | 800 H 128 |
| Pine Grove CA | Indian Grinding Rock State Historic Park | 209-296-7488 | 14881 Pine Grove - Volcano Road |
| Pioneertown CA | Pioneertown | 760-964-6549 | Pioneertown Road |
| Piru CA | Lake Piru Marina | 805-521-1231 | 4780 Piru Canyon Road |
| Pismo Beach CA | Pismo Beach Premium Outlets | 805-773-4661 | 333 Five Cities Drive, Suite 100 |
| Placerville CA | Abel's Apple Acres | 530-626-0138 | 2345 Carson Rd. |
| Placerville CA | Apple Creek Ranch | 530-644-5073 | 2979 Carson Rd. |
| Placerville CA | Auriga Wine Cellars | 530-621-0700 | 4520 Pleasant Valley Road |
| Placerville CA | Boa Vista Orchards | 530-622-5522 | 2952 Carson Rd. |
| Placerville CA | Boeger Winery | 530-622-8094 | 1709 Carson Road |
| Placerville CA | Gold Hill Vineyard | 530-626-6522 | 5660 Vineyard Lane |
| Placerville CA | High Hill Ranch | 530-644-1973 | 2901 High Hill Rd. |
| Placerville CA | Hooverville Orchards | 530-622-2155 | 1100 Wallace Rd. |
| Placerville CA | Lava Cap Winery | 530-621-0175 | 2221 Fruitridge Road |
| Placerville CA | Placerville Downtown Area | | Main Street & Hwy 49 |
| Placerville CA | Sierra Vista Winery & Vineyard | 530-622-7841 | 4560 Cabernet Way |
| Plymouth CA | Convergence Vineyards | 209-245-3600 | 14650 H 124 |
| Plymouth CA | Deaver Vineyards | 209-245-4099 | 12455 Steiner Road |

| | | | |
|---|---|---|---|
| Plymouth CA | Montevina Wines | 209-245-6942 | 20680 Shenandoah School Road |
| Plymouth CA | Nine Gables Vineyard & Winery | 209-245-3949 | 10778 Shenandoah Road |
| Plymouth CA | Renwood Winery | 209-245-6979 | 12225 Steiner Road |
| Plymouth CA | Sobon Winery | 209-245-6554 | 14430 Shenandoah Rd |
| Pollock Pines CA | Harris Tree Farm | 530-644-2194 | 2640 Blair Road |
| Rancho Cordova CA | Nimbus Fish Hatchery | 916-358-2884 | 2001 Nimbus Rd |
| Rancho Cucamonga CA | Victoria Gardens | 909-463-2830 | 12505 North Mainstreet |
| Redding CA | Kent's Meat and Grocery and Kathy's Deli | 530-365-4322 | 8080 Airport Road |
| Redwood Valley CA | Elizabeth Vineyards | 707-485-9009 | 8591 Colony Drive |
| Redwood Valley CA | Gabrielli Winery | 707-485-1221 | 10950 West Road |
| Riverside CA | Citrus State Historic Park | 909-780-6222 | Van Buren Blvd. |
| Rutherford CA | Frogs Leap Winery | 707-963-4704 | 8815 Conn Creek Road |
| Rutherford CA | Mumm Napa Winery | 800-686-6272 | 8445 Silverado Trail |
| Rutherford CA | Sullivan Vineyards | 707-963-9646 | 1090 Galleron Rd |
| Sacramento CA | Capitol Park-Self-Guided Walk | 916-324-0333 | 10th and L Streets |
| Sacramento CA | Downtown Plaza | 915-442-4000 | 547 L Street |
| Sacramento CA | Old Sacramento Historic Area | 916-442-7644 | between I and L Streets |
| Sacramento CA | Scribner Boat Rentals | 916-744-1803 | 9051 River Road |
| Sacramento CA | Top Hand Ranch Carriage Rides | 916-655-3444 | Old Sacramento |
| Saint Helena CA | Frenchie Winery (at Raymond Vineyards) | 707-963-3141 | 849 Zinfandel Lane |
| San Diego CA | Action Sport Rentals | 619-275-8945 | 1775 Mission Bay |
| San Diego CA | Aqua Adventures Kayak Center | 619-523-9577 | 1548 Quivira Way |
| San Diego CA | Cinderella Carriage Rides | 619-239-8080 | |
| San Diego CA | Family Kayak Adventure Center | 619-282-3520 | 4217 Swift Avenue |
| San Diego CA | Gaslamp Quarter Guided Walking Tour | 619-233-4692 | 410 Island Avenue |
| San Diego CA | Horton Plaza Shopping Center | 619-239-8180 | 324 Horton Plaza |
| San Diego CA | Old Town State Historic Park | 619-220-5422 | San Diego Ave & Twiggs St |
| San Diego CA | San Pasqual Winery | 858-270-7550 | 5151 Santa Fe Street |
| San Diego CA | SeaWorld of California-Kennels | 619-226-3901 | 1720 South Shore Rd. |
| San Diego CA | Seaforth Boat Rentals | 619-223-1681 | 1641 Quivira Road |
| San Diego CA | Westfield UTC Mall | 858-546-8858 | 4545 La Jolla Village Drive, Suite E-25 |
| San Francisco CA | Barbary Coast Trail | 415-775-1111 | |
| San Francisco CA | Coit Tower | 415-362-0808 | 1 Telegraph Hill Blvd |
| San Francisco CA | Extranominal Tours | 866-231-3752 | 690 Fifth Street (cross street Townsend) |
| San Francisco CA | Fisherman's Wharf Shopping | | Jefferson Street |
| San Francisco CA | Fort Point National Historic Site | 415-556-1693 | Fort Mason, Building 201 |
| San Francisco CA | Ghirardelli Square Shopping Center | 415-775-5500 | 900 North Point Street |
| San Francisco CA | Pac Bell Park | 415-972-2000 | 24 Willie Mays Plaza |
| San Francisco CA | Vampire Tour of San Francisco | 866-4-BITTEN (424-8836) | Nob Hill, Corner of California and Tayor Streets |
| San Francisco CA | Westfield San Francisco Center | 415-512-6776 | 865 Market Street |
| San Jose CA | Ron's Tours / Pedicab Service | 408-859-8961 | Call to Arrange. |
| San Jose CA | Santana Row | 408-551-4611 | 368 Santana Row |
| San Luis Obispo CA | San Luis Obispo Botanical Garden | 805-546-3501 | Post Office Box 4957 |
| San Miguel CA | The Rios-Caledonia Adobe | 805-467-3357 | 700 S. Mission Street |
| San Pedro CA | Catalina Classic Cruises | 800-641-1004 | Berth 95 |
| Santa Barbara CA | La Cumbre Plaza | 805-687-3500 | 120 South Hope Avenue |
| Santa Barbara CA | Municipal Winemakers | 805-931 MUNI (6864) | 28 Anacapa Street |
| Santa Barbara CA | Oreana Winery | 805-962-5857 | 205 Anacapa Street |
| Santa Barbara CA | Santa Barbara Botanical Garden | 805-682-4726 | 1212 Mission Canyon Road |
| Santa Barbara CA | State Street Shopping Area | 805-963-2202 | 100-700 State Street |
| Santa Barbara CA | Stearns Wharf | 805-897-1961 | Cabrillo Blvd |
| Santa Barbara CA | Stearns Wharf Vinters | 805-966-6624 | 217-G Stearns Wharf |
| Santa Barbara CA | TJ Paws Pet Wash | 805-687-8772 | 2601 De La Vina Street |
| Santa Cruz CA | De Laveaga Park Disc Golf | | Branciforte |
| Santa Cruz CA | Harbor Water Taxis | 831-475-6161 | Lake Avenue |
| Santa Cruz CA | Lighthouse Point Surfer's Museum | 831-420-6289 | W. Cliff Dr |
| Santa Cruz CA | Santa Cruz Harley Davidson Motorcyles | 831-421-9600 | 1148 Soquel Ave |
| Santa Rosa CA | Deloach Vineyards | 707-526-9111 | 1791 Olivet Road |
| Santa Rosa CA | Hanna Winery | 707-575-3371 | 5353 Occidental Road |
| Santa Rosa CA | Martini and Prati Wines | 707-823-2404 | 2191 Laguna Road |
| Santa Rosa CA | Matanzas Creek Winery | 707-528-6464 | 6097 Bennet Valley Road |
| Santa Ynez CA | LinCourt Vineyards | 805-688-8381 | 343 North Refugio Rd |
| Sebastopol CA | Taft Street Winery | 707-823-2404 | 2030 Barlow Lane |
| Shasta CA | Shasta State Historic Park | 530-243-8194 | 15312 H 299 W |

| | | | |
|---|---|---|---|
| Simi Valley CA | Simi Valley Town Center Mall | 805-581-1430 | 1555 Simi Town Center Way |
| Sky Forest CA | Children's Forest | 909-338-5156 | Keller Peak Road |
| Solvang CA | Buttonwood Farm Winery | 805-688-3032 | 1500 Alamo Pintado Rd |
| Solvang CA | D'Alfonso-Curran Wines | 805-693-8864 | 1557 Mission Drive/H 246 |
| Solvang CA | Lucas and Lewellen Winery | 805-686-9336 | 1645 Copenhagen Drive |
| Solvang CA | Mandolina Wines | 888-777-6663 | 1665 Copenhagen Drive |
| Solvang CA | Solvang Horsedrawn Streetcars | | P.O. Box 531 |
| Solvang CA | Solvang Village | 800-468-6765 | 1500-2000 Mission Drive |
| Sonoma CA | Bartholomew Park Winery | 707-935-9511 | 1000 Vineyard Ln |
| Sonoma CA | Sebastiani Vineyards and Winery | 800-888-5532 | 389 Fourth Street East |
| Sonoma CA | Small Lot Wine Tours | 707-294-2232 | Various |
| South Lake Tahoe CA | Tahoe Keys Boat Rentals | 530-544-8888 | 2435 Venice Drive E. |
| South Lake Tahoe CA | Tahoe Sport Fishing | 530-541-5448 | 900 Ski Run Boulevard |
| South Lake Tahoe CA | Tallac Historic Site | | Highway 89 |
| St Helena CA | Beringer Vineyards | 707-963-4812 | 2000 Main Street |
| St Helena CA | Casa Nuestra Winery | 866-844-WINE | 3451 Silverado Trail North |
| St Helena CA | Rustridge | 707-965-2871 | 2910 Lower Chiles Valley Rd |
| St Helena CA | V. Sattui Winery | 707-963-7774 | 1111 White Lane |
| St Helena CA | V. Sattui Winery | 707-963-7774 | 1111 White Lane |
| Sutter Creek CA | Sutter Creek | 209-267-5647 | Highway 49 |
| Sutter Creek CA | Sutter Creek Wine Tasting | 209-267-5838 | 85 Main Street |
| Tahoe City CA | Reel Deal Sport Fishing & Lake Tours | 530-318-6272 | P.O. Box 1173 |
| Tahoe City CA | Truckee River Raft Rentals | 530-581-0123 | 185 River Road |
| Temecula CA | Baily Vineyard | 951-676-WINE (9463) | 33440 La Serena Way |
| Temecula CA | Europa Village Winery | 888-383-8767 | 33475 La Serena Way |
| Temecula CA | Falkner Winery | 951-676-8231 | 40620 Calle Contento |
| Temecula CA | Filsinger Vineyards and Winery | 909-302-6363 | 39050 De Portola Rd |
| Temecula CA | Maurice Carrie Vineyard | 951-676-1711 | 34225 Rancho California Road |
| Temecula CA | Miramonte Winery | 951-506-5500 | 33410 Rancho California Road |
| Temecula CA | Oak Mountain Winery | 951-699-9102 | 36522 Via Verde |
| Temecula CA | Old Town Temecula | | Front Street |
| Temecula CA | Stuart Cellars | 888-260-0870 | 33515 Rancho California Road |
| Temecula CA | Tesoro Winery | 951-308-0000 | 28475 Old Town Front Street |
| Temecula CA | Van Roekel Winery | 909-699-6961 | 34567 Rancho California Rd |
| Temecula CA | Wine Country Wedding Chapel | 951-760-3399 | 41973 6th Steet |
| Templeton CA | Venteux Vineyards | 805-369-0127 | 1795 Las Tablas Road |
| Tulelake CA | Medicine Lake Highlands | 530-233-5811 | Forest Road 49 |
| Tulelake CA | Volcanic Historic Loop | 530-233-5811 | State Route 139 |
| Tuttletown CA | Mark Twain Cabin | | Jackass Hill Rd. |
| Universal City CA | Universal Studios Kennel | 818-508-9600 | Hollywood Frwy (Hwy 101) |
| Vacaville CA | The Nut Tree | 707-447-6000 | 1681 East Monte Vista Avenue |
| Valencia CA | Six Flags Magic Mountain | 661-255-4100 | 26101 Magic Mountain Parkway |
| Valley Center CA | Bates Nut Farm | 760-749-3333 | 15954 Woods Valley Road |
| Ventura CA | Albinger Archaeological Museum | 805-648-5823 | 113 East Main Street |
| Ventura CA | Ventura Harbor Village | 805-644-0169 | 1559 Spinnaker Drive |
| Ventura CA | Ventura Pier | | 668 Harbor Blvd |
| Walnut Creek CA | Broadway Plaza Shopping Center | 925-939-7600 | 1275 Broadway Plaza |
| West Hollywood CA | Sunset Plaza | 310-652-2622 | 8600 - 8700 Sunset Boulevard (at Sunset Plaza Drive), |
| Westlake Village CA | The Dogs Gallery | 818-707-8070 | 31139 Via Colinas, Suite 204 |
| Windsor CA | Martinell Vineyards | 707-525-0570 | 3360 River Road |
| Windsor CA | Mutt Lynch Winery | 707-942-6180 | 9050 Windsor Road |
| Wishon CA | Millers Landing Resort - Bass Lake | 559-642-3633 | 37976 Road 222 |
| Yermo CA | Calico Ghost Town | 760-254-2122 | PO Box 638 |
| Yorkville CA | Meyer Family Cellars | 707-895-2341 | 19750 H 128 |
| Yorkville CA | Yorkville Cellars | 707-894-9177 | 25701 H 128 |
| Yountville CA | Domain Chandon | 707-944-2280 | One California Drive |
| Yountville CA | Hill Family Estate | 707-944-9580 | 6512 Washington Street |
| Yreka CA | Blue Goose Steam Excursion Train | 530-842-4146 | 300 East Miner Street |

**Colorado Listings**

| | | | |
|---|---|---|---|
| Aurora CO | Cherry Creek Marina Boat Rentals | 303-779-6144 | Cherry Creek State Park |
| Bond CO | Colorado River Runs | 800-826-1081 | Star Route, Box 32 |
| Boulder CO | Boulder Creek Winery | 303-516-9031 | 6440 Odell Place |
| Boulder CO | Bus Transport | 303-441-3266 | 1739 Broadway Street/H 7 |

| | | | |
|---|---|---|---|
| Boulder CO | Twenty Ninth Street Mall | 303-449-1189 | 1710 29th Street |
| Burlington CO | Kit Carson Carousel | | Kit Carson County Fairgrounds |
| Canon City CO | Buckskin Joe Frontier Town and Railway | 719-275-5149 | 1193 Fremont County Road 3A |
| Canon City CO | Royal Gorge Bridge & Park | 719-275-7507 | 4218 Fremont County Road 3A |
| Castle Rock CO | Outlets at Castle Rock | 303-688-4495 | 5050 Factory Shops Blvd |
| Castle Rock CO | The Castle Rock Outlet Stores | 303-688-4495 | 5050 Factory Shops Blvd |
| Cimarron CO | Cimarron Railroad Exhibit | 970-641-2337 | Off H 50 |
| Clark CO | Steamboat Lake Marina | 970-879-7019 | P. O. Box 867/County Road 62 |
| Colorado Springs CO | Adventures Out West | 800-755-0935 | 1680 S 21Street Street |
| Colorado Springs CO | Ghost Town Wild West Museum | 719-634-0696 | 400 S 21st Street |
| Colorado Springs CO | Pictures on the Promenade | 719-265-6264 | 1885 Briargate Parkway |
| Colorado Springs CO | Pikes Peak Toll Road | 719-385-PEAK | P.O. Box 1575-MC060 |
| Colorado Springs CO | Prominade Shops at Briargate | 719-265-6264 | 1885 Briargate Parkway |
| Cripple Creek CO | The Pikes Peak Heritage Center at Cripple Creek | 719-689-3315 | 9283 S H 67 |
| Denver CO | Cherry Creek Mall | | 3000 E First Avenue |
| Denver CO | Denver Pavilions | 303-260-6000 | 15th Street and Tremont |
| Denver CO | Larimer Square | | Larimer Street |
| Denver CO | Rocky Mountain Audio Guides, LLC | 303-898-7073 | P.O. Box 22963 |
| Denver CO | State Capitol Grounds | 303-866-2604 | 200 E Colfax |
| Durango CO | Horse Gulch Trail | 800-463-8726 | off 3rd Street and 8th/9th Avenue |
| Durango CO | Outlaw River and Jeep Tours | 970-259-1800 | 555 Main Avenue |
| Durango CO | Rent A Wreck of Durango | 970-259-5858 | 21760 Highway 160 West |
| Fort Collins CO | Grave of Annie the Railroad Dog | | 201 Peterson St |
| Golden CO | Buffalo Bills Gravesite and Museum | 303-526-0744 | 987 1/2 Look-Out Mountain Road |
| Golden CO | Lookout Mountain Park | 303-964-2589 | Lookout Mountain Road |
| Golden CO | The Colorado Trail | 303-384-3729 | 710 10th Street, Room 210 (Foundation Office) |
| Gunnison CO | Elk Creek Marina | 970-641-0707 | 24830 H 50 |
| Gunnison CO | Lake Fork Marina | 970-641-3048 | Lake Fork |
| Gunnison CO | Monarch Crest Tram | 719-539-4091 | H 50 between Salida and Gunnison |
| Idaho Springs CO | Argo Gold Mill and Museum | 303-567-2421 | 2350 Riverside Drive |
| Idaho Springs CO | Argo Gold Mine and Mill | 303-567-2421 | I 70 |
| La Junta CO | Bent's Old Fort National Historic Site | 719-383-5010 | 35110 Highway 194 East |
| Littleton CO | Aspen Grove Lifestyle Center | 303-794-0640 | 7301 S Santa Fe Drive |
| Littleton CO | Aspen Grove Shopping Center | 303-794-0640 | 7301 S Santa Fe Drive |
| Loveland CO | Loveland Promendade Shops | 970-461-1285 | 5971 Sky Pond Drive |
| Loveland CO | Outlets at Loveland | 970-663-1916 | 5661 McWhinney Blvd |
| Loveland CO | Promenade Shops at Centerra | 970-461-1285 | Centerra Parkway at Sky Pond Drive |
| Loveland CO | Promenade Shops at Centerra | 970-461-1285 | Centerra Parkway at Sky Pond Drive |
| Manitou Springs CO | Manitou Cliff Dwellings Museum | 719-685-5242 | Cliff Dwelling Road |
| Morrison CO | Dinosaur Ridge | 303-697-3466 | 16831 West Alameda Parkway |
| Ouray CO | Colorado West Jeep Tours | 800-648-JEEP (5337) | 701 Main Street/H 550 |
| Ouray CO | San Juan Scenic Jeep Tours | 970-325-0089 | 210 7th Avenue |
| Ouray CO | Switzerland of America Jeep Tours & Rentals | 970-325-4484 | 226 7th Avenue |
| Palisade CO | Colorado Cellars Winery | 970-464-7921 | 3553 E Road |
| Pueblo CO | Riverwalk of Pueblo | 719-583-4277 | S Union Avenue |
| Pueblo CO | The Farmers' Market at the Riverwalk | 719-595-0242 | W 1st Street |
| Red Feather Lakes CO | Sundance Trail Guest Ranch | 800-357-4930 | 17931 Red Feather Lakes Rd |
| Salida CO | Monarch Crest Tram | 719-539-4091 | H 50 between Salida and Gunnison |
| Silverthome CO | Outlets at Silverthorne | 866-746-7686 | 246-V Rainbow Drive |
| Snowmass Village CO | Aspen Gondola | 877-282-7736 | Center of town |
| Snowmass Village CO | Blazing Adventures | 800-282-7238 | P. O. Box 5068 |
| Steamboat Springs CO | Amaze'n Steamboat | 970-870-8682 | 1255 S Lincoln Avenue |
| Steamboat Springs CO | Silver Bullet Gondola Rides | 970-879-0740 | Gondola Square |
| Telluride CO | Dave's Mountain Tours | 970-728-9749 | P.O. Box 2736 |
| Telluride CO | The Gondola | 888-353-5473 | San Juan Street |
| Vallecito Lake CO | Vallecito Lake Trails | 970-247-1573 | |

## Connecticut Listings

| | | | |
|---|---|---|---|
| Brookfield CT | DeGrazia Vineyards | 203-775-1616 | 131 Tower Road |
| Clinton CT | Chamard Vineyards | 860-664-0299 | 115 Cow Hill Road |
| Glastonbury CT | Connecticut Audubon Center | 860-633-8402 | 1361 Main St |
| Hartford CT | State Historic Preservation Museum | 860-566-3005 | 59 S Prospect Street |

| | | | |
|---|---|---|---|
| Litchfield CT | Haight-Brown Vineyard | 860-567-4045 | 29 Chestnut Hill Road |
| Mystic CT | Denison Pequotsepos Nature Center | 860-536-1216 | 109 Pequotsepos Rd |
| Mystic CT | Downtown Mystic | 866-572-9578 | 14 Holmes Street |
| Mystic CT | Mystic Seaport | 860-572-0711 | 75 Greenmanville Avenue |
| Mystic CT | Mystic Seaport - The Museum of America and the Sea | 860-572-0711 | 75 Greenmanville Ave |
| Mystic CT | Olde Mistic Village | 860-536-4941 | 27 Coogan Blvd |
| Mystic CT | Olde Mistick Village | 860-536-4941 | 27 Coogan Blvd #2C |
| New London CT | Connecticut College Arboretum | 860-447-1911 | 270 Mohegan Ave |
| New Milford CT | The Silo at Hunt Hill Farm | 860-355-0300 | 44 Upland Road |
| New Preston CT | Hopkins Vineyard and Winery | 860-868-7954 | 25 Hopkins Road |
| Norfolk CT | Norfolk Chamber Music Festival | 203-432-1966 | Routes 44 and 272 |
| Old Lyme CT | Florence Griswold Museum | 860-434-5542 | 96 Lyme Street |
| Old Lyme CT | Florence Griswold Museum | 860-434-5542 | 96 Lyme St |
| Pomfret Center CT | Connecticut Audubon Center | 860-928-4948 | 189 Pomfret Street |
| Sharon CT | Sharon Audubon Center | 860-364-0520 | 325 Cornwall Bridge/H 4 |
| South Windsor CT | The Promenade Shops At Evergreen Walk | 860-432-3398 | 503 Evergreen Way |
| Stonington CT | Stonington Vineyards | 860-535-1222 | 523 Taugwonk Road |
| Weathersfield CT | Webb-Deane-Stevens Museum | 860-529-0612 | 211 Main Street |
| West Cornwall CT | Clarke Outdoors Canoe Rental | 860-672-6365 | 163 H 7 |
| Woodbury CT | The Glebe House Museum and Gertrude Jekyll Garden | 203-263-2855 | 49 Hollow Road |

**D.C. Listings**

| | | | |
|---|---|---|---|
| Washington DC | Capitol River Cruises | 301-460-7447 | 31st and K St, NW |
| Washington DC | Doggie Happy Hour at Cantina Marina | 202-554-8396 | 600 Water Street SW |
| Washington DC | FDR Memorial | | National Mall |
| Washington DC | Fletcher's Boat House | 202-244-0461 | 4940 Canal Rd NW |
| Washington DC | Gangplank on the Potomac | 202-554-5000 Ext. 11 | 600 Water Street SW |
| Washington DC | Jefferson Memorial | | National Mall |
| Washington DC | Lincoln Memorial | | National Mall |
| Washington DC | National Mall | | Independence Ave and 14th St. |

**Delaware Listings**

| | | | |
|---|---|---|---|
| Dover DE | Air Mobility Command Museum | 302-677-5938 | 1301 Heritage Road |
| Lewes DE | Fisherman's Wharf by the Drawbridge | 302-645-8862 | Anglers Road |
| Lewes DE | Lil Angler Charters | 302-645-8688 | Angler Road |
| Rehoboth Beach DE | Tanger Outlets | 302-226-9223 | 36470 Seaside Outlet Drive |
| Smyrna DE | Bombay Hook National Wildlife Refuge | 302) 653-6872 | 2591 Whitehall Neck Road |
| Wilmington DE | Christina River Boat Company Inc. | 302-530-5069 | 201 A Street |
| Wilmington DE | Rockwood Museum | 302-761-4340 | Washington Street Extension |
| Wilmington DE | The Shipyard Shops | 302-425-5000 | 900 South Madison Street |
| Wilmington DE | Trolley Square Shopping Center | 302-428-1040 | 21A Trolley Square |

**Florida Listings**

| | | | |
|---|---|---|---|
| Belleview FL | The Land Bridge Trailhead | 352-236-7143 | H 475 A |
| Big Pine Key FL | Blue Hole - Big Pine | 305-872-2239 | Watson Blvd |
| Big Pine Key FL | Jack Watson's Nature Trail | 305-872-2239 | MM 30.5 H 1 |
| Big Pine Key FL | National Key Deer Refuge | 305-872-0774 | 175-179 Key Deer Blvd |
| Boca Raton FL | Mizner Park | 561-362-0606 | 327 West Plaza Real |
| Bradenton FL | De Soto National Memorial | 941-792-0458 | P. O. Box 15390 |
| Bradenton FL | Hunsader U-Pick Farms | 941-322-2168 | 5500 C.R. 675 |
| Cape Canaveral FL | Kennedy Space Center Tours - Kennels | 407-452-2121 | S.R. 405 |
| Celebration FL | Celebration | | US 192 and I-4 |
| Clearwater FL | Murielle Winery | 727-561-0336 (voice mail) | 13131 56th Court, Suite 305 |
| Clermont FL | Lakeridge Winery | 352-394-8627 | 19239 H 27N |
| Coopertown FL | Coopertown Airboat Tours | 305-226-6048 | US-41 |
| Coral Gables FL | Village of Merrick Park Shopping Plaza | 305-529-0200 | 358 Avenue San Lorenzo |
| Crystal River FL | Crystal River State Archeological Site | 352-795-3817 | 3400 N. Museum Point |
| Delray Beach FL | Carnival Flea Market | 561-499-9935 | 5283 W Atlantic Avenue/H 806 |
| Destin FL | HarborWalk Village | 850-0269-0235 | Harbor Blvd |
| Ellenton FL | Ellenton Premium Outlets | 941-723-1150 | 5461 Factory Shops Blvd |

| | | | |
|---|---|---|---|
| Estero FL | Coconut Point Mall | 239-992-9966 | 23106 Fashion Drive, Suite 107 |
| Estero FL | Coconut Point Mall | 239-992-9966 | 23106 Fashion Drive |
| Estero FL | Miromar Outlet Mall | 239-948-3766 | 10801 Corkscrew Road, Suite 199 |
| Estero FL | Shoppes of Grande Oak | | 20321 Grand Oak Shoppes |
| Fernandina Beach FL | Amelia River Cruises/Charters and the Cumberland Ferry | 904-261-9972 | 1 North Front Street |
| Fort Lauderdale FL | Club Nautico | 954-467-6000 | 801 Seabreeze Blvd |
| Fort Lauderdale FL | Fort Lauderdale Riverwalk | 954-761-5784 | 2nd St and 4th Ave |
| Fort Lauderdale FL | Las Olas District | | Las Olas Blvd and Federal Hwy |
| Fort Myers FL | Bell Tower Mall | 239-489-1221 | Daniels Parkway and H/41 |
| Fort Myers FL | Manatee World Boat Tours | 239-693-1434 | 16991 State Road 31 |
| Fort Myers Beach FL | Key West Express Ferry | 888-539-2628 | 2200 Main Street |
| Gainesville FL | Kanapaha Botanical Gardens | 352-372-4981 | 4700 SW 58th Drive |
| Gulf County FL | St.Vincent Island - Shuttle Services | 850-229-1065 | Indian Pass Boat Launch, Hwy C-30B |
| Homestead FL | Coral Castle | 305-248-6345 | 28655 S Dixie H/H 1/5 |
| Islamorada FL | Theatre of the Sea | 305-664-2431 | 84721 H 1, MM 84.5 H 1 |
| Jacksonville FL | Fort Caroline National Memorial | 904-641-7155 | 12713 Ft. Caroline Road |
| Jacksonville FL | Kingsley Plantation | 904-251-3537 | 11676 Palmetto Avenue |
| Jacksonville FL | Marjorie Harris Carr Cross Florida Greenway | 850-245-2052 | |
| Jacksonville FL | Riverside Arts Market | | 715 Riverside Avenue/H 211 |
| Key Biscayne FL | Club Nautica | 305-361-9217 | 4000 Crandon Blvd |
| Key Largo FL | Dirty Waters Charters | 305-304-2212 | 322 Bay View Avenue |
| Key West FL | Duval Street Shopping District | | Duval Street |
| Key West FL | Fish Monster | 305-432-0047 | PO Box 2580 |
| Key West FL | Key West Aquarium | 305-296-2051 | 1 Whitehead St |
| Key West FL | Key West Tropical Forest & Garden | 305-296-1504 | 5210 College Road |
| Key West FL | Lazy Dog Outfitters, Kayaks and Boat Charters | 305-293-9550 | 5114 Overseas Highway |
| Key West FL | Mallory Square | 305-296-4557 | 1 Whitehead St |
| Key West FL | No Worries Charters | 305-393-2402 | Eisenhower Drive, Garrison Bight Marina |
| Key West FL | Southernmost Point Monument | | Whitehead St and South Street |
| Key West FL | Stephen Huneck Art Gallery | 305-295-7616 | 218 Whitehead St |
| Kissimmee FL | Big Toho Airboat Rides | 888-937-6843 | 100 Lakeshore Blvd |
| Kissimmee FL | Kissimmee Air Museum | 407-870-7366 | 233 N Hoagland Blvd |
| Kissimmee FL | Old Town | 407-396-4888 | 5570 W Irlo Bronson Memorial H/H 192 |
| Lake Buena Vista FL | Best Friends Pet Care at Disney's Port Orleans Resort | 877-493-9738 | 2510 Bonnet Creek Parkway |
| Lake Worth FL | Hoffman Chocolate Shop and Gardens | 561-433-GIFT | 5190 Lake Worth Rd |
| Land O Lakes FL | Florida Estates Winery | 813-996-2113 | 25241 State Rd 52 |
| Largo FL | Florida Botanical Gardens | 727-582-2100 | 12175 125th Street N |
| Largo FL | Heritage Village | 727-582-2123 | 11909 125th Street N |
| Longwood FL | Wekiva Island | 407-862-1500 | 1014 Miami Springs Drive |
| Miami FL | Bal Harbour Shopping Center | 305-866-0311 | 9700 Collins Ave |
| Miami FL | Fruit and Spice Park | 305-247-5727 | 24801 SW 187th Avenue |
| Miami FL | Monty's Marina | 305-854-7997 | 2560 S Bayshore Dr |
| Miami Beach FL | Art Deco Self-Guided Walking Tour | 305-672-2014 | 1001 Ocean Drive |
| Miami Beach FL | Club Nautico Power Boat Rentals | 305-858-6258 | 300 Alton Rd Ste 112 |
| Miami Beach FL | Lincoln Road Shops | 305-531-3442 | Lincoln Road |
| North Fort Myers FL | The Shell Factory and Nature Park | 239-995-2141 | 2787 North Tamiami Trail/H 41 |
| Orlando FL | Sea World - Kennel | 888-800-5447 | 7007 Sea World Drive |
| Orlando FL | Spring Fiesta in the Park | 407-649-3152 | 195 N Rosalind Avenue |
| Ormond Beach FL | Bruce Rossmeyer's Destination Daytona | 866-642-3464 | 1635 N Highway1 |
| Palm Beach FL | Worth Avenue Shopping District | | Worth Avenue |
| Panama City Beach FL | Pier Park | 850-236-9974 | 600 Pier Park Drive |
| Pensacola FL | Fort Barrancas | 850-455-5167 | Pensacola Navel Air Station |
| Plant City FL | Dinosaur World | 813-717-9865 | 5145 Harvey Tew Road |
| Pompano Beach FL | Festival Flea Market Mall | 800-353-2627 | 2900 W Sample Road/H 834 |
| Port St Joe FL | Constitution Convention Museum State Park | 850-229-8029 | 200 Allen Memorial Way |
| Port St Joe FL | Port St Joe Marina | 850-227-9393 | 340 Marina Drive |
| Port St Joe FL | Seahorse Water Safaris | 850-227-1099 | 340 Marina Drive |
| Silver Springs FL | Silver Springs Nature Park | 352-236-2121 | 5656 E Silver Springs Blvd/H 40 |
| Singer Island FL | Palm Beach Water Taxi | 561-683-TAXI (8294) | 98 Lake Drive |

365

| | | | |
|---|---|---|---|
| St Augustine FL | Fountain of Youth | 904-829-3168 | 11 Magnolia Ave. |
| St Augustine FL | Ghost Walk - Spirits of St. Augustine | 904-829-2391 | St. George Street |
| St Augustine FL | Ghostly Encounters Walking Tour | 800-404-2531 | 3 Aviles Street |
| St Augustine FL | St Augustine Lighthouse | 904-829-0745 | 81 Lighthouse Avenue |
| St Augustine FL | St Augustine Scenic Cruise | 904-824-1806 | St Augustine Municipal Marina |
| St Augustine FL | St. Augustine Historic Downtown | | St. George St |
| St Augustine FL | St. Augustine Transfer Co. Carriages | 904-829-2391 | Avenida Menendez and Hypolita St. |
| St Pete Beach FL | Shell Key Shuttle | 727-360-1348 | 801 Pass-A-Grille Way |
| St Petersburg FL | Florida Orange Groves Inc and Winery | 800-338-7923 | 1500 Pasadena Ave South |
| St Petersburg FL | Saturday Morning Farmers' Market | 727-455-4921 | First Avenue South and First Street. |
| Stuart FL | B and A Flea Market | 772-288-4915 | 2885 SE H 1 |
| Tallahassee FL | Downtown MarketPlace | 850-224-3252 | Park Avenue and Monroe Street |
| Tallahassee FL | Goodwood Museum & Gardens | 850-877-4202 | 1600 Miccosukee Rd |
| Tallahassee FL | Mission San Luis | 850-245-6406 | 2100 West Tennessee Street |
| Tallahassee FL | The Cotton Trail | | |
| Tallahassee FL | The Native Trail | | |
| Tallahassee FL | The Quail Trail | | |
| Tamiami FL | Wings Over Miami Air Museum | 305-233-5197 | 14710 128th Street SW |
| Tampa FL | Adventure Island - Kennel | 888-800-5447 | 4500 Bougainvillea Avenue |
| Tampa FL | Busch Gardens - Kennel | 888-800-5447 | 3605 Bougainvillea Avenue |
| Tampa FL | Hyde Park Village | 813-251-3500 | Swann and Dakota Avenues |
| Tarpon Springs FL | St Nicholas Boat Line | 727-942-6225 | 693 Dodecanese Blvd |
| Titusville FL | Space Shuttle and Rocket Launches | 321-867-4636 | Kennedy Space Center |
| West Palm Beach FL | City Place | 561-366-1000 | 700 S Rosemary Avenue |
| Winter Park FL | Hip Dog Canine Aquatic Rehabilitation and Fitness Ctr. | 407-628-1476 | P. O. Box 793/4965 N Palmetto Avenue |
| Winter Park FL | Winter Park Shopping District | | Park Avenue and Osceola Ave |

**Georgia Listings**

| | | | |
|---|---|---|---|
| Atlanta GA | Atlanta Preservation Center | 404-876-2041 | 327 Saint Paul Ave Se |
| Atlanta GA | Bark in the Park | 404-733-5000 | Piedmont Park |
| Atlanta GA | Centennial Olympic Park | 404-222-PARK | 265 Park Avenue West |
| Darien GA | Preferred Outlets at Darien | 912-437-8360 | 1111 Magnolia Bluff Way SW |
| Dawsonville GA | North Georgia Premium Outlets | 706-216-3609 | 800 H 400 S |
| Fort Oglethorpe GA | Chickamauga and Chattanooga National Military Park | 706-866-9241 | 3370 Lafayette Road |
| Fort Pulaski GA | Fort Pulaski National Monument | 912-786-5787 | On H 80E |
| Helen GA | Anna Ruby Falls | 706-878-1448 | 3453 Anna Ruby Falls Road |
| Helen GA | Charlemagne's Kingdom | 706-878-2200 | 8808 N Main Street/H 17/75 |
| Jekyll Island GA | Mini Golf | 912-635-2648 | Beachview Drive |
| Jekyll Island GA | Victoria's Carriages | 912-635-9500 | Stable Road |
| Kennesaw GA | Kennesaw Mountain National Battlefield Park | 770-427-4686 | 900 Kennesaw Mountain Drive |
| Pine Mountain GA | Pine Mountain Wild Animal Safari Kennels | 706-663-8744 | 1300 Oak Grove Road |
| Plains GA | Jimmy Carter National Historic Site | 229-824-4104 | 300 North Bond Street |
| Savannah GA | Ghost Talk Ghost Walk | 912-233-3896 | On Abercorn between Congress and Bryan |
| Savannah GA | Old Fort Jackson | 912-232-3945 | 1 Fort Jackson Road |
| Savannah GA | Savannah Riverfront Area | 912-644-6400 | River Street |
| St Simons GA | Fort Frederica National Monument | 912-638-3639 | 6515 Frederica Road |
| Stone Mountain GA | Stone Mountain Park | 770-498-5600 | Highway 78 |
| Stone Mountain GA | Stone Mountain Village | 770-879-4971 | Main Street |
| Washington GA | Callaway Plantation | 706-678-7060 | 2160 Lexington Road |
| Young Harris GA | Crane Creek Vineyards | 706-379-1236 | Crane Creek Road |

**Hawaii Listings**

| | | | |
|---|---|---|---|
| Aiea HI | The 'Aiea Loop Trail | 808-973-9782 | End of Aiea Heights Drive |
| Honolulu HI | Aloha Tower Marketplace | 808-566-2337 | 1 Aloha Tower Drive |
| Honolulu HI | Island Air | 800-652-6541 | 99 Kapalulu Place |
| Honolulu HI | Ka Iwi State Scenic Shoreline | 808-587-0300 | Kalaniana'ole H/H 72 |
| Honolulu HI | Koko Marina Center | 808-395-4737 | 7192 Kalanianaole H, Suite #A-143 / H 72 |
| Honolulu HI | Kuliouou Ridge Hiking Trail | 808 973-9782 | Kala`au Place |

| Honolulu HI | Pacific Aviation Museum Pearl Harbor | 808-441-1000 | Hangar 37, Ford Island 319 Lexington Blvd |
| Honolulu HI | The Ward Center | 808-591-8411 | Ala Moana Blvd/H 92 |
| Honolulu HI | Ualaka'a Trail | 808-587-0300 | Off Round Top Drive off Makiki Street |
| Honolulu HI | Wa'ahila Ridge (Mount Olympus) Hiking Trail | 808-973-9782 | End of Ruth Place, via Peter Street from St. Louis Drive off Wai'alae Avenue |
| Kaaawa HI | Kapa'ele'ele Trail | 808-973-9782 | 52-222 Kamehameha H/H 83 |
| Kahana HI | Nakoa Trail | 808-973-9782 | 52-222 Kamehameha H/H 83 |
| Kailua HI | Aikahi Park Shopping | 808-735-8822 | 25 Kaneohe Bay Drive |
| Kailua HI | Maunawili Falls Hiking Trail | 808-973-9782 | Maunawili Road |
| Kapolei HI | Halekuai Center | | 563 Farrington H/H 93 |
| Kula HI | Haleakala Ridge Trail | 808-587-0300 | Waipoli Road |
| Kula HI | Polipoli Trail | 96790 | Waipoli Road |
| Kula HI | Redwood Trail | 808-587-0300 | Waipoli Road |
| Lihue HI | Kauai Path | 808-639-1018 | P. O. Box 81 |
| Manoa Valley HI | Manoa Falls Trail | 808-973-9782 | End of Manoa Road |
| Maui HI | Ke Ala Loa O Maui/Piilani Trail | 808-587-0300 | Waianapanapa Road |

## Idaho Listings

| Bonners Ferry ID | Copper Falls Self-Guided Nature Trail | 208-267-5561 | Forest Road 2517 |
| Bonners Ferry ID | Deep Creek Trail | 208-267-3888 | 287 Westside Road |
| Bonners Ferry ID | Kootenai National Wildlife Refuge | 208-267-3888 | 287 Westside Road/H 18 |
| Bonners Ferry ID | West Fork Lake and Mountain Trail #347 | 208-765-7223 | Road #2466 |
| Caldwell ID | Ste Chapelle Winery | 877-783-2427 | 19348 Lowell Rd |
| Challis ID | Custer Motorway | 208-756-5100 | West end of Main Street/H 93 |
| Challis ID | Land of the Yankee Fork State Park | 208-879-5244 | H 75 and H 93 |
| Eagle ID | The Winery at Eagle Knoll | 208-286-9463 | 3705 North Hwy 16 |
| Elk City ID | Elk City Wagon Road/Nez Perce National Forest | 208-842-2245 | HC01, Box 416 |
| Hope ID | Diamond Charters | 208-265-2565 | PO Box 153 |
| Horseshoe Bend ID | Cascade Raft Company | 208-793-2221 | 7050 H 55 |
| Idaho Falls ID | A Whispering Giant | 208-523-1010 | 850 Lincoln Road |
| Idaho Falls ID | Trackside Mall | 208-523-9111 | 301 Poulson Avenue |
| Kellogg ID | Silver Mountain Gondola | 208-783-1111 | 610 Bunker Avenue |
| Kune ID | Indian Creek (Stowe) Winery | 208-922-4791 | 1000 North McDermott Rd |
| Lewiston ID | Kirkwood Historic Ranch | 208-628-3916 | Kirkwood Road |
| McCall ID | Backwoods Adventures | 208-469-9067 | P. O. Box 1976 |
| McCall ID | Mile High Marina | 208-634-8605 | 1300 E Lake Street |
| McCall ID | Payette National Forest/Lake Fork Trail | 208-634-0700 | 800 W Lakeside Avenue |
| Riggins ID | Heavens Gate Observation Site/Hells Canyon | 208-628-3916 | Forest Road 517 |
| Ririe ID | Cress Creek Nature Trail | 208-523-1012 | E Heise Road |
| Salmon ID | Sacajawea Interpretive Cultural and Education Center | 208-756-1188 | 60 H 28 |
| Sandpoint ID | North Idaho Native Plant Arboretum | | Ella Avenue and Ontario Street |
| Sandpoint ID | Pend Oreille Divide Trail #67 | 208-765-7223 | Lunch Peak Road 1091 |
| Sandpoint ID | Pend d'Oreille Winery | 877-452-9011 | 220 Cedar St |
| Sandpoint ID | Sandpoint Marine & Motorsports | 208-263-5128 | Highway95 |
| Sandpoint ID | Schweitzer Mountain | 800-831-8810 | 10,000 Schweitzer Mountain Road |
| Spencer ID | Spencer Opal Mine | 208-374-5476 | Main Street |

## Illinois Listings

| Albany IL | Albany Indian Mounds State Historic Site | 309-788-0177 | S Cherry Street and 12th Avenue |
| Alto Pass IL | Alto Vineyards | 618-893-4898 | Hwy 127 |
| Arthur IL | Great Pumpkin Patch | 217-543-2394 | RR1 Box 100 |
| Aurora IL | Chicago Premium Outlets | 630-585-2200 | 1650 Premium Outlets Blvd |
| Batavia IL | Fermi National Accelerator Lab | 630-840-3351 | P.O. Box 500/Pine Street or Batavia Road |
| Belknap IL | Cache River Basin Vineyards and Winery | 618-658-2274 | 315 Forman Lane |
| Belleville IL | Eckert's Orchards | 618-233-0513 | 951 S Greenmount Road |
| Bourbonnais IL | Perry Farm Park | 815-933-9905 | 459 N Kennedy Drive/H 45-H 52 |
| Carbondale IL | Grammer Orchards | 618-684-2471 | 4140 Dutch Ridge Road |
| Carbondale IL | Kite Hill Winery | 618-684-5072 | 83 Kite Hill Road |
| Champaign IL | Alto Vineyards | 217-356-4784 | 4210 N Duncan Rd |

| | | | |
|---|---|---|---|
| Chicago IL | Antique Coach and Carriage Company | 773-735-9400 | 700 North Michigan |
| Chicago IL | Buckingham Fountain | 312-742-7529 | In Grant Park |
| Chicago IL | Chicago Horse and Carriage Rides | 312-953-9530 | Michigan Avenue |
| Chicago IL | Chicago White Sox Dog Day | 866-769-4263 | 333 W. 35th Street |
| Chicago IL | Chicagoland Canoe Base | 773-777-1489 | 4019 N Narragansett Avenue |
| Chicago IL | Mercury Canine Cruises | 312-332-1353 | Michigan Ave. & Wacker Dr. |
| Chicago IL | Navy Pier | 312-595-7437 | 600 East Grand Avenue |
| Chicago IL | Of Mutts and Men | 773-477-7171 | 2149 W. Belmont |
| Chicago IL | Pedway: Downtown Chicago Pedestrian Walkway System | 312-744-5000 | Downtown |
| Chicago IL | Retail Stores | | See comments for details. |
| Chicago IL | Riverwalk Gateway/Riverwalk | 312-744-6630 | Lake Shore Drive |
| Chicago IL | Seadog Cruises at Navy Pier | 888-840-6317 | 600 E. Grand (Entrance on Illinois) |
| Chicago IL | Shoreline Sightseeing Boat Tours | 312-222-9328 | Illinois Street |
| Chicago IL | Step in Time Carriages | 773-501-7011 | 830 N Michigan Avenue |
| Cobden IL | Owl Creek Vineyard | 618-893-2557 | 2655 Water Valley Road |
| Collinsville IL | Cahokia Mounds State Historic Site | 618-346-5160 | 30 Ramey Street |
| Dixon IL | John Deere Historic Site | 815-652-4551 | 8393 S Main |
| Dixon IL | Ronald Reagan Boyhood Home | 815-288-5176 | 810 S Hennepin Avenue |
| El Paso IL | Furrow Vineyard | 866-880-9463 | 1131 H 251 |
| Elizabeth IL | Long Hollow Scenic Overlook | 800-747-9377 | H 20 |
| Evanston IL | Ladd Arboretum | 847-448-8256 | 2024 Mc Cormick Blvd |
| Evanston IL | Shakespeare Garden at Northwestern University | 847-491-3741 | 633 Clark Street |
| Galena IL | Fever River Outfitters | 815-776-9425 | 525 Main Street |
| Galena IL | Galena Cellars Winery | 800-397-9463 | 4746 N Ford Road |
| Galena IL | Galena Cellars Winery and Vineyard | 800-397-9463 | 515 South Main St |
| Galena IL | Galena Trolley Tours | 815-777-1248 | 314 S Main |
| Galena IL | President Ulysses S. Grant Home State Historic Park | 815-777-3310 | 500 Bouphillier Street |
| Galena IL | Wooded Wonderland Country Store and Sawmill | 815-777-3426 | 610 S Devil's Ladder Road |
| Galesburg IL | Carl Sandburg State Historic Site | 309-342-2361 | 313 E Third Street |
| Galesburg IL | Seminary Street Shopping District | 309-342-1000 | Seminary Street |
| Geneva IL | Geneva Commons | 630-262-0044 | 602 Commons Drive |
| Geneva IL | Geneva Commons Outdoor Shopping Mall | 630-262-0044 | 602 Commons Drive |
| Geneva IL | The Fabyan Villa Museum | 630-232-4811 | 1511 S Batavia Avenue/H 31 |
| Glenview IL | Glenview Farmers' Market | 847-657-1506 | Wagner Road |
| Grafton IL | Aeries Riverview Winery | 618-786-VIEW (8439) | 600 Mulberry Street |
| Grafton IL | Piasa Winery | 618-786-9463 | 211 W Main Street /H 100 |
| Grafton IL | Piasa Winery | 618-786-WINE | 211 West Main St |
| Greenup IL | Cameo Vineyards | 217-923-9963 | 400 Mill Rd |
| Greenup IL | Cumberland County Covered Bridge | 217-923-3401 | Embarras River |
| Gurnee IL | Six Flags Great America Kennel | 847-249-4636 | 542 N H 21 |
| Hartford IL | The Lewis and Clark State Historic Site | 618-251-5811 | 1 Lewis and Clark Trail/H 3 |
| Huntley IL | Prime Outlets | 847-669-9100 | 11800 Factory Shops Blvd |
| Joliet IL | Joliet Iron Works Historic Site | 815-724-3760 | E Columbia Street |
| Lincoln IL | Lincoln Farmers' Market | | 316 S Kickapoo Street |
| Long Grove IL | Historic Long Grove Shopping District | 847-634-9440 | Old McHenry Road |
| Makanda IL | Makanda Boardwalk | 800-526-1500 | Makanda Road |
| Manhattan IL | Manhattan Farmers' Market | 815-478-3811 | Wabash Street |
| Moline IL | Channel Cat Water Taxi | 309-788-3360 | 13th Street |
| Moline IL | Channel Cat Water Taxi | 309-788-3360 | 13th Street |
| Monticello IL | Monticello Railway Museum | 217-762-9011 | 993 Iron Horse Road |
| Mount Vernon IL | GenKota Winery | 618-246-WINE (9463) | 301 N 44th Street |
| Niles IL | The Leaning Tower of Niles | 847-647-8222 | 6300 W Touhy Avenue |
| Oak Brook IL | Graue Mill and Museum | 630-655-2090 | 3800 S. York Road |
| Oak Park IL | Hemingways Birthplace | 708-848-2222 | 339 N Oak Park |
| Oak Park IL | Oak Park Self-Guided Walking Tours | 708-848-1500 | 158 N Forest Avenue |
| Olney IL | Fox Creek Vineyards | 618-392-0418 | 5502 North Fox Rd |
| Ottawa IL | Starved Rock Adventures | 815-434-9200 | 1 Dee Bennett Road/H 34 |
| Pana IL | Coal Creek Pioneer Village | 217-562-4240 | Fairgrounds Road |
| Peoria IL | Carriage Classics | 309-579-2833 | Main Street and Water Streets |
| Pomona IL | Pomona Winery | 618-893-2623 | 2865 Hickory Ridge Rd |
| Pomona IL | Von Jakob Vineyard | 618-893-4500 | 1309 Sadler Rd |

| | | | |
|---|---|---|---|
| Red Bud IL | Lau-Nae Winery | 618-282-9463 | 1522 State Route 3 |
| Red Bud IL | Lau-Nae Winery, Inc. | 618-282-WINE (9463) | 1522 H 3 |
| Rockford IL | Klehm Arboretum and Botanic Garden | 815-965-8146 | 2715 S Main Street/H 2 |
| Roselle IL | Lynfred Winery | 630-529-9463 | 15 S Roselle Road |
| Sandwich IL | Fox Valley Winery | 815-786-3124 | 120 South Main St |
| Springfield IL | Lincoln's Tomb State Historic Site | 217-782-2717 | 1500 Monument Avenue/Oak Ridge Cemetary |
| Springfield IL | Pampered Pet Center | 217-483-9106 | 3401 Gateway Drive |
| St Charles IL | Concerts in the Park at Lincoln Park | 630-513-6200 | W Main Street/H 64 |
| St Charles IL | Pride of the Fox Riverfest | 630-377-6161 | Main Street/H 64 |
| St Charles IL | Sculptures in the Park in Mt. St. Mary Park | 630-513-4316 | H 31/Geneva Road |
| St Charles IL | St Charles Holiday Homecoming and Electric Christmas Parade | 630-516-5386 | Main Street/H 64 |
| St Charles IL | St Charles Paddlewheel Riverboats | 630-584-2334 | 2 North Avenue |
| Stewardson IL | Vahling Vineyards | 217-682-5409 | Mode Road/400 N |
| Tuscola IL | Tanger Outlet | 217-253-2282 | 4045 Tuscola Blvd |
| Union IL | Illinois Railway Museum | 815-923-4000 | 7000 Olson Road |
| Urbana IL | University of Illinois Arboretum | 217-333-7579 | Lincoln Avenue, Urbana Champaign Campus |
| Urbana IL | University of Illinois Campus | 217-333-4666 | 1401 W Green Street |
| Vienna IL | Shawnee Winery | 618-658-8400 | 200 Commercial Street |
| Waterloo IL | Schorr Lake Vineyards | 618-939-3174 | 1032 S Library St |
| Whittington IL | Pheasant Hollow Winery | 618-629-2302 | 14931 State Hwy 37 |

**Indiana Listings**

| | | | |
|---|---|---|---|
| Bloomington IN | Indiana University Campus | 812-856-4648 | 300 N Jordan Avenue |
| Bloomington IN | Lake Monroe Boat Rental | 812-837-9909 | 4855 H 446 |
| Bloomington IN | Oliver Winery | 812-876-5800 | 8024 H 37N |
| Borden IN | Huber Orchard and Winery | 812-923-9813 | 19816 Huber Road |
| Columbus IN | Irwin Gardens | 812-378-2622 | 5th Street and Layfette Avenue |
| Elkhart IN | Amish Heritage Driving Tour | 574-262-8161 | 219 Caravan Drive |
| Elkhart IN | National New York Central Railroad Museum | 574-294-3001 | 721 S Main Street |
| French Lick IN | Indiana Railway Museum and Train Ride | 800-74-TRAIN | 8594 H 56W |
| Hagerstown IN | Wilbur Wright Birthplace | 765-332-2495 | 1525 N 750 E |
| Indianapolis IN | Blue Ribbon Carriage Company | 317-631-4169 | 1311 S. Drover St |
| Indianapolis IN | Crown Hill Cemetery | 317-925-3800 | 700 W. 38th St. |
| Indianapolis IN | Fountain Square | 317-686-6010 | 1105 Prospect Street |
| Indianapolis IN | Garfield Park Conservatory | 317-327-7184 | 2450 S. Shelby St |
| Indianapolis IN | Indiana World War Memorial | 317-232-7615 | 5 Block Memorial Plaza |
| Indianapolis IN | Medal of Honor Memorial in White River State Park | 317-233-2434 | 801 W. Washington St |
| Indianapolis IN | Soldiers and Sailors Monument | 317-232-7615 | Monument Circle |
| Kendallville IN | Mid-America Windmill Museum | 260-347-5273 | 732 S Allen Chapel Road |
| Lincoln City IN | Lincoln Boyhood National Memorial | 812-937-4541 | 3027 E South Street |
| Linn Grove IN | Swiss Heritage Village and Museum | 260-589-8007 | 1200 Swiss Way |
| Mauckport IN | Squire Boone Caverns and Village | 812-732-4381 | 100 Squire Boone Road SW |
| Nashville IN | T.C. Steele's State Historic Site | 812-988-2785 | 4220 T.C. Steele Rd. |
| Peru IN | Grissom Air Museum | 765-689-8011 | 1000 W Hoosier Blvd |
| Plainfield IN | Chateau Thomas Winery | 317-837-WINE (9463) | 6291 Cambridge Way |
| Santa Claus IN | Holiday World Theme Park Kennel | 877-463-2645 | 452 E Christmas Blvd |
| South Bend IN | University of Notre Dame Campus | 574-631-5726 | S Dixie Way/H 31/933 |
| Valparaiso IN | Taltree Arboretum & Gardens | 219-462-0025 | 71 N 500 W |
| Vincennes IN | George Rogers Clark National Historical Park | 812-882-1776, ext 210 | 401 S 2nd Street |

**Iowa Listings**

| | | | |
|---|---|---|---|
| Amana IA | Amana Colonies | 319-622-7622 | 622 46th Avenue (Visitor's Bureau) |
| Bedford IA | Taylor County Historical Museum and Round Barn | 712-523-2041 | 1001 W Pollock Avenue/H 2 W |
| Bloomfield IA | Pioneer Ridge Nature Area and Nature Center | 641-682-3091 | 1339 H 63 |

|  |  |  |  |
|---|---|---|---|
| Burlington IA | Starr's Cave Park and Preserve | 319-753-5808 | 11627 Starr's Cave Road |
| Cedar Falls IA | Hartman Reserve Nature Center | 319-277-2187 | 657 Reserve Drive |
| Cedar Rapids IA | Czech Village | 319-364-0001 | 16th Ave SW |
| Cedar Rapids IA | Indian Creek Nature Center | 319-362-0664 | 6665 Otis Road SE |
| Clear Lake IA | Iowa Trolley Park | 641-357-7433 | 3429 Main Avenue |
| Clive IA | Clive Greenbelt Trail | 515-223-5246 | 156th Street |
| Creston IA | Union County Historical Village & Museum | 515-782-4247 | McKinley Street |
| Decorah IA | Seed Savers Exchange/Heritage Farm | 563-382-5990 | 3074 N Winn Road |
| Des Moines IA | Des Moines Farmers Market | 515-286-4919 | 4th and Court Streets |
| Des Moines IA | Fort Des Moines | 888-828-FORT (3678) | 75 E Army Post Road |
| Des Moines IA | Four-Mile Greenway Trail | 515-266-1563 | Copper Creek Drive |
| Des Moines IA | Salisbury House and Gardens | 515-274-1777 | 4025 Tonawanda Drive |
| Des Moines IA | The Great Western Trail | 515-323-5300 | Valley Drive |
| Dubuque IA | Mines of Spain | 563-556-0620 | 8991 Bellevue Heights |
| Dyersville IA | Field of Dreams Movie Site | 888-875-8404 | 28995 Lansing Road |
| Fort Dodge IA | Fort Museum and Frontier Village | 515-573-4231 | South Kenyon and Museum Road |
| Fredericksburg IA | Hawkeye Buffalo Ranch | 563-237-5318 | 3034 Pembroke Avenue |
| Greenfield IA | Iowa Aviation Museum | 641-343-7184 | 2251 Airport Road |
| Harpers Ferry IA | Effigy Mounds National Monument | 563-873-3491 | 151 H 76 |
| Hawarden IA | Calliope Village | 712-551-2403 | 19th Street and Avenue E |
| Indianola IA | Buxton Park Arboretum | 515-961-9420 | N Buxton Street and W Girard Avenue |
| Knoxville IA | Marion County Historical Village | 641-842-5526 | Willetts Drive |
| Leighton IA | Tassel Ridge Winery | 641-672-WINE (9463) | 1681 220th Street |
| Lime Springs IA | Lidtke Mill Historical Site | 563-566-2893 | Mill Street |
| Long Grove IA | Dan Nagle Walnut Grove Pioneer Village | 563-328-3283 | 18817 290th Street |
| Lorimor IA | Mount Pisgah/Mormon Trail | 641-782-7021 | H 169 |
| Maharishi Vedic City IA | Maharishi Vedic City Self-Guided Walking | 641-472-9580 | 1734 Jasmine Avenue (The Raj Hotel) |
| Maharishi Vedic City IA | Vedic Observatory | 641-472-9580 | 1734 Jasmine Avenue (Visitors Center at The Raj) |
| Mason City IA | Kinney Pioneer Museum | 641-423-1258 | H 122 W at airport entrance |
| Mason City IA | Lime Creek Nature Center | 641-423-5309 | 3501 Lime Creek Road |
| Monticello IA | Riverside Gardens | 319-465-6384 | 441 E 3rd Street |
| Mount Pleasant IA | Old Threshers Park and Campground | 319-385-8937 | 405 E Threshers Road |
| N Liberty IA | North Liberty Farmers' Market | 319-626-5716 | 520 W Cherry Street |
| Nashua IA | The Old Bradford Pioneer Village | 641-435-2567 | H 346 East |
| Odebolt IA | Prairie Pedlar | 712-668-4840 | 1609 270th Street |
| Oelwein IA | Hub City Heritage Railway Museum | 319-283-1939 | 26 Second Avenue SW |
| Pella IA | Pella Historical Village | 641-628-4311 | 507 Franklin Street |
| Pella IA | The Molengracht Plaza | 877-954-8400 | Main Street |
| Polk City IA | Big Creek Boat Rental | 515-984-6083 | 8550 NW 142nd Avenue |
| Princeton IA | Buffalo Bill Cody Homestead | 563-225-2981 | 28050 230th Avenue |
| Red Oak IA | Heritage Hill Tour | 712-623-4821 | First and Coolbaugh Streets |
| Rockford IA | Fossil and Prairie Park Preserve and Center | 641-756-3490 | 1227 215th Street |
| Ruthven IA | Lost Island Prairie Wetland Nature Center | 712-837-4866 | 3259 355th Avenue |
| Shenandoah IA | Iowa Walk of Fame | 712-246-3455 | Sheridan Avenue |
| Sioux City IA | Dorothy Pecaut Nature Center | 712-258-0838 | 4500 Sioux River Road/H 12 |
| Sioux City IA | Milwaukee Railroad Shops Historic District | 712-276-6432 | 3400 Sioux River Road/H12 |
| Sioux City IA | Sergeant Floyd Monument | 712-279-0198 | 2601 S Lewis Blvd |
| South Amana IA | Ackerman Winery | 319-622-3379 | 4406 220th Trail/H 220 |
| South Amana IA | The Barn Museum | South Amana | 413 P Street |
| St Ansgar IA | Bel-Aire Estates Winery | 641-420-7092 | 4351 Dancer Avenue |
| Storm Lake IA | Buena Vista County Wind Farm | 712-732-3780 | 119 W 6th Street |
| Urbandale IA | Living History Farms | 515-278-5286 | 2600 111th Street |
| Wapello IA | Toolesboro Mound Group | 319-523-8381 | 6568 Toolesboro Road |
| West Bend IA | Grotto of the Redemption | 515-887-2371 | 300 N Broadway |
| West Branch IA | Herbert Hoover Presidential Library, Museum and Birthplace Cottage | 319-643-5301 | 210 Parkside Drive |
| West Des Moines IA | Historic Valley Junction | 515-222-3642 | 5th Street |
| West Des Moines IA | Jordan Creek Trail | 515-222-3444 | Off the E. P. True Parkway |
| Williamsburg IA | Tanger Outlet Center | 319-668-2885 | 150 Tanger Drive |

## Kansas Listings

| | | | |
|---|---|---|---|
| Abilene KS | Heritage Center of Dickinson County | 785-263-2681 | 412 S Campbell |
| Antiock KS | Overland Park Arboretum and Botanical Gardens | 913-685-3604 | 8909 W 179th Street |
| Atchison KS | Amelia Earhart Birthplace Museum | 913-367-4217 | 223 NTerrace Street |
| Atchison KS | Forest of Friendship | 913-367-1419 | 17862 274th Rd |
| Dodge City KS | Fort Dodge Kansas State Soldier's Home | 620-227-2121 | 714 Sheridan |
| Dodge City KS | The Dodge City Trail of Fame | 620-561-1925 | P. O. Box 1243 |
| Fort Scott KS | Fort Scott National Historic Site | 620-223-0310 | 2 S Main Street |
| Hays KS | Stone Gallery and Scupture Tour | 785-625-7619 | 107 ½ West 6th |
| Hiawatha KS | Brown County Agriculture Museum | 785-742-3702 | 301 E Iowa |
| Kansas City KS | Grinter Place State Historic Site | 913-299-0373 | 1400 S 78th Street |
| Kansas City KS | The Boulevard Drive-In | 913-262-2414 | 1051 Merriam Lane/H 12 |
| Kansas City KS | The Legends at Village West | 913-788-3700 | 1843 Village West Parkway |
| Larned KS | Fort Larned National Historic Site | 620-285-6911 | H 156 |
| Lawrence KS | University of Kansas | 785-864-2700 | Jayhawk Boulevard |
| Lenexa KS | Legler Barn Museum | 913-492-0038 | 14907 W 87th Street Parkway |
| Liberal KS | Dorothy's House/Land of Oz | 316-624-7624 | 567 East Cedar |
| Olathe KS | The Prairie Center | 913-856-7669 | 26325 W 135th |
| Somerset KS | Sumerset Ridge Winery | 913-491-0038 | 29725 Somerset Road |
| Stafford KS | Quivira National Wildlife Refuge | 620-486-2393 | 1434 NE 80th Street |
| Topeka KS | Old Prairie Town at Ward Meade Park | 785-368-3888 | 124 NW Fillmore |
| Wichita KS | Bradley Fair | 316-630-9990 | 2000 N Rock Road |
| Wichita KS | Lake Afton Public Observatory | 316-978-7827 | MacArthur Road and 247th St W |
| Wichita KS | Old Town Wichita | 316-262-3555 | E 2nd Street N |

## Kentucky Listings

| | | | |
|---|---|---|---|
| Barbourville KY | Dr. Thomas Walker State Historic Site | 606-546-4400 | 4929 H 459 |
| Bardstown KY | Central Kentucky Canoe and Kayak | 502-507-9364 | |
| Bowling Green KY | Civil War Discovery Trail | 800-326-7465 | 352 Three Springs Road (Visitor Center) |
| Bowling Green KY | Lost River Cave and Valley | 270-393-0077 | 2818 Nashville Road/H 31W |
| Cadiz KY | Elk and Bison Prairie | 270-924-2000 | The Trace Road |
| Cave City KY | Dinosaur World | 270-773-4345 | 711 Mammoth Cave Rd |
| Clermont KY | Bernheim Arboretum | 502-955-8512 | 2499 H 245 |
| Covington KY | Elegant Carriages | 937-903-5156 | 10 West Rivercenter Blvd |
| Covington KY | Mainstasse Village | 859-491-0458 | |
| Crestview Hills KY | Crestview Hills Town Center | 859-341-4353 | 2791 Town Center Boulevard |
| Frankfort KY | Kentucky State Capitol Grounds | 502-564-3449 | 700 Capitol Avenue |
| Frankfort KY | Kentucky Vietnam Veterans Memorial | 800-960-7200 | Coffee Tree Road |
| Georgetown KY | Factory Stores of America | 502-868-0682 | 401 Outlet Center Drive |
| Georgetown KY | The Official Kentucky-Japan Friendship Garden | 502-316-4554 | N Broadway Street/H 25 |
| Harrodsburg KY | Shaker Village of Pleasant Hill | 800-734-5611 | 3501 Lexington Road/H 68 |
| Hodgenville KY | Abraham Lincoln Birthplace National Historic Site | 270-358-3137 | 2995 Lincoln Farm Road/H 31E |
| Lexington KY | American Saddlebred Museum | 859-259-2746 | 4093 Iron Works Pkwy |
| Lexington KY | Chrisman Mill Winery | 859-264-WINE (9463) | 2300 Sir Barton Way, Suite #175 |
| Lexington KY | Kentucky Horse Park | 800-678-8813 | 4089 Ironworks Parkway |
| Lexington KY | Talon Winery and Vineyards | 859-971-3214 | 7086 Tates Creek Road/H 1974 |
| Lexington KY | University of Kentucky Campus | 859-323-6371 | 410 Administration Drive |
| Louisville KY | Riverside - The Farnsley-Moremen Landing | 502-935-6809 | 7410 Moorman Street |
| Louisville KY | The Old Louisville Walking Tour | 502-635-5244 | 218 W Oak Street (Visitor Center) |
| Midway KY | Equus Run Vineyards | 859-846-9463 | 1280 Moores Mill Road |
| Newport KY | Elegant Carriages | 937-903-5156 | 1 Levee Way |
| Perryville KY | Perryville Battlefield State Historic Site | 859-332-8631 | 1825 Battlefield Road |
| Renfro Valley KY | Bittersweet Cabin Museum | 606-256-0715 | H 25 |
| Springfield KY | Lincoln Homestead State Park | 859-336-7461 | 5079 Lincoln Park RoadH 528 |
| Stearns KY | Barthell Coal Mining Camp | 606-376-8749 | 552 Barthell Road |
| Whitesburg KY | Little Shepherd Trail | 606-573-4156 | H 119 |
| Wickliffe KY | Wickliffe Mounds State Historic Site | 270-335-3681 | 94 Green Street/H 60 |

## Louisiana Listings

| | | | |
|---|---|---|---|
| Alexandria LA | Kent Plantation | 318-487-5998 | 3601 Vayou RapidesH 496 |
| Baton Rouge LA | BREC's Bluebonnet Swamp | 225-757-8905 | 10503 North Oak Hills Parkway |
| Baton Rouge LA | Louisiana State Capitol | 225-342-7317 | 900 North Third Street on State Capital Drive |
| Baton Rouge LA | Perkins Rowe Shopping District | 225-761-6905 | 10107 Park Row Avenue |
| Calcasieu and Cameron parishes LA | Creole Nature Trail | 800-456-7952 | H 27 |
| Clinton LA | Casa De Sue Winery | 225-405-4692 | 12324 St Helena |
| Darrow LA | Houmas House Plantation and Gardens | 225-473-9380 | 40136 H 942 |
| DeQuincy LA | DeQuincy Railroad Museum Park | 337-786-2823 | 400 Lake Charles Avenue |
| Folsom LA | Landry Vineyards | 985-294-7790 | 11650 Tantela Ranch Rd |
| Frogmore LA | Frogmore Cotton Plantation | 318-757-2453 | 11054 H 84 |
| Jackson LA | Feliciana Cellars | 225-634-7982 | 1848 Charter St |
| Kraemer LA | Torres Cajun Swamp Tours | 985-633-7739 | 105 Torres Road |
| Lafayette LA | Atchafalaya Experience | 337-261-5150 | 338 N Sterling Street |
| Layfayette LA | The Real French Destination Scenic Byway | 800-4BYWAYS option 3 | H 93 |
| Marksville LA | Marksville State Historic Site | 318-253-8954 | 837 Martin Luther King Drive |
| Napoleonville LA | Madewood Plantation | 800-375-7151 | 4250 H 308 |
| New Orleans LA | Algiers Ferry | 504-376-8100 | Canal Street |
| New Orleans LA | Bloody Mary's Tours | 504-523-7684 | 4905 Canal Street (meet outside) |
| New Orleans LA | Buggy Rides | | Decatur Street at Jackson Square |
| New Orleans LA | French Quarter District | 504-522-7226 | Canal Street to Esplanade Avenue up to Rampart Street |
| New Orleans LA | Ghost City Tours | 888-859-5375 | 643 Magazine Street, Suite 304 |
| New Orleans LA | Good Old Days Buggies Inc | 504-523-0804 | 1229 Saint Thomas Street |
| New Orleans LA | Haunted History Tours | 504-861-2727 | 97 Fontainebleau Dr. |
| New Orleans LA | Historic New Orleans Walking Tours, Inc | 504-947-2120 | 2727 Prytania St. Suite 8 |
| New Orleans LA | Jazz Walk of Fame | 504-589-4841 | Algiers Point |
| Shreveport LA | Gardens of the American Rose Center | 318-938-5402 | 8877 Jefferson Paige Road |
| Shreveport LA | Just Pets Gourmet | 318-798-5858 | 7030 Youree Drive |
| Slidell LA | Pearl River Eco-Tours | 866-59-SWAMP (597-9267) | 55050 H 90 |
| St Francisville LA | Audubon State Historic Site and Oakley House | 225-635-3739 | 11788 H 965 |
| St Francisville LA | Rosedown Plantation State Historic Site | 225-635-3332 | 12501 H 10 |
| Vacherie LA | Laura Plantation | 225-265-7690 | 2247 H 18 |
| W Monroe LA | Tractor Supply Company | 318-329-1123 | 201 Mane Street |

## Maine Listings

| | | | |
|---|---|---|---|
| Bar Harbor ME | Acadia Outfitters | 207-288-8118 | 106 Cottage Street |
| Bar Harbor ME | Bar Harbor Downtown Shopping District | 800-345-4617 | Downtown Bar Harbor |
| Bar Harbor ME | Downeast Windjammer Cruises | 207-288-4585 | Bar Harbor Pier |
| Bar Harbor ME | Wildwood Stables Carriage Tours | 207-276-3622 | Route 3 |
| Belfast ME | Water Walker Sea Kayaks | 207-338-6424 | 152 Lincolnville Avenue |
| Bethel ME | Bethel Nordic Ski Center | 207-824-3880 | 786 Intervale Road |
| Boothbay ME | Boothbay Railway Village | 207-633-4727 | 586 Wiscasset Road /H 29 |
| Boothbay Harbor ME | Balmy Day Cruises | 207-633-2284 | 42 Commercial Street/Pier 8 |
| Boothbay Harbor ME | Cap'n Fish Boat Tours | 207-633-3244 | 65 Atlantic Avenue |
| Boothbay Harbor ME | Tidal Transit Kayak Company | 207-633-7140 | 18 Granary Way |
| Camden ME | Lively Lady Too Boat Tours | 207-236-6672 | Bay View Landing Wharf |
| Camden ME | Schooner Lazy Jack II | 207-230-0602 | Camden Public Landing |
| Camden ME | Schooner Olad | 207-236-2323 | Camden Harbor/Camden Public Landing |
| Freeport ME | Wolfe's Neck Farm | 207-865-4469 | 184 Burnett Rd |
| Greenville ME | Northwoods Outfitters | 207-695-3288 | 5 Lily Bay Road |
| Kennebunkport ME | Gallery on Chase Hill | 207-967-0049 | 10 Chase Hill Road |
| Kennebunkport ME | Seashore Trolley Museum | | 195 Log Cabin Road |
| Kittery ME | Kittery Premium Outlets | 207-439-6548 | 375 H 1 |
| Milbridge ME | Robertson Sea Tours and Adventures | 207-546-3883 | Milbridge Marina |
| New Harbor ME | Hardy Boat Cruises | 207-677-2026 | 132 H 32 |

| | | | |
|---|---|---|---|
| Northeast Harbor ME | Beal and Bunker Mail Boat Ferry | 207-244-3575 | Harbor Drive |
| Phippsburg ME | Fort Popham State Historic Site | 207-389-1335 | 10 Perkins Farm Lane |
| Portland ME | Casco Bay Lines Boats | 207-74-7871 | 56 Commercial Street |
| Portland ME | Greater Portland Landmarks Walking Tours | 207-774-5561 | 165 State Street/H 77 |
| Portland ME | Maine Narrow Gauge Railroad Co. and Museum | 207-828-0814 | 58 Fore Street |
| Portland ME | Old Port Waterfront District | 207-772-6828 | Congress Street |
| Portland ME | Portland Discovery Land and Sea Tours | 207-774-0808 | 170 Commercial Street |
| Portland ME | The Maine Narrow Gauge Railroad | 207-828-0814 | 58 Fore Street |
| Round Pond ME | Salt Water Charters | 207-677-6229 | Town Landing Road/Round Pond Dock |
| South Freeport ME | Atlantic Seal Cruises | 207-865-6112 | 25 Main Street |
| Southwest Harbor ME | Masako Queen Fishing Company | 207-244-5385 | Beal's Wharf |
| Stonington ME | Old Quarry Ocean Adventures | 207-367-8977 | 130 Settlement Road |
| Stonington ME | The Stonington Farmers Market | | School Street |
| Wells ME | World Within Sea Kayaking | 207-646-0455 | 746 Ocean Avenue |
| Winterport ME | Winterport Winery | 207-223-4500 | 279 South Main St |

## Maryland Listings

| | | | |
|---|---|---|---|
| Annapolis MD | Annapolis Digital Walking Tours | 410-267665 | 99 Main Street |
| Annapolis MD | Annapolis Harbor Center | 410-266-5857 | 2472 Solomon's Island Road/H2 |
| Annapolis MD | Annapolis Maritime Museum | 410-295-0104 | 723 2nd Street |
| Annapolis MD | Annapolis Small Boat Rentals | 410-268-2628 | 808 Boucher Avenue |
| Annapolis MD | Annapolis Trolley Tours | 410-626-6000 | 99 Main Street |
| Annapolis MD | First Sunday Arts Festival | 410-741-3267 | Calvert Street and West Street |
| Annapolis MD | Roots and Tides Driving Tour | 866-639-3526 | H 2 (begins; other Highways follow) |
| Annapolis MD | Summer at City Dock Concerts | 410-268-1636 | Main Street |
| Annapolis MD | Watermark | 410-263-0033 | end of Dock Street |
| Annapolis MD | Watermark Cruises | 800-569-9622 | 1 Dock Street |
| Annapolis MD | eCruisers llc | 443-497-4769 | PO Box 5647 |
| Baltimore MD | Baltimore Adventures | 410-342-2004 | 1001 Fell Street |
| Baltimore MD | Cylburn Arboretum | 410-367-2217 | 4915 Greenspring Avenue |
| Baltimore MD | Farmers Market at the Avenue | 410-931-0411 | Honeygo Blvd |
| Baltimore MD | Henderson's Wharf Marina | 410-342-2004 | 1001 Fell Street |
| Baltimore MD | Heritage Walk Self-Guided Walking Tour | 877-BALTIMORE(225-8466) | 401 Light Street/H2 |
| Baltimore MD | Maryland Sled Dog Adventures LLC | 443-562-5736 | |
| Baltimore MD | Seadog Cruises | 866-845-7245 | 561 Light Street/H 2 |
| Baltimore MD | The Original Fell's Point Ghost Walk Tour | 410-522-7400 | P. O. Box 38140 |
| Baltimore MD | Westminster Cemetery | 410-706-2072 | 509 W. Fayette Street |
| Bel Air MD | Bel Air Farmers' Market | 410-879-9500 | 1310 Somerville Road |
| Cambridge MD | Dorchester Arts Center Walking Tours | 410-228-7782 | 120 High Street |
| Catonsville MD | Benjamin Banneker Historical Park and Museum | 410-887-1081 | 300 Oella Avenue |
| Chestertown MD | Virginia Gent Decker Arboretum | 800-422-1782 ext/7726 | 300 Washington Avenue/H 213 |
| Crisfield MD | Tangier Island Cruises | 410-968-2338 | 1001 West Main Street/H 413 |
| Cumberland MD | George Washington's Headquarters | 301-777-5132 | Greene Street |
| Easton MD | Historical Society of Talbot County | 410-822-0773 | 25 S Washington Street |
| Edgewater MD | Historic London Town and Gardens | 410-222-1919 | 839 Londontown Road |
| Ellicott City MD | Ghost Tours | 410-313-8141 | 8267 Main Street |
| Frederick MD | The Monocacy National Battlefield | 301-662-3515 | 5201 Urbana Pike/H 355 |
| Galesville MD | Duffy Electric Boats Sales/Rentals | 443-433-2129 | P.O. Box 254 |
| Grantsville MD | Spruce Forest Artisan Village | 301-895-3332 | 177 Casselman Road |
| Hagerstown MD | Prime Outlets | 888-883-6288 | 495 Prime Outlets Boulevard |
| Havre de Grace MD | The Skipjack Martha Lewis | 410-939-4078 | South end of Union Avenue/Tidings Park |
| Knoxville MD | River and Trail Outfitters | 301-695-5177 | 604 Valley Road |
| Oakland MD | Bill's Marine Service Boat Rentals | 301-387-5536 | 20721 Garrett H/H 219 |
| Red House MD | Red House School Country Mall | 301-334-2800 | 3039 Garrett Highway/H 219 |
| Scotland MD | Point Lookout Confererate Monument | 301-872-5688 | 11175 Point Lookout Road |
| Sharpesburg MD | Antietam National Battlefield | 301-432-5124 | 5831 Dunker Church Road |
| Solomons MD | Bunky's Charter Boats | 410-326-3241 | 14448 Solomons Island Road S |
| St Michaels MD | St. Michaels Harbor Shuttle | 410-924-2198 | 101 N Harbor Road |

| | | | |
|---|---|---|---|
| Tilghman MD | Dockside Express Cruises | 888-312-7847 | Phillips Wharf |
| Tilghman Island MD | Tilghman Island Marina | 410-886-2500 | 6140 Mariners Court |

**Massachusetts Listings**

| | | | |
|---|---|---|---|
| Boston MA | Bay State Cruise Company | 617-748-1428 | The Pier at the World Trade Center |
| Boston MA | Black Heritage Trail | 617-725-0022 | 46 Joy Street |
| Boston MA | Boston African American National Historic Site | 617-742-5415 | 14 Beacon Street Ste 503 |
| Boston MA | Boston Harbor Cruises | 617-227-4320 | 1 Long Wharf |
| Boston MA | Downtown Crossing Shopping Center | 617-482-2139 | 59 Temple Place |
| Boston MA | Faneuil Hall Marketplace | | North St and Merchants Row |
| Boston MA | Freedom Trail | | Tremont and Temple |
| Boston MA | Horse and Carriage (Bridal Carriage) | 781-871-9224 | Faneuil Hall Marketplace |
| Boston MA | Secret Tour of Boston's North End | 617-720-2283 | Four Battery Street |
| Boston MA | The Cheers Building-Outside View | | 84 Beacon St |
| Brookline MA | John F Kennedy National Historic Site | 617-566-7937 | 83 Beals Street |
| Cambridge MA | Harvard Square Shopping Center | 617-491-3434 | JFK Street at Massachusetts Avenue |
| Cambridge MA | Harvard University Campus | 617-495-1000 | 1350 Massachusetts Avenue/Harvard Square |
| Cambridge MA | Longfellow National Historic Site | 617-876-4491 | 105 Brattle Street |
| Chester MA | Chester Hill Winery | 413-354-2340 | 47 Lyon Hill Road |
| Chestnut Hill MA | Boston College Campus | 617-552-8000 | 140 Commonwealth Avenue |
| Concord MA | Concord Guides & Press Walking Tours | 978-287-0897 | P.O. Box 1335 |
| Concord MA | Minute Man National Historical Park | | Rt 2A and I-95 |
| Deerfield MA | Historic Deerfield Village | 413-775-7214 | Old Main Street |
| East Boston MA | City Water Taxi's Island Romp for Dogs | 617-633-9240 | Long Wharf/Columbus Park |
| East Sandwich MA | Green Briar Nature Center | 508-888-6870 | 6 Discovery Hill |
| Falmouth MA | Martha's Vineyard Ferry | 508-548-4800 | 75 Falmouth Heights Road |
| Gloucester MA | Cape Ann Whale Watch | 978-283-5110 | 415 Main Street |
| Gloucester MA | Dogtown Common | | Dogtown Road at Cherry |
| Hyannis MA | Hy-Line Harbor Cruises | 508-790-0696 | Ocean Street Docks |
| Hyannis MA | Hyannisport Harbor Cruises | 508-778-2600 | Ocean Street Dock |
| Lee MA | Windy Knoll Farm | 413-243-0989 | 40 Stringer Avenue |
| Nantucket MA | Nantucket Regional Transit Authority (NRTA) | 508-228-7025 | 22 Federal Street |
| New Marlborough MA | Les Trois Emme Winery and Vineyard | 413-528-1015 | 8 Knight Road |
| Newton MA | Charles River Canoe & Kayak | 617-965-5110 | 2401 Common Wealth Avenue |
| North Adams MA | The Mohawk Trail | 413-743-8127 | P. O. Box 1044 |
| North Weymouth MA | Pilgrim Congregational Church | 781-337-2075 | 24 Athens Street |
| Onset MA | Cape Cod Canal Cruise | 508-295-3883 | Town Pier |
| Orleans MA | Goose Hummock Outdoor Center | 508-255-2620 | 13 Old County Road |
| Provincetown MA | Bay State Cruise Company | 617-748-1428 | MacMillan Pier |
| Provincetown MA | Flyer's Boat Rentals | 508-487-0898 | 131 Commercial Street |
| Richmond MA | Hilltop Orchards & Furnace Brook Winery | 413-698-3301 | 508 Canaan Road/H 295 |
| Salem MA | Haunted Footsteps Ghost Tour | 978-645-0666 | 8 Central Street |
| Salem MA | Salem Trolley | 978-744-5469 | 2 New Liberty Street |
| Salem MA | Salem Walking Tour | | |
| Salem MA | Salem Willows Amusement Park | 978-745-0251 | 171-185 Fort Avenue |
| Shelburne Falls MA | Bridge of Flowers | 413-625-2526 | 16-22 Water Street |
| Wellfleet MA | Wellfleet Drive-in Movie Theater | 508-349-7176 | 51 H 6 |
| West Tisbury MA | West Tisbury Farmer's Markets | 508-693-0085 | State Road |
| Worcester MA | Blackstone River Bikeway | 401-762-0250 | Worcester Square |
| Wrentham MA | Wrentham Village Premium Outlets | 508-384-0600 | One Premium Outlets Blvd |

**Michigan Listings**

| | | | |
|---|---|---|---|
| Ada MI | Ada Farmers Market | | 7239 Thornapple River Drive |
| Ann Arbor MI | Argo Canoe Livery | 734-794-6000 X 42530 | 1055 Longshore Drive |
| Ann Arbor MI | Border to Border Trail | 734-971-6337 | P.O. Box 8645 |
| Ann Arbor MI | Cobblestone Farm Museum | 734-994-2928 | 2781 Packard Road |
| Ann Arbor MI | Gallup Park Livery | 734-662-9319 | 3000 Fuller Road |
| Ann Arbor MI | Nichols Arboretum | 734-647-7600 | 1600 Washington Heights |
| Ann Arbor MI | Skip's Huron River Canoe Livery | 734-769-8686 | 3780 Delhi Court |
| Ann Arbor MI | Yellow Cab | 734-663-3355 | 2050 Commerce Ann Arbor |

| | | | |
|---|---|---|---|
| Augusta MI | W.K. Kellogg Experiment Station | 269-731-4597 | 7060 N. 42nd Street |
| Bad Axe MI | Pioneer Log Cabin Village | 989-269-8325 | 210 S Hanselman Street |
| Baldwin MI | Shrine of the Pines | 231-745-7892 | 8962 S H 37 |
| Baroda MI | Round Barn Winery | 269-422-1617 | 10981 Hills Road |
| Bay City MI | Appledore Tall Ships | 989-895-5193 | 901 Saginaw Street |
| Birmingham MI | Birmingham Principal Shopping District | 248-530-1200 | Woodward Avenue/H 1 |
| Bridgeport MI | Price Nature Center | 989-790-5280 | 6685 Sheridan Road |
| Buchanan MI | Tabor Hill Winery | 800-283-3363 | 185 Mt Tabor Road |
| Capac MI | Blueridge Blueberry Farm | 810-395-2245 | 16276 Donald Road |
| Caspian MI | Iron County Historical Museum | 906-265-2617 | Brady at Museum Drive |
| Cedar MI | Bel Lago Vineyards and Winery | 231-228-4800 | 6530 S Lake Shore Drive/H 643 |
| Cedar MI | Longview Winery | 231-228-2880 | 8697 Good Harbor Trail |
| Chelsea MI | Chelsea Farmers' Market | 734-475-1145 | Park Street |
| Clinton Township MI | The Mall at Partridge Creek | 586-416-3839 | 17420 Hall Road/H 59 |
| Clinton Township MI | The Mall at Partridge Creek | 586-226-0330 | 17420 Hall Road/H 59 |
| Copper Harbor MI | Delaware Mine | 906-289-4688 | H 41 |
| Copper Harbor MI | Sunset Cruises | 906-289-4437 | 5th Street at Waterfront Landing |
| Davison MI | Johnny Panther Quests | 810-653-3859 | 8065 E Coldwater Rd |
| Dearborn MI | University of Michigan - Dearborn Campus | 734 764-1817 | 4901 Evergreen Road |
| Detroit MI | Bray's Charter Boat Service | 313-273-9183 | 14767 Riverside Blvd |
| Detroit MI | Rivard Plaza | 313-566-8200 | 1340 E Atwater Street |
| Detroit MI | The Detroit RiverFront Conservancy | 313-566-8200 | Renaissance Center |
| Drummond Island MI | Drummond Island Yacht Haven | 800-543-4743 | 33185 S Water Street |
| East Lansing MI | Michigan State University Campus | 517-355-1855 | South Harrison Road |
| Eau Claire MI | Tree-Mendus Fruit Farm | 269-782-7101 | 9351 E Eureka Road |
| Flint MI | Crossroads Village and Huckleberry Railroad | 801-736-7100 | 6140 Bray Road |
| Flushing MI | Almar Orchard | 810-659-6568 | 1431 Duffield Road |
| Grand Rapids MI | Downtown Center | 616-459-8287 | Monroe Center St NW at Ionia Ave NW |
| Grand Rapids MI | Grand River Sculpture and Fish Ladder | 616-459-8287 | Grand River at Front and Fourth NW |
| Hancock MI | The Quincy Mine/A Keweenaw Heritage Site | 906-482-3101 | 49750 H 41 |
| Harrison Township MI | Eddie's Drive-in | 586-469-2345 | 36111 Jefferson Avenue |
| Hickory Corners MI | Gilmore Car Club Museum | 269-671-5089 | 6865 W Hickory Road |
| Holland MI | Holland Town Center | 616-396-1808 | 12330 James Street |
| Holland MI | Nelis Dutch Village | 616-396-1475 | 12350 Jane Street |
| Howell MI | Tanger Outlets | 517-545-0500 | 1475 N Burkhart |
| Kalamazoo MI | Husted Farm | 269-372-1237 | 9191 W Main |
| Kalamazoo MI | Kalamazoo Mall and Arcadia Creek Festival Place | 269-344-0795 | S Kalamazoo Mall |
| Kalamazoo MI | Peterson and Sons Natural Wines | 269-626-9755 | 9375 E P Avenue |
| Lansing MI | Frandor Shopping Center | 517-351-8300 | 416 Frandor Avenue, Suite 103 |
| Lansing MI | Michigan Princess | 517-627-2154 | At Grand River Park |
| Lansing MI | Planet Walk | 517-702-6730 | On the Riverwalk between Michigan Avenue & Potters Park |
| Leland MI | Good Harbor Vineyards | 231-256-7165 | 34 S Manitou Trail/H 22 |
| Ludington MI | White Pine Village | 231-843-4808 | 1687 S Lakeshore Drive |
| Mackinac Island MI | Mackinac Island | 800-454-5227 | Accessible by ferry |
| Mackinac Island MI | Mackinac Island Carriage Tours | 906-847-3307 | Main Street |
| Mackinaw City MI | Arnold Mackinac Island Ferry | 800-5420-8528 | 801 South Huron Street |
| Mackinaw City MI | Colonial Michilimackinac | 231-436-4100 | Nicolet Street |
| Mackinaw City MI | Historic Mill Creek | 231-436-4100 | Huron Avenue H 23 |
| Midland MI | Midland Public Dog Park | 989-837-6930 | Ann and Ashman Streets |
| Milford MI | Heavner Canoe Rental | 248-685-2379 | 2775 Garden Road |
| Monroe MI | River Raisin Battlefield | 734-243-7136 | 1403 E Elm Avenue |
| Montaque MI | Happy Mohawk Canoe Livery | 231-894-4209 | 735 Fruitvale Road |
| Munising MI | Pictured Rock Cruises Kennels | 906-387-2379 | City Dock (P. O. Box 355) |
| Munising MI | Seaberg Pontoon Rentals LLC | 906-387-2685 | 1330 Commercial Street |
| Munising MI | Shipwreck Boat Tours Kennels | 906-387-4477 | 1204 Commercial Street |
| Muskegon MI | Dog Star Ranch | 231-766-0444 | 4200 Whitehall Road |
| Muskegon MI | Dog Star Ranch | 866-766-0444 | 4200 Whitehall Road |
| Newberry MI | Two Hearted Canoe Trips | 906-658-3357 | 9706 County Road 423/Mouth of Two Heart Road |
| Paradise MI | Great Lakes Shipwreck Museum | 888-492-3747 | 18335 Whitefish Point Road |
| Paw Paw MI | Warner Vineyards | 800-756-5357 | 706 S Kalamazoo Street/H 40 |

| | | | |
|---|---|---|---|
| Port Austin MI | Tip-A-Thum Canoe Rental | 989-738-7656 | 2475 Port Austin Road/H 25 |
| Richland MI | Braelock Farm | 269-629-9884 | 9124 N 35th Street |
| Rochester MI | Spectacular Strolls | 248-608-8352 | |
| Rochester Hills MI | Meadow Brook Hall and Gardens | 248-370-3140 | 480 S Adams Road/Oakland University Campus |
| Rockford MI | AAA Rogue River Canoe Rental | 616-866-9264 | 49 E Bridge Street |
| Rockford MI | Rockford and Squires Street Square | 616-866-2000 | 12 Squires Street Square |
| Saline MI | Saline Farmers Market | 734-429-3518 | South Ann Arbor Street |
| Sault Ste. Marie MI | Soo Locks Boat Tours Kennels | 800-432-6301 | Dock 1, 1157 E Portage Ave/Dock 2, 515 E Portage Ave |
| Soo Junction MI | Toonerville Trolley and Riverboat | 888-778-7246 | |
| St Johns MI | Andy T's Farms | 989-224-7674 | 3131 S Bus H 27 |
| St Johns MI | Uncle John's Cider Mill | 989-224-3686 | 8614 N H 127 |
| Thompsonville MI | Michigan Legacy Art Park at Crystal Mountain | 800-9687686 | 12500 Crystal Mountain Drive |
| Tipton MI | Hidden Lake Gardens | 517-431-2060 | 6214 Monroe Road/H 50 |
| Traverse City MI | Brys Estate Vineyard and Winery | 231-223-9303 | 3309 Blue Water Road |
| Traverse City MI | Preferred Outlets | 231-941-9211 | 3639 Market Place Circle |
| Traverse City MI | Sail and Power Boat Rental | 231-922-9336 | 615 Front Street |
| Waterford MI | Drayton Plains Nature Center | 248-674-2119 | 2125 Denby Drive |
| Wellston MI | Pine River Paddlesport Center | 231-862-3471 | 9590 S Grandview H/H 37S |
| West Branch MI | Tanger Outlet Center | 989-345-2594 | 2990 Cook Road #28 |
| White Cloud MI | Loda Lake Wildflower Sanctuary | 231-745-4631 | Fletch Avenue |
| Ypsilanti MI | Blue Cab | 734-547-2222 | |

**Minnesota Listings**

| | | | |
|---|---|---|---|
| Baxter MN | Northland Arboretum | 218-829-8770 | 14250 Conservation Drive |
| Duluth MN | Fitger's Brewery Complex | 218-279-2739 | 600 East Superior Street |
| Excelsior MN | Excel Boat Club Boat Rentals | 952-401-3880 | 141 Minnetonka Blvd |
| Grand Marais MN | Anderson Aero | 218-387-1687 | 80 Skyport Lane |
| International Falls MN | Rainy Lake Houseboats | 218-286-5391 | 2031 Town Road 488 |
| Lanesboro MN | Scenic Valley Winery | 507-467-2958 | 101 Copy Street E |
| Mankato MN | The Paw Pet Resort | 507-625-7070 | 1741 Premier Drive |
| Medford MN | Medford Outlet Center | 507-455-2042 | 6750 W Frontage Road |
| Minneapolis MN | Chain of Lakes Byway | 612 230-6400 | 2117 West River Road (MN Park and Recreation) |
| Minneapolis MN | Midwest Mountaineering | 612-339-3433 | 309 Cedar Avenue |
| Minneapolis MN | Minneapolis Sculpture Garden | 612-375-7600 | 1750 Hennepin |
| Minneapolis MN | Nicollet Mall | 888-676-6757 | Between Washinton Avenue S and 13th Street S |
| Minneapolis MN | St Anthony Falls Heritage Trail | 612-661-4800 | Plymouth/8th Avenue Bridge to Franklin Avenue Bridge |
| Minneapolis MN | The Hitching Company | 612-338-7777 | 925 N 5th Street |
| Minneapolis MN | Upper St Anthony Falls Lock and Dam | 877-552-1416 | 1 Portland Avenue S |
| Montevideo MN | Historic Chippewa City | 320-269-7636 | 151 Arnie Anderson Drive |
| Montevideo MN | Olof Swensson Farm | 320-269-7636 | 115 H 15 SE |
| Morton MN | Birch Coulee Battlefield | 507-697-6321 | 32469 H 2 |
| Orr MN | Ebels Voyageur Houseboats | 218-374-3571 | 10326 Ash River Trail |
| Park Rapids MN | Summerhill Farm | 218-732-3865 | 24013 H 71 |
| Pipestone MN | Pipestone National Monument | 507-825-5464 | 36 Reservation Avenue |
| Plummer MN | Two Fools Vineyard and Winery | 218-465-4655 | 12501 240th Avenue SE |
| Rochester MN | Miracle Mile Shopping Center | 507-288-2455 | 115 16th Avenue NW |
| Rochester MN | Quarry Hill Nature Center | 507-281-6114 | 701 Silver Creek Road NE |
| Rochester MN | Silver Lake Boat and Bike Rentals | 507-261-9049 | 700 W Silver Lake Drive NE |
| St Paul MN | Jackson Street Roundhouse Railway Museum and Other Sites | 651-228-0263 | 193 Pennsylvania Ave E |
| Tower MN | Vermilion Houseboats | 218-753-3548 | 9482 Angus Road/H 77 |
| Worthington MN | Pioneer Village | 507-376-3125 | 501 Stower Drive |
| Zimmerman MN | Sherburne National Wildlife Refuge | 763-389-3323 | 17076 293rd Avenue/H 9 |

**Mississippi Listings**

| | | | |
|---|---|---|---|
| Bay St Louis MS | Old Town Bay St Louis | 800-466-9048 | 1928 Depot Way |
| Belzoni MS | Wister Gardens | 662-247-3025 | 1440 H 7 |
| Biloxi MS | The Biloxi Shrimping Trip | 228-385-1182 | 693 Beach Blvd |
| Cleveland MS | Historic Downtown Cotton Row | 800-295-7473 | Cotton Row |

| Grenada MS | Historic Walking Tours | 662-226-2571 | 95 SW Frontage Road |
| Gulfport MS | Prime Outlets at Gulfport | 228-867-6100 | 10000 Factory Shop Blvd |
| Hattiesburg MS | All American Rose Garden | 601-266-4491 | 118 College Drive |
| Holly Springs MS | Holly Springs Driving Tour | 662-252-2515 | 104 East Gholson Avenue |
| Jackson MS | Civil Rights Driving Tour | 601-960-1891 | 111 E Capitol Street |
| Jackson MS | Mississippi Museum of Art "Dog Day Afternoons" | 601-960-1515 | 380 S Lamar Street |
| Long Beach MS | Wolf River Canoe and Kayak | 228-452-7666 | 21652 Tucker Road |
| Madison MS | Cypress Swamp | 800-305-7417 | MP 122 Natchez Trace Parkway |
| Natchez MS | Emerald Mound Broken Arrows | 601-43-2111 | 66 Emerald Mound Road |
| Natchez MS | Forks of the Road Slave Market Site | 800-647-6724 | Intersection of D'Evereux Drive, Saint Catherine Street and Liberty Road |
| Natchez MS | Grand Village of the Natchez Indians | 601-446-6502 | 400 Jefferson Davis Blvd |
| Natchez MS | Southern Carriage Tours | 800-647-6724 | 200 State Street |
| Pascagoula MS | Scranton Nature Center | 228-938-6612 | 3928 Nathan Hale Avenue |
| Port Gibson MS | Grand Gulf Military Park | 601-437-5911 | 12006 Grand Gulf Road |
| Tupelo MS | Brices Cross Roads National Battlefield Site | 800-305-7417 | 2680 Natchez Trace Parkway/H 370 |
| Tupelo MS | Chickasaw Village | 662-680-4027 | Natchez Trace Parkway |
| Tupelo MS | Elvis Presley Birthplace | 662-841-1245 | 306 Elvis Presley Drive |
| Tupelo MS | Tupelo National Battlefield | 800-305-7417 | 2680 Natchez Trace Parkway |
| Vicksburg MS | Mississippi River Boat Tours | 866-807-2628 | 1208 Levee Street |
| Vicksburg MS | Vicksburg Factory Outlets | 601-636-7434 | 4000 S Frontage Road |
| Vicksburg MS | Vicksburg National Cemetery | 601-636-0583 | 3201 Clay Street |
| Vicksburg MS | Vicksburg National Military Park | 601-636-0583 | 3201 Clay Street |

**Missouri Listings**

| Altenburg MO | Tower Rock Winery | 573-824-5479 | 10769 Highway A |
| Ash Grove MO | Nathan Boone's Homestead | 417-751-3266 | 7850 N State Hwy V |
| Augusta MO | Mount Pleasant Winery | 636-482-4419 | 5634 High St |
| Berger MO | Bias Vineyards and Winery | 800-905-2427 | 3166 Highway B |
| Boonville MO | Boone's Lick State Historic Site | 660-837-3330 | H 187 |
| Branson MO | Factory Merchants Outlet Center | 417-335-6686 | 1000 Pat Nash Drive |
| Branson MO | Stone Hill Winery | 888-926-WINE | 601 State Hwy 165 |
| Branson MO | The Shoppes at Branson Meadows | 417-339-2580 | 2651 Shepard of the Hills |
| Branson West MO | Talking Rocks Cavern | 417-272-3366 | 423 Ferry Cave Lane |
| Brazeau MO | Hemman Winery | 573-824-6040 | 13022 Hwy C |
| Burfordville MO | Bollinger Mill State Historic Site | 573-243-4591 | 113 Bollinger Mill Rd |
| Camdenton MO | Bridal Cave and Thunder Mountain Park | 573-346-2676 | 526 Bridal Cave Rd |
| Camdenton MO | Lake of the Ozarks Marina | 573-873-3705 | H 5 N, Niangua Arm |
| Columbia MO | Stephens College in Missouri | 800-876-7207 | 1200 E Broadway |
| Commerce MO | River Ridge Winery | 573-264-3712 | 850 County Rd 321 |
| Defiance MO | Chandler Hill Vineyards | 636-798-2675 | 596 Defiance Road |
| Eagle Rock MO | The Promised Land Zoo | 417-342-4800 | 32297 H 86 |
| Eureka MO | Six Flags St Louis | 636-938-4800 | I-44 & Six Flag Rd |
| Florida MO | Mark Twain Birthplace State Historical Site | 573-565-3449 | 37352 Shrine Road |
| Fulton MO | Auto World Museum | 573-642-2080 | 200 Peacock Drive |
| Hannibal MO | Mark Twain Riverboat | 573-221-3222 | Center Street Landing |
| Hermann MO | Adam Puchta Winery | 573-486-5596 | 1947 Frene Creek Road |
| Hermann MO | Hermannhof Vineyards | 800-393-0100 | 330 E First Street/H 100 |
| Hermann MO | Stone Hill Winery | 573-486-2129 | 1110 Stonehill Hwy |
| Holts Summit MO | Summit Lake Winery | 573-896-9966 | 1707 South Summit Dr |
| Independence MO | Harry S. Truman Farm Home | 816-254-2720 | 223 North Main Street |
| Jefferson City MO | Missouri Veterinary Museum | 573-636-8737 | 2500 Country Club Drive |
| Jefferson City MO | Native Stone Vineyard and Bull Rock Brewery | 573-584-8600 | 4301 Native Stone Rd |
| Kansas City MO | Country Club Plaza | 816-753-0100 | 4750 Broadway |
| Kansas City MO | Country Club Plaza | 816-561-3456 | 310 Ward Pkwy |
| Kansas City MO | Walk and Tour Westport | 816-561-1821 | 4000 Baltimore |
| Kansas City MO | Westport Plaza Farmers Market | 913-432-4101 | Wyoming Street and Westport Road |
| Lebanon MO | Factory Stores of America | 417-588-4142 | 2020 Evergreen Parkway |
| Lees Summit MO | Stonehaus Farm Winery | 816-554-8800 | 24607 NE Colburn Rd |
| Lone Jack MO | Bynum Winery | 816-566-2240 | 13520 South Sam Moore Rd |
| Mound City MO | Squaw Creek National Wildlife Refuge | 660-442-3187 | H 159S |
| Osage Beach MO | Blue Moon Marina, Inc | 573-348-3178 | 5395 Bruce Lane |

| | | | |
|---|---|---|---|
| Osage Beach MO | Osage Beach Premium Outlets | 573-348-2065 | 4540 H 54 |
| Osage Beach MO | Osage Premium Outlets | 573-348-2065 | 4540 H 54 |
| Park Hills MO | Missouri Mines State Historic Site | 573-431-6226 | 75 H 32 |
| Puxico MO | Mingo National Wildlife Refuge | 573-222-3589 | 24279 H 51 |
| Republic MO | Wilson's Creek National Battlefield | 417-732-2662 ext. 227 | 6424 W Farm Road 182/Elm Street |
| Springfield MO | Fantastic Caverns | 417-833-2010 | 4872 N Farm Rd 125 |
| Springfield MO | Japanese Stroll Garden | 417-864-1049 | 2400 S Scenic Avenue |
| St Charles MO | Lewis and Clark Boat House and Nature Center | 636-947-3199 | 1050 Riverside Drive |
| St James MO | Ferrigno Winery | 573-265-7742 | 17301 State Route B |
| St James MO | Heinrichhaus Vineyards and Winery | 573-265-5000 | 18500 State Route U |
| St James MO | Meremec Vineyards | 877-216-WINE | 600 State Road Rte B |
| St Joseph MO | Pony Express National Memorial | 816-279-5059 | 914 Penn Street |
| St Louis MO | Gateway Riverboat Cruises | 314-621-4040 | 800 N. First St. |
| St Louis MO | Kirkwood Farmers' Market | 314-822-0084 | 130 E. Jefferson Avenue |
| St Louis MO | Laclede's Landing Self Guided Walking tour | 314-241-5875 | Laclede's Landing Blvd |
| St Louis MO | Laumeier Sculpture Park | 314-821-1209 | 12580 Rott Road |
| St Louis MO | Museum of Transportation | 314-965-7998 | 3015 Barrett Station Rd |
| St Louis MO | The American Kennel Club Museum of the Dog | 314-821-3647 | 1721 S Mason Road |
| St Louis MO | The Boathouse in Forest Park | 314-367-2224 | 6101 Government Dr |
| St Louis MO | Ulysses S. Grant National Historical Site | 314-842-3298 | 7400 Grant Rd |
| Ste Genevieve MO | Cave Vineyard | 573-543-5284 | 21124 Cave Rd |
| Ste Genevieve MO | Chaumette Vineyards and Winery | 573-747-1000 | 24345 State Route WW |
| Steelville MO | Peaceful Bend Vineyard | 573-775-3000 | 1942 Hwy T |
| Stover MO | Grey Bear Vineyards | 573-377-4313 | 25992 Hwy T |
| Sumner MO | Swan Lake National Wildlife Refuge | 660-856-3323 | 16194 Swan Lake Avenue |
| University City MO | St. Louis Walk of Fame | 314-727-7827 | Delmar Boulevard |
| Washington MO | La Dolce Vita Vineyard and Winery | 636-239-0399 | 72 Forest Hills Drive |
| Wellington MO | New Oak Vineyards | 816-240-2311 | 11644 Flourney School Rd |

**Montana Listings**

| | | | |
|---|---|---|---|
| Anaconda MT | Cable Mine Ghost Town | 406-563-3357 | H 10A/H 1 |
| Big Sky MT | The Historic Crail Ranch | 406-995-2160 | 2110 Spotted Elk Road |
| Bigfork MT | Pointer Scenic Cruises | 406-837-5617 | 452 Grand Drive |
| Billings MT | Big Sky Sedan | 406-256-9793 | 314 N 20th Street |
| Billings MT | Billings Trolley and Bus Company | 406-252-1778 | 1509 Rosebud Lane |
| Bozeman MT | Bohart Ranch Cross Country Ski Center | 406-586-9070 | 16620 Bridger Canyon Road/H 86 |
| Browning MT | Camp Disappointment | 406-338-4015 | H 2 |
| Columbia Falls MT | Flathead Lake Winery | 406-387-WINO (9466) | 29 Golden Eagle Street |
| Garnet MT | Garnet Ghost Town | 406-728-1695 | Off Bear Gultch Road |
| Helena MT | Rimini Ghost Town | 406-442-4120 | Rimini Road |
| Libby MT | Kootenai Falls and Swinging Bridge | 406-293-3608 | MP 21 (between Libby and Troy) |
| Lolo MT | Traveler's Rest State Park | 406-273-4253 | 6717 Highway12 W |
| Missoula MT | Historic Missoula Downtown Walking Tour | 406-543-4238 | Downtown sites |
| Moiese MT | National Bison Range: | 406-644-2211 | 58355 Bison Range Road |
| Nevada City MT | Nevada City Ghost Town | 406-843-5247 | H 287 |
| Virginia City MT | Historic Tour Company | 406-843-5421 | Wallace Street/H 287 |
| Virginia City MT | Virginia City Ghost Town | 406-843-5247 | H 287 |
| Virginia City MT | Virginia City Overland Stagecoach | 406-843-5200 | Wallace Street/H 287 |

**Nebraska Listings**

| | | | |
|---|---|---|---|
| Alliance NE | Carhenge | | 2141 County Road 59/H 87 |
| Alliance NE | Dobby's Frontier Town | 308-762-4321 | 320 E 25th Street |
| Alliance NE | Sallows Arboretum | 308-762-2384 | 11th and Niobrara |
| Blair NE | Black Elk/Neihardt Park | 402-533-4455 | College Drive |
| Comstock NE | Second Wind Ranch | 800-658-4443 | H 21C |
| Elm Creek NE | Chevyland U.S.A. Auto Museum | 308-856-4208 | 7245 Buffalo Creek Road |
| Fairbury NE | McDowell's Tomb "Magic Etched in Stone" | 402-729-3000 | 566th Avenue |

| | | | |
|---|---|---|---|
| Fremont NE | Fremont and Elkhorn Valley Railroad and Nebraska Railroad Museum | 402-727-0615 | 1835 N Somers Avenue |
| Gering NE | Farm and Ranch Museum | 308-436-1989 | H 92 |
| Gering NE | Robidoux Pass and Robidoux Trading Post | 308-436-6886 | Carter Canyon Road |
| Grand Island NE | Stolley Park | 308-385-5444 | Stolley Park Road |
| Grand Island NE | Stuhr Museum of the Prairie Pioneer | 308-385-5316 | 3133 W H 34 |
| Gretna NE | Nebraska Crossings Outlet Stores | 402-332-4940 | 14333 S H 31 |
| Harrison NE | Agate Fossil Bed National Monument | 308-436-9760 | 301 River Road |
| Harrison NE | Warbonnet Battlefield | 308-432-0300 | Hat Creek Road |
| Kearney NE | Apple Acres | 308-893-2845 | 7460 W 100th Street |
| Kearney NE | Great Platte River Road Archway | 877-511-ARCH (2724) | 3060 E 1st Street |
| Lexington NE | Heartland Museum of Military Vehicles | 308-324-6329 | 606 Heartland Road |
| Lexington NE | Mac's Creek Vineyards and Winery | 308-324-0440 | 43315 Road 757 |
| Lincoln NE | Deer Springs Winery | 402-327-8738 | 16255 Adams Street |
| Lincoln NE | Lester F Larsen Tractor Test and Power Museum | 402-472-8389 | 35th and Fair Streets |
| Lincoln NE | Veterans Memorial Garden | 402-441-7847 | 3200 Veterans Memorial Drive |
| Lynch NE | Old Baldy - The Tower | 402-569-3143 | Off H 12 |
| Macy NE | Blackbird Scenic Overlook | 402-837-5391 | H 75 |
| Mitchell NE | Prairie Vine Vineyard & Winery | 308-623-2955 | 1463 17th Avenue |
| Nebraska City NE | Arbor Day Farm | 402-873-8733 | 2700 Sylvan Road |
| Nebraska City NE | Arbor Lodge State Historical Park and Arboretum | 402-873-7222 | 2600 Arbor Avenue |
| Nebraska City NE | Factory Stores of America | 402-873-7727 | 1001 H 2 |
| Nebraska City NE | Kimmel Orchard and Vineyard | 402-873-5293 | 5995 G Road |
| Neligh NE | Antelope County Pioneer Jail Museum | 402-887-5046 | 509 L Street |
| North Platte NE | Bailey Railroad Yard and Golden Spike Tower and Visitor Center | 308-660-3776 | 1249 N Homestead Road |
| Omaha NE | Gerald R Ford Birthsite and Gardens | 402-444-5955 | 3202 Woolworth Avenue |
| Omaha NE | Heartland of America Park and Fountain | 402-444-5900 | 8th and Douglas Streets |
| Omaha NE | Joslyn Castle | 402-595-2199 | 3902 Davenport Street |
| Omaha NE | Lewis and Clark National Historic Trail | 402-661-1804 | 601 Riverfront Drive |
| Omaha NE | Mormon Trail Center at Historic Winter Quarters | 402-453-9372 | 3215 State Street |
| Omaha NE | Old Market Shopping District | 402-346-4445 | Farnam to Jackson Streets/10th to 13th Streets |
| Omaha NE | One Pacific Place | 402-399-8049 | 103rd and Pacific Street |
| Pawnee City NE | SchillingBridge Winery and Microbrewery | 402-852-2400 | 62193 710th Road |
| Raymond NE | James Arthur Vineyards | 402-783-5255 | 2001 W Raymond Rd |
| Scotia NE | Happy Jack Peak and Chalk Mine | 308-245-3276 | NE H 11 |
| Springfield NE | Soaring Wings Vineyard | 402-253-2479 | 17111 S 138th Street |
| Trenton NE | Massacre Canyon Monument and Visitor Center | 308-539-1736 | H 34 |
| Winnebago NE | Honoring-the-Clans Sculpture Garden and Cultural Plaza | 402-846-5353 | Ho-Chunk Plaza |

**Nevada Listings**

| | | | |
|---|---|---|---|
| Beatty NV | Rhyolite Ghost Town | 760-786-3200 | off Highway 374 |
| Henderson NV | District at Green Valley Ranch | 702-564-8595 | 2240 Village Walk Drive |
| Lake Tahoe NV | North South Lake Tahoe Boat Rentals | 888-312-1116 | |
| Las Vegas NV | Camp Bow Wow | 702-255-2267 | 5175 S Valley View Blvd |
| Las Vegas NV | Historic Spring Mountain Ranch | 702-875-4141 | State Route 159 |
| Las Vegas NV | Las Vegas Strip Walking Tour | | 3300-3900 Las Vegas Blvd. |
| Las Vegas NV | Old Las Vegas Mormon Fort | 702-486-3511 | 500 E Washington Ave |
| Las Vegas NV | Tivoli Village | 702-570-7400 | 440 S Rampart Blvd |
| Las Vegas NV | Town Square Las Vegas | 702-269-5000 | 6605 Las Vegas Blvd S |
| Sparks NV | Legends Outlets Sparks | 775-358-3800 | 1310 Scheels Dr |
| Sparks NV | Legends at Sparks Marina | 775-358-3800 | 1310 Scheels Drive |
| Sparks NV | Scraps Dog Bakery at Sparks Marina | 775-358-9663 | 325 Harbour Cove Drive |
| Stateline NV | Borges Sleigh and Carriage Rides | 775-588-2953 | P.O. Box 5905 |
| Tonopah NV | Tonopah Historic Mining Park | 775-482-9274 | 520 McCullough Avenue |
| Virginia City NV | Comstock Firemen's Museum | 775-847-0717 | 117 S. C St. |
| Virginia City NV | Gold Panning Lessons | | C Street |
| Virginia City NV | Happy Hoofers Carriage Service | 775-848-4421 | |

| | | | |
|---|---|---|---|
| Virginia City NV | Masonic and Mt St Mary's Cemeteries | 775-847-0281 | Just out of town |
| Virginia City NV | TNT Stagecoach Rides | 775-721-1496 | F Street across from the Railroad |
| Virginia City NV | Virginia & Truckee Railroad Co. | 775-847-0380 | 565 S. K Street |
| Virginia City NV | Virginia City | 775-847-0311 | Hwy 341 |
| Virginia City NV | Virginia City Tractor Tram | | C Street |

### New Hampshire Listings

| | | | |
|---|---|---|---|
| Center Conway NH | Saco Bound Canoe Rental | 603-356-5251 | 2561 E Main Street |
| Concord NH | Concord Downtown Shopping District | 603-226-2150 | Main Streets and surrounding streets |
| Cornish NH | Saint-Gaudens National Historic Site | 603-675-2175 | 139 Saint-Gaudens Road |
| Freeport NH | Muddy Paw Sled Dog Kennel | 207-865-4469 | 184 Burnett Rd |
| Gilford NH | Gunstock Mountain Resort | 1-800-GUNSTOCK (486-7862) | 719 Cherry Valley Road |
| Gorham NH | Mount Washinton Auto Road | 603-466-3988 | Mount Washinton Auto Road |
| Intervale NH | Hartmann Model Railroad Museum | 603-356-9922 | 15 Town Hall Road/H 16 |
| Intervale NH | Mountain Washington Valley Ski Touring and Snowshoe Foundation | 603-356-9920 | 279 H 16/302 |
| Jackson NH | Jackson Ski Touring Foundation | 603-383-9355 | 153 Main Street |
| Pinkham Notch NH | Wildcat Mountain Gondola | 603-466-3326 | H 16 |
| Portsmouth NH | Portsmouth Guided Walking Tours | 603-436-3988 | 500 Market Street |
| Rye NH | Granite State Whale Watch | 603-964-5545 | PO Box 768 |
| St-Lunaire-Griquet NH | L'Anse aux Meadows National Historic Site | 709-623-5229 | Viking Trail/H 436 |
| Wolfeboro NH | Wet Wolfe Watercraft Rentals | 603-271-3254 | 17 Bay Street |

### New Jersey Listings

| | | | |
|---|---|---|---|
| Atco NJ | Amalthea Cellars | 856-768-8585 | 209 Vineyard Road |
| Atlantic City NJ | The Civil Rights Garden | 609-347-0500 | Martin Luther King Blvd. |
| Bayonne NJ | Dogtopia of Bayonne | 201-437-WOOF (9663) | 188-190 Avenue E |
| Bayville NJ | Blackbeards Cave Entertainment Center | 732-286-4414 | 136 H 9 |
| Belvidere NJ | Four Sisters Winery | 908-475-3671 | 783 H 519 |
| Blairstown NJ | Double D Guest Ranch | 908-459-9044 | 81 Mount Hermon Road |
| Bridgeton NJ | Dutch Neck Village | 856-451-2188 | 97 Trench Road |
| Cape May NJ | Cape May Whale Watcher | 609-884-5445 | 2nd Avenue & Wilson Drive |
| Cape May NJ | Cape May Winery and Vineyard | 609-884-1169 | 711 Town Bank Road |
| Cape May NJ | Historic Cold Spring Village | 609-898-2300 | 720 H 9S |
| Cape May NJ | Miss Chris Marina | 609-884-3351 | 1218 Wilson Drive |
| Chatsworth NJ | Mick's Canoe and Kayak Rental | 609-726-1380 | 3107 H 563 |
| Chatsworth NJ | Pine Barrens Canoe Rental | 609-726-1515 | 3260 H 563 |
| Chester NJ | Alstede Farms | 908-879-7189 | 84 H 513 (Old Route 24), |
| Cream Ridge NJ | Cream Ridge Winery | 609-259-9797 | 145 H 539 |
| Eatontown NJ | Bliss Price Arboretum and Wildlife Sanctuary | 732-389-7621 | North side of Wykcoff Road/H 537 |
| Elizabeth NJ | Elizabeth Avenue Farmers Market | 908-965-0660 | Union Square Plaza at Elizabeth Avenue and High Street |
| Farmingdale NJ | Allaire Village | 732-919-3500 | 4265 Atlantic Avenue |
| Flemington NJ | Liberty Village Premium Outlets | 908-782-8550 | One Church Street |
| Hamilton NJ | Sayen House and Gardens | 609-890-3543 | 155 Hughes Drive |
| Hammonton NJ | Tomasello Winery | 800-MMM-WINE (666-9463) | 225 N White Horse Pike/H 30 |
| Holmdel NJ | A. Casola Farms | 732-332-1533 | 178 Hwy 34 |
| Jackson NJ | Rova Farm Resort | 732-928-0928 | 120 Cassville Road |
| Lafayette NJ | Olde LaFayette Village Shopping Center | 973-383-8323 | 75 H 15q |
| Lake Hopatcong NJ | Dow's Boat Rental | 973-663-3826 | 145 Nolan's Point Rd |
| Landing NJ | Lakes End Marina | 973-398-5707 | 91 Mount Arlington Blvd |
| Landisville NJ | Bellview Winery | 856-697-7172 | 150 Atlantic Street |
| Manalapan NJ | Monmouth Battlefield State Park | 732-462-9616 | 347 Freehold Road |
| Medford NJ | Lewis W Barton Arboretum at Medford Leas | 609-654-3000 | One Medford Leas Way |
| Metuchen NJ | Metuchen Farmers' Market | 732-548-2964 | Pearl Street |
| Millville NJ | Glasstown Arts District | 800-887-4957 | 22 N High Street |
| Montague NJ | Westfall Winery | 973-293-3428 | 141 Clove Road |

| Mount Laurel NJ | Rancocas Woods Village of Shops | 856-235-0758 | 114 Creek Road |
|---|---|---|---|
| Mullica Hill NJ | Heritage Vineyards of Richwood | 856-589-4474 | 480 Mullica Hill Road |
| New Brunswick NJ | The Rutgers Gardens at Rutgers University | 732-932-8451 | 112 Ryders Lane |
| Newark NJ | New Jersey Transit | 973-491-7000 | 1 Penn Plaza E |
| North Cape May NJ | Turdo Vineyards and Winery | 609-898-3424 | 3911 Bayshore Road |
| Ocean City NJ | Bay Cats | 609-391-7960 | 316 Bay Avenue |
| Ogdensburg NJ | Sterling Hill Mining Museum | 973-209-7212 | 30 Plant Street |
| Piscataway NJ | East Jersey Olde Towne Village | 732-745-3030 | 1050 River Road |
| Princeton NJ | Morven Museum and Gardens | 609-683-4495 | 55 Stockton Street |
| Princeton NJ | Princeton Canoe and Kayak Rental | 609-452-2403 | 483 Alexander Street |
| Princeton NJ | Princeton University Campus | 609-258-1766 | Nassau Street |
| Ringoes NJ | Unionville Vineyards | 908-788-0400 | 9 Rocktown Road |
| Ringwood NJ | Long Pond Ironworks Historic District | 973-962-7031 | 1304 Sloatsburg Road, c/o Ringwood State Park |
| Robbinsville NJ | Silver Decoy Winery | 609-371-6000 | 610 Perrineville Road |
| Rosenhayn NJ | Bisconte Farms | 856-455-3405 | 350 Morton Avenue |
| Shamong NJ | Valenzano Winery | 609-268-6731 | 1320 Old Indian Mills Road |
| Shrewbury NJ | Anthropologie | 732-842-0762 | 617 Broad Street/H 35 |
| Trenton NJ | Trenton Battle Monument | 609-737-0623 | N Broad Street/H 206 |
| West Orange NJ | Edison National Historic Site | 973-736-0551 | Main Street and Lakeside Avenue |

**New Mexico Listings**

| Albuquerque NM | ABQ Uptown Growers Market | 505-865-3533 | Uptown Loop Rd NE |
|---|---|---|---|
| Albuquerque NM | Albuquerque Museum's Historic Old Town Walking Tours | 505-243-7255 | 2000 Mountain Road NW |
| Albuquerque NM | New Mexico Ghost Tours | 505-249-7827 | 303 Romero Street NW |
| Albuquerque NM | Petroglyph National Monument | 505-899-0205 | 6001 Unser Boulevard NW |
| Aztec NM | Aztec Museum and Pioneer Village | 505-334-9829 | 125 N Main Avenue |
| Belen NM | The Harvey House Museum | 505-861-0581 | 104 North First Street |
| Cerrillos NM | Old Coal Mine Museum | 505-438-3780 | 2846 H 14 |
| Chimayo NM | High Road Market Place | 505-351-1078 | HC 64 Box 12/Santuario Drive |
| Espanola NM | Estrella Del Norte Vineyard | 505-455-2826 | 106 N Shining Sun |
| Farmington NM | Four Corners Monument | 928-871-6647 | Navajo Reservation |
| Fort Sumner NM | Fort Sumner State Monument | 505-355-2573 | 3647 Billy the Kid Road |
| Gallup NM | Gallup Cultural Center | 505-863-4131 | 201 E H 66 |
| Holloman AFB NM | White Sands National Monuments | 505-679-2599 | PO Box 1086 |
| La Mesa NM | Stahmann Pecan Farms | 505-526-8974 | 22505 H 28 |
| La Union NM | LaVina Winery | 505-882-7632 | 4201 South Highway 28 |
| Las Cruces NM | Blue Teal Tasting Room | 866-336-7360 | 1720 Avenida de Mesilla |
| Lincoln NM | Lincoln Historic Town | | Highway 380 |
| Madrid NM | Old Coal Mine Museum | 505-473-0743 | 2846 Highway 14 |
| Mesilla NM | The Shops at Mesilla | 575-523-5561 | Calle del Norte and various side streets |
| Mountainair NM | Salinas Pueblo Missions National Monument | 505-847-2585 | PO Box 517 |
| Placitas NM | Anasazi Fields | 505-867-3062 | 26 Camino de los Pueblitos |
| Placitas NM | Sandia Man Cave | 505-281-3304 | Cibola National Forest |
| Roseburg NM | Shakespeare Ghost Town | 505-542-9034 | Ghost Town Road |
| Roswell NM | International UFO Museum & Research Center | 505-625-9495 | 114 N. Main Street |
| Santa Fe NM | El Camino Real de Tierra Adentro National Historic Trail | 505-988-6888 | 1100 Old Santa Fe Trail |
| Santa Fe NM | Galloping Galleries | 505-988-7016 | 22B Stacy Rd |
| Santa Fe NM | Historic Walking Tour of Santa Fe | 505-986-8388 | San Francisco Street |
| Santa Fe NM | Old Spanish National Historic Trail | 505-988-6888 | 1100 Old Santa Fe Trail |
| Santa Fe NM | Santa Fe National Historic Trail | 505-988-6888 | 1100 Old Santa Fe Trail |
| Santa Fe NM | Santa Fe Premium Outlets | 505-474-4000 | 8380 Cerrillos Rd Ste 412 |
| Santa Fe NM | Shops at Sanbusco | 505-989-9390 | 500 Montezuma Ave |
| Santa Fe NM | State Capitol Grounds | 505-986-4589 | 491 Old Santa Fe Trail |
| Santa Fe NM | Trail of Tears National Historic Park | 505-988-6888 | 1100 Old Santa Fe Trail |
| Socorro NM | Very Large Array (VLA) Radio Telescope | 505-835-7000 | U.S. Hwy 60 |
| Steins NM | Steins Railroad Ghost Town | 505-542-9791 | Interstate 10, Exit 3 |
| Tularosa NM | Tularosa Vineyards | 505-585-2260 | 23 Coyote Canyon Rd |
| Velarde NM | Black Mesa Winery | 800-852-6372 | 1502 State Hwy 68 |
| Watrous NM | Fort Union National Monument | 505-425-8025 | Po Box 127 |

## New York Listings

| | | | |
|---|---|---|---|
| Albany NY | Hudson River Way Pedestrian Bridge | 518-434-2032 | Broadway |
| Albany NY | Stuyvesant Plaza | 518-482-8986 | 1475 Western Avenue |
| Alexandria Bay NY | Uncle Sam Boat Tours | 315-482-2611 | 47 James Street |
| Aquebogue NY | Paumanok Vineyards | 631-722-8800 | 1074 Main Road/H 25 |
| Aurora NY | Long Point Winery | 315-364-6990 | 1485 Lake Road |
| Baiting Hollow NY | Baiting Hollow Farm Vineyard | 631-369-0100 | 2114 Sound Avenue |
| Ballston Spa NY | Bliss Glad Farm | 518-885-9314 | 129 Hop City Road |
| Barryville NY | Indian Head Canoes | 800-874-2628 | 3883 H 97 |
| Bellport NY | Outlets at Bellport | 631-286-3872 | Farber Drive |
| Bolton Landing NY | Lake George Kayak Company | 518-644-9366 | 3 Boathouse Ln |
| Branchport NY | Hunt Country Vineyards | 315-595-2812 | 4021 4021 Italy Hill Road |
| Brooklyn NY | New York City Boardwalks | 212-NEW-YORK | Various |
| Buffalo NY | Theodore Roosevelt Inaugural National Historic Site | 716-884-0095 | 641 Delaware Avenue |
| Burdett NY | Catharine Valley Winery | 607-546-5300 | 4201 H 414 |
| Canandaigua NY | Wilhelmus Estate Winery | 585-394-2860 | 3627 E Lake Road/H 364 |
| Central Valley NY | Woodbury Common Premium Outlets | 845-928-4000 | 498 Red Apple Court |
| Clinton Corners NY | Clinton Vineyards | 845-266-5372 | 450 Schultzville Road |
| Cutchogue NY | Bedell Cellars | 631-734-7537 | 36225 Main Road/H 25 |
| Cutchogue NY | Castello di Borghese Vineyard & Winery | 631-734-5111 | 17150 H 48 |
| Cutchogue NY | Peconic Bay Winery | 631-734-7361 | 31320 Main Rd |
| Dundee NY | McGregor Vineyard | 800-272-0192 | 5503 Dutch Street |
| Dundee NY | Woodbury Vineyards-Senaca Lake | 866-331-9463 | 4141 State Route 14 |
| Elmira NY | Walking Tour of Elmira | 607-733-4924 | 353 Davis Street |
| Elmira NY | Woodlawn Cemetery - Mark Twain's Burial Site | 607-732-0151 | 1200 Walnut Street |
| Fly Creek NY | Fly Creek Cider Mill and Orchard | 607-547-9692 | 288 Goose Street |
| Forestville NY | Merritt Estate Winery | 888-965-4800 | 2264 King Rd |
| Fort Montgomery NY | Fort Montgomery State Historical Site | 845-446-2134 (Summer) | 690 H 9W |
| Fredonia NY | Woodbury Vineyards | 716-679-9463 | 3215 S Roberts Road |
| Gardiner NY | Whitecliff Vineyard | 845-255-4613 | 331 McKinstry Road |
| Gardiner NY | Wright's Apple Farm | 845-255-5300 | 699 H 208 |
| Geneva NY | Roy's Marina | 315-789-3094 | 4398 Clark's Point/H 14 |
| Geneva NY | White Springs Winery | 315-781-9463 | 4200 H 14 |
| Geneva NY | White Springs Winery | 315-781-9463 | 4200 H 14 |
| Germantown NY | Clermont State Historic Site | 518-537-4240 | One Clermont Avenue |
| Ghent NY | The Hudson-Chatham Winery | 518-392-WINE (9463) | 1900 H 66 |
| Hammondsport NY | North Country Kayak and Canoe Rentals | 607-868-7456 | 16878 West Lake Road/H 54A |
| Hector NY | Hazlitt 1852 | 607-546-9463 | 5712 H 414 |
| Herkimer NY | Herkimer Diamond Mine | 800-562-0897 | 4601 H 28N |
| Howes Cave NY | Howe Caverns | 518-296-8900 | 255 Discovery Drive |
| Hyde Park NY | Vanderbilt Mansion - FDR Homesite | 800-337-8474 | 4079 Albany Post Road |
| Inlet NY | Mountainman Outdoor Supply Company | 315-357-6672 | 221 H 28 |
| Interlaken NY | Americana Vineyards and Winery and Crystal Lake Cafe | 607-387-6804 | 4367 E Covert Road |
| Interlaken NY | Lucas Vineyards | 800-682-WINE (9463) | 3862 H 150 |
| Ithaca NY | Cornell Botanic Gardens | 607-255-3020 | 1 Plantations Road |
| Ithaca NY | Tiohero Tours Boat Cruises | 866-846-4376 | 435 Old Taughannock Blvd |
| Jamesport NY | Jamesport Vineyards | 631-722-5256 | 1216 Main Road /H 25 |
| Jamesport NY | Jason's Vineyard | 631-238-5801 | 1785 Main Road/H 25 |
| Kinderhook NY | Martin Van Buren National Historic Site | 518-758-9589 | 1013 Old Post Road |
| King Ferry NY | King Ferry WineryTM Inc | 315-364-5100 | 658 Lake Road |
| Kingston NY | Hudson River Maritime Museum | 845-338-0071 | 50 Rondout Landing |
| Lake George NY | Lake George Plaza Factory Outlets Center | 518-798-7234 | H 9 |
| Lodi NY | Lamoreaux Landing Wine Cellars | 607-582-6011 | 9224 H 414 |
| Lodi NY | Wagner Vineyards, Brewery, and Ginney Lee Restaurant | 607-582-6450 | 9322 H 414 |
| Manhasset NY | Americana Manhasset | 516-627-2277 | 2060 Northern Boulevard at Searingtown Road |

| | | | |
|---|---|---|---|
| Marlboro-on-Hudson NY | Benmarl Vineyards and Winery at Slate Hill | 845-236-4265 | 156 Highland Avenue |
| Mattituck NY | Macari Vineyards | 631-298-0100 | 150 Bergen Avenue |
| Mattituck NY | Sherwood House Vineyards | 631-298-1396 | 2600 Oregon Road |
| Mattituck NY | Sherwood House Vineyards | 631-298-1396 | 2600 Oregon Road |
| Millbrook NY | Millbrook Winery | 845-677-8383 | 26 Wing Road |
| Millerton NY | Hudson Valley DockDogs | 914-631-1470 | 639 Smithfield Road |
| Mount Tremper NY | Kaatskill Kaleidoscope | 877-688-2828 | 5340 Rt. 28 |
| New York NY | Brooklyn Bridge Self-Guided Walk | | Park Row |
| New York NY | Federal Hall National Memorial | 212-825-6888 | 26 Wall Street |
| New York NY | Free Tours by Foot | 646-450-6831 | 112 Suffolk St. |
| New York NY | General Grant National Monument | 212-666-1640 | Riverside Drive and 122nd St |
| New York NY | Horse & Carriage Rides | | 59th Street and Fifth Avenue |
| New York NY | NY's Long Island Rail Road | 212-867-6149 | Throughout Region |
| New York NY | NYC Dog Walking Tour | 914-633-7397 | various (see below) |
| New York NY | New York City Boardwalks | 212-NEW-YORK | Various |
| New York NY | South Street Seaport | 212-732-8257 | South Street |
| New York NY | Statue of Liberty National Monument | 212-363-3200 | Liberty Island |
| New York NY | TV Broadcasts | | various (see below) |
| New York NY | Theodore Roosevelt Birthplace National Historic Site | 212-260-1616 | 28 East 20th Street |
| New York NY | Time Warner Center | 212-823-6000 | 10 Columbus Circle |
| New York NY | Times Square Walking Tour | 212-768-1560 | 1560 Broadway |
| New York NY | William Secord Gallery | 212-249-0075 | 52 East 76th Street |
| Niagara Falls NY | Niagara Falls State Park | 716-278-1796 | Robert Moses Parkway |
| Olcott NY | Carousel Park | 716-778-7066 | 5979 Main Street |
| Old Chatham NY | Old Chatham Sheepherding Company | 888-SHEEP-60 (743-3760) | 155 Shaker Museum Road |
| Old Forge NY | Water Safari Enchanted Forest | 315-369-6145 | 3138 H 28 |
| Oyster Bay NY | Sagamore Hill Estate | 516-922-4447 | 20 Sagamore Hill Road |
| Patchgue NY | Rainbow Rides Transportation | 631-737-7300 | 414 W Sunrise H #285 |
| Peconic NY | Pindar Vineyards | 631-734-6200 | 37645 Main Road/H 25 |
| Penn Yan NY | Anthony Road Wine Company | 800-559-2182 | 1020 Anthony Road |
| Penn Yan NY | Fox Run Vineyards | 315-536-4616 | 670 H 14 |
| Penn Yan NY | Fox Run Vineyards | 315-536-4616 | 670 H 14 |
| Penn Yan NY | Prejean Winery | 315-536-7524 | 2634 Route 14 |
| Penn Yan NY | Red Tail Ridge Winery | 315-536-4580 | 846 H 14 |
| Phoenicia NY | Phoenicia Library | 845-688-7811 | 48 Main Street/H 214 |
| Pine Bush NY | Baldwin Vineyards | 845-744-2226 | 176 Hardenburgh Road |
| Poughkeepsie NY | The Walkway Over the Hudson State Historic Park | 845-834-2867 | Parker Avenue |
| Prattsville NY | Pratt Rock Park | 518-299-3395 | H 23 |
| Rhinebeck NY | Old Rhinebeck Aerodrome | 845-752-3200 | 42 Old Stone Church Road |
| Riverhead NY | Martha Clara Vineyards | 631-298-5502 | 6025 Sound Avenue |
| Riverhead NY | Tanger Outlet Center | 631-369-2732 | 1770 W Main Street |
| Rochester NY | VRA Imperial Limousine, Inc. | 800-303-6100 | |
| Rome NY | Erie Canal Village | 315-337-3999 | 5789 New London Road /H 46 & 49 |
| Rome NY | Fort Stanwix National Monument | 315-338-7730 | 112 E Park Street |
| Romulus NY | Buttonwoodgrove Winery | 607-869-9760 | 5986 State Route 89 |
| Saranac NY | Adirondack Lakes and Trails Outfitters | 518-891-7450 | 541 Lake Flower AvenueH 86 |
| Saranac Lake NY | St Regis Canoe Outfitters | 518-891-1838 | 73 Dorsey Street |
| Saratoga Springs NY | Downtown Saratoga Springs | | Broadway Avenue/H 9/29/50 (and surrounding streets) |
| Saratoga Springs NY | Point Breeze Marina | 518-587-3397 | 1459 H 9P |
| Saratoga Springs NY | Saratoga Arts Center | 518-584-4132 | 320 Broadway Avenue/H 9/50 |
| Saratoga Springs NY | Saratoga Boatworks | 518-584-2628 | 549 Union Avenue |
| Saratoga Springs NY | Saratoga Horse and Carriage | 518-584-8820 | P. O. Box 5184 |
| Saratoga Springs NY | Yaddo Gardens | 518-584-0746 | H 9P/P. O. Box 395 |
| Schuylerville NY | Saratoga Apple, Inc. | 518-695-3131 | 1174 H 29 |
| Seneca Falls NY | Montezuma National Wildlife Refuge | 315-568-5987 | 3395 Route 5 and 20 East |
| Seneca Falls NY | Montezuma Winery | 315-568-8190 | 2981 Auburn Road/H 5/20 |
| Sheridan NY | Willow Creek Winery | 716-934-9463 | 2627 Chapin Rd Box 54 |
| Skaneateles NY | Skaneateles Historical Walking Tour | 315-685-1360 | The Creamery, 28 Hannum Street |
| Sleepy Hollow NY | Sleepy Hollow Cemetery | 914-631-0081 | 540 N Broadway |
| Southampton NY | Long Island Hampton Jitney | 631-283-4600 | 395 County Road 39A |
| Southhold NY | Croteaux Vineyards | 631-765-6099 | 1450 S Harbor Road |

| Southold NY | Eagle's Neck Paddling Company | 631-765-3502 | 49295 Main Road/ H25 |
| Stamford NY | Catskill Scenic Trial | 607-652-2821 | Railroad Avenue and South Street |
| Staten Island NY | Staten Island Ferry | 718-727-2508 | 1 Bay Street |
| Tannersville NY | The Mountain Top Arboretum | 518-589-3903 | H 23C and Maude Adams Road |
| Tappan NY | The De Wint House, George Washington Historical Site | 845-359-1359 | 20 Livingston Street |
| Victor NY | Ganondagan State Historic Site | 585-742-1690 | 1488 H 444 |
| Warwick NY | Warwick Valley Winery | 845-258-4858 | 114 Little York Road |
| Washingtonville NY | Brotherhood America's Oldest Winery | 845-496-3661 | 100 Brotherhood Plaza Drive |
| Water Mill NY | Duck Walk Vineyards | 631-726-7555 | 231 Montauk H |
| Waterloo NY | Waterloo Premium Outlets | 315-539-1100 | 655 H 318 |
| Westfield NY | Johnson Estate Winery | 716-326-2191 | 8419 W Main Road |
| Westport NY | Westport Marina | 800-626-0342 | 20 Washington Street |
| Williamsville NY | The Canine Rehabilitation Center of Western New York | 716-634-0000 | 6551 Main St. Williamsville |
| Wilmington NY | Whiteface Mountain Veterans Memorial Highway | 518-523-1655 | 5021 RT 86 |
| Woodstock NY | Woodstock Byrdcliffe | 845-679-2079 | Upper Byrdcliffe Road |

### North Carolina Listings

| Asheville NC | Asheville Historic Trolley Tour | 888-667-3600 | 151 Haywood Street/Asheville Visitor Center |
| Asheville NC | Asheville Urban Trail | 828-258-0710 | 2 South Pack Square (Pack Place) |
| Asheville NC | Biltmore Estate | 800-624-1575 | 1 Approach Road |
| Asheville NC | Biltmore Village | 888-561-5437 | Biltmore Plaza |
| Asheville NC | Craggy Gardens | 828-298-0398 | Milepost 364 Blue Ridge Parkway |
| Asheville NC | Ghost Hunters of Asheville Tours | 828-779-HUNT (4868) | 1 Battery Park Avenue (Haywood Park Hotel) |
| Asheville NC | Grove Arcade Public Market | 828-252-7799, ext.302 | 1 Page Avenue |
| Asheville NC | North Carolina Arboretum | 828-665-2492 | 100 Fredrick |
| Asheville NC | Shakespeare in the Park | 828-254-5146 | 100 Gay Street |
| Atlantic Beach NC | Sea Water Marina | 252-726-1637 | 400 Atlantic Beach Causeway |
| Banner Elk NC | Lees-McRae College | 800-280-4LMC (4562) | 191 Main Street/H 194 |
| Beaufort NC | Beaufort Historic Site | 252-728-5225 | 150 Turner Street |
| Beaufort NC | Good Fortune Sail Charters | 252-241-6866 | 600 Front Street |
| Blowing Rock NC | Blowing Rock | 828-295-7111 | H 321 S |
| Blowing Rock NC | Tanger Shoppes on the Parkway | 828-295-4444 | H 321 |
| Blowing Rock NC | Tweetsie Railroad | 828-264-9061 | 300 Tweetsie Railroad Lane |
| Boone NC | Wahoo's Adventures | 828-262-5774 | H 321S |
| Boonville NC | RagApple Lassie Vineyards | 336-367-6000 | 3724 RagApple Lassie Lane |
| Burlington NC | Burlington Outlet Village | 336-227-2872 | 2839 Corporation Parkway |
| Canton NC | Old Pressley Sapphire Mine | 828-648-6320 | 240 Pressley Mine Road |
| Chapel Hill NC | Historic Chapel Hill | 919-942-7818 | 610 E Rosemary Street |
| Chapel Hill NC | The North Carolina Botanical Garden | 919-962-0522 | Old Mason Farm Road |
| Charlotte NC | Carowinds Amusement Park | 704-588-2600 | 14523 Carowinds |
| Charlotte NC | Carowinds Theme Park | 803-548-5300 | 14523 Carowinds Park Road |
| Cherokee NC | Smoky Mountain Gold and Ruby Mine | 828-497-6574 | H 441 North |
| Corolla NC | Corolla Wild Horses | 252-453-8002 | 1126 Old Schoolhouse Lane |
| Corolla NC | Currituck Beach Lighthouse | 252-453-4939 | H 12 |
| Corolla NC | Rick's Jeep Adventures | 252-489-4878 | 610 Currituck Clubhouse Drive |
| Creswell NC | Somerset Place | 252-797-4560 | 2572 Lake Shore Road |
| Creswell NC | The Davenport Homestead | 252-793-3248 | 2637 Mt Tabor Road |
| Currie NC | Moores Creek Bridge | 910-283-5591 | 40 Patriots Hall Drive |
| Dobson NC | Black Wolf Vineyards | 336-374-2532 | 283 Vineyard Lane |
| Durham NC | Duke Homestead | 919-477-5498 | 2828 Duke Homestead Road |
| Durham NC | Duke University | 919-684-3701 | Duke University Road |
| Durham NC | Durham Downtown Walking Tour | 919-687-0288 | 101 East Morgan Street |
| Durham NC | Lap it Up Canine Swim and Activity Center | 919-455-6001 | 5420 H 55 |
| Fayetteville NC | Fayetteville Technical Community College Campus | 910-678-8400 | 2201 Hull Road |
| Flat Rock NC | Carl Sandburg Historical Park | 828-693-4178 | 81 Carl Sandburg Lane |
| Four Oaks NC | Bentonville Battlefield State Historic Site | 910-594-0789 | 5466 Harper House Road |
| Franklin NC | Gold City Gem Mine | 828-369-3905 | 9410 Sylva Road |

384

| Graham NC | Benjamin Vineyards and Winery | 336-376-1080 | 6516 Whitney Raod |
|---|---|---|---|
| Hatteras Island NC | Pea Island National Wildlife Refuge | 252-987-2394 | 14500 H 12 @ MM #31 |
| Henderson NC | The Raleigh Road Outdoor Theatre | 252-438-6959 | 3336 Raleigh Road/BH 1 |
| Hendersonville NC | Historic Johnson Farm | 828-891-6585 | 3346 Hayward Road |
| High Point NC | Piedmont Environmental Center | 336-883-8531 | 1220 Penny Road |
| Highlands NC | Highlands Botanical Garden | 828-526-2602 | 930 Horse Cove Road |
| Highlands NC | Highlands Nature Center and Botanical Gardens | 828-526-2623 | 930 Horse Cove Road |
| Jamestown NC | Mendenhall Plantation | 33-454-3819 | 603 W Main Street |
| Jarvisburg NC | Sanctuary Vineyards: | 252-491-2387 | 7005 Caratoke H/H 158 |
| Jarvisburg NC | Weeping Radish Farm Brewery | 252-491-5205 | 6810 Caratoke H/H 158 |
| Kannapolis NC | Cannon Village | 704-938-3200 | 200 West Avenue (Visitor Center) |
| Kannapolis NC | Dale Earnhardt Plaza and Statue | 704-938-3200 | Dale Earnhardt Blvd/H 3 |
| Knotts Island NC | Moonrise Bay Vineyard | 252-429-9463 | 134 Moonrise Bay Landing |
| Lake Toxaway NC | Lake Toxaway Marine | 828-877-3155 | 15885 Rosman H/H 64/281 |
| Linville NC | Grandfather Mountain | 828-733-4337 | near Blue Ridge Parkway |
| Little Switzerland NC | Emerald Village Mining Museum | 828-ROK-MINE (765-6463) | 331 McKinney Mine Road |
| Manteo NC | Fort Raleigh National Historic Site | 252-473-5772 | 1401 National Park Drive |
| Manteo NC | Manteo Beaches | 252-441-5508 | N Virginia Dare Trail/H 12 |
| Manteo NC | Outer Banks Air Charters | 252-256-2322 | 400 Airport Road |
| Manteo NC | The Roanoke Marshes Lighthouse | 252-475-1750 | 207 Queen Elizabeth Avenue |
| Manteo NC | Wright Brothers National Memorial | 252-441-7430 | 1401 National Park Drive |
| Mebane NC | Winery at Iron Gate Farm | 919-304-9463 | 2540 Lynch Store Road |
| Midland NC | Reed Gold Mine State Historic Site | 704-721-4653 | 9621 Reed Mine Road |
| Mount Gilead NC | Town Creek Indian Mound | 910-439-6802 | 509 Town Creek Mound Road |
| Nags Head NC | Tanger Outlet | 252-441-5634 | 7100 S Croatan H/H 158 |
| New Bern NC | Barnacle Bob's Boat and Jet Ski Rentals | 252-634-4100 | Sheraton Marina |
| New Bern NC | Heritage Walking Tours | 800-437-5767 | 203 S Front Street |
| New Bern NC | On the Wind Sailing Cruises | 252-322-5804 | 104 Marina Drive |
| Ocracoke NC | Cottage Ghost Tales and Murder Mysteries | 252-928-6300 | 170 Howard Street |
| Ocracoke NC | Ghost Tours and Walking Tours | 252-928-5541 | 170 Howard Street |
| Ocracoke NC | Ocracoke Pony Pen | 252-473-2111 | Hwy 12 |
| Ocracoke NC | Ocracoke Sports Fishing Charters | 252-928-4841 | PO Box 429 |
| Ocracoke NC | Restless Native Boat Rentals | 252-928-1421 | 109 Lighthouse Road |
| Ocracoke Village NC | The Anchorage Inn Marina | 252-928-6661 | 180 Irvin Garrish H/H 12 |
| Pittsboro NC | Fearrington Village | 919-542-2121 | 2000 Fearrington Village Center |
| Raleigh NC | Art Space | 919-821-2723 | 201 E Davie Street |
| Raleigh NC | Cameron Village Shopping Center | 919-821-1350 | 1900 Cameron Street |
| Raleigh NC | City Market | 919-821-1350 | Person and Martin Streets |
| Raleigh NC | Raleigh Little Theatre Rose Garden | 919-821-4579 | 301 Pogue Street |
| Raleigh NC | The Raleigh Flea Market | 919-899-FLEA (3532) | 1025 Blue Ridge Road |
| Salem NC | Old Salem | 336-721-7350 | 601 Old Salem Road |
| Sanford NC | House in the Horseshoe | 910-947-2051 | 288 Alston House Road |
| Smithfield NC | Carolina Premium Outlets | 919-989-8757 | 1025 Industrial Park Drive |
| Southern Pines NC | Weymouth Woods-Sandhills Nature Preserve | 910-692-2167 | 1024 Ft. Bragg Road |
| Weaverville NC | Vance Birthplace | 828-645-6706 | 911 Reems Creek Rd. |
| Westfield NC | Hanging Rock River Trips | 336-593-8283 | 3466 Moores Spring Road |
| Winnabow NC | Orton Plantation Gardens | 910-371-6851 | 9149 Orton Road SE |

**North Dakota Listings**

| Bismarck ND | Chateau De Mores State Historic Site | 701-623-4355 | 612 E Boulevard Avenue |
|---|---|---|---|
| Bismarck ND | Chief Lookings Earthlodge Village Interpretive Trail | 701-222-6455 | Burnt Boat Drive |
| Bismarck ND | George Bird Rotary Park Arboretum Trail | 701-222-6455 | Divide Avenue and College Drive |
| Churchs Ferry ND | Garden Dwellers Farm | 701-351-2520 | 7th and Summit Streets |
| Dickinson ND | Crooked Crane Trail | 701-456-2074 | 8th Street SW |
| Dickinson ND | Prairie Outpost Park | 701-456-6225 | 200 Museum Drive |
| Dunseith ND | International Peace Garden | 701-263-4390 | RR 1, Box 116/H 3 |
| Fargo ND | Celebrity Walk of Fame | 701-282-3653 | 2001 44th Street S |
| Fargo ND | Fargo Air Museum | 701-293-8043 | 1609 19th Avenue N/H 81 |
| Fort Yates ND | Fort Yates Historical Site | 701-222-4308 | Standing Rock Avenue |

| | | | |
|---|---|---|---|
| Grand Forks ND | Japanese Gardens | 701-746-2750 | 3300 11th Avenue South |
| Grand Forks ND | The Greenway/ Grand Forks Park District | 701-746-2750 | 1210 7th Avenue S |
| Medora ND | Maah Daah Hey Trail (Association) | 701-227-7800 | P. O. Box 156 |
| Medora ND | Painted Canyon Visitor Center | 701-575-4020 | 7 miles East of Medora on I-94 |
| Minot ND | Riverwalk of Minot | 701-857-8206 | 1020 South Broadway |
| New Town ND | Crow Flies High Butte Overlook | 701-627-4812 | H 23 |
| Riverdale ND | Misty the Mermaid | 701-654-7636 | 300 2nd Street |
| Stanton ND | Knife River Indian Villages | 701-745-3300 | 564 H 37 |
| Valley City ND | Medicine Wheel Park | 800-532-8541 | Winter Show Drive |
| Valley City ND | Scenic Bridges Tour | 701-845-1891 | 250 W Main Street/H 52 |
| Watford City ND | Little Missouri National Grasslands (N Ranger District) | 701-250-4443 | 1901 S Main Street W |
| Watford City ND | Little Missouri National Grasslands (N Ranger District) | 701-250-4443 | 1901 S Main Street W |
| Williston ND | Missouri-Yellowstone Confluence Interpretive Center | 701-572-9034 | 15349 39th Lane NW |

## Ohio Listings

| | | | |
|---|---|---|---|
| Canal Winchester OH | Blacklick Creek Greenways Trail | 614-891-0700 | 7680 Wright Road |
| Chagrin Falls OH | Chagrin Falls Main Street | 440-247-4470 | Main Street |
| Chillicothe OH | Disc Golf Course - Great Seal State Park | 740-663-2125 | 635 Rocky Road |
| Cincinnati OH | Cincinnati Nature Center | 513-831-1711 | 4949 Tealtown Road |
| Cincinnati OH | Elegant Carriages | 937-903-5156 | 501 Vine Street |
| Cincinnati OH | Northside Farmers Market | 513-614-3671 | 4104 Hamilton Avenue |
| Cincinnati OH | Withrow Nature Preserve | 513-521-7275 | 7075 Five Mile Rd |
| Cleveland OH | Gordon Square Farmers Market | 216-233-8300 | W 65th Street and Clinton Avenue |
| Cleveland OH | Tower City Center | 216-623-4750 | 230 W. Huron Road |
| Columbus OH | Polaris Fashion Place | 614-846-1500 | 1500 Polaris Parkway |
| Coshocton OH | Historic Roscoe Village | 740-622-9310 | Hill Street |
| Groveport OH | Loop Trails | 614-891-0700 | 3860 Bixby Road |
| Hilliard OH | Heritage Park, Multi-Use Trail | 614-891-0700 | 7262 Hayden Run Road |
| Jeffersonville OH | Jeffersonville Outlet Mall | 740-948-9090 | 8000 Factory Shops Blvd |
| Kirtland OH | Holden Arboretum | 440-946-4400 | 9500 Sperry Road |
| Lancaster OH | Farmers Flea Market | 740-974-7991 | Route 33, 10 mi. s. of Lancaster |
| Lancaster OH | Historic Lancaster | 740-653-8251 | 1 North Broad Street |
| Logan OH | Hocking Hills Canoe Livery | 740-385-0523 | 12789 St. Rt. 664 South |
| Logan OH | Hocking Valley Canoe Livery | 740-385-8685 | 31251 Chieftain Drive |
| Logan OH | Lake Logan Boat Rentals | 740-380-9233 | 30443 Lake Logan Road |
| Lyndhurst OH | Legacy Village | 216-382-3871 | 25001 Cedar Road |
| Mason OH | Deerfield Towne Center | 513-770-0273 | 5503 Deerfield Blvd |
| Nelsonville OH | Robbins Crossing at Hocking College | 740-753-3591 | 3301 Hocking Parkway |
| Port Clinton OH | African Safari Wildlife Park | 800-521-2660 | 267 Lightner Road |
| Port Clinton OH | Miller Ferries to Put-in-Bay | 800-500-2421 | 5174 E Water Street/H 53 |
| Put-in-Bay OH | Kayak the Bay, Ltd | 419-967-0796 | 760 Bayview Ave |
| Put-in-Bay OH | Put-in-Bay Tour Train | 419-285-4855 | Box 190 |
| Ripley OH | Kinkead Ridge Winery | 937-392-6077 | 904 Hamburg Street |
| Rockbridge OH | Barnebey Pet Trail | 614-891-0700 | 185 Clear Creek Road |
| Rockbridge OH | Old Man River Canoe Livery | 866-380-0510 | 10653 Jackson Street |
| Sandusky OH | Cedar Point Amusement Park Kennels | 419-627-2350 | One Cedar Point Drive |
| Westerville OH | Goldenrod Pet Trail | 614-891-0700 | 4265 E Dublin-Granville Road |
| Westlake OH | Crocker Park Shopping Center | 440-871-6880 | 25 Main St. |
| Worthington OH | Olde Worthington | | High Street (near SR 161) |
| Worthington OH | Pooch Parade | 614-473-9244 | High St and SR 161 |
| Worthington OH | Worthington Farmers Market | 614-891-6293 | High Street |

## Oklahoma Listings

| | | | |
|---|---|---|---|
| Anadarko OK | Woods and Water Winery | 580-588-2515 | Route 3 Box 160 C |
| Bartlesville OK | Woolaroc Museum and Wildlife Preserve | 918-336-0307 | H 123 |
| Beggs OK | Natura Vineyards and Winery | 918-756-9463 | 8500 North 245 Rd |
| Big Cabin OK | Cabin Creek Vineyards and Winery | 918-783-5218 | 32153 South 4360 Rd |
| Bristow OK | Nuyaka Creek Winery | 918-756-8485 | 35230 South 177th West Ave |
| Caney OK | Cimarron Cellars Winery | 580-889-5997 | 1280 S. US Highway 69/75 |
| Cheyenne OK | Washita Battlefield National Historic Site | 580-497-2742 | RR 1 Box 55A/On H 47A |
| Claremore OK | Claremore Lake Park | 918-341-1238 | E Blue Starr Drive |

| | | | |
|---|---|---|---|
| Claremore OK | The Rogers State University Conservation Education Reserve | 918-341-4147 | 1701 W Will Rogers Blvd/H 88 |
| Davis OK | Arbuckle Wilderness | 580-369-3383 | Route 1 Box 63 |
| Elk City OK | Old Town Museum Complex | 580-225-6266 | 2717 W 3rd Street |
| Enid OK | Railroad Museum of Oklahoma | 580-233-3051 | 702 N Washington Street |
| Fort Gibson OK | Fort Gibson Historic Site | 918-478-4088 | 907 N Garrison/H 80 |
| Fort Sill OK | Fort Sill National Historic Landmark & Missile Park | 580-442-5123 | 437 Quanah Road |
| Grove OK | Har-Ber Village | 918-786-6446 | 4404 W 20th Street |
| Grove OK | Lendonwood Gardens | 918-786-2938 | Harbor Road |
| Heavener OK | Heavener Runestone State Park | 918-653-2241 | 18365 Runestone Road |
| Jet OK | Salt Plains National Wildlife Refuge | 580-626-4794 | Route 1 Box 76 |
| Lexington OK | Canadian River Vineyards and Winery | 405-872-5565 | 7050 Slaughterville Rd |
| Luther OK | Tres Suenos Vineyards and Winery | 405-277-7089 | 19691 East Charter Oak Rd |
| Norman OK | The University of Oklahoma Campus | 405-325-2151 | 1000 Asp Avenue |
| Oklahoma City OK | Bricktown Canal and Entertainment District | 405-236-8666 | West Reno and N Hudson Avenues |
| Oklahoma City OK | Casady Square Shopping Center | 405-843-7474 | W Britton Road and N Pennsylvania Avenue |
| Oklahoma City OK | Route 66 Boathouse | 405-552-4040 | 3115 E Overholser Drive |
| Oklahoma City OK | Stockyard City | 405-235-8675 | 1305 S Agnew Avenue |
| Oklahoma City OK | The Boathouse District | 405-552-4040 | 725 S Lincoln Blvd |
| Oologah OK | Will Rogers Birthplace Ranch | 918-275-4201 | 9501 E 380 Road |
| Pawnee OK | Pawnee Bill's Wild West Show | 918-762-2513 | 1141 Pawnee Bill Road |
| Perry OK | Cherokee Strip Museum | 580-336-2405 | 2617 W Fir Avenue |
| Ringwood OK | Indian Creek Village Winery | 580-883-4919 | RR 2 Box 174 |
| Tulsa OK | Gardens at Gilcrease Museum | 918-596-2700 | 1400 Gilcrease Museum Road |
| Tulsa OK | Utica Square Shopping Center | 918-742-5531 | 1579 E 21st Street S |

**Oregon Listings**

| | | | |
|---|---|---|---|
| Astoria OR | Fort Astoria | 503-325-6311 | 15th and Exchange Streets |
| Beaverton OR | Cooper Mountain Vineyards | 503-649-0027 | 9480 SW Grabhorn Road |
| Bend OR | Wanoga Sno-Park | 541-383-4000 | On H 46, 14 miles SW of Bend |
| Carlton OR | Anne Amie Vineyards | 503-864-2991 | 6580 NE Mineral Springs Road |
| Carson OR | Wind River Experimental Forest/Arboretum | 509-427-3200 | 1262 Hemlock Road |
| Coos Bay OR | New Carissa Shipwreck | 800-547-7842 | North Spit Beach |
| Depoe Bay OR | Dockside Charters Whale Watching | 541-765-2445 | PO Box 1308/ Coast Guard Place |
| Dundee OR | Sokol Blosser Winery | 503-864-2282 | 5000 Sokol Blosser Lane |
| Eugene OR | King Estate Winery | 541-942-9874 | 80854 Territorial Road |
| Gaston OR | Elk Cove Vineyards | 503-985-7760 | 27751 NW Olson Road |
| Haines OR | Eastern Oregon Museum | 541-856-3380 | 610 3rd Street |
| Hillsboro OR | Oak Knoll Winery | 530-648-8198 | 29700 SW Burkhalter Rd. |
| Monmouth OR | Airlie Winery | 503-838-6013 | 15305 Dunn Forest Road |
| Newberg OR | Rex Hill Vineyards | 800-739-4455 | 30835 N H 99W |
| Newport OR | Agate Beach Golf Course | 541-265-7331 | 4100 N Coast H/H 101 |
| Port Orford OR | Prehistoric Gardens | 541-332-4463 | 36848 H 101S |
| Portland OR | Bridgeport Village | 503-968-8940 | 7455 SW Bridgeport Road |
| Portland OR | Crystal Springs Rhododendron Garden | 503-771-8386 | SE 28th Avenue and Woodstock |
| Portland OR | Hoyt Arboretum | 503-865-8733 | 4000 SW Fairview Blvd |
| Portland OR | Oaks Park Amusement Park | 503-233-5777 | 7100 SE Oaks Parkway |
| Portland OR | Peninsula Rose Garden | 503-823-7529 | 700 N Portland Blvd |
| Portland OR | Portland Farmers' Markets | 503-241-0032 | 240 N Broadway, Suite 129 |
| Portland OR | Portland Saturday Market | 503-222-6072 | 108 West Burnside |
| Portland OR | Portland Walking Tours | 503-774-4522 | SW Broadway and Salmon |
| Portland OR | The Grotto | 503-254-7371 | NE 85th and Sandy Blvd. |
| Portland OR | The Pearl District | 503-227-8519 | Between 6th and 19th Avenues & W Bernside Street and Naito Parkway |
| Portland OR | The Sniff Dog Hotel | 503-208-2366 | 1828 NW Raleigh Street |
| Portland OR | TriMet Transit | 503-238-RIDE (7433) | Various |
| Princeton OR | Malheur Field Station | 541-493-2629 | 34848 Sodhouse Lane |
| Redmond OR | Peterson Rock Gardens | 541-382-5574 | 7930 SW 77th Street |
| Roseburg OR | Hillcrest Vineyards | 541-673-3709 | 240 Vineyard Lane |
| Roseburg OR | Spangle Vineyards | 541-679-9654 | 491 Winery Lane |
| Rouge River OR | Rouge River Palmerton Arboretum | 541-582-4401 | W Evans Creek Road |

| | | | |
|---|---|---|---|
| Salem OR | Ankeny Vineyard Winery | 503-378-1498 | 2565 Riverside Road S |
| Salem OR | Reed Opera House | 503-391-4481 | 189 Liberty Street NE |
| Silverton OR | The Oregon Garden | 877-674-2733 | 879 W Main Street |
| Sunriver OR | Sunriver Nature Center | 541-593-4394 | 57245 River Road |
| The Dalles OR | Dalles Farmer Market | 541-490-6420 | City Park, Union and E 5th Street |

### PR Listings

| | | | |
|---|---|---|---|
| Jayuya PR | Enscribed Rock | 800-866-7827 | H 144, Km 7.8 (dept. of tourism) |
| Mayaguez PR | USDA-ARS Tropical Agriculture Research Station | 787-831-3435 | 2200 Pedro Albizu Campos Avenue |
| San Juan PR | Castillo de San Cristobal | 787-729-6777 | Calle Norzagaray |
| San Juan PR | Castillo de San Felipe del Morro | 787-729-6777 | Calle del Morro |
| San Juan PR | Old San Juan Walking Tour | 787-750-0000 | |
| San Juan PR | Walking Tour of Old San Juan | 787-605-9060 | P.O. Box 9021692 |
| Utado PR | Caguana Indian Ceremonial Park | 787-894-7325 | H 11 at km 12.3 |

### Pennsylvania Listings

| | | | |
|---|---|---|---|
| Allenwood PA | Reptiland | 570-538-1869 | 18628 H 15 |
| Annville PA | Union Canal Canoe Rental | 717-838-9580 | 1929 Blacks Bridge Road |
| Apollo PA | Roaring Run Natural Area | 724-238-1200 | end of Canal Road |
| Ashland PA | Ashland Coal Mine and Steam Train | 570-325-3850 | 19th and Oak Streets |
| Beaver Falls PA | Air Heritage Museum | 724-843-2820 | 35 Piper Street |
| Bedford PA | Old Bedford Village | 800-238-4347 | 220 Sawblade Road |
| Bethlehem PA | Burnside Plantation | 610-868-5044 | 1461 Schoenersville Road |
| Bethlehem PA | Colonial Industrial Quarter | 610-691-6055 | 459 Old York Road |
| Bird-in-hand PA | Aaron and Jessica's Buggy Rides | 717-768-8828 (barn phone) | 3121A Old Philadelphia Pike/H 340 |
| Bird-in-hand PA | Abe's Buggy Rides | 717-392-1794 | 2596 Old Philadelphia Pike |
| Birdsboro PA | Daniel Boone Homestead | 610-582-4900 | 400 Daniel Boone Road |
| Center Valley PA | The Promenade Shops at Saucon Valley | 610-791-9707 | 2845 Center Valley Parkway |
| Center Valley PA | The Promenade Shops at Saucon Valley | 610-791-9707 | 2845 Center Valley Parkway |
| Chadds Ford PA | Brandywine Battlefield Historic Site | 610-459-3342 | H 1 |
| Chadds Ford PA | Glen Eagle Square | 610-558-8000 | H 202 at Springhill Road |
| Chalkhill PA | Christian W. Klay Winery | 724-439-3424 | 412 Fayette Spring Road |
| Dingmans Ferry PA | Kittatinny Canoes | 800-356-2852 | 2130 H 739 |
| Easton PA | Moyer Aviation | 610-258-0473 | 3800 Sullivan Trail |
| Elverson PA | Hopewell Furnace National Historic Site | 610-582-8773 | 2 Mark Bird Lane |
| Elysburg PA | Knoebel's Amusement Park | 800-ITS-4FUN | Route 487 |
| Farmington PA | Fort Necessity National Battlefield | 724-329-5805 | 1 Washington Parkway |
| Gallitzin PA | Allegheny Portage Railroad National Heritage Site | 814-886-6150 | 110 Federal Park Road/H 22 |
| Gettysburg PA | Eisenhower National Historic Site | 717-338-9114 | 97 Taneytown Road |
| Gettysburg PA | Gettysburg Ghost Tours | 717-338-1818 | 47 Steinwehr Avenue/H 15 |
| Gettysburg PA | Gettysburg National Military Park | 717-334-1124 | |
| Gettysburg PA | Gettysburg Village | 717-337-9705 | 1863 Gettsyburg Village Drive |
| Glen Mills PA | Newlin Grist Mill | 610-459-2359 | 219 S Cheyney Road |
| Grove City PA | Prime Outlets at Grove City | 724-748-4770 | 1911 Leesburg Grove City Road/H 208 |
| Harrisburg PA | Pennsylvania State Capitol Complex | 717-787-6810 | N 3rd and State Streets |
| Hermitage PA | Avenue of the Flags, Hillcrest Memorial Park | 724-346-3818 | 2619 East State Street |
| Hershey PA | Hersheypark Amusement Park Kennels | 800-HERSHEY (437-7439) | 100 W Hershey Park Drive |
| Hershey PA | The Outlets at Hershey | 717-520-1236 | 150 Hershey Park Drive |
| Intercourse PA | Carriage Rides at Kitchen Kettle Village | 717-768-8261 | Route 340 |
| Intercourse PA | Kitchen Kettle Village | 717-768-8261 | 3529 Old Philadelphia Pike |
| Jeannette PA | Bushy Run Battlefield | 724-527-5584 | 151 Bushy Field Road |
| Jim Thorpe PA | The Switch Back Trail | 570-325-8255 | Railroad Station |
| King of Prussia PA | Valley Forge National Historical Park | 610-783-1077 | 1400 North Outer Line Drive |
| Kutztown PA | Dutch Hex Tour | 800-HEX-TOUR (439-8687) | Old Route 22 |
| Lahaska PA | Peddler's Village | 215-794-4000 | 81 Peddler Village Road |
| Lahaska PA | Penn's Purchase Factory Outlet Village | 215-794-2232 | H 202 |
| Lancaster PA | Tanger Outlet | 717-392-7260 | 311 Stanley K. Tanger Blvd |

| Lancaster PA | The Amish Farm and House | 717-394-6185 | 2395 Covered Bridge Drive (for GPS: 2395 Lincoln H E) |
| Lancaster PA | Wheatland - The Estate of President James Buchanan | 717-392-8721 | 1120 Marietta Avenue |
| Moosic PA | Shoppes at Montage | 570-341-3271 | 1035 Shoppes Blvd |
| New Castle PA | Harlansburg Station Transportation Museum | 724-652-9002 | 424 Old Route 19 |
| North East PA | Penn Shore Vineyards | 814-725-8688 | 10225 E Lake Road |
| North East PA | Winery at Mazza | 814-725-8695 | 11518 E Lake Road |
| Orrtanna PA | Adams County Winery | 717-334-4631 | 251 Peach Tree Road |
| Orrtanna PA | Adams County Winery | 717-334-4631 | 251 Peach Tree Road |
| Philadelphia PA | Ben Franklin Bridge | | 5th St and Vine St |
| Philadelphia PA | Ben Franklin's Grave | | 5th St and Arch St |
| Philadelphia PA | Edgar Allan Poe National Historic Site | 215-597-8780 | 532 N Seventh Street |
| Philadelphia PA | Gloria Dei Church National Historic Site | 215-389-1513 | Columbus Blvd and Christian Street |
| Philadelphia PA | Horse and Carriage Rides at Independence Mall | | At the Liberty Bell Pavilion |
| Philadelphia PA | Independence National Historic Park | | Market St and 5th St |
| Philadelphia PA | South Street District | | South St and 2nd Ave |
| Philadelphia PA | Thaddeus Kosciuszko National Memorial | 215-597-9618 | 301 Pine Street |
| Pittsburgh PA | Station Square | 412-261-2811 | 100 W Station Square Drive |
| Point Marion PA | Friendship Hill National Historic Site | 724-725-9190 | 223 New Geneva Road |
| Scranton PA | Steamtown National Historic Site | 570-340-5206 | 150 South Washington Avenue |
| Smicksburg PA | Windgate Vineyards | 814-257-8797 | 1998 Hemlock Acres Road |
| Somerset PA | Georgian Place | 814-443-3818 | 317 Georgian Place |
| Somerset PA | Glades Pike Winery | 814-445-3753 | 2208 Glades Pike/H 31 |
| Tannersville PA | The Crossing Premium Outlets | 570-629-4650 | 1000 H 611 |
| Titusville PA | Oil Creek and Titusville Railroad | 814-676-1733 | 409 S Perry Street |
| Upper Black Eddy PA | Bucks County Trolley Company | 610-982-5200 | 1469 River Road/H 32 |
| Washington Crossing PA | Washington Crossing Historical Park | 215-493-4076 | 1112 River Road |
| Weatherly PA | Eckleys Miners Village | 570-636-2070 | 2 Eckley Main Street |
| Wellsboro PA | Pine Creek Outfitters and Rentals | 570-724-3003 | 5142 H 6 |
| West Chester PA | Northbrook Canoe Company | 610-793-2279 | 1810 Beagle Road |
| Wrightstown PA | Carousel Village at Indian Walk | 215-598-0707 | 591 Durham Road/H 413 |
| Wyomissing PA | VF Outlets Village | 610-378-0408 | 801 Hill Avenue |

## Rhode Island Listings

| Little Compton RI | Sakonnet Vineyards | 401-635-8486 | 162 W Main Road |
| Newport RI | Cliff Walk | 401-421-5055 | Memorial Blvd/H 138A |
| Newport RI | Gansett Cruises | 401-787-4438 | Private Dock at the Inn on Long Wharf, 142 Long Wharf, |
| Newport RI | Newport Historical Society | 401-846-0813 | 82 Touro Street |
| Newport RI | Newport Tour & Guide Company | 401-864-0392 | |
| Newport RI | Ten-Mile Drive | | Ocean Avenue |
| Newport RI | Touro Synagogue National Historic Site | 401-847-4794 | 85 Touro Street |
| Portsmouth RI | Greenvale Vineyard | 401-847-3777 | 582 Wapping Road |
| Providence RI | New England Fast Ferry | 617-748-1428 | 8 Point Street |
| Providence RI | Providence Preservation Society Walking Tours | 401-831-7440 | 21 Meeting Street |
| Providence RI | RIHS Walking Tours of Providence | 401-331-8575 | 52 Power Street |
| Providence RI | Roger Williams National Memorial | 401-521-7266 | 282 North Main Street |
| Woonsocket RI | Blackstone River Valley National Heritage Corridor | 401-762-0250 | One Depot Square |

## South Carolina Listings

| Aiken SC | Hopeland Gardens | 803-642-7630 | 135 Dupree Place |
| Beech Island SC | Redcliffe Plantation State Historic Site | 803-827-1473 | 181 Redcliffe Road |
| Blacksburg SC | Overmountain Victory National Historic Trail | 864-936-3477 | 2635 Park Road |
| Bluffton SC | Tanger Factory Outlet Center | 843-689-6767 | 1414 Fording Island Rd # B9 |
| Cayce SC | Adventure Carolina | 803-796-4505 | 1107 State Street/H 2 |
| Charleston SC | Battery and White Point Gardens | 843-853-8000 | East Battery Street and Murray Blvd. |
| Charleston SC | Carolina Polo and Carriage Company | 843-577-6767 | 181 Church St (In lobby of Doubletree Hotel) and 16 Hayne St |
| Charleston SC | Charleston Strolls | 843-766-2080 | 115 Meeting Street |

| | | | |
|---|---|---|---|
| Charleston SC | Magnolia Plantation and Gardens | 843-571-1266 | 3550 Ashley River Road |
| Charleston SC | Palmetto Carriage Works | 843-723-8145 | 40 N Market Street |
| Charleston SC | The Original Charleston Walks and Ghost Tours | 843-577-3800 | 58 1/2 Broad Street |
| Charleston SC | Tour Charleston Ghost Tours | 843-577-3800 | 45 Broad Street Suite 200 |
| Clemson SC | South Carolina Botanical Garden | 864-656-3405 | Perimeter Road |
| Clinton SC | Musgrove Mill State Historic Site | 864-938-0100 | 398 State Park Road |
| Columbia SC | African-American Historical Museum | 803-734-2430 | 1100 Gervais Street |
| Columbia SC | Historic Columbia Foundation Tours | 803-252-1770, ext. 24 | Main Street |
| Columbia SC | River Runner Outdoor Center | 803-771-0353 | 905 Gervais Street/H 1/378 |
| Dillon SC | South of the Border | 843-774-2411 | H 301 N |
| Fort Mill SC | Charlotte Knights-Dog Day Game | 704-357-8071 | Gold Hill Road (Exit 88 off I-77) |
| Gaffney SC | Cowpens National Battlefield | 864-461-2828 | 4001 Chesnee H/H 11 |
| Gaffney SC | Prime Outlets | 864-902-9900 | 1 Factory Shops Blvd |
| Georgetown SC | Captain Sandy's Tours | 843-527-4106 | 343 Ida Drive |
| Georgetown SC | Swamp Fox Tours | 843-527-1112 | 600 Front Street |
| Greenwood SC | Emerald Farm | 864-223-2247 | 409 Emerald Farm Road |
| Hartsville SC | Kalmia Gardens | 843-383-8145 | 1624 W Carolina Avenue/H 151 |
| Hilton Head SC | Daufuskie Island Ferry | 843-342-8687 | Broad Creek Marina, Mathews Dr. |
| Hilton Head SC | The Mall at Shelter Cove | 843-686-3090 | 24 Shelter Cove Lane |
| Hilton Head SC | The Promenade Shops at Saucon Valley | 843-686-3090 | H 278 at MM8 |
| Hilton Head Island SC | Adventure Cruises Inc | 843-785-4558 | 1 Shelter Cove Lane |
| Hilton Head Island SC | Runaway Charters | 843-689-2628 or cell # 843-384-6511 | Hudson Road (Charley's Crab Restaurant Docks) |
| Hilton Head Island SC | Vagabond Cruise | 843-342-2345 | 149 Lighthouse Road |
| Hopkins SC | Congaree Swamp Canoe Tours | 803-776-4396 | 100 National Park Road |
| Isle of Palms SC | Barrier Island Eco Tours | 843-886-5000 | 50 41st Avenue |
| Moncks Corner SC | Cypress Gardens | 843-553-0515 | 3030 Cypress Gardens Road/H 9 |
| Mount Pleasant SC | Boone Hall Plantation and Gardens | 843-571-1266 | 1235 Long Point Road |
| Mount Pleasant SC | Coastal Expeditions Kayak Rentals | 843-884-7684 | 514B Mill Street |
| Myrtle Beach SC | Hammock Shop Complex | 843-237-9122 | 9600 N Kings H/H 17 |
| North Myrtle Beach SC | Barefoot Landing | 843-272-8349 | 4898 H 17S |
| Orangeburg SC | Edisto Memorial Gardens | 803-533-6020 | 250 Riverside Drive SW |
| Pinopolis SC | Blackwater Adventures | 843-761-1850 | 1944 Pinopolis Road/H 5 |
| Ridgeland SC | Jasper County Farmer's Market | 843-726-8127 | 9985 Jacob Smart Blvd/H 17 (1/2 mile S of Downtown) |
| Rock Hill SC | Glencairn Garden | 803-329-5620 | 725 Crest St |
| Sheldon SC | Oyotunji Village | 843-846-8900 | 56 Bryant Lane |
| Sullivan Island SC | Fort Moultrie National Historic Site | 843-883-3123 | 1214 Middle Street |
| Union SC | Rose Hill Plantation State Historic Site | 864-427-5966 | 2677 Sardis Road |
| Wadmalaw Island SC | Bohicket Boat - Adventure and Tour Co. | 843-559-3525 | 2789 Cherry Point Road |
| Wilson SC | The Wilson Farmers Market | 252-237-0111 | 2331 H 301S |
| York SC | Windy Hill Orchard and Cider Mill | 803-684-0690 | 1860 Black H/H 5 |

**South Dakota Listings**

| | | | |
|---|---|---|---|
| Aberdeen SD | Kuhnert Arboretum | 605-626-7015 | E Melgaard Road/H 19W |
| Columbia SD | Sand Lake National Wildlife Refuge | 605-885-6320 | 39650 Sand Lake Drive |
| Crazy Horse SD | Crazy Horse Mountain Memorial | 605-673-4681 | 12151 Avenue Of The Chiefs |
| Custer SD | The Flintstones Bedrock City Theme Park | 605-673-4079 | US Highways 16 and 385 |
| Deadwood SD | Boondocks | 605-578-1186 | 21559 H 385 |
| Deadwood SD | Historic Downtown Deadwood | 605-578-1876 | Main Street |
| Edgemont SD | Centennial Trail | 605-255-4515 | Off H 385/Wind Cave National Park |
| Hill City SD | Black Hills Central Railroad | 605-574-2222 | 222 Railroad Avenue |
| Hill City SD | Prairie Berry Winery | 605-574-3898 | 23837 H 385, PO Box 8 |
| Kadoka SD | Badlands Petrified Gardens | 605-837-2448 | 23104 H 248 |
| Keystone SD | Mt. Rushmore National Memorial | 605-574-2523 | 13000 Highway 244 |
| Kimball SD | SD Tractor Museum | 605-778-6421 | 201 W Cemetery Road |
| Lead SD | Homestake Mining Company | 605-584-3110 | 160 West Main Street/H 85 |
| Lead SD | President's Park | 605-584-9925 | 104 Galena Street |
| Mitchell SD | Corn Palace (Outside View Only) | 605-995-8427 | 612 North Main Street |
| Mitchell SD | Mitchell Prehistoric Indian Village | 605-996-5473 | 3200 Indian Village Road |
| Mitchell SD | Prehistoric Indian Village | 605-995-1017 | 3200 Indian Village Road |
| Mobridge SD | Ft Leavenworth Monument | 605-845-2387 | W H 12 |
| Mobridge SD | Sitting Bull Monument | 605-845-2387 | H 1806 |

| | | | |
|---|---|---|---|
| Montrose SD | Porter Sculpture Park | 605-853-2266 | 25700 451st Avenue |
| Murdo SD | 1880 Town | 605-344-2259 | I-90 at exit 170 |
| Murdo SD | Pioneer Auto Show | 605-669-2691 | I 90 & US 83 |
| Piedmont SD | Petrified Forest of the Black Hills | 605-787-4884 | 8220 Elk Creek Road |
| Pierre SD | Lewis and Clark National Historic Trail | 605-773-3458 | 900 Governor's Drive (SD Cultural Heritage Center) |
| Pierre SD | Pierre Historic Homes Driving Tour | 605-224-7361 | 800 W Dakota |
| Pierre SD | Pierre Loop Trail | 605-773-7445 | http://ci.pierre.sd.us/parks/trailmaps.shtm |
| Pierre SD | State Capitol Grounds | 605-773-3765 | 500 E Capitol Avenue |
| Rapid City SD | Bear Country U.S.A. | 605-343-2290 | 13820 South Highway 16 |
| Rapid City SD | Berlin Wall | 605-394-4175 | In Memorial Park |
| Rapid City SD | Reptile Gardens | 605-342-5873 | Highway 16 |
| Rapid City SD | South Dakota Air and Space Museum | 605-385-5188 | off I-90 |
| Rapid City SD | Thunderhead Underground Falls | 605-343-0081 | 10940 W. Highway 44 |
| Sioux Falls SD | Falls Park Farmers' Market | | 309 E Falls Park Drive |
| Sioux Falls SD | Great Bear Recreation Park | 605-367-4309 | 2401 W 49th Street |
| Sioux Falls SD | Historic Downtown Sioux Falls | 605-338-4009 | Phillips Avenue |
| Sioux Falls SD | Self-Guided Historic Walking Tours | 605-367-4210 | 200 W 6th Street and N Main (Old Court House) |
| Spearfish SD | Spearfish Canyon Scenic Byway | 605-673-9200 | MP 10.5 at Colorado Boulevard and Scenic Byway/H 14A |
| Yankton SD | Lewis and Clark Marina | 605-665-3111 | 43527 Shore Drive |

**Tennessee Listings**

| | | | |
|---|---|---|---|
| Antioch TN | 4 Corners Boat Rentals | 651-641-9523 | 4027 LaVergne Couchville Pike |
| Blountville TN | Tri-Cities Factory Stores of America | 423-323-6866 | 354 Shadowtown Road |
| Chattanooga TN | Chattanooga Choo Choo | 800-TRACK-29 (872-2529) | 1400 Market Street/H 8 |
| Chattanooga TN | Ruby Falls at Lookout Mountain | 423-821-2544 | 1720 S Scenic H/H 148 |
| Chattanooga TN | South Chickamauga Creek Greenway | 423-643-6888 | varied |
| Chattanooga TN | The Walnut Street Walking Bridge | | Walnut Street |
| Chattanooga TN | Walnut Street Bridge | 423-643-6079 | Walnut Street |
| Clarksville TN | Beachaven Vineyards Winery | 931-645-8867 | 1100 Dunlop Lane, Clarksville, TN 37040 |
| Crossville TN | Stonehaus Winery Inc | 931-484-9463 | 2444 Genesis Rd # 103 |
| Dover TN | Fort Donelson National Battlefield | 931-232-5706 | PO Box 434 |
| Dover TN | Fort Donelson National Cemetery | 931-232-5706 | PO Box 434 |
| Franklin TN | Factory At Franklin | 615-791-1777 | 230 Franklin Road/H 6/31 |
| Franklin TN | Historic Carnton Plantation | 615-794-0903 | 1345 Carnton Lane |
| Gatlinburg TN | Mountain Mall | 865-436-5935 | 611 Parkway Suite F15/H 71/441 |
| Gatlinburg TN | Smoky Mountain Winery | 865-436-7551 | 450 Cherry Street, Ste. #2 |
| Gatlinburg TN | The Salt and Pepper Shaker Museum | 888-778-1802 | 461 Brookside Village Way |
| Goodlettsville TN | Long Hollow Winery and Vineyards | 615-859-5559 | 665 Long Hollow Pike/H 174 |
| Grand Junction TN | National Bird Dog Museum | 731-764-2058 | 505 H 57W |
| Greeneville TN | Andrew Johnson National Historic Site | 423-638-3551 | 121 Monument Ave |
| Hampshire TN | Amber Falls Winery & Cellars | 931-285-0088 | 794 Ridgetop Road |
| Jackson TN | Casey Jones Village | 931-296-7700 | 56 Casey Jones Lane |
| Kingsport TN | Bays Mountain Nature Preserve | 423-229-9447 | 853 Bays Mountain Park Road |
| Knoxville TN | Ijams Nature Center | 865-577-4717 | 2915 Island Home Avenue |
| Knoxville TN | Marble Springs Historic Farmstead | 865-573-5508 | 1220 W Governor John Sevier H/H 168 |
| Lafayette TN | Red Barn Winery and Vineyard | 615-688-6012 | 1805 Tanyard Road |
| Lakeland TN | Lakeland Factory Outlet Mall | 901-386-3180 | 3536 Canada Road |
| Lebanon TN | Prime Outlets | 615-444-0433 | One Outlet Village Boulevard |
| Lebanon TN | Prime Outlets of Lebanon | 615-444-0433 | One Outlet Village Blvd |
| Lookout Mountain TN | Rock City Gardens | 706-820-2531 | I-24, Exit 174 or 178 |
| Manchester TN | Beachaven Vineyards and Winery | 931-645-8867 | 426 Ragsdale Road |
| Memphis TN | Carriage Tours of Memphis | 901-527-7542 | 393 North Main Street |
| Memphis TN | Memphis Farmers Market | 901-575-0540 | S Front Street at E GE Patterson |
| Memphis TN | Memphis Riverboats Inc. | 901-527-BOAT (2628) | 45 Riverside Drive |
| Memphis TN | University of Memphis: Chucalissa Archaeological Museum | 901-785-3160 | 1987 Indian Village Drive |
| Morristown TN | David Crockett Tavern and Museum | 423-587-9900 | 2106 Morningside Drive |
| Mount Juliet TN | Providence MarketPlace | 615-773-2298 | 401 S Mt Juliet Road/H 171 |

| | | | |
|---|---|---|---|
| Murfreesboro TN | Cannonsburgh Village | 615-890-0355 | 312 S Front Street |
| Murfreesboro TN | Discovery Center At Murfree Spring | 615-890-2300 | 502 SE Broad Street |
| Murfreesboro TN | Stones River National Battlesite | 615-893-9501 | 3501 Old Nashville Highway |
| Murfreesboro TN | The Avenue Murfreesboro | 615-893-4207 | 2615 Medical Center Parkway |
| Nashville TN | BiCentennial Mall State Park | 615-741-5800 | 598 James Robertson Pkwy |
| Nashville TN | CityWalk | 615-862-7970 | |
| Nashville TN | Fort Nashborough | 615-862-8400 | 100 1st Avenue N |
| Nashville TN | Fort Negley | 615-862-8470 | 1100 Fort Negley Blvd |
| Nashville TN | Horse and Carriages | | Broadway and 1st St |
| Nashville TN | Legends Corner | 615-248-6334 | 428 Broadway |
| Nashville TN | Nashville City Cemetery | 615-862-8400 | 1001 Fourth Avenue S |
| Nashville TN | Nashville Downtown Partnership | 615-743-3090 | 150 Fourth Avenue North, Suite G-150 |
| Nashville TN | Nashville Ghost Tours | 615-884-3999 | 600 Union Square |
| Nashville TN | The Fontanel Mansion | 615-724-1600 | 4225 Whites Creek Pike/H 65/431 |
| Nashville TN | Woodbine Farmers Market | 615-977-6543 | 384 Thompson Lane |
| Pigeon Forge TN | Alabama Touring Bus | 865-908-8777 | 2050 Parkway |
| Pigeon Forge TN | Dollywood Amusement Park Kennels | 865-428-9488 | 1020 Dollywood Lane |
| Pigeon Forge TN | Mountain Valley Vineyards | 865-453-6334 | 2174 Parkway/H 441 |
| Pigeon Forge TN | Pigeon Forge Factory Outlet Mall | 865-428-2828 | 2850 Parkway/H 321/441 |
| Pigeon Forge TN | Tanger Factory Outlet | 865-428-7002 | 161 E Wears Valley Road/H 321 |
| Portland TN | Sumner Crest Winery | 615-325-4086 | 5306 Old H 52 |
| Sevierville TN | Tanger Outlets at Five Oaks | 865-453-1053 | 1645 Parkway |
| Shiloh TN | Shiloh National Cemetery | 731-689-5696 | 1055 Pittsburg Landing |
| Shiloh TN | Shiloh National Military Park | 731-689-5696 | 1055 Pittsburg Landing Road |
| Sparta TN | White County Farmers Market | 931-836-3438 | Liberty Square and Maple Street |
| Springfield TN | Chateau Ross Winery | 615-654-9463 | 5823 Fulton Road |
| Townsend TN | Little River Railroad and Lumber Company | 865-428-0099 | H 321 |
| Winchester TN | Franklin County Old Jail | 931-967-0524 | 400 Dinah Shore Blvd/H 41 |

**Texas Listings**

| | | | |
|---|---|---|---|
| Abilene TX | Fort Phantom Hill | 325-677-1309 | H 600 N |
| Adrian TX | Adrian Lions Farm & Ranch Museum | 806-267-2828 | H 66 |
| Amarillo TX | Amarillo Botanical Gardens | 806-352-6513 | 1400 Streit Street |
| Amarillo TX | Cadillac Ranch | | Old Route 66 |
| Amarillo TX | Route 66 Historic District | 806-374-8474 | 401 S Buchanan Street |
| Arlington TX | Six Flags Over Texas - Kennel | 817-530-6000 | 2201 Road to Six Flags |
| Athens TX | East Texas Arboretum and Botanical Society | 903-675-5630 | 1601 Patterson |
| Austin TX | Austin Carriage Service | 512-243-0044 | various downtown locations |
| Austin TX | Cedar Park Farmer to Market | | 11200 Lakeline Mall Drive |
| Austin TX | Congress Avenue Bridge Bats | 512-416-5700 | 305 South Congress Avenue |
| Austin TX | Zilker Botanical Gardens | 512-477-8672 | 2220 Barton Springs Drive |
| Austin TX | Zilker Park Boat Rentals | 512-327-1388 | 2201 Barton Springs Road |
| Bee Cave TX | Hill Country Galleria | 512-263-0001 | 12700 Hill Country Blvd |
| Big Spring TX | Hangar 25 Air Museum | 432-264-1999 | 1911 Apron Drive |
| Brenham TX | Pleasant Hill Winery | 979-830-VINE | 1441 Salem Rd |
| Brownsville TX | Brownsville Heritage Trail | 9565463721 | 650 FM 802/E Rueben M Torres Sr Blvd |
| Brownsville TX | Palo Alto Battlefield | 956-541-2785 | Paredes Line Road and H 511 |
| Buffalo Gap TX | Buffalo Gap Historic Village | 325-572-3365 | 133 N William |
| Burnet TX | Highland Lakes CAF Air Museum | 512-756-2226 | H 281 at Burnet Municiple Airport |
| Canutillo TX | Zin Valle Vineyards | 915-877-4544 | 7315 H 28 |
| Canyon TX | Elkins Ranch Cowboy Morning | 806-488-2100 | RR2 Box 289 |
| Canyon Lake TX | Fawn Crest Vineyards | 830-935-2407 | 1370 Westside Circle |
| Cedar Hill TX | Penn Farm Agricultural History Center | 972-291-3900 | 1570 W H 82 |
| Clarendon TX | Bar H Working Dude Ranch | 806-874-2634 | 12064 Bar H Ranch Road |
| Concordia TX | Concordia Cemetery | 915-562-7062 | 3700 W Yandell Street |
| Corpus Christi TX | Captain Clark's Flagship | 361-884-8306 | Peoples Street T-Head Marina |
| Corpus Christi TX | Corpus Christi Botanical Gardens | | 8545 South Staples Street |
| Corpus Christi TX | South Texas Botanical Gardens | 361-852-2100 | 8545 S Staples/H 2444 |
| Corsicana TX | Corsicana Pioneer Village | 903-654-4846 | 912 W Park Avenue |
| Dallas TX | Highland Park Village | 214-443-9898 | 47 Highland Park Village |
| Dallas TX | McKinney Avenue Trolley | 214-855-5267 | McKinney Avenue |
| Dallas TX | Old City Park | 214-428-5448 | 1717 Gano St. |
| Dallas TX | Party Animals Carriage Rides | 214-441-9996 | Market Street-West End Area |

| | | | |
|---|---|---|---|
| Dallas TX | Pioneer Plaza | 214-953-1184 | Young Street and Griffin Street |
| Dallas TX | The Shops at Park Lane | 214-369-0860 | 8070 Park Ln |
| Dallas TX | West Village Shopping Center | 469-547-9650 | 3699 McKinney Ave |
| Del Rio TX | Val Verde Winery | 830-775-9714 | 100 Qualia Drive |
| Devine TX | Shooting Star Museum | 830-931-3837 | 5445 CR 5710 |
| El Paso TX | Chamizal National Memorial | 915-532-7273 | 800 S San Marcial Street |
| El Paso TX | Las Palmas Marketplace | 915-633-8841 | 1317 George Dieter |
| El Paso TX | Railroad and Transportation Museum | 915-422-3240 | 400 W San Antonio Avenue |
| Fort Davis TX | Fort Davis National Historic Site | 432-426-3224 | 101 Lieutenant Henry Flipper Drive |
| Fort Worth TX | Stockyards Station | 817-624-4741 | |
| Fort Worth TX | Vintage Flying Museum | 817-624-1935 | 505 NW 38th Street Hangar 33 S |
| Fredericksburg TX | Chisholm Trail Winery | 830-990-2675 | 2367 Usener Road |
| Galveston TX | Caribbean Breeze Boat Rental | 409-740-0400 | 1723 61st Street |
| Galveston TX | Island Carriages | 409-765-6951 | Pier 21 or 22 |
| Garland TX | Firewheel Town Center | 972-675-1041 | 245 Cedar Sage Dr |
| Gonzales TX | Gonzales Pioneer Village | 210-672-2157 | 2122 N St Joseph Street/H 183 |
| Houston TX | Houston Arboretum and Nature Center | 713-681-8433 | 4501 Woodway Drive |
| Humble TX | Mercer Arboretum and Botanic Gardens | 281-443-8731 | 22306 Aldine Westfield Road |
| Huntsville TX | Sam Houston's Grave-Oakwood Cemetery | 936-291-9726 | 7600 H 76S |
| Idalou TX | Apple Country-Hi Plains Orchards | 806-892-2961 | 12206 E H 62 |
| Ingleside TX | Dolphin Connection | 361-776-2887 | off 1069 |
| Iowa Park TX | Wichita Falls Vineyards and Wine | 940-855-2093 | 3399 B Peterson Rd South |
| Jacksonville TX | Lookout Mountain Camping | 903-586-2217 | 43822 H 69N |
| Johnson City TX | Lyndon B. Johnson National Historical Park | 830-868-7128 | Lady Bird Lane |
| La Grange TX | Monument Hill and Kreische Brewery State Historic Sites | 979-968-5658 | 414 H Loop 92 |
| La Porte TX | San Jacinto Battleground | 281-479-2431 | 3523 Highway 134 |
| Lubbock TX | American Museum of Agriculture | 806-744-3786 | 1501 Canyon Lake Drive |
| Lubbock TX | American Wind Power Center | 806-747-8734 | 1701 Canyon Lake Drive |
| Lubbock TX | Llano Estacado Winery | 806-745-2258 | 3426 E H 85 |
| McKinney TX | Chestnut Square Historical Park | 972-562-8790 | 315 S Chestnut Street |
| McKinney TX | Happy Trails Horse-Drawn Carriage Service | 214-662-6705 | |
| Midland TX | George W Bush Childhood Home | 432-685-1112 | 1412 W Ohio Avenue |
| Midland TX | The Permian Basin Petroleum Museum | 432-683-4403 | 1500 I 20 W |
| Nacogdoches TX | Millard's Crossing Historic Village | 936-564-6631 | 6020 North Street (B H 59 N) |
| Nacogdoches TX | Stephen F. Austin Mast Arboretum | 936-468-1832 | Wilson Drive |
| Needville TX | George Observatory | 281-242-3055 | 21901 H 762 |
| New Braunfels TX | Dry Comal Creek Vineyards | 830-885-4076 | 1741 Herbelin Road |
| Oak Island TX | Frascone Winery | 800-920-2248 | 311 Bayside Dr |
| Odessa TX | Odessa Meteor Crater | 432-381-0946 | 3100 Meteor Crater Road |
| Orange TX | Piney Woods Country Wines | 409-883-5408 | 3408 Willow Street |
| Paint Rock TX | Pictographs of Painted Rocks | 325-732-4376 | Box 186/On H 83 |
| Parker TX | Southfork Ranch | 972-442-7800 | 3700 Hogge Road |
| Plano TX | Heritage Farmstead Museum | 972-881-0140 | 1900 W 15th Street |
| Rusk TX | Maydelle Country Wines | 903-795-3915 | RR4 Box 19102 |
| San Angelo TX | Fort Concho Museum | 325-481-2646 | 630 S Oakes St |
| San Antonio TX | La Villita | | King Phillip Walk |
| San Antonio TX | Market Square - El Mercado | 210-207-8600 | W. Commerce Street |
| San Antonio TX | Pearl Farmers Market | 210-212-7260 | 300 E Grayson Street |
| San Antonio TX | Riverwalk | 210-207-3000 | South Alamo |
| San Antonio TX | San Antonio Missions National Historical Park | 210-932-1001 | 6701 San Jose Drive |
| San Antonio TX | Sea World | 210-523-3000 | 10500 Sea World Drive |
| San Antonio TX | Sisters Grimm Nightly Ghost Tour | 210-638-1338 | 300 Alamo Plaza |
| San Antonio TX | Six Flags Fiesta Texas - Kennels | 210-697-5050 | 17000 I 10W |
| San Antonio TX | Texas Transportation Museum | 210-490-3554 | 11731 Wetmore Road |
| San Antonio TX | Veterans Memorial Plaza | 800-447-3372 | 100 Auditorium Circle |
| San Antonio TX | Westover Marketplace | 210-494-3338 | At Intersection H Loop 410 & H 151 |
| San Antonio TX | Yellow Rose Carriage Co. | 210-337-6495 | Crockett Street |
| San Elizario TX | The Mission Trail Art Market | 915-594-8424 | 1500 Main Street/Veteran's Memorial Plaza |
| Sisterdale TX | Sister Creek Vineyards | 830-324-6704 | 1142 Sisterdale Road/H 473 |
| Southlake TX | Southlake Town Square | 817-329-5566 | 256 Main St #244 |
| Spicewood TX | Spicewood Vineyards | 830-693-5328 | 1419 Burnet County Rd |
| Spring TX | Rummy's Beach Club | 713-446-3805 | 22111 Fields Lane |

| | | | |
|---|---|---|---|
| Stonewall TX | Becker Vineyards | 830-644-2681 | 464 Becker Farms Road |
| Stonewall TX | Woodrose Winery | 830-644-2111 | 662 Woodrose Lane |
| Tarrant TX | Lightcatcher Winery | 817-237-2626 | 6435A Nine Mile Bridge Rd |
| Tow TX | Fall Creek Vineyards | 325-379-5361 | 1820 County Rd 222 |
| Umbarger TX | Buffalo Lake National Wildlife Refuge | 806-499-3382 | H 168 |
| Uncertain TX | Caddo Lake Steamboat Company | 903-789-3978 | 328 Bois D'Arc Lane |
| Vega TX | Oldham County Farm and Ranch Heritage Museum | 806-267-2828 | H 66 |
| Washington TX | Washington-on-the-Brazos State Historic Site | 936-878-2214 | 12300 Park Road 12 |
| Weatherford TX | Clark Gardens Botanical Park | 940-682-4856 | 567 Maddux Road |

**Utah Listings**

| | | | |
|---|---|---|---|
| Brigham City UT | Transcontinental Railroad National Back Country Byway | 801-471-2209 | P. O. Box 897 |
| Bullfrog UT | Lake Powell Houseboats | 888-896-3829 | MM 31 H 276 |
| Eureka UT | Tintic Mining Museum | 435-433-6842 | 241 W Main Street |
| Farmington UT | Lagoon Amusement Park and Pioneer Village | 801-451-8000 | 375 N Lagoon Drive |
| Kanab UT | Frontier Movie Town | | 297 W Center Street |
| Kaysville UT | Utah Botanical Center | 801-593-8969 | 725 South Sego Lily Drive |
| Moab UT | Red River Canoe Company | 800-753-8216 | 1371 Main Street/N H 191 |
| Promontory UT | Golden Spike National Historical Site | 435-471-2209 | 6200 N 22300 W |
| Salt Lake City UT | California National Historic Trail | 801-741-1012 | 324 South State Street Ste 200 |
| Salt Lake City UT | Carriage for Hire | 801-363-8687 | across from Crossroads Mall |
| Salt Lake City UT | City Creek Center | 801-521-2012 | 50 S Main Street |
| Salt Lake City UT | KUTV2 Main Street News Studio | 801-973-3000 | 299 South Main Street |
| Salt Lake City UT | Olympic Cauldron Park | 801-972-7800 | 451 South 1400 East |
| Salt Lake City UT | Oregon National Historic Trail | 801-741-1012 | 324 South State Street Ste 200 |
| Salt Lake City UT | Pony Express National Historic Trail | 801-741-1012 | 324 South State Street Ste 200 |
| Salt Lake City UT | Pony Express Trail National Back Country Byway | 801-977-4300 | BLM, 2370 South 2300 W |
| Salt Lake City UT | The Gateway Shopping District | 801-456-0000 | 400 W 100 S |
| Salt Lake City UT | Wheeler Historic Farm | 801-264-2241 | 6351 S 900 E |
| Stansbury Park UT | Benson Grist Mill | 435-882-7678 | 325 H 138 |
| West Jordan UT | Gardner Village Shopping Center | 801-566-8903 | 1100 W 7800 S |

**Vermont Listings**

| | | | |
|---|---|---|---|
| Bennington VT | Apple Barn and Country Bake Shop | 802-447-7780 | 604 H 7S |
| Bennington VT | Bennington Battle Monument | 802-447-0550 | 15 Monument Circle |
| Brattleboro VT | Vermont Canoe Touring Center | 802-257-5008 | 451 Putney Road |
| Burlington VT | Church Street Marketplace | 802-863-1648 | 2 Church Street |
| Burlington VT | Church Street Marketplace | 802-863-1648 | Church Street |
| Burlington VT | Ethan Allen Homestead Park Area | 802-865-4556 | 1 Ethan Allen Homestead, Suite 1 |
| Cambridge VT | Boyden Valley Winery | 802-644-8151 | 64 H 104 |
| Essex VT | Essex Shoppes and Cinema | 802-657-2777 | 21 Essex Way |
| Hardwick VT | Jeudevine Falls Nature and Event Center | 802-472-5486 | 2259 Crafstbury Road |
| Middlebury VT | Robert Frost Interpretive Trail | 802-388-4362 | H 125 |
| Putney VT | Harlow's Sugar House | 802-387-5852 | 563 Bellows Falls Road |
| South Hero VT | Allenholm Farm | 802-372-5566 | 150 South Street |
| South Hero VT | Apple Island Marina | 802-372-3922 | H 2 |
| St Johnsbury VT | Stephen Huneck Gallery at Dog Mountain | 800-449-2580 | 143 Parks Road |
| Stowe VT | Gondola Skyride at Stowe Mountain Resort | 802-253-3500 | 5781 Mountain Road/H 108 |
| Wilmington VT | Green Mountain Flagship Company | 802-464-2975 | 389 H 9 West |
| Woodstock VT | Sugarbush Farm | 802-457-1757 | 591 Sugarbush Farm Road |

**Virginia Listings**

| | | | |
|---|---|---|---|
| Abingdon VA | Historic Main Street | 276-676-2282 | Main Street |
| Abingdon VA | The Cave House | 276-628-7721 (store) | 279 E Main Street/H 11 |
| Abingdon VA | White's Mill | 276-628-2960 | White's Mill Road |
| Alexandria VA | Alexandria's Footsteps to the Past Walking Tours | 703-683-3451 | 221 King Street |

| | | | |
|---|---|---|---|
| Alexandria VA | Doggie Happy Hour | 703-549-6080 | 480 King Street |
| Alexandria VA | Fort Ward Museum and Historic Site | 703-838-4848 | 4301 W Braddock Road |
| Alexandria VA | George Washington's Grist Mill and Distillery | 703-780-2000 | Mt Vernon Memorial H/H 235 |
| Alexandria VA | Old Town Horse and Carriage | 703-765-8976 | Duke St |
| Alexandria VA | Potomac Riverboat Co. Canine Cruises | 703-548-9000 | Cameron and Union Streets |
| Alexandria VA | Woodlawn Plantation | 703-780-4000 | 9000 Richmond H/H 1 |
| Amherst VA | Rebec Vineyards | 434-946-5168 | 2229 North Amherst Highway |
| Amissville VA | Unicorn Winery | 540-349-5885 | 489 Old Bridge Rd |
| Appomattox VA | Appomattox Court House NHP | 434-352-8987 | Hwy 24, PO Box 218 |
| Arlington VA | Arlington National Cemetery | | Memorial Drive |
| Arlington VA | Iwo Jima Memorial | | |
| Bentonville VA | Downriver Canoe Company | 540-635-5526 | 884 Indian Hollow Road |
| Broad Run VA | Pearmund Cellars | 540-347-3475 | 6190 Georgetown Road |
| Brookneal VA | Red Hill - The Patrick Henry National Memorial | 434-376-2044 | 1250 Red Hill Road |
| Chantilly VA | Sully Historic Site | 703-437-1794 | 3601 Sully Road |
| Charlottesville VA | Blenheim Vineyards | 434-293-5366 | 31 Blenheim Farm |
| Charlottesville VA | Charlottesville Historic Downtown Mall | 434-977-1783 | Downtown Charlottesville |
| Charlottesville VA | Jefferson Vineyards | 434-977-3042 | 1353 Thomas Jefferson Parkway |
| Charlottesville VA | Thomas Jefferson's Monticello Estate | 434-984-9822 | 931 Thomas Jefferson Parkway |
| Chesapeake VA | Dismal Swamp Canal Trail | 757-382-CITY (2489) | Dominion Blvd and Old Route 17 (North Trailhead) |
| Chincoteague VA | Chincoteague Ponies at the Carnival Grounds | | Carnival Grounds |
| Colonial Beach VA | Ingleside Vineyards | 804-224-8687 | 5872 Leedstown Road |
| Delaplane VA | Barrel Oak Winery | 703-798-8308 | 3623 Grove Lane/H 55 |
| Delaplane VA | Barrel Oak Winery LLC (BOW). | 540-364-6402 | 3623 Grove Lane |
| Delaplane VA | Three Fox Vineyards | 540-364-6073 | 10100 Three Fox Lane |
| Delaplane VA | Three Fox Vineyards | 540-364-6073 | 10100 Three Fox Lane |
| Doswell VA | Kings Dominion Amusement Park Kennels | 804-876-5400 | 16000 Theme Park Way |
| Fincastle VA | Fincastle Vineyard and Winery | 540-591-9000 | 203 Maple Ridge Lane |
| Floyd VA | Chateau Morrisette Winery | 540-593-2865 | 287 Winery Road SW |
| Floyd VA | Villa Appalaccia | 540-593-3100 | 752 Rock Castle Gorge |
| Forest VA | Thomas Jefferson's Poplar Forest Estate | 434-525-1806 | 1008 Poplar Forest Drive |
| Fredericksburg VA | Chancellorsville Battlefield | 540-786-2880 | 9001 Plank Road |
| Fredericksburg VA | Fredericksburg Battlefield Park | 540-373-6122 | 1013 Lafayette Blvd |
| Fredericksburg VA | Gari Melchers Home and Studio | 540-654-1015 | Belmont, 224 Washington Street |
| Fredericksburg VA | George Washington's Ferry Farm | 540-373-3381 | 268 Kings Hwy/H 3 |
| Fredericksburg VA | Kenmore Plantation and Gardens | 540-373-3381 | 1201 Washington Ave |
| Glen Allen VA | James River Cellars | 804-550-7516 | 11008 Washington Highway |
| Gordonsville VA | Horton Vineyards | 540-832-7440 | 6399 Spotwood Trial |
| Hardy VA | Booker T. Washington National Monument | 540-721-2094 | 12130 Booker T. Washington H |
| Huntly VA | Rappahannock Cellars Vineyard | 540-635-9398 | 14437 Hume Road |
| Irvington VA | White Fences Vineyard | 804-761-4866 | 170 White Fence Drive |
| Jamestown VA | Historic Jamestown | 757-898-2410 | Colonial Parkway |
| Keswick VA | Keswick Vineyards | 434-244-3341 | 1575 Keswick Winery Drive |
| Leesburg VA | Leesburg Corner Premium Outlets | 703-737-3071 | 241 Fort Evans Road NE |
| Leesburg VA | Tarara Winery | 703-443-9836 | 13648 Tarara Lane |
| Lexington VA | Hull's Drive-In | 540-463-2621 | Rr 5 |
| Lexington VA | Lexington Antique and Craft Mall | 540-463-9511 | 1495 N Lee Hwy/H 11 |
| Lexington VA | Lexington Carriage Company | 540-463-5647 | 106 E Washington Street |
| Manassas VA | Manassas National Battlefield | 703-361-1339 | 6511 Sudley Road |
| Max Meadows VA | Fort Chiswell Outlets | 276-637-6214 | Factory Outlet Drive |
| Middleburg VA | Chrysalis Vineyards | 800-235-8804 | 23876 Champe Ford Rd |
| Mount Vernon VA | Mount Vernon | 703-780-2000 | George Washington Pkwy |
| Natural Bridge VA | Natural Bridge | 540-291-2121 | 15 Appledore Lane |
| Newport News VA | Endview Plantation | 757-887-1862 | 362 Yorktown Road |
| Newport News VA | Mariner's Museum | 757-596-2222 | 100 Museum Drive |
| Norfolk VA | Kayak Adventure Rentals | 757-480-1999 | 110 W Randall Avenue |
| Petersburg VA | Petersburg National Battlefield | 804-732-3531 | 1539 Hickory Hill Drive |
| Pocahontas VA | Pocahontas Exhibition Coal Mine and Museum | 276-945-9522 | Centre Street |
| Portsmouth VA | Portsmouth Olde Towne Walking Tour | 757-393-5111 | 6 Crawford Parkway |
| Purcellville VA | Breaux Vineyards | 540-668-6299 | 36888 Breaux Vineyards Lane |
| Raphine VA | Rockbridge Vineyard | 540-377-6204 | 35 Hillview Lane |

| Reston VA | Reston Town Center | 703-689-4699 | 11900 Market Street |
|---|---|---|---|
| Richmond VA | Hollywood Cemetery | 804-648-8501 | 412 S Cherry Street |
| Richmond VA | Richmond National Battlefield | 804-226-1981 | 470 Tredegar Street |
| Richmond VA | Riverfront District and Canal Walk | 804-788-6466 | N 14th and E Cary Street |
| Richmond VA | Stony Point Fashion Park | 804-560-SHOP | 9200 Stony Point Parkway |
| Richmond VA | The Market Umbrella Markets | | Forest Hill Avenue and 42nd Street |
| Richmond VA | Virginia State Capitol | 804-698-1788 | Bank Street |
| Stafford VA | Potomac Point Winery | 540-446-2266 | 275 Decatur Road |
| Staunton VA | Historic Staunton Guided and Self-Guided Walking Tours | 540-332-3971 | 35 S New Street/H 250 |
| Staunton VA | Woodrow Wilson Library and Birthplace | 540-885-0897 | 18-24 N Coalter Street |
| Stephens City VA | Family Drive-In Theatre | 540-514-6145 | 5890 Valley Pike |
| Tangier Island VA | Tangier Island Buggy Tours | | Tangier Pier |
| Virginia Beach VA | Two Brothers Dog Wash | 757-497-9274 | 426 Newtown Road |
| Waterford VA | 8 Chains North | 571-439-2255 | 38593 Daymont Lane |
| Waterford VA | Waterford Village | 540-882-3018 | Main Street |
| Waynesboro VA | Blue Ridge Parkway Auto Tour | 828-271-4779 | Blue Ridge Parkway, Milepost 0 |
| Waynesboro VA | Blue Ridge Parkway Auto Tour | 828-271-4779 | Blue Ridge Parkway, Milepost 0 |
| Williamsburg VA | Busch Gardens Kennels | 800-343-7946 | 1 Busch Garden Blvd |
| Williamsburg VA | Colonial Williamsburg | | |
| Williamsburg VA | Mini-Golf America | 757-229-7200 | 1901 Richmond Rd |
| Williamsburg VA | Prime Outlets | 757-565-0702 | 5715-62A Richmond Road |
| Williamsburg VA | The College of William and Mary | 757-221-4000 | Grigsby Drive |
| Winchester VA | African-American Heritage Driving Tour | 540-542-1326 | 1360 S Pleasant Valley Road |
| Winchester VA | Battle of Third Winchester Driving Tour | 540-542-1326 | 1360 S Pleasant Valley Road |
| Winchester VA | Deer Meadow Wines | 800-653-6632 | 199 Vintage Lane |
| Winchester VA | Follow the Apple Trail Auto Tour | 540-542-1326 | 1360 S Pleasant Valley Road |
| Winchester VA | Old Town Mall | 877-871-1326 | Loudoun Street |
| Winchester VA | Stonewall Jackson's Headquarters Museum | 540-667-3242 | 415 N Braddock Street/H 522/11 |
| Winchester VA | Washington's Office Museum | 540-662-4412 | 32 W Cork Street |
| Woodford VA | Stonewall Jackson Shrine | 804-633-6076 | 12019 Stonewall Jackson Road/H 606 |
| Yorktown VA | Historic Yorktown | 757-898-2410 | Historical Tour Drive |
| Yorktown VA | Yorktown Riverwalk Landing | 757-890-3300 | Water Street |

## Washington Listings

| Bainbridge Island WA | Bainbridge Island Vineyards | 206-842-9463 | 8989 Day Road East |
|---|---|---|---|
| Ballard WA | Carl English Jr Botanical Garden | 206-783-7059 | 3015 NW 54th Street |
| Bellingham WA | Sehome Hill Arboretum | 360-676-6985 | 25th Street and McDonald Parkway |
| Bellingham WA | Victoria San Juan Cruises | 800-443-4552 | 355 Harris Avenue, Ste 104 |
| Blaine WA | M.V. Plover Ferry | 360-332-5742 | Marine Drive / Blaine Moorage Dock at Gate II |
| Chehalis WA | Chehalis-Centralia Railroad | 360-748-9593 | 1101 Sylvenus Street |
| Chelan WA | Chelan Airways | 509-682-5555 | 1328 West Woodin Ave/H Alt 97 |
| Chelan WA | Lady of the Lake Boat Ride | 888-682-4584 | 1418 W Wooden Avenue/H 97A |
| Chelan WA | The Tour Boat | 509-682-8287 | Lake Chelan Marina |
| Chewelah WA | 49 Degrees North Mountain Resort | 509-935-6049 | 3311 Flowery Trail Road |
| Clarkston WA | Snake Dancer Excursions | 509-758-8927 | 1550 Port Drive, Suite B (Below Roosters Landing) |
| Everson WA | Mt Baker Vineyards | 360-592-2300 | 4298 Mt Baker H |
| Federal Way WA | Marlene's | 253-839-0933 | 2565 S Gateway Center Place |
| Friday Harbor WA | San Juan Island National Historic Park | 360-378-2902 | 125 Spring Street |
| Hoodsport WA | Hoodsport Winery | 360-877-9894 | 23522 N H 101 |
| Kenmore WA | Kenmore Air Seaplanes | 800-543-9595 | 6321 Northeast 175th |
| Kennewick WA | Badger Mountain Vineyard and Powers Winery | 800-643-WINE (9463) | 1106 N Jurupa Street |
| Leavenworth WA | Tube Leavenworth | 509-548-TUBE (8823) | 220 9th St. #104 |
| Newport WA | Bead Lake Trail | 800-832-1355 | Forest Road |
| Ocean Park WA | Willapa Bay Oyster House Interpretive Center | 360-665-4547 | 3311 275th Street |
| Paterson WA | Columbia Crest Winery | 509-875-2061 | Columbia Crest Drive |
| Port Angeles WA | Black Diamond Winery | 360-457-0748 | 2976 Black Diamond Road |
| Port Angeles WA | Harbinger Winery | 360-452-4262 | 2358 H 101W |
| Port Angeles WA | Olympic National Park | 360-565-3130 | 600 East Park Avenue |
| Port Angeles WA | Rite Bros Aviation | 360-452-6226 | 1406 Fairchild International Airport |

| | | | |
|---|---|---|---|
| Port Townsend WA | Puget Sound Express/Point Hudson Marina | 360-385-5288 | 227 Jackson Street |
| Port Townsend WA | Sidewalk Tours | 360-385-1967 | Old City Hall |
| Ruston WA | Fort Nisqually | 253-591-5339 | 5400 N Pearl Street |
| Seattle WA | Ballard Sunday Farmer's Market | 206-851-5100 | Ballard Avenue N between Vernon Place NW & 22nd Avenue NW |
| Seattle WA | Blake Island Adventure Cruise/Tillicum Village | 206-933-8600 | 2992 SW Avalon Way |
| Seattle WA | Broadway Sunday Farmers Market | 206-547-2278 | 10th Avenue E and E Thomas Street |
| Seattle WA | Columbia City Farmers Market | 206-547-2278 | 4801 Rainier Avenue S |
| Seattle WA | Dog Gone Taxi | 888-761-8626 | Throughout City |
| Seattle WA | Emerald Country Carriages | 425-868-0621 | Piers 55-56 |
| Seattle WA | Fun Forest Amusement Park | 206-728-1586 | 305 Harrison Street |
| Seattle WA | Kubota Garden | 206-684-4584 | 9817 55th Avenue S |
| Seattle WA | Lake Washington Ship Canal and Ballard Locks | 206-783-7059 | 3015 NW 54th St. |
| Seattle WA | Magnolia Farmers Market | 206-547-2278 | 2550 34th Avenue W |
| Seattle WA | Pike Place Market | 206-682-7453 | First and Pike |
| Seattle WA | Pioneer Square | | First Street and Yesler Way |
| Seattle WA | Seattle Center | 206-684-7200 | Mercer Street and Broad St. |
| Seattle WA | Seattle Ferry Service | 206-713-8446 | Valley Street and Terry Avenue N |
| Seattle WA | The Center for Wooden Boats | 206-382-2628 | 1010 Valley Street |
| Seattle WA | University Village Shopping Center | 206-447-5744 | 2690 NE University Village |
| Seattle WA | Vancouver Farmers Market | 206-547-2278 | 505 W 8th Street |
| Seattle WA | Washington Park Arboretum | 206-543-8800 | 4300 Arboretum Drive E |
| Seattle WA | Woodland Park Rose Garden | 206-684-4863 | 700 N 50th Street |
| Sequim WA | The Water Limousine | 360-457-4491 | W Sequim Bay Road |
| Snoqualmie WA | Northwest Railway Museum | 425-888-3030 | 38625 SE King Street |
| Union Gap WA | Central Washington Agricultural Museum | 509-457-8735 | 4508 Main Street |
| Vancouver WA | Fort Vancouver National Historic Site | 800-832-3599 | 612 E Reserve St |
| Vancouver WA | Fort Vancouver National Historical Reserve | 360-696-7655 | 1501 E Evergreen Blvd |
| Vancouver WA | McLoughlin House National Historic Site | 800-832-3599 | 612 E Reserve St |
| Vancouver WA | Vancouver Farmers Market | 360-737-8298 | 8th and Ester Streets |
| Vashon WA | Palouse Winery | 206-567-4994 | 12431 Vashon Island Hwy SW |
| Walla Walla WA | Whitman Mission National Historic Site | 509-522-6357 | 328 Whitman Mission Road |
| Yakima WA | McAllister Museum of Aviation | 509-457-4933 | 2008 S 16th Avenue |

**West Virginia Listings**

| | | | |
|---|---|---|---|
| Arthurdale WV | Arthurdale Heritage | 304-864-3959 | H 92 |
| Berkeley Springs WV | Berkeley Springs Walking Tour | 800-447-8797 | 127 Fairfax Street |
| Berkeley Springs WV | Washington Heritage Trail | 800-447-8797 | 127 Fairfax Street (Visitor Center) |
| Crab Orchard WV | Daniel Vineyards | 304-252-9750 | 200 Twin Oaks Road |
| Harpers Ferry WV | Appalachian National Scenic Trail | 304-535-6278 | Harpers Ferry Center |
| Harpers Ferry WV | Appalachian Trail in West Virginia | 304-535-6331 | Off Sandy Hook Road |
| Harpers Ferry WV | Ghost Tours of Harpers Ferry | 304-725-8019 | 175 High Street |
| Harpers Ferry WV | Harpers Ferry National Historical Park | 304-535-6029 | P.O. Box 65 |
| Harpers Ferry WV | O' Be JoyFull" Historical Tours & Entertainment | 732-801-0381 | 175 High Street |
| Lewisburg WV | Historic Downtown Lewisburg | 304-645-4333 | 209 W Washington Street |
| Summersville WV | The Kirkwood Winery | 888-4WV-WINE (498-9463) | 45 Winery Lane/Phillips Run Road |

**Wisconsin Listings**

| | | | |
|---|---|---|---|
| Alma WI | Fun'N the Sun Houseboat Rentals | 888-343-5670 | S2221 H 35 |
| Baileys Harbor WI | Lynn's Fishing Charter | 920-854-5109 | Ridges Road |
| Baraboo WI | Mirror Lake Rentals | 608-254-4104 | E10320 Fern Dell Road |
| Baraboo WI | Tanger Outlet Center | 608-253-5380 | 210 Gasser Road |
| Bayside WI | Community Bark | 414-DOG-WASH (364-9274) | 326 W Brown Deer Road/H 32 |
| Beloit WI | Beloit River Walk | 608-364-2929 | Riverside Drive |
| Bristol WI | Pringle Nature Center | 262-857-8008 | 9800 160th Avenue/H MB |
| Chetek WI | Stardust Drive-In Theater | 715-458-4587 | 995 22nd St |

| | | | |
|---|---|---|---|
| Cochrane WI | Prairie Moon Garden and Museum | 608-687-9511 | S2727 Prairie Mood Road |
| Door County WI | The Salmon Depot Charter Fishing | 800-345-6701 | Box 141, Billy's Harbor |
| Ephraim WI | Stiletto Sailing Cruises | 920-854-7245 | 9993 H 42 |
| Fish Creek WI | Classic Boat Tours of Door County | 920-421-2080 | 9145 Spring Road |
| Fish Creek WI | Lautenbach's Orchard Country | 920-868-3479 | 9197 H 42 |
| Gillsrock WI | Island Clipper | 920-854-2972 | 12731 H 42 |
| Green Bay WI | Fox River Trail | 920-448-4466 | Porlier and Adams Streets |
| Jacksonport WI | Simon Creek Vineyard and Winery | 920-746-9307 | 5896 Bochek Road |
| La Pointe WI | Bog Lake Outfitters | 715-747-2685 | 2848 School House Road |
| La Pointe WI | Madeline Island Ferry | 715-747-2051 | 100 Main Street |
| Lac du Flambeau WI | Waswagoning Indian Village | 715-588-3560 | H 47 |
| Lake Delton WI | Lost Canyon Horse Carriage Tours | 608-254-8757 | 720 Canyon Road |
| Madison WI | State Street Shopping Area | 800-373-6376 | State Street |
| Madison WI | University of Wisconsin Botanical Garden | 608-263-2400 | University Avenue |
| Madison WI | University of Wisconsin Campus | 608-263-2400 | 21 N Park Street |
| Madison WI | Wiconsin State Capitol Grounds | 608-266-0382 | 2 E Main Street |
| Marshfield WI | Jusrustic park | http://www.jurustic.com/ | M222 Sugar Bush Lane |
| Milwaukee WI | Blue Max Charters | 414-828-1094 | 740 N Plankinton |
| Milwaukee WI | Henry Aaron State Trail | 414-263-8559 | 2300 N Martin Luthur King Jr Drive (Dept.of Natural Resources) |
| Milwaukee WI | Historic Third Ward District | 414-287-4100 | North Milwaukee Street/H 32 |
| Milwaukee WI | Milwaukee Boat Line | 414-294-9450 | 505 N RiverWalk Way |
| Milwaukee WI | Movies Under the Stars | 414-276-6696 | North Old World 3rd Street |
| Milwaukee WI | Riverwalk | 414-287-4100 | Riverwalk Row (several connecting streets) |
| New Glarus WI | Swiss Village Museum | 608-527-2317 | 612 7th Avenue |
| New Munster WI | New Munster Wildlife Area | 888-WDNRINFo (1-888-936-7463) | 34315 Geneva Road |
| North Freedom WI | Mid-Continent Railway Museum | 608-522-4261 | E8948 Diamond Hill Road |
| Pleasant Prairie WI | Prime Outlets | 262-857-2101 | 11211 120th Avenue |
| Prairie Du Sac WI | Wollersheim Winery | 800-VIP-WINE (847-9463) | 7876 H 188 |
| Racine WI | River Bend Nature Center | 262-639-0930 | 3600 N Green Bay Road |
| Sister Bay WI | Shoreline Charters at Sister Bay Village Marina | 920-854-4707 | 12747 H 42 |
| Sturgeon Bay WI | Boat Door County | 920-743-2337 | 3662 N Duluth Avenue |
| Sturgeon Bay WI | Boat Door County | 800-231-5767 | 1627 Memorial Dr |
| Sturgeon Bay WI | Door Peninsula Winery | 920-743-7431 | 5608 H 42 |
| Sturgeon Bay WI | Snug Harbor Inn and Marina | 920-743-2337 | 1627 Memorial Drive |
| Sturgeon Bay WI | The Chicago Fireboat-Legend Cruises, LLC | 920-495-6454 | 120 N Madison Avenue |
| Sturgeon Bay WI | The Chicago Fireboat-Legend Cruises, LLC | 920-495-6454 | 120 N Madison Avenue |
| Washington Island WI | Rock Island Ferry | 920-847-3322 | Jackson Harbor Road |
| Washington Island WI | Washington Island Ferry | 800-223-2094 | Northport Pier |
| Wisconsin Dells WI | Dells Army Ducks | 608-254-6080 | 1550 Wisconsin Dells Parkway |
| Wisconsin Dells WI | Dells Boat Tours | 608-254-8555 | 1890 Wisconsin Dells Parkway |
| Wisconsin Dells WI | Dells Mining Company | 608-253-7002 | 1480 Wisconsin Dells Parkway/H 12/23 |
| Wisconsin Dells WI | Original Wisconsin Ducks | 608-254-8751 | 1890 Wisconsin Dells Parkway |

**Wyoming Listings**

| | | | |
|---|---|---|---|
| Banner WY | Fort Phil Kearny State Historic Site | 307-684-7629 | 528 Wagon Box Road |
| Casper WY | Casper Downtown Shopping District | 800-852-1889 | 992 N Poplar Street (Visitor Bureau) |
| Casper WY | Casper Walking Tours and Ghost Tours | 307-267-7243 | 330 S Center Suite 414 |
| Casper WY | Fort Caspar Museum | 307-235-8462 | 4001 Fort Caspar Road |
| Casper WY | Platte River Parkway | 307-577-7162 | P.O Box 1228 |
| Cheyenne WY | Capitol City Cab | 307-632-8294 | 2504 E 7th Street |
| Cheyenne WY | Cheyenne Botanic Gardens | 307-637-6458 | 710 S Lions Park Drive |
| Cheyenne WY | Cheyenne Street Railway Trolley | 800-426-5009 | 121 W 15th Street |
| Cheyenne WY | Cheyenne Taxi Service | 307-638-4530 | 2504 E 8th Street |
| Cheyenne WY | Historic Downtown Walking Tour | 307-778-3133 | 121 W 15th Street |
| Cody WY | Cody Trolley Tours | 307-527-7043 | Corner of 12th Street and Sheridan Ave |
| Cody WY | Paul Stock Nature Trail | 307-587-0400 | 801 Spruce Drive |

| | | | |
|---|---|---|---|
| Cody WY | River Runners of Wyoming | 307-527-7238 | 1491 Sheridan Avenue/H 14/16/20 |
| Evansville WY | Independence Rock State Historic Site | 307-577-5150 | Milepost 63 H 220 |
| Fort Bridger WY | Fort Bridger State Historic Site | 307-782-3842 | 37000 Business Loop I 80 |
| Fort Laramie WY | Fort Laramie National Historic Site | 307-837-2221 | 965 Gray Rocks Road |
| Glendo WY | Hall's Glendo Marina | 307-735-4216 | 383 Glendo Park Road |
| Green River WY | Buckboard Marina | 307-875-6927 | H 530/Flaming Gorge Lake (HCR 65, Box 100) |
| Guernsey WY | Oregon Trail Ruts and Register Cliff | 307-777-6323 | S Wyoming Avenue |
| Jackson WY | Amaze'n Jackson Hole | 307-734-0455 | 85 Snow King Ave |
| Jackson WY | Gaper Guide | 307-733-4626 | 145 W Gill Avenue |
| Jackson WY | National Elk Refuge | 307-733-9212 | 532 N Cache Street (Visitor Center)/H 26/89/191 |
| Jackson Hole WY | Wild West Jeep Tours | 307-733-9036 | P.O. Box 7506 |
| Kemmerer WY | Fossil Butte National Monument | 307-877-4455 | 864 Chicken Creek Road |
| Laramie WY | Ames Monument | 307-777-6323 | Monument Road |
| Laramie WY | Snowy Range Scenic Byway | 307-745-2300 | H 130 |
| Laramie WY | University Of Wyoming Campus | 307-766-1121 | 1000 E University Avenue |
| Laramie WY | Wyoming Territorial Prison | 307-745-6161 | 975 Snowy Range Road |
| Lovell WY | Medicine Wheel National Historic Landmark | 307-548-6541 | Forest Road |
| Lovell WY | Yellowtail Wildlife Habitat Management Area | 307-527-7125 | H 14/16/20 |
| Lusk WY | Historic Hat Creek Stage Station | 307-334-2950 | H 85 |
| Pine Bluffs WY | University of Wyoming Archaeological Dig Site | 307-245-3695 | Muddy Creek Drive |
| Pinedale WY | Museum of the Mountain Man | 307-367-4101 | 700 E Hennick Street |
| Rawlins WY | Wyoming Frontier Prison Museum | 307-324-4422 | 500 W Walnut Street |
| Rock Springs WY | Pilot Butte Wild Horse Scenic Loop | 307-352-0256 | County Road 53 north of Rock Springs |
| Sheridan WY | Trail End State Historic Site | 307-674-4589 | 400 Clarendon Avenue |
| South Pass WY | South Pass City State Historic Site | 307-332-3684 | 125 South Pass Main |

# Canada

## Alberta Listings

| | | | |
|---|---|---|---|
| Calgary AB | Calaway Amusement Park Kennel | 403-290-1875 | 245033 Range Road 33 |
| Calgary AB | Calgary Downtown Walking Tour (including Stephen Ave) | 403-215-1570 | 320 8th Avenue SE, Suite 720 (Calgary Downtown Association) |
| Calgary AB | Calgary Transit | Call Center: 403-262-1000 | Varied routes |
| Calgary AB | Eau Claire Festival Market | 403-264-6450 | 200 Barclay Parade SW |
| Calgary AB | Fort Calgary Historic Park | 403-290-1875 | 750 9th Avenue SE |
| Calgary AB | Kensington Village | 403-215-1570 | 10th Street NW |
| Calgary AB | Uptown 17th Shopping Center | 403-245-1703 | 17th Avenue SW |
| Edmonton AB | Downtown Walking Tours | 780-424-4085 | 9990 Jasper Avenue (World Trade Centre street front office) |
| Edmonton AB | South Edmonton Common | 780-466-2221 | 10180 111th Street |
| Fort McMurray AB | MacDonald Island Park | 888-281-MIPS (6477) | 1 C.A. Knight Way |
| Jasper AB | Athabasca Glacier | 780-852-6176 | H 93 |
| Jasper AB | Jasper Carriage Company | 780-852-RIDE (7433) | P.O. Box 1200 |
| Jasper AB | Jasper Tramway | 866-850-8726 (TRAM) | Box 418 |
| Lethbridge AB | Fort Whoop-up Interpretive Centre | 403-329-0444 | P. O. Box 1074 |
| Longview AB | Bar U Ranch National Historic Site | 403-395-2212 | H 22, Foothills # 31 |
| Nanton AB | Big Sky Garden Railway | 403-646-1190 | 2121 18th Street |
| Nanton AB | The Nanton Lancaster Society Air Museum | 403-646-2270 | H 2 Southbound at 17th Street |
| Skagway AB | Chilkoot Trail National Historic Site of Canada | 800-661-0486 | Dyea Road |
| Wetaskiwin AB | Reynolds-Alberta Museum | 780-361-1351 | H 13W (P.O. Box 6360) |

## British Columbia Listings

| | | | |
|---|---|---|---|
| 108 Mile House BC | 108 Mile House Heritage Site | 250-791-5288 | 4690 Telqua Drive |
| Abbotsford BC | Trethewey House Heritage Museum | 604-853-0313 | 2313 Ware Street |
| Boston Bar BC | Hell's Gate Airtram | 604-867-9277 | 43111 Trans Canada Highway |
| Boston Bar BC | Hell's Gate Airtram | 604-867-9277 | 43111 Trans Canada Highway |
| Campbell River BC | Northwest Seaplanes | 800-690-0086 | 3050 Spit Road |
| Clinton BC | South Cariboo Historical Museum | 250-459-2442 | 1419 Cariboo H |
| Dawson Creek BC | Alaska Highway Mile Zero Sign | 250-782-9595 | 900 Alaska Hwy |
| Fort Nelson BC | Fort Nelson Heritage Museum | 250-774-3536 | Mile 300 Alaska H |
| Fort St John BC | Heritage Kiosk Walking Tour | 250-785-3033 | 9523 100th Street (Ft St John Visitor Center) |
| Fort Steele BC | Fort Steele | 250-417-6000 | 9851 H 93/95 |
| Fort Steele BC | Fort Steele Heritage Town | 250-417-6000 | 9851 H 93/95 |
| Golden BC | Golden Farmers' Market | 250-344-5678 | 10 Avenue N/H 95 |
| Langley BC | Ft Langley Village Farmers' Market | 604-728-2080 | 23433 Mavis Avenue |
| Mount Washington BC | Mount Washington Alpine Resort | 250-338-1515 | 1 Strathcona Parkway |
| North Vancouver BC | Capilano Suspension Bridge and Park | 604-985-7474 | 3735 Capilano Road |
| Osoyoos BC | Nk'Mip Cellars | 250-495-2985 | 1400 Rancher Creek Road |
| Port Hardy BC | Sea Legend Water Taxi Services | 250-949-6541 | Hardy Bay Road |
| Prince George BC | Railway and Forestry Museum | 250-563-7351 | 850 River Road |
| Prince Rupert BC | Skeena Kayaking Rentals and Tours | 250-624-4393 | 1534 11th Ave East |
| Rosedale BC | Minter Gardens | 604-794-7191 | 52892 Bunker Road |
| Sidney BC | The British Columbia Aviation Museum | 250-655-3300 | 1910 Norseman Road |
| Tofino BC | Tofino Sea-Kayaking Co | 250-725-4222 | 320 Main Street |
| Vancouver BC | AquaBus Ferries | 604-689-5858 | 230-1333 Johnston Street/Granville Island |
| Vancouver BC | Granville Island | 604-666-6655 | |
| Vancouver BC | Historic Gastown | 604-683-5650 | Water Street |
| Vancouver BC | Historic Gastown Guided Walking Tours | 604-683-5650 | Water and Carrall Streets |
| Vancouver BC | Main Street Station Farmers Market | 604-879-FARM (3276) | Main Street between Terminal and National Avenues |
| Vancouver BC | Sam Kee Building | | Pender Street |
| Vancouver BC | Vancouver Winter Farmers' Market | 604-879-FARM (3276) | E 30th Avenue and Ontario Street/Nat Bailey Stadium |
| Vancouver Island BC | The Butchart Gardens | | |
| Victoria BC | Adam's Fishing Charters | 250-370-2326 | Wharf Street |
| Victoria BC | Alcheringa Gallery | 250-383-8224 | 665 Fort Street |
| Victoria BC | Discover the Past Walking Tours | 250-384-6698 | 812 Wharf Street |
| Victoria BC | Grandpas Antique Photo Studio | 250-920-3800 | 1252 Wharf Street |
| Victoria BC | Great Pacific Adventures | 250-386-2277 | 450 Swift Street |
| Victoria BC | Kabuki Kabs | 250-385-4243 | 526 Discovery Street |
| Victoria BC | Ocean River Sports | 250-381-4233 | 1824 Store Street |
| Victoria BC | Tally Ho Horse and Carriage | 866-383-5067 | Belleville and Menzies Streets |
| Victoria BC | Victoria Carriage Tours | 250-383-2207 | Menzies and Belleville Street |
| Victoria BC | Victoria Harbour Ferry and Tours | 250-708-0201 | 1234-N Wharf Street |
| Whistler BC | Whistler Village | 800-WHISTLER (944-7853) | Village Stroll |

## Manitoba Listings

| | | | |
|---|---|---|---|
| Brandon MB | Assiniboine Riverbank Trail System | 204-729-2141 | #1-545 Conservation Drive/Riverbank Discovery Center |
| Brandon MB | Eleanor Kidd Gardens | 204-729-2141 | 18th Street N/H 10 and John Avenue |
| Brandon MB | Manitoba Agricultural Hall Of Fame | 204-728-3736 | 1129 Queens Avenue |
| Steinbach MB | Mennonite Heritage Village | 204-326-9661 | H 12N |
| Winnipeg MB | Assiniboine Park and the Leo Mol Sculpture Garden | 204-986-5717 | 460 Assiniboine Park Drive |
| Winnipeg MB | Cityplace | 204 989-1817 | 333 St Mary Avenue at Hargrave Street |
| Winnipeg MB | Exchange District | 204-942-6716 | Main Street |
| Winnipeg MB | Exchange District Guided Walking Tours | 204-942-6716 | King Street and Bannatyne Avenue |
| Winnipeg MB | Historic District of St Boniface | 866-808-8338 | Provencher Blvd/H 57 and surrounding streets |
| Winnipeg MB | Splash Dash Boats | 204-783-6633 | 1 Forks Market Road |

## New Brunswick Listings

| | | | |
|---|---|---|---|
| Fredericton NB | Guided Heritage Walking Tours | 506-460-2129 | 397 Queen Street |
| Fredericton NB | Haunted Hike | 506-457-1975 | 745 George Street |
| Fredericton NB | Historic Garrison District | 506-460-2041 | 457 Queen Street |
| Fredericton NB | Time Travel Tours | 506-460-2129 | 397 Queen Street |
| Hampton NB | Osprey Adventures | 506-832-6025 | 1075 Main Street/Lighthouse Park River Center |
| Hampton NB | Zelda's River Adventures | 506-653-0726 | 55 Randall Drive |
| Hartland NB | Hartland Covered Bridge | 506-375-4357 | H 2 between H 105 and H 103 |
| Hopewell Cape NB | Hopewell Rocks | 877-734-3429 | 131 Discovery Road |
| Moncton NB | Wharf Village Shoppes and Restaurant | 506-858-8841 | 50 Magic Blvd |
| Richmond Corner NB | Maliseet Trail | 800-526-7070 | 109 Tourist Bureau Road |
| St Edouard de Kent NB | Irving Eco-Centre - La Dune de Bouctouche | 506-743-2600 | 1932 H 475 |
| St John NB | Carleton Martello Tower National Historic Site of Canada | 506-636-4011 | 454 Whipple Street |
| St John NB | Gibson Creek Canoeing | 506-672-8964 | 821 Anderson Drive |
| St John NB | Irving Nature Park | 506-653-7367 | Sand Cove Road |
| St John NB | Reversing Falls Visitor Information Centre | 506-658-2937 | 200 Bridge Road/H 100 (Visitor Information Centre) |
| St John NB | Rockwood Park Stables | 506-633-7659 | PO Box 686 Stn Main |
| St John NB | Turn of the Century Trolley Tours | 506-633-7659 | |
| St John NB | Walking Tour of Old Saint John | 866-463-8639 | 15 Market Square |
| Woodstock NB | Woodstock Walking Tour | 506-328-9706 | 679 Main Street |

## Newfoundland Listings

| | | | |
|---|---|---|---|
| Bishop's Falls NF | Bishop's Falls Trestle | 709-258-2228 | |
| Bishop's Falls NF | Jiggs' Fun Farm | 709-258-5229 | H 350 |
| Fleur de Lys NF | Dorset Soapstone Quarry National Historic Site | 709-253-2126 | H 410/Baie Verte Peninsula |
| Fleur de Lys NF | Fleur de Lys Trails | 709-253-2126 | H 410/Baie Verte Peninsula |
| Gander NF | North Atlantic Aviation Museum | 709-256-2923 | H 135 |
| St Johns NF | Bowring Park | 709-576-8601 | 305 Waterford Bridge Road |
| St Johns NF | Dee Jay Charters | 709-753-8687 (in season) 709-726-2141 (all year) | Harbour Drive |

## Nova Scotia Listings

| | | | |
|---|---|---|---|
| Bear River NS | Bear River Vineyards | 902-467-4156 | 133 Chute Road |
| Canning NS | Blomidon Estate Winery | 902-582-7565 | 10318 H 221 |
| Dartmouth NS | Dartmouth Heritage Walk | 902-490-4000 | Alderney Drive |
| Halifax NS | Halifax Citadel National Historic Site | 902-426-5080 | 5425 Sackeille |
| Halifax NS | Tall Ship Silva | 902-429-9463 | Lower Water Street/H 102 |
| Hubbards NS | Peers' Fancy Sailing Charters | 902-476-4437 | St Margaret's Bay Rd |
| Lower West Pubnico NS | Nova Scotia Historic Acadian Village | 902-762-2530 | Old Church Road |
| Port Maitland NS | Port Maitland Provincial Beach Park | 800-565-0000 | 3297 Main Shore Road |
| Port Maitland NS | Tight Lines Guide Service | 902-649-2428 | Box 44 |
| Sydney NS | Smart Shop Place | 902-564-5777 | 314 Charles Street |
| Yarmouth NS | Deep Sea Fishing Charters | 902-742-2713 | R.R.#5, Box 2003 |

## Ontario Listings

| | | | |
|---|---|---|---|
| Amherstburg ON | Fort Malden National Historic Site | 519-736-5416 | 100 Laird Avenue |
| Belle River ON | Captain Dan Charters | 519-982-8934 | Lake Street |
| Bracebridge ON | Muskoka Rails Museum | 705-646-9711 | 14 Gray Road |
| Burlington ON | Royal Botanical Gardens | 905-527-1158 | 680 Plains Road W |
| Gananoque ON | 1000 Islands Kayaking Company | 613-329-6265 | P. O. Box 166 |
| Gananoque ON | Houseboat Holidays | 613-382-2842 | RR 3 |
| Gravenhurst ON | Swift Canoe and Kayak | 800-661-1429 | 2394 H 11N |
| Hamilton ON | Dundurn Castle | 905-546-2872 | 610 York Blvd |
| Hamilton ON | Hamilton Museum of Steam and Technology | 905-546-4797 | 900 Woodward Avenue |

| | | | |
|---|---|---|---|
| Kingston ON | Kingston Public Market and Craft Fair | 613-546-49291 | 216 Ontario Street |
| Kingston ON | Kingston's Waterfront Pathway | 613-546-0000 | E King Street |
| Kingston ON | Portsmouth Village | 613-546-0000 | King Street and surrounding streets |
| Kingston ON | Wolfe Island Ferry Service | 613-548-7227 | Ontario and Barrack Streets |
| Kingsville ON | Mastronardi Estate Winery | 519-733-9463 | 1193 Concession 3 E |
| Kingsville ON | Pelee Island Winery | 519-724-2469 | 455 Seacliff Drive/ H 20 |
| LaSalle ON | Windsor Crossing Premium Outlets | 519-972-7111 | 1555 Talbot Road/H 3 |
| Landsdowne ON | 1000 Islands Boat Tours | 613-659-3350 | 574 1000 Islands Parkway |
| Leamington ON | Pelee Island Ferry | 800-661-2220 | 500 Erie Street |
| London ON | Fanshawe Pioneer Village | 519-457-1296 | 1424 Clarke Road |
| London ON | Springbank Park | 519-661-5575 | 929 Springbank Drive |
| Morrisburg ON | Upper Canada Village | 613-543-4328 | 13740 H 2 |
| Niagara Falls ON | Niagara Falls | 800-563-2557 | off Queen Elizabeth Way |
| Niagara on the Lake ON | Konzelmann Estate Winery | 905-935-2866 | 1096 Lakeshore Road, RR#3 |
| Niagara-on-the-Lake ON | Marynissen Estates | 905-468-7270 | 1209 Concession 1, RR #6 |
| Ottawa ON | Parliament Hill | 613-992-4793 | Parliament Hill |
| Ottawa ON | Rideau Canal and Trail | 613-239-5234 | 90 Wellington Street |
| Ottawa ON | Stony Swamp Conservation Area | 613-239-5000 | Hunt Club Road |
| Parry Sound ON | Georgian Nordic Ski and Canoe Club | 705-746-5067 | 9 Mile Bay Road |
| Portland ON | Bayview Yacht Harbour | 613-272-2787 | 2785 H 15 |
| Portland ON | Big Rideau Lake Boat Rentals | 613-880-9288 | 15 Water Street |
| Portland ON | Len's Cove Marina | 613-272-2581 | 1 Water Street |
| Renfrew ON | Storyland | 613-432-2222 | 793 Storyland Road |
| Sault Ste. Marie ON | Sault Ste. Marie Canal National Historic Site | 705-941-6262 | 1 Canal Drive |
| Tobermory ON | Chi-Cheemaun Ferry/Tobermory Terminal | 519 596 2510 | 8 Eliza Street |
| Toronto ON | Black Creek Pioneer Village | 416-736-1733 | 1000 Murray Ross Parkway |
| Toronto ON | Centreville Amusement Park | 416-203-0405 | Centre Island |
| Toronto ON | City Walks Guided Tours | 416-966-1550 | Call to arrange. |
| Toronto ON | Great Lakes Schooner Company | 416-203-2322 | Queen's Quay |
| Toronto ON | Harbourfront Centre | 416-973-3000 | York and John Quays |
| Toronto ON | PawsWay | 416-360-PAWS (7297) | 245 Queens Quay, North Building |
| Toronto ON | Toronto Islands Park | 416-392-8186 | |
| Vineland ON | Vineland Estates Winery | 888-VINELAND (846-3526) | 3996 Moyer Road |
| Virgil ON | Hillebrand Estates Winery | 905-468-7123 | 1249 Niagara Stone Road/H 55 |

**Prince Edward Island Listings**

| | | | |
|---|---|---|---|
| Cavendish PE | Green Gables Heritage Site | 902-963-7874 | 8619 H 6 |
| Charlottetown PE | Northumberland Ferries Ltd. | 877-635-SAIL (7245) | 94 Water Street, Box 634 |
| Charlottetown PE | Prince Edward Air Ltd. | 902-566-4488 | 250 Brackley Point Road |

**Quebec Listings**

| | | | |
|---|---|---|---|
| Beauport PQ | Parc de la Chute-Montmorency | 418-663-3330 | 2490, avenue Royale |
| Montreal PQ | Caleche Andre Boisrt | 450-653-0751 | St Lawrence Blvd at De La Commune |
| Montreal PQ | Caleche Lucky Luc | 514-934-6105 | |
| Montreal PQ | Circuit des Fantoms du Vieux Ghost Tours | 514-868-0303 | 469 Francis Xavier |
| Montreal PQ | Lachine Canal National Historic Site | 514-283-6054 | East to West across Montreal |
| Montreal PQ | Place Jacques Cartier and Vieux Montreal | | Rue St-Paul E at Place Jacques Cartier |
| Montreal PQ | Tours Kaleidoscope | 514-990-1872 | 6592, Chateaubriand |
| Pointe-Claire PQ | Geordie Charters | 514-695-2552 | 20 Westwood Drive Pointe-Claire |
| Quebec PQ | Association des guides touristiques de Quebec | 418-624-2851 | |
| Quebec PQ | CSA Historical Walking Tour | 418-692-3033 | 4, rue Toussaint |
| Quebec PQ | Fortifications of Québec National Historic Site | 418-648-7016 | 100 Saint-Louis St. |
| Quebec PQ | Horse and Carriage Tours | 418-683-9222 | Place d'Armes or rue d'Auteuil |
| Quebec PQ | Le Promenade des Ecrivains (Writer's Walking Tour) | 418-264-2772 | 1588, avenue Bergemont |
| Quebec PQ | Le Promenades du Vieux-Quebec | 418-692-6000 | 43, rue De Buade |

| Quebec PQ | Parc Nautique de Cap-Rouge Boat Rentals | 418-641-6148 | 4155, chemin de la Plage-Jacques-Cartier |
|---|---|---|---|
| Quebec PQ | Quebec - Levis Ferry | 418-644-3704 | Rue Dalhousie, Lower Town |
| Quebec PQ | Rue du Tresor Open Air Artist District | 418-259-7453 | Rue du Tresor |
| Quebec PQ | Voir Quebec Walking Tours | 418-694-2001 | 12, rue Ste-Anne |
| Quebec City PQ | Ghost Tours of Quebec | 418-692-9770 | 85, rue St-Louis |
| St-Joseph-du-Lac PQ | La Roche des brises Vineyard | 450-472-2722 | 2007, rue Principale |
| Val-David PQ | Santa Claus Village | 819-322-2146 | 987 Marin |

**Saskatchewan Listings**

| Battleford SK | Fort Battleford National Historic Site | 306-937-2621 | 13th Street and Central Avenue |
|---|---|---|---|
| Lumsden SK | Corn Maiden Market at Lincoln Gardens | 306-731-3133 | On H 20 between Lumsden and Craven |
| Maple Creek SK | Fort Walsh National Historic Site | 306-662-2645 | H 271 (PO Box 278) |
| Rosthern SK | Batoche National Historic Site | 306-423-6227 | H 225 |
| Rosthern SK | Seager Wheeler National Historic Site | 306-232-5959 | Seager Wheeler Road |
| Saskatoon SK | Berry Barn | 306-978-9797 | 830 Valley Rd |
| Saskatoon SK | Wanuskewin Heritage Park | 306-931-6767 | RR4 Penner Road |

**Yukon Listings**

| Dawson City YU | Dawson City Yukon River Trail | 867-993-5575 | |
|---|---|---|---|
| Dawson City YU | Jack London Cabin and Interpretive Museum | 867-993-5575 | 8th Avenue and Firth Street |
| Faro YU | Dena Cho Trail | 867-994-2728 | Campbell Street (Campbell Region Interpretive Centre) |
| Haines YU | Alaska Chilkat Bald Eagle Preserve | 907-465-4563 | Haines H/H 7 |
| Klukshu YU | Klukshu Village | 867-634-7279 | Haines H/H 3 |
| Ross River YU | Canol Footbridge | | Canol Road |
| Watson Lake YU | Signpost Forest | | |
| Whitehorse YU | Whitehorse Fishway | 867-633-5965 | Nisutlin Drive |
| Whitehorse YU | Yukon Conservation Society Guided Nature Walks | 867-668-5678 | 302 Hawkins Street |

Chapter 6

# Dog-Friendly Outdoor Dining

Dog-Friendly Outdoor Dining - Please always call ahead to make sure an establishment is still dog-friendly

## Alabama Listings

| | | | |
|---|---|---|---|
| Auburn AL | Ariccia | 334-821-8200 | 241 S College Street |
| Auburn AL | Smoothie King | 334-887-1882 | 1499 S College Street, # A |
| Birmingham AL | Chipotle | 205-982-4833 | 1759 Montgomery H S/H 3/31 |
| Birmingham AL | Chipotle | 205-991-4846 | 4719 H 280 S |
| Birmingham AL | Jason's Deli | 205-877-8477 | 583 Brookwood Village |
| Birmingham AL | Johnny Rockets | 205-298-0700 | 331 Summit Blvd |
| Birmingham AL | Organic Harvest Market and Cafe | 205-978-0318 | 1580 Montgomery Hwy/H 31 |
| Birmingham AL | The Cantina | 205-323-6980 | 2901 Second Avenue S |
| Daphne AL | Moe's Original BBQ | 251-625-7427 | 6423 Park Dr |
| Fairhope AL | Fairhope Restaurant | 251-928-6226 | 62 S Church Street |
| Fairhope AL | Original Ben's Jr. | 251-928-1211 | 552 N Section Street/H 98 |
| Fairhope AL | Panini Pete's Cafe and Bakeshoppe | 251-929-0122 | 42 1/2 South Section Street, Suite 2/H 3 |
| Fayetteville AL | Ozark Natural Foods and Deli | 479-521-7558 | 1554 N College Avenue/H 71/180 |
| Hoover AL | Cajun Steamer | 205-985-7785 | 180 Main Street |
| Hoover AL | Jason's Deli | 205-987-8740 | 3032 John Hawkins Parkway/H 150 |
| Huntsville AL | Bandito Burrito | 256-534-0866 | 3017 Governors Drive SW |
| Huntsville AL | Jason's Deli | 256-883-7300 | 4800 Whitesburg Drive Suite 4 |
| Huntsville AL | Jason's Deli | 256-971-5325 | 1395 Enterprise Way |
| Huntsville AL | Stanlieo's Sub Villa | 256-837-7220 | 605 Jordan Lane |
| Mobile AL | Callaghan's Irish Social Club | 251-433-9374 | 916 Charleston Street |
| Mobile AL | Panera Bread | 251-342-5101 | 3691 Airport Blvd # D |
| Mobile AL | Panera Bread | 251-634-9604 | 750 Schillinger Road S |
| Mobile AL | Tropical Smoothie Cafe | 251-378-5648 | 9 Du Rhu Drive |
| Mobile AL | Tropical Smoothie Cafe | 251-634-3454 | 570 Schillinger Road S |
| Mobile AL | True Midtown Kitchen | 251-433-2253 | 1104 Dauphin Street |
| Montgomery AL | Jason's Deli | 334-409-9890 | 1520 Eastern Blvd, #12 /H 8/53/80 |
| Orange Beach AL | Cosmos Restaurant and Bar | 251-948-WOOF (9663) | 25753 Canal Road/H 180 |
| Prattville AL | Tropical Smoothie Cafe | 334-285-4545 | 2790 Legends Parkway |
| Troy AL | Sonic | 334-807-0011 | 1140 Hwy 231 South |
| Tuscaloosa AL | Chipotle - University of Alabama | 205-391-0140 | 1800 McFarland Blvd, Suite 608/H 6/82 |
| Tuscaloosa AL | Jason's Deli | 205-752-6192 | 2300 E McFarland Blvd, Suite 10 /H 6/82 |
| Tuscaloosa AL | Smoothie King | 205-462-3664 | 1403 University Blvd, Suite 1 |

## Alaska Listings

| | | | |
|---|---|---|---|
| Anchorage AK | Artic Roadrunner | 907-561-1245 | 5300 Old Sewar H |
| Anchorage AK | Great Harvest Bread Co. | 907-274-3331 | 570 E Benson Blvd |
| Anchorage AK | L'Aroma Bakery and Deli | 907-274-9797 | 900 W 13th Avenue |
| Anchorage AK | L'aroma | 907-336-5704 | 9900 Old Seward H |
| Anchorage AK | Middleway Cafe | 907-272-6433 | 1200 W Northern Lights Blvd |
| Anchorage AK | New Sagayaas City Market | 907-274-6173 | 900 W 13th Avenue |
| Anchorage AK | Pizza Olympia | 907-561-5264 | 2809 Spenard Rd |
| Anchorage AK | Spenard's Roadhouse | 907-770-7623 | 1049 W Northern Lights Blvd |
| Anchorage AK | Yes Bistro | 907-258-1113 | 3801 Debarr Road |
| Chicken AK | Chicken Creek Outpost and Cafe | 520-413-1480 (internet phone -Skype) | Chicken Loop Rd |
| Douglas AK | The Island Pub | 907-364-1595 | 1102 2nd Street |
| Fairbanks AK | C and J Drive In | 907-452-3159 | 2233 S Cushman Street |
| Fairbanks AK | Gambardella's Pasta Bella | 907-456-3417 | 706 2nd Avenue |
| Girdwood AK | Coast Pizzeria | 907-783-0122 | Corner of Alyeska and Seward H |
| Girdwood AK | Jack Sprat | 907-783-5225(JACK) | 165 Olympic Mountain Loop |
| Haines AK | Mountain Market & Cafe | 907-766-3340 | 151 3rd Ave Haines Hwy |

| Halibut Cove AK | The Saltry | 907-399-2683 | Docking Station |
| Homer AK | Cosmic Kitchen | 907-235-6355 | 510 E Pioneer Avenue |
| Homer AK | Fresh Sourdough Express Bakery and Cafe | 907-235-7571 | 1316 Ocean Drive |
| Homer AK | Two Sisters Bakery | 907-235-2280 | 233 E Bunnell Avenue |
| Juneau AK | Silverbow Inn and Bakery | 907-586-4146 | 120 2nd Street |
| Juneau AK | Twisted Fish Company | 907-463-5033 | 550 S Franklin Street |
| Ketchikan AK | Burger Queen | 907-225-6060 | 518 Water Street/H7 |
| Ketchikan AK | Ocean View Restaurant | 907-225-7566 | 3159 Tongass Avenue/H 7 |

**Arizona Listings**

| Avondale AZ | Chipotle - 99th Ave & McDowell | 623-907-1122 | 9925 W McDowell Road |
| Avondale AZ | Jamba Juice | 623-478-9250 | 10110 W McDowell Road, Bldg 6, Suite 120 |
| Bisbee AZ | Jimmy's Hot Dog Company | 520-432-5911 | 938 W H 92 |
| Buckeye AZ | Chipotle - Sundance Town Center | 623-691-6919 | 944 S Watson Road |
| Bullhead City AZ | El Palacio Restaurant & Cantina | 928-763-2494 | 1885 Hwy 95 |
| Cave Creek AZ | Big Earl's Greasy Eats | 480-575-7889 | 6135 E Cave Creek Road |
| Chandler AZ | 24 Carrots Natural Food and Juice Bar | 480-753-4411 | 6140 W Chandler Blvd |
| Chandler AZ | BJ's Restaurant and Brewhouse | 480-917-0631 | 3155 W.Chandler Blvd |
| Chandler AZ | BLD | 480-779-8646 | 1920 W Germann Road |
| Chandler AZ | Chipotle - Alma School & Queen Creek | 480-786-1122 | 2895 Alma School Road |
| Chandler AZ | Chipotle - Chandler Fashion | 480-899-5049 | 3157 W Chandler Blvd, Suite 2 |
| Chandler AZ | Chipotle - Chandler Pavillions | 480-783-0200 | 890 N 54th Street |
| Chandler AZ | Coffee Bean & Tea Leaf | 480-899-2005 | 2560 W. Chandler Blvd #1 |
| Chandler AZ | El Palacio Restaurant & Cantina | 480-802-5770 | 2950 E. Germann Road |
| Chandler AZ | Firehouse Subs | 480-726-8200 | 3245 W Ray Road, Suite 1 |
| Chandler AZ | Jamba Juice | 480-857-9852 | 2095 N Alma School Road, Suite 12 |
| Chandler AZ | Jason's Deli | 480-705-9266 | 7230 W Ray Road |
| Chandler AZ | San Tan Brewing Company | 480-917-8700 | 8 South San Marcos Place |
| Chandler AZ | Tropical Smoothie Cafe | 480-883-1234 | 4015 S. Arizona Avenue/H 87 |
| Flagstaff AZ | Campus Coffee Bean | 928-556-0660 | 1800 S. Milton |
| Flagstaff AZ | Late for the Train | 928-779-5975 | 107 N San Francisco Street |
| Flagstaff AZ | Macy's European Coffeehouse | 928-774-2243 | 14 S Beaver Street |
| Flagstaff AZ | New Jersey Pizza Company | 928-774-5000 | 2224 E Cedar Avenue, #C6 |
| Gilbert AZ | Chipotle - 202 & Gilbert | 480-963-8585 | 3757 S Gilbert Road, Suite #110 |
| Gilbert AZ | Chipotle - Cooper & Baseline | 480-632-1875 | 1546 N. Cooper Road |
| Gilbert AZ | Chipotle - Warner & Gilbert | 480-892-8307 | 1084 S. Gilbert Road, Suite 104 |
| Gilbert AZ | Jamba Juice | 480-782-0378 | 3765 S Gilbert Road, Suite 104 |
| Gilbert AZ | Jason's Deli | 480-813-1358 | 1065 E Baseline Road , Suite 101 |
| Gilbert AZ | Johnny Rockets | 480-722-1848 | 2270 E Williams Field Road, Bldg. B #101 |
| Glendale AZ | Johnny Rockets | 623-877-2977 | 9390 W Hanna Drive |
| Glendale AZ | Starbucks | 623-362-9288 | 20249 North 67th Ave #B |
| Glendale AZ | Starbucks | 623-878-1717 | 7410 W Bell Rd #310 |
| Goodyear AZ | Clubhouse Grill | 623-535-4857 | 14175 W Indian School Rd C01 |
| Goodyear AZ | Tropical Smoothie Cafe | 623-414-4064 | 13375 W Mcdowell Road |
| Lake Havasu City AZ | Javelina Cantina | 928-855-8226 | 1420 McCulloch Drive |
| Lake Havasu City AZ | Mudshark Brewery | 928-453-2981 | 210 Swanson Ave |
| Lake Havasu City AZ | Oasis Grill | 928-854-3223 | 401 English Village |
| Mesa AZ | BJ's Restaurant and Brewhouse | 480-324-1675 | 6622 E. Superstition Springs Blvd |
| Mesa AZ | Chipotle - Power & 202-Gateway Crossing | 480-988-6935 | 4984 S Power Road, Suite 107 |
| Mesa AZ | Chipotle - Superstition Springs | 480-654-3400 | 6602 E Superstition Springs Blvd |
| Mesa AZ | Dos Gringos Mexigrill | 480-633-5525 | 1958 S Greenfield |
| Mesa AZ | Firehouse Subs | 480-539-4322 | 3420 E. Baseline Road., Suite 101 |
| Mesa AZ | Honey Baked Ham and Co and Cafe | 480-854-3300 | 6736 E Baseline Rd |
| Mesa AZ | Jamba Juice | 480-380-3590 | 1804 S Signal Butte, Suite 104 |
| Mesa AZ | Salty Senorita | 480-632-TACO (8226) | 1860 S Stapley Drive |
| Mesa AZ | The Mesa Monastery | 480-474-4477 | 4810 East McKillips |
| Mesa AZ | Tropical Smoothie Cafe | 480-325-7680 | 6614 E. Baseline Road |
| Mesa AZ | Tropical Smoothie Cafe | 623-810-9511 | 2832 N Power Road |
| Mesa AZ | Uncle Bears Bar and Grill | 480-986-2228 | SW corner of Baseline & Ellsworth |
| Peoria AZ | BJ's Restaurant and Brewhouse | 623-772-6470 | 9748 W. Northern Avenue |
| Peoria AZ | Chipotle - Arrowhead Fountains | 623-487-1907 | 16680 N. 83rd Avenue |

| Peoria AZ | Chipotle - Happy Valley | 623-362-1252 | 9940 W Happy Valley Parkway |
|---|---|---|---|
| Peoria AZ | Coffee Bean & Tea Leaf | 623-776-9680 | 7407 W. Bell Road, #2 |
| Peoria AZ | Salty Senorita | 623-979-GUAC (4822) | 8011 W Paradise Lane |
| Phoenix AZ | Aunt Chiladas | 602-944-1286 | 7330 North Dreamy Draw Drive |
| Phoenix AZ | BJ's Restaurant and Brewhouse | 480-538-0555 | 21001 N Tatum Blvd |
| Phoenix AZ | Breadcrafters | 602-494-4442 | 12635 Tatum Blvd |
| Phoenix AZ | Chakra 4 Vegetarian Restaurant | 602-283-1210 | 4773 N. 20th Street |
| Phoenix AZ | Chipotle - 44th St. & Thomas | 602-522-2394 | 4423 E Thomas Road |
| Phoenix AZ | Chipotle - Camelback | 602-274-4455 | 1660 E Camelback Road |
| Phoenix AZ | Chipotle - Metro Center | 602-944-5060 | 3039 W. Peoria Avenue |
| Phoenix AZ | Chipotle - Nortera | 623-215-0900 | 2470 W Happy Valley Road |
| Phoenix AZ | Chipotle - South Mountain | 602-283-9500 | 2415 E Baseline Road |
| Phoenix AZ | Coffee Bean & Tea Leaf | 602-404-6446 | 20235 N. Cave Creek Road |
| Phoenix AZ | Duck and Decanter | 602-274-5429 | 1651 East Camelback Road |
| Phoenix AZ | Duke's Sports Bar and Grill | 480-675-9724 | 7607 E McDowell Road |
| Phoenix AZ | Honey Baked Ham and Co and Cafe | 602-996-0600 | 4635 E Cactus Road |
| Phoenix AZ | Humble Pie | 602-229-1289 | 333 N 7th Street |
| Phoenix AZ | Humble Pie | 480-502-2121 | 21050 N Tatum Blvd |
| Phoenix AZ | Jamba Juice | 480-706-8500 | 4302 E Ray Road |
| Phoenix AZ | Jason's Deli | 602-870-8611 | 10217 N Metro Parkway W |
| Phoenix AZ | Morning Glory Restaurant | 602-276-8804 | 6106 S 32nd Street |
| Phoenix AZ | NYPD Pizza | 602-294-6969 | 1949 E Camelback Rd |
| Phoenix AZ | O.H.S.O. Eatery and nano-Brewery | 602-955-0358 | 4900 E Indian School Road |
| Phoenix AZ | Pita Jungle | 602-955-PITA (7482) | 4340 E Indian School Road |
| Phoenix AZ | Pomegranate Cafe | 480-706-7472 | 4025 E. Chandler Blvd, Suite 28 |
| Phoenix AZ | Red Robin | 623-581-8635 | 2501 W Happy Valley Road |
| Phoenix AZ | Rico's American Grill | 602-997-5850 | 7677 N 16th Street |
| Phoenix AZ | Rubio's Fresh Mexican Grill | 602-508-1732 | 4340 E. Indian School Rd., Ste. 1 |
| Phoenix AZ | Rubio's Fresh Mexican Grill | 602-867-1454 | 4747 East Bell Road #17 |
| Phoenix AZ | St Francis | 602-200-8111 | 111 E Camelback Road |
| Phoenix AZ | The Capital Grille | 602-952-8900 | 2502 E. Camelback Rd. |
| Phoenix AZ | The Farm at S Mountain/Morning Glory Cafe | 602-276-6360 | 6106 South 32nd Street |
| Phoenix AZ | True Food Kitchen | 602-774-3488 | 2502 E Camelback Road #135 |
| Phoenix AZ | Z Pizza | 602-254-4145 | 111 W Monroe Street |
| Phoenix AZ | Z Pizza | 602-234-3289 | 53 W Thomas Road |
| Phoenix AZ | Z Pizza | 602-765-0511 | 13637 N Tatum Blvd |
| Queen Creek AZ | Chipotle - Rittenhouse | 480-214-9200 | 21172 S Ellsworth Loop Road |
| Queens Creek AZ | Uncle Bears Bar and Grill | 480-882-3177 | NW corner of Rittenhouse & Ocotillo Road |
| Scottsdale AZ | Chipotle - 92nd & Shea | 480-860-6901 | 9301 E Shea Blvd #F102 |
| Scottsdale AZ | Chipotle - Downtown Scottsdale | 480-684-1090 | 4513 N Scottsdale Road |
| Scottsdale AZ | Chipotle - Hayden & Royal Palm | 480-556-0475 | 8320 N Hayden Road |
| Scottsdale AZ | Chipotle - Maloney | 480-367-1218 | 15425 N Scottsdale Road |
| Scottsdale AZ | Chipotle - Thompson Peak | 480-661-5650 | 15035 N Thompson Peak Parkway |
| Scottsdale AZ | Coffee Bean & Tea Leaf | 480-941-7059 | 4032 N. Miller Road, Suite 102 |
| Scottsdale AZ | Coffee Bean & Tea Leaf | 480-607-3146 | 16211 N Scottsdale Road, Suite A-5 |
| Scottsdale AZ | Dos Gringos Scottsdale Cantina | 480-423-3800 | 4209 N Craftsman Court |
| Scottsdale AZ | Fresh Mint | 480-443-2556 | 13802 N Scottsdale Road, Suite 161 |
| Scottsdale AZ | Humble Pie | 480-556-9900 | 6149 N Scottsdale Road |
| Scottsdale AZ | Jason's Deli | 480-443-3811 | 10605 N. Scottsdale Road |
| Scottsdale AZ | Rubio's Fresh Mexican Grill | 480-575-7280 | 32415 N. Scottsdale Road, Ste. C |
| Sedona AZ | Chocolatree | 928-282-2997 | 1595 W H 89A |
| Sedona AZ | Cucina Rustica | 928-284-3010 | 7000 H 179 |
| Sedona AZ | Open Range Grill and Tavern | 928-282-0002 | 320 N H 89A |
| Sedona AZ | The Grille at ShadowRock at the Hilton Sedona | 928-284-4040 | 90 Ridge Trail Dr |
| Sedona AZ | Troia's Pizza Pasta Amore | 928-282-0123 | 1885 W H 89A |
| Sierra Vista AZ | Landmark Cafe | 520-459-4624 | 400 W Fry Blvd |
| Sierra Vista AZ | Sonic Drive-In | 520-458-4530 | 3640 E Fry Blvd |
| Surprise AZ | Big Buddha Chinese Restaurant | 623-266-3328 | 16572 W Greenway Road #115 |
| Surprise AZ | Chipotle - Surprise | 623-544-2363 | 13869 W Bell Road #107 |
| Tempe AZ | Coffee Bean & Tea Leaf | 480-966-0252 | 2000 E. Rio Salado Parkway, #1158 |
| Tempe AZ | Green Vegetarian Restaurant | 480-941-9003 | 2240 N Scottsdale Road |
| Tempe AZ | Jamba Juice | 480-491-5252 | 1827 E Guadalupe Road |

| | | | |
|---|---|---|---|
| Tempe AZ | Pier 54 | 480-820-0660 | 5394 S Lakeshore Drive |
| Tempe AZ | Pita Jungle | 480-804-0234 | 1250 E Apache Blvd |
| Tempe AZ | Rubio's Fresh Mexican Grill | 480-897-3884 | 1712 East Guadalupe Rd., Ste. 109 |
| Tempe AZ | Tropical Smoothie Cafe | 480-496-4200 | 8707 S. Priest Drive |
| Tombstone AZ | O.K. Cafe | 520-457-3980 | 220 E. Allen Street |
| Tucson AZ | BJ's Restaurant and Brewhouse | 520-690-1900 | 4270 N. Oracle Road/H 77 |
| Tucson AZ | BJ's Restaurant and Brewhouse | 520-512-0330 | 5510 E Broadway Blvd |
| Tucson AZ | Cafe Passe | 520-624-4411 | 415 N 4th Avenue |
| Tucson AZ | Chipotle - Foothills Mall | 520-544-3868 | 7555 N La Cholla Blvd |
| Tucson AZ | Chipotle - Grant & Swan | 520-326-1009 | 4774 E Grant Road |
| Tucson AZ | Chipotle - Park Place Mall | 520-908-7440 | 5870 E Broadway Blvd |
| Tucson AZ | Chipotle - Tucson Mall | 520-888-0444 | 235 W Wetmore Road |
| Tucson AZ | Chipotle - University Square | 520-628-7967 | 905 E University Blvd Unit 149 |
| Tucson AZ | Cup Cafe | 520-622-8848 | 311 E Congress Street |
| Tucson AZ | Eclectic Cafe | 520-885-2842 | 7053 E Tanque Verde Road |
| Tucson AZ | Eegee's | 520-881-3280 | 4510 E Speedway |
| Tucson AZ | Famous Sam's Restaurant and Bar | 520-531-9464 | 8058 North Oracle Rd |
| Tucson AZ | Ghini's | 520-326-9095 | 1803 E Prince Rd |
| Tucson AZ | Honey Baked Ham | 520-544-2121 | 7090 N Oracle/H 77 |
| Tucson AZ | Honey Baked Ham | 520-745-0700 | 5350 E Broadway |
| Tucson AZ | Jamba Juice | 520-293-6080 | 235 W Wetmore Road, Suite 121 |
| Tucson AZ | Johnny Rockets | 520-622-2245 | 825 E University, Suite 121 |
| Tucson AZ | Li'l Abner's Steakhouse | 520-744-2800 | 8501 North Silverbell Rd |
| Tucson AZ | Mama's Famous Pizza and Heros | 520-297-3993 | 7965 North Oracle Rd |
| Tucson AZ | Revolutionary Grounds Books and Coffee | 520-620-1770 | 606 N 4th Avenue |
| Tucson AZ | Schlotzsky's Deli | 520-741-2333 | 3270 East Valencia |
| Tucson AZ | Thai China Bistro | 520-325-5185 | 5121 East Grant Rd |
| Tucson AZ | The Cereal Boxx | 520-622-BOXX (2699) | 943 E University Blvd |
| Tucson AZ | The Cup Cafe (in Hotel Congress) | 520-798-1618 | 311 E Congress St |
| Tucson AZ | The Tasteful Kitchen | 520-250-9600 | 722 N Stone Avenue |
| Williams AZ | Cruiser's Cafe | 928-635-2445 | 233 West Route 66 |
| Williams AZ | The Route 66 Place | 928-635-0266 | 417 East Route 66 |
| Yuma AZ | Julieanna's Patio Cafe | 928-317-1961 | 1951 W 25th St |

**Arkansas Listings**

| | | | |
|---|---|---|---|
| Conway AR | Tropical Smoothie Cafe | 501-764-4800 | 705 Club Lane #109 |
| Eureka Springs AR | New Delhi Cafe | 479-253-2525 | 2 N Main Street/H 23 |
| Fort Smith AR | Firehouse Subs | 479-452-4468 | 7805-C Rogers Avenue/H 22 |
| Hot Springs AR | Angel's Italian Restaurant | 501-609-9323 | 600 Central Avenue/H 7 |
| Hot Springs AR | The Boathouse | 501-525-8585 | 4904 Central Avenue/H 7 |
| Jacksonville AR | Tropical Smoothie Cafe | 501-241-2233 | 140 John Hardin Drive #29 |
| Jonesboro AR | Tropical Smoothie Cafe | 870-935-2233 | 2007 E. Nettleton Avenue |
| Little Rock AR | Jason's Deli | 501-954-8700 | 301 Shackleford Road , Suite H1A |
| Little Rock AR | Leo's Greek Castle | 501-666-7414 | 2925 Kavanaugh Blvd |
| Little Rock AR | The Root Cafe | 501-414-0423 | 1500 S Main Street |
| Little Rock AR | Thirst N' Howl | 501-379-8189 | 14710 Cantrell Road/H 10 |
| Little Rock AR | Tropical Smoothie Cafe | 501-851-9555 | 12007 Maumelle Blvd/H 100 |
| Little Rock AR | Tropical Smoothie Cafe | 501-224-2233 | 10221 N Rodney Parham Road |
| Little Rock AR | Za Za Pizza and Salad | 501-661-9292 | 5600 Kavanaugh Blvd |
| N Little Rock AR | Jason's Deli | 501-945-7700 | 4209 E McCain Blvd |

**California Listings**

| | | | |
|---|---|---|---|
| Alameda CA | Jamba Juice | 510-521-1112 | 2306 S Shore Center |
| Alameda CA | Tucker's Super-Creamed Ice Cream | 510-522-4960 | 1349 Park Street |
| Albany CA | Cugini Restaurant | 510-558-9000 | 1556 Solano Ave |
| Albany CA | Schmidts Pub | 510-525-1900 | 1492 Solano Avenue |
| Alhambra CA | Diner on Main | 626-281-3488 | 201 W Main Street |
| Aliso Viejo CA | Z Pizza | 949-425-0102 | 26921 Aliso Creek Road |
| Anaheim CA | Chipotle | 714-283-3092 | 8182 E Santa Ana Canyon Road |
| Anaheim CA | Coffee Bean & Tea Leaf | 714-772-4861 | 2002 E Lincoln Blvd |
| Anaheim CA | Johnny Rockets | 714-491-1800 | 321 W Katella Avenue #320 |
| Anaheim CA | Rubios Baja Grill | 714-999-1525 | 520 N Euclid St |
| Anaheim CA | Subway Sandwiches | 714-535-3444 | 514 N Euclid Street |
| Anaheim Hills CA | Baja Fresh Mexican Grill | 714-685-9386 | 5781 E. Santa Ana Canyon Rd. |

| Anaheim Hills CA | Z Pizza | 714-998-4171 | 5745 E Santa Ana Canyon Road |
| Aptos CA | Bittersweet Bistro | 831-662-9899 | 787 Rio Del Mar Blvd |
| Aptos CA | Cole's Bar-B-Q | 831-662-1721 | 8059 Aptos Street |
| Arcadia CA | Matt Denny's Ale House | 626-462-0250 | 145 E Huntington Dr |
| Arnold CA | Giant Burger | 209-795-1594 | 846 Highway 4 |
| Arroyo Grande CA | Baja Fresh Mexican Grill | 805-474-8900 | 929 Rancho Pkwy |
| Arroyo Grande CA | Jamba Juice | 805-481-8930 | 926 Rancho Parkway |
| Arroyo Grande CA | Old Village Grill | 805-489-4915 | 101 E. Branch St |
| Auburn CA | Bootleggers Tavern and Grill | 530-889-2229 | 210 Washington St |
| Auburn CA | Ikeda's | 530-885-4243 | 13500 Lincoln Way |
| Auburn CA | La Bou | 530-823-2303 | 2150 Grass Valley Hwy |
| Auburn CA | Max's | 530-823-6297 | 11960 Heritage Oak Place |
| Auburn CA | Tio Pepe's | 530-888-6445 | 216 Washington Street |
| Avila Beach CA | The Customs House | 805-595-7555 | 404 Front Street |
| Azusa CA | Jamba Juice | 626-334-1268 | 832 E Alosta Avenue |
| Bakersfield CA | Baja Fresh Mexican Grill | 661-587-8700 | 9660 Hageman Rd. |
| Bakersfield CA | Baja Fresh Mexican Grill | 661-665-2252 | 9000 Ming Ave. |
| Bakersfield CA | Black Angus | 661-324-0814 | 3601 Rosedale Highway |
| Bakersfield CA | Cafe Med | 661-834-4433 | 4809 Stockdale Hwy |
| Bakersfield CA | Chipotle | 661-335-0400 | 4950 Stockdale H |
| Bakersfield CA | Filling Station | 661-323-5120 | 1830 24th Street |
| Bakersfield CA | Jamba Juice | 661-322-6722 | 5180 Stockdale Hwy #AB |
| Bakersfield CA | Jamba Juice | 661-829-1830 | 9360 Rosedale H/H 58 |
| Bakersfield CA | Los Hermanos | 661-328-1678 | 3501 Union Ave |
| Bakersfield CA | Los Hermanos | 661-835-7294 | 8200 Stockdale Hwy #N |
| Bakersfield CA | Patio Mexican Grill | 661-587-6280 | 13001 Stockdale Hwy |
| Bakersfield CA | Rosemary's Family Creamery | 661-395-0555 | 2733 F Street |
| Bakersfield CA | Sequoia Sandwich Company | 661-323-2500 | 1231 18th Street |
| Bakersfield CA | Sonic Drive In | 661-324-9100 | 1402 23rd Street |
| Bakersfield CA | Sonic Drive-In | 661-587-9400 | 13015 Stockdale Hwy |
| Bakersfield CA | Sub Station | 661-323-2400 | 5464 California Ave |
| Bakersfield CA | Subway | 661-366-3300 | 8346 East Brundage Lane |
| Bakersfield CA | The Gourmet Shoppe | 661-834-5522 | 4801 Stockdale Hwy |
| Balboa CA | Ruby's Diner | 949-675-7829 | #1 Balboa Pier |
| Barstow CA | Baja Fresh Mexican Grill | 760-253-2505 | 2854 Lenwood Rd |
| Barstow CA | El Pollo Loco | 760-253-5222 | 2820 Lenwood Road |
| Belmont CA | Coyote Cafe | 650-595-1422 | 1003 Alameda de las Pulgas |
| Belmont Shore CA | Coffee Bean & Tea Leaf | 562-930-0246 | 4925 E Second Street |
| Ben Lomond CA | Spanky's | 831-336-8949 | 9520 H 9 |
| Benicia CA | Jamba Juice | 707-748-1203 | 804-A Southampton Road |
| Berkeley CA | Cafe Trieste | 510-548-5198 | 2500 San Pablo Ave |
| Berkeley CA | Chipotle | 510-526-6047 | 1050 Gilman Street |
| Berkeley CA | Chipotle | 510-548-0340 | 2311 Telegraph Ave. |
| Berkeley CA | Crepevine | 510-705-1836 | 1600 Shattuck Avenue |
| Berkeley CA | Espresso Roma Café at the French Hotel | 510-548-9930 | 1538 Shattuck Ave |
| Berkeley CA | Gather | 510-809-0400 | 2200 Oxford Street |
| Berkeley CA | Homemade Cafe | 510-845-1940 | 2454 Sacramento St |
| Berkeley CA | La Mediterranee | 510-540-7773 | 2936 College Avenue |
| Berkeley CA | Pasta Shop | 510-528-1786 | 1786 4th Street |
| Berkeley CA | Riva Cucina | 510-841-RIVA (7482) | 800 Heinz Avenue |
| Berkeley CA | Tacubaya | 510-525-5160 | 1788 4th Street |
| Berkeley CA | Whole Foods Market | 510-649-1333 | 3000 Telegraph Ave. |
| Beverly Hills CA | Baja Fresh Mexican Grill | 310-858-6690 | 475 N. Beverly Drive |
| Beverly Hills CA | Chipotle | 310-824-4180 | 1077 Broxton Avenue |
| Beverly Hills CA | Chipotle | 310-273-8265 | 244 South Beverly Drive |
| Beverly Hills CA | Coffee Bean & Tea Leaf | 310-278-1865 | 445 N Beverly Drive |
| Beverly Hills CA | Coffee Bean & Tea Leaf | 323-852-9988 | 8328 Wilshire Blvd |
| Beverly Hills CA | Coffee Bean & Tea Leaf | 310-274-7801 | 233 S. Beverly Drive |
| Beverly Hills CA | Joan's on 3rd | 323-655-2285 | 8350 W Third Street |
| Beverly Hills CA | Kings Road Expresso Cafe | 323-655-9044 | 8361 Beverly Blvd |
| Beverly Hills CA | The Lazy Daisy | 310-859-1111 | 9010 Wilshire Blvd |
| Beverly Hills CA | Urth Cafe | 310-205-9311 | 267 S Beverly Dr |
| Big Bear Lake CA | Alpine High Country Cafe | 909-866-1959 | 41546 Big Bear Blvd |
| Big Bear Lake CA | BLT's Restaurant | 909-866-6659 | 41799 Big Bear Blvd |
| Big Bear Lake CA | Big Bear Mountain Brewery | 909-866-2337 | 40260 Big Bear Blvd |
| Big Bear Lake CA | Jasper's Smokehouse and Steaks | 909-866-2434 | 607 Pine Knot Avenue |

| Big Bear Lake CA | Nottingham's Restaurant and Tavern | 909-866-4644 | 40797 Lakeview Drive |
|---|---|---|---|
| Big Bear Lake CA | Village Pizza | 909-866-8505 | 40568 Village Dr |
| Big Sur CA | Big Sur Coast Gallery & Cafe | 831-667-2301 | 49901 H 1 |
| Bishop CA | Pizza Factory | 760-872-8888 | 970 N Main Street/H 6/395 |
| Blue Lake CA | Mad River Brewing Company | 707-668-4151 | 195 Taylor Way |
| Bolinas CA | Coast Cafe | 415-868-2298 | 46 Wharf Road |
| Boonville CA | Boonville Hotel/Table 128 | 707-895-2210 | 14050 H 128 |
| Boonville CA | Mosswood Market Cafe | 707-895-3635 | 14111 H 128 Suite A |
| Borrego Springs CA | The Red Ocotillo | 760-767-7400 | 818 Palm Canyon Drive |
| Brea CA | Baja Fresh Mexican Grill | 714-671-9992 | 2445 Imperial Hwy. Suite H |
| Brea CA | Coffee Bean & Tea Leaf | 714-255-8026 | 1080 E. Imperial H/H 90, #E-2 |
| Brea CA | Lazy Dog Restaurant & Bar | 714-529-9300 | 240 S State College Blvd |
| Brea CA | Schlotzsky's Deli | 714-256-1100 | 2500 E. Imperial Hwy #196 |
| Brentwood CA | San Gennaro Cafe | 310-476-9696 | 140 Barrington Place |
| Burbank CA | Baja Fresh Mexican Grill | 818-841-4649 | 877 N. San Fernando Blvd. |
| Burbank CA | Chipotle | 818-842-0622 | 135 E Palm Avenue |
| Burbank CA | Coffee Bean & Tea Leaf | 818-842-2394 | 340 N San Fernando Blvd |
| Burbank CA | Priscilla's Coffee and Tea | 818-843-5707 | 4150 W Riverside Street, Suite A |
| Burlingame CA | Copenhagen Bakery and Cafe | 650-342-1357 | 1216 Burlingame Ave |
| Burlingame CA | Crepevine | 650-344-1310 | 1310 Burlingame Avenue |
| Burlingame CA | Urban Bistro | 650-347-7687 | 270 Lorton Avenue |
| Calabasas CA | Baja Fresh Mexican Grill | 818-591-2262 | 23697 Calabasas Parkway |
| Calabasas CA | Coffee Bean & Tea Leaf | 818-225-1887 | 23635 Calabasas Road |
| Calistoga CA | Buster's BBQ | 707-942-5605 | 1207 Foothills Blvd |
| Calistoga CA | Home Plate Cafe | 707-942-5646 | 2448 Foothill Blvd |
| Camarillo CA | Baja Fresh Mexican Grill | 805-383-6884 | 1855 Daily Drive |
| Camarillo CA | Coffee Bean & Tea Leaf | 805-383-7767 | 824 Arneil Road |
| Camarillo CA | Old Town Cafe | 805-484-5500 | 2050 E. Ventura Blvd |
| Camarillo CA | Panda Express | 805-987-3368 | 199 W Ventura Blvd |
| Camarillo CA | The Way Point Cafe | 805-388-2535 | 325 Durley Avenue |
| Camarillo CA | Topper's Pizza | 805-385-4444 | 520 Arneill Rd |
| Cambria CA | Las Cambritas | 805-927-0175 | 2336 Main Street |
| Cambria CA | Madeline's | 805-927-4175 | 788 Main St |
| Camino CA | Mountain Mike's Pizza | 530-644-6000 | 3600 Carson Rd #C |
| Camp Pendleton CA | Johnny Rockets | 760-829-1258 | 15103 Mainside Center |
| Campbell CA | Aqui Cal-Mex | 408-374-2784 | 201 East Campbell Ave |
| Campbell CA | Baja Fresh Mexican Grill | 408-377-2600 | 1976 S. Bascom Ave |
| Campbell CA | Chipotle | 408-371-5284 | 1815 S Bascom Avenue |
| Campbell CA | Rock Bottom Restaurant & Brewery | 408-377-0707 | 1875 S Bascom Ave |
| Campbell CA | Stacks | 408-376-3516 | 139 E Campbell Ave |
| Campbell CA | Yiassoo | 408-559-0312 | 2180 S Bascom Ave |
| Capitola CA | Gayle's Bakery and Rosticceria | 831-462-1200 | 504 Bay Avenue |
| Carlsbad CA | Cafe Elysa | 760-434-4100 | 3076 Carlsbad Blvd |
| Carlsbad CA | Coffee Bean & Tea Leaf | 760-720-1381 | 2508 El Camino Real Suite F |
| Carlsbad CA | Coffee Bean & Tea Leaf | 760-634-3268 | 1935 Calle Barcelona, #176 |
| Carlsbad CA | Gregorio's Restaurant | 760-720-1132 | 300 Carlsbad Village Dr #208 |
| Carlsbad CA | Mas Fina Cantina | 760-434-3497 | 2780 State Street |
| Carlsbad CA | O'Sullivan's Irish Pub and Restaurant | 760-729-7234 | 640 Grand Ave |
| Carlsbad CA | Vigilucci's Cucina Italiana | 760-434-2500 | 2943 State Street |
| Carlsbad CA | Vinaka Cafe | 760-720-7890 | 300 Carlsbad Village Dr #211 |
| Carlsbad Village CA | Tom Giblin's Irish Pub | 760-729-7234 | 640 Grand Avenue |
| Carmel CA | Allegro Gourmet Pizzeria | 831-626-5454 | 3770 The Barnyard |
| Carmel CA | Anton and Michel | 831-624-2406 | Mission Street and 7th Avenue |
| Carmel CA | Casanova Restaurant | 831-625-0501 | Mission & 5th |
| Carmel CA | Forge in the Forest | 831-624-2233 | 5th and Junipero, SW Corner |
| Carmel CA | Hog's Breath Inn | 831-625-1044 | San Carlos St and 5th Ave |
| Carmel CA | Nico's | 831-624-6545 | San Carlos St and Ocean Ave |
| Carmel CA | PortaBella | 831-624-4395 | Ocean Ave |
| Carmel CA | R. G. Burgers | 831-626-8054 | 201 Crossroads Shopping Village |
| Carmel CA | The Forge In the Forest | 831-624-2233 | Fifth and Junipero Avenues |
| Carmel Valley CA | Cachagua General Store | 831-659-1857 | 18840 Cachagua Rd |
| Carmel Valley CA | Cafe Stravaganza | 831-625-3733 | 241 The Crossroads |
| Carmel Valley CA | Plaza Linda | 831-659-4229 | 9 Del Fino Pl |
| Carmel Valley CA | The Corkscrew Cafe | 831-659-8888 | 55 W Carmel Valley Rd |
| Carmel-by-the-Sea CA | Carmel Belle | 831-624-1600 | SW Corner of San Carlos and Ocean |

| Carmel-by-the-Sea CA | Flaherty's Seafood Grill & Oyster Bar | Oyster Bar 831-624-0311 / Seafood Grill 831-625-1500 | 6th Avenue between San Carlos & Dolores |
|---|---|---|---|
| Carmel-by-the-Sea CA | Village Corner Mediterranean Bistro | 831-624-3588 | Dolores & 6th Avenue |
| Carmichael CA | Bella Bru Coffee Co | 916-485-2883 | 5038 Fair Oaks Blvd |
| Carnelian Bay CA | Old Post Office Coffee Shop | 530-546-3205 | 5245 North Lake Blvd |
| Carpinteria CA | Crushcakes & Cafe | 805-684-4300 | 4945 Carpinteria Avenue |
| Carpinteria CA | The Coffee Bean & Tea Leaf | 805-745-5861 | 4991 Carpinteria Avenue |
| Castro Valley CA | Chipotle | 510-582-8643 | 3369 Castro Valley Blvd |
| Cathedral City CA | Michael's Cafe | 760-321-7197 | 35955 Date Palm Drive |
| Century City CA | The Coffee Bean & Tea Leaf | 310-286-2273 | 2000 Avenue of the Stars #100 |
| Cerritos CA | Lazy Dog Restaurant & Bar | 562-402-6644 | 278 Los Cerritos Center |
| Cerritos CA | The Coffee Bean & Tea Leaf | 562-865-9713 | 12550 Artesia Blvd |
| Chico CA | Baja Fresh Mexican Grill | 530-896-1077 | 2072 E. 20th St. |
| Chico CA | Bellachinos | 530-892-2244 | 800 Bruce Road |
| Chico CA | Cal Java | 530-893-2662 | 2485 Notre Dame Blvd. |
| Chico CA | Celestino's Pasta and Pizza | 530-345-7700 | 1354 East Ave |
| Chico CA | Chipotle | 530-343-8707 | 620 Mangrove Avenue |
| Chico CA | El Patron | 530-343-9779 | 1354 East Ave |
| Chico CA | Jamba Juice | 530-345-5355 | 201 Broadway Street |
| Chico CA | S & S Organic Produce and Natural Foods | 530-343-4930 | 1924 Mangrove Avenue |
| Chico CA | Shubert's Ice Cream | 530-342-7163 | 178 E 7th Street |
| Chico CA | Spiteri's Delicatessen | 530-891-4797 | 971 East Avenue |
| Chino CA | Blue Fire Grill | 909-591-8783 | 5670 Schaefer Avenue |
| Chino Hills CA | Chipotle | 909-548-3721 | 13920 City Center Drive, Suite 4005 |
| Chino Hills CA | Jamba Juice | 909-591-8019 | 3660 Grand Avenue, Suite F |
| Chula Vista CA | Jamba Juice | 619-409-9840 | 555 Broadway, Suite 135 |
| Chula Vista CA | Jamba Juice | 619-656-5030 | 2275 Otay Lakes Road, #117 |
| Citrus Heights CA | Chipotle | 916-967-7881 | 5851 Sunrise Blvd |
| Clairemont CA | Cucina Italiana | 858-274-9732 | 4705-A Clairemont Drive |
| Claremont CA | Aruffo's Italian Cuisine | 909-624-9624 | 126 Yale Ave |
| Claremont CA | Espiau's Restaurant | 909-621-1818 | 109 Yale Ave |
| Claremont CA | Some Crust Bakery | 909-621-9772 | 119 Yale Avenue |
| Claremont CA | The Coffee Bean & Tea Leaf | 909-624-2147 | 101 N. Indian Hill, # 105 |
| Claremont CA | The Loving Hut | 909-621-1668 | 175 N Indian Hill Blvd, Building A 102 |
| Claremont CA | Village Grill | 909-626-8813 | 148 Yale Ave |
| Clayton CA | Skipolini's Pizza | 925-672-1111 | 1033 Diablo St |
| Clovis CA | Chipotle | 559-298-4708 | 1210 Shaw Avenue |
| Clovis CA | Jamba Juice | 559-325-8974 | 775 W Herndon Avenue, Suite 100 |
| Coloma CA | Argonaut Cafe | 530-626-7345 | Hwy 49 |
| Coloma CA | Sutter Center Market | 530-626-0849 | 378 Highway 49 |
| Concord CA | Lazy Dog Restaurant & Bar | 925-849-1221 | 1961 Diamond Blvd |
| Corona CA | Jamba Juice | 951-371-9450 | 2620 Tuscany Street, Suite 106 |
| Corona Del Mar CA | Baja Fresh Mexican Grill | 949-760-8000 | 3050 E. Coast Hwy |
| Corona Del Mar CA | Coffee Bean & Tea Leaf | 949-673-7062 | 2933 Coast H E, Space 3A/H 1 |
| Coronado CA | Burger Lounge | 619-435-6835 | 922 Orange Avenue/H 75 |
| Coronado CA | Cafe 1134 | 619-437-1134 | 1134 Orange Ave |
| Coronado CA | McP's Irish Pub and Grill | 619-435-5280 | 1107 Orange Avenue |
| Coronado CA | Spiro's Gyros | 619-435-1225 | 1201 First Street |
| Corte Madera CA | A.G. Ferrari Foods | 415-927-4347 | 107 Corte Madera Town Ctr |
| Corte Madera CA | Baja Fresh Mexican Grill | 415-924-8522 | 100 Corte Madera Town Center |
| Corte Madera CA | Book Passage Bookstore and Cafe | 415-927-1503 | 51 Tamal Vista |
| Costa Mesa CA | Baja Fresh Mexican Grill | 949-675-2252 | 3030 Harbor Blvd |
| Costa Mesa CA | Chipotle | 949-646-1288 | 2300 Harbor Blvd |
| Costa Mesa CA | Side Street Cafe | 949-650-1986 | 1799 Newport Blvd Ste A105 |
| Costa Mesa CA | The Coffee Bean & Tea Leaf | 949-722-9673 | 1835 Newport Blvd. # B122 |
| Cotati CA | Redwood Cafe | 707-795-7868 | 8240 Old Redwood Highway |
| Crescent City CA | Los Compadres Mexican Food | 707-464-7871 | 457 Highway 101 |
| Cromberg CA | Neighbors Bar-B-Que | 530-836-1365 | 58421 H 70 |
| Culver City CA | Baja Fresh Mexican Grill | 310-280-0644 | 10768 Venice Blvd |
| Cupertino CA | Baja Fresh Mexican Grill | 408-257-6141 | 20735 Stevens Creek Blvd |
| Cupertino CA | Cafe Society | 408-725-8091 | 21265 Stevens Creek Blvd #202 |
| Cupertino CA | Lazy Dog Restaurant & Bar | 408-359-4690 | 19359 Stevens Creek Blvd |
| Cupertino CA | Whole Foods Market | 408-257-7000 | 20830 Stevens Creek Blvd. |
| Daly City CA | Chipotle | 650-757-4587 | 213 Westlake Center |

| | | | |
|---|---|---|---|
| Daly City CA | Jamba Juice | 650-992-2610 | 127 Serramonte Center |
| Dana Point CA | Luxe Restaurant & Martini Bar | 949-276-4990 | 24582 Del Prado # A/H 1 |
| Dana Point CA | Wind and Sea | 949-496-6500 | 34699 Golden Lantern |
| Davis CA | Ali Baba Middle Eastern Restaurant | 530-758-2251 | 220 3rd Street |
| Davis CA | Cafe Bernardo Davis | 530-750-5101 | 234 D Street |
| Davis CA | Chipotle | 530-758-3599 | 227 E Street |
| Davis CA | Davis Food Co-op | 530-758-2667 | 620 G Street |
| Davis CA | Dos Coyotes | 530-753-0922 | 1411 W Covell Blvd |
| Davis CA | Dos Coyotes | 530-758-1400 | 2191 Cowell Blvd |
| Davis CA | Jamba Juice | 530-757-8499 | 500 1st Street #3 |
| Davis CA | Mishka's | 530-759-0811 | 514 2nd Street |
| Davis CA | Posh Bagels | 530-753-6770 | 206 F Street |
| Davis CA | Redrum Burger | 530-756-2142 | 978 Olive Drive |
| Davis CA | Steve's Place Pizza, Pasta & Grill | 530-758-2800 | 314 F Street |
| Davis CA | Subway | 530-753-2141 | 4748 Chiles Rd |
| Davis CA | Sudwerk | 530-758-8700 | 2001 2nd Street |
| Death Valley CA | Panamint Springs Resort | 775-482-7680 | 40440 H 190 |
| Del Mar CA | Americana | 858-794-6838 | 1454 Camino Del Mar |
| Del Mar CA | Del Mar Rendezvous | 858-755-2669 | 1555 Camino Del Mar Suite # 102 |
| Del Mar CA | En Fuego Cantina & Grill | 858-792-6551 | 1342 Camino del Mar |
| Del Mar CA | Pacifica Breeze Cafe | 858-509-9147 | 1555 Camino Del Mar #209 |
| Del Mar CA | Smashburger | 858-461-4105 | 1555 Camino Del Mar |
| Del Mar CA | Stratford Court Cafe | 858-792-7433 | 1307 Stratford Court |
| Del Mar CA | The Coffee Bean & Tea Leaf | 858-481-6229 | 2689 Via de la Valle, Suite E |
| Downey CA | Lazy Dog Restaurant & Bar | 562-354-4910 | 8800 Apollo Way |
| Downey CA | The Coffee Bean & Tea Leaf | 562-904-7016 | 8550 Firestone Blvd |
| Dublin CA | Baja Fresh Mexican Grill | 925-556-9199 | 4550 Tassajara Rd. |
| Dublin CA | Chipotle | 925-828-4361 | 7020 Amador Plaza Road |
| Dublin CA | Lazy Dog Restaurant & Bar | 925-361-3690 | 4805 Hacienda Dr |
| Dunsmuir CA | Cafe Maddalena | 530-235-2725 | 5801 Sacramento Avenue |
| Dunsmuir CA | Cornerstone Bakery & Cafe | 530-235-4677 | 5759 Dunsmuir Avenue |
| El Dorado Hills CA | Bella Bru Coffee Company | 916-933-5454 | 3941 Park Drive #50 |
| El Dorado Hills CA | Juice It Up | 916-941-7140 | 4355 Town Center Blvd, #113 |
| El Dorado Hills CA | Mama Ann's Deli & Bakery | 916-939-1700 | 4359 Town Center Blvd #111 |
| El Dorado Hills CA | Steve's Place Pizza & Pasta | 916-939-2100 | 3941 Park Drive, #100 |
| El Segundo CA | Chipotle | 310-426-1437 | 307 N Sepulveda Blvd |
| Elk Grove CA | Baja Fresh Mexican Grill | 916-691-2252 | 7419 Laguna Blvd. Ste 220 |
| Elk Grove CA | Chipotle | 916-478-2360 | 7440 Laguna Blvd. #124 |
| Elk Grove CA | Dos Coyotes | 916-687-3790 | 8519 Bond Road, Suite 100 |
| Emeryville CA | Jamba Juice | 415-288-9980 | 5761 Christie Avenue |
| Encinitas CA | Baja Fresh Mexican Grill | 760-633-2262 | 194 El Camino Real Blvd |
| Encinitas CA | Beachside Bar & Grill | 760-942-0738 | 806 S Coast Highway101 |
| Encinitas CA | Bentley's Steak and Chop House | 760-632-9333 | 162 S Rancho Santa Fe Rd |
| Encinitas CA | Chipotle | 760-635-3863 | 268 North El Camino Real |
| Encinitas CA | Encinitas Cafe | 760-632-0919 | 531 S Coast Hwy 101 |
| Encinitas CA | Firenze Trattoria | 760-944-9000 | 162 S Rancho Santa Fe Road |
| Encinitas CA | Jamba Juice | 760-943-9751 | 272-A N El Camino Real |
| Encinitas CA | Mr. Peabody's | 760-753-7192 | 136 Encinitas Blvd |
| Encinitas CA | Peace Pies | 760-479-0996 | 133 Daphne Street |
| Encino CA | Baja Fresh Mexican Grill | 818-907-9998 | 16542 Ventura Blvd |
| Encino CA | Coffee Bean & Tea Leaf | 818-386-0935 | 16101 Ventura Blvd. Suite 180 |
| Encino CA | Johnny Rockets | 818-981-5900 | 16901 Ventura Blvd |
| Encino CA | The Coffee Bean & Tea Leaf | 818-906-9551 | 17301-1 Ventura Blvd |
| Escondido CA | Baja Fresh Mexican Grill | 760-480-9997 | 890 W Valley Parkway |
| Escondido CA | Centre City Cafe | 760-489-6011 | 2680 S Escondido Blvd |
| Escondido CA | Charlie's Family Restaurant | 760-738-1545 | 210 N Ivy Street |
| Escondido CA | Chipotle | 760-740-9043 | 1282 Auto Park Way |
| Etiwanda CA | Johnny Rockets | 909-463-2800 | 7800 Kew Avenue |
| Eureka CA | Hana Sushi Restaurant | 707-444-3318 | 2120 4th Street |
| Eureka CA | Los Bagels | 707-442-8525 | 403 Second Street |
| Eureka CA | Starbucks Coffee | 707-445-2672 | 1117 Myrtle Avenue |
| Fairfax CA | Fairfax Scoop | 415-453-3130 | 63 Broadway Blvd |
| Fairfax CA | Iron Springs Pub and Brewery | 415-485-1005 | 765 Center Blvd |
| Fairfield CA | Baja Fresh Mexican Grill | 707-432-0460 | 1450 Travis Blvd |
| Felton CA | Rocky's Cafe | 831-335-4637 | 6560 H 9 |
| Folsom CA | Chipotle | 916-983-9374 | 1001 E Bidwell Street Suite 160 |
| Folsom CA | Coffee Republic | 916-987-8001 | 6610 Folsom Auburn Rd |

| Folsom CA | Jamba Juice | 916-985-0164 | 13389 Folsom Blvd. #400 |
|---|---|---|---|
| Folsom CA | Panera Bread | 916-984-4953 | 380 Palladio Parkway, #301 |
| Folsom CA | Pinkberry | 916-983-3550 | 280 Palladio Pkwy #933 |
| Folsom CA | Pizzeria Classico | 916-351-1430 | 702 Sutter St |
| Folsom CA | Rubio's Baja Grill | 916-983-0645 | 2776 E Bidwell Street |
| Folsom CA | Snook's Candies and Ice Cream | 916-985-0620 | 731 Sutter Street |
| Fontana CA | Coffee Bean & Tea Leaf | 909-349-0811 | 16215 Sierra Lakes Parkway |
| Fontana CA | Jamba Juice | 909-823-6303 | 16635 Sierra Lakes Parkway, Suite 100 |
| Forestville CA | Russian River Pub | 707-887-7932 | 11829 River Road |
| Forestville CA | Russian River Vineyards and the Corks Restaurant | 707-887-3344 | 5700 Gravenstein H N/H 116 |
| Fort Bragg CA | Home Style Cafe | 707-964-6106 | 790 S. Main Street |
| Fort Bragg CA | Laurel Deli | 707-964-7812 | 401 N Main Street |
| Fort Bragg CA | Mendocino Cookie Company | 707-964-0282 | 303 N Main St |
| Fort Bragg CA | Piaci Pub and Pizzeria | 707-961-1133 | 120 W. Redwood Avenue |
| Fort Bragg CA | Silver's at the Wharf | 707-964-4283 | 32260 N Harbor Dr |
| Fortuna CA | Shotz Coffee | 707-725-8000 | 1665 Main Street |
| Foster City CA | Baja Fresh Mexican Grill | 650-358-8632 | 1031 East Hillsdale Blvd. |
| Foster City CA | El Torito Mexican Restaurant and Cantina | 650-574-6844 | 388 Vintage Park Drive |
| Fountain Valley CA | Chipotle | 951-817-0447 | 18951 Brookhurst |
| Fountain Valley CA | The Coffee Bean & Tea Leaf | 714-438-0138 | 18011 Newhope Street, Suite G |
| Fremont CA | Chipotle | 510-979-9397 | 5565 Auto Mall Parkway |
| Fresno CA | Baja Fresh Mexican Grill | 559-431-8811 | 7675 N. Blackstone |
| Fresno CA | Chipotle | 559-225-1166 | 5128 North Palm Ave |
| Fresno CA | Dai Bai Dang Restaurant | 559-448-8894 | 7736 N Blackstone Ave |
| Fresno CA | Jamba Juice | 559-271-7493 | 3696 W Shaw Avenue |
| Fresno CA | Jamba Juice | 559-433-6970 | 1512 E Champlain Drive, #101 |
| Fresno CA | Jamba Juice | 559-261-2619 | 190 Paseo del Centro |
| Fresno CA | Jamba Juice | 559-456-0518 | 570 S Clovis Avenue, Suite 105 |
| Fresno CA | Revue News | 559-499-1844 | 620 E. Olive Avenue |
| Fresno CA | TGI Fridays | 559-435-8443 | 1077 E. Herndon Avenue |
| Fresno CA | The Loving Hut | 559-237-4052 | 1495 N Van Ness Avenue |
| Fresno CA | Whole Foods Market | 559-241-0300 | 650 West Shaw Avenue |
| Fullerton CA | Chipotle | 714-525-2121 | 501 N State College |
| Fullerton CA | Coffee Bean & Tea Leaf | 714-447-4160 | 205 Orangefair Avenue, Space 11A |
| Fullerton CA | Tropical Smoothie Cafe | 714-680-3008 | 229 E. Common Wealth Avenue |
| Glen Ellen CA | Garden Court Cafe & Bakery | 707-935-1565 | 13875 Sonoma Highway 12 |
| Glendale CA | The Coffee Bean & Tea Leaf | 818-242-4074 | 300A N Glendale Avenue |
| Glendale CA | The Coffee Bean & Tea Leaf | 818-956-8303 | 1500 Canada Blvd, Unit C |
| Glendale CA | The Coffee Bean & Tea Leaf | 818-242-6123 | 763 Americana Way |
| Glendora CA | Chipolte | 909-595-7063 | 1365 E East Hillsdale Street, Suite 700 |
| Glendora CA | Z Pizza | 909-599-4500 | 1365 E Gladstone Street |
| Goleta CA | Baja Fresh Mexican Grill | 805-685-9988 | 7127 Hollister Ave. |
| Goleta CA | Hollister Brewing Company | 805-968-2810 | 6980 Market Place Drive |
| Goleta CA | The Coffee Bean & Tea Leaf | 805-696-6845 | 5745 Calle Real |
| Goleta CA | The Natural Cafe | 805-692-2363 | 5892 Hollister Avenue |
| Granite Bay CA | La Bou | 916-791-2142 | 4110 Douglas Blvd |
| Grass Valley CA | Bubba's Bagels | 530-272-8590 | 11943 Nevada City Hwy |
| Grass Valley CA | Cousin Jack Pasty Company | 530-272-9230 | 100 S Auburn St |
| Greenbrae CA | Jamba Juice | 415-925-8470 | 301 Bon Air Shopping Center |
| Guerneville CA | Main Street Station Ristorante, Cabaret & Pizzeria, | 707-869-0501 | 16280 Main Street |
| Guerneville CA | Roadhouse Restaurant at Dawn Ranch Lodge | 707-869-0656 | 16467 River Road |
| Half Moon Bay CA | Half Moon Bay Brewery | 650-728-2739 | 390 Capistrano Road |
| Half Moon Bay CA | Half Moon Bay Coffee Company | 650-726-3664 | 20 Stone Pine Rd #A |
| Half Moon Bay CA | It's Italia Pizzeria | 650-726-4444 | 401 Main Street |
| Half Moon Bay CA | Three-Zero Cafe | 650-728-1411 | 9850 Cabrillo Hwy N |
| Hanford CA | Jamba Juice | 559-587-2710 | 186 N 12th Avenue, Suite 113 |
| Healdsburg CA | Barndiva | 707-431-0100 | 231 Center Street |
| Healdsburg CA | Dry Creek General Store | 707-433-4171 | 3495 Dry Creek Rd |
| Healdsburg CA | Giorgio's Pizzeria | 707-433-1106 | 25 Grant Avenue |
| Hollywood CA | Birds Cafe-Bar | 323-465-0175 | 5925 Franklin Avenue |
| Hollywood CA | In-N-Out Burgers | 800-786-1000 | 7009 Sunset Blvd. |
| Hollywood CA | Johnny Rockets | 323-465-4456 | 6801 Hollywood Blvd |
| Hollywood CA | La Poubelle Bistro and Bar | 323-465-0807 | 5907 Franklin Avenue |
| Hollywood CA | The Cat and Fiddle | 323-468-3800 | 6530 Sunset Blvd |

| | | | |
|---|---|---|---|
| Hollywood CA | The Coffee Bean & Tea Leaf | 323-467-7785 | 6922 Hollywood Blvd, #103 |
| Huntington Beach CA | Corner Bakery Cafe | 714-891-8400 | 7621 Edinger Ave Ste 110 |
| Huntington Beach CA | Johnny Rockets | 714-901-1100 | 7801 Edinger Avenue |
| Huntington Beach CA | Kahoots Pet Store | 714-842-1841 | 18681 Main St |
| Huntington Beach CA | Slaters | 714-594-5730 | 8082 Adams Ave |
| Huntington Beach CA | Spark Woodfire Grill | 714-960-0996 | 300 Pacific Coast H |
| Huntington Beach CA | The Coffee Bean & Tea Leaf | 714-375-9274 | 17969 Beach Blvd |
| Huntington Beach CA | The Coffee Bean & Tea Leaf | 714-960-1582 | 200 Main Street, Suite 109 |
| Huntington Beach CA | The Park Bench Cafe | 714-842-0775 | 17732 Goldenwest Street |
| Huntington Beach CA | Z Pizza | 714-968-8844 | 10035 Adams Avenue |
| Huntington Beach CA | Z Pizza | 714-536-3444 | 19035 Golden West Avenue, Huntington Beach, CA - ( |
| Idyllwild CA | Cafe Aroma | 951-659-5212 | 54750 North Circle Drive |
| Idyllwild CA | Joanne's Restaurant and Bar | 951-659-0295 | 25875 N Village Drive |
| Imperial Beach CA | Katy's Cafe | 619-863-5524 | 704 Seacoast Drive |
| Inverness CA | Vladimir's Czechoslovakian Restaurant | 415-669-1021 | 12785 Sir Francis Drake Blvd. |
| Irvine CA | Baja Fresh Mexican Grill | 714-508-7777 | 13248 Jamboree Rd. |
| Irvine CA | Chipotle | 949-753-0554 | 81 Fortune Drive Suite 107 |
| Irvine CA | Chipotle | 714-508-2463 | 3955 Irvine Blvd |
| Irvine CA | Coffee Bean & Tea Leaf | 714-505-0498 | 13786-B Jamboree Road |
| Irvine CA | Coffee Bean & Tea Leaf | 949-651-9903 | 5653 Alton Parkway |
| Irvine CA | Corner Bakery Cafe | 714-734-8270 | 13786 Jamboree Rd |
| Irvine CA | Johnny Rockets | 949-753-8144 | 73 Fortune Drive |
| Irvine CA | Lazy Dog Restaurant & Bar | 714-731-9700 | 13290 Jamboree Rd |
| Irvine CA | Mother's Market & Kitchen | 949-752-6667 | 2963 Michelson Drive |
| Irvine CA | Philly's Best | 949-857-2448 | 4250 Barranca Parkway #R |
| Irvine CA | The Coffee Bean & Tea Leaf | 949-660-1332 | 17595 Harvard Avenue, #B |
| Irvine CA | The Coffee Bean & Tea Leaf | 949-453-1815 | 71 Fortune Drive, #844 |
| Irwindale CA | Picasso's Cafe Bakery and Catering Co | 626-969-6100 | 6070 N. Irwindale Ave. |
| Jackson CA | Mel & Faye's Drive In | 209-223-0853 | 205 N. State Hwy 49 |
| Jamestown CA | Historic National Hotel | 209-984-3446 | 18187 Main St |
| Jamestown CA | Pizza Plus | 209-984-3700 | 18251 Main St |
| Julian CA | Apple Alley Bakery | 760-765-2532 | 2122 Main Street |
| Julian CA | Buffalo Bills | 760-765-1560 | 2603 B Street |
| Julian CA | Julian Pie Company | 760-765-2449 | 2225 Main Street |
| Julian CA | The Bailey Wood Pit Barbecue | 760-765-3757 | Main and A Streets |
| Julian CA | The Julian Grille | 760-765-0173 | 2224 Main Street |
| Julian CA | The Rongbranch Restaurant | 760-765-2265 | 2722 Washington St |
| Julian CA | Wynola Pizza Express | 760-765-1004 | 4355 H 78/79 |
| Kings Beach CA | Brockway Bakery | 530-546-2431 | 8710 North Lake Blvd |
| Kings Beach CA | Char-Pit | 530-546-3171 | 8732 N Lake Blvd |
| La Canada CA | Pinkberry | 818-952-0128 | 712 Foothill Blvd |
| La Crescenta CA | Baja Fresh Mexican Grill | 818-541-0568 | 2637 Foothill Blvd |
| La Crescenta CA | Jeremy's | 818-248-7772 | 3009 Honolulu Avenue |
| La Habra CA | Chipotle | 714-526-0800 | 1202 S Idaho Street, Unit A |
| La Jolla CA | Burger Lounge | 858-456-0196 | 1101 Wall Street |
| La Jolla CA | Cass Street Café and Bakery | 858-454-9094 | 5550 La Jolla Blvd |
| La Jolla CA | Chipotle | 858-554-1866 | 8657 Villa La Jolla |
| La Jolla CA | Girard Gourmet | 858-454-3321 | 7837 Girard Avenue |
| La Jolla CA | Harry's Coffee Shop | 858-454-7381 | 7545 Girard Avenue |
| La Jolla CA | Rubio's | 858-546-9377 | 8855 Villa La Jolla Drive |
| La Jolla CA | The 910 Restaurant and Bar | 858-454-2181 | 910 Prospect St |
| La Jolla CA | Whole Foods Market | 858-642-6700 | 8825 Villa La Jolla Drive |
| La Jolla CA | Yummy Maki Yummy Box | 858-587-9848 | 3211 Holiday Ct # 101A |
| La Jolla CA | Zenbu Sushi Bar & Restaurant | 858-454-4540 | 7660 Fay Avenue |
| La Mesa CA | Chipotle | 619-589-2258 | 8005 Fletcher Parkway |
| La Quinta CA | Chipotle | 760-564-3079 | 79-174 H 111, Suite 101 |
| La Quinta CA | The Coffee Bean & Tea Leaf | 760-771-8012 | 79-024 H 111, Suite 101 |
| La Verne CA | Aoki Japanese Restaurant | 909-593-2239 | 2307 D Street |
| La Verne CA | Cafe Allegro | 909-593-0788 | 2124 3rd Street |
| La Verne CA | Jamba Juice | 909-392-4927 | 1614 Foothill Blvd/H 66 |
| Ladera Ranch CA | Z Pizza | 949-347-8999 | 25672 Crown Valley Parkway |
| Lafayette CA | Baja Fresh Mexican Grill | 925-283-8740 | 3596 Mt. Diablo Blvd. |
| Lafayette CA | Chow Restaurant | 925-962-2469 | 53 Lafayette Circle |
| Lafayette CA | Uncle Yu's Szechuan | 925-283-1688 | 999 Oak Hill Rd |
| Laguna Beach CA | Food Village | 949-464-0060 | 211-217 Broadway St |
| Laguna Beach CA | Madison Squar and Garden Cafe | 949-494-0137 | 320 N Coast Hwy |

| Laguna Beach CA | Zinc Cafe and Market | 949-494-6302 | 350 Ocean Avenue |
| Laguna Hills CA | Baja Fresh Mexican Grill | 949-360-4222 | 26548 Moulton Park Way |
| Laguna Hills CA | Coffee Bean & Tea Leaf | 949-583-9216 | 24155 Laguna Hills Mall #1635 |
| Laguna Hills CA | Lulu's Creperie Cafe | 949-855-2222 | 24781 Alicia Parkway, Suite E |
| Laguna Niguel CA | Z Pizza | 949-481-3948 | 32371 Golden Lantern Street |
| Lake Elsinore CA | Coffee Bean & Tea Leaf | 951-245-4374 | 29263 Central Avenue, Suite P6 |
| Lake Forest CA | Chipotle | 949-830-9091 | 22379 El Toro Road |
| Lake Forest CA | Chipotle | 949-587-1550 | 23645 El Toro Road |
| Lake Forest CA | Jamba Juice | 949-587-9891 | 23628 El Toro Road |
| Lake Forest CA | The Coffee Bean & Tea Leaf | 949-458-1907 | 23647 El Toro Road, Suite E |
| Lake Tahoe CA | Jamba Juice | 530-544-8890 | 4000 Lake Tahoe Blvd. #33 |
| Lakewood CA | Chipotle | 562-790-8786 | 5310 Lakewood Blvd/H 19 |
| Lancaster CA | Camille's Sidewalk Cafe | 661-940-5878 | 43901 15th Street W |
| Lancaster CA | Giovanni's Italian Deli & Delights | 661-729-1300 | 42035 10th Street W |
| Larkspur CA | Left Bank | 415-927-3331 | 507 Magnolia Avenue |
| Laytonville CA | The Chief Smokehouse | 707-984-6770 | 44400 N Hwy 101 |
| Little River CA | Wild Fish Restaurant | 949-720-9925 | 7750 N Highway 1 |
| Livermore CA | Baja Fresh Mexican Grill | 925-245-9888 | 2298 Las Positas |
| Livermore CA | First Street Ale House | 925-371-6588 | 2086 1st Street |
| Livermore CA | Manpuku | 925-371-9038 | 4363 First Street |
| Livermore CA | Olive Tree Café and Catering | 925-960-0636 | 7633 Southfront Road |
| Livermore CA | Panama Red Coffee Co. | 925-245-1700 | 2115 First Street |
| Lone Pine CA | Pizza Factory | 760-876-4707 | 301 S Main Street/H 395 |
| Long Beach CA | Chipotle | 562-597-0469 | 1800 Ximeno Avenue |
| Long Beach CA | Coffee Bean & Tea Leaf | 562-598-2198 | 6471 E Pacific Coast H/H 1 |
| Long Beach CA | Coffee Bean & Tea Leaf | 562-492-9020 | 4105 S Atlantic Avenue, Suite A |
| Long Beach CA | Coffee Bean & Tea Leaf | 562-429-4139 | 6344 Spring Street, Suite 1 |
| Long Beach CA | Coffee Bean & Tea Leaf | 562-494-3514 | 1996 Ximeno Avenue, Space 101 |
| Long Beach CA | Coffee Bean & Tea Leaf | 562-985-3477 | 1212 Bellflower Blvd |
| Long Beach CA | Johnny Rockets | 562-983-1332 | 245 Pine Avenue |
| Long Beach CA | Kafe Neo | 562-987-1210 | 2800 E. 4th St. |
| Long Beach CA | Omelette Inn | 562-437-5625 | 108 W 3rd Street |
| Long Beach CA | Roots Gourmet | 562-795-7668 (ROOT) | 6473 E. Pacific Coast H/H 1 |
| Long Beach CA | Royal Cup Cafe | 562-363-6069 | 194 Marina Drive #101 |
| Long Beach CA | Royal Cup Cafe | 562-987-1027 | 994 Redondo Avenue |
| Long Beach CA | Royal Cup Cafe | 562-987-1027 | 994 Redondo Avenue |
| Long Beach CA | Stefano's | 562-437-2880 | 429-C Shoreline Village Drive |
| Long Beach CA | The Small Cafe | 562-434-0226 | 5656 E 2nd st |
| Long Beach CA | Whole Foods Market | 562-598-8687 | 6550 E. Pacific Coast Highway |
| Long Beach CA | Z Pizza | 562-987-4500 | 4612 E 2nd Street |
| Long Beach CA | Z Pizza | 562-498-0778 | 5718 E 7th Street |
| Los Angeles CA | Alcove | 323-644-0100 | 1929 Hillhurst Avenue |
| Los Angeles CA | Baja Fresh Mexican Grill | 323-436-3844 | 7919 Sunset Blvd. |
| Los Angeles CA | Baja Fresh Mexican Grill | 323-549-9080 | 5757 Wilshire Blvd. |
| Los Angeles CA | Chipotle | 213-765-9068 | 3748 S Figueroa Street |
| Los Angeles CA | Chipotle | 323-857-0608 | 110 S Fairfax Avenue |
| Los Angeles CA | Coffee Bean & Tea Leaf | 213-381-6853 | 3183 Wilshire Blvd #115A |
| Los Angeles CA | Coffee Bean & Tea Leaf | 213-388-9763 | 3810 Wilshire Blvd Suite 110C |
| Los Angeles CA | Coffee Bean & Tea Leaf | 213-622-9748 | 801 W 7th Street |
| Los Angeles CA | Coffee Bean & Tea Leaf | 213-749-5746 | 210 E Olympic Blvd, #102 |
| Los Angeles CA | Coffee Bean & Tea Leaf | 310-234-8411 | 10401 Santa Monica Blvd |
| Los Angeles CA | Coffee Bean & Tea Leaf | 323-962-7078 | 6255 W Sunset Blvd, Suite 170 |
| Los Angeles CA | Coffee Bean & Tea Leaf | 310-282-9907 | 9541 W Pico Blvd |
| Los Angeles CA | Coffee Bean & Tea Leaf | 310-442-1019 | 11698 San Vicente Blvd |
| Los Angeles CA | Coffee Bean & Tea Leaf | 310-914-9564 | 11913 W Olympic Blvd |
| Los Angeles CA | Fred's 62 | 323-667-0062 | 1850 N Vermont Ave |
| Los Angeles CA | Golden Road Brewing | 213-373-HOPS (4677) | 5410 W San Fernando Road |
| Los Angeles CA | Good Microbrew and Grill | 323-660-3645 | 922 Lucille Avenue |
| Los Angeles CA | Griffith Park snack stand | | Vermont Ave |
| Los Angeles CA | Hollywood Blvd restaurants | | Hollywood Blvd. |
| Los Angeles CA | Home | 323-669-0211 | 2500 Riverside Drive |
| Los Angeles CA | Il Capriccio on Vermont | 323-662-5900 | 1757 N Vermont Avenue |
| Los Angeles CA | Jamba Juice | 310-476-5823 | 11911 San Vincente Blvd, #100 |
| Los Angeles CA | Johnnie's New York Pizza | 310-553-1188 | 10251 Santa Monica Blvd |
| Los Angeles CA | Johnny Rockets | 213-687-8206 | 131 S Central Avenue |

| | | | |
|---|---|---|---|
| Los Angeles CA | Lala's Argentine Grill""; | 323-934-6838 | 7229 Melrose Avenue |
| Los Angeles CA | Le Figaro Bistro | 323-662-1587 | 1802 N Vermont Avenue |
| Los Angeles CA | Leaf Organics | 310-397-0700 | 11938 W Washington Blvd |
| Los Angeles CA | Lulu's Cafe | 323-938-6095 | 7149 Beverly Blvd |
| Los Angeles CA | Mel's Drive-In | 310-854-7200 | 8585 Sunset Blvd. |
| Los Angeles CA | Millie's Restaurant | 323-664-0404 | 3524 W Sunset Blvd |
| Los Angeles CA | The Coffee Bean & Tea Leaf | 323-469-4684 | 135 N Larchmont |
| Los Angeles CA | The Coffee Bean & Tea Leaf | 213-745-4963 | 3726 S. Figueroa Street |
| Los Angeles CA | The Coffee Bean & Tea Leaf | 213-627-3816 | 645 W 9th Street, #108 |
| Los Angeles CA | The Coffee Bean & Tea Leaf | 323-263-9317 | 209 S Mednik Avenue |
| Los Angeles CA | The Coffee Bean & Tea Leaf | 310-470-4226 | 1500 Westwood Blvd |
| Los Angeles CA | The Coffee Bean & Tea Leaf | 310-473-6618 | 11049 Santa Monica Blvd |
| Los Angeles CA | The Coffee Bean & Tea Leaf | 323-913-3457 | 2081 Hillhurst Avenue |
| Los Angeles CA | The Coffee Bean & Tea Leaf | 310-313-0259 | 3470 S Sepulveda Blvd |
| Los Angeles CA | The Coffee Bean & Tea Leaf | 310-842-9330 | 10401 Venice BlvdH 187 |
| Los Angeles CA | The Coffee Bean & Tea Leaf | 310-815-1255 | 1845 S La Cienega Blvd |
| Los Angeles CA | The Coffee Bean & Tea Leaf | 323-857-0461 | 6333 W 3rd Street, E-11 |
| Los Angeles CA | The Coffee Bean & Tea Leaf | 323-934-1449 | 7235 Beverly Blvd |
| Los Angeles CA | The Coffee Bean & Tea Leaf | 323-934-7277 | 5979 W Third Street |
| Los Angeles CA | The Coffee Bean & Tea Leaf | 310-665-9814 | 8601 S Lincoln Blvd, Suite 140/H 1 |
| Los Angeles CA | The Coffee Bean & Tea Leaf | 323-851-8392 | 7915 Sunset Blvd |
| Los Angeles CA | The Coffee Bean & Tea Leaf | 310-441-1705 | 10897 Pico Blvd |
| Los Angeles CA | The Coffee Bean & Tea Leaf | 213-689-8087 | 601 W 5th Street, #R1 |
| Los Angeles CA | The Coffee Bean & Tea Leaf | 310-535-5596 | 909 Sepulveda Blvd, Suite 135/ H1 |
| Los Angeles CA | Tiago Coffee Bar and Kitchen | 323-466-5600 | 7080 Hollywood |
| Los Angeles CA | Toast Bakery Cafe Inc | 323-655-5018 | 8221 W 3rd St |
| Los Angeles CA | Whole Foods Market | 310-824-0858 | 1050 S. Gayley |
| Los Angeles CA | Whole Foods Market | 323-964-6800 | 6350 West 3rd Street |
| Los Angeles CA | Whole Foods Market | 323-848-4200 | 7871 West Santa Monica Blvd. |
| Los Angeles CA | Whole Foods Market | 310-826-4433 | 11737 San Vicente Blvd. |
| Los Angeles CA | Whole Foods Market | 310-996-8840 | 11666 National Boulevard |
| Los Angeles CA | Wirtshaus | 323-931-9291 | 345 N La Brea Ave |
| Los Feliz CA | Home | 323-665-HOME (4663) | 1760 Hillhurst Avenue |
| Los Gatos CA | Happy Hound | 408-358-2444 | 15899 Los Gatos Blvd |
| Los Gatos CA | Whole Foods Market | 408-358-4434 | 15980 Los Gatos Blvd. |
| Los Gatos CA | Willow Street Pizza | 408-354-5566 | 20 S. Santa Cruz Ave |
| Lower Lake CA | Vigilance Winery | 707-994-9656 | 13888 Point Lakeview Road |
| Madera CA | IHOP Restaurant | 559-675-5179 | 2201 W Cleveland Avenue |
| Malibu CA | Malibu Cafe | 818-540-2400 | 327 South Latigo Canyon |
| Malibu CA | The Coffee Bean & Tea Leaf | 310-456-5771 | 3835 Cross Creek Road #7 |
| Mammoth Lakes CA | Base Camp Cafe | 760-934-3900 | 3325 Main Street |
| Mammoth Lakes CA | Looney Bean Roasting Company | 760-934-1345 | 26 Old Mammoth Rd |
| Mammoth Lakes CA | Paul Schat's Bakery | 760-934-6055 | 3305 Main Street |
| Mammoth Lakes CA | Roberto's Mexican Cafe | 760-934-3667 | 271 Old Mammoth Road |
| Mammoth Lakes CA | Side Door Cafe | 760-934-5200 | 1000 Canyon Blvd #229 |
| Manhattan Beach CA | Johnny Rockets | 310-536-9464 | 1550 Rosecrans Ave. |
| Manhattan Beach CA | The Coffee Bean & Tea Leaf | 310-546-3359 | 3008 Sepulveda Blvd/H 1 |
| Manhattan Beach CA | The Coffee Bean & Tea Leaf | 310-374-9396 | 1133 Artesia Blvd |
| Manteca CA | Chipotle | 209-823-1017 | 1440 Hulsey Way |
| Marina Del Rey CA | Baja Fresh Mexican Grill | 310-578-2252 | 13424 Maxella Avenue |
| Marina Del Rey CA | Coffee Bean & Tea Leaf | 310-823-0858 | 13420 Maxella, Suite C20 |
| Marina Del Rey CA | The Coffee Bean & Tea Leaf | 310-821-1068 | 4020 S Lincoln Blvd, Space D/H 1 |
| Marina del Rey CA | Chipotle | 310-821-0059 | 4718 Admiralty Way |
| Mendocino CA | Frankie's Mendocino | 707-937-2436 | 44951 Ukiah Street |
| Mendocino CA | Mendo Burgers | 707-937-1111 | 10483 Lansing Street |
| Mendocino CA | Mendocino Cafe | 707-937-2422 | 10451 Lansing St |
| Menlo Park CA | Left Bank | 650-473-6543 | 635 Santa Cruz Avenue |
| Middletown CA | Mountain High Coffee and Books | 707-928-0461 | 16295 H 175 |
| Millbrae CA | Chipotle | 650-259-9301 | 135 S El Camino Real |
| Milpitas CA | Bento Xpress | 408-262-7544 | 23 N. Milpitas Blvd |
| Mission Viejo CA | Baja Fresh Mexican Grill | 949-347-9033 | 27620 Marguerite Pkwy Ste C |
| Mission Viejo CA | Skimmer's Panini Cafe | 949-855-8500 | 25290 Marguerite Parkway |
| Mission Viejo CA | Taco Mesa | 949-364-1957 | 27702 Crown Valley Parkway |
| Modesto CA | Baja Fresh Mexican Grill | 209-545-4111 | 3801 Pelandale Ave |
| Modesto CA | Baja Fresh Mexican Grill | 209-238-0222 | 801 Oakdale Road Ste |
| Modesto CA | Barkin' Dog Grill | 209-572-2341 | 940 11th Street |

| | | | |
|---|---|---|---|
| Monrovia CA | Peach Cafe | 626-599-9092 | 141 E Colorado Blvd |
| Monrovia CA | The Coffee Bean & Tea Leaf | 626-301-0317 | 102 S Myrtle Avenue |
| Monrovia CA | The Coffee Bean & Tea Leaf | 626-657-1404 | 702 E Huntington Drive |
| Montecito CA | Pierre Lafond Montecito Deli | 805-565-1504 | 516 San Ysidro Road |
| Monterey CA | Abalonetti Seafood Trattoria | 831-373-1851 | 57 Fishermans Wharf |
| Monterey CA | Ambrosia India Bistro | 831-641-0610 | 565 Abrego Street |
| Monterey CA | Archie's Hamburgers & Breakfast | 831-375-6939 | 125 Ocean View Blvd. |
| Monterey CA | Bubba Gump Shrimp Co. | 831-373-1884 | 720 Cannery Row |
| Monterey CA | Cafe Fina | 831-372-5200 | 47 Fishermans Wharf #1 |
| Monterey CA | Domenico's on the Wharf | 831-372-3655 | 50 Fishermans Wharf #1 |
| Monterey CA | East Village Coffee Lounge | 831-373-5601 | 498 Washington St |
| Monterey CA | Ghiradelli Ice Cream | 831-373-0997 | 660 Cannery Row |
| Monterey CA | Indian Summer | 831-372-4744 | 220 Olivier Street |
| Monterey CA | Louie Linguini's | 831-648-8500 | 660 Cannery Row |
| Monterey CA | Paluca Trattoria | 831-373-5559 | 6 Fishermans Wharf #1 |
| Monterey CA | Parker-Lusseau Pastries | 831-641-9188 | 539 Hartnell Street |
| Monterey CA | Peter B's Brewpub | 831-649-4511 | 2 Portola Plaza |
| Monterey CA | Pino's Italian Cafe & Ice Cream | 831-649-1930 | 211 Alvarado St |
| Monterey CA | Tarpy's Road House | 831-647-1444 | 2999 Monterey Salinas Hwy #1 |
| Monterey CA | Whole Foods Market | 831-333-1600 | 800 Del Monte Center |
| Montgomery CA | Bubba Gump Shrimp Company Restaurant | 831-373-1884 | 720 Cannery Row |
| Montrose CA | The Coffee Bean & Tea Leaf | 818-249-7848 | 3701 Ocean View Blvd |
| Montrose CA | Zeke's Smokehouse Restaurant | 818-957-7045 | 2209 Honolulu Avenue |
| Moorpark CA | Jamba Juice | 805-529-7381 | 2944 Tapo Canyon Road, #H |
| Moorpark CA | The Natural Cafe | 805-523-2016 | 840 New Los Angeles Avenue #A-2/H 23/118 |
| Moreno Valley CA | Jamba Juice | 951-697-8880 | 12430 Day Street, Suite C-4 |
| Morgan Hill CA | Chipotle | 408-776-8505 | 775 Cochrane Road, Bldg C |
| Morgan Hill CA | Jamba Juice | 408-465-2456 | 317 Vineyard Town Center Way |
| Morgan Hill CA | Rosy's at the Beach | 408-778-0551 | 17320 Monterey Road |
| Morro Bay CA | Dorn's Original Breakers Cafe | 805-772-4415 | 801 Market Ave |
| Moss Beach CA | Moss Beach Distillery | 650-728-5595 | 140 Beach Way @ Ocean Blvd |
| Mount Shasta CA | Lalo's Mexican Restaurant | 530-926-5123 | 520 N Mount Shasta Blvd |
| Mountain View CA | Amici's East Coast Pizza | 650-961-6666 | 790 Castro Street |
| Mountain View CA | Cafe Baklava | 650-969-3835 | 341 Castro Street |
| Mountain View CA | Chipotle | 650-969-6528 | 2400 Charleston Road |
| Mountain View CA | Clarkes Charcoal Broiler | 650-967-0851 | 615 W El Camino Real |
| Mountain View CA | Hobee's | 650-968-6050 | 2312 Central Expressway |
| Mountain View CA | La Salsa Restaurant | 650-917-8290 | 660 San Antonio Rd |
| Mountain View CA | Le Boulanger | 650-961-1787 | 650 Castro St #160 |
| Mountain View CA | Posh Bagel | 650-968-5308 | 444 Castro Street #120 |
| Mountain View CA | Steak Out | 650-209-0383 | 383 Castro Street |
| Napa CA | Angele | 707-252-8115 | 540 Main Street |
| Napa CA | Bistro Don Giovanni | 707-224-3300 | 4110 Howard Street |
| Napa CA | Napa General Store Restaurant | 707-259-0762 | 540 Main Street |
| Napa CA | Sweetie Pies | 707-257-7280 | 520 Main Street |
| Needles CA | Juicy's River Cafe | 760-326-2233 | 2411 W Broadway St |
| Nevada City CA | Broad Street Bistro | 530-265-4204 | 426 Broad St |
| Nevada City CA | California Organics | 530-265-9392 | 135 Argall Way |
| Nevada City CA | New Moon Cafe | 530-265-6399 | 203 York Street |
| Newark CA | Chipotle | 510-742-8010 | 34883 Newark Blvd |
| Newbury Park CA | Baja Fresh Mexican Grill | 805-376-0808 | 1015 Broadbeck Dr. |
| Newbury Park CA | The Natural Cafe | 805-498-0493 | 1714 Newbury Road, Suite R |
| Newport Beach CA | Baja Fresh Mexican Grill | 949-759-0010 | 1324 Bison Avenue |
| Newport Beach CA | Cafe Beau Soleil | 949-640-4402 | 953 Newport Center Drive |
| Newport Beach CA | Charlie's Chili | 949-675-7991 | 102 McFadden Place |
| Newport Beach CA | Jamba Juice | 949-852-6500 | 4341 MacArthur Blvd, #A |
| Newport Beach CA | Park Avenue Cafe | 949-673-3830 | 501 Park Avenue |
| Newport Beach CA | The Coffee Bean & Tea Leaf | 949-719-0524 | 1316 Bison Avenue |
| Newport Beach CA | Top Dog Barkery | 949-759-3647 | 924 Avocado Ave |
| Newport Beach CA | Wilma's Patio | 949-675-5542 | 203 Marine Avenue |
| Newport Beach CA | Z Pizza | 949-715-1117 | 7956 E Pacific Coast H/H 1 |
| Newport Beach CA | Z Pizza | 949-760-3100 | 2549 Eastbluff Drive |
| Newport Beach CA | Z Pizza | 949-219-9939 | 1616 San Miguel Drive- |
| Newport Beach CA | Z Pizza | 949-723-0707 | 3423 Via Lido |
| Norco CA | Rubio's Baja Grill | 951-898-3591 | 110 Hidden Valley Pkwy |
| North Highlands CA | Jamba Juice | 916-344-4108 | 4981 Watt Avenue |

| | | | |
|---|---|---|---|
| Northridge CA | Jamba Juice | 818-893-1256 | 9012 Balboa Blvd |
| Northridge CA | The Coffee Bean & Tea Leaf | 818-360-8299 | 18705 Devonshire Street |
| Northridge CA | Whole Foods Market | 818-363-3933 | 19340 Rinaldi |
| Novato CA | Baja Fresh Mexican Grill | 415-897-4122 | 924 Diablo Ave. |
| Novato CA | La Pinata | 415-892-1471 | 940 7th Street |
| Novato CA | Moylans Brewing Company | 415-898-4677 | 15 Rowland Way |
| Oakhurst CA | Pizza Factory | 559-683-2700 | 40120 Highway 41 #B |
| Oakland CA | Crepevine | 510-658-2026 | 5600 College Avenue |
| Oakland CA | Fentons Creamery & Restaurant | 510-658-7000 | 4226 Piedmont Avenue |
| Oakland CA | Filippo's | 510-601-8646 | 5400 College |
| Oakland CA | Heinolds First & Last Chance | 510-839-6761 | 56 Jack London Sq |
| Oakland CA | Italian Colors Ristorante | 510-482-8094 | 2220 Mountain Boulevard |
| Oakland CA | Posh Bagel | 510-597-0381 | 4037 Piedmont Avenue |
| Oakland CA | Urban Legend Cellars | 510-545-4356 | 621 4th Street |
| Occidental CA | Howard's Cafe | 707-874-2838 | 3811 Bohemian H |
| Ocean Beach CA | Bar-B-Que House | 619-222-4311 | 5025 Newport Avenue |
| Ocean Beach CA | Tower Two Beach Cafe | 619-223-4059 | 5083 Santa Monica Avenue # 1B |
| Oceanside CA | Chipotle | 760-721-6904 | 2611 Vista Way |
| Oceanside CA | Don's Country Kitchen | 760-722-7337 | 1938 Coast Highway |
| Oceanside CA | Hill Street Coffee House | 760-966-0985 | 524 S Coast Hwy |
| Oceanside CA | Jamba Juice | 760-433-6719 | 2619 Vista Way, Suite B-2 |
| Ojai CA | Agave Maria's | 805-646-6353 | 106 S Montgomery St |
| Ojai CA | Deer Lodge Tavern | 805-646-4256 | 2261 Maricopa Hwy |
| Ojai CA | Full of Beans | 805-640-8500 | 11534 N Ventura Avenue/H 33 |
| Ojai CA | Jim & Rob's Fresh Grill | 805-640-1301 | 535 E Ojai Ave |
| Ojai CA | Rainbow Bridge Natural Foods Market | 805-646-4017 | 211 East Matilija Street |
| Ojai CA | Sea Fresh Seafood | 805-646-7747 | 533 E. Ojai Avenue/H 150 |
| Olympic Valley CA | Auld Dubliner | 530-584-6041 | The Village at Squaw Valley |
| Ontario CA | Baja Fresh Mexican Grill | 909-484-6200 | 929 N. Milliken Ave Ste C |
| Ontario CA | In-N-Out Burger | 800-786-1000 | 1891 E. G Street |
| Ontario CA | Jamba Juice | 909-476-8008 | 990 Ontario Mills Drive |
| Orange CA | Byblos Mediterranean Cafe | 714-538-7180 | 129 W Chapman Ave |
| Orange CA | Chipotle | 714-283-5010 | 2202 N Tustin Avenue |
| Orange CA | Jamba Juice | 714-769-3151 | 20 City Blvd W K #5 |
| Orange CA | Johnny Rockets | 714-385-0086 | 20 City Blvd |
| Orange CA | Krispy Kreme Doughnuts | 714-769-4330 | 330 The City Dr S |
| Orange CA | Lazy Dog Restaurant & Bar | 714-769-7020 | 1623 West Katella Ave. |
| Orange CA | The Coffee Bean & Tea Leaf | 714-283-0088 | 2202 N. Tustin Street, Suite C |
| Orange CA | The Loving Hut | 714-464-0544 | 237 S Tustin Street |
| Orange CA | Two's Company | 714-771-7633 | 22 Plaza Square |
| Orinda CA | Shelby's | 925-254-9687 | 2 Theater Square |
| Oxnard CA | Baja Fresh Mexican Grill | 805-988-7878 | 2350 Vineyard Ave |
| Oxnard CA | Café Amri | 805-983-3026 | 2000 Outlet Center Dr #295 |
| Oxnard CA | Lazy Dog Restaurant & Bar | 805-351-4888 | 598 Town Center Drive |
| Oxnard CA | Sea Fresh Restaurant | 805-204-0974 | 3550 Harbor Blvd |
| Oxnard CA | The Coffee Bean & Tea Leaf | 805-485-8112 | 2180 N Rose Avenue |
| Oxnard CA | The Coffee Bean & Tea Leaf | 805-984-7162 | 1191 S Victoria Avenue |
| Oxnard CA | Topper's Pizza | 805-385-4444 | 2100 S. Saviers Rd |
| Oxnard CA | Topper's Pizza | 805-385-4444 | 2701 Peninsula Rd |
| Oxnard CA | Topper's Pizza | 805-385-4444 | 111 E. Gonzales Rd |
| Pacific Grove CA | Bagel Bakery | 831-649-6272 | 1132 Forest Ave |
| Pacific Grove CA | First Awakenings | 831-372-1125 | 125 Ocean View Blvd #105 |
| Pacific Grove CA | Toasties Cafe | 831-373-7543 | 702 Lighthouse Ave |
| Pacific Palisades CA | The Coffee Bean & Tea Leaf | 310-230-2587 | 15278 Antioch Street |
| Palm Desert CA | The Coffee Bean & Tea Leaf | 760-674-9056 | 73400 El Paseo Drive #9 |
| Palm Springs CA | Chipotle | 760-325-0346 | 2465 East Palm Canyon Drive, Bldg. 11, Ste. 1110 |
| Palm Springs CA | Coffee Bean & Tea Leaf | 760-325-9402 | 100 N Palm Canyon Drive/H 111 |
| Palm Springs CA | Hair of the Dog English Pub | 760-323-9890 | 238 N Palm Canyon Dr |
| Palm Springs CA | Native Foods | 760-416-0070 | 1775 E. Palm Canyon Drive |
| Palm Springs CA | Nature's Health Food and Café | 760-323-9487 | 555 South Sunrise Way |
| Palm Springs CA | New York Pizza Delivery | 760-778-6973 | 260 N. Palm Canyon Drive |
| Palm Springs CA | Peabody's Coffee Bar | 760-322-1877 | 134 S Palm Canyon Dr |
| Palm Springs CA | Pomme Frite | 760-778-3727 | 256 S. Palm Canyon Drive |
| Palm Springs CA | Shermans Deli and Bakery | 760-325-1199 | 401 Tahquitz Canyon Way |
| Palm Springs CA | Spencer's Restaurant | 760-327-3446 | 701 West Baristo Road |
| Palm Springs CA | Starbucks | 760-323-8023 | 682 S. Palm Canyon Drive |

| Palmdale CA | Baja Fresh Mexican Grill | 661-947-1682 | 39332 10th St. W. |
|---|---|---|---|
| Palmdale CA | Chipotle | 661-266-0944 | 1125 Rancho Vista |
| Palmdale CA | The Coffee Bean & Tea Leaf | 661-273-7441 | 39605 10th Street W, Unit D |
| Palo Alto CA | Baja Fresh Mexican Grill | 650-424-8599 | 3990 El Camino Real |
| Palo Alto CA | Coupa Cafe | 650-322-6872 | 538 Ramona Street |
| Palo Alto CA | Crepevine | 650-323-3900 | 367 University Avenue |
| Palo Alto CA | Izzy's Brooklyn Bagels | 650-329-0700 | 477 S California Ave |
| Palo Alto CA | Joanie's Cafe | 650-326-6505 | 447 S California Ave |
| Palo Alto CA | Spalti Ristorante | 650-327-9390 | 417 S California Ave |
| Palo Alto CA | St. Michael's Alley | 650-326-2530 | 140 Homer Avenue |
| Palo Alto CA | Whole Foods Market | 650-326-8676 | 774 Emerson Street |
| Pasadena CA | All India Cafe | 626-440-0309 | 39 S Fair Oaks Ave |
| Pasadena CA | Baja Fresh Mexican Grill | 626-792-0446 | 899 E. Del Mar |
| Pasadena CA | Chipotle | 626-229-9173 | 246 S Lake Avenue |
| Pasadena CA | Chipotle | 626-351-6017 | 3409 E Foothill Blvd |
| Pasadena CA | Coffee Bean & Tea Leaf | 626-449-5499 | 18 S Fair Oaks |
| Pasadena CA | Il Fornaio | 626-683-9797 | 24 W Union |
| Pasadena CA | Jones Coffee Roasters | 626-564-9291 | 693 S Raymond Avenue |
| Pasadena CA | Kabuki Japanese Restaurant | 626-568-9310 | 88 W. Colorado Blvd. |
| Pasadena CA | Lucky Baldwins Trappiste | 626-844-0447 | 1770 E Colorado Blvd |
| Pasadena CA | Mi Piace | 626-795-3131 | 25 E Colorado Blvd |
| Pasadena CA | The Coffee Bean & Tea Leaf | 626-744-9370 | 415 S Lake Avenue, Suite 108 |
| Paso Robles CA | Big Bubba's BBQ | 805-238-6272 | 1125 24th Street |
| Paso Robles CA | Big Bubba's Bad BBQ | 805-238-6272 | 1125 24th St |
| Paso Robles CA | Chubby Chandler's | 805-239-2141 | 1304 Railroad St. |
| Paso Robles CA | Good Ol' Burgers | 805-238-0655 | 1145 24th St |
| Paso Robles CA | Good Ol' Burgers | 805-238-0655 | 1145 24th Street |
| Paso Robles CA | Jamba Juice | 805-227-0826 | 96 Niblick Road |
| Paso Robles CA | Odyssey World Café | 805-237-7516 | 1214 Pine St |
| Paso Robles CA | Panolivo Family Bistro | 805-239-3366 | 1344 Park Street |
| Paso Robles CA | Pappy McGregor's Irish Pub | 805-238-7070 | 1122 Pine Street |
| Paso Robles CA | Thomas Hill Organics Bistro & Wine Lounge | 805-226-5888 | 1305 Park St |
| Petaluma CA | Apple Box | 707-762-5222 | 224 B Street |
| Petaluma CA | Della Fattoria | 707-763-0161 | 141 Petaluma Blvd N |
| Pine Grove CA | 88 Burgers | 209-296-7277 | 19845 State Highway 88 |
| Pinole CA | Jamba Juice | 510-669-1321 | 2794 Pinole Valley Road |
| Pismo Beach CA | Mo's Smokehouse BBQ | 805-773-6193 | 221 Pomeroy Ave |
| Pismo Beach CA | Seaside Cafe and Bakery | 805-773-4360 | 1327 Shell Beach Road |
| Pismo Beach CA | The Coffee Bean & Tea Leaf | 805-773-6420 | 354 Five Cities Drive |
| Pittsburg CA | Chipotle | 925-754-3270 | 4418 Century Blvd |
| Placerville CA | Jamba Juice | 530-344-1675 | 3987 Missouri Flat Road, Suite 300 |
| Placerville CA | Noah's Ark | 530-621-3663 | 535 Placerville Drive |
| Placerville CA | Pizza Factory | 530-644-6043 | 4570 Pleasant Valley Road |
| Placerville CA | Quiznos Sub | 530-622-7878 | 3967 Missouri Flat Road |
| Placerville CA | Teriyaki Junction | 530-295-1413 | 1216 Broadway |
| Placerville CA | The Cellar at Smith Flat House | 530-621-1003 | 2021 Smith Flat Road |
| Playa Vista CA | The Coffee Bean & Tea Leaf | 310-862-5725 | 13020 Pacific Promenade, Suite 9 |
| Pleasant Hill CA | Chipotle | 925-674-0615 | 60 Crescent Drive |
| Pleasanton CA | Baci Restaurant | 925-600-0600 | 500 Main Street |
| Pleasanton CA | Baja Fresh Mexican Grill | 925-251-1500 | 2457 Stoneridge Mall Ste. |
| Pleasanton CA | Bob's House | 925-847-1700 | 5321 Hopyard Road |
| Pleasanton CA | Erik's Deli | 925-847-9755 | 4247 Rosewood Drive |
| Pleasanton CA | Handles | 925-399-6690 | 855 Main Street |
| Plymouth CA | Cafe at the Park | 209-245-6981 | 18265 Hwy 49 |
| Plymouth CA | Marlene and Glen's Diner | 209-245-5778 | 18726 Highway 49 |
| Point Reyes Station CA | Cowgirl Creamery | 415-663-9335 | 80 Fourth Street |
| Pollock Pines CA | Burger Barn & Cafe | 530-344-7167 | 6404 Pony Express Trail |
| Port Hueneme CA | Chinese Dumpling House | 805-985-4849 | 575 W. Channel Islands Blvd. |
| Porter Ranch CA | Baja Fresh Mexican Grill | 818-831-3100 | 19701 Rinaldi St. |
| Porter Ranch CA | Z Pizza | 818-363-2600 | 19300 Rinaldi Street |
| Porterville CA | Jamba Juice | 559-784-0196 | 1395 W Henderson Avenue |
| Poway CA | Chipotle | 858-748-9200 | 13495 Poway Road |
| Princeton CA | Half Moon Bay Brewing Company | 650-728-BREW (2739) | 390 Capistrano Rd |
| Quincy CA | Sweet Lorraine's | 530-283-5300 | 384 W Main Street/H 70 |
| Ragged Point CA | Ragged Point Restaurant | 805-927-5708 | 19019 H 1 |

| | | | |
|---|---|---|---|
| Rancho Bernardo CA | Baja Fresh Mexican Grill | 858-592-7788 | 11980-11976 Bernardo Plaza Dr. |
| Rancho Cucamonga CA | Chipotle | 909-476-8424 | 10811 Foothill Blvd/Historic H 66 |
| Rancho Cucamonga CA | Chipotle | 909-476-7863 | 11334 4th Street |
| Rancho Cucamonga CA | Coffee Bean & Tea Leaf | 909-483-2544 | 8140 Haven Avenue, Suite 100 |
| Rancho Cucamonga CA | Corner Bakery Cafe | 909-803-2600 | 12375 N Main Street |
| Rancho Cucamonga CA | Johnny Rockets | 909-463-2800 | 7800 Kew Avenue |
| Rancho Cucamonga CA | Lazy Dog Restaurant & Bar | 909-987-4131 | 11560 4th Street |
| Rancho Cucamonga CA | Panera Bread | 909-919-7999 | 8055 Haven Avenue |
| Rancho Mirage CA | Baja Fresh Mexican Grill | 760-674-9380 | 71-800 Highway 111, Ste A-116 |
| Rancho Penasquitos CA | Cafe 56 | 858-484-5789&8206 | 13211 Black Mountain Rd |
| Redding CA | Bartel's Giant Burger | 530-243-7313 | 75 Lake Blvd E/ H 299 |
| Redding CA | Burrito Bandito | 530-222-6640 | 8938 Airport Road |
| Redding CA | Chipotle | 530-223-9292 | 961 Dana Drive |
| Redding CA | In-n-Out | 800-786-1000 | 1275 Dana Dr |
| Redding CA | Jamba Juice | 530-243-1736 | 3455 Placer Street, Unit B |
| Redding CA | Manhattan Bagel | 530-222-2221 | 913 Dana Drive |
| Redding CA | Sandwichery | 530-246-2020 | 1341 Tehama Street |
| Redding CA | Togos | 530-222-9212 | 1030 East Cypress Avenue Ste B |
| Redlands CA | Chipolte | 909-307-8424 | 625 Orange Street |
| Redlands CA | Jamba Juice | 909-792-0900 | 27510 Lugonia Avenue, Suite F |
| Redlands CA | The Coffee Bean & Tea Leaf | 909-798-0454 | 528 Orange Street |
| Redondo Beach CA | The Coffee Bean & Tea Leaf | 310-316-2416 | 1617 Pacific Coast H, #103/H 1 |
| Redondo Beach CA | Whole Foods Market | 310-376-6931 | 405 N. Pacific Coast Hwy. |
| Redwood City CA | Cafe La Tartine | 650-474-2233 | 830 Middlefield Road |
| Redwood City CA | Chipotle | 650-216-9325 | 861 Middlefield Road |
| Redwood City CA | City Pub | 650-363-2620 | 2620 Broadway |
| Redwood City CA | Talk of Broadway | 650-368-3295 | 2096 Broadway Street |
| Redwood City CA | The Sandwich Spot | 650-299-1300 | 2420 Broadway Street |
| Redwood City CA | Whole Foods Market | 650-367-1400 | 1250 Jefferson Avenue |
| Reedley CA | Jamba Juice | 559-637-1496 | 765 N Reed Avenue |
| Riverside CA | Antonious Pizza | 951-682-9100 | 3737 Main Street |
| Riverside CA | The Coffee Bean & Tea Leaf | 951-684-3803 | 3712 Mission Inn Avenue, Suite N-4 |
| Rocklin CA | Baja Fresh Mexican Grill | 916-772-1600 | 2210 Sunset Blvd. |
| Rohnert Park CA | Baja Fresh Mexican Grill | 707-585-2252 | 451 Rohnert Pk. Expressway West |
| Rohnert Park CA | Golden B Cafe | 707-585-6185 | 101 Golf Course Drive |
| Roseville CA | Baja Fresh Mexican Grill | 916-773-2252 | 1850 Douglas Blvd |
| Roseville CA | Cafe Elletti | 916-774-6704 | 2240 Douglas Blvd |
| Roseville CA | Chipotle | 916-786-9218 | 3988 Douglas Blvd |
| Roseville CA | Chipotle | 916-788-8282 | 781 Pleasant Grove Blvd |
| Roseville CA | Chipotle | 916-783-8841 | 1136 Galleria Blvd |
| Roseville CA | Dos Coyotes | 916-772-0775 | 2030 Douglas Blvd Suite 4 |
| Roseville CA | Mas Mexican Food | 916-773-3778 | 1563 Eureka Roa |
| Roseville CA | Quizno's Classic Subs | 916-787-1940 | 1228 Galleria Blvd #130 |
| Roseville CA | Togo's Eatery | 916-782-4546 | 1825 Douglas Blvd |
| Roseville CA | Z Pizza | 916-786-9797 | 3984 Douglas Blvd |
| Rutherford CA | Rutherford Grill | 707-963-1792 | 1180 Rutherford Road |
| Sacramento CA | Ambrosia Cafe & Catering | 916-444-8129 | 1030 K Street |
| Sacramento CA | Annabelle's Pizza-Pasta | 916-448-6239 | 200 J Street |
| Sacramento CA | Baja Fresh Mexican Grill | 916-564-2252 | 2100 Arden Way |
| Sacramento CA | Baja Fresh Mexican Grill | 916-920-5201 | 2600 Gateway Oaks Dr. |
| Sacramento CA | Bella Bru Cafe and Catering | 916-928-1770 | 4680 Natomas Blvd |
| Sacramento CA | Cafe Bernardo | 916-443-1180 | 2726 Capitol Avenue |
| Sacramento CA | Cafe Bernardo / R15 | 916-930-9191 | 1431 R Street |
| Sacramento CA | Cafe Bernardo Midtown / Monkey Bar | 916-443-1180 | 2726 Capitol Avenue |
| Sacramento CA | Chipotle | 916-861-0620 | 2878 Zinfandel Drive |
| Sacramento CA | Chipotle | 916-444-8940 | 1831 Capitol Avenue |
| Sacramento CA | Chipotle | 916-485-6305 | 3328 El Camino Avenue |
| Sacramento CA | Chipotle | 916-646-4571 | 1729 Howe Avenue |
| Sacramento CA | Chipotle | 916-487-1125 | 2517 Fair Oaks Blvd |
| Sacramento CA | Chipotle | 916-334-5200 | 5040 Auburn Blvd |
| Sacramento CA | Danielle's Creperie | 916-972-1911 | 3535 B Fair Oaks Blvd |
| Sacramento CA | Dos Coyotes | 916-452-5696 | 6450 Folsom Blvd #110 |
| Sacramento CA | Jamba Juice | 916-927-2051 | 2600 Gateway Oaks, #300 |
| Sacramento CA | Jamba Juice | 916-419-6092 | 4640 Natomas Blvd, #120 |
| Sacramento CA | La Bou | 916-369-7824 | 10395 Rockingham Dr |
| Sacramento CA | Magpie Cafe & Catering | 916-452-7594 | 1409 R Street Suite 102 |

| | | | |
|---|---|---|---|
| Sacramento CA | Original Pete's Pizza, Pasta and Grill | 916-442-6770 | 2001 J Street |
| Sacramento CA | Pyramid Alehouse | 916-498-9800 | 1029 K Street |
| Sacramento CA | River City Brewing Company | 916-447-2739 | 545 Downtown Plaza Ste 1115 |
| Sacramento CA | Rubicon Brewing Company | 916-448-7032 | 2004 Capitol Avenue |
| Sacramento CA | Sacramento Natural Foods Cooperative | 916-455-2667 | 1900 Alhambra Blvd. |
| Sacramento CA | Spataro Restaurant and Bar | 916-440-8888 | 1415 L Street |
| Sacramento CA | Streets of London Pub | 916-498-1388 | 1804 J Street |
| Sacramento CA | Ten 22 | 916-441-2211 | 1022 Second Street |
| Sacramento CA | The Bread Store | 916-557-1600 | 1716 J Street |
| Sacramento CA | Whole Foods Market | 916-488-2800 | 4315 Arden Way |
| Salinas CA | Jamba Juice | 831-449-3200 | 1552-A N Main Street |
| San Anselmo CA | Java Hub Cafe | 415-451-4928 | 60 Greenfield Avenue |
| San Bernardino CA | Baja Fresh Mexican Grill | 909-890-1854 | 745 E. Hospitality Lane Ste C |
| San Bernardino CA | Chipotle | 909-799-9420 | 1092 Hospitality Lane, Suite B |
| San Bernardino CA | Jamba Juice | 909-796-6012 | 1078 E Hospitality Lane, Suite F |
| San Carlos CA | Chipotle | 650-598-0847 | 1135 Industrial Road, Suite C |
| San Carlos CA | Santorini | 650-637-8283 | 753 Laurel Street |
| San Clemente CA | Baja Fresh Mexican Grill | 949-361-4667 | 979 Avenida Pico |
| San Clemente CA | Italian Cravings | 949-492-2777 | 105 S Ola Vis |
| San Clemente CA | The Cellar | 949-492-3663 | 156 Avenida Del Mar |
| San Clemente CA | Z Pizza | 949-498-3505 | 1021 Avenida Pico |
| San Diego CA | Acapulco Restaurant | 619-260-8124 | 2467 Juan Street |
| San Diego CA | Baja Fresh Mexican Grill | 619-222-3399 | 3369 Rosecrans |
| San Diego CA | Baja Fresh Mexican Grill | 858-277-5700 | 3737 Murphy Cyn Rd |
| San Diego CA | Baja Fresh Mexican Grill | 619-295-1122 | 845 Camino De La Reina |
| San Diego CA | Bare Back Grill | 858-274-7117 | 4640 Mission Blvd |
| San Diego CA | Bull's Smokin' BBQ | 619-276-2855 | 1127 W Morena Blvd |
| San Diego CA | Burger Lounge | 619-237-7878 | 1608 India Street |
| San Diego CA | Burger Lounge | 619-955-5727 | 528 5th Avenue |
| San Diego CA | Burger Lounge | 619-487-1183 | 406 University Avenue |
| San Diego CA | Burger Lounge | 619-584-2929 | 4116 Adams Avenue |
| San Diego CA | Champagne French Bakery Cafe | 858-792-2222 | 12955 El Camino Real |
| San Diego CA | Chipotle | 619-209-3688 | 734 University Avenue Suite C |
| San Diego CA | Chipotle | 619-491-0481 | 1025 Camino De La Reina, Suite 2 |
| San Diego CA | Chipotle | 858-274-3093 | 1504 Garnet Avenue |
| San Diego CA | Chipotle | 619-222-0508 | 3680 Rosecrans Street |
| San Diego CA | Chipotle | 858-586-2147 | 8250 Mira Mesa Blvd, Suite G |
| San Diego CA | Chipotle SDSU | 619-265-2778 | 5842 Hardy Avenue |
| San Diego CA | Coffee Bean & Tea Leaf | 858-715-0278 | 5657 Balboa Avenue |
| San Diego CA | Coffee Bean & Tea Leaf | 858-505-9909 | 9343 Clairemont Mesa Blvd |
| San Diego CA | El Indio | 619-299-0333 | 3695 India Street |
| San Diego CA | Elephant & Castle Pub | 619-234-9977 | 1355 N Harbor Drive |
| San Diego CA | Fig Tree Cafe Restaurant & Catering | 858-274-2233 | 5119 Cass Street |
| San Diego CA | Fred's Mexican Cafe | 619-858-TACO (8226) | 2470 San Diego Avenue |
| San Diego CA | Indigo Grill | 619-234-6802 | 1536 India Street |
| San Diego CA | Jamba Juice | 858-490-5177 | 1774 Garnet Avenue #D |
| San Diego CA | Jamba Juice | 858-487-1500 | 11738 Carmel Mountain Road, #178 |
| San Diego CA | King's Fish House | 619-574-1230 | 825 Camino de la Reina |
| San Diego CA | Korky's Ice Cream and Coffee | 619-297-3080 | 2371 San Diego Avenue |
| San Diego CA | Lazy Dog Restaurant & Bar | 619-481-6191 | 1202 Camino Del Rio N |
| San Diego CA | Mitch's Seafood | 619-222-8787 | 1403 Scott Street |
| San Diego CA | Oggi's Pizza | 619-640-1072 | 2245 Fenton Parkway |
| San Diego CA | Pampas Argentine Grill | 858-278-5971 | 8690 Aero Drive Suite 105 |
| San Diego CA | Panera Bread | 858-385-9066 | 12156 Carmel Mountain Road |
| San Diego CA | Peace Pies | 619-223-2880 | 4230 Voltaire Street |
| San Diego CA | Saffron Thai Grilled Chicken | 619-574-0177 | 3137 India Street |
| San Diego CA | Sally's Seafood on the Water | 619-358-6740 | 1 Market Place |
| San Diego CA | Slaters | 619-398-2600 | 2750 Dewey Rd #193 |
| San Diego CA | The Coffee Bean & Tea Leaf | 619-574-7588 | 120 W Washington, Suite B |
| San Diego CA | The Coffee Bean & Tea Leaf | 619-238-8047 | 160 W Broadway |
| San Diego CA | The Coffee Bean & Tea Leaf | 619-299-5072 | 925 C Camino De La Reina |
| San Diego CA | The Coffee Bean & Tea Leaf | 858-385-7895 | 10550 Craftsman Way, Suite #187 |
| San Diego CA | The Coffee Bean & Tea Leaf | 858-592-7348 | 12070 Caramel Mountain Road, Suite 296 |
| San Diego CA | The Coffee Bean & Tea Leaf | 858-350-9673 | 12730 Carmel Country Road |
| San Diego CA | The Patio on Lamont Street | 858-412-4648 | 4445 Lamont Street |

| | | | |
|---|---|---|---|
| San Diego CA | Trattoria Fantastica | 619-234-1735 | 1735 India Street |
| San Diego CA | Twisted Vine Bistro | 858-780-2501 | 7845 Highland Village Place |
| San Diego CA | Whole Foods Market | 619-294-2800 | 711 University Avenue |
| San Diego CA | Zia's | 619-234-1344 | 1845 India Street |
| San Dimas CA | Roady's Restaurant | 909-592-0980 | 160 W. Bonita Ave |
| San Francisco CA | Absinthe Brasserie and Bar | 415-551-1590 | 398 Hayes Street |
| San Francisco CA | Alaturca Restaurant | 415-345-1011 | 869 Geary Street |
| San Francisco CA | B44 Bistro | 415-986-6287 | 44 Belden Place |
| San Francisco CA | Baja Fresh Mexican Grill | 415-369-9760 | 30 Fremont St |
| San Francisco CA | Beach Chalet Brewery & Restaurant | 415-386-8439 | 1000 Great Highway @ Ocean Beach |
| San Francisco CA | Blissful Bites | 415-750-9460 | 397 Arguello Blvd |
| San Francisco CA | Blue Danube Coffee House | 415-221-9041 | 306 Clement St |
| San Francisco CA | Cafe De La Presse | 415-398-2680 | 352 Grant Ave |
| San Francisco CA | Calzone's | 415-397-3600 | 430 Columbus Ave |
| San Francisco CA | Chipotle | 415-278-0461 | 525 Market Street |
| San Francisco CA | Chipotle | 415-512-8113 | 126 New Montgomery Street |
| San Francisco CA | Cioppino's | 415-775-9311 | 400 Jefferson Street |
| San Francisco CA | Coffee Bean and Tea Leaf | 415-447-9733 | 2201 Fillmore St |
| San Francisco CA | Coffee Roastery | 415-922-9559 | 2191 Union Street |
| San Francisco CA | Crepevine | 415-431-4646 | 216 Church Street |
| San Francisco CA | Crepevine | 415-681-5858 | 624 Irving Street |
| San Francisco CA | Dolores Park Cafe | 415-621-2936 | 18th and Dolores |
| San Francisco CA | Farley's | 415-648-1545 | 1315-18th Street |
| San Francisco CA | Flippers | 415-552-8880 | 482 Hayes Street |
| San Francisco CA | Ghirardelli Ice Cream Fountain | 415-771-4903 | Ghirardelli Square/900 N Point Street |
| San Francisco CA | Jamba Juice | 415-864-7105 | 2300 16th Street, #245 |
| San Francisco CA | Jamba Juice | 415-616-9949 | 152 Kearny Street |
| San Francisco CA | Jamba Juice | 415-703-6011 | 2014 Market Street |
| San Francisco CA | La Mediterranee | 415-431-7210 | 288 Noe Street |
| San Francisco CA | Lou's Pier 47 Restaurant | 415-771-5687 | 300 Jefferson St |
| San Francisco CA | Martha & Brothers Coffee Company | 415-648-1166 | 1551 Church Street |
| San Francisco CA | Panta Rei | 415-591-0900 | 431 Columbus |
| San Francisco CA | Park Chow | 415-665-9912 | 1240 9th Avenue |
| San Francisco CA | Peet's Coffee and Tea | 415-563-9930 | 2197 Fillmore St |
| San Francisco CA | Plant Organic Cafe;""; Downtown Cafe | 415-693-9730 | 101 California Street |
| San Francisco CA | Plant Organic Cafe;""; Marina | 415-931-2777 | 3352 Steiner Street |
| San Francisco CA | Plant Organic Cafe;""; Pier 3 | 415-984-0437 | Pier 3, Suite 108, The Embarcadero |
| San Francisco CA | Plouf | 415-986-6491 | 40 Belden Place |
| San Francisco CA | Pluto's Fresh Food | 415-775-8867 | 3258 Scott St |
| San Francisco CA | Pompei's Grotto | 415-776-9265 | 340 Jefferson St |
| San Francisco CA | Public House | 415-644-0240 | 24 Willie Mays Plaza |
| San Francisco CA | Rogue Ales Public House | 415-362-7880 | 673 Union |
| San Francisco CA | The Curbside Cafe | 415-929-9030 | 2417 California St |
| San Jose CA | Amato Pizzeria | 408-997-7727 | 6081 Meridian Avenue #A |
| San Jose CA | Aqui Cal-Mex | 408-362-3456 | 5679 Snell Avenue |
| San Jose CA | Baja Fresh Mexican Grill | 408-436-5000 | 1708 Oakland Road |
| San Jose CA | Bill's Cafe | 408-294-1125 | 1115 Willow Street |
| San Jose CA | Britannia Arms | 408-278-1400 | 173 W Santa Clara Street |
| San Jose CA | Camille's Sidewalk Cafe | 408-436-5333 | 90 Skyport Drive |
| San Jose CA | Casa Vicky's Catering and Cafe | 408-995-5488 | 792 E Julian St |
| San Jose CA | Chipotle | 408-288-9172 | 975 The Alameda/H 82, Suite 10 |
| San Jose CA | Chipotle | 408-453-6115 | 1751 N First Street |
| San Jose CA | Chipotle | 408-369-8163 | 2007 Camden Avenue, #50 |
| San Jose CA | Fu Kee Chinese Restaurant | 408-225-3218 | 121 Bernal Road |
| San Jose CA | Grande Pizzeria | 408-292-2840 | 150 E San Carlos Street |
| San Jose CA | Johnny Rockets | 408-977-1414 | 150 S First Street, # 115 |
| San Jose CA | Johnny Rockets | 408-229-1414 | 840 Blossom Hill |
| San Jose CA | Left Bank | 408-984-3500 | 377 Santana Row, Suite 1100 |
| San Jose CA | Noah's Bagels | 408-371-8321 | 1578 S Bascom Ave |
| San Jose CA | Pasta Pomodoro | 408-241-2200 | 378 Santana Row #1130 |
| San Jose CA | Pizza Antica | 408-557-8373 | 334 Santana Row #1065 |
| San Jose CA | Poor House Bistro | 408-292-5837 | 91 S Autumn Street/H 82 |
| San Jose CA | Sam's BBQ | 408-297-9151 | 1110 S Bascom Avenue |
| San Jose CA | Siena Bistro | 408-271-0837 | 1359 Lincoln Avenue |
| San Jose CA | Straits | 408-246-6320 | 333 Santana Row |
| San Jose CA | The Loft Bar and Bistro | 408-291-0677 | 90 S Second Street |
| San Jose CA | Willow Street Wood Fired Pizza | 408-971-7080 | 1072 Willow St |

| | | | |
|---|---|---|---|
| San Juan Bautista CA | JJ's Homemade Burgers | 831-623-1748 | 100 The Alameda |
| San Juan Capistrano CA | L'Hirondelle Restaurant | 949-661-0425 | 31631 Camino Capistrano |
| San Juan Capistrano CA | Z Pizza | 949-429-8888 | 32341 Camino Capistrano |
| San Luis Obispo CA | Baja Fresh Mexican Grill | 805-544-5450 | 1085 Higuera Street |
| San Luis Obispo CA | Jamba Juice | 805-549-0733 | 890 Marsh Street |
| San Luis Obispo CA | Novo Restaurant | 805-543-3986 | 726 Higuera Street |
| San Luis Obispo CA | Splash Cafe | 805-544-7567 | 1491 Monterey Street |
| San Marcos CA | Jamba Juice | 760-471-9404 | 591 Grand Avenue, Suite 100 |
| San Marcos CA | Old California Coffee House | 760-744-2112 | 1080 W. San Marcos Blvd #176 |
| San Mateo CA | Chipotle | 650-627-9245 | 1062 Foster City Blvd |
| San Mateo CA | Whole Foods Market | 650-358-6900 | 1010 Park Place |
| San Pedro CA | The Lighthouse Deli | 310-548-3354 | 508 W 39th Street |
| San Rafael CA | Jamba Juice | 415-491-7700 | 266 Northgate One |
| San Rafael CA | Ristorante La Toscana | 415-492-9100 | 3751 Redwood Hwy. |
| San Rafael CA | The Lighthouse Diner | 415-721-7700 | 1016 Court Street |
| San Ramon CA | Baja Fresh Mexican Grill | 925-866-6667 | 132 Sunset Drive |
| San Ramon CA | Whole Foods Market | 925-355-9000 | 100 Sunset Drive |
| San Ramon CA | Z Pizza | 925-328-0525 | 3141-D Crow Canyon Place |
| San Simeon CA | San Simeon Restaurant | 805-927-4604 | 9520 Castillo Dr. |
| Sanger CA | Jamba Juice | 559-876-3026 | 775 Bethel Avenue, Suite 108 |
| Santa Ana CA | Chipotle | 714-754-7380 | 3705 S Bristol Street |
| Santa Ana CA | The Coffee Bean & Tea Leaf | 714-542-5307 | 2264 17th Street |
| Santa Ana CA | The Coffee Bean & Tea Leaf | 714-667-7840 | 2783 N Main Street |
| Santa Ana CA | Z Pizza | 714-437-1111 | 3941 South Bristol |
| Santa Barbara CA | Baja Fresh Mexican Grill | 805-687-9966 | 3851 State Street |
| Santa Barbara CA | Chipotle | 805-730-9195 | 723 State Street |
| Santa Barbara CA | Coffee Bean & Tea Leaf | 805-565-7559 | 3052 De La Vina |
| Santa Barbara CA | Crushcakes & Cafe | 805-963-9353 | 1315 Anacapa Street |
| Santa Barbara CA | Dargan's Irish Pub | 805-568-0702 | 18 E. Ortega Street |
| Santa Barbara CA | Emilio's Restaurant | 805-966-4426 | 324 W Cabrillo Blvd |
| Santa Barbara CA | Fresco Cafe | 805-967-6037 | 3987 State Street, #B |
| Santa Barbara CA | Intermezzo | 805-966-9463 | 813 Anacapa Street |
| Santa Barbara CA | Java Station | 805-681-0202 | 4447 Hollister Avenue |
| Santa Barbara CA | Le Cafe Stella | 805-569-7698 | 3302 McCaw Avenue |
| Santa Barbara CA | Mesa Cafe | 805-966-5303 | 1972 Cliff Drive/H 225 |
| Santa Barbara CA | Pascucci's Restaurant | 805-963-8123 | 729 State Street |
| Santa Barbara CA | Pizza Mizza | 805-564-3900 | 140 S Hope Avenue, Suite 102A |
| Santa Barbara CA | Renaud's Patisserie & Bistro | 805-892-2800 | 1324 State Street |
| Santa Barbara CA | Renaud's Patisserie & Bistro | 805-569-2400 | 3315 State Street |
| Santa Barbara CA | Santa Barbara Shellfish Company | 805-966-6676 | 230 Stearns Wharf |
| Santa Barbara CA | The Brewhouse | 805-884-4664 | 229 W Montecito Street |
| Santa Barbara CA | The Coffee Bean & Tea Leaf | 310-260-0044 | 1209 Coast Village Road |
| Santa Barbara CA | The Coffee Bean & Tea Leaf | 805-966-2442 | 811 State Street |
| Santa Barbara CA | The Coffee Bean & Tea Leaf | 805-569-1809 | 3052 De La Vina |
| Santa Barbara CA | The Natural Cafe | 805-962-9494 | 508 State Street |
| Santa Barbara CA | The Natural Cafe | 805-563-1163 | 361 Hitchcock Way |
| Santa Barbara CA | Tupelo Junction Cafe | 805-899-3100 | 1218 State Street |
| Santa Barbara CA | Vices & Spices | 805-687-7196 | 3558 State Street |
| Santa Clara CA | Baja Fresh Mexican Grill | 408-588-4060 | 3950 Rivermark Plaza |
| Santa Clara CA | Pizz'a Chicago | 408-244-2246 | 1576 Halford Ave |
| Santa Clara CA | Red Robin Gourmet Burgers | 408-855-0630 | 3906 Rivermark Plaza |
| Santa Clara CA | Tony & Alba's Pizza & Pasta | 408-246-4605 | 3137 Stevens Creek Blvd |
| Santa Clarita CA | Jamba Juice | 661-284-6347 | 27061 McBean Parkway |
| Santa Clarita CA | The Big Oaks | 661-296-5656 | 33101 Bouquet Canyon Road |
| Santa Cruz CA | Aldo's Harbor Restaurant | 831-426-3736 | 616 Atlantic Avenue |
| Santa Cruz CA | Black China Cafe and Bakery | 831-460-1600 | 1121 Soquel Avenue |
| Santa Cruz CA | Cafe Limelight | 831-425-7873 | 1016 Cedar St |
| Santa Cruz CA | Cole's Bar-B-Q | 831-476-4424 | 2590 Portola Drive |
| Santa Cruz CA | Engfer's Pizza | 831-429-1856 | 537 Seabright Avenue |
| Santa Cruz CA | Firefly Coffee House | 801-598-3937 | 131 A Front Street |
| Santa Cruz CA | Harbor Bay | 831-475-4948 | 535 7th Avenue |
| Santa Cruz CA | Joe's Pizza and Subs | 831-426-5955 | 841 N Branciforte Avenue |
| Santa Cruz CA | Kelly's French Bakery | 831-423-9059 | 402 Ingalls Street, Santa Cruz, Ca 95060: |
| Santa Cruz CA | Las Palmas Taco Bar | 831-429-1220 | 55 Front Street |
| Santa Cruz CA | Mamma Lucia Cafe Bar Pizzeria | 831-458-2222 | 1618 Mission Street |
| Santa Cruz CA | Pleasure Pizza | 831-475-4999 | 4000 Portola Drive |

| | | | |
|---|---|---|---|
| Santa Cruz CA | River Cafe | 831-420-1280 | 415 River Street, Suite K |
| Santa Cruz CA | Woodstock's Pizza | 831-427-4444 | 710 Front Street |
| Santa Maria CA | Jamba Juice | 805-922-3240 | 530 E Betteravia Road, Suite A-3 |
| Santa Maria CA | The Natural Cafe | 805-937-2735 | 2407 S Broadway/H 135 |
| Santa Monica CA | Babalu | 310-395-2500 | 1002 Montana Avenue |
| Santa Monica CA | Baja Fresh Mexican Grill | 310-393-9313 | 720 Wilshire Blvd. |
| Santa Monica CA | Blue Plate | 310-260-8877 | 1415 Montana Avenue |
| Santa Monica CA | Cezanne | 310-395-9700 | 1740 Ocean Avenue |
| Santa Monica CA | Coffee Bean & Tea Leaf | 310-260-0044 | 200 Santa Monica Blvd |
| Santa Monica CA | Jinky's | 310-917-3311 | 1447 2nd Street |
| Santa Monica CA | The Coffee Bean & Tea Leaf | 829 Wilshire Blvd | 829 Wilshire Blvd |
| Santa Monica CA | The Coffee Bean & Tea Leaf | 310-394-9737 | 1312 Third Street Promenade |
| Santa Monica CA | The Coffee Bean & Tea Leaf | 310-396-6706 | 3150 Ocean Park Blvd |
| Santa Monica CA | The Coffee Bean & Tea Leaf | 310-392-1406 | 2901 Main Street |
| Santa Monica CA | The Coffee Bean & Tea Leaf | 310-581-7991 | 1804 Lincoln Blvd |
| Santa Monica CA | True Food Kitchen | 310-593-8300 | 395 Santa Monica Place, Suite 172 |
| Santa Rosa CA | Flying Goat Coffee | 707-575-1202 | 10 4th Street |
| Santa Rosa CA | Jamba Juice | 707-527-5501 | 2360 Mendocino Avenue |
| Santa Rosa CA | Lita's Cafe | 707-575-1628 | 1973 Mendocino Avenue |
| Santa Rosa CA | Sunnyside Tokyo | 707-526-2652 | 3800 Sebastopol Road |
| Santa Rosa CA | Sweet Spot Pub & Lounge | 707-528-7566 | 619 Fourth Street |
| Santa Rosa CA | Whole Foods Market | 707-575-7915 | 1181 Yulupa Ave. |
| Santa Ysabel CA | Dudley's Bakery | 760-765-0488 | 30218 H 78 |
| Santa Ysabel CA | Jeremy's on the Hill | 760-765-1587 | 4354 California 78 |
| Santee CA | Jamba Juice | 619-448-2746 | 9828 Mission Gorge Road |
| Saratoga CA | La Fondue | 408-867-3332 | 14550 Big Basin Way |
| Sausalito CA | Anchorage 5 | 415-331-8329 | 475 Gate 5 Road |
| Sausalito CA | Poggio Trattoria | 415-332-7771 | 777 Bridgeway |
| Sausalito CA | Scoma's | 415-332-9551 | 588 Bridgeway |
| Sausalito CA | Taste of Rome | 415-332-7660 | 1000 Bridgeway |
| Seal Beach CA | River's End Cafe | 562-431-5558 | 15 1st Street |
| Seal Beach CA | The Coffee Bean & Tea Leaf | 562-596-4006 | 347 Main Street, Suite A |
| Seal Beach CA | Z Pizza | 562-493-3440 | 12430 Seal Beach Blvd |
| Seaside CA | Jamba Juice | 831-583-9696 | 2160 California Ave |
| Sebastopol CA | Whole Foods Market | 707-829-9801 | 6910 McKinley St. |
| Shell Beach CA | Zorro's Cafe and Cantina | 805-773-ZORO (9676) | 927 Shell Beach Road |
| Sherman Oaks CA | Baja Fresh Mexican Grill | 818-789-0602 | 14622 Ventura Blvd. |
| Sherman Oaks CA | Whole Foods Market | 818-382-3700 | 4520 Sepulveda Boulevard |
| Sherman Oaks CA | Whole Foods Market | 818-762-5548 | 12905 Riverside Drive |
| Shingletown CA | Higher Ground Coffee | 530-474-1913 | 28526 Highway44 |
| Sierra City CA | Herrington's Sierra Pines Resort Restaurant | 530-862-1151 | 104 Main Street/H 49 |
| Simi Valley CA | Baja Fresh Mexican Grill | 805-581-6001 | 2679 Tapo Cyn Rd |
| Simi Valley CA | Chipotle | 805-584-0514 | 1263 Simi Town Center Way |
| Simi Valley CA | Jamba Juice | 805-522-1055 | 2944 Tapo Canyon Road, #H |
| Simi Valley CA | The Coffee Bean & Tea Leaf | 805-582-0566 | 2944-G Tapo Canyon Road |
| Simi Valley CA | The Natural Cafe | 805-527-2272 | 2667 Tapo Canyon Road, Unit G |
| Simi Valley CA | Topper's Pizza | 805-385-4444 | 2408 Erringer Rd |
| Solana Beach CA | Beach Grass Cafe | 858-509-0632 | 159 S H 101 |
| Solana Beach CA | Jamba Juice | 858-755-2056 | 689-D Lomas Santa Fe Drive |
| Solvang CA | Bit O'Denmark | 805-688-5426 | 473 Alisal Road |
| Solvang CA | Cali Love Wine | 805-688-1678 | 1651 Copenhagen Drive |
| Solvang CA | Fresco Valley Cafe | 805-688-8857 | 442 Atterdag Road |
| Solvang CA | Giovanni's Italian Restaurant | 805-688-1888 | 1988 Old Mission Drive |
| Solvang CA | Olsen's Danish Village Bakery | 805-688-6314 | 1529 Mission Drive |
| Solvang CA | Panino | 805-688-0608 | 475 First Street |
| Solvang CA | River Grill at The Alisal | 805-688-7784 | 150 Alisal Rd |
| Solvang CA | Subway | 805-688-7650 | 1641 Mission Dr |
| Solvang CA | The Belgian Cafe | 805-688-6630 | 1671 Copenhagen Drive |
| Solvang CA | The Big Bopper | 805-688-6018 | 1510 Mission Drive |
| Solvang CA | The Mustard Seed Restaurant | 805-688-1318 | 1655 Mission Drive/H 246 |
| Solvang CA | The Solvang Brew Company | 805-688-2337 | 1547 Mission Street/H 246 |
| Solvang CA | The Touch | 805-686-0222 | 1635 Mission Drive |
| Solvang CA | Tower Pizza | 805-688-3036 | 436 Alisal Rd, Units C + D |
| Solvang CA | Viking Garden Restaurant | 805-688-1250 | 446C Alisal Rd |

| Solvang CA | Wandering Dog Wine Bar | 805-686-9126 | 1539 C Mission Drive/H 246 |
| Sonoma CA | Centre Du Vin | 707-996-9779 | 480 First Street East |
| Sonoma CA | La Casa | 707-996-3406 | 121 E Spain Street |
| Sonora CA | Pine Tree Restaurant | 209-536-6065 | 19601 Hess Ave |
| Soquel CA | Michael's on Main | 831-479-9777 | 2591 Main Street |
| South Lake Tahoe CA | Big Daddy's Burgers | 530-541-3465 | 3490 Lake Tahoe Blvd/H 50 |
| South Lake Tahoe CA | Izzy's Burger Spa | 530-544-5030 | 2591 Highway 50 |
| South Lake Tahoe CA | Meyer's Downtown Cafe | 530-573-0228 | 3200 Highway 50 |
| South Lake Tahoe CA | Nikkis Restaurant | 530-541-3354 | 3469 Lake Tahoe Blvd |
| South Lake Tahoe CA | Sno-Flake Drive In | 530-544-6377 | 3059 Harrison |
| South Lake Tahoe CA | Sprouts Health Foods | 530-541-6969 | 3125 Harrison Avenue |
| South Pasadena CA | Fair Oaks Pharmacy and Soda Fountain | 626-799-1414 | 1526 Mission St |
| South Pasadena CA | The Coffee Bean & Tea Leaf | 626-403-2141 | 700 S Fair Oaks, #A |
| St Helena CA | Ristorante Tra Vigne | 707-963-4444 | 1050 Charter Oak Avenue |
| St Helena CA | Tra Vigne Cantinetta | 707-963-4444 | 1050 Charter Oak Avenue |
| Stanton CA | Rubio's | 714-827-6495 | 7063 Katella Ave |
| Stinson Beach CA | Parkside Cafe | 415-868-1272 | 43 Arenal Avenue |
| Stinson Beach CA | Sand Dollar Restaurant | 415-868-0434 | 3458 Shoreline Highway |
| Stockton CA | Baja Fresh Mexican Grill | 209-477-5024 | 5350 Pacific Ave |
| Stockton CA | Chipotle | 209-476-7217 | 4940 Pacific Avenue |
| Studio City CA | Jamba Juice | 818-769-6705 | 10955 Ventura Blvd |
| Studio City CA | Le Pain Quotidien | 818-986-1929 | 13045 Ventura Blvd |
| Studio City CA | The Coffee Bean & Tea Leaf | 818-506-4620 | 12050 Ventura Blvd, C-104 |
| Studio City CA | The Coffee Bean & Tea Leaf | 818-783-8068 | 12930 Ventura Blvd, #122 |
| Studio City CA | The Coffee Bean & Tea Leaf | 818-763-7271 | 12501 W Ventura Blvd |
| Summerland CA | The Summerland Beach Cafe | 805-969-1019 | 2294 Lillie Avenue |
| Sun Valley CA | Big Jim's | 818-768-0213 | 8950 Laurel Canyon Blvd |
| Sunnyvale CA | Chipotle | 408-773-1304 | 324 W El Camino Real/H 82 |
| Susanville CA | Frosty Mill | 530-257-5894 | 605 Ash Street |
| Tahoe City CA | Rosie's Cafe | 530-583-8504 | 571 North Lake Blvd |
| Tahoe City CA | Tahoe House Bakery and Gourmet Store | 530-583-1377 | 625 W Lake Blvd |
| Tahoe City CA | The Blue Agave | 530-583-8113 | 425 N Lake Blvd |
| Tarzana CA | The Coffee Bean & Tea Leaf | 818-776-1178 | 18505 Ventura Blvd |
| Tarzana CA | The Coffee Bean & Tea Leaf | 951-694-0723 | 31938 Temecula Parkway, Suite D/H 79 |
| Temecula CA | Applebees | 951-506-7852 | 32175 H 79 |
| Temecula CA | Baja Fresh Mexican Grill | 909-719-1570 | 40688 Winchester Rd |
| Temecula CA | Bushfire Grill | 951-296-0190 | 40665 Winchester Rd |
| Temecula CA | Cafe Daniel | 951-676-8408 | 28601 Old Town Front Street |
| Temecula CA | Carol's Restaurant | 951-676-9243 | 33440 La Serena Way |
| Temecula CA | Chili's | 951-694-0099 | 27645 Ynez Road |
| Temecula CA | Chipotle | 951-506-1734 | 40573 Margarita Road |
| Temecula CA | Front Street Bar and Grill | 951-676-9567 | 28699 Old Town Front Street |
| Temecula CA | Lazy Dog Restaurant & Bar | 951-719-1884 | 40754 Winchester Road |
| Temecula CA | Marie Callender's | 951-699-9339 | 29363 Rancho California Rd |
| Temecula CA | Natural Pet Food Market, Dog Park Cafe and Encore Grooming & Spaw | 951-308-4545 | 31795 Rancho California Road |
| Temecula CA | Outback Steakhouse | 951-719-3700 | 40275 Winchester Road/H 79 |
| Temecula CA | Scarcella's Italian Grille | 951-676-5450 | 27525 Ynez Rd |
| Temecula CA | Temecula Pizza Company | 951-694-9463 | 44535 Bedford Ct # D |
| Temecula CA | Texas Lil's Mesquite Grill | 951-699-5457 | 28495 Old Town Front St |
| Thousand Oaks CA | Baja Fresh Mexican Grill | 805-778-0877 | 595 N Moorpark Rd |
| Thousand Oaks CA | Chipotle | 805-499-3561 | 935 Broadbeck Drive |
| Thousand Oaks CA | Johnny Rockets | 805-778-0780 | 322 W Hillcrest |
| Thousand Oaks CA | Lazy Dog Restaurant & Bar | 805-449-5206 | 172 West Hillcrest Drive |
| Thousand Oaks CA | The Coffee Bean & Tea Leaf | 805-497-7467 | 487 N Moorpark Road Unit 3 |
| Thousand Oaks CA | The Coffee Bean & Tea Leaf | 805-241-2499 | 1772-A E Avenida De Los Arboles |
| Thousand Oaks CA | Thousand Oaks Meat Locker | 805-495-3211 | 2684 E Thousand Oaks Blvd |
| Thousand Oaks CA | Topper's Pizza | 805-385-4444 | 1416 N. Moorpark Rd. |
| Thousand Oaks CA | Z Pizza | 818-991-4999 | 5776 Lindero Canyon Road |
| Tiburon CA | Three Degrees Restaurant at The Lodge at Tiburon | 415-435-3133 | 1651 Tiburon Blvd/H 131 |
| Toluca Lake CA | Baja Fresh Mexican Grill | 818-762-7326 | 10760 Riverside Drive |
| Toluca Lake CA | Priscilla's Gourmet Cafe | 818-843-5707 | 4150 Riverside Dr |
| Toluca Lake CA | The Coffee Bean & Tea Leaf | 818-763-4815 | 10121 Riverside Drive |
| Toluca Lake CA | The Coffee Bean & Tea Leaf | 818-763-3387 | 4444 Lankershim Blvd. #114 |
| Tomales CA | Tomales Bakery | 707-878-2429 | 27000 Highway One |

| | | | |
|---|---|---|---|
| Topanga CA | Abuelitas Restaurant | 310-455-8788 | 137 South Topanga Canyon Blvd |
| Torrance CA | Chipotle | 310-530-0690 | 24631 Crenshaw Blvd Unit A |
| Torrance CA | Johnny Rockets | 310-214-4051 | 3525 Carson Street, Suite 75 |
| Torrance CA | Lazy Dog Restaurant & Bar | 310-921-6080 | 3525 West Carson Street |
| Torrance CA | The Coffee Bean & Tea Leaf | 310-792-8630 | 21300 B Hawthorne Blvd/H 107 |
| Torrance CA | The Coffee Bean & Tea Leaf | 310-530-5443 | 25345 Crenshaw Blvd, Suite B |
| Torrance CA | Whole Foods Market | 310-257-8700 | 2655 Pacific Coast Highway |
| Tracy CA | Baja Fresh Mexican Grill | 209-834-2252 | 1855 W. 11th Street |
| Truckee CA | The Squeeze In | 530-587-9814 | 10060 Donner Pass Road |
| Tulare CA | Jamba Juice | 559-686-1857 | 1681 Hillman Street |
| Turlock CA | Chipotle | 209-656-7647 | 3090 Countryside Drive |
| Tustin CA | Chipotle | 714-665-6730 | 13348 Newport Avenue |
| Tustin CA | Jamba Juice | 714-505-2582 | 2937 E Camino Real #B |
| Tustin CA | Tustin Brewing Company | 714-665-2337 | 13011 Newport Avenue |
| Tustin CA | Whole Foods Market | 714-731-3400 | 14945 Holt Ave. |
| Tustin CA | Z Pizza | 714-734-9749 | 12932 Newport Avenue |
| Upland CA | Chipotle | 909-579-0999 | 1092 North Mountain Avenue |
| Upland CA | Molly's Souper | 909-982-1114 | 388 N 1st Avenue |
| Upland CA | Molly's Souper | 909-982-1114""; | 220 E A Street |
| Upland CA | Molly's Souper | 909-982-1114 | 388 N 1st Ave |
| Upland CA | Qdoba Mexican Grill | 909-932-0090 | 1902 N Campus Avenue |
| Upland CA | Z Pizza | 909-949-1939 | 1943-C N Campus Avenue |
| Upper Lake CA | Blue Wing Saloon and Cafe | 707-275-2233 | 9520 Main Street |
| Vacaville CA | Baja Fresh Mexican Grill | 707-446-6736 | 150 Nut Tree Parkway |
| Vacaville CA | Fentons Creamery & Restaurant at the Nut Tree | 707-469-7200 | E Monte Vista Avenue |
| Vacaville CA | Jamba Juice | 707-455-7302 | 1651 E Monte Vista Avenue, Suite 101 @ Nut Tree Village |
| Valencia CA | Baja Fresh Mexican Grill | 661-254-6060 | 23630 W. Valencia Blvd. |
| Valencia CA | Chipotle | 916-600-9477 | 28102 Newhall Ranch Road |
| Valencia CA | Jamba Juice | 661-222-3174 | 25888 The Old Road |
| Valencia CA | Johnny Rockets | 661-291-2590 | 24425 Town Center Drive |
| Valencia CA | Lazy Dog Restaurant & Bar | 661-253-9996 | 24201 Valencia Blvd |
| Valencia CA | Lucille's Smokehouse BBQ | 661-255-1227 | 24201 Valencia Blvd |
| Valencia CA | The Coffee Bean & Tea Leaf | 661-702-1760 | 28291 Newhall Ranch Road |
| Valencia CA | The Coffee Bean & Tea Leaf | 661-291-1134 | 24201 Valencia Blvd, Space #3648 |
| Vallejo CA | Jamba Juice | 707-645-8912 | 165 Plaza Drive #709 |
| Van Nuys CA | Springboc Bar and Grill | 818-988-9786 | 16153 Victory Blvd |
| Venice CA | Baja Fresh Mexican Grill | 310-392-3452 | 245 Main Street |
| Venice CA | The Terrace | 310-578-1530 | 7 Washington Blvd |
| Ventura CA | Anacapa Brewing Company | 805-643-BEER (2337) | 472 E Main Street |
| Ventura CA | Baja Fresh Mexican Grill | 805-650-3535 | 4726-2 Telephone Road |
| Ventura CA | Cafe Nouveau | 805-648-1422 | 1497 E Thompson Blvd |
| Ventura CA | Chipotle | 805-650-6627 | 1145 S Victoria Avenue |
| Ventura CA | Chipotle | 805-654-0143 | 488 S Mills Road |
| Ventura CA | Golden Egg Cafe | 805-641-2866 | 2009 East Main Street |
| Ventura CA | Lassen Ventura Market and Deli | 805-644-6990 | 4071 E Main Street |
| Ventura CA | Nature's Grill | 805-643-7855 | 566 E Main Street |
| Ventura CA | RedBrick Pizza Ventura | 805-658-2828 | 4990 Telephone Road |
| Ventura CA | Spasso Cucina Italiana | 805-643-2777 | 1140 Seaward Avenue |
| Ventura CA | The Coffee Bean & Tea Leaf | 805-639-0795 | 1780 S Victoria Avenue, Suite A |
| Ventura CA | The Coffee Bean & Tea Leaf | 805-644-6000 | 4360 E Main Street, Suite 3 |
| Ventura CA | The Wharf | 805-648-5035 | 980 E Front Street |
| Ventura CA | Tony's Pizzeria | 805-643-8425 | 186 E Thompson Blvd |
| Ventura CA | Topper's Pizza | 805-385-4444 | 3940 E. Main St. |
| Visalia CA | Jamba Juice | 559-713-0704 | 2028 S Mooney M-1/H 63 |
| Vista CA | Baja Fresh Mexican Grill | 760-643-0110 | 620 Hacienda Dr. |
| Vista CA | Chipotle | 760-639-0529 | 30 Main Street |
| Vista CA | Jamba Juice | 760-599-0215 | 1661-A S Melrose Drive |
| Walnut CA | Chipolte | 909-595-1502 | 21710-A Valley Blvd |
| Walnut Creek CA | Baja Fresh Mexican Grill | 925-947-0588 | 1271-1273 S. California Blvd. |
| Walnut Creek CA | Chipotle | 925-935-9307 | 1158 Locust Street |
| Walnut Creek CA | Pacific Bay Coffee Co and Micro-Roastry | 925-935-1709 | 1495 Newell Ave |
| Watsonville CA | El Alteno | 831-768-9876 | 323 Main Street |
| West Covina CA | Chipolte | 626-967-6680 | 143 N Barranca # A |

| | | | |
|---|---|---|---|
| West Covina CA | Lazy Dog Restaurant & Bar | 626-480-8603 | 1440 Plaza Drive |
| West Hills CA | Baja Fresh Mexican Grill | 818-704-4267 | 22815 Victory Blvd. Ste C |
| West Hills CA | The Coffee Bean & Tea Leaf | 818-704-5867 | 6401 Platt Avenue |
| West Hollywood CA | Argyle Terrace at The Sunset Tower Hotel | 323-654-7100 | 8358 Sunset Blvd |
| West Hollywood CA | Basix Cafe | 323-848-2460 | 8333 Santa Monica Blvd. |
| West Hollywood CA | Burger Lounge | 310-289-9250 | 8539 W Sunset Blvd |
| West Hollywood CA | Eveleigh | 424-239-1630 | 8752 Sunset Blvd |
| West Hollywood CA | Jamba Juice | 323-512-0552 | 7100 Santa Monica Blvd |
| West Hollywood CA | Joey's Cafe | 323-822-0671 | 8301 Santa Monica Blvd/H 2 |
| West Hollywood CA | Le Pain Quotidien | 310-854-3700 | 8607 Melrose Avenue |
| West Hollywood CA | Marix West Hollywood | 323-656-8800 | 1108 N. Flores Street |
| West Hollywood CA | The Coffee Bean & Tea Leaf | 310-659-4592 | 8793 Beverly Blvd |
| West Hollywood CA | The Coffee Bean & Tea Leaf | 310-659-8207 | 8735 Santa Monica Blvd/H 2 |
| West Hollywood CA | The Coffee Bean & Tea Leaf | 310-659-1890 | 8789 Sunset Blvd |
| West Hollywood CA | Urth Cafe | 310-659-0628 | 8565 Melrose Ave |
| West Hollywood CA | Z Pizza | 310-360-1414 | 8869 Santa Monica Blvd/H 2 |
| Westlake Village CA | Baja Fresh Mexican Grill | 818-889-1347 | 30861 Thousand Oaks Blvd. |
| Westlake Village CA | Jamba Juice | 805-778-0854 | 2749 Agoura Road |
| Westlake Village CA | The Coffee Bean & Tea Leaf | 805-497-1256 | 968 S Westlake Blvd, Suite 6 |
| Westminster CA | Lazy Dog Restaurant & Bar | 714-500-1140 | 16310 Beach Blvd |
| Westwood CA | The Coffee Bean & Tea Leaf | 310-208-8018 | 950 Westwood Blvd |
| Whittier CA | Baja Fresh Mexican Grill | 562-464-5900 | 13582 Whittier Blvd |
| Whittier CA | The Coffee Bean & Tea Leaf | 562-696-8452 | 7201 Greenleaf Avenue |
| Willow Glen CA | Aqui Cal-Mex | 408-995-0381 | 1145 Lincoln Ave. |
| Woodland CA | Jamba Juice | 530-406-0486 | 1897 E Gibson Road, Suite E |
| Woodland CA | Steve's Place Pizza Pasta | 530-666-2100 | 714 Main Street |
| Woodland Hills CA | Baja Fresh Mexican Grill | 818-888-3976 | 19960 Ventura Blvd. |
| Woodland Hills CA | Baja Fresh Mexican Grill | 818-347-9033 | 5780 Canoga Avenue |
| Woodland Hills CA | Chipotle | 818-710-0466 | 5430 Topanga Canyon Blvd |
| Woodland Hills CA | Jamba Juice | 818-340-5770 | 22815 Victory Blvd, #B |
| Woodland Hills CA | Pickwick's Pub | 818-340-9673 | 21010 Ventura Blvd |
| Woodland Hills CA | The Coffee Bean & Tea Leaf | 818-716-7981 | 21851 Ventura Blvd |
| Woodland Hills CA | The Coffee Bean & Tea Leaf | 818-346-4863 | 19732 Ventura Blvd |
| Woodland Hills CA | The Coffee Bean & Tea Leaf | 818-348-2609 | 5780 Canoga Avenue, Suite F |
| Yorba Linda CA | The Coffee Bean & Tea Leaf | 202-483-3000 | 18503 Yorba Linda Blvd, #A |
| Yountville CA | Bistro Jeanty | 707-944-0103 | 6510 Washington Street |
| Yountville CA | Hurley's Restaurant | 707-944-2345 | 6518 Washington Street |
| Yuba City CA | Chipotle | 530-671-1581 | 1005 Gray Avenue |
| Yuba City CA | Sonic Drive-in | 530-671-3736 | 981 Grey Avenue |
| Yuba City CA | The City Cafe | 530-671-1501 | 667 Plumas Street |

**Colorado Listings**

| | | | |
|---|---|---|---|
| Aspen CO | Grateful Deli | 970-925-6647 | 233 E Main Street |
| Aurora CO | Jason's Deli | 303-991-2311 | 5440 South Parker, #K /H 83 |
| Aurora CO | Udi's Bread Cafe at Anschutz - Fitzsimmons | 303-340-3388 | 12700 E 19th Avenue, Bldg. P-15 |
| Boulder CO | Asher Brewing Company | 303-530-1381 | 4699 Nautilus Court, Suite 104 |
| Boulder CO | Boulder Beer | 303-444-8448 | 2880 Wilderness Place |
| Boulder CO | Firehouse Subs | 303-440-7827 | 1695 29th Street |
| Boulder CO | Half Fast Subs | 303-449-0404 | 1215 13th Street |
| Broomfield CO | Jason's Deli | 303-465-2882 | 549 Flatiron Blvd, Bldg 40 Suite H |
| Colorado Springs CO | Caspian Cafe | 719-528-1155 | 4375 Sinton Road |
| Colorado Springs CO | Jamba Juice | 719-598-1939 | 3730 Bloomington Street |
| Colorado Springs CO | Jamba Juice | 719-574-8787 | 3730 Bloomington Street |
| Colorado Springs CO | Jason's Deli | 719-302-0234 | 7455 N Academy Blvd |
| Colorado Springs CO | Nosh | 719-635-6674 | 121 S Tejon Street |
| Colorado Springs CO | Pizzeria Rustica | 719-632-8121 | 2527 W Colorado Avenue |
| Colorado Springs CO | Poor Richard's Restaurant | 719-632-7721 | 324 1/2 N. Tejon Street |
| Colorado Springs CO | Starbuck's | 719-594-9405 | 1605 Briargate Parkway |
| Colorado Springs CO | Ted's Montana Grill | 719-598-6195 | 1685 Briargate Parkway |
| Denver CO | Baja Fresh | 303-296-1800 | 9991 8th Street, #107 |
| Denver CO | Corner Bakery Cafe | 303-572-0170 | 500 16th Street |
| Denver CO | Denver's Washington Park Grille | 303-777-0707 | 1096 S Gaylord St |
| Denver CO | Jamba Juice | 303-892-1361 | 701 16th Street |
| Denver CO | Jamba Juice | 303-691-5066 | 1685 S Colorado Blvd |
| Denver CO | Jason's Deli | 303-243-5599 | 702 16th Street |

| | | | |
|---|---|---|---|
| Denver CO | Johnny Rockets | 303-399-5522 | 3000 E 1st Street |
| Denver CO | Rubios Baja Grille | 303-765-0636 | 703 S Colorado Blvd |
| Denver CO | St Mark's Coffeehouse | 303-322-8384 | 2019 E 17th Ave |
| Denver CO | The Market | 303-534-5140 | 1445 Larimer Street |
| Denver CO | Udi's Bread Cafe at Stapleton | 303-329-8888 | 7357 E 29th Avenue |
| Denver CO | Udi's Bread Cafe on Broadway | 303-657-1600 | 101 E 70th Avenue |
| Denver CO | Wall Street Deli | 303-296-6277 | 1801 California Street |
| Durango CO | Cyprus Cafe | 970-385-6884 | 725 East Second Avenue |
| Durango CO | Durango Natural Foods Deli | 970-247-8129 | 575 East 8th Avenue |
| Durango CO | Guido's Favorite Foods | 970-259-5028 | 1201 Main Avenue |
| Durango CO | Homeslice Pizza | 970-259-5551 | 441 E College Drive |
| Durango CO | Just Bo's Pizza and Rib Company | 970-259-0010 | 1301 Florida Road |
| Durango CO | Magpie's Newsstand Cafe | 970-259-1159 | 707 Main Street |
| Durango CO | Serious Texas BBQ | 970-247-2240 | 3535 N Main Avenue/H 550 |
| Durango CO | Serious Texas Bar-B-Q II | 970-259-9507 | 650 S Camino Del Rio/H 550 |
| Englewood CO | Jamba Juice | 303-996-6667 | 901 W Hampden Avenue, Suite 101/H 285 |
| Englewood CO | Jason's Deli | 303-708-1448 | 9525 E County Line Road |
| Estes Park CO | Molly B's | 970-586-2766 | 200 Moraine Avenue |
| Estes Park CO | Notchtop Bakery & Cafe | 970-586-0272 | 459 E Wonderview Avenue |
| Estes Park CO | Wild Rose Restaurant | 970-586-2806 | 157 West Elkhorn Ave. |
| Fort Collins CO | Jason's Deli | 970-204-9203 | 1538 E Harmony Road/H 68 |
| Fort Collins CO | Tasty Harmony | 970-689-3234 | 130 S Mason Street |
| Golden CO | Jamba Juice | 303-271-0667 | 14237 W Colfax Avenue |
| Greenwood Village CO | Jamba Juice | 303-740-8116 | 8547 E Arapahoe Road, #K |
| Greenwood Village CO | Jason's Deli | 720-489-8900 | 5302 DTC Blvd , Suite 400 |
| Highlands Ranch CO | Jamba Juice | 720-344-2950 | 9315 Dorchester Street, Unit G 104 |
| Highlands Ranch CO | Rubios Baja Grille | 303-471-6222 | 3620 Highlands Ranch Parkway |
| Lakewood CO | Jamba Juice | 720-974-3216 | 7161 W Alaska Drive |
| Lakewood CO | Johnny Rockets | 303-215-7100 | 14500 W Colfax Avenue |
| Leadville CO | Cookies with Altitude | 303-720-3683 | 717 1/2 Harrison AvenueH 24 |
| Loveland CO | Serious Texas Bar-B-Q III | 970-667-1415 | 201 W 71st Street |
| Manitou Springs CO | The Garden of the God Trading Post and Cafe | 719-685-9045 | 324 Beckers Lane |
| Montrose CO | Don Jilberto's | 970-252-8279 | 16367 S Townsend Avenue # 14/H 550 |
| Montrose CO | El Jimador Mexican Restaurant | 970-249-8990 | 1201 S Townsend Ave |
| Montrose CO | Heidis Brooklyn Deli | 970-240-2044 | 1521 Oxbow Circle |
| Montrose CO | Ted Nelson's Steakhouse | 970-252-0262 | 697 Cobble Drive |
| Pueblo CO | Angelo's Pizza Parlor And-a-more | 719-544-8588 | 105 E River Street |
| Pueblo CO | Bingo Burger | 719-225-8366 | 101 Central Plaza |
| Pueblo CO | Gold Dust Saloon | 719-545-0741 | 217 S Union Avenue |
| Pueblo CO | Wireworks Coffeehouse | 719-543-3000 | 103 S. Union Ave #110 |
| Redstone CO | Crystal Club Cafe | 970-963-9515 | 467 Redstone Blvd |
| Steamboat Springs CO | Rio Grande Restaurant | 970-871-6277 | 628 Lincoln Avenue/H 40 |
| Vail CO | Bully Ranch Restaurant | 970-479-5460 | 20 Vail Rd |

**Connecticut Listings**

| | | | |
|---|---|---|---|
| Bethel CT | Molten Java | 203-739-0313 | 213 Greenwood Ave |
| Fairfield CT | The Pantry | 203-259-0400 | 1580 Post Road |
| Guilford CT | The Place | 203-453-9276 | 901 Boston Post Road |
| Hartford CT | Costa del Sol | 860-296-1714 | 901 Wethersfield Ave |
| Hartford CT | First & Last Bakery Cafe | 860-956-7000 | 920 Maple Ave |
| Hartford CT | Hot Tomato's Restaurant | 860-249-5100 | 1 Union Place |
| Hartford CT | Lena's First & Last Pizzeria | 860-232-4481 | 2053 Park St |
| Hartford CT | Red Rock Tavern | 860-246-4527 | 369 Capitol Ave |
| Hartford CT | Salute | 860-899-1350 | 100 Trumbull St #2 |
| Hartford CT | The Half Door | 860-232-7827 | 270 Sisson Ave |
| Hartford CT | Tisane Euro-Asian Cafe | 860-523-5417 | 537 Farmington Ave |
| Hartford CT | Trinity Restaurant | 860-728-9822 | 243 Zion St |
| Hartford CT | Wood-n-Tap Bar & Grill | 860-232-8277 | 99 Sisson Ave |
| New Haven CT | Basta Trattoria | 203-772-1715 | 1006 Chapel Street |
| New Haven CT | Claire's Corner Copia | 203-562-3888 | 1000 Chapel Street |
| South Norwalk CT | Burger Bar & Bistro | 203-853-2037 | 60 N Main St |
| South Windsor CT | Johnny Rockets | 860-432-0048 | 101 Evergreen Walk |

Dog-Friendly Outdoor Dining - Please always call ahead to make sure an establishment is still dog-friendly

## D.C. Listings

| | | | |
|---|---|---|---|
| Washington DC | Art and Soul Restaurant | 202-393-7777 | 415 New Jersey Ave NW |
| Washington DC | Bangkok Bistro | 202-337-2424 | 3251 Prospect Street NW |
| Washington DC | Busboys and Poets | 202-789-2227 | 1025 5th Street NW |
| Washington DC | Busboys and Poets | 202-387-7638 | 2021 14th Str NW |
| Washington DC | Busboys and Poets | 202-726-0856 | 235 Carroll St NW |
| Washington DC | Busboys and Poets | 202-646-7230 | 625 Monroe St NE |
| Washington DC | Cafe Milano | 202-333-6183 | 3251 Prospect St NW |
| Washington DC | Café Olé | 202-244-1330 | 4000 Wisconsin Ave NW |
| Washington DC | Cantina Marina | 202-554-8396 | 600 Water St. SW |
| Washington DC | Chef Geoff's (New Mexico Ave) | 202-237-7800 | 3201 New Mexico Ave NW |
| Washington DC | Chipotle | 202-299-9111 | 2600 Connecticut Avenue NW |
| Washington DC | Chipotle | 202-466-4104 | 1837 M Street NW |
| Washington DC | Fusion Grill | 202-546-3874 | 515 8th St |
| Washington DC | Grillfish | 202-331-7310 | 1200 New Hampshire Ave NW |
| Washington DC | Grillfish | 202-331-7310 | 1200 New Hampshire Ave NW |
| Washington DC | Larry's Lounge | 202-483-1483 | 1840 14th Street NW |
| Washington DC | Logan at the Heights | 202-797-7227 | 3115 14th Street NW |
| Washington DC | Mai Thai | 202-452-6870 | 3251 Prospect St NW |
| Washington DC | Paper Moon | 202-965-6666 | 1073 31st St NW |
| Washington DC | Park Place Gourmet II | 202-783-4496 | 1634 I St NW # 2006 |
| Washington DC | Patisserie Poupon | 202-342-3248 | 1645 Wisconsin Avenue NW |
| Washington DC | Red Derby | 202-291-5000 | 3718 14th St NW |
| Washington DC | RedRocks Firebrick Pizzeria | 202-506-1402 | 1036 Park Road NW |
| Washington DC | Scion Restaurant | 202-833-8899 | 2100 P St NW |
| Washington DC | The Heights | 202-797-7227 | 3115 14th St NW |
| Washington DC | The Sacraficial Lamb | 202-797-2736 | 1704 R Street NW |
| Washington DC | Union Pub | | 201 Massachusetts Ave NE |
| Washington DC | Wonderland Ballroom | 202-232-5263 | 1101 Kenyon St NW |

## Delaware Listings

| | | | |
|---|---|---|---|
| Centreville DE | Buckley's Tavern | 302-656-9776 | 5812 Kennett Pike/H 52 |
| Dewey Beach DE | Sharky's Grill | 302-226-3116 | Hwy 1 and Read Street |
| Lewes DE | Arena's Cafe | 302-644-0370 | 17314 N Village Main Blvd |
| Lewes DE | Gilligan's Waterfront Restaurant and Bar | 302-644-7230 | 134 Market Street |
| Newark DE | Iron Hill Brewery | 302-266-9000 | 147 E Main Street/H 2/273 |
| Newark DE | Santa Fe Mexican Grill | 302-369-2500 | 190 East Main Street/H 2 |
| Rehoboth Beach DE | Arena's Deli & Bar | 302-227-1272 | 149 Rehoboth Avenue/H 15 |
| Rehoboth Beach DE | Arena's Deli & Bar | 302-226-CAFE (2233) | 4113 H 1 |
| Rehoboth Beach DE | Big Fish Grill | 302-227-FISH (3474) | 4117 H 1 |
| Rehoboth Beach DE | Cypress | 302-260-9527 | 37 Wilmington Ave |
| Rehoboth Beach DE | Rigby's Bar & Grill | 302-227-6080 | 404 Rehoboth Avenue/H 1/15 |
| Wilmington DE | Catherine Rooney's | 302-654-9700 | 1616 Delaware Avenue, Trolley Square |

## Florida Listings

| | | | |
|---|---|---|---|
| Altamonte Springs FL | Tropical Smoothie Cafe | 407-294-0098 | 851 S H 434 |
| Atlantic Beach FL | Joseph's Pizza | 904-270-1122 | 30 Ocean Blvd |
| Atlantic Beach FL | Ocean 60 Restaurant & Wine Bar | 904-247-0060 | 60 Ocean Blvd |
| Atlantic Beach FL | Poe's Tavern | 904-241-7637 | 363 Atlantic Blvd/H 1A/A1AN/10 |
| Ave Maria FL | Tropical Smoothie Cafe | 239-867-4492 | 5072 Annunciation Circle |
| Belleair Bluffs FL | Bonefish Grill | 727-518-1230 | 2939 W Bay Drive |
| Belleview FL | B.D. Beans Coffee Company | 352-245-3077 | 5148 SE Abshier Blvd/H 25/27/441 |
| Boca Raton FL | Einstein Bros Bagels | 561-477-0667 | 9795 Glades Rd |
| Boca Raton FL | GreenWise Market | 561-544-2422 | 21230 Saint Andrews Blvd |
| Boca Raton FL | Jamba Juice | 561-994-0236 | 694 Yamato Road |
| Boca Raton FL | Kapow Noodle Bar | 561-347-7322 | 431 Plaza Real |
| Boca Raton FL | Lion and Eagle English Pub | 561-447-7707 | 2401 N Federal Hwy |
| Boca Raton FL | Shake Shack | 561-923-0847 | 1400 Glades Road |
| Boca Raton FL | TooJay's Gourmet Deli | 561-241-5903 | 5030 Champion Blvd |
| Boca Raton FL | TooJay's Gourmet Deli | 561-997-9911 | 3013 Yamato Road |

| | | | |
|---|---|---|---|
| Boca Raton FL | Tucker Dukes | 561-717-8153 | 1658 N Federal Hwy |
| Bonita Springs FL | The Fish House | 239-495-5770 | 4665 Bonita Beach Road |
| Boynton Beach FL | Pei Wei Asian Diner | 561-364-1830 | 1750 N Congress Avenue/H 807 |
| Boynton Beach FL | TooJay's Gourmet Deli | 561-740-7420 | 801 N Congress Avenue/H 807 |
| Bradenton FL | Smoothie King | 941-758-1000 | 3543 53rd Avenue W |
| Brandon FL | Tropical Smoothie Cafe | 813-689-6200 | 2330 W. Brandon Blvd/H 60 |
| Cape Coral FL | Jason's Deli | 239-458-8700 | 2311 Santa Barbara |
| Cape Coral FL | Longboards at Cape Harbour | 239-542-0123 | 5785 Cape Harbour Drive |
| Cedar Key FL | Big Deck Raw Bar | 352-543-9992 | 331 Dock St |
| Clearwater FL | Clearwater Wine Co | 727-446-8805 | 483 Mandalay Ave # 113 |
| Clearwater FL | Island Way Grill | 727-461-6617 | 20 Island Way |
| Clearwater FL | Jason's Deli | 727-793-0446 | 25801 H 19 N |
| Clearwater FL | O'Keefes Tavern | 727-442-9034 | 1219 S Fort Harrison Ave |
| Clearwater FL | Rumba Island Bar & Grill | 727-446-7027 | 1800 Gulf-to-Bay Blvd |
| Clearwater FL | Sea Dog Brewing Company | 727-466-4916 | 26200 US Hwy 19 N |
| Clearwater FL | Tropical Smoothie Cafe | 727-536-1800 | 2695 Roosevelt Blvd |
| Clearwater FL | Wildflower Cafe | 727-447-4497 | 1465 S Fort Harrison Ave, #105 |
| Cocoa FL | Sonic Drive-in | 321-631-4121 | 1112 Clearlake Road/H 501 |
| Cocoa Beach FL | Long Doggers | 321-613-0002 | 350 W Cocoa Beach Cswy |
| Cocoa Beach FL | The Pig & Whistle | 321-799-0724 | 240 N Orlando Ave |
| Cocoa Beach FL | The Tiny Turtle | 321-446-7361 | 249 Minutemen Causeway |
| Coconut Grove FL | Burgers Lokal Beer - Coconut Grove | 305-442-3377 | 3190 Commodore Plaza |
| Coconut Grove FL | The Spillover | 305-456-5723 | 2911 Grand Ave |
| Cooper City FL | Beverly Hills Cafe | 954-434-2220 | 5544 S. Flamingo Road |
| Coral Gables FL | SAWA Restaurant and Lounge | 305-447-6555 | 360 San Lorenzo Ave, #1500 |
| Coral Springs FL | Jamba Juice | 954-575-2228 | 2816 University Drive/H 817 |
| Dania Beach FL | The Field Irish Pub and Eatery | 954-964-5979 | 3281 Griffin Road |
| Daytona Beach FL | Martini's Chophouse | 386-763-1090 | 1815 S. Ridgewood Avenue |
| Deerfield Beach FL | Bru's Room Sports Grill | 954-420-5959 | 123 NE 20th Avenue |
| Deerfield Beach FL | Tucker Dukes | 954-708-2035 | 1101 South Powerline Road |
| Delray Beach FL | Beer Trade Co | 561-808-7304 | 145 NE 4th Ave |
| Delray Beach FL | Boston's On The Beach | 561-278-3364 | 40 S Ocean Blvd |
| Delray Beach FL | Chipotle | 561-276-2093 | 520 Linton Blvd, Suite 101/H 811 |
| Delray Beach FL | City Oyster & Sushi Bar | 561-272-0220 | 213 E Atlantic Ave |
| Delray Beach FL | Ellie's Catering & Banquet | 561-276-7716 | 2410 N Federal Hwy |
| Delray Beach FL | Lilo's | 561-272-8049 | 814 East Atlantic Avenue |
| Destin FL | Dewey Destin's Seafood & Restaurant | 850-837-7525 | 9 Calhoun Avenue |
| Destin FL | Hammerhead's Bar and Grille | 850-351-1997 | 137 Fisherman's Cove |
| Destin FL | Harry T's | 850-654-4800 | 46 Harbor Blvd |
| Dunedin FL | Dunedin Brewery | 727-736-0606 | 937 Douglas Avenue |
| Dunedin FL | Dunedin Brewery | 727-736-0606 | 937 Douglas Ave |
| Dunedin FL | Eddie's Bar & Grill | 727-734-2300 | 1283 Bayshore Blvd/H 19 |
| Dunedin FL | Marina Cafe | 727-733-2151 | 148 Marina Plaza |
| Dunedin FL | Mike & Lisa's Cricketers | 727-736-1322 | 2634 Bayshore Blvd/H 19 |
| Dunedin FL | Sams Fresh Seafood Restaurant | 727-736-1179 | 900 Broadway/Alt 19 |
| Fernandina Beach FL | 29 South | 904-277-7919 | 29 S 3rd Street |
| Fernandina Beach FL | Cafe Karibo | 904-277-5269 | 27 N 3rd Street |
| Fernandina Beach FL | Happy Tomato | 904-321-0707 | 7 S. 3rd St. |
| Fernandina Beach FL | Sandy Bottoms | 904-310-6904 | 2910 Atlantic Avenue/H A1A/1A |
| Fort Lauderdale FL | 33rd and Dine French Cafe | 954-630-0235 | 3330 NE 33rd Street |
| Fort Lauderdale FL | Briny Riverfront Pub | 954-376-4742 | 305 S Andrews Avenue |
| Fort Lauderdale FL | Coconuts | 954-525-2421 | 429 Seabreeze Blvd/H 1A |
| Fort Lauderdale FL | Colada | 954-368-4705 | 525 N Federal Highway |
| Fort Lauderdale FL | Doc B's Fresh Kitchen | 754-900-2401 | 452 N Federal Highway |
| Fort Lauderdale FL | Einstein's Bros Bagels | 954-462-1132 | 19 N Federal H/H 1/5 |
| Fort Lauderdale FL | Einstein's Bros Bagels | 954-463-1717 | 1499 SE 17th Street Causeway/H 1A |
| Fort Lauderdale FL | Einsteins Bagel | 954-565-2155 | 3200 N Federal Hwy |
| Fort Lauderdale FL | Georgie's Alibi | 954-565-2526 | 2266 Wilton Drive/NE 4th AvenueH 811 |
| Fort Lauderdale FL | Indigo Restaurant | 954-467-0045 | 620 E Las Olas Blvd |
| Fort Lauderdale FL | Jamba Juice | 954-630-3638 | 3200N Federal H/H 1 |
| Fort Lauderdale FL | Kitchenetta | 954-567-3333 | 2850 N Federal H/H 1/5 |
| Fort Lauderdale FL | Panera Bread | 954-567-5925 | 1762 North Federal H/H 1/5 |
| Fort Lauderdale FL | Rino's Tuscan Grill | 954-766-8700 | 1105 E Las Olas Blvd |
| Fort Lauderdale FL | Starbucks | 954-791-7265 | 6781 W Broward Blvd |
| Fort Lauderdale FL | Stromboli Pizza | 954-472-2167 | 801 S University Dr |
| Fort Lauderdale FL | The Floridian | 954-463-4041 | 1410 East Las Olas Boulevard |

| | | | |
|---|---|---|---|
| Fort Lauderdale FL | The Riverside Market and Cafe | 954-358-8333 | 608 SW 12th Avenue |
| Fort Lauderdale FL | Tokyo Sushi | 954-767-9922 | 1499 SE 17th Street/H 1A |
| Fort Lauderdale FL | Tropical Smoothie Cafe | 954-523-2268 | 1922 Cordova Road |
| Fort Myers FL | Bistro 41 | 239-466-4141 | 13499 S Cleveland Avenue |
| Fort Myers FL | Jason's Deli | 239-590-9994 | 13550 Reflections Parkway, #1-101 |
| Fort Myers FL | TGI Fridays at the Bell Tower Shops | 239-489-2401 | 13499 S Cleveland Ave # 223/H 41/45 |
| Fort Myers FL | Tropical Smoothie Cafe | 239-931-3100 | 9377 Six Mile Cypress Parkway, Suite 100 |
| Fort Myers Beach FL | Parrot Key Caribbean Grill | 239-463-3257 | 2500 Main Street |
| Fort Myers Beach FL | The Fish House and Restaurant | 239-765-6766 | 7225 Estero Blvd |
| Fort Walton Beach FL | Tropical Smoothie Cafe | 850-864-4991 | 312 NW Racetrack Road/H 188 |
| Fort Worth FL | Dave's Last Resort and Raw Bar | 561-588-5208 | 632 Lake Ave |
| Gainesville FL | Firehouse Subs | 352-336-0419 | 3221 SW 35th Blvd |
| Gotha FL | Yellow Dog Eats Cafe | 407-296-0609 | 1236 Hempel Ave |
| Gulfport FL | Boca Bay Grill | 727-201-8280 | 2834 Beach Blvd S |
| Gulfport FL | Tangelo's | 727-894-1695 | 3121 Beach Blvd |
| Gulfport FL | Tangelos Grille | 727-894-1695 | 3121 Beach Blvd South |
| Harbour Island FL | Café Dufrain | 813-275-9701 | 707 Harbour Post Drive |
| Harmony FL | Harmony Town Tavern/Greensides Restaurant | 407-891-2630 | 7251 Five Oaks Drive/H 192 |
| Hollywood FL | Chillbar | 954-647-8505 | 1940 N 30th Rd |
| Hollywood FL | Einstein's Bros Bagels | 954-989-4500 | 5341 Sheridan Street/H 822 |
| Hollywood FL | Einstein's Bros Bagels | 954-893-8701 | 340 N Park Road |
| Hollywood FL | Jamba Juice | 954-437-9404 | 11053 Pines Blvd, Unit 422 |
| Hollywood FL | Jimbo's Sand Bar | 954-927-9560 | 6200 N Ocean Dr |
| Hollywood FL | Lola's on Harrison | 954-927-9851 | 2032 Harrison Street |
| Hollywood FL | Nakorn Japanese and Thai Restaurant | 954-921-1200 | 1935 Harrrison Street |
| Hollywood FL | Tipsy Boar | 954-920-2627 | 1906 Harrison St |
| Hudson FL | Sam's Hudson Beach Restaurant | 727-868-1971 | 6325 Clark Street |
| Indian Rocks Beach FL | Crabby Bills Loading Dock | 727-595-4825 | 401 Gulf Blvd |
| Indian Shores FL | Pub Waterfront Restaurant | 727-595-3172 | 20025 Gulf Boulevard |
| Indian Shores FL | The Pub Waterfront Restaurant | 727-595-3172 | 20025 Gulf Blvd/H 689 |
| Jacksonville FL | Bistro Aix | 904-398-1949 | 1440 San Marco Blvd |
| Jacksonville FL | Brick Restaurant | 904-387-0606 | 3585 Saint Johns Avenue/H 211 |
| Jacksonville FL | Cinco de Mayo Restaurant | 904-329-2892 | W Independent Drive - Jacksonville Landing |
| Jacksonville FL | Firehouse Subs | 904-886-2179 | 10131-8 San Jose Blvd/H 13 |
| Jacksonville FL | Hurricane's Grille and Wings | 904-393-7933 | 1615 Hendricks Avenue/H 13 |
| Jacksonville FL | Jason's Deli | 904-620-0707 | 4375-15 Southside Blvd/H 115 |
| Jacksonville FL | Taverna | 904-398-3005 | 1986 San Marco Blvd |
| Jacksonville FL | The Brick Restaurant | 904-387-0606 | 3585 St Johns Avenue/H 211 |
| Jacksonville FL | Tropical Smoothie Cafe | 904-399-1514 | 1808 Hendricks Avenue/H 13 |
| Jacksonville FL | Tropical Smoothie Cafe | 904-646-9727 | 8221 Southside Blvd |
| Jacksonville Beach FL | Cruisers Grill | 904-270-0356 | 319 23rd Avenue S |
| Jacksonville Beach FL | Jason's Deli | 904-246-7585 | 2230 3rd Street/H A1A |
| Jacksonville Beach FL | Tropical Smoothie Cafe | 904-242-4940 | 1230 Beach Blvd/H 212 |
| Jensen Beach FL | Tropical Smoothie Cafe | 772-692-8088 | 2491 S. Federal H/H 1 |
| Jupiter FL | Nature's Way Cafe | 561-743-0401 | 103 S H 1 |
| Jupiter FL | TooJay's Gourmet Deli | 561-627-5555 | 4050 H 1 |
| Jupiter FL | Tropical Smoothie Cafe | 561-748-4457 | 6671 W Indiantown Road - Suite 52 |
| Jupiter FL | Tropical Smoothie Cafe | 561-624-8775 | 5440 Military Trail |
| Key Largo FL | Key Largo Conch House | 305-453-4844 | 100211 Overseas Hwy |
| Key Largo FL | Key Largo Fisheries | 305-451-3784 | 1313 Ocean Bay Dr |
| Key Largo FL | Skipper?s Dockside | 305-453-9794 | 528 Caribbean Dr |
| Key West FL | Amigo's Tortilla Bar | 305-292-2009 | 425 Greene Street |
| Key West FL | Blue Heaven | 305-296-8666 | 729 Thomas St |
| Key West FL | Bo's Fish Wagon | 305-294-9272 | 801 Caroline St |
| Key West FL | Casablanca Bogart | 305-296-0815 | 904 Duval St |
| Key West FL | Dante's | 305-293-5123 | 951 Caroline Street |
| Key West FL | Fat Tuesday's | 305-296-9373 | 305 Duval Street |
| Key West FL | Harpoon Harry's | 305-294-8744 | 832 Caroline Street |
| Key West FL | Hogs Breath Saloon | 305-296-4222 | 400 Front Street |
| Key West FL | Hurricane Joe's Seafood Bar and Grill | 305-294-0200 | Hurricane Hole Marina Mile Marker 4 |
| Key West FL | Louie's Backyard | 305-294-1061 | 700 Waddell Avenue |
| Key West FL | Old Town Mexican Cafe | 305-296-7500 | 609 Duval St |
| Key West FL | Outback Steakhouse | 305-292-0667 | 3230 N Roosevelt Blvd/H1 |
| Key West FL | Pepe's Cafe and Steakhouse | 305-294-7192 | 806 Caroline Street |

| | | | |
|---|---|---|---|
| Key West FL | Pepe?s Cafe & Steakhouse | 305-294-7192 | 806 Caroline St |
| Key West FL | Salsa Loca | 305-292-1865 | 623-625 Duval Street |
| Key West FL | Sarabeth?s Keywest | 305-293-8181 | 530 Simonton St |
| Key West FL | Schooner Wharf Bar | 305-292-9520 | 202 William Street |
| Key West FL | Six-Toed Cat | 305-294-3318 | 823 Whitehead Street/H 1/5 |
| Kissimmee FL | Johnny Rockets | 407-870-5310 | 3230 N John Young Parkway |
| Kissimmee FL | Pei Wei Asian Diner | 407-846-0829 | 2501 W Osceola Parkway |
| Lady Lake FL | Johnny Rockets | 352-259-0051 | 976 Old Mill Run |
| Lake Mary FL | Dexter's of Lake Mary | 407-805-3090 | 950 Promenade Avenue |
| Lake Mary FL | TooJay's Gourmet Deli | 407-833-0848 | 3577 Lake Emma Road |
| Lake Park FL | Casper's On Park | 561-791-6179 | 850 Park Ave |
| Lake Sumter Landing FL | TooJay's Gourmet Deli | 352-430-0410 | 1129 Canal Street |
| Lake Worth FL | Nature's Way Cafe | 561-721-0232 | 517 N Lake Avenue/H 802 |
| Lake Worth FL | TooJay's Gourmet Deli | 561-582-8684 | 419 Lake Avenue/H 802 |
| Lakeland FL | Smoothie King | 863-647-9602 | 3423 S Florida Avenue |
| Lakeland FL | Tropical Smoothie Cafe | 863-686-9474 | 116 S. Tennessee Avenue |
| Largo FL | Einstein's Bros Bagels | 727-533-0800 | 5395 E Bay Drive, Suite 104 (H 686) |
| Largo FL | Tropical Smoothie Cafe | 727-216-2120 | 1001 W Bay Drive |
| Lauderdale-by-the-Sea FL | The Village Grill & The Village Pump | 954-776-5092 | 4404 El Mar Drive |
| Lighthouse Point FL | The Nauti Dawg Marina Cafe | 954-941-0246 | 2841 Marina Cir |
| Lynn Haven FL | Tropical Smoothie Cafe | 850-271-2120 | 504 W H 390 |
| Madeira Beach FL | Bamboo Beach Bar & Grill | 727-398-5401 | 13025 Village Blvd |
| Madeira Beach FL | The Brown Boxer Pub & Grille | 727-391-1704 | 15000 Madeira Way |
| Matlacha FL | Bert's Bar and Grill | 239-282-3232 | 4271 Pine Island Road/H 78 |
| Melbourne FL | Coaster's Pub | 321-779-BREW | 971A E. Eau Gallie Blvd |
| Melbourne FL | Mustard's Last Stand | 321-951-3469 | 415 E New Haven Avenue |
| Melbourne FL | Mustard's Last Stand | 321-254-5776 | 1288 N Harbor City Blvd/H 1 |
| Melbourne FL | Tropical Smoothie Cafe | 321-952-5575 | 1520 S. Babcock Street |
| Melbourne FL | Tropical Smoothie Cafe | 321-454-2303 | Melbourne Village Plaza, 1270 N. Wickham Road #1 |
| Miami FL | Catalina Hotel and Beach Club | 305-674-1160 | 1732-1756 Collins Avenue |
| Miami FL | Jamba Juice | 305-273-5536 | 7704 N Kendall Drive |
| Miami FL | Johnny Rockets | 305-444-1000 | 3036 Grand Ave |
| Miami FL | Johnny Rockets | 305-538-2115 | 728 Ocean Drive |
| Miami FL | Johnny Rockets | 305-252-8181 | 8888 SW 136th Street |
| Miami FL | LoKal Burgers | 305-442-3377 | 3190 Commodore Plaza |
| Miami FL | Michael's Genuine Food & Drink | 305-573-5550 | 130 N.E. 40th Street |
| Miami FL | Wall's Old Fashioned Ice Cream | 305-740-9830 | 8075 SW 67th Ave |
| Miami FL | Wood Tavern | 305-748-2828 | 2531 NW 2nd Ave |
| Miami Beach FL | Baires Grill | 305-538-1116 | 1116 Lincoln Road |
| Miami Beach FL | Fratelli la Bufala | 305-532-0700 | 437 Washington Avenue |
| Miami Beach FL | Nexxt Cafe | 305-532-6643 | 700 Lincoln Road |
| Miami Beach FL | Taste Bakery Cafe | 305-695-9930 | 900 Alton Road |
| Miami Lakes FL | Beverly Hills Cafe | 305-558-8201 | 7321 Miami Lakes Drive |
| Miami Lakes FL | Elevation Burger | 786-517-5775 | 16010 NW 57th Avenue, Suite 13B/H 823 |
| Mount Dora FL | Pizza Amore | 352-383-0090 | 116 E 5th Avenue/H 46 |
| Naples FL | D'Amico & Sons | 239-430-0955 | 4691 9th St N |
| Naples FL | EJ's Bayfront Cafe | 239-353-4444 | 469 Bayfront Pl |
| Naples FL | Fred's Diner | 239-431-7928 | 2700 Immokalee Road |
| Naples FL | Jason's Deli | 239-593-9499 | 2700 Immokalee Road , Suite 1 & 2 |
| Naples FL | M Waterfront Grill | 239-263-4421 | 4300 Gulf Shore Blvd. N |
| Naples FL | McCormick & Schmick's Seafood Restaurant | 239-591-2299 | 9114 Strada Place |
| Naples FL | Tropical Smoothie Cafe | 239-591-2241 | 13585 Tamiami Trail N Unit #19/H 41 |
| Navarre FL | Tropical Smoothie Cafe | 850-936-1320 | 8646 Navarre Parkway/H 30/98 |
| Neptune Beach FL | Sliders Seafood Grille | 904-246-0881 | 218 1st Street |
| New Smyrna Beach FL | Cafe Heavenly | 386-427-7475 | 115 Flagler Avenue |
| New Smyrna Beach FL | Cafe Verde | 386-957-3958 | 301 Flagler Ave |
| New Smyrna Beach FL | Clancy's Cantina | 386-428-4500 | 301 Flagler Ave |
| New Smyrna Beach FL | Gnarly Surf Bar & Grill | 386-957-3844 | 114 Flagler Ave |
| New Smyrna Beach FL | New Smyrna Steakhouse | 386-424-9696 | 723 E 3rd Ave |
| New Smyrna Beach FL | Norwood's Restaurant & Wine Shop | 386-428-4621 | 400 E 2nd Ave |
| New Smyrna Beach FL | That's Amore Restaurant | 386-957-4956 | 103 S Pine St |
| New Smyrna Beach FL | The Taco Shack | 386-428-9882 | 642 N Dixie Fwy |
| North Miami Beach FL | Chipotle | 305-947-2779 | 14776 Biscayne Blvd/H 1/5 |

| North Miami Beach FL | Jamba Juice | 305-948-9919 | 13505 Biscayne Blvd, Bay #28/H 1 |
|---|---|---|---|
| North Redington Beach FL | Conch Republic Grill | 727-320-0536 | 16699 Gulf Blvd |
| North Redington Beach FL | Sweet Sage Cafe | 727-391-0453 | 16725 Gulf Blvd |
| Ocala FL | Firehouse Subs | 352-873-7827 | 2701 H 200, Suite 108 |
| Ocala FL | Harry's Seafood and Grille | 352-840-0900 | 24 SE 1st Avenue |
| Ocala FL | Ker's WingHouse | 352-671-7880 | 2145 E Silver Springs Blvd/H 40 |
| Ocoee FL | TooJay's Gourmet Deli | 407-798-2000 | 10185 W Colonial Drive/H 50 |
| Orlando FL | Casey's on Central | 407-648-4218 | 50 East Central Blvd |
| Orlando FL | Dexter's of Thornton Park | 407-629-1150 | 808 Washington Street |
| Orlando FL | Eola Wine Company | 407-481-9100 | 500 E Central Blvd. in Orlando |
| Orlando FL | Jason's Deli | 407-425-3562 | 25 W Crystal Lake Street, #151 |
| Orlando FL | Johnny Rockets | 407-903-0762 | 9101 International Drive |
| Orlando FL | K Restaurant Wine Bar | 407-872-2332 | 2401 Edgewater Drive |
| Orlando FL | NYPD Pizza | 407-293-8880 | 2589 S Hiawassee Road |
| Orlando FL | Pei Wei Asian Diner | 407-563-8777 | 3011 E Colonial Drive/H 50 |
| Orlando FL | QDOBA Mexican Grill | 407-238-4787 | 12376 Apopka Vineland Road/H 535 |
| Orlando FL | Smoothie King | 407-380-3333 | UCF, Student Union, Pegasus Circle, Bldg 52 |
| Orlando FL | Stardust Video & Coffee | 407-623-3393 | 1842 E Winter Park Road |
| Orlando FL | TooJay's Gourmet Deli | 407-894-1718 | 2400 E Colonial Drive |
| Orlando FL | TooJay's Gourmet Deli | 407-355-0340 | 7600 Dr Phillips Blvd |
| Orlando FL | TooJay's Gourmet Deli | 407-249-9475 | 715 N Alafaya Trail |
| Orlando FL | Tropical Smoothie Cafe | 407-839-0830 | 63 W Washington Street |
| Orlando FL | Tropical Smoothie Cafe | 407-704-8205 | 12789 Waterford Lakes Parkway |
| Orlando FL | Wildside BBQ | 407-872-8665 | 700 E Washington Street |
| Ormond Beach FL | Daytona Pig Stand | 386-898-0360 | 1633 N Highway1 |
| Ormond Beach FL | The Black Sheep Pub | 386-673-5933 | 890 S. Atlantic Avenue/H 1A |
| Palm Bay FL | Tropical Smoothie Cafe | 321-725-6535 | 4700 Babcock Street., Unit 9 |
| Palm Beach Gardens FL | GreenWise Market | 561-514-5175 | 11231 Legacy Avenue |
| Palm Beach Gardens FL | TooJay's Gourmet Deli | 561-622-8131 | 11701 Lake Victoria Gardens |
| Palm Beach Gardens FL | Tropical Smoothie Cafe | 561-624-4513 | 4276 Northlake Blvd |
| Palm Harbor FL | Consciousness Blossoms | 727-789-1931 | 3390 Tampa Road/H 584 |
| Palm Harbor FL | Einstein's Bros Bagels | 727-771-9448 | 33119 H 19N |
| Palm Harbor FL | Smoothie King | 727-232-1299 | 4956 Ridgemoor Blvd |
| Palmetto FL | Riverhouse Reef and Grill | 941-729-0616 | 995 Riverside Drive |
| Panama City Beach FL | Salty Sue's | 850-234-8485 | 17501 Back Beach Rd |
| Pembroke Pines FL | Chipotle | 954-433-9918 | 15880 Pines Blvd/H 820/Hollywood Blvd |
| Pembroke Pines FL | Jamba Juice | 954-885-9050 | 2024 N Flamingo Road |
| Pembroke Pines FL | Jason's Deli | 954-438-1280 | 14200 Pines Blvd/H 820 |
| Pembroke Pines FL | Lime Fresh Mexican Grill | 954-436-4700 | 601 SW 145th Terrace |
| Pensacola FL | Sunset Grille | 850-492-1063""; | 14050 Canal A Way |
| Pensacola FL | Tropical Smoothie Cafe | 850-332-6601 | 5147 Bayou Blvd/H 296 |
| Pensacola FL | Tuscan Oven Pizzeria | 850-484-6836 | 4801 N 9th Avenue/H 289 |
| Pensacola Beach FL | Surf Burger | 850-932-1417 | 500 Quietwater Beach Blvd |
| Plantation FL | Einstein's Bros Bagels | 954-370-3105 | 8500 W Broward Blvd/H 842 |
| Plantation FL | Einstein's Bros Bagels | 954-423-3030 | 989 Nob Hill Road |
| Plantation FL | TooJay's Gourmet Deli | 954-423-1993 | 801 S University Drive/H 817 |
| Pompano Beach FL | Bru's Room Sports Grill | 954-785-2227 | 235 S Federal H |
| Pompano Beach FL | Galuppi's | 954-785-0226 | 1103 N Federal H/H 1 |
| Ponce Inlet FL | Hidden Treasure Rum Bar & Grill | 386-761-9271 | 4940 S Peninsula |
| Ponte Vedra Beach FL | Pusser's Caribbean Grille | 904-280-7766 | 816 H A1A North |
| Port Charlotte FL | Jason's Deli | 941-235-3354 | 1100 El Jobean Road #128 |
| Port St Joe FL | Dockside Cafe | 850-229-5200 | 342 Marina Drive |
| Port St Lucie FL | Tropical Smoothie Cafe | 772-380-9494 | 9182 S. Federal H/H 1 |
| Port St Lucie FL | Tropical Smoothie Cafe | 772-621-4504 | 1707 NW St Lucie W Blvd #122 |
| Port St Lucie FL | Tropical Smoothie Cafe | 772-621-4504 | 1707 NW St. Lucie West Blvd |
| Port St Lucie FL | Tropical Smoothie Cafe | 772-344-6960 | 10628 S.W. Village Parkway |
| Riverview FL | Acropolis | 813-654-2255 | 6108 Winthrop Town Center Avenue |
| Riverview FL | Green Iguanna | 813-643-7800 | 6264 Winthrop Town Center Avenue |
| Safety Harbor FL | Café Orlando | 727-723-1116 | 500 Main Street/H 590 |
| Saint Augustine FL | Harry's Seafood Bar & Grille | 904-824-7765 | 46 Avenida Menendez |
| Sandestin FL | Johnny Rockets | 850-650-3100 | 625 Grand Blvd., Space E-107 |
| Sanford FL | Hollerbach's Willow Tree Cafe | 407-321-2204 | 205 E First Street |
| Sanford FL | QDOBA Mexican Grill | 407-330-3039 | 202 W Lake Mary Blvd |
| Sanford FL | Riverwalk Pizzeria | 407-328-0018 | 350 E. Seminole Blvd |

| | | | |
|---|---|---|---|
| Sarasota FL | Barnacle Bill's Seafood | 941-365-6800 | 1526 Main Street |
| Sarasota FL | Chipotle | 941-957-6406 | 1707 S Tamiami Trail/H 41/45 |
| Sarasota FL | Columbia Restaurant | 941-388-3987 | 411 St Armands Circle |
| Sarasota FL | Jason's Deli | 941-351-5999 | 5231 University Parkway |
| Sarasota FL | Madfish Grill | 941-377-3474 | 4059 Cattlemen Rd |
| Sarasota FL | Marina Jack | 941-365-4232 | 2 Marina Plaza |
| Sarasota FL | O'leary's Tiki Bar and Grill | 941-953-7505 | 5 Bayfront Drive/H 41/45 |
| Sarasota FL | Old Salty Dog | 941-349-0158 | 5023 Ocean Blvd |
| Sarasota FL | Old Salty Dog II | 941-388-4311 | 1601 B Ken Thompson Parkway |
| Sarasota FL | The Breakfast House | 941-366-6860 | 1817 Fruitville Road/H 780 |
| Sarasota FL | The Old Salty Dog I | 941-349-0158 | 5023 Ocean Blvd |
| Sarasota FL | Tropical Smoothie Cafe | 941-365-8423 | 1900 Main Street |
| Seminole FL | Einstein's Bros Bagels | 727-392-8515 | 11234 Park Blvd |
| Siesta Key FL | Old Salty Dog | 941-388-4311 | 1601 Ken Thompson Pkwy |
| South Beach FL | Shake Shack | 305-434-7787 | 1111 Lincoln Road |
| South Miami FL | Chipotle | 305-668-3831 | 6290 S Dixie H |
| South Miami FL | Johnny Rockets | 305-663-1004 | 5701 Sunset Drive/H 986 |
| South Stuart FL | Tropical Smoothie Cafe | 772-283-7377 | 6134 S.E Federal H/H 1 |
| St Augustine FL | Beaches at Vilano | 904-829-0589 | 254 Vilano Rd |
| St Augustine FL | Cafe Cordova | 904-827-1888 | 95 Cordova Street |
| St Augustine FL | Carrabba's Italian Grill | 904-819-9093 | 155 H 312 W |
| St Augustine FL | Crispers | 904-825-9901 | 200 CBL Drive FL |
| St Augustine FL | Cruisers Grill | 904-824-6993 | 3 St. George Street |
| St Augustine FL | Firehouse Subs | 904-819-1808 | 200 Cobblestone Drive |
| St Augustine FL | Florida Cracker Cafe | 904-829-0397 | 81 St. George Street |
| St Augustine FL | Harry's Seafood Bar Grille | 904-824-7765 | 46 Avenida Menendez |
| St Augustine FL | Hot Shot Bakery & Cafe | 904-824-7898 | 47 Cordova St |
| St Augustine FL | La Pentola | 904-824-3282 | 58 Charlotte Street |
| St Augustine FL | Love Tree Cafe | 904-823-1818 | 6 Cordova Street |
| St Augustine FL | Milltop Tavern | 904-829-2329 | 19 1/2 Saint George Street |
| St Augustine FL | Old City House Inn and Restaurant | 904-826-0184 | 115 Cordova Street |
| St Augustine FL | Sonic Drive Inn | 904-808-4788 | 704 E Geoffrey Street |
| St Augustine FL | The Reef | 904-824-8008 | 4100 Coastal H/H 1A |
| St Augustine FL | Tropical Smoothie Cafe | 904-461-9090 | 112 Seagrove Main Street |
| St John FL | Tropical Smoothie Cafe | 904-829-9292 | 2245 H 210 W |
| St Pete Beach FL | Ninas Cafe | 727-367-1397 | 9524 Blind Pass Rd |
| St Pete Beach FL | Sea Critters Cafe | 727-360-3706 | 2007 Pass-A-Grille Way |
| St Pete Beach FL | Skidders | 727-360-1029 | 5799 Gulf Blvd/H 699 |
| St Petersburg FL | 400 Beach Seafood and Tap House | 727-896-2400 | 400 Beach Drive NE |
| St Petersburg FL | BellaBrava | 727-895-5515 | 204 Beach Drive |
| St Petersburg FL | Biff's Burger & Buffy's BBQ | 727-522-0088 | 3911 49th North |
| St Petersburg FL | Burrito Boarder | 727-209-0202 | 17 3rd Street/H 687 |
| St Petersburg FL | Cassis American Brasserie | 727-827-2927 | 170 Beach Dr NE |
| St Petersburg FL | Ceviches Tapas Bar & Restaurant | 727-209-2299 | 10 Beach Dr |
| St Petersburg FL | Ceviches Tapas Bar & Restaurant | 727-209-2299 | 10 Beach Dr |
| St Petersburg FL | Chattaway | 727-823-1594 | 358 22nd Avenue S |
| St Petersburg FL | Chattaway Drive-In | 727-823-1594 | 358 22nd Ave S |
| St Petersburg FL | Corned Beef Corner | 727-347-3921 | 4040 Park St North |
| St Petersburg FL | Einstein's Bros Bagels | 727-578-9800 | 9346 4th Street N/H 92/687 |
| St Petersburg FL | El Cap | 727-521-1314 | 3500 4th Street/H 92/687 |
| St Petersburg FL | Fish Tales | 727-821-3474 | 1500 2nd Street S |
| St Petersburg FL | Foxy's Cafe | 727-363-3699 | 160 107th Ave |
| St Petersburg FL | Fresco's Waterfront Bistro | 727-894-4429 | 300 2nd Avenue NE |
| St Petersburg FL | Parkshore Grill | 727-896-3463 | 300 Beach Drive |
| St Petersburg FL | Parkshore Grill | 727-896-9463 | 300 Beach Dr |
| St Petersburg FL | Pei Wei Asian Diner | 727-347-1351 | 1402 66th Street |
| St Petersburg FL | Tavern at Bayboro | 727-821-1418 | 121 7th Avenue S |
| St Petersburg FL | The Cafe @ARTpool Gallery | 727-324-3878 | 2030 Central Ave |
| St Petersburg FL | Tropical Smoothie Cafe | 727-821-3100 | 1201 4th Street N/H 92/687 |
| St Petersburg FL | Tropical Smoothie Cafe | 727-573-1425 | 150 Fountain Parkway N |
| Stuart FL | Pei Wei Asian Diner | 772-219-0466 | 2101 SE Federal H/H 1/5 |
| Stuart FL | TooJay's Gourmet Deli | 772-287-6514 | 2504 SE Federal H/H 1/5 |
| Stuart FL | Tropical Smoothie Cafe | 772-220-2995 | 1989 SE Federal H/H1 |
| Sunrise FL | Chipotle | 954-858-1961 | 129 NW 136th Avenue |
| Tallahassee FL | Andrew's Capital Grill & Bar | 850-222-3444 | 228 S Adams Street |
| Tallahassee FL | Black Dog Cafe | 850-224-2518 | 229 Lake Ella Drive |
| Tallahassee FL | Food,Glorious Food | 850-224-9974 | 1950 Thomasville Rd |

| | | | |
|---|---|---|---|
| Tallahassee FL | New Leaf Market | 850-942-2557 | 1235 Apalachee Parkway |
| Tallahassee FL | Nuberri Frozen Yogurt | 850-222-2374 | 101 North Blair Stone Road |
| Tallahassee FL | Pepper's Mexican Grill & Cantina | 850-877-2020 | 1140 Capital Circle SE #15 |
| Tallahassee FL | QDOBA Mexican Grill | 850-671-3334 | 1594 Governor's Square Blvd #2 |
| Tallahassee FL | Sage Restaurant | 850-270-9396 | 3534 Maclay Blvd. |
| Tallahassee FL | Sweet Pea Cafe | 850-692-3476 | 832 W Tharpe Street |
| Tallahassee FL | Tropical Smoothie Cafe | 850-412-9100 | 209 N. Magnolia Drive |
| Tallahassee FL | Tropical Smoothie Cafe | 850-894-4980 | 1415 Timberlane Road. Unit 323 |
| Tamarac FL | Einstein's Bros Bagels | 954-718-6088 | 5705 N University Drive/H 817 |
| Tampa FL | Bagels Plus | 813-971-9335 | 2706 E Fletcher Ave |
| Tampa FL | Bernini Restaurant | 813-248-0099 | 1702 E 7th Ave |
| Tampa FL | Columbia Cafe | 813-229-5511 | 801 Old Water Street |
| Tampa FL | Einstein's Bros Bagels | 813-871-1074 | 619 S Dale Mabry H/H 92 |
| Tampa FL | Einstein's Bros Bagels | 813-968-8868 | 10802 N Dale Mabry H/H 597 |
| Tampa FL | Evos | 813-258-EVOS (3867) | 609 S Howard Avenue |
| Tampa FL | Gaspar's Grotto | 813-248-5900 | 1805 E 7th Avenue |
| Tampa FL | GreenWise Market | 813-250-0129 | 2401 W Azeele Street |
| Tampa FL | GrillSmith | 813-250-3850 | 1108-D S Dale Mabry H |
| Tampa FL | MacDinton's Irish Pub & Restaurant | 813-251-8999 | 405 S Howard Avenue |
| Tampa FL | Mad Dogs and Englishmen | 813-832-3037 | 4115 S Macdill Ave |
| Tampa FL | Pei Wei Asian Diner | 813-207-1190 | 217 S Dale Mabry/H 92 |
| Tampa FL | Pei Wei Asian Diner | 813-960-2031 | 12927 N Dale Mabry H/H 597 |
| Tampa FL | Pour House at Grand Central | 813-402-2923 | 1208 E. Kennedy Blvd, Suite #112 |
| Tampa FL | QDOBA Mexican Grill | 813-984-4650 | 5001A E Fowler Avenue/H 582 |
| Tampa FL | Rolling Oats Market and Cafe | 813-873-7428 | 1021 N MacDill Avenue |
| Tampa FL | Sail Pavilion | 813-274-8511 | 333 S Franklin Street |
| Tampa FL | Smoothie King | 813-250-3888 | 2205 W Swann Avenue |
| Tampa FL | The Bungalow | 813-253-3663 | 2202 W. Kennedy Blvd/H 60 |
| Tampa FL | TooJay's Gourmet Deli | 813-348-4101 | 2223 NW Shore Blvd |
| Tarpon Springs FL | Costa's | 727-938-6890 | 521 Athens Street |
| Titusville FL | Bruster's Ice Cream | 321-385-0400 | 855 Cheney Hwy |
| Venice FL | TJ Carney's | 941-480-9244 | 231 W Venice Avenue |
| Vero Beach FL | Osceola Bistro | 772-569-1299 | 2045 13th Avenue |
| Wellington FL | Chipotle | 561-204-2816 | 1000 H 7, Suite 2 |
| Wellington FL | Jason's Deli | 561-333-1263 | 2605 H 7 |
| Wellington FL | Pei Wei Asian Diner | 561-753-6260 | 10610, Bay 10, Forest Hill Blvd |
| West Palm Beach FL | Chipotle | 561-688-8951 | 2380 Palm Beach Lakes Blvd |
| West Palm Beach FL | Copper Blues Rock Club and Kitchen | 561-404-4101 | 550 S. Rosemary Ave |
| West Palm Beach FL | Darbster | 561-586-2622 | 8020 S Dixie Hwy |
| West Palm Beach FL | Dixie Grill and Bar | 561-586-3189 | 5101 S Dixie Hwy |
| West Palm Beach FL | Kapow Noodle Bar | 561-246-3827 | 519 Clematis St |
| West Palm Beach FL | Nature's Way Cafe | 561-622-0440 | 9920 H A1A |
| West Palm Beach FL | The Chickpea | 561-855-7028 | 400 Clematis St |
| Wilton Manors FL | The Alchemist | 954-673-4614 | 2430 NE 13th Ave |
| Winter Park FL | Bosphorous | 407-644-8609 | 108 Park Avenue S |
| Winter Park FL | Dexter's of Winter Park | 407-629-1150 | 558 W New England Avenue |
| Winter Park FL | Eola Wine Company | 407-647-9103 | 136 S Park Avenue |
| Winter Park FL | Luma on Park | 407-599-4111 | 290 S Park Avenue |
| Winter Park FL | Park Plaza Gardens | 407-645-2475 | 319 S Park Avenue |
| Winter Park FL | The Wine Room | 407-696-WINE (9463) | 270 S Park Avenue |
| Winter Park FL | Three Ten Park South | 407-647-7277 | 310 S Park Ave |

## Georgia Listings

| | | | |
|---|---|---|---|
| Alpharetta GA | Chipotle | 678-867-9459 | 5250 Windward Parkway |
| Alpharetta GA | Jason's Deli | 770-619-2300 | 3070 Windward Plaza , SuiteT |
| Alpharetta GA | Z Pizza | 678-205-4471 | 5315 Windward Parkway |
| Athens GA | Heirloom Market and Cafe | 706-354-7901 | 815 N Chase Street |
| Athens GA | Jason's Deli | 706-425-4950 | 140 Alps Road, Suite 56 |
| Atlanta GA | 4th & Swift | 678-904-0160 | 621 N Avenue NE |
| Atlanta GA | 5 Seasons Westside | 404-875-3232 | 1000 Marietta Street |
| Atlanta GA | Anis Cafe and Bistro | 404-233-9889 | 2974 Grandview Avenue |
| Atlanta GA | Brewhouse Cafe | 404-525-7799 | 401 Moreland Avenue NE |
| Atlanta GA | Bruster's Real Ice Cream | 404-320-7166 | 2095 LaVista Rd NE/H 236 |
| Atlanta GA | Chipotle | 404-869-7921 | 3424 Piedmont Road/H 237 |

| | | | |
|---|---|---|---|
| Atlanta GA | Chipotle | 404-685-3531 | 718 Ponce de Leon Avenue/H 8/29/78 |
| Atlanta GA | Chipotle | 404-252-2998 | 5920 Roswell Road |
| Atlanta GA | Chipotle | 404-929-9907 | 2963 N Druid Hills Road NE |
| Atlanta GA | Chipotle | 770-916-0788 | 2973 Cobb Parkway/H 3/41 |
| Atlanta GA | Chipotle | 770-677-5542 | 123 Perimeter Center W |
| Atlanta GA | Corner Bakery Cafe | 404-816-5100 | 3368 Peachtree Rd. NE |
| Atlanta GA | Crooked Tree Café | 770-333-9119 | 2355 Cumberland Parkway, Suite 110 |
| Atlanta GA | Dakota Blue | 404-589-8002 | 454 Cherokee Ave SE |
| Atlanta GA | Firehouse Subs | 404-347-9912 | 537 10th Street NW |
| Atlanta GA | Jason's Deli | 404-231-3333 | 3330 Piedmont Road NE |
| Atlanta GA | Jason's Deli | 404-843-8212 | 5975 Roswell Road/H 9 |
| Atlanta GA | Jason's Deli | 770-671-1555 | 4705 Ashford Dunwoody Road, A-2 |
| Atlanta GA | Jason's Deli | 770-432-4414 | 1109 Cumberland Mall, #136 |
| Atlanta GA | Johnny Rockets | 404-525-7117 | 50 Upper Alabama |
| Atlanta GA | Johnny Rockets | 404-231-5555 | 5 W Paces Ferry Road NW |
| Atlanta GA | Nancy G's Cafe | 404-705-8444 | 4920 Roswell Rd |
| Atlanta GA | Park Tavern | 404-249-0001 | 500 10th Street NE |
| Atlanta GA | Sevananda Food Coop | 404-681-2831 | 467 Moreland Avenue NE |
| Atlanta GA | The Farm Burger | 404-816-0603 | 3365 Piedmont Road |
| Atlanta GA | The Shed at Glenwood | 404-835-4363 | 475 Bill Kennedy Way |
| Augusta GA | Panera Bread | 706-738-8922 | 254 Robert Daniel Parkway |
| Augusta GA | The Pizza Joint | 706-774-0037 | 1245 Broad Street/H 25 |
| Buford GA | Chipotle | 678-482-4355 | 3350 Buford Drive, Suite B 260/H 20 |
| Columbus GA | Jason's Deli | 706-494-8857 | 5555 Whittlesey Blvd |
| Darien GA | Skipper's Fish Camp | 912-437-FISH (3474) | 85 Screven Street |
| Decatur GA | Mojo Pizza | 404-373-1999 | 657 E Lake Drive |
| Decatur GA | The Farm Burger | 404-378-5077 | 4108 W Ponce De Leon |
| Decatur GA | Universal Joint | 404-373-6260 | 906 Oakview Road |
| Duluth GA | Chipotle | 678-584-0011 | 2040 Pleasant Hill Road |
| Duluth GA | Chipotle | 770-623-1724 | 11720 Medlock Bridge Road/H 141 |
| Duluth GA | Jason's Deli | 678-957-1973 | 11720 Medlock Bridge Road #150 /H 141 |
| Duluth GA | Z Pizza | 770-817-0526 | 11720 Medlock Bridge Road/H 141 |
| Evans GA | Panera Bread | 706-860-1580 | 4237 Washington Road/H 104 |
| Gainesville GA | Firehouse Subs | 770-533-7415 | 333 Shallowford Road NW, Suite D |
| Lawrenceville GA | Chipotle | 678-985-9290 | 860 Duluth H, Suite 320/H 120 |
| Marietta GA | Marietta Pizza Company | 770-419-0900 | 3 Whitlock Avenue SW/H 120 |
| McDonough GA | PJ's Cafe' | 770-898-5373 | 30 Macon Street/H 23/42 |
| Norcross GA | The Loving Hut | 678-421-9191 | 6385 Spalding Drive, Suite E |
| Roswel GA | Zest Sushi and Tapas | 678-461-6788 | 957 Canton St |
| Roswell GA | Chipotle | 770-642-0710 | 10800 Alpharetta H/H 9/120 |
| Sandy Springs GA | 5 Seasons Brewing Company;""; The Prado | 404-255-5911 | 5600 Roswell Road |
| Sandy Springs GA | Teela Taqueria | 404-459-0477 | 227 Sandy Springs Place, Suite 506 |
| Savannah GA | Beetnix Superfoods and Juice Bar | 912-231-9643 | 18 E Broughton St |
| Savannah GA | Brighter Day Natural Foods | 912-236-4703 | 1102 Bull Street |
| Savannah GA | Cha Bella Patio Bar and Grill | 912-790-7888 | 102 E Broad Street |
| Savannah GA | Firehouse Subs | 912-920-4161 | 8108 Abercorn Street, Suite 430/H 204 |
| Savannah GA | J Christopher's | 912-236-7494 | 122 E Liberty St |
| Savannah GA | Kayak Kafe | 912-233-6044 | One E Broughton Street |
| Savannah GA | Sentient Bean | 912-232-4447 | 13 E Park Avenue |
| Savannah GA | The Coffee Fox | 912-401-0399 | 102 W Broughton St |
| Savannah GA | Vinnie VanGoGo's | 912-233-6394 | 317 W Bryan Street |
| Savannah GA | Wild Wing Cafe | 912-790-WING (9464) | 27 Barnard Street |
| Savannah GA | World Of Beer | 912-443-1515 | 112 W Broughton St |
| Tucker GA | Jason's Deli | 770-493-4020 | 4073 Lavista Road/H 236 |
| Valdosta GA | Tropical Smoothie Cafe | 229-247-5599 | 1525 Baytree Road |
| Vinings GA | Meehan's Public House | 770-433-1920 | 2810 Paces Ferry Road |
| Warner Robins GA | Firehouse Subs | 478-542-9967 | 206 Russell Parkway, Suite 100 |

**Hawaii Listings**

| | | | |
|---|---|---|---|
| Aiea HI | Jamba Juice | 808-484-1519 | 99115 Aiea Heights Drive, #135 |
| Haleiwa HI | Waialua Bakery | 808-341-2838 | 66-200 Kamehameha H |
| Hanalei HI | Polynesia Cafe | 808-826-1999 | 5-5190 Kuhio H/H 560 |

| | | | |
|---|---|---|---|
| Honolulu HI | Barefoot Beach Cafe | 808-924-2233 | 2699 Kalakaua Ave |
| Honolulu HI | Diamond Head Cove Health Bar | 808-732-8744 | 3045 Monsarrat Avenue # 5 |
| Honolulu HI | Grondin: French-Latin Kitchen | 808-566-6768 | 62 N Hotel St |
| Honolulu HI | Grondin: French-Latin Kitchen | 8085666768 | 62 N Hotel St |
| Honolulu HI | Jamba Juice | 808-585-8359 | 130 Merchant Street #111 |
| Honolulu HI | Le Bistro | 808-373-7990 | 5730 Kalanianaloe H/H 72 |
| Honolulu HI | Nico's at Pier 38 Restaurant & Fish Market | 808-540-1377 | 1133 N Nimitz H/H 92 |
| Honolulu HI | Pindan Foods | 808-489-4557 | 131 Kaiulani Ave |
| Honolulu HI | The Greek Marina Restaurant | 808-396-8441 | 7192 Kalanianaole H/H 72 |
| Honolulu HI | The Wedding Cafe | 808-591-1005 | 1050 Ala Moana Blvd/H 92 |
| Honolulu HI | Town Restaurant | 808-735-5900 | 3435 Waialae Ave #104 |
| Honolulu HI | Z Pizza | 808-596-0066 | 1200 Ala Moana Blvd/H 92 |
| Kailua HI | Jamba Juice | 808-263-0975 | 539 Kailua Road/H 61 |
| Kailua-Kona HI | Jamba Juice | 808-327-6900 | 74-5588 Palani Road |
| Kailua-Kona HI | Kanaka Kava | 808-327-1660 | 75-5803 Alii Dr #6b |
| Kapolei HI | Starbucks | 808-674-8735 | 563 Farrington H #101/H 93 |
| Kihei HI | Jamba Juice | 808-891-8874 | 274 Piikea Avenue, #105/H 61 |
| Kihei HI | Taqueria Cruz | 808-875-2910 | 2395 S Kihei Road |
| Koloa HI | Puka Dog Hawaiian Style Hot Dog | 808-742-6044 | 2360 Kiahuna Plantation Drive |
| Kula HI | Grandma's Maui Coffee | 808-878-2140 | 9232 Kula H/H 37 |
| Lahaina HI | Penne Pasta Cafe | 808-661-6633 | 180 Dickenson Street |
| Lanai City HI | Cafe 565 | 808-565-6622 | 408 8th Street |
| Lanai City HI | Pele's Other Garden | 808-565-9628 | 811 Houston Street |
| Lanai City HI | The Blue Ginger Cafe | 808-565-6363 | 409 7th Street |
| Lihue HI | Kalapaki Beach Hut | 808-246-6330 | 3474 Rice Street/H 51 |
| Waianae HI | Jamba Juice | 808-628-6797 | 86-120 Farrington H, Unit #5/H 93 |
| Waikiki HI | Hula Dog Hawaiian Style | 808-634-2834 | 2301 Kuhio Avenue #334 |
| Waipahu HI | Jamba Juice | 808-680-9223 | 94-673 Kupuohi Street |

**Idaho Listings**

| | | | |
|---|---|---|---|
| Ammon ID | The Cellar | 208-525-9300 | 3520 E 17th Street |
| Boise ID | Baja Fresh | 208-327-0099 | 992 N Milwaukee |
| Boise ID | Baja Fresh Mexican Grill | 208-331-1100 | 980 Broadway Avenue/On H 20/26 |
| Boise ID | Big Bun Drive In | 208-375-5361 | 5816 W Overland Road |
| Boise ID | Highlands Hollow Brewhouse | 208-343-6820 | 2455 Harrison Hollow Lane |
| Boise ID | Jamba Juice | 208-658-1765 | 7709 W Overland Road, Suite 150 |
| Boise ID | Jamba Juice | 208-938-2102 | 13681 W McMillan Road |
| Boise ID | Mazzah Mediterranean | 208-333-2566 | 1772 W State Street |
| Boise ID | Mazzah Mediterranean Grill | 208-333-2223 | 404 E Parkcenter Blvd |
| Boise ID | Quiznos | 208-389-1177 | 2237 University Drive |
| Boise ID | Smashburger | 208-319-0090 | 8247 Franklin Road |
| Boise ID | Westside Drive-in | 208-342-2957 | 1939 W State Street |
| Boise ID | Wiseguy Pizza Pie | 208-336-7777 | 570 Main Street |
| Bonners Ferry ID | Under the Sun Organic Bistro and Coffee Bar | 208-267-6467 | 7178 Main Street |
| Coeur D' Alene ID | Rep Cafe | 208-930-4922 | 3330 N Grand Millane |
| Coeur d' Alene ID | Jamba Juice | 208-664-3206 | 202 W Ironwood Drive, Suite E |
| Coeur d'Alene ID | Pilgrim's Natural Foods Market and Deli | 208-676-9730 | 1316 N 4th Street |
| Dover ID | Dover Bay Cafe | 208-265-6467 | 204 S 4th Street |
| Driggs ID | Tony's Italian Grille | 208-354-8829 | 634 N Main Street/H 33 |
| Hailey ID | Wiseguy Pizza Pie | 208-788-8688 | 121 N Main Street Suite 3B/H 75 |
| Hope ID | Old Ice House Pizzeria & Bakery | 208-264-5555 | 140 W. Main Street |
| Idaho Falls ID | Jamba Juice | 208-542-0231 | 1803 S 2500 E |
| Ketchum ID | Rico's Pizza | 208-726-RICO (7426) | 200 N Main |
| Ketchum ID | Wiseguy Pizza Pie | 208-726-0737 | 460 Sun Valley Road |
| McCall ID | Bistro 45 Wine Bar and Cafe | 208-634-4515 | 1101 N 3rd Street/H 55 |
| McCall ID | Mile High Marina | 208-634-8605 | 1300 E Lake Street |
| McCall ID | Salmon River Brewery | 208-634-4SRB (4772) | 300 W Colorado Street |
| Meridian ID | Baja Fresh | 208-855-2468 | 1440 N Eagle Road |
| Pocatello ID | Jamba Juice | 208-478-9852 | 1103 Yellowstone Avenue/H 91 |
| Ponderay ID | Laughing Dog Brewing Co. | 208-263-9222 | 1109 Fontaine Dr |
| Sandpoint ID | Chimney Rock Grill | 208-255-3071 | 10,000 Schweitzer Mountain Road |
| Sandpoint ID | Ivano's Caffe | 208-263-0211 | 102 S First Avenue/Highway95 |

| | | | |
|---|---|---|---|
| Sandpoint ID | Mojo Coyote Cafe | 208-255-3071 | 10,000 Schweitzer Mountain Road |
| Sandpoint ID | Pine Street Bakery | 208-263-9012 | 710 Pine Street |
| Sandpoint ID | Zip's Drive-in | 208-255-7600 | 1301 Highway 2 |
| Twin Falls ID | Dunken's Microbrewery | 208-733-8114 | 102 Main Avenue N |

**Illinois Listings**

| | | | |
|---|---|---|---|
| Algonquin IL | Chipotle | 847-458-1030 | 412 S Randall Road |
| Algonquin IL | Jamba Juice | 847-854-2240 | 1515 S. Randall Road |
| Aurora IL | Jamba Juice | 630-585-1290 | 4430 Fox Valley Center Drive |
| Barrington IL | Tropical Smoothie Cafe | 847-277-7590 | 500 N. Hough Street/H 59 |
| Bloomingdale IL | Chipotle | 630-893-2108 | 396 W Army Trail Road |
| Bloominton IL | Chipotle | 309-661-4355 | 305 N Veterans Parkway, Suite 101/H 55 |
| Bolingbrook IL | Chipotle | 630-759-9359 | 274 S Weber Road |
| Braidwood IL | Polka Dot Drive-in | 815-458-3377 | 222 N Front St/H 53 |
| Carbondale IL | Neighborhood Co-op Grocery | 618-529-3533 | 1815 W Main Street/H 13 |
| Chicago IL | Bistrot Margot | 312-587-3660 | 1437 N Wells Street |
| Chicago IL | Brownstone Tavern | 773-528-3700 | 3937 N Lincoln Avenue |
| Chicago IL | Charmers | 773-743-2233 | 1500 W Jarvis Avenue |
| Chicago IL | Chicago Raw Food | 312-831-2729 | 131 N Clinton Street, Suite 7 |
| Chicago IL | Chipotle | 312-587-7753 | 291 E Ontario |
| Chicago IL | Chipotle | 773-661-0250 | 2717 N Elston Avenue |
| Chicago IL | Chipotle | 773-935-5710 | 2000 N Clybourn Avenue |
| Chicago IL | Chipotle | 773-935-6744 | 2256 N Orchard Avenue |
| Chicago IL | Chipotle | 773-465-9281 | 6600 N Sheridan Road |
| Chicago IL | Chipotle | 773-281-1492 | 610 W Diversey |
| Chicago IL | Chipotle | 773-348-5388 | 1025 W Belmont Avenue |
| Chicago IL | Cody's Public House | 773-528-4050 | 1658 W Barry Ave |
| Chicago IL | Corner Bakery | 312-263-4258 | 188 W. Washington Street |
| Chicago IL | Dunlay's on Clark | 773-883-6000 | 2600 North Clark Street |
| Chicago IL | Erie Cafe | 312-266-2300 | 536 W Erie Street |
| Chicago IL | Four Moon Tavern | 773-929-6666 | 1847 W Roscoe Street |
| Chicago IL | Jake Melnicks Corner Tap | 312-266-0400 | 41 E Superior St |
| Chicago IL | Kitsch'n on Roscoe | 773-248-SERA (7372) | 2005 W. Roscoe Street |
| Chicago IL | Mahoney's Pub & Grille | 312-733-2121 | 551 N Ogden Avenue |
| Chicago IL | Morgan Street Cafe | 312-850-0292 | 111 S Morgan |
| Chicago IL | O'Donavan's Restaurant | 773-478-2100 | 2100 West Irving Park Road |
| Chicago IL | Orange Restaurant | 773-248-0999 | 2011 West Roscoe |
| Chicago IL | Parline's | 773-561-8573 | 1754 W Balmoral Ave |
| Chicago IL | Perennial Virant | 312-981-7070 | 1800 N Lincoln Avenue |
| Chicago IL | Rockit Bar and Grill | 773-645-4400 | 3700 N Clark Street |
| Chicago IL | Swim Cafe | 312-492-8600 | 1357 W. Chicago Ave |
| Chicago IL | The Daily Bar and Grill | 773-561-6198 | 4560 N Lincoln Avenue |
| Chicago IL | Uncommon Ground | 773-929-3680 | 3800 N Clark Street |
| Chicago IL | Via Veneto Ristorante | 773-267-0888 | 6340 N Lincoln Ave |
| Chicago IL | Wishbone | 312-850-2663 | 1001 W Washington Blvd |
| Crystal Lake IL | Chipotle | 815-444-1532 | 5006 Northwest H/H 14 |
| DeKalb IL | Chipotle | 815-756-3715 | 1013A W Lincoln H/H 38 |
| Decatur IL | Panera Bread | 217-872-6435 | 255 E Ash Avenue |
| Deer Park IL | Jamba Juice | 847-438-4928 | 21690 W Long Grove Road, Unit B |
| Deerfield IL | Chipotle | 847-948-7902 | 675 Deerfield Road |
| Edwardsville IL | Bull & Bear Grill & Bar | 618-655-9920 | 1071 S H 157 |
| Effingham IL | Firefly Grill | 217-342-2002 | 1810 Avenue of Mid America |
| Evanston IL | Hartigan's Ice Cream Shoppe | 847-491-1232 | 2909 Central Street |
| Evanston IL | Oceanique | 847-864-3435 | 505 Main Street |
| Evanston IL | Sarkis' Cafe | 847-328-9703 | 2632 Gross Point Rd |
| Fairview Heights IL | Chipotle | 618-398-6655 | 6415 N Illinois Street/H 159 |
| Galena IL | Kaladi's 925 Coffee Bar | 815-776-0723 | 309 S Main Street |
| Geneva IL | Chipotle | 630-208-7430 | 1441 S Randall Road, Suite D |
| Geneva IL | Chipotle | 630-588-9728 | 811 Butterfield Road, Suite 101/H 56 |
| Geneva IL | Jamba Juice | 630-262-9455 | 1544 Commons Drive |
| Glen Ellyn IL | Chipotle | 630-469-4035 | 695 Roosevelt Road/H 38 |
| Glencoe IL | Foodstuffs | 847-835-5105 | 338 Park Avenue |
| Glencoe IL | Little Red Hen | 847-835-4900 | 653 Vernon Avenue |
| Gurnee IL | Chipotle | 847-406-4003 | 6040 Gurnee Mills Blvd E |

| | | | |
|---|---|---|---|
| Highland Park IL | Cafe Central | 847-266-7878 | 455 Central Avenue |
| Highland Park IL | Chipotle | 847-433-6453 | 1849 Green Bay Road |
| Highland Park IL | Hot Tamales | 847-433-4070 | 493 Central Avenue |
| Highland Park IL | Little Szechwan | 847-433-7007 | 1900 First Street |
| Hoffman Estates IL | Chipotle | 847-649-5800 | 4600 Hoffman Blvd |
| Kildeer IL | Chipotle | 847-438-3835 | 20505 N. Rand Road/H 12 |
| La Grange IL | Chipotle | 630-627-6610 | 18 W 050 22nd Street |
| La Grange IL | Chipotle | 708-588-9652 | 1 S La Grange Road |
| Lockport IL | Public Landing Restaurant and Banquet Center | 815-838-6500 | 200 W 8th Street |
| Lombard IL | Tropical Smoothie Cafe | 630-652-0500 | 2770 Highland Avenue |
| Melrose Park IL | Chipotle | 708-731-5800 | 1401 W North Avenue/H 64 |
| Moline IL | Dead Poets Espresso | 309-736-7606 | 1525 3rd Avenue A |
| Naperville IL | Chipotle | 630-718-9420 | 22 E Chicago Avenue |
| Naperville IL | Jason's Deli | 630-955-1179 | 1739 Freedom Drive |
| Naperville IL | Johnny Rockets | 630-428-8525 | 2835 Showplace Drive, Suite 115 |
| Oak Lawn IL | Chipotle | 630-469-4035 | 6230-B W 95th Street/H 12/20 |
| Oak Park IL | Barclay's American Grill | 708-848-4250 | 1120 Pleasant Street |
| Oak Park IL | Buzz Cafe | 708-524-2899 | 905 S. Lombard Avenue |
| Oak Park IL | Chipotle | 708-524-8211 | 1132 W Lake Street |
| Oakland IL | Jason's Deli | 708-233-0368 | 6260 W 95th Street/H 12/20 |
| Oglesby IL | Moore's Root Beer Stand | 815-883-9254 | 225 Columbia Avenue |
| Oglesby IL | Starved Rock Lodge Veranda | 815-667-4211 | 2668 East 873 Road |
| Oregon IL | Jay's Drive In | 815-732-2396 | 107 W Washington Street/H 64 |
| Orland Park IL | Jamba Juice | 708-364-1054 | 15159 S LaGrange Road, #400/H 45 |
| Oswego IL | Chipotle | 630-554-3508 | 2432 H 34 |
| Peoria IL | Jalapeno's Bar, Grill, and Patio | 309-691-3599 | 4620 N University Street |
| Peoria IL | Panera Bread | 309-682-3300 | 2601 W Lake Avenue |
| Peoria IL | Panera Bread | 309-692-8400 | 1101 W Bird Blvd |
| Rock Island IL | Cool Beanz Coffeehouse | 309-558-0909 | 1325 30th Street |
| Rockford IL | Chipotle | 815-397-8688 | 751 S Perryville Road |
| Rockford IL | Mary's Market Cafe and Bakery | 815-986-3300 | 2636 McFarland Road |
| Rockford IL | Mary's Market Cafe and Bakery | 815-394-0765 | 1659 N Alpine Road |
| Rockford IL | Meg's Daily Grind | 815-316-8785 | 1141 N Alpine Road |
| Rolling Meadows IL | Chipotle | 847-439-2430 | 1211 Golf Road/H 58 |
| Rosemont IL | Chipotle | 847-299-9201 | 7020 Mannheim Road/H 12/45 |
| S Elgin IL | Chipotle | 847-931-4172 | 348 Randall Road |
| Schaumburg IL | Chipotle | 847-839-8580 | 2558 W Schaumburg Road |
| Schaumburg IL | Jason's Deli | 847-240-0516 | 1530 McConnor Parkway |
| Shaumburg IL | Jamba Juice | 847-995-1445 | 601 N Martingale, #310 |
| Skokie IL | Chipotle | 847-679-0025 | 9408 Skokie Blvd/H 41 |
| Springfield IL | Augies Front Burner | 217-544-6979 | 109 S 5th Street |
| Springfield IL | Chipotle | 217-321-0500 | 2579 W Wabash Avenue/H 54 |
| Springfield IL | Maldaner's Restaurant | 217-522-4313 | 222 S 6th Street |
| Springfield IL | Panera Bread | 217-529-6200 | 3019 S Dirksen Parkway |
| Springfield IL | Panera Bread | 217-726-5070 | 3101 W White Oaks Drive |
| St Charles IL | Chipotle | 630-587-9033 | 3821 E Main Street/H 64 |
| Tinley Park IL | Chipotle | 708-407-7500 | 15980 S Harlem Avenue/H 43 |
| Urbana IL | Crane Alley | 217-384-7526 | 115 W Main Street |
| Urbana IL | Strawberry Fields | 217-328-1655 | 306 W Springfield |
| Vernon Hills IL | Chipotle | 847-478-0883 | 375 N Milwaukee Avenue/H 21 |
| Vernon Hills IL | Jason's Deli | 847-680-1869 | 545 Lakeview Parkway |
| Warrenville IL | Chipotle | 630-836-0016 | 28251 Diehl Road |
| Warrenville IL | Jamba Juice | 630-393-0159 | 28341 Diehl Road |
| Waukegan IL | Chipotle | 847-406-5770 | 940 S Waukegan Road |
| West Dundee IL | Chipotle | 847-426-2183 | 201 N 8th Street/H 31 |
| Westmont IL | Chipotle | 630-920-1890 | 300 E Ogden Avenue/H 34 |
| Wheaton IL | Firehouse Subs | 630-221-0101 | 272 Danada Square W |
| Wheaton IL | Jamba Juice | 630-221-1573 | 278 Danada Square W |
| Wheeling IL | Chipotle | 847-520-6353 | 1572 W Lake Cook Road |
| Willowbrook IL | Chipotle | 630-560-7900 | 7173 Kingery H/H 83 |
| Wilmette IL | The Noodle Cafe | 847-251-2228 | 708 12th Street |
| Woodstock IL | Expressly Leslie Vegetarian Specialties | 815-338-2833 | 110 S. Johnson Street |

**Indiana Listings**

| | | | |
|---|---|---|---|
| Avon IN | Chipotle | 317-271-1481 | 10403 E H 36 |

| | | | |
|---|---|---|---|
| Bloomington IN | Chipotle | 812-330-1435 | 420 E Kirkwood Avenue |
| Carmel IN | Cafe Patachou | 317-569-0965 | 4733 126th Street |
| Carmel IN | Chipotle | 317-816-0033 | 2420 E 146th Street |
| Columbus IN | Tropical Smoothie Cafe | 812-375-1100 | 3135 25th Street |
| Elkhart IN | Pete's Simonton Lake Tavern | 574-264-9033 | 51426 H 19 |
| Fort Wayne IN | Chipotle | 260-432-6364 | 4210 W Jefferson Blvd |
| Fort Wayne IN | Chipotle | 260-483-6074 | 910 E Coliseum Blvd/H 30/37/930 |
| Fort Wayne IN | Three Rivers Food Co-op | 260-424-8812 | 1612 Sherman Street |
| Goshen IN | Maple City Market | 574-534-2355 | 314 S Main Street/H 15 |
| Greenwood IN | Johnny Rockets | 317-881-6240 | 1251 H 31N, Room R100 |
| Indianapolis IN | Boogie Burger | 317-255-2450 | 1904 Broad Ripple Ave |
| Indianapolis IN | Cafe Patachou | 317-632-0765 | 225 West Washington Street |
| Indianapolis IN | Cafe Patachou | 317-925-2823 | 4901 North Pennsylvania Street |
| Indianapolis IN | Chatham Tap | 317-917-8425 | 719 Massachusetts Ave |
| Indianapolis IN | Chipotle | 317-815-9017 | 1560 E 86th Street |
| Indianapolis IN | Chipotle | 317-575-8292 | 4625 E 96th Street |
| Indianapolis IN | Chipotle | 317-415-0136 | 3340 W 86th Street |
| Indianapolis IN | El Arado Mexican Grill | 317-632-2076 | 1063 Virginia Ave |
| Indianapolis IN | Firehouse Subs | 317-334-1471 | 3516 W 86th Street |
| Indianapolis IN | Front Page Tavern | 317-631-6682 | 310 Massachusetts Avenue |
| Indianapolis IN | Greek Island Restaurant | 317-636-0700 | 906 S. Meridian Street |
| Indianapolis IN | Johnny Rockets | 317-578-8015 | 6020 E 82nd Street |
| Indianapolis IN | La Margarita Restaurant and Tequila Bar | 317-384-1457 | 1043 Virginia Avenue, Suite 1 |
| Indianapolis IN | Mikado Japanese Restaurant | 317-972-4180 | 148 S Illinois Street |
| Indianapolis IN | Panera Bread | 317-542-7450 | 9145 E 56th Street |
| Indianapolis IN | Panera Bread | 317-334-7800 | 2902 W 86th Street |
| Indianapolis IN | Plump's Last Shot | 317-257-5867 | 6416 Cornell Avenue |
| Indianapolis IN | Ralston's Drafthouse | 317-493-1143 | 635 Massachusetts Ave. |
| Indianapolis IN | The Milano Inn Restaurant | 317-264-3585 | 231 S College Ave |
| Indianapolis IN | Whole Foods Market | 317-706-0900 | 1300 E 86th Street |
| Indianapolis IN | Yats | 317-253-8817 | 5363 North College Ave |
| Kokomo IN | Chipotle | 765-743-4804 | 1201 S Reed Road/H 31 |
| Lafayette IN | McAlister's Deli | 765-449-2300 | 100 S Creasy Lane, Suite 1000 |
| Merrillville IN | Chipotle | 219-755-4292 | 1948 Southlake Mall |
| Merrillville IN | Jamba Juice | 219-736-6191 | 2493 Southlake Mall, Unit 2495A |
| Michigan City IN | Ryan's Irish Pub | 219-872-0361 | 4461 S Franklin St. |
| Mishawaka IN | Chipotle | 574-271-3353 | 5545 N Main Street |
| Mooresville IN | Zedeco Grill | 317-834-3900 | 11 E Main |
| Noblesville IN | Firehouse Subs | 317-773-7333 | 17053 Mercantile Blvd |
| Richmond IN | Chipotle | 765-966-3292 | 3726 National Road E/H 40/E Main Street |
| S Bend IN | Jamba Juice | 574-232-0970 | 1234 N Eddy Street, Suite 107 |
| W Lafayette IN | Chipotle | 765-743-4804 | 200 W State Street/H 26 |

**Iowa Listings**

| | | | |
|---|---|---|---|
| Amana IA | Millstream Brewing Company | 319-622-3672 | 835 48th Avenue |
| Coralville IA | New Pioneer Food Co-op and Bakehouse | 319-358-5513 | 1101 2nd Street/H 6 |
| Davenport IA | Thunder Bay Grille | 563-386-2722 | 6511 N Brady Street |
| Decorah IA | Oneota Community Co-op | 563-382-4666 | 312 W Water Street |
| Iowa City IA | Atlas | 319-341-7700 | 127 Iowa Avenue |
| Iowa City IA | Chipotle | 319-338-1194 | 201 S Clinton, Suite 112 |
| Iowa City IA | New Pioneer Food Co-op | 319-338-9441 | 22 S Van Buren Street |
| Urbandale IA | Panera Bread | 515-253-9223 | 2839 86th Street |
| W Des Moines IA | Chipotle | 515-422-9800 | 1551 Valley West Drive, Suite 224 |
| W Des Moines IA | Jason's Deli | 515-222-9797 | 3910 University Avenue |
| Waukee IA | LT Organic Farm | 515-987-3561 | 3241 Ute Avenue |

**Kansas Listings**

| | | | |
|---|---|---|---|
| Kansas City KS | Chipotle - Legends | 913-299-9221 | 1813 Village W Parkway Q101 |
| Kansas City KS | Grinders | 816-472-5454 | 417 E 18th Street |
| Kansas City KS | MeMa's Old-Fashioned Bakery | 913-299-9121 | 1829 Village W Parkway |
| Lawrence KS | Chipotle - Mass | 785-843-8800 | 911 Massachusetts Street |
| Lawrence KS | Chipotle - West Lawrence | 785-843-1510 | 4000 W 6th Avenue/H 40 |
| Lawrence KS | Community Mercantile Co-Op | 785-843-8544 | 901 Iowa Street/H 59 |
| Lawrence KS | Jason's Deli | 785-842-5600 | 3140 S Iowa Street, #110 /H 10/59 |

| | | | |
|---|---|---|---|
| Lenexa KS | Chipotle - 95th & Quivira | 913-492-4610 | 12150 W 95th Street |
| Lenexa KS | La Peep | 913-492-6644 | 7936 Quivira Road |
| Lenexa KS | Spin Pizza | 913-438-SPIN (7746) | 9474 Renner Blvd |
| Manhattan KS | Chipotle - Manhattan | 785-587-8029 | 606 N Manhattan Avenue |
| Mission KS | Chipotle - Johnson Drive | 913-261-3530 | 6864 Johnson Drive |
| Olathe KS | Chipotle - Northridge | 913-393-3319 | 15100 W 119th Street |
| Olathe KS | Chipotle - Southgate | 913-829-4399 | 20080 W 153rd Street |
| Olathe KS | Jason's Deli | 913-498-2255 | 16535 W. 119th Street |
| Olathe KS | Jason's Deli | 913-825-4422 | 16535 W. 119th Street |
| Olathe KS | Spin Pizza | 913-764-SPIN (7746) | 14230 W 119th Street |
| Overland Park KS | Barley's Brewhaus | 913-663-4099 | 11924 W 119th Street |
| Overland Park KS | Chipotle - Corp Woods | 913-469-6620 | 9900 College Blvd Unit 16 |
| Overland Park KS | Firehouse Subs | 913-451-6200 | 7521 W 119th Street |
| Overland Park KS | Jason's Deli | 913-498-2255 | 12010 Metcalf Avenue |
| Overland Park KS | LePeep | 913-661-9441 | 7218 College Blvd |
| Overland Park KS | Spin Pizza | 913-451-SPIN (7746) | 6541 W 119th Street |
| Prairie Village KS | Cafe Provence | 913-384-5998 | 3936 W 69th Terrace |
| Prairie Village KS | La Peep | 913-948-9100 | 5400 W 95th Street |
| Prairie Village KS | The Blue Moose Bar and Grill | 913-722-9463 | 4160 W 71st Street |
| Shawnee KS | Barley's Brewhaus | 913-268-5160 | 16649 Midland Drive |
| Shawnee Mission KS | Sonic Drive-In | 913-901-8511 | 8905 Santa Fe Dr |
| Topeka KS | Chipotle - Wanamaker | 785-273-3692 | 2040 SW Wanamaker Road |
| Topeka KS | Jason's Deli | 785-478-4144 | 6121 SW 12th Street #400 |
| Wichita KS | Buffalo Wild Wings Grill and Bar | 316-636-9464 | 3236 N Rock Road |
| Wichita KS | Chipotle - Hillside | 316-612-6931 | 515 N Hillside |
| Wichita KS | Chipotle - New Market | 316-722-4300 | 2241 N Maize Road, Suite 111 |
| Wichita KS | Chipotle - Rock Road | 316-631-3892 | 3015 N Rock Road |
| Wichita KS | Jason's Deli | 316-721-4993 | 7447 W 21st Street, #141 |
| Wichita KS | Jason's Deli | 316-636-4447 | 2000 N Rock Road, Suite 108 |

**Kentucky Listings**

| | | | |
|---|---|---|---|
| Bowling Green KY | 440 Main Restaurant and Bar | 270-793-0450 | 440 E Main Avenue |
| Crescent Springs KY | Chipotle | 859-341-8111 | 525 Buttermilk Pike |
| Florence KY | Chipotle | 859-371-3002 | 7915 Dream Street |
| Lexington KY | Chipotle | 859-389-6643 | 345 S Limestone |
| Lexington KY | Chipotle | 859-268-1142 | 2905 Richmond Road |
| Lexington KY | Chipotle | 859-263-2611 | 1869 Plaudit Place |
| Lexington KY | Firehouse Subs | 859-226-0111 | 535 S Upper Street, Suite 175/H 27 |
| Lexington KY | Good Foods Market & Cafe | 859-278-1813 | 455 Southland Dr # D |
| Lexington KY | Jean Farris Winery and Bistro | 859-263-WINE (9463) | 6825 Old Richmond Road/H 25/421 |
| Lexington KY | Stella's Kentucky Deli | 859-255-DELI (3354) | 143 Jefferson Street |
| Lexington KY | Stella's Kentucky Deli | 859 255-DELI (3354) | 143 Jefferson Street |
| Lexington KY | Tropical Smoothie Cafe | 859-269-2233 | 1060 Chinoe Road |
| Lexington KY | West Sixth Brewing | 859-951-6006 | 501 W 6th St |
| Louisville KY | Jason's Deli | 502-412-4101 | 410 N Hurstbourne Parkway, Suite 100 /H 1747 |
| Louisville KY | Moe's Southwest Grill | 502-491-1800 | 2001 S Hurstbourne Parkway |
| Owensboro KY | Famous Bistro | 270-686-8202 | 102 W 2nd Street/H 60 |
| Versailles KY | Wallace Station Deli & Bakery | 859-846-5161 | 3854 Old Frankfort Pike |

**Louisiana Listings**

| | | | |
|---|---|---|---|
| Baton Rouge LA | Bistro Byronz | 225-218-1433 | 5412 Government Street |
| Baton Rouge LA | Jason's Deli | 225-926-7788 | 2531 Citiplace Court |
| Baton Rouge LA | Jason's Deli | 225-293-9099 | 6725 Siegen Lane, Suite X |
| Baton Rouge LA | Lucy's Retired Surfer Bar and Restaurant | 225-361-0372 | 151 3rd Street |
| Baton Rouge LA | The Bulldog - Baton Rouge | 225-303-9400 | 4385 Perkins Road/H 427 |
| Baton Rouge LA | Tropical Smoothie Cafe | 225-408-2290 | 13200 Airline H/H 61 |
| Bossier City LA | Firehouse Subs | 318-747-6344 | 3011 Airline Drive |
| La Provence LA | La Provence | 985-626-7662 | 25020 H 190 |

| Lafayette LA | Jason's Deli | 337-216-0194 | 149 Arnould Blvd |
| Lafayette LA | Tropical Smoothie Cafe | 337-456-3933 | 458 Heymann Blvd |
| Lake Charles LA | Pujo Street Cafe | 337-439-2054 | 901 Ryan Street |
| New Orleans LA | CC's Community Coffee House | 504-482-9865 | 2800 Esplanade Avenue |
| New Orleans LA | Cafe Amelie | 504-412-8965 | 912 Royal Street |
| New Orleans LA | Cafe Envie | 504-524-3689 | 1241 Decatur St |
| New Orleans LA | Cafe Lafitte in Exile | 504-522-8397 | 901 Bourbon St |
| New Orleans LA | Chartres House Cafe | 504-586-8383 | 601 Chartres |
| New Orleans LA | Claire's Pour House | 504-558-8980 | 233 Decatur Street |
| New Orleans LA | Gazebo Cafe | 504-525-8899 | 1018 Decatur St |
| New Orleans LA | Jamba Juice | 504-304-4210 | 930 Poydras Street |
| New Orleans LA | Lucy's Retired Surfer's Bar | 504-523-8995 | 701 Tchoupitoulas Street |
| New Orleans LA | Parkway Bakery & Tavern | 504-482-3047 | 538 Hagan Avenue |
| New Orleans LA | Poppy's Crazy Lobster | 504-569-3380 | 500 Port of New Orleans Place Suite 83 |
| New Orleans LA | The Bulldog | 504-891-1516 | 3236 Magazine Street |
| New Orleans LA | The Bulldog - Mid-City | 504-488-4191 | 5135 Canal Blvd |
| New Orleans LA | The Bulldog - Uptown | 504-891-1516 | 3236 Magazine Street |
| New Orleans LA | The Green Goddess | 504-301-3347 | 307 Exchange Place |
| New Orleans LA | The Louisiana Pizza Kitchen | 504-522-9500 | 95 French Market Place |
| New Orleans LA | The Market Cafe | 504-527-5000 | 1000 Decatur St |
| Ruston LA | Smoothie King | 318-251-8181 | 1100 Cooktown Road |
| Shreveport LA | Firehouse Subs | 318-798-6547 | 7230 Youree Drive, Suite 113/H 1 |
| Slidell LA | Tropical Smoothie Cafe | 985-643-3328 | 2040 E Gause Blvd/H 190 |

**Maine Listings**

| Bar Harbor ME | Adelmann's Deli | 207-288-0455 | 224 Main St |
| Bar Harbor ME | Bar Harbor Whale Watch Co. | 207-288-2386 | 1 West Sreet |
| Bar Harbor ME | Blaze Restaurant | 207-801-2755 | 198 Main St |
| Bar Harbor ME | Cafe This Way | 207-288-4483 | 14 1/2 Mt Desert Street/H 3 |
| Bar Harbor ME | Cherrystones Restaurant | 207-801-2290 | 185 Main St |
| Bar Harbor ME | China Joy Restaurant | 207-288-8666 | 195 Main Street |
| Bar Harbor ME | Fish House Grill | 207-288-3070 | 1 West Street |
| Bar Harbor ME | Jack Russell Pub | 207-288-5214 | 102 Eden Street/H 3 |
| Bar Harbor ME | Jordon Pond House Restaurant | 207-276-3316 | Route 3 |
| Bar Harbor ME | Mama DiMatteo's | 207-288-3666 | 34 Kennebec Place |
| Bar Harbor ME | McKays Public House | 207-288-2002 | 231 Main Street/H 3 |
| Bar Harbor ME | Paddy's Irish Pub | 207-801-3786 | 50 West St |
| Bar Harbor ME | Pat's Pizza | 207-288-5117 | 51 Rodick St |
| Bar Harbor ME | Poor Boy's Gourmet Restaurant | 207-288-4148 | 300 Main St |
| Bar Harbor ME | Rupununi | 207-288-2886 | 119 Main St |
| Bar Harbor ME | Siam Orchid | 207-288-9669 | 30 Rodick St |
| Bar Harbor ME | Side Street Cafe | 207-801-2591 | 49 Rodick St |
| Bar Harbor ME | Stewman's Lobster Pound | 207-288-0346 | 35 West Street |
| Bar Harbor ME | The Chart Room | 207-288-9740 | 565 Eden St |
| Bar Harbor ME | The Looking Glass Restaurant | 207-288-5663 | 50 Eden St |
| Bass Harbor ME | Seafood Ketch | 207-244-7463 | 47 Shore Rd |
| Boothbay ME | Boothbay Lobster Wharf | 207-633-4900 | 97 Atlantic Avenue |
| Boothbay Harbor ME | The Lobster Dock | 207-633-7120 | 49 Atlantic Avenue |
| Brunswick ME | Fat Boy Drive-in | 207-729-9431 | 111 Bath Road/H 24 |
| Cape Porpoise Harbor ME | Cape Pier Chowder House | 207-967-0123 | 79 Pier Road |
| Ellsworth ME | Finelli's Pizza | 207-664-0230 | 12 Downeast H/H 1 |
| Mount Desert ME | Abel's Lobster Pound | 207-276-5827 | 13 Abels Ln |
| Oquossoc ME | The Gingerbread House | 207-864-3602 | 55 Carry Road, Rangeley Lk |
| Portland ME | Beals Old Fashioned Ice Cream | 207-828-1335 | 12 Moulton St |
| Portland ME | Gritty McDuffs | 207-772-BREW (2739) | 396 Fore Street |
| Portland ME | Portland Lobster Company | 207-775-2112 | 180 Commercial Street/H 1 |
| Portland ME | Sebago Brewpub | 207-775-2337 | 164 Middle Street |
| Portland ME | The Flatbread Company | 207-772-8777 | 72 Commercial Street/H 1 |
| South Freeport ME | Johnny Rockets | 207-865-6070 | 1 Freeport Village, Suite 300 |
| Southwest Harbor ME | Eat a Pita Restaurant | 207-244-4344 | 326 Main St |
| Southwest Harbor ME | The Captains Galley at Beal Lobster Pier | 207-244-3202 | 182 Clark Point Rd |

**Maryland Listings**

442

| | | | |
|---|---|---|---|
| Annapolis MD | Baltimore Coffee and Tea | 410-573-5792 | 890 Bestgate Road |
| Annapolis MD | Buddy's Crabs and Ribs | 410-626-1100 | 100 Main Street |
| Annapolis MD | Davis's Pub | 410-268-7432 | 400 Chester Ave |
| Annapolis MD | Grump's Cafe | 410-267-0229 | Bay Ridge Plaza 117 Hillsmere Drive |
| Annapolis MD | Harry Browne's Restaurant | 410-263-4332 | 66 State Cir |
| Annapolis MD | Johnny Rockets | 410-897-0717 | 1084 Annapolis Mall |
| Annapolis MD | Kilwins Chocolate & Ice Cream | 410-263-2601 | 128 Main St |
| Annapolis MD | Ledo's Pizza | 410-295-3030 | 505 S Cherry Grove Ave |
| Annapolis MD | McBride Gallery | 410-267-7077 | 215 Main St |
| Annapolis MD | Pusser's Caribbean Grille | 410-626-0004 | 80 Compromise Street |
| Annapolis MD | Rams Head Tavern | 410-268-4545 | 33 West Street |
| Annapolis MD | Red Red Wine Bar | 410-990-1144 | 189B Main Street |
| Annapolis MD | Reynolds Tavern | 410-295-9555 | 7 Church St. |
| Annapolis MD | Stan and Joe's Saloon | 410-263-1993 | 37 West Street/H 450 |
| Annapolis MD | The Federal House Bar & Grille | 410-268-2576 | 22 Market Space |
| Annapolis MD | The Greene Turtle | 410-266-7474 | 177 Jennifer Rd |
| Annapolis MD | W.R. Chance & Son Jewelers | 410-263-2404 | 110 Main St |
| Aspen Hill MD | Chipotle | 301-598-2215 | 13501 Connecticut Avenue |
| Baltimore MD | Baba's Mediterranean Kitchen | 410-727-7482 | 745 East Fort Avenue |
| Baltimore MD | Bo Brooks Restaurant & Catering | 410-558-0202 | 2701/150 Lighthouse Point |
| Baltimore MD | Bonjour | 410-372-0238 | 6070 Falls Rd |
| Baltimore MD | Chipotle | 410-837-8353 | 621 E Pratt Street |
| Baltimore MD | Chipotle | 410-377-7728 | 6314 York Road/H 45 |
| Baltimore MD | City Cafe | 410-539-4252 | 1001 Cathedral St |
| Baltimore MD | Crush Restaurant | 443-278-9001 | 510 E Belvedere Ave |
| Baltimore MD | Dangerously Delicious Pies | 410-522-PIES (7437) | 1036 Light Street |
| Baltimore MD | Ethel and Ramone's | 410-664-2971 | 1615 Sulgrave Ave |
| Baltimore MD | Frank & Nic's West End Grille | 410-685-6800 | 511 W Pratt St |
| Baltimore MD | Greene Turtle | 410-342-4222 | 722 S Broadway |
| Baltimore MD | Hersh's Pizza & Drinks | 443-438-4948 | 1843 Light St |
| Baltimore MD | Iggies Pizza | 410-528-0818 | 818 N Calvert Street |
| Baltimore MD | Los Amigos Authentic Mexican Restaurant | 410-444-4220 | 5506 Harford Rd |
| Baltimore MD | Max's Taphouse | 888-675-6297 | 737 S Broadway |
| Baltimore MD | Metropolitan | 410-234-0235 | 904 S Charles St |
| Baltimore MD | No Idea Tavern | 410-685-4332 | 1649 S Hanover St |
| Baltimore MD | Patterson Perk | 410-534-1286 | 2501 Eastern Avenue |
| Baltimore MD | Pub Dog Pizza & Drafthouse | 410-727-6077 | 20 East Cross Street |
| Baltimore MD | Riptide by the Bay | 410-732-3474 | 1718 Thames St |
| Bethesda MD | Chipotle | 301-907-9077 | 7600 Old Georgetown Road |
| Bethesda MD | Chipotle | 301-214-2410 | 10400 Old Georgetown Road |
| Bethesda MD | Jaleo | 301-913-0003 | 7271 Woodmont Ave |
| Bowie MD | Chipotle | 301-262-4580 | 15500 Excelsior Drive |
| Bowie MD | Chipotle | 301-464-4517 | 10201 Martin Luther King Jr H/H 704 |
| Callaway MD | Bear Creek Open Pit BBQ | 301-994-1030 | 21030 Point Lookout Road/H 5 |
| Cambridge MD | Snappers Waterfront Cafe | 410-228-0112 | 112 Commerce Street |
| Chesapeake City MD | Bayard House | 410-885-5040 | 11 Bohemia Avenue |
| Chevy Chase MD | Chipotle | 301-654-6661 | 4471 Willard Avenue |
| College Park MD | Chipotle | 240-582-0015 | 7332 Baltimore Avenue/H 1 |
| Columbia MD | Chipotle | 410-997-1083 | 6181 Old Dobbin Lane |
| Columbia MD | Tropical Smoothie Cafe | 410-730-6564 | 6455 Dobbin Road, Suite 35 |
| Crisfield MD | The Waterman Inn | 410-968-2119 | 901 W Main Street/H 413 |
| Cumberland MD | City Lights | 301-722-9800 | 59 Baltimore St |
| Cumberland MD | Gianni's Pizza and Wings | 301-729-3737 | 15712 McMullen H/H 220 |
| Deep Creek Lake MD | Lakeside Creamery | 301-387-2580 | 20282 Garrett H/H 219 |
| Edgewater MD | Chipotle Mexican Grill | 410-956-7484 | 3046 Solomons Island Rd #200 |
| Fells Point MD | The Point in Fells | 410-327-7264 | 1738 Thames Street |
| Frederick MD | Chipotle | 301-846-0933 | 5223 Buckeystown Pike |
| Frederick MD | Firehouse Subs | 301-668-6301 | 5100 Buckeystown Pike, Suite 194/H 85 |
| Frederick MD | La Paz | 301-694-8980 | 51 South Market Street |
| Gaithersburg MD | Chipotle | 240-632-1228 | 564 N Frederick Avenue |
| Gaithersburg MD | Chipotle | 301-926-3875 | 96 Main Street |
| Grambrills MD | Chipotle | 410-451-4161 | 2503 Brandermill Blvd |
| Greenbelt MD | Chipotle | 301-982-6722 | 5506 Cherrywood Lane |
| Hagerstown MD | Chipotle | 240-420-8010 | 18003 Garland Groh Blvd |

| | | | |
|---|---|---|---|
| Hyattsville MD | Elevation Burger | 301-985-6869 | 5501 Baltimore Avenue/H 1 |
| Laurel MD | Chipotle | 301-604-2241 | 14354 Baltimore Avenue/H1 |
| Lexington Park MD | Chipotle | 240-725-0330 | 22720 Three Notch Road/H 235 |
| Lutherville MD | Chipotle | 410-308-2616 | 1830 York Road/H 45 |
| McHenry MD | Canoe on the Run | 301-387-5933 | 2622 Deep Creek Drive |
| Mechanicsville MD | Bert's 50's Diner | 301-884-3837 | 28760 Three Notch Road/H 5/235 |
| Middletown MD | The Main Cup Cafe | 301-371-4433 | 14 W Main Street/H 40 |
| Ocean City MD | Dumser's Dairyland Drive-In | 410-524-1588 | 4901 Coastal Hwy |
| Ocean City MD | Macky's Bayside Bar and Grill | 410-723-5565 | 54th Street on the Bay |
| Ocean City MD | Micky Fins Bar & Grill | 410-213-9033 | 12952 Inlet Isle Ln |
| Ocean City MD | Smoker's BBQ Pit | 410-213-0040 | 9711 Stephen Decatur Hwy |
| Ocean City MD | The Bayside Skillet | 410-524-7950 | 7701 Coastal Hwy |
| Potomac MD | Elevation Burger | 301-838-4010 | 12525 Park Potomac Avenue, Bldg G, Unit D |
| Rockville MD | Chipotle | 301-838-9222 | 14925 Shady Grove Road |
| Rockville MD | Chipotle | 301-881-2600 | 11830 Rockville Pike #17B |
| S Chesapeake City MD | Chesapeake Inn | 410-885-2040 | 605 Second Street/H 286 |
| Savage MD | Rams Head Tavern Savage Mill | 301-604-3454 | 8600 Foundry St Ste 2065 |
| Severna Park MD | Chipotle | 410-315-9501 | 575 Ritchie H/H 2 |
| Silver Spring MD | Chipotle | 301-586-0430 | 12060 Cherry Hill Road |
| Silver Spring MD | Chipotle | 301-608-3688 | 907 Ellsworth Avenue |
| Silver Spring MD | Denizens Brewing Company | 301-557-9818 | 1115 East-West Highway |
| Silver Spring MD | Eggspectation | 301-585-1700 | 923 Ellsworth Drive |
| Silver Spring MD | The Daily Dish | 301-588-6300 | 8301 Grubb Road |
| St Michaels MD | Ava's Pizzeria & Wine Bar | 410-745-3081 | 409 S Talbot St |
| St Michaels MD | St Michaels Crab House | 410-745-3737 | 305 Mulberry Street |
| Towson MD | Chipotle | 410-296-1742 | 801 Goucher Blvd |
| Waldorf MD | Chipotle | 301-632-6959 | 3250 Crain H/H 301 |

**Massachusetts Listings**

| | | | |
|---|---|---|---|
| Amesbury MA | The Flatbread Company | 978-834-9800 | 5 Market Square |
| Amherst MA | Rao's Coffee Roasting Company | 413-253-9441 | 17 Kellogg Avenue |
| Beverly MA | Rawbert's Organic Cafe | 978-922-0004 | 294 Cabot Street/H 22 |
| Bolton MA | Slater's Restaurant of Bolton | 978-779-6680 | 356 Main St |
| Boston MA | Chipotle | 617-236-4950 | 148 Brookline Avenue |
| Boston MA | Coppa | 617-391-0902 | 253 Shawmut Ave |
| Boston MA | Da Vinci | 617-350-0007 | 162 Columbus Ave |
| Boston MA | Gaslight Brasserie Du Coin | 617-422-0224 | 560 Harrison Ave |
| Boston MA | Hamersley's Bistro | 617-423-2700 | 553 Tremont St. |
| Boston MA | Tremont 647 | 617-266-4600 | 647 Tremont S |
| Boston MA | Whole Foods Market | 617-375-1010 | 15 Westland Avenue |
| Brewster MA | Cobie's Clam Shack | 508-896-7021 | 3260 Main St |
| Brookline MA | Dorado Tacos and Cemitas | 617-566-2100 | 401 Harvard Street |
| Brookline MA | The Fireplace | 617-975-1900 | 1634 Beacon St. |
| Cambridge MA | Bambara Restaurant | 617-868-4444 | 25 Edwin H Land Boulevard |
| Cambridge MA | Cambridge Brewing Company | 617-494-1994 | 1 Kendall Square, Bldg 100 |
| Cambridge MA | Chipotle | 617-491-0677 | One Brattle Square |
| Cambridge MA | Henrietta's Table | 617-661-5005 | One Bennett Street |
| Concord MA | Country Kitchen | 978-371-0181 | 181 Sudbury Road |
| Dedham MA | Chipotle | 781-329-2332 | 176 Providence H |
| Fiskdale MA | Pioneer Brewing Company | 508-347-7500 | 195 Arnold Road |
| Framingham MA | Chipotle | 508-879-0823 | 1 Worcester Road/H 9 |
| Gloucester MA | Virgilios Italian Bakery | 978-283-5295 | 29 Main Street |
| Hyannis MA | Alberto's Ristorante | 508-778-1770 | 360 Main St |
| Hyannis MA | Barbyann's | 508-775-9795 | 120 Airport Rd |
| Lexington MA | Dabin Restaurant | 781-860-0171 | 10 Muzzey St #1 |
| Mansfield MA | Chipotle | 508-339-2061 | 287 School Street |
| Marlborough MA | Chipotle | 508-480-8412 | 237 Boston Post Road W/H 20 |
| Mashpee MA | Starbuck's Coffee House | 508-477-5806 | 38 Nanthan Ellis Hwy |
| Mashpee MA | The Tea Shoppe | 508-477-7261 | 13 Steeple Street |
| Medford MA | Chipotle | 781-393-6871 | 616 Fellsway/H 28 |
| Nantucket MA | Centre Street Bistro | 508-228-8470 | 29 Centre St |
| Nantucket MA | Cisco Brewers | 508-325-5929 | 5 Bartlett Farm Rd |
| Nantucket MA | Espresso To Go | 508-228-6930 | 1 Toombs Court |
| Nantucket MA | Something Natural | 508-228-0504 | 50 Cliff Road |
| Newburyport MA | Revitalive Cafe | 978-462-0639 | 50 Water Street |

| | | | |
|---|---|---|---|
| North Dartmouth MA | Tropical Smoothie Cafe | 508-858-5456 | 85A Faunce Corner Mall Road |
| Norwood MA | Chipotle | 781-762-2550 | 1415 Boston-Providence H/H 1 |
| Oak Bluffs MA | Carousel Ice Cream Factory | 508-693-7582 | 15 Circuit Avenue |
| Peabody MA | Chipotle | 978-531-4875 | 210 Andover Street, Suite E194A/H 114 |
| Plymouth MA | Lobster Hut | 508-746-2270 | 25 Town Wharf |
| Provincetown MA | Bubala's by the Bay | 508-487-0773 | 183 Commercial St #185 |
| Provincetown MA | Governor Bradford Restaurant | 508-487-2781 | 312 Commercial St |
| Provincetown MA | Patio American Grill | 508-487-4003 | 328 Commercial St |
| Provincetown MA | Pepe's Wharf Restaurant | 508-487-8717 | 371 Commercial St |
| Provincetown MA | Waydowntown Restaurant | 508-487-8800 | 265 Commercial St |
| Quincy MA | Chipotle | 617-328-0413 | 60 Newport Avenue |
| Rockport MA | Helmut's Strudel Shop | 978-546-2824 | 69 Bearskin Neck |
| Rockport MA | Roy Moore Lobster Company | 978-546-6696 | 39 Bearskin Neck |
| Rockport MA | The Lobster Pool | 978-546-7808 | 329 Granite Street/H 127 |
| Salem MA | Gulu Gulu Cafe | 978-740-8882 | 247 Essex St |
| Salem MA | The Lobster Shanty | 978-745-5449 | 25 Front Street @ Artist's Row |
| Saugus MA | Chipotle | 781-231-0175 | 444 Broadway Space |
| Shrewsbury MA | Chipotle | 508-752-1726 | 97 Boston Turnpike/H 9 |
| Somerville MA | Chipotle | 617-500-9373 | 276 Elm Street |
| Southbridge MA | Vienna Restaurant (and Historic Inn) | 508-764-0700 | 14 South Street |
| Vineyard Haven MA | Net Result | 508-693-6071 | 79 Beach Rd |
| Wellfleet MA | P.J.'s Family Restaurant | 508-349-2126 | H 6 and School Street |
| Westborough MA | Chipotle | 508-366-0653 | 1 Oak Street |
| Woburn MA | Chipotle | 781-933-5450 | 112 Commerce Way |

## Michigan Listings

| | | | |
|---|---|---|---|
| Ann Arbor MI | Amadeus Cafe | 734-665-8767 | 122 E Washington Street |
| Ann Arbor MI | Arbor Brewing Company | 734-213-1393 | 114 E Washington Street |
| Ann Arbor MI | Aut Bar | 734-994-3677 | 315 Braun Court |
| Ann Arbor MI | Cafe Felix | 734-662-8650 | 204 S Main Street |
| Ann Arbor MI | Chipotle | 734-975-9912 | 3354 E Washtenaw Avenue/I 94/H 23 |
| Ann Arbor MI | Chipotle | 734-327-3710 | 235 S State Street |
| Ann Arbor MI | Chipotle | 734-794-0600 | 858 Briarwood Circle |
| Ann Arbor MI | Connor O'Neill's Irish Pub and Restaurant | 734-665-2968 | 318 S Main Street |
| Ann Arbor MI | Gratzi | 734-663-5555 | 326 S Main Street |
| Ann Arbor MI | Monahan's Seafood | 734-662-5118 | 415 N Fifth Ave - 1st Floor |
| Ann Arbor MI | Palio | 734-930-6100 | 347 S Main Street |
| Ann Arbor MI | Panera Bread | 734-213-5800 | 5340 Jackson Road |
| Ann Arbor MI | Panera Bread | 734-222-4944 | 903 W Eisenhower Parkway |
| Ann Arbor MI | Panera Bread | 734-677-0400 | 3205 Washtenaw Avenue |
| Ann Arbor MI | People's Food Co-op and Cafe Verde | 734-994-9174 | 216 N 4th Avenue |
| Ann Arbor MI | Real Seafood Company | 734-769-7738 | 341 S Main |
| Ann Arbor MI | Silvio's Organic Pizza | 734-214-6666 | 715 N. University Avenue |
| Ann Arbor MI | Zingerman's Deli | 734-663-3354 | 422 Detroit St |
| Ann Arbor MI | Zingerman's Roadhouse | 734-663-3663 | 2501 Jackson Ave |
| Ann Arbor MI | aut BAR | 734-994-3677 | 315 Braun Court |
| Birmingham MI | Brooklyn Pizza | 248-258-6690 | 111 Henrietta |
| Birmingham MI | Schakolad Chocolate Factory | 248-723-8008 | 167 N Old Woodward Avenue |
| Chelsea MI | Mike's Deli | 734-475-5980 | 114 W Middle Street |
| Chelsea MI | Zou Zou's Cafe | 734-433-4226 | 101 Main Street/H 52 |
| Chesterfield MI | Panera Bread | 586-598-5728 | 51490 Gratiot Avenue |
| Clarkston MI | Tropical Smoothie Cafe | 248-922-9000 | 6459 Dixie H/H24 |
| Clio MI | Tropical Smoothie Cafe | 810-564-9993 | 5105 W. Vienna Road/H 57 |
| Dearborn MI | A & W Family Restaurant | 313-271-1676 | 210 Town Center Dr |
| Detroit MI | Avalon International Breads | 313-832-0008 | 422 W Willis Street |
| Detroit MI | Brooklyn Pizza | 248-258-6690 | 111 Henrietta St |
| Detroit MI | Chelis Chili Bar and Restaurant | 313-961-1700 | 47 E Adams Avenue |
| E Lansing MI | Chipotle | 517-333-3680 | 539 E Grand River/H 43 |
| Fenton MI | Tropical Smoothie Cafe | 810-714-4888 | 4009 Owen Road |
| Flint MI | Tropical Smoothie Cafe | 810-733-2100 | 2103 S. Linden Road |
| Grand Blanc MI | Tropical Smoothie Cafe | 810-953-2233 | 2383 E. Hill Road |
| Grand Rapids MI | Noto's Old World Restaurant | 616-493-6686 | 6600 28th Street SE |
| Grand Rapids MI | Panera Bread | 616-363-9100 | 2044 Celebration Drive NE |
| Grand Rapids MI | The Electric Cheetah | 616-451-4779 | 1015 Wealthy Street SW |
| Kentwood MI | Chipotle | 616-885-1520 | 3610 28th Street SE/H 11 |

| | | | |
|---|---|---|---|
| Lansing MI | Chipotle | 517-323-2069 | 5330 W Saginaw H, Suite 208/H 43/I 69 |
| Lansing MI | Panera Bread | 517-332-9183 | 310 N Clippert Street |
| Lansing MI | Panera Bread | 517-703-9340 | 5330 W Saginaw H/H 43 |
| Livonia MI | Tropical Smoothie Cafe | 734-427-5500 | 30971 Five Mile Road |
| Mackinac Island MI | Bistro on the Greens | 906-847-3312 | One Lakeshore Drive |
| Mackinac Island MI | Dog House at Windermere Point | 906-847-3301 | 7498 Main St |
| Mackinac Island MI | Feedbag | 906-847-3593 | Surrey Hills |
| Mackinac Island MI | Fort Mackinac Tea Room | 906-847-6327 | 7127 Huron Road |
| Mackinac Island MI | Lakeside Marketplace/Freighters Deli | 906-847-3312 | One Lakeshore Drive |
| Mackinac Island MI | Lucky Bean Coffeehouse | 248-342-2988 | 7383 Market St |
| Mackinac Island MI | Round Island Bar and Grill | 800-833-7711 | 6633 Main St |
| Mackinac Island MI | Ryba's Fudge Shop | 906-847-4065 | 7245 Main St |
| Mackinac Island MI | Verandah at Carriage House | 906-847-3321 | 7485 Main Street |
| Mackinaw Island MI | Mary's Bistro | 906-847-9911 | Main Street/H 185 |
| Mackinaw Island MI | Mary's Bistro | 906-847-0354 | 7463 Main Street |
| Manistee MI | Boathouse Grill | 231-723-2300 | 440 River Street |
| Manistee MI | Goody's Juice and Java | 231-398-9580 | 343 River Street |
| Marquette MI | Border Grill | 906-228-5228 | 180 S McClellan Avenue |
| Mount Pleasant MI | Tropical Smoothie Cafe | 989-317-4800 | 2332 S Mission Street |
| Oxford MI | Red Knapps American Grill | 248-628-1200 | 2 N Washington Street/H 24 |
| Petoskey MI | Chandler's | 231-347-2981 | 215 1/2 Howard Street |
| Rochester Hills MI | Chipotle | 248-853-2850 | 2611 Rochester Road/H 150 |
| Royal Oak MI | Cafe Muse | 248-544-4749 | 418 S Washington Avenue |
| Royal Oak MI | Chipotle | 248-658-3100 | 32824 Woodward Avenue/H 1 |
| Saginaw MI | Tropical Smoothie Cafe | 989-249-0499 | 5815 Bay Road/H 84 |
| Saline MI | Mickey's Dairy Twist Ice Cream | 734-429-4450 | 751 W Michigan Avenue |
| Saugatuck MI | Pumpernickel's Eatery | 269-857-1196 | 202 Butler Street |
| Sault Ste. Marie MI | Cup of the Day | 906-635-7272 | 406 Ashmun Street |
| Shelby Township MI | Panera Bread | 586-532-1520 | 14121 Hall Road |
| Southfield MI | Chipotle | 248-658-3100 | 26147 Evergreen Road |
| St Joseph MI | Caffe Tosi | 269-983-3354 | 516 Pleasant Street |
| St Joseph MI | Qdoba | 269-982-0001 | 2909 Niles Avenue |
| Sterling Heights MI | Chipotle | 586-532-1139 | 13975 Lakeside Circle |
| Traverse City MI | Oryana Community Co-op | 231-947-0191 | 260 E 10th Street |
| Troy MI | Chipotle | 248-816-5103 | 3129 Crooks Road |
| W Bloomfield MI | Chipotle | 248-539-9014 | 6753 Orchard Lake Road |
| Ypsilanti MI | Harvest Moon Cafe | 734-434-8100 | 5484 W Michigan/H 12 |

**Minnesota Listings**

| | | | |
|---|---|---|---|
| Apple Valley MN | Chipotle | 952-997-2211 | 7638 W 150th Street |
| Bemidji MN | Harmony Natural Foods | 218-751-2009 | 117 3rd Street NW |
| Blaine MN | Chipotle | 763-780-3138 | 10450 Baltimore Street NE |
| Bloomington MN | Chipotle | 952-884-5721 | 10629 France Avenue S |
| Brooklyn Park MN | Chipotle | 763-315-5936 | 7631 Jolly Lane |
| Burnsville MN | Chipotle | 952-435-3176 | 728 County Road 42 W |
| Champlin MN | Mavericks Wood Grill | 763-576-8150 | 11328 W River Rd |
| Chanhassen MN | Chipotle | 952-294-0301 | 560 W 79th |
| Chanhassen MN | Lakewinds Natural Foods | 952-697-3366 | 435 Pond Promenade |
| Coon Rapids MN | Chipotle | 763-421-3455 | 3455 River Rapids Drive NW |
| Crystal MN | Chipotle | 763-535-3303 | 5608 W Broadway Avenue |
| Duluth MN | Chester Creek Cafe | 218-724-6811 | 1902 East 8th Street |
| Eden Prairie MN | Chipotle | 952-934-5955 | 13250 Technology Drive |
| Edina MN | Chipotle | 952-926-6651 | 6801 York Avenue S |
| Elk River MN | Chipotle | 763-441-3662 | 18201 Carson Circle NW |
| Ely MN | The Front Porch Coffee and Tea Company | 218-365-2326 | 343 E Sheridan Street/H 1/169 |
| Golden Valley MN | Chipotle | 763-544-2530 | 515 Winnetka Avenue N |
| Hastings MN | Chipotle | 651-437-3196 | 1769 N Frontage Road |
| Hopkins MN | Chipotle | 952-935-0044 | 786 Mainstreet |
| Mankato MN | Chipotle | 507-388-1222 | 1600 Warren Street |
| Maple Grove MN | Chipotle | 763-494-5005 | 7750 Main Street N |
| Maple Grove MN | Chipotle | 763-420-5173 | 9881 Maple Grove Parkway N |
| Minneapoli MN | Linden Hills Co-op | 612-922-1159 | 2813 W 43rd Street |
| Minneapolis MN | 331 Bar | 612-331-1746 | 331 13th Avenue NE/H 47 |
| Minneapolis MN | Chipotle | 612-659-7955 | 1040 Nicollet Avenue |
| Minneapolis MN | Chipotle | 612-377-6035 | 2600 Hennepin Avenue |

| | | | |
|---|---|---|---|
| Minneapolis MN | Chipotle | 612-331-6330 | 225 Hennepin Avenue E |
| Minneapolis MN | Chipotle | 612-378-7078 | 800 Washington Avenue SE |
| Minneapolis MN | Chipotle | 612-789-5000 | 2701 39th Avenue NE, Suite 128 |
| Minneapolis MN | Chipotle | 612-659-7830 | 229 Cedar Avenue S |
| Minneapolis MN | Chipotle Mexican Grill | 612-331-6330 | 225 Hennepin Avenue E |
| Minneapolis MN | Corner Coffee | 612-338-2002 | 514 N 3rd St Suite 102 |
| Minneapolis MN | Eastside Food Co-op | 612-788-0950 | 2551 Central Avenue NE/H 65 |
| Minneapolis MN | Jamba Juice | 612-836-0622 | 3060 Excelsior Blvd |
| Minneapolis MN | Lucia's Restaurant | 612-825-1572 | 1432 W 31st Street |
| Minneapolis MN | Parkway Pizza | 612-729-9090 | 4457 42nd Avenue S |
| Minneapolis MN | The Bad Waitress | 612-872-7575 | 2 E. 26th Street |
| Minneapolis MN | The Craftsman Restaurant | 612-722-0175 | 4300 Lake Street |
| Minneapolis MN | Town Hall Brewery | 612-339-8696 | 1430 Washington Avenue SE |
| Minneapolis MN | View Calhoun | 612-920-5000 | 2730 West Lake Street |
| Minnetonka MN | Chipotle | 952-252-4900 | 12509 Wayzata Blvd |
| Minnetonka MN | Lakewinds Natural Foods | 952-473-0292 | 17501 Minnetonka Blvd |
| Oak Park Heights MN | Chipotle | 651-439-3390 | 13315 60th Street N |
| Owatonna MN | Central Park Coffee Co. | 507-451-4242 | 113 N Cedar Avenue |
| Plymouth MN | Chipotle | 763-544-2530 | 3425 Vicksburg Lane N |
| Rochester MN | Chipotle | 507-288-9171 | 3780 Marketplace NW |
| Rochester MN | Chipotle | 507-529-5484 | 1201 S Broadway/H 63 |
| Roseville MN | Chipotle | 651-633-2300 | 860 Rosedale Center Plaza |
| Savage MN | Tropical Smoothie Cafe | 952-226-1633 | 8330 Egan Drive |
| Shakopee MN | Chipotle | 952-403-6336 | 8094 Old Carriage Court N |
| St Peter MN | St Peter Food Co-op and Deli | 507-934-4880 | 119 W Broadway |
| St Cloud MN | Chipotle | 320-253-7014 | 3959 2nd Street S |
| St Louis Park MN | Chipotle | 952-922-1970 | 5480 Excelsior Blvd |
| St Paul MN | Chipotle | 651-291-5411 | 29 5th Street W |
| St Paul MN | Chipotle | 651-602-0560 | 867 Grand Avenue |
| St Paul MN | Chipotle | 651-699-1000 | 2082 Ford Parkway |
| St Paul MN | Eagle Street Grill and Pub | 651-225-1382 | 174 W 7th Street/H 5 |
| St Paul MN | Jamba Juice | 651-695-0080 | 1577 Grand Avenue |
| St Paul MN | Sweeneys (Que Pasa) | 612-396-0701 | 96 N Dale Street |
| St Paul MN | The Happy Gnome | 651-287-2018 | 498 Selby Avenue |
| St Paul MN | Trotter's Cafe | 651-645-8950 | 232 N Cleveland Avenue |
| St Paul MN | W.A. Frost and Company | 651-224-5715 | 374 Selby Avenue |
| Stillwater MN | River Market Community Co-op | 651-439-0366 | 221 N Main Street, Suite 1/H 95 |
| Tofte MN | Bluefin Grill | 218-663-6200 ext. 2 | 7192 H 61W |
| Tofte MN | Coho Cafe | 218-663-8032 | 7126 H 61W |
| Vadnais Heights MN | Chipotle | 651-486-7129 | 925 E County Road E/H 244 |
| Wayzata MN | Chipotle | 952-473-7100 | 1313 Wayzata Blvd |
| West St Paul MN | Chipotle | 651-552-2110 | 1857 Robert Street |
| White Bear Lake MN | Washington Square Bar & Grill | 651-407-7162 | 4736 Washington Square |
| Woodbury MN | Chipotle | 651-738-9366 | 7455 Currell Blvd #116 |
| Woodbury MN | Chipotle | 651-777-2155 | 2303 White Bear Avenue H |
| Woodbury MN | Chipotle | 651-739-1164 | 9965 Hudson Road |
| Woodbury MN | Jamba Juice | 651-731-9412 | 8362 Tamarack Village, #123 |

**Mississippi Listings**

| | | | |
|---|---|---|---|
| Biloxi MS | Mary Mahoney's | 228-374-0163 | 110 Rue Magnolia Blvd |
| Biloxi MS | The Balmoral Inn | 800-393-9131 | 120 Balmoral Avenue |
| Horn Lake MS | Sonic Drive In | 662-280-0900 | 2344 Goodman Road W/H 302 |
| Jackson MS | Jason's Deli | 601-206-9191 | 1067 County Line Road |
| Southaven MS | Firehouse Subs | 662-349-5940 | 7111 Southcrest Parkway, Suite 11 |

**Missouri Listings**

| | | | |
|---|---|---|---|
| Chesterfield MO | Jason's Deli | 636-536-6868 | 17245 Chesterfield Airport Road |
| Clayton MO | Chipotle | 314-725-5650 | 1 N Central |
| Columbia MO | Chipotle | 573-875-6622 | 306 S 9th Street |
| Columbia MO | Chipotle | 573-875-0067 | 2540 Broadway Bluffs Drive |
| Columbia MO | International Cafe | 573-449-4560 | 209 Hitt Street |
| Ellisville MO | Chipotle | 636-527-9116 | 15836 Manchester Road/H 100 |
| Independence MO | Chipotle | 816-795-0590 | 18880 E Valley View Parkway |
| Jefferson City MO | Chipotle | 573-634-3532 | 1400 Missouri Blvd |

| | | | |
|---|---|---|---|
| Kansas City MO | Aixois | 816-333-3305 | 301 E 55th Street |
| Kansas City MO | Blue Bird Bistro | 816-221-7559 | 1700 Summit St |
| Kansas City MO | Cafe Al Dente | 816-472-9444 | 412 Delaware Street, # D |
| Kansas City MO | Chipotle | 816-421-4342 | 1370 Walnut Street |
| Kansas City MO | Chipotle | 816-931-8006 | 1713 W 39th Street |
| Kansas City MO | Chipotle | 816-756-5158 | 4851 Main Street |
| Kansas City MO | Chipotle | 816-942-6274 | 13127 State Line Road |
| Kansas City MO | Chipotle | 816-746-0050 | 8600 N Boardwalk Avenue |
| Kansas City MO | Firehouse Subs | 816-997-9555 | 4167 Sterling Avenue |
| Kansas City MO | Panera Bread Company | 816-931-8181 | 4700 Pennsylvania Avenue |
| Kansas City MO | Shields Manor Bistro | 816-858-5557 | 121 Main Street |
| Kansas City MO | Spin Pizza | 816-561-SPIN (7746) | 4950 Main Street |
| Kansas City MO | The Farmhouse | 816-569-6032 | 300 Delaware Street |
| Kirkwood MO | Graham's Grill and Bayou Bar | 314-965-2003 | 612 W Woodbine Avenue |
| Lee's Summit MO | Chipotle | 816-246-0505 | 1716 NW Chipman Road |
| Lee's Summit MO | Spin Pizza | 816-246-SPIN (7746) | 1808 D NW Chipman Road |
| Liberty MO | Chipotle | 816-415-2801 | 8700 N Flintlock Road |
| O'Fallon MO | Chipotle | 636-240-7276 | 2028 H K;; Suite 112 |
| Osage Beach MO | Backwater Jack's | 573-348-6639 | 4341 Beach Drive |
| Osage Beach MO | Miller's Landing | 573-348-5268 | MM 28 1/2 Runabout Drive |
| Overland MO | Woofie's Hot Dogs | 314-426-6291 | 1919 Woodson Rd |
| Richmond Heights MO | OR Smoothie & Cafe | 314-647-8881 | 6654 Clayton Road |
| Saint Peters MO | Shamrocks Pub n Grill | 636-939-2000 | 4177 Veterans Memorial Parkway |
| Springfield MO | Chipotle | 417-831-2159 | 1211 E St Louis Street |
| Springfield MO | Chipotle | 417-883-1944 | 3356 S Campbell Avenue |
| Springfield MO | McAlister's Deli | 417-866-2331 | 2445 N Kansas Expressway |
| Springfield MO | Springfield Brewing Co | 417-832-TAPS (8277) | 301 S Market Avenue |
| Springfield MO | Tropical Smoothie Cafe | 417-887-6600 | 3811 S. Campbell Avenue |
| St Louis MO | Boathouse Restaurant in Forest Park | 314-367-2224 | 6101 Government Dr. |
| St Louis MO | Chipotle | 314-238-0300 | 1255 S Kirkwood Road |
| St Louis MO | Coffee Cartel | 314-454-0000 | 2 Maryland Plaza |
| St Louis MO | Hammerstones Restaurant | 314-773-5565 | 2028 S 9th Street |
| St Louis MO | Niche | 314-773-7755 | 1831 Sidney Street |
| St Louis MO | Sanctuaria | 314-535-9700 | 4198 Manchester @ the corner of Manchester and Boyle |
| St Louis MO | Whole Foods Market | 314-968-7744 | 1601 S Brentwood Blvd |
| St Louis MO | Wild Flower Restaurant & Catering | 314-367-9888 | 4590 Laclede Avenue |

**Montana Listings**

| | | | |
|---|---|---|---|
| Billings MT | Fuddruckers | 406-656-5455 | 2011 Overland Avenue |
| Billings MT | The Rex | 406-245-7477 | 2401 Montana Avenue |
| Billings MT | The Windmill Restaurant | 406-252-8100 | 3429 TransTech Way |
| Bozeman MT | Co-op Downtown | 406-922-2667 | 44 E Main Street |
| Bozeman MT | The Emerson Grill | 406-586-5247 | 207 W Olive Street |
| Bozeman MT | The Nova Cafe | 406-587-3973 | 312 E. Main Street |
| Bozeman MT | Vera Fare Cafe | 406-922-0888 | 2251 W Kagy |
| Butte MT | Bonanza Steakhouse | 406-723-6662 | 1040 S Montana Street/I 15/90 |
| Helena MT | Riley's Irish Pub | 406-495-9067 | 15 W 6th Avenue |
| Missoula MT | Bernice's Bakery | 406-728-1358 | 190 S 3rd W |
| Missoula MT | Big Dipper Ice Cream | 406-543-5722 | 631 S Higgins Avenue/Highway12 |
| Missoula MT | Fuddruckers | 406-721-4577 | 2805 N Reserve Street |
| Missoula MT | Hunter Bay Coffee Bar | 406-830-3388 | 101 E Front Street |
| Missoula MT | Tropical Smoothie Cafe | 406-543-1141 | 1300 S. Reserve Street |
| Stevensville MT | The New Coffee Mill | 406-777-2939 | 225 Main Street |
| West Yellowstone MT | Petes Rocky Mountain Pizza and Pasta | 406-646-7820 | Canyon Street and Madison Ave. |
| Whitefish MT | McGarry's Roadhouse | 406-862-6223 | 510 Wisconsin Avenue |

**Nebraska Listings**

| | | | |
|---|---|---|---|
| Bellevue NE | Chipotle | 402-291-3035 | 10403 S 15th Street |
| Lincoln NE | Art and Soul Restaurant | 402-483-1744 | 5740 Hidcote Dr |
| Lincoln NE | Chipotle | 402-474-1133 | 232 N 13th Street |
| Lincoln NE | Chipotle | 402-420-2801 | 2801 Pine Lake Road |

Dog-Friendly Outdoor Dining - Please always call ahead to make sure an establishment is still dog-friendly

| | | | |
|---|---|---|---|
| Lincoln NE | MaGGiE's | 402-477-3959 | 311 N 8th Street |
| Lincoln NE | Open Harvest Natural Foods Cooperative Grocery | 402-475-9069 | 1618 South Street |
| Lincoln NE | Parthenon Restaurant | 402-423-2222 | 5500 S 56th Street #100 |
| Omaha NE | Chipolte | 402-498-3633 | 3605 N 147th Street |
| Omaha NE | Chipotle | 402-391-9979 | 201 S 72nd Street |
| Omaha NE | Chipotle | 402-697-4903 | 13203 W Center Road/H 38 |
| Omaha NE | Chipotle | 402-334-7006 | 2717 S 177th Street |
| Omaha NE | Chipotle Mexican Grill | 402-391-9979 | 201 S 72nd Street |
| Omaha NE | Chipotle Mexican Grill | 402-498-3633 | 3605 N 147th Street, # 111 |
| Omaha NE | Chipotle Mexican Grill | 402-697-4903 | 13203 W Center Road/H 38 |
| Omaha NE | Dante Pizzeria Napoletana | 402-932-3078 | 16901 Wright Plaza |
| Omaha NE | Goldberg's II Dundee | 402-556-2006 | 2936 S 132nd Street |
| Omaha NE | Jason's Deli | 402-551-2233 | 7010 Dodge Street/H 6 |
| Omaha NE | Jason's Deli | 402-932-5544 | 12320 L Street/H 92/275 |
| Omaha NE | Qdoba | 402-934-9680 | 1110 S. 71st Street |
| Papillion NE | Tropical Smoothie Cafe | 402-614-9050 | 7902 Towne Center Parkway #109 |

**Nevada Listings**

| | | | |
|---|---|---|---|
| Boulder City NV | Milo's Best Cellars | 702-293-9540 | 538 Nevada Way |
| Carson City NV | Comma Coffee | 775-883-2662 | 312 S. Carson Street |
| Carson City NV | Johnny Rockets | 775-883-2607 | 4600 Snyder Avenue/H 518 |
| Carson City NV | Johnny Rockets | 775-883-2607 | 4600 Snyder Avenue #B/H 518 |
| Carson City NV | Mom and Pops Diner | 775-884-4411 | 224 S. Carson St. |
| Charleston NV | Tropical Smoothie Cafe | 702-304-1931 | 6350 W. Charleston Blvd/H 159 |
| Henderson NV | Baja Fresh Mexican Grill | 702-450-6551 | 675 Mall Ring Circle |
| Henderson NV | Chipotle - St. Rose | 702-361-6438 | 10251 S Eastern Avenue |
| Henderson NV | Chipotle - Sunset Station | 702-436-7740 | 1311 W Sunset Road |
| Henderson NV | The Brooklyn Bagel | 702-260-9511 | 1500 N. Green Valley Parkway |
| Henderson NV | The Coffee Bean & Tea Leaf | 702-260-3075 | 2220 Village Walk Drive |
| Incline Village NV | T's Rotisserie | 775-831-2832 | 901 Tahoe Blvd |
| Las Vegas NV | Baja Fresh Mexican Grill | 702-699-8920 | 1380 E Flamingo Rd |
| Las Vegas NV | Baja Fresh Mexican Grill | 702-948-4043 | 8780 W Charleston Blvd # 100 |
| Las Vegas NV | Baja Fresh Mexican Grill | 702-838-4100 | 7501 W Lake Mead Blvd # 100 |
| Las Vegas NV | Baja Fresh Mexican Grill | 702-563-2800 | 9310 S Eastern Ave |
| Las Vegas NV | Chipotle | 702-436-9177 | 4530 S Maryland Parkway |
| Las Vegas NV | Chipotle - Belz | 702-270-1973 | 7370 S Las Vegas Blvd/H 604 |
| Las Vegas NV | Chipotle - Rock Springs | 702-233-3199 | 7175 W. Lake Mead |
| Las Vegas NV | Chipotle - Sahara Pavilion | 702-252-4013 | 2540 S Decatur Blvd |
| Las Vegas NV | Chipotle - The Arroyo | 702-361-0203 | 7340 Arroyo Crossing Parkway, Suite 100 |
| Las Vegas NV | Chipotle - The Cannery | 702-633-4463 | 2546 E Craig Road, Suite 100 |
| Las Vegas NV | Einstein Brothers Bagels | 702-254-0919 | 9031 W. Sahara Ave |
| Las Vegas NV | Firehouse Subs | 702-893-3473 | 9555 S Eastern Avenue, Suite 130 |
| Las Vegas NV | Grape Vine Cafe | 702-228-9463 | 7501 W Lake Mead Blvd #120 |
| Las Vegas NV | Havana Grill | 702-932-9310 | 8878 S Eastern Ave #100 |
| Las Vegas NV | Holly's Cuppa | 702-778-7750 | 9265 S Cimarron Rd #115 |
| Las Vegas NV | In-N-Out Burger | 800-786-1000 | 2900 W. Sahara Ave. |
| Las Vegas NV | It's A Grind | 702-360-4232 | 8470 W Desert Inn Rd |
| Las Vegas NV | Jamba Juice | 702-633-0097 | 1121 S Decatur Blvd |
| Las Vegas NV | Jamba Juice | 702-457-7015 | 2675 S Eastern Avenue, Suite 400 |
| Las Vegas NV | Jason's Deli | 702-366-0130 | 100 City Parkway |
| Las Vegas NV | Lazy Dog Restaurant & Bar | 702-941-1920 | 6509 Las Vegas Blvd. South |
| Las Vegas NV | Lazy Dog Restaurant & Bar | 702-727-4784 | 1725 Festival Plaza Dr |
| Las Vegas NV | Mountain Springs Saloon | 702-875-4266 | Highway 160 |
| Las Vegas NV | Rainbow's End Natural Foods | 702-737-1338 | 1100 E Sahara Avenue, Suite #120 |
| Las Vegas NV | Starbucks | 702-369-5537 | 395 Hughes Center Drive |
| Las Vegas NV | TGI Fridays | 702-889-1866 | 4570 W Sahara Avenue/H 589 |
| Las Vegas NV | The Coffee Bean & Tea Leaf | 702-998-0216 | 9091 W Sahara Avenue |
| Las Vegas NV | The Coffee Bean & Tea Leaf | 702-220-6820 | 6115 S Rainbow Blvd, Suite 101 |
| Las Vegas NV | The Coffee Bean & Tea Leaf | 702-944-5029 | 4550 S Maryland Parkway, Suite A |
| Las Vegas NV | The Coffee Bean & Tea Leaf | 702-944-0030 | 7291 W Lake Mead Drive |
| Las Vegas NV | The Coffee Bean & Tea Leaf | 702-785-0419 | 3645 S Towncenter Drive, Suite 101 |
| Las Vegas NV | The Coffee Bean & Tea Leaf | 702-838-5661 | 10834 W Charleston Blvd |
| Las Vegas NV | Triple George Grill | 702-384-2761 | 201 N 3rd St #120 |
| Las Vegas NV | Tropical Smoothie Cafe | 603-509-3000 | Lowes & Kohl's Plaza |

| | | | |
|---|---|---|---|
| Las Vegas NV | Tropical Smoothie Cafe | 702-616-1931 | 10612 S. Eastern Avenue |
| Las Vegas NV | Tropical Smoothie Cafe | 702-207-1931 | 9440 W. Sahara Blvd |
| Las Vegas NV | Tropical Smoothie Cafe | 702-247-6208 | 6555 S. Jones Blvd, #110 |
| Las Vegas NV | Tropical Smoothie Cafe | 702-450-1931 | 7291 S Eastern Avenue |
| Las Vegas NV | Tropical Smoothie Cafe | 702-257-1931 | 7580 S. Las Vegas Blvd |
| Las Vegas NV | Tropical Smoothie Cafe | 702-365-1931 | 7660 W Cheyenne Avenue |
| Las Vegas NV | Tropical Smoothie Cafe | 702-869-0603 | 10260 W. Charleston Blvd/H 159 |
| Las Vegas NV | Tropical Smoothie Cafe | 702-629-3692 | 4262 Blue Diamond Road, #103 |
| Las Vegas NV | Tropical Smoothie Cafe | 702-242-1931 | 4165 S. Grand Canyon Drive, # 106 |
| Las Vegas NV | Tropical Smoothie Cafe | 702-459-8000 | 5035 S Fort Apache Road |
| Las Vegas NV | Whole Foods Market | 702-254-8655 | 8855 West Charleston Blvd. |
| Las Vegas NV | Whole Foods Market | 702-942-1500 | 7250 W. Lake Mead Blvd |
| North Las Vegas NV | Jamba Juice | 702-633-0097 | 1829 W Craig Road, Unit 3/H 573 |
| Reno NV | 4th Street Bistro | 775-323-3200 | 3065 W 4th Street |
| Reno NV | Archie's Grill | 775-322-9595 | 2195 N. Virginia St. |
| Reno NV | Baja Fresh Mexican Grill | 775-826-8900 | 5140 Kietzke Ln. |
| Reno NV | Jamba Juice | 775-828-5483 | 5140 Kietzke Lane |
| Reno NV | Java Jungle | 775-329-4484 | 246 W. 1st Street |
| Reno NV | My Favorite Muffin & Bagel Cafe | 775-333-1025 | 340 California Ave. |
| Reno NV | Peg's Glorified Ham & Eggs | 775-329-2600 | 420 S. Sierra St. |
| Reno NV | Riverview Café | 877-743-6233 | 1 Lake Street |
| Reno NV | Sup Restaurant | 775-324-4787 | 719 S Virginia Street |
| Reno NV | The Squeeze In | 775-787-2700 | 5020 Las Brisas Blvd |
| Reno NV | The Stone House | 775-284-3895 | 1907 S Arlington Avenue |
| Reno NV | Walden's Coffee Co. | 775-787-3307 | 3940 Mayberry Drive |
| Reno NV | Walden's Coffee House | 775-787-3307 | 3940 Mayberry Drive |
| Reno NV | Wild River Grille | 775-284-7455 | 17 S Virginia Street, # 180/H 395 |
| Reno NV | Z Pizza | 775-828-6565 | 4796 Caughlin Parkway |
| Reno NV | Zpizza | 775-828-6565 | 3600 Warren Way |
| Sparks NV | Sunset Cove Coffee and Wine House | 775-657-8505 | 325 Harbour Cove Drive |
| Virginia City NV | Virginia City Coffee House | 775-847-0159 | North C Steet |
| Virginia City NV | Virginia City Jerky Company | 775-847-7444 | 204 C St |

**New Hampshire Listings**

| | | | |
|---|---|---|---|
| Bedford NH | T- Bones | 603-641-6100 | 25 South River Rd |
| Concord NH | Concord Cooperative Market Celery Stick Cafe | 603-225-6840 | 24 S Main Street |
| Jackson Village NH | Wildcat Inn & Tavern | 603-356-8700 | H 16A/Village Road |
| Keene NH | Luca's Mediterranean Café | 603-358-3335 | 10 Central Square |
| Lebanon NH | The Co-op Food Store | 603-643-2667 | 12 Centerra Parkway |
| Newington NH | Chipotle | 603-433-5981 | 45 Gosling Road |
| North Conway NH | Black Cap Grille | 603-356-2225 | 1498 White Mountain Hwy |
| North Conway NH | The Flatbread Company | 603-356-4470 | 2760 White Mountain H/H 16/302 |
| Northwood NH | Susty's | 603-942-5862 | 159 1st New Hampshire Turnpike |
| Portsmouth NH | Annabelle's Natural Ice Cream | 603-436-3400 | 49 Ceres Street |
| Portsmouth NH | Popovers | 603-431-1119 | 8 Congress Street |
| Portsmouth NH | Portsmouth (Redhook) Brewery and Cataqua | 603-430-8600 | 35 Corporate Drive |
| Portsmouth NH | The Juicery | 603-431-0693 | 51 Hanover Street |
| Portsmouth NH | Works Bakery Cafe | 603-431-4434 | 9 Congress Street |
| West Ossipee NH | Yankee Smokehouse | 603-539-7427 | H 16 and H 25W |

**New Jersey Listings**

| | | | |
|---|---|---|---|
| Asbury Park NJ | Lance & Debbies Wonder Bar | 732-502-8886 | 1213 Ocean Ave |
| Atlantic City NJ | Johnny Rockets | 609-340-0099 | Park Place and Boardwalk |
| Barnegat NJ | Sweet Jenny's Ice Cream Parlor | 609-698-2228 | 107 S Main Street/H 9 |
| Belmar NJ | Federico's Pizza and Restaurant | 732-774-8448 | 700 Main St |
| Bradley Beach NJ | Bagel International | 732-775-7447 | 48 Main St |
| Bridgewater NJ | Chipotle | 908-231-0398 | 640 Commons Way |
| Cape May NJ | Blue Pig Tavern at Congress Hall | 609-884-8422 | 251 Beach Ave |
| Cape May NJ | Jackson Mountain Cafe | 609-884-5648 | 400 Washington Street |
| Cape May NJ | Zoe's Beachfront Eatery | 609-884-1233 | Beach & Stockton Place |
| Clifton NJ | Chipotle | 973-916-0040 | 380 H 3W |
| E Hanover NJ | Chipotle | 973-599-1370 | 368 H 10W |
| East Hanover NJ | Baja Fresh | 973-952-0080 | 136 H 10 |

| Edgewater NJ | Jamba Juice | 201-941-4000 | 905 River Road |
| Fort Lee NJ | Tast Eatery | 201-313-8278 | 1224 Anderson Avenue |
| Frenchtown NJ | The Frenchtown Inn | 908-996-3300 | 7 Bridge Street |
| Frenchtown NJ | What's Brewing at Maria's | 908-996-7258 | 52 Bridge Street |
| High Bridge NJ | Circa Restaurant | 908-638-5560 | 37 Main Street |
| Hoboken NJ | Arthur's Steak House | 201-656-5009 | 237 Washington Street |
| Hoboken NJ | Helmer's Restaurant | 201-963-3333 | 1306 Washington Street |
| Hoboken NJ | Johnny Rockets | 201-659-2620 | 134 Washington Street |
| Hoboken NJ | Margherita's Pizzeria and Cafe | 201-222-2400 | 740 Washington St |
| Hoboken NJ | Panera Bread | 201-876-3233 | 308 Washington St |
| Hoboken NJ | Sushi Lounge | 201-386-1117 | 200 Hudson Street |
| Lambertville NJ | De Anna's Restaurant | 609-397-8957 | 54 N Franklin Street |
| Lambertville NJ | Hamilton's Grill Room at the Porkyard | 609-397-4343 | 8 Coryell Street |
| Moorestown NJ | Chipotle | 856-235-0991 | 640 Jefferson Road/H 252 |
| Morristown NJ | Morristown Deli | 973-267-3766 | 7 Elm St |
| Morristown NJ | Morristown Deli & Restaurant | 973-267-3766 | 7 Elm Street |
| Mount Holly NJ | Olde World Bakery | 609-265-1270 | 1000 Smithville Road |
| Mount Holly NJ | Robin's Nest Restaurant and the Crow Bar | 609-261-6149 | 2 Washington Street |
| N Brunswick NJ | Jamba Juice | 732-227-0490 | 652 Shoppes Blvd |
| Normandy Beach NJ | Labrador Lounge | 732-830-5770 | 3581 H 35 N |
| North Brunswick NJ | Chipotle | 732-342-7272 | 524 Shoppes Blvd |
| North Long Branch NJ | Windmill Hot Dogs | 732-870-6098 | 200 Ocean Avenue |
| Ocean City NJ | Bashful Banana Cafe and Bakery | 609-398-9677 | 944 Ocean City Boardwalk |
| Secaucus NJ | Chipotle | 201-223-0562 | 700 Plaza Drive |
| Springfield NJ | Chipotle | 973-376-0152 | 101 H 22E |
| Stockton NJ | Cravings | 609-397-2911 | 10 Risler Street |
| Stockton NJ | Stockton Inn Restaurant and Tavern | 609-397-1250 | 1 Main Street |
| Tenafly NJ | Café Angelique | 201-541-1010 | 1 Piermont Road |
| W Caldwell NJ | Chipotle | 973-226-6421 | 749 Bloomfield Avenue |
| Wayne NJ | Chipotle | 973-237-1390 | 70 Willowbrook Blvd |

**New Mexico Listings**

| Albuquerque NM | Annapurna's World Vegetarian Restaurant | 505-262-2424 | 2201 Silver Avenue SE |
| Albuquerque NM | Annapurna's World Vegetarian Restaurant | 505-254-2424 | 7520 4th Street NW |
| Albuquerque NM | Chama River Brewing Company | 505-342-1800 | 4939 Pan American H NE/I 25 |
| Albuquerque NM | El Patio de Albuquerque | 505-268-4245 | 142 Harvard Drive SE |
| Albuquerque NM | El Patron Restaurant and Cantina | 505-275-0223 | 10551 Montgomery Blvd |
| Albuquerque NM | Firehouse Subs | 505-797-4554 | 8050 Academy Road |
| Albuquerque NM | Flying Star Cafe | 505-255-6633 | 3416 Central AVe SE |
| Albuquerque NM | Flying Star Cafe | 505-344-6714 | 4026 Rio Grande NW |
| Albuquerque NM | Flying Star Cafe | 505-275-8311 | 4501 Juan Tabo NE |
| Albuquerque NM | Flying Star Cafe | 505-923-4211 | 8000 Paseo Del Norte NE/H 423 |
| Albuquerque NM | Flying Star Cafes | 505-255-6633 | 3416 Central Ave NE |
| Albuquerque NM | Fuddruckers | 505-344-7449 | 4855 Pan American W H NE |
| Albuquerque NM | Geckos Bar and Tapas | 505-262-1848 | 3500 Central Avenue SE/H 66 |
| Albuquerque NM | Il Vicino | 505-266-7855 | 3403 Central Avenue NE |
| Albuquerque NM | Kelly's Brew Pub | 505-262-2739 | 3222 Central Avenue SE/H 66 |
| Albuquerque NM | La Montanita Co-op | 505-242-8800 | 2400 Rio Grande Blvd NW |
| Albuquerque NM | La Montanita Co-op | 505-265-4631 | 3500 Central SE/H 66 |
| Albuquerque NM | La Quiche Parisienne Bistro | 505-242-2808 | 401-A Copper Avenue NW, Albuquerque |
| Albuquerque NM | O'Niells Irish Pub | 505-293-1122 | 3301 Juan Tabo Blvd NE |
| Albuquerque NM | Pars Cuisine | 505-345-5156 | 4320 The 25 Way NE |
| Albuquerque NM | Satellite Coffee | 505-254-3800 | 2300 Central Avenue NE |
| Albuquerque NM | Satellite Coffee | 505-899-1001 | 1642 Alameda Blvd NW/H 528 |
| Albuquerque NM | Seasons Rotisserie & Grill | 505-766-5100 | 2031 Mountain Road, San Felipe Plz |
| Albuquerque NM | Sonic Drive-In | 505-243-7880 | 531 Bridge Blvd SW |
| Albuquerque NM | Sonic Drive-In | 505-897-7538 | 220 Alameda Blvd NW |
| Albuquerque NM | Sonic Drive-in | 505-292-6979 | 11715 Central Avenue NE/Historic H 66 |
| Albuquerque NM | St. Clair Winery & Bistro | 505-243-9916 | 901 Rio Rancho Blvd NW |
| Albuquerque NM | The Grove Cafe and Market | 505-248-9800 | 600 Central Avenue SE, Suite A |
| Albuquerque NM | The Standard Diner | 505-243-1440 | 320 Central Avenue SE |
| Albuquerque NM | Whole Foods Market | 505-856-0474 | 5815 Wyoming Blvd NE |
| Chimayo NM | Rancho de Chimayo | 505-351-4444 | County Road 98/H 98 |
| Corrales NM | Flying Star Cafe | 505-938-4717 | 10700 Corrales Road |

| | | | |
|---|---|---|---|
| Corrales NM | Indigo Crow | 505-898-7000 | 4515 Corrales Road/H 448 |
| Credar Crest NM | Beyond Grounds | 505-281-2000 | 12220 N H 14 |
| Deming NM | St Clair Winery Tasting Room: | 575-546-1179 | 1325 De Baca Road |
| Jemez Springs NM | The Laughing Lizard Inn and Cafe | 505-753-3211 | 17526 H 4 |
| Las Cruces NM | Caliche's Frozen Custard | 575-521-1161 | 131 Roadrunner Parkway |
| Las Cruces NM | International Delights | 575-647-5956 | 1245 El Paseo Road |
| Las Cruces NM | Spirit Winds Coffee Bar | 575-521-1222 | 2260 S Locust Street |
| Ruidoso NM | Grill Caliente | 575-630-0224 | 2800 Sudderth Dr |
| Santa Fe NM | 315 Restaurant | 505-986-9190 | 315 Old Santa Fe Trail |
| Santa Fe NM | Annapurna's World Vegetarian Restaurant | 505-988-9688 | 1620 St. Michael's Drive |
| Santa Fe NM | Counter Culture | 505-995-1105 | 930 Baca Street |
| Santa Fe NM | Downtown Subscription | 505-983-3085 | 376 Garcia Street |
| Santa Fe NM | La Casa Sena | 505-988-9232 | 125 E Palace Avenue |
| Santa Fe NM | La Montanita Co-op | 505-984-2853 | 913 W Alameda Street |
| Santa Fe NM | O'Keeffe Cafe | 505-986-2008 | 217 Johnson Street |
| Santa Fe NM | The Burrito Company | 505-982-4453 | 111 Washington Avenue |
| Santa Fe NM | The Gate House | 505-992-0957 | 150 E DeVargas |
| Santa Fe NM | The Shed | 505-982-9030 | 113 1/2 E Palace Avenue |
| Santa Fe NM | Whole Foods Market | 505-992-1700 | 753 Cerrillos Road |
| Silver City NM | Vicki's Eatery | 575-388-5430 | 107 W Yankie Street |
| Taos NM | Alley Cantina | 575-758-2121 | 121 Teresina Lane |
| Taos NM | Doc Martin's Restaurant at the Historic Taos Inn | 575-758-1977 | 125 Paseo Del Pueblo Norte/H 68 |
| Taos NM | Gutiz | 575-758-1226 | 812B Paseo Del Pueblo Norte/H 64 |
| Taos NM | La Cueva Cafe | 575-758-7001 | 135 Paseo Del Pueblo Sur/H 68 |
| Taos Ski Valley NM | Tim's Stray Dog Cantina | 575-776-2894 | 105 Sutton Place |

**New York Listings**

| | | | |
|---|---|---|---|
| Astoria NY | Bareburger | 718-204-7167 | 23-01 31st St |
| Brooklyn NY | Brooklyn-Heights Deli | 718-643-1361 | 292 Henry St |
| Brooklyn NY | The Gate | 718-768-4329 | 321 5th Avenue |
| Brooklyn NY | The JakeWalk | 347-599-0294 | 282 Smith St |
| Buffalo NY | Lexington Co-operative Market | 716-886-COOP (2667) | 807 Elmwood Avenue |
| Buffalo NY | O3 Downtown | 716-551-0136 | 739 Elmwood Avenue |
| Callicoon NY | Matthews on Main | 845-887-5636 | 19 Lower Main Street |
| Carle Place NY | Chipotle | 516-877-7720 | 135 Old Country Road |
| Chappaqua NY | Crabtree's Kittle House Restaurant and Inn | 914-666-8044 | Eleven Kittle Road |
| Darien Center NY | Minty Wellness | 585-591-39339 | 1961 Church Road |
| E Northport NY | Tropical Smoothie Cafe | 631-486-4455 | 532 Larkfield Road |
| East Hampton NY | Nichol's | 631-324-3939 | 100 Montauk H |
| East Hampton NY | The Living Room | 631-324-5006 | 207 Main Street |
| Elmira NY | The Green Star Natural Foods Market | 607-273-8213 | 215 N Cayuga Street |
| Farmingdale NY | Chipotle | 631-845-4598 | 901 Broad Hollow Road/H 110 |
| Garden City NY | Grimaldi's Restaurant | 516-294-6565 | 980 Franklin Avenue |
| Hicksville NY | Chipotle | 516-822-4074 | 215 N Broadway |
| Huntington NY | Tropical Smoothie Cafe | 631-424-8767 | 61 Wall Street |
| Ithaca NY | Blue Stone Bar and Grill | 607-272-2371 | 110 N Aurora Street |
| Ithaca NY | Madeline's Restaurant | 607-277-2253 | 215 East State Street, The Commons |
| Lake George NY | Christie's on the Lake | 518-668-2515 | 6 Christie Lane |
| Lake George NY | King Neptune's Pub and Night Club | 518-668-2017 | 1 Kurosaka Lane |
| Lake George NY | Lake George Barnsider Restaurant | 518-668-5268 | Route 9 South Lake George |
| Lake Placid NY | Bazzi's Pizza | 518-523-9056 | 138 Main St |
| Long Island City NY | The Creek and the Cave | 718-706-8783 | 1093 Jackson Ave |
| Manhattan NY | Drop Off Service | 212-260-2914 | 211 Avenue A |
| Mount Kisco NY | Johnny Rockets | 914-244-4450 | 360 N Bedford Road/H 117 |
| New Hartford NY | Peter's Cornucopia | 315-724-4998 | 38 New Hartford Shopping Center |
| New Paltz NY | The Bakery | 845-255-8840 | 13-A North Front Street |
| New York NY | 71 Irving | 212-995-5252 | 71 Irving Pl |
| New York NY | Bangkok House | 212-541-5943 | 360 W 46th Street |
| New York NY | Bistro Chat Noir | 212-794-2428 | 22 E 66th St |
| New York NY | Boat Basin Café | 212-496-5542 | West 79th St |
| New York NY | Brio | 212-980-2300 | 137 E 61st St |
| New York NY | Chipotle | 212-682-9860 | 150 E 44th Street |
| New York NY | Chipotle | 212-755-9754 | 150 E 52nd Street |
| New York NY | Cinema Cafe On 34th Street | 212-689-9022 | |

| | | | |
|---|---|---|---|
| New York NY | Da Rosina Ristorante | 212-977-7373 | 342 W 46th St |
| New York NY | Dinosaur Bar-B-Que | 212-694-1777 | 700 W 125th St |
| New York NY | Fetch | 212-289-2700 | 1649 Third Avenue |
| New York NY | Firehouse | 212-787-FIRE (3473) | 522 Columbus Avenue |
| New York NY | Fred's NYC | 212-579-3076 | 476 Amsterdam Ave |
| New York NY | French Roast | 212-799-1533 | 2340 Broadway (between 84th St & 85th St) |
| New York NY | Il Porto | 212-791-2181 | 11 Fulton Street |
| New York NY | Les Enfant Terrible | 212-777-7518 | 37 Canal Street |
| New York NY | P J Clarke's on the Hudson | 212-285-1500 | 250 Vesey Street |
| New York NY | Rocking Horse Cafe | 212-463-9511 | 182 8th Ave |
| New York NY | San Martin Restaurant | 212-832-0888 | 143 E 49th Street |
| New York NY | Shake Shack | 212-889-6600 | Madison Ave & E 23rd St |
| New York NY | Sidewalk Cafe | 212-473-7373 | 94 Avenue A |
| New York NY | The Park | 212-352-3313 | 118 10th Avenue |
| New York NY | Zucchero E Pomodori | 212-585-2100 | 1431 2nd Ave |
| New York City NY | The Coffee Bean & Tea Leaf | 212-535-1022 | 1469 3rd Avenue |
| Newburgh NY | Cena 2000 Restorante and Bar | 845-561-7676 | 50 Front Street |
| Niagara Falls NY | Papa Leo's Pizzeria | 716-731-5911 | 2265 Niagara Falls Blvd. |
| Nyack NY | Lanterna Tuscan Bistro | 845-353-8361 | 3 S Broadway |
| Oswego NY | Rudy's Lakeside | 315-343-2671 | Washington Blvd |
| Plainview NY | Quiznos | 516-942-5188 | 1161 Old Country Road |
| Potsdam NY | Potsdam Food Co-op | 315-265-4630 | 24 Elm Street |
| Rochester NY | Muddy Waters Coffee House | 585-730-7949 | 752 S Goodman Street |
| Seneca Falls NY | Downtown Deli | 315-568-9943 | 53 Falls Street/H 5 |
| Smithtown NY | Napper Tandy's | 631-360-0606 | 15 East Main Street/H 25 |
| Syracuse NY | Dinosaur Barbecue | 315-476-4937 | 246 W Willow Street |
| Syracuse NY | Pastabilities | 315-474-1153 | 311 S Franklin Street |
| Warwick NY | Pané Café | 845-258-4858 | 114 Little York Road |

**North Carolina Listings**

| | | | |
|---|---|---|---|
| Arden NC | Black Forest Restaurant | 828-687-7980 | 2155 Hendersonville Road/H 25 |
| Asheville NC | 12 Bones Smokehouse | 828-253-4499 | 5 Riverside Drive |
| Asheville NC | Asheville Pizza and Brewing Company | 828-254-1281 | 675 Merrimon Avenue |
| Asheville NC | Avenue M | 828-350-8181 | 791 Merrimon Ave |
| Asheville NC | Bavarian Restaurant & Biergarten | 828-645-8383 | 332 Weaverville H/H 19 |
| Asheville NC | Carmel's Restaurant and Bar | 828-252-8730 | Corner of Page Avenue and Battery Park |
| Asheville NC | City Bakery Cafe | 828-252-4426 | 60 Biltmore Avenue/H 25 |
| Asheville NC | Earth Fare Natural Food Market | 828-253-7656 | 66 Westgate Parkway |
| Asheville NC | Fig Restuarant | 828-277-0889 | 18 Brook Street/H 25 |
| Asheville NC | Hannah Flannigan's Pub | 828-252-1922 | 27 Biltmore Avenue/H 25 |
| Asheville NC | Jason's Deli | 828-252-7006 | 5 Westgate Parkway, Suite 100 |
| Asheville NC | Nine Mile Restaurant | 828-505-3121 | 233 Montford Ave, Asheville, NC 28804 |
| Asheville NC | Over Easy Cafe | 828-236-3533 | 32 Broadway |
| Asheville NC | Posana Cafe | 828-505-3969 | One Biltmore Avenue |
| Asheville NC | Sunny Point Cafe and Bakery | 828-252-0055 | 626 Haywood Road |
| Asheville NC | The Laughing Seed Cafe | 828-252-3445 | 40 Wall Street |
| Asheville NC | Urban Burrito | 828-251-1921 | 640 Merrimon Avenue |
| Asheville NC | Vinnie's Neighborhood Italian | 828-253-1077 | 641 Merrimon Avenue/H 25 |
| Asheville NC | West End Bakery | 828-252-9378 | 757 Haywood Road/BH 19/23 |
| Asheville NC | YoLo Frozen Yogurt | 828-255-4515 | 505 Merrimon Avenue/H 25 |
| Barco NC | Currituck BBQ Company | 252-453-6618 | 4467 Caratoke H/H 158 |
| Beaufort NC | Front Street Grill at Stillwater | 252-728-4956 | 300 Front St #5 |
| Carrboro NC | Panzanella | 919-929-6626 | 200 Greensboro Street |
| Carrboro NC | The Cafe at Weaver Street Market | 919-929-0010 | 101 E Weaver Street |
| Cary NC | Ruckus Pizza | 919-851-3999 | 8111-208 Tryon Woods Drive |
| Cary NC | Taziki's Mediterranean Cafe | 919-415-0447 | 302 Colonades Way #201 |
| Chapel Hill NC | Carolina Brewery | 919-942-1800 | 460 W Franklin Street |
| Chapel Hill NC | Chipotle | 919-942-2091 | 301 W Franklin Street |
| Chapel Hill NC | Il Palio Restorante | 919-929-4000 | 1505 E Franklin Street |
| Chapel Hill NC | Nantucket Grill & Bar | 919-402-0077 | 5925 Farrington Road |
| Charlotte NC | Angry Ale's Neighborhood Bar & Grill | 704-525-3663 | 1600 Montford Drive |
| Charlotte NC | Boardwalk Billy's Raw Bar & Ribs | 704-503-7427 | 9005-2 JM Keynes Drive |

| | | | |
|---|---|---|---|
| Charlotte NC | Brixx Pizza | 704-347-2749 | 225 E 6th Street |
| Charlotte NC | Brixx Pizza | 704-376-1000 | 1801 Scott Avenue |
| Charlotte NC | Brixx Pizza | 704-295-0707 | 7814 Fairview Road |
| Charlotte NC | Brooklyn Pizza Parlor | 704-542-5439 | 7725 Colony Road |
| Charlotte NC | Burgers & Bagels | 704-525-5295 | 4327 Park Road Bldg 25 |
| Charlotte NC | Chipotle | 704-366-7280 | 2921 Providence Road, Suite 100/H 16 |
| Charlotte NC | Dog Bar NoDa | 704-370-3595 | 3307 N Davidson Street |
| Charlotte NC | Fuel Pizza | 704-350-1680 | 214 N Tryon |
| Charlotte NC | Fuel Pizza | 704-376-3835 | 1501 Central Avenue |
| Charlotte NC | Fuel on the Green | 704-370-2755 | 500 S College Street |
| Charlotte NC | Harvest Moon Grille | 704-342-1193 | 235 N. Tryon Street |
| Charlotte NC | Jason's Deli | 704-688-1004 | 210 E Trade Street, Suite C240 |
| Charlotte NC | Jason's Deli | 704-676-5858 | 1600 E Woodlawn Road, Suite 200 |
| Charlotte NC | Jason's Deli | 704-921-1545 | 3509 David Cox Road, Suite A |
| Charlotte NC | Maria Bonita's Cantina & Grill | 704-542-6165 | 7741 Colony Road |
| Charlotte NC | Moe's Southwest Grill | 704-377-6344 | 1500 East Blvd. |
| Charlotte NC | Shane's Rib Shack | 704-509-6553 | 9330 Center Lake Drive, Suite 100 |
| Charlotte NC | Shane's Rib Shack | 704-503-3113 | 440-E Mc Cullough Drive |
| Charlotte NC | Smelly Cat Coffee House | 704-374-9656 | 514 E 36th Street |
| Charlotte NC | Starbucks | 704-338-9911 | 1401 East Blvd |
| Charlotte NC | The Common Market | 704-332-7782 | 1515 S Tryon St |
| Charlotte NC | Thomas Street Tavern | 704-376-1622 | 1218 Thomas Ave. |
| Charlotte NC | Tony's Pizza | 704-541-8225 | 14027 Conlan Circle |
| Charlotte NC | Upstream | 704-556-7730 | 6902 Phillips Place |
| Charlotte NC | Wolfman Pizza | 704-552-4979 | 8418 Park Rd |
| Charoltte NC | Luna's Living Kitchen | 704-333-0008 | 2102 South Blvd |
| Coinjock NC | Coinjock Marina Restaurant | 252-453-3271 | 321 Waterlily Road |
| Cornelius NC | Alton's Kitchen & Cocktails | 704-655-2727 | 19918 North Cove Road in Jetton Village |
| Cornelius NC | Brooklyn South Neighborhood Pizzeria | 704-896-2928 | 19400 Jetton Road |
| Cornelius NC | Lucky Dog Bark & Brew | 704-896-5550 | 19607 Statesville Rd |
| Corolla NC | Bacchus Wine and Cheese | 252-453-4333 | 891 Albacore Street |
| Corolla NC | Steamer's Shellfish To Go | 252-453-3305 | 798 Sunset Blvd # B |
| Davidson NC | Fuel Pizza | 704-655-3835 | 402 S Main Street |
| Duck NC | Aqua S Restaurant | 252-261-9700 | 1174 Duck Road/H 12 |
| Duck NC | Duck's Cottage Coffee and Books | 252-261-5510 | 1240 Duck Road/H 12 |
| Durham NC | 604 W Morgan | 919-680-6333 | 604 W Morgan Street/H 70 |
| Durham NC | Chipotle | 919-309-2901 | 2608 Erwin Road |
| Durham NC | Fullstream Brewery | 919-682-BEER (2337) | 726 Rigsbee Avenue |
| Durham NC | Jason's Deli | 919-493-3350 | 725 Eden Way N, Suite # 714 |
| Durham NC | Nantucket Grill & Bar | 919-484-8162 | 5826 Fayetteville Road |
| Durham NC | Sunset Grille | 919-544-8585 | 5850 Fayetteville Road # 101 |
| Durham NC | The Meridian Cafe | 919-361-9333 | 2500 Meridian Parkway, Suite 130 |
| Durham NC | The Original Q Shack | 919-402-4227 | 2510 University Drive |
| Durham NC | Toast | 919-683-2183 | 345 W Main Street |
| Durham NC | Tyler's Taproom | 919-433-0345 | 324 Blackwell Street |
| Fayetteville NC | Jason's Deli | 910-860-0253 | 419 Cross Creek Mall |
| Grandy NC | Mels Diner | 252-457-1010 | 6684 Caratoke H/H 158 |
| Greensboro NC | Chipotle | 336-292-4410 | 5402 Sapp Road |
| Greensboro NC | Chipotle | 336-272-5503 | 1420 Westover Terrace |
| Greensboro NC | Jason's Deli | 336-297-9195 | 3326 W. Friendly Avenue, Suite 140 |
| Greensboro NC | Natty Greene's Pub & Brewing Company | 336-274-1373 | 345 S Elm Street |
| Greenville NC | Barley's Taproom | 864-232-3706 | 25 W Washington Street |
| Hatteras NC | Harbor Deli | 252-986-2500 | 58058 H 12 |
| Hendersonville NC | Henderson Community Co-op | 828-693-0505 | 715 Old Spartanburg H |
| Hickory NC | Firehouse Subs | 828-327-8800 | 2423 N Center Street/H 127 |
| High Point NC | Liberty Steak House and Brewery | 336-882-4677 | 914 Mall Loop Road |
| High Point NC | Uptowne Tavern | 336-883-0030 | 1807 N Main Street/H 311 |
| Huntersville NC | Fox and Hound Pub and Grill | 704-895-4504 | 8711 Lindholm Drive |
| Huntersville NC | Jason's Deli | 704-895-2505 | 16639 Birkdale Commons Parkway, Suite 120 |
| Indian Trail NC | Panera Bread | 704-882-5663 | 14035 Independence Blvd/H 74 |
| Kitty Hawk NC | BK Shuckers | 252-261-7800 | 4020 North Croatan Hwy |
| Kitty Hawk NC | Jimmy's Buffet | 252-261-4973 | 4117 N Croatan H/H 158 |
| Marion NC | Switzerland Cafe & General Store | 828-765-5289 | 9440 H 226A |

| | | | |
|---|---|---|---|
| Mathews NC | Panera Bread | 704-846-4003 | 1904 Matthews Township Parkway/H 51 |
| Matthews NC | Chipotle | 704-845-9406 | 1909 Matthews Township Parkway/H 51 |
| Mooresville NC | Brooklyn Boys Neighborhood Pizzeria | 704-696-2697 | 119-A Market Place Avenue |
| Mooresville NC | Tony's Pizza | 704-658-1926 | 688-F Bluefield Road |
| Nags Head NC | Mulligan's Raw Bar & Grille | 252-480-2000 | 4005 S Croatan Hwy |
| Nags Head NC | Sonic Drive-in | 252-441-9030 | 5205 S Croatan H/H 158 |
| Nags Head NC | Sooey's BBQ At Jockey's Ridge | 252-449-6465 | 3919 S Croatan H/H 158 |
| Nags Head NC | Tropical Smoothie Cafe | 252-441-3500 | 2236 S Croatan H, Unit #2 |
| New Bern NC | Bear Town Market (BTM) | 252-637-0022 | 402 S Front Street |
| New Bern NC | Morgan's Tavern & Grill | 252-636-2430 | 235 Craven Street |
| New Bern NC | Persimmons Waterfront Restaurant | 252-514-0033 | 100 Pollock Street |
| New Bern NC | Port City Java | 252-633-7900 | 323 Middle Street |
| Northport NC | Napper Tandy's | 631-757-4141 | 229 Laurel Avenue |
| Ocracoke NC | Jolly Roger Pub and Marina | 252-928-3703 | 396 Irvin Garrish H/H 12 |
| Pineville NC | Jason's Deli | 704-541-1228 | 10610 Centrum Parkway |
| Pittsboro NC | Carolina Brewery | 919-545-2330 | 120 Lowes Drive, Suite 100 |
| Poplar Branch NC | Diggers Diner | 252-453-0971 | 5658 Caratoke H/H 158 |
| Raleigh NC | 618 Bistro | 919-787-9100 | 4035 Lake Boone Trail |
| Raleigh NC | Armadillo Grill | 919-546-0555 | 439 Glenwood Avenue |
| Raleigh NC | Bella Monica Restaurant | 919-881-9778 | 3121 Edwards Mill Road |
| Raleigh NC | Cafe Carolina and Bakery | 919-821-7117 | 401 Daniels Street |
| Raleigh NC | Chipotle | 919-877-8554 | 6102 Falls of Neuse Road/H 2000 |
| Raleigh NC | Chipotle | 919-781-5115 | 6602 Glenwood Avenue/H 70 |
| Raleigh NC | Cloos' Coney Island | 919-834-3354 | 2233 Avent Ferry Road #102 |
| Raleigh NC | Flying Saucer Draught Emporium | 919-821-7468 | 328 W Morgan St |
| Raleigh NC | Helios | 919-838-5177 | 413 Glenwood Avenue |
| Raleigh NC | Jason's Deli | 919-855-9898 | 909 Spring Forest Road, Suite 100 |
| Raleigh NC | Jason's Deli | 919-572-9996 | 8421 Brier Creek Parkway, #101 |
| Raleigh NC | Lilly's Pizza | 919-833-0226 | 1813 Glenwood Avenue |
| Raleigh NC | Midtown Grille | 919-782-9463 | 4421-115 Six Forks Road |
| Raleigh NC | MoJoe's Burger Joint | 919-832-6799 | 620 Glenwood Avenue |
| Raleigh NC | Morning Times | 919-836-1204 | 10 E Hargett Street |
| Raleigh NC | Nantucket Grill & Bar | 919-870-1955 | 1145 Falls River Avenue |
| Raleigh NC | Napper Tandy's | 919-833-5535 | 126 N West Street |
| Raleigh NC | New World Coffee House | 919-786-0091 | 4112 Pleasant Valley Road #124 |
| Raleigh NC | Ruckus Pizza | 919-835-2002 | 2233-112 Avent Ferry Road |
| Raleigh NC | Sosta Cafe | 919-833-1006 | 130 E Davie Street |
| Raleigh NC | The Brickhouse Sports Restaurant and Pub | 919-829-3666 | 3801 Hillsborough Street/H 54 |
| Raleigh NC | The Players Retreat | 919-755-9589 | 105 Oberlin Road |
| Raleigh NC | The Third Place | 919-834-6566 | 1811 Glenwood Avenue |
| Raleigh NC | The Village Draft House | 919-833-1373 | 428 Daniels Street |
| Raleigh NC | Tropical Smoothie Cafe | 919-755-2222 | 1028 Oberlin Road |
| Raleigh NC | Tropical Smoothie Cafe | 919-803-5991 | 8111 Creedmoor Road/H 50 |
| Raleigh NC | Tuscan Blu | 919-834-5707 | 327 W Davie Street |
| Raleigh NC | Vic's Ristorante Italiano | 919-829-7090 | 331 Blake Street |
| Raleigh NC | Vivace | 919-787-7747 | 4209 Lassiter Mill Road |
| Raleigh NC | Z Pizza | 919-844-0065 | 9630 Falls of the Neuse Road |
| Raleigh NC | Zely & Ritz | 919-828-0018 | 301 Glenwood Avenue, Suite 100 |
| Salisbury NC | Outback Steakhouse | 704-637-1980 | 1020 E Innes St |
| Southern Shores NC | Tropical Smoothie Cafe | 252-441-9996 | 5385 N. Virginia Dare Trail/H 12 |
| Southport NC | Trolley Stop | 910-457-7017 | 111A S Howe Street/H 211 |
| Spindale NC | Barley's Taproom and Pizzeria | 828-288-8388 | 115 W Main Street |
| Statesville NC | Big Shotz Tavern | 704-838-8755 | 1531-A Cinema Drive |
| Surf City NC | New York Corner Deli | 910-328-2808 | 206 N Topsail Drive |
| Wilmington NC | Aubriana's | 910-763-7773 | 115 S Front Street |
| Wilmington NC | Brasserie Du Soleil | 910-256-2226 | 1908 Eastwood Road |
| Wilmington NC | Brixx | 910-256-9677 | 6801 Main Street |
| Wilmington NC | Catch | 910-799-3847 | 6623 Market Street |
| Wilmington NC | Fat Tony's Italian Pizza | 910-343-8881 | 131 N Front Street |
| Wilmington NC | Flaming Amy's Burrito Barn | 910-799-2919 | 4002 Oleander Drive/H 76 |
| Wilmington NC | The Coastal Roaster | 910-399-4701 | 5954 Carolina Beach Road, Unit 170/H 421 |
| Wilmington NC | The Fish House Grill | 910-256-3693 | 1410 Airlie Road |
| Wilmington NC | Tidal Creek Cooperative Market | 910-799-2667 | 5329 Oleander Drive/H 76 |

| | | | |
|---|---|---|---|
| Wilmington NC | Tokyo 101 | 910-399-3101 | 880 Town Center Drive |
| Winston-Salem NC | Chipotle | 336-245-2522 | 128 Hanes Mall Circle |
| Winston-Salem NC | Firehouse Subs | 336-293-6230 | 205 S Stratford Road/H 158 |
| Winston-Salem NC | Foothills Brewing | 336-777-3348 | 638 W 4th Street |
| Winston-Salem NC | Mooney's Mediterranean | 336-722-4222 | 101 W 4th Street |
| Winston-Salem NC | Mozelle's Fresh | 336-703-5400 | 878 W 4th Street |
| Wrightsville Beach NC | South Beach Grill | 910-256-4646 | 100 S Lumina Avenue |
| Wrightsville Beach NC | Trolly Stop | 910-256-3421 | 94 S Lumina Avenue |

**North Dakota Listings**

| | | | |
|---|---|---|---|
| Dickinson ND | Serendipity Coffee House | 701-483-1946 | 789 State Avenue |
| Medora ND | Medora Fudge & Ice Cream Depot | 701-623-4444 | 201 Broadway |

**Ohio Listings**

| | | | |
|---|---|---|---|
| Akron OH | Chipotle | 330-374-0204 | 825 W Market Street/H 18 |
| Athens OH | Chipotle | 740-592-3656 | 41 S Court Street |
| Beavercreek OH | Chipotle | 937-426-2611 | 4473 Walnut Street |
| Bellefontaine OH | Subway Sandwiches & Salads | 937-592-3000 | 800 S. Main Street |
| Berlin OH | Java Jo Coffee Bar | 330-893-9211 | 4860 East Main Street |
| Bexley OH | Chipotle | 614-236-8733 | 2484 E Main Street/H 40 |
| Bowling Green OH | Chipotle | 419-353-4534 | 1558 E Wooster Street/H 64 |
| Canton OH | Chipotle | 330-493-1648 | 5097 Dressler Road NW |
| Centerville OH | Chipotle | 937-432-6950 | 1051 Miamisburg-Centerville Road/H 725 |
| Centerville OH | Flavors Eatery | 937-434-6336 | 865 E Franklin Street |
| Centerville OH | Tropical Smoothie Cafe | 937-434-8699 | 6241 Far Hills Avenue/H 48 |
| Centerville OH | Tropical Smoothie Cafe | 937-291-9250 | 988 Miamisburg Centerville |
| Chillicothe OH | Chipotle | 740-773-4333 | 1290 N Bridge Street Suite A/H 159 |
| Cincinnati OH | ALREDDY Coffee & Cafe | 513-563-4550 | 11083 Reading Road |
| Cincinnati OH | Arlin's Bar & Restaurant | 513-751-6566 | 307 Ludlow Avenue |
| Cincinnati OH | Chipotle | 513-579-9900 | 1 Fountain Square Plaza |
| Cincinnati OH | Chipotle | 513-631-3800 | 3725 Paxton Avenue |
| Cincinnati OH | Chipotle | 513-351-0100 | 4402 Montgomery Road |
| Cincinnati OH | Chipotle | 513-281-8600 | 2507 W Clifton Avenue |
| Cincinnati OH | Chipotle | 513-931-9333 | 8375 Winton Road |
| Cincinnati OH | Chipotle | 513-469-1980 | 11257 Reed Hartman H |
| Cincinnati OH | Chipotle | 513-554-0911 | 2552 Cunningham Drive |
| Cincinnati OH | Chipotle | 513-947-8201 | 4397 Glen Este-Withamsville Road |
| Cincinnati OH | Chipotle | 513-385-2156 | 9430 Colerain Avenue |
| Cincinnati OH | Firehouse Subs | 513-583-8800 | 4750 Fields Ertel Road |
| Cincinnati OH | The Firehouse Grill | 513-733-FIRE (3473) | 4785 Lake Forest Drive |
| Cincinnati OH | The Loving Hut | 513-731-2233 | 6227 Montgomery Road/H 3/22 |
| Cleveland OH | Bar Cento & McNulty's Bier Market | 216-274-1010 | 1948 W 25th Street |
| Cleveland OH | Bar Cento & McNulty's Bier Markt | 216-274-1010 | 1948 W 25th Street |
| Cleveland OH | Chipotle | 216-661-6750 | 3471 Steelyard Drive |
| Cleveland OH | Crop Bistro and Bar | 216-696-CROP (2767) | 2537 Lorain Avenue |
| Cleveland OH | Fire | 216-921-3473 | 13220 Shaker Square |
| Cleveland OH | Fire Food and Drink | 216-916-3473 | 13220 Shaker Square |
| Cleveland OH | Great Lake Brewing Company | 216-771-4404 | 2516 Market Avenue |
| Cleveland OH | LaBodega | 216-621-7075 | 869 Jefferson |
| Cleveland OH | Liquid Planet | 216-631-2266 | 11002 Clifton Blvd/H 2/6/20 |
| Cleveland OH | Liquid Planet | 440-835-8006 | 224 Crocker Park Blvd |
| Cleveland OH | Market Avenue Wine Bar | 216-696-WINE (9463) | 2521 Market Avenue |
| Cleveland Heights OH | Liquid Planet | 216-791-3700 | 12413 Cedar Road |
| Columbus OH | Bodega | 614-299-9399 | 1044 N High Street |
| Columbus OH | Chipotle | 614-789-0920 | 6079 Parkcenter Circle |
| Columbus OH | Chipotle | 614-921-8206 | 1835 Hilliard Rome Road |
| Columbus OH | Chipotle | 614-263-5547 | 4489 N High Street |
| Columbus OH | Chipotle | 614-228-5488 | 401 N Front Street |
| Columbus OH | Chipotle | 614-337-8044 | 4034 Townsfair Way |
| Columbus OH | Chipotle | 614-853-4245 | 1528 Georgesville Road |
| Columbus OH | Chipotle | 614-472-3720 | 4750 Morse Road |

| | | | |
|---|---|---|---|
| Columbus OH | Chipotle | 614-433-0221 | 154 Hutchinson Avenue |
| Columbus OH | Chipotle | 614-781-1320 | 1140 Polaris Parkway |
| Columbus OH | City Barbecue | 614-538-8890 | 2111 West Henderson Road |
| Columbus OH | Katalina's Cafe Corner | 614-294-2233 | 1105 Pennsylvania Ave |
| Columbus OH | La Chatelaine French Bakery | 614-488-1911 | 1550 West Lane Avenue |
| Columbus OH | La Chatelaine French Bakery & Bistro | 614-488-1911 | 1550 W Lane Ave |
| Columbus OH | Max and Ermas | 614-840-9466 | 1515 Polaris Parkway |
| Columbus OH | Northstar Cafe | 614-298-9999 | 951 N High Street |
| Columbus OH | Northstar Cafe | 614-532-5444 | 4015 Townsfair Way |
| Columbus OH | Spagio Restaurant | 614-486-1114 | 1295 Grandview Avenue |
| Cuyahoga Falls OH | Chipotle | 330-920-1295 | 371 Howe Avenue |
| Dayton OH | Chipotle | 937-222-2238 | 1211 Brown Street |
| Dayton OH | Chipotle | 937-890-0473 | 6759 Miller Lane |
| Dayton OH | Milanos | 937-222-7072 | 1820 Brown Street |
| Dayton OH | Tropical Smoothie Cafe | 937-395-3525 | 2307 Far Hills Avenue/H 48 |
| Dublin OH | Jason's Deli | 614-336-3853 | 225 W Bridge Street |
| Elyria OH | Chipotle | 440-324-5723 | 1615 W River Road N |
| Fairlawn OH | Chipotle | 330-670-8393 | 3890 Medina Road |
| Fairview Park OH | Chipotle | 440-356-3109 | 21029 Center Ridge Road/H 20/113 |
| Findlay OH | Chipotle | 419-424-0905 | 15067 H 224 |
| Forest Park OH | Chipotle | 513-671-3000 | 350 Forest Fair Drive |
| Garfield Heights OH | Chipotle | 216-662-6402 | 9761 Vista Way |
| Grandview Heights OH | Jason's Deli | 614-291-7246 | 775 Yard Street, #190 |
| Grove City OH | Chipotle | 614-801-0784 | 1671 Stringtown Road |
| Hamilton OH | Chipotle | 513-737-3403 | 3335 Princeton Road, Suite 109 |
| Hilliard OH | Chipotle | 614-527-7049 | 3670 Fishinger Blvd |
| Holland OH | Chipotle | 419-867-1875 | 6658 Airport H/H2 |
| Huber Heights OH | Chipotle | 937-242-6900 | 7767 Old Troy Pike |
| Hudson OH | Chipotle | 330-342-0669 | 5 Atterbury Blvd |
| Jeffersonville OH | Chipotle | 740-948-2151 | 12478 H 35 NW |
| Lakewood OH | Chipotle | 216-221-9100 | 14881 Detroit Avenue |
| Lancaster OH | Chipotle | 740-689-9627 | 1608 N Memorial Drive |
| Lancaster OH | Fatcat Pizza | 740-687-1966 | 323 Washington Avenue |
| Lancaster OH | Four Reasons Bakery & Deli | 740-654-2253 | 135 W Main Street |
| Lancaster OH | Panera Bread | 740-654-8902 | 1374 Ety Road NW |
| Logan OH | Grandma Faye's Grocery | 740-385-9466 | 20507 H 664 S |

**Oklahoma Listings**

| | | | |
|---|---|---|---|
| Edmond OK | Chipotle - Edmond | 405-341-6765 | 1569 S Broadway/H 77 |
| Edmond OK | Jamba Juice | 405-844-4582 | 8 E 33rd Street #A |
| Norman OK | Jamba Juice | 405-292-3700 | 100 E Alameda Street |
| Norman OK | My Cool Greens | 405-701-5000 | 3700 W Robinson Street |
| Oklahoma City OK | Earl's Barbecue | 405-272-9898 | 216 Johnny Bench Drive |
| Oklahoma City OK | Green Goodies | 405-842-2288 | 5840 N Classen Blvd, Suite 5 |
| Oklahoma City OK | Jamba Juice | 405-749-2617 | 12311 N May Avenue |
| Oklahoma City OK | Musashi's | 405-602-5623 | 4315 N Western Avenue |
| Oklahoma City OK | Museum Cafe | 405-235-6262 | 415 Couch Drive |
| Oklahoma City OK | My Cool Greens | 405-841-COOL (2665) | 6475 Avondale Drive |
| Oklahoma City OK | My Cool Greens | 405-286-9304 | 14201 N May Avenue, Suite 209 |
| Oklahoma City OK | Oliveto Italian Bistro | 405-735-5553 | 1301 S I-35 Service Rd |
| Oklahoma City OK | Rococo | 405-528-2824 | 2824 N Pennsylvania Avenue |
| Oklahoma City OK | Rococo | 405-212-4577 | 12252 N May Avenue |
| Oklahoma City OK | Vito's Ristorante | 405-848-4867 | 7521 N May Avenue |
| Owasso OK | Jamba Juice | 918-272-9496 | 9025 N 121st E Avenue |
| Tulsa OK | Firehouse Subs | 918-249-3473 | 6630 S. Memorial Drive |
| Tulsa OK | Jamba Juice | 918-488-9696 | 5956 S Yale Avenue |
| Tulsa OK | Ti Amo | 918-499-1919 | 6024-A S Sheridan |
| Tulsa OK | Tropical Smoothie Cafe | 918-938-7747 | 7460 S. Olympia Avenue |

**Oregon Listings**

| | | | |
|---|---|---|---|
| Aloha OR | Burgerville | 503-690-0299 | 1245 NW 185th Avenue |
| Astoria OR | Astoria Cooperative | 503-325-0027 | 1355 Exchange Street |
| Beaverton OR | Burgerville | 503-293-0817 | 9385 SW Allen Blvd |
| Beaverton OR | Chipotle | 503-620-9700 | 9120 SW Hall Blvd, Suite D |

| | | | |
|---|---|---|---|
| Beaverton OR | Jamba Juice | 503-533-2050 | 18021 NW Evergreen Parkway, #D |
| Beaverton OR | McMenamins Cedar Hills | 503-641-0151 | 2927 SW Cedar Hills Blvd |
| Beaverton OR | McMenamins Murray & Allen | 503-644-4562 | 6179 SW Murray Blvd |
| Beaverton OR | Monteaux's Public House | 503-439-9942 | 16165 SW Regatta Lane |
| Beaverton OR | New Seasons Markets | 503-641-4181 | 3495 SW Cedar Hills Blvd |
| Bend OR | Anthony's Homeport | 541-389-8998 | 475 SW Powerhouse Dr |
| Bend OR | Big Island Kona Mix Plate | 541-633-7378 | 680 SW Powerhouse Dr #1004 |
| Bend OR | Brother Jon's Public House | 541-306-3321 | 1227 NW Galveston Ave |
| Bend OR | Crux Fermentation Project | 541-385-3333 | 50 SW Division St, |
| Bend OR | Greg's Grill | 541-382-2200 | 395 SW Powerhouse Dr |
| Bend OR | Jamba Juice | 541-647-2235 | 63455 N H 97, Suite 72 |
| Bend OR | Jamba Juice | 541-388-1916 | 2680 NE H 20, Suite D3 |
| Bend OR | Parrilla Grill | 541-617-9600 | 635 NW 14th St |
| Bend OR | Zydeco Kitchen & Cocktails | 541-312-2899 | 919 Bond St |
| Canby OR | Burgerville | 503-266-2568 | 909 SW 1st Avenue/H 99E |
| Cannon Beach OR | Lumberyard Rotisserie and Grill | 503-436-0285 | 264 E 3rd Street |
| Cannon Beach OR | Pizza A' Fetta | 503-436-0333 | 231 N Hemlock Street |
| Corvallis OR | First Alternative | 541-452-3115 | 2855 NW Grant Avenue |
| Corvallis OR | First Alternative | 541-753-3115 | 1007 SE 3rd Street/H 99W |
| Corvallis OR | Jamba Juice | 541-752-0096 | 1580 NW 9th, Suite 105 |
| Corvallis OR | McMenamin's Corvallis | 541-758-6044 | 420 NW Third Street/BH 99W |
| Gresham OR | Burgerville | 503-665-0931 | 2975 NE Hogan Drive |
| Gresham OR | Highland Pub & Brewery | 503-665-3015 | 4225 SE 182nd Avenue |
| Happy Valley OR | New Seasons Markets | 503-558-9214 | 15861 SE Happy Valley Town Center Drive |
| Hillsboro OR | Burgerville | 503-648-7787 | 2401 NE Cornell Road |
| Hillsboro OR | Chipotle | 503-533-0275 | 2048 NW Stucki Avenue |
| Hillsboro OR | Jamba Juice | 503-648-3925 | 7204 NE Cornell Road, Bldg No. cos357 |
| Hillsboro OR | New Seasons Markets | 503-648-6968 | 1453 NE 61st Avenue |
| Hillsboro OR | Orenco Station Grill | 503-844-9119 | 6195 NE Cornell Road |
| Keizer OR | Jamba Juice | 503-485-0472 | 2555 Jorie Lane, Suite 104 |
| Lake Oswego OR | Burgerville | 503-684-8142 | 15650 SW Upper Boones Ferry Road |
| Lake Oswego OR | Jamba Juice | 503-635-4444 | 3 Monrow Parkway, Suite #Z1 |
| Lake Oswego OR | New Seasons Markets | 503-496-1155 | 3 SW Monroe Parkway |
| Lincoln City OR | Lighthouse Brewpub | 541-994-7238 | 4157 N H 101 |
| Lincoln City OR | Nelscott Cafe | 541-994-6100 | 3237 SW Highway 101 |
| Monmouth OR | Burgerville | 503-838-6096 | 615 E Main Street |
| Newberg OR | Burgerville | 503-538-0914 | 2514 Portland Road/H 99W |
| Newport OR | Ocean Bleu Cafe at Gino's Fish Market | 541-265-2424 | 808 SW Bay Blvd |
| Newport OR | Rogue Ale Public House | 541-265-3188 | 748 SW Bay Blvd |
| Oregon City OR | Burgerville | 503-655-0013 | 1900 Molalla Drive |
| Portland OR | Allan's Authentic Mexican Restaurant | 503-629-1764 | 18365 NW West Union Road |
| Portland OR | Bagdad Theater & Pub | 503-467-7521 | 3702 SE Hawthorne Blvd |
| Portland OR | Baja Fresh Mexican Grill | 503-595-2252 | 1121 W. Burnside St. |
| Portland OR | Baja Fresh Mexican Grill | 503-331-1000 | 1505 NE 40th Ave |
| Portland OR | Barley Mill Pub | 503-231-1492 | 9 SE Hawthorne |
| Portland OR | Berlin Inn German Restaurant and Bakery | 503-236-6761 | 3131 SE 12th and Powell |
| Portland OR | Biscuits Cafe | 503-372-5579 | 4744 NW Bethany Blvd, B-1 |
| Portland OR | Blue Moon Tavern & Grill | 503-223-3184 | 432 NW 21st |
| Portland OR | Burgerville | 503-239-5942 | 3432 SE 25th Avenue/H 26 |
| Portland OR | Burgerville | 503-286-8600 | 8671 N Ivanhoe Street |
| Portland OR | Burgerville | 503-255-2815 | 8218 NE Glisan Street |
| Portland OR | Burgerville | 503-252-1804 | 4229 NE 122nd Avenue |
| Portland OR | Burgerville | 503-235-6858 | 1135 NE Martin Luther King Jr Blvd |
| Portland OR | Burgerville | 503-253-0553 | 429 SE 122nd Avenue |
| Portland OR | Burgerville | 503-762-1648 | 16211 SE Division Street |
| Portland OR | Burgerville | 503-777-7078 | 3504 SE 92nd Avenue |
| Portland OR | Burgerville | 503-655-3932 | 19119 SE McLoughlin Blvd/H 99E |
| Portland OR | Casa Colima | 503-892-9944 | 6319 SW Capitol H/H 10 |
| Portland OR | Chipotle | 503-274-2002 | 1948 SW Broadway |
| Portland OR | Chipotle | 503-241-7475 | 240 SW Yamhill |
| Portland OR | Chipotle | 503-287-8242 | 704 NE Weidler Street |
| Portland OR | City Thai | 503-293-7335 | 6341 S.W. Capitol Highway |
| Portland OR | Crackerjacks | 503-222-9069 | 2788 NW Thurman @ 28th Avenue |
| Portland OR | Equinox Restaurant | 503-460-3333 | 830 N Shaver Street |
| Portland OR | Food Front Cooperative Grocery | 503-222-5658 | 2375 NW Thurman Street |

| | | | |
|---|---|---|---|
| Portland OR | Food Front Cooperative Grocery | 503-546-6559 | 6344 SW Capitol H/H 10 |
| Portland OR | Fulton Pub & Brewery | 503-246-9530 | 0618 SW Nebraska Street |
| Portland OR | Goose Hollow at the Cove | 503-228-7010 | 1927 SW Jefferson |
| Portland OR | Greater Trumps | 503-235-4530 | 1520 SE 37th Avenue |
| Portland OR | Jake's Famous Crawfish | 503-226-1419 | 401 SW 12th Ave. |
| Portland OR | Jamba Juice | 503-287-3523 | 10131 NE Cascade Parkway |
| Portland OR | Jamba Juice | 503-252-3233 | 1307 NE 102nd Avenue, Suite 1 |
| Portland OR | Joy Wok Cafe | 503-297-8989 | 7331 SW Barnes Road |
| Portland OR | Kells Irish Pub | 503-227-4057 | 112 SW 2nd Avenue |
| Portland OR | La Costita Restaurant II | 503-293-1899 | 7405 SE Barbur Blvd, Suite 110 |
| Portland OR | Lucky Labrador Beer Hall | 503-517-4352 | 1945 NW Quimby Street |
| Portland OR | Lucky Labrador Brew Pub | 503-236-3555 | 915 SE Hawthorne Blvd |
| Portland OR | Lucky Labrador Public House | 503-244-2537 | 7675 SW Capitol Hwy |
| Portland OR | Lucky Labrador Tap Room | 503-505-9511 | 1700 N Killingsworth |
| Portland OR | MacTarnahan's Taproom | 503-228-5269 | 2730 NW 31st Avenue |
| Portland OR | McMenamin's Mall 205 | 503-254-5411 | 9710 SE Washington Street |
| Portland OR | New Seasons Market | 503-230-4949 | 1214 SE Tacoma Street |
| Portland OR | New Seasons Markets | 503-445-2888 | 1954 SE Division Street |
| Portland OR | New Seasons Markets | 503-288-3838 | 5320 NE 33rd Avenue |
| Portland OR | New Seasons Markets | 503-236-4800 | 4034 SE Hawthorne Blvd |
| Portland OR | New Seasons Markets | 503-292-6838 | 7300 SW Beaverton-Hillsdale H/H 10 |
| Portland OR | Oak Hills Brewpub | 503-645-0286 | 14740 NW Cornell Road |
| Portland OR | Old Market Pub & Brewery | 503-244-0450 | 6959 SW Multnomah Blvd |
| Portland OR | Pearls Bakery | 503-827-0910 | 102 NW 9th Ave, Portland 92709 |
| Portland OR | Ringler's Annex | 503-221-0098 | 1223 SW Stark Street |
| Portland OR | Seasons and Regions Seafood | 503-244-6400 | 6660 SW Capitol H |
| Portland OR | St. Johns Theater & Pub | 503-283-8520 | 8203 N. Ivanhoe Street |
| Portland OR | The Blue Moon Tavern and Grill | 503-223-3184 | 432 NW 21st Ave |
| Portland OR | The Rams Head | 503-221-0098 | 2282 NW Hoyt |
| Portland OR | The Three Degrees Restaurant at RiverPlace Hotel | 503-295-6166 | 1510 SW Harbor Way |
| Portland OR | Tin Shed Garden Cafe | 503-288-6966 | 1438 NE Alberta St |
| Portland OR | Whole Foods | 503-288-3414 | 3535 15th Ave. |
| Portland OR | Whole Foods | 503-232-6601 | 2825 East Burnside Street |
| Portland OR | Widmer Brothers Gasthaus | 503-281-3333 | 955 N Russell Street |
| Portland OR | Zeus Cafe | 503-384-2500 | 303 SW 12th Avenue (Enter on Stark Street) |
| Roseburg OR | Roseburg Station Pub & Brewery | 541-672-1934 | 700 SE Sheridan Street |
| Salem OR | Boon's Treasury | 503-399-9062 | 888 Liberty Street NE |
| Salem OR | Jamba Juice | 503-391-6251 | 2910 Commercial Street SE |
| Salem OR | Jamba Juice | 503-585-5544 | 515 Taggert Drive NW, Suite 110 |
| Salem OR | Jamba Juice | 503-566-7045 | 3096 Lancaster Drive NE/H 213 |
| St Helens OR | Burgerville | 503-397-5885 | 715 S Columbia River H/H 30 |
| The Dalles OR | Burgerville | 541-298-5753 | 118 W 3rd Street |
| The Dalles OR | Holstein's | 541-298-2326 | 3rd and Taylor |
| Tigard OR | Jamba Juice | 503-639-4505 | 7136 SW Hazel Fern Road |
| Tigard OR | McMenamins Greenway Pub | 503-590-1865 | 12272 SW Scholls Ferry Road |
| Tualatin OR | Chipotle | 503-692-5709 | 7003 SW Nyberg Street |
| Tualatin OR | Jamba Juice | 503-692-4328 | 7137 SW Nyberg Street |
| W Linn OR | Burgerville | 503-635-7339 | 18350 Willamette Drive/H 43 |
| Wilsonville OR | Jamba Juice | 503-570-9119 | 8261 SW Wilsonville Road, Suite B |
| Wood Village OR | Jamba Juice | 503-492-9467 | 22401 NE Glisan Street, Suite A |

**Pennsylvania Listings**

| | | | |
|---|---|---|---|
| Allentown PA | Fegley's Brew Works | 610-433-7777 | 812-816 W Hamilton Street |
| Ardmore PA | Chipolte | 610-649-3061 | 133 W Lancaster Avenue/H 30 |
| Bethel Park PA | Panera Bread | 412-854-2007 | 5243 Library Road |
| Bethlehem PA | The Brew Works | 610-882-1300 | 569 Main Street |
| Bethlehem Townplace PA | Geakers Drive In | 610-419-4869 | 6th Street and Freemansburg Avenue |
| Bloomsburg PA | Panera Bread | 570-380-1230 | 76 Lunger Drive |
| Clarks Summit PA | State Street Grill | 570-585-5590 | 114 S State Street/H 6/11 |
| Collegeville PA | Elevation Burger | 610-831-1360 | 201 Plaza Drive |
| Conshohocken PA | Spring Mill Cafe | 610-828-2550 | 164 Barren Hill Road |
| Dickson City PA | Panera Bread | 570-489-6707 | 1101 Commerce Blvd |
| Easton PA | Panera Bread | 610-253-4340 | 4442 Southmont Way |
| Elysburg PA | Ponduce Farms | 570-799-5888 | 270 White Church Road |

| | | | |
|---|---|---|---|
| Exton PA | Appetites on Main | 610-594-2030 | 286 Main Street |
| Exton PA | The Brickside Grill | 610-321-1600 | 540 Wellington Square |
| Gettysburg PA | Friendly's Restaurant | 717-337-1426 | 445 Steinwehr Avenue/H 15 |
| Gettysburg PA | Hunt's Fresh Cut Fries | 717-334-4787 | 61 Steinwehr Avenue |
| Gettysburg PA | O'Rorkes | 717-334-2333 | 44 Steinwehr Ave |
| Glenshaw PA | The Hartwood Restaurant and Whispers Pub | 412-767-3500 | 3400 Harts Run Road |
| Greensburg PA | Chipotle | 724-838-7591 | 2000 Lincoln Place |
| Harrisburg PA | Chipotle | 717-614-1504 | 5106-I Jonestown Road/H 22 |
| Intercourse PA | Kettle House Cafe | 717-768-8261 | Route 340 |
| Kennett Square PA | Kennett Square Inn | 610-444-5687 | 201 E State Street |
| King of Prussia PA | Baja Fresh | 610-337-2050 | 340 W DeKalb Pike |
| King of Prussia PA | Starbucks | 610-768-5130 | 140 West DeKalb Pike |
| Lancaster PA | Isaac's Restaurant and Deli | 717-394-5544 | 25 N Queen Street/H 72 |
| Lancaster PA | Tropical Smoothie Cafe | 717-397-1827 | 15 E King Street/H 462 |
| Lititz PA | Tropical Smoothie Cafe | 717-560-1490 | 235 Bloomfield Drive |
| Montoursville PA | Johnson's Cafe | 570-368-8351 | 334 Broad Street |
| Moosic PA | Panera Bread | 570-941-0946 | 1151 Shoppes Blvd |
| Mount Lebanon PA | Il Pizzaiolo | 412-344-4123 | 703 Washington Rd |
| New Hope PA | Triumph Brewing Company | 215-862-8300 | 400 Union Square |
| North Wales PA | Chipotle | 215-368-8740 | 30 Airport Square |
| Northumberland PA | Front Street Station | 570-473-3626 | 2 Front Street |
| Philadelphia PA | 1 Shot Coffee | 215-627-1620 | 1040 N 2nd Street |
| Philadelphia PA | Cafe Zesty | 215-483-6226 | 4382 Main St |
| Philadelphia PA | Cantina Dos Segundos | 215-629-0500 | 931 N Second Street |
| Philadelphia PA | Cantina Los Caballitos | 215-755-3550 | 1651 E Passyunk Avenue |
| Philadelphia PA | Caribou Cafe | 215-625-9535 | 1126 Walnut St |
| Philadelphia PA | Cebu Restaurant and Bar | 215-629-1100 | 123 Chestnut Street |
| Philadelphia PA | Chipotle | 215-222-0632 | 3925 Walnut Street, Suite 128/H 3 |
| Philadelphia PA | Chipotle | 215-878-0452 | 4030 City Avenue/H 1 |
| Philadelphia PA | Devon's Seafood | 215-546-5940 | 225 18th St F1 1 |
| Philadelphia PA | Fork | 215-625-9425 | 306 Market Street |
| Philadelphia PA | Gold Standard Cafe | 215-727-8247 | 4800 Baltimore Avenue/H 13 |
| Philadelphia PA | Le Bus | 215-487-2663 | 4266 Main St |
| Philadelphia PA | O'Neal's Pub | 215-574-9495 | 611 S 3rd Street |
| Philadelphia PA | Pat's King of Steaks | 215-468-1546 | 1237 E Passyunk Ave |
| Philadelphia PA | Philadelphia Java Company | 215-928-1811 | 518 4th St |
| Philadelphia PA | Sabrina's Cafe | 215-636-9061 | 1804 Callowhill Street |
| Philadelphia PA | Tavern 17 | 215-790-1799 | 220 S 17th Street |
| Philadelphia PA | The Abbaye | 215-627-6711 | 637 N 3rd Street |
| Philadelphia PA | The Continental | 215-923-6069 | 134 Market Street |
| Philadelphia PA | Valley Green Inn | 215-247-1730 | Springfield Ave and Wissahickon |
| Philadelphia PA | White Dog Cafe | 215-386-9224 | 3420 Sansom Street |
| Phoenixville PA | Franco's Italian Restaurant | 610-933-0880 | 226 Bridge Street |
| Pittsburg PA | Pino's Contemporary Italian Restaurant & Wine Bar | 412-661-3651 | 6739 Reynolds Street |
| Pittsburgh PA | Atria's Restaurant and Tavern | 412-322-1850 | 103 Federal Street |
| Pittsburgh PA | Cafe Zinho | 412-363-1500 | 238 Spahr St |
| Pittsburgh PA | Chipotle | 412-621-1993 | 4800 Baum Blvd/H 380 |
| Pittsburgh PA | Chipotle | 412-655-8271 | 509 Clairton Blvd/H 51 |
| Pittsburgh PA | Chipotle | 412-367-4902 | 4861 McKnight Road/H 19 |
| Pittsburgh PA | Chipotle | 412-787-3227 | 300 McHolme Drive |
| Pittsburgh PA | Jerome Bettis' Grill 36 | 412-224-6287 | 375 N Shore Drive |
| Pittsburgh PA | Mullaney's Harp and Fiddle | 412-642-6622 | 2329 Penn Avenue |
| Pittsburgh PA | Panera Bread | 412-799-0210 | 942 Freeport Road #114 |
| Pittsburgh PA | Roland's Seafood Grill | 412-261-3401 | 1904 Penn Ave |
| Plains Township PA | DQ Grill and Chill Restaurant | 570-270-0947 | 1245 H 315 |
| Plymouth Meeting PA | Chipolte | 610-834-5795 | 500 W Germantown Pike, Suite 2200 |
| Stroudsburg PA | Everybody's Cafe | 570-424-0896 | 905 Main Street |
| Stroudsburg PA | Panera Bread | 570-476-6740 | 900 Shoppes at Stroud |
| Swarthmore PA | Swarthmore CO-OP | 610-543-9805 | 341 Dartmouth Avenue |
| University Park PA | Berkey Creamery at PSU | 814-865-7535 | 119 Food Science Building |
| W Chester PA | Iron Hill Brewery | 610-738-9600 | 3 W Gay Street/H 3 |
| Warrington Township PA | Chipotle | 215-343-8656 | 1515 Main Street |
| West Chester PA | Chipotle | 610-344-7042 | 101 Turner Lane |
| West Chester PA | Four Dogs Tavern | 610-692-5702 | 1300 W Strasburg Road/H 162 |
| Whitehall PA | Panera Bread | 610-433-8101 | 2669 MacArthur Road/H 145 |

| | | | |
|---|---|---|---|
| Wilkes-Barre PA | Panera Bread | 570-825-8077 | 3570 Wilkes Barre Commons |
| Willow Grove PA | Chipotle | 215-659-8108 | 2618 Moreland Road/H 63 |
| Wynnewood PA | Elevation Burger | 610-645-7704 | 50 E Wynnewood Road |

**Rhode Island Listings**

| | | | |
|---|---|---|---|
| Cranston RI | Johnny Rockets | 401-228-7833 | 400 New London Turnpike, Suite 100 /H 2 |
| East Greenwich RI | Chianti's Italian Cuisine | 401-884-3810 | 195 Old Forge Road |
| Jamestown RI | East Ferry Market and Deli | 401-423-1592 | 47 Conanicus Avenue |
| Jamestown RI | Slice of Heaven | 401-423-9866 | 32 Narragansett Avenue |
| Jamestown RI | Trattoria Simpatico | 401-423-3731 | 13 Narragansett Avenue |
| Middletown RI | Flo's Clam Shack | 401-847-8141 | 4 Wave Avenue/H 138 |
| Middletown RI | Frosty Freeze | 401-846-1697 | 496 East Main Road/H 138 |
| Newport RI | Canfield House Restaurant and Pub | 401-847-0416 | 5 Memorial Blvd |
| Newport RI | Kilwins Chocolate, Fudge, and Ice Cream Shop | 401-619-3998 | 262 Thames Street |
| Newport RI | Malt on Broadway | 401-619-1667 | 150 Broadway |
| Newport RI | Nikolas Pizza | 401-849-6611 | 38 Memorial Blvd/H 138 |
| Newport RI | O'Brien's Pub | 401-849-6623 | 501 Thames Street |
| Newport RI | Salvation Army Cafe | 401-847-2620 | 140 Broadway |
| Newport RI | Sardella's Restaurant | 401-849-6312 | 30 Memorial Blvd |
| Newport RI | The Landing on Bowen's Wharf | 401-847-4514 | 30 Bowen's Wharf |
| Newport RI | The Pier | 401-847-3645 | 10 Howard Wharf |
| Providence RI | Amy's Place | 401-274-9966 | 214 Wickenden Street |
| Providence RI | Cable Car Cinema | 401-272-3970 | 204 S Main |
| Providence RI | Hemenway's | 401-351-8570 | 121 S Main Street |
| Providence RI | India Restaurant | 401-421-2600 | 1060 Hope St |
| Providence RI | Joe's American Bar and Grill | 401-270-4737 | 148 Providence Place |
| Providence RI | Luxe Burger | 401-621-LUXE (5893) | 5 Memorial Drive |
| Providence RI | Rick's Roadhouse | 401-272-7675 | 370 Richmond St |
| Smithfield RI | Terrazza Restaurant | 401-233-3223 | 645 Douglas Pike |
| Tiverton RI | Gray's Ice Cream | 401-624-4500 | 16 East Street |
| Warwick RI | Chipotle | 401-821-3007 | 969 Bald Hill Road/H 2 |

**South Carolina Listings**

| | | | |
|---|---|---|---|
| Aiken SC | Malia's | 803-643-3086 | 120 Laurens Street |
| Anderson SC | Firehouse Subs | 864-222-3702 | 3321 N Main Street, Suite D/H 28/76/178 |
| Beaufort SC | Firehouse Subs | 843-379-3443 | 2219 Boundary Street/H 21 |
| Beaufort SC | Hemmingway's Bistro | 843-521-4480 | 920 Bay St |
| Charleston SC | 39 Rue de Jean | 843-722-8881 | 39 John Street |
| Charleston SC | Daniel Island Grille | 843-377-8750 | 259 Seven Farms Drive |
| Charleston SC | Firehouse Subs | 843-766-9111 | 1836 Ashley River Road, Suite I/H 61 |
| Charleston SC | Juanita Greenberg's | 843-723-NACHO(6224) | 439 King Street |
| Charleston SC | The Bubba Gump Shrimp Co. Restaurant & Market | 843-723-5665 | 99 S Market St |
| Charleston SC | The HydeOut at Dolphin Cove Marina | 843-745-0426 | 2079 Austin Avenue |
| Columbia SC | Firehouse Subs | 803-749-5535 | 150-A Harbison Blvd |
| Columbia SC | Firehouse Subs | 803-736-9680 | 4546 Hardscrabble Road |
| Columbia SC | Panera Bread | 803-647-9722 | 6080 Garners Ferry Road/H 76/378 |
| Columbia SC | Panera Bread | 803-407-5773 | 1007 Bower Parkway |
| Columbia SC | Panera Bread | 803-865-8460 | 631-6 Promenade Place |
| Columbia SC | Rosewood Market & Deli | 803-765-1083 | 2803 Rosewood Drive |
| Columbia SC | Rossa's | 803-787-3949 | 4840 Forest Drive/H 12 |
| Columbia SC | The Salty Nut | 803-256-4611 | 2000A Greene Street |
| Columbia SC | Tropical Smoothie Cafe | 803-781-6535 | 1150 Bower Parkway |
| Columbia SC | Yesterday's Restaurant and Tavern | 803-799-0196 | 2030 Devine Street |
| Columbia SC | Z Pizza | 803-708-4703 | 1004 Gervais Street/H 1/378 |
| Columbia SC | Za's Pizza | 803-771-7334 | 2930 Devine Street |
| Conway SC | Tropical Smoothie Cafe | 843-234-5670 | 201 Graduate Road |
| Greenville SC | Chipotle | 864-234-6460 | 4 Market Point Drive |
| Greenville SC | Firehouse Subs | 864-297-2535 | 3935 Pelham Road, Suite E |
| Greenville SC | High Cotton | 864-335-4200 | 550 S Main Street at RiverPlace |

| Greenville SC | Jason's Deli | 864-284-9870 | 824 Woods Crossing Road |
|---|---|---|---|
| Greenville SC | Smoke on the Water | 864-232-9091 | 1 Augusta Street |
| Greenville SC | Soby's | 864-232-7007I 85 | 207 S Main Street |
| Greenville SC | Strossner's Bakery and Cafe | 864-233-3996 | 21 Roper Mountain Road |
| Hilton Head Island SC | Bistro 17 at Shelter Cove Marina | 843-785-5517 | 17D Harborside Lane |
| Hilton Head Island SC | Black Marlin Bayside Grill and Hurricane Bar | 843-785-4950 | 86 Helmsman Way # 103 |
| Hilton Head Island SC | Hinchey's Chicago Bar and Grill | 843-686-5959 | 36 S Forest Beach Drive |
| Hilton Head Island SC | Skillets Cafe | 843-785-3131 | 1 N Forest Beach Dr J1 |
| Hilton Head Island SC | Up The Creek Pub | 843-681-DOCK (3625) | 18 Simmons Road |
| Hilton Head Isle SC | Bistro 17 | 843-785-5517 | 17 Harbourside Ln |
| Mount Pleasant SC | Dog and Duck Food and Spirits | 843-881-3056 | 624 A Longpoint Road |
| Myrtle Beach SC | Bay Naturals Healthy Market and Kitchen | 843-448-0011 | 7611 N Kings H/H 17 |
| Myrtle Beach SC | Firehouse Subs | 843-626-9111 | 1211 38th Avenue N |
| Myrtle Beach SC | Liberty Steak House and Brewery | 843-626-4677 | 1321 Celebrity Circle/Broadway at the Beach |
| North Augusta SC | Firehouse Subs | 803-279-5534 | 1237 Knox Avenue N/H 121 |
| North Charleston SC | DIG in the Park | 843-225-5201 | 1049 E Montague Avenue |
| North Myrtle Beach SC | Johnny Rockets | 843-361-0191 | 4712-A Highway 17 S |
| North Myrtle Beach SC | Molly Darcy's Irish Pub & Restaurant | 843-272-5555 | 1701 S Ocean Blvd |
| Rock Hill SC | Panera Bread | 803-329-0200 | 526 John Ross Parkway |
| Simpsonville SC | P. Simpson's Hometown Grill | 864-757-9691 | 111 N Main Street |
| Spartanburg SC | Jason's Deli | 864-574-0202 | 1450 W.O. Ezell Blvd/H29 |
| Sullivan's Island SC | Poe's Tavern | 843-883-0083 | 2210 Middle Street |

**South Dakota Listings**

| Custer SD | Flintstones Drive-In | 605-673-4079 | US Highways 16 and 385 |
|---|---|---|---|
| Custer SD | Wrangler Cafe | 605-673-4271 | 302 Mt. Rushmore Rd. |
| Deadwood SD | Buffalo Steakhouse | 605-578-1300 | 658 Main Street |
| Keystone SD | Ruby House Restaurant | 605-666-4404 | 126 Winter Street |
| Lead SD | Cheyenne Crossing General Store and CafÃ_x0083_Â© | 605-584-3510 | 21415 H/14A/85 |
| Rapid City SD | Flying T Chuckwagon | 605-342-1905 | 8971 S H 16 |
| Rapid City SD | Mostly Chocolates | 605-341-2264 | 1919 Mount Rushmore Rd # 1/H 16 |
| Rapid City SD | Sonic Drive-In | 605-716-3663 | 2316 Mount Rushmore Road/H 16 |
| Rapid City SD | Stonewalls Espresso Cafe | 605-342-6100 | 5955 S H 16 |
| Rapid City SD | Subway | 605-341-0387 | 2415 Mount Rushmore Rd # 2/H 16 |
| Rapid City SD | The Corn Exchange Restaurant & Bistro | 605-343-5070 | 727 Main Street/I 90/H 79 |
| Rapid City SD | Thirsty's | 605-343-3104 | 819 West Main Street |
| Sioux Falls SD | Bagel Boy | 605-336-8366 | 3200 E 26th Street |
| Sioux Falls SD | Bagel Boy | 605-334-3212 | 1911 S Minnesota Avenue |
| Sioux Falls SD | Mixed | 605-271-2161 | 2604 S Louise Avenue |
| Sioux Falls SD | Sanaas Gourmet Mediterranean | 605-275-2516 | 401 E 8th Street #100 |
| Spearfish SD | Bay Leaf Cafe | 605-642-5462 | 126 W Hudson Street |
| Spearfish SD | Green Bean Coffeehouse | 605-717-3636 | 304 N. Main Street |

**Tennessee Listings**

| Bartlett TN | YoLo Frozen Yogurt | 901-266-5111 | 5985 Stage Road #30/H 15 |
|---|---|---|---|
| Chattanooga TN | Aretha Frankensteins | 423-265-SOUL (7685) | 518 Tremont Street, Chattanooga, TN |
| Chattanooga TN | Big River Grille | 423-267-2739 | 222 Broad Street |
| Chattanooga TN | Blue Orleans | 423-757-0088 | 1463 Market Street/H 8 |
| Chattanooga TN | Brix Nouveau Wine and Cheese Bar | 423-488-2926 | 301 Cherokee Blvd/H 8 |
| Chattanooga TN | Buffalo Wild Wings | 423-634-0468 | 120 Market Street |
| Chattanooga TN | Clumpies Ice Cream | 423-267-5425 | 26 Frazier Avenue # B |
| Chattanooga TN | Dipped Fresh | 423-490-9334 | 221 River Street |
| Chattanooga TN | Easy Bistro & Bar | 423-266-1121 | 203 Broad Street |
| Chattanooga TN | Firehouse Subs | 423-893-3473 | 6025 E Brainerd Road, Suite 110/H 320 |
| Chattanooga TN | Food Works | 423-752-7487 | 205 Manufacturers Road |
| Chattanooga TN | Greenlife Grocery and Deli | 423-702-7300 | 301 Manufacturer's Road |
| Chattanooga TN | Greyfriar's Coffee | 423-267-0376 | 406-B Broad Street |
| Chattanooga TN | Hair of the Dog Pub | 423-265-4615 | 334 Market Street/H 8 |

| | | | |
|---|---|---|---|
| Chattanooga TN | Jason's Deli | 423-296-1096 | 2115 Gunbarrel Road |
| Chattanooga TN | Marco's Italian Bistro | 423-710-2568 | 417 Frazier Avenue |
| Chattanooga TN | Moccasin Bend Brewing Company Tasting Room | 423-821-6392 | 4015 Tennessee Avenue/H 58 |
| Chattanooga TN | Sluggo's North Vegetarian Cafe | 423-752-5224 | 501 Cherokee Blvd/H 8 |
| Chattanooga TN | Stone Cup Cafe | 888-698-4404 | 330 Frazier Avenue |
| Chattanooga TN | Subway | 423-266-6727 | 208 Frazier Avenue |
| Chattanooga TN | Terra Nostra Tapas and Wine | 423-634-0238 | 105 Frazier Avenue |
| Chattanooga TN | The Blue Plate | 423-648-6767 | 191 Chestnut Street, unit B |
| Chattanooga TN | The Ice Cream Show | 423-702-5173 | 105 Walnut Street |
| Chattanooga TN | The Terminal Brew House | 423-752-8090 | No. 6 14th Street |
| Chattanooga TN | Tropical Smoothie Cafe | 423-475-5124 | 1925 Gunbarrel Road |
| Chattanooga TN | Vine Street Market | 423-266-8463 | 1313 Hanover Street |
| Cordova TN | Tropical Smoothie Cafe | 901-755-5588 | 1625 N. Germantown Parkway/H 177 |
| Elizabethton TN | Sonic Drive-in | 423-547-0084 | 1003 W. Elk Avenue/H 91/321 |
| Gatlinburg TN | Howard's Restaurant | 865-436-3600 | 976 Parkway/H 71/441 |
| Gatlinburg TN | Subway | 865-436-6792 | 223 Airport Rd |
| Germantown TN | Swanky's Taco Shoppe | 901-737-2088 | 6641 Poplar Avenue/H 57/72 |
| Johnson City TN | Luke's Pizza | 423-328-0186 | 3111 W Market Street/H 411 |
| Johnson City TN | Sonic Drive-in | 423-975-0015 | 3300-A W Market Street/H 411 |
| Johnson City TN | Sonic Drive-in | 423-283-0146 | 2619 N Roan Street |
| Knoxville TN | Barley's Taproom and Pizzeria | 865-521-0092 | 200 E Jackson Avenue |
| Knoxville TN | Bistro By The Tracks | 865-558-9500 | C215 Brookview Centre Way |
| Knoxville TN | Calhoun's on the River | 865-673-3400 | 400 Neyland Drive/H 158 |
| Knoxville TN | Cool Beans Restaurant & Tavern | 865-522-6417 | 1817 Lake Avenue |
| Knoxville TN | Cosmo's Cafe | 865-584-8739 | 5107 Kingston Pike/H 1/11/70 |
| Knoxville TN | Firehouse Subs | 865-673-0864 | 1708 W Cumberland Avenue/H 1/11/70 |
| Knoxville TN | Jason's Deli | 865-247-5222 | 2120 Cumberland Avenue/H 1/11 |
| Knoxville TN | Jason's Deli | 865-357-3354 | 133 N Peters Road |
| Knoxville TN | Oodles Uncorked | 865-521-0600 | 18 Market Square SW |
| Knoxville TN | Pelancho's Mexican Grill | 865-694-9060 | 1516 Downtown W Blvd |
| Knoxville TN | Seasons Innovative Bar and Grille | 865-392-1121 | 11605 Parkside Dr |
| Knoxville TN | Shonos In City | 865-544-5800""; | 5 Market Square |
| Knoxville TN | Soccer Taco | 865-544-4471 | 9 Market Square |
| Knoxville TN | Soccer Taco | 865-588-2020 | 6701 Kingston Pike/H 1/11/70 |
| Knoxville TN | The Downtown Grill & Brewery | 865-633-8111 | 424 S Gay Street |
| Knoxville TN | The French Market | 865-540-4372 | 530 S Gay Street |
| Knoxville TN | The Plaid Apron Cafe | 865-247-4640 | 1210 Kenesaw Avenue |
| Knoxville TN | The Tomato Head | 865-637-4067 | 12 Market Square |
| Knoxville TN | The Tomato Head | 865-584-1075 | 7240 Kingston Pike, Suite 172 |
| Knoxville TN | Tropical Smoothie Cafe | 865-246-1041 | 4839 Kingston Pike/H 1/11/70 |
| Knoxville TN | Urban Bar and Corner Cafe | 865-546-2800 | 109 N Central Street |
| Memphis TN | Bleu Restaurant and Lounge | 901-334-5950 | 221 S 3rd Street |
| Memphis TN | Brookhaven Pub and Grill | 901-680-8118 | 695 W Brookhaven Circle |
| Memphis TN | Cafe Eclectic | 901-725-1718 | 603 N. McLean Blvd |
| Memphis TN | Cafe Society | 901-722-2177 | 208 N Evergreen Street |
| Memphis TN | Celtic Crossing | 901-274-5151 | 903 S Cooper Street |
| Memphis TN | Central BBQ | 901-272-9377 | 2249 Central Avenue |
| Memphis TN | Chipotle Mexican Grill | 901-416-1944 | 5865 H 72, Suite 104 |
| Memphis TN | El Porton | 901-452-7330 | 65 S Highland Street |
| Memphis TN | Firehouse Subs | 901-373-9200 | 6606 Charlotte Pike, Suite 101/H 24/70 |
| Memphis TN | Fuel Cafe | 901-725-9025 | 1761 Madison Avenue |
| Memphis TN | Jason's Deli | 901-685-3333 | 1199 Ridgeway Road |
| Memphis TN | Java Cabana | 901-272-7210 | 2170 Young Avenue |
| Memphis TN | Memphis Pizza Cafe | 901-726-5343 | 2087 Madison Avenue, Overton Square |
| Memphis TN | Napa Cafe | 901-683-0441 | 5101 Sanderlin Avenue |
| Memphis TN | Tropical Smoothie Cafe | 901-791-9251 | 2105 Union Avenue/H 23/64/79 |
| Memphis TN | Tropical Smoothie Cafe | 901-791-9027 | 7960 Winchester Road |
| Memphis TN | Tropical Smoothie Cafe | 901-757-3637 | 1779 Kirby Parkway |
| Memphis TN | YoLo Frozen Yogurt | 901-343-0438 | 6 S Cooper Street |
| Memphis TN | YoLo Frozen Yogurt | 901-683-0190 | 559 Erin Drive |
| Nashville TN | 12 South Tap Room | 615-463-7552 | 2318 12th Avenue S |
| Nashville TN | Acorn Restaurant | 615-320-4399 | 114 28th Avenue N |
| Nashville TN | Baja Fresh | 615-341-0100 | 1720 W End Avenue |

| | | | |
|---|---|---|---|
| Nashville TN | Baja Fresh | 615-279-1620 | 2116 Green Hills Village Drive |
| Nashville TN | Batter'd & Fried Boston Seafood House | 615-226-9283 | 1008 Woodland Street |
| Nashville TN | Blackstone Restaurant & Brewery | 615-327-9969 | 1918 W End Avenue/H 70S |
| Nashville TN | Bongo Java | 615-385-5282 | 2007 Belmont Blvd |
| Nashville TN | Bruegger's Bagel Bakery | 615-327-0055 | 422 21st Avenue S |
| Nashville TN | Bruegger's Bagel Bakery | 615-352-1128 | 5305 Harding Rd |
| Nashville TN | Chago's Cantina | 615-386-0106 | 2015 Belmont Blvd |
| Nashville TN | Chipotle Mexican Grill | 615-320-1693 | 2825 West End Avenue/H 1/70S |
| Nashville TN | FLYTE World Dining and Wine | 615-255-6200 | 718 Division Street |
| Nashville TN | Fido's | 615-777-3436 | 1812 21st Avenue S/H 106/431 |
| Nashville TN | Gerst Haus | 615-244-8886 | 301 Woodland Street |
| Nashville TN | Grins Vegetarian Cafe | 615-322-8571 | 2421 Vanderbilt Place |
| Nashville TN | Jack's Bar-B-Que | 615-254-5715 | 416A Broadway/H 24/70 |
| Nashville TN | Jackson's Bar and Bistro | 615-385-9968 | 1800 21st Avenue |
| Nashville TN | Park Cafe | 615-383-4409 | 4403 Murphy Road |
| Nashville TN | Pizza Perfect | 615-329-2757 | 1602 21st Avenue S |
| Nashville TN | Quiznos | 615-313-7842 | 315 Deadrick Street, Suite 140 |
| Nashville TN | The Turnip Truck Natural Market | 615-650-3600 | 970 Woodland Street |
| Pigeon Forge TN | Baskin Robbins Ice Cream | 865-453-3337 | 3668 Parkway |
| Spindale TN | Barley's Taproom | 828-288-8388 | 115 W Main/H 74/221 |
| Townsend TN | Subway | 865-448-6909 | 8213 State Highway 73 |

**Texas Listings**

| | | | |
|---|---|---|---|
| Abilene TX | Jason's Deli | 325-692-1975 | 3490 Catclaw Drive |
| Abilene TX | Quiznos | 325-674-2107 | 216 McGlothin Campus Center |
| Addison TX | Chipotle - Addison | 972-243-9088 | 3771 Belt Line Road |
| Addison TX | Humperdinks | 972-484-3051 | 3820 Belt Line Rd |
| Addison TX | Lazy Dog Restaurant & Bar | 469-754-1300 | 5100 Beltline Rd |
| Allen TX | Chipotle - Allen | 972-747-1731 | 103 Central Expressway N |
| Allen TX | Jason's Deli | 972-727-3440 | 906 W McDermott Drive, #100 |
| Amarillo TX | 7 Grill & Bar | 806-358-2222 | 3130 S Soncy Rd |
| Amarillo TX | Chipotle Mexican Grill | 806-576-0764 | 2414 S Georgia St |
| Amarillo TX | Jason's Deli | 806-353-4440 | 7406 W 34th Avenue |
| Amarillo TX | Ruby's Tequila | 806-463-7829 | 2001 S. Georgia |
| Amarillo TX | The 806 Coffee + Lounge | 806-322-1806 | 2812 SW 6th Ave |
| Amarillo TX | The Big Texan Steak Ranch | 806-372-6000 | 7701 E I-40 |
| Arlington TX | Chipotle - UTA | 817-860-0010 | 1390 S Cooper Street, Suite #100/H 157 |
| Arlington TX | Firehouse Subs | 817-466-1227 | 1001 W Arbrook Blvd |
| Arlington TX | Jason's Deli | 817-860-2888 | 780 Road to Six Flags |
| Arlington TX | Jason's Deli | 817-557-3311 | 951 W I-20, Suite 109 |
| Austin TX | Austin Java Company | 512-476-1829 | 1206 Parkway |
| Austin TX | Austin Terrier | 512-369-3751 | 3435 Greystone Dr |
| Austin TX | BB Rover's Cafe and Pub | 512-335-9504 | 12636 Research Blvd. |
| Austin TX | Banger's Sausage House & Beer Garden | 512-386-1656 | 79 Rainey St |
| Austin TX | Banger's Sausage House & Beer Garden | 512-386-1656 | 79 & 81 Rainey St |
| Austin TX | Billy's on Burnet | 512-407-9305 | 2105 Hancock Street |
| Austin TX | Bouldin Creek Coffee House | 512-416-1601 | 1501 S 1st Street |
| Austin TX | Carmelo's Italian Restaurant | 512-477-7497 | 504 East 5th St. |
| Austin TX | Carrabba's Italian Grill | 512-345-8232 | 11590 Research Blvd. |
| Austin TX | Casa De Luz Austin | 512-476-2535 | 1701 Toomey Road |
| Austin TX | Cherrywood Coffee House | 512-538-1991 | 1400 E. 38 1/2 St |
| Austin TX | Chipotle - 45th and Lamar | 512-419-9898 | 4400 N Lamar Blvd #101 |
| Austin TX | Chipotle - Lakeline Mall | 512-331-8700 | 11301 Lakeline Blvd |
| Austin TX | Chipotle - Mueller | 512-495-9083 | 1201 Barbara Jordan Blvd, Suite 1300 |
| Austin TX | Chipotle - Parmer & McNeil | 512-996-9538 | 6301 W Parmer Lane, Suite 201 |
| Austin TX | Chipotle - Parmer & Metric | 512-837-0114 | 1700 W Parmer Lane, Suite 200 |
| Austin TX | Chipotle - Southpark Meadows | 512-291-1057 | 9600 S I 35 |
| Austin TX | Chipotle - Stassney | 512-707-0969 | 610 E Stassney Lane |
| Austin TX | Chipotle - Sunset Valley | 512-892-4222 | 5400 Brodie Lane |
| Austin TX | Chipotle - Westbank | 512-329-8600 | 3300 Bee Caves Road #670 |
| Austin TX | Cipollina | 512-477-5211 | 1213 West Lynn St. |
| Austin TX | Contigo | 512-614-2260 | 2027 Anchor Ln |
| Austin TX | Crown and Anchor Pub | 512-322-9168 | 2911 San Jacinto Blvd |
| Austin TX | Dog & Duck Pub | 512-479-0598 | 406 West 17th Street |
| Austin TX | El Mercado | 512-477-7689 | 1302 South 1st St |

| | | | |
|---|---|---|---|
| Austin TX | Flying Saucer | 512-454-8200 | 815 W 47th Street |
| Austin TX | Ginger Man Pub | 512-473-8801 | 304 W. Fourth Street |
| Austin TX | Green Man Mesquite BBQ & More | 512-479-0485 | 1400 Barton Springs Road |
| Austin TX | Jason's Deli | 512-328-0200 | 3300 Bee Caves Road |
| Austin TX | Jason's Deli | 512-280-0990 | 9600 S I-35, Suite D-500 |
| Austin TX | Jo's Coffee | 512-444-3800 | 1300 S. Congress Avenue |
| Austin TX | Max's Wine Dive | 512-904-0111 | 207 San Jacinto Blvd |
| Austin TX | Moonshine Patio Bar & Grill | 512-236-9599 | 303 Red River Street |
| Austin TX | Moonshine Patio Bar & Grill | 512-236-9599 | 303 Red River St |
| Austin TX | North by North West Restaurant and Brewery | 512-467-6969 | 10010 N. Capitol of Texas Hwy. |
| Austin TX | Opal Divines | 512-733-5353 | 12709 Mopac and Parmer Lane |
| Austin TX | P Terry's Burger Stand | 512-473-2217 | 404 S Lamar Blvd |
| Austin TX | Phils Ice House | 512-524-1212 | 5620 Burnet Road |
| Austin TX | Picnik Austin | 737-226-0644 | 4801 Burnet Rd |
| Austin TX | Red River Cafe | 512-472-0385 | 2912 Medical Arts |
| Austin TX | Red's Porch | 512-440 REDS (7337) | 3508 S. Lamar Blvd {around back}/H 343 |
| Austin TX | Ross' Old Austin Cafe | 512-835-2414 | 11800 N Lamar Blvd/H 275 |
| Austin TX | Scholz Beer Garden | 512-474-1958 | 1607 San Jacinto Blvd. |
| Austin TX | Spider House | 512-480-9562 | 2908 Fruth St. |
| Austin TX | Texas Land and Cattle Steakhouse | 512-451-6555 | 6007 North IH 35 |
| Austin TX | The Coffee Bean & Tea Leaf | 512-351-8680 | 221 S Lamar Blvd |
| Austin TX | The Coffee Bean & Tea Leaf | 512-382-9701 | 3724 N Lamar Blvd |
| Austin TX | The Coffee Bean & Tea Leaf | 512-322-9820 | 2402 Guadalupe Street, Suite C |
| Austin TX | The Coffee Bean & Tea Leaf | 512-394-9010 | 5701 W Slaughter Lane, Suite A170 |
| Austin TX | The Coffee Bean & Tea Leaf | 512-494-4041 | 3220 Amy Donovan Plaza, Suite 100 |
| Austin TX | The Coffee Bean & Tea Leaf | 512-219-9256 | 13376 N H 183, Suite 800 |
| Austin TX | The Coffee Bean & Tea Leaf | 512-351-8676 | 1000 E 41st Street, Suite 180 |
| Austin TX | The Gingerman Pub | 512-473-8801 | 301 Lavaca |
| Austin TX | The Tavern | 512-320-8377 | 922 W 12th Street |
| Austin TX | Torchy's Tacos Spicewood | 512-291-7277 | 4211 Spicewood Springs Road |
| Austin TX | Uncle Billy's | 512-476-0100 | 1530 Barton Springs Road |
| Austin TX | Yard Bar | 512-900-3773 | 6700 Burnet Rd |
| Beaumont TX | Luke's Icehouse | 409-347-8139 | 2325 Calder Ave |
| Cedar Park TX | Tropical Smoothie Cafe | 512-259-5472 | 1465 E Whitestone Blvd |
| College Station TX | Blackwater Draw Brewing Co | 979-703-6170 | 303 Boyett St |
| College Station TX | Chipotle - College Station | 979-260-2282 | 815 W University Drive |
| College Station TX | Genghis Grill | 979-260-6800 | 700 University Drive |
| College Station TX | Grub Burger Bar | 979-268-1041 | 980 University Dr E |
| College Station TX | Jamba Juice | 979-846-6200 | 980 University Drive E, Suite 300 |
| College Station TX | Jason's Deli | 979-764-2929 | 1404 Texas Avenue S |
| College Station TX | Veritas Wine & Bistro | 979-268-3251 | 830 University Dr East |
| Coppell TX | Chipotle - Coppell | 972-393-2156 | 104 Denton Tap Road |
| Corpus Christi TX | Executive Surf Club | 361-884-7873 | 306 N Chaparral |
| Corpus Christi TX | Harrison's Landing | 361-881-8503 | 108 Peoples St T-Head St |
| Corpus Christi TX | Jamba Juice | 361-906-2474 | 5425 S Padre Island Drive, #114/H 358 |
| Corpus Christi TX | Seawall Food & Spirits | 361-726-3533 | 520 S Shoreline |
| Corpus Christi TX | Sonic Drive-In | 361-949-7886 | 14401 South Padre Island Drive |
| Corpus Christy TX | Jason's Deli | 361-980-8300 | 5325 Saratoga Blvd #200 /H 357 |
| Dallas TX | Bolsa Market--Cafe--Wine Bar | 214-367-9367 | 614 W Davis Street |
| Dallas TX | Breadwinner Cafe and Bakery | 214-351-3339 | 5560 W Lovers Lane #260 |
| Dallas TX | Cafe Brazil | 214-461-8762 | 3847 Cedar Springs Rd |
| Dallas TX | Cafe Brazil | 214-747-2730 | 2815 Elm Street |
| Dallas TX | Café Toulouse | 214-520-8999 | 3314 Knox Street |
| Dallas TX | Campisi's | 214-752-0141 | 1520 Elm Street, Suite 111 |
| Dallas TX | Chipotle - Central Expressway | 214-890-0903 | 11613 N Central Expressway, Suite 100 |
| Dallas TX | Chipotle - Knox Street | 214-302-2500 | 4502 McKinney Avenue |
| Dallas TX | Chipotle - McKinney | 214-871-3100 | 2705 McKinney Avenue |
| Dallas TX | Chipotle - North Dallas | 972-934-8580 | 5290 Beltline Road, Suite, 102A |
| Dallas TX | Chipotle - Preston Center | 214-691-7755 | 8301 Westchester Drive |
| Dallas TX | Chipotle - Preston Forest | 972-789-1900 | 11930 Preston Road/H 289 |
| Dallas TX | Chipotle - Upper Greenville | 469-232-0963 | 7700 N. Central Expressway |
| Dallas TX | Chipotle - West End | 214-939-5272 | 208 N Market Street |
| Dallas TX | Chipotle Mexican Grill | 214-871-3100 | 2705 McKinney Ave |
| Dallas TX | Chipotle Mexican Grill | 214-691-7755 | 8301 Westchester Drive |

| | | | |
|---|---|---|---|
| Dallas TX | Corner Bakery Cafe | 972-407-9131 | 7615 Campbell Rd |
| Dallas TX | Dream Cafe | 214-954-0486 | 2800 Routh Street |
| Dallas TX | Elevation Burger | 214-360-0088 | 8611 Hillcrest Road, Suite 195 |
| Dallas TX | Gloria's Restaurant | 214-874-0088 | 3715 Greenville Avenue |
| Dallas TX | Goodfriend Beer Garden & Burger House | 214-324-3335 | 1154 Peavy Rd |
| Dallas TX | Hunky's | 214-522-1212 | 4000 Cedar Springs Rd |
| Dallas TX | Jamba Juice | 214-363-6828 | 8421 Westchester Drive |
| Dallas TX | Jamba Juice | 972-665-0425 | 18204 Preston Road, #E2 |
| Dallas TX | Jason's Deli | 214-821-7021 | 5400 E Mockingbird Lane |
| Dallas TX | Jason's Deli | 214-739-1800 | 7412 Greenville Avenue |
| Dallas TX | Jason's Deli | 972-818-3354 | 18111 Dallas Parkway #100 |
| Dallas TX | LG Taps | 972-807-9329 | 3619 Greenville Ave |
| Dallas TX | La Calle Doce | 214-941-4304 | 415 W 12th Street |
| Dallas TX | La Calle Doce | 214-824-9900 | 1925 Skillman St. |
| Dallas TX | Lee Harvey's | 214-428-1555 | 1807 Gould Street |
| Dallas TX | Mutts Canine Cantina | 214-377-8723 | 2889 Cityplace W Blvd |
| Dallas TX | Parigi's Restaurant | 214-521-0295 | 3311 Oak Lawn Avenue, Suite 102 |
| Dallas TX | Ristorante Bugatti | 214-350-2470 | 3802 West Northwest Hwy |
| Dallas TX | San Francisco Rose | 214-826-2020 | 3024 Greenville Ave |
| Dallas TX | Slaters | 214-888-0158 | 2817 Greenville Ave |
| Dallas TX | State and Allen Lounge | 214-239-1990 | 2400 Allen Street in Uptown - Dallas, Texas 75204 |
| Dallas TX | TCBY Frozen Yogurt | 214-821-5757 | 6402 E. Mockingbird Lane |
| Dallas TX | The Ginger Man Pub | 214-754-8771 | 2718 Boll Street |
| Dallas TX | Truck Yard | 469-500-0139 | 5624 Sears St |
| Dallas TX | Twisted Root Burger Company | 214-741-ROOT (7668) | 2615 Commerce Street |
| Dallas TX | Zini's Pizzeria | 214-599-2600 | 4001 Cedar Springs Road |
| Denton TX | Chipotle - Denton | 940-565-0990 | 1800 S Loop 288 |
| Denton TX | Fuzzy's Taco Shop | 940-380-TACO (8226) | 115 Industrial Street |
| El Paso TX | Block - Table & Tap | 915-351-0775 | 4172 N Mesa St |
| El Paso TX | Cafe Central | 915-545-2233 | 109 N Oregon Street # 1 |
| El Paso TX | El Tenedor | 915-727-9789 | 414 E San Antonio Dr |
| El Paso TX | Hope and Anchor | 925-533-8010 | 4012 N Mesa St |
| El Paso TX | Ripe | 915-584-7473 | 910 E Redd Rd |
| El Paso TX | Salt Box pours & provisions | 915-307-3222 | 204 Boston Ave |
| El Paso TX | The Hoppy Monk | 915-307-3263 | 4141 N Mesa St |
| El Paso TX | The Kitchen at 150 Sunset | 915-585-1150 | 150 E Sunset Rd |
| Euless TX | Lazy Dog Restaurant & Bar | 682-738-0861 | 2521 State Highway 121 |
| Fort Worth TX | Chadra Mezza | 817-9CHADRA (817-924-2372) | 1622 Park Place Avenue |
| Fort Worth TX | Chipotle - Bryant Irvin | 817-735-4506 | 4484 Bryant Irvin Road |
| Fort Worth TX | Chipotle - Fort Worth | 817-348-8530 | 3000 W 7th Street |
| Fort Worth TX | Chipotle - Trinity Commons | 817-735-8355 | 3050 S Hulen Street, Unit C |
| Fort Worth TX | Chipotle Mexican Grill | 817-348-8530 | 3000 W 7th Street |
| Fort Worth TX | Chipotle Mexican Grill | 817-735-8355 | 3050 S. Hulen Street, Unit C |
| Fort Worth TX | Fred's Texas Cafe | 817-332-0083 | 915 Currie St |
| Fort Worth TX | Fuzzy's Taco Shop | 817-924-7943 | 2917 W Berry Street |
| Fort Worth TX | Fuzzy's Taco Shop | 817-831-TACO (8226) | 2719 Race Street |
| Fort Worth TX | Fuzzy's Taco Shop at Alliance | 817-750-8226 | 9180 North Freeway, Suite 500 |
| Fort Worth TX | Jamba Juice | 817-870-1001 | 400 Main Street |
| Fort Worth TX | Jamba Juice | 817-370-6478 | 4801 Overton Ridge |
| Fort Worth TX | Jason's Deli | 817-738-7144 | 6244 Camp Bowie Blvd/H 377 |
| Fort Worth TX | Jason's Deli | 817-370-9187 | 5100 Overton Ridge Blvd |
| Fort Worth TX | Jason's Deli | 817-750-0151 | 9517 Sage Meadow Trail |
| Fort Worth TX | Love Shack | 817-740-8812 | 817 Matisse Lane |
| Fort Worth TX | Mash'd | 817-882-6723 | 2948 Crockett St |
| Fort Worth TX | Mimi's Cafe | 817-731-9644 | 5858 SW Loop 820 |
| Fort Worth TX | Rodeo Goat | 817-877-4628 | 2836 Bledsoe St |
| Fort Worth TX | The Bearded Lady | 817-349-9832 | 1229 7th Ave |
| Fort Worth TX | The Gingerman Pub | 817-886-2327 | 3716 Camp Bowie Blvd |
| Fort Worth TX | Tumbleweeds Sports Bar | 817-626-5225 | 1008 NE Loop 820 |
| Fort Worth TX | Waters Texas | 817-984-1110 | 301 Main St |
| Fort Worth TX | Ye Olde Bull and Bush Pub | 817-731-9206 | 2300 Montgomery Street |
| Fredericksburg TX | Altdorf's Biergarden | 830-997-7865 | 301 West Main Street |

| | | | |
|---|---|---|---|
| Fredericksburg TX | Hondo's | 830-997-1633 | 312 W Main Street/H 87/290 |
| Fredericksburg TX | Silver Creek-Beer Garden & Grill | 830-990-4949 | 310 E Main Street/H 87/290 |
| Fredericksburg TX | West End Pizza | 830-990-8646 | 232 W Main St |
| Frisco TX | Chipotle - Preston Ridge | 972-668-1540 | 3401 Preston Road, #2/H 289 |
| Frisco TX | Jason's Deli | 972-377-8652 | 8520 H 121 |
| Galveston TX | Mosquito Cafe | 409-763-1010 | 628 14th St |
| Galveston TX | Mosquito Cafe | 409-763-1010 | 628 14th Street |
| Galveston TX | Olympia the Grill at Pier 21 | 409-765-0021 | 100 21st St |
| Galveston TX | Porch Cafe | 855-223-2526 | 1625 E Beach Dr |
| Galveston TX | Sonic Drive-In | 409-740-9009 | 6502 Seawall Boulevard |
| Galveston TX | Stuttgarden Tavern On The Strand | 409-497-4972 | 2110 Strand St |
| Galveston TX | Yaga's Cafe and Bar | 409-762-6676 | 2314 Strand |
| Garland TX | Chipotle - Firewheel | 972-530-5811 | 4170 Lavon DriveH 78 |
| Georgetown TX | Chipotle - Republic Square | 512-868-0941 | 900 N. Austin Avenue |
| Grand Prairie TX | Jamba Juice | 972-606-8655 | 3040 W Camp Wisdom Road, Suite 100 |
| Grapevine TX | Jason's Deli | 817-421-0566 | 1270 William D Tate Avenue #100 |
| Highland Park TX | Jamba Juice | 972-966-0285 | 3180 H 407, Suite #510 |
| Houston TX | Becks Prime | 713-266-9901 | 2615 Augusta Drive |
| Houston TX | Boondoggle's Pub and Pizzeria | 281-326-BREW | 4106 Nasa Rd |
| Houston TX | Chatter's Cafe and Bistro | 713-864-8080 | 140 S Heights Blvd |
| Houston TX | Chipotle - Katy | 281-646-8588 | 1260 Fry Road |
| Houston TX | Chipotle - Louetta Road | 281-812-0451 | 10905 Louetta Road |
| Houston TX | Chipotle - Med Center | 713-666-9769 | 6600 Fannin Street |
| Houston TX | Chipotle - Mid-Westheimer | 713-784-4246 | 8401 Westheimer Road, Bldg. A, Suite 100 |
| Houston TX | Chipotle - NW Marketplace | 713-996-9047 | 13768 NW Freeway |
| Houston TX | Chipotle - Reliant Park | 713-630-8100 | 8505 S Main Street/H 90 |
| Houston TX | Chipotle - Richmond & Sage | 832-675-0086 | 5176 Richmond Avenue |
| Houston TX | Chipotle - Theater District | 713-225-6633 | 909 Texas Avenue |
| Houston TX | Chipotle - Village Place | 713-666-9769 | 5600 Kirby #N-1 |
| Houston TX | Chipotle - Willowbrook | 832-237-2449 | 7600 FM 1960 Road W |
| Houston TX | Edison | 281-501-3780 | 4203 Edison |
| Houston TX | Firehouse Subs | 281-647-7827 | 17758 Katy H, Suite F-1/H 90/I 10 |
| Houston TX | Fox and Hound English Pub and Grille | 281-589-2122 | 11470 Westheimer Road |
| Houston TX | Gingerman's | 713-526-2770 | 5607 Morningside Dr |
| Houston TX | Gratifi Kitchen + Bar | 832-203-5950 | 302 Fairview St |
| Houston TX | Heights Bier Garten | 713-862-4940 | 1433 N Shepherd Dr |
| Houston TX | Henderson Heights | 713-714-8367 | 908 Henderson St |
| Houston TX | Hickory Hollow BBQ | 713-869-6300 | 101 Heights Blvd |
| Houston TX | Jason's Deli | 713-739-1200 | 1200 Smith Street, #110 |
| Houston TX | Jason's Deli | 713-522-2660 | 2530 University Blvd |
| Houston TX | Jason's Deli | 713-975-7878 | 5860 Westheimer Road |
| Houston TX | Jason's Deli | 713-975-7878 | 5860 Westheimer Road |
| Houston TX | Jason's Deli | 281-444-7515 | 5403-D FM 1960 |
| Houston TX | Jason's Deli | 281-531-1999 | 14604 Memorial Drive |
| Houston TX | Jason's Deli | 281-858-7500 | 7010 H 6 N |
| Houston TX | Jason's Deli | 713-467-2007 | 10321-A Katy H |
| Houston TX | Jason's Deli | 713-520-6728 | 2611 S. Shepherd Square |
| Houston TX | Jason's Deli | 713-522-2660 | 23530 University Blvd |
| Houston TX | McCormick and Schmick's Seafood Restaurant | 713-840-7900 | 1151 Uptown Park Blvd. |
| Houston TX | Panera Bread Bakery and Cafe | 281-469-5623 | 12220 Farm Road 1960 |
| Houston TX | Presidio | 832-740-4574 | 911 W 11th St |
| Houston TX | Red Mango | 713-463-3830 | 801 Town & Country Blvd, Suite A |
| Houston TX | Soto's Cantina | 281-955-5667 | 10609 Grant Road |
| Houston TX | The Ginger Man Pub | 713-526-2770 | 5607 Morningside |
| Houston TX | The Red Lion | 713-782-3030 | 2316 S Shephard Drive |
| Houston TX | Tila's Restaurant and Bar | 713-522-7654 | 1111 S Shepard Dr |
| Houston TX | Underdogs Pub | 713-410-5660 | 4212 Washington Ave |
| Houston TX | West Alabama Icehouse | 713-528-6874 | 1919 West Alamaba |
| Houston TX | Z Pizza | 713-432-7219 | 4010 Bissonnet St |
| Humble TX | Chipotle - Deerbrook | 281-446-1077 | 10035 FM 1960 Bypass W, Suite F-2 |
| Hurst TX | Chipotle - North East Mall | 817-595-3875 | 1312 W Pipeline |
| Irving TX | Chipotle - Las Colinas | 972-501-9925 | 7717 N MacArthur Blvd |
| Irving TX | Chipotle - Las Colinas South | 972-957-3100 | 118 E John Carpenter H/H 114 |

| | | | |
|---|---|---|---|
| Irving TX | Jamba Juice | 972-401-3800 | 6440 N MacArthur Blvd |
| Katy TX | Jamba Juice | 281-574-1646 | 23501 Cinco Ranch Blvd |
| Katy TX | Jason's Deli | 281-693-3354 | 21953 F Katy H |
| Killeen TX | Firehouse Subs | 254-680-3473 | 1000 Lowes Blvd, #400 |
| Leon Springs TX | Fralo's Art of Pizza | 210-698-6616 | 23651 H WW |
| Lewisville TX | Chipotle - N Lewisville | 469-549-4964 | 722 Main Street |
| Lewisville TX | Chipotle - Vista Ridge | 972-315-3694 | 2605 S Stemmons H |
| Lewisville TX | Jason's Deli | 972-459-2905 | 500 E FM 3040, Suite 318 |
| Live Oak TX | The Lion and the Rose | 210-547-3000 | 8211 Agora Parkway #112 |
| Longview TX | Jason's Deli | 903-663-5161 | 103 W Loop 281, #201 |
| Lubbock TX | Apple Tree Cafe and Bakery | 806-799-7715 | 3501 50th St |
| Lubbock TX | BushHog's | 806-863-4647 | 16202 Tx-493 Lp |
| Lubbock TX | Firehouse Subs | 806-747-9600 | 411 University Avenue, Suite 200 |
| Lubbock TX | Fuzzy's Taco Shop | 806-740-TACO (8226) | 2102 Broadway Street |
| Lubbock TX | Jason's Deli | 806-799-8660 | 4001 S Loop 289 |
| Lubbock TX | The Lantern Tavern | 806-785-2280 | 3502 Slide Rd |
| McKinney TX | Chipotle - 380 Town Crossing | 972-548-1542 | 2014 W University Drive |
| McKinney TX | Chipotle - Eldorado | 972-542-7337 | 2811 Craig Drive |
| McKinney TX | Jason's Deli | 972-542-9393 | 1681 N Central Expressway |
| Mesquite TX | Chipotle - Mesquite | 972-686-9078 | 1715 N Town East Blvd |
| Midland TX | Flat Belly Organics | 432-699-1410 | 3326 N Midkiff Road |
| Midland TX | Fuddruckers | 432-362-4330 | 4511 N Midkiff Road # C22 |
| Midland TX | Jason's Deli | 432-682-2200 | 4610 N Garfield Road |
| Midland TX | Natural Foods Market and the Strawberry Cafe | 432-699-4048 | 2311 W Wadley Avenue |
| New Braunfels TX | Jason's Deli | 830-620-7000 | 280 N Business IH 35 , Suite 400 |
| North Richland Hills TX | Chipotle - N Richland Hills | 817-428-9770 | 9127 Blvd 26, Suite, 100/H 26 |
| Pasadena TX | Chipotle - Pasadena | 281-991-1600 | 5759 Fairmont Parkway |
| Pasadena TX | Jason's Deli | 713-946-3354 | 3905 Spencer H |
| Pearland TX | Jamba Juice | 713-340-2278 | 2810 Business Center Drive, Suite 138 |
| Plano TX | Chipotle - Collin Creek | 972-423-5115 | 1009 N Central Expressway |
| Plano TX | Chipotle - Park & Preston | 469-467-9900 | 4901 W Park Blvd, Suite 539 |
| Plano TX | Jamba Juice | 972-398-6550 | 5700 Legacy Drive, #A2 |
| Plano TX | Jamba Juice | 972-424-5015 | 1201 E Spring Creek Parkway, Suite 180 |
| Plano TX | Jason's Deli | 972-578-2520 | 925 N Central Expressway |
| Plano TX | Jason's Deli | 972-519-0022 | 4801 W Parker Road |
| Plano TX | Lazy Dog Restaurant & Bar | 469-609-1570 | 8401 Preston Rd |
| Richardson TX | Chipotle - Telecom Corridor | 972-907-1712 | 293 W Campbell Road |
| Richardson TX | Jason's Deli | 972-437-9156 | 101 S Coit Road |
| Rockwell TX | Chipotle - Rockwall | 972-722-0445 | 951 E I 30 |
| Round Rock TX | Chipotle - Round Rock | 512-828-0788 | 150 Sundance Parkway |
| Round Rock TX | Jamba Juice | 512-863-6649 | 200 University Blvd, Suite 240 |
| Round Rock TX | Third Base Sports Bar and Restaurant | 512-388-BASE (2273) | 3107 S IH 35 Suite 810 |
| San Antonio TX | Bella On The River | 210-404-2355 | 106 River Walk St |
| San Antonio TX | Cappy's | 210-828-9669 | 5011 Broadway Ave |
| San Antonio TX | Charlie Wants a Burger Sports Bar | 210-227-0864 | 223 Losoya Street |
| San Antonio TX | Chipotle - Alamo Heights | 210-832-9812 | 3928 Broadway Street |
| San Antonio TX | Chipotle - Huebner Oaks | 210-699-4392 | 11745 I 10W |
| San Antonio TX | Chipotle - Quarry | 210-493-2875 | 1201 N Loop 1604 W |
| San Antonio TX | Chipotle - Quarry | 210-832-9444 | 7322 Jones Maltsberger |
| San Antonio TX | Chipotle - San Pedro | 210-340-0571 | 438 NW Loop 410, Suite 101 |
| San Antonio TX | Chipotle - Vineyard | 210-493-2875 | 1201 N Loop 1604 W |
| San Antonio TX | Chipotle Mexican Grill | 210-832-9812 | 3928 Broadway Street |
| San Antonio TX | Chipotle Mexican Grill | 210-340-0571 | 438 NW Loop 410, Suite 101 |
| San Antonio TX | Chipotle Mexican Grill | 210-521-0672 | 8227 H 151, Suite 105 |
| San Antonio TX | Crumpets Restaurant and Bakery | 210-821-5600 | 3920 Harry Wurzback Rd |
| San Antonio TX | Firehouse Subs | 210-490-7610 | 1802 N H Loop 1604 E, Suite 104 |
| San Antonio TX | Flying Saucer | 210-696-5080 | 11255 Huebner Road |
| San Antonio TX | Fralo's Art of Pizza | 210-698-6616 | 23651 IH 10 West |
| San Antonio TX | Green Vegetarian Cuisine at Pearl Brewery | 210-320-5865 | 200 E Grayson St |
| San Antonio TX | Guadalajara Grill | 210-222-1992 | 301 S. Alamo Street |
| San Antonio TX | Jamba Juice | 210-824-0050 | 290 E Basse Road, A |
| San Antonio TX | Jason's | 210-690-3354 | 9933 I 10 W |

| | | | |
|---|---|---|---|
| San Antonio TX | Jason's Deli | 210-524-9288 | 25 NE Loop 410 |
| San Antonio TX | Jason's Deli | 210-545-6888 | 1141 N. Loop 1604 E |
| San Antonio TX | Jason's Deli | 210-647-5000 | 5819 NW Loop 410 |
| San Antonio TX | La Tuna Icehouse | 210-224-8862 | 100 Probandt/H 536 |
| San Antonio TX | Los Patios | 210-655-6171 | 2015 Northeast Loop 410 |
| San Antonio TX | Luther's Cafe | 210-223-7727 | 1425 N Main Avenue |
| San Antonio TX | Madhatters Tea House and Cafe | 210-212-4832 | 320 Beauregard |
| San Antonio TX | Osteria Il Sogno | | 200 E Grayson St |
| San Antonio TX | Pugel's | 210-467-5062 | 3502 N Saint Mary's St |
| San Antonio TX | Quarry Cantina | 210-290-8066 | 7310 Jones Maltsberger Road |
| San Antonio TX | Rita's On The River | 210-227-7482 | 245 E Commerce Street |
| San Antonio TX | Sangria On the Burg | 210-265-3763 | 5115 Fredericksburg Rd |
| San Antonio TX | Stella's Public House | 210-277-7047 | 1414 S Alamo St |
| San Antonio TX | Sushihana Japanese Restaurant | 210-340-7808 | 1810 NW Military Hwy |
| San Antonio TX | Taco Garage | 210-826-4405 | 8403 Broadway Street |
| San Antonio TX | The Cove | 210-227-2683 | 606 W Cypress |
| San Antonio TX | The Friendly Spot | (210) 224-BEER (2337) | 943 S. Alamo Street |
| San Antonio TX | The Friendly Spot Ice House | 210-224-2337 | 943 S Alamo St |
| San Antonio TX | The Landing | 210-223-7266 | 123 Losoya St |
| San Antonio TX | The Luxury | 210-354-2274 | 103 E Jones Ave |
| San Antonio TX | The Original Mexican Restaurant | 210-224-9951 | 102 W Crockett Street |
| San Antonio TX | Tito's Mexican Restaurant | 210-212-TACO (8226) | 955 S Alamo Street |
| San Antonio TX | Tong's Thai Restaurant | 210-829-7345 | 1146 Austin Hwy |
| San Antonio TX | Tycoon Flats | 210-320-0819 | 2926 N St. Mary's Street |
| San Antonio TX | Yellowfish Sushi | 210-614-3474 | 9102 Wurzbach Rd |
| San Antonio TX | Zuni Grill | 210-227-0864 | 223 Losoya St. |
| San Marcos TX | Johnny Rockets | 512-392-7499 | 3939 I/35 S #915 |
| South Padre Island TX | Yummies Coffee Shack | 956-761-2526 | 708 Padre Blvd |
| Southlake TX | Chipotle - Southlake | 817-459-0939 | 3010 E Southlake Blvd |
| Southlake TX | Jamba Juice | 817-416-9971 | 222 State Street |
| Spicewood TX | Angel's Icehouse | 512-264-3777 | 21815 Texas 71 |
| Spring TX | Tapped Drafthouse & Kitchen | 281-719-0360 | 20444 Kuykendahl Rd |
| Sugar Land TX | Jason's Deli | 281-565-3737 | 15275 SW H |
| Sugarland TX | Chipotle - Sugarland | 281-980-6622 | 2280 Lone Star Drive |
| Tomball TX | Craft Grill | 281-255-2396 | 25219 Kuykendahl Rd |
| Tyler TX | Jason's Deli | 903-561-5380 | 4913 S Broadway Avenue/H 69 |
| Victoria TX | La Hacienca Mexican Grill | 361-570-6800 | 7702 N Navarro St. |
| Waco TX | Bare Arms Brewing | 254-759-8480 | 2515 La Salle Ave |
| Waco TX | Jamba Juice | 254-751-1689 | 4300 W Waco Drive/H 84 |
| Waco TX | Lula Jane' | 254-366-0862 | 406 Elm St |
| Waco TX | Mad Hasher Waco | | 210 S. University Parks |
| Waco TX | The Grape | 254-772-1866 | 2006 N Valley Mills Drive |
| Watauga TX | Chipotle - Watauga | 817-577-0208 | 7604 Denton H/H 377 |
| Webster TX | Jamba Juice | 281-316-9965 | 528 W Bay Area Blvd, Suite 300 |
| Webster TX | Jason's Deli | 281-338-8000 | 541 W Bay Area Blvd |
| Woodlands TX | Chipotle - Woodlands | 281-296-2772 | 9595 Six Pines Drive |
| Woodlands TX | Johnny Rockets | 281-419-9002 | 9595 Six Pines Drive |

**Utah Listings**

| | | | |
|---|---|---|---|
| Cottonwood Heights UT | Chipotle - Fort Union | 801-943-3525 | 6924 S Park Centre Drive |
| Kanab UT | Escobar's Mexican Restaurant | 435-644-3739 | 373 E 300 S/H 89 |
| Kanab UT | Laid Back Larry's | 435-644-3636 | 98 S 100 E/H 89 |
| Kanab UT | Rocking V Cafe | 435-644-8001 | 97 W Center Street/H 89 |
| Marysvale UT | The Prospector Cafe | 435-326-4281 | 50 S. Hwy 89 |
| Midvale UT | Firehouse Subs | 801-561-3117 | 1008 E Ft. Union Blvd |
| Ogden UT | Great Harvest Bread Co | 801-394-6800 | 272 25th Street |
| Ogden UT | Two Bit Street - Club Cafe & Antiques | 801-393-1225 | 126 Historic 25th Street |
| Park City UT | Whole Foods Market | 435-575-0200 | 1748 W Redstone Center Drive |
| Salt Lake City UT | Chipotle - Sandy | 801-571-8547 | 10387 S State Street/H 89 |
| Salt Lake City UT | Chipotle - Sugarhouse | 801-467-1311 | 1011 E 2100 S |
| Salt Lake City UT | Citris Grill | 801-466-1202 | 2991 E 3300 S/H 171 |
| Salt Lake City UT | Les Madeleines | 801-355-2294 | 216 E 500 S |
| Salt Lake City UT | Liberty Heights Fresh Cafe | 801-58-FRESH (583-7374) | 1290 S 1100 E |

| | | | |
|---|---|---|---|
| Salt Lake City UT | Log Haven Restaurant | 801-272-8255 | 6451 E Mill Creek Canyon Road |
| Salt Lake City UT | Noodle and Company | 801-466-8880 | 1152 E 2100 S |
| Salt Lake City UT | Penny Ann's Cafe | 801-935-4760 | 1810 South Main Street |
| Salt Lake City UT | Rubios Baja Grille | 801-363-0563 | 358 S 700 E, Suite F |
| Salt Lake City UT | Rubios Baja Grille | 801-466-1220 | 1160 E 2100 S |
| Salt Lake City UT | Toaster's | 801-328-2928 | 151 W 200 S |
| Salt Lake City UT | Vertical Diner | 801-484-8378""; | 2280 Southwest Temple |
| West Bountiful UT | Chipotle - West Bountiful | 801-295-5140 | 135 N 500 W |

**Vermont Listings**

| | | | |
|---|---|---|---|
| Brandon VT | Cafe Provence | 802-247-9997 | 11 Center Street |
| Brattleboro VT | Top of the Hill Grill | 802-258-9178 | 632 Putney Road |
| Burlington VT | City Market, Onion River Co-op | 802-861-9700 | 82 S Winooski Avenue/H 7 |
| Burlington VT | Lake Champlain Chocolates | 802-864-1807 | 750 Pine Street |
| Burlington VT | Sweetwaters | 802-864-9800 | 120 Church Street |
| Burlington VT | Vermont Pub & Brewery | 802-865-0500 | 144 College Street |
| Manchester VT | Brasserie L'Oustau de Provence | 802-768-8538 | 1716 Depot Street |
| Putney VT | Putney Food Co-op | 802-387-5866 | 8 Carol Brown Way |
| S Burlington VT | Quiznos Sub | 802-864-0800 | 1335 Shelburne Road |
| Stowe VT | The Solstice at Stowe Mountain Lodge | 802-760-4735 | 7412 Mountain Road/H 108 |
| Vienna VT | Chipotle | 703-255-1100 | 213 Maple Avenue E/H 123 |
| Winchester VT | Piccadilly Pub | 540-535-1899 | 125 E Piccadilly Street |

**Virginia Listings**

| | | | |
|---|---|---|---|
| Alexandria VA | Baja Fresh | 703-823-2888 | 3231 Duke Street |
| Alexandria VA | Caboose Cafe & Bakery | 703-566-1283 | 2419 Mount Vernon Avenue |
| Alexandria VA | Chipotle | 703-660-9214 | 6770 Richmond H/H 1 |
| Alexandria VA | Chipotle | 703-370-2152 | 4531 Duke Street/H 236 |
| Alexandria VA | Chipotle | 703-924-6018 | 5955 Kingstowne Towne Center |
| Alexandria VA | Dairy Godmother | 703-683-7767 | 2310 Mount Vernon Avenue |
| Alexandria VA | Five Guys Burgers and Fries | 703-549-7991 | 107 N Fayette Street |
| Alexandria VA | Foxfire Grill | 703-914-9280 | 6550 Little River Turnpike |
| Alexandria VA | Gadsby's Tavern | 703-548-1288 | 138 N Royal Street |
| Alexandria VA | Jackson 20 New American Tavern | 703-842-2790 | 480 King Street |
| Alexandria VA | Overwood Restaurant and Bar | 703-535-3340 | 220 N Lee Street |
| Alexandria VA | Taqueria Poblano | 703-548-8226 | 2400-B Mount Vernon Ave |
| Alexandria VA | Tropical Smoothie Cafe | 703-354-0940 | 6552-A Little River Turnpike/H 236 |
| Alexandria VA | Z Pizza | 703-600-1193 | 3217 Duke Street |
| Arlington VA | Asia Bistro & Bar | 703-413-2002 | 1301 S Joyce St |
| Arlington VA | California Pizza Kitchen | 703-412-4900 | 1201 S Hayes St |
| Arlington VA | Chasin' Tails | 703-538-2565 | 2200 N Westmoreland St #103 |
| Arlington VA | Chipotle | 703-294-6669 | 1735 N Lynn Street |
| Arlington VA | Chipotle | 703-920-8779 | 2231 Crystal Drive, Suite 100 |
| Arlington VA | Faccia Luna | 703-276-3099 | 2909 Wilson Blvd |
| Arlington VA | House of Steep | 703-567-1589 | 3800 Lee Hwy |
| Arlington VA | Il Raddiccio | 703-276-2627 | 1801 Clarendon Blvd |
| Arlington VA | La Cate D'Or Cafe | 703-538-3033 | 6876 Lee Hwy |
| Arlington VA | Lyon Hall | 703-741-7636 | 3100 N. Washington Blvd |
| Arlington VA | Mexicali Blues Restaurant & Bar | 703-812-9352 | 2933 Wilson Blvd |
| Arlington VA | Nando's Peri Peri | 571-858-9953 | 1301 S Joyce St |
| Arlington VA | Quiznos | 703-248-8888 | 2201 Wilson Blvd |
| Arlington VA | Quiznos | 703-248-9585 | 1555 Wilson Blvd |
| Arlington VA | Rappahannock Coffee | 703-271-0007 | 2406 Columbia Pike |
| Arlington VA | Rhodeside Grill | 703-243-0145 | 1836 Wilson Blvd |
| Arlington VA | Rocklands Barbeque & Grilling Company | 703-528-9663 | 3471 Washington Blvd |
| Arlington VA | Saigon Saigon | 703-412-0822 | 1101 S Joyce St |
| Arlington VA | Samuel Beckett's Irish Pub | 703-379-0122 | 2800 S Randolph St |
| Arlington VA | Sine Irish Pub & Restaurant | 703-415-4420 | 1301 S Joyce St |
| Arlington VA | T.H.A.I. in Shirlington | 703-931-3203 | 4029 Campbell Avenue |
| Arlington VA | The Boulevard Wood Grille | 703-875-9663 | 2901 Wilson Blvd |
| Arlington VA | The Greene Turtle | 703-741-0901 | 900 N Glebe Rd |
| Arlington VA | The Liberty Tavern | 703-465-9360 | 3195 Wilson Blvd |
| Arlington VA | Withlows | 703-276-9693 | 2854 Wilson Blvd |
| Arlington VA | World of Beer | 703-962-6982 | 901 N Glebe Rd |

| | | | |
|---|---|---|---|
| Ashburn VA | Chipotle | 703-729-9530 | 43660 Yukon Drive |
| Ashburn VA | Tropical Smoothie Cafe | 571-291-9089 | 43670 Greenway Corporate Drive, Suite # 126 |
| Ballston VA | Chipotle | 703-243-9488 | 4300 Wilson Blvd |
| Carrollton VA | Tropical Smoothie Cafe | 757-745-7700 | 13609 Carrollton Blvd # 1 |
| Centerville VA | Tropical Smoothie Cafe | 703-815-1455 | 13609 Carrollton Blvd/H 17/32/258 |
| Centreville VA | Chipotle | 703-830-1438 | 6317 Multiplex Drive |
| Chantilly VA | Baja Fresh | 703-378-3804 | 13940 Lee-Jackson Memorial Highway |
| Chantilly VA | Chipotle | 703-961-0688 | 14416 Chantilly Crossing Lane |
| Chantilly VA | Quiznos | 703-817-1244 | 13661 Lee Jackson Memorial H |
| Charlottesville VA | Bang! | 434-984-2264 | 213 Second Street SW |
| Charlottesville VA | Beer Run | 434-984-BEER (2337) | 156 Carlton Road, Suite 203 |
| Charlottesville VA | Blue Light Grill and Raw Bar | 434-295-1223 | 120 E Main Street |
| Charlottesville VA | Chipotle | 434-872-0212 | 953 Emmet Street |
| Charlottesville VA | Downtown Grille | 434-817-7080 | 201 W Main Street |
| Charlottesville VA | The Ivy Inn Restaurant | 434-977-1222 | 2244 Old Ivy Road |
| Charlottesville VA | The Mudhouse | 434-984-6833 | 213 W Main Street |
| Charlottesville VA | Tropical Smoothie Cafe | 434-975-2233 | 1954 Rio Hill Center |
| Charlottesville VA | Zocalo Restaurant | 434-977-4944 | 201 E Main Street |
| Chesapeake VA | Firehouse Subs | 757-410-5982 | 1217 Battlefield Blvd N/H 168 |
| Clarendon VA | Baja Fresh | 703-528-7010 | 2815 Clarendon Blvd |
| Clifton VA | The Kings Head | 703-266-9181 | 5774 Union Mill Road |
| Fairfax VA | Baja Fresh | 703-352-1792 | 12150 Fairfax Town Center |
| Fairfax VA | Chipotle | 703-934-7099 | 11062 Lee H/H 29 |
| Fairfax VA | Chipotle | 703-288-3890 | 11939 Grand Commons Avenue |
| Fairfax VA | Chipotle | 703-222-1117 | 13042 Fair Lakes Shopping Center |
| Fairfax VA | Courtside Thai Restaurant | 703-934-8880 | 3981 Chain Bridge Road/H 123 |
| Fairfax VA | Coyote Grill Cantina | 703-591-0006 | 10266 Main Street/H 236 |
| Falls Church VA | Chipotle | 571-423-5150 | 8191 Strawberry Lane |
| Falls Church VA | Chipotle | 703-534-6464 | 6299 Seven Corners Center |
| Falls Church VA | Clare and Don's Beach Shack, | 703-532-9283 | 130 N Washington Street/H 29/237 |
| Falls Church VA | Z Pizza | 703-536-6969 | 1051 W Broad Street/H 7 |
| Fredericksburg VA | Castiglias | 540-373-6650 | 324 William Street |
| Fredericksburg VA | Chipotle | 540-548-4554 | 3051 Plank Road |
| Gainesville VA | Chipotle | 571-248-8036 | 5025 Wellington Road |
| Gainesville VA | Z Pizza | 703-753-7492 | 7929 Hertiage Hunt Drive |
| Glen Allen VA | Chipotle | 804-553-0335 | 1070 Virginia Center Parkway |
| Glen Allen VA | Chipotle | 804-290-7804 | 10501 W Broad Street |
| Hampton VA | Chipotle | 757-826-7890 | 3510 Von Schilling Drive |
| Herndon VA | Bagel Cafe | 703-318-7555 | 300 Elder St |
| Herndon VA | Baja Fresh | 703-793-0878 | 2405 Centerville Road |
| Herndon VA | Chipotle | 703-435-3324 | 1144 Elden Street/H 228 |
| Herndon VA | Manhattan Pizza | 703-481-6580 | 2320-C Woodland Crossing Drive |
| Irvington VA | The Local | 804-438-9356 | 4337 Irvington Road/H 200 |
| Leesburg VA | Manhattan Pizza | 703-669-4020 | 659 Potomac Station Drive |
| Leesburg VA | South Street Under | 703-771-9610 | 203 Harrison St SE |
| Lexington VA | Pure Eats | 540-462-6000 | 107 North Main Street |
| Lexington VA | Sweet Treats Bakery | 540-463-3611 | 19 W Washington St |
| Lexington VA | The Red Hen | 540-464-4401 | 11 E Washington Street |
| Lorton VA | Z Pizza | 703-372-1538 | 9451 Lorton Market Street |
| Lynchburg VA | Firehouse Subs | 434-237-2290 | 4018 Wards Road/H 29 |
| Manassas VA | Baja Fresh | 703-365-2077 | 8099 Sudley Road |
| Manassas VA | Chipotle | 703-365-0213 | 7311 Sudley Road/H 234 |
| Manassas VA | Chipotle | 703-530-0010 | 9511 Liberia Avenue |
| Manassas VA | Z Pizza | 703-580-8100 | 12817 Galveston Court |
| McLean VA | Chipotle | 703-288-3890 | 8092 Tysons Corner Center |
| Midlothian VA | Chipotle | 804-744-5242 | 13300 Rittenhouse Drive |
| Midlothian VA | Tropical Smoothie Cafe | 804-763-2900 | 4501 Commonwealth Centre Parkway |
| Newport News VA | Chipotle | 757-882-8313 | 12300 Jefferson Avenue/H 143 |
| Newport News VA | Tropical Smoothie Cafe | 757-833-6256 | 12551 Jefferson Avenue |
| Newport News VA | Tropical Smoothie Cafe | 757-240-5458 | 12368 Warwick Blvd, A-109 |
| Newport News VA | Tropical Smoothie Cafe | 757-595-0600 | 4191 William Styron Square |
| Norfolk VA | Kincaid's Fish, Chop, and Steak House | 757-622-8000 | 300 Monticello Avenue, Suite 147 (MacArthur Center) |
| Norfolk VA | Pasha Mezze | 757-627-1317 | 340 W 22nd Street |
| Norfolk VA | Tropical Smoothie Cafe | 757-455-5694 | 1153 N. Military H/H 13 |

| | | | |
|---|---|---|---|
| Norfolk VA | Tropical Smoothie Cafe | 757-455-5694 | 1153 N. Military H/H 13 |
| Norfolk VA | Tropical Smoothie Cafe | 757-440-7580 | 4316 Monarch Way |
| Norfolk VA | Tropical Smoothie Cafe | 757-440-7580 | 4316 Monarch Way |
| Oakton VA | Tropical Smoothie Cafe | 703-496-5535 | 2918 Chain Bridge Road/H 123 |
| Purcellville VA | Tropical Smoothie Cafe | 540-338-6703 | 609 E. Main Street/H 7 |
| Reston VA | Chipotle | 703-435-0888 | 12152 Sunset Hills Road |
| Reston VA | Clyde's of Reston | 703-787-6601 | 11905 Market Street |
| Richmond VA | Acacia | 804-562-0138 | 2601 W Cary Street |
| Richmond VA | Chipotle | 804-254-9425 | 810 W Grace Street |
| Richmond VA | Chipotle | 804-282-4081 | 4930 W Broad Street/H 250 |
| Richmond VA | Chipotle | 804-360-8033 | 11728 W Broad Street |
| Richmond VA | Chipotle | 804-272-6322 | 9200 Stony Point Parkway |
| Richmond VA | Chipotle | 804-379-2791 | 11440 Midlothian Turnpike |
| Richmond VA | Chipotle Mexican Grill | 804-272-6322 | 9200 Stony Point Parkway |
| Richmond VA | Fresca on Addison | 804-359-TOFU (8638) | 22 S Addison Street |
| Richmond VA | Jason's Deli | 804-323-9390 | 7115 Forest Hill Avenue |
| Richmond VA | Panera Bread | 804-560-9700 | 9200 Stony Point Parkway, Suite 158D |
| Richmond VA | Poe's Pub | 804-648-2120 | 2706 E Main Street/H 60/5 |
| Richmond VA | Smoothie King | 804-355-9934 | 3152 W Cary Street |
| Richmond VA | The Home Team Grill | 804-254-7360 | 1630 W Main/H 147 |
| Roanoke VA | Awful Arthur's | 540-344-2997 | 2229 Colonial Avenue SW |
| Springfield VA | Z Pizza | 703-313-8181 | 6699-B Frontier Drive |
| Staunton VA | Cranberries | 540-885-4755 | 7 S New Street |
| Staunton VA | Wright's Dairy-Rite | 540-886-0435 | 346 Greenville AvenueH 250 |
| Sterling VA | Chipotle | 703-421-5079 | 21031 Tripleseven Road |
| Sterling VA | Tropical Smoothie Cafe | 703-430-1700 | 20995 Davenport Drive |
| Suffolk VA | Firehouse Subs | 757-638-3473 | 6255 College Drive, Suite K/H 135 |
| Suffolk VA | Tropical Smoothie Cafe | 757-539-7774 | 1201 N. Main Street/H 32/460 |
| Virginia Beach VA | Tropical Smoothie Cafe | 757-747-1941 | 4312 Holland Road |
| Virginia Beach VA | Abby Road Restaurant and Pub | 757-425-6330 | 203 22nd Street |
| Virginia Beach VA | Chipotle | 757-671-9460 | 300 Constitution Drive/H 58 |
| Virginia Beach VA | Croc's 19th Street Bistro | 757-428-5444 | 620 19th Street |
| Virginia Beach VA | Jason's Deli | 757-456-5481 | 4554 Virginia Beach Blvd, Suite 980 /H 58 |
| Virginia Beach VA | Tropical Smoothie Cafe | 757-965-6965 | 2865 Lynnhaven Drive |
| Virginia Beach VA | Tropical Smoothie Cafe | 757-422-3970 | 211 25th Street |
| Virginia Beach VA | Tropical Smoothie Cafe | 757-333-6700 | 2728 N. Mall Drive |
| Virginia Beach VA | Tropical Smoothie Cafe | 757-200-0500 | 4001 Virginia Beach Blvd/H 58 |
| Virginia Beach VA | Tropical Smoothie Cafe | 757-430-0144 | 2165 General Booth Blvd/H 615 |
| Virginia Beach VA | Tropical Smoothie Cafe | 757-313-7350 | 401 N Great Neck Road/H 279 |
| Virginia Beach VA | Tropical Smoothie Cafe | 757-460-3350 | 4701 Shore Drive |
| Virginia Beach VA | Tropical Smoothie Cafe | 757-313-7230 | 1255 Fordham Drive |
| Virginia Beach VA | Z Pizza | 757-368-9090 | 3376 Princess Anne Road/H 165 |
| Warrenton VA | Tropical Smoothie Cafe | 540-428-1818 | 251 W Lee H/H 29/211 |
| Williamsburg VA | Aroma's | 757-221-6676 | 431 Prince George St |
| Williamsburg VA | Firehouse Subs | 757-208-0688 | 1430 Richmond Road, Suite 1105/H 60 |
| Williamsburg VA | Pierce's Bar-B-Que | 757-565-2955 | 447 Rochambeau Dr |
| Winchester VA | Chipotle | 540-667-9534 | 2012 Pleasant Valley Road |
| Winchester VA | Tropical Smoothie Cafe | 540-667-0002 | 152 Market Street |
| Woodbridge VA | Chipotle | 703-490-9746 | 2457 Prince William Parkway |

**Washington Listings**

| | | | |
|---|---|---|---|
| Anacortes WA | Brown Lantern | 360-293-2544 | 412 Commercial Avenue |
| Auburn WA | Pick Quick Drive-In | 253-248-1949 | 1132 Auburn Way N |
| Bainbridge Island WA | Bainbridge Thai Cuisine | 206-780-2403 | 330 Madison Avenue S |
| Bainbridge Island WA | Emmy's VegeHouse | 206-855-2996 | 100 Winslow Way W |
| Bainbridge Island WA | Pegasus Coffee House | 206-842-6725 | 131 Parfitt Way |
| Battle Ground WA | Burgerville | 360-687-7308 | 217 W Main Street |
| Bellevue WA | 520 Bar & Grill | 425-450-0520 | 10146 Main Street |
| Bellevue WA | Amore Chocolates | 425-453-4553 | 10149 Main Street |
| Bellevue WA | Chipotle | 425-467-0660 | 10503 NE 4th Street |
| Bellingham WA | Community Food Coop | 360-734-8158 | 315 Westerly Road |
| Camas WA | Burgerville | 360-834-3289 | 518 NE 3rd Avenue |
| Centralia WA | Burgerville | 360-736-5212 | 818 Harrison Avenue |
| Cle Elum WA | Pioneer Coffee | 509-674-4100 | 121 Pennsylvania Avenue |

472

| | | | |
|---|---|---|---|
| Edmonds WA | The Dining Dog | 425-314-4612 | 9635 Firdale Avenue N |
| Everett WA | Jamba Juice | 425-513-1656 | 305 SE Everett Mall Way, Suite 30/H 99 |
| Federal Way WA | Chipotle | 253-945-8287 | 31827 Pacific Highway S/H 99 |
| Fife WA | Pick Quick Drive-In | 253-922-5599 | 4306 Pacific H E |
| Friday Harbor WA | Friday's Crabhouse | 360-378-8801 | 65 Front Street |
| Friday Harbor WA | SJ Coffee Roasting Company | 360-378-4443 | 18 Cannery Landing |
| Friday Harbor WA | The Bean Cafe | 360-370-5858 | 150B First Street |
| Friday Harbor WA | Vic's Driftwood Drive In | 360-378-VICS (8427) | 25 2nd Street |
| Issaquah WA | Chipotle Mexican Grill | 425-837-9100 | 775 NW Gilman Blvd |
| Kelso WA | Burgerville | 360-501-4354 | 600 W Main Street |
| Kent WA | Chipotle | 253-850-3777 | 512 Ramsay Way |
| Kent WA | Jamba Juice | 253-852-4078 | 417 Ramsay Way, Suite 107 |
| Kent WA | Jamba Juice | | 417 Ramsay Way, Suite 107 |
| Kent WA | Johnny Rockets | 253-854-1573 | 418 Ramsey Way |
| Kirkland WA | Hector's Restaurant | 425-827-4811 | 112 Lake St S |
| Kirkland WA | Olive You and the Tervelli Ultralounge | 425-250-1555 | 89 Kirkland Avenue |
| Lacey WA | Jamba Juice | 360-459-1162 | 1350 Marvin Road NE, Suite F |
| Lynnwood WA | Chipotle | 425-776-7549 | 4120 196th Street, Suite 150 |
| Lynnwood WA | Jamba Juice | 425-640-7297 | 3000 184th Street, #870 |
| Manson WA | Blueberry Hills Farm and Restaurant | 509-687-2379 | 1315 Washington Street |
| Mercer Island WA | Bennett's Pure Food Bistro | 206-232-2759 | 7650 SE 27th Street |
| Okremos WA | Gilbert and Blake's | 517-349-1300 | 3554 Okemos Road |
| Olympia WA | The Flaming Eggplant Cafe | 360-867-5092 | 2700 Evergreen Parkway NW |
| Redmond WA | Chipotle Mexican Grill | 425-558-5868 | 17875 Redmond Way/H 202 |
| Redmond WA | Victors Celtic Coffee Company | 425-881-6451 | 7993 Gilman Street |
| Seattle WA | Bark! Espresso | 206-364-0185 | 11335 Roosevelt Way NE |
| Seattle WA | Belltown Pub | 206-448-6210 | 2322 1st Ave |
| Seattle WA | Cafe Campagne | 206-728-2233 | 1600 Post Alley |
| Seattle WA | Cedarbrook Lodge Restaurant & Bar | 206-901-9268 | 18525 36th Avenue South |
| Seattle WA | Chipotle | 206-362-0285 | 401 NE Northgate Way, Suite 1119 |
| Seattle WA | Chipotle - The Ave | 206-547-4644 | 4231 University Way NE |
| Seattle WA | Duchess Tavern | 206-527-8606 | 2827 NE 55th St |
| Seattle WA | Essential Baking Company and Cafe | 206-545-0444 | 1604 N 34th Street |
| Seattle WA | Essential Baking Company and Cafe | 206-328-0078 | 2719 E Madison Street |
| Seattle WA | Fiddler's Inn Pub & Restaurant | 206-525-0752 | 9219 35th Avenue Northeast |
| Seattle WA | Fiddler's Inn Pub & Restaurant | 206-525-0752 | 9219 35th Ave NE |
| Seattle WA | Five Hooks Fish Grill | 206-403-1263 | 2232 Queen Anne Ave N |
| Seattle WA | Great Harvest Bread | 206-365-4778 | 17171 Bothell Way NE # A121/H 522 |
| Seattle WA | Great Harvest Bread Co. | 206-524-4873 | 5408 Sand Point Way NE/H 513 |
| Seattle WA | Hangar Cafe | 206-762-0204 | 6261 13th Ave S |
| Seattle WA | India Bistro Ballard | 206-783-5080 | 2301 NW Market Street |
| Seattle WA | Jamba Juice | 206-522-3063 | 2690 NE 49th Street |
| Seattle WA | Jamba Juice | 206-935-4408 | 2600 SW Barton Street, #A4 |
| Seattle WA | Johnny Rockets | 206-522-5282 | 2685 NE University Street #D3 |
| Seattle WA | La Isla Seattle | 206-789-0516 | 2320 NW Market Street |
| Seattle WA | Le Rêve Bakery & Café | 206-623-7383 | 1805 Queen Anne Ave N |
| Seattle WA | Liberty | 206-323-9898 | 517 15th Ave E |
| Seattle WA | Lombardi's Cucina | 206-783-0055 | 2200 N.W. Market Street |
| Seattle WA | Lottie's Lounge | 206-725-0519 | 4900 Rainier Avenue S/H 167 |
| Seattle WA | Matador Restaurant & Tequila Bar | 206-297-2855 | 2221 NW Market St |
| Seattle WA | Mulleadys Irish Pub and Restaurant | 206-283-8843 | 3055 21st Avenue W |
| Seattle WA | Norm's Eatery & Ale House | 206-547-1417 | 460 N 36th St |
| Seattle WA | Norm's Eatery and Ale House | 206-547-1417 | 460 N 36th Street |
| Seattle WA | Pink Door | 206-443-3241 | 1919 Post Aly |
| Seattle WA | Portage Bay Cafe | 206-547-8230 | 4130 Roosevelt Way NE |
| Seattle WA | Sip and Ship | 206-789-4488 | 1752 NW Market Street |
| Seattle WA | Stumbling Goat | 206-784-3535 | 6722 Greenwood Avenue N |
| Seattle WA | Summit Public House | 206-324-7611 | 601 Summit Ave E Ste 102 |
| Seattle WA | The Barking Dog Alehouse | 206-782-2974 | 705 NW 70th Street |
| Seattle WA | The Blue Saucer | 206-453-4955 | 9127 Roosevelt Way NE |
| Seattle WA | The Dray | 206-453-4527 | 708 NW 65th St |
| Seattle WA | The Lookout Bar & Grill | 206-329-0454 | 757 Bellevue Ave E |
| Seattle WA | The Luna Park Cafe | 206-935-7250 | 2918 SW Avalon Way |
| Seattle WA | The Twilight Exit | 206-324-7462 | 2514 E Cherry St |
| Seattle WA | Thrive Cafe | 206-525-0300 | 1026 NE 65th Street, #A102 |

| | | | |
|---|---|---|---|
| Snohomish WA | Grilla Bites | 360-568-7333 | 1020 1st Street, Suite 104 |
| Spokane WA | Didier's Yogurt & More | 509-466-8434 | 10410 N Division St |
| Spokane WA | Main Market Co-op | 509-458-COOP (2667) | 44 W Main Avenue |
| Spokane WA | Sante Restaurant & Charcuterie | 509-315-4613 | 404 W Main Avenue |
| Spokane WA | Sante Restaurant & Charcuterie | 509-315-4613 | 404 W Main Avenue |
| Tukwila WA | Chipotle | 425-207-0300 | 17250 Southcenter Parkway |
| Vancouver WA | Burgerville | 360-696-0308 | 2200 E Fourth Plain Blvd |
| Vancouver WA | Burgerville | 360-892-9781 | 10903 NE Fourth Plain Blvd |
| Vancouver WA | Burgerville | 360-944-6230 | 8320 NE Vancouver Plaza Drive |
| Vancouver WA | Burgerville | 360-892-9781 | 10903 NE Fourth Plain Blvd |
| Vancouver WA | Burgerville | 360-694-4971 | 7401 E Mill Plain Blvd |
| Vancouver WA | Burgerville | 360-567-1550 | 6700 NE 162nd Avenue/H 500 |
| Vancouver WA | Burgerville | 360-254-9301 | 11704 SE Mill Plain Blvd |
| Vancouver WA | Burgerville | 360-574-1981 | 9909 NE H 99 |
| Vancouver WA | Chipotle | 360-256-2355 | 915 SE 164th Avenue |
| Vancouver WA | Jamba Juice | 360-260-5061 | 8101 NE Parkway Drive, Suite D-6 |
| Vancouver WA | Jamba Juice | 360-718-2169 | 16501 SE Mill Plain Blvd, Suite 102 |
| Vancouver WA | McMenamins East Vancouver | 360-254-3950 | 1900 NE 162nd, Suite B107 |
| W Seattle WA | Beveridge Place Pub | 206-932-9906 | 6413 California Avenue SW |
| Woodinville WA | Molbaks Nursery and Cafe | 425-483-5000 | 13625 NE 175th Street |
| Woodland WA | Burgerville | 360-225-7965 | 1120 Lewis River Road |

**West Virginia Listings**

| | | | |
|---|---|---|---|
| Beckley WV | Pasquale Mira Restaurant | 304-255-5253 | 224 Harper Park Drive |
| Berkeley Springs WV | Maria's Garden and Inn | 304-258-2021 | 42 Independence Street |
| Charleston WV | Ellen's Homemade Ice Cream | 304-343-6488 | 225 Capitol Street |
| Martinsburg WV | Tropical Smoothie Cafe | 304-264-4445 | 171 Retail Commons Parkway |
| Thomas WV | The Purple Fiddle | 304-463-4040 | 21 East Avenue |

**Wisconsin Listings**

| | | | |
|---|---|---|---|
| Appleton WI | Acoco Coffee | 920-993-1458 | 500 W College Avenue |
| Appleton WI | Angels | 920-993-8847 | 1401 E John Street |
| Appleton WI | Aspen Coffee and Tea | 920-882-9336 | 107 E College Avenue/H 125 |
| Appleton WI | Brewed Awakenings | 920-882-9336 | 107 E College Avenue |
| Baileys Harbor WI | Harbor Fish Market & Grille | 920-839-9999 | 8080 Hwy 57 |
| Baileys Harbor WI | Harbor Fish Market and Grille | 920-839-9999 | 8080 H 57 |
| Beloit WI | Bushel and Peck's Local Market | 608-363-3911 | 328 State Street |
| Brookfield WI | Cafe Manna | 262-790-2340 | 3815 N Brookfield Road |
| Brookfield WI | Chipotle | 262-781-3692 | 3705 N 124th Street |
| Brookfield WI | Chipotle | 262-796-0463 | 15375 Bluemound Road/H 18 |
| Egg Harbor WI | Blue Horse Bistro | 920-868-1471 | 4158 Main Street |
| Egg Harbor WI | The Bistro at Liberty Square | 920-868-4800 | 7755 H 42 |
| Ellison Bay WI | The Viking Grill | 920-854-2998 | 12029 H 42 |
| Elm Grove WI | The Grove Restaurant | 262-814-1890 | 890 Elm Grove Road |
| Fish Creek WI | Gibraltar Grill | 920-868-4745 | 3993 Main Street/H 42 |
| Fish Creek WI | Pelletier's | 920-868-3313 | 4199 Main Street |
| Fish Creek WI | Sweetie Pie's | 920-868-2743 | 9106 H 42 |
| Fitchburg WI | Laredo's Fitchburg | 608-274-7370 | 2935 Fish Hatchery Road |
| Glendale WI | Panera Bread | 414-962-4775 | 5595 Port Washington Road |
| Grand Chute WI | Chipotle | 920-636-4300 | 111 N Mall Drive |
| Hales Corner WI | Chipotle | 414-427-1667 | 5794 S 108th Street |
| La Crosse WI | Rudy's Drive In Restaurant | 608-782-2200 | 1004 La Crosse Street/H 16 |
| Madison WI | Bandung Indonesian Restaurant | 608-255-6910 | 600 Williamson Street |
| Madison WI | Chipotle | 608-826-0919 | 8422 Old Sauk Road |
| Madison WI | Chipotle | 608-242-7334 | 4628 E Washington Avenue/H 151 |
| Madison WI | Come Back In | 608-258-8619 | 508 E Wilson Street |
| Madison WI | Harvest Restaurant | 608-255-6075 | 21 N. Pinckney Street |
| Madison WI | Hawk's Bar and Grill | 608-256-4295 | 425 State Street |
| Madison WI | Kabul Restaurant | 608-256-6322 | 541 State Street |
| Madison WI | Marigold Kitchen | 608-661-5559 | 118 S Pinckney Street |
| Madison WI | Panera Bread | 608-826-0808 | 601 Junction Road |
| Madison WI | Willy Street Co-op | 608-251-6776 | 1221 Williamson Street |
| Menasha WI | WeatherVane Restaurant | 920-725-2824 | 186 Main Street |
| Menomonie WI | Menomonie Market Food Co-op | 715-235-6533 | 521 2nd Street, E |

| | | | |
|---|---|---|---|
| Middleton WI | Capital Brewery | 608-836-7100 | 7734 Terrace Avenue |
| Middleton WI | Chipotle Mexican Grill | 608-826-0919 | 8422 Old Sauk Road |
| Middleton WI | Claddagh | 608-833-5070 | 1611 Aspen Commons |
| Middleton WI | Johnny's Italian Steakhouse | 608-831-3705 | 8390 Market St. |
| Milwaukee WI | Alterra Cafe At the Lake | 414-223-4551 | 1701 N Lincoln Memorial Drive |
| Milwaukee WI | Apollo Cafe | 414-272-2233 | 1310 E Brady Street |
| Milwaukee WI | Beans & Barley | 414-278-7878 | 1901 E North Avenue/H 32 |
| Milwaukee WI | Beer Belly's | 414-481-5520 | 512 W Layton Avenue |
| Milwaukee WI | Brewed Cafe | 414-276-2739 | 1208 E Brady Street |
| Milwaukee WI | Cafe Hollander | 414-963-6366 | 2608 N Downer Avenue |
| Milwaukee WI | Cafe Hollander | 414-475-6771 | 7677 W State Street/H 181 |
| Milwaukee WI | Chipotle | 414-223-4710 | 600 E Ogden Avenue |
| Milwaukee WI | Chipotle | 414-389-1380 | 3232 S 27th Street/H 41 |
| Milwaukee WI | Coast | 414-727-5555 | 931 E Wisconsin Avenue |
| Milwaukee WI | Crazy Water | 414-645-2606 | 839 S 2nd Street |
| Milwaukee WI | Milwaukee Waterfront Deli | 414-220-9300 | 761 N Water Street |
| Milwaukee WI | Nomad World Pub | 414-224-8111 | 1401 E Brady Street |
| Milwaukee WI | Paddy's Pub | 414-223-3496 | 2339 N Murray Ave |
| Milwaukee WI | Regano's Roman Coin | 414-278-9334 | 1004 East Brady St |
| Milwaukee WI | Riverwalk Bistro | 414-272-4200 | 223 N Water Street |
| Milwaukee WI | Riverwest Cooperative | 414-264-7933 | 733 E Clarke Street |
| Milwaukee WI | Rock Bottom Restaurant and Brewery | 414-276-3030 | 740 N Plankinton Ave, #1 |
| Milwaukee WI | The Hi Hat Garage | 414-220-8090 | 1701 N Arlington Place |
| Milwaukee WI | The Palomino | 414-747-1007 | 2491 S Superior Street |
| Milwaukee WI | The Wicked Hop | 414-223-0345 | 345 N Broadway |
| Milwaukee WI | The Yard at Iron Horse Hotel | 414-374-4766 | 500 W Florida Street |
| Minocqua WI | The Vine | 715-614-5920 | 203 Front Street |
| Minoqua WI | Minoqua Island Cafe | 715-356-6977 | 314 Oneida Street/H 51 |
| Mount Pleasant WI | Chipotle | 262-632-0985 | 5720 Washington Avenue/H 20 |
| Neenah WI | Zuppas, Market, Cafe, and Catering | 920-720-5045 | 1540 S Commercial Street |
| Newport WI | O'Brien's Pub | 401-849-6623 | 501 Thames St |
| Oshkosh WI | A & W | 920-233-4677 | 2187 W 9th Avenue |
| Oshkosh WI | Ardy and Ed's Drive In | 920-231-5455 | 2413 S Main Street/H 45 |
| Oshkosh WI | Leon's Frozen Custard | 920-231-7755 | 121 W Murdock |
| Racine WI | Freddie's Friki Tiki | 262-635-0533 | 207 Gas Light Drive |
| Shorewood WI | Einstein Brothers Bagels | 414-962-9888 | 4301 N Oakland Avenue |
| Shorewood Hills WI | Panera Bread | 608-442-9994 | 3416 University Avenue |
| Stevens Point WI | Emy J's | 715-345-0471 | 1009 First Street |
| Sturgeon Bay WI | Gilmo's | 920-824-5440 | 3600 H CC |
| Sturgeon Bay WI | Stone Harbor Restaurant and Pub | 920-746-9004 | 107 N 1st Avenue |
| Sturgeon Bay WI | Waterfront Mary's | 920-743-3690 | 3662 N Duluth Avenue |
| Washington Island WI | Deer Run Pub | 920-847-2017 | 1885 Michigan Road |
| Waupaca WI | Clear Water Harbor | 715-258-2866 | N2757 H QQ |
| Wauwatosa WI | Chipotle | 414-258-6649 | 2711 N Mayfair Road, Suite A/H 100 |
| Wauwatosa WI | Hector's | 414-258-5600 | 7118 W State Street |
| Wisconsin Dells WI | Brat House Grill | 608-254-8505 | 49 Wisconsin Dells Parkway S/H 12/23 |
| Wisconsin Dells WI | Culver's Restaurant | 608-253-9080 | 312 Broadway |
| Wisconsin Dells WI | Culvers of Lake Delton | 608-253-3195 | 1070 Wisconsin Dells Parkway/H 12/23 |
| Wisconsin Dells WI | Mexicali Rose | 608-254-6036 | 195 H 13 |
| Wisconsin Dells WI | Sand Bar | 608-253-3073 | 130 Washington Ave |
| Woodruff WI | Anthony's Restaurante | 715-358-1999 | 1419 H 47 |

**Wyoming Listings**

| | | | |
|---|---|---|---|
| Casper WY | Bosco's Italian Restaurant | 307-265-9658 | 847 E A Street |
| Cheyenne WY | Chipotle Mexican Grill | 307-632-6200 | 1508 Dell Range Blvd |
| Cheyenne WY | Shadows Pub & Grill | 307-634-7625 | 115 W 15th Street |
| Cody WY | Grizzly Creek Coffee Co | 307-527-7238 | 1491 Sheridan Avenue/H 14/16/20 |
| Cody WY | Outpost Restaurant | 307-527-5510 | 4 Van Dyke Road |
| Cody WY | Silver Dollar Bar | 307-527-7666 | 1313 Sheridan Avenue/H 14/16 |
| Jackson WY | Bon Appe Thai | 307-734-0245 | 245 W Pearl Street |
| Jackson WY | Cafe Genevieve | 307-732-1910 | 135 East Broadway |
| Jackson WY | Pica's Mexican Taqueria | 307-734-4457 | 1160 Alpine Lane |
| Laramie WY | Bailey's Restaurant and Patio | 307-742-6411 | 2410 E Grand Avenue/H 30 |
| Sheridan WY | Lulu's Cafe | 307-674-5858 | 118 N Brooks |

| | | | |
|---|---|---|---|
| Sheridan WY | Sidewalk Cafe | 307-673-3195 | 1333 W 5th Street/H 330 |
| Wilson WY | Pearl Street Bagels | 307-739-1261 | Fish Creek Center |

**Canada Listings**

**Alberta Listings**

| | | | |
|---|---|---|---|
| Calgary AB | Ranchman's Cookhouse and Dancehall | 403-253-1100 | 9615 Macleod Trail SW |
| Jasper AB | Cafe Mondo | 780-852-9676 | 616 Patricia Street |

**British Columbia Listings**

| | | | |
|---|---|---|---|
| Abbotsford BC | Lepp Farm Market | 604-851-LEPP (851-5377) | 33955 Clayburn Road |
| Abbotsford BC | Wired Monk | 604-746-3683 | #111-1975 McCallum Road |
| Abbotsford BC | Wired Monk | 604-746-1136 | #100 1910 N. Parallel Road |
| Boston Bar BC | Simon's Café | 604-867-9277 | 43111 Trans Canada H |
| Coquuitlam BC | BG Urban Grill | 604-945-9494 | 2991 Lougheed Highway |
| Kelowna BC | The Rotten Grape | 250-717-8466 | 231 Bernard Avenue |
| New Westminster BC | The Hide Out Cafe | 604-521-3344 | 716 Carnarvon Street |
| Port Hardy BC | A&W Restaurant | 250-949-2345 | 8950 Granville Street |
| Port Hardy BC | Captain Hardy's | 250-949-7133 | 7145 Market Street |
| Prince Rupert BC | Cowpuccino's Coffee House | 250-627-1395 | 25 Cow Bay Road |
| Prince Rupert BC | Javadotcup | 250-622-2822 | 516 Third Avenue W |
| Tofino BC | Caffe Vincente | 250-725-2599 | 441 Campbell Street/H 4 |
| Tofino BC | SOBO Good Food To Go | 250-725-2341 | 311 Neill |
| Vancouver BC | Aphrodite's | 604-733-8308 | 3598 W 4th Avenue |
| Vancouver BC | Bread Garden Bakery Cafe | 604-638-3982 | 889 West Pender Street |
| Vancouver BC | Don Francesco Ristorante | 604-685-7770 | 860 Burrard Street |
| Vancouver BC | Le Gavroche Restaurant | 604-685-3924 | 1616 Alberni Street |
| Victoria BC | Cafe Brio | 250-383-0009 | 944 Fort Street |
| Victoria BC | Noodle Box | 250-360-1312 | 626 Fisgard St |
| Victoria BC | Pagliacci's | 250-386-1662 | 1011 Broad Street |
| Victoria BC | Saigon Harbor Vietnamese Restaurant | 250-386-3354 | 1012 Blanshard St |
| West Vancouver BC | BG Urban Grill | 604-925-0181 | 550 Park Royal North |
| Williams Lake BC | Joey's Grill | 250-398-8727 | 177 Yorston Street |

**New Brunswick Listings**

| | | | |
|---|---|---|---|
| St John NB | Infusion Tea Room | 506-693-8327 | 41 Charlotte Street |

**Ontario Listings**

| | | | |
|---|---|---|---|
| Kingston ON | Pan Chanco | 613-544-7790 | 44 Princess Street/H 2 |
| Markham ON | Carmelina | 905-477-7744 | 7501 Woodbine Avenue |
| Ottawa ON | Carmello's | 613-563-4349 | 300 Sparks Street |
| Toronto ON | Charlotte Room Restaurant | 416-591-1738 | 19 Charlotte Street |
| Toronto ON | Mitzi's Cafe and Gallery | 416-588-1234 | 100 Sorauren Avenue |
| Toronto ON | The Longest Yard Restaurant and Bar | 416-480-9273 | 535 Mount Pleasant Road |
| Toronto ON | Whistler's Grille and Cafe Bar | 416-421-1344 | 995 Broadview Avenue |

**Prince Edward Island Listings**

| | | | |
|---|---|---|---|
| Charlottetown PE | Fishbone's | 902-628-6569 | 136 Richmond Street |
| Charlottetown PE | Water Prince Corner Shop | 902-368-3212 | 141 Water Street |

**Quebec Listings**

| | | | |
|---|---|---|---|
| Montreal PQ | Brioche Lyonnaise | 514-842-7017 | 1593 St. Denis Street |
| Montreal PQ | Byla Byla | 514-368-1888 | 1395, Avenue Dollard Verdun/Lasalle, Lachine |
| Montreal PQ | Jardin Asean Garden | 514-487-8868 | 5828 Sherbrooke West |
| Quebec PQ | Chez Rabelais | 418-694-9460 | 2, rue du Petit-Champlain |
| Quebec PQ | Le Buffet de l'Antiquaire | 418-692-2661 | 95 rue Saint-Paul |

476

**Saskatchewan Listings**

| Regina SK | 13th Ave Food & Coffee House | 306-522-3111 | 3136 13th Avenue |
| Regina SK | Copper Kettle Restaurant | 306-525-3545 | 1953 Scarth Street |

**Yukon Listings**

| Beaver Creek YU | Buckshot Betty's Restaurant and Rooms | 867-862-7111 | 1202 Alaska H |
| Dawson City YU | The Jack London Dining Room | 867-993-5346 | Corner of Second and Queen |
| Haines Junction YU | Madley's General Store | 867-634-2200 | Box 5371 |
| Haines Junction YU | The Village Bakery | 867-634-BUNS (2867) | Corner of Logan and Kluane Streets |

Chapter 7

# Off-Leash Dog Parks

## Alabama Listings

| Cullman AL | Heritage City Park Dog Park | 334-365-9997 | 200 South Court Street |
| Daphne AL | Daphne Dog Park | 251-621-3703 | Whispering Pines Road |
| Fairhope AL | Fairhope Dog Park | 251-928-2136 | 701 Volanta Avenue |
| Prattville AL | Cooter's Pond Dog Park | 334-365-9997 | 1844 Cooters Pond Road |

## Alaska Listings

| Anchorage AK | Conners Lake Park | 907-343-8118 | Jewel Lake Road |
| Anchorage AK | Far North Bicentennial Park | 907-343-4355 | Campbell Airstrip Road |
| Anchorage AK | Russian Jack Springs Park | 907-343-8118 | 6th Avenue and Boniface Parkway |
| Anchorage AK | University Lake Park | 907-343-8118 | Bragaw Street and University Lake Drive |

## Arizona Listings

| Avondale AZ | Avondale Friendship Dog Park | 623-333-2400 | 12325 W McDowell Road |
| Casa Grande AZ | A Leash on Life Dog Park | 520-421-8600 | Pinal Ave at Rodeo Rd |
| Chandler AZ | Nozomi Dog Park | 480-782-2727 | 250 S. Kyrene Rd |
| Chandler AZ | Shawnee Dog Park | 480-782-2727 | 1400 W. Mesquite |
| Chandler AZ | Snedigar Bark Park | 480-782-2727 | 4500 S. Basha Rd |
| Flagstaff AZ | Barkmaster Dog Park | | 3150 N. Alta Vista |
| Flagstaff AZ | Thorpe Park Bark Park | 928-779-7690 | 600 N. Thorpe Road |
| Fountain Hills AZ | Desert Vista Off-Leash Dog Park | 480-816-5152 | 11800 North Desert Vista |
| Gilbert AZ | Cosmo Dog Park | 480-503-6200 | 2502 E. Ray Road |
| Gilbert AZ | Dog Park at Crossroads | 480-503-6200 | 2155 E. Knox Rd |
| Glendale AZ | Foothills Park Dog Park | 623-930-2820 | 57th Avenue and Union Hills Drive |
| Glendale AZ | Northern Horizon Dog Park | 623-930-2820 | 63rd and Northern Avenue |
| Glendale AZ | Sahuaro Ranch Dog Park | | 63rd Avenue |
| Goodyear AZ | Roscoe Dog Park | 623-882-7537 | 15600 W Roeser |
| Lake Havasu City AZ | Lions Dog Park @ London Bridge Beach | 928-453-8686 | 1340 McCulloch Blvd. |
| Marana AZ | Silverbell District Dog Park | | 7548 N Silverbell Road |
| Mesa AZ | Quail Run Park Dog Park | 480-644-2352 | 4155 E. Virginia |
| Oro Valley AZ | James D. Kriegh Dog Park | 520-229-5050 | 23 W Calle Concordia |
| Payson AZ | The Payson Off-Leash Dog Park | 928-474-2216 ext.109 | McLane Road |
| Phoenix AZ | Grovers Basin Dog Park | 602-262-6696 | 20th Street at Grovers Ave |
| Phoenix AZ | Mofford Sports Complex Dog Park | 602-261-8011 | 9833 N. 25th Avenue |
| Phoenix AZ | PetsMart Dog Park | 602-262-6971 | 21st Avenue |
| Phoenix AZ | Phoenix Sky Harbor International Airport | 602-273-3300 | E Sky Harbor Blvd |
| Phoenix AZ | RJ Dog Park at Pecos Park | 602-262-6862 | 48th Street |
| Phoenix AZ | Steele Indian School Dog Park | 602-495-0739 | 7th Street at Indian School Road |
| Prescott AZ | Willow Creek Dog Park | 928-777-1100 | Willow Creek Road |
| Prescott Valley AZ | Mountain Valley Dog Park | 928-759-3090 | 8600 E Nace Lane |
| Sahuarita AZ | Anamax Off-Leash Dog Park | 520-625-2731 | 17501 S. Camino de las Quintas |
| Scottsdale AZ | Chaparral Park Dog Park | 480-312-2353 | 5401 N. Hayden Road |
| Scottsdale AZ | Horizon Park Dog Park | 480-312-2650 | 15444 N. 100th Street |
| Scottsdale AZ | Vista del Camino Park Dog Park | 480-312-2330 | 7700 E. Roosevelt Street |
| Sedona AZ | Sedona Dog Park | 928-301-0226 | NW Corner of Carruth and Soldiers Pass Roads |
| Surprise AZ | Surprise Dog Park | 623-266-4500 | 15930 N. Bullard Avenue |
| Tempe AZ | Creamery Park | 480-350-5200 | 8th Street and Una Avenue |
| Tempe AZ | Creamery Park Dog Park | 480-350-5200 | 8th St. & Una |
| Tempe AZ | Jaycee Park | 480-350-5200 | 5th Street and Hardy Drive |
| Tempe AZ | Jaycee Park Dog Park | 480-350-5200 | 5th St. and Hardy Dr. |
| Tempe AZ | Mitchell Park | 480-350-5200 | Mitchell Drive and 9th Street |
| Tempe AZ | Mitchell Park Dog Park | 480-350-5200 | Mitchell Dr. & 9th St. |
| Tempe AZ | Papago Park | 480-350-5200 | Curry Road and College Avenue |
| Tempe AZ | Papago Park Dog Park | 480-350-4311 | Curry Rd. and College Ave. |
| Tempe AZ | Tempe Sports Complex Dog Park | 480-350-5200 | Warner Rd & Hardy Dr |

| Tempe AZ | Tempe Sports Complex Dog Park | 480-350-4311 | 8401 S. Hardy Dr. |
|---|---|---|---|
| Tucson AZ | Christopher Columbus Dog Park | 520-791-4873x0 | 4600 N. Silverbell |
| Tucson AZ | Gene C. Reid Park Off-Leash Area | 520-791-3204 | 900 S. Randolph Way |
| Tucson AZ | Jacobs Dog Park | 520-791-4873x0 | 3300 N. Fairview Ave. |
| Tucson AZ | McDonald District Park Off-Leash Area | 520-877-6000 | 4100 N. Harrison Road |
| Tucson AZ | Northwest Center Off-Leash Dog Park | 520-791-4873x0 | 2075 N. 6th Ave |
| Tucson AZ | Palo Verde Park Off-Leash Area | 520-791-4873 | 300 S. Mann Avenue |
| Tucson AZ | Udall Dog Park | 520-791-5930 | 7290 E. Tanque Verde |
| Yuma AZ | The Bark Park | 928-373-5243 | 1705 E. Palo Verde Street |

**Arkansas Listings**

| Mountain Home AR | Mountain Home Dog Park | | 1831 Rossi Road |
|---|---|---|---|

**California Listings**

| Angels Camp CA | JD's Bark Park | 209-736-0404 | 3069 Highway 49 S |
|---|---|---|---|
| Aptos CA | Polo Grounds Dog Park | 831-454-7900 | 2255 Huntington Avenue |
| Arcadia CA | Arcadia Dog Park | 626-574-5400 | Second Avenue and Colorado Blvd |
| Arroyo Grande CA | Elm Street Dog Park | | 380 Elm Street |
| Atascadero CA | Heilmann Dog Park | | |
| Auburn CA | Ashley Memorial Dog Park | 530-887-9993 | Auburn Ravine Road (back of Ashford Park) |
| Bakersfield CA | Centennial Park Off-Leash Dog Park | 661-326-3866 | On Montclair north of Stockdale Hwy |
| Bakersfield CA | Kroll Park Off-Leash Dog Park | 661-326-3866 | Kroll Way and Montalvo Dr |
| Bakersfield CA | University Park Off-Leash Dog Park | 661-326-3866 | University Ave east of Columbus |
| Bakersfield CA | Wilson Park Off-Leash Dog Park | 661-326-3866 | Wilson Road and Hughes Lane |
| Belmont CA | Cipriani Dog Park | 650-365-3524 | 2525 Buena Vista Avenue |
| Berkeley CA | Cesar Chavez Park Off-Leash Dog Area | 510-981-6700 | 11 Spinnaker Way |
| Berkeley CA | Ohlone Dog Park | | Hearst Avenue |
| Bishop CA | Bishop Dog Park | | 690 N Main Street /H 395 |
| Buena Park CA | Bellis Park Dog Park | 714-236-3860 | 7171 8th Street |
| Burlingame CA | Bayside Park Dog Park | 650-558-7300 | 1125 South Airport Blvd |
| Calabasas CA | Calabasas Bark Park | | Las Virgines Road |
| Cambria CA | Cambria Dog Park | | Main Street and Santa Rosa Creek Rd |
| Campbell CA | Los Gatos Creek County Dog Park | 408-866-2105 | 1250 Dell Avenue |
| Carlsbad CA | Ann D. L'Heureaux Memorial Dog Park | 760-434-2825 | Carlsbad Village Drive |
| Carmichael CA | Carmichael Park and Dog Park | 916-485-5322 | Fair Oaks Blvd & Grant Ave |
| Castro Valley CA | Earl Warren Dog Park | 510-881-6700 | 4660 Crow Canyon |
| Chico CA | DeGarmo Dog Park | | Leora Court |
| Chico CA | Lower Bidwell Park Off-Leash Hours | 530-891-4671 | Various Entrances |
| Chula Vista CA | Dog Park at Otay Ranch Town Center | 619-656-9100 | Eastlake Pkwy At Olympic Pkwy |
| Chula Vista CA | Montevalle Park Dog Park | 619-691-5269 | 840 Duncan Ranch Road |
| Citrus Heights CA | C-Bar-C Dog Park | 916-725-1585 | Oak Avenue east of Fair Oaks |
| Claremont CA | Pooch Park | | 100 S. College Avenue |
| Concord CA | Newhall Community Park Paw Patch | 925-671-3329 | Turtle Creek Road |
| Concord CA | Paw Patch in Newhall Community Park | 925-671-3329 | Clayton Rd & Newhall Pkwy |
| Corona CA | Butterfield Park Dog Park | 909-736-2241 | 1886 Butterfield Drive |
| Corona CA | Corona Dog Park | 888-636-7387 | Butterfield Drive and Smith Avenue |
| Corona CA | Harada Heritage Dogs Park | 888-636-7387 | 13100 65th Street |
| Costa Mesa CA | Bark Park Dog Park | 949-73-4101 | Arlington Dr |
| Culver City CA | Culver City Off-Leash Dog Park | 310-390-9114 | Duquesne Ave near Jefferson Blvd |
| Davis CA | Toad Hollow Dog Park | 530-757-5656 | 1919 Second Street |
| Dublin CA | Dougherty Hills Dog Park | 925-833-6600 | Stagecoach Road and Amador Valley Blvd |
| East Camarillo CA | Camarillo Grove Dog Park | 805-482-1996 | off Camarillo Springs Road |
| El Cajon CA | Wells Park & Off-Leash Dog Park | 619-441-1680 | 1153 E. Madison Ave |
| Elk Grove CA | Elk Grove Dog Park | 916-405-5600 | 9950 Elk Grove Florin Rd |
| Elk Grove CA | Laguna Dog Park | 916-405-5600 | 9014 Bruceville Rd |
| Encinitas CA | Encinitas Park | | D Street |
| Encino CA | Sepulveda Basin Dog Park | 818-756-7667 | 17550 Victory Blvd. |
| Escondido CA | Mayflower Dog Park | | 3420 Valley Center Road |
| Fair Oaks CA | Phoenix Dog Park | 916-966-1036 | 9050 Sunset Ave |
| Folsom CA | FIDO Field Dog Park | 916-355-7283 | 1780 Creekside Drive |

| | | | |
|---|---|---|---|
| Foster City CA | Foster City Dog Park | | Foster City Blvd at Bounty |
| Fremont CA | Central Park Dog Park | 510-494-4800 | 1110 Stevenson Blvd |
| Fresno CA | Basin AH1 Dog Park and Pond | 559-621-2900 | 4257 W. Alamos |
| Fresno CA | Woodward Park Dog Park | 559-621-2900 | E. Audubon Drive |
| Fullerton CA | Fullerton Pooch Park | 714-738-6575 | S Basque Avenue |
| Fullerton CA | Fullerton Pooch Park | 714-738-6575 | 201 S Basque Ave |
| Garden Grove CA | Garden Grove Dog Park | 714-741-5000 | 13601 Deodara Dr |
| Glen Ellen CA | Elizabeth Anne Perrone Dog Park | 707-565-2041 | 13630 Sonoma H/H 12 |
| Grass Valley CA | Condon Park Dog Park | 530-273-9268 | 660 Minnie Street |
| Grass Valley CA | Grass Valley Dog Park | 530-273-9268 | 660 Minnie Street |
| Half Moon Bay CA | Half Moon Bay Dog Park | 650-560-9822 | Wavecrest Rd |
| Half Moon Bay CA | Half Moon Bay Dog Park | 650-726-8297 | Wavecrest Road |
| Highland CA | Aurantia Dog Park | 909-864-6861 | Greenspot Road |
| Huntington Beach CA | Huntington Beach Central Park | 714-536-5486 | 18000 Goldenwest St |
| Huntington Beach CA | Huntington Beach Dog Park | 949-536-5672 | Edwards Street |
| Irvine CA | Central Bark | 949-724-7740 | 6405 Oak Canyon |
| Irvine CA | Irvine Central Bark Dog Park | 949-724-6833 | 6405 Oak Canyon |
| La Crescenta CA | La Crescenta Dog Park | 818-249-5940 | 3901 Dunsmore Avenue |
| La Mesa CA | Harry Griffen Park | 619-667-1307 | 9550 Milden Street |
| Laguna Beach CA | Laguna Beach Dog Park | | 20672 Laguna Canyon Road |
| Laguna Beach CA | Laguna Beach Dog Park | | Laguna Canyon Rd at El Toro Rd |
| Laguna Niguel CA | Laguna Niguel Pooch Park | | Golden Latern |
| Lake Elsinore CA | Canyon Hills Community Park | 951-674-3124 | 34360 Canyon Hills Road |
| Lancaster CA | Hull Park Dog Park | 661-723-6000 | 30th Street W |
| Larkspur CA | Canine Commons | 415-927-5110 | Doherty, East of Magnolia |
| Lincoln CA | Auburn Ravine Dog Park | 916-624-6808 | 1300 Green Ravine Dr |
| Livermore CA | Del Valle Dog Run | 510-562-PARK | Del Valle Road |
| Livermore CA | Livermore Canine Parks | | Murdell Lane |
| Loma Linda CA | Loma Linda Dog Park | | Beaumont Ave and Mountain View Ave. |
| Long Beach CA | Recreation Park Dog Park | 562-570-3100 | 7th St & Federation Dr |
| Los Angeles CA | Barrington Dog Park | 310-476-4866 | 333 South Barrington Avenue |
| Los Angeles CA | Griffith Park Dog Park | 323-913-4688 | North Zoo Drive |
| Los Angeles CA | Herman Park Dog Park | 323-255-0370 | 5566 Via Marisol |
| Los Angeles CA | Laurel Canyon Park | | 8260 Mulholland Dr. |
| Los Angeles CA | Runyon Canyon Park | 323-666-5046 | Mulholland Hwy |
| Los Angeles CA | Silverlake Dog Park | | 2000 West Silverlake Blvd. |
| Mill Valley CA | Mill Valley Dog Park | | Sycamore Ave At Camino Alto |
| Milpitas CA | Dog Park at Ed Levin | 408-262-6980 | 3100 Calveras Blvd. |
| Milpitas CA | Humane Society Silicon Valley | 408-262-2133 x164 | 901 Ames Avenue |
| Moraga CA | Rancho Laguna Park | 925-888-7045 | 2101 Camino Pablo |
| Morgan Hill CA | Morgan Hill Off-Leash Dog Park | 408-779-3451 | Edumundson Avenue |
| Morro Bay CA | Jodi Giannini Family Dog Park at Del Mar Park | | Ironwood Avenue |
| Mountain View CA | Mountain View Dog Park | | Shoreline Blvd at North Rd |
| Napa CA | Canine Commons Dog Park | 707-257-9529 | Dry Creek Rd at Redwood Rd |
| Napa CA | Shurtleff Park Dog Park | 707-257-9529 | Shetler Avenue |
| North Hollywood CA | Whitnall Off-Leash Dog Park | 818-756-8190 | 5801 1/2 Whitnall Highway |
| Novato CA | Dogbone Meadow at O'Hair Park | | Novato Blvd at Sutro |
| Oak Park CA | Oak Canyon Dog Park | | 5600 Hollytree Drive |
| Oakland CA | Hardy Dog Park | 510-238-PARK | 491 Hardy Street |
| Ocean Beach CA | Dusty Rhodes Dog Park | 619-236-5555 | Sunset Cliffs Blvd. |
| Oceanside CA | Oceanside Dog Park | 760-757-4357 | 2905 San Luis Rey Rd |
| Oceanside CA | San Diego Humane Society and SPCA Dog Park | 760-757-4357 | 2905 San Luis Rey Road |
| Ojai CA | Soule Dog Park | 805-654-3951 | 310 Soule Park Drive |
| Orange CA | Yorba Dog Park | 714-633-2980 | 190 S Yorba Street |
| Orcutt CA | Orcutt Community Park Dog Park | 805-934-6211 | 5800 S. Bradley |
| Oxnard CA | College Park Dog Park | 805-385-7950 | 3250 S Rose Avenue |
| Oxnard CA | College Park Dog Park | 805-385-7950 | 3200 S Rose Avenue |
| Palm Desert CA | Civic Center Dog Park | 760-346-0611 | 73-510 Fred Waring Dr |
| Palm Desert CA | Joe Mann Dog Park | 888-636-7387 | California Drive |
| Palm Desert CA | Palm Desert Civic Center Park | 888-636-7387 | Fred Waring |
| Palm Springs CA | Palm Springs Dog Park | 888-636-7387 | 222 Civic Drive N |
| Palo Alto CA | Greer Dog Park | 650-329-2261 | 1098 Amarillo Avenue |
| Palo Alto CA | Hoover Park | 650-329-2261 | 2901 Cowper St |

| | | | |
|---|---|---|---|
| Palo Alto CA | Mitchell Park/Dog Run | 650-329-2261 | 3800 Middlefield Rd |
| Pasadena CA | Alice Frost Kennedy Off-Leash Dog Area | 626-744-4321 | 3026 East Orange Grove Blvd |
| Paso Robles CA | Sherwood Dog Park of Paso Robles | 805-239-9326 | 290 Scott Street |
| Petaluma CA | Rocky Memorial Dog Park | 707-778-4380 | W. Casa Grande Road |
| Pinole CA | Pinole Dog Park | 510-741-2999 | 3790 Pinole Valley Road |
| Pleasanton CA | Muirwood Dog Exercise Area | 925-931-5340 | 4701 Muirwood Drive |
| Poway CA | Poway Dog Park | | 13094 Civic Center Drive |
| Poway CA | The Poway Dog Park | 858-668-4673 | 13094 Civic Center Drive |
| Rancho Cucamonga CA | Etiwanda Creek Dog Park | | 5939 East Avenue |
| Redding CA | Benton Dog Park | 530-941-8200 | 1700 Airpark Drive |
| Redding CA | Benton Dog Park | 530-941-8200 | 1700 Airpark Drive |
| Redondo Beach CA | Redondo Beach Dog Park | 310-376-9263 | Flagler Lane and 190th |
| Redwood City CA | Shores Dog Park | | Radio Road |
| Richmond CA | Point Isabel Dog Park | 888-327-2757 | 2701 Isabel Street |
| Richmond CA | Point Isabel Regional Shoreline | 510-562-PARK | Isabel Street |
| Rio Linda CA | Westside Dog Park | 916) 991-5929 | 810 Oak Lane |
| Riverside CA | Carlson Dog Park | 888-636-7387 | At the foot of Mt. Rubidoux |
| Riverside CA | Pat Merritt Dog Park | 888-636-7387 | Limonite Frontage Road |
| Riverside CA | Riverwalk Dog Park | 951-358- 7387 | Pierce Street and Collett Avenue |
| Roseville CA | Marco Dog Park | 916-774-5950 | 1800 Sierra Gardens Drive |
| S Lake Tahoe CA | Bijou Dog Park | | 1201 Al Tahoe Blvd |
| Sacramento CA | Bannon Creek Dog Park | 916-264-5200 | Bannon Creek Drive near West El Camino |
| Sacramento CA | Bradshaw Dog Park | 916-368-7387 | 3839 Bradshaw Road |
| Sacramento CA | Glenbrook Dog Park | | 8500 La Riviera Drive |
| Sacramento CA | Granite Park Dog Park | 916-264-5200 | Ramona Avenue near Power Inn Rd |
| Sacramento CA | Howe Dog Park | 916-927-3802 | 2201 Cottage Way |
| Sacramento CA | North Natomas Regional Park Dog Park | | 2501 New Market Drive |
| Sacramento CA | Partner Park Dog Park | 916-264-5200 | 5699 South Land Park Drive |
| Sacramento CA | Regency Community Park Dog Park | | 5500 Honor Parkway |
| Sacramento CA | Sutter's Landing Dog Park | 916-875-6961 | 20 28th Street |
| Sacramento CA | Tanzanite Community Park Dog Park | 916-808-5200 | Tanzanite Dr at Innovator Dr |
| San Anselmo CA | Redhill Community Dog Park | | Shaw Drive or Sunny Hills Drive |
| San Bernardino CA | Wildwood Dog Park | | 536 E. 40th St |
| San Bruno CA | San Bruno Dog Park | 650-877-8868 | Commodore Lane and Cherry Ave |
| San Carlos CA | Heather Dog Exercise Area | 650-802-4382 | 2757 Melendy Drive |
| San Carlos CA | Pulgas Ridge Off-Leash Dog Area | 650-691-1200 | Edmonds Road and Crestview Drive |
| San Clemente CA | Baron Von Willard Dog Park | | 301 Avenida La Pata |
| San Diego CA | Balboa Park Dog Run | 619-235-1100 | Balboa Dr |
| San Diego CA | Capehart Dog Park | 619-525-8212 | Felspar at Soledad Mountain Rd |
| San Diego CA | Doyle Community Park | 619-525-8212 | 8175 Regents Road |
| San Diego CA | Grape Street Park Off-Leash Area | 619-525-8212 | Grape Street at Granada Ave |
| San Diego CA | Kearny Mesa Dog Park | 619-525-8212 | 3170 Armstrong Street |
| San Diego CA | Maddox Dog Park | 619-525-8212 | 7815 Flanders Dr |
| San Diego CA | Rancho Bernardo Off-Leash Park | 858-538-8129 | 18448 West Bernardo Drive |
| San Diego CA | Rancho Peasquitos Park | 619-221-8901 | Salmon River Road at Fairgrove Lane |
| San Diego CA | Torrey Highlands Park | 619-525-8212 | Landsdale Drive at Del Mar Heights Road |
| San Dimas CA | San Dimas Dog Park | 909-394-6230 | 301 Horsethief Canyon Rd |
| San Francisco CA | Alamo Square Off Leash Dog Park | 415-831-2084 | Scott Street, between Hayes and Fulton Streets |
| San Francisco CA | Alta Plaza Off Leash Dog Park | 415-831-2084 | Steiner and Clay Street |
| San Francisco CA | Bernal Heights Dog Play Area | 415-831-2084 | Bernal Heights and Esmerelda |
| San Francisco CA | Buena Vista Dog Play Area | 415-831-2084 | Buena Vista West at Central Avenue |
| San Francisco CA | Corona Heights | 415-831-2084 | 16th and Roosevelt |
| San Francisco CA | Crocker Amazon Dog Play Area | 415-831-2084 | At Geneva Avenue and Moscow Street |
| San Francisco CA | Delores Park South Dog Play Area | 415-831-2700 | 19th Street and Delores Street |
| San Francisco CA | Eureka Valley Dog Play Area | 415-831-6810 | 100 Collingwood Street |
| San Francisco CA | Fort Miley Off Lead Dog Area | 415-561-4700 | Point Lobos and 48th Avenues |
| San Francisco CA | Glen Canyon Park Off Leash Dog Area | 415-337-4705 | 400 O'Shaughnessy Blvd |
| San Francisco CA | Golden Gate Park Off Leash Dog Areas | 415-751-8987 | Sloat & Great Highway |
| San Francisco CA | Head & Brotherhood Dog Park | 415-831-2700 | Head St & Brotherhood Way |
| San Francisco CA | Jefferson Square Off Lead Dog Park | 415-831-2084 | Eddy and Laguna Streets |
| San Francisco CA | Lafayette Park Dog Play Area | 415-831-2084 | Washington/Clay/Laguna |
| San Francisco CA | McLaren Park Geneva Dog Play Area | 415-831-2084 | 1600 Geneva Avenue |
| San Francisco CA | Mountain Lake Dog Play Area | 415-666-7005 | 12th Avenue and Lake Street |

| | | | |
|---|---|---|---|
| San Francisco CA | Pine Lake Dog Play Area - Stern Grove Trail | 415-252-6252 | Between H 1(Stern Grove) and Wawona (Pine Lake) |
| San Francisco CA | Pine Lake Park Dog Play Area | 415-831-2700 | Sloat Boulevard & Vale Street |
| San Francisco CA | Portrero Hill Mini Park Dog Play Area | 415-695-5009 | 22nd Street and Arkansas |
| San Francisco CA | St Mary's Off Leash Dog Park | 415-695-5006 | 95 Justin Drive |
| San Francisco CA | Stern Grove Dog Play Area | 415-252-6252 | 19th Avenue and Wawona Avenue |
| San Francisco CA | Upper Douglass Dog Play Area | 415-831 | 27th and Douglass Streets |
| San Francisco CA | Upper Noe Dog Play Area | 415-831-2084 | 30th and Church Street |
| San Francisco CA | Walter Haas Playground and Dog Park | 415-831-2084 | Diamond Heights and Addison Street |
| San Jose CA | Delmas Dog Park | 408-535-3570 | Park Avenue and Delmas Avenue |
| San Jose CA | Fontana Dog Park | 408-535-3570 | Golden Oak Way at Castello Drive |
| San Jose CA | Hellyer Park/Dog Run | 408-225-0225 | Hellyer Ave |
| San Jose CA | Miyuki Dog Park | 408-277-4573 | Santa Teresa Boulevard |
| San Jose CA | Roy M. Butcher Dog Park | 408-277-2757 | Camden Avenue at Lancaster Drive |
| San Jose CA | Ryland Dog Park | 408-535-3570 | First Street at Bassett Street |
| San Jose CA | Saratoga Creek Dog Park | 650-499-6387 | Graves Avenue |
| San Jose CA | Watson Park Dog Park | | Jackson Avenue & 22nd St |
| San Luis Obispo CA | El Chorro Regional Park and Dog Park | 805-781-5930 | Hwy 1 |
| San Luis Obispo CA | Laguna Lake Dog Park | 805-781-7300 | 504 Madonna Road |
| San Luis Obispo CA | Nipomo Park Off-Leash Area | 805-781-5930 | W. Tefft St and Pomery Rd |
| San Marcos CA | Hollandia Off Leash Dog Park | 760-744-900 | 12 Mission Hills Court |
| San Marcos CA | Montiel Off Leash Dog Park | 760-744-1050 | 2290 Montiel Road |
| San Marcos CA | San Elijo Hills Community Bark Park | 760-798-1765 | Elfin Forest Road |
| San Marcos CA | San Elijo Off Leash Dog Park | 760-744-1050 | 1105 Elfin Forest Road |
| San Marcos CA | Sunset Off Leash Dog Park | 760-744-9000 | 909 Puesta Del Sol- East Entrance |
| San Pedro CA | Knoll Hill Off-Leash Dog Park | 310-514-0338 | 200 Knoll Drive |
| San Rafael CA | Field of Dogs | | Civic Center Drive behind the Marin County Civic Center |
| San Ramon CA | Del Mar Dog Park | 925-973-3200 | Del Mar and Pine Valley |
| San Ramon CA | Memorial Park Dog Run | 925-973-3200 | Bollinger Canyon Road at San Ramon Valley Blvd |
| Santa Barbara CA | Douglas Family Preserve | 805-564-5418 | Linda Street |
| Santa Barbara CA | Santa Barbara Off-Leash Areas | 805-564-5418 | Various |
| Santa Clara CA | Raymond G. Gamma Dog Park | 408-615-3140 | 888 Reed Street |
| Santa Clara CA | Santa Clara Dog Park | 408-615-3144 | 3450 Brookdale Drive |
| Santa Cruz CA | Frederick Street Park Dog Park | 831-420-5270 | 168 Frederick Street (Frederick at Broadway) |
| Santa Cruz CA | Grant Park Dog Park | 831-420-5270 | 180 Grant Street |
| Santa Cruz CA | Ocean View Park | 831-420-5270 | 102 Ocean View Avenue |
| Santa Cruz CA | Pacheco Dog Park | 831-420-5270 | Pacheco Avenue and Prospect Heights |
| Santa Cruz CA | University Terrace Dog Run | 831-420-5270 | Meder Street and Nobel Drive |
| Santa Cruz CA | University Terrace Park | 831-420-5270 | Nobel Drive and Meder Street |
| Santa Maria CA | Woof-Pac Park | 805-896-2344 | 300 Goodwin Rd |
| Santa Monica CA | Airport Dog Park | 310-458-8411 | 3201 Airport Avenue |
| Santa Monica CA | Joslyn Park Dog Park | 310-458-8974 | 633 Kensington Road |
| Santa Monica CA | Memorial Park | 310-450-1121 | 1401 Olympic Blvd |
| Santa Monica CA | Pacific Street Dog Park | 310-450-6179 | Main and Pacific Street |
| Santa Rosa CA | DeTurk Round Barn Dog Park | 707-543-3292 | 819 Donahue Street |
| Santa Rosa CA | Doyle Community Park Dog Park | 707-543-3292 | 700 Doyle Park Drive |
| Santa Rosa CA | Galvin Community Park Dog Park | 707-543-3292 | 3330 Yulupa Avenue |
| Santa Rosa CA | Northwest Community Dog Park | 707-543-3292 | 2620 W. Steele Lane |
| Santa Rosa CA | Rincon Valley Community Park Dog Park | 707-543-3292 | 5108 Badger Road |
| Sausalito CA | Sausalito Dog Park | | Bridgeway and Ebbtide Avenues |
| Scotts Valley CA | Scotts Valley Dog Park | 831-438-3251 | Bluebonnet Road |
| Seal Beach CA | Arbor Dog Park | 562-799-9660 | Lampson Avenue at Heather St. |
| Sebastopol CA | Sebastopol Dog Park | 707-823-7262 | 500 Ragle Rd |
| Sierra Madre CA | Sierra Madre Dog Park | 626-355-5278 | 611 E. Sierra Madre Blvd |
| Simi Valley CA | Simi Dog Park | | 2151 Lost Canyons Drive |
| Sonoma CA | Ernie Smith Community Park Dog Park | 707-539-8092 | 18776 Gilman Drive |
| South Sacramento CA | Jacinto Creek Park Dog Park | | 8600 W Stockton Blvd |
| Stockton CA | BarkleyVille Dog Park | 209-937-8206 | 5505 Feather River Drive |
| Sunnyvale CA | Las Palmas Park - Dog Park | 408-730-7506 | 850 Russett Drive |
| Temecula CA | Redhawk Dog Park | 951-694-6444 | 44747 Redhawk Parkway |
| Templeton CA | Vineyard Dog Park | 805-239-4437 | 1010 Semillon Lane |
| Thousand Oaks CA | Conejo Creek Dog Park | 805-495-6471 | 1350 Avenida de las Flores |
| Union City CA | Drigon Dog Park | 510-471-3232x702 | Mission Blvd at 7th Street |

| | | | |
|---|---|---|---|
| Upland CA | Baldy View Dog Park | 909-931-4280 | 11th Street at Mountain Ave. |
| Vallejo CA | Wardlaw Dog Park | | Redwood Pkwy at Ascot Pkwy |
| Venice CA | Westminster Dog Park | 310-392-5566 | 1234 Pacific Ave |
| Ventura CA | Arroyo Verde Park | 805-658-4740 | Foothill and Day Road |
| Ventura CA | Camino Real Park | 805-658-4740 | At Dean Drive and Varsity Street |
| Visalia CA | Cody Kelly Bark Park | | Plaza Drive and Airport Road |
| Visalia CA | Seven Oaks Bark Park | 559-713-4586 | 900 S Edison Street |
| Walnut Creek CA | Walnut Creek Dog Park | 925-671-3329 | 301 N San Carlos Drive |
| Watsonville CA | Pinto Lake Dog Park | 831-454-7900 | 757 Green Valley Road |
| West Sacramento CA | Sam Combs Dog Park | 916-617-4620 | 205 Stone Blvd |
| Yuba City CA | Off-Leash Dog Park | 530-329-1997 | 2050 Wild River Drive |

**Colorado Listings**

| | | | |
|---|---|---|---|
| Arvada CO | West Arvada Dog Park | 303-421-3487 | 17975 West 64th Parkway |
| Aurora CO | Grandview Park Dog Park | 303-739-7160 | 17500 E. Salida Street |
| Boulder CO | Chautauqua Park | 303-441-3440 | Grant and Baseline Streets |
| Boulder CO | East Boulder Park | 303-413-7258 | 5660 Sioux Drive |
| Boulder CO | Foothills Park Dog Park | 303-413-7258 | Cherry Ave at 7th St |
| Boulder CO | Howard Hueston Dog Park | 303-413-7258 | 34th Street |
| Boulder CO | Valmont Dog Park | 303-413-7258 | 5275 Valmont Road |
| Brighton CO | Happy Tails Dog Park | 303-655-2049 | 1111 Judicial Center Drive |
| Broomfield CO | Broomfield County Commons Dog Park | 303-464-5509 | 13th and Sheridan Blvd |
| Castle Rock CO | Glendale Open Space Dog Park | 303-660-7495 | 100 Third Street |
| Colorado Springs CO | Bear Creek Dog Park | | 21st Street and Rio Grande Street |
| Colorado Springs CO | Cheyenne Meadows Dog Park | 719-385-2489 | Charmwood Dr. and Canoe Creek Dr. |
| Colorado Springs CO | Garden of the Gods Park Off-Leash Area | 719-385-2489 | Gateway Road |
| Colorado Springs CO | Palmer Park Dog Park | 719-385-2489 | 3650 Maizeland Road |
| Colorado Springs CO | Rampart Park Dog Park | 719-385-2489 | 8270 Lexington Drive |
| Colorado Springs CO | Red Rock Canyon Off-Leash Dog Loops | 719-385-2489 | 31st Street at Highway 24 |
| Conifer CO | Beaver Ranch Bark Park | 303-829-1917 | 11369 Foxton Rd |
| Denver CO | Berkeley Park Dog Park | 720-913-0696 | Sheridan and West 46th |
| Denver CO | Denver International Airport | 303-342-2000 | 8500 Pena Blvd |
| Denver CO | Fuller Dog Park | 720-913-0696 | Franklin and East 29th |
| Denver CO | Green Valley Ranch East Dog Park | 720-913-0696 | Jebel and East 45th |
| Denver CO | Greenway Dog Park | 720-913-0696 | E 22nd Ave and Syracuse St |
| Denver CO | Jason Street Dog Park | 303-698-0076 | 666 South Jason Street |
| Denver CO | Kennedy Dog Park | 720-913-0696 | Hampden and South Dayton |
| Durango CO | Durango Dog Park | 970-385-2950 | Highway 160 at Highway 550 |
| Eagle CO | Eagle Ranch Dog Park | 970-328-6354 | Sylvan Lake Rd at Lime Park Dr |
| Englewood CO | Centennial Park Off-Leash Area | 303-762-2300 | 4630 S. Decatur |
| Englewood CO | Duncan Park Off-Leash Area | 303-762-2300 | 4800 S. Pennsylvania |
| Englewood CO | Englewood Canine Corral | 303-762-2300 | 4848 S. Windermere |
| Englewood CO | Jason Park Off-Leash Area | 303-762-2300 | 4200 S. Jason |
| Englewood CO | Northwest Greenbelt Off-Leash Area | 303-762-2300 | Tejon at W Baltic Pl |
| Estes Park CO | Estes Valley Dog Park | 970-586-8191 | off Highway 36 |
| Fort Collins CO | Fossil Creek Dog Park | 970-221-6618 | 5821 South Lemay Avenue |
| Fort Collins CO | Soft Gold Dog Park | 970-221-6618 | 520 Hickory Street |
| Fort Collins CO | Spring Canyon Dog Park | 970-221-6618 | Horsetooth Road |
| Grand Junction CO | Canyon View Dog Park | 970-254-3846 | Interstate 70 at 24 Road |
| Littleton CO | Chatfield's Dog Off-Leash Area | 303-791-7275 | 8000 S Platte Canyon Road |
| Longmont CO | Longmont Dog Park #1 | 303-651-8447 | 21st and Francis |
| Longmont CO | Longmont Dog Park #2 | 303-651-8447 | Airport Road at St Vrain Rd |
| Louisville CO | Louisville Community Park Dog Park | 303-335-4735 | 955 Bella Vista Drive |
| Morrison CO | Lakewood Dog Park | | 15900 W Alameda Parkway/H 26 |
| Westminster CO | Westminster Hills Dog Park | 303-658-2400 | 105th Avenue and Simms Street |
| Windsor CO | Poudre Pooch Park | 970-674-3500 | Eastman Park Dr at 7th Street |

**Connecticut Listings**

| | | | |
|---|---|---|---|
| Colchester CT | Colchester Dog Park | 860-537-7295 | 99 Old Amston Rd |
| Danielson CT | Mitchell D. Phaiah Dog Park | 860-204-9561 | 78 Quinebaug Drive |
| Granby CT | Granby D.O.G.G.S. Park | 860-653-0173 | 215 Salmon Brook Street/H 202 |
| Groton CT | The Central Bark Dog Park | 860-441-6600 | 821 Gold Star Highway |
| Hamden CT | Hamden Dog Park at Bassett | | On Waite Street at Ridge Road |
| Manchester CT | Manchester Dog Park | | Mt Nebo Park, Spring Street |
| Milford CT | Eisenhower Park Dog Run | 203-783-3280 | North Street |

| | | | |
|---|---|---|---|
| Norwich CT | Estelle Cohn Memorial Dog Park | 860-367-2660 | 261 Asylum Street |
| Norwich CT | Pawsitive Park Dog Park, Estelle Cohn Memorial Dog Park | 860-367-7271 | 261 Asylum Street |
| Ridgefield CT | Ridgefield Bark Park | | Prospect Ridge Road |
| Southbury CT | Southbury Dog Park | | 236 Roxbury Road |
| Wethersfield CT | Wethersfield Dog Park | 860-721-2890 | 154 Prospect St |

**D.C. Listings**

| | | | |
|---|---|---|---|
| Washington DC | Glover Park Dog Park | | 39th St and W Street NW |

**Delaware Listings**

| | | | |
|---|---|---|---|
| Bear DE | Lums Pond Dog Area | 302-368-698 | |
| Wilmington DE | Brandywine Dog Park | 302-577-7020 | North Park Drive at North Adams |
| Wilmington DE | Carousel Park Off-Leash Area | 302-995-7670 | 3700 Limestone Rd |
| Wilmington DE | Rockford Park Dog Park | 302-577-7020 | Rockford Rd at Tower Road |
| Wilmington DE | Talley Day Bark Park | 302-395-5654 | 1300 Foulk Road |

**Florida Listings**

| | | | |
|---|---|---|---|
| Apoka FL | Doctors Dog Park | 407-703-1741 | 21 N Highland Avenue |
| Boca Raton FL | Mizner Bark Dog Park | 561-393-7821 | 751 Banyan Trail |
| Bonita Beach FL | Dog Beach | 239-461-7400 | County Road 865 |
| Bradenton FL | Happy Trails Canine Park | 941-742-5923 | 5502 33rd Avenue Drive W |
| Cape Coral FL | Wagging Tails Dog Park | 239-549-4606 | 5505 Rose Garden Road |
| Casselberry FL | Pawmosa Dog Park | 407-262-7720 | 140 Plumosa Avenue |
| Clearwater FL | Crest Lake Dog Park | 727-562-4800 | 201 Glenwood Avenue |
| Clearwater FL | Enterprise Dog Park | 727-562-4800 | 2671 Enterprise Road |
| Clearwater FL | Sand Key Park Paw Playground | 727-588-4852 | 1060 Gulf Blvd. |
| Cocoa Beach FL | Lori Wilson Park Dog Park | 321-868-1154 | 1500 N Atlantic Avenue/H A1A |
| Coconut Grove FL | Dog Chow Dog Park | 954-570-9507 | 2400 S Bayshore Drive |
| Coral Springs FL | Dr. Paul's Pet Care Center Dog Park | 954-346-4428 | 2575 Sportsplex Drive |
| Coral Springs FL | Dr. Steven G. Paul Dog Park | 954-346-4428 | 2575 Sportsplex Drive |
| Debary FL | Gemini Springs Dog Park | 386-736-5953 | 37 Dirksen Drive |
| Deland FL | Barkley Square Dog Park | 386-736-5953 | 1010 N Ridgewood Avenue |
| Delray Beach FL | Lake Ida Dog Park | 561-966-6600 | 2929 Lake Ida Road |
| Deltona FL | Keysville Dog Park | | 2461 Keysville Avenue |
| Estero FL | Estero Corkscrew Dog Park | 239-498-0415 | 9200 Corkscrew Palms Blvd |
| Estero FL | K-9 Corral at Estero Park | 239-498-0415 | 9200 Corkscrew Palms Blvd |
| Fernandina Beach FL | The Nassau Humane Society Dog Park | 904-491-1511 | 641 Airport Road |
| Flagler Beach FL | Bark Park | 386-439-4006 | 711 John Anderson H |
| Flagler Beach FL | Wadsworth Park Dog Park | 386-313-4020 | 2200 Moody Blvd/H 100 |
| Fort Lauderdale FL | Bark Park At Snyder Park | 954-828-3647 | 3299 S.W. 4th Avenue |
| Fort Myers FL | Barkingham Park | 239-338-3288 | 9800 Buckingham Road |
| Hialeah FL | Amelia Earhart Bark Park | 305-769-2693 | 401 E. 65th Street |
| Holly Hill FL | Riviera Oaks Dog Park | 386-671-1240 | 980 Alabama Avenue |
| Hollywood FL | Poinciana Dog Park | 954-921-3404 | 1301 S 21st Avenue |
| Jacksonville FL | Dogwood Park | 904-296-3636 | 7407 Salisbury Rd South |
| Jacksonville Beach FL | Paws Dog Park | 904-513-9240 | Penman Road S |
| Key West FL | Higgs Beach Dog Park | 305-809-3765 | White Street and Atlantic Blvd |
| Kissimmee FL | KUA Canine Cumbie Court | 407-933-9838 | 2318 Agate St |
| Largo FL | Walsingham Park Paw Playground | 727-549-6142 | 12615 102nd Avenue North |
| Lutz FL | Carolyn Meeker Dog Park | 813-635-3500 | 122 1st Avenue SW |
| Marco Island FL | Canine Cove Dog Park | 239-642-1666 | 1361 Andalusia Terrace, Marco Island |
| Melbourne FL | Wickham Park Dog Park | 321-255-4307 | 2500 Parkway Drive |
| Miami FL | East Greynolds Park | 305-945-3425 | 16700 Biscayne BlvdH 1/5 |
| Miami FL | Tropical Dog Park | 305-226-8316 | 7900 SW 40 Street |
| Miami FL | West Kendall District Park Bark Park | | 11255 SW 157TH Ave |
| Miami Beach FL | Flamingo Bark Park | 305-673-7224 | 13th Street and Michigan Avenue |
| Miami Beach FL | North Shore Open Space Park | 305-673-7720 | Collins Avenue and 78th Street |
| Miami Beach FL | Pinetree Bark Park | 305-673-7730 | 4400 Pinetree Drive |
| Miami Beach FL | Washington Avenue Bark Park | 305-673-7766 | 201 2nd Street |
| Mount Dora FL | Mount Dora Dog Park | 352-735-7183 | East end of 11th Avenue |
| Naples FL | Rover Run Dog Park | 239-566-2367 | 1895 Veterans Park Drive |
| New Smyrna Beach FL | New Smyrna Beach Dog Park | 800-541-9621 | 2641 Paige Avenue |
| North Fort Myers FL | Pooch Park | 239-656-7748 | 1297 Driftwood Drive |

| | | | |
|---|---|---|---|
| North Miami Beach FL | Northeast Dog Park | 305-673-7730 | 16700 Biscayne Blvd/H 1/5 |
| Ocala FL | Millennium Dog Park | | 2513 SE 32nd Avenue |
| Orlando FL | Downey Dog Park | 407-249-6195 | 10107 Flowers Avenue |
| Orlando FL | Dr. Phillips Dog Park | 407-254-9037 | 8249 Buenavista Woods Blvd |
| Orlando FL | Meadow Woods Dog Park | 407-858-4725 | 1751 Rhode Island Woods Circle |
| Orlando FL | Yucatan Dog Park | 407-254-9160 | 6400 Yucatan Drive |
| Palm Bay FL | Palm Bay Regional Park Off-Leash Dog Park | 321-868-1154 | 1951 Malabar Road NW |
| Palm Coast FL | Holland Park Dog Park | 386-986-2323 | Florida Park Drive |
| Palm Coast FL | Holland Park Dog Park | 386-986-2323 | Florida Park Drive |
| Palm Harbor FL | Chestnut Park Paw Playground | 727-669-1951 | 2200 East Lake Road |
| Pembroke Pines FL | Johnson Street Dog Park | 954-435-6525 | 9751 Johnson Street |
| Plantation FL | Happy Tails Dog Park at Seminole Park | 954-452-2510 | 6600 SW 16th Street |
| Ponce Inlet FL | Happy Trails Dog Park | 386-236-2150 | 4680 S Peninsula Drive |
| Port Orange FL | Seemore Dog Park | 386-506-5852 | 5959 S Spruce Creek Road |
| Port St John FL | Port St John Dog Park | | Fay Lake Wilderness Park |
| Sanford FL | Paw Park of Historic Sanford | 407-330-5688 | 427 S. French Avenue |
| Satellite Beach FL | E. Lorraine Gott Dog Park | 321-777-8004 | 750 Jamaica Boulevard |
| Sebastian FL | Sebastian Bark Park | | Keen Terrace |
| Seffner FL | Mango Dog Park | 813-975-2160 | 11717 Claypit Road |
| Seminole FL | Boca Ciega Park Paw Playground | 727-588-4882 | 12410 74th Ave. N |
| Spring Hill FL | Rotary Centennial Dog Park | 352-754-4027 | 10375 Sandlor Street |
| St Augustine FL | Paws Dog Park | 904-209-0655 | 1595 Wildwood Drive |
| Sunny Isles Beach FL | Haulover Beach Bark Park | 305-947-3525 | 10800 Collins Avenue |
| Sunrise FL | Barkham at Markham Park | 954-389-2000 | 16001 W H 84 |
| Tallahassee FL | San Luis Dog Park | | 1560 San Luis Rd |
| Tallahassee FL | Tom Brown Park Off-Leash Dog Park | 850-891-3966 | 501 Easterwood Dr |
| Tampa FL | Al Lopez Dog Park | 813-274-8615 | 4810 North Himes |
| Tampa FL | Curtis Hixon Waterfront Dog Park | 813-274-8615 | 600 N Ashley Drive |
| Tampa FL | Davis Islands Dog Park | 813-274-8615 | 1002 Severn |
| Tampa FL | Palma Ceia | 813-274-8615 | San Miguel & Marti |
| Tarpon Springs FL | Anderson Park Paw Playground | 727-943-4085 | 39699 U.S. Highway 19 North |
| Tavares FL | Dog Park at Aesop's Park | 352-742-6477 | 501 E Caroline Street |
| Tavares FL | Lake Idamere Dog Park | | 3861 H 19 |
| Tierra Verde FL | Fort DeSoto Park Paw Playground | 727-582-2267 | 3500 Pinellas Bayway South |
| Titusville FL | Marina Park Dog Park | 321-264-5105 | 501 Marina Road |
| Venice FL | Paw Park and South Brohard Beach | 941-486-2626 | S Harbor Drive |
| Vero Beach FL | Vero Beach Dog Park | | 3481 Indian River Drive E |
| Vero Beach FL | Vero Dog Park | | 3451 Indian River Drive East |
| Wellington FL | Wellington Dog Park | 561-791-4005 | 2975 Greenbriar Blvd |
| West Palm Beach FL | Pooch Pines Dog Park | 561-966-6600 | 7715 Forest Hill Blvd/H 882 |
| Winter Garden FL | West Orange Dog Park | 407-656-3299 | 12400 Marshall Farms Road |
| Winter Park FL | Fleet Peeples Park Dog Park | 407-740-8897 | South Lakemont Avenue |

**Georgia Listings**

| | | | |
|---|---|---|---|
| Acworth GA | Pitner Road Dog Park | 770-528-8890 | 2450 Pitner Road |
| Alpharetta GA | Waggy World Dog Park | 678-297-6100 | 175 Roswell Street |
| Athens GA | Memorial Park Dog Park | 706-613-3580 | 293 Gran Ellen Drive |
| Athens GA | Sandy Creek Park Dog Parks | 706-613-3800 | 400 Bob Holman Rd |
| Athens GA | Southeast Clarke Park Dog Park | 706-613-3871 | 4440 Lexington Road |
| Atlanta GA | Hartsfield, Jackson, Atlanta International Airport | 404-209-2920 | N Terminal Parkway |
| Atlanta GA | Piedmont Park Off Leash Dog Park | 404-875-7275 | Park Drive |
| Augusta GA | The Pendleton King Park Bark Park | 706-821-2300 | 1600 Troupe Street |
| Cumming GA | Fowler Dog Park | 770-886-4088 | 4110 Carolene Way |
| Cumming GA | Windermere Dog Park | 770-781-2215 | 3355 Windermere Parkway |
| Dalton GA | Lakeshore Dog Park | 706-278-5404 | 1212 Dennard Dr |
| Dunwoody GA | Brook Run Dog Park | 678-234-4428 | 4770 N. Peachtree Road |
| Dunwoody GA | Brook Run Dog Park | 404-371-2631 | 4770 N. Peachtree Rd |
| Gainesville GA | Laurel Park Dog Park | 770-535-8280 | 3100 Old Cleveland Hwy |
| Lawrenceville GA | Ronald Reagan Dog Park | | 2777 Five Forks Trickum Rd |
| Macon GA | Macon Dog Park | 478-742-5084 | Chestnut and Adams |
| Marietta GA | Sweat Mountain Dog Park | 770-591-3160 | 4346 Steinhauer Road |
| Marietta GA | Sweat Mountain Dog Park | 770-591-3160 | 4346 Steinhauer Road |
| Milton GA | Wolfbrook Private Dog Park and Club | 770-772-0440 | 13665 New Providence Rd |
| Norcross GA | Graves Dog Park | 770-822-8840 | 1540 Graves Rd |

| | | | |
|---|---|---|---|
| Norcross GA | Pinckneyville Dog Park | 770-822-8840 | 4758 S Old Peachtree Road |
| Roswell GA | Leita Thompson Dog Park | 770-641-3760 | 1355 Woodstock Rd |
| Savannah GA | Savannah Dog Park | | 41st and Drayton St |
| Smyrna GA | Burger Dog Park | 770-431-2842 | 680 Glendale Pl |
| Stone Mountain GA | Red Dog Park | 770-879-4971 | 3rd and 4th Streets |
| Tybee GA | City of Tybee Dog Park | 912-786-4573 | Van Home and Fort Streets |

**Hawaii Listings**

| | | | |
|---|---|---|---|
| Honolulu HI | McInerny Dog Park | 808-946-2187 | 2700 Waialae Avenue |
| Honolulu HI | Mililani Dog Park | 808-946-2187 | 95-1069 Ukuwai St |
| Honolulu HI | Moanalua Dog Park | 808-831-7105 | 2900 Moanalua Road |
| Honolulu HI | Moanalua Dog Park | | Moanalua Park Rd and Hahiole St |
| Honolulu HI | Oahu Dog-Friendly Parks (Leashes Required) | 808-946-2187 | Various |
| Honolulu HI | The Bark Park | | Diamond Head Rd at 18th Avenue |
| Hui 'Ilio HI | Hawai'i Kai Dog Park | | Keahole Street |
| Lihue HI | Freddie's Dog Park | 808-632-0610 | 3-825 Kaumualii H/H 50 |
| Mililani HI | Mililani Dog Park | | 95-1069 Ukuwai Street |
| Waikiki HI | Ala Wai K9 Playground | | Ala Wai Blvd |

**Idaho Listings**

| | | | |
|---|---|---|---|
| Boise ID | Military Reserve Flood Basin Dog Off-Leash Area | 208-384-4060 ext. 333 | 750 Mountain Cove Road |
| Boise ID | Military Reserve Off-Leash Park | 208-384-4240 | Mountain Cove Road and Reserve St |
| Boise ID | Morris Hill Park | 208-384-4060 ext 338 | 10 Roosevelt Street |
| Boise ID | Morris Hill Park | | 10 Roosevelt Street |
| Boise ID | Pine Grove Park | | 8995 W Shoup Drive |
| Boise ID | Ridge to Rivers Trails | 208-384-4060 ext. 333 | Boise Foothills |
| Coeur d'Alene ID | Central Bark | | Atlas Road and Nez Perce Drive, in Coeur d'Alene |
| Dover ID | The Balto Dog Park | | Tank Hill |
| Idaho Falls ID | Snake River Animal Shelter Dog Park | 208-529-1117 | 3250 Lindsay Blvd |
| Meridian ID | Storey Bark Park | 208-888-3579 | 430 E. Watertower Lane |
| Moscow ID | Moscow Dog Park Idaho | | 2019 White Avenue |
| Nampa ID | Amity Dog Park | 208-468-5858 | 2nd Street S and E Amity Avenue |
| Pocatello ID | Bartz Field | | 921 S. 8th Avenue |
| Salmon ID | Island Park Dog Park | 208-756-3214 | At Main and Highway93 |
| Sandpoint ID | Pend Oreille Dog Park | | 895 Kootenai Cutoff Road |

**Illinois Listings**

| | | | |
|---|---|---|---|
| Aurora IL | Aurora West Forest Preserve | 630-232-5980 | Hankes Road |
| Chicago IL | Challenger Playlot Dog Park | 312-742-PLAY | 1100 W. Irving Park Rd |
| Chicago IL | Churchill Field Park Dog Park | 312-742-PLAY | 1825 N. Damen Ave. |
| Chicago IL | Coliseum Park Dog Park | 312-742-PLAY | 1466 S. Wabash Ave. |
| Chicago IL | Grant Park Bark Park | 312-742-PLAY | 9th and Columbus |
| Chicago IL | Hamlin Park Dog Park | 312-742-PLAY | 3035 N. Hoyne Ave. |
| Chicago IL | Noethling Park Dog Park - Wiggly Field | 312-742-PLAY | 2645 N. Sheffield Ave. |
| Chicago IL | Puptown Dog Park in Margate Park | 312-742-PLAY | 4921 N. Marine Drive |
| Chicago IL | River Park Dog Park | 312-742-PLAY | 5100 N. Francisco Ave |
| Chicago IL | Walsh Park Dog Park | 312-742-PLAY | 1722 N. Ashland Ave. |
| Chicago IL | Wicker Park Dog Park | 312-742-PLAY | 1425 N. Damen Ave. |
| Dundee IL | Schweitzer Woods | 630-232-5980 | 16N690 Sleepy Hollow Road |
| Lake Forest IL | Prairie Wolf Dog Exercise Area | 847-367-6640 | S Waukegan Road/H 43 |
| Lake Villa IL | Duck Farm Dog Exercise Area | 847-367-6640 | Grand Avenue (Route 132), east of Route 83 |
| Libertyville IL | Independence Grove Dog Exercise Area | 847-367-6640 | N Milwaukee Avenue |
| Naperville IL | Whalon Lake Dog Park | 815-727-8700 | Royce Road |
| Peoria IL | Bradley Dog Park | | 1314 Park Road |
| Peoria IL | Vicary Bottoms Dog Exercise Area | 309-682-6684 | Kickapoo Creek Road |
| Shorewood IL | Hammel Woods Dog Park | 815-727-8700 | DuPage River Access on E Black Road |
| Springfield IL | Riverside Park Dog Run | | 4115 Sandhill |
| Springfield IL | Stuart Park Dog Park | 217-544-1751 | W Jefferson Street and Winch Road |

| | | | |
|---|---|---|---|
| St Charles IL | East Side Sports Complex Dog Park | 630-513-4316 | Commerce Drive |
| St Charles IL | Fox River Bluff & Fox River Bluff West Forest Preserve | 630-232-5980 | H 25 and H 31 |
| St Charles IL | James O. Breen Community Dog Park | 630-513-4316 | Campton Hills and Peck Roads |
| Urbana IL | Urbana Dog Park | 217-344-9583 | 1501 E. Perkins Rd. |
| Wauconda IL | Lakewood Dog Exercise Area | 847-367-6640 | Fairfield Road |

**Indiana Listings**

| | | | |
|---|---|---|---|
| Crown Point IN | Dogwood Run at Lemon Lake County Park | 219-945-0543 | 6322 W. 133rd Avenue |
| Fishers IN | Pierson Bark Park | 317-577-BARK (2275) | 11787 E 131st Street |
| Fort Wayne IN | Pawster Park Pooch Playground | 260-427-6000 | Winchester Road and Bluffton Road |
| Goshen IN | Robert Nelson Dog Park | | 60376 C.R. 13 |
| Highland IN | Wicker Memorial Park | 219-838-3420 | 8554 Indianapolis Boulevard |
| Indianapolis IN | Bark Park | 317-327-7076 | 11300 E Prospect Street |
| Indianapolis IN | Bark Park | 317-327-7161 | 1550 Broad Ripple Avenue |
| Indianapolis IN | Eagle Creek Park | 317-327-PARK (7275) | 7840 W 56th Street |
| Kokomo IN | Mehlig Dog Park | 765-456-7275 | 1701 W. Carter St. |
| Kokomo IN | Mohr Dog Park | 765-456-7275 | 2302 Saratoga Ave |
| Lafayette IN | Shamrock Park Dog Park | 765-225-8388 | Wabash Avenue |
| Michigan City IN | Creek Ridge County Park Dog Park | 219-325-8315 | 7943 W 400 North |
| Muncie IN | ARF (Animal Rescue Fund) Park | 765-282-2733 (ARFF) | 1209 W Riggin Road |
| Valparaiso IN | Canine Country Club | 219-548-3604 | 3556 Sturdy Road |
| Westville IN | Bluhm County Park Dog Park | 219-325-8315 | 3855 South 1100 W |

**Iowa Listings**

| | | | |
|---|---|---|---|
| Ankeny IA | Ankeny Dog Park | | 1155 SW Ankeny Road |
| Bettendorf IA | Crow Creek Dog Park | 563-344-4113 | 4800 N Devils Glen Road |
| Cedar Falls IA | Cedar Falls Paw Park | 319-273-8624 | S Main and Hwy 58 Overpass |
| Cedar Rapids IA | Cheyenne Park Off-Leash Area | 319-286-5760 | 1500 Cedar Bend Lane SW |
| Clinton IA | Prairie Pastures Dog Park | 563-242-9088 | 3923 N 3rd Street |
| Clinton IA | Prairie Pastures Dog Park at Soaring Eagle Nature Center | 563-243-3022 | 3923 North 3rd Street |
| Indianola IA | Indianola Off-Leash Dog Playground | 515-480-9746 | S K Street and W 17th Avenue |
| Iowa City IA | Thornberry Off-Leash Dog Park | 319-356-5107 | Foster Road |
| Ottumwa IA | Ottumwa Bark Park | | U.S. Highway 34 |
| Runnells IA | Rover's Ranch Dog Park | 515-967-6768 | 200 SE 108th Street |
| Sioux City IA | Lewis and Clark Dog Park | 712-279-6311 | 5015 Correctionville Road |
| Washington IA | Sunset Dog Park | 319-653-6584 | S H Avenue |
| Washington IA | Washington Sunset Dog Park | 319-653-6584 | 915 W Main Street |
| Waterloo IA | Pat Bowlsby Off-Leash Dog Park | 319-291-4370 | 1320 Campbell Avenue |
| West Des Moines IA | Raccoon River Dog Park | 515-222-3444 | 2500 Grand Avenue |
| West Des Moines IA | Racoon River Dog Park | 515-222-3444 | 2500 Grand Avenue |

**Kansas Listings**

| | | | |
|---|---|---|---|
| De Soto KS | Kill Creek Streamway Park | 913-831-3355 | 33460 West 95th St |
| Hays KS | Hays Dog Park | | 1376 Highway 183 |
| Hutchinson KS | Hutchinson Dog Park | | 1501 S Severance |
| Lawrence KS | Mutt Run | 785-832-3405 | 1330 East 902 Road |
| Manhattan KS | Stretch Dog Park | 785-539-7941 | 5800 A River Pond Road |
| Olathe KS | Heritage Park | 913-831-3355 | 16050 Pflumm |
| Overland Park KS | Thomas S. Stoll Memorial Dog Park | 913-831-3355 | 12500 W. 119th Street |
| Shawnee KS | Shawnee Mission Park | 913-831-3355 | 7900 Renner Rd/87th St |
| Topeka KS | Bark Park (Gage Park) | 785-368-3838 | 10th and Gage St |

**Kentucky Listings**

| | | | |
|---|---|---|---|
| Ashland KY | Ashland Boyd County Dog Park | | Fraley Field |
| Covington KY | Kenton County Paw Park | | 3950 Madison Pike |
| Fort Thomas KY | Highland Hills Dog Park | 859-781-1700 | 199 Mayfield Avenue |
| Lexington KY | Coldstream Dog Park | | 1875 Newtown Pike |

| | | | |
|---|---|---|---|
| Lexington KY | Jacobson Dog Park | | 4001 Athens-Boonesboro Road |
| Lexington KY | Masterson Station Dog Park | | Leestown Road/H 421 |
| Lexington KY | Wellington Dog Park | | New Circle Road |
| Louisville KY | Cochran Hill Dog Run | 502-291-6873 | Cochran Hill Road |
| Louisville KY | Sawyer Dog Park | 502-291-6873 | Freys Hill Road |
| Louisville KY | Vettiner Dog Run | 502-291-6873 | Mary Dell Road |
| Milford KY | Kennel Resorts | | 5825 Meadowview Drive |

**Louisiana Listings**

| | | | |
|---|---|---|---|
| Baton Rouge LA | Burbank Dog Park at Burbank Sports Complex | 225-272-9200 | 12400 Burbank Drive/H 42 |
| Baton Rouge LA | Forest Park Dog Park | 225-752-1853 | 13950 Harrell's Ferry Road |
| Baton Rouge LA | Raising Cane's Dog Park - Brooks Community Park | 225-272-9200 | 1442 City Park Avenue |
| Baton Rouge LA | Raising Cane's Dog Park at Forest Community Park | 225-272-9200 | 13900 Harrells Ferry Road |
| Baton Rouge LA | Raising Cane's Dog Park at Greenwood Community Park | 225-272-9200 | 13350 H 19 |
| Lake Charles LA | Bark du Lac Dog Park | 337-502-5214 | Pine St and Ryan St |
| Lake Charles LA | Calcasieu Parish Animal Control Public Dog Park | 337-439-8879 | 5500-A Swift Plant Rd. |
| Lake Charles LA | Enos Derbonne Sports Complex Dog Park | 337-502-5214 | 7903 Lake Street |

**Maine Listings**

| | | | |
|---|---|---|---|
| Belfast ME | Belfast Dog Park | | Lincolnville Avenue |
| Kennebunk ME | Kennebunk Dog Park | 207-985-3244 | 36 Sea Road |
| Lewiston ME | Robin's Garden and Dog Park | | 55 Strawberry Avenue |
| Ogunquit ME | Ogunquit Dog Park | | Spring Hill Road off Berwick Road |
| Old Orchard Park ME | Old Orchard Beach Dog Park | 207-934-0860 | Memorial Park at 1st St. |
| Portland ME | Capisic Dog Park | 207-874-8793 | Capisic Street |
| Portland ME | Eastern Promenade Park Off-Leash Area | 207-874-8793 | Cutter Street |
| Portland ME | Hall School Woods | 207-874-8793 | 23 Orono Road |
| Portland ME | Jack School Dog Run | 207-874-8793 | North St. and Washington Ave. |
| Portland ME | Pine Grove Park | 207-874-8793 | Harpswell Road |
| Portland ME | Portland Arts & Technology School Dog Run | 207-874-8793 | 196 Allen Avenue |
| Portland ME | Riverton Park | 207-874-8793 | Riverside Street |
| Portland ME | University Park | 207-874-8793 | Harvard Street |
| Portland ME | Valley Street Park | 207-874-8793 | Valley St. |
| Seal Harbor ME | Little Long Pond Leash-Free Area | 207-288-3338 | Peabody Drive |

**Maryland Listings**

| | | | |
|---|---|---|---|
| Annapolis MD | Broadneck Park | 410-222-7317 | 618 Broadneck Road |
| Annapolis MD | Quiet Waters Dog Park | 410-222-1777 | 600 Quiet Waters Park Rd |
| Baltimore MD | Canton Dog Park | 410-396-7900 | Clinton & Toone Streets |
| Bowie MD | Bowie Dog Park | | Northview Drive and Enfield Drive |
| Boyds MD | Black Hills Regional Park Dog Park | 301-972-9396 | 20930 Lake Ridge Rd |
| Ellicott City MD | Worthington Park | 410-313-PARK (7275) | 8170 Hillsborough Road |
| Gaithersburg MD | Green Run Dog Park | | Bickerstaff Rd and I-370 |
| Germantown MD | Ridge Road Recreational Dog Park | 301-972-9396 | 21155 Frederick Road |
| Laurel MD | Dr. Bruce Morley Dog Playground | 240-294-1307 | 8103 Sandy Spring Rd |
| Ocean City MD | Ocean City Dog Park | | 94th Street |
| Owings Mills MD | BARC Park (Baltimore Animal Recreation Center) | 410-887-3630 | Reisterstown Road |
| Pasadena MD | Downs Park | 410-222-7000 | 8311 John Downs Loop |
| Rockville MD | Cabin John Dog Park | 301-495-2525 | 7400 Tuckerman Lane |
| Salisbury MD | Salisbury Dog Park | 410-334-3031 | 430 North Park Drive |
| Silver Spring MD | Wheaton Regional Park Dog Exercise Area | 301-680-3803 | 11717 Orebaugh Ave |

**Massachusetts Listings**

| | | | |
|---|---|---|---|
| Boston MA | Boston Common Off-Leash Dog Hours | 617-635-4505 | Beacon Street/H 2 |

| | | | |
|---|---|---|---|
| Boston MA | Peters Park Dog Run | | E. Berkeley and Washington St. |
| Cambridge MA | Danehy Park | 617-349-4800 | 99 Sherman Street |
| Cambridge MA | Fort Washington Park | | Waverly Street |
| Egremont MA | French Park Dog Park | 413-528-0182 | Baldwin Hill Road |
| Falmouth MA | Falmouth Dog Park | 508-524-5247 | 257 Brick Kiln Road (near the PAL building) |
| Hingham MA | Stoddard's Neck Dog Run | | Route 3A |
| Medway MA | Medway Dog Park | | Cottage Street and Village Street |
| Oak Bluffs MA | Trade Winds Preserve | 508-693-0072 | County Road |
| Provincetown MA | Pilgrim Bark Park | 508-487-1325 | Corner of Shank Painter Road and H 6 |
| Saugus MA | Breakheart Reservation Dog Park | 781-233-0834 | 177 Forest Street |
| Sharon MA | Sharon Dog Park | | East Foxboro Street |
| Somerville MA | Nunziato Field Dog Park | | 22 Vinal Avenue |

**Michigan Listings**

| | | | |
|---|---|---|---|
| Ada MI | Shaggy Pines Dog Park | 616-676-9464 | 3895 Cherry Lane SE |
| Bay City MI | Bay County Central Bark Park | | 800 Livingston Street |
| Birmingham MI | Lincoln Hills Dog Park | 248-530-1800 | 2666 W 14 Mile Road |
| Canton MI | Cherry Hill Village Dog Park | 734-394-5310 | 500 S Ridge Road |
| Clinton Township MI | Clinton Township Dog Park | 586-286-9336 | Romeo Plank Rd |
| East China Township MI | East China Township Dog Park | 810-989-6960 | 701 Recor Road |
| East Lansing MI | Northern Tail Dog Park | 517-319-6809 | 6400 Abbot Road |
| Frankenmuth MI | Frankenmuth Hund Platz | 989-652-3440 | 624 E Tuscola |
| Grand Rapids MI | Pet Supplies Plus Dog Park | | Lyon Avenue NE and Benjamin Avenue NE |
| Holland MI | Park Township Dog Park | 800-506-1299 | 1286 Ottawa Beach Road |
| Howell MI | E-Z Dog Park and Training Center | 810-599-6669 | 230 Norlynn Dr |
| Jackson MI | Paw Playground | 517-787-7387 | 1515 Carmen Drive |
| Kalamazoo MI | Meadow Run Dog Park | 269-353-4736 | 900 8th Street |
| Kalamazoo City MI | Fairmount Dog Park | 269-337-8191 | 1108 N Prairie Street |
| Lake Orion MI | Orion Oaks Dog Park | 248-858-0906 | 2301 Clarkston Road |
| Lansing MI | Soldan Dog Park | | 1601 East Cavanaugh Road |
| Madison Heights MI | Red Oaks Dog Park | 888-OCPARKS | 31353 Dequindre Road |
| Midland MI | Midland Dog Park | 989-837-6930 | Currie Parkway and Golfside Drive |
| Mount Clemens MI | Mt Clemens Dog Park (Behnke Dog Park) | | 300 N Groesbeck Highway |
| Pinckney MI | The Arise Community Dog Park | 734-878-1928 | 11211 Dexter-Pinckney Road |
| Portage MI | Bark Park | 269-324-9663 | 6604 Lovers Lane |
| Royal Oak MI | Cummingston Park Dog Run | 248-246-3300 | Torquay & Leafdale |
| Royal Oak MI | Mark Twain Park Dog Run | 248-246-3300 | 4600 North Campbell |
| Royal Oak MI | Quickstad Park Dog Run | 248-246-3300 | Marais between Normandy & Lexington |
| Royal Oak MI | Wagner Park Dog Run | 248-246-3300 | Detroit Ave, between Rochester and Main |
| Saline MI | Mill Pond Dog Park | | W. Bennett St |
| Saugatuck MI | Tails 'N Trails Dog Park | 269-857-7721 | 134th Avenue |
| Vicksburg MI | Prairie View County Park | 269-649-4737 | 899 E U Avenue |
| Vicksburg MI | Prairie View Dog Park | 269-649-4737 | 899 East U Avenue |
| Westland MI | Wayne County Parks Dog Park | | Hawthorne Ridge west of Merriman |
| Wixom MI | Lyon Oaks Dog Park | 248-858-0906 | 52221 Pontiac Trail |

**Minnesota Listings**

| | | | |
|---|---|---|---|
| Andover MN | Coons Rapids Dog Park | 763-767-6462 | Hanson Boulevard and 133rd Avenue |
| Benson MN | Waggin' Tails Dog Park | 320-808-3497 | H 12 and 22nd Street |
| Bloomington MN | Bloomington Off-leash Dog Park | 952-563-8892 | Nesbitt Ave and W 110th St |
| Burnsville MN | Alimagnet Dog Park | | 1200 Alimagnet Parkway |
| Coates MN | Dakota Woods Dog Park | 651-437-3191 | 16470 Blaine Ave. |
| Duluth MN | Keene Creek Dog Park | 218-730-4300 | I-35 and Grand Ave |
| Eden Prairie MN | Bryant Lake Regional Park Dog Park | 763-694-7764 | 6800 Rowland Road |
| Faribault MN | White Sands Dog Park | 507-334-2064 | 900 Lyndale Avenue N/H 21 |
| Hanover MN | Crow-Hassan Park Reserve Off-Leash Area | 763-694-7860 | 11629 Crow-Hassan Park Road |
| Mankato MN | Kiwanis Dog Park at Kiwanis Recreation Area | 507-387-8649 | Highway 169, north of the intersection of Highway 169 and Highway 14 |
| Maplewood MN | Battle Creek Dog Park | 651-748-2500 | Lower Afton Rd E at McKnight Rd S |
| Minneapolis MN | Franklin Terrace Off-Leash Rec Area | 612-230-6400 | Franklin Terrace at SE Franklin Ave |

| | | | |
|---|---|---|---|
| Minneapolis MN | Lake of the Isles Off-Leash Rec Area | 612-230-6400 | Lake of the Isles Pkwy at W. 28th St |
| Minneapolis MN | Loring Park Off-Leash Dog Park | | Maple St at Harmon Place |
| Minneapolis MN | Minneapolis - St Paul Airport Dog Park | 612-230-6400 | 6040 28th Ave S. |
| Minneapolis MN | Minnehaha Off-Leash Rec Area | 612-230-6400 | 54th St and Hiawatha Ave |
| Minneapolis MN | St. Anthony Parkway Off-Leash Rec Area | 612-230-6400 | St. Anthony Parkway |
| Minneapolis MN | Victory Prairie Dog Park | 612-230-6400 | 4701 N Russell Avenue |
| Osseo MN | Elm Creek Dog Off-Leash Area | 763-559-9000 | Elm Creek Rd at Zachary Lane N |
| Prior Lake MN | Cleary Lake Regional Park Dog Park | 763-559-9000 | Eagle Creek Ave SE at Texas Ave |
| Rockford MN | Lake Sarah Regional Park Off-Leash Area | 763-559-9000 | S Lake Sarah Dr at W Lake Sarah Drive |
| Roseville MN | Woodview Off-Leash Area | 651-748-2500 | Kent St at Larpenteur Ave W |
| Shoreview MN | Rice Creek North Trail Corridor Off-Leash Area | 651-748-2500 | Lexington Avenue at County Road J |
| St Paul MN | Arlington Arkwright Off-Leash Dog Area | 651-266-8989 | Arlington Ave E at Arkwright St |
| Victoria MN | Carver Park Reserve Off-Leash Dog Park | 763-694-7650 | 7025 Victoria Drive |
| White Bear MN | Otter Lake Regional Park Dog Park | 651-748-2500 | County Rd H2 E at Otter Lake Rd |
| Woodbury MN | Andy's Bark Park | | 11664 Dale Road |

**Mississippi Listings**

| | | | |
|---|---|---|---|
| Petal MS | Petal Dog Park | 601-554-5440 | Dawson Cut Off |
| Starkville MS | Starkville Dog Park | | N Jackson Street |
| Starkville MS | The Starkville Dog Park | 662-323-2294 | 405 Lynn Lane |
| Tupelo MS | Tupelo Dog Park | | Veterans Blvd (N. of the Eastwood Softball Complex) |

**Missouri Listings**

| | | | |
|---|---|---|---|
| Arnold MO | Arnold Dog Park | 636-282-2380 | Bradley Beach Road and Jeffco Blvd |
| Branson MO | Elmo & Rosalea Marrs Memorial Dog Park | 417-335-2368 | 524 Stockstill Lane |
| Chesterfield MO | The Eberwein Dog Park | | 1627 Old Baxter Road |
| Columbia MO | Twin Lakes Recreation Area | 573-445-8839 | 2500 Chapel Hill Road |
| Defiance MO | Broemmelsiek Park | 636-949-7535 | Schwede and Wilson Roads |
| Kansas City MO | Penn Valley Off-Leash Park | 816-784-5030 | W. 28th St. and Wyandotte St. |
| Kansas City MO | Penn Valley Off-Leash Park | 816-513-7500 | Pershing Road and Main Street |
| Kansas City MO | Wayside Waifs Bark Park | 816-761-8151 | 3901 Martha Truman Rd |
| Springfield MO | Cruse Dog Park | 417-864-1049 | 2100 W Catalpa Street |
| St Charles MO | DuSable Dog Park | 636-949-3372 | 2598 N Main Street |
| St Louis MO | Frenchtown Dog Park | | S 10th and Emmet Streets |
| St Louis MO | Lambert-St. Louis International Airport | 314-426-8000 | Lambert International Blvd |
| St Louis MO | Lister Dog Park | | Taylor Rd and Olive St |
| St Louis MO | Shaw Neighborhood Dog Park | | Thurman and Cleveland Ave |
| St Louis MO | Southwest City Dog Park - Member Only | | Jamieson Avenue |
| St Louis MO | Taylor Dog Park | | Taylor Rd |
| St Louis MO | Water Tower Dog Park | 314-552-9000 | S Grand and Russel Blvds |
| Wentzville MO | Quail Ridge Park | | Quail Ridge Rd |

**Montana Listings**

| | | | |
|---|---|---|---|
| Bozeman MT | Bozeman Dog Park | 406-582-3200 | 501 Haggerty Ln |
| Bozeman MT | Peets Hill - Burke Park | 406-582-3200 | S. Church and E. Story |
| Livingston MT | Moja Campbell Dog Park | 406-222-2111 | View Vista Drive |
| Missoula MT | Fort Missoula Canine Campus | | Fort Missoula Rd |
| Missoula MT | Jacob's Island Park Dog Park | 406-721-7275 | off VanBuren Street |
| Missoula MT | Jacobs Island Bark Park | | Van Buren St |
| Red Lodge MT | Double Ditch Dog Park | | Remington Ranch Road |

**Nebraska Listings**

| | | | |
|---|---|---|---|
| Hastings NE | Hastings Dog Park | 402-461-2324 | E South Street/H 6 |
| Kearney NE | Meadowlark North Dog Park | 308-237-4644 | 30th Avenue at 39th Street |
| Las Vegas NE | Winding Trails Park | 702-633-1171 | S Buffalo Drive and Oakey Boulevard |
| Lincoln NE | Rickman's Run (Holmes Lake Dog Run) | 402-441-7847 | 70th Street & Van Dorn Street |
| Norfolk NE | Off-Leash Dog Recreation Area | 402-844-2000 | 2201 South 13th Street |
| North Platte NE | Waggin' Tails Dog Park | 308-535-6772 | S McDonald Street |
| Omaha NE | Hefelinger Park Dog Park | 402-444-5900 | 112th Street and West Maple Road |

| | | | |
|---|---|---|---|
| Scottsbluff NE | Common Grounds Dog Park | 308-630-6238 | Off S Beltline Road |
| Scottsbluff NE | Scottsbluff Dog Park | 308-630-6238 | S Beltline Road |

**Nevada Listings**

| | | | |
|---|---|---|---|
| Henderson NV | Acacia Park Dog Park | 702-267-4000 | S Gibson Road and Las Palmas Entrada |
| Henderson NV | Dos Escuelas Park Dog Park | 702-267-4000 | 1 Golden View Street |
| Las Vegas NV | All American Park | 702-317-7777 | 121 E Sunset Road |
| Las Vegas NV | Barkin' Basin Park | 702-229-6297 | Alexander Road and Tenaya Way |
| Las Vegas NV | Centennial Hills Dog Park | 702-229-6297 | Buffalo Drive and Elkhorn Road |
| Las Vegas NV | Children's Memorial Park | 702-229-6718 | 6601 W Gowan Road |
| Las Vegas NV | Desert Breeze Dog Run | | 8425 W. Spring Mtn. Road |
| Las Vegas NV | Desert Inn Dog Park | 702-455-8200 | 3570 Vista del Monte |
| Las Vegas NV | Dog Fancier's Park | 702-455-8200 | 5800 E. Flamingo Rd. |
| Las Vegas NV | Justice Myron E. Leavitt Family Park (formerly known as Jaycee Park) | 702-229-6718 | E St Louis Avenue and Eastern Avenue |
| Las Vegas NV | Lorenzi Park | 702-229-4867 | 3075 W Washington Avenue |
| Las Vegas NV | Molasky Park Dog Run | 702-455-8200 | 1065 E. Twain Ave |
| Las Vegas NV | Police Memorial Park | 702-229-6297 | Cheyenne Avenue and Metro Academy Way |
| Las Vegas NV | Shadow Rock Dog Run | 702-455-8200 | 2650 Los Feliz on Sunrise Mountain |
| Las Vegas NV | Silverado Ranch Park Dog Park | 702-455-8200 | 9855 S. Gillespie |
| Las Vegas NV | Sunset Park Dog Run | 702-455-8200 | 2601 E. Sunset Rd |
| Las Vegas NV | Woofter Park | 702-633-1171 | Rock Springs and Vegas Drive |
| Reno NV | Link Piazzo Dog Park | 775-823-6501 | 4740 Parkway Drive |
| Reno NV | Rancho San Rafael Regional Park | 775-785-4512 | 1595 North Sierra Street |
| Reno NV | Sparks Marina Dog Park and Beach | 775-353-2376 | 300 Howard Drive |
| Reno NV | Virginia Lake Dog Park | 775-334-2099 | Lakeside Drive |
| Reno NV | Whitaker Dog Park | 775-334-2099 | 550 University Terrace |

**New Hampshire Listings**

| | | | |
|---|---|---|---|
| Conway NH | Mt. Washington Valley Dog Park | 603-447-3811 | 223 E Main Street |
| Derry NH | Derry Dog Park | 603-432-6100 | 45 Fordway |
| Portsmouth NH | South Mill Pond Portsmouth Dog Park | 603-431-2000 | South Mill Pond |

**New Jersey Listings**

| | | | |
|---|---|---|---|
| Barnegat Light NJ | Barnegat Light Dog Park/Beach | 609-494-9196 | W 10th Street |
| Bayonne NJ | Dennis P. Collins Dog Park | 201-858-7181 | 1st Street at Kennedy Blvd |
| Bedminster NJ | Bedminster Dog Park | 908-212-7014 | River Road at Rt 206 |
| Berkeley Township NJ | RJ Miller Airpark Dog Park | 732-506-9090 | Route 530 |
| Cape May NJ | Cape May Dog Park | 609-884-9525 | 705 Lafayette Street |
| Cherry Hill NJ | Cooper River Dog Park | 856-795-PARK | North Park Drive at Cuthbert Blvd |
| Cherry Hill NJ | Pooch Park in Cooper River Park | 856-225-5431 | North Park Drive |
| Flemington NJ | The Hunterdon County Off-Leash Dog Area | 908-782-1158 | 1020 State Route 31 |
| Hamilton NJ | Veteran's Park Dog Park | | Kuser Road |
| Hoboken NJ | Church Square Dog Run | | 4th and 5th, between Garden and Willow |
| Hoboken NJ | Elysian Park Dog Run | | Hudson between 10th and 11th |
| Hoboken NJ | Stevens Park Dog Run | | Hudson between 4th and 5th |
| Jersey City NJ | Van Vorst Dog Run | 201-433-5127 | Jersey Avenue and Montgomery Street |
| Lakewood NJ | Ocean County Park Dog Park | 732-506-9090 | Route 88 |
| Leonia NJ | Overpeck County Park Dog Run | 201-336-7275 | Fort Lee Road |
| Lincroft NJ | Thompson Park Dog Park | 732-842-4000x4256 | 805 Newman Springs Road |
| Lyndhurst NJ | Riverside County Park Dog Run | 201-336-7275 | Riverside Ave |
| Medford NJ | Freedom Park Dog Park | 609-654-2512 | Union Street at Main Street |
| Millburn NJ | Essex County South Mountain Dog Park | 973-268-3500 | Crest Drive |
| North Bergen NJ | Braddock Park Dog Park | 201-915-1386 | Bergenline Ave at 81st |
| Ocean City NJ | Ocean City Dog Park | | 45th Street and Haven Avenue |
| Oceanport NJ | Wolf Hill Off Leash Dog Park | 732-229-7025 | 3 Crescent Place |
| Princeton NJ | Rocky Top Private Dog Park | 732-297-6527 | 4106 Route 27 |
| West Windsor NJ | Mercer County Park | 609-448-1947 | Old Trenton Road at Robbinsville Rd |
| Westfield NJ | Echo Lake Dog Park | 908-527-4900 | Rt 22 |

| | | | |
|---|---|---|---|
| Woodcliff Lake NJ | Wood Dale County Park Dog Run | 201-336-7275 | Prospect Avenue |

**New Mexico Listings**

| | | | |
|---|---|---|---|
| Albuquerque NM | Coronado Dog Park | 505-768-1975 | 301 McKnight Ave. NW |
| Albuquerque NM | Los Altos Dog Park | 505-768-1975 | 821 Eubank Blvd. NE |
| Albuquerque NM | Montessa Park Off-Leash Area | 505-768-1975 | 3615 Los Picaros Rd SE |
| Albuquerque NM | Rio Grande Triangle Park Dog Park | 505-873-6620 | Iron Avenue |
| Albuquerque NM | Roosevelt Park Dog Park | 505-873-6620 | Hazeldine Avenue |
| Albuquerque NM | Santa Fe Village Dog Park | 505-768-1975 | 5700 Bogart St. NW |
| Albuquerque NM | Tom Bolack Urban Forest Dog Park | 505-873-6620 | Haines Avenue |
| Albuquerque NM | USS Bullhead Dog Park | 505-768-1975 | 1606 San Pedro SE |
| Deming NM | Deming Dog Park | | Granite St at E.J. Hooten Park |
| Deming NM | Raymond Reed Blvd Dog Park | | Raymond Reed Blvd across from Soccer Fields |
| Las Cruces NM | Las Cruces Dog Park | 575-541-2200 | N Hermosa Street (between E Hadley and Griggs Avenues) |
| Rio Rancho NM | Rainbow Dog Park | | Southern Blvd at Atlantic |
| Santa Fe NM | Frank Ortiz Park Off-Leash Area | 505-955-2100 | Camino Las Crucitas |

**New York Listings**

| | | | |
|---|---|---|---|
| Albany NY | Department of General Services Off Lead Area | 518-434-CITY (2489) | Erie Blvd |
| Albany NY | Hartman Road Dog Park | 518-434-CITY (2489) | Hartman Road |
| Albany NY | Normanskill Farm Dog Park | 518-434-CITY (2489) | Mill Road/Delaware Avenue |
| Albany NY | Westland Hills Dog Park | 518-434-CITY (2489) | Anthony Street |
| Ballston Spa NY | Kelly Park Dog Run | 518-885-9220 | Ralph Street & Malta Ave |
| Bronx NY | Ewen Park Dog Run | 212-NEW-YORK | Riverdale to Johnson Aves., South of West 232nd St. |
| Bronx NY | Hackett Park Dog Run | 212-NEW-YORK | Riverdale Ave. and W. 254th Street |
| Bronx NY | Pelham Bay Park Dog Run | 212-NEW-YORK | Middletown Rd. & Stadium Ave., Northwest of Parking Lot |
| Bronx NY | Seton Park Dog Run | 212-NEW-YORK | West 232nd St. & Independence Ave. |
| Bronx NY | Van Cortlandt Park Dog Run | 212-NEW-YORK | West 251st Street & Broadway |
| Bronx NY | Williamsbridge Oval Dog Run | 212-NEW-YORK | 3225 Reservoir Oval East |
| Brooklyn NY | Adam Yauch Park Palmetto Playground Dog Run | 212-NEW-YORK | Atlantic Ave, Furman, Columbia, State Streets |
| Brooklyn NY | Brooklyn Bridge Park Dog Run | 212-NEW-YORK | Adams Street and N/S Plymouth St |
| Brooklyn NY | Cooper Park Dog Run | 212-NEW-YORK | Olive St at Maspeth Ave |
| Brooklyn NY | DiMattina Park Dog Run | 212-NEW-YORK | Hicks, Coles and Woodhull Streets |
| Brooklyn NY | Dyker Beach Park Dog Run | 212-NEW-YORK | 86th Street from 7th Ave to 14th Ave |
| Brooklyn NY | Hillside Park Dog Run | 212-NEW-YORK | Columbia Heights & Vine Street |
| Brooklyn NY | J J Byrne Memorial Park Dog Run | 212-NEW-YORK | 3rd to 4th Streets between 4th and 5th Ave |
| Brooklyn NY | Manhattan Beach Dog Run | 212-NEW-YORK | East of Ocean Avenue, North Shore Rockaway inlet |
| Brooklyn NY | McCarren Park Dog Run | 212-NEW-YORK | Nassau Ave, Bayard, Leonard & N. 12th Sts |
| Brooklyn NY | McGolrick Park Dog Run | 212-NEW-YORK | North Henry Street at Driggs Ave |
| Brooklyn NY | Owls Head Park Dog Run | 212-NEW-YORK | Shore Pkwy, Shore Rd, Colonial Rd, 68th Street |
| Brooklyn NY | Prospect Park | 212-NEW-YORK | |

| | | | |
|---|---|---|---|
| Brooklyn NY | Seth Low Playground Dog Run | 212-NEW-YORK | Avenue P, Bay Parkway, W. 12th Street |
| Buffalo NY | The Barkyard | 716-218-0303 | D A R Drive |
| Cornwall NY | Cornwall Bark Park | 360-778-7000 | 15 Muser Drive |
| E Hampton NY | Springs Dog Park | 631-324-2417 | Three Mile Harbor Road |
| Elmsford NY | Elmsford Dog Park | | North Everts at Winthrop Avenue |
| Forest Park NY | Forest Park Dog Run | 212-NEW-YORK | Park Lane South & 85th Street |
| Hamburg NY | Rootie's Run | 716-649-7700 | 2900 Lakeview Road |
| Huntington NY | West Hills County Park Dog Run | 631-854-4423 | Sweet Hollow Rd at Old Country Road |
| Jamesville NY | Jamesville Beach Park Off-Leash Area | | South Street at Coye Rd |
| Lido Beach NY | Nickerson Beach Park Dog Run | 516-571-7700 | Merrick Road at Wantagh Avenue |
| Liverpool NY | Wegmans Good Dog Park | | Route 370 |
| Montebello NY | Kakiat Park Dog Park | 845-364-2670 | 668 Haverstraw Road |
| Montgomery NY | The Dog Park | 845-457-4900 | Grove Street |
| Montgomery NY | Thomas Bull Memorial Dog Park | 845-457-4900 | H 416 |
| Mount Tremper NY | Emerson Resort & Spa Dog Park | 877-688-2828 | 5340 H 28 |
| New City NY | Kennedy Dells Dog Park | 845-364-2670 | 355 North Main Street |
| New Rochelle NY | Paws Place in Ward Acres Park | | Broadfield Rd at Quaker Ridge Road |
| New York NY | Andrew Haswell Green Park Dog Run (East River Esplanade) | 212-NEW-YORK | East River at East 60th Street |
| New York NY | Carl Schurz Park Dog Run | 212-NEW-YORK | East End Ave.between 84th and 89th Street |
| New York NY | Central Park Off-Leash Hours and Areas | 212-NEW-YORK | |
| New York NY | Chelsea Waterside Park Dog Run | 212-627-2020 | 22nd St and 11th Avenue |
| New York NY | Coleman Playground Dog Run | 212-NEW-YORK | Pike St at Monroe St |
| New York NY | DeWitt Clinton Park Dog Run | 212-NEW-YORK | Between 10th and 11th Ave at 52nd and 54th |
| New York NY | Fish Bridge Park Dog Run | 212-NEW-YORK | Dover St., between Pearl & Water St. |
| New York NY | Fort Tryon Park Dog Run | 212-NEW-YORK | Margaret Corbin Drive, Washington Heights |
| New York NY | Highbridge Park Dog Run | 212-NEW-YORK | Amsterdam at Fort George Avenue |
| New York NY | Hudson River Park - Chelsea Waterside Dog Park | 212-NEW-YORK | W 44th Street at Pier 84 |
| New York NY | Hudson River Park - Leroy Street Dog Park | 212-NEW-YORK | Leroy Street at Pier 40 |
| New York NY | Inwood Hill Park Dog Run | 212-NEW-YORK | Dyckman St and Payson Ave |
| New York NY | J. Hood Wright Dog Run | 212-NEW-YORK | Fort Washington & Haven Aves., West 173rd St. |
| New York NY | Madison Square Park Dog Run | 212-NEW-YORK | Madison Ave. To 5th Ave. between East 23rd St. & East 26th St. |
| New York NY | Marcus Garvey Park Dog Run | 212-NEW-YORK | Madison Ave at East 120th Street |
| New York NY | Morningside Park Dog Run | 212-NEW-YORK | Morningside Avenue between 114th and 119th Streets |
| New York NY | Other New York City Off-Leash Areas | 212-NEW-YORK | |
| New York NY | Other New York City Off-Leash Areas | 212-NEW-YORK | |
| New York NY | Peter Detmold Park Dog Run | 212-NEW-YORK | West Side of FDR Drive between 49th and 51st |
| New York NY | Riverside Park Dog Runs | 212-NEW-YORK | Riverside Dr at W 72nd,87th, and 105th |
| New York NY | Robert Moses Park Dog Run | 212-NEW-YORK | 41st Street and 1st Ave. |
| New York NY | Sirius Dog Run | | Liberty St and South End Avenue |
| New York NY | St Nicholas Park Dog Run | 212-NEW-YORK | St Nicholas Ave at 135th Street |
| New York NY | Theodore Roosevelt Park Dog Run | 212-NEW-YORK | Central Park West and W 81st St. |
| New York NY | Thomas Jefferson Park Dog Run | 212-NEW-YORK | East 112th Street at FDR Drive |

| | | | |
|---|---|---|---|
| New York NY | Tompkins Square Park Dog Run | 212-NEW-YORK | 1st Ave and Ave B between 7th and 10th |
| New York NY | Union Square Dog Run | 212-NEW-YORK | Union Square |
| New York NY | Washington Sq. Park Dog Run | | Washington Sq. South |
| Ossining NY | Ossining Dog Park | 914-941-3189 | 235 Cedar Lane |
| Owego NY | Rebecca Weitsman Memorial Dog Park | 607-687-1199 | 359 Hickories Park Rd |
| Poughkeepsie NY | See Spot Run Off Leash Area | 845-452-1972 | 110 Overlook Road |
| Queens NY | Alley Pond Park Dog Run | 212-NEW-YORK | Alley Picnic Field Number 12 |
| Queens NY | Cunningham Park Dog Run | 212-NEW-YORK | 193rd Street between Aberdeen Road and Radnor Road |
| Queens NY | Doughboy Plaza Windmuller Park Dog Run | 212-NEW-YORK | Woodside Ave., 54-56 Sts. |
| Queens NY | K-9 Dog Run in Forest Park | 212-NEW-YORK | Park Lane South at 85th Street |
| Queens NY | Little Bay Dog Run | 212-NEW-YORK | Cross Island Parkway between Clearview Expwy and Utopia Parkway |
| Queens NY | Murray Playground Dog Run | 212-NEW-YORK | 21st Street & 45th Road on the SE side of park |
| Queens NY | Sherry Park Dog Run | 212-NEW-YORK | Queens Boulevard, 65 Place and the BQE |
| Queens NY | Underbridge Playground Dog Run | 212-NEW-YORK | 64th Ave and 64th Road on Grand Central Parkway service road |
| Queens NY | Veterans Grove Dog Run | 212-NEW-YORK | Judge & Whitney on the south side of the park |
| Rome NY | Bark Park | 315-339-7656 | 500 Chestnut Street |
| Roslyn NY | Christopher Morley Park Dog Run | 516-571-8113 | Searingtown Road |
| Seaford NY | Cedar Creek Dog Run | 516-571-7470 | Merrick Road at Wantagh Avenue |
| Sleepy Hollow NY | Kingsland Point Park Dog Park | 914-366-5104 | Palmer Ave at Munroe Ave |
| Smithtown NY | Blydenburgh County Park Dog Park | 631-854-4949 | Veterans Memorial Highway |
| Staten Island NY | Silver Lake Park Dog Run | 212-NEW-YORK | Victory Blvd just within Silver Lake Park |
| Staten Island NY | Wolfe's Pond Park Dog Run | 212-NEW-YORK | End of Huguenot & Chester Avenues |
| Wantagh NY | Wantagh Park Dog Run | 516-571-7460 | Kings Road at Canal Place |
| White Plains NY | Bark Dog Park | 914-422-1336 | Brockway Place at South Kensico Road |

## North Carolina Listings

| | | | |
|---|---|---|---|
| Asheville NC | Azalea Dog Park | 828-259-5800 | 395 Azalea Road |
| Asheville NC | French Broad River Park Dog Park | 828-259-5800 | 508 Riverview Dr., Asheville, NC 28806 |
| Charlotte NC | Barkingham Park | 704-432-4280 | 2900 Rocky River Road |
| Charlotte NC | Barkingham Park Dog Park - Reedy Creek | 704-336-3854 | 2900 Rocky River Rd. |
| Charlotte NC | Fetching Meadows Dog Park | 704-336-3854 | McAlpine Park |
| Charlotte NC | Frazier Park Dog Park | 704-432-4280 | 1201 W 4th Street Extension |
| Charlotte NC | Ray's Fetching Meadow | 704-432-4280 | 8711 Monroe Road |
| Charlotte NC | William R. Davie District Park | 704-541-9880 | 4635 Pineville-Matthews Road/H 51 |
| Cornelius NC | Swaney Pointe K-9 Park | 704-432-4280 | 18441 Nantz Road Cornelius |
| Gastonia NC | George Poston Park Dog Park | 704-922-2162 | 1101 Lowell Spencer Mountain Road |
| Greensboro NC | Bark Park | 336-545-5343 | 3905 Nathaneal Greene Drive |
| Kinston NC | Rotary Dog Park | 252-939-3332 | H 55/11 S |
| Raleigh NC | Carolina Pines | 919-831-6640 | 2305 Lake Wheeler Road/H 1375 |
| Raleigh NC | Millbrook Exchange Off Leash Dog Park | 919-872-4156 | 1905 Spring Forest Road |
| Raleigh NC | Oakwood Dog Park | | 910 Brookside Drive |
| Roanoke Rapids NC | Halifax County Visitors Center Dog Run | 800-522-4282 | 260 Premier Blvd |
| Roanoke Rapids NC | Halifax County Visitors Center Dog Run | 800-522-4282 | 260 Premier Blvd |
| Southern Pines NC | Martin Dog Park | 910-692-2463 | 350 Commerce Avenue |
| Wilmington NC | Wilmington Dog Park at Empie | 910-341-3237 | Independence Blvd at Park Avenue |

## North Dakota Listings

| | | | |
|---|---|---|---|
| Fargo ND | Village West Dog Park | | 45th Street |
| Grand Forks ND | Roaming Paws | 218-779-5037 | Lincoln Drive |

## Ohio Listings

| | | | |
|---|---|---|---|
| Brunswick OH | Brunswick Dog Park | | Cross Creek Rd at Rt 303 |
| Cincinnati OH | Clark Field Dog Park | | Clark Avenue & W. 11th Street |
| Cincinnati OH | Fido Field | | 630 Eggleston Ave |
| Cincinnati OH | Kellogg Park Dog Field | 513-357-6629 ext. 1 | 6701 Kellogg Avenue/H 52 |
| Cincinnati OH | Mt. Airy Forest Dog Park | 513-352-4080 | Westwood Northern Blvd. |
| Cincinnati OH | Otto Armleder Memorial Dog Park | | 5057 Wooster Pike |
| Cincinnati OH | Red Dog Park | | 5081 Madison Rd |
| Columbus OH | Big Walnut Dog Park | 614-645-3300 | 5000 E Livingston Avenue |
| Deerfield OH | Schappacher Dog Park | 513-701-6958 | 4686 Old Irwin-Simpson Rd |
| Delaware OH | Companion Club Dog Park | 740-881-2000 | 6306 Home Road |
| Dublin OH | Nando's Dog Park | | Cosgray and Shier Rings Road |
| Eastlake OH | Eastlake Dog Park | | 35740 Lakeshore Blvd at Woodland Park |
| Gahanna OH | Alum Creek Dog Park | 614-342-4250 | Hollenback Road |
| Gahanna OH | Pizzurro Dog Park | 614-855-3860 | 940 Pizzuro Park Way |
| Grove City OH | Wagtail Trail | 614-891-0700 | Off Georgesville Wrightsville Road |
| Huron OH | Erie MetroBark Park | 419-625-7783 x221 | 3109 Hull Rd |
| Lakewood OH | Lakewood Dog Park | | 1699 Valley Parkway |
| Lewis Center OH | Alum Creek Dog Park | | 3992 Hollenback Road |
| Marblehead OH | Bark Until Dark Dog Park | 419-732-3039 | 310 S. Bridge Rd. (SR 269) |
| Mason OH | Schappacher Park Dog Run | 513-701-6958 | 4686 Old Irwin Simpson Road |
| Medina OH | Medina Memorial Dog Park | | East Homestead St & N Harmony St. |
| Milford OH | Bark Park at Miami Meadows Park | | 1546 State Route 131 |
| Milford OH | Kennel Resorts | 513-831-7297 | 5825 Meadowview Drive |
| Newtown OH | WagsPark Dog Park | 513-322-5432 | 3810 Church Street |
| South Euclid OH | City of South Euclid Dog Park | | Monticello Blvd & South Belvoir Blvd |
| South Euclid OH | South Euclid Dog Park | | Monticello Blvd & South Belvoir Blvd |
| Stow OH | Double Dog Day Care & Indoor Dog Park | 330-968-4272 | 3073 Graham Road |
| Symmes OH | Symmes Township Dog Park | 513-683-6644 | 11600 N Lebanon Rd |
| Twinsburg OH | Twinsburg Dog Park | 216-233-5277 | Liberty Road & Abrams Dr. |
| Wellston OH | Lake Alma State Park | 740-384-4474 | 422 Lake Alma Road |
| West Chester OH | Wiggly Field | 513-759-7304 | 8070 Tylersville Road |
| Westerville OH | Westerville Bark Park | | 708 Park Meadow Road |
| Xenia OH | Scout Burnell-Garbrecht Dog Park | 937-562-7440 | 210 Fairground Road |

## Oklahoma Listings

| | | | |
|---|---|---|---|
| Bartlesville OK | Cooper Dog Park | | 2400 Adams Blvd/H 60 |
| Del City OK | Wiggly Field | | E Reno Avenue |
| Norman OK | Norman Community Dog Park | | Robinson and 12th St NE |
| Oklahoma City OK | Paw Park | 405-782-4311 | Grand Blvd. and Lake Hefner Parkway |
| Tulsa OK | Biscuit Acres at Hunter Park | 918-596-7275 | 5804 E 91 Street |
| Tulsa OK | Joe Station Bark Park | | 2279 Charles Page Blvd |
| Yukon OK | Pets and People Dog Park | | 701 Inla |

## Oregon Listings

| | | | |
|---|---|---|---|
| Ashland OR | The Dog Park | 541-488-6002 | Nevada and Helman Streets |
| Beaverton OR | Hazeldale Park Dog Park | | Off 196th, N of Farmington |
| Bend OR | Awbrey Butte Resevoir Off-Leash Area | 541-388-5435 | NW 10th and Trenton |
| Bend OR | Big Sky Dog Park | 541-389-7275 | 21690 NE Neff Road |
| Bend OR | Hollinshead Community Park | 541-388-5435 | 1235 NE Jones Road |
| Bend OR | Overturf Butte Reservoir | 541-388-5435 | Skyliner Summit Loop |
| Bend OR | Pine Nursery Community Park | 541-388-5435 | Yeoman Road |
| Bend OR | Ponderosa Community Park | 541-388-5435 | 225 SE 15th Street |
| Bend OR | Riverbend Dog Park | 541-388-5435 | 799 SW Columbia Street |
| Bend OR | Ruffwear Dog Park | 800-829-2442 | 13000 SW Century Drive |
| Canby OR | Molalla River State Park Off-Leash Area | 800-551-6949 | Canby Ferry Road |
| Corvallis OR | Bald Hill Park Dog Park | 541-766-6918 | Oak Creek Drive |
| Corvallis OR | Chip Ross Park Dog Park | 541-766-6918 | Lester Avenue |
| Corvallis OR | Crystal Lake Sports Field Dog Park | 541-766-6918 | Crystal Lake Drive |
| Corvallis OR | Martin Luther King Jr Park Dog Park | 541-766-6918 | Walnut Boulevard |

| Corvallis OR | Willamette Park Dog Park | 541-766-6918 | SE Goodnight Avenue |
| Corvallis OR | Woodland Meadow Park Dog Park | 541-766-6918 | Circle and Witham Hill Drive |
| Estacada OR | Milo McIver State Park Off-Leash Area | 503-630-7150 | Springwater Road |
| Eugene OR | Alton Baker Park Off-Leash Area | 541-682-4800 | Leo Harris Parkway |
| Eugene OR | Amazon Park Off-Leash Area | 541-682-4800 | Amazon Parkway |
| Eugene OR | Armitage Park Dog Park | 541-689-1503 | 90064 Coburg Road |
| Eugene OR | Candlelight Park Off-Leash Area | 541-682-4800 | Royal Avenue |
| Eugene OR | Wayne Morse Family Farm Off-Leash Area | 541-682-4800 | 595 Crest Drive |
| Hillsboro OR | Hondo Dog Park | 503-681-6120 | 4499 NW 229th Avenue (Near Hillsboro Stadium) |
| McMinnville OR | McMinnville Dog Park | 503-434-7359 | 1900 NE Riverside Drive |
| Medford OR | Bear Creek Park Dog Park | 541-774-2400 | Highland Drive |
| Milwaukie OR | North Clackamas Park | 503-794-8002 | 5440 SE Kellog Ck Drive |
| Newport OR | Agate Beach Neighborhood and Dog Park | 541-265-7783 | 185 NW 60th Street |
| Newport OR | Wilder Dog Park | 541-265-7783 | NE 50th Street |
| Portland OR | Brentwood Park Dog Park | 503-823-PLAY | 60th Street and Duke |
| Portland OR | Chimney Dog Park | 503-823-7529 | 9360 N. Columbia Blvd |
| Portland OR | Delta Park Off-Leash Area | 503-823-7529 | N. Expo Road & Broadacre |
| Portland OR | East Delta Park Off-Leash Area | 503-823-7529 | N. Union Court |
| Portland OR | Gabriel Park and Off-Leash Area | 503-823-7529 | SW 45 Ave and Vermont |
| Portland OR | Normandale Off-Leash Area | 503-823-7529 | NE 57th Ave at Halsey St |
| Portland OR | Portland's Unfenced Off-Leash Dog Areas | 503-823-PLAY | Various |
| Portland OR | Rooster Rock State Park Off-Leash Area | 503-695-2261 | I-84 |
| Roseburg OR | Happy Tails Dog Park | 541-440-1188 | 100 SE Templin St |
| Salem OR | Minto-Brown Island Park | 503-588-6336 | 2200 Minto Island Road |
| Salem OR | Orchard Heights Park | 503-588-6336 | 1165 Orchard Heights Road NW |
| Tigard OR | Ash Street Dog Park | 503-639-4171 | 12770 SW Ash Avenue |
| Tigard OR | Potso Dog Park | 503-639-4171 | Wall Street at Hunziker Street |
| Tigard OR | Summerlake Park Dog Park | 503-639-4171 | 11450 SW Winterlake Drive |
| Warrenton OR | Warrenton Dog Park | 503-861-3669 | NW Warrenton Drive/H 104 |
| West Linn OR | Mary S. Young Dog Park | 503-557-4700 | Hwy 43 |
| Wilsonville OR | Memorial Park Off-Leash Dog Park | 503-682-3727 | 8100 SW Wilsonville Road |

**Pennsylvania Listings**

| Beaver Falls PA | Bradys Run Park Dog Park | 724-770-2060 | 121 Bradys Run Road |
| Bellevue PA | Bellevue Dog Woods | | Memorial Park, Bellevue Road |
| Conneaut Lake PA | Conneaut Lake Bark Park | 814-382-2267 | 12810 Foust Road |
| Fayetteville PA | Norlo Dog Park | | W Main Street |
| Fort Washington PA | Mondaug Bark Park | | 1130 Camphill Road |
| Hanover PA | West Manheim Dog Park | | St. Bartholomew Road |
| Harrisburg PA | Lower Paxton Dog Park | | Dowhower and Union Deposit Roads |
| Horsham PA | Horsham Dog Park | 215-290-1917 | 1013 Horsham Road/H 463 |
| Lancaster PA | Beau's Dream Dog Park at Buchanan Park | | Buchanan Avenue and Race Avenue |
| Levittown PA | Falls Township Community Dog Park | 215-949-9000 ext. 220 or 221 | 9125 Millcreek Road |
| Library PA | South Park Dog Park | 412-350-7275 | Corrigan Drive at South Park |
| McKeesport PA | White Oak Dog Park | 412-350-7275 | Route 48 |
| Mechanicsburg PA | Lower Allen Dog Park | 717-975-7575 | 4075 Lisburn Road |
| Monroeville PA | Heritage Park Dog Park | 412-350-7275 | 2364 Saunders Station Road |
| Morrisville PA | Morrisville Dog Park | | S Delmorr and E Philadelphia Avenues |
| North Wales PA | Bark Park | | Welsh Road (H 63) and Bell Run Blvd |
| Philadelphia PA | Chester Avenue Dog Park | 215-748-3440 | Chester Ave and 48th |
| Philadelphia PA | Eastern State Dog Pen | | Corinthian Ave & Brown St |
| Philadelphia PA | Orianna Hill Dog Park | 215-423-4516 | North Orianna St, between Poplar and Wildey |
| Philadelphia PA | Pretzel Park Dog Run | | Cresson St |
| Philadelphia PA | Schuylkill River Park Dog Run | | 25th St between Pine and Locust |
| Philadelphia PA | Seger Dog Park | | 11th Street between Lombard and South St. |
| Pittsburgh PA | Frick Park Dog Park | 412-255-2539 | 6750 Forbes Avenue |
| Pittsburgh PA | Hartwood Acres Dog Park | 412-767-9200 | Middle Road |
| Pittsburgh PA | Upper Frick Dog Park | | Beechwood and Nicholson |
| Scranton PA | Connell Dog Park | | 800 Gibbons Street |
| Wyncote PA | Curtis Dog Park | | Church Road (H 73) and Greenwood Avenue |

| | | | |
|---|---|---|---|
| Wyncote PA | Curtis Dog Park | | 1250 W. Church Road |
| York PA | Canine Meadows | | Mundis Race Road |

**Rhode Island Listings**

| | | | |
|---|---|---|---|
| Barrington RI | Barrington Dog Park | 401-253-7482 | Rt 103 |
| Newport RI | Newport Dog Park | 401-845-5800 | Connell Highway |
| Pawtucket RI | Pawtucket Dog Park | 401-728-0500 | Newport Avenue/H 1 |
| Pawtucket RI | Pawtucket Dog Park | 401-728-0500 | Newport Avenue/H 1 |
| Providence RI | Dexter Training Ground Dog Park | | Dexter Street |
| Providence RI | Gano Street Dog Park | 401-785-9450 | Gano Street and Power |
| Warwick RI | Warwick City Dog Park | 401-738-2000 | 199 Shamrock Dr |

**South Carolina Listings**

| | | | |
|---|---|---|---|
| Charleston SC | Hampton Park Off-Leash Dog Park | | corner of Rutledge and Grove |
| Charleston SC | James Island County Park Dog Park | 843-795-PARK (7275) | 871 Riverland Drive |
| Columbia SC | NOMA Bark Park | | 1111 Parkside Drive |
| Columbia SC | Sesquicentennial State Park | 803-788-2706 | 9564 Two Notch Rd |
| Hilton Head SC | Chaplin Dog Park | 843-785-7616 | William Hilton Parkway/H 278 |
| Hilton Head SC | Chaplin Dog Park (Best Friends) | | Off Hwy 40 |
| Isle of Palms SC | Isle of Palms Dog Park | 843-886-8294 | 29th Ave behind Rec Center |
| Little River SC | Waggin' Tails Dog Park | 843-281-3800 | 50 Citizens Circle |
| Mount Pleasant SC | Palmetto Islands County Park Dog Park | 843-572-PARK (7275) | 444 Needlerush Parkway |
| Myrtle Beach SC | Myrtle Beach Barc Parc | 843-918-1000 | Kings Hwy at Mallard Lake Drive |
| North Charleston SC | Wannamaker County Park Dog Park | 843-572-PARK (7275) | 8888 University Blvd |

**South Dakota Listings**

| | | | |
|---|---|---|---|
| Sioux Falls SD | Lien Park Off-Leash Area | 605-367-6076 | North Cliff Avenue |
| Sioux Falls SD | Spencer Park Off-Leash Area | | 3501 South Cliff Avenue |
| Spearfish SD | Spearfish Off Leash Dog Park | 605-642-1333 | Roughlock Ln |

**Tennessee Listings**

| | | | |
|---|---|---|---|
| Chattanooga TN | Chattanooga Chew Chew Canine Park | | 1801 Carter Street |
| Clarksville TN | Heritage Park Bark Park | 931-645-7476 | 1241 Peachers Mill Road |
| Cookeville TN | Wag'n Tails of Cookeville Indoor/Outdoor Park | 931-528-2298 | 310 Newman Drive |
| Hixson TN | Greenway Farm Dog Park | 423-757-2143 | 5051 Gann Store Road |
| Hixson TN | Greenway Farms Dog Park | 423-425-6311 | 5051 Gann Store Road |
| Knoxville TN | Dogwood Park @ Victor Ashe Park | 865-215-1413 | 4901 Bradshaw Road |
| Knoxville TN | PetSafe Downtown Dog Park | 311 | Summit Hill Drive and Central Avenue |
| Knoxville TN | PetSafe Village Dog Park | 865-777-DOGS (3647) | 10427 Electric Avenue |
| Murfreesboro TN | Murfreesboro Bark Park | | 1540 W College Street |
| Nashville TN | Centennial Dog Park | 615-862-8400 | 31st Avenue and Park Plaza |
| Nashville TN | Centennial Dog Park | | 2900 Parthenon Avenue |
| Nashville TN | Edwin Warner Dog Park | 615-862-8400 | Vaughn Gap Road at Old Hickory Blvd |
| Nashville TN | Shelby Park | 615-862-8400 | South 20th and Shelby |

**Texas Listings**

| | | | |
|---|---|---|---|
| Abilene TX | Camp Barkeley Dog Park | | 2070 Zoo Lane |
| Arlington TX | Tails 'N Trails Dog Park | | 950 SE Green Oaks Blvd |
| Austin TX | Auditorium Shores Off-Leash Area | 512-974-6700 | 920 W. Riverside Drive |
| Austin TX | Davis White Northeast District Park Off-Leash Area | 512-974-6700 | 5909 Crystalbrook Drive |
| Austin TX | Emma Long Metro Park Off-Leash Area | 512-974-6700 | 1600 City Park Rd. |
| Austin TX | Far West Off-Leash Area | 512-974-6700 | Far West at Great Northern Blvd |
| Austin TX | Norwood Estate Off-Leash Area | 512-974-6700 | I-35 and Riverside Drive |
| Austin TX | Onion Creek District Park Off-Leash Area | 512-974-6700 | 6900 Onion Creek Drive |
| Austin TX | Red Bud Isle | | 3401 Redbud Trail |
| Austin TX | Red Bud Isle Off-Leash Area | 512-974-6700 | 3401 Red Bud Trail Unit Circle |
| Austin TX | Shoal Creek Dog Park | 512-974-6700 | 2600-2799 Lamar Blvd. |

| | | | |
|---|---|---|---|
| Austin TX | Shoal Creek Greenbelt-Central | 512-854-7275 | 2631 Shoal Creek Blvd (address for parking near off-leash site) |
| Austin TX | Walnut Creek Metropolitan Park Off-Leash Area | 512-974-6700 | 12138 North Lamar Blvd. |
| Austin TX | West Austin Park Off-Leash Area | 512-974-6700 | 1317 W 10th Street |
| Austin TX | Zilker Off-Leash Area | 512-974-6700 | 2100 Barton Springs Rd. |
| Baytown TX | Baytown Bark Park | 713-865-4500 | 4334 Crosby Cedar Bayou Road |
| College Station TX | University Dog Park | | 300 Park Road |
| Dallas TX | Wagging Tail Dog Park | 214-670-4100 | 5841 Keller Springs Road |
| Dallas TX | White Rock Dog Park | 214-670-8895 | 8000 Mockingbird Lane |
| Denton TX | Wiggly Field at Lake Forest Park | 940-349-8731 | 1400 E Ryan Road |
| Euless TX | Villages of Bear Creek Dog Park | 817-685-1429 | Bear Creek Parkway |
| Fairview TX | The Village at Allen Canine Commons Dog Park | 972-678-4939 | 329 Town Place |
| Fort Worth TX | Fort Woof Off-Leash Dog Park | 817-871-7638 | 3500 Gateway Park Drive |
| Grand Prairie TX | Central Bark | | 2222 W Warrior Trail |
| Grand Prairie TX | Paw Pals of Grand Prairie Dog Park | | 2222 W Warrior Trl |
| Houston TX | Congressman Bill Archer Park | 281-496-2177 | 3201 H 6 N |
| Houston TX | Danny Jackson Dog Park | 281-496-2177 | Westpark Drive (just east of Loop 610) |
| Houston TX | Ervan Chew Park Dog Park | 713-845-1000 | 4502 Dunlavy |
| Houston TX | Maxey Park Dog Park | | 601 Maxey Road |
| Houston TX | Millie Bush Dog Park | 713-755-6306 | Westheimer Parkway |
| Houston TX | TC Jester Dog Park | 713-865-4500 | 4201 TC Jester W |
| Houston TX | Tanglewood Bark Park | 713-865-4500 | Bering and Woodway |
| Irving TX | City of Irving Dog Park | 972-721-2256 | 4140 Valley View Lane |
| Leander TX | Devine Lake Off Leash Area | 512-528-9909 | 1000 Maple Creek |
| McAllen TX | McAllen Dog Park | | Tamarack Ave and 5th Street |
| Midland TX | Hogan's Dog Run | 432-685-7424 | 1201 E Wadley |
| North Richland Hills TX | Tipps Canine Hollow | 817-427-6620 | 7804 Davis Boulevard |
| Plano TX | Jack Carter Park Dog Park | 972-941-7250 | Pleasant Valley Drive |
| Round Rock TX | Round Rock Dog Depot (Dog Park) | 512-218-5540 | 800 Deerfoot Drive |
| San Antonio TX | Madison Square Dog Park | | 400 Lexington Avenue |
| San Antonio TX | McAllister Dog Park | 210-207-3000 | 13102 Jones-Maltsberger |
| San Antonio TX | Pearsall Park Dog Park | 210-207-3000 | 4700 Old Pearsall Road |
| San Antonio TX | Phil Hardberger Park Dog Park | 210-207-3284 | 13203 Blanco Road |
| Webster TX | Bay Area Doggy Park | 713-865-4500 | 7500 Bay Area Blvd |

**Utah Listings**

| | | | |
|---|---|---|---|
| Salt Lake City UT | Herman Franks Park | | 700 E 1300 S |
| Salt Lake City UT | Jordan Park | 801-972-7800 | 1060 South 900 West |
| Salt Lake City UT | Lindsey Gardens | 801-972-7800 | 9th Avenue and M Street |
| Salt Lake City UT | Memory Grove Park Off-Leash Park | 801-972-7800 | 485 N. Canyon Road |
| Salt Lake City UT | Parley's Gulch | 801-269-7499 | 2700 East Salt Lake City |
| Sandy UT | Sandy City Dog Park | 801-568-2900 | 9980 South 300 East |
| South Ogden UT | South Ogden Dog Park | | 4150 South Palmer Drive |
| St George UT | J.C. Snow Dog Park | 435-627-4500 | 900 S 400 E |
| Taylorsville UT | Millrace Off-Leash Dog Park | 801-963-5400 | 5400 South at 1100 West |

**Vermont Listings**

| | | | |
|---|---|---|---|
| Burlington VT | Starr Farm Dog Park | 802-864-0123 | Starr Farm Rd |
| Burlington VT | Waterfront Dog Park at Urban Reserve | 802-865-7247 | near Moran Building |
| Colchester VT | Niquette Bay State Park | 802-893-5210 | 274 Raymond Road |
| Hartford VT | Watson Upper Valley Dog Park | 802-295-5036 | H 14 W |
| Martinsville VT | SPCA of Henry County | 276-638-PAWS (7297) | 132 Joseph Martin H |

**Virginia Listings**

| | | | |
|---|---|---|---|
| Alexandria VA | Ben Brenman Dog Park | 703-838-4343 | at Backlick Creek |
| Alexandria VA | Braddock Road Dog Run Area | 703-838-4343 | SE Corner of Braddock Rd and Commonwealth |
| Alexandria VA | Chambliss Street Dog Run Area | 703-838-4343 | Chambliss St |
| Alexandria VA | Chinquapin Park Dog Run Area | 703-838-4343 | Chinquapin Park East of Loop |
| Alexandria VA | Duke Street Dog Park | 703-838-4343 | 5000 block of Duke Street |
| Alexandria VA | Fort Ward Park Offleash Dog Run | 703-838-4343 | East of Park Road |

| | | | |
|---|---|---|---|
| Alexandria VA | Fort Williams Dog Run Area | 703-838-4343 | Between Ft Wiliams and Ft Williams Parkway |
| Alexandria VA | Founders Park Dog Run Area | 703-838-4343 | Oronoco St and Union St |
| Alexandria VA | Hooff's Run Dog Run Area | 703-838-4343 | Commonwealth between Oak and Chapman St |
| Alexandria VA | Montgomery Park Dog Park | 703-838-4343 | Fairfax and 1st Streets |
| Alexandria VA | Monticello Park Dog Run Area | 703-838-4343 | Monticello Park |
| Alexandria VA | Simpson Stadium Dog Park | 703-838-4343 | Monroe Avenue |
| Alexandria VA | Tarleton Park Dog Run Area | 703-838-4343 | Old Mill Run west of Gordon St |
| Alexandria VA | W&OD Railroad Dog Run Area | 703-838-4343 | Raymond Avenue |
| Alexandria VA | Windmill Hill Park Dog Run Area | 703-838-4343 | Gibbon and Union Streets |
| Annandale VA | Mason District Dog Park | | 6621 Columbia Pike |
| Arlington VA | Benjamin Banneker Park Dog Run | | 1600 Block North Sycamore |
| Arlington VA | Fort Barnard Dog Park | | Corner of South Pollard St and South Walter Reed Drive |
| Arlington VA | Glencarlyn Dog Park | | 301 South Harrison St |
| Arlington VA | Madison Community Center Dog Park | | 3829 North Stafford St |
| Arlington VA | Shirlington Dog Park | | 2601 South Arlington Mill Drive |
| Arlington VA | Towers Dog Park | | 801 South Scott St |
| Charlottesville VA | Darden Towe Park | 434-296-5844 | 1445 Darden Towe Park Road |
| Chesapeake VA | Chesapeake City Dog Park | 757-382-6411 | 900 Greenbrier Parkway |
| Chesapeake VA | Western Branch Park | 757-382-6411 | 4437 Portsmouth Blvd |
| Herndon VA | Chandon Dog Park | | 900 Palmer Drive |
| Norfolk VA | Brambleton Dog Park | 757-441-2400 | Booth Street and Malloy Ave |
| Norfolk VA | Cambridge Crescent Dog Park | 757-441-2400 | Cambridge Place and Cambridge Place |
| Norfolk VA | Dune Street Dog Park | 757-441-2400 | 400 block Dune St |
| Oakton VA | Blake Lane Dog Park | | 10033 Blake Lane |
| Reston VA | Baron Cameron Dog Park | | 11300 Baron Cameron Avenue |
| Richmond VA | Barker Field Dog Park | 804-646-5733 | South Boulevard |
| Richmond VA | Church Hill Dog Park (Chimborazoo) | 804-646-0954 | 2900 E Grace Street |
| Richmond VA | Ruff House Dog Park at Rockwood Park | 804-748-1623 | 3401 Courthouse Road |
| Springfield VA | South Run Dog Park | | 7550 Reservation Drive |
| Virginia Beach VA | Red Wing Park Dog Park | 757-437-2038 | 1398 General Booth Blvd. |
| Virginia Beach VA | Woodstock Park Dog Park | 757-366-4538 | 5709 Providence Rd. |

**Washington Listings**

| | | | |
|---|---|---|---|
| Bainbridge Island WA | Eagledale Park Off-Leash Dog Park | 206-842-2306 | 5055 Rose Avenue NE |
| Ballard WA | Golden Gardens Dog Park | 206-684-4075 | 8498 Seaview Place NW |
| Ballard WA | Golden Gardens Park Dog Park | 206-684-4075 | 8498 Seaview Place NW |
| Bellevue WA | Robinswood Off-Leash Dog Corral | 425-452-6881 | 2430 148th Ave SE |
| Bonney Lake WA | Viking Park Off-Leash Dog Park | 253-447-4334 | 18902 E 82nd Street E |
| Bremerton WA | Bremerton Bark Park | 360-473-5305 | 1199 Union Avenue |
| Brush Prairie WA | Lucky Dog Park | 360-619-1111 | NE 149th Street and NE 101st Place |
| Burley WA | Bandix Dog Park | | Bandix Road SE at Burley-Olalla Rd |
| Coupeville WA | Patmore Pit Off-Leash Area | 360-321-4049 | Patmore Rd At Keystone Hill Rd |
| Everett WA | Loganberry Lane Off-Leash Area | 425-257-8300 | 18th Ave. W. |
| Everett WA | Lowell Park Off-Leash Area | 425-257-8300 | 46th St at S 3rd Ave. |
| Federal Way WA | French Lake Dog Park | 253-835-6901 | 31531 1st Ave S |
| Freeland WA | Marguerite Brons Dog Park | 360-321-4049 | WA 525 at Bayview Rd |
| Friday Harbor WA | Eddie and Friends Dog Park | 360-378-4953 | Mullis Street |
| Issaquah Highlands WA | Bark Park | 425-507-1107 | 2702 Magnolia Street |
| Lakewood WA | Fort Steilacoom Park Off-Leash Area | | 8714 87th Avenue SW |
| Longview WA | Gerhart Gardens Off-Leash Dog Park | 360-442-5000 | 200 Freedom Rd |
| Marysville WA | Strawberry Fields for Rover | 360-651-0633 | 6102 152nd Street NE |
| Mercer Island WA | Luther Burbank Dog Park | 206-236-3545 | 2040 84th Avenue SE |
| Mountlake Terrace WA | Mountlake Terrace Dog Park | 425 776 9173 ext. 1109 | 53rd Avenue W and 228th Street SW |
| Oak Harbor WA | Clover Valley Dog Park | 360-321-4049 | Oak Harbor at Ault Field Rd |
| Oak Harbor WA | Technical Dog Park | 360-321-4049 | Technical Park at Goldie Rd |
| Port Angeles WA | Port Angeles Dog Park | | 1469 W Lauridsen Blvd |
| Port Orchard WA | Howe Farm Historic Park and Off-Leash Dog Area | 360-337-5350 | Long Lake Rd at Sedgwick Rd |
| Poulsbo WA | Raab Dog Park | 360-779-9898 | 18349 Caldart Ave |
| Puyallup WA | Puyallup Dog Park | 253-841-4321 | 1700 12th Avenue SW |
| Redmond WA | Marymoor Park Off-Leash Area | 206-205-3661 | 6046 West Lake |
| Richland WA | Paws-Ability Place | 509-942-7529 | 350 Keene Road |

| | | | |
|---|---|---|---|
| Sammamish WA | Beaver Lake Park Off-Leash Area | 425-295-0500 | SE 24th Street at 244th Avenue SE |
| Seatac WA | Grandview Park Dog Park | 425-881-0148 | |
| Seattle WA | Dr. Jose Rizal Park Off-Leash Area | 206-684-4075 | 1007 12th Avenue S |
| Seattle WA | Genesee Park Dog Park | 206-684-4075 | 46th Avenue S & S Genesee Street |
| Seattle WA | I-5 Colonnade Dog Park | 206-684-4075 | E. Howe Street at Lakeview Blvd |
| Seattle WA | I-90 "Blue Dog Pond" Off-Leash Area | 206-684-4075 | S Massachusetts |
| Seattle WA | Northacres Park Off-Leash Area | 206-684-4075 | 12718 1st Ave NE |
| Seattle WA | Plymouth Pillars Dog Park | 206-684-4075 | Boren Avenue at Pike Street |
| Seattle WA | Regrade Park Off-Leash Area | 206-684-4075 | 2251 3rd Avenue |
| Seattle WA | Sand Point Magnuson Park Dog Off-Leash Area | 206-684-4946 | 7400 Sand Point Way NE |
| Seattle WA | Westcrest Park | 206-684-4075 | 8806 8th Avenue SW |
| Seattle WA | Woodland Park Off-Leash Area | 206-684-4075 | 1000 N 50th St |
| Sedro-Woolley WA | Bark Park | 360-855-1661 | 710 Front Street |
| Sequim WA | Sequim Dog Park | 360-681-2371 | 202 N Blake Avenue |
| Snoqualmie WA | The Three Forks Natural Area Off-Leash Dog Park | 425-888-1555 | 39912 SE Park Street |
| Spokane WA | SCRAPS Dog Park | 509-477-2532 | 26715 E Spokane Bridge Rd |
| Spokane WA | Spok Animal Dog Park | 509-534-8133 | S A Street & Riverside Avenue |
| Tacoma WA | Rogers Park Off-Leash Dog Park | 253-305-1060 | E L St At E Wright Ave |
| Vancouver WA | Pacific Community Park Dog Park | 360-619-1123 | NE 18th Street between NE 164th and 172nd Avenues |
| Vancouver WA | Ross Off-Leash Rec Area | 360-619-1111 | NE Ross St at NE 18th St |
| West Seattle WA | Westcrest Park and Off-Leash Dog Park | | 9000 8th Avenue SW |

**West Virginia Listings**

| | | |
|---|---|---|
| Charleston WV | East End Dog Park | 592 Washington Street, East |
| Eleanor WV | Eleanor Dog Park at Putnam Park | Putnam County Park |
| Fairmont WV | FIDO's Backyard | East Marion Park |
| Hurricane WV | Valley Dog Park | 2 Valley Park Rd |
| Morgantown WV | Krepps Park Dog Park | Krepps Park |
| Morgantown WV | Stanley's Spot Dog Park | Pleasant Street and Spruce Street |
| Waverly WV | Mountwood Park Dog Park | Mountwood Park |

**Wisconsin Listings**

| | | | |
|---|---|---|---|
| Appleton WI | Outagamie County Dog Park | | French Road and Highway OO |
| Brookfield WI | Brookfield Dog Park | | River Rd |
| Cross Plains WI | Indian Lake Pet Exercise Area | 608-266-4711 | Hwy 19 |
| Eau Claire WI | Eau Claire Dog Park | 715-839-4923 | 4503 House Rd |
| Egg Harbor WI | Harbor Hounds Dog Park | | Church St |
| Grafton WI | Muttland Meadows Dog Park | | 789 Green Bay Road |
| Green Bay WI | Brown County Park and Pet Exercise Area | 920-448-4466 | Highway 54 |
| Janesville WI | Palmer Park Pet Exercise Area | | Palmer Park |
| Janesville WI | Rock River Parkway Pet Exercise Area | | Rock River Parkway |
| Johnson Creek WI | Jefferson County Dog Park | | Hwy 26 |
| Madison WI | Brittingham Park Dog Park | 608-266-4711 | 401 West Shore Dr |
| Madison WI | Quann Park Dog Park | 608-266-4711 | 1802 Expo Drive |
| Madison WI | Sycamore Park Dog Park | 608-266-4711 | 4517 Sycamore Park |
| Madison WI | Token Creek Park Pet Exercise Area | 608-266-4711 | Hwy 51 |
| Madison WI | Warner Park Dog Park | 608-266-4711 | Sheridan Drive |
| Madison WI | Yahara Heights Pet Exercise Area | 608-266-4711 | 5428 State Highway 113 |
| Marshfield WI | Marshfield Dog Park Paws 'N Play | | S Peach Ave & 21st Street |
| Mequon WI | Katherine Kearny Carpenter Dog Run | | N Katherine Dr |
| Middleton WI | Middleton Pet Exercise Area | 608-266-4711 | County Highway Q S of Hwy K |
| Milton WI | Tails n Trails Dog Park | 608-868-6900 | John Paul Road and Vincent Street |
| Milwaukee WI | Runway Dog Exercise Area | | 1214 E Rawson Ave |
| Oshkosh WI | Winnebago County Community Park Dog Park | 920-232-1960 | 501 East County Road Y |
| Portage WI | Standing Rock Park Dog Exercise Area | 715-346-1433 | Standing Rocks Road |
| Sister Bay WI | Sister Bay Dog Park | 920-854-4118 | Autumn Court |
| Stevens Point WI | Point Dog Park | | 601 Mason Street |
| Stoughton WI | Viking Park Pet Exercise Area | 608-266-4711 | Highway N |
| Sun Prairie WI | Sun Prairie Pet Exercise Area | 608-266-4711 | S. Bird Street |
| Tomahawk WI | Tomahawk Area Dog Park | | SARA Park |

| | | | |
|---|---|---|---|
| Verona WI | Prairie Moraine Parkway Pet Exercise Area | 608-266-4711 | County Hwy PB |
| Waupaca WI | Waupaca County Dog Park | 715-258-6243 | Hwy K |
| Waupun WI | Waupun Dog Park | 920-324-7900 | 903 N Madison Street |
| Wausau WI | Mountain Park Dog Exercise Area | 715-261-1550 | Stewart Avenue (H 52) and 17th Avenue |
| Weston WI | Weston Dog Park | 715-359-9988 | 6100 Rogan Lane |

**Wyoming Listings**

| | | | |
|---|---|---|---|
| Cheyenne WY | Nancy Mockler Community Dog Park | 307-632-6655 | 800 SW Drive |

# Canada Listings

**Alberta Listings**

| | | | |
|---|---|---|---|
| Acadia AB | Acadia Off-Leash Areas | 403-268-2489 | Various |
| Altadore AB | Altadore Off-Leash Areas | 403-268-2489 | Various |
| Bankview AB | Bankview Off-Leash Areas | 403-268-2489 | Various |
| Beaverdam AB | Beaverdam Off-Leash Areas | 403-268-2489 | Various |
| Beddington Heights AB | Beddington Heights Off-Leash Areas | 403-268-2489 | Various |
| Belgravia AB | Belgravia Off-Leash Area | 780-496-1475 | Saskatchewan Dr at University Ave |
| Bowness AB | Bowness Off-Leash Areas | 403-268-2489 | Various |
| Braeside AB | Braeside Off-Leash Areas | 403-268-2489 | Various |
| Brentwood AB | Brentwood Off-Leash Areas | 403-268-2489 | Various |
| Briar Hill AB | Briar Hill Off-Leash Areas | 403-268-2489 | Various |
| Bridgeland AB | Bridgeland Off-Leash Areas | 403-268-2489 | Various |
| Britannia AB | Britannia Off-Leash Areas | 403-268-2489 | Various |
| Calgary AB | Bowmont Park Home Road Off-Leash Area | 403-268-2489 | Home Road at 52 St NW |
| Calgary AB | Bowmont Park Silver Springs Gate Off-Leash Area | 403-268-2489 | SilverView Dr and SilverView Way NW |
| Callingwood North AB | West Jasper Place Park Off-Leash Area | 780-496-1475 | 69 Ave at 172 St |
| Cambrian Heights AB | Cambrian Heights Off-Leash Areas | 403-268-2489 | Various |
| Coach Hill AB | Coach Hill Off-Leash Areas | 403-268-2489 | Various |
| Collingwood AB | Collingwood Off-Leash Areas | 403-268-2489 | Various |
| Crescent Heights AB | Crescent Heights Off-Leash Areas | 403-268-2489 | Various |
| Cromdale AB | Cromdale Off-Leash Area | 780-496-1475 | Kinnard Ravine at 78 St. |
| Deer Ridge AB | Deer Ridge Off-Leash Areas | 403-268-2489 | Various |
| Diamond Cove AB | Diamond Cove Off-Leash Areas | 403-268-2489 | Various |
| Dunluce AB | Orval Allen Park Off-Leash Area | 780-496-1475 | 127 St South of 162 Ave |
| Eagleridge AB | Eagleridge Off-Leash Areas | 403-268-2489 | Various |
| East Village AB | East Village Off-Leash Areas | 403-268-2489 | Various |
| Edgemont AB | Edgemont Off-Leash Areas | 403-268-2489 | Various |
| Edmonton AB | Buena Vista Great Meadow Off-Leash Area | 780-496-1475 | Buena Vista Dr and Valleyview Cres NW |
| Edmonton AB | Jackie Parker Park Off-Leash Area | 780-496-1475 | Whitemud Dr and 50 St. |
| Elbow Park AB | Elbow Park Off-Leash Areas | 403-268-2489 | Various |
| Elboya AB | Elboya Off-Leash Areas | 403-268-2489 | Various |
| Fairview AB | Fairview Off-Leash Areas | 403-268-2489 | Various |
| Falconridge AB | Falconridge Off-Leash Areas | 403-268-2489 | Various |
| Forest Lawn Industrial AB | Forest Lawn Off-Leash Areas | 403-268-2489 | Various |
| Glenbrook AB | Glenbrook Off-Leash Areas | 403-268-2489 | Various |
| Greenview AB | Greenview Off-Leash Areas | 403-268-2489 | Various |
| Hawkwood AB | Hawkwood Off-Leash Areas | 403-268-2489 | Various |
| Haysboro AB | Haysboro Off-Leash Areas | 403-268-2489 | Various |
| Hidden Valley AB | Hidden Valley Off-Leash Areas | 403-268-2489 | Various |
| Huntington Hills AB | Huntington Hills Off-Leash Areas | 403-268-2489 | Various |
| Inglewood AB | Inglewood Off-Leash Areas | 403-268-2489 | Various |
| Jasper AB | Jasper Off-Leash Area | 780-852-3356 | Highway 93A and Sleepy Hollow Road |
| Lake Bonavista AB | Lake Bonavista Off-Leash Areas | 403-268-2489 | Various |
| Lakeview AB | Lakeview Off-Leash Areas | 403-268-2489 | Various |
| Lauderdale AB | Grand Trunk Park Off-Leash Area | 780-496-1475 | 127 Ave at 109 St |

| | | | |
|---|---|---|---|
| Lynnwood Ridge AB | Lynnwood Ridge Off-Leash Areas | 403-268-2489 | Various |
| Mapleridge AB | Mapleridge Off-Leash Areas | 403-268-2489 | Various |
| Marlborough AB | Marlborough Off-Leash Areas | 403-268-2489 | Various |
| Martindale AB | Martindale Off-Leash Areas | 403-268-2489 | Various |
| Mayland Heights AB | Mayland Heights Off-Leash Areas | 403-268-2489 | Various |
| Montgomery AB | Montgomery Off-Leash Areas | 403-268-2489 | Various |
| North Haven AB | North Haven Off-Leash Areas | 403-268-2489 | Various |
| Ogden AB | Ogden Off-Leash Areas | 403-268-2489 | Various |
| Parkland AB | Parkland Off-Leash Areas | 403-268-2489 | Various |
| Pineridge AB | Pineridge Off-Leash Areas | 403-268-2489 | Various |
| Pumphill AB | Pumphill Off-Leash Areas | 403-268-2489 | Various |
| Queensland AB | Queensland Off-Leash Areas | 403-268-2489 | Various |
| Ramsay AB | Ramsay Off-Leash Areas | 403-268-2489 | Various |
| Ranchlands AB | Ranchlands Off-Leash Areas | 403-268-2489 | Various |
| Renfrew AB | Renfrew Off-Leash Areas | 403-268-2489 | Various |
| Riverbend AB | Riverbend Off-Leash Areas | 403-268-2489 | Various |
| Riverdale AB | Riverdale Off-Leash Areas | 403-268-2489 | Various |
| Rosedale AB | Rosedale Off-Leash Areas | 403-268-2489 | Various |
| Roxboro AB | Roxboro Off-Leash Areas | 403-268-2489 | Various |
| Rundle AB | Rundle Off-Leash Areas | 403-268-2489 | Various |
| Sandstone AB | Sandstone Off-Leash Areas | 403-268-2489 | Various |
| Scarboro AB | Scarboro Off-Leash Areas | 403-268-2489 | Various |
| Scenic Acres AB | Scenic Acres Off-Leash Areas | 403-268-2489 | Various |
| Shaganappi AB | Shaganappi Off-Leash Areas | 403-268-2489 | Various |
| Silver Springs AB | Silver Springs Off-Leash Areas | 403-268-2489 | Various |
| Southwood AB | Southwood Off-Leash Areas | 403-268-2489 | Various |
| Spruce Cliff AB | Spruce Cliff Off-Leash Areas | 403-268-2489 | Various |
| Strathcona AB | Strathcona Off-Leash Areas | 403-268-2489 | Various |
| Sunalta AB | Sunalta Off-Leash Areas | 403-268-2489 | Various |
| Thorncliffe AB | Thorncliffe Off-Leash Areas | 403-268-2489 | Various |
| Varsity AB | Varsity Off-Leash Areas | 403-268-2489 | Various |
| Wellington AB | Wellington Off-Leash Area | 780-496-1475 | West of 141 St from 137 Ave to 132 Ave |
| Willowpark AB | Willowpark Off-Leash Areas | 403-268-2489 | Various |
| Woodbine AB | Woodbine Off-Leash Areas | 403-268-2489 | Various |

**British Columbia Listings**

| | | | |
|---|---|---|---|
| Burnaby BC | Confederation Park Off-Leash Area | 604-294-7450 | Willingdon Avenue |
| South Burnaby BC | Burnaby Fraser Foreshore Park Off-Leash Area | 604-294-7450 | Byrne Road |
| Vancouver BC | Balaclava Park Off-Leash Dog Park | 604-257-8689 | 4594 Balaclava Street |
| Vancouver BC | Charleson Park Off-Leash Dog Park | 604-257-8400 | 999 Charleson Street |
| Vancouver BC | Cooper's Park Off-Leash Dog Park | 604-257-8400 | 1020 Marinaside Crescent |
| Vancouver BC | Dusty Greenwell Park Off-Leash Dog Park | 604-257-8613 | 2799 Wall Street |
| Vancouver BC | Falaise Park Off-Leash Dog Park | 604-257-8613 | 3434 Falaise Avenue |
| Vancouver BC | Fraserview Golf Course Off-Leash Dog Park | 604-257-8613 | 8101 Kerr Street |
| Vancouver BC | George Park Off-Leash Dog Park | 604-257-8689 | 500 E 63rd Avenue |
| Vancouver BC | Jones Park Off-Leash Dog Park | 604-257-8613 | 5350 Commercial Street |
| Vancouver BC | Killarney Park Off-Leash Dog Park | 604-257-8613 | 6205 Kerr Street |
| Vancouver BC | Kingscrest Park Off-Leash Dog Park | 604-257-8613 | 4150 Knight Street |
| Vancouver BC | Locarno Park Off-Leash Dog Park | 604-257-8689 | NW Marine Drive and Trimble Street |
| Vancouver BC | Musqueam Park Off-Leash Dog Park | 604-257-8689 | 4000 SW Marine Drive |
| Vancouver BC | Nat Bailey Stadium Off-Leash Dog Park | 604-257-8689 | 4601 Ontario Street |
| Vancouver BC | Nelson Park Off-Leash Dog Park | 604-257-8400 | 1030 Bute Street |
| Vancouver BC | Oak Meadows Dog Park | 604-257-8689 | 899 W 37th Ave |
| Vancouver BC | Queen Elizabeth Park Off-Leash Dog Park | 604-257-8689 | 4600 Cambie Street |
| Vancouver BC | Quilchena Park Off-Leash Dog Park | 604-257-8689 | 4590 Magnolia Street |
| Vancouver BC | Sparwood Park Off-Leash Dog Park | 604-257-8613 | 6998 Arlington Street |
| Vancouver BC | Stanley Park Dog Park for Small Dogs Only | 604-257-8400 | Stanley Park Shuffleboard Court Area |
| Vancouver BC | Strathcona Park Off-Leash Dog Park | 604-257-8613 | 857 Malkin Avenue |
| Vancouver BC | Sunrise Park Off-Leash Dog Park | 604-257-8613 | 1950 Windermere Street |
| Vancouver BC | Sunset Park Off-Leash Dog Park | 604-257-8689 | 300 E 53rd Avenue |
| Vancouver BC | Tecumseh Park Off-Leash Dog Park | 604-257-8613 | 1751 E 45th Avenue |

| | | | |
|---|---|---|---|
| Vancouver BC | Valdez Park | 604-257-8689 | 3210 W 22nd Avenue |
| Victoria BC | Alexander Park Off-Leash Area | 250-361-0600 | |
| Victoria BC | Arbutus Park Off-Leash Area | 250-361-0600 | Washington Street |
| Victoria BC | Oswald Park Off-Leash Area | 250-361-0600 | Stroud Rd at Gosworth Rd |
| Victoria BC | Redfern Park Off-Leash Area | 250-361-0600 | Redfern St at Leighton Ave |
| Victoria BC | Topaz Park Off-Leash Area | 250-361-0600 | Topaz at Blanshard |
| Victoria BC | Victoria West Park Off-Leash Area | 250-361-0600 | Wilson St at Bay St |

**Manitoba Listings**

| | | | |
|---|---|---|---|
| Brandon MB | East End Paw Park | 204-729-2150 | 11 Street East & Victoria Avenue East |
| Brandon MB | Hanbury Hill Pooch Park | 204-729-2150 | 600 Braecrest Drive |
| Brandon MB | The Doggie Diamond | 204-729-2148 | 2720 Park Ave |
| Winnipeg MB | Bourkevale Dog Park | 204-986-7623 | 100 Ferry Rd |
| Winnipeg MB | Juba Park Off-Leash Area | 204-986-7623 | Bannatyne Ave at Ship St. |
| Winnipeg MB | Kilcona Park Off-Leash Area | 204-986-7623 | Lagimodiere Blvd at Springfield Road |
| Winnipeg MB | King's Park Park Off-Leash Area | 204-986-7623 | King's Drive at Kilkenny Drive |
| Winnipeg MB | Little Mountain Park Off-Leash Area | 204-986-7623 | Klimpke Road at Farmers Rd |
| Winnipeg MB | Maple Grove Park Off-Leash Area | 204-986-7623 | 190 Frobisher Road |
| Winnipeg MB | St. Boniface Industrial Park Off-Leash Area | 204-986-7623 | Mazenod Rd at Camile Sys |
| Winnipeg MB | Sturgeon Road Dog Park | 204-986-7623 | Sturgeon Rd at Silver Avenue |
| Winnipeg MB | Westview Park Off-Leash Area | 204-986-7623 | Midland Street and Saskatchewan Avenue |
| Winnipeg MB | Woodsworth Park Off-Leash Area | 204-986-7623 | King Edward Ave at Park Lane |

**Nova Scotia Listings**

| | | | |
|---|---|---|---|
| Halifax NS | Point Pleasant Park Off-Leash Area | | Point Pleasant Dr at Tower Rd |

**Ontario Listings**

| | | | |
|---|---|---|---|
| Ancaster ON | Cinema Park | 905-546-2424 ext. 2045 | Golf Links Road |
| Barrie ON | DOLRA (Dog Off Leash Recreation Area) | 705-726-4242 | Sunnidale Road |
| Dundas ON | Little John Park | 905-546-2424 ext. 2045 | Lynden Avenue (behind Wentworth Lodge) |
| Hamilton ON | Hamilton Dog Park | 905-546-2424 ext. 2045 | 245 Dartnall Road |
| Hawkesbury ON | Hawkesbury Dog Park in Cyr de Lasalle Park | 613-632-0106 | 571 Main Street |
| London ON | Greenway Off-Leash Dog Park | | Springbank Dr at Greenside Ave |
| London ON | Pottersburg-FIDO Dog Park | | Hamilton Rd at Gore Rd |
| London ON | Stoney Creek Off-Leash Dog Park | | Adelaide St N. at Windermere |
| Mississauga ON | Totoredaca Leash Free Park | | 2715 Meadowvale Blvd |
| Orillia ON | Clayt French Dog Park | 705-325-1311 | Atlantis Drive |
| St Thomas ON | Lions Club Dog Park | | 25 Talbot Street |
| Stratford ON | Stratford Dog Park | | Packham Road |
| Toronto ON | Dog Park - High Park | 416-397-8186 | 1873 Bloor Street |

**Quebec Listings**

| | | | |
|---|---|---|---|
| Lachine Borough PQ | Autoroute 20 at 55e Avenue Off-Leash Area | 514-637-7587 | Autoroute 20 at 55e Avenue |
| Lachine Borrough PQ | Promenade du rail Off-Leash Area | 514-637-7587 | rue Victoria between 10e and 15e |
| Lachine Borrough PQ | Rue Victoria and 28e Avenue Off-Leash Area | 514-637-7587 | Rue Victoria and 28e Avenue |
| Lachine Borrough PQ | Rue Victoria and 40e Avenue Off-Leash Area | 514-637-7587 | Rue Victoria and 40e Avenue |
| Lachine Borrough PQ | Rue des Erables Off-Leash Area | 514-637-7587 | Rue des Erables at Rue Emile-Pominville |
| Lachine Borrough PQ | Stoney Point River Park Off-Leash Area | 514-637-7587 | Between 45e and 56e Avenues |
| Montreal PQ | Notre-Dame-de-Grace Park | 514-637-7587 | Girouard and Sherbrooke West |
| Westmount PQ | King George Park Off-Leash Area | 514-989-5200 | Cote St. Antoine and Murray |

**Saskatchewan Listings**

| | | | |
|---|---|---|---|
| Saskatoon SK | Off Leash Dog Parks | 306-975-2611 | Various si |

Chapter 8

# Emergency Veterinarians

## Alabama Listings

| | | | |
|---|---|---|---|
| Auburn AL | Auburn University Critical Care Program | 334-844-4690 | College of Veterinary Medicine |
| Birmingham AL | Emergency and Specialty Animal Clinic | 205-967-7389 | 2864 Acton Rd |
| Birmingham AL | Red Mountain Animal Clinic | 205-326-8080 | 2148 Green Springs Highway |
| Huntsville AL | Animal Emergency Clinic of North Alabama | 256-533-7600 | 2112 Memorial Pkwy SW |
| Mobile AL | Animal Emergency Clinic | 251-476-2020 | 2811 Airport Blvd |
| Montgomery AL | Animal Emergency Clinic | 334-264-5555 | 1231 Perry Hill Rd # C |
| Tuscaloosa AL | Indian Hills Animal Clinic | 205-345-1231 | 200 Mcfarland Circle North |

## Alaska Listings

| | | | |
|---|---|---|---|
| Anchorage AK | Diamond Animal Hospital | 907-562-8384 | 2545 E. Tudor Road |
| Anchorage AK | Pet Emergency Treatment | 907-274-5636 | 2320 E. Dowling Rd |
| Cantwell AK | Cantwell Veterinary Services | 907-768-2228 | Denali Hy |
| Fairbanks AK | After Hours Veterinary Emergency Clinic | 907-479-2700 | 8 Bonnie Ave |
| Homer AK | Homer Veterinary Clinic | 907-235-8960 | 326 Woodside Avenue |
| Juneau AK | Southeast Alaska Animal Medical Center | 907-789-7551 | 8231 Glacier Highway |
| Kenai AK | Kenai Veterinary Hospital | 907-283-4148 | 10976 Kenai Spur Hwy |
| Seward AK | Seward Animal Clinic | 907-224-5500 | Mile 3 1/2 Seward Hwy |
| Sitka AK | Sitka Animal Hospital | 907-747-7387 | 209 Jarvis St |
| Wasilla AK | All Creatures Veterinary Clinic | 907-376-7930 | 4360 Snider Drive |
| Wasilla AK | Wasilla Veterinary Clinic | 907-376-3993 | |

## Arizona Listings

| | | | |
|---|---|---|---|
| Bullhead City AZ | Spirit Mountain Animal Hospital | 928-758-3979 | 1670 E Lakeside Dr |
| Flagstaff AZ | Flagstaff Animal Hospital | 928-779-4565 | 2308 E. Route 66 |
| Flagstaff AZ | Westside Veterinary Clinic | 928-779-0148 | 963 West Route 66 Suite 230 |
| Gilbert AZ | Emergency Animal Clinic | 480-497-0222 | 86 West Juniper Ave. |
| Kingman AZ | Kingman Animal Hospital | 928-757-4011 | 1650 Northern Ave. |
| Kingman AZ | Stockton Hill Animal Hospital | 928-757-7979 | 4335 Stockton Hill Rd |
| Page AZ | Page Animal Hospital | 928-645-2816 | 87th South 7th Avenue |
| Peoria AZ | Emergency Animal Clinic | 623-974-1520 | 9875 W. Peoria Ave. |
| Phoenix AZ | Emergency Animal Clinic | 602-995-3757 | 2260 W. Glendale Ave. |
| Scottsdale AZ | Emergency Animal Clinic | 480-949-8001 | 14202 N. Scottsdale Rd. #163 |
| Sedona AZ | Oak Creek Small Animal Clinic | 928-282-1195 | 3130 West Highway 89A |
| Sierra Vista AZ | New Frontier Animal Medical Center | 520-459-0433 | 2045 Paseo San Luis |
| Tucson AZ | Southern Arizona Veterinary Specialty and Emergency Center | 520-888-3177 | 141 East Fort Lowell Road |
| Tucson AZ | Southern Arizona Veterinary Specialty and Emergency Center | 520-888-3177 | 7474 E Broadway Blvd |
| Willcox AZ | Willcox Veterinary Clinic | 520-384-2761 | 889 N Taylor Rd |
| Window Rock AZ | Navajo Nation Veterinary Clinics | | P.O. Box 4889 |
| Window Rock AZ | Navajo Nation Veterinary Clinics | | P.O. Box 4889 |
| Window Rock AZ | Navajo Nation Veterinary Clinics | | P.O. Box 4889 |
| Yuma AZ | Desert Veterinary Clinic | | 995 South 5th Avenue |

## Arkansas Listings

| | | | |
|---|---|---|---|
| El Dorado AR | Ralson Animal Hospital | 870-863-4194 | 3500 North Jefferson |
| Fort Smith AR | Fort Smith Animal Emergency Clinic | 479-649-3100 | 4301 Regions Park Dr # 3 |
| Hot Springs AR | Hot Springs Animal Hospital | 501-623-2411 | 1533 Malvern Avenue |
| Hot Springs AR | Lake Hamilton Animal Hospital | 501-767-8503 | 1525 Airport Road |
| Jonesboro AR | Vetcare | 870-972-5320 | 619 W Parker Rd |
| Little Rock AR | Animal Emergency Clinic | 501-224-3784 | 801 John Barrow Rd |
| Mountain Home AR | Spring Park Animal Hospital | 870-425-6201 | 404 Highway 201 North |
| North Little Rock AR | Animal Emergency & Specialty Clinic | 501-224-3784 | 8735 Sheltie Dr, Ste G |
| Springdale AR | Animal Emergency Clinic of Northwest Arkansas | 479-927-0007 | 1110 Mathias Drive Suite E |

## California Listings

| | | | |
|---|---|---|---|
| Anaheim CA | Yorba Regional Animal Hospital | 714-921-8700 | 8290 E. Crystal Drive |
| Arroyo Grande CA | Central Coast Pet Emergency Clinic | 805-489-6573 | 1558 W Branch St |
| Bakersfield CA | Kern Animal Emergency Clinic | 661-322-6019 | 4300 Easton Dr #1 |
| Berkeley CA | Pet Emergency Treatment Service | 510-548-6684 | 1048 University Ave |
| Big Bear City CA | Bear City Animal Hospital | 909-585-7808 | 214 Big Bear Blvd W |
| Big Bear City CA | VCA Lakeside Animal Hospital | 909-866-2021 | 42160 N Shore Dr |
| Bishop CA | Bishop Veterinary Hospital | 760-873-5801 | 1650 N. Sierra Highway |
| Buellton CA | Valley Pet Emergency Clinic | 805-688-2334 | 914 W Highway 246 |
| Campbell CA | United Emergency Animal Clinic | 408-371-6252 | 911 Dell Avenue |
| Carson City NV | Carson Tahoe Veterinary Hospital | 775-883-8238 | 3389 S. Carson Street |
| Concord CA | Veterinary Emergency Clinic | 925-798-2900 | 1410 Monument Blvd |
| Culver City CA | Affordable Emergency Clinic | 310-397-4883 | 5558 Sepulveda Blvd |
| Davis CA | UC Davis Medical Teaching Hospital | 530-752-1393 | One Shields Avenue |
| Diamond Bar CA | East Valley Emergency Pet Clinic | 909-861-5737 | 938 N Diamond Bar Blvd |
| El Monte CA | Emergency Pet Clinic | 626-579-4550 | 3254 Santa Anita Ave |
| Escondido CA | Animal Urgent Care | 760-738-9600 | 2430-A S. Escondido Blvd |
| Fair Oaks CA | Greenback Veterinary Hospital | 916-725-1541 | 8311 Greenback Lane |
| Fremont CA | Ohlone Veterinary Emergency | 510-657-6620 | 1618 Washington Blvd |
| Fresno CA | Veterinary Emergency Services | 559-486-0520 | 1639 N Fresno St |
| Garden Grove CA | Orange County Emergency Pet Hospital | 714-537-3032 | 12750 Garden Grove Blvd |
| Glendale CA | Animal Emergency Clinic | 818-247-3973 | 831 Milford St |
| Granada Hills CA | Affordable Animal Emergency Clinic | 818-363-8143 | 16907 San Fernando Mission |
| Grand Terrace CA | Animal Emergency Clinic | 909-783-1300 | 12022 La Crosse Ave |
| Lancaster CA | Animal Emergency Clinic | 661-723-3959 | 1055 W Avenue M #101 |
| Long Beach CA | Evening Pet Clinic | 562-422-1223 | 6803 Cherry Ave |
| Los Angeles CA | Animal Emergency Clinic | 310-473-1561 | 1736 S Sepulveda Blvd #A |
| Los Angeles CA | Eagle Rock Emergency Pet Clinic | 323-254-7382 | 4252 Eagle Rock Blvd |
| Mammoth Lakes CA | Alpen Veterinary Hospital | 760-934-2291 | 217 Sierra Manor Rd |
| Mammoth Lakes CA | High Country Veterinary Hospital | 760-934-3775 | 148 Mountain Blvd |
| Mission Viejo CA | Animal Urgent Care Clinic | 949-364-6228 | 28085 Hillcrest |
| Modesto CA | Veterinary Medical Clinic | 209-527-8844 | 1800 Prescott Rd |
| Montclair CA | Emergency Pet Clinic of Pomona | 909-981-1051 | 8980 Benson Ave |
| Monterey CA | Monterey Peninsula - Salinas Emergency Vet | 831-373-7374 | 2 Harris Court Suite A1 |
| Monterey CA | Monterey Peninsula - Salinas Emergency Vet | 831-373-7374 | 2 Harris Court Suite A1 |
| Norwalk CA | Crossroads Animal Emergency Hospital | 562-863-2522 | 11057 Rosecrans Ave |
| Oakhurst CA | Hoof and Paw Veterinary Hospital | 559-683-3313 | 41149 Highway 41 |
| Oakhurst CA | Oakhurst Veterinary Hospital | 559-683-2135 | 40799 Highway 41 |
| Palo Alto CA | Emergency Veterinary Clinic | 650-494-1461 | 3045 Middlefield Rd |
| Pasadena CA | Animal Emergency Clinic | 626-564-0704 | 2121 E Foothill Blvd |
| Roseville CA | Pet Emergency Center | 916-783-4655 | 1100 Atlantic St |
| Sacramento CA | Emergency Animal Clinic | 916-362-3146 | 9700 Business Park Dr #404 |
| Sacramento CA | Sacramento Emergency Vet Clinic | 916-922-3425 | 2201 El Camino Ave |
| San Diego CA | Animal ER of San Diego | 858-569-0600 | 5610 Kearny Mesa Rd |
| San Diego CA | Animal Emergency Clinic | 858-748-7387 | 13240 Evening Creek Dr S |
| San Diego CA | Emergency Animal Clinic | 619-299-2400 | 2317 Hotel Cir S # A |
| San Francisco CA | All Animals Emergency Hospital | 415-566-0531 | 1333 9th Ave |
| San Jose CA | Emergency Animal Clinic | 408-578-5622 | 5440 Thornwood Dr. |
| San Leandro CA | Alameda County Emergency Pet Hospital | 510-352-6080 | 14790 Washington Ave |
| San Rafael CA | Pet Emergency & Specialty | 415-456-7372 | 901 Francisco Blvd E |
| Santa Barbara CA | CARE Hospital | 805-899-2273 | 301 E. Haley St. |
| Santa Cruz CA | Santa Cruz Veterinary | 831-475-5400 | 2585 Soquel Dr |
| Sherman Oaks CA | Emergency Animal Clinic | 818-788-7860 | 14302 Ventura Blvd |
| Shingle Springs CA | Mother Lode Pet Emergency Clinic | 530-676-9044 | 4050 Durock Rd |
| South Lake Tahoe CA | Avalanche Natural Health Office for Pets and Kennel | 530-541-3551 | 964 Rubicon Trail |
| Stockton CA | Associated Veterinary Emergency Hospital | 209-952-8387 | 3008 E Hammer Lane #115 |
| Studio City CA | Animal Emergency Center | 818-760-3882 | 11730 Ventura Blvd |
| Sun City CA | Menifee Valley Animal Clinic | 951-672-8077 | 26900 Newport Rd # 105 |
| Sun City CA | Sun City Veterinary Clinic | 951-672-1802 | 27994 Bradley Rd # J |
| Temecula CA | Emergency Pet Clinic | 909-695-5044 | 27443 Jefferson Ave |
| Thousand Oaks CA | Pet Emergency Clinic | 805-492-2436 | 2967 N Moorpark Rd |

| Thousand Palms CA | Animal Emergency Clinic | 760-343-3438 | 72374 Ramon Rd |
| Ventura CA | Pet Emergency Clinic | 805-642-8562 | 2301 S Victoria Ave |
| Ventura CA | Veterinary Medical and Surgical Group | 805-339-2290 | 2199 Sperry Avenue |

**Colorado Listings**

| Arvada CO | Animal Urgent Care | 303-420-7387 | 7851 Indiana St |
| Aspen CO | Aspen Animal Hospital | 970-925-2611 | 301 Aabc |
| Basalt CO | Valley Emergency Pet Care | 970-927-5066 | 180 Fiou Lane |
| Boulder CO | Boulder Emergency Pet Clinic | 303-440-7722 | 1658 30th Street |
| Colorado Springs CO | Animal Emergency Care Center | 719-578-9300 | 3775 Airport Rd. and Academy Blvd. |
| Colorado Springs CO | Animal Emergency Care Center North | 719-260-7141 | 5520 North Nevada Avenue #150 |
| Durango CO | Durango Animal Hospital | 970-247-3174 | 2461 Main Ave |
| Fort Collins CO | Fort Collins Veterinary Emergency Hospital | 970-484-8080 | 816 S. Lemay Ave. |
| Grand Junction CO | Veterinary Emergency Center | 970-255-1911 | 1660 North Ave |
| Lakewood CO | Access Animal Critical Care | 303-239-1200 | 1597 Wadsworth Blvd |
| Pueblo CO | Animal Emergency Room | 719-595-9495 | 225 E 4th St |
| Westminster CO | Northside Emergency Pet Clinic | 303-252-7722 | 945 West 124th Avenue |

**Connecticut Listings**

| Avon CT | Farmington Valley Veterinary Emergency Hospital | 860-674-1886 | 9 Avonwood Rd |
| Bolton CT | East of the River Veterinary Emergency Clinic | 860-646-6134 | 222 Boston Turnpike |
| Bridgeport CT | A-1 Emergency Animal Hospital | 203-334-5548 | 2727 Main St |
| Danbury CT | Animal Emergency Clinic of Danbury | 203-790-6383 | 22 Newtown Rd |
| New Haven CT | New Haven Central Hospital for Veterinary Medicine | 203-865-0878 | 843 State Street |
| Oakdale CT | Veterinary Emergency Treatment Services | 860-444-8870 | 8 Enterprise Lane |

**D.C. Listings**

| Washington DC | Friendship Hospital for Animals | 202-363-7300 | 4105 Brandywine St NW |

**Delaware Listings**

| Dover DE | Delmarva Animal Emergency Center | 302-697-0850 | 1482 E Lebanon Rd |
| Wilmington DE | Veterinary Emergency Center of Delaware | 302-691-3647 | 1212 East Newport Pike |

**Florida Listings**

| Boca Raton FL | Calusa Veterinary Center | 561-999-3000 | 6900 Congress Avenue |
| Boynton Beach FL | PetPB Animal Emergency Center | 561-752-3232 | 2246 North Congress Ave |
| Brandon FL | Animal Emergency Clinic of Brandon | 813-684-3013 | 693 W. Lumsden Rd. |
| Casselberry FL | Veterinary Emergency Clinic | 407-644-4449 | 195 Concord Drive |
| Cooper City FL | Animal Medical Center at Cooper City | 954-432-5611 | 9410 Stirling Road |
| Delray Beach FL | Atlantic Animal Hospital Emergency Clinic | 561-272-1552 | 10160 La Reina Dr. |
| Doral FL | Animal Emergency Clinic of Doral | 305-598-1234 | 9589 NW 41st St |
| Fort Myers FL | Emergency Veterinary Clinic | 239-939-5542 | 2045 Collier Avenue |
| Fort Pierce FL | Animal Emergency & Referral Center | 772-466-3441 | 3984 SO. US 1 |
| Gainesville FL | University of Florida Veterinary Medical Center | 352-392-2235 | 2015 SW 16th Ave |
| Jacksonville FL | Animal ER | 904-642-4357 | 3444 Southside Blvd, Suite 101 |
| Jacksonville Beach FL | Emergency Pet Clinic | 904-223-8000 | 14185 Beach Blvd |
| Key West FL | Animal Hospital - Olde Key West | 305-296-5227 | 6150 2nd Street |
| Lakeland FL | Veterinary Emergency Clinic | 863-665-3199 | 3609 Highway 98 South |
| Leesburg FL | Veterinary Emergency Clinic | 352-728-4440 | 33040 Professional Drive |
| Melbourne FL | Animal Emergency & Critical Care Center | 321-725-5365 | 2281 W Eau Gallie Blvd |
| Miami FL | Animal Emergency Clinic South | 305-251-2096 | 8429 SW 132nd St |
| Miami FL | Emergency Animal Clinic | 305-754-7000 | 570 NW 103RD St |
| Miami FL | Jonicer Emergency Animal Clinic | 305-757-3030 | 570 NW 103rd St |
| Miami FL | Miami Emergency and Critical Center | 305-598-0157 | 8601 SW 72nd St |
| Miami FL | Miami Pet Emergency | 305-273-8100 | 114 NE 108th St |
| Naples FL | Emergency Pet Hospital of Collier County | 239-263-8010 | 6530 Dudley Drive |
| Niceville FL | Emergency Veterinary Clinic | 850-729-3335 | 212 Government Ave |

| | | | |
|---|---|---|---|
| Oakland Park FL | Animal Emergency Trauma Center | 954-670-8823 | 2200 W Oakland Park Blvd |
| Ocala FL | Ocala Animal Emergency Hospital | 352-840-0044 | 1815 NE Jacksonville Rd |
| Orange Park FL | Clay-Duval Pet Emergency Clinic | 904-264-8281 | 275 Corporate Way |
| Orlando FL | Animal Emergency Center | 407-273-3336 | 7313 Lake Underhill Rd |
| Orlando FL | Veterinary Emergency Clinic | 407-438-4449 | 2080 Principal Row |
| Palm Harbor FL | Animal Emergency Hospital of Countryside | 727-786-5755 | 30606 Us Highway 19 N |
| Pensacola FL | Veterinary Emergency Referral Center | 850-477-3914 | 4800 N. Davis Highway |
| Sarasota FL | Sarasota Veterinary Emergency | 941-923-7260 | 7519 S Tamiami Trl |
| St Augustine FL | Animal Emergency Hospital of St. Johns | | 2505 Old Moultrie Rd |
| St Augustine FL | Veterinary Emergency Service of St Johns County | 904-824-1414 | 195 San Marco Ave |
| St Augustine FL | Vilano Mobile Vet | 904-315-1331 | Various |
| St Petersburg FL | Animal Emergency Clinic | 727-323-1311 | 3165 22nd Ave N |
| Stuart FL | Pet Emergency & Critical Care | 772-781-3302 | 2239 S Kanner Hwy |
| Tallahassee FL | Allied Veterinarians Emergency Hospital | 850-222-0123 | 2324 Centerville Rd |
| Tallahassee FL | Northwood Animal Hospital | 850-385-8181 | 1818-B North Martin Luther King Blvd. |
| Tampa FL | Tampa Bay Veterinary Emergency Clinic | | 238 E Bears Ave |
| West Palm Beach FL | Pet Emergency of Palm Beach County | 561-691-9999 | 3816 Northlake Blvd |
| Winter Haven FL | Veterinary Healthcare Associates | 863-324-3340 | 3025 Dundee Rd |

**Georgia Listings**

| | | | |
|---|---|---|---|
| Athens GA | University of Georgia Vet Teaching Hospital | 706-542-3221 | Carlton St at DW Brooks Dr |
| Atlanta GA | Georgia Veterinary Specialists | 404-459-0903 | 455 Abernathy Rd NE |
| Augusta GA | Augusta Animal Emergency | 706-733-7458 | 208 Hudson Trace |
| Columbus GA | Animal Emergency Center | 706-324-6659 | 2507 Manchester Expressway |
| Decatur GA | Animal Emergency Center of Decatur | 404-371-9774 | 217 N. McDonough Street |
| Gainesville GA | An-Emerg | 770-534-2911 | 275 #3 Pearl Nix Pkwy |
| Macon GA | Animal Emergency Care | 478-750-0911 | 2009 Mercer University Dr |
| Marietta GA | Cobb Emergency Veterinary Clinics | 770-424-9157 | http://www.decaturanimaler.com |
| Sandy Springs GA | Animal Emergency Center of Sandy Springs | 404-252-7881 | 228 Sandy Springs Place, NE |
| Savannah GA | Savannah Veterinary Emergency Clinic | 912-355-6113 | 5509 Waters Ave |
| Savannah GA | Veterinary Specialists of the Southeast | 912-354-6681 | 335 Stephenson Ave |
| St Simons Island GA | Tyler Animal Hospital | 912-342-4108 | 132 Airport Rd |
| Tucker GA | DeKalb-Gwinnett Animal Emergency Clinic | 770-491-0661 | 6430 Lawrenceville Hwy |
| Woodstock GA | Cherokee Emergency Veterinary Clinic | 770-924-3720 | 7800 Highway 92 |

**Hawaii Listings**

| | | | |
|---|---|---|---|
| Hilo HI | East Hawaii Veterinary Center | 808-959-2273 | 111 E.Puainako St. A-109 |

**Idaho Listings**

| | | | |
|---|---|---|---|
| Idaho Falls ID | Idaho Falls Emergency Vet Clinic | 208-552-0662 | 3120 S Woodruff Ave |
| Ketchum ID | Sun Valley Animal Center | 208-726-7777 | P.O. Box 177 |
| Meridian ID | WestVet Emergency & Specialty Center | | 3085 E. Magic View Drive, Suite 110 |
| Post Falls ID | North Idaho Pet Emergency Clinic | 208-777-2707 | 2700 E Seltice Way |
| Sandpoint ID | North Idaho Animal Hospital | 208-265-5700 | 1020 S Ella |
| Twin Falls ID | Twin Falls Veterinary Clinic & Hospital | 208-736-1727 | 2148 4th Avenue East |

**Illinois Listings**

| | | | |
|---|---|---|---|
| Bloomington IL | Animal Emergency Clinic | 309-665-5020 | 2505 E Oakland Avenue |
| Carbondale IL | Lakeside Veterinary Hospital | 618-529-2236 | 2001 Sweets Dr. |
| Chicago IL | Chicago Veterinary Emergency Services | 773-281-7110 | 3123 North Clybourn |
| Dolton IL | Dolton Veterinary Emergency Service | 708-849-2608 | 15022 Lincoln Ave |
| Galena IL | Galena Square Veterinary Clinic | 815-777-2592 | 984 James St |
| Lisle IL | Emergency Veterinary Service | 630-960-2900 | 820 Ogden Ave |
| Mokena IL | Animal Emergency of Mokena | 708-326-4800 | 19110 S. 88th Ave |
| Northbrook IL | Animal Emergency Referral Center | 847-564-5775 | 1810 Skokie Blvd |
| Peoria IL | Tri-County Animal Emergency | | 1800 North Sterling |
| Rockford IL | Animal Emergency Clinic of Rockford | 815-229-7791 | 4236 Maray Drive |

| | | | |
|---|---|---|---|
| Schaumburg IL | Animal Emergency Services | 847-885-3344 | 1375 N. Roselle Road |
| Springfield IL | Animal Emergency Clinic | 217-698-0870 | 1333 Wabash Ave |

**Indiana Listings**

| | | | |
|---|---|---|---|
| Evansville IN | All Pet Emergency Clinic | 812-422-3300 | 104 S Heidelbach Ave |
| Fort Wayne IN | Northeast Indiana Veterinary Emergency and Specialty Hospital | 260-426-1062 | 5818 Maplecrest Road |
| Indianapolis IN | Animal Emergency Center | 317-849-4925 | 8250 Bash St |
| Indianapolis IN | Indianapolis Veterinary Emergency Center | 317-782-4418 | 5425 Victory Drive |
| Lafayette IN | Animal Emergency Clinic | 765-449-2001 | 1343 Sagamore Pkwy N |
| Mishawaka IN | Animal Emergency Clinic | 574-259-8387 | 2324 Grape Rd |
| Schererville IN | Calumet Emergency Vet Clinic | 219-865-0970 | 216 W Lincoln Hwy |
| South Bend IN | Animal Emergency Clinic | 574-272-9611 | 17903 State Rd 23 |
| South Bend IN | Western Veterinary Clinic | 574-234-3098 | 25190 SR 2 |
| Terre Haute IN | Animal Emergency Clinic | 812-242-2273 | 1238 S 3rd St |

**Iowa Listings**

| | | | |
|---|---|---|---|
| Ames IA | Iowa State University Veterinary Teaching Hospital | 515-294-1500 | 1600 S 16th St |
| Bettendorf IA | Animal Emergency Center | 563-344-9599 | 1510 State Street |
| Bettendorf IA | Bettendorf Veterinary Hospital | 563-332-8387 | 3510 Belmont Rd |
| Cedar Rapids IA | Eastern Iowa Veterinary Specialty Center | 319-841-5160 | 755 Capital Dr SW |
| Des Moines IA | Iowa Veterinary Specialties | 515-280-3051 | 6110 Creston Avenue |
| Iowa City IA | Bright Eyes & Bushy Tails Veterinary Hospital | 319-351-4256 | 3030 Northgate Dr |

**Kansas Listings**

| | | | |
|---|---|---|---|
| Dodge City KS | Dodge City Veterinary Clinic | | 1920 E Trail Street |
| Goodland KS | Prairieland Animal Clinic | | 204 N Caldwell St |
| Lawrence KS | Clinton Parkway Animal Hospital | 785-841-3131 | 4340 Clinton Parkway |
| Manhattan KS | Kansas State University Veterinary Hospital | 785-532-5690 | Kimball Ave at Denison Ave |
| Meriden KS | Meriden Animal Hospital | 785-484-3358 | 7146 K-4 Hwy |
| Mission KS | Mission MedVet | 913-722-5566 | 5914 Johnson Drive |
| Overland Park KS | Emergency Veterinary Clinic of Greater KC | 913-649-5314 | 10333 Metcalf Ave |
| Overland Park KS | Veterinary Specialty and Emergency Center | 913-642-9563 | 11950 West 110th Street |
| Russell KS | Town and Country Animal Hospital | 785-483-2435 | 655 S Van Houten St |
| Salina KS | Animalcare ER | | 645 S Ohio St |
| Topeka KS | Emergency Animal Clinic | 785-272-2926 | 839 SW Fairlawn Rd |
| Wichita KS | Emergency Veterinary Clinic | 316-262-5321 | 727 S Washington St |

**Kentucky Listings**

| | | | |
|---|---|---|---|
| Bowling Green KY | Snodgrass Veterinary Medical Center | 270-781-5041 | 6000 Scottsville Road |
| Lexington KY | AA Small Animal Emergency Service | 859-276-2505 | 200 Southland Drive |
| Louisville KY | Jefferson Animal Hospital | 866-689-0233 | 4504 Outer Loop |
| Louisville KY | Louisville Veterinary | 502-244-3036 | 12905 Shelbyville Rd Suite 3 |
| Taylor Mill KY | OKI Veterinary Emergency and Critical Care | 606-261-9900 | 5052 Old Taylor Mill Rd |

**Louisiana Listings**

| | | | |
|---|---|---|---|
| Alexandria LA | Crossroads Animal Emergency | 318-427-1292 | 5405 North Blvd |
| Baton Rouge LA | Animal Emergency Clinic | 225-927-8800 | 7353 Jefferson Hwy |
| Baton Rouge LA | Baton Rouge Pet Emergency Hospital | 225-925-5566 | 1514 Cottondale Dr |
| Baton Rouge LA | LSU Veterinary Teaching Hospital | 225-578-9600 | Skip Bertman Drive |
| Lafayette LA | Lafayette Animal Emergency Clinic | 337-989-0992 | 206 Winchester Dr |
| Lake Charles LA | Pet Emergency Clinic | 337-562-0400 | 1501 W Mcneese St |
| Metairie LA | Animal Emergency Clinic | 504-835-8508 | 1955 Veterans Memorial Blvd |
| Metairie LA | Southeast Veterinary Emergency Clinic | 504-219-0444 | 400 N. Causeway Blvd |
| Shreveport LA | Animal Emergency Clinic | 318-227-2345 | 2421 Line Ave |
| Terrytown LA | Westbank Pet Emergency Clinic | 504-392-1932 | 1152 Terry Pkwy |
| West Monroe LA | Animal Emergency Clinic of NE Louisiana | 318-410-0555 | 102 Downing Pines Rd |

## Maine Listings

| | | | |
|---|---|---|---|
| Arundel ME | York County Veterinary Emergency & Referral Center | 207-284-9911 | 20 Hill Rd |
| Bar Harbor ME | Acadia Veterinary Hospital | 207-288-5733 | 21 Federal St |
| Brewer ME | Eastern Maine Emergency Veterinary Clinic | 207-989-6267 | 15 Dirigo Dr |
| Ellsworth ME | Ellsworth Veterinary Hospital | 207-667-3437 | 381 State St |
| Lewiston ME | Animal Emergency Clinic-Mid Maine | 207-777-1110 | 37 Strawberry Ave |
| Portland ME | Animal Emergency Clinic | 207-878-3121 | 739 Warren Ave |
| South Thomaston ME | Harbor Road Veterinary Hospital | 207-354-0266 | 626 Saint George Road |

## Maryland Listings

| | | | |
|---|---|---|---|
| Annapolis MD | Anne Arundel Veterinary Emergency Clinic | 410-224-0331 | 808 Bestgate Rd |
| Baltimore MD | Eastern Animal Hospital | 410-633-8808 | 6404 Eastern Ave |
| Baltimore MD | Falls Road Animal Hospital | 410-825-9100 | 6314 Falls Road |
| Easton MD | Midshore Veterinary Service | 410-820-9229 | 602 Dutchmans Lane |
| Frederick MD | Frederick Emergency Vet | | 434 Prospect Blvd |
| Glendale MD | Beltway Emergency Animal Hospital | 301-464-3737 | 11660 Annapolis Rd |
| Hollywood MD | Three Notch Veterinary Hospital | 301-373-8633 | 44215 Airport View Drive |
| Huntingtown MD | Allied Partners Veterinary Emergency Service | 410-414-8250 | 4135 Old Town Road, Suite B |
| LaVale MD | LaVale Veterinary Hospital | 301-729-6084 | 913 National Highway |
| Ocean City MD | Ocean City Animal Hospital | 410-213-1170 | 11843 Ocean Gateway |
| Rockville MD | Metropolitan Emergency Animal Clinic | 301-770-5225 | 12106 Nebel St |
| Urbana MD | Greenbriar Veterinary Hospital | 301-874-8880 | 3051 Thurston Road |
| Waldorf MD | Southern Maryland Veterinary Referral Service | 301-638-0988 | 3485 Rockefeller Court |

## Massachusetts Listings

| | | | |
|---|---|---|---|
| Boston MA | Angell Animal Medical Center - Boston | 617-522-7282 | 350 South Huntington Avenue |
| Edgartown MA | Vineyard Veterinary Clinic | 508-627-5292 | 276 Edgartown Vineyard Hvn Rd |
| Nantucket MA | Offshore Animal Hospital - Nantucket | 508-228-1491 | 21 Crooked Lane |
| North Andover MA | Essex County Veterinary Referral Hospital | 978-725-5544 | 247 Chickering Road |
| Orleans MA | Animal Hospital of Orleans | 508-255-1194 | 65 Finlay Road |
| Pittsfield MA | Animal ER (Pittsfield Veterinary Hospital) | 413-997-3425 | 1634 West Housatonic St |
| South Deerfield MA | Veterinary Emergency & Specialty Hospital | 413-665-4911 | 141 Greenfield Road |
| South Dennis MA | Cape Animal Referral and Emergency Center | 508-398-7575 | 79 Theophilus Smith Rd |
| Springfield MA | Western Massachusetts Veterinary Emergency Service | 413-783-0603 | 1235 Boston Rd |
| Swansea MA | Bay State Vet Emergency Services | 508-379-1233 | 76 Baptist St |
| Walpole MA | Tufts Veterinary Emergency Treatment | 508-668-5454 | 525 South Street |
| Waltham MA | Veterinary Specialty Center of New England | 781-684-8387 | 180 Bear Hill Rd |
| West Bridgewater MA | New England Animal Medical Center | 508-580-2515 | 595 West Center Street |
| Woburn MA | Massachusetts Veterinary Referral Hospital | 781-932-5802 | 20 Cabot Road |

## Michigan Listings

| | | | |
|---|---|---|---|
| Ann Arbor MI | Animal Emergency Clinic | 734-971-8774 | 4126 Packard Road |
| Carrollton Township MI | Great Lakes Pet Emergency Hospital | 989-752-1960 | 1220 Tittabawassee Road |
| Detroit MI | Animal Emergency Room | 313-255-2404 | 24429 Grand River Ave |
| East Lansing MI | Michigan State University Veterinary Teaching Hospital | 517-353-5420 | Wilson Rd at Bogue St |
| Flint MI | Animal Emergency Hospital of Flint | 810-238-7557 | 1007 S. Ballenger Hwy. |
| Grand Rapids MI | Animal Emergency Hospital | 616-361-9911 | 3260 Plainfield Av NE |
| Harbor Springs MI | Bay Pines Veterinary Clinic | 231-347-1383 | 8769 M 119 |
| Kalamazoo MI | Southwest Michigan Veterinary Referral Center | 269-381-5228 | 3301 S. Burdick St. |

| | | | |
|---|---|---|---|
| Mackinac Island MI | Mackinac Island Veterinary Clinic | 906-847-3737 | 1st MCKNC Is |
| Madison Heights MI | Veterinary Emergency Service East | 248-547-4677 | 28223 John R |
| Marquette MI | Animal Medical Center of Marquette | 906-226-7400 | 3145 Wright Street |
| Milford MI | Veterinary Care Specialists | 248-684-0468 | 205 Rowe Road |
| Plymouth MI | Veterinary Emergency Service West | 734-207-8500 | 40850 Ann Arbor Rd |
| Sault Ste Marie MI | Animal Kingdom Veterinary Clinic | 906-635-1200 | 305 West 3 Mile Road |
| Sault Ste Marie MI | Sault Animal Hospital | 906-635-5910 | 2867 Ashmun Street |
| Traverse City MI | Companion Animal Hospital | 231-935-1511 | 1885 Chartwell Drive |

**Minnesota Listings**

| | | | |
|---|---|---|---|
| Albert Lea MN | Albert Lea Veterinary Clinic | 507-373-8161 | 401 Saint Thomas Ave |
| Blaine MN | Midwest Veterinary Specialty Group | 763-754-5000 | 11850 Aberdeen Street NE |
| Coon Rapids MN | Affiliated Emergency Veterinary Service | 763-754-9434 | 1615 Coon Rapids Blvd |
| Duluth MN | Affiliated Emergency Veterinary Service | 218-302-8000 | 2314 W. Michigan St. |
| Eden Prairie MN | Affiliated Emergency Veterinary Service | 952-942-8272 | 7717 Flying Cloud Drive |
| Fergus Falls MN | Fergus Falls Animal Care Clinic | 218-736-6961 | 112 N Cascade St |
| Golden Valley MN | Affiliated Emergency Veterinary Service | 763-529-6560 | 4708 Highway 55 |
| Jackson MN | Jackson Veterinary Clinic | 507-847-2010 | 210 1st St |
| Kasson MN | K-M Regional Veterinary Hospital | 507-634-8000 | 200 5TH ST SE |
| Luverne MN | Rock Veterinary Clinic | 507-283-9524 | 1295 101st Street |
| Rochester MN | Affiliated Emergency Veterinary Service | 507-424-3976 | 121 23rd Ave SW |
| St Cloud MN | Affiliated Emergency Veterinary Service | 320-258-3481 | 4180 Thielman Ln |

**Mississippi Listings**

| | | | |
|---|---|---|---|
| Biloxi MS | Gulf Coast Veterinary Emergency Hospital | 228-392-7474 | 13095 Hwy 67 |
| Gulfport MS | Gulfport Veterinary Hospital | 228-865-0575 | 204 Pass Rd |
| Hattiesburg MS | Emergency Vets | 601-450-3838 | 6335 US Highway 49 #40 |
| Jackson MS | Animal Emergency Clinic | 601-352-8383 | 607 Monroe Street |
| Meridian MS | Till-Newell Animal Hospital | 601-485-8049 | 200 Highway 45 North |
| Tupelo MS | Tupelo Small Animal Hospital | 662-840-0210 | 2096 South Thomas St |

**Missouri Listings**

| | | | |
|---|---|---|---|
| Bridgeton MO | Animal Emergency Clinic | 314-739-1500 | 12501 Natural Bridge Rd |
| Columbia MO | University of Missouri Veterinary Teaching Hospital | 573-882-7821 | 379 East Campus Drive |
| Kansas City MO | Animal Emergency Center | 816-455-5430 | 8141 N Oak Trfy |
| Lees Summit MO | Animal ER and Refer | 816-554-4990 | 3495 NE Ralph Powell Rd |
| Springfield MO | Emergency Veterinary Clinic of Southwest Missouri | 417-890-1600 | 400 S. Glenstone Ave. |
| St Louis MO | Animal Emergency Clinic | 314-822-7600 | 9937 Big Bend Blvd |
| Wildwood MO | Veterinary Emergency Referral Center | | 16457 Village Plaza View Dr |

**Montana Listings**

| | | | |
|---|---|---|---|
| Billings MT | Animal Clinic of Billings | 406-252-9499 | 10th St.West & Ave. B |
| Billings MT | Granite Peak Veterinary Hospital | 406-655-1122 | Shilo at Grand Avenue |
| Bozeman MT | Animal Medical Center | 406-587-2946 | 216 N. 8th Ave |
| Bozeman MT | Montana Veterinary Hospital | 406-586-2019 | 6588 Tawny Brown Lane |
| Glendive MT | Dawson County Veterinary Clinic | 406-377-6554 | 2210 W Towne St |
| Great Falls MT | Big Sky Animal Medical Center | 406-761-8387 | 5101 North Star Boulevard |
| Missoula MT | Missoula Veterinary Clinic | 406-251-2400 | 3701 Old US Highway 93 |
| West Yellowstone MT | High West Veterinary Services | 406-646-4410 | 201 S Canyon St |

**Nebraska Listings**

| | | | |
|---|---|---|---|
| Alliance NE | Alliance Animal Clinic | 308-762-4140 | 903 Flack Ave |
| Chadron NE | Panhandle Veterinary Clinic | 308-432-2020 | 985 So. Hwy385 |
| Grand Island NE | Stolley Park Veterinary Hospital | 308-384-6272 | 3020 W. Stolley Park Road |
| Kearney NE | Cottonwood Veterinary Clinic | 308-234-8118 | 5912 2nd Ave West |
| Lincoln NE | Belmont Veterinary Center | 402-435-4947 | 2200 Cornhusker Hwy |
| Lincoln NE | Veterinary Emergency Services of Lincoln | 402-489-6800 | 3700 South 9th Street |
| Norfolk NE | Companion Animal Veterinary Clinic | 402-379-1200 | 1113 Riverside Boulevard |
| North Platte NE | America's Heartland Animal Center | 308-532-4880 | 220 West Fremont Drive |
| Ogallala NE | Animal Clinic & Pharmacy | 308-284-2182 | 105 W O St |

| | | | |
|---|---|---|---|
| Ogallala NE | Baltzell Veterinary Hospital | 308-284-4313 | 1710 W 4th St |
| Omaha NE | Animal Emergency Clinic | 402-504-1731 | 15791 W Dodge Rd |
| Omaha NE | Emergency Animal Clinic | 402-339-6232 | 9664 Mockingbird Dr |
| Pine Bluffs WY | Bluffs Veterinary Clinic | 307-245-9263 | 722 West 7th Street |
| Scottsbluff NE | Animal Health Center | 308-635-0116 | 190624 Highway 26 |
| Scottsbluff NE | Pioneer Animal Clinic | 308-635-3188 | 1905 East 20th St |
| South Sioux City NE | South Sioux Animal Hospital | 402-494-3844 | 301 West 29th St. |
| Valentine NE | Cherry County Veterinary Clinic | 402-376-3750 | 604 E C St |

**Nevada Listings**

| | | | |
|---|---|---|---|
| Bullhead City AZ | Spirit Mountain Animal Hospital | 928-758-3979 | 1670 E Lakeside Dr |
| Carson City NV | Carson Tahoe Veterinary Hospital | 775-883-8238 | 3389 S. Carson Street |
| Elko NV | Elko Veterinary Clinic | 775-738-6116 | 1850 Lamoille Hwy |
| Ely NV | White Pine Veterinary Clinic | 775-289-3459 | 159 MC Gill Hwy |
| Las Vegas NV | Animal Emergency Service | 702-457-8050 | 1914 E Sahara Ave |
| Las Vegas NV | Las Vegas Animal Emergency Hospital | 702-822-1045 | 5231 W. Charleston Boulevard |
| Mesquite NV | Virgin Valley Veterinary Hospital | 702-346-4401 | 660 Hardy Way Suite #44 |
| Reno NV | Animal Emergency Center | 775-851-3600 | 6425 S Virginia St |
| Winnemucca NV | Keystone Veterinary Hospital | 775-623-5100 | 1050 Grass Valley Rd |

**New Hampshire Listings**

| | | | |
|---|---|---|---|
| Brentwood NH | Veterinary Emergency & Surgery Hospital | 603-642-9111 | 168 Crawley Falls Rd |
| Concord NH | Capital Area Veterinary Emergency Service | 603-227-1199 | 22 Bridge Street |
| Littleton NH | Littleton Veterinary Clinic | 603-444-0132 | 59 W Main St |
| Manchester NH | Veterinary Emergency Center of Manchester | 603-666-6677 | 336 Abby Road |
| Meredith NH | Meredith Place Veterinary Emergency Hospital | 603-279-1117 | 8 Maple Street, Suite 2 |
| North Conway NH | North Country Animal Hospital | 603-356-5538 | 2237 West Side Road |
| Portsmouth NH | The Veterinary Emergency Center of NH | 603-431-3600 | 15 Piscataqua Drive |

**New Jersey Listings**

| | | | |
|---|---|---|---|
| Cape May NJ | Cape May Veterinary Hospital | 609-884-1729 | 694 Petticoat Creek Lane |
| Cherry Hill NJ | Red Bank Veterinary Hospital | 856-429-4394 | 1425 East Marlton Pike |
| Fairfield NJ | Animal Emergency & Referral Associates | 973-788-0500 | 1237 Bloomfield Ave |
| Forked River NJ | Veterinary Emergency Services | 609-693-6900 | 720 Lacey Rd |
| Freehold NJ | Emergency Veterinary Care | 732-845-0200 | 44 Thoreau Dr |
| Iselin NJ | Central Jersey Veterinary Emergency Services | 732-283-3535 | 643 Lincoln Hwy |
| Linwood NJ | Red Bank Veterinary Hospital | 609-926-5300 | 535 Maple Avenue |
| Lyndhurst NJ | New Jersey Veterinary Emergency Services | 201-438-7122 | 724 Ridge Road |
| Mount Laurel NJ | Animal Emergency Service of South Jersey | 856-727-1332 | 220 Moorestown - Mount Laurel Road |
| Newton NJ | Newton Veterinary Hospital | 973-383-4321 | 116 Hampton House Road |
| Princeton NJ | Princeton Animal Hospital | 609-951-0400 | 726 Alexander Rd |
| Tinton Falls NJ | Garden State Veterinary Specialists | 732-922-0011 | One Pine Street |

**New Mexico Listings**

| | | | |
|---|---|---|---|
| Albuquerque NM | Veterinary Emergency & Specialty Center | 505-884-3433 | 4000 Montgomery Blvd NE |
| Angel Fire NM | Angel Fire Small Animal Hospital | 575-377-3165 | 3382 Mountain View Blvd |
| Carlsbad NM | Carlsbad Animal Clinic | 575-887-3653 | 103 E Blodgett St |
| Deming NM | Deming Animal Clinic | 505-546-2621 | 2117 Columbus Rd SE |
| Gallup NM | Red Rock Animal Hospital | 505-722-2251 | 816 South Boardman |
| Las Cruces NM | Veterinary Emergency Services | 505-527-8100 | 162 Wyatt Drive |
| Las Cruces NM | Veterinary Emergency Services | 575-527-8100 | 1700 E Lohman Ave |
| Roswell NM | Country Club Animal Hospital | 575-623-9191 | 301 W Country Club Rd |
| Santa Fe NM | Emergency Veterinary Clinic | 505-984-0625 | 2001 Vivigen Way |
| Santa Fe NM | Emergency Veterinary Clinic of Santa Fe | 505-984-0625 | 1311 Calle Nava |
| Socorro NM | Animal Haven Veterinary Clinic of Socorro | | 1433 Frontage Rd NW |
| Taos NM | Salazar Road Veterinary Clinic | 575-758-9115 | 1025 Salazar Rd |

| | | | |
|---|---|---|---|
| Tucumcari NM | Tucumcari Animal Hospital | 575-461-3900 | 101 N 10th St |
| Window Rock AZ | Navajo Nation Veterinary Clinics | | P.O. Box 4889 |

## New York Listings

| | | | |
|---|---|---|---|
| Baldwinsville NY | Veterinary Emergency Center | 315-638-3500 | 2115 Downer Street Rd |
| Briarcliff Manor NY | Animal Health Center | | 438 North state Rd. |
| Brooklyn NY | Veterinary Emergency & Referral Group | 718-522-9400 | 318 Warren St |
| Cheektowaga NY | Greater Buffalo Veterinary Emergency Clinic | 716-839-4044 | 4821 Genesee Street |
| Commack NY | Animal Emergency Services | 631-462-6044 | 6230 Jericho Tpke # C |
| East Syracuse NY | Veterinary Medical Center of Central NY | 315-446-7933 | 5841 Bridge Street, Suite 200 |
| Elmhurst NY | Elmhurst Animal Emergency Hospital | 718-426-4444 | 8706 Queens Blvd |
| Farmingdale NY | Veterinary Emergency Service | 631-249-2899 | 2233 Broadhollow Rd |
| Forest Hills NY | NYC Veterinary Specialists - Queens | 718-263-0099 | 107-28 71st Road |
| Gansevoort NY | Northway Animal Emergency Clinic | 518-761-2602 | 35 Fawn Road |
| Grand Island NY | Grand Island Small Animal Hospital | 716-773-7646 | 2323 Whitehaven Rd |
| Ithaca NY | Cornell University Hospital for Animals | 607-253-3060 | Cornell Campus |
| Kingston NY | Animal Emergency Clinic of the Hudson Valley | 845-336-0713 | 1112 Morton Blvd |
| Latham NY | Capital District Animal Emergency Clinic | 518-785-1094 | Rt. 2, 222 Troy-Schenectady Rd |
| Middletown NY | Orange County Animal Emergency Service | 845-692-0260 | 517 Route 211 East |
| New York NY | Animal Medical Center - 24 hours | 212-838-8100 | 510 East 62nd Street |
| New York NY | At Home Veterinary | 646-688-3087 | At Your Location |
| New York NY | NYC Veterinary Specialists | 212-767-0099 | 410 West 55th Street |
| Orchard Park NY | Orchard Park Veterinary Medical Center | 716-662-6660 | 3930 North Buffalo Road |
| Plainview NY | Long Island Veterinary Specialists | 516-501-1700 | 163 South Service Rd |
| Poughkeepsie NY | Animal Emergency Clinic of the Hudson Valley | 845-471-8242 | 84 Patrick Ln |
| Ray Brook NY | High Peaks Animal Hospital | 518-891-4410 | 1087 Route 86 |
| Rochester NY | Animal Emergency Service | | 825 White Spruce Blvd |
| Saranac Lake NY | Adirondack Park Pet Hospital | 518-891-3260 | 25 Brandy Brook Avenue |
| Selden NY | Animal Emergency Services | 631-698-2225 | 280-L Middle Country Rd. |
| Staten Island NY | Veterinary Emergency Center | 718-720-4211 | 1293 Clove Road |
| Vestal NY | Vestal Veterinary Hospital | 607-754-3933 | 2316 Vestal Parkway East |
| Westbury NY | Nassau Animal Emergency Group | 516-333-6262 | 740 Old Country Road |
| Westmoreland NY | Rome Area Veterinary Emergency | 315-853-2408 | 4769 State Route 233 |
| Yonkers NY | Animal Specialty Center | 914-457-4000 | 9 Odell Plaza |

## North Carolina Listings

| | | | |
|---|---|---|---|
| Asheville NC | Regional Emergency Animal Care Hospital | 828-665-4399 | 677 Brevard Rd |
| Durham NC | Triangle Veterinary Emergency Clinic | 919-489-0615 | 3319 Durham Chapel Hill Blvd |
| Fayetteville NC | Animal Urgent Care | 910-864-2844 | 3635 Sycamore Dairy Rd |
| Greensboro NC | Happy Tails Emergency Veterinary Clinic | 336-288-2688 | 2936 Battleground Avenue |
| Greenville NC | Pet Emergency Clinic of Pitt County | 252-321-1521 | 2207-A Evans Street |
| Huntersville NC | Carolina Veterinary Specialists | 704-932-1182 | 12117 Statesville Road |
| Jacksonville NC | Jacksonville Veterinary Hospital | 910-455-3838 | 1200 Hargett St |
| Kannapolis NC | Cabarrus Emergency Veterinary Clinic | 704-932-1182 | 1317 South Cannon Blvd |
| Kitty Hawk NC | Coastal Animal Hospital | 252-261-3960 | 3616 N. Croatan Hwy |
| Matthews NC | Emergency Veterinary Clinic | 704-844-6440 | 2440 Plantation Center Drive |
| Raleigh NC | After Hours Emergency Clinic | 919-781-5145 | 409 Vick Ave |
| Raleigh NC | Quail Corners Animal Hospital | 919-876-0739 | 1613 E Millbrook Rd |
| Wilmington NC | Animal Emergency Hospital of Wilmington | 910-791-7387 | 5333 Oleander Dr |
| Wilson NC | East Carolina Veterinary Emergency Treatment Services | 252-265-9920 | 4909-D Expressway Dr |

## North Dakota Listings

| | | | |
|---|---|---|---|
| Bismarck ND | Bismarck Animal Clinic & Hospital | 701-222-8255 | 1414 E Calgary Ave |
| Bismarck ND | Pinehurst Veterinary Hospital | 701-222-0551 | 755 Interstate Ave |
| Devils Lake ND | Lake Region Veterinary Service | 701-662-3321 | Highway 2 E |
| Dickinson ND | West Dakota Veterinary Clinic | 701-483-0240 | 93 21st St E |
| Dickinson ND | Yost Veterinary Clinic | 701-483-4863 | 1171 E Villard St |

| | | | |
|---|---|---|---|
| Fargo ND | Animal Health Clinic | 701-237-9310 | 1441 South University Drive |
| Fargo ND | Red River Animal Emergency | 701-478-9299 | 1401 Oak Manor Ave S # 2 |
| Grand Forks ND | Kindness Animal Hospital | 701-772-7289 | 4400 32nd Avenue |
| Jamestown ND | Prairie Veterinary Hospital | 701-252-9470 | 1305 Business Loop E |
| Jamestown ND | Southwood Veterinary Clinic | 701-252-3430 | 833 18th St SW |
| Minot ND | Minot Veterinary Clinic | 701-852-4831 | 3010 Burdick Expy E |
| Williston ND | Kitterz Total Pet Veterinary | 701-774-7979 | 308 26th St W |
| Williston ND | Western Veterinary Clinic | 701-572-7878 | # 85W, Highway 2 |

## Ohio Listings

| | | | |
|---|---|---|---|
| Akron OH | Akron Veterinary Referral & Emergency Center | 330-665-4996 | 1321 Centerview Circle |
| Bedford OH | Veterinary Referral Clinic & Emergency Center | 216-831-6789 | 5035 Richmond Rd |
| Canton OH | Stark County Veterinary Emergency Clinic | | 2705 Fulton Dr NW |
| Cincinnati OH | CARE Center Emergency Vet | 513-530-0911 | 6995 East Kemper Rd. |
| Cincinnati OH | Emergency Veterinary Clinic | 513-561-0069 | 4779 Red Bank Rd |
| Cincinnati OH | Grady Veterinary Hospital | 513-931-8675 | 9255 Winton Rd |
| Cleveland OH | Animal Emergency Clinic West | 216-362-6000 | 5320 W 140th St |
| Columbus OH | Capital Veterinary Referral & Emergency Center | 614-870-0480 | 5230 Renner Road |
| Columbus OH | Capital Veterinary Referral and Emergency Center | 614-351-5290 | 3578 W Broad St |
| Columbus OH | Ohio State University Veterinary Hospital | 614-292-3551 | 601 Vernon L. Tharp Street |
| Dayton OH | Centerville Veterinary Emergency Hospital | 937-434-0260 | 6880 Loop Rd |
| Dayton OH | Dayton Emergency Veterinary Hospital | 937-293-2714 | 2714 Springboro Rd West |
| Findlay OH | Findlay Animal Hospital | 419-423-7232 | 2141 Bright Rd |
| Girard OH | After Hours Animal Emergency Clinic | 330-530-8387 | Placement on map is approximate |
| Logan OH | Hocking Hills Animal Clinic | 740-380-7387 | 1978 E Front St |
| Lorain OH | Animal Emergency Center | 440-240-1400 | 5152 Grove Ave |
| Lorain OH | Animal Emergency Center | 440-240-1400 | 5152 Grove Ave |
| Mentor OH | Animal Emergency Clinic Northeast | 440-255-0770 | 8250 Tyler Boulevard |
| Parkersburg WV | Animal Veterinary Emergency | 304-428-8387 | 3602 E 7th St # B |
| Toledo OH | Animal Emergency & Critical | 419-473-0328 | 2785 W Central Avenue |
| Westerville OH | Animal Care Clinic of Central Ohio | 614-882-4728 | 25 Collegeview Rd |
| Worthington OH | Medvet Medical and Cancer Center for Pets | 614-846-5800 | 300 E. Wilson Bridge Rd |

## Oklahoma Listings

| | | | |
|---|---|---|---|
| Elk City OK | Circle M Animal Hospital | 580-225-4321 | 1420 E Highway 66 |
| Lawton OK | Midtown Animal Hospital | 580-353-3438 | 1101 SW Park Ave |
| Moore OK | After Hours Emergency Pet Hospital | 405-703-1741 | 9225 S Interstate 35 St |
| Norman OK | Animal Emergency Center of Norman | 405-360-7828 | 2121 McKown Drive |
| Oklahoma City OK | Animal Emergency Center | 405-631-7828 | 931 SW 74th Street |
| Oklahoma City OK | Neel Veterinary Hospital | 405-947-8387 | 2700 N. MacArthur Blvd |
| Stillwater OK | Oklahoma State University Vet | 405-744-8468 | 1 Bvmth |
| Tulsa OK | Animal Emergency Center | 918-665-0508 | 7220 E 41st Street |

## Oregon Listings

| | | | |
|---|---|---|---|
| Albany OR | River's Edge Pet Medical Center | 541-924-1700 | 202 NW Hickory Street |
| Bend OR | Animal Emergency Center of Central Oregon | 541-385-9110 | 1245 SE 3rd Street #C3 |
| Clackamas OR | Northwest Veterinary Specialists | 503-656-3999 | 16756 SE 82nd Drive |
| Corvallis OR | Williamette Veterinary Clinic | 541-753-2223 | 1562 SW 3rd Street |
| Medford OR | Southern Oregon Veterinary Specialists | 541-282-7711 | 3265 Biddle Road |
| Portland OR | Northwest Hospital | 503-228-7281 | 1945 NW Pettygrove |
| Portland OR | Southeast Hospital | 503-262-7194 | 10564 SE Washington Street #205 |
| Portland OR | VCA Southeast Portland Animal Hospital | 503-255-8139 | 13830 SE Stark Street |
| Salem OR | Salem Veterinary Emergency Clinic | 503-588-8082 | 3215 Market Street NE |
| Springfield OR | Emergency Veterinary Hospital | 541-746-0112 | 103 W. Q Street |
| Tualatin OR | Emergency Veterinary Clinic | 503-691-7922 | 19314 SW Mohave Court |

## Pennsylvania Listings

| Erie PA | Northwest PA Pet Emergency Center | 814-866-5920 | 429 West 38th Street |
|---|---|---|---|
| Lancaster PA | Pet Emergency Treatment Services | 717-295-7387 | 930 North Queen Street |
| Langhorne PA | Veterinary Specialty and Emergency Center | 215-750-7884 | 1900 W. Old Lincoln Hwy |
| Malvern PA | Veterinary Referral Center | 610-647-2950 | 340 Lancaster Ave |
| Malvern PA | Veterinary Referral Center & Emergency Service | 610-647-2950 | 340 Lancaster Ave |
| Mechanicsburg PA | Animal Emergency Medical Center | 717-796-2334 | 11 Willow Mill Park Rd |
| Monroeville PA | Avets | 412-373-4200 | 4224 Northern Pike |
| Philadelphia PA | Penn Veterinary Hospital (Ryan Veterinary Hospital) | 215-746-8387 | 3800 Spruce St |
| Pittsburgh PA | Pittsburgh Veterinary Specialists | 412-366-3400 | 807 Camp Horne Road |
| Pittston PA | Animal Emergency & Referral Hospital | 570-655-3600 | 755 South Township Blvd. |
| Scotrun PA | Pocono Veterinary Emergency & Critical Care | 570-620-1800 | 19 Scotrun Ave |
| Springfield PA | AAA Veterinary Emergency Hospital | 610-328-1301 | 820 W Springfield Rd |
| State College PA | Mt Nittany Veterinary Hospital | 814-237-4272 | 200 Elmwood St |
| Warrington PA | Bucks County Veterinary Emergency Trauma Services | 215-918-2200 | 968 Easton Road |
| Watsontown PA | Animal Emergency Center | 570-742-7400 | 395 Susquehanna Trl |
| Wexford PA | Bradford Hills Veterinary Hospital | 724-935-5827 | 13055 Perry Highway |
| Whitehall PA | Valley Central Veterinary Referral Center | | 210 Fullerton Avenue |
| York PA | Animal Emergency Clinic | 717-767-5355 | 1640 S Queen St |

## Rhode Island Listings

| Block Island RI | Block Island Veterinary Service | 401-466-8500 | Cooneymus Rd |
|---|---|---|---|
| East Greenwich RI | Ocean State Veterinary Specialists | 401-886-6787 | 1480 South Country Trail |
| Middletown RI | Newport Animal Hospital | 401-849-3400 | 333 Valley Rd |
| Warwick RI | Emergency Veterinary Service of Rhode Island | 401-732-1811 | 205 Hallene Road |

## South Carolina Listings

| Columbia SC | South Carolina Veterinary Emergency Care | 803-798-3837 | 3924 Fernandina Rd |
|---|---|---|---|
| Florence SC | VCA Pee Dee Animal Hospital | 843-662-9223 | 815 2nd Loop Road |
| Greenville SC | Animal Emergency Clinic | 864-232-1878 | 393 Woods Lake Road |
| Mount Pleasant SC | Veterinary Emergency Care | 843-216-7554 | 930 Pine Hollow Rd |
| Myrtle Beach SC | Animal Emergency Hospital of The Strand | 843-445-9797 | 303 Highway 15 Suite 1 |
| North Charleston SC | Greater Charleston Emergency Veterinary Clinic | 843-744-3372 | 3163 W Montague Ave |
| North Charleston SC | Veterinary Specialists of the Southeast | 843-566-0023 | 3169 West Montague Avenue |

## South Dakota Listings

| Aberdeen SD | Animal Health Clinic | 605-229-1691 | 704 S Melgaard Rd |
|---|---|---|---|
| Chamberlain SD | Mid River Veterinary Clinic | 605-234-6562 | 1950 E King Ave |
| Fort Pierre SD | Oahe Veterinary Clinic | 605-223-2562 | 118 E Missouri Ave #1 |
| Hot Springs SD | Fall River Veterinary Clinic | 605-745-3786 | Fall River Road |
| Huron SD | Huron Veterinary Hospital | 605-352-6063 | 340 4th St NW |
| Kadoka SD | Kadoka Veterinary Clinic | 605-837-2436 | 1004 Main Street |
| Mitchell SD | Lakeview Veterinary Clinic | 605-996-3242 | 2020 W Havens Ave |
| Mobridge SD | Oahe Veterinary Hospital | 605-845-3634 | 721 20th St E |
| Pierre SD | Animal Clinic of Pierre | 605-224-1075 | 118 E Missouri Ave #1 |
| Rapid City SD | Dakota Hills Veterinary Clinic | 605-342-7498 | 1571 Hwy 44 |
| Rapid City SD | Emergency Veterinary Hospital | 605-342-1368 | 1655 E 27th St |
| Rapid City SD | Noahs Ark Animal Hospital | 605-343-3225 | 1315 Mount Rushmore |
| Sioux Falls SD | Dale Animal Hospital | 605-371-3791 | 3642 Southeastern Ave |
| Sioux Falls SD | Veterinary Emergency Hospital | 605-977-6200 | 3508 South Minnesota Avenue Suite 104 |
| Sturgis SD | Sturgis Veterinary Hospital | 605-347-4436 | 2421 Vanocker Canyon Rd |
| Wall SD | Golden Veterinary Service | 605-279-2077 | 308 James Ave |
| Watertown SD | Howard Veterinary Clinic | 605-882-4188 | 1400 N Highway 20 |

## Tennessee Listings

| | | | |
|---|---|---|---|
| Alcoa TN | Midland Pet Emergency Center | 865-982-1007 | 235 Calderwood St. |
| Blountville TN | Airport Pet Emergency Clinic | 423-279-0574 | 2436 Highway 75 |
| Brentwood TN | Pet Emergency Treatment Service | 615-333-1212 | 1668 Mallory Lane |
| Chattanooga TN | River Vet Emergency Clinic | | 2132 Amnicola Hwy |
| Cordova TN | PetMed Emergency Center | 901-624-9002 | 830 N. Germantown Parkway Suite 105 |
| Jackson TN | Jackson Pet Emergency Center | 731-660-4343 | 8 Yorkshire Cv |
| Knoxville TN | Pet Emergency Clinic | 865-637-0114 | 1819 Ailor Ave |
| Livingston TN | Ragland and Riley Veterinary Hospital | 931-498-3153 | 3207 Cookeville Hwy |
| Memphis TN | Animal Emergency Center | 901-323-4563 | 3767 Summer Avenue |
| Murfreesboro TN | Animal Medical Center | 615-867-757 | 234 River Rock Blvd |
| Nashville TN | Nashville Pet Emergency Clinic | 615-383-2600 | 2000 12th Ave S |
| Talbott TN | Five Rivers Pet Emergency | 423-581-9492 | 6057 W Andrew Johnson Hwy # 1 |

## Texas Listings

| | | | |
|---|---|---|---|
| Amarillo TX | Small Animal Emergency Clinic | 806-352-2277 | 4119 Business Park Dr |
| Arlington TX | I-20 Emergency Animal Clinic | 817-478-9238 | 5820 W. Interstate 20 |
| Austin TX | Austin Vet - Emergency | 512-459-4336 | 4106 North Lamar Blvd |
| Austin TX | Emergency Animal Hospital - North | 512-331-6121 | 12034 Research Blvd - Suite 8 |
| Austin TX | Emergency Animal Hospital - South | 512-899-0955 | 4434 Frontier Trail |
| Beaumont TX | Southeast Texas Animal Emergency Clinic | 409-842-3239 | 3420 W Cardinal Dr |
| Carrollton TX | Emergency Pet Clinic of North Texas | 972-323-1310 | 1712 W. Frankford Road Suite #108 |
| Corpus Christi TX | Northwest Animal Emergency Center | 361-242-3337 | 11027 Leopard St |
| El Paso TX | Animal Emergency Center | 915-545-1148 | 2101 Texas Ave |
| El Paso TX | El Paso Animal Emergency Center | 915-545-1148 | 1220 Airway Blvd |
| Euless TX | Animal Freeway Animal Emergency Clinic | 817-571-2088 | 411 N Main St |
| Fort Stockton TX | Southwest Vet Clinic | 432-336-7048 | 3010 W Dickinson Blvd |
| Fort Worth TX | Metro West Emergency Veterinary Center | 817-731-3734 | 3201 Hulen Street |
| Grapevine TX | Animal Emergency Hospital | | 2340 W Southlake Blvd |
| Houston TX | Animal Emergency Center of West Houston | 832-593-8387 | 4823 Highway 6 North |
| Houston TX | Animal Emergency Clinic | 713-693-1100 | 1111 West Loop South Suite 200 |
| Houston TX | Animal Emergency Clinic SH 249 | 281-890-8875 | 19311 SH 249 |
| Houston TX | Veterinary Emergency Referral Group | 713-932-9589 | 8921 Katy Freeway |
| Longview TX | East Texas Pet Emergency Clinic | 903-759-8545 | 812 Gilmer Road |
| Lubbock TX | Small Animal Emergency Clinic | 806-797-6483 | 5103 34th St # A |
| Odessa TX | Permian Basin Emergency Veterinary Clinic | 432-561-8301 | 13528 W Highway 80 E |
| Richardson TX | Emergency Animal Clinic | 972-479-9110 | 401 W. Pres Bush Tpke, Ste 113 |
| Round Rock TX | Animal Emergency Clinic of Central Texas | 512-671-6252 | 2000 N Mays St # 112 |
| San Angelo TX | Animal Emergency Hospital | 325-653-8781 | 59 E Avenue L |
| San Antonio TX | Animal Emergency Room | 210-737-7380 | 4315 Fredericksburg Road #2 |
| San Antonio TX | Emergency Pet Clinic | 210-822-2873 | 8503 Broadway, Suite 105 |
| San Antonio TX | I-10 Pet Emergency | 210-691-0900 | 10822 Fredericksburg Road |
| Sonora TX | Sonora Animal Hospital | 325-387-2481 | 300 N Service Rd |
| Vernon TX | Vernon Veterinary Clinic | 940-552-5548 | |
| Waco TX | Animal Emergency Clinic - Waco | 254-753-0905 | 4900 Steinbeck Bend Dr |
| Wichita Falls TX | Colonial Park Veterinary Hospital | 940-691-0261 | 4713 Taft Blvd |

## Utah Listings

| | | | |
|---|---|---|---|
| Cedar City UT | Color Country Animal Hospital | 435-865-7264 | 390 N 4050 W |
| Cedar City UT | Southern Utah Animal Hospital | 435-586-6216 | 1203 N Main St |
| Clearfield UT | Animal Emergency Center | 801-776-8118 | 2465 N Main St # 5 |
| Kanab UT | Kanab Veterinary Hospital | 435-644-2400 | 484 S 100 E |
| Moab UT | Moab Veterinary Clinic | 435-259-8710 | 4575 Spanish Valley Drive |
| Orem UT | Veterinary Emergency Services | 801-426-8727 | 525 S State St |
| Park City UT | White Pine Veterinary Clinic | 435-649-7182 | 2100 West Rasmussen Road |
| Salt Lake City UT | Central Valley Veterinary Hospital | 801-487-1321 | 55 East Miller Avenue |
| Salt Lake City UT | Cottonwood Animal Hospital | 801-278-3367 | 6360 Highland Dr |
| Sandy UT | Animal Emergency South | 801-572-4357 | 10572 S 700 E |
| St George UT | Southwest Animal Emergency Clinic | 435-627-2522 | 435 N 1680 E |

| St George UT | Southwest Animal Emergency Clinic | 435-627-2522 | 435 N 1680 E |
| Wendover UT | A Visiting Veterinarian | 435-665-7704 | 479 E Wendover Blvd |

**Vermont Listings**

| Middlesex VT | Onion River Animal Hospital | 802-223-7765 | 36 Three Mile Bridge Road |
| Newbury VT | River Valley Veterinary Hospital | 802-866-5922 | 3890 Route 5 North |
| Rutland VT | Rutland Veterinary Clinic | 802-773-2779 | 90 E. Pittsford Road |
| Williston VT | Burlington Emergency Veterinary Service | 802-863-2387 | 200 Commerce St |

**Virginia Listings**

| Alexandria VA | Alexandria Animal Hospital and Veterinary Emergency Service | 703-751-2022 | 2660 Duke Street |
| Ashburn VA | Emergency Vet | 571-223-0811 | 20207 Birdsnest Pl |
| Charlottesville VA | Veterinary Emergency Treatment Service | 434-973-3519 | 370 Greenbrier Drive Suite A-2 |
| Chesapeake VA | Greenbrier Veterinary Emergency Clinic | 757-366-9000 | 1100 Eden Way North, Suite 101B |
| Fairfax VA | Pender Veterinary Centre and Emergency Clinic | 703-591-3304 | 4001 Legato Road |
| Fairfax VA | SouthPaws Veterinary Center | 703-752-9100 | 8500 Arlington Blvd |
| Lawrenceville VA | Greensville Veterinary Clinic Emergency | 434-848-2876 | 2024 Lawrenceville Plank Rd |
| Leesburg VA | Animal Emergency Hospital Leesburg | 703-777-5755 | 165 Fort Evens Rd NE |
| Lynchburg VA | Animal Emergency & Critical Care | 434-846-1504 | 3432 Odd Fellows Road |
| Manakin-Sabot VA | Veterinary Referral & Critical Care | 804-784-8722 | 1596 Hockett Road |
| Manassas VA | Prince William Emergency Veterinary Clinic | 703-361-8287 | 8610 Centreville Road |
| Midlothian VA | Veterinary Emergency Center South | 804-353-9000 | 2460 Colony Crossing Place |
| Roanoke VA | Emergency Veterinary Service of Roanoke | 540-563-8575 | 4902 Frontage Rd NW |
| Springfield VA | Springfield Emergency Pet Hospital | 703-451-8900 | 6651 Backlick Rd |
| Vienna VA | Hope Center | 703-281-5121 | 140 Park Street SE |
| Virginia Beach VA | Beach Veterinary Emergency Center | 757-468-4900 | 1124 Lynnhaven Parkway, Suite C |
| Virginia Beach VA | Tidewater Animal Emergency & Referral Center | 757-499-5463 | 364 South Independence Blvd |
| Williamsburg VA | James City Veterinary Clinic | 757-220-0226 | 95 Brookwood Drive |
| Winchester VA | Valley Emergency Veterinary Clinic | 540-662-7811 | 164 Garber Ln |
| Yorktown VA | Emergency Veterinary Clinic | 757-874-8115 | 1120 George Wash Mem Hwy |

**Washington Listings**

| Auburn WA | After Hours Animal Emergency Clinic | 253-939-6272 | 718 Auburn Way N |
| Bellevue WA | After Hours Animal Emergency Clinic | 425-641-8414 | 2975 156th Ave SE |
| Bellingham WA | Bellingham Animal Emergency Care | 360-758-2200 | 317 Telegraph Road |
| Lacey WA | Olympia Pet Emergency | 360-455-5155 | 3011 Pacific Ave. SE |
| Mount Vernon WA | Pet Emergency Center | 360-848-5911 | 14434 Avon Allen Road |
| Pasco WA | Pet Emergency Service | 509-547-3577 | 8913 Sandifur Pkwy |
| Pullman WA | Washington State University Veterinary Hospital | 509-335-0711 | Washington State University |
| Seattle WA | Animal Critical Care and Emergency Services | 206-364-1660 | 11536 Lake City Way NE |
| Seattle WA | Emerald City Emergency Clinic | 206-634-9000 | 4102 Stone Way N |
| Seattle WA | Five Corners Animal Hospital | 206-243-2982 | 15707 1st Ave S |
| Spokane WA | Pet Emergency Clinic | 509-326-6670 | 21 E Mission Ave |
| Tacoma WA | Animal Emergency Clinic | 253-474-0791 | 5608 South Durango St |
| Vancouver WA | Clark County Emergency Veterinary Service | 360-694-3007 | 6818 NE Fourth Plain Blvd |
| Vancouver WA | St Francis 24 Hour Pet Hospital | 360-253-5446 | 12010 NE 65th St |
| Yakima WA | Pet Emergency Service of Yakima | 509-452-4138 | 510 W Chestnut Ave |

**West Virginia Listings**

| Fairmont WV | North Central WV Veterinary Emergency Clinic | 304-363-2227 | Ih 79 # 139 |
| Morgantown WV | After Hours Veterinary Clinic | 304-599-3111 | 149 N Main St |
| Parkersburg WV | Animal Veterinary Emergency | 304-428-8387 | 3602 E 7th St # B |
| South Charleston WV | Animal Emergency Clinic | 304-768-2911 | 5304 MacCorkle Av SW |

**Wisconsin Listings**

| | | | |
|---|---|---|---|
| Ashland WI | Ashland Area Veterinary Clinic | 715-682-4199 | 2700 Farm Rd |
| Eau Claire WI | Oakwood Hills Animal Hospital | 715-835-0112 | 4616 Commerce Valley Road |
| Glendale WI | Animal Emergency Center | 414-540-6710 | 2100 W. Silver Spring Drive |
| Grafton WI | Wisconsin Veterinary Referral Center | 262-546-0249 | 1381 Port Washington Road |
| Green Bay WI | Green Bay Animal Emergency Center | 920-494-9400 | 933 Anderson Drive, Suite F |
| Madison WI | Veterinary Emergency Service - East | 608-222-2455 | 4902 East Broadway |
| Madison WI | Veterinary Specialty & Emergency Care | 608-845-0002 | 1848 Waldorf Boulevard |
| Middleton WI | Veterinary Emergency Service - Middleton | 606-831-1101 | 1612 N. High Point Road, Suite 100 |
| Mosinee WI | Emergency Vet of Central Wisconsin | 715-693-6934 | 1420 Kronenwetter Dr |
| Port Washington WI | Lakeshore Veterinary Specialists | 262-268-7800 | 207 W. Seven Hills Rd. |
| Sheboygan WI | Animal Clinic & Emergency Hospital | 920-565-2125 | 2734 Calumet Dr |
| Waukesha WI | Wisconsin Veterinary Referral Center | 866-542-3241 | 360 Bluemound Road |

**Wyoming Listings**

| | | | |
|---|---|---|---|
| Casper WY | Animal Hospital of Casper | 307-266-1660 | 2060 Fairgrounds Road |
| Cheyenne WY | Cheyenne Pet Clinic | 307-635-4121 | 3740 E. Lincolnway |
| Cody WY | Advanced Veterinary Care Center | 307-527-6828 | 1901 Demaris Dr |
| Cody WY | Lifetime Small Animal Hospital | 307-587-4324 | 2627 Big Horn Ave |
| Evanston WY | Bear River Veterinary Clinic | 307-789-5230 | 619 Almy Road 107 |
| Evanston WY | MJB Animal Clinic | 307-789-4289 | 2301 Wasatch Rd |
| Green River WY | Animal Clinic of Green River | 307-875-9827 | Animal Clinic of Green River |
| Jackson WY | Jackson Hole Veterinary Clinic | 307-733-4279 | 2950 W Big Trail Dr |
| Jackson WY | Spring Creek Animal Hospital | 307-733-1606 | 1035 West Broadway |
| Jackson WY | Teton Veterinary Clinic | 307-733-2633 | 1225 Gregory Ln |
| Laramie WY | Alpine Animal Hospital | 307-745-7341 | 610 Skyline Rd |
| Pine Bluffs WY | Bluffs Veterinary Clinic | 307-245-9263 | 722 West 7th Street |
| Rawlins WY | Hones Veterinary Services | 307-324-9999 | 519 W Spruce St |
| Rock Springs WY | Mountainaire Animal Clinic | 307-362-1440 | 1801 Yellowstone Road |
| Sheridan WY | Bischoff Veterinary Services | 307-674-4500 | 241 Centennial Ln |
| Sheridan WY | Crook County Veterinary Services | 307-283-2115 | Stock Tank Highway 14 |
| Sheridan WY | Moxey Veterinary Hospital | 307-672-5533 | 1650 Commercial Ave |
| Thermopolis WY | Hot Springs Veterinary Clinic | 307-864-5553 | 827 S 6th St |

**Canada Listings**

**Alberta Listings**

| | | | |
|---|---|---|---|
| Calgary AB | Care Center Animal Hospital | 403-541-0815 | 7140 - 12th Street S.E. |
| Edmonton AB | Edmonton Veterinarian's Emergency Clinic | 780-433-9505 | 11104 102 Ave NW |

**British Columbia Listings**

| | | | |
|---|---|---|---|
| Coquitlam BC | Central Animal Emergency Clinic | 604-931-1911 | 812 Roderick Avenue |
| Dawson Creek BC | Dawson Creek Veterinary Clinic | 250-782-1080 | 238 116 Avenue |
| Langley BC | Animal Emergency Clinic of the Fraser Valley | 604-514-1711 | #306-6325 204th St |
| Vancouver BC | Vancouver Animal Emergency Clinic | 604-734-5104 | 1590 West 4th Ave |
| Victoria BC | Central Victoria Veterinary Hospital | 250-475-2495 | 760 Roderick Street |

**Manitoba Listings**

| | | | |
|---|---|---|---|
| Winnipeg MB | Pembina Veterinary Hospital | 204-452-9427 | 400 Pembina Highway |

**New Brunswick Listings**

| | | | |
|---|---|---|---|
| Moncton NB | The Oaks Veterinary Medical & Emergency Referral Center | 506-854-6257 | 565 Mapleton Road |

**Newfoundland Listings**

| | | | |
|---|---|---|---|
| St Johns NF | St John's Veterinary Hospital | 709-722-7766 | 335 Freshwater Road |

**Nova Scotia Listings**

| | | | |
|---|---|---|---|
| Dartmouth NS | Metro Animal Emergency Clinic | 902-468-0674 | 201 Brownlow Avenue |

**Ontario Listings**

| | | | |
|---|---|---|---|
| Burlington ON | Burgess Veterinary Emergency Clinic | 905-637-8111 | 775 Woodview Road |
| Oakville ON | Veterinary Emergency Hospital | 905-829-9444 | 2285 Bristol Circle |
| Toronto ON | Veterinary Emergency Clinic - North | 416-226-3663 | 280 Sheppard Ave |
| Toronto ON | Veterinary Emergency Clinic - South | 416-920-2002 | 920 Yonge St |

**Quebec Listings**

| | | | |
|---|---|---|---|
| Montreal PQ | Veterinary Clinic - Villeray - Papineau | 514-593-6777 | 7655 Papineau Avenue |

**Saskatchewan Listings**

| | | | |
|---|---|---|---|
| Martensville SK | Martensville Veterinary Hospital | 306-933-2677 | Hwy 12 |

**Yukon Listings**

| | | | |
|---|---|---|---|
| Whitehorse YU | Alpine Veterinary Medical Center | 867-633-5700 | 107 Copper Road |
| Whitehorse YU | Copper Road Veterinary Clinic | 867-633-5184 | 128B Copper Road |